DATE DUE

			PRINTED IN U.S.A.

THE ENCYCLOPEDIA OF

Country Music

THE ENCYCLOPEDIA OF

Country Music

The Ultimate Guide to the Music

Compiled by the staff of the Country Music Hall of Fame
and Museum

Edited by Paul Kingsbury

with the assistance of Laura Garrard, Daniel Cooper, and John Rumble

NEW YORK   OXFORD

OXFORD UNIVERSITY PRESS

1998

Oxford University Press

Oxford   New York
Athens Auckland Bangkok Bogotá Buenos Aires
Calcutta Cape Town Chennai Dar es Salaam
Delhi Florence Hong Kong Istanbul Karachi
Kuala Lumpur Madrid Melbourne Mexico City
Mumbai Nairobi Paris São Paulo Singapore
Taipei Tokyo Toronto Warsaw

and associated companies in
Berlin   Ibadan

Copyright © 1998 by the Country Music Foundation

Published by Oxford University Press, Inc.
198 Madison Avenue, New York, New York 10016

Oxford is a registered trademark of Oxford University Press

Library of Congress Cataloging-in-Publication Data
The encyclopedia of country music: the ultimate guide to the music/
compiled by the staff of the Country Music Hall of Fame and Museum;
edited by Paul Kingsbury with the assistance of
Laura Garrard, Daniel Cooper, and John Rumble.
p. cm. Includes bibliographical references.
ISBN 0-19-511671-2
1. Country music—Encyclopedias. I. Kingsbury, Paul.
II. Garrard, Laura. III. Cooper, Daniel (Daniel C.). IV. Rumble, John.
ML102.C7E54 1998   781.642'03—dc21   97-51362

1 3 5 7 9 8 6 4 2

Printed in the United States of America
on acid-free paper

CONTENTS

FOREWORD

I first became acquainted with the Country Music Foundation in the mid-1970s, when Bill Ivey, the CMF's director at that time, made me a tape of 1950s and 1960s recordings by the Louvin Brothers that he thought I might like. I hadn't asked him to make that tape, but he was right—I did like the songs. A *lot*. Ira and Charlie Louvin were not just exquisite harmony singers, they were also masterful songwriters whose songs are still being recorded to this day.

Through that little courtesy, I gradually came to find out that the Country Music Foundation is one of America's great natural resources. In addition to operating the Country Music Hall of Fame and Museum (probably the premier music museum in the world), the CMF's staff oversee a massive archive of country music recordings, photographs, films, and publications. They're collecting country music today so that our grandchildren—and their grandchildren—will know why we love it so, where it came from, and what country music tells us about ourselves.

The people who work for the CMF really care about country music. All of it—from the oldest old-time fiddle tunes on up to what's happening on Nashville's Music Row right now. I've learned a lot from those folks. And just as with that first tape, they're still passing that passion and knowledge on.

This encyclopedia represents the culmination of several years of hard work and dedication. As with everything they do, the staff of the Country Music Hall of Fame and Museum have put this book together with a genuine love and concern for the music. They've brought in experts from all over to make this encyclopedia the best it can be. It's truly a labor of love, and I'm proud to be associated with it.

I hope you find that it brings you a little closer to the music you love and leads you down paths that bring more music into your life.

—EMMYLOU HARRIS

INTRODUCTION

What is country music?

That is a question fans, performers, and businesspeople have been asking and debating, in one form or another, for most of the twentieth century. Many styles of music now fall under the broad rubric known as country music: old-time, honky-tonk, western swing, Cajun, bluegrass, rockabilly, country-pop, country-rock, folk-country, new traditionalism, hot country, and even insurgent or alternative country. The reason that country music exists as such a catchall category of music can be found in the music's commercial origins.

Country music came into being as a genre of music in the early 1920s when record companies began seeking new audiences to sell recordings to. Since the turn of the twentieth century, record companies had been made in the big city and catered to big-city tastes with the marching tunes of John Philip Sousa, the arias of Enrico Caruso, the hammy show tunes of Al Jolson, and the orchestral jazz of Paul Whiteman. When radio became a commercial reality in 1920, the new entertainment medium immediately cut into sales of record companies, especially in the cities, where radio stations first thrived. The reason was simple economics. After the initial investment in a radio set, to listen to a radio was free, of course. Records, on the other hand, cost at least 75 cents apiece, sometimes as much as $1.25.

It was time for record companies to find new niche markets, and they found them quickly in two previously underserved and unexploited markets: black audiences and rural white audiences. To reach black record buyers, the record companies sought out black blues and jazz performers to make "race records," as they were then called. For their rural white counterparts, the record companies sought genuine rustic talent in the hills and hollows of the rural Southeast: fiddlers, stringbands, singers of old folk ballads, gospel quartets. These sorts of performers and their music became the foundation of what has come to be known as country music. In the beginning, though, this white rural music was known by many different names as the record companies struggled to define the new and lucrative market they had discovered, labeling their new series variously Old Time Tunes (OKeh Records), Old Time Melodies of the Sunny South (Victor), Special Records for Southern States (Vocalion), Familiar Tunes (Columbia), and finally and most typically, Hillbilly Music. Somehow the audiences found the music and responded.

The first country music "hit" was Fiddlin' John Carson's "The Little Old Log Cabin in the Lane" b/w "The Old Hen Cackled and the Rooster's Going to Crow," released in July 1923 by OKeh Records. By early 1925, country music had its first million seller with Vernon Dalhart's recording of "The Wreck of the Old 97" b/w "The Prisoner's Song" for Victor Records. It has been said that by the early 1930s it was commonplace in general stores across the South to hear this familiar refrain: "Let me have a pound of butter, a dozen eggs, and the latest Jimmie Rodgers record."

But even if businessmen in a way "created" country music by identifying various strains of rural music and getting them to their rightful audience, they never completely controlled it. Because it was music, after all, it had meaning for its audience far beyond whatever the businessmen had ever intended. Music can be sold like a commodity (like breakfast cereal), but it is never merely consumed, and it is appreciated in an entirely different way than a simple disposable commodity.

As musicians and fans grew accustomed to the idea of hillbilly music, they began ascribing to the music its own traditions and codes. By the time of Hank Williams, the genre was established enough that the great country songwriter felt he could state unequivocally what characterized the music (then known as "folk").

"Folk music is sincere," Williams said in 1952. "There ain't nothin' phony about it. When a folksinger sings a sad song, he's sad. He means it. The tunes are simple and easy to remember, and they're sincere with them.

"I judge a song by its lyrics," he added. "A song ain't nothin' in the world but a story just wrote with music to it."

A few years later, hillbilly/folk music would become known as country & western, and then simply as country. But even as its name changed, its bedrock values remained. Country music is simple music. It is a music of nostalgia and sentiment. It is a music that speaks of the tension between sin and salvation. It is a music of human stories, hopes, and failings.

Today country music is also big business, accounting for more than $2 billion in annual record sales by 1995. In addition, as writer Peter Applebome has noted, "With 2,400 radio stations, country is on 1,600 more stations than the next most popular format, news talk. Each week, 70 million Americans listen to country radio, leading its nearest rival, adult contemporary, by almost 19 million listeners."

By the 1990s, country music had broken out of its original marketing niche. No longer was country music simply rural music made for rural listeners. A case in point is Garth Brooks, a college marketing major from suburban Oklahoma who had sold more than 62 million records by 1997, meaning not only that his sales placed him in the same elite echelon as the Beatles and Elvis Presley but also that Brooks reached the same mass audience that had embraced those famous rock & rollers. Country music has become— as the businessmen on Nashville's Music Row are fond of calling it—America's music.

One indication of how far country music has come is the very existence of an institution such as the Country Music Foundation. Formed in 1964 by the state of Tennessee as a charitable educational organization, the CMF is the governing body of the Country Music Hall of Fame and Museum, which opened in 1967. Today the Country Music Foundation and its museum constitute the largest and most active popular music research center in the world, with a full-time staff of thirty-five. In addition to the Hall of Fame, the CMF offers journalists and researchers a massive library of recordings and printed material covering the full history of country music. The heart of the library's holdings is a collection of 250,000 country recordings. Thousands of films, videotapes, books, periodicals, and microfilms round out the collection. Dozens of network television productions and such films as *Coal Miner's Daughter* and *Tender Mercies* have used the research facilities at the CMF. In addition to its museum and library programs, the Country Music Foundation reissues historic recordings on its own record label, publishes books, conducts educational programs in schools, and actively investigates issues related to contemporary and historical country music performance.

Speaking for the staff of the Country Music Hall of Fame and Museum, we believe it is high time for an encyclopedia that does justice to the music. To that end we enlisted some 150 authorities on the music to help us compile this book, which we believe is the most comprehensive, thorough, responsible, and accurate encyclopedia of country music to date. In addition to making sure that each of the encyclopedia's entries was written by an acknowledged expert on the subject, the staff of the Hall of Fame rigorously fact-checked each entry for accuracy. Going far beyond the work of previous books, the staff verified every birth name, birthplace, birth date, and death date by vital-records searches, contacts with surviving family, musicians' union records, genealogical searches on the Internet, and personal conversations with living performers and their representatives. We have chosen to limit this vital-records information to birthplace, birth date, and date of death, reasoning that place of death is generally of far less importance, for biographical purposes, than birthplace.

A few words about the parameters of the encyclopedia: This compendium focuses on North American country music, primarily commercial country music of the United States. Although we acknowledge that thriving country music scenes exist outside the United States, their performers are not treated here.

Ralph Waldo Emerson said there is no history, only biography, and this encyclopedia certainly subscribes to that dictum. The entries herein are primarily biographical ones on performers, with entries also devoted to important songwriters, businesspeople, and radio personalities. In addition, there are entries for important radio and television programs, substyles of country music, instruments used in the music, music organizations, and record companies. Unfortunately, not every person or entity that could have been mentioned is included in this encyclopedia. We had to set some limits to make this encyclopedia usable and affordable. Therefore we have focused on those people and entities that in our judgment have had the most impact on the history of the music. In some cases we have chosen to include performers such as Emmett Miller, John Denver, and the Eagles, who are not squarely in the country music tradition. Our rationale in these cases has been to include those whose influence within and on the realm of country music has been significant, even if the performers never considered themselves a part of country music.

Informing our choices has been the Country Music Foundation Library and Media Center and its staff. For more than twenty-five years the Hall of Fame has offered a reference service out of the Library and Media Center. Annually, the Reference Department responds to some 2,500 telephone inquiries and 300 to 400 letters. In addition, the Reference Department and other staff work to answer questions and provide footage and photographs for national television news programs, music businesses across the nation, and even for country entertainers who want to research old records and career histories. All of these years of research and reference experience inform the work in this encyclopedia—from the overall choice of entries down to the checking of every last, minute fact. For these reasons, we believe this encyclopedia to be the most useful and accurate on the music to date.

How to use this encyclopedia:

1. The entries are titled and alphabetized by the most commonly used name for that person or organization (e.g., The Big Bopper rather than J. P. Richardson, ASCAP rather than American Society for Composers, Authors, and Publishers). Wherever possible, full names for individuals and business enterprises have been included within the body of the entries.
2. Cross-references to other entries are indicated within entry texts by names in small capitals.
3. Most artist entries are followed by brief listings of representative recordings. These are not intended to be comprehensive but to suggest where one might best begin to investigate the works of the artist.
4. See the appendices in the back for important tables of record sales and major awards.
5. If you simply cannot find enough information within these pages, we encourage you to visit us in Nashville at the Country Music Hall of Fame and Museum, where we take pleasure in answering your questions personally.

—PAUL KINGSBURY

ACKNOWLEDGMENTS

Over the past four years, this encyclopedia has required the dedication of many people, all of whom deserve recognition for their significant contributions to this work. Our thanks go first of all to the writers who contributed to this book; they are experts in the field, and they responded enthusiastically to the challenge to compile the most authoritative encyclopedia in the country field. Thanks to the Board of Trustees and the hardworking staff of the Country Music Foundation for aiding the production of this volume in innumerable ways. For farsighted guidance and support, thanks to former CMF director Bill Ivey and acting director Kyle Young. Thanks in particular go to Country Music Hall of Fame and Museum staff past and present who worked hard to ensure the accuracy and relevance of each of the encyclopedia's entries: especially Kent Henderson, Bob Pinson, Ronnie Pugh, and John Rumble. Other staff members who made valuable contributions include Jonita Aadland, Sally Allen, Steve Betts, Lauren Bufferd, William P. Davis, Chris Dickinson, Lauren Finney, Linda Gross, Bob Kramer, Mark Medley, Becky Miley, Chris Skinker, Alan Stoker, and the staff of Hatch Show Print. For help in compiling our invaluable databases, thanks to the CMF's John Knowles. For administrative assistance, thanks to Kelley Sallee Snead. Thanks also to our energetic and dedicated team of interns over the past four years: Amanda James, Rob Porter, Shannon Becker, Charlotte Walker, and Kara Furlong. For contributions of incalculable value at every stage of the project, thanks to Daniel Cooper. My personal gratitude and appreciation go to Laura Garrard and Ashley LaRoche, each of whom managed this project on a daily basis and kept it running smoothly—Ashley from April 1995 to June 1996, and Laura from July 1996 to its completion. Laura was particularly involved in assisting with editing the final manuscript. Finally, thanks to Jonathan Wiener, Soo Mee Kwon, and Maribeth Anderson Payne at Oxford University Press for their unstinting support of this project and their considerable editorial expertise.

—PAUL KINGSBURY
EDITOR

THE ENCYCLOPEDIA OF

Country Music

Abbott Records

established in Hollywood, California, fall 1951

Hollywood-based Abbott Records was an important independent label in country music in the early 1950s. It was founded by FABOR ROBISON, primarily to promote the career of country singer JOHNNY HORTON. The name Abbott came from Robison's partner, a drugstore owner who put up part of the funding. Though Horton had no major hits on Abbott, Robison soon found and recorded artists such as JIM REEVES, who had his first #1 hit, "Mexican Joe," on the label, and MITCHELL TOROK, whose record "Caribbean" was a #1 country hit in 1953. Many of Abbott's artists, as well as studio musicians, were drawn from Shreveport's KWKH and its LOUISIANA HAYRIDE show. By 1954 Robison had turned most of his attention to a new label, FABOR RECORDS.
—*Stacey Wolfe*

Jean and Julian Aberbach (*see* Hill & Range)

Nathan Abshire

b. Gueydan, Louisiana, June 27, 1913; d. May 13, 1981

Cajun accordionist Nathan Abshire learned much of his music from his parents and an uncle, all of whom played the accordion. He was also strongly influenced by pioneer Creole accordionist Amédé Ardoin, with whom he often played dances. Abshire began his performing career at age eight, when he appeared at a dance hall in Mermentau Cove. In the 1930s he recorded for BLUEBIRD RECORDS with the Rayne-Bo Ramblers, but the 1940s saw a decline in the popularity of the accordion in Cajun music, and Abshire's career suffered as a result.

In 1949 Abshire helped revive the popularity of the accordion with his hit recording of "Pine Grove Blues" on the O.T. label. He followed this with other moderately successful recordings, such as "Pine Grove Boogie," "La Valse de Holly Beach," and "Shamrock Waltz," but was unable to duplicate the success of "Pine Grove Blues." Abshire's career enjoyed another upturn when he was discovered by folk music enthusiasts during the folk music revival of the 1960s and 1970s. One of the best-loved and most influential figures in Cajun music, he remained a favorite on the folk festival circuit right up until his death in 1981.
—*Charlie Seemann*

REPRESENTATIVE RECORDINGS

The Best of Nathan Abshire (Swallow, 1991); *French Blues* (Arhoolie, 1993)

Academy of Country Music (*see* ACM)

Accordion

The accordion is an instrument made of an airtight box in which a bellow pushes air through *free reeds*. A free reed is a tongue made of metal or wood, attached at one end over a close-fitting opening through which the free end vibrates when air passes over it. The period from 1818 to 1848 was the time of development of a whole new group of musical instruments, the free reed instruments, today represented by the accordion, the harmonium, and the HARMONICA.

In the early nineteenth century, much experimentation was done in developing effective reed instruments. The single-row melodeon, the lap organ, and the Viennese Physharmonica were a few of the first experiments. One of the earliest popular accordions was the concertina, an instrument with an octagonally shaped body, a very complete chromatic scale of notes (divided between the two sides of the body), and double-action reeds (the tone is different according to whether the air is drawn or blown through the reeds). This instrument was perfected in 1844 by Charles Wheatstone of England. The first famed player of this instrument was the Italian Giulio Regondi, followed by the Englishman Richard Blagrove.

In the twentieth century, the accordion gained its greatest popularity in 1910 when various makers, notably Mariano Dallapé of Italy, began to make the reeds out of steel. Steel reeds have steadier pitch and a much greater volume, thus giving them the bite and power to hold the attention of an audience. The popular types of accordion in this century are the single-row diatonic, a small rectangular instrument with one row of double-action reeds; the double row, larger with two rows of double-action or diatonic reeds; the triple row with three rows of double-action reeds; the triple row with a chromatic scale (a scale containing all the accidental, or sharp and flat, notes); and lastly the piano-key accordion, a large accordion with single-action reeds (reeds that make the same tone whether played by pushing or drawing air through them) and a piano-style keyboard. The piano-key accordion was first developed in Vienna and Paris and later adopted in Italy and Germany.

The accordion has been used in several styles of country music, particularly the western songs of the singing cowboys and in Cajun music. Sally Ann Forrester even played the instrument briefly in BILL MONROE's Blue Grass Boys during the early 1940s. Probably the most famous accordionist in country music has been bandleader PEE WEE

KING. In the mid-1800s German settlers introduced the diatonic accordion to the Acadian population of southwestern Louisiana, and it soon became a key ingredient of the Cajun sound. Among its famous practitioners have been JOE FALCON, IRY LEJEUNE, LAWRENCE WALKER, NATHAN ABSHIRE, Octa Clark, and Clifton Chenier. More recently, Zachary Richard, Steve Riley, Wayne Toups, and this author's husband, MARC SAVOY, have carried on the tradition of the accordion in Cajun music. —*Ann Allen Savoy*

ACE

established in Nashville, Tennessee, November 4, 1974; ended September 25, 1981

Following the October 14, 1974, CMA Awards Show, which saw Australian pop star OLIVIA NEWTON-JOHN win the Female Vocalist of the Year award, GEORGE JONES and TAMMY WYNETTE hosted a meeting of twenty-two other country artists at their home in Nashville. Artists attending included BILL ANDERSON, JIM ED BROWN, BRENDA LEE, BARBARA MANDRELL, DOLLY PARTON, CAL SMITH, HANK SNOW, MEL TILLIS, CONWAY TWITTY, PORTER WAGONER, DOTTIE WEST, and FARON YOUNG. A week later this group announced the formation of the Association of Country Entertainers (ACE), an organization restricted to country performers. Ostensibly, these Nashville-based artists organized to look after the specific interests of entertainers and to bolster the CMA's efforts in promoting country music growth worldwide. They announced that they were primarily concerned about inadequate entertainer representation in the CMA's board of directors and problems with country radio's playlists. But owing to the timing of the organization's formation, and public statements made ten days after their first meeting, many observers concluded that ACE had been formed to protest the increasing acceptance of pop singers in the country community and that ACE was opposed to change. In fact, ACE convened a screening committee to determine the country credentials of prospective ACE members.

Two years later, on November 4, 1976, ACE presented a more carefully refined set of views during a press conference that focused attention on problems arising from short radio playlists and suggested a need for additional choice in country radio formats. ACE never had adequate funding to do its job, and the office closed in 1981.

The artists most active in ACE were all connected with the GRAND OLE OPRY. They included GRANDPA JONES, ERNEST TUBB, VIC WILLIS, JEAN SHEPARD, HANK SNOW, ROY WIGGINS, Patsy Stoneman, JUSTIN TUBB, DEL WOOD, Oscar Sullivan, GEORGE MORGAN, WILMA LEE & STONEY COOPER, CONNIE SMITH, BARBARA MANDRELL, Charlie Louvin, Bill Carlisle, Jesse McReynolds, BILLY GRAMMER, and JIMMY DICKENS. —*Paul W. Soelberg*

ACM

established in Los Angeles, California, 1964

A trade organization formed by Tommy Wiggins, EDDIE MILLER, and Chris & Mickey Christensen, the Academy of Country Music's stated goal "to enhance and promote the growth of country music" was undertaken by a combined membership of performers and fans. Many key forces in West Coast country, including TEX WILLIAMS, JOHNNY BOND, and CLIFFIE STONE, served as academy presidents; EDDIE DEAN and JIMMY WAKELY were also very active in the

organization, which aggressively focused on California-based country artists for its first ten years.

Initially known as the Country & Western Music Academy, the organization gave out its first awards in 1965, two years before the rival CMA adopted a similar program. Among the 1965 winners, determined by popular membership vote, were BUCK OWENS, BONNIE OWENS, MERLE HAGGARD, and ROGER MILLER. By 1974 the organization had been renamed the Academy of Country Music, and its awards show was broadcast nationally on ABC. In 1979 the ACM's BILL BOYD and Gene Weed moved the show to NBC, where it has since aired to high ratings annually.

—*Jonny Whiteside*

Roy Acuff

b. Maynardville, Tennessee, September 15, 1903; d. November 23, 1992

Named the King of Country Music by baseball great Dizzy Dean, Roy Claxton Acuff emerged as a star during the early 1940s. He helped intensify the star system at the GRAND OLE OPRY and remained its leading personality until his death. In so doing, he formed the bridge between country's rural stringband era and the modern era of star singers backed by fully amplified bands. In addition, he cofounded ACUFF-ROSE PUBLICATIONS with songwriter FRED ROSE, thus laying an important cornerstone of the Nashville music industry.

Although he helped bring country music to the city and to the world of big business, Acuff came from a rural, folk-based background. His father farmed while also serving as Maynardville's postmaster and as pastor of the town's Baptist church. As a youth, Acuff soaked in music of all sorts: folk ballads and fiddle tunes learned from neighbors and kin, hymns learned from itinerant school instructors, recordings of early country artists, and even some of the classical vocal training pursued by his sister Sue after the family moved to Fountain City, a Knoxville suburb. But Acuff's real love at the time was sports; in high school he lettered in football, basketball, and baseball.

Roy Acuff

After graduation, Acuff turned down a scholarship to nearby Carson-Newman College and worked temporarily at a variety of jobs, including that of railroad "call boy," the one responsible for rounding up other workers as the need arose. He also played semiprofessional baseball and boxed informally. Early in 1929, major-league baseball scouts recruited Acuff for training camp, but his collapse during a game—an aftereffect of an earlier sunstroke—prompted a nervous breakdown and sidelined him for most of 1930.

During his recuperation, Acuff began to practice his fiddle, and in 1932 he worked a medicine show tour of the Tennessee-Virginia mountains that fired his enthusiasm for show business. Next, he began playing square dances and other gatherings with various local musicians, including Lonnie Wilson and BEECHER "PETE" KIRBY, who would both become longtime members of his band. Radio broadcasts on Knoxville's WROL and WNOX broadened his experience. It was a WROL announcer, in fact, who named Acuff's band the Crazy Tennesseans. His radio fame caught the attention of AMERICAN RECORD CORPORATION (ARC) producer W. R. CALAWAY, who brought the band to Chicago to cut their first twenty numbers in 1936. Follow-up sessions yielded recordings released on a series of department-store labels, budget priced for Depression-era buyers.

Acuff lost no time trying to gain a spot on the Grand Ole Opry, but the Opry's GEORGE D. HAY repeatedly refused his services until promoter J. L. FRANK intervened in Acuff's behalf. A 1937 guest shot produced no results, but another, on February 5, 1938, did the trick when Acuff's performance of the classic "The Great Speckled Bird" generated sacks of fan mail. J. L. Frank suggested a new band name, the Smoky Mountain Boys, and Opry executives HARRY STONE and DAVID STONE immediately put the singer at the center of a budding star system, pushing Acuff's trademark song "Wabash Cannon Ball" equally hard. Stylistically, his clear, heartfelt vocals modernized the era's predominantly stringband sound just enough to seem innovative and traditional at the same time.

Early in the 1940s, Acuff zoomed to the top of his field with help from WSM's 50,000-watt transmitter, Opry promotion, and his status as headliner of the *Prince Albert Show*, the Opry's NBC network segment begun in October 1939. Fast-selling songbooks, hit records for the OKeh label such as "Wreck on the Highway" and "Fireball Mail," mushrooming gate receipts on the road, and appearances in a series of films all boosted his income to the $200,000 mark in 1942. In that year he proved himself a business leader by forming Acuff-Rose Publications—legally a partnership between Acuff's wife, Mildred, and Fred Rose—a company that laid the foundation for music publishing in Nashville while providing the Acuffs with their greatest source of wealth.

Acuff's star did not shine as brightly during the late 1940s. The rise of honky-tonk, exemplified by the Opry's ERNEST TUBB, and a smoother, pop-oriented brand of country music personified by EDDY ARNOLD were eclipsing Acuff's old-time sound. But his music remained highly popular, and he remained an important star in country music's growing constellation of hitmaking artists. Although he left the Opry during 1946–47 in a salary dispute, he returned to host the *Royal Crown Cola Show* segment. He also opened a recreational park near Clarksville, Tennessee; ran—unsuccessfully—for the governorship of Tennessee on the Republican ticket in 1948; and made his first international tour with an Opry troupe, which performed at U. S. military bases in Europe in 1949. His subsequent travels outside the U.S. mainland included Alaska, Korea, Japan, the Caribbean, and the Mediterranean.

By the early fifties, Acuff could easily have retired from the recording studio and the road, but he remained active, recording for CAPITOL, DECCA, MGM, and after 1957, HICKORY RECORDS, a label he formed with Fred Rose and WESLEY ROSE in 1953. His records charted occasionally during the 1950s, but his annual sales generally amounted to a small, if steady, 25,000 copies. Combined with falling road show receipts during the late fifties and early sixties, his modest sales prompted him to temporarily incorporate a snare drum and electric guitar into his band, but these experiments were ultimately dropped in a return to his standby all-acoustic sound. After he suffered serious injuries in a July 1965 car wreck that also nearly killed band member SHOT JACKSON, he began to speak of retiring from the road, though he would continue to make personal appearances for some time to come.

In 1971 Acuff received a substantial boost by participating in the famous *Will the Circle Be Unbroken* album project, which featured the NITTY GRITTY DIRT BAND and a number of country artists. This added to the exposure he'd gained on the college circuit during the folk music revival of the 1960s. Other testaments to his continuing popularity were the 1974 chartmaking records "Back in the Country" and "Old Time Sunshine Song," written by Acuff-Rose singer-songwriter EDDY RAVEN.

Although appearances on *Hee Haw* and TV specials also helped to keep Acuff in the public eye, his primary showcase continued to be the Grand Ole Opry. The Roy Acuff Theater at OPRYLAND, the Roy Acuff Museum (housing his collection of instruments and other memorabilia), and his long-held role as the Opry's senior statesman gave him a status that no Opry star has surpassed.

Acuff was elected the first living member of the Country Music Hall of Fame in 1962. —*John Rumble*

REPRESENTATIVE RECORDINGS

Columbia Historic Edition (Columbia, 1985); *The Essential Roy Acuff* (Columbia, 1992)

Acuff-Rose Publications
established in 1942

As Nashville's first country music publishing company, Acuff-Rose Publications was a key player in the city's emergence as a music center beginning in the early 1940s. The company was organized in 1942 by GRAND OLE OPRY star ROY ACUFF and Nashville songwriter FRED ROSE. Acuff put up $25,000 he had saved from songbook sales, while Rose contributed his personal songwriting catalogue as capital. As it turned out, Rose, who ran the firm, never had to touch Acuff's working capital, due to Acuff-Rose's earnings from early hits with BOB WILLS, Acuff, and BOB ATCHER. After the war, the company had continued success with such artists as CURLY FOX & TEXAS RUBY, EDDY ARNOLD, and PAUL HOWARD, all of whom scored hits with Acuff-Rose material.

Acuff-Rose's most significant connection, however, was with HANK WILLIAMS. He began publishing songs regularly through Acuff-Rose in 1946 and signed an exclusive writer's contract with the company in 1948. In addition, Rose steered Williams to a profitable recording contract with MGM, beginning in 1947. Besides Williams's own country hits, Rose and his son WESLEY ROSE, who joined the firm in 1945 as general manager, secured numerous lucrative recordings of Williams's songs by pop acts. Other memorable Acuff-Rose copyrights of the late 1940s and early 1950s included "Tennessee Waltz," a country hit for PEE WEE KING and a pop smash for Patti Page, and "Chattanoogie Shoe Shine Boy," a dual-market chart-topper for RED FOLEY.

During these same years, Acuff-Rose pioneered in advocating songwriters' interests. In 1948 the Roses worked out the "Nashville Plan" with BMI to secure performance royalties for songwriters. Acuff-Rose would pay writers a portion of its BMI earnings, and BMI would reimburse the company. In 1953 Acuff and the Roses established HICKORY RECORDS as an outlet for rising songwriters and recording artists. (In 1959 the Acuff-Rose Artists Corporation joined the complex.)

Wesley Rose successfully ran the firm after his father died in 1954. From the late 1950s into the early 1970s, Acuff-Rose remained a power in the country and pop fields, helping to develop singers and songwriters such as the EVERLY BROTHERS, MARTY ROBBINS, DON GIBSON, JOHN D. LOUDERMILK, ROY ORBISON, MICKEY NEWBURY, EDDY RAVEN, and DALLAS FRAZIER. (Earlier, Acuff-Rose had been responsible for bringing ace songwriters BOUDLEAUX AND FELICE BRYANT to Nashville.) Beginning in 1957, Acuff-Rose set up offices abroad. The company's development of new writers and artists waned after the early 1970s, but the firm's impressive catalogue continued to generate hits, making it an attractive purchase by Gaylord Broadcasting in 1985, when Acuff-Rose became part of Gaylord's Opryland Music Group.

—*John Rumble*

Kay Adams
b. Knox City, Texas, April 9, 1941

During the mid-1960s, Princetta Kay Adams recorded a series of concept albums in the hard-country style popularized by BAKERSFIELD legends BUCK OWENS and MERLE HAGGARD. *Wheels and Tears* (1966) is perhaps the best of Adams's records. A collection of truck driving songs sung from a woman's point of view, it included the minor (but enduring) hit single "Little Pink Mack."

Raised in Vernon, Texas, Adams moved to Bakersfield in 1964. There she met producer CLIFFIE STONE, who signed her to the Tower label, a subsidiary of CAPITOL RECORDS. Adams's first single for Tower, "Honky-Tonk Heartache" (1964), earned her the 1965 ACADEMY OF COUNTRY MUSIC award for Most Promising Female Vocalist (Merle Haggard won Most Promising Male Vocalist honors the same year). Adams starred in a country music opera (*The Legend of Johnny Brown*, 1966) and appeared in the road shows of Owens and Haggard. She subsequently recorded for Capitol, Granite, Ovation, and Frontline. In 1996, after years of relative professional inactivity, Adams teamed up with Nashville neo-honky-tonkers BR5-49 to record "Mama Was a Rock (Daddy Was a Rolling Stone)" for *Rig Rock Deluxe*, a collection of truck driving songs compiled by Jeremy Tepper of DIESEL ONLY RECORDS and Jake Guralnick for the Upstart label. —*Bill Friskics-Warren*

REPRESENTATIVE RECORDINGS

Wheels and Tears (Tower, 1966); *A Devil Like Me Needs an Angel Like You* with Dick Curless (Tower, 1966)

Trace Adkins
b. Springhill, Louisiana, January 13, 1962

Trace Adkins, a six-foot-six Louisiana honky-tonk baritone singer, earned his first #1 single and platinum album in 1997, the same year he was named Top New Male Artist by the ACM.

Adkins began singing in the gospel quartet New Commitment while attending a Sarepta, Louisiana, high school. The quartet recorded two albums for an independent label: *The New Commitment Quartet* (1979) and *The Best of the New Commitment Quartet* (1980). After graduating from high school, Adkins played defensive end for Louisiana Tech University's football team and studied petroleum technology. A knee injury ended his sports career after two years, so he spent the next eight years working in the oil industry as a derrick man and pipe fitter. He joined a band called Bayou that won a regional talent contest and competed in the national finals in Nashville. The band played clubs in Texas, Louisiana, New Mexico, and Mississippi for four years.

Adkins became unhappy with his musical career and returned to the drilling rigs. But he did have the foresight to have an injured pinky finger set in a permanent bend so he could continue to play guitar. He moved to Nashville in August 1992 and decided to make music a full-time career. He was introduced to CAPITOL Nashville president SCOTT HENDRICKS, who signed Adkins to the label after seeing him perform at a Mount Juliet bar, Tillie's.

Adkins's debut album, *Dreamin' Out Loud*, was produced by Hendricks and released in June 1996. Adkins penned his own debut single, "There's a Girl in Texas," which was a Top Twenty hit, and followed that with the Top Five hit "Every Light in the House." He earned his first #1 in 1997 with "(This Ain't No) Thinkin' Thing." Adkins released his second album, *Big Time*, in September 1997, and it was certified gold in early 1998. The album contains the ballad "The Rest of Mine," which Adkins cowrote and sang at his May 1997 wedding to Rhonda Forlaw. The song reached #2 in December 1997.

—*Beverly Keel*

REPRESENTATIVE RECORDINGS

Dreamin' Out Loud (Capitol, 1996); *Big Time* (Capitol, 1997)

AFM
established in New York, New York, November 6, 1896

The American Federation of Musicians (AFM) was originally chartered in New York with Owen Miller as president. He resolved to improve musicians' wages, employment hours, and benefits. Today there are some 125,000 members nationwide.

For more than half a century, only three presidents had headed the union: Joseph Weber, who served thirty-nine years; Frank Carothers (1914–15), and James C. Petrillo (1940–58). Petrillo called a strike against record labels, effective August 1, 1942, halting recordings. In September 1943 Decca became the first label to come to agreement with the union, establishing a performance trust fund to aid out-of-work musicians. A second strike, on January 1, 1948, was settled to the satisfaction of the AFM on December 14, 1948. Steve Young was voted national AFM president in June 1995.

Nashville Local 257 was chartered December 11, 1902, with Joe Miles as president. GEORGE W. COOPER JR. held the branch presidency the longest, serving successively from 1937 to 1973. HAROLD BRADLEY, elected in December 1990, is now president. With its growth as a major recording center, Nashville has become the sixth-largest union branch in North America, with nearly 4,000 members.

AFM Los Angeles was chartered March 15, 1897; and AFM Chicago was chartered September 17, 1901.

—*Walt Trott*

AFRS

established fall 1943

The Armed Forces Radio Service (AFRS) was a special program of the U.S. military created to boost the morale of U.S. servicemen overseas. The AFRS accomplished this by creating and distributing to troops 16-inch radio transcription discs providing timely information, education, and, importantly, entertainment. These transcriptions offered AFRS-produced fare, network radio broadcasts, and, starting in 1945, commercial recordings of current pop, jazz, Latin, classical, and country music. Among the important country music programs in the AFRS library are the AFRS-created *Melody Roundup* series of more than 2,000 fifteen-minute shows (originally distributed at the rate of four per week) and Nashville's long-running GRAND OLE OPRY, which was used for more than twenty-five years. Although AFRS was officially established in the fall of 1943 as a branch of the Special Services Division, in reality the SSD had already been providing the unique service one commonly associates with AFRS since summer 1942.

AFRS discs were heard on naval vessels (including submarines), in the field via mobile fifty-watt suitcase units, at military hospitals abroad, and in the United States through closed-circuit broadcasts, short wave and AFRS-developed station transmissions, and even on foreign station broadcasts via airtime provided gratis or on a lease basis. By 1945 more than 800 AFRS outlets were sharing a weekly mailing of 200 sets of discs from AFRS's primary production center, Los Angeles.

AFRS's entertainment programming emphasized music, but not to the exclusion of comedy, drama, and sports. And this philosophy has continued right up into the television era as the AFRS has become the AFRTS (Armed Forces Radio and *Television* Service). Since 1953, TV programs have been distributed to troops via film, videotape, and satellite. Meanwhile, AFRTS radio programming, which was originally distributed on 16-inch discs, was issued on 12-inch microgroove LPs beginning in the early 1960s, and then on cassettes as of 1994. By the late 1990s, satellite radio programming feeds to AFRTS made the need for discs and cassettes almost inessential.

—*Bob Pinson*

AFTRA

established in New York, New York, August 1, 1937

The American Federation of Television and Radio Artists (AFTRA) is a national union representing television and radio artists, including announcers, actors, dancers, singers, and broadcasters. Chartered in 1937 with actor Eddie Cantor as president, today it is an 82,000-member organization, headquartered in New York City. The Los Angeles chapter, also chartered in 1937, boasts some 30,000 members. Susan Boyd is president of AFTRA-L.A., dealing largely with TV, radio, and phonograph recordings. The Nashville chapter, founded in 1961, is 1,500 members strong and acts as local representative for the Screen Actors Guild in regard to locally produced motion pictures, commercials, and TV shows. Randall Himes has been executive director since 1986.

Country has a strong voice in the chapter. Past presidents Jim Ferguson and Louis Nunley still perform regularly. Nunley and ANITA KERR (both of the Anita Kerr Singers) are among the local founding members. Ferguson and Nunley are past national vice presidents. "We are the only phonograph-driven local in the United States," Himes said in 1995. "We process more session reports than any other AFTRA local. We have jurisdiction for audio- and videotapes . . . our blanket [license] fee is a contribution to the Performers Benefit Fund, which we instituted as part of our negotiations with the OPRY." —*Walt Trott*

Rhett Akins

b. Valdosta, Georgia, October 13, 1969

A fairly new hitmaking artist, Thomas Rhett Akins can be considered both a prolific writer and a hitmaking singer. He grew up in Valdosta, Georgia, and played the guitar as a boy, forming a band with his brothers before he was eleven years old. In 1992 he came to Nashville and was eventually signed by DECCA.

On his January 1995 debut album, *A Thousand Memories*, Akins co-wrote nine of its ten songs, including the #1 single "That Ain't My Truck" and the ballad "She Said Yes." Two other songs on the album hit the Top Forty: "What They're Talking About" and "I Brake for Brunettes."

This first effort firmly established Akins as a member of the New Country club, or a youthful singer walking the line between country-rock and a cleaned-up version of honkytonk. Most of Akins's material focused on lighthearted themes that appealed to his representative age group, as found in the song "That Ain't My Truck."

Akins received an additional career boost with his first tour in 1995, opening for REBA McENTIRE. His second DECCA album, *Somebody New*, released in June 1996, also produced a #1 single, "Don't Get Me Started," co-written by Akins. This album reflected the work of a maturing artist and emphasized slower-tempoed songs dealing with the topic of personal relationships. Propelled by his early chart success, Akins was named one of *Country America* magazine's Top New Stars of 1995. Akins was also a finalist in the New Country Artist category at the 1995 American Music Awards. —*Bob Paxman*

REPRESENTATIVE RECORDINGS

A Thousand Memories (Decca, 1995); *Somebody New* (Decca, 1996); *What Livin's All About* (Decca, 1998)

Alabama

Jeffrey Alan Cook b. Fort Payne, Alabama, August 27, 1949
Teddy Wayne Gentry b. Fort Payne, Alabama, January 22, 1952
Mark Joel Herndon b. Springfield, Massachusetts, May 11, 1955
Randy Yeull Owen b. Fort Payne, Alabama, December 13, 1949

When the ACADEMY OF COUNTRY MUSIC and *Cashbox* magazine both named Alabama Artist of the Decade in 1989, it

Alabama: (from left) Jeff Cook, Randy Owen, Teddy Gentry, and Mark Herndon

reflected how thoroughly the quartet had dominated commercial country music in the eighties. As of 1995, Alabama has sold more than 57 million albums worldwide, has scored forty-one #1 hits, and has won 160 music awards, including the COUNTRY MUSIC ASSOCIATION's Entertainer of the Year award for three consecutive years, 1982–84.

Unlike vocal groups such as the OAK RIDGE BOYS and the STATLER BROTHERS, Alabama was a self-contained band—they handled all the instruments as well as all the vocals, an unprecedented phenomenon at the upper reaches of the country charts. Although session musicians contributed to Alabama's recordings, guitarist Randy Owen, bassist Teddy Gentry, drummer Mark Herndon, and guitarist Jeff Cook acquitted themselves as competent if not virtuosic players on the band's busy tour schedule. By successfully applying the rock & roll model of the self-contained band to country music, Alabama paved the way for such acts as RESTLESS HEART, SHENANDOAH, and the MAVERICKS.

Owen and Gentry are first cousins who grew up within walking distance of each other on farms outside Fort Payne, Alabama. Distant cousin Jeff Cook lived in town, and as teenagers the three relatives formed a band called Wildcountry. In 1973 they quit their day jobs and played their blend of Allman Brothers–style southern rock and country-pop throughout the South, most notably at the Bowery in Myrtle Beach, South Carolina. In 1977 Wildcountry changed its name to Alabama and in 1979 hired rock & roller Herndon as its permanent drummer. Alabama recorded for the small labels GRT and MDJ in the late seventies and even scored Top Forty country hits for MDJ with "I Wanna Come Over" in 1979 and "My Home's in Alabama" in 1980. That won the group an invitation to the "New Faces" show at Nashville's annual Country Radio Seminar, and their popular performance there quickly won them a contract with RCA, which they signed on April 11, 1980.

Alabama's first single for RCA, "Tennessee River," began a streak of twenty-one consecutive #1 singles between 1980 and 1987. Among the more memorable singles in that run were "Feels So Right" (1981, pop Top Twenty), "Love in the First Degree" (1981, pop Top Twenty), and "The Closer You Get" (1983, pop Top Thirty, Grammy winner). In addition, the albums *Feels So Right* (1981), *Mountain Music* (1982), *The Closer You Get . . .* (1983), *Roll On* (1984), *40 Hour Week* (1985), and *Greatest Hits* (1986) all went platinum and broke into the Top Thirty pop album charts.

Since 1982 Alabama has sponsored the June Jam, a full-day music festival in a forty-acre field behind Fort Payne High School. With Alabama as the annual headliner, the June Jam has drawn as many as 60,000 fans at a time and has raised more than $3 million for local charities.

Despite Alabama's immense commercial success, the band has never fared well with the critics, who have complained about its vacuous songwriting and watered-down, middle-of-the-road arrangements. Typical was the *Baltimore Sun* argument that Alabama "renders country music all but indistinguishable from pop" and thus "trivializes some of country's most hallowed traditions."

Alabama revisited its Myrtle Beach days and its roots in the r&b-flavored beach music of the Carolinas by cutting the 1997 album *Dancin' on the Boulevard.* —*Geoffrey Himes*

REPRESENTATIVE RECORDINGS

Feels So Right (RCA, 1981); *Mountain Music* (RCA, 1982); *The Closer You Get . . .* (RCA, 1983); *40 Hour Week* (RCA, 1985); *American Pride* (RCA, 1992); *Dancin' on the Boulevard* (RCA, 1997)

Pat Alger
b. LaGrange, Georgia, September 23, 1947

In the early 1990s, Patrick J. Alger emerged as one of Nashville's most successful and perceptive songwriters. Merging a literate folkie's touch for insightful social commentary with MUSIC ROW's knack for catchy songcraft, he has written four #1 hits for superstar GARTH BROOKS. Alger was born in LaGrange, Georgia, and he set his career in motion in 1973 when he moved to Woodstock, New York, where he joined the Woodstock Mountain Revue, a loose-knit group that included John Sebastian, Paul Butterfield, Eric Andersen, JIM ROONEY, Bill Keith, and Happy & Artie Traum. He also recorded a duet album with Artie Traum: *From the Heart* (Rounder, 1980).

Alger's initial success as a songwriter came in 1980, when Livingston Taylor recorded his "First Time Love," which became a Top Ten adult-contemporary hit. The following year, Alger moved to Nashville; his early cuts included contributions to NANCI GRIFFITH ("Once in a Very Blue Moon" and "Lone Star State of Mind"), DON WILLIAMS ("True Love"), TRISHA YEARWOOD ("Like We Never Had a Broken Heart"), and HAL KETCHUM ("Small Town Saturday Night"). KATHY MATTEA scored hits with Alger's "Goin' Gone," "She Came from Fort Worth," and "A Few Good Things Remain."

Upon moving to Nashville, Alger also met up with Woodstock cohort Jim Rooney, a partner in the publishing company Forerunner Music, Inc., along with Garth Brooks's producer ALLEN REYNOLDS. This connection brought Alger together with Brooks, for whom he co-wrote the #1 hits "Unanswered Prayers," "The Thunder Rolls," "What She's Doing Now," and "That Summer." He was named ASCAP Songwriter of the Year in 1992, and from 1995 to 1997 he served as president of the NSAI board. Alger also has released two solo albums, *True Love and Other Stories* on SUGAR HILL and *Seeds* on LIBERTY.

—*Michael McCall*

Deborah Allen
b. Memphis, Tennessee, September 30, 1953

Deborah Allen (born Deborah Lynn Thurmond) had a successful career as a Nashville songwriter before achieving popularity as a performer. In 1978 she began collaborating with Rafe Van Hoy, producing hits for JOHN CONLEE, LEE GREENWOOD, JANIE FRICKE, and TANYA TUCKER. She and Van Hoy married in 1982.

A former Memphis beauty queen, Allen migrated to Music City at age nineteen. After stints at OPRYLAND and as a backup singer for ROY ORBISON, she began recording duets with the deceased JIM REEVES in 1979. Allen added the ethereal harmonies to Reeves's tracks, and three of these tunes, including "Don't Let Me Cross Over," became Top Ten country hits.

Allen's country-pop style, marked by a wall of sound and soulful singing, was showcased in her 1983 RCA hit "Baby I Lied." Three more chart successes followed in 1984.

Allen cultivated a disarmingly open sexual image, posing in unclothed innocence and holding an apple on the jacket of her 1980 CAPITOL debut album *Trouble in Paradise*. This trend continued with the Allen-in-bed cover photo of her 1984 RCA album *Let Me Be the First*. In 1987 Allen's RCA album *Telepathy* featured a Madonna-like image and a title tune by the artist then known as Prince.

In 1992 Allen re-emerged in the country field on the GIANT label, using her blended Memphis-Nashville style to good effect.

—*Mary A. Bufwack*

REPRESENTATIVE RECORDINGS

Cheat the Night (RCA, 1983); *Delta Dreamland* (Giant, 1993)

Jules Verne Allen
b. Waxahachie, Texas, April 1, 1883; d. 1945

Jules Verne Allen was one of the few early SINGING COWBOYS who had actually been a working cowboy. His classic performances of songs such as "'Long Side the Santa Fe Trail," "The Dying Cowboy," and "The Days of '49" are considered to be some of the finest examples of authentic traditional cowboy songs ever captured on record.

Allen began ranch work at age ten in his native Ellis County, Texas. He worked at a number of jobs, including horse wrangler, and eventually became an experienced all-around "hand." He participated in a number of trail drives from the Mexican border to the railroad shipping centers in Montana. During this time he began to play guitar and learn cowboy songs, which he would perform for his fellow ranch hands. After a stint in the military during World War I, he returned to ranch work, but decided to try singing professionally instead. During the 1920s he began performing over radio stations WFAA in Dallas, KFI and KNX in Los Angeles, and WOAI and KTSA in San Antonio, calling himself "the Original Singing Cowboy," "Longhorn Luke," and "Shiftless." His San Antonio sponsor, the Longhorn Portland Cement Company, published a little songbook titled *Cowboy Songs Sung by Longhorn Luke and His Cowboys*.

Allen began his brief recording career in 1928, cutting three songs, "Little Joe the Wrangler," "Jack O' Diamonds," and "Po' Mourner," for Victor. His six Victor sessions of 1928–29 resulted in a total of twenty-four recorded performances. In 1933 the Naylor Company published *Cowboy Lore*, a book Allen had put together of thirty-six cowboy songs along with tidbits of information about ranch life. Though his recording contract was not renewed, Allen continued to perform on the radio and appear at rodeos for a number of years.

—*Charlie Seemann*

REPRESENTATIVE RECORDING

Jules Allen, The Texas Cowboy (Folk Variety, 1973)

Red Allen
b. Pigeon Roost, Kentucky, February 12, 1930; d. April 3, 1993

A singer-guitarist with a high, mountain-flavored voice, Harley "Red" Allen was an influential figure in BLUEGRASS from the 1950s onward. His early career, centered in the Dayton, Ohio, area, included small-label recordings, and radio and club appearances with mandolinist Frank Wakefield and banjo player Noah Crase. Allen teamed with the OSBORNE BROTHERS in 1956, performing on the WWVA JAMBOREE. Before their partnership ended in 1958, they recorded sixteen sides for MGM RECORDS, among which "Once More" is considered a landmark in the development of sophisticated three-part vocal harmony.

In the 1960s Allen moved to Washington, D.C., often working and recording with Wakefield, including a 1963 performance at CARNEGIE HALL. His hard-driving style attracted young urban bluegrass enthusiasts DAVID GRISMAN, BILL KEITH, and Peter (Roberts) Kuykendall, who were members of Allen's Kentuckians before launching their own careers. In the 1960s Allen worked with EARL SCRUGGS during LESTER FLATT's recuperation from surgery; in 1969 Allen performed and recorded in Lexington, Kentucky, with banjo player J. D. CROWE and mandolinist DOYLE LAWSON.

Before failing health forced his semiretirement in the 1980s, Allen recorded with his sons, Neil (d. 1974), Ronnie, Greg, and Harley (now a Nashville singer-songwriter), and with later versions of the Kentuckians.

—*Frank and Marty Godbey*

REPRESENTATIVE RECORDINGS

The Osborne Brothers, 1956–1968 (Bear Family, 1995); *Bluegrass* (Folkways, 1963) with Frank Wakefield

Rex Allen

b. Willcox, Arizona, December 31, 1920

The last, and arguably the best vocalist (although EDDIE DEAN and KEN CURTIS could justifiably contend) of the SINGING COWBOYS, Rex Elvie Allen possessed a voice of astonishing range and strength. Allen first found work as an entertainer during World War II, before being called to fill the singing cowboy slot (following in the illustrious footsteps of GENE AUTRY, EDDIE DEAN, and BOB ATCHER) at the NATIONAL BARN DANCE in 1945.

A trip to Hollywood followed, and the first of Allen's nineteen films for Republic, *The Arizona Cowboy*, was released in 1950; his last, *The Phantom Stallion* (1954), is considered the final singing cowboy film, marking the end of an era in American music and film. He later starred in a television series called *Frontier Doctor*, and his resonant, authoritative speaking voice became one of the most familiar in America thanks to a long association with Walt Disney as a narrator of more than fifty films and television shows, as well as hundreds of commercials. Allen is now semiretired, living in his native Arizona, and as a founder of the Western Music Association, he acts as today's elder statesman of western music.

Allen's recording career began with MERCURY in Chicago in 1945, and although his voice was best suited to western ballads, he occasionally appeared on the country charts, notably with "Crying in the Chapel" (1953) and "Don't Go Near the Indians" (1962).

Each of Rex Allen's three sons entered the entertainment business, and his eldest, Rex Jr. (born August 23, 1947), made a significant mark on the country charts in the 1970s and 1980s. Rex Jr. is still actively recording and touring and has six Top Ten hits on WARNER BROS. RECORDS. In 1995 Rex Sr. and Rex Jr. teamed up for the Warner Western album *The Singing Cowboys*.

—*Douglas B. Green*

REPRESENTATIVE RECORDINGS

Rex Allen: The Hawaiian Cowboy (Bear Family, 1986); *Under Western Skies* (Decca, 1956, reissued on Stetson, 1987); *Rex Allen Jr. & Rex Allen Sr.: The Singing Cowboys* (Warner Western, 1995)

Rosalie Allen

b. Old Forge, Pennsylvania, June 27, 1924

Known as the Queen of the Yodelers, Rosalie Allen was born Julie Marlene Bedra, one of eleven children of Polish parents living in the coal fields of Pennsylvania.

Her story is a classic tale of the Depression. At the age of nine she worked and boarded in a restaurant and sent her earnings home. Fascinated with singing and listening to the radio, she defied her parents and hit the road with a touring hillbilly band at age thirteen, after winning a contest.

At nineteen Allen was becoming known for her elaborate yodeling. Her arrival in New York City in 1943 with DENVER DARLING's Swing Billies cowboy troupe marked the start of her solo career. With many male entertainers drafted, she became one of the female radio pioneers, finding popularity as the first female country disc jockey with her *Prairie Stars* show on New York's WOV (1944–56). She made the transition to TV with a country program (1949–53) and was the owner of New York City's first country record shop. She also wrote columns for fan magazines.

Allen made soundies (short films of performances) in the mid-1940s, and she also appeared in a 1949 feature film *Village Barn*. She recorded with RCA VICTOR in the late 1940s; titles included "Guitar Polka," "Yodel Boogie," and her biggest hit, "He Taught Me to Yodel." Her yodeling was at its decorative best in duets with ELTON BRITT.

—*Mary A. Bufwack*

REPRESENTATIVE RECORDINGS

Queen of the Yodelers (Cattle, 1983); *The Cowboy's Sweetheart* (Cowgirlboy, 1990)

Allen Brothers (Austin and Lee)

Austin Ambrose Allen b. Sewanee, Tennessee, February 7, 1901; d. January 5, 1959

Lee William Allen b. Sewanee, Tennessee, June 1, 1906; d. February 24, 1981

One of the first successful BROTHER DUETS in country recordings, the Allen Brothers combined the blues, vaudeville, and folk music of the Chattanooga area into a distinctive style that made them one of the most influential old-time acts. Unlike later brother acts such as the BLUE SKY BOYS or the MONROE BROTHERS, who featured sentimental and gospel songs, the Allens preferred rowdy, double-entendre material such as their biggest hit, "Salty Dog Blues." In fact, the Allens were so adept at performing white blues that in 1927, Columbia mistakenly released their "Laughin' and Cryin' Blues" in the "race" series instead of the "old-time" series. (Not seeing the humor in it, the Allens sued and promptly moved to the Victor label.)

The Allens toured widely, and between 1926 and 1934 they recorded for COLUMBIA, Victor, and ARC, a total of some eighty-nine sides that included hits such as "Roll Down the Line" (1930) and "Jake Walk Blues" (about the Jamaica Ginger poisoning scare, 1930). After 1934, on the heels of an unsuccessful stint in legitimate theater, both brothers left the business. Reissues of their work in the 1970s spurred new interest in their music, and Lee Allen made a brief comeback before his death in 1981. Austin died in 1959.

—*Charles Wolfe*

REPRESENTATIVE RECORDINGS

Chattanooga Boys (Old Timey, circa 1975); *Whiter Shade of Blues* (Sony Legacy, 1993)

Shelly Lee Alley

b. Colorado County, Texas, July 6, 1894; d. June 1, 1964

Remembered chiefly today as the writer of JIMMIE RODGERS's 1931 classic "Traveling Blues," and for his 1930s western swing recordings, fiddler Shelly Lee Alley was a pop bandleader who switched to country at midcareer.

After leading a military orchestra in San Antonio during World War I, Alley spent the 1920s fronting early radio and dance orchestras in the Dallas–Fort Worth area. After he made Rodgers's acquaintance and the latter recorded "Traveling Blues" (with Alley and brother Alvin providing twin fiddles) and "Gambling Barroom Blues," Alley began to concentrate on string music. He led the original SWIFT JEWEL COWBOYS in Houston in 1933 and then took his own Cowboys to XEPN at Eagle Pass. The emergence of western swing in the mid-thirties provided Alley with an opportunity to combine his pop/jazz sensibilities with stringband instrumentation.

Alley recorded an odd mix of ballads ("My Precious Darling") and off-color blues ("She Just Wiggled Around") for Vocalion, OKEH, and BLUEBIRD, using musicians such as CLIFF BRUNER and TED DAFFAN, but never attained the level of success he felt his talent merited. He gave up performing after 1946, but wrote songs until his death, including MOON MULLICAN's "Broken Dreams" (1947) and BIFF COLLIE's and Little Marge's "Why Are You Blue?"(1950), and as late as 1955 had a single release on the Jet label. "Traveling Blues" was revived by LEFTY FRIZZELL (1951) and later MERLE HAGGARD. Alley's stepson is multi-instrumentalist western swing legend Clyde Brewer, who now leads the Houston-based Original River Road Boys.
—*Kevin Coffey*

REPRESENTATIVE RECORDINGS

Wanderers Swing (Krazy Kat, 1994), British reissue containing a 1946 recording by Alley; *Nite Spot Blues* (Krazy Kat, 1998) (British various-artists reissue containing two 1937 recordings by Alley)

Joe Allison
b. McKinney, Texas, October 3, 1924

As radio personality, publishing and recording executive, and songwriter, Joe Marion Allison made numerous contributions to country music from the late 1930s to the mid-1970s. After attending an Oklahoma junior college, he broke into radio as a country and pop announcer and manager for several Texas stations during the late 1940s, broadening his musical education during several tours with TEX RITTER. In 1949 he moved to Nashville to become an influential disc jockey on WMAK.

Through the early 1950s Allison divided his time between Nashville and Pasadena, California, where for a time he succeeded TENNESSEE ERNIE FORD on KXLA. In Nashville Allison worked TV and radio on WSM and WSIX. In 1953 he helped to found the Country Music Disc Jockeys Association (CMDJA), forerunner of CMA. Late in the decade he moved to Hollywood to co-produce *Country America*, a first-class country-pop TV show aired over the ABC network.

Early in the sixties, Allison held down two jobs: professional manager for the Hollywood-based publishing company CENTRAL SONGS, and country recording chief for LIBERTY RECORDS, where he produced early recordings by HANK COCHRAN and WILLIE NELSON, among others, and helped to revive BOB WILLS's career as well. During these same years, Allison not only began a long-running international radio show over the Armed Forces Radio Network

but also wrote and produced a series of sales presentations for CMA, which helped convince conventions of advertisers and broadcasters to program country music and thus played a vital role in country radio's expansion. For this he received CMA's Founding President's Award in 1964.

By 1967 Allison had become an independent producer and began to turn out hits such as "The Tips of My Fingers" and "Yesterday When I Was Young" with ROY CLARK and "Smoky the Bar" with HANK THOMPSON. From 1970 to 1972, Allison headed the country department for Paramount in Nashville, and signed both Tommy Overstreet and JOE STAMPLEY. From 1972 to 1974 Allison worked in a parallel capacity with CAPITOL, developing RED STEAGALL and producing *Tex Ritter: An American Legend*, the star's final LP.

Allison was also instrumental in launching both CMA and the Country Music Foundation (CMF). Allison was a 1978 inductee into the NSAI Songwriter's Hall of Fame for numbers such as the FARON YOUNG hit "Live Fast, Love Hard, Die Young" and the JIM REEVES classic "He'll Have to Go." By the early 1980s Allison retired from music, and today he is an antiques dealer.
—*John Rumble*

Amazing Rhythm Aces

Though they were one of the most innovative bands of the 1970s and early 1980s, the commercial span of the Memphis-based Amazing Rhythm Aces was relatively brief. They are best remembered for a handful of hits for ABC Records, including "Third Rate Romance" (which made both the pop and country Top Twenty in 1975), "Amazing Grace (Used to Be Her Favorite Song)" (1975), and "The End Is Not in Sight (The Cowboy Tune)" (1976). The group's distinction came from its blend of country, rock, and r&b.

Founding members included Russell Smith (b. Nashville, Tennessee, June 17, 1949) on guitar and lead vocals; Barry "Byrd" Burton on guitar and dobro; Billy Earhart III on keyboards; Jeff Davis on bass; and Butch McDade on drums. In 1976 the act won a Grammy for Best Country Performance by a Duo or Group with Vocal. Guitarist Duncan Cameron joined the band in 1977 and later became a member of SAWYER BROWN.

In 1979 the Amazing Rhythm Aces moved briefly to COLUMBIA RECORDS and the following year to WARNER BROS. RECORDS, but they had no more hits and had disbanded by 1981. Since then, Russell Smith has flourished as a Nashville songwriter and has made occasional solo outings (for CAPITOL in 1984, and for Columbia in 1989). In the 1990s he recorded and performed in the humorous country band Run C&W along with ex-EAGLE Bernie Leadon, Vince Melamed, and Jim Photoglo. In 1996 Smith, Earhart, Davis, McDade, and newcomer Danny Parks re-formed the Aces and began to record and tour. Their recent albums, released through Smith's Breaker Productions, are *Ride Again, Volume 1* (1996) and *Out of the Blue* (1997).
—*Bob Allen*

REPRESENTATIVE RECORDINGS

Too Stuffed to Jump (ABC, 1976); *The Amazing Rhythm Aces* (ABC, 1979)

American Federation of Musicians (*see* AFM)

American Federation of Television and Radio Artists (*see* AFTRA)

American Record Corporation

New York–based American Record Corporation (ARC) had a life span of ten years (1929–38). Founded in July 1929 (primarily through a merger of the Regal and Cameo label complexes), ARC, in turn, was bought by Consolidated Film Industries (CFI) in October 1930. As an autonomous subsidiary, ARC acquired the Brunswick Record Corporation (BRC) division from Warner Brothers Pictures' Brunswick *Radio* Corporation entity (December 1931) and purchased the Columbia Phonograph Company from Grigsby-Grunow (1934).

Via BRC came rights to the Vocalion and Melotone labels, in addition to the Brunswick name itself. While Vocalion and BRUNSWICK label product was marketed under BRC's banner, ARC disregarded such rights to the COLUMBIA and OKEH names, conveyed through Columbia Phonograph, and chose instead to market recordings on Melotone, Perfect, Banner (sold by W. T. Grant stores), Oriole (McCrory's), and Romeo (S. H. Kress). Each ARC release featured identical song couplings on the relevant labels. Sears Roebuck also leased ARC/BRC-derived product for its CONQUEROR label from the early to late 1930s, but Conqueror's couplings often differed from those on the ARC/BRC labels.

During its heyday, ARC/BRC was a major marketer of recorded pop, blues, and country performances, competing successfully with RCA, DECCA, and others. ART SATHERLEY and his protégé, DON LAW, headed up A&R responsibilities for country and blues product, establishing an artist slate of such stalwarts as ROY ACUFF, GENE AUTRY, Big Bill Broonzy, Bill & Cliff CARLISLE, CHUCK WAGON GANG, AL DEXTER, RED FOLEY, Blind Boy Fuller, Robert Johnson, the LIGHT CRUST DOUGHBOYS, PATSY MONTANA, the PRAIRIE RAMBLERS, and BOB WILLS, to name several.

In December 1938, CFI sold its ARC/BRC subsidiary to Columbia Broadcasting System, thus allowing CBS to acquire rights to the COLUMBIA record label name, as well as OKeh. CBS then retired the ARC labels. Due to a licensing violation, Brunswick/Vocalion reverted to WARNER BROS., in 1940, which subsequently sold those label names and catalogues to Decca the following year. —*Bob Pinson*

American Society of Composers, Authors, and Publishers (*see* ASCAP)

Americana Record Chart
established January 20, 1995

Instituted by *Gavin*, a weekly San Francisco–based music trade publication, the Americana chart gives radio exposure to country and roots-oriented performers whose music is perceived by programmers as not suited to either mainstream country stations or the Adult Album Alternative (AAA) format.

The brainchild of former *Gavin* editor Rob Bleetstein, the Americana chart first appeared on January 20, 1995, with forty-seven radio stations reporting from across the United States. The number of Americana stations—those that play at least twelve hours of alternative country music each week—has since grown to seventy-nine, two thirds of these being commercial stations, the remaining one third broadcasting as public radio affiliates. By contrast, approximately 2,600 U.S. stations play mainstream country music.

Geared more toward artists and artist development than narrowly defined, hit-seeking playlists, the music heard on Americana stations is considerably diverse. During one particular week, for example, pioneering cowpunks JASON & THE SCORCHERS appeared on the Americana chart alongside country legend JOHNNY CASH, Texas songster ROBERT EARL KEEN, and bluegrass sensation ALISON KRAUSS. But other than Krauss and Cash (whose music used to be a staple of mainstream country radio), few Americana artists have had much of a commercial impact. In contrast to mainstream country superstars such as GARTH BROOKS and ALAN JACKSON, whose albums sell in the millions, Americana artists typically register sales of 5,000 to 100,000 units.

Although *Gavin*'s Americana chart has thus far made only a modest impression on the record industry, it nonetheless has named and given expression to a grassroots movement within country music—one that is attracting a growing number of listeners. —*Bill Friskics-Warren*

Bill Anderson
b. Columbia, South Carolina, November 1, 1937

Equally successful as singer and composer, James William Anderson III has thirty-seven Top Ten *Billboard* singles as artist and has earned more than fifty BMI songwriter awards. His breathy, conversational tenor earned him the nickname "Whisperin' Bill," a sobriquet bestowed by comedian Don Bowman.

While earning a degree in journalism, Anderson worked his way through the University of Georgia as DJ (WJJC Commerce), sportswriter (*DeKalb New Era*), and performer. In 1957 Anderson recorded "City Lights" for TNT Records in San Antonio, Texas. This honky-tonk-themed song found its way to COLUMBIA'S RAY PRICE, whose May 29, 1958, recording became a #1 country hit on the *Billboard* charts.

Signed within weeks to DECCA, Anderson recorded his first session for the label in August 1958 and joined the

Bill Anderson

GRAND OLE OPRY in 1961. He wrote many of his #1 hits, including "Mama Sang a Song," "Still" (a pop Top Ten), "I Get the Fever," and "My Life." He helped discover CONNIE SMITH and wrote her #1 breakthrough, "Once a Day" (1964), plus five Top Ten follow-ups. Others scoring substantial hits with Anderson tunes include JIM REEVES, ROGER MILLER, HANK LOCKLIN, KITTY WELLS, PORTER WAGONER, and CAL SMITH. His songs breathed new life into the careers of LEFTY FRIZZELL ("Saginaw, Michigan"), CHARLIE LOUVIN ("I Don't Love You Anymore"), and JEAN SHEPARD ("Slippin' Away"). His "Tip of My Fingers" made the Top Ten for himself (1960), ROY CLARK (1963), EDDY ARNOLD (1966), and STEVE WARINER (1992). Revivals of Anderson songs worked for MICKEY GILLEY ("City Lights," #1, 1974) and CONWAY TWITTY ("I May Never Get to Heaven," #1, 1979).

Anderson's hit "Po' Folks" inspired both his band name and a restaurant chain, for which he is spokesperson. His duet partners have included JAN HOWARD ("For Loving You," #1) and Mary Lou Turner ("Sometimes," #1). In 1995 Anderson coauthored "Which Bridge to Burn" with VINCE GILL.

The tall, versatile entertainer hosted his own syndicated 1960s TV series for nine years (1965–73); was the first country star to host a 1970s network game show (ABC's *The Better Sex*); and hosted TNN's *Fandango* for six years (1983–89). He now cohosts TNN's *Backstage at the Opry* show on Saturday nights. Anderson starred in several low-budget, country-oriented films such as *Las Vegas Hillbillies* (1966); is the author of a 1989 autobiography and a 1993 memoir, the humorous *I Hope You're Living As High on the Hog As the Pig You Turned Out to Be;* and still writes a *Country Song Round-Up* magazine column.

Anderson's last hit as an artist was "I Can't Wait Any Longer" (#4, 1978). After nearly twenty-five years at Decca/MCA, he left the label in 1982 and has since recorded for Southern Tracks and Curb. —*Walt Trott*

REPRESENTATIVE RECORDINGS

Still (Decca, 1963, out of print); *For Loving You* (MCA, 1969, with Jan Howard)*; The Bill Anderson Story* (MCA, 1972, out of print); *Bill Anderson's Greatest Hits, Volume 2* (MCA, 1973)*; Best of Bill Anderson* (Curb, 1991)

John Anderson
b. Orlando, Florida, December 13, 1954

John Anderson's voice and songwriting typify the NEW TRADITIONALISM with which he was first associated in the late 1970s and early 1980s. His vocal sound and songs have a distinct and modern quality while remaining firmly rooted in the honky-tonk music styles of the 1950s—most notably that of LEFTY FRIZZELL.

After playing with a rock band in high school, John David Anderson moved to Nashville in 1971. There he worked the Nashville club scene and signed as a writer with AL GALLICO. Anderson recorded one single for the independent Ace of Hearts label in 1974, then signed with WARNER BROS. in 1977. He did not enjoy a Top Ten hit until early 1981, however, when his "1959" went to #7.

Anderson's early- to mid-eighties Warner Bros. albums contained such solid modern material as his wonderful rendition of BILLY JOE SHAVER's "I'm Just an Old Chunk of Coal" (#4, 1981) and "I Just Came Home to Count the Memories" (#7, 1981), in addition to covers of honky-tonk

John Anderson

classics such as Frizzell's "I Love You a Thousand Ways" (1983). Featuring hard-core country arrangements and highlighting Anderson's plaintive voice and distinctive phrasing, these albums were both commercially and critically successful, placing Anderson alongside contemporaries GEORGE STRAIT and RICKY SKAGGS as an effective purveyor of contemporary country music that remained traditional.

Anderson's biggest hit during this part of his career was the 1983 novelty song "Swingin'." Co-written by Anderson and Lionel Delmore, it became a chart-topping phenomenon, the CMA single of the year, and a jukebox favorite (it is currently the #30 jukebox hit of all time, according to the Amusement and Music Operators Association). That same year, Anderson won the CMA Horizon award.

Anderson's career faded during the late 1980s and early 1990s as his singles found little success on country radio and his albums began to stray more toward r&b and southern rock. A brief stint with MCA proved relatively unproductive, but in 1992 Anderson re-emerged as a force in country music with the impressive album *Seminole Wind*. Recorded for BNA ENTERTAINMENT, *Seminole Wind* spawned such hit singles as the title track (#2, 1992) and the wonderful chart-topper "Straight Tequila Night." He recorded three more albums for BNA—*Solid Ground* (1993), *Country 'til I Die* (1995), and *Paradise* (1996)—before leaving the label. A subsequent record deal with MERCURY resulted in the 1997 release *Takin' the Country Back,* hailed by some as signaling yet another career comeback for Anderson.

—*Mark Fenster*

REPRESENTATIVE RECORDINGS

Greatest Hits (Warner Bros., 1984); *Seminole Wind* (BNA, 1992)

Liz Anderson

b. Roseau, Minnesota, March 13, 1930

Best known for her songwriting, Elizabeth Jane Haaby Anderson penned, among many other tunes, the MERLE HAGGARD classics "(My Friends Are Gonna Be) Strangers" and "The Fugitive" (co-written with her husband, Casey).

Anderson played mandolin at age eight and performed duets with her brother. She married Casey at age sixteen and had daughter LYNN ANDERSON at seventeen. The Andersons moved to California in 1951, and though Liz wrote often, she didn't do so commercially until 1958. JACK MCFADDEN worked with Casey and was able to get Liz's songs to DEL REEVES and ROY DRUSKY. Her success with Haggard's "(My Friends Are Gonna Be) Strangers" (also a hit for Drusky) brought her a BMI award in 1965 and gained the attention of RCA's CHET ATKINS, who signed her to the label. The Andersons soon moved to Nashville.

Anderson's image as a sweet, domestic mother contrasted with her witty songwriting and performances. Top Ten hits included "The Game of Triangles" (1966, with BOBBY BARE and NORMA JEAN) and "Mama Spank" (1967). She sang about her husband as "Ekcedrin Headache #99," and her divorce songs "Go Now, Pay Later" and "So Much for Me, So Much for You" were unashamedly tough and spirited.

Five of Lynn Anderson's early hits were penned by Liz, and in 1968 the mother-daughter team recorded a duet, "Mother May I." In the 1980s Liz and Casey co-hosted a Nashville Network TV travel show, *Side by Side*.

—*Mary A. Bufwack*

REPRESENTATIVE RECORDINGS

Cookin' Up Hits (RCA, 1967); *Husband Hunting* (RCA, 1970)

Lynn Anderson

b. Grand Forks, North Dakota, September 26, 1947

Lynn (Rene) Anderson's 1970 hit "Rose Garden" ushered in a decade in which women country performers achieved significant crossover success and national fame.

Raised in Sacramento, California (and an accomplished equestrienne since childhood), Anderson was offered a contract with the Chart label after performing backup with her mother, the singer and songwriter LIZ ANDERSON, on recordings for RCA. Lynn had her first Top Ten record, "If I Kiss You (Will You Go Away)," in 1967, and she performed regularly on TV, on *The Lawrence Welk Show*, in 1967 and 1968.

In 1968 Lynn married Glenn Sutton, the Grammy-winning songwriter who also produced her hit records. Her 1970 COLUMBIA recording of "Rose Garden," a JOE SOUTH song, became her first country chart topper. The record also hit #3 pop and earned Anderson a Grammy award. This was followed in 1971 by recognition of Anderson as the COUNTRY MUSIC ASSOCIATION's Female Vocalist of the Year. To date, "Rose Garden" has sold 16 million copies worldwide.

Anderson's chart success was substantial, with nearly sixty chart singles and eighteen Top Ten hits. Divorced from Sutton in 1977, she continued to throw herself into her career. As the decade progressed she stretched stylistically from upbeat songs such as "What a Man My Man Is" to more poignant fare such as "I've Never Loved Anyone More."

Always photogenic, Anderson found additional popularity on TV and in her stage shows with designer costuming. In 1977 she had her own TV special on CBS, and in 1980, as she donned a skintight, white satin cowgirl outfit, she was to be Columbia's answer to DOLLY PARTON and BARBARA MANDRELL. However, Anderson married Louisiana oilman Harold Stream and retired to raise a family. She filed for divorce in 1982, citing physical abuse, and returned to performing. Custody litigation was no help to her career, though she released two quality albums in 1983 and 1988. Her 1992 *Cowboy's Sweetheart* album is a compilation demonstrating her love of western music.

—*Mary A. Bufwack*

REPRESENTATIVE RECORDINGS

Lynn Anderson's Greatest Hits (Columbia, 1972, 1992); *What She Does Best* (Mercury, 1988)

Pete Anderson

b. Detroit, Michigan, July 23, 1948

Originally a blues player, Pete Anderson became known as a country musician and producer when he and DWIGHT YOAKAM joined forces in the early eighties. Anderson says that he remembers seeing ELVIS PRESLEY on Ed Sullivan's television show and deciding "that would be a good job to have," but that he was really drawn to the playing of guitarist Scotty Moore.

Anderson started playing seriously a few years later, during the folk revival of the 1960s, beginning in a jug band. "As a teenager," he has said, "my interests passed through the folk blues, discovering who all the names on the records were, from Robert Johnson to Bobby 'Blue' Bland." Moving to Los Angeles in 1976, he produced a single for Fantasy Records by the r&b vocal group the Gliders and issued blues singles under his own name on his Dem-O label. He made a living playing in country bars around Los Angeles, and it was at one such gig, at J. R.'s in Chatsworth, that Yoakam first sat in with Anderson's band. "He was real young as a vocalist, then, but his writing was great," Anderson has remarked. The two started working together in 1981. Yoakam's *Guitars, Cadillacs, Etc., Etc.* EP was released on the tiny Oak label in 1984, and the following year Yoakam signed with WARNER BROS. RECORDS, beginning a very successful string of albums all produced by Anderson. Anderson also co-produced the two *A Town South of Bakersfield* compilations of young Los Angeles–based country performers, and subsequent full albums by George Highfill and ROSIE FLORES and an unreleased project by JIM LAUDERDALE—all, like Yoakam, alumni of those influential collections.

In addition to producing and playing on all of Yoakam's albums to date, Anderson has produced albums by Michelle Shocked, the Meat Puppets, Steve Forbert, Danny Tate, and Blue Rodeo. Anderson also produced the duet "Crying" by ROY ORBISON and K. D. LANG, which won a 1988 Grammy Award for the Best Country Vocal Collaboration. Starting his own Little Dog imprint in 1994, Anderson has released his own solo album (*Working Class*) on the label, as well as albums by rock singer Anthony Crawford and country singer JOY LYNN WHITE.

— *Todd Everett*

REPRESENTATIVE RECORDINGS

Working Class (Little Dog, 1994); *Dogs in Heaven* (Little Dog, 1997)

The Andy Griffith Show

The Andy Griffith Show, a popular comedy about life in mythical Mayberry, North Carolina, premiered on CBS-TV in 1960. A spin-off from an episode of Danny Thomas's *Make Room for Daddy* that featured Griffith as a small-town sheriff, it garnered several Emmys during its eight-year run.

The program's peaceful, southern setting made it easy for Griffith and his producers to work traditional music into the script. Griffith, a North Carolina native, had a deep-rooted love of folk music and was featured playing his D-18 Martin guitar in countless episodes. Professional musicians also guested on the show frequently. Fiddler CURLY FOX, Salty Holmes, and the California-based Country Boys all appeared in the "Folk Music Collector" episode. The Country Boys—consisting of CLARENCE AND ROLAND WHITE, Leroy Mac, and Roger Bush, who played four fictional brothers on the program—made a second appearance later that year.

Proof of the show's impact on folk and bluegrass was evident when the DILLARDS succeeded the Country Boys as the show's occasional musical guests. Exposure as the Darling Family sent sales of the Dillards' ELEKTRA album *Back Porch Bluegrass* through the roof and helped bluegrass gain a crop of young, new fans. The show signed off in 1968 but is syndicated and appears several times a day throughout the United States. —*Chris Skinker*

ARC (*see* American Record Corporation)

Arista Records
established in New York, New York, 1974

One of the first major labels to open a Nashville office during country's popularity boom in the late 1980s, Arista Records was soon also one of the most successful. A subsidiary of the New York–based Bertelsmann Music Group (BMG), Arista was founded by its current CEO, Clive Davis, in 1974. Davis named TIM DUBOIS head of Arista Nashville in 1989, and the label found immediate success with ALAN JACKSON's *Here in the Real World.*

DuBois concentrated on signing and developing new artists, and by mid-1995 Arista had received gold, platinum, or multiplatinum certifications for seventeen of the label's approximately three dozen albums. The label's roster has included, among other acts, PAM TILLIS, BROOKS & DUNN, DIAMOND RIO, STEVE WARINER, BLACKHAWK, the TRACTORS, and BR5-49. In its first five years Arista Nashville sold more than 40 million copies of thirty-four releases.

Arista launched Arista Texas, based in Austin, Texas, in 1993, with a roster that included Tejano band La Diferenzia, FREDDY FENDER, and FLACO JIMENEZ. In early 1995 Arista spun off a sister label, Career Records, with former Arista artist LEE ROY PARNELL and new signee Brett James; the Career imprint folded in October 1997. Arista also acquired Christian label Reunion Records (later sold to Zomba in 1996), which included Michael W. Smith and Kathy Troccoli on its roster. —*Brian Mansfield*

Aristocratic Pigs (*see* Fisher Hendley)

Arkie the Arkansas Woodchopper
b. near Knob Noster, Missouri, March 2, 1907; d. June 23, 1981

After previously working at KMBC in Kansas City, Luther W. Ossenbrink joined the WLS NATIONAL BARN DANCE in 1929 as Arkie the Arkansas Woodchopper. He was still performing on the show when it went off the air in 1960, and he was one of several *National Barn Dance* veterans who moved to WGN to work the *WGN Barn Dance* until that show also folded in about 1971. A fiddler, guitar player, singer, and square dance caller, he endeared himself to audiences with his ability (and sometimes inability) to maintain his composure while fellow musicians good-naturedly heckled him. His recordings of mostly cowboy songs between 1928 and 1941—for COLUMBIA, GENNETT, ARC, and OKEH—sold well but failed to establish him as a major recording artist. —*Wayne W. Daniel*

Armed Forces Radio and Television Service (*see* AFRS)

Eddy Arnold
b. Henderson, Tennessee, May 15, 1918

Perhaps more than any other artist, Eddy Arnold personifies country music's adaptation to the modern, urban world, and its transition from folk-based sounds, styles, and images to pop-influenced ones. He is also one of country music's most prolific hitmaking artists, regularly placing songs high in the charts from the 1940s through the 1960s, and scoring Top Ten hits as late as 1980.

Richard Edward Arnold came from a large farming family in Chester County, Tennessee, which accounts for

Eddy Arnold

his later stage name, the "Tennessee Plowboy." He took an interest in music early on. His cousin lent him a Sears, Roebuck Silvertone guitar, which he learned to play with help from his mother and an itinerant musician, and he listened to records by GENE AUTRY, Bing Crosby, and JIMMIE RODGERS on a wind-up Victrola. Often Arnold slipped away to some private spot to sing. He also sang at school near Jackson, Tennessee, and in church. "I discovered I could speak to people through songs in a way I never could by just talking," Arnold later reflected.

Arnold's father died when Eddy was eleven, and the next fall, creditors auctioned the family farm; thus the Arnolds became sharecroppers during the Great Depression. Arnold's singing at candy pulls, socials, and barbecues for $1 a night helped supplement the family income while providing some relief from daily toil. In these circumstances he jumped at the chance to pursue music professionally. Beginning at age seventeen, he worked on radio and in beer joints in Jackson, Tennessee, while also serving as as an undertaker's driver. Next he moved to radio work in Memphis and St. Louis, singing and performing rube comedy as well.

Arnold's prospects brightened when he joined PEE WEE KING's Golden West Cowboys as a featured singer in 1940. With King, he worked the GRAND OLE OPRY and the famous CAMEL CARAVAN tour of military bases in the United States and Central America. With his popularity rising, he struck out on his own in 1943, broadcasting on WSM daytime shows and eventually the Opry. WSM station manager HARRY STONE also worked with Chicago publisher Fred Forster to bring Arnold to the attention of RCA RECORDS, and the singer recorded his first session for the label in WSM's studios in December 1944. Meanwhile, he began to work show dates at churches and schools.

Arnold's early releases sold well, and he dominated the *Billboard* country charts for the remainder of the decade with hits such as "That's How Much I Love You" (1946), "I'll Hold You in My Heart (Till I Can Hold You in My Arms)" (1947), "Anytime" (1948), and "Bouquet of Roses" (1948). Many of his hits crossed over into the pop market, thus paving the way for later crossover acts, such as JIM REEVES and PATSY CLINE. With help from his then manager, TOM PARKER, Arnold became host of the Mutual Network's Purina-sponsored segment of the Opry and of Mutual's *Checkerboard Jamboree,* a noontime show shared with Ernest Tubb and broadcast from a Nashville theater. Recorded radio shows widened Arnold's exposure, as did the live CBS Network series *Hometown Reunion,* undertaken with the DUKE OF PADUCAH after Arnold left the Opry in 1948 following a salary dispute. In 1949 and 1950 Arnold appeared in the Columbia films *Feudin' Rhythm* and *Hoedown,* respectively. Soon his earnings from recordings and road shows—together with a lucrative publishing arrangement with HILL AND RANGE SONGS—enabled him to diversify his investments and build a fine home in Brentwood, Tennessee. He was determined never to be poor again, and he succeeded.

By the time he played the Sahara Hotel in Las Vegas in 1953—making him one of the first country stars to work the Vegas scene—Arnold was also pioneering as a country television performer. He appeared on *The Milton Berle Show* in 1949 and hosted summer replacement series in 1952 and 1953 for Perry Como and Dinah Shore, respectively. *Eddy Arnold Time,* a series made in Chicago, appeared in 1955, and *The Eddy Arnold Show,* shot in Springfield, Missouri, followed in 1956.

During country music's late-1950s slump, Arnold's record sales fell off, as did his personal appearances, and he considered retiring from music. In fact, he was on the verge of a new wave of popularity, as he traded his Tennessee Plowboy image for an uptown, sophisticated one. By the mid-1950s his somewhat plaintive singing style had already begun to mellow, and songs such as "I Really Don't Want to Know" (1954), recorded without the earlier trademark steel parts of LITTLE ROY WIGGINS, and a new version of "Cattle Call" (1955), recorded with an orchestra, anticipated the pop-oriented groove he would later establish with hits such as "What's He Doing in My World" (1965), "Make the World Go Away" (1965), and numerous other #1 records. In the mid-1960s, under the management of Gerard Purcell, Arnold began to wear tuxedos and make personal appearances with orchestras. His nightclub and TV work increased markedly, and his discs charted abroad as well, paving the way for international tours.

In 1966 Arnold was elected to the COUNTRY MUSIC HALL OF FAME, in 1967 he won the CMA's coveted Entertainer of the Year Award, and in 1984 he received the ACM's Pioneer Award. In 1970 RCA honored him for reaching the 60 million figure in lifetime record sales, a number that reportedly topped 80 million by 1985. In 1993 RCA released the album *Then and Now,* marking Arnold's fiftieth year with the label, an association interrupted only briefly from 1973 to 1975, when Arnold recorded for MGM. He continued to tour heavily during the seventies and beyond, and as of 1998 Arnold, now with CURB RECORDS, was still playing occasional show dates. —*John Rumble*

REPRESENTATIVE RECORDINGS

The Best of Eddy Arnold (RCA, 1966); *Legendary Performer* (RCA, 1983); *The Last of the Love Song Singers: Then and Now* (RCA, 1993)

Jimmy Arnold
b. Fries, Virginia, June 11, 1952; d. December 26, 1992

A tattooed mountain man whose outlaw ways often overshadowed his prodigious talent, James Edward Arnold was a bluegrass multi-instrumentalist whose most enduring legacy remains a Civil War concept album, *Southern Soul.*

The only son of a Pentecostal cotton mill hand, Arnold became a child prodigy on a Silvertone banjo ordered from a Sears catalog. At thirteen he recorded his first record, a cover of "Make Me a Pallet on the Floor," for Stark; at sixteen, his rendition of "Old Joe Clark" won first prize at the GALAX Old Time Fiddlers' Convention, held annually in southwestern Virginia near his native Fries. As a teen on the bluegrass festival circuit, Arnold fell under the spell of old-time fiddler TOMMY JARRELL, who taught him Civil War–era songs that Jarrell had learned from Confederate veterans. Stints with Cliff Waldron & the New Shades of Grass, CHARLIE MOORE & the Dixie Partners, and KEITH WHITLEY's New Tradition established Arnold's reputation as a brilliant multi-instrumentalist—and notorious boozer—of the Washington, D.C., bluegrass scene. He spent the later 1970s as a fiddler with Judy Lynn in Las Vegas; during rambling forays into Texas, New Orleans, and Mexico he added harmonica and Spanish dobro, among other instruments, to his vast musical arsenal. In the early 1980s Arnold relocated to the Washington, D. C. area, where his encyclopedic grasp of southern styles—from Appalachian reels to WESTERN SWING to New Orleans blues—

stunned audiences at shows that often included veteran fiddler Tex Logan. "Everything that's in me comes out through my music," Arnold told *Washingtonian* magazine at the time.

Arnold recorded several solo instrumental records on REBEL in the 1970s, including his banjo tour de force, *Strictly Arnold* (1974), and made frequent sideman appearances, most notably as fiddle player on master dobroist Mike Auldridge's *Eight-String Swing* (Sugar Hill, 1982). But Arnold's definitive work remains *Southern Soul* (Rebel, 1983), a Civil War concept album recorded near the Chancellorsville battlefield outside Fredericksburg, Virginia. Revealing himself a gifted singer and composer, Arnold weaved autobiographical fragments into a first-person song cycle about a Confederate soldier. The record featured original compositions, Civil War–era tunes, Charlie Moore's "Rebel Soldier," and The Band's "The Night They Drove Old Dixie Down." Using extensive studio overdubs, Arnold provided most of the instrumental back up on the critically acclaimed album, which proved a commercial dud. Bouts with the law and the bottle sabotaged Arnold's later career, which was littered with unfinished projects—including tribute sessions to idols JIMMIE RODGERS, Leadbelly, and HANK WILLIAMS—that may yet see posthumous release. Arnold was planning a comeback that included an East European tour when he died of heart failure at age forty.
—*Eddie Dean*

REPRESENTATIVE RECORDINGS

Strictly Arnold (Rebel, 1974); *Jimmy Arnold Guitar* (Rebel, 1977); *Southern Soul* (Rebel, 1983)

Charline Arthur
b. Henrietta, Texas, September 2, 1929; d. November 27, 1987

Though none of her single releases—for BULLET, RCA, Republic, or any number of smaller labels—ever made the *Billboard* charts, Charline Arthur, with her gutsy, blues-flavored vocal style and brassy stage presence, had more influence on her times than her obscurity might suggest. Among her fans were ELVIS PRESLEY and PATSY CLINE.

Born Charline Highsmith to an impoverished Pentecostal preacher and his guitar-playing wife, Arthur began her career in the mid-1940s singing at radio station KPLT in Paris, Texas. In 1948 she married bass player Jack Arthur, who became her manager. In 1949 Bullet Records released her self-penned song "I've Got the Boogie Blues." When COLONEL TOM PARKER happened to hear Arthur singing at station KERM in Kermit, Texas (where she was also a DJ), he brought her to the attention of the influential New York music publishing firm HILL & RANGE. Hill & Range signed her as a songwriter in 1952 and in turn brought Arthur to RCA Records, which signed her in January 1953. She was produced at RCA first by STEVE SHOLES and later by CHET ATKINS, with whom the tempestuous singer claimed to have had a serious personality clash. Among the country boogie and honky-tonk records she recorded for RCA were "Kiss the Baby Goodnight," "I'm Having a Party All by Myself," "Leave My Man Alone," and "Just Look, Don't Touch, He's Mine." In 1955 she was named runner-up to KITTY WELLS in *Country & Western Jamboree* magazine's annual "DJ Choice" poll.

After she left RCA in 1956, the archly temperamental singer ceased to be a presence in country music, although she did continue recording sporadically into the 1970s.

When Arthur died in rural Idaho in 1987 she'd been living for quite a few years on a modest $335-a-month disability pension.
—*Bob Allen*

REPRESENTATIVE RECORDING

Welcome to the Club (Bear Family, 1986)

Emry Arthur
b. Wayne County, Kentucky, ca. 1900; d. August 1966

As a vocalist, Emry Arthur cut more than eighty sides for Vocalion, Paramount, and DECCA from January 1928 to January 1935. More than half were solos, while on others he performed in duet with various partners and as part of his own Arthur's Sacred Singers group. Arthur played guitar and harmonica; one Vocalion release of his harmonica solos labeled him "The Jack Harmonica Player."

Arthur's music was folk-rooted in his southern Kentucky family heritage. His father, Harry B. Arthur, was a locally known bass singer, and a brother, Henry (who assisted Emry on some cuts), played fiddle and steel guitar. Another relation, William Rexroat, led the locally based Cedar Crest Singers, who also recorded in January 1929 for Vocalion.

Although born in Kentucky, Arthur lived most of his life in Indianapolis, Indiana, where he died in 1966.
—*Bob Pinson*

REPRESENTATIVE RECORDING

I Am a Man of Constant Sorrow (Old Homestead, 1987)

ASCAP
established in New York, New York, February 1914

The American Society of Composers, Authors, and Publishers—ASCAP—was founded in New York City in February 1914. Modeled upon France's SACEM, ASCAP sought to enforce the stipulation of the 1909 Copyright Act that requires payment to creators of music (composers, lyricists—which "Authors" is taken to mean—and publishers) for the "public, nondramatic performance" of their works. ASCAP collects license fees from music users (hotels, clubs, restaurants, motion picture producers, broadcasters, and now commercial users of the Internet) on behalf of its members, to whom it distributes all income above operating expenses—half to writer members and half to publisher members. ASCAP negotiates its license fees with music users, and these fees vary widely: local radio stations pay less than broadcast networks, and a tavern pays less than a big-city hotel. Distribution is based on the number and kind of music performances logged with the ASCAP survey. Performances of a song on radio stations that pay ASCAP a $25,000 per year license will be worth five times as much as performances on a station that pays $5,000 per year.

ASCAP began with 170 writers and twenty-two publishers and has grown in its eighty-plus years to a total membership in excess of 40,000. ASCAP now licenses all kinds of music but strongly emphasized classical music and Tin Pan Alley pop in its early years. Within the country field, its biggest early writers were GENE AUTRY, FRED ROSE, and BOB WILLS. ASCAP still licenses such country standards as "Blue Eyes Crying in the Rain," "Cattle Call," and "Tumbling Tumbleweeds."

ASCAP came to Nashville in the 1950s with a branch office for Alabama and Tennessee headed by Asa W. Bush in the West End building. Juanita Jones led a Nashville branch office when it was established in 1963, the same year ASCAP gave its first country music awards. By that time various forces, including competition from rival BMI, had led ASCAP to open up its membership policies and broaden its logging procedures. Plans were announced for the first ASCAP building on MUSIC ROW in October 1968, about the time Ed Shea became southern regional director for ASCAP. This building, at the corner of Seventeenth and Division opened in 1969 and was replaced by a newer, multistory complex at the same site in January 1992. Shea became national coordinator of public affairs for ASCAP in 1980–81, at which time CONNIE BRADLEY replaced him as southern regional director.

In recent years ASCAP has strengthened its country music presence with songs from such writers as RODNEY CROWELL, Rory Bourke, Bob Morrison, Randy Goodrum, DON SCHLITZ, CLINT BLACK, GARTH BROOKS, Bill Rice, PAT ALGER, DON HENRY, Jon Vezner, ALAN JACKSON, and Bob McDill.   —*Ronnie Pugh*

Clarence "Tom" Ashley
b. Bristol, Tennessee, September 29, 1895; d. June 2, 1967

A respected musician and comedian from eastern Tennessee, Clarence "Tom" Ashley recorded as a soloist and with various bands during the late 1920s and early 1930s; he successfully resumed his career during the urban folk revival of the early 1960s.

Although Ashley (born Clarence Earl McCurry) was taught banjo and traditional ballads by his aunts at an early age, his musical education largely stemmed from itinerant musicians who lodged at his mother's boardinghouse. By 1913 he was an all-around entertainer, telling jokes, singing, and playing banjo and guitar with horse-drawn medicine shows throughout the Cumberlands. Young ROY ACUFF reportedly served an apprenticeship under Ashley during one tour in the early 1920s.

Ashley first recorded for GENNETT in February 1928. Country record producers quickly recognized his abilities as a utility singer and musician. VICTOR'S RALPH PEER recruited him for four CAROLINA TARHEELS sessions in 1928–29; COLUMBIA recorded him in 1929–30 as a soloist and with Byrd Moore and His Hot Shots. During the early 1930s he recorded for the AMERICAN RECORD CORPORATION labels. Ashley basically retired from entertaining by 1943, although he occasionally worked as a comedian with the CHARLIE MONROE and STANLEY BROTHERS shows.

After meeting old-time music enthusiasts RALPH RINZLER and Eugene Earle at the 1960 Union Grove Fiddlers' Convention, Ashley realized that many young folk musicians and collectors treasured his original recordings. He resumed singing and playing banjo; for his first recording session in nearly thirty years, Ashley recruited a guitarist neighbor, DOC WATSON, to accompany him. In 1961 Ashley, Watson, Clint Howard, and Fred Price formed a band to play at colleges, clubs, and folk festivals.
—*Dave Samuelson*

REPRESENTATIVE RECORDING

The Original Folkways Recordings of Doc Watson and Clarence Ashley (Smithsonian/Folkways, 1994), 2 CDs

Ashley's Melody Makers

Ashley's Melody Makers, an Ozark stringband, were also known as Ashley's Melody Men. The group played for local occasions in the Arkansas Ozarks, with a fluid lineup that changed slightly at almost every performance. Their leader was steel guitarist Hobart Ashley (1895–1969) of Marshall, Arkansas. Other members included Anson Fuller (1907–36), fiddle; Homer Treat (b. 1910), banjo; Vern Baker (1905–73), guitar; Hugh Ashley (b. 1915), guitar; and Gerald Ashley (b. 1917). The latter two were Hobart's sons. This band had three recording sessions: the first two in Memphis in October 1929 and June 1930, the last in Dallas in February 1932. At these sessions they recorded mainly songs written by Hugh Ashley (who later wrote "One Step at a Time" for BRENDA LEE, "The Old Fiddler" for BILL MONROE, and "What Would You Do? (If Jesus Came to Your House") for PORTER WAGONER, although the band did record the traditional song "Methodist Pie." Ashley's Melody Makers are important representatives of the Ozark stringband tradition.   —*W. K. McNeil*

REPRESENTATIVE RECORDING

Echoes of the Ozarks, Volume 1 (County, 1970) reissue of 1929 sides: "Bath House Blues" and "Searcy County Rag"

Jesse Ashlock
b. Walker County, Texas, February 22, 1915; d. August 9, 1976

Jesse Thedford Ashlock was already a well-known, revered western swing fiddler by the time BOB WILLS & His Texas Playboys recorded his first songwriting efforts, in 1941. Ashlock's "Please Don't Leave Me" and "My Life's Been a Pleasure" produced a double-sided smash for Wills and established him as an important songwriter as well as musician.

In 1930, at age fifteen, Ashlock was apprenticing behind Wills at Crystal Springs, west of Fort Worth. In addition to Wills, Ashlock idolized and emulated jazz violinist Joe Venuti. In 1932 Ashlock became a member of MILTON BROWN's seminal Musical Brownies. With CECIL BROWER, Ashlock formed the first significant twin fiddle team in western swing and helped pioneer the genre. By 1935 he was in Tulsa with Wills and, from then until 1941—except for a brief stretch in Texas with BILL BOYD, ROY NEWMAN, and others—his hot fiddling was an important element in Wills's early sound.

Ashlock worked intermittently with Wills after World War II and recorded with Sam Nichols, PORKY FREEMAN, and others. He continued to score as a songwriter, penning Wills's classics "The Kind of Love I Can't Forget" (1946) and "Still Water Runs the Deepest" (1947). A capable vocalist, Ashlock also recorded under his own name for COLUMBIA in 1947. He drifted into obscurity until the western swing revival of the seventies. Based in AUSTIN at his death, he guested with youngsters such as Alvin Crow and ASLEEP AT THE WHEEL and performed with the reformed Texas Playboys.   —*Kevin Coffey*

REPRESENTATIVE RECORDINGS

Bob Wills & His Texas Playboys: The Golden Era (Columbia Historic Edition, 1987); *Bob Wills: Fiddle* (Country Music Foundation, 1987); *Hillbilly Fever, Volume One: Western Swing* (Rhino, 1995, reissue contains one 1947 recording by Ashlock)

Ernie Ashworth

b. Huntsville, Alabama, December 15, 1928

Ernest Bert Ashworth made his mark as a songwriter and GRAND OLE OPRY performer in the 1950s and early 1960s. His first radio job was at his hometown station of WBHP in 1948; he moved up to Nashville two years later. WESLEY ROSE signed him as an ACUFF-ROSE songwriter and placed him with the MGM label in 1955, where he recorded as "Billy Worth" into 1957 with no chart impact. During this time Ashworth also wrote songs recorded by JIMMY DICKENS, CARL SMITH, and JOHNNY HORTON. After a more successful stint with DECCA (1960–62) that led to three Top Twenty hits, Ashworth signed with the Acuff-Rose subsidiary label HICKORY. Between 1957 and 1964 he commuted to Nashville from Huntsville, where he worked by day at the Redstone Arsenal defense plant. In 1963 he scored his first (and only) #1 hit with JOHN D. LOUDERMILK's "Talk Back Trembling Lips," which showcased his yearning tenor to great effect. The bouncy breakthrough record earned him Most Promising Artist awards from *Cashbox* and *Billboard* in 1963. Nevertheless, he hung on to his Huntsville day job until he joined the Grand Ole Opry in March 1964. The following year he appeared in the musical comedy film *The Farmer's Other Daughter.* Though he placed records on the charts through 1970, they came with decreasing frequency and impact. He continues to perform at the Grand Ole Opry and now owns radio station WSLV in Ardmore, Tennessee.　　　—*Walt Trott*

REPRESENTATIVE RECORDING

Greatest Hits (Curb, 1991)

Asleep At The Wheel

Though known for their pivotal role in the western swing revival, Asleep At The Wheel was the brainchild of two high school rock musicians: Ray Benson Siefert (b. March 16, 1951) and Reuben "Lucky Oceans" Gosfield (b. April 22, 1951). They formed Asleep At The Wheel in about 1969, when they moved from the Philadelphia area to tiny Paw Paw, West Virginia, and played locally. The bands' musicians came and went, but a young Virginia high school graduate named Chris O'Connell and singer-songwriter Leroy Preston stayed on. The group drew inspiration from both honky-tonk music and BOB WILLS–styled western swing.

A 1972 move to Berkeley, California, brought two years of playing bars, and their meeting pianist Jim Haber, known professionally as "Floyd Domino." They signed with United Artists Records that year, but the group's debut LP wasn't successful. In 1974 they moved to AUSTIN, TEXAS, just as that city's music scene was gaining national attention. A 1974 LP for EPIC fizzled. But after they signed with CAPITOL in 1975, they had a hit single with *The Letter That Johnny Walker Read* and released their classic *Texas Gold* LP, which revealed their matured mix of country, r&b, and western swing. The band expanded with a full horn section and added big band swing to their sound, spreading western swing's appeal nationwide. In 1978 their Capitol LP cut of Count Basie's instrumental "One O'clock Jump" won them a Grammy for Best Country Instrumental Performance.

Through the 1980s, they recorded for MCA, Stony Plain, Epic, and ARISTA, where they were the first to record the future BROOKS & DUNN hit "Boot Scootin' Boogie." They next moved to LIBERTY, where they recorded their acclaimed 1993 all-star tribute to Bob Wills with various former Texas Playboys. One instrumental from that album, *Red Wing,* won them another Grammy.

With only Benson remaining from the original band, the act left Liberty (renamed Capitol Nashville) in 1995. Asleep at the Wheel also celebrated its twenty-fifth anniversary that year with an AUSTIN CITY LIMITS special, reuniting many former band members. In addition, the group won a Grammy, Best Country Instrumental Performance, for a song off their album *The Wheel Keeps on Rollin':* "Hightower," a song that features BÉLA FLECK, JOHNNY GIMBLE, and others.

The group recently signed with a new Sony imprint called Lucky Dog and released a live album called *Back to the Future Now: Live from Arizona Charlie's, Las Vegas* (1997).　　　—*Rich Kienzle*

REPRESENTATIVE RECORDINGS

Texas Gold (Capitol, 1975); *A Tribute to the Music of Bob Wills and His Texas Playboys* (Liberty, 1993); *Comin' Right At Ya* (United Artists, 1973); *Collision Course* (Capitol, 1978); *Still Swingin'* (Liberty, 1993), 3 CDs

Association of Country Entertainers (*see* ACE)

Asylum Records

established 1970; Nashville branch established 1992

Asylum Records began under the wing of ATLANTIC in 1970 and entered the country marketplace in 1992 with an unusually strong commitment to artistic vision. With record producer KYLE LEHNING heading the operation in its early years, the label signed such critically acclaimed acts as GUY CLARK and EMMYLOU HARRIS as well as soon-to-be acclaimed artists such as BOB WOODRUFF.

Emphasis on the artist had been Asylum's hallmark especially since 1971, when entertainment mogul David Geffen—then still in his twenties—formed the label. Asylum quickly became a company of note with a roster that included the EAGLES, Jackson Browne, and Joni Mitchell, as well as LINDA RONSTADT, who scored numerous country/pop crossover hits with Asylum during the 1970s.

An affiliate of ELEKTRA RECORDS, Asylum became Elektra's first country outlet in nearly a decade when the Nashville office opened in 1992. The label's penchant for art came with a price, however, as it earned only one Top Ten single—BROTHER PHELPS' 1993 release "Let Go"—during its first three years in business. Asylum's commercial fortunes later improved with the success of BRYAN WHITE and KEVIN SHARP, while MANDY BARNETT's 1996 debut found favor with critics. Also in 1996, Joe Mansfield came on board as Asylum's co-president (with Kyle Lehning) and CEO. Lehning and Mansfield left Asylum in 1998; their successor, Evelyn Shriver, became the first female president of a major Music Row label.　　—*Tom Roland*

Bob Atcher

b. Hardin County, Kentucky, May 11, 1914; d. October 31, 1993

Robert Owen Atcher is best remembered through his hit recordings of the early 1940s and later appearances on Chicago's WLS *NATIONAL BARN DANCE.* Adept at folk, country, and cowboy material, he typically prefaced each song with a descriptive story while softly strumming open chords on his guitar.

Early successes on Louisville radio brought Atcher to Chicago in 1932; he remained there for most of his career. In 1939 he began recording for Vocalion. His first hit was a cover of "I'm Thinking Tonight of My Blue Eyes," punctuated by sobs and screams; other successes included "Cool Water" and "You Are My Sunshine." Many of Atcher's early records were duets with Loeta Applegate, who was billed as "Bonnie Blue Eyes."

In 1942 Atcher shared billing with popular bandleader Ben Bernie on CBS Radio's *Wrigley Spearmint Show.* He later hosted many Chicago-based network radio shows of his own, and in 1949 he joined the *National Barn Dance.* For years he remained one of Chicago's busiest performers. He eventually cut back his performing schedule, although he remained a *Barn Dance* regular through the show's 1960–71 tenure on WGN. From 1959 to 1975 he served as mayor of Schaumburg, Illinois.

Atcher's brother Randy (b. December 7, 1918; Tip Top, Kentucky) worked with Bob before World War II, then later developed a strong regional following of his own around Louisville.   —*Dave Samuelson*

Chet Atkins
b. Luttrell, Tennessee, June 20, 1924

No single country instrumentalist has achieved the notoriety and respect that Chester Burton Atkins has. He has influenced country, rock, and jazz musicians—from JERRY REED to George Harrison, Duane Eddy, and Earl Klugh—for nearly half a century. Many hit records he produced during his days at RCA are now classics.

Atkins grew up in the hills near a tiny, remote eastern Tennessee town called Luttrell. James Atkins, his father, was an itinerant music teacher who had previously been married. His wife Ida, Chester's mother, sang and played piano. After the Atkinses divorced, Ida Atkins remarried, in 1932, and Chester began to learn guitar and fiddle, often playing with his brother and sister and their stepfather, Willie Strevel. A 1936 asthma attack forced Chester to relocate to the improved climate at his father's Georgia farm, where, on one night in the late 1930s, he first heard MERLE TRAVIS playing guitar over WLW in Cincinnati. Travis's thumb-and-finger-picking style fascinated Atkins, who created his own thumb-and-two-finger variation.

After attending high school in Georgia, Atkins landed a job at WNOX in Knoxville, fiddling for the team of singer BILL CARLISLE and comic ARCHIE CAMPBELL. WNOX executive Lowell Blanchard heard Chester's guitar playing and began featuring him on the *MIDDAY MERRY-GO-ROUND,* the station's popular daily barn dance show. Atkins broadened his repertoire though listening sessions in the station's music library. In 1945 he briefly joined WLW in Cincinnati; then in early 1946 he worked with JOHNNIE & JACK in Raleigh, North Carolina, before moving to Chicago, where RED FOLEY, leaving the WLS *NATIONAL BARN DANCE* to host the GRAND OLE OPRY's *Prince Albert Show,* hired Atkins and took him to Nashville. There he made his first solo recording, "Guitar Blues," for the local BULLET label.

Moving on to KWTO in Springfield, Missouri, Atkins received his nickname "Chet" from station official SI SIMAN. Other officials there, believing that his style was too polished for "hillbilly" music, eventually fired him. Meanwhile, however, Siman tried to interest record companies in Atkins, and RCA Victor's STEVE SHOLES signed him as a singer and guitarist in 1947. In about 1948 Chet returned to WNOX, working first with HOMER & JETHRO and then joining Maybelle and the CARTER SISTERS as lead guitarist. They subsequently worked at KWTO before relocating to Nashville to join the Opry in 1950.

With FRED ROSE's help, Chet became one of Nashville's early "A-Team" of session musicians, recording with everyone from WADE RAY to HANK WILLIAMS and WEBB PIERCE. He also appeared on the Opry as a solo act. His first chart hit, a cover of the pop hit "Mister Sandman," came in 1955, followed by a hit guitar duet with HANK SNOW on "Silver Bell."

Through the 1950s, Atkins's relationship with STEVE SHOLES evolved into that of trusted protégé. Initially Chet organized sessions, and if Sholes, who was based in New York, couldn't come to Nashville, Atkins produced the records himself. In 1955 Sholes made him manager of RCA's new Nashville studio, which eventually led to an RCA vice-presidential position.

After rock & roll set back country record sales, Atkins's production skills came to the foreground. Intent on making country records appeal to pop and country audiences, he—along with OWEN BRADLEY at DECCA, DON LAW at COLUMBIA, and KEN NELSON at CAPITOL—began to produce singers backed by neutral rhythm sections and to replace steel guitars and fiddles with vocal choruses, a style later known as the NASHVILLE SOUND. Atkins transformed hard-country RCA artists JIM REEVES and DON GIBSON by producing hits for both that successfully crossed over into the pop market. Among the many acts he produced successfully were EDDY ARNOLD, SKEETER DAVIS, BOBBY BARE, and FLOYD CRAMER. In 1965 Atkins took a major step forward by signing African-American country singer CHARLEY PRIDE to RCA. In that same year Atkins enjoyed his own biggest hit single with "Yakety Axe," an adaptation of Nashville studio musician BOOTS RANDOLPH's hit "Yakety Sax."

Atkins produced a constant stream of solo RCA albums during these years. As he hired additional producers at RCA, he cut back his own production work to focus on

Chet Atkins

recording, and Atkins made albums with other fine RCA guitarists: HANK SNOW, Jerry Reed, Merle Travis, and LES PAUL. In 1973 Atkins was elected to the COUNTRY MUSIC HALL OF FAME, and from 1967 to 1988 he won the CMA's Instrumentalist of the Year eleven times. In 1982 he relinquished his RCA executive role and left RCA to record for COLUMBIA in 1983. Frequent collaborations with younger players, such as British rock guitarist Mark Knopfler, reflected his desire to remain contemporary. In 1993 Atkins received a Lifetime Achievement Award from the National Academy of Recording Arts and Sciences (NARAS), placing him among such musical greats as Louis Armstrong, Ray Charles, Leonard Bernstein, and Paul McCartney. In 1997 Atkins won a Grammy award, Country Instrumental Performance, for the 1996 song "Jam Man."

—*Rich Kienzle*

REPRESENTATIVE RECORDINGS

The Essential Chet Atkins (RCA, 1996); *Galloping Guitar* (Bear Family, 1993) 4 CDs; *Chester and Lester* (with Les Paul) (RCA, 1976); *A Session with Chet Atkins* (RCA, 1954); *Alone* (RCA, 1973)

Atlantic Records
established in New York, New York, 1947

Atlantic Records began primarily as a jazz and r&b label; by the mid-1990s its Nashville branch epitomized the country music mainstream. TRACY LAWRENCE, NEAL MCCOY, and JOHN MICHAEL MONTGOMERY comprised the label's core, each with albums selling more than 1 million copies. The Atlantic group CONFEDERATE RAILROAD also sold over 1 million.

Founded by Herb Abramson and Ahmet Ertegun, who were joined by Jerry Wexler in 1953, Atlantic occasionally flirted with country music, releasing singles by DOTTIE WEST and Dale Hawkins in 1962, for instance. The label first operated a Nashville office from 1972 to 1974 under the direction of Rick Sanjek; its roster included WILLIE NELSON, JOHN PRINE, Doug Sahm, and HENSON CARGILL. Prompted by BILLY JOE ROYAL's success on the Atlantic America subsidiary between 1985 and 1988, Atlantic reopened Nashville offices in 1989 with RICK BLACKBURN and Nelson Larkin at the helm; Blackburn later became president of the division. The initial roster also included Robin Lee and Girls Next Door.

Under Blackburn, Atlantic succeeded with a combination of marketing savvy and a small, radio-friendly roster. Lawrence and McCoy both joined in 1991, Montgomery and Confederate Railroad in 1992. Mila Mason's debut CD appeared on Atlantic in 1996. —*Brian Mansfield*

Austin, Texas

Ever since the early 1970s, when WILLIE NELSON and others made Austin, Texas, a well-known music locale, the city's musical history has been a healthy reminder that country is not synonymous with Nashville. Long before it attained national notoriety as a country music center, Austin had several country music clubs such as the Broken Spoke, Split Rail, and Skyline Club (where both HANK WILLIAMS and JOHNNY HORTON gave "last" performances). Threadgill's Bar, housed in a converted filling station on the edge of town in North Austin, was a bridge between the country music of the fifties and the eclectic, youth-oriented country-rock music of the seventies. Kenneth Threadgill, the proprietor, was a JIMMIE RODGERS-style yodeler who encouraged other people to sing. In the early sixties Threadgill's became a microcosm of the later country music scene when spillovers from the University of Texas folk music club (including Janis Joplin) began mixing their personas and repertoires with the older styles of country music that had long been present there.

In the late sixties the Vulcan Gas Company club became a meeting place for hippies and college students and such local rock bands as the Thirteenth Floor Elevators, Shiva's Headband, and others. When the Vulcan folded, the Armadillo World Headquarters, housed in a vacant armory building, replaced it in 1970 as the center of countercultural music activity. Musicians of varying stripes were already coming to Austin, and during the early 1970s remnants of the rock music scene (and a few ex-folkies such as JERRY JEFF WALKER) began to bring together the disparate strains of country, bluegrass, urban folk, blues, and rock music. Two groups, Greezy Wheels and Freda & the Firedogs (the latter headed by pianist and blues singer Marcia Ball), were pioneers in this attempt at musical fusion, but they were soon joined by Doug Sahm, MICHAEL MARTIN MURPHEY, B. W. Stevenson, Steve Fromholz, WILLIS ALAN RAMSEY, and others. The Armadillo World Headquarters became the central locus of the emerging fusion of rock and country music, but after February 1973, the Soap Creek Saloon also became an active arena for musicians. The performers began adopting cowboy names and dress in order to establish identities that seemed consonant with the Texas Hill Country. Jim Franklin, who had already been painting armadillo posters for Shiva's Headband, and Kerry Awn, who created the Soap Creek calendars, contributed greatly to the imagery that surrounded Austin music with their depictions of longhorn steers, cactus, sagebrush, armadillos, and longneck beers.

As the Austin musical mix gained notoriety, observers were hard-pressed to find a name that sufficiently encompassed the emerging musical culture. "Redneck rock" and "cosmic cowboy music" were terms that were sometimes affixed to the city's varied styles. The most often used term, "progressive country," was introduced in 1973 by Austin radio station KOKE-FM to describe the wide-ranging mixture of records played by its disc jockeys. A stockbroker and ardent music fan, Townsend Miller was also a strong contributor to the idea of Austin as a "musical colony." He began touting the city's music in a local newspaper column and in music magazines. A thriving music scene already existed, then, when Willie Nelson moved to the city in late 1971. He, Jerry Jeff Walker, Marcia Ball, ASLEEP AT THE WHEEL, Alvin Crow, KINKY FRIEDMAN, Steve Fromholz, and frequent visitor WAYLON JENNINGS made the laid-back Austin scene famous throughout the nation. Nelson's giant outdoor festivals, held first at nearby Dripping Springs and later at other Texas locations, lent even greater notoriety to the Austin musical culture while also bringing together musicians as diverse as LEON RUSSELL and ROY ACUFF.

Since 1987 Austin has hosted the annual South by Southwest Music and Media Conference, one of the nation's preeminent music industry gatherings. Nevertheless, Austin's prominence as a country music capital has declined since the 1980s, partly because the city never built a recording complex that could augment its numerous live performance venues. With the notable exceptions of Willie Nelson and Jerry Jeff Walker, very few of the Austin musicians even had recording contracts during the highly publicized events of the seventies. Music, however, is still extremely popular in Austin, and some notable country music personalities, such as Walker, Asleep at the Wheel, the Austin Lounge Lizards, JUNIOR BROWN, JIMMIE DALE GILMORE, and TISH HINOJOSA still make the city their chief base of operations. —*Bill C. Malone*

Austin City Limits
established in Austin, Texas, summer 1975; first aired fall 1976

Austin City Limits is a long-running, influential music series produced for public television in Austin, Texas, and shot at the KLRU-TV studio on the University of Texas campus. The series was launched to help expose Austin's "cosmic cowboy" progressive country music to the world at large. It was developed by Bill Arhos, then program director for KLRU-TV (now general manager for the public station and executive producer of *Austin City Limits*). After a pilot featuring WILLIE NELSON, the first program paired ASLEEP AT THE WHEEL with a reunion of the Texas Playboys, BOB WILLS's famous band.

The series has since featured a wide range of Austin artistry extending well beyond country, along with nationally known performers in the country-folk, roots-music, and singer-songwriter veins. Among the most significant artists to have appeared on the program are RAY CHARLES, ROY ORBISON, B. B. King, EMMYLOU HARRIS, and NEIL YOUNG. Among the artists more commonly associated with Austin, NANCI GRIFFITH, JIMMIE DALE GILMORE, and Stevie Ray Vaughan were featured on the program well before they had achieved national notoriety.

"We try to come up with a mix or balance of original music that reflects a variety of styles that are uniquely American," explained Terry Lickona, who has been booking and producing the program since 1978.

The program has long been a favorite with artists, both for the concert format that keeps the focus on music and for the enthusiasm of the Austin audience. GARTH BROOKS, ALAN JACKSON, and VINCE GILL are among the many musicians who were regular viewers of the series long before they were invited to appear on it. During his years on the Texas club circuit, Lyle Lovett was such a regular in the audience that when he finally appeared as a performer, the program (as an insider joke) inserted a shot of him watching from the crowd.

Although *Austin City Limits* was once among the primary vehicles of television exposure for country artists, the boom in the music's popularity and the proliferation of cable TV programming has meant more competition among TV shows for top country talent. The series has responded by featuring a wider variety of performers such as ROBBIE FULKS, the Indigo Girls, and HAL KETCHUM. Country music continues to be an essential element in its programming, but in diminished concentration. —*Don McLeese*

Gene Autry
b. Tioga, Texas, September 29, 1907

While he was unquestionably the best-selling c&w artist from the early days of the Depression through the close of World War II, Gene Autry was also much more. His status as a top box-office attraction in motion pictures brought his music to the attention of a vast audience otherwise unfamiliar with country music. In addition, his success as a

Gene Autry

SINGING COWBOY launched an entire genre of movies and paved the way for successful rivals such as ROY ROGERS and TEX RITTER.

Orvon Gene Autry, grandson of a Baptist minister, was born in a farmhouse near Tioga to Delbert and Elnora Autry. He first performed as a boy soprano in his grandfather's church choir. Subsequently he mastered a $12 Sears mail-order guitar, which he used to accompany his singing at local events. When the Autrys moved to Oklahoma, young Gene took a job as relief telegrapher for the St. Louis & Frisco railroad, where he eventually met Jimmy Long, an older fellow railroader who also made music on the side and had ideas about cutting records. Inspired by Long (and possibly by a chance, encouraging encounter with humorist Will Rogers), nineteen-year-old Autry took a leave of absence from his job to make the rounds of New York City record companies, auditioning with his versions of the current Gene Austin and Al Jolson hits.

Befriended by fellow Oklahomans Johnny and FRANKIE MARVIN, then pop singers recording in New York, Gene made test records for EDISON and VICTOR before being urged to return home and gain experience as a performer. He spent two years (1928–29) on Tulsa's KVOO, billed as "Oklahoma's Yodeling Cowboy" and singing JIMMIE RODGERS's then-current hits before returning to New York in October 1929, just days before the market crashed. He began recording with a vengeance, cutting masters for five different companies, each of which issued records on several labels for chain-store distribution. For two years he recorded prolifically, covering Rodgers's hits and performing other songs in that style. Ironically, stardom came the first time he broke away from the Rodgers mold, recording "That Silver-Haired Daddy of Mine" as a duet with Jimmy Long for the ARC family of labels and its A&R man ART SATHERLEY. Lilting and sentimental in the tradition of the turn-of-the-century parlor ballad, the song became a major hit and propelled Autry to a radio career on Chicago's WLS, beginning with his first morning broadcast on December 1, 1931, on his own show *Conqueror Record Time.* Urged by Satherley, Autry focused on western songs and attire, and recorded his first western songs in 1933. In addition, WLS announcer Anne Williams created skillful word-pictures building Autry's cowboy image, which was reinforced by his hit recordings of "The Last Roundup" and "Cowboy's Heaven."

In the summer of 1934 Gene and his wife, Ina (Jimmy Long's niece), and his friend Lester "SMILEY" BURNETTE, musician-composer-comedian with the Autry radio troupe, drove to California, where the singing cowboy was to make a guest appearance in the Republic Pictures western movie *In Old Santa Fe.* His own series of films began the following year (with the science fiction serial *The Phantom Empire*), and by 1937 exhibitors voted Autry the #1 box-office attraction in westerns, a position he would retain for years to come.

Hit records, such as "Tumbling Tumbleweeds," "Mexicali Rose," "Take Me Back to My Boots and Saddle," "Gold Mine in the Sky," "South of the Border (Down Mexico Way)," "Back in the Saddle Again," and "Be Honest With Me," abounded. His smooth, relaxed baritone voice extended his appeal to devotees of mainstream pop music, while the down-home warmth of his delivery assured the country audience he never ceased to be one of them. The virtual antithesis of today's vocalists, he adhered to the melody line with a total absence of vocal gymnastics or bluesy embellishments, with his clear, emotionless delivery evoking both sincerity and serenity.

His screen presence, as gentle and reassuring as his singing style, offered comfort and inspiration to a Depression-weary audience. Invariably cast as himself—that is, Gene Autry—a good-natured and unassuming country singer, he was no superhero, but rather a guileless young man who triumphed over all odds by virtue of his innate goodness. Charismatic and handsome astride his horse Champion, Autry filled his movies with humor (Smiley Burnette was his usual comic sidekick), music, and a minimum of gunplay. In 1940 he was voted the fourth most popular Hollywood star, outpolling Tyrone Power and James Cagney.

Wrigley sponsored the Autry CBS radio series *Melody Ranch* from 1940 through 1956, interrupted only during Autry's service in the Army Air Corps during World War II (he joined voluntarily on July 26, 1942, during a *Melody Ranch* broadcast and served as a transport plane pilot in the Pacific Theater for three years). The postwar years brought more million-selling records, including "Here Comes Santa Claus" (1947), "Rudolph, the Red-Nosed Reindeer" (1949), and "Peter Cottontail" and "Frosty the Snow Man" (both 1950). Autry produced his own feature films from 1947 through 1953 and, shrewdly judging the importance of the new medium (television), became the first major star to appear in his own filmed TV series. *The Gene Autry Show,* produced by Autry's Flying A Produc-

tions, was sponsored on CBS-TV by Wrigley from July 23, 1950, through August 7, 1956.

Fulfilling a lifelong fantasy, Autry became owner of the Los Angeles (now California) Angels baseball team in December 1960. Although he continued to perform sporadically during the next five years, he left the arena before country singers' personal appearances were termed "concerts" and before it became commonplace to attribute artistic genius to country or rock artists. Lavish praise for his talent and his impact on our popular culture has been slow in coming, but he continues to be idolized by generations, including many younger country singers who patterned their lives after his and who cheered his 1969 induction into the COUNTRY MUSIC HALL OF FAME.

—*Jonathan Guyot Smith*

REPRESENTATIVE RECORDINGS

Blues Singer, 1929–1931: "Booger Rooger Saturday Nite!" (Columbia/Legacy, 1996); *Essential Gene Autry, 1933–1946* (Columbia/Legacy, 1992); *The Christmas Cowboy* (LaserLight, 1993); *Back in the Saddle Again* (Encore, 1977); *22 Legendary Hits* (Sony/Time Warner, 1996)

Hoyt Axton
b. Duncan, Oklahoma, March 25, 1938

Singer-songwriter and movie actor Hoyt Wayne Axton came by his talent and ambition quite naturally. His mother, Mae Boren Axton (b. Bardwell, Texas, September 14, 1914; d. April 9, 1997) wrote the early ELVIS PRESLEY hit "Heartbreak Hotel" as well as tunes recorded by PATSY CLINE, HANK SNOW, CONWAY TWITTY, and others. For years Mae Axton was a fixture in Nashville's music community as a TV and radio personality, public relations person, journalist, and friend to the stars.

Hoyt Axton began his career as a country-flavored folksinger in the Southern California coffeehouse scene. He made his first significant mark as a songwriter with "Greenback Dollar," an early 1960s hit for the Kingston Trio that has since become a modern folk standard (several other, unrelated folk- and country songs have shared this title). Another Axton original, "The Pusher," was a major hit for the rock group Steppenwolf and was prominently featured in the soundtrack of the 1969 film *Easy Rider.*

Axton recorded for several small record labels beginning in 1961 but had no significant chart action until the mid-1970s. His highest entry in the country charts came with his 1974 Top Ten novelty hit "Boney Fingers" on A&M Records

Axton flourished in the early 1970s, recording for A&M, MCA, and later his own label, Jeremiah. His songs "Joy to the World" and "Never Been to Spain" were big pop hits for the rock group Three Dog Night. Axton also produced country-rockers Commander Cody & The Lost Planet Airmen's album *Tales from the Ozone.* He signed briefly with ELEKTRA in the early eighties but had scant chart action. Through the years Axton has also appeared in a number of feature films, most notably *The Black Stallion* (1979) and *Gremlins* (1984). —*Bob Allen*

REPRESENTATIVE RECORDINGS

Joy to the World (Capitol, 1971); *Snowblind Friend* (MCA, 1977)

B·B·B·B·   ·B·B·B·B

The Bailes Brothers

Kyle O. Bailes b. Kanawha County, West Virginia, May 7, 1915; d. March 3, 1996

John Jacob Bailes b. Kanawha County, West Virginia, June 24, 1918; d. December 21, 1989

Walter Butler Bailes b. Kanawha County, West Virginia, January 17, 1920

Homer Abraham Bailes Jr. b. Kanawha County, West Virginia, May 8, 1922

The Bailes Brothers carried the harmony duet tradition of the thirties into the next two decades. Though there were four brothers, they usually worked in combinations of two. Reared in poverty by a proud, determined, widowed mother on the outskirts of Charleston, West Virginia, various brothers struggled to make it on radio stations in their home state but had little success until John and Walter worked at WSAZ-Huntington in 1942. Two years later ROY ACUFF helped them secure a spot on the GRAND OLE OPRY and a contract with COLUMBIA RECORDS. Their original songs, such as "Dust on the Bible" and "I Want to Be Loved," also helped further their popularity.

At the end of 1946 the brothers went to KWKH in Shreveport, where they helped initiate the *LOUISIANA HAYRIDE* and gave support to the fledgling career of HANK WILLIAMS. By this time brother Homer had joined on fiddle and Kyle on bass. When Walter joined the ministry in 1947, Homer replaced him in the duo. The act broke up at the end of 1949, but John and Walter reformed as a gospel duo in 1953 and recorded for King. In later years various combinations of the brothers got together for occasional recordings and appearances, especially Kyle and Walter, the latter releasing material on his Loyal and White Dove labels. At different times, Homer, John, and Walter also did solo sessions. —*Ivan M. Tribe*

REPRESENTATIVE RECORDINGS

The Bailes Brothers (Johnnie & Homer): Early Radio Volumes I & II (Old Homestead, 1975, 1976); *The Bailes Brothers (Johnnie & Walter): Early Radio Favorites* (Old Homestead, 1977)

DeFord Bailey

b. Smith County, Tennessee, December 14, 1899; d. July 2, 1982

A pioneer member of the GRAND OLE OPRY and the program's first black star, DeFord Bailey was one of the Opry's most popular early performers. GEORGE D. HAY dubbed him the "Harmonica Wizard" and reported that Bailey's "Pan American Blues"—a country blues rendition of a fast-moving locomotive, the Pan American Express—inspired the actual naming of the Opry.

A harmonica virtuoso, Bailey recorded in 1927 for CO-LUMBIA (unissued) and BRUNSWICK, and in 1928 for VICTOR, in the first recording sessions that ever took place in Nashville. There, as almost always, he used the simple Hohner Marine Band harmonica. His "harp" classics included "Ice Water Blues," "Old Hen Cackle," "Fox Chase," "Lost John," "Muscle Shoals Blues," "Up Country Blues," "Evening Prayer Blues," and his train tunes. When he played the guitar and banjo, he did so in a unique left-handed, upside-down style.

The grandson of a skilled Smith County fiddler, Bailey moved to Nashville in 1918. His introduction to radio broadcasting came in 1925 on WDAD, Nashville's pioneer station. A few weeks later, with strong encouragement from harmonicist DR. HUMPHREY BATE, he came to WSM ra-

DeFord Bailey

dio, and except for a brief period in 1928–29 on WNOX in Knoxville, he was an Opry regular for nearly fifteen years.

One evening in 1927, following an NBC radio network broadcast of classical music over WSM, Hay introduced a live performance by Bailey by saying that for the past hour listeners had been hearing "grand opera," but now they would be treated to something more down-home, a "Grand Ole Opry." The term stuck, and WSM's *Barn Dance* had a new name.

Bailey performed virtually every Saturday night while frequently going out during the week on road shows throughout the South and Midwest with UNCLE DAVE MACON, the DELMORE BROTHERS, BILL MONROE, ROY ACUFF, and other WSM artists. Bailey was always well received by the white audiences they entertained, but in this heyday of Jim Crow, Bailey faced real hardships in finding accommodations and meals.

Bailey was able to adjust to and deal with the indignities of segregation, but his firing by WSM in 1941 was more devastating to him; although still extremely popular, he had become victim of a BMI-ASCAP performance licensing conflict that disallowed his playing his favorite tunes on the air. Having previously shined shoes, operated a barbecue stand, and rented out rooms in his home for extra money, he now turned to these activities to make a living for himself, his wife, and their three children. He never stopped playing his harp, but rarely performed publicly for the next forty years. When he agreed to perform on the Opry in February 1974, it became the occasion for the first annual Old Timers Show.   —*David C. Morton*

Razzy Bailey
b. Five Points, Alabama, February 14, 1939

The musical style that took Rasie Michael Bailey to the top of the charts in the early 1980s reflects what he heard while growing up on his family's southern farm. The singings held in Bailey's house were country, but he also became fascinated with the rhythm & blues of the black farmhands. The genres would later merge in Bailey's singing, guitar playing, and songwriting.

Bailey played with a country band after graduating from high school but later worked in sales during a musical dry spell. He formed a pop trio called Daily Bread in 1958 and recorded for MGM RECORDS in the early 1970s. In 1976 Bailey's song "9,999,999 Tears" provided a career jolt when DICKEY LEE took it to #3 on the country charts. After efforts on small labels, Bailey signed as an artist with RCA RECORDS, and his first RCA release, "What Time Do You Have to Be Back to Heaven," reached the Top Ten in 1978. That ignited an eleven-year chart run that peaked in 1980–81 with five #1 hits, including "Loving Up a Storm" and "She Left Love All Over Me." Bailey later recorded for MCA and SOA Records.   —*Gerry Wood*

REPRESENTATIVE RECORDING
Greatest Hits (RCA, 1983)

Baillie & the Boys
Kathie Baillie b. Morristown, New Jersey, February 20, 1951
Michael Bonagura b. Newark, New Jersey, March 26, 1953

Kathie Baillie was among a group of women who fronted country-rock bands in the 1980s. Her yearning soprano voice led Baillie & the Boys into the country Top Ten in 1987 with "Oh Heart," co-written with DON SCHLITZ. The group scored a total of seven Top Ten records between 1987 and 1991.

Baillie & the Boys began as a trio consisting of Baillie, Michael Bonagura, and Alan LeBoeuf. Bonagura and LeBoeuf had been in a group together in 1968, and when Bonagura met Baillie, their voices blended well. The trio got its start in 1973 in New York City, providing studio backup and singing commercials.

Baillie and Bonagura married in 1977 and decided to try for success in Nashville in 1980. LeBoeuf joined them later. Many years of work followed, in which Bonagura waited tables and Baillie was an aerobics instructor and receptionist. Each had songwriting contracts, and they found opportunities to sing back up on records by ANNE MURRAY, VINCE GILL, and RANDY TRAVIS. Their efforts resulted in an RCA recording contract in 1986.

After LeBoeuf left in 1988, Baillie and Bonagura were billed as a husband-wife duo, with both writing more extensively. *Lovin' Every Minute*—a 1996 recording project with Roger McVay—is on Intersound.   —*Mary A. Bufwack*

REPRESENTATIVE RECORDING
The Best of Baillie and the Boys (RCA, 1991)

Kenny Baker
b. Jenkins, Kentucky, June 26, 1926

For nearly twenty years, bluegrass patriarch BILL MONROE introduced sideman Kenneth Baker as "the greatest fiddler in bluegrass music." Monroe wasn't exaggerating simply because Baker worked for him. Few musicians have had the impact on bluegrass Baker has had. His jazzy, swinglike arrangements of traditional numbers, smooth long-bow technique, and ability to write freshly original tunes have made him a favorite on the bluegrass circuit for four decades.

A third-generation fiddler from the coal mining town of Jenkins, Kentucky, Baker picked up the family fiddle at about age eight but soon switched over to guitar. Baker's father, Thaddeus, reportedly did not think his son capable of doing justice to old-time fiddle tunes such as "Grey Eagle" and "Lost John."

After dropping out of high school while in his teens, Baker enlisted in the navy during World War II and served in the Pacific Theater. After his discharge, Baker returned to Jenkins and took a day job with Consolidated Coal Company. He was playing local dances when DON GIBSON hired him in 1953. Bill Monroe first saw Baker while working with Gibson on Knoxville's *Tennessee Barn Dance* and promptly offered Baker a job.

In 1956 Baker joined Monroe's band. Two years later he and Bobby Hicks twin-fiddled on the Monroe instrumentals "Scotland" and "Panhandle Country." Baker also cut a handful of sides with Austin Wood for the Sure label.

With the responsibilities of raising a family, Baker left the band and returned to the mines, where income was steady. He rejoined Monroe's band for less than a year, in 1962–63—just long enough to bring singer DEL MCCOURY and banjo player BILL KEITH into the fold. Baker left in about June 1963 and rejoined for the final time in 1967.

That same year Baker recorded the album *High Country* with Joe Greene for COUNTY RECORDS. Baker's first solo album, *Portrait of a Bluegrass Fiddler*, was released on County in 1968. His most popular recording is probably his tribute album to his boss, *Kenny Baker Plays Bill Monroe* (County, 1976).

Baker left Monroe in 1985 and joined forces with dobro player JOSH GRAVES. He toured and recorded with Graves, banjo player Eddie Adcock, and mandolinist Jesse McReynolds as The Masters. Still touring and recording with Graves, Baker spends his spare time working on his farm just outside of Nashville. —*Chris Skinker*

REPRESENTATIVE RECORDINGS

Portrait of a Bluegrass Fiddler (County, 1968); *Kenny Baker Plays Bill Monroe* (County, 1976)

Bakersfield

Bakersfield, in California's Kern County, spawned and exported so much country music from the 1940s through the 1970s that, by the late 1960s, some observers called it "Nashville West." (BUCK OWENS countered: "We call Nashville Bakersfield East.") The seeds for this phenomenon were sown by the Depression-era tide of migrants from Oklahoma, Texas, and Arkansas into the agriculture- and oil-rich San Joaquin Valley (as author Nicholas Dawidoff has noted, today Kern County grows more crops than all but two of America's counties and produces more oil than all but three of the world's *countries*). By the time their Texas-born hero BOB WILLS settled in the San Fernando Valley in 1945, Bakersfield had such dance halls as the Beardsley Garden & Rhythm Rancho to host the era's western swing bands and the huge crowds they drew. Radio station KGEE began broadcasts of BILL WOODS & the Orange Blossom Playboys in 1946, and the local scene perked up with the opening of such "drinking and fighting" clubs as the Corral and the Blackboard. It was in such places that the scaled-down, amped-up version of western swing and honky-tonk later dubbed the "Bakersfield sound" was honed in the 1950s. This harder-edged musical style contrasted with—and commercially rivaled—the smoother NASHVILLE SOUND, then in its ascendancy in the East. Bill Woods's band was a proving ground through which BILLY MIZE, Buck Owens, and MERLE HAGGARD passed. Other key players on the scene were FERLIN HUSKY, TOMMY COLLINS, and the influential but underrated WYNN STEWART.

The 1950s was the era when the creative spark ignited Bakersfield. However, it wasn't until the mid-sixties, when Buck Owens built his Bakersfield-based empire (radio stations, publishing companies, and the management of local talent, including Merle Haggard for a time), that the notion of Bakersfield as an upstart country music center spread. For all Buck's local boosterism, he and his hometown's finest musicians still made the one-hundred-mile drive south to Hollywood to record. RED SIMPSON and a few other Bakersfield-based artists enjoyed hits well into the 1970s, but the hopes of "Nashville West" were never realized. However, the Los Angeles alternative country artists of the 1980s viewed 1960s Bakersfield as the embodiment of a golden age. As a tribute, producer Pete Anderson delivered two anthologies of L.A. alternative country acts called *A Town South of Bakersfield Volumes I & II* in 1985 and 1988. The crowning glory of the Bakersfield consciousness of the 1980s was the DWIGHT YOAKAM–Buck Owens duet "Streets of Bakersfield," a #1 hit in 1988.

—*Mark Humphrey*

Dewey Balfa

b. Grand Louis, Louisiana, March 20, 1927; d. June 17, 1992

Dewey Balfa and his brothers provided some of the best examples of traditional Cajun music ever put on record. Their unique style of toning down the accordion and featuring the fiddles, and of taking the words of old ballads and putting them to dance hall–type arrangements, made their music richly varied and broad in scope.

Dewey Balfa and his eight brothers and sisters were born into the family of sharecropper Charles Balfa, and it was from their father and grandmother Marie Richard that Dewey and his brothers learned much of their music. In 1948 Dewey, Will, and Harry Balfa formed a band, the Musical Brothers, with accordionist Hadley Fontenot. They played at local dances, and for many years hosted a live weekend radio program at Mouche's Lounge in Basile.

In 1964 Dewey Balfa performed at the Newport Folk Festival in Rhode Island; three years later he returned to the festival with brothers Will and Rodney (both of whom would die in a car wreck in 1979), along with daughter Nelda and Hadley Fontenot. The Balfas recorded for Swallow and other labels, and Dewey Balfa became known as a major ambassador of the Cajun culture. —*Ann Allen Savoy*

REPRESENTATIVE RECORDINGS

The Balfa Brothers Play Traditional Cajun Music Volumes 1 & 2 (Swallow, 1987); *J'ai Vu le Loup* (Rounder, 1988)

David Ball

b. Rock Hill, South Carolina, July 9, 1953

After years on the fringes of Austin's and Nashville's progressive music scene, David Ball finally found commercial success in the mid-1990s with a solid brand of Texas honky-tonk music exemplified by his 1994 WARNER BROS. album *Thinkin' Problem.*

The son of a Baptist minister, Ball began appearing on the folk festival circuit while still in high school. During the 1970s, he joined forces with Walter Hyatt and DesChamps Hood in an eclectic Austin-based trio, Uncle Walt's Band, which played a blend of stringband, swing, and pop harmony music that was ahead of its time; Ball played string bass in the band. In Austin Ball became deeply enamored of RANDY TRAVIS's 1985 breakthrough album *Storms of Life*, and of the western swing bands that he heard around Austin.

Ball's initial attempt to enter the Nashville scene in the late 1980s was disastrous. Signed to RCA RECORDS in 1987, he cut nearly two albums' worth of material in 1988 and 1989, most of which went unreleased at the time. None of his three RCA singles that were released went higher than #46.

But after a hiatus, Ball found new life, and a new sense of direction in the honky-tonk vein as both a writer and a musician. *Thinkin' Problem* was produced by Blake Chancey, and the honky-tonk title tune, which hit #2 on the *Billboard* country chart, was one of 1994's surprise hits. Unfortunately, Ball's equally strong follow-up album, *Starlite Lounge,* did not produce any hits to rival the impact of "Thinkin' Problem." —*Bob Allen*

REPRESENTATIVE RECORDINGS

David Ball (RCA, 1994); *Thinkin' Problem* (Warner Bros., 1994); *Starlite Lounge* (Warner Bros., 1996)

Ballads

In modern country, the term *ballad* is often used (rather vaguely) to refer to any slow, emotive love song, a usage borrowed from popular music of the big band era. In a more holistic sense, however, the term *ballad* refers to a specific song type that has been a staple of country music from its earliest days. In the folk music that formed the foundation for much country music, the ballad was a narrative song—one that told a story. Many originated in England, Scotland, and Ireland, and ballads such as "Barbara Allen," "The House Carpenter," and "The Wexford Girl," many of which dealt with murder and romance, became as popular in America as in England. By the early nineteenth century Americans were developing their own native ballads, some circulated orally, others by broadsides (sheets of paper or small cards) and in cheap songsters, or songbooks. These pieces have been studied and classified by scholar Malcolm Laws and are generally known as Laws ballads.

In the 1920s a new type of ballad emerged, one written by commercial songwriters for specific use on the first generation of country records, and referred to by the record industry as the "event song." Many of these were first cousins to the older broadside ballads, which often dealt with recent historical or topical events. As early as 1924, with ERNEST STONEMAN's OKeh recording of "The Sinking of the Titanic" and VERNON DALHART's Victor recording of "The Wreck of the Old 97," pioneer country recording artists had set the stage for this new style. When Dalhart's disc went on to become country's first million-seller, the companies began falling all over themselves to find and issue more such ballads.

The year 1925 was the high-water mark for such efforts, with Dalhart's recording of "The Death of Floyd Collins," about a caver trapped in a Kentucky sand cave, and "Little Mary Phagan," about a sensational murder in Georgia, selling more than 300,000 copies for COLUMBIA. In fact, of the seven best-selling Columbia records for 1925, only two did not have some sort of event song. These ranged from "The Scopes Trial" to "The Santa Barbara Earthquake," both events that were still dominating the headlines. Among the songwriters who specialized in these songs were Atlanta evangelist REV. ANDREW JENKINS, Memphis native BOB MILLER, and then Dalhart partner CARSON ROBISON.

The commercial boom in event songs was short-lived, and within a couple of years other types of country songs were dominating the field. Through the 1920s and 1930s, companies and singers repeatedly tried to resurrect topical songs, with pieces such as "The Death of Jimmie Rodgers" (GENE AUTRY), "The Fate of Will Rogers and Wiley Post" (Bob Miller), and "Amelia Earhart's Last Flight" (RED RIVER DAVE). In the 1940s, folk-based murder ballads such as "The Hills of Roane County" (the BLUE SKY BOYS, BILL MONROE) and "Tragic Romance" (GRANDPA JONES, the MORRIS BROTHERS, COWBOY COPAS) achieved widespread popularity.

In the 1960s, on the heels of the folk music revival, a new cycle of ballads began appearing on the charts. Sometimes called "saga songs," they included items such as "The Battle of New Orleans" (JIMMY DRIFTWOOD, JOHNNY HORTON) and MARTY ROBBINS's remarkable "El Paso." LEFTY FRIZZELL's "The Long Black Veil" so successfully copied the old folk ballad style that many assumed this commercially written number was a genuine traditional folksong.

Though most modern country songs are technically lyrics—songs that express emotion and are highly subjective—the older ballad forms and techniques continue to infuse and influence modern songwriters, as evidenced in DON SCHLITZ's "The Gambler," a monster hit for superstar KENNY ROGERS. And many of the ballads themselves continue to survive in repertoires of bluegrass and more traditional country singers.

—*Charles Wolfe*

A. V. Bamford
b. Havana, Cuba, April 5, 1909

Alfred Vincent Bamford was a major promoter of concerts during the surge in popularity of country music in the 1950s. He came to the United States at age fourteen. After attending military school in Pennsylvania, the University of Alabama, and New York University, Bamford sold radio advertising and managed radio stations before entering the concert booking field in San Francisco in the late 1930s. He promoted shows for Benny Goodman, Tommy Dorsey, and others before switching to country music in the late 1940s, when he worked for BOB WILLS. Promoter OSCAR DAVIS introduced Bamford to JIM DENNY, who represented GRAND OLE OPRY acts, and Bamford soon became one of country music's top promoters. He was promoting HANK WILLIAMS's shows at the time of Hank's death, and he handled early country music dates for ELVIS PRESLEY. In later years, Bamford owned and managed several country music radio stations.

—*Al Cunniff*

Moe Bandy
b. Meridian, Mississippi, February 12, 1944

From the time he made his breakthrough record "I Just Started Hatin' Cheatin' Songs Today" in 1974 and until he left the COLUMBIA label in 1986, Marion Franklin Bandy Jr. seldom strayed from the Texas honky-tonk style on which he was nurtured. With a smooth and crisply articulated vocal style, performed to the accompaniment of fiddles and pedal steel guitar, Bandy thrived commercially at a time when most country musicians were experimenting with country-pop sounds and striving for crossover acceptance. His clean-cut, choirboy looks stood in dramatic contrast to the long string of songs about hurting, drinking, and cheating that he placed on the country charts.

Bandy grew up in San Antonio listening to the music of visiting country stars and to his father's band, the Mission City Playboys. His first commercially released recording was the self-penned "Lonely Lady" on the Satin label in 1964. Ten years later he was working as a sheet metal worker and playing music in local clubs at night, when Nashville producer Ray Baker became his manager. Baker and Bandy independently produced a recording of "I Just Started Hatin' Cheatin' Songs Today" on the Footprint label and eventually got it released on the independent Atlanta label GRC, where it became a Top Twenty hit. After signing with Columbia Records in 1975, several hits followed, including "It Was Always So Easy to Find an Unhappy Woman" and "Bandy the Rodeo Clown," both written by WHITEY SHAFER, and "Hank Williams, You Wrote My Life," from the pen of PAUL CRAFT. In the post-Columbia years, Bandy has strayed often from the honky-tonk style and has enjoyed only indifferent success. His recordings with JOE STAMPLEY (1979–85), which exploited the stereotype of the southern "good ole boy," were marked generally by good humor and self-mockery. Bandy now appears at his own Americana Theater in BRANSON, Missouri.

—*Bill C. Malone*

REPRESENTATIVE RECORDINGS

Greatest Hits (Columbia, 1982); *Greatest Hits* (Curb, 1990)

Banjo

Generically, banjos are plucked or strummed stringed instruments whose distinctive tone stems from the strings being supported by a bridge that rests on a tightly stretched skin membrane. Historically, American banjos are descendants of a broadly related family of lutes developed in West Africa from earlier Middle Eastern models. The slave trade brought banjo prototypes to the New World, where such powerful transforming forces as nineteenth-century minstrelsy and mass manufacture changed the banjo and its associated playing styles many times over.

The family of banjos today includes four-string tenors (similar to the standard banjo but with a shorter neck and no fifth string), plectrums (so called because they are played with a plectrum, and in form identical to the standard banjo but with no fifth string), and six-string guitar-banjos. Most common now is the five-string banjo, on which the "fifth string" is a short string usually tuned to function as a high drone or "chanterelle." Five-string banjos may be found in open-back folk or old-time types using gut or steel strings and also in resonator-backed variations, almost always steel-strung. Banjos may be fretted or fretless, acoustic or electric, mass-manufactured or individually handcrafted.

The banjo is visually and aurally one of the most recognizable instruments associated with country music. To early recordings and broadcasts of country music the banjo brought not only its distinctive frailing or finger-picked sounds, but also its African and minstrel connotations. In both the nineteenth-century minstrel show and the early twentieth-century country music show, banjo players typically played comedy roles and were often musically marginal, although they were significant symbolically and for their tonal contributions within an ensemble. Beginning in the 1940s, Pete Seeger's revival of the five-string banjo to accompany folk music began to introduce the instrument to new northern and urban audiences. At the same time, the emergent sound of bluegrass music, built in large part around the stylistic breakthrough into a smooth three-finger picking style of EARL SCRUGGS, began to stimulate yet another renaissance for this ancient instrument. Today the banjo is enormously popular around the world, particularly the five-string form played in bluegrass and other forms of folk and country music. —*Thomas A. Adler*

Bar X Cowboys

Founded by fiddler Ben Christian (1885–1956) in Houston in 1932, the prolific and long-lived Bar X Cowboys were the city's first organized country dance band. More musically conservative than most western swing bands in the area, the Cowboys responded less to jazz and blues than their contemporaries, and their straightforward approach ensured their popularity, especially in the German communities west of Houston. The band first recorded for DECCA in 1937. It recorded for BLUEBIRD in the years 1940–41, by which time steel guitarist-composer TED DAF-

FAN had been added to its lineup. Bandleader Ben Christian departed in 1940 to form his own group, with his brother Elwood "Elmer" Christian (1892–1970) taking the helm, although JERRY IRBY, who replaced guitarist-vocalist Chuck Keeshan in 1941, was the band's front man until 1947. Irby's replacement, Paul Brown (b. 1911), bought the Bar X Cowboys from Elmer Christian in 1949 and kept a band going through the early fifties. The group recorded for several small concerns after the war, including Globe, Macy's, and Nucraft, its biggest hit coming with "Cocain Blues [*sic*]," on the Eddy's label in 1948.   —*Kevin Coffey*

REPRESENTATIVE RECORDINGS

Stompin' at the Honky-Tonk (String, 1978) (various-artists reissue containing a 1937 recording by the Bar X Cowboys); *Western Swing, Volume Three* (Old Timey, 1975) (various-artists reissue containing a 1940 recording by the Bar X Cowboys); *Cat'n Around* (Krazy Kat, 1992) (various-artists reissue containing a 1949 recording by the Bar X Cowboys)

Bobby Bare

b. Lawrence County, near Ironton, Ohio, April 7, 1935

Innovative and smart, funny and very laid back, Robert Joseph Bare has taken an eclectic approach to music that has variously identified him as a storyteller, humorist, folkie, and country OUTLAW. In addition, his instinct for songs (he is described by longtime friend WAYLON JENNINGS as "the best songhound in the world") has led to associations with many of country music's greatest songwriters, including KRIS KRISTOFFERSON, BILLY JOE SHAVER, MICKEY NEWBURY, BOB MCDILL, TOM T. HALL, HARLAN HOWARD, and RODNEY CROWELL. Numerous collaborative efforts with the eccentric songwriter-author-cartoonist SHEL SILVERSTEIN are among Bare's most notable artistic achievements.

Born and raised on a hillside farm at the southernmost tip of Ohio, Bare moved to Springfield as a teenager, and

Bobby Bare

it was there that his musical career began. Arriving in the Los Angeles area in December 1953, he soon became friends with steel guitarist SPEEDY WEST, songwriter Harlan Howard, and singer-songwriter WYNN STEWART.

Bare recorded briefly for the CAPITOL and CHALLENGE labels in the mid-fifties and was signed to write songs for Opal Music. He had just been drafted into the army in November 1958 when he agreed to help an old friend, Bill Parsons, record some demos for a possible record deal. At the session, Bare sang an unfinished song, "All-American Boy," intending for Parsons to learn and record it later. The acetates were copied at Cincinnati's Fraternity Records studio, and Fraternity decided to release the demo as it was. By the time Bare had finished basic training several weeks later, the record was a huge pop hit, eventually rising to #2. Ironically, Parsons was credited as both singer and writer because of Bare's preexisting contracts with Challenge and Opal.

Bare continued to record for Fraternity for the next several years until he signed with CHET ATKINS and RCA in early 1962. The following year, Bare's version of the MEL TILLIS-DANNY DILL song "Detroit City" became his first Top Ten country hit (also a Top Twenty pop hit) and earned him a Grammy for Best Country & Western Recording. Subsequent hits with "500 Miles Away from Home," "Miller's Cave," and "Four Strong Winds" closely associated him with the folk music movement of the early 1960s. He moved to Nashville in 1964.

During the sixties, along with his solo RCA albums, Bare recorded two LPs with SKEETER DAVIS, one with NORMA JEAN and LIZ ANDERSON, and another with the British country group the Hillsiders. He recorded for MERCURY in 1970–72, then returned to RCA. In 1973 he cut his first album with Silverstein, *Lullabys, Legends and Lies*, which produced a #2 hit duet with his five-year-old son, Bobby Jr. ("Daddy, What If"), and his first #1 song, "Marie Laveau."

Bare has since recorded for COLUMBIA and EMI, and in the mid-eighties he was the host of the critically acclaimed *Bobby Bare and Friends* TV show on THE NASHVILLE NETWORK. —*Dale Vinicur*

REPRESENTATIVE RECORDINGS

All-American Boy (Bear Family Records, 1994) (4 discs); *Margie's at the Lincoln Park Inn* (RCA, 1969); *Lullabys, Legends and Lies* (RCA, 1973); *Hard Time Hungrys* (RCA, 1975); *Drunk & Crazy* (Columbia, 1980)

Benny Barnes
b. Beaumont, Texas, January 1, 1936; d. August 27, 1987

As a youth, Ben Milam Barnes Jr. sang for Beaumont civic groups, but family tradition coaxed him to become an oilfield roughneck during his teens. After an oil-rig injury, Barnes pursued his musical leanings and landed a job singing with guitar in a local lounge.

In 1956 Benny Barnes, now an exponent of classic honky-tonk country, was invited to participate on a STARDAY RECORDS session of fellow Beaumont resident GEORGE JONES, which prompted an on-the-spot audition for Barnes singing "Poor Man's Riches." Barnes's 1957 Starday release of the song charted #2 in *Billboard* and led to his late 1950s stint on Shreveport's *LOUISIANA HAYRIDE*.

Ultimately Barnes recorded for many companies, including MERCURY and RCA. "Poor Old Me," "Penalty," "Yearning," and "Gold Records in the Snow" (a tribute to

BUDDY HOLLY, J. P. Richardson, and Ritchie Valens) are among his successful recordings. —*Bob Pinson*

Max D. Barnes
b. Hardscratch, Iowa, July 24, 1936

Max Duane Barnes emerged in the eighties as one of MUSIC ROW's leading songwriters with concise, miniature dramas such as "Storms of Life" and "Chiseled in Stone." Raised in Nebraska, Barnes attended Omaha South High. Jobs as a farmhand, carpenter, and long-distance trucker instilled in him an abiding respect for the struggles of the working class. His music career began in earnest with his self-penned record "Ribbons of Steel," released on John Denny's JED label in 1971. After signing a publishing contract with the Denny family's CEDARWOOD firm in 1972, Barnes moved to Nashville on May 1, 1973. His first song to hit the charts came in 1979 with CONWAY TWITTY's recording of "Don't Take It Away." It was followed by another Twitty hit, "Redneckin', Love Makin' Night" (1981), written with Barnes's friend and frequent co-writer Troy Seals. Other Barnes-Seals collaborations include "Who's Gonna Fill Their Shoes" (GEORGE JONES, 1985), "Storms of Life" (RANDY TRAVIS, 1985), "Ten Feet Away" (KEITH WHITLEY, 1986), and "I Won't Need You Anymore (Always and Forever)" (Travis, 1987). Barnes has enjoyed particular success co-writing with VERN GOSDIN. Their compositions include "Do You Believe Me Now" (1987) and "Chiseled in Stone" (1988), the 1989 CMA Song of the Year. Barnes took the Song of the Year award again in 1992 with "Look at Us," written with VINCE GILL. Barnes attributes his long run of success to a simple rule of thumb: "I try to write so there's no confusion. Country music is for ordinary people. That's what I am, and I don't ever want to get above that."

Barnes's son Max Troy Barnes (b. October 25, 1962) is a successful tunesmith in his own right. Among his hit songs are "Love, Me" (COLLIN RAYE, 1991), "Before You Kill Us All" (Randy Travis, 1994), and "Way Down Deep" (Vern Gosdin, 1983), a collaboration with Barnes Sr. —*Kent Henderson*

Mandy Barnett
b. Crossville, Tennessee, September 28, 1975

When twenty-one-year-old Amanda Carol "Mandy" Barnett celebrated the release of her debut album in 1996, she was already a country music celebrity, having found both critical and popular acclaim portraying PATSY CLINE in the RYMAN AUDITORIUM's theater production of *Always . . . Patsy Cline*. During her two-season run (1994–95), Barnett's vocal impression of Cline astounded many country fans and critics.

Although her childhood included a stint as secretary of a chapter of the Future Farmers of America and as a homecoming queen, Barnett's one goal was to sing. When she was ten, she won the Best Country Act contest at Dollywood, the famed Pigeon Forge, Tennessee, theme park. An offer of employment at Dollywood followed, and by the time she was twelve, Barnett was visiting Nashville regularly to sing on the ERNEST TUBB Record Shop's Midnite Jamboree.

After being invited by JUSTIN TUBB to perform on the GRAND OLE OPRY, Barnett began making the rounds of Nashville's clubs to sing for industry executives. By age thirteen she had been signed to Universal Records by famed producer-executive JIMMY BOWEN, who subsequently took her with him to LIBERTY RECORDS. She spent five years in a developmental deal that allowed her the opportunity to learn what kind of music she wanted to sing.

Released from the Liberty contract, Barnett was signed to ASYLUM RECORDS in 1995 by label president KYLE LEHNING, the producer who had helped launch RANDY TRAVIS's career. Her debut Asylum album, *Mandy Barnett,* afforded her the opportunity to demonstrate the breadth of her vocal prowess and musical vision. Though not a major commercial success, the album was generally well received by critics.

In 1997 Barnett moved to the Sire label and was working on a new album with Hall of Fame producer OWEN BRADLEY before his death on January 7, 1998.

—*Janet E. Williams*

REPRESENTATIVE RECORDING

Mandy Barnett (Asylum, 1996)

Bashful Brother Oswald
b. Sevier County, Tennessee, December 26, 1911

The shimmery cry of Bashful Brother Oswald's dobro was an essential part of the signature sound of ROY ACUFF's Smoky Mountain Boys for more than a half century. Oswald also sang high harmony with Acuff, frailed banjo, and did rube comedy with the Smoky Mountain Boys, but his distinctive dobro lines on such 1940s classics as "The Wreck on the Highway" are Oswald's true legacy. His Hawaiian-style playing underlined the pathos of such Acuff performances as "The Precious Jewel," and it was Oswald's persistent presence on radio, record, and stage that saved the dobro, a missing link between acoustic Hawaiian and electric steel guitars, from likely oblivion after World War II preempted production.

Beecher Ray Kirby was one of the eleven children of George Wesley Kirby, who provided for his brood by barbering, moonshining, and leading shape-note "singing schools." In 1929 Beecher, who preferred to be called Pete, left the Great Smoky Mountains for Flint, Michigan, to join an uncle working at the Buick factory. The Depression kept Kirby off the assembly line, but it was in Flint that he encountered a Hawaiian guitarist named Rudy Waikiki whose playing he emulated. He bought a metal National Hawaiian guitar and in 1933 was performing in Chicago-area bars, theaters, and burlesque houses by night while working as a fry cook at the Century of Progress Exposition by day.

Kirby was back on native turf in 1936, working at a Knoxville bakery and occasionally filling in for dobroist Clell Summey (a.k.a. Cousin Jody) in Roy Acuff's Crazy Tennesseans. Acuff remembered him and sent for him from Nashville after Summey and other members of his band, renamed the Smoky Mountain Boys, quit on New Year's Day 1939. Kirby first appeared on the GRAND OLE OPRY on January 7, 1939. Later that year Acuff dubbed him Bashful Brother Oswald when singer-banjoist Rachel Veach ("Queen of the Hills") joined Acuff's troupe. An unescorted female was considered scandalous by enough of Acuff's audience to require the ruse of a "brother" in the band as Veach's guardian.

Bashful Brother Oswald was the sole member of the 1939 Smoky Mountain Boys still accompanying Acuff at the time of his death in 1992. Oswald was finally inducted into the Grand Ole Opry on January 21, 1995.

—*Mark Humphrey*

REPRESENTATIVE RECORDINGS

Brother Oswald (Rounder, 1976); *The Best of Oswald* (Country Heritage, 1986; reissued by Rounder, 1995)

Dr. Humphrey Bate
b. Castalian Springs, Sumner County, Tennessee, May 25, 1875;
d. June 12, 1936

GEORGE D. HAY called Dr. Humphrey Bate "the Dean of the GRAND OLE OPRY," and for the first decade of the show it was Dr. Bate's colorful band, the Possum Hunters, that served as the Opry's musical anchor. Dr. Bate's band was also the first to play country music over Nashville radio (in 1925) and the first to play on WSM radio. Dr. Bate was a close friend of Opry founder Hay and was responsible for getting on the show numerous other pioneer performers, such as the CROOK BROTHERS and DEFORD BAILEY.

Dr. Bate was a genuine country doctor, a graduate of Vanderbilt who enjoyed classical music. At heart, though, he was a skilled harmonica player who had learned much of his repertoire on his father's middle Tennessee plantation; by World War I he was running two or three separate bands. Dr. Bate's groups were large by stringband standards—often containing two fiddles, two guitars, a banjo, a harmonica, a cello, and a bowed bass. His repertoire, some of which he preserved on record for BRUNSWICK in 1928, included "Old Joe," "Greenback Dollar," and "Going Uptown" (the first sheet music published by an Opry star). Key members of the Possum Hunters included fiddlers Oscar Stone and Bill Barret as well as banjoist Walter Ligget. Dr. Bate's records, numbering only twelve sides, are generally considered to be among the finest and most complex of any in old-time music.

Dr. Bate died in 1936, though his band continued to play on the Opry. His son Buster performed on the show for a few years, and his daughter Alcyone Bate Beasley remained a singer on WSM throughout the 1950s.

—*Charles Wolfe*

REPRESENTATIVE RECORDING

Nashville: The Early String Bands, Volumes 1 and 2 (County, 1976)

Eddie Bayers
b. Pautaxant, Maryland, January 28, 1949

One of the top studio drummers of country music's modern era, Edward Howard Bayers Jr. received his career break when he was employed by record producer JIM ED NORMAN to work on the soundtrack for the movie *URBAN COWBOY.* Bayers played on MICKEY GILLEY's "Stand By Me" and ANNE MURRAY's "Could I Have This Dance," both #1 hits from *Urban Cowboy,* and his more recent credits have included ALAN JACKSON's "Here in the Real World" and VINCE GILL's "When I Call Your Name." At one time Bayers was the drummer on the top eleven country albums and top thirteen country singles listed in *Billboard.*

The son of a fighter pilot, Bayers grew up living in such varied locations as a Maryland air force base (where he was born), San Diego, and North Africa. Originally a keyboard player, he shifted to drums as his primary instrument once he became a fixture on the Nashville music scene in the mid-1970s.

In the mid-1980s Bayers nearly lost his place among the top session players when he suffered a broken left wrist. The injury kept him out of work for a year, and after his recovery several producers were reticent about hiring him, believing his skills had deteriorated.

Most of the industry disagreed. During the 1990s Bayers received the ACADEMY OF COUNTRY MUSIC's top drummer honor five straight years, and he was nominated as the COUNTRY MUSIC ASSOCIATION's musician of the year four times.
—*Tom Roland*

Bean Blossom
established in Bean Blossom, Indiana, June 1967

The event now referred to as the Granddaddy of Bluegrass Festivals started when BILL MONROE staged his first weekend event in June 1967 at his music park in Bean Blossom, Indiana. In planning the festival, Monroe was following the lead of promoter CARLTON HANEY, who staged similar events in 1965 and 1966. Washington, D.C.–area DJ and promoter Don Owens and BILL CLIFTON had also organized one-day bluegrass events, in 1960 and 1961, respectively.

Prior to the founding of Bean Blossom, the local Brown County Jamboree, started by area businessmen, had been entertaining the populace since 1931. Local talent usually played the weekend shows. In 1951 Monroe purchased the Jamboree's property and hired his brother Birch as the Jamboree's manager. Bill Monroe booked many of his peers at the GRAND OLE OPRY, including ROY ACUFF, ERNEST TUBB, and KITTY WELLS. He also provided a venue for older artists such as FIDDLIN' ARTHUR SMITH and CLAYTON MCMICHEN.

In the late 1970s and early 1980s Monroe expanded the festival to ten days. Beginning in about 1977, Monroe added a second annual festival, usually scheduled near his birthday, on September 13.

Bill Monroe's Bean Blossom festival, continued by his son James since Monroe's 1996 death, is the longest-running bluegrass festival in the United States and has inspired countless others.
—*Chris Skinker*

BeauSoleil (*see* Michael Doucet & BeauSoleil)

Jim Beck
b. Marshall, Texas, August 11, 1916; d. May 3, 1956

Jim Beck was a Dallas recording engineer who, but for a tragic accident, might well have changed the course of country music. As it was, his brief stint in the limelight, 1950–56, made an important impact on a number of artists, including LEFTY FRIZZELL, RAY PRICE, BILLY WALKER, and others; indeed, any singer from the Southwest who came up in the 1950s knew of Beck's legendary Dallas studio and the hits produced there. When COLUMBIA A&R man DON LAW began his work to revamp the old Columbia catalogue in the early 1950s, he recorded more in Beck's studio than in Nashville or New York, and for a time it seemed that Dallas might emerge as the country recording center.

By all accounts, Beck was something of a self-taught en-

gineering genius who had built a working radio station in his bedroom by the time he was fourteen. During World War II he got more experience in the army with broadcasting and recording techniques; in 1945 he returned to Dallas and built his first recording studio to do contract work. At first his main client was the army itself, but soon, to support his studio, he had to go to work as an announcer at KRLD, then developing into a powerful country station through the *BIG D JAMBOREE*. It was there that Beck learned to appreciate country music.

Beck eventually borrowed enough money to open a regular studio on Ross Avenue in Dallas, where he made the first demo recordings of Lefty Frizzell. These not only launched Frizzell's career (the singer would use the Beck studio to do most of his early hits) but also brought Beck to the attention of Columbia's Don Law, who began to use his operation as the primary base for Columbia's country product. The word spread, as Beck also engineered for Nashville's BULLET label, SYD NATHAN's KING label, as well as for IMPERIAL and DECCA. Artists going through his studio ranged from Ray Price to Fats Domino, and from Sid King to classical pianist Gregor Sandor. His contacts allowed Beck to make regular trips to New York to look over the latest innovations in sound technology there; often he would return to Dallas, reproduce the changes, and make improvements in them.

Beck's star in the music industry was still rising when he died tragically in 1956; he had been cleaning his recording machine heads with carbon tetrachloride and had forgotten to open the windows for ventilation. The poison lodged in his system, and he died a few weeks later.
—*Charles Wolfe*

Barry Beckett
b. Birmingham, Alabama, February 4, 1943

After a lengthy stint as a member of the acclaimed house rhythm section at the Fame recording studio in Muscle Shoals, Alabama, keyboardist Barry Edward Beckett went on to become a prominent Nashville-based producer, with credits ranging from Etta James and Bob Seger to CONFEDERATE RAILROAD, LORRIE MORGAN, and EMILIO.

Beckett was playing in a lounge band in Pensacola, Florida, when he met "Papa Don" Schroeder, a local disc jockey and sometime record producer. Schroeder brought Beckett to Muscle Shoals, where Beckett's first hit session was James and Bobby Purify's "I'm Your Puppet" (Bell Records, 1966). "About a year later," Beckett recalled, "[producer] Rick Hall was about to expand Fame studios, and the musicians asked me if I'd like to come up and play with them, full-time."

The Fame rhythm section, which then included Jimmy Johnson, David Hood, Roger Hawkins, Junior Lowe, and Beckett, played on hits including Wilson Pickett's "Land of 1,000 Dances," Aretha Franklin's "I Never Loved a Man," and Percy Sledge's "When a Man Loves a Woman." Later, Beckett, Johnson, Hawkins, and Hood opened their own Muscle Shoals Recording Studios, where they backed Paul Simon (*There Goes Rhymin' Simon*), BOB DYLAN (*Slow Train Coming*), and Bob Seger (*Night Moves*).

After producing hits including Mary MacGregor's "Torn Between Two Lovers" (Ariola America, 1976) and the Sanford-Townsend Band's "Smoke from a Distant Fire" (Warner Bros., 1977), Beckett moved to Nashville in 1982, where he became director of A&R for WARNER

BROS.'s country division and co-produced HANK WILLIAMS JR. with JIM ED NORMAN.

After leaving Warner Bros. to produce independently, Beckett worked with ALABAMA, ASLEEP AT THE WHEEL, Kenny Chesney, JASON & THE SCORCHERS, DELBERT MCCLINTON, NEAL MCCOY, K. T. OSLIN, LEE ROY PARNELL, and EDDY RAVEN, among others. In the early 1990s Beckett began producing international rock acts, including Brendan Croker, Feargal Sharkey, and the Waterboys. —*Todd Everett*

Bob Beckham

b. Stratford, Oklahoma, July 8, 1927

Robert Joseph Beckham has been active in Nashville publishing circles since he began as a song plugger for LOWERY MUSIC in 1961. After a stint with SHELBY SINGLETON Music, he joined COMBINE MUSIC in 1964, becoming president in 1966. There he helped build the careers of DOLLY PARTON, KRIS KRISTOFFERSON, RAY STEVENS, JERRY REED, Dennis Linde, and TONY JOE WHITE, among others.

Beckham started in entertainment with a traveling show at age eight. He worked in movies (*Junior G Men, Star Maker*) in California but returned to Oklahoma in 1940, attending school before he became an army paratrooper at seventeen. After a postwar stint as an electrician, he worked in radio with Arthur Godfrey, enjoyed two Top Forty pop hits as a singer ("Just As Much As Ever," "Crazy Arms"), and toured with BRENDA LEE before settling in Nashville in 1959.

Through hard work and shrewd, pioneering deals for uses of songs in commercials, he built Combine into a major publishing company before its 1986 sale to the SBK music publishing firm. In 1990 he established HoriPro Music, a part of Taiyo Music, Japan's biggest publisher, and has operated it since then. —*John Lomax III*

Carl Belew

b. Salina, Oklahoma, April 21, 1931; d. October 31, 1990

Carl Robert Belew is best remembered for writing "Am I That Easy to Forget," "Lonely Street," "Stop the World (And Let Me Off)," "What's He Doing in My World," and "That's When I See the Blues (In Your Pretty Brown Eyes)." As a farm boy, he began playing guitar as a pastime and worked his way to the West Coast in the early 1950s. After stints at *TOWN HALL PARTY* and *The CLIFFIE STONE Show* in 1956, he joined the cast of the *LOUISIANA HAYRIDE* in 1957. As an artist, Belew began his recording career with FOUR STAR RECORDS in 1955, moving on to DECCA in 1958, RCA in 1962, and MCA in 1970. His three biggest hits as a recording artist were "Am I That Easy to Forget" (#9, 1959), "Hello Out There" (#8, 1962), and "Crystal Chandelier" (#12, 1965). He died of cancer in 1990. —*Walt Trott*

REPRESENTATIVE RECORDING

Twelve Shades of Belew (RCA, 1968, out of print)

Bellamy Brothers

Homer Howard Bellamy b. Darby, Florida, February 2, 1946
David Milton Bellamy b. Darby, Florida, September 16, 1950

For many years one of country music's most popular duos, the Bellamy Brothers first made their mark with the smooth and upbeat crossover hit "Let Your Love Flow," which peaked at #1 on the pop charts in 1976. As their career veered toward country in the late 1970s, they enjoyed one more big crossover hit, the craftily titled "If I Said You Have a Beautiful Body Would You Hold It Against Me." The title came from a line David Bellamy heard Groucho Marx use on his TV series *You Bet Your Life*.

The Bellamys grew up in west-central Florida, in an area surrounded by cattle ranches and orange groves. Homer Bellamy, their father, was a musician who encouraged his sons to take up music. They were also influenced by the records of ELVIS PRESLEY, BUDDY HOLLY, RICKY NELSON, and the EVERLY BROTHERS, by migrant Jamaican orange-pickers, and by the Beatles-led "British Invasion" of the 1960s.

The Bellamy Brothers first performed in 1958 with their father at the Rattlesnake Roundup in San Antonio, Florida. They later formed various groups in which they played Top Forty, country, and soul music. In the late 1960s they migrated to Atlanta, where they saw such acts as the Allman Brothers and Frank Zappa. "Oddly enough," recalled Howard, "that era was probably the most influential in our lives."

Eventually the brothers returned to the ranch, where David concentrated on songwriting. One night they came home late, and rather than wake their parents, they spent the night in the adjoining bunkhouse. Howard woke up with a chicken snake in his sleeping bag. That gave David the idea for "Spiders and Snakes," which became a major pop hit for JIM STAFFORD in 1974.

Encouraged by the song's success, the Bellamys moved to Los Angeles, where Howard became Stafford's road manager. Stafford's manager Phil Gernhard helped the brothers work out a record deal on Warner/CURB RECORDS. "Let Your Love Flow" quickly became an international hit.

The Bellamys' country career grew slowly, however, until "Beautiful Body" hit #1 in 1979. Subsequent singles ran an eclectic gamut from "Redneck Girl" (1982) to such cultural explorations as the probing and sensitive "Old Hippie" (1985) and "Kids of the Baby Boom" (1987).

Seeking complete artistic freedom and control of their music, Howard and David formed Bellamy Brothers Records in 1992 and continued their chart presence with such singles as "Cowboy Beat." They also stage an annual Snake, Rattle & Roll Jam near their Darby, Florida, home, a charity fund raiser in behalf of such recipients as the Children's Miracle Network and efforts to save the endangered manatee and Florida panther. —*Gerry Wood*

REPRESENTATIVE RECORDINGS

The Bellamy Brothers (Warner/Curb, 1976); *Greatest Hits, Volume 1* (Warner/Curb, 1982); *Rebels Without a Clue* (MCA/Curb, 1988); *Rip off the Knob* (Bellamy Brothers, 1993)

Richard Bennett

b. Chicago, Illinois, July 22, 1951

Richard Bennett has made his mark on modern country music as a session guitarist and as a producer. In both cases he has combined a strong respect for country's traditions with a knack for remaking those traditions afresh.

Born in Chicago, Bennett was reared in a household full of music. His mother sang light opera on the radio; his father was an amateur accordionist. At age eight, the family moved to Phoenix, where young Richard began taking guitar lessons from music shop owner Forrest Skaggs, former host of the *Arizona Hayride* barn dance. Through Skaggs's connections and those of session guitarist Al Casey, Bennett began playing guitar in Los Angeles recording sessions in 1968. Among the hundreds of pop and rock artists he backed on record through 1975 were Peggy Lee, Johnny Mathis, Barbra Streisand, Helen Reddy, Billy Joel, and Neil Diamond.

In the early 1980s, Bennett began making semiregular trips to Nashville to play sessions for BRENDA LEE, ROSANNE CASH, GEORGE STRAIT, and others. In 1985, at STEVE EARLE's urging, Bennett moved to Nashville to participate on Earle's *Guitar Town* album as lead guitarist and coproducer. *Guitar Town* proved to be a watershed in Bennett's career, as his muscular guitar playing received notice in the press and in the Nashville music industry. Since that critically acclaimed work, Bennett has produced or coproduced records for JO-EL SONNIER, MARTY BROWN, EMMYLOU HARRIS, Bill Miller, KIM RICHEY, and MARTY STUART. He has continued to make appearances as a session guitarist for a number of artists and has recorded and toured with rock artist Mark Knopfler. —*Paul Kingsbury*

Ed Benson
b. Nashville, Tennessee, February 18, 1945

Edwin W. Benson Jr. became executive director of the CMA in January 1992, following the retirement of JO WALKER-MEADOR. Benson had joined the CMA in August 1979 as its first associate executive director. He also opened the first international office for the CMA in London in 1982.

Benson is a native Nashvillian who comes from the prominent Benson music family; his great-grandfather John T. Benson established the first gospel music publishing company in Nashville, in 1902. Later the family established Benson publishing and recordings. Ed Benson worked for the Benson Company from 1970 to 1978. Benson graduated from Vanderbilt in 1967 with a B.A. in business administration.

In addition to his work with the CMA, Benson has served on numerous civic and business boards and has been a longtime member of most of Nashville's music organizations. —*Don Cusic*

Matraca Berg
b. Nashville, Tennessee, February 3, 1964

Though a respected performer in her own right, Matraca Maria Berg has found greater success writing songs for other artists. Country stars ranging from REBA MCENTIRE ("The Last One to Know," 1987) to DEANA CARTER ("Strawberry Wine," 1996) have topped the charts with Berg's material, and her songs have been covered by nearly every contemporary female country singer, including PATTY LOVELESS, TRISHA YEARWOOD, SUZY BOGGUSS, and LINDA RONSTADT.

One of the few performer-songwriters to grow up in Nashville, Berg is the daughter of the late session singer-songwriter Icee Berg. From the time Matraca had her first #1 hit as a songwriter in 1982 (T. G. SHEPPARD and KAREN BROOKS's "Faking Love," co-written with BOBBY BRADDOCK), she's been one of the most successful songwriters in Music City, ultimately winning the CMA's Song of the Year award

in 1997 for "Strawberry Wine" (co-written with Gary Harrison).

As an RCA recording artist, Berg has fared less well, at least commercially. Her first two singles, "Baby, Walk On" and "The Things You Left Undone," both peaked at #36 in 1990, but subsequent RCA releases failed to reach the Top Forty. Her album *Sunday Morning to Saturday Night* appeared on Rising Tide in 1997. Berg is married to Jeff Hanna of the NITTY GRITTY DIRT BAND. —*Brian Mansfield*

REPRESENTATIVE RECORDINGS
Lying to the Moon (RCA, 1990); *The Speed of Grace* (RCA, 1993)

Byron Berline
b. Caldwell, Kansas, July 6, 1944

A fiddle virtuoso, Byron Berline has been a prominent figure in bluegrass circles since the 1960s. He was reared on a Kansas farm near the Oklahoma border. His mother played the piano, and his father was an accomplished old-time fiddler in the Texas contest tradition. Byron was playing the fiddle by age five and won his first contest when he was ten. He grew up listening to the great southwestern fiddlers, such as Benny Thomasson and ECK ROBERTSON. While he was a student at the University of Oklahoma he formed his first band, the Cleveland County Ramblers, with three classmates, and began learning to play bluegrass. He joined the DILLARDS in 1963, with whom he recorded the classic *Pickin' and Fiddlin'* for Elektra. In 1967 he became a member of BILL MONROE's Bluegrass Boys for a few months before joining the army. After he left the service in 1969 he became a much-sought-after session musician in Los Angeles, where he even recorded with the Rolling Stones. He later played with a series of groups, including Hearts and Flowers, the Dillard and Clark Expedition, and most notably COUNTRY GAZETTE. He has continued to have a successful career as session musician, composer, and fiddler in some of the hottest West Coast bluegrass aggregations. —*Charlie Seemann*

REPRESENTATIVE RECORDINGS
Pickin' and Fiddlin' (Elektra, 1965); *Jumpin' the Strings* (Sugar Hill, 1990); *(California) Traveler* (Sugar Hill, 1992)

John Berry
b. Aiken, South Carolina, September 14, 1959

Had John Edward Berry, a chart-topping 1990s country artist, begun his career in the 1970s, he likely would have been regarded as a rock singer-songwriter in the vein of Peter Frampton. By the 1990s, country had absorbed many of the musical values of 1970s pop, and few singers showed the influence as dramatically as Berry. His concerts regularly featured covers of songs by the Doobie Brothers and Bruce Springsteen, and the performance of HANK SNOW's 1963 hit "Ninety Miles an Hour (Down a Dead End Street)" that appeared on his second album owed as much to Meat Loaf as it did to the Singing Ranger.

A native of South Carolina but raised in Georgia, Berry began playing guitar at twelve and writing songs at seventeen, but not until a motorcycle accident crushed both his legs at age twenty-two did he decide to pursue a music career seriously. His shows became a regular part of post-football-game life in the university town of Athens, Georgia, and he won his region's competition in the Marlboro Country Music Roundup two years running. Also, Berry released six albums independently before signing with LIBERTY RECORDS. (CAPITOL RECORDS eventually reissued two of them.)

In the spring of 1994 Berry had another harrowing medical experience not long after the release of his first Liberty album, when a brain cyst was diagnosed after he passed out at the hospital following the birth of his second child. On the night of the surgery to drain the cyst, his wife, Robin (who often worked as his backup singer), learned that "Your Love Amazes Me" had become Berry's first #1 single. The song went on to win Song of the Year honors from the TNN/Music City News Songwriters Awards and the Nashville Songwriters Association International. (Berry received a Grammy nomination for his performance of the song.)

John Berry, the singer's first album for Capitol/Liberty, was certified gold, and his second contained the singles "If I Had Any Pride Left at All" and "I Think About It All the Time." He released a Christmas album, *O Holy Night,* in 1995, and *Faces* in September 1996. —*Brian Mansfield*

REPRESENTATIVE RECORDINGS

John Berry (Liberty, 1993); *Standing on the Edge* (Capitol, 1994)

Hattie Louise "Tootsie" Bess (*see* Tootsie's)

The Beverly Hill Billies

From their initial appearance over station KMPC on April 6, 1930, the Beverly Hill Billies quickly became the most popular country music act in Southern California, and this popularity opened the door to a much wider acceptance of country music on the West Coast. They were the creation of KMPC station manager/announcer Glen "Mr. Tallfeller" Rice and fellow announcer John McIntire. Beginning with that first group appearance, Rice informed the listening audience that a band of hillbillies had been found far back in the hills of Beverly, adding that he had persuaded them to ride in each night to perform on his radio station—a myth that was accepted at face value by many of the station's listeners.

Combining the talents of accordionist "Zeke Manners" (Leo Mannes), guitarist Tom "Pappy" Murray, vocalist "Ezra Longnecker" (Cyprian Paulette), and fiddler "Hank Skillet" (Henry Blaeholder), the Hill Billies were a sensation soon after taking to the air, drawing crowds into the tens of thousands with their old heart songs, striking solos, strong harmonies, and comedy routines. The group made its first recordings for the Brunswick label on April 25, 1930, and continued to record for the label through September 1932. That same month the Hill Billies left KMPC for KTM. The group also appeared in several western movies with Charles Starrett, RAY WHITLEY, GENE AUTRY, and TEX RITTER.

Changes, brought about by friction within the group, and the appearance of two strong L.A.-area competitors, STUART HAMBLEN's Lucky Stars and the SONS OF THE PIONEERS, caused interest in the Hill Billies to wane, although they continued to have a following until near the start of World War II. Other talents featured at some point with the group were singer ELTON BRITT (Jimmy Baker), guitarist "Lem Giles" (Aleth Hansen), guitarist "Charlie Slater" (Charles Quirk), guitarist and singer Ashley Dees, and singers Hubert Walton, Marjorie Bauersfeld, Stuart Hamblen, and Lloyd Perryman.

In 1963 members of the group sued and won a settlement from the TV producers of CBS's *THE BEVERLY HILLBILLIES* for name infringement. —Ken Griffis

The Beverly Hillbillies

CBS-TV's *The Beverly Hillbillies* is one of the most successful situation comedies in television history. Premiering in the fall of 1962, it exposed millions of Americans to bluegrass music each week via its theme song, performed by FLATT & SCRUGGS. Initially the duo was ambivalent about doing "The Ballad of Jed Clampett," as the word "hillbilly" had a derogatory connotation among country musicians. After viewing the pilot episode, however, Flatt & Scruggs decided to record the song for television broadcast. Then, at the suggestion of Scruggs's wife, Louise, they recorded and released "The Ballad of Jed Clampett" as a COLUMBIA RECORDS single in 1962. The song went to the top of the *Billboard* charts, making it the first bluegrass song to reach #1. Through 1968 Flatt & Scruggs made yearly appearances on the program. As a result of the show, the duo's popularity increased dramatically and banjo sales soared.

Singer-guitarist ROY CLARK made a handful of guest appearances after Flatt & Scruggs disbanded in 1969. As Cousin Roy, Clark would appear wearing an outrageous plaid suit and armed with a guitar full of hot licks. Superbly cast, the show's principals included actor-dancer Buddy Ebsen as widower Jed Clampett, Irene Ryan as Granny, Donna Douglas as Elly May, and Max Baer Jr. as the nitwit nephew Jethro. Raymond Bailey as banker Milburn Drysdale and Nancy Kulp as Drysdale's assistant Jane Hathaway provided excellent support. In 1971 the show ceased production, but it continues to air in syndication. —*Chris Skinker*

Shelia Shipley Biddy
b. Scottsville, Kentucky, October 2, 1952

In 1993, Shelia Shipley Biddy became the first woman to run a major country record label when she was named senior vice president/general manager of the newly revived DECCA RECORDS. (Decca, whose roster once included KITTY WELLS, LORETTA LYNN, and PATSY CLINE, had been folded into parent company MCA in 1973.) Known for her expertise in radio promotion, Shipley Biddy is responsible for daily label operations as well as guiding the careers of such acts as MARK CHESNUTT, RHETT AKINS, Gary Allan, Lee Ann Womack, and Chris Knight.

In 1976 Shipley Biddy joined MONUMENT RECORDS as an administrative assistant and worked there for three years before moving to RCA. She joined MCA in 1984 as director of sales and marketing and was named director of national promotion a year later. She became senior vice president of national promotion in 1992, working with such acts as VINCE GILL, REBA MCENTIRE, WYNONNA JUDD, and GEORGE STRAIT. During her tenure at MCA Nashville, the label increased its chart share from 11 percent to 28 percent and was named Country Label of the Year by *Billboard* for seven years. Shipley Biddy helped the label earn more than 120 #1 singles. —*Beverly Keel*

The Big Bopper (J. P. Richardson)
b. Sabine Pass, Texas, October 24, 1930; d. February 3, 1959

Jiles Perry Richardson Jr., a.k.a. the Big Bopper, is chiefly remembered for perishing in the same plane crash that took the lives of Ritchie Valens and BUDDY HOLLY; as a result, Richardson's accomplishments as a singer and country songwriter have been overlooked.

A career DJ, Richardson joined KTRM in Beaumont, Texas, in about 1949. He first recorded for J. D. MILLER in Crowley, Louisiana, although the tracks went unissued at the time. Then he recorded "Beggar to a King" (later a hit for HANK SNOW) and "Crazy Blues" for Mercury-Starday Records (1957).

In June 1958, as the partnership between Mercury and Starday was dissolving, Richardson recorded "Chantilly Lace" for PAPPY DAILY's D Records. The record was issued under the pseudonym "The Big Bopper" (a name Richardson used to host an r&b show on KTRM). After strong sales in Texas, Mercury leased it, and it rose to #6 on the pop charts. Richardson quit KTRM in December 1958 to work show dates; two months later, he was dead.

Richardson also wrote "Running Bear" for Johnny Preston, as well as "White Lightnin'" and "Treasure of Love," both recorded by GEORGE JONES.   —*Colin Escott*

REPRESENTATIVE RECORDING

Helloo Baby! The Best of the Big Bopper (Rhino, 1989)

Big D Jamboree
established in Dallas, Texas, fall 1948

Not as long-lived nor as fabled as many of country music's Saturday night barn dances, Dallas's *Big D Jamboree* was nevertheless an important regional broadcast that propelled several artists toward national prominence and proved a key venue for both touring acts and area talent.

Begun in 1946 as the *Texas State Barn Dance* by radio personality Uncle Gus Foster and Dallas club owner Slim McDonald, and using coproducer Ed McLemore's wrestling arena, the Sportatorium, the show was rechristened the *Lone Star Jamboree* when it began airing on WFAA radio, probably in late 1947. The show was renamed *Big D Jamboree* when it began broadcasting on KRLD in the fall of 1948. Hosted and coproduced by KRLD's Johnny Hicks and its original host, KLIF disc jockey Big Al Turner (who would be replaced by John Harper), the show featured regional stars such as the CALLAHAN BROTHERS, Riley Crabtree, and Gene O'Quin.

Over the next decade, on both radio and television, the *Jamboree* served as springboard for artists such as O'Quin, BILLY WALKER, and SONNY JAMES, as well as providing a valuable outlet for regionally based stars such as HANK LOCKLIN and CHARLINE ARTHUR and for national touring acts. The LIGHT CRUST DOUGHBOYS, usually billed as the Country Gentlemen, served as house band for many years. Johnny Hicks left the show in 1959, but it continued in some form into the mid-1960s; its subsequent hosts included LAWTON WILLIAMS and former *LOUISIANA HAYRIDE* host Horace Logan. In 1963 STARDAY RECORDS released an album of live recordings from the show, which enjoyed a brief but unsuccessful revival in about 1970.   —*Kevin Coffey*

Binkley Brothers Dixie Clodhoppers
Amos Binkley b. Cheatham County, Tennessee, March 30, 1895; d. October 1985
Gale Binkley b. Cheatham County, Tennessee, May 7, 1896; d. April 1979

One of JUDGE GEORGE D. HAY's famed "hoedown bands" that helped start the GRAND OLE OPRY, the Binkley Brothers brought to the Nashville media the clean, precise instrumental style of west-central Tennessee—the same area that later produced artists such as ARTHUR SMITH and HOWDY FORRESTER. They were watchmakers and jewelry repairmen by day, but they were featured on both WSM and rival station WLAC from 1926 until 1938. Gale was a contest-winning fiddler, while brother Amos was a banjoist. Their guitar player was Tom Andrews, and for much of their career their vocalist was Jack Jackson the Strolling Yodeler, the single most popular radio singer in Nashville during the early 1930s.

In 1928 the Binkley Brothers earned a footnote in history by becoming the first artists to make commercial records in Nashville. They recorded for VICTOR in the YMCA building, doing numbers such as "Watermelon Hanging on the Vine" and "Give Me Back My Fifteen Cents." These first sides were rejected, however. A few days later they joined forces with Jack Jackson and recorded a series of more successful sides, including a classic of old-time music, "I'll Rise When the Rooster Crows."

When the Binkleys decided to quit the Opry in 1939, their place was taken by a new stringband called BILL MONROE & the Blue Grass Boys.   —*Charles Wolfe*

REPRESENTATIVE RECORDING

Nashville: The Early String Bands, Volumes 1 & 2 (County, 1976)

Clint Black
b. Long Branch, New Jersey, February 4, 1962

Clint Patrick Black possesses one of the finest honky-tonk voices ever to come out of Texas. His versatile baritone can croon smoothly up high and can growl ominously down low. He also has the square jaw and high cheekbones of a matinee idol. The first gift has given him the potential to be one of the finest traditionalist singers of his generation, but it has sometimes conflicted with the crossover stardom made possible by the second.

Black was born in New Jersey but raised in Houston, listening to everything from his father's favorites, such as GEORGE JONES and LEFTY FRIZZELL, to his schoolmates' heroes, such as Dire Straits and Yes. By age fifteen Black was strumming an acoustic guitar and singing for friends and neighbors. He dropped out of high school to work as an ironworker and fishing guide by day and as a one-man bar band by night.

By 1986 Black was working the Houston-Galveston circuit steadily and had formed a songwriting partnership with Hayden Nicholas, a fellow struggling singer. In 1987 Black was offered $250 to sell one of his songs outright, and though he needed the money, he decided he needed a manager more. A week later Houston record promoter Sammy Alfano introduced him to Z. Z. Top manager Bill

Ham, who was looking for a country act. Within six months Ham had signed Black with RCA.

Black wrote ten songs—five of them with Nicholas—on his 1989 debut album, *Killin' Time,* and co-producers JAMES STROUD and MARK WRIGHT gave it an old-fashioned honky-tonk and western swing feel, albeit with crisp, state-of-the-art fidelity. The album received glowing reviews, topped the country album charts for twenty-eight weeks, yielded four consecutive #1 singles ("Better Man," "Killin' Time," "Nobody's Home," and "Walkin' Away"), and was eventually certified triple-platinum.

On the strength of this showing, Black won the 1989 CMA Horizon Award and the 1990 CMA Award for Best Male Vocalist. He followed up those successes with 1990's *Put Yourself in My Shoes,* a double-platinum album that also produced two number-one singles: "Loving Blind" and "Where Are You Now." He was inducted as a member of the GRAND OLE OPRY in 1991.

After his 1990–91 New Year's Eve show at the Houston Summit, Black met TV personality Lisa Hartman backstage. They began to date, and in October 1991 they married. The following January, Black hired his mother-in-law, Jonni Hartman, as his personal assistant. A month later he announced a split with manager Ham. Black claimed Ham had trapped him into a contract with unreasonably high commissions and failed to provide proper accounting. Ham countered that he had taken an obscure Houston bar singer and turned him into one of the biggest stars in the music industry.

As the acrimonious split made its way through the lawyers, Black continued his career. *Put Yourself in My Shoes* had been criticized for containing too many country-pop numbers and too much filler, but *The Hard Way* was hailed as a return to form. Released in 1992 amid the lawsuits, it sent three singles to the Top Five: "We Tell Ourselves" (#2), "Burn One Down" (#4), and "When My Ship Comes In" (#1). *The Hard Way* was also the first album on which Black was credited as co-producer with Stroud.

By now, Black's tours had become multimedia extravaganzas. His 1992 tour, for instance, featured an elaborate Utah desert set and closed-circuit TV screens. Likewise, his albums had become balancing acts between his hard-country roots and his pop-country tendencies. When the album *No Time to Kill* was released in 1993, critics complained that the quality of the songwriting was tailing off as well. Nonetheless, Black enjoyed a #3 hit with the title track and a #2 hit on his duet with WYNONNA JUDD, "A Bad Goodbye." The two singers followed it up with the "Black and Wy" tour. Also in 1993, Black's version of "Desperado" became one of the most popular radio cuts from the tribute album *Common Thread: The Songs of the Eagles.*

In 1994 Black ventured into acting, appearing in *Wings* on TV and in *Maverick* in the movies. That same year he released two albums, *One Emotion* and *Looking for Christmas,* and the former yielded five Top Three singles: "Untanglin' My Mind," "Wherever You Go," "Summer's Comin'," "Life Gets Away," and "One Emotion." Nicholas, who had maintained his partnership with Black since the Houston bar days, co-wrote all but the first, which Black co-wrote with his hero MERLE HAGGARD.

After the supporting tour, however, Black decided to take a long vacation. The time off extended through 1996, when he released his *Greatest Hits,* which included a dozen old singles, three new songs, and a new, live version of "Desperado." In 1997 Black released the album *Nothin' but the Taillights.* —*Geoffrey Himes*

Clint Black

REPRESENTATIVE RECORDINGS

Killin' Time (RCA, 1989); *Put Yourself in My Shoes* (RCA, 1990); *The Hard Way* (RCA, 1992); *No Time to Kill* (RCA, 1993); *One Emotion* (RCA, 1994)

Black Artists in Country Music

When CHARLEY PRIDE first broke into the country charts in 1966, he was often asked how it felt to be a black man singing "white" music. His reply: "I'm not a black man singing white man's music. I'm an American singing American music." Although country music has been viewed as a white man's province, black influences in country have been profound, and black musicians have played prominent roles in its development. In fact, folklorist D. K. Wilgus has defined country music as a combination of black and white folk and popular styles that emerged as a commercial idiom in the 1920s.

Long before this, however, the process of black-white American musical interchange was well under way. Slave fiddlers were noted as early as the eighteenth century, and, of course, the banjo—later to become integral to old-time and bluegrass music—was of African origin. Black spirituals, plantation work songs, and minstrel songs all made their way into white folk and commercial traditions that nurtured early country music, just as ragtime, jazz, and blues were to do in the late nineteenth and early twentieth centuries. Indeed, black and white musicians—especially in the South, where the black population was most heavily concentrated—often shared songs and styles, especially in the realms of blues and stringband music. Judging from the southern origins of recent black country acts, the region's importance to racial musical interchange is still strong.

White country musicians influenced by blacks are numerous indeed. Two early examples are JIMMIE RODGERS, who absorbed the music of black railroad workers and recorded with such black musicians as Clifford Gibson and Louis Armstrong, and JIMMIE DAVIS, who borrowed heavily from blues and also recorded with black sideman Oscar Woods. During the 1920s, black Kentuckian Arnold Schultz, widely acknowledged as a major source of the modern thumb-style guitar, performed with BILL MONROE and other white country musicians and ultimately inspired CHET ATKINS and MERLE TRAVIS through his influence on white guitarists Kennedy Jones and MOSE RAGER. Black stringbands continued to influence whites into the thirties; Bo Chatman and his Mississippi Sheiks first popularized "Sittin' on Top of the World," later recorded by BOB WILLS and Monroe. By far the most significant black country star before World War II was the GRAND OLE OPRY's DEFORD BAILEY, a diminutive harmonica player whose song "Pan American Blues" inspired Opry founder GEORGE D. HAY's naming of the show in 1927.

After World War II, rhythm & blues proved to be a major source of inspiration for many country acts, including King Records' MOON MULLICAN, who recorded with black drummer Calvin "Eagle Eye" Shields and worked closely with black producer HENRY GLOVER. Artists like BILL HALEY, ELVIS PRESLEY, JOHNNY CASH, and CARL PERKINS, of course, made r&b a building block for rock & roll. Black artist BIG AL DOWNING joined in the ROCKABILLY trend as well, recording on his own and backing WANDA JACKSON.

In the early 1960s, r&b superstar RAY CHARLES broadened country's exposure in the pop mainstream by recording the albums *Modern Sounds in Country and Western Music* and *Modern Sounds in Country and Western Music, Volume 2*, which were filled with country standards such as DON GIBSON's "I Can't Stop Loving You." Esther Phillips, O. C. Smith, and numerous other black singers followed Charles's lead by scoring major pop hits with country material.

The first black artist to make it big as a modern country act, however, was Charley Pride, a Sledge, Mississippi, native who is the most successful black country artist ever. RCA was cautious in marketing him to country's largely white audience at first, but he went on to Grand Ole Opry stardom and mass acceptance with sixty-seven chart records between 1966 and 1992 (fifty-two of them Top Ten). With a gravelly voice reminiscent of ERNEST TUBB, Pride brought a grit and honesty to stage and studio that made him the CMA's 1971 and 1972 Male Vocalist of the Year and Entertainer of the Year in 1971. Pride's success paved the way for other black country singers such as LINDA MARTELL, who in 1969 became the first black female country singer to work the Opry.

Although Pride has been called the "Jackie Robinson of country music," no black country artist who followed him has approached his level of stardom. HONKY-TONK stylist STONEY EDWARDS, from Seminole, Oklahoma, had fifteen country chart singles between 1971 and 1980, including the moving "Blackbird," a black family's advice to a son to claim his musical and moral heritage as a country musician. Still, major stardom eluded Edwards, as it did Ruby Falls and singer-songwriter O. B. McCLINTON.

Black artists active in country music during the eighties mainly crossed over from the pop field. Ray Charles hit with "I Didn't See a Thing" (a duet with George Jones) in 1983–84 and "Seven Spanish Angels" (a pairing with Willie Nelson) in 1984. Pop star Lionel Richie wrote the #1 coun-

try and pop hit "Lady" (1980) for Kenny Rogers and hit #10 country himself with "Deep River Woman" (recorded with Alabama) in 1987. Pop hitmaker Dobie Gray made a pop-to-country chart transition during the late eighties as well.

Despite these successes and the links they forged with wider audiences, black singers trying to come up through country music have fared poorly during the eighties and nineties. Nisha Jackson, of Tyler, Texas, was signed to Capitol after winning a TNN "You Can Be a Star" contest in 1987, but the label released only one recording and dropped her in 1990. Cleve Francis, a cardiologist from Jennings, Louisiana, caught Liberty mogul Jimmy Bowen's eye in 1991 and released three albums, but poor sales led to Francis's departure from the roster and return to medicine four years later. Although the uncertain fortunes facing any artist doubtless played their part, Jackson has explained black country singers' problems partly in terms of music executives' conservatism (if not racism) and failure to market black artists aggressively.

Early in 1995, however, Francis began to publicize recent survey data showing that some 17 percent to 24 percent of black adults over age eighteen listen to country music, a figure that reveals an underserved market of some 5 million to 7 million listeners. To what extent country music executives will seek to tap this potential—and use black artists to do so—remain to be seen but the recent signings of black recording acts Wheels (Warner Bros.) and Trini Triggs (Curb) are hopeful signs, as is the 1998 Warner Bros. boxed set *From Where I Stand: The Black Experience in Country Music,* which reviews the contributions of black performers to country music since the 1920s.

—*John Rumble*

Rick Blackburn
b. Cincinnati, Ohio, November 16, 1942

With the exception of about a year and a half, Rick Blackburn has helmed major labels in Nashville since 1980. He is currently president of Atlantic Records Nashville, where he oversees the entire operation and an artist roster that includes the multiplatinum acts JOHN MICHAEL MONTGOMERY, TRACY LAWRENCE, CONFEDERATE RAILROAD, and NEAL McCOY.

Blackburn's career began in 1964 when, after graduating from the University of Cincinnati, he worked in pop radio and distribution. He moved to Chicago in 1965 to promote pop records for MERCURY RECORDS and then EPIC RECORDS a year later. Blackburn transferred to Epic's New York office in 1968 to become director of merchandising, formed the CBS-distributed Ode Records (with Herb Alpert and Lou Adler) in Los Angeles in 1970, and moved back to New York as director of national sales and distribution. He then migrated to Nashville in 1974 as general manager of MONUMENT RECORDS. Two years later Blackburn accepted the position of vice president of marketing for CBS's Nashville division, and by 1980 he had climbed to vice president and general manager.

Under his leadership, CBS jumped from fourth in country market share to #1. Mainstays such as Ricky Skaggs, MERLE HAGGARD, ROSANNE CASH, EXILE, RICKY VAN SHELTON, CHET ATKINS, and VERN GOSDIN came to the label during his tenure. When Japanese conglomerate Sony bought CBS in November 1987, Blackburn had already decided to leave the label to form Venture Entertainment, a publishing/management/production partnership with Blake Mevis.

But Blackburn did not stay away from the record business for long. On August 7, 1989, Atlantic opened its doors in Nashville, and Blackburn was named vice president of operations and head of the Nashville division. His utilization of research and music testing has helped the label launch four platinum acts: Montgomery, Lawrence, McCoy, and Confederate Railroad. —*Michael Hight*

Blackface Minstrelsy

In the 1830s Thomas D. Rice and George Washington Dixon established what became that century's most popular type of American popular theater when they masked their whiteness in blackface makeup and dressed, danced, sang, played, spoke, joked, and acted somewhat after the manner of African Americans. By so doing they were developing musical theater along racial lines, whereas class had figured prominently earlier in the century, principally in theater that featured the popular country rube stereotype. Quickly the form grew in size, and by midcentury a typical minstrel show featured a team of blackface performers (four to six initially; dozens or more later in the century) who presented whole evenings of entertainment. By this time, too, minstrelsy had become essentially derogatory in its representation of African Americans, especially to northern, urban audiences.

Although minstrelsy's heyday was in the nineteenth century, it enjoyed considerable popularity well into the middle years of the twentieth century. The influence of minstrelsy reached into many parts of popular culture, not least of which was the development of country music. In obvious ways, the hillbilly persona employed by many in country music (e.g., GRANDPA JONES, STRINGBEAN, ARCHIE CAMPBELL, even MINNIE PEARL) is a direct legacy of the rube plays. Several songs from the early minstrel tradition became barn-dance staples, especially "Zip Coon" (known more widely as "Turkey in the Straw") and "Old Dan Tucker." And many are the early stars of country music who gained valuable stage experience while performing (in blackface) in traveling medicine shows, which by convention included blackface performers. CLAYTON MCMICHEN of the Skillet Lickers frequently appeared in such shows. Both JIMMIE RODGERS and BOB WILLS were accomplished blackface performers, which gave them better reason to perform in blues-inflected styles. ROY ACUFF performed in blackface. BILL MONROE, like many other such artists, worked alongside blackface comics and may himself have appeared as such.

Minstrelsy's comedic style also came over to country music. Blackface humor typically featured a patter of low-order puns and jokes from complementary comics (typically named Bones and Tambo), a device that has served country music performance to the present. A popular early-period blackface Bones/Tambo duo, JAMUP & HONEY, headlined one of the popular GRAND OLE OPRY tent shows in the early 1940s. A midcentury comedy duo, HOMER & JETHRO, even sported something like "fright wigs" (popular among minstrels a hundred years earlier), although they performed exclusively in whiteface.

The format of minstrelsy directly influenced the performance of early country music as well. The *Boone County Jamboree*, broadcast by WLW-Cincinnati, often arrayed the performers in a semicircle onstage for the whole performance, exactly as the minstrel show did; a "shout," featuring all the performers concluded the evening in lively fashion, much like the "walkaround" ended a minstrel show. Lasses White, who organized the Friday night minstrel show for WSM in the 1920s, brought his craft to the Grand Ole Opry as its first blackface performer. By the mid-1930s the Opry had absorbed aspects of minstrelsy's performance conventions, many of which are still in evidence today. Country music's most obvious link to minstrelsy in its more recent history is provided by the television show *HEE HAW*, which in structure, humor, characterization, and, in many ways, music, was a minstrel show in "rube-face."

Blackface entertainment was endemic right at the time country music was being formed, so it is not surprising that many aspects of one genre would have migrated to the other. Minstrelsy, like country music, was also by, for, and about common people who occupied lower social echelons, one ostensibly about black people, the other about white. It is surely significant that both minstrelsy and country music were at their most expressive (and popular) when they acknowledged that American culture, especially among common people, follows from the races knowing and understanding each other, and giving expression to the possibility of accommodation. —*Dale Cockrell*

BlackHawk

Henry Paul b. Kingston, New York, August 25, 1949
David Ray "Dave" Robbins b. Atlanta, Georgia, May 26, 1959
Van Stephenson b. Hamilton, Ohio, November 4, 1953

When the trio BlackHawk released their first album in early 1994, syncopated rhythms marked the CD's smoothly crafted country-pop, and the band members ranged in age from thirty-four to forty-four. Lead vocalist–mandolinist Henry Paul had been a member of the southern-rock group the Outlaws and leader of the Henry Paul Band; keyboardist Dave Robbins and guitarist Van Stephenson had co-written songs for Restless Heart with TIM DUBOIS ("Let the Heartache Ride," "Bluest Eyes in Texas"), and for DAN SEALS, POCO, and Eric Clapton. Stephenson had also had a Top Forty pop hit in 1984 with "Modern Day Delilah."

Already songwriting acquaintances, the three began performing together at DuBois's suggestion and signed with ARISTA RECORDS. BlackHawk's first single, "Goodbye Says It All," debuted in *Billboard* on November 20, 1993. It and four more singles ("Every Once in a While," "I Sure Can Smell the Rain," "Down in Flames," and "That's Just About Right") from *BlackHawk* hit the Top Ten; "Every Once in a While" reached #2 *Billboard* in 1994. *BlackHawk* was certified platinum March 9, 1995; that same year, their follow-up album, *Strong Enough*, yielded the Top Five hits "I'm Not Strong Enough to Say No" and "Like There Ain't No Yesterday." —*Brian Mansfield*

REPRESENTATIVE RECORDINGS

BlackHawk (Arista, 1994); *Strong Enough* (Arista, 1995); *Love and Gravity* (Arista, 1997)

Randy Blake (*see* Suppertime Frolic)

Frank Blevins
b. Smyth County, Virginia, February 25, 1911

The music of Walter Franklin Blevins not only embodies the traditions of Appalachian fiddling but also reflects the influences of technology and social change that helped shape country music in the years preceding World War II. Raised in Ashe County, North Carolina, Blevins learned to play violin as a child and formed a stringband in his teenage years with his brother Edd on guitar and neighbor Fred Miller on banjo. The trio, billed as Frank Blevins & His Tar Heel Rattlers, traveled to Atlanta in 1927 and 1928 to record old-time mountain songs for the COLUMBIA Phonograph Company.

After moving to Marion, Virginia, in 1929, Blevins became a protégé of folklorist Annabel Morris Buchanan and was twice champion fiddler at the annual White Top Folk Festival. At the 1933 festival, Frank and Edd Blevins teamed with banjoist Jack Reedy in a special program for visiting First Lady Eleanor Roosevelt, who awarded them top honors for best band performance.

The group expanded in 1934 with the addition of guitarist Corwin Matthews, dubbing themselves the Southern Buccaneers. Led by Frank Blevins's dynamic fiddling and singing, the Southern Buccaneers reigned as the foremost country stringband in southwestern Virginia throughout the 1930s, with a diverse repertoire and frequent radio broadcasts. The death of Edd Blevins in 1944 signaled the end of Frank Blevins's professional fiddling career, though he continued to make music informally for another two decades. —*Marshall Wyatt*

REPRESENTATIVE RECORDINGS

It'll Never Happen Again: Old Time String Bands, Volume 1 (Marimac, 1985), cassette; *Goin' Up Town: Old Time String Bands, Volume 2* (Marimac, 1985), cassette; *Music from the Lost Provinces* (Old Hat, 1997)

Blue Sky Boys
William A. Bolick b. Hickory, North Carolina, October 28, 1917
Earl A. Bolick b. Hickory, North Carolina, November 16, 1919; d. April 19, 1998

It is not enough to describe Bill and Earl Bolick as simply one of country music's many BROTHER DUETS. Their beautifully crafted vocal harmonies, tasteful mandolin and guitar accompaniment, and repertoire of mostly traditional ballads and gospel songs put them in a class by themselves. Their understated vocals, characterized by Earl's baritone lead and Bill's tenor harmony, nevertheless conveyed a pathos and sincerity that have rarely been equaled in country music, and their influence can still be heard in the singing of such modern duos as JIM & JESSE McReynolds and Charles & Robert Whitstein.

The Bolicks began singing on radio in North Carolina in 1935, and in 1936 began a recording career with RCA VICTOR that lasted (except for their military service during World War II) until their retirement in 1951. They named themselves the Blue Sky Boys in tribute to the Blue Ridge Mountains ("the Land of the Sky"), which lay west of the Bolicks' North Carolina home. After military service, they resumed their career in 1946 on WGST in Atlanta, but thereafter played on a series of radio stations and shows, including the LOUISIANA HAYRIDE in Shreveport. On their postwar recordings and radio shows, they also employed a fiddler, most often Curly Parker, who sang a third part in their trios. In the 1960s they gave concerts at a few university campuses and bluegrass festivals, and recorded some highly praised albums for STARDAY and CAPITOL. Excellent recordings made from home recordings or radio tran-

scriptions also have been released on the COUNTY, ROUNDER, and Copper Creek labels. —*Bill C. Malone*

REPRESENTATIVE RECORDINGS

Are You from Dixie? Great Country Brother Teams of the 1930s (RCA, 1988); *In Concert, 1964* (Rounder, 1989)

Bluebird Cafe

Founded in 1982 as a lunch and music spot in a strip mall, the Bluebird Cafe quickly evolved into the premier Nashville listening room for singer-songwriters. KATHY MATTEA, PAM TILLIS, T. GRAHAM BROWN, TRISHA YEARWOOD, FAITH HILL, the Indigo Girls, and GARTH BROOKS all played to the 120-capacity room before moving on to national stardom. Longer, and harder to catalogue, is the list of songs first given a public performance at the club before going on to become major country and pop hits, among them the Grammy-winning "Where've You Been" written by Bluebird regulars Jon Vezner and DON HENRY.

CBS Television's *48 Hours* news program visited the club to document an audition for the Bluebird's renowned Sunday writers' night, and feature film *The Thing Called Love,* directed by Peter Bogdanovich and starring the late River Phoenix, set several scenes in the club. The Bluebird is popular with songwriters because owner Amy Kurland and her staff demand quiet attention to performances, and great care is given to the quality of sound reproduction. In-the-round sessions are regular features in which three or four songwriters play facing each other in the middle of the club and are surrounded by the audience. The arrangement creates intimacy between performers and audience, and encourages the easy sharing of original work. The practice dates from 1987, when DON SCHLITZ, PAUL OVERSTREET, Fred Knobloch, and THOM SCHUYLER pioneered the presentation. A year and a half later, Pam Tillis, Ashley Cleveland, Karen Staley, and Tricia Walker countered with a popular women-in-the-round arrangement.

Owner Kurland also has taken Bluebird-style shows on the road: to the Disney Institute in Orlando, Florida, and to the Bottom Line in New York. "I want to make it clear to the world that songwriters are artists in themselves," Kurland says. —*Jay Orr*

Bluebird Records
established April 1933

Bluebird Records was a budget-line subsidiary of RCA VICTOR RECORDS. From the early 1920s, nonclassical 78-rpm records had been marketed to sell for as little as 20¢ to 35¢, but the RCA Victor label had held fast to a 75¢ retail price for all its records. As the Depression deepened, RCA Victor had second thoughts, and—after test-marketing the Sunrise, Timely Tunes, Electradisk, and Bluebird labels in various marketing styles—decided to sell Bluebird recordings at 35¢. The first regular release appeared in April 1933—six months before England's DECCA RECORDS debuted their American imprint, also priced at 35¢.

Bluebird's releases were a mix of dance bands, blues, and country reissues from the RCA Victor catalogue. Soon after RCA noted the strong sales response to Bluebird's low prices, all RCA "race" and country products appeared solely on Bluebird. RCA had no staff for this label; RCA personnel in Camden, New Jersey, handled all Bluebird functions. The vast majority of Bluebird's country recordings were cut by remote recording touring units that ventured south four or five times annually. Country artists who contributed to the label's heavy sales were the BLUE SKY BOYS, DELMORE BROTHERS, the Mainers, BILL BOYD, the MONROE BROTHERS, the CARTER FAMILY, and ELTON BRITT.

The label continued an aggressive release program until 1942, when an AFM recording strike—along with a government ban against increasing list pricing—caused RCA to begin phasing out the budget label, which went out of existence in about 1950. RCA Victor's use of the Bluebird label name was far from over, however. In 1953 RCA used the Bluebird name for a budget line of classical 12-inch LPs, and in 1956 for a line of children's records. In 1970 Bluebird was once again revived as a label for a series of vintage music on long-playing records. The name is still in use for CD releases of mostly jazz and blues reissues.

—*Brad McCuen*

Bluegrass

Bluegrass is a traditionally oriented country music initially created as the stringband sound of BILL MONROE & His Blue Grass Boys, which became widely imitated and evolved into a distinctive musical genre. Singer, songwriter, and mandolin player Monroe (1911–96) formed his band in 1938, naming it in honor of his home state of Kentucky, the Blue Grass State. Monroe had intended simply to develop a sound that differentiated him from other performers, but he soon spawned admirers who patterned their music after his.

There has been considerable debate over what constitutes bluegrass, yet the music has certain recognizable characteristics. Its many varieties are all artistic descendants of Monroe's sound. Bluegrass combines elements of old-time mountain modal music and ballad singing, square dance fiddling (with some western swing influence), blues, gospel music, and Tin Pan Alley songwriting. It is a jazz-influenced performance format in which instrumental soloists take turns playing improvisational variations on the melody while at other times backing the vocals or instrumental solos. Bluegrass bands generally consist of a five-string banjo (played in a syncopated, finger-picking style), fiddle, mandolin, six-string guitar, and bass, with occasional use of resophonic slide guitar (dobro) or additional fiddles or guitars. Aside from occasional use of electric bass and/or harmonica, bluegrass is an acoustic stringband music. Vocalists typically also play an instrument and sing in keys pitched to their upper ranges. These pitches, bluegrass singers' austere, tight-throated style, and the mournfully lyrical themes that permeate much of the music have caused bluegrass to be dubbed "the high lonesome sound." Close-harmony duets, trios, and quartets are often featured. As in most country music, the upbeats (second and fourth beats) are emphasized, but bluegrass has a distinctive timing that surges slightly ahead of or anticipates the main beat to create an energized effect (the opposite of jazz or blues, often played slightly behind the main beat for drama).

The first Blue Grass Boys lineup contained fiddle, mandolin, guitar, and bass, and Monroe often stated that his band sound was built around fiddling and a surging tempo. However, some critics hold that bluegrass was truly defined by the addition of syncopated banjo picking, and that the 1946–48 edition of the Blue Grass Boys (combining Monroe with EARL SCRUGGS on banjo, LESTER FLATT on guitar, CHUBBY WISE on fiddle, and Joel Price or Birch Monroe on bass) was the first true bluegrass band and perhaps the finest.

The evolution of bluegrass into a recognizable genre started as early as 1946, when the STANLEY BROTHERS began performing covers of Monroe material while retaining the feel of old-time mountain music in their sound. In 1948 FLATT & SCRUGGS founded their own band, the Foggy Mountain Boys, emphasizing the banjo and smoother lead vocals while de-emphasizing Monroe-style mandolin and modal melodic or harmonic lines. Bluegrass developed regional shadings in the 1950s, 1960s, and 1970s: JIMMY MARTIN, RED ALLEN, and others adopted elements of honky-tonk music while playing in midwestern bars catering to transplanted southern industrial workers; in Washington, D.C., a geographical and political meeting point for the nation, the COUNTRY GENTLEMEN and the SELDOM SCENE mixed southern sensibilities and northern folk-pop influences; in Nashville, GRAND OLE OPRY bluegrassers such as the OSBORNE BROTHERS and JIM & JESSE employed elements of mainstream country; and California saw both the traditionalism of the Hillmen or High Country and the adventurous eclecticism of the DILLARDS.

Monroe did not name his music "bluegrass" (a term now written as one word). Although a 1950 songbook published by Bill Monroe Music, Inc., was titled *Bill Monroe's Blue Grass Country Songs,* until the mid- to late 1950s most Monroe-influenced performers referred to what they played simply as "country" or "hillbilly" music. But during this period disc jockeys and music historians recognized that Monroe's admirers were playing a distinctive style of roots-based acoustic music that was becoming rapidly differentiated from country as a whole. To describe this new category, they began using the word "bluegrass," a reference to the name of Monroe's band. There is also evidence that during this period fans of Flatt & Scruggs wished to hear songs the duo had performed with Monroe's group but, aware of frictions between the bands, did not mention Monroe's name but simply requested "some of those Blue Grass songs." Whatever the case, the term's late development bears witness to the fact that bluegrass, although traditionally rooted, is a modern commercial music. Thus the use of "bluegrass" as a generic label for mountain folk music is incorrect.

The market for bluegrass withered in the late 1950s due to the rise of rock & roll and electrified country, although individual bands, notably Flatt & Scruggs and the Osborne Brothers, prospered with their polished presentations and ability to appeal to crossover audiences. Bluegrass rebounded in the early 1960s, when it was embraced as a type of traditional music by the national folk music revival. The music also advanced with the development of bluegrass festivals as separate entities from country or folk shows that included only token bluegrass acts in their lineups.

Singer-promoter BILL CLIFTON staged an all-bluegrass program on July 4, 1961, in Luray, Virginia, but the three-day gathering at Fincastle, Virginia, on September 3–5, 1965, organized by country music promoter CARLTON HANEY with the assistance of folklorist RALPH RINZLER, is considered the first true bluegrass festival. As the festivals proliferated, they provided bands with increased bookings and record sales opportunities, reinforced the bluegrass community's sense of identity, and attracted many curious first-time listeners who became loyal fans. (As of this writing there are some 600 bluegrass festivals held around the world each year.) Bluegrass has also benefited from grassroots clubs that promote shows and from such publications as *Bluegrass Unlimited* (founded in 1966), which disseminate information about performers, new recordings, and upcoming events. Although bluegrass has largely functioned as a niche music supported by hobbyists, the International Bluegrass Music Association, a trade organization founded in Owensboro, Kentucky, in 1985, has boosted the music's business activities and professional image.

Many of those who discovered bluegrass in the 1960s and 1970s were young, innovative musicians who mixed elements of jazz, pop, and rock with bluegrass to create what is broadly called "newgrass." Early practitioners were the NEW GRASS REVIVAL, the New Deal String Band, and Breakfast Special—all of whom built on earlier experiments of the Osborne Brothers, the Country Gentlemen, and the Dillards. To some, the movement helped prevent bluegrass from ossifying into a museum piece. To others, newgrass was dissonant and thoroughly unrelated to the music established by Monroe. Time has softened these positions as the progressive banjo stylings of BILL KEITH, Tony Trischka, BELA FLECK, and others have become familiar to mainstream fans, and young experimentalists have gained respect for the considerable technical virtuosity of Monroe, Scruggs, and other bluegrass pioneers.

An overseas bluegrass boom began in the 1970s, most notably in Japan and Europe. Monroe-Stanley-styled bluegrass reemerged as a vital force in the 1980s with the popularity of DEL MCCOURY, the JOHNSON MOUNTAIN BOYS, and other traditionally oriented acts, while the Nashville-influenced music of such groups as the Lonesome River Band represented another style of bluegrass. The most striking trend of the 1990s was the emergence of popular female performer-bandleaders in this previously male-dominated music, notably ALISON KRAUSS (the most successful bluegrass performer, male or female, of the decade), Kathy Chiavola, LAURIE LEWIS, and LYNN MORRIS.

—*Richard D. Smith*

The Bluegrass Alliance

In the late 1960s, the Louisville-based Bluegrass Alliance attracted young, urban audiences to bluegrass by means of their instrumental prowess and unusual mixture of material. Their adaptations of pop and rock songs excited a new generation of bluegrass fans for whom "cabins" and "mountains" had little relevance.

The definitive unit—Dan Crary, guitar; Danny Jones, mandolin; Lonnie Peerce, fiddle; Buddy Spurlock, banjo; and Harry "Ebo Walker" Shelor, bass—showcased Crary's lead guitar, a novelty at the time. The group's first nonregional performance of note was at Camp Springs, North Carolina, in 1969.

Recordings for American Heritage and appearances on the emerging festival circuit followed; by 1970, Crary, Jones, and Spurlock had left, replaced by Tony Rice, guitar; SAM BUSH, mandolin; and Courtney Johnson, banjo. In 1971, again at Camp Springs, Rice played the event with both the Alliance and the new band J. D. CROWE and the New South, of which he was a key member.

Soon replacing Rice in the Alliance was Curtis Burch, who then joined Bush, Shelor, and Johnson in forming the NEW GRASS REVIVAL in the fall of 1971. The Alliance still continued, with Peerce filling empty slots from a seemingly endless list of talented young musicians, among whom was

future star VINCE GILL. The Bluegrass Alliance has not been active since the 1980s, however.

—*Frank and Marty Godbey*

REPRESENTATIVE RECORDING
The Bluegrass Alliance (American Heritage, ca. 1970)

The Bluegrass Cardinals
Don Parmley b. Monticello, Kentucky, October 19, 1933
David Parmley b. Alameda, California, February 2, 1959

A popular bluegrass outfit since the 1970s, the Bluegrass Cardinals trace their origins to banjo player Don Parmley's move to Los Angeles in the 1950s. Parmley provided soundtrack banjo for the BEVERLY HILLBILLIES television program (although LESTER FLATT & EARL SCRUGGS played the show's famous theme), and he also worked with the Golden State Boys, an early sixties group that included Rex & VERN GOSDIN and CHRIS HILLMAN.

The Bluegrass Cardinals developed in the early 1970s when Parmley and mandolinist Randy Graham were playing together. Parmley's teenage son David sang and played bass, and the three worked local jobs, including Disneyland. When David moved to guitar, the group added fiddler Dennis Fetchet and bassist Bill Bryson.

Promoting their first album, released on Briar, the Cardinals toured the East in 1976. The Parmleys and Graham then relocated near Washington, D.C., a decision celebrated with the 1977 release of the ROUNDER RECORDS album *Welcome to Virginia*. Their instrumental skill, their vocals (Graham's intense tenor, David's rich lower lead, Don's harmony), and their ability to personalize any material into a distinctive Cardinal sound made them immediate bluegrass favorites. The band recorded a series of well-received albums for CMH and Sugar Hill, then formed their BGC label.

Among Cardinal alumni are fiddlers Warren Blair, Mike Hartgrove, and Tim Smith; mandolinists Herschel Sizemore, Larry Stephenson, and Norman Wright; and tenor-singing bass player Ernie Sykes. In 1992 David Parmley left the band, but the Cardinals, led by Don Parmley, continued on the bluegrass circuit until January 1997.

—*Frank and Marty Godbey*

REPRESENTATIVE RECORDINGS
What Have You Done for Him (BGC, 1992); *My Kinda Grass* (BGC, 1994)

BMG (*see* RCA Victor Records)

BMI (Broadcast Music, Inc.)
established in New York, New York, 1940

BMI (the well-known acronym for Broadcast Music, Inc.) is one of America's largest music licensing firms, its purpose being to collect and distribute monies paid to the creators and publishers of music for public performance rights. For decades since its inception BMI was the major licenser of country music and remains, with ASCAP, one of the two major such licensers.

BMI was established with headquarters at New York City in 1940 by leaders of the national radio industry unhappy with that industry's stalled contract negotiations with ASCAP. Previously the only major U.S. licenser of musical public performance rights, ASCAP had proposed doubling radio's payment rates. Rather than agree to the new terms, the broadcasters created their own music licensing firm, BMI, and ceased playing ASCAP tunes for most of 1941.

Late in 1941 the large radio stations and broadcast networks (NBC, CBS, and Mutual) settled with ASCAP, but BMI continued to grow by leaps and bounds because of its open-door policy toward music that had not gotten much support from ASCAP: primarily country, blues, and r&b. Country music prospered during and after World War II; meanwhile, BMI grew to 6,300 licensees and 1,362 affiliated publishers by 1950. BMI's logging system, which took into account more local programming (not only networks) and record plays (in addition to live performances) was also beneficial to country writers and publishers. Also, more than a few country writers and publishers got a start in the business with monies advanced from BMI in return for their affiliation.

BMI and ASCAP feuded in the courts and the trade press for much of BMI's first two decades, but all the while BMI established a strong position in those fields of music where ASCAP had once stood alone: motion picture soundtracks, pop, jazz, even classical. Rock & roll proved a big boost to BMI's fortunes during and after the mid-1950s; its worth as music was yet another bone of contention with ASCAP.

Attorney Sydney M. Kaye was BMI's founder, organizer, and first president, though several persons were influential in its early growth—Robert Sour, George Marlo, Carl Haverlin, Thea Zavin, and ROBERT J. BURTON among them. BMI has given country music awards since 1953, and its first Nashville offices were established in 1958 by FRANCES WILLIAMS PRESTON, a former WSM receptionist. Ground was broken by BMI in 1963 for what became the first Music Row office in Nashville of any music licensing firm. Ms. Preston became BMI's president and CEO in 1986, succeeding longtime president Edward Cramer. ROGER SOVINE is vice president in charge of the newly enlarged Nashville office, where much of BMI's overall operation moved in 1995.

BMI counts many country songwriters and publishers among its 160,000 members. Throughout much of its history, all of the best-known country publishers (ACUFF-ROSE, CEDARWOOD, FOUR STAR, HILL AND RANGE, Moss Rose, PAMPER, and TREE) and many of the most important country writers (BILL ANDERSON, HARLAN HOWARD, KRIS KRISTOFFERSON, LORETTA LYNN, ROGER MILLER, WILLIE NELSON, DOLLY PARTON, ERNEST TUBB, and HANK WILLIAMS, to name a select few) affiliated with BMI. The majority of country music's best-known standards are lodged within BMI's growing catalogue of approximately 3 million songs. In recent years, however, ASCAP has become an equal competitor in many respects. —*Ronnie Pugh*

BNA Entertainment
established in Nashville, Tennessee, April 1991

BNA began as a sister label to RCA RECORDS, with Ric Pepin at the helm for three years. BMG executive JOE GALANTE reorganized BNA into part of the RCA Label Group, and it was run by Vice President and General Manager Randy Goodman until he was succeeded by Butch Waugh in 1996. The label experienced instant success with the comeback effort of JOHN ANDERSON (1991–96) and has developed a strong artist lineup that currently includes LORRIE MORGAN (1991–), Kenny Chesney (1994–), K. T. OSLIN (1996–), LONESTAR (1995–), MINDY MCCREADY (1996–), Ray Vega (1997–), and Jason Sellers (1997–). BNA has dropped the following acts: the Remingtons (1991–93), Lisa Stewart (1992–94), DOUG SUPERNAW (1993–95), the KENTUCKY HEADHUNTERS (1996–97), and Kim Hill (1995).
—*Clark Parsons*

Dock Boggs
b. West Norton, Virginia, February 7, 1898; d. February 7, 1971

Dock Boggs was perhaps the most emotionally deep and certainly the least musically tractable of all traditional country singers—"hillbilly" or "old-time" they called his music when he first recorded it in 1927. His professional career as an entertainer ended in the early 1930s, with the onset of the Great Depression. Boggs went back to the coal mines of southwestern Virginia and eastern Kentucky, where he had worked since 1910 and where he would continue until 1954, when his age left him unable to find a job. In 1963 he was recorded again by Mike Seeger of the NEW LOST CITY RAMBLERS, eventually cutting three albums for the Folkways label and performing around the country on the festival circuit of the folk revival. Boggs's story can be seen as typical of that of many performers of traditional music, black or white—the sort of artists whose generally forgotten but somewhat persistent work was first collected on Harry Smith's landmark 1952 *Anthology of American Folk Music*. And yet Boggs's life and music raise the question of whether such categories as "traditional" or "folk" or even "country" are of any use at all when confronted with music as powerful and as strange as that Dock Boggs left behind.

He was born Moran Lee Boggs, the youngest of ten children, in West Norton, Virginia, in 1898, and died on his birthday in nearby Needmore in 1971. Both spots were on the edges of Norton, a coal mining center and in 1927 the site of a mass audition of "mountain talent" held by the BRUNSWICK label. Boggs's father, formerly a mountain farmer, was a blacksmith, and also a singer who could read music; various of Boggs's siblings sang and played the banjo, the instrument that would become his. Many of his most striking performances—"Pretty Polly," "Country Blues," and others—were utterly traditional in origin. In this sense Boggs personified the folk strain of country music in both his life and his art. When, after passing the Brunswick audition, he traveled to New York to record, he had never been out of his home mountains.

Nevertheless, Boggs's "Country Blues"—a variant of "Hustlin' Gamblers" or "Darlin' Corey"—is no more traditional in Boggs's performance than HANK WILLIAMS's 1949 "Alone and Forsaken." Boggs is not frailing his banjo, but picking the strings and sliding the notes toward blues, into discord and disharmony. The old song, it seems, is being sung for the first time, or the last. It is the same with "Down South Blues" or "Sugar Baby," performances Boggs derived from records by northern, urban blues singers such as Sara Martin. The momentum of the playing seems to overtake the singer's cadence, and the result is an awful suspense. *Get it over with,* the banjo says in the murder fable "Pretty Polly." *Not yet,* the singer replies.

In this sense, Boggs is no traditionalist, but again, like Williams, a modernist—that is, as a solitary individual who can no longer fall back on the comforts and assurances of an unquestioned religion; an immutable family; a stable, rural society; or a predictable economy, Boggs confronted the world directly and as it was, naked, with a music so strong, cruel, and unforgiving of its own sinfulness that it could repel any belief brought to it. —*Greil Marcus*

REPRESENTATIVE RECORDINGS

Dock Boggs: His Twelve Original Recordings (1927 & 1929) (Folkways, 1983), produced by Mike Seeger with a comprehensive essay by Barry O'Connell; *Dock Boggs* (Folkways, 1963), produced by Mike Seeger.; *Dock Boggs, Volume 2* (Folkways, 1965), produced by Mike Seeger; *Dock Boggs, Volume 3* (Folkways, 1970), produced by Mike Seeger. These albums are out of print, but available on cassette, as single copies, from Smithsonian Folkways Records, Smithsonian Institution, 955 L'Enfant Plaza 2600, Washington, D.C. 20560 (tel. 202-287-3262). The following recording is available. *Dock Boggs: Country Blues, Complete Early Recordings, 1927–1929* (Revenant, 1998)

Noel Boggs
b. Oklahoma City, Oklahoma, November 14, 1917; d. August 30, 1974

One of the smoothest and most influential western swing steel guitarists, Noel Edwin Boggs played and recorded with almost every major artist in the genre, from BOB WILLS and SPADE COOLEY to BILL BOYD, TOMMY DUNCAN, and HANK PENNY. Admired by his peers for his full tone and innovative tunings, Boggs was a supreme stylist.

His early experience was in Oklahoma, but he got his first big break in New Orleans, a job with Hank Penny's Radio Cowboys. Boggs recorded with the group for Vocalion in 1939, his solo work indicating he was already moving away from the established BOB DUNN style of western swing steel and into new territory. By 1940 Boggs was back in Oklahoma City, backing JIMMY WAKELY, with whom he worked often throughout his career.

In 1944 Boggs joined Bob Wills & His Texas Playboys in California and quickly established himself as a star sideman, recording the classic "Texas Playboy Rag" in January 1945. Boggs was with Spade Cooley's large western swing group by 1946 and worked several stints with Cooley over the next decade, recording classics such as "Boggs Boogie" (1947). He also recorded with T. TEXAS TYLER, WADE RAY, and others and became a charter member of Tommy Duncan's Western All-Stars in 1948. During the mid-fifties Boggs led his own trio and recorded for COLUMBIA, releasing his signature "Steelin' Home" in 1954. He drifted into obscurity in the 1960s, unfortunately dying just as western swing was experiencing a revival. —*Kevin Coffey*

REPRESENTATIVE RECORDINGS

Hillbilly Fever, Volume 1: Western Swing (Rhino, 1995) (various-artists reissue containing five recordings featuring Boggs); *Noel Boggs Quintet: Magic Steel Guitar* (Shasta, 1976) (reissue of 1958 release)

Suzy Bogguss
b. Aledo, Illinois, December 30, 1956

Susan Kay Bogguss took a unique route to her success in the country music field of the 1990s. Singing at age five and playing drums as a teen, she cultivated her folk brand of country listening to LINDA RONSTADT and EMMYLOU HARRIS. Bogguss majored in art at Illinois State University, plan-

Suzy Bogguss

ning to make jewelry. But exposed to art, drama, and music, she began performing. She eventually stayed on the road for five years, traveling in a camper from Massachusetts to Wyoming.

In 1984 Bogguss recorded an album to sell at performances. She traveled to Nashville and left the album at stars' homes, then returned in 1985 and got a job singing in a restaurant near Music Row. She made demo tapes for songwriters, and she married one of those songwriters, Doug Crider, in 1986. After Bogguss landed the headlining slot at the Dollywood theme park in Pigeon Forge, Tennessee, talent scouts from CAPITOL RECORDS heard her and the homemade cassette she was peddling from the Dollywood stage and offered her a contract.

Bogguss's 1989 Capitol debut album, *Somewhere Between,* had only minor success, as did the follow-up. But her third Capitol album, *Aces,* released in 1991, was her breakthrough. The fine songs showcased the strength and versatility of her voice, and "Outbound Plane" and "Aces" were Top Ten hits. "Drive South," from her 1992 *Voices in the Wind* album, climbed to #2 on the *Billboard* charts, and that year she received the CMA Horizon award.

Her 1994 album *Simpatico,* recorded with guitarist CHET ATKINS, was a critical success. Atkins had contributed liner notes for Bogguss's first Capitol album, and in 1990 they had collaborated on a holiday single. They had also spent many hours just playing together and swapping songs they loved. Their duet album covered material ranging from JIMMIE RODGERS to Elton John.

Bogguss's *Give Me Some Wheels* (1996) followed a two-year break during which she devoted time to raising her son Ben. —*Mary A. Bufwack*

REPRESENTATIVE RECORDINGS

Greatest Hits (Liberty, 1994); *Simpatico* (Liberty, 1994)

Bill and Earl Bolick (*see* Blue Sky Boys)

James Bonamy

b. Winter Park, Florida, April 29, 1972

James Bonamy has parlayed the necessary elements of style and substance for country success in the youth-oriented 1990s. Bonamy possesses a soft, romantic voice that fits his singing style, which blends country and pop leanings. The Florida-born vocalist is also a virtual "made-for-video" artist, with darkly handsome looks and a muscular, athletic build. The total package helped to earn him a spot in a summer musical revue at Nashville's OPRYLAND theme park, after first performing regularly in Orlando in his early twenties. Bonamy's debut album in 1995 on EPIC RECORDS, *What I Live to Do*, yielded only moderate chart success until the release of the single "I Don't Think I Will." The smooth ballad, at times delivered in a register barely above a whisper, became a #1 hit, supported by a well-choreographed and -executed music video.

"I Don't Think I Will" established Bonamy as an artist capable of tackling emotionally complex ballads, even with his relative youth and limited life experience. He's also shown other dimensions in choice of material, delving into occasional traditional and also dance club–inspired tunes. In 1997 Bonamy received a nomination from the ACADEMY OF COUNTRY MUSIC as Top New Male Artist.   —*Bob Paxman*

REPRESENTATIVE RECORDINGS

What I Live to Do (Epic, 1995); *Roots and Wings* (Epic, 1997)

Eddie Bond

b. Memphis, Tennessee, July 1, 1933

Edward James Bond was one of the few Memphis rockabillies actually born in the city. Being in the right place at the right time didn't translate into a successful recording career, though.

Bond led bands steadily from 1952 (early band members included future Nashville session musicians John Hughey and REGGIE YOUNG), and he began recording country music in 1955 for Ekko Records. Switching to MERCURY and to rockabilly in 1956, he briefly seemed to be a hepcat contender with records such as "Slip Slip Slippin' In," "Boppin' Bonnie," and "Rockin' Daddy." Continuing to record prolifically for ever-smaller labels, Bond started a parallel career as a DJ, concert promoter, club owner, and radio station owner.

Bond had a fascination with the career of lawman Buford Pusser from Finger, Tennessee, and eulogized him on several releases before the Pusser legend, such as it was, was enshrined in the 1973 movie *Walking Tall;* Bond contributed to the movie's soundtrack. In 1974 Bond ran unsuccessfully for sheriff of Shelby County (which includes Memphis).   —*Colin Escott*

REPRESENTATIVE RECORDING

Rockin' Daddy (Bear Family, 1993)

Johnny Bond

b. Enville, Oklahoma, June 1, 1915; d. June 12, 1978

Laconic, humorous, and self-deprecating, Johnny Bond was one of the true gentlemen of western music as well as an important songwriter and musician. Reared in south-central Oklahoma, Cyrus Whitfield Bond moved in 1937 to

Johnny Bond

Oklahoma City, where he formed a trio with JIMMY WAKELY and Scotty Harrell, known as the Bell Boys after their sponsor, the Bell Clothing Company. Regional success followed, and the inevitable move to Hollywood came in 1939, where they appeared in a ROY ROGERS film, *Saga of Death Valley.* They landed a spot on GENE AUTRY's CBS *Melody Ranch* radio show in 1940 and stayed together until Wakely's solo career took off. Meanwhile, they pulled a clever musical scam: They recorded for DECCA as the Jimmy Wakely Trio and for COLUMBIA as Johnny Bond & the Cimarron Boys.

Although he composed hundreds of songs ("I Wonder Where You Are Tonight," "Love Gone Cold," "Your Old Love Letters," "Tomorrow Never Comes," "Those Gone and Left Me Blues," and many others, mostly in the country idiom), Bond is best remembered for his western classic "Cimarron," which he composed in Oklahoma City as a theme song for the Bell Boys. As a recording artist he enjoyed moderate success, from his earliest recordings in 1941 through the 1950s, and even placed a few hits high on the charts during the late 1940s. In 1965 Bond's recording career briefly revived with STARDAY and the novelty drinking song "10 Little Bottles," which he had first recorded for Columbia in 1951.

Whereas Wakely's career was meteoric, Bond's was steadier: He remained a mainstay of the *Melody Ranch* cast until the show's end in 1956, and his distinctive acoustic guitar runs became an Autry trademark on radio and record. He had small parts in many films, recorded frequently, began a music publishing business with TEX RITTER, spent nearly a decade as host and writer on the television show *TOWN HALL PARTY,* and in his later years became an author as well, writing a brief autobiography and a biography of Tex Ritter.   —*Douglas B. Green*

Johnny Bond's Best (Harmony, 1964, out of print)

Bonnie Lou
b. Towanda, Illinois, October 27, 1924

Singer Mary Kath was known throughout the tristate area of Ohio, Kentucky, and Indiana simply as Bonnie Lou. The central Illinois native developed an interest in music at a young age. By age eleven she was playing both fiddle and guitar and began working on her Swiss yodel. Kath started her professional radio career at Peoria radio station WMBD in 1939. In 1940 she moved to WJBC in Bloomington, Illinois, and upon high school graduation in 1942 she moved to KMBC in Kansas City. Billed as Sally Carson, she performed as a soloist and as a member of the Rhythm Rangers on the *Brush Creek Follies*.

In the spring of 1945 Kath moved to WLW in Cincinnati. Station manager Bill McCluskey changed her name to Bonnie Lou and added her to the *MIDWESTERN HAYRIDE* cast. There she won many fans both as a soloist and as a member of the Trailblazers. By 1953 she had her first chart single, "Seven Lonely Days," on KING RECORDS. The follow-up, "The Tennessee Wig Walk," also broke into the country Top Ten. Bonnie Lou stayed with the *Hayride* until 1966.

WLW programmed several live shows from the 1950s through the mid-1970s. Bonnie Lou performed on several of these, including the station's morning variety program, *The Paul Dixon Show,* and Ruth Lyons's noontime program, *The 50-50 Club*. Bonnie Lou has lived in retirement for the most part since the early 1980s, occasionally appearing on local television and commercials. —*Chris Skinner*

Boone County Jamboree (*see* Midwestern Hayride)

Boone Creek (*see* Ricky Skaggs)

Border Radio

The term "border radio" refers to an American broadcasting industry that sprang up on Mexico's northern border in the early 1930s and flourished for half a century. High-powered transmitters on Mexican soil, beyond the reach of U.S. regulators, blanketed North America. Early on, hillbilly music proved to be one of the most effective mediums for pulling mail and moving merchandise; in turn, the border stations played a significant role in popularizing country music during the crucial pre– and post–World War II growth years.

Mexico accommodated these "outlaw" media folk, some of whom had been denied United States broadcasting licenses, because Canada and the United States had divided the long-range radio frequencies between themselves, allotting none to Mexico.

The first border station, XED, began broadcasting from Reynosa, Tamaulipas, in 1930. Owned for a time by Houston theater owner and philanthropist Will Horwitz, XED hosted occasional performances by Horwitz's friend JIMMIE RODGERS.

DR. JOHN R. BRINKLEY opened XER (later called XERA) in Villa Acuña, Coahuila, the following year. Brinkley also obtained XED, changing the name to XEAW. In 1939 he sold XEAW to Carr Collins, owner of CRAZY WATER CRYSTALS. According to Collins's son Jim, W. LEE "PAPPY" O'DANIEL was part owner of the station. The Mexican government confiscated XERA in 1941 and tried to confiscate XEAW shortly thereafter, but Collins moved his equipment north of the border.

Engineer Bill Branch and businessman C. M. Bres operated XEPN in Piedras Negras in the 1930s. And Iowan Norman Baker, whose experimental cancer treatments made him a controversial figure, broadcast from his station XENT in Nuevo Laredo.

Border station power generally ranged from 50,000 to 500,000 watts. Sometimes listeners claimed to enjoy the broadcasts without a radio, receiving the powerful signal on dental work, bedsprings, and barbed wire. American network programs were often lost in the ether when a Mexican border outlet was broadcasting near its frequency.

HANK THOMPSON, who grew up in Waco, Texas, in the 1930s, said the American-Mexican stations "were about the only ones where you could hear country music most all the time." Thompson and other listeners heard COWBOY SLIM RINEHART, PATSY MONTANA, the CARTER FAMILY, the PICKARD FAMILY, Pappy O'Daniel's Hillbilly Boys, Roy "Lonesome Cowboy" Faulkner, SHELLY LEE ALLEY, and others. Performers broadcast live and via transcription disc, sometimes syndicating a show on several of the maverick stations.

Important postwar stations included XEG in Monterrey and XERF in Ciudad Acuña. WEBB PIERCE, JIM REEVES, and other stars appeared live in the studio with XERF DJ Paul Kallinger. In a colorful exaggeration that could hold a nugget of truth, Pierce said country music "might not have survived if it hadn't been for border radio."

Some border musicians, such as Dallas "Nevada Slim" Turner, filled several functions, such as singing cowboy, evangelist, and pitchman. "Only three things will sell on the border," said Turner, "health, sex, and religion." Many country music shows on *la frontera* radio combined all three.

In 1986, after years of waning influence, the border stations were dealt a crippling blow by an international broadcasting agreement between the United States and Mexico that allowed both Mexican and American broadcasters to use the other country's clear-channel frequencies for low-powered stations in the evening. That meant that the signals of the border stations would be drowned out in many communities by local broadcasts, effectively putting an end to the era of high-powered, far-ranging radio. —*Gene Fowler*

Chris Bouchillon
b. Oconee County, South Carolina, 1895; d. early 1970s

One of the most enduring bits of country comedy is a spoken lyric that begins, "If you want to get to Heaven, let me tell you how to do it." Over the years it has been popularized by WOODY GUTHRIE, CURLY FOX, GRAND OLE OPRY star ROBERT LUNN, and many others. It is usually called "The Talking Blues" or "The Original Talking Blues," and it is a rare example of a song that became a musical genre. Though its ultimate origins probably lie in nineteenth-century vaudeville, the artist who first made it famous was a bespectacled, pipe-smoking comedian named Christopher Allen Bouchillon (pronounced BUSH-alon).

The son of a mountain banjo player, Bouchillon grew

up near an iron foundry in Greenville, South Carolina; as a teenager he performed with his brothers Uris and Charlie, recording briefly as the Greenville Trio. In 1926 Chris recorded his "Talking Blues" for COLUMBIA; A&R chief FRANK WALKER later claimed he told Bouchillon to talk through the song because he didn't like Bouchillon's singing voice. Friends, however, insist Bouchillon himself came up with the style after spending hours listening to African-American performers in the area. Issued in February 1927, the disc sold almost 100,000 copies—a huge hit by 1920s standards. Several of his later efforts also became best-sellers: "Born in Hard Luck" did well, as did "My Fat Girl" and a singing effort, "Hannah" (later revived by a MEL TILLIS rewrite as "Honey [Open That Door]" and turned into a #1 hit by RICKY SKAGGS).

Bouchillon seemed uninterested in exploiting his hit records and did not tour or try radio. In later years, seemingly unaware of how influential his work had been, he operated a dry cleaning shop and lived in relative obscurity. He died in a nursing home in the early 1970s.

—*Charles Wolfe*

REPRESENTATIVE RECORDING

Chris Bouchillon: The Original Talking Blues Man (Old Homestead, 1987)

Jimmy Bowen

b. Santa Rita, New Mexico, November 30, 1937

Few individuals have had as big an impact on the Nashville music industry as James Allen Bowen, an outspoken, controversial, and colorful maverick who relocated to Music City from Los Angeles in 1977. During his now forty-year career, he has been a DJ, hit pop artist, publishing employee, record label A&R head, record producer, and finally, the Nashville boss of such major labels as (in chronological order) MGM, MCA, ELEKTRA/ASYLUM, WARNER BROS., MCA (again), Universal, CAPITOL, LIBERTY, and PATRIOT RECORDS.

Bowen grew up in Dumas, Texas, starting his career as a teenage DJ. By eighteen he was playing bass and singing with Buddy Knox & the Rhythm Orchids, a rockabilly group that scored pop smashes with "Party Doll" (#1, 1957), sung by Knox, and "I'm Stickin' with You" (#14), sung by Bowen.

Bowen forsook performing in 1959 and moved to Los Angeles, where he had remarkable success with Frank Sinatra, Sammy Davis Jr., and Dean Martin. Bowen produced fifteen gold albums with Martin, including his best-known hit, "Everybody Loves Somebody" (#1 pop, 1964), and crafted legendary Sinatra records such as "Strangers in the Night" (#1 pop, 1966) and "That's Life" (#4 pop, 1967). He also started his own record label, A.M.O.S., where he worked with, among others, KENNY ROGERS and future EAGLES Don Henley and Glenn Frey.

In 1977 Bowen moved to Nashville and apprenticed at TOMPALL GLASER's studio, then known as "Outlaw Central." Bowen spent about three years there, working first with MEL TILLIS and immediately scoring major hits with him. Shortly afterward he began producing HANK WILLIAMS JR. and helped launch that performer's career into a new, more commercial direction.

During the 1980s Bowen's production whirlwind peaked, delivering hits for a huge variety of artists, among them CONWAY TWITTY, GEORGE STRAIT, REBA MCENTIRE, the BELLAMY BROTHERS, CRYSTAL GAYLE, JOHN ANDERSON, and WAYLON JENNINGS. Known for dramatically slashing artist rosters upon taking control of a label (he let go twenty-nine of fifty-three acts on the combined Elektra/Warner roster in 1984), he nevertheless endeared himself to many artists. He set an important precedent in Nashville by co-producing most of the records with the artists above, giving them a key role in their recordings for the first time— "freeing the slaves," as he called it. As of late 1995, such collaborations had resulted in the incredible total of 227 Top Twenty singles, 197 of which landed in the Top Ten, with sixty-seven hitting #1. He also produced forty-five Top Ten albums, twenty of them #1s, earning at least twenty gold and a dozen platinum records, a total that will doubtless increase due to catalogue sales in subsequent years.

Bowen tried hard to help Nashville diversify its musical output and was, with BOB BECKHAM, an invaluable figure in the establishment of the Nashville Music Association (now the Nashville Entertainment Association), a group dedicated to stimulating Music City's noncountry side.

He was the key person in upgrading the sound quality of Nashville records to compete with pop recordings, boasting that he had "taught the hillbillies how to make a $40,000 album for $150,000." He was the city's most vocal early advocate for digital recording and began transferring the MCA label's country catalogue to CD as early as 1984. In addition, a number of Bowen employees have gone on to become major figures in the industry, among them JIM ED NORMAN, TONY BROWN, Martha Sharp, Nick Hunter, and JAMES STROUD.

He established the *MCA Masters Series* in 1986, empowering Brown to oversee recordings of deserving noncountry artists, primarily instrumentalists, then created his own label in 1988, Universal Records. When MCA terminated that venture, Bowen moved to CAPITOL RECORDS along with most of the Universal roster, renaming the Nashville divi-

Jimmy Bowen

sion Liberty Records. Bowen was instrumental in guiding the rise of GARTH BROOKS, working closely with the EMI corporate brass in New York to make Brooks a priority and overseeing the marketing of Brooks's second and third albums, *No Fences* and *Ropin' the Wind*, the two biggest-selling albums in country history.

Bowen had better working relationships with the corporate higher-ups on both coasts than other Nashville labels. However, late in 1994 his luck ran out. Despite the success both men had enjoyed, his relationship with Brooks soured, and he became entangled in disputes with EMI's top brass in New York. His time on the golf course increased as he seemed to lose interest in the label. Personal health problems (thyroid cancer) also took their toll. In early 1995 he put his Nashville house on the market and moved to Maui to recuperate and to work on his autobiography, *Rough Mix*, published by Simon & Schuster in 1997.

Throughout his nearly twenty years in Nashville, Bowen was remarkably skilled at delegating tasks. He frequently produced two or more acts simultaneously, working with a personally trained corps of recording engineers, often by directing the early recording stages from a mobile phone on his golf cart, then listening to the rough mixes at night, before showing up at the studio to immerse himself in the final mixing of the album. He always seemed to be the central figure in the Music City rumor mill and was not above starting some of the rumors himself, particularly toward the end of his various contracts.   —*John Lomax III*

Boxcar Willie

b. Sterratt, Texas, September 1, 1931

Lecil Travis Martin was forty-four years old when he donned a hobo costume and turned down-home vocals and a throbbing railroad whistle into a million-dollar telemarketing act. Though it took him years to break through, Boxcar Willie aimed for a music career almost from the beginning. Encouraged by a fiddle-playing father, he was singing on local Texas radio by age ten and had performed in honky-tonks by thirteen. At sixteen he had played a stint at the *BIG D JAMBOREE*. After two tours of duty and a decade as an air force C-5 pilot, he spent two years in Lincoln, Nebraska, performing on a local live TV show. Beginning in 1960, as Marty Martin, he worked as a DJ at KGEM–Boise, Idaho, for almost ten years. In 1970 he moved back to Texas, where he worked on and off as a pilot, mechanic, and DJ. In the fall of 1975, while living in Fort Worth, he began performing in hobo costume as Boxcar Willie and appeared on the local *Grapevine Opry*. In 1978 Scottish promoter Drew Taylor engaged him as the opening act for a star in a series of shows in the United Kingdom. When the name artist bowed out, Taylor gambled on Boxcar Willie as the headliner. The Texan's booming vocal style and hobo persona caught on with British audiences. In April 1979, without benefit of a major label or a hit single, Boxcar Willie appeared at England's Wembley International Country Music Festival and was named Most Promising International Artist, though still largely unknown in the States.

Shortly afterward Boxcar Willie had four albums top the English country charts and won both the British CMA International Entertainer of the Year and Best Song (for *Daddy Was a Railroad Man*) awards. He continued this run of success in the United States in 1980 with his *King of the Road* album for Main Street Records, eventually selling some 3 million copies worldwide, almost exclusively via television marketing. As a result, readers of *Music City News* voted Boxcar Willie Most Promising Male Artist of 1981. He debuted at the GRAND OLE OPRY on June 19, 1980, and joined the Opry cast on February 21, 1981.

Of the ten singles Boxcar Willie placed in the *Billboard* charts between 1980 and 1984, his best was "Bad News" (#36, 1982). In 1986 he became one of the first artists to open a theater in BRANSON, Missouri, where he still performs regularly in addition to visits to the Grand Ole Opry.   —*Walt Trott*

REPRESENTATIVE RECORDINGS

King of the Road (Main Street, 1980); *Boxcar Willie* (Column One, 1981)

Boy Howdy

Jeffrey Steele b. Burbank, California, August 27, 1961
Cary Park b. Stockton, California, June 3, 1959
Larry Park b. Stockton, California, March 14, 1956
Hugh Wright b. Keokuk, Iowa, November 18, 1951

Boy Howdy was a Southern California–based band consisting of bassist/lead vocalist Jeffrey Levasseur Steele, guitar-playing brothers Larry and Cary Park, and drummer Hugh Wright. They met at a Los Angeles club and formed in 1990. After playing the California club circuit for nearly two years, the band was signed to CURB RECORDS in 1992 and soon thereafter released their debut album, *Welcome to Howdywood*.

The members of Boy Howdy brought different backgrounds to the group setting. The Park brothers' father, Ray Park, played bluegrass in the 1960s duo of Vern & Ray and had taught his sons a variety of musical styles, including jazz and country. Wright was a professionally trained jazz/blues musician who earned a degree from the Iowa State University School of Music. Steele, who wrote or co-wrote most of the original material, took his influences from sixties rock bands such as the Kinks, along with California bands such as the EAGLES. He was essentially the group's focal point, a charismatic figure both onstage and in the band's videos.

The band first debuted over a radio station in Southern California, KZLA-Burbank, and released a single in 1991, "When Johnny Comes Marchin' Home Again." This song gained them a contract with CURB RECORDS. The album *Welcome to Howdywood* generated the band's first hit single, "A Cowboy's Born with a Broken Heart," which received mild airplay. What most impressed reviewers was the group's expert musicianship, both individually and collectively.

Boy Howdy received a nomination from the ACADEMY OF COUNTRY MUSIC in 1993, for Best New Vocal Group. In 1994 Boy Howdy released the single "She'd Give Anything," which was the title cut off their second album. The song, co-written by Steele, went to the #4 spot on *Billboard* country charts. They were not able to match this level of success, however, with their 1995 follow-up album, *Bigger Fish to Fry;* it failed to produce a major chart single. Boy Howdy eventually disbanded in 1996, with Steele pursuing a solo career.   —*Bob Paxman*

REPRESENTATIVE RECORDING

She'd Give Anything (Curb, 1994)

BR5-49: (from left) Don Herron, Chuck Mead, "Smilin'" Jay McDowell, "Hawk" Shaw Wilson, and Gary Bennett

Bill & Jim Boyd

Bill Boyd b. Fannin County, Texas, September 29, 1910;
d. December 7, 1977
Jim Boyd b. Fannin County, Texas, September 28, 1914;
d. March 11, 1993

Bill Boyd's Cowboy Ramblers are usually considered one of the four major western swing bands of the prewar era, along with BOB WILLS & His Texas Playboys, MILTON BROWN & His Musical Brownies, and the LIGHT CRUST DOUGHBOYS. William Lemuel Boyd was known as the King of the Instrumentals for cutting classics such as "Under the Double Eagle" (1935), "New Spanish Two-Step" (1938), and "Lone Star Rag" (1949) during a prolific association with RCA VICTOR. Brother Jim Boyd—who had a longer career than Bill—served as his right-hand man for most of the Cowboy Ramblers' existence, which spanned two decades, from the early thirties through the mid-fifties.

Bill Boyd was essentially a country singer-guitarist whose first incarnation of the Cowboy Ramblers, formed at Dallas's WRR in about 1932, was oriented toward cowboy songs and old-time tunes. Under the influence of Fort Worth's Musical Brownies, Boyd gravitated steadily toward western swing, sharing personnel such as fiddler Art Davis and banjoist Walker Kirkes, with ROY NEWMAN's jazzy WRR stringband. Boyd's recording bands were rarely like his daily radio and road bands. For his BLUEBIRD (and later RCA Victor) recordings he borrowed jazz-minded men such as Knocky Parker and Marvin Montgomery from the Light Crust Doughboys and other bands, recording a far different repertoire and style than his live performances featured. In the early forties Boyd's repertoire became more weighted toward originals or songs that Boyd owned a piece of; if these compositions did not always measure up to the material Boyd had played previously, they were nevertheless always performed expertly.

Partly owing to his sister, Janie Hamilton, who deftly handled his publicity, Bill Boyd remained a viable major label act far longer than many of his contemporaries. In the early forties he even appeared in a series of western films.

"Lone Star Rag" was his last hit in 1949, and after leaving RCA in 1951 he recorded for TNT and for STARDAY before fading from the scene.

Arguably a far better singer and musician than his brother, Jim Boyd played extensively with Roy Newman's band, worked the first of many stints with the Light Crust Doughboys in 1938–39, and led his own Men of the West, recording for RCA, 1949–51. Jim remained musically active until shortly before his death. —*Kevin Coffey*

REPRESENTATIVE RECORDINGS

Bill Boyd's Cowboy Ramblers (Bluebird, 1976); *Bill Boyd & His Cowboy Ramblers, 1934–1947* (Texas Rose, 1982)

BR5-49

Gary Bennett b. Las Vegas, Nevada, October 9, 1964
Donald John Herron Jr. b. Steubenville, Ohio, September 23, 1962
Jay Michael McDowell b. Bedford, Indiana, June 11, 1969
Charles Lynn Mead b. Nevada, Missouri, December 22, 1960
Randall Edward Shaw Wilson b. Topeka, Kansas, July 10, 1960

From 1994 to 1996, BR5-49 stepped up from playing for tips in downtown Nashville to become one of the most talked-about acts in country music. The neo-hillbilly boogie quintet, with a deep affection for all genres of American roots music, and the group's long run at Robert's Western World at 416 Broadway touched off a street-level industry buzz that landed them on the cover of the trade magazine *Billboard* before they had a record deal.

Originally, BR5-49 had coalesced around the talents of front men Gary Bennett and Chuck Mead, a pair of singer-songwriter-guitarists who began working together at Robert's in early 1994. The group takes its name from Junior Samples's used-car salesman routine on *Hee Haw*. BR5-49 went through various personnel changes before the current lineup, which includes drummer "Hawk" Shaw Wilson, bassist "Smilin' " Jay McDowell, and multi-instrumentalist Don Herron, solidified in the spring of 1995. By then, their four-hour sets at Robert's, a combination bar and western wear store, had become standing-room-only affairs. Their high-energy mixture of classic country covers (WEBB PIERCE, FARON YOUNG, JOHNNY HORTON, etc.) and original tunes spearheaded a downtown Nashville music revival that made national news. Journalists and music industry insiders flocked to Robert's, and on October 13, 1995, after much hype and speculation, the band was signed to ARISTA-Nashville. A *Live from Robert's* minialbum was released in April 1996, followed in September by an eponymous full-length album. The debut single off the latter album, a cover of the MOON MULLICAN hit "Cherokee Boogie," was nominated for a Grammy. The album crested just inside the Top Forty, leaving the question open at the close of 1996 as to how much a history-conscious band that played for tips in a Nashville boot store might or might not affect the course of country music. —*Daniel Cooper*

REPRESENTATIVE RECORDINGS

BR5-49 Live from Robert's (Arista, 1996); *BR5-49* (Arista, 1996)

Bobby Braddock
b. Auburndale, Florida, August 5, 1940

One of Nashville's most admired songwriters, Robert Valentine Braddock moved to Nashville in September 1964; he took a job as MARTY ROBBINS's piano player in January 1965. Later that same year, Braddock landed his first cut when Robbins recorded "While You're Dancing." Braddock signed his first publishing contract with TREE INTERNATIONAL in 1966.

In the late 1960s Braddock parlayed a relationship with producer BILLY SHERRILL into hits by TAMMY WYNETTE, GEORGE JONES, and many other Sherrill-produced artists. Classic songs of Braddock's include "D-I-V-O-R-C-E" (Wynette, 1968), "Golden Ring" (Jones & Wynette, 1976), "He Stopped Loving Her Today" (Jones, 1980), and "Time Marches On" (Tracy Lawrence, 1996). Other artists who charted with Braddock tunes include JOHN ANDERSON, TANYA TUCKER, TRACY LAWRENCE, LACY J. DALTON, MARK CHESNUTT, JOHNNY DUNCAN, and JOHNNY PAYCHECK.

In addition to songwriting, Braddock has recorded for MGM, COLUMBIA, MERCURY, ELEKTRA, and RCA with minor chart impact. His offbeat, slightly askew sense of humor was perhaps best portrayed on the RCA album *Hardpore Cornography*. —*Kent Henderson*

REPRESENTATIVE RECORDINGS

Love Bomb (Elektra, 1980, out of print); *Hardpore Cornography* (RCA, 1983, out of print)

Connie Bradley
b. Fayetteville, Tennessee, October 1, 1945

Connie Bradley is southern executive director for the American Society of Composers, Authors, and Publishers (ASCAP), a position she has held since 1980. Her Nashville branch of the performing rights agency is responsible for signing songwriters and publishers in a twenty-state area.

Born Connie Darnell, Bradley grew up in Shelbyville, Tennessee, and worked for Nashville's WLAC-TV, Famous Music/DOT RECORDS, the Bill Hudson & Associates public relations firm, and RCA RECORDS before she joined ASCAP in 1976. She has served on the boards of numerous music and community organizations; she served as the CMA's chairman of the board in 1989.

Bradley has won numerous awards, including Lady Executive of the Year (1985) from the National Women Executives and the Community Salesperson of the Year (1992) honor from the Tennessee Association of Sales Professionals. Bradley is the wife of JERRY BRADLEY and the daughter-in-law of the late country music pioneer OWEN BRADLEY. —*Don Cusic*

Harold Bradley
b. Nashville, Tennessee, January 2, 1926

Harold Ray Bradley, considered the "Dean of Nashville Session Guitarists," grew up in Nashville, and his first instrument was the tenor banjo. Older brother OWEN BRADLEY suggested that his younger brother learn guitar, though. Harold was playing amplified jazz guitar by 1943, and Owen got him a summer job playing lead guitar with ERNEST TUBB's Texas Troubadours. After his service in the U.S. Navy from 1944 to 1946, Harold returned to Nashville to study music and play in Owen's dance band. His first country recording session came in 1946, when he recorded with PEE WEE KING's Golden West Cowboys in Chicago. As recording activities increased in Nashville, Harold's studio workload grew. His acoustic rhythm guitar opened RED FOLEY's 1950 hit "Chattanoogie Shoe Shine Boy."

Though he is a capable lead guitarist, Harold's studio specialty was rhythm work. On many sessions, he was part of a studio guitar triumvirate with lead specialists HANK GARLAND and GRADY MARTIN. Garland specialized in jazzy licks, Martin in funkier leads. After Garland's disabling 1961 accident, Harold took Garland's place, and RAY EDENTON played rhythm guitar chores. His rhythm playing wasn't always apparent when listening to recordings, although his parts were essential contributions. Occasionally he did play lead parts that stood out. For example, he played the opening banjo notes (the instrument was tuned like a guitar) on JOHNNY HORTON's 1959 hit "The Battle of New Orleans."

After operating two small recording studios in town in the early 1950s, Harold and Owen opened Bradley Film and Recording on Sixteenth Avenue South, in 1955. After COLUMBIA RECORDS purchased the Bradley studio in 1962,

Harold Bradley

Owen and his son Jerry opened Bradley's Barn east of Nashville in tiny Mount Juliet, Tennessee.

In addition to his studio achievements, Harold was the first president of Nashville's chapter of the National Academy of Recording Arts and Sciences. In the 1980s he toured with FLOYD CRAMER and served as bandleader for SLIM WHITMAN. He also produced Irish country singer Sandy Kelly and EDDY ARNOLD's later RCA albums. As president of Nashville's chapter of the American Federation of Musicians since 1991, Bradley has helped establish a union presence in Branson, Missouri. —*Rich Kienzle*

REPRESENTATIVE RECORDINGS

Bossa Nova Goes to Nashville (Columbia, 1963); *Misty Guitar* (Columbia, 1963)

Jerry Bradley

b. Nashville, Tennessee, January 30, 1940

As the son of famed Nashville recording pioneer OWEN BRADLEY, Jerry Bradley was groomed to succeed in the music business. After working for a number of years as a publisher with his father's Forest Hills Music, he succeeded CHET ATKINS as head of RCA RECORDS' Nashville office in 1973. At the time, Atkins's influence still loomed large over RCA, and Bradley was eager to make his own mark. He glimpsed his opportunity in the burgeoning OUTLAW movement in country music in the mid-1970s. Bradley put together an album package consisting of cuts by WAYLON JENNINGS, some by Jennings's wife, JESSI COLTER, and others by WILLIE NELSON and TOMPALL GLASER, and released it in 1976 as *Wanted: The Outlaws*. It shortly became country music's first album to be certified platinum for sales of 1 million copies. Nashville executives had traditionally viewed their business as having a low sales ceiling, but the success of the platinum-selling *Wanted: The Outlaws* changed all that.

Bradley was eventually succeeded as RCA Nashville chief by JOE GALANTE. Bradley went on to head the OPRYLAND MUSIC GROUP, which grew out of GAYLORD ENTERTAINMENT's acquisition of the ACUFF-ROSE publishing catalogues. —*Chet Flippo*

Owen Bradley

b. Westmoreland, Tennessee, October 21, 1915; d. January 7, 1998

William Owen Bradley produced the hits of a half dozen Country Music Hall of Famers. He built the first music business on Music Row and is the only country producer who has been nominated for an Academy Award. In addition, Bradley was an architect of the NASHVILLE SOUND.

The Bradley family moved to Nashville when Owen was a boy. He was fascinated with music and learned harmonica, steel guitar, trombone, piano, vibraphone, and organ. He was working professionally as a musician by age fifteen.

By the late 1930s Bradley was leading his own band, which eventually included future pop stars Snooky Lanson and Kitty Kallen as vocalists. He broadcast on WLAC during 1937–40, then became a regular on WSM. DECCA executive PAUL COHEN noted Bradley's studio skills during his recording visits to Nashville, and in 1947 he hired Bradley to lead the label's sessions there.

In addition to those duties and co-writing songs such as ROY ACUFF's 1942 hit "Night Train to Memphis," Bradley found time for his own recording career. "Zeb's Mountain

Owen Bradley

Boogie," issued as by "Brad Brady and His Tennesseans," launched BULLET RECORDS in 1946. Bradley's group had additional hits on Coral in 1949 ("Blues Stay Away from Me") and in 1950 ("The Third Man Theme").

One of Bradley's first big production successes was RED FOLEY's 1950 million seller "Chattanoogie Shoe Shine Boy." In that same year BILL MONROE rejoined Decca, and Bradley soon began producing a string of bluegrass classics. He started working with honky-tonk masters ERNEST TUBB and WEBB PIERCE in 1947 and 1952, respectively. He also led the session that revolutionized female country music, KITTY WELLS's 1952 blockbuster "It Wasn't God Who Made Honky-Tonk Angels."

Owen and his brother HAROLD BRADLEY were among the first to build independent recording studios in Nashville. Paul Cohen was contemplating relocating Decca's country headquarters to Dallas, but in 1955, Bradley promised him a Nashville recording center in an old house at 804 Sixteenth Avenue South; the Bradleys later added an army Quonset hut film and recording studio behind it.

Ironically, the earliest hits from Bradley Studios weren't all Decca recordings. Rented to other labels, the studio became the birthplace of SONNY JAMES's "Young Love" and Gene Vincent's "Be-Bop-a-Lula" (both CAPITOL, 1956), MARTY ROBBINS's "Singing the Blues" (COLUMBIA, 1956), CONWAY TWITTY's "It's Only Make Believe" (MGM, 1958), Mark Dinning's "Teen Angel" (MGM, 1959), and JOHNNY HORTON's "The Battle of New Orleans" (Columbia, 1959), to name but a few.

Owen Bradley was named head of Decca's Nashville division in 1958, from which position he helped shape the evolution of the Nashville Sound. In addition to turning out hits by Decca's country acts, Bradley also produced a Grammy-winning record for folk star BURL IVES (1962) and attracted Dixieland clarinetist Pete Fountain and pop organist Lenny Dee to Nashville. Bradley himself scored pop hits for Decca in 1957 ("White Silver Sands") and 1958 ("Big Guitar").

Bradley's finest productions for Decca were with female vocalists. He produced numerous Top Ten hits with Kitty Wells, and his collaborations with PATSY CLINE remain the standard against which female country records are measured to this day. BRENDA LEE had twelve Top Ten pop hits produced by Bradley in the early 1960s, and he also produced the fifty-plus hits that made LORETTA LYNN a country legend.

By the early 1960s Bradley's studio was hosting 700 sessions annually and had been joined by similar businesses in a district that would come to be known as Music Row. CO-LUMBIA RECORDS bought the studio from Bradley in 1962 and built the label's Nashville headquarters around it. Columbia continued to use that studio for recording until 1982.

In 1965 Bradley converted a Mount Juliet, Tennessee, barn into another studio. "Bradley's Barn," as it was called, was used by Gordon Lightfoot, Joan Baez, the Beau Brummels, and other pop acts. Meanwhile, Bradley continued to sign important artists to Decca, most notably Conway Twitty.

Bradley was inducted into the COUNTRY MUSIC HALL OF FAME in 1974. He stepped down as a label head in 1976 (by which time Decca had been completely absorbed into MCA) to become an independent producer and work with his publishing firm, Forest Hills Music. He built yet another studio (on the same site) after Bradley's Barn was destroyed by fire in 1980.

Actress Sissy Spacek portrayed Loretta Lynn in the 1980 movie *Coal Miner's Daughter;* the soundtrack, produced by Bradley, received an Academy Award nomination. In 1985 Jessica Lange portrayed Patsy Cline in the film *Sweet Dreams;* again, Bradley produced the soundtrack. Canadian K. D. LANG came to Nashville in 1987 to record *Shadowland: The Owen Bradley Sessions.* The album sold 1 million copies.

In the 1990s Bradley produced records for Marsha Thornton, Brenda Lee, and Pete Fountain, and went into semiretirement. The Recording Academy gave him its Governors Award at a 1995 gala, and the reactivated Decca label saluted him with a 1996 compilation called *The Nashville Sound.*

Bradley fathered a musical dynasty. Son Jerry led RCA's Nashville operations for a time, then took the reins of the OPRYLAND MUSIC GROUP, where grandson Clay also works. Daughter Patsy is at BMI; nephew Bobby is a studio engineer. Daughter-in-law Connie is the head of Nashville's AS-CAP office. Younger brother Harold became the most recorded session guitarist in history, and the president of the Nashville musicians' union.

When Owen Bradley died in 1998 his funeral service was held at the RYMAN AUDITORIUM. —*Robert K. Oermann*

Paul Brandt
b. Calgary, Alberta, Canada, July 21, 1972

Paul Brandt burst onto the country music scene in 1996 with his three-octave baritone and self-penned ballads. His debut single, "My Heart Has a History," reached the Top Five in July 1996, followed by "I Do" (#2) in October 1996.

Brandt grew up singing in church and began playing guitar in ninth grade. He began writing songs and entering talent contests in high school while listening to CLINT BLACK, GEORGE STRAIT, and DWIGHT YOAKAM. Although he won the $1,000 prize at the 1992 Calgary Stampede and

found success in other U.S. and Canadian talent competitions, he simultaneously pursued another career, in nursing. His father is a paramedic, so when Paul's mother returned to school to become a registered nurse, Paul soon followed.

Brandt spent two years at Alberta's Children's Hospital, often working with terminally ill children, but his medical career was cut short after he won Best Original Canadian Country Song for "Calm Before the Storm" in a nationwide contest sponsored by the Society of Composers, Authors, and Music Publishers of Canada (SOCAN), a performance rights society. Among the music executives in attendance was Warner Music Canada's Kim Cooke, who contacted Brandt. Brandt sent a tape to WARNER BROS.' Nashville office and soon got a message from Warner vice president Paige Levy, who had signed Dwight Yoakam to Warner/Reprise. Warner Bros. eventually signed Brandt, and the label released his debut album, *Calm Before the Storm,* in August 1996. Produced by Josh Leo, the album contains six songs either written or co-written by Brandt.
—*Beverly Keel*

REPRESENTATIVE RECORDINGS

Calm Before the Storm (Warner Bros., 1996); *Outside the Frame* (Warner Bros., 1997)

Branson, Missouri

The Ozark Mountains community of Branson, in southwestern Missouri, is one of America's most popular and distinctive resort and entertainment areas, attracting more than 5.8 million visitors in 1994. Since the 1960s, the town has grown into a major live performance center for the music industry, where stars of country, pop, and big band music perform to enthusiastic audiences from April through October. As of 1995, entertainers including GLEN CAMPBELL, MEL TILLIS, JIM STAFFORD, MICKEY GILLEY, CHARLEY PRIDE, Tony Orlando, BOXCAR WILLIE, and Bobby Vinton were headlining at their own theaters there, while VINCE GILL, BARBARA MANDRELL, KENNY ROGERS, and LORRIE MORGAN, to name a few, performed at a 4,000-seat, state-of-the-art facility called the Grand Palace.

Branson was a tourism center before the live music boom. Tours of Marvel Cave (now part of the area's largest employer, the theme park Silver Dollar City) have brought visitors to Branson for more than one hundred years. The region has flourished as a fishing and camping haven since the 1920s, and water sports are popular in the three lakes that surround Branson.

The first live performance attraction in Branson started more than thirty years ago with a hillbilly jamboree called Baldknobbers (named for a turn-of-the-century Ozarks vigilante gang). Built in 1967, Presley's Jubilee was the first theater on 76 Country Boulevard, known locally as "The Strip." Branson has since grown to accommodate more than thirty local venues with a combined total of more than 50,000 indoor theater seats and 21,500 amphitheater seats.

In the early 1990s the town's booming popularity as a country music tourism destination caught the attention of the national media, which portrayed Branson as threatening Nashville's dominant position as a country music mecca. Though the threat later appeared exaggerated, Branson has continued to hold a preeminent position among national tourism destinations. Among other hon-

ors, Branson was listed as one of the Top Ten U.S. "hot spots" for 1995 by the American Society of Travel Agents.
—*Janet E. Williams*

Rod Brasfield
b. Smithville, Mississippi, August 22, 1910; d. September 12, 1958

From 1947 to 1958, Rodney Leon Brasfield was the premier comedian at the GRAND OLE OPRY and very likely in country music. He began his career as straight man for his brother Lawrence (known as "Boob") during several years with Bisbee's Dramatic Shows, one of many such troupes that traversed the South during the late 1800s and early 1900s. Brasfield served one year in the army air corps during World War II, but returned to Bisbee's because of a nagging childhood back injury. Boob eventually wound up playing "Uncle Cyp" on Springfield, Missouri's, *OZARK JU-BILEE* television program (1955–60).

While working the road in the Southeast, Brasfield was recruited by GEORGE D. HAY for the Grand Ole Opry in 1944. By this time Brasfield was playing both comic and straight parts and became an immediate hit with the show's stage and radio audiences, especially with Opry TENT SHOWS. With his trademark baggy suit, button shoes, beat-up hat, rubbery face, and clacking false teeth, he could have the audience laughing before he spoke a word. Playing the drawling bumpkin to the hilt, he had a finely honed sense of timing and worked easily with host RED FO-LEY on the Opry's NBC network segment beginning in 1947, when Brasfield replaced the DUKE OF PADUCAH in this regard. Much of their comedy contrasted the tall, broad-shouldered Foley with the diminutive Brasfield, who skillfully milked running gags by deferentially addressing the singer as "Mr. Foley" and complaining good-naturedly

Rod Brasfield

about the sweltering summer heat in the RYMAN AUDITO-RIUM.

Audiences instinctively sympathized with Brasfield's hapless character, a good ole country boy who was constantly unlucky. Like MINNIE PEARL, with whom he frequently teamed from 1948 until his death, he often poked fun at country life—always with good humor. Reinforcing his small-town identity, he took his moniker, the Hohenwald Flash, from the name of a Tennessee town southwest of Nashville. Brasfield and Pearl's comic exchanges (in which they alternated in delivering punch lines—that is, neither was the straight man) were not only broadcast on the Opry radio show but also televised on a series of ABC network shows made by Opry acts in 1955 and 1956. In addition, Brasfield did comedy routines with singer-comedienne June Carter. Brasfield's role as Andy Griffith's sidekick in the 1957 film *A Face in the Crowd* hinted at a film career that might have been. A victim of heart failure and a widely known problem with alcohol, Brasfield was elected to the COUNTRY MUSIC HALL OF FAME in 1987.
—*John Rumble*

Thom Bresh
b. Hollywood, California, February 23, 1948

Versatility has distinguished the career of Thomas Charles Bresh, who has been a singer, songwriter, and impressionist, and who at age three was billed as "Hollywood's Youngest Stunt Man." But Bresh's command of fingerstyle guitar is perhaps his most natural talent, since Bresh is the son of MERLE TRAVIS.

This was an open secret for years, only publicized since the deaths of Travis and Hollywood photographer Bud Bresh. Bresh grew up knowing Travis as a family friend from whom he never took lessons. However, Bresh says, "I could play everything he did when I was about thirteen years old. . . . I inherited a heavy thumb from Merle." When he was sixteen, Bresh replaced ROY CLARK in HANK PENNY's band and made an unsuccessful bid for pop success with his 1963 recording debut, "Pink Dominoes." Working with Penny in Vegas, Bresh played guitar, banjo, and trumpet, and did impressions. A stint running a Seattle recording studio yielded Bresh's 1972 novelty "D. B. Cooper, Where Are You?" His biggest chart success came four years later, with the JIMMY BOWEN–produced "Homemade Love" on the short-lived Los Angeles–based Farr label. It is Bresh's only entry into the country Top Ten.

Subsequent recordings in the 1970s and 1980s for ABC/DOT and LIBERTY brought Bresh little commercial success. He hosted a Canadian television series, *Nashville Swing*, for a time before moving to Music City in 1983. Bresh has in recent years highlighted his relation to Travis and displays his inherent guitar skills in recordings for Scotty Moore's Belle Meade label.   —*Mark Humphrey*

REPRESENTATIVE RECORDINGS

Son of a Guitar Pickin' Man (Belle Meade, 1993); *Next Generation* (Belle Meade, 1994)

David Briggs
b. Florence, Alabama, March 16, 1943

When David Paul Briggs moved to Nashville in 1964, at twenty-one, he had established a significant career as a session musician. Briggs began working as a teenager at Rick Hall's Fame studio in Muscle Shoals and helped shape classics such as Arthur Alexander's "You Better Move On" and Jimmy Hughes's "Steal Away." "The only reason I ended up playing piano in Muscle Shoals was because nobody else there was good enough," he has said. "I was the best of the worst."

Signed to DECCA by OWEN BRADLEY as a singer-songwriter in 1962, Briggs had some success but returned to sessions because "I could get paid in two weeks." In 1965 he played piano on ELVIS PRESLEY's recording of "Love Letters," beginning a twelve-year association with Presley. In 1969 Briggs opened Quadrafonic Studios in Nashville with Norbert Putnam.

Briggs has also been successful in production, arranging, publishing, jingle writing, and performing with Area Code 615. His session credits include ALABAMA, Bob Seger, HANK WILLIAMS JR., NEIL YOUNG, REBA MCENTIRE, LINDA RONSTADT, WILLIE NELSON, B. B. King, DOLLY PARTON, James Brown, ERNEST TUBB, ROY ORBISON, and MARTY ROBBINS.

In 1985 he and Will Jennings started a publishing company, Willin' David Music, and soon after published the Academy Award–winning "Up Where We Belong" and Steve Winwood's "Higher Love." Briggs has had his own studio on Music Row, House of David, since 1980.

—John Lomax III

Dr. John R. Brinkley
b. Beta, North Carolina, July 8, 1885; d. May 26, 1942

In the 1930s and early 1940s, John Romulus Brinkley owned a super-powered BORDER RADIO station that reached most of North America with hillbilly music and cowboy songs.

A 1915 graduate of Kansas City's Eclectic Medical Institute, Brinkley set up practice in Milford, Kansas, where he became rich and famous in the Roaring Twenties for pioneering a controversial rejuvenation operation in which he implanted slivers of billy goat sex glands into the human body. "A man is only as old as his glands," the goateed and diamond-studded physician told listeners of his Kansas radio station KFKB.

Medical and radio authorities drove Brinkley out of the Sunflower State, but not before he almost won the Kansas governorship in 1930, running on the slogan "Let's pasture the goats on the statehouse lawn." Undaunted, the maverick medicine man moved to the Rio Grande badlands, establishing the second border radio station, XER (later XERA), broadcasting at more than 100,000 watts from Villa Acuña, Mexico, just across the border from Del Rio, Texas, in 1931. Among the performers who worked at his station were the CARTER FAMILY, from 1938 to 1942.

Brinkley moved his hospital to Del Rio in 1933 and switched his medical practice from goat glands to an equally controversial prostate treatment. His early advertising proved so effective, however, that listeners remembered him long after his death as "the Goat Gland Man." In the radio business, he pioneered the use of prerecorded programming through electrical transcription discs. He built a palatial Spanish Mission–style home in Del Rio (which still stands) that *Texas Centennial* magazine described in 1936 as "the showplace of the Southwest." Along with splashing fountains and colored lights that spelled his name, the grounds contained Galapagos turtles and other exotic sights.

A 1939 libel suit against the American Medical Association, which Brinkley lost, began the fall of his peculiar empire. Dissatisfied patients sued for malpractice. The Mexican government confiscated his radio station. The IRS hit him for back taxes. Bankrupt, Brinkley was slated to stand trial for mail fraud when he died in San Antonio. But for decades afterward, radio fans chuckled at an old Texas joke that HANK THOMPSON told me: "What's the fastest thing on four legs? A goat passing the Brinkley Hospital."

—Gene Fowler

Bristol, Tennessee-Virginia

A small city in extreme northeastern Tennessee and southwestern Virginia, Bristol has had an amazing impact on the history of country music. Its strategic location has, since the 1920s, placed it at the crossroads of several key musical traditions. In 1927 talent scout RALPH PEER set up temporary recording studios on State Street to record for the Victor Company (predecessor to RCA-VICTOR) a series of recordings that included the first made by the CARTER FAMILY and JIMMIE RODGERS, as well as important recordings by other artists from Tennessee, Virginia, West Virginia, and Kentucky. The success of these records helped make country a viable commercial commodity. From the first, the city fathers of Bristol encouraged this activity, and in early 1928 an editorial in a Bristol newspaper chronicled the number of local musicians who were recording. Peer returned to the town for a follow-up session in the summer of 1928, and rival COLUMBIA records set up sessions in nearby Johnson City.

Further support for the music came in 1929, when local businessman W. A. Wilson opened radio station WOPI and began to feature live local music. By the late 1940s a second station, WCYB, began to feature the new bluegrass sounds of FLATT & SCRUGGS, the STANLEY BROTHERS, and CARL STORY. Two important regional record companies emerged to help chronicle the area's music: Jim Stanton's RICH-R-TONE label, which recorded the Stanley Brothers and WILMA LEE & STONEY COOPER in the late 1940s; and Joe Morrell's Shadow label, which did everything from old-time stringbands to rhythm and blues in the 1950s.

Bristol has continued to support and celebrate its musical heritage. In the 1990s the town organized the Bristol Country Music Association and staged a series of local concerts. Though the historical building where Ralph Peer made his first recordings no longer stands, a huge mural celebrating the event appears on the side of a building near State Street. Nearby, East Tennessee State University has a traditional music program that has trained a number of young acoustic musicians.

—Charles Wolfe

Elton Britt
b. Zack, Arkansas, June 27, 1913; d. June 23, 1972

Elton Britt (real name James Elton Baker) was the first country musician to be awarded a gold record and one of the greatest yodelers ever. The youngest child of Martella and James Baker, he was what is now known as a "blue baby" and was plagued with heart trouble all his life. At age ten he started playing music on a mail order guitar he bought from Montgomery Ward. Impressed with JIMMIE RODGERS, he taught himself to yodel by listening to the Singing Brakeman's 78s.

Breath control he learned as a swimmer enabled Britt to

maintain an extremely long yodel. Recruited out of Arkansas by the BEVERLY HILL BILLIES, he joined the group and journeyed to Los Angeles in 1930. "Little Elton," as he was then billed, remained with the Hill Billies for several years, during which time he acquired the name Britt. He also probably made his first commercial recordings with this band. Beginning in August 1933 he recorded for ARC as part of the Wenatchee Mountaineers, a band that included his brothers Vern and Arl. His first success was "Chime Bells" in 1934 (he had a bigger hit with it in 1948), and by 1939 he had signed with RCA VICTOR. His RCA hits included "Someday" (1946), "Detour" (1946), "Candy Kisses" (1949), and "Quicksilver" (1950, a duet with Rosalie Allen). But his biggest hit was his 1942 recording of "There's a Star Spangled Banner Waving Somewhere," which reportedly sold 4 million copies and earned Britt the aforementioned gold record.

In the 1930s and 1940s Britt appeared in three movies, but they did little to advance his career. By the 1950s he entered into the first of many retirements, though he signed with ABC-Paramount at the close of the decade. In 1960 he made an unsuccessful run for president on the Democratic ticket. Eight years later, again with RCA, he had his last Top Forty success with a seven-minute yodeling song, "The Jimmie Rodgers Blues." Shortly before starting a concert tour in 1972 Britt died of a heart attack. Although he recorded extensively, relatively little of Britt's work remains in print today.
—*W. K. McNeil*

Broadcast Music Incorporated (*see* BMI)

Garth Brooks

b. Luba, Oklahoma, February 7, 1962

Troyal "Garth" Brooks is not only the biggest country music star in the 1990s, he is also the most popular new musical act in the United States. Between 1989 and 1996, 60 million of his albums have sold, and his concerts have tallied up similar record-breaking numbers. Along the way, he has set a new standard for success in country music while being the primary protagonist in giving the genre a higher media profile. In the 1990s, country music moved once again into the mainstream of American entertainment. More than anyone, Brooks is responsible for taking it there.

Brooks was the sixth and last child to join the family of Troyal and Colleen Brooks. Though his mother appeared on the OZARK JUBILEE in the 1950s and recorded for two small labels, Brooks didn't pick up a guitar until high school. While attending Oklahoma State University, he started performing in nightclubs, concentrating largely on songs by James Taylor, Dan Fogelberg, Billy Joel, and Bob Seger while mixing in the occasional tune by GEORGE STRAIT or other country hitmakers of the 1980s.

His first trip to Nashville in 1985 ended in quick disappointment. He returned two years later with his newlywed, the former Sandy Mahl. This time he found encouragement. He hooked up with MUSIC CITY veteran Bob Doyle, who left an executive position at ASCAP to form a publishing company with Brooks as his first major client. Doyle and Pam Lewis teamed to manage the hopeful artist. Jim Foglesong of CAPITOL RECORDS signed him eight months after Garth arrived in Nashville this second time.

Capitol Records introduced Brooks to veteran pro-

Garth Brooks

ducer ALLEN REYNOLDS, who had worked with KATHY MATTEA, DON WILLIAMS, and CRYSTAL GAYLE. Reynolds gently altered Brooks's singing style, encouraging him to stop belting out ballads in a full-throated, operatic style similar to that of LEE GREENWOOD and Gary Morris and, instead, instructed him to use a more relaxed, natural voice. The change brought out an intimate, subtly dramatic tone in Brooks's voice, which he used to great effect on two of his early hit ballads, "If Tomorrow Never Comes" and "The Dance." With his first album—*Garth Brooks*, his most traditional country effort to date—Brooks also established his credentials as an unusually evocative songwriter. He wrote or co-wrote his first three hits, "Much Too Young (To Feel This Damn Old)," "If Tomorrow Never Comes," and "Not Counting You." He has written more than half of the hits on ensuing albums.

Sales of Brooks's first album initially were strong but not spectacular: It sold 500,000 copies in the first year. But after the release of "The Dance" in the spring of 1990, along with a music video debut, sales doubled within a month. The release that summer of his second album, *No Fences*, indicated the record-breaking success to come when, fueled by the popularity of the hit "Friends in Low Places," it sold more than 700,000 copies within its first ten days in stores. His third album, *Ropin' the Wind*, made American music history by gaining orders of 4 million copies before its release and by becoming the first album by a country singer to debut at #1 on the *Billboard* pop charts. By 1991 his initial three albums had sold a mind-boggling 30 million copies.

Forget country music comparisons; Brooks was surpassing sales figures racked up by the Beatles, Michael Jackson, and Bruce Springsteen. When Brooks entered country music, platinum sales of 1 million copies were big news, and only a handful of artists had achieved double-platinum status. To say his sales figures were unprecedented is an understatement; he had reached levels no one thought possible for a country music performer.

In addition to his radio hits, "Garthmania" was fueled by the athletic performer's explosive stage show. An acknowledged fan of 1970s rock acts—Kiss, Kansas, and Queen—Brooks added an arena-rock flash to his performances, utilizing dramatic lighting effects while busting guitars, swinging from ropes, dousing himself and his band in water, and raucously tearing across the stage while exhorting the crowd and beating his chest. His ticket sales rivaled those of such grand rock tours as those put on by the Rolling Stones, the EAGLES reunion, and the Grateful Dead.

By the mid-1990s Brooks seemed to be settling into a musical formula: His albums repeatedly combined melodramatic ballads, high-speed country-rock, and the occasional swing or honky-tonk tune, with a cowboy song regularly thrown in for its down-to-earth effect. He also understood the value of a controversial song: From the banned video of "The Thunder Rolls," a song that vividly discussed the horrors of domestic violence, to the gay rights statement nestled into "We Shall Be Free," to the cheeky wordplay of "Papa Loved Mama" and "Bury the Hatchet," Brooks took chances, courted contention, and gained media attention. Though album sales for *The Chase*, *In Pieces*, and *Fresh Horses* tailed off a bit from those of *No Fences* and *Ropin' the Wind*, Brooks still managed to capture the public's attention while compiling sales numbers that were the envy of pop and country performers alike.

On August 7, 1997, Brooks performed in New York's Central Park before a live audience estimated to be 250,000. The concert was also broadcast on HBO. Conflicts with his Capitol label reportedly resulted in a corporate shake-up and delayed the release of his album *Sevens*, which went on sale November 25, 1997.

—*Michael McCall*

REPRESENTATIVE RECORDINGS

No Fences (Liberty, 1990); *Ropin' the Wind* (Liberty, 1991); *Sevens* (Liberty, 1997)

Karen Brooks
b. Dallas, Texas, April 29, 1954

For her uncommonly literary and sophisticated recordings in the realm of progressive country, real-life cowgirl Karen Brooks apparently has earned a trip back to the farm. When she was named the ACADEMY OF COUNTRY MUSIC's Best New Female Vocalist in 1983, the coltish singer-songwriter seemed to be on the verge of a major breakthrough. Yet "Faking Love," an improbable pairing with the countrypolitan T. G. SHEPPARD that reached #1 that year, has proven to be her only contact with the Top Ten.

A product of AUSTIN's vibrant musical marketplace, Brooks moved to California in the late 1970s at the invitation of RODNEY CROWELL. In addition to harmonizing with Crowell, she gained recognition as the composer of "Tennessee Rose" (EMMYLOU HARRIS) and "Couldn't Do Nothing Right" (ROSANNE CASH). By 1982 Brooks had relocated to the Nashville area and signed with WARNER BROS. RECORDS. Karen's debut album (*Walk On*) yielded several modest hit singles and introduced the soaring balladry that has evoked comparison with ROY ORBISON's legendary minidramas. But the commercial failure of two subsequent LPs silenced Brooks until 1992, when she resurfaced on MERCURY with longtime collaborator Randy Sharp. *That's Another Story*, highlighted by Brooks's sassy rap on "Baby I'm the One," quickly vanished as well.   —*Pete Loesch*

REPRESENTATIVE RECORDINGS

Walk On (Warner Bros., 1982); *That's Another Story* (Mercury, 1992), with Randy Sharp

Brooks & Dunn
Kix Brooks b. Shreveport, Louisiana, May 12, 1955
Ronnie Dunn b. Coleman, Texas, June 1, 1953

Kix Brooks had recorded an album for CAPITOL RECORDS and written hits for other country artists, and Ronnie Dunn had won a national country talent competition, when the two paired up. ARISTA Nashville chief TIM DUBOIS urged them to join forces to become the high-energy country duo of Brooks & Dunn. The team released its first album, *Brand New Man*, in 1991. Five years, three more albums, and 14 million in sales later, Brooks & Dunn became the first duo in history to be named Entertainer of the Year by both the ACADEMY OF COUNTRY MUSIC and the COUNTRY MUSIC ASSOCIATION.

Leon Eric "Kix" Brooks III gravitated to music at an early age. He grew up on the same Shreveport, Louisiana, street as Billie Jean Horton, who had been married to both HANK WILLIAMS SR. and JOHNNY HORTON. Brooks's first paying performance was at age twelve with Horton's daughter, and he still lists Williams and Horton as key influences. Brooks worked the Louisiana club circuit before leaving for stretches in Alaska and Maine. He moved to Nashville in 1979 to pursue a country career, and his budding talents were nurtured by respected songman and producer Don Gant. A single for independent country label Avion, "Baby, When Your Heart Breaks Down," went to #73 in 1983, but Brooks fared better as a writer, penning #1 hits such as

Brooks & Dunn: Kix Brooks (left) and Ronnie Dunn

"I'm Only in It for the Love" for JOHN CONLEE (1983) and "Modern Day Romance" for the NITTY GRITTY DIRT BAND (1985). He signed with CAPITOL Nashville and released an album in 1989. A single, "Sacred Ground," did not do well, but the song went on to become a hit in 1992 for MCBRIDE & THE RIDE.

After studying theology at Abilene Christian College in his native Texas, Ronnie Gene Dunn moved with his parents to Tulsa, Oklahoma, where he fronted the house band at Duke's Country, a popular nightclub. Dunn recorded for Churchill Records, owned by Oklahoma talent agent JIM HALSEY, and charted with "It's Written All Over Your Face" (1983) and "She Put the Sad in All His Songs" (1984). Drummer Jamie Oldaker, who played with Eric Clapton before joining the TRACTORS, entered Dunn in a Marlboro country talent contest. His victory led to recording sessions with up-and-coming engineer-producer SCOTT HENDRICKS; he also gained national exposure while touring as a member of the Marlboro Country Music Tour.

Hendricks brought Dunn to DuBois's attention, and the label chief introduced him to Brooks over lunch, suggesting that they try to write and record together. Pleased with the results, DuBois offered them a record deal as a duo. Their first album, *Brand New Man,* issued August 31, 1991, sold 5 million copies and yielded the #1 hits "Brand New Man," "My Next Broken Heart," "Neon Moon," and "Boot Scootin' Boogie." Written by Dunn, "Boot Scootin' Boogie" already had been recorded by ASLEEP AT THE WHEEL, but the song became a smash for Brooks & Dunn and inspired a country line dance of the same name as well as a remixed dance version. The record helped set off a country dance craze. *Brand New Man* remained on the charts for more than five years and became the best-selling album in history for a country duo.

In 1992, just over a year since the release of their first album, the COUNTRY MUSIC ASSOCIATION named Brooks & Dunn Vocal Duo of the Year, an award they won each year from 1992 to 1997. Under the continuing guidance of producer-songwriter Don Cook, their fortunes climbed higher with the release of their second album, *Hard Workin' Man,* in 1993, which sold 4 million copies and generated the hits "We'll Burn That Bridge" (#2), "She Used to Be Mine" (#1), and "That Ain't No Way To Go" (#1). The duo's 1994 release, *Waitin' on Sundown,* sold 2 million copies and included chart-toppers "She's Not the Cheatin' Kind," "Little Miss Honky-Tonk," and "You're Gonna Miss Me When I'm Gone."

The duo's fourth album, *Borderline,* released in 1996, pushed them to even greater heights. A cover of the B. W. Stevenson hit "My Maria" became the first #1 single and helped sell tickets to the duo's headlining concerts, making them one of the top touring acts of the year. Borderline had sold 2 million copies and remained in the Top Ten of the country album charts as of February 1997. The CMA named Brooks & Dunn Vocal Duo of the Year for the fifth consecutive year in 1996, and both the CMA and the ACADEMY OF COUNTRY MUSIC gave them their highest prize, Entertainer of the Year.

An outstanding country singer, Dunn handles most of the lead vocals, with Brooks supplying harmonies. In concert, Brooks plays the animated crowd rouser, sometimes leaving the stage during a number to dance with audience members. Both men continue to write for publishing house Sony/ATV Tree, collaborating on their hits and occasionally coming up with songs for other artists. Dunn was named *Billboard*'s Country Songwriter of the Year in 1995

and BMI's Country Songwriter of the Year in 1996. Brooks & Dunn teamed with REBA MCENTIRE for an eighty-five-city tour in 1997 and released their album *The Greatest Hits Collection* in that same year.

—*Jay Orr*

REPRESENTATIVE RECORDINGS

Brand New Man (Arista, 1991); *Hard Workin' Man* (Arista, 1993); *Waitin' On Sundown* (Arista, 1994); *Borderline* (Arista, 1996); *The Greatest Hits Collection* (Arista, 1997)

Brother Duets

Brother vocal duets have thrived in country music since the early thirties. Similar vocal timbres, common word pronunciations, familiarity with each other's singing style, and shared cultural origins help to explain siblings' ability to phrase and harmonize so well. With the appearance in 1925 of electrical microphones, replacing the old acoustical horns in recording, the subtleties of harmony singing could at last be preserved on record and disseminated.

Brother teams also learned from and were inspired by the music of other duets who were not brothers. Thanks to the powerful signal of station WLS, two NATIONAL BARN DANCE acts—MAC & BOB (Lester McFarland and Robert Gardner) and KARL & HARTY (Karl Davis and Hartford Connecticut Taylor)—exerted a powerful musical influence, as their mandolin and guitar playing, close harmony, and a repertoire of old-time songs were broadcast far and wide in the 1920s and 1930s. Almost as a consequence, the heyday of brother duet singing followed in the late thirties when the MONROE BROTHERS (Charlie and Bill), the CALLAHAN BROTHERS (Bill and Joe), the BLUE SKY BOYS (Bill and Earl Bolick), the DELMORE BROTHERS (Alton and Rabon), the SHELTON BROTHERS (Bob and Joe), the Morris Brothers (Wiley and Zeke), the DIXON BROTHERS (Dorsey and Howard), and similar acts became prominent on radio and recordings. Although the mandolin was generally the preferred lead instrument, other instruments, such as Rabon Delmore's tenor guitar and Howard Dixon's Hawaiian guitar, also figured prominently in the music of these duos.

The BAILES BROTHERS (first as Walter and Johnnie, and later as Johnnie and Homer) added their soulful sound to the genre in the 1940s. The number of brother duets has declined since that time, but the tradition has never disappeared. In fact, the quality and influence of this tradition probably reached its peak in the 1950s with the marvelous and highly influential singing of the LOUVIN BROTHERS (Charlie and Ira), the WILBURN BROTHERS (Doyle and Teddy), and the EVERLY BROTHERS (Don and Phil). The style could even be detected in the sixties in the singing of the Beatles. Today the brother duet style endures in the singing of such performers as JIM & JESSE McReynolds and the Whitstein Brothers (Charles and Robert).

—*Bill C. Malone*

REPRESENTATIVE RECORDING

Are You from Dixie? Great Country Brother Teams of the 1930s (RCA, 1988)

Brother Phelps

Calvin Douglas Phelps b. Cardwell, Missouri, February 16, 1960
Ricky Lee Phelps b. Cardwell, Missouri, October 8, 1953

Doug and older brother Ricky Lee Phelps found country music fame as members of the KENTUCKY HEADHUNTERS.

Not content making the rock-influenced music for which the HeadHunters were known, the pair formed Brother Phelps with the intention of recording more straight-ahead country music.

Ricky Lee Phelps was the family rebel who grew his hair long and escaped from his small-town upbringing in the 1970s. Heading west, he played the club circuit with his band and would occasionally send home tapes of his music. Viewing his brother as a role model, Doug Phelps memorized the tunes, and when Ricky Lee made a visit home in 1976, Doug surprised him by singing perfect harmonies.

Doug left home in 1981 to work with singer RONNIE MC-DOWELL. One year later, Ricky Lee relocated to Nashville and landed a job in the band Sweetwater. In 1986 Doug and McDowell band alumnus Greg Martin were experimenting musically with Martin's cousins Richard and Fred Young. Ricky Lee joined the group, which became the Kentucky HeadHunters.

Soon the HeadHunters were selling millions of albums, winning awards, and touring nonstop. By late 1991 all five members were exhausted and decided to take a break. Reconvening in early 1992, they discovered they had grown apart musically. Doug and Ricky Lee Phelps announced their intention to leave the group to concentrate on music with a more traditional country flavor. As Brother Phelps, they landed on ASYLUM RECORDS. Their breezy debut single, "Let Go," landed in the Top Ten. Other singles included "Were You Really Livin'"; "Eagle Over Angel"; and, from their second Asylum release, "Anyway the Wind Blows."

In 1997 Doug Phelps rejoined the Kentucky Head-Hunters.
—*Janet E. Williams*

REPRESENTATIVE RECORDINGS

Let Go (Asylum, 1993); *Anyway the Wind Blows* (Asylum, 1995)

Cecil Brower
b. Bellevue, Texas, November 28, 1914; d. November 21, 1965

One of the architects of western swing and the man who established its fundamental fiddle style, Cecil Lee Brower was a classically trained violinist with an ear cocked toward jazz and country when MILTON BROWN persuaded him to join his Musical Brownies in 1933. Brower left the Southern Melody Boys, with whom he and Kenneth Pitts played arranged duets and Brower had begun improvising choruses in the manner of jazz violinist Joe Venuti. With the Brownies, Brower teamed with JESSE ASHLOCK, forming the first identifiably western swing twin fiddle team.

Over the next few years Brower set the basic model for western swing fiddle with a fluid style full of essential tricks of the trade such as "rocking the bow." He was the fiddler on all of Brown's recordings from 1934 through 1936, successfully teaming with CLIFF BRUNER at the last of these sessions. After Brown's death in 1936 Brower worked for bandleader ROY NEWMAN in Dallas and also recorded with BOB WILLS and BILL BOYD during this time. After a stint with pop bandleader Ted Fio Rito, Brower returned to Texas in 1939 and worked until World War II with the LIGHT CRUST DOUGHBOYS, reteaming with old cohort Kenneth Pitts.

Brower served in the coast guard, and after the war he worked with the HI FLYERS before leading his own Kilocycle

Cowboys in Odessa in the years 1946 to 1949. Stints with LEON MCAULIFFE and AL DEXTER followed; then Brower moved to Springfield, Missouri, to work with RED FOLEY on TV's *Jubilee, U.S.A.* He followed Foley to Nashville and became an in-demand session musician before joining JIMMY DEAN, with whom he was playing when he died from a bleeding ulcer following a show at Carnegie Hall.
—*Kevin Coffey*

REPRESENTATIVE RECORDINGS

Milton Brown & His Brownies: Pioneer Western Swing Band (1935–36) (MCA, 1982); *Bill Boyd's Cowboy Ramblers* (Bluebird, 1976)

Hylo Brown
b. River, Kentucky, April 20, 1922

Frank "Hylo" Brown Jr.—nicknamed for his broad vocal range—was one of the most admired BLUEGRASS voices of the mid- to late fifties. Born in the Kentucky mountains and reared in an atmosphere of traditional music, young Frank Brown migrated with his family to Springfield, Ohio, during World War II. For some years thereafter he worked in a factory and played music on the local scene, including radio programs at WPFB in nearby Middletown. In 1954 his composition "Lost to a Stranger" came to the attention of KEN NELSON, who signed him to a CAPITOL RECORDS contract. Most of his recordings used acoustic, bluegrass-style accompaniment and were well received by fans of traditional sounds. Brown worked the WWVA JAMBOREE for a time and then became a featured opening act with the FLATT & SCRUGGS band. For three years Hylo then led his own bluegrass band, the highly regarded Timberliners (mandolinist Red Rector, fiddler Tater Tate, banjoist Jim Smoak, and bassist Joe Phillips), with whom he worked a series of TV shows for MARTHA WHITE FLOUR. The group appeared at the 1959 NEWPORT FOLK FESTIVAL, where they backed Earl Scruggs. Later he rejoined Flatt & Scruggs and afterward toured for many years as a solo act. Brown cut four albums for STARDAY in the early sixties and six more for the Rural Rhythm label later in the decade. He has become increasingly inactive in recent years, following retirement to his native Kentucky.
—*Ivan M. Tribe*

REPRESENTATIVE RECORDING

Hylo Brown & the Timberliners, 1954–1960 (Bear Family, 1992), 2 CDs

Jim Ed Brown
b. Sparkman, Arkansas, April 1, 1934

James Edward Brown rose to fame with his sisters Bonnie and Maxine recording for RCA RECORDS as THE BROWNS trio from 1954 until 1967. Jim Ed's success was not limited to the trio, however. As a solo act for RCA, he began placing hits on the charts in 1965 with "I Just Heard from a Memory Last Night." His Top Ten country hits include "Pop A Top" (1967), "Morning" (1970), Southern Loving" (1973), "Sometime Sunshine" (1973), and "It's That Time of Night" (1974).

In 1976 he began recording duets with Helen Cornelius (b. Hannibal, Missouri, December 6, 1941). A year later they won the CMA award for 1977 Vocal Duo of the Year.

Their best-known hits are "I Don't Want to Have to Marry You" (1976), "Saying Hello, Saying I Love You, Saying Goodbye" (1976), "Lying in Love with You" (1979), and "Fools" (1979). In addition to joining the GRAND OLE OPRY as a member of the Browns in 1963, Jim Ed hosted TNN's *You Can Be a Star* talent show in the 1980s.   —*Stacey Wolfe*

REPRESENTATIVE RECORDING

The Essential Jim Ed Brown (RCA, 1997)

Junior Brown

b. Cottonwood, Arizona, June 12, 1952

Jamieson "Junior" Brown is an idiosyncratic, formidable musician who helped define the difference between AUSTIN's "alternative" approach to country music and Nashville's commercial mainstream in the 1990s. With his cowboy hat, deep baritone, bent sense of humor, and total command of 1940s–70s country, Brown would seem to be a throwback to an earlier era. (He calls the years 1962 to 1974 the "renaissance" of country music, and one of his songs is titled "My Baby Don't Dance to Nothing but ERNEST TUBB.") While his retrobilly shtick is amusing, Brown is also a clever songwriter and a virtuosic guitarist, known to toss Jimi Hendrix acid-blues licks into country instrumentals such as "Sugarfoot Rag." He is the inventor of the guit-steel, a double-necked instrument combining the qualities of an electric guitar and a steel guitar, and for a time during the 1980s he taught guitar with LEON MCAULIFFE and ELDON SHAMBLIN at Rodgers State College in Oklahoma.

Brown's family moved around the country a lot when he was young, and though his father played piano, Brown took to guitar at an early age. Growing up in the sixties, he drew from sources as varied as the Isley Brothers' r&b and Ernest Tubb's TV show. After playing the clubs around Albuquerque, New Mexico, and elsewhere, Brown arrived in Austin in 1979 and worked as a lead guitarist and pedal steel player in various country bands. It wasn't until he put together his own band featuring his wife, Tanya Rae (whom he met at Rodgers State College), on rhythm guitar and vocals that folks began to take notice of Brown's regular appearances at Austin's Continental Club. His self-produced first album, *12 Shades of Brown,* was picked up for international distribution by England's Demon label in 1990. Following a 1992 SRO performance at Austin's South by Southwest music conference, Brown was signed to CURB RECORDS in Nashville, which rereleased *12 Shades of Brown* along with the newly recorded album *Guit with It* in 1993. Brown's remake of RED SIMPSON's "Highway Patrol," originally included on *Guit with It,* dented the country charts in 1995 after Curb released a remixed version (from the minialbum *Junior High*) with an accompanying video. The following year he won the CMA's Music Video of the Year award for "My Wife Thinks You're Dead," but the single itself never cracked the Top Forty. Brown is probably too eccentric to convert the majority of mainstream country fans, but his cult-hero reputation has continued to grow.   —*Rick Mitchell*

REPRESENTATIVE RECORDINGS

12 Shades of Brown (Curb, 1993); *Guit with It* (Curb, 1993); *Semi Crazy* (Curb, 1996)

Marty Brown

b. Maceo, Kentucky, July 25, 1965

When he released his debut album, *High and Dry,* in 1991, Dennis Marty Brown was more than just another country traditionalist; he was a throwback to an earlier time. Fresh off a tobacco farm in eastern Kentucky, Brown offered the unvarnished drawl and twang of his heroes HANK WILLIAMS and JIMMIE RODGERS. Brown proved too country for country radio, but he sent the critics scrambling for superlatives.

Brown had been sleeping behind an air-conditioning unit in a Music Row alley and knocking on doors by day when BMI's Kurt Denny signed him to the performing rights agency and began promoting Brown's career. The improbable story went nationwide on a 1991 segment of CBS-TV's *48 Hours.* That led to a record deal with MCA and the debut album, which balanced Hank Williams–style honky-tonk with the sort of bouncy confections FELICE AND BOUDLEAUX BRYANT whipped up for the EVERLY BROTHERS. He promoted the album in 1991 with an unconventional tour of Wal-Mart stores in forty-five cities, playing "his acoustic guitar, live and in-person, somewhere between Ladies Apparel and Consumer Electronics," as the press release put it.

The reviews and Wal-Mart shows did little to impress country radio, so Brown's second album, *Wild Kentucky Skies* (1993), was a more diverse effort, featuring lush love songs and a ghostly, extravagantly produced elegy for his grandmother ("She's Gone") as well as vintage HONKY-TONK and ROCKABILLY. When that didn't sell, Brown went back to his first love and filled his third album, *Cryin', Lovin', Leavin',* with catchy Everly-ish romps and poignant Hank-ish ballads. It didn't sell either, and Brown was dropped by MCA. He resurfaced in 1996 on the HIGHTONE label with *Here's to the Honky-Tonks.*   —*Geoffrey Himes*

REPRESENTATIVE RECORDINGS

High and Dry (MCA, 1991); *Cryin', Lovin', Leavin'* (MCA, 1994)

Milton Brown

b. Stephenville, Texas, September 8, 1903; d. April 18, 1936

Widely regarded as one of the originators of the music known today as western swing, vocalist-bandleader Milton Brown was largely responsible for establishing the genre in the early 1930s. Though not as familiar to modern audiences as his contemporary BOB WILLS, Brown, along with his influential band the Musical Brownies, introduced many elements to western swing recordings: the 2/4 dance rhythm of New Orleans jazz, twin fiddles playing in harmony, slapped bass fiddle, jazz piano, and the first amplified instrument in country music, BOB DUNN's steel guitar. During a sensational three-and-a-half-year career, the Brownies became the Southwest's preeminent stringband, only to see their fortunes collapse when their leader died after an automobile accident.

Brown had been singing since he was a small boy in Stephenville. After moving to Fort Worth in 1918, he accompanied his father, a breakdown fiddler, at local house dances. He formed a small vocal group in 1927, building a repertoire of popular standards. At a house dance in 1930,

Milton Brown & His Musical Brownies

Brown met Wills and guitarist Herman Arnspiger. The three began playing on radio as the Aladdin Laddies and later as the original LIGHT CRUST DOUGHBOYS.

In September 1932 Brown formed the Musical Brownies. Original personnel included Brown, vocals; younger brother Derwood on guitar; JESSE ASHLOCK, fiddle; Wanna Coffman, bass; and OCIE STOCKARD, tenor banjo. Shortly after, jazz pianist Fred "Papa" Calhoun joined, followed by swing fiddler CECIL BROWER. Other key additions included amplified steel guitarist Bob Dunn (1934) and fiddler CLIFF BRUNER (1935). The Brownies played a daily radio program on KTAT (1932–35) and WBAP (1935–36) and barnstormed the state playing dances. Their regular Saturday night dances at Fort Worth's Crystal Springs Dancing Pavilion became *de rigueur* for their legion of fans.

Brown also introduced a new kind of singing to Texas country music. His style was smooth, rhythmic, sophisticated, and highly improvisatory, more jazz than country, and similar to that of Cab Calloway or Jack Teagarden. He established recorded western swing's initial repertoire of jazz, blues, and pop songs, introducing to the genre such staples as "Right or Wrong," "Corrine Corrina," and "Sitting on Top of the World" through recording sessions for BLUEBIRD (1934) and DECCA (1935–36). The Brownies' April 4, 1934, Bluebird session is considered to have been history's first true western swing recording session.

On the morning of April 13, 1936, Brown was injured in an automobile accident that killed his passenger, a sixteen-year-old girl. An untreated punctured lung resulted in pneumonia, which caused Brown's death on April 18 at age thirty-two. The funeral drew an estimated 3,500 mourners.
—*Cary Ginell*

REPRESENTATIVE RECORDINGS

Milton Brown & His Musical Brownies: The Complete Recordings (Texas Rose, 1995), 5 discs; *Under the Double Eagle: Great Western Swing Bands of the 1930's, Volume 1* (RCA, 1990); *Pioneer Western Swing Band* (MCA, 1982); *Taking Off!* (String, 1977)

T. Graham Brown
b. Atlanta, Georgia, December 30, 1954

Born Anthony Graham Brown, this Georgia-raised singer dabbled in southern beach music (as half of a duo called Dirk & Tony), soul music (in the late 1970s with a band called Rack of Spam), and OUTLAW country (in a DAVID ALLAN COE–inspired eight-piece ensemble called Reo Diamond) before he hit the country charts in 1985.

Recording for CAPITOL RECORDS, Graham had a dozen chart singles between 1985 and 1991, including three #1s: "Hell and High Water" (1986), "Don't Go to Strangers" (1987), and "Darlene" (1988). His r&b-style mainstream country was captured most vividly on recordings such as his 1991 cover of "With This Ring" (originally a 1967 pop hit for the Platters) and his rendition of Otis Redding's "Sittin' on the Dock of the Bay," which was released in Germany.

Brown often infuses his music and stage presentations with an irrepressible spirit of extroversion. (As a practical joke, he once cut off RALPH EMERY's tie while appearing on the TNN TV show *Nashville Now*.)

Before moving to Nashville in 1982, Brown, a former Georgia all-state high school baseball pitcher, also attended classes and played baseball at the University of Georgia. In Nashville he quickly found work singing demo recordings for Music Row publishers.

Though by the mid-1990s Brown was without a major label recording contract, his voice has continued to get a wide hearing through his work singing jingles for TV ads for McDonald's, Taco Bell, and Miller and Budweiser Beers. Additionally he has appeared in several feature films, including *Greased Lightning* (starring Richard Pryor), *Heartbreak Hotel, The Farm*, and *The Curse* (starring JOHN SCHNEIDER).
—*Bob Allen*

REPRESENTATIVE RECORDINGS

I Tell It Like It Used to Be (Capitol, 1986); *Greatest Hits* (Capitol, 1990)

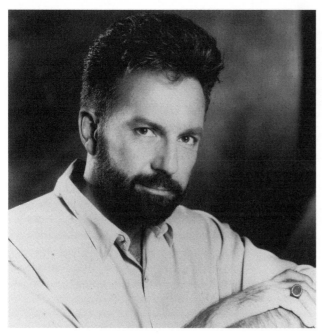

Tony Brown

Tony Brown
b. Greensboro, North Carolina, December 11, 1946

If Nashville's Music Row had a mayor, Tony Brown, president of MCA RECORDS Nashville, could get elected. In an April 1996 cover story, the *Los Angeles Times Magazine* crowned him "The King of Nashville." And Brown has made *Entertainment Weekly*'s annual ranking of the one hundred most powerful people in the entertainment industry. The North Carolina native earned his reputation with business savvy, discerning musical taste, a winning personality, a strong sense of civic responsibility, and keenly honed musical skills. As a producer, he has overseen platinum and multiplatinum albums by VINCE GILL, GEORGE STRAIT, REBA MCENTIRE, and WYNONNA, among others. TRACY BYRD, RODNEY CROWELL, Gill, PATTY LOVELESS, McEntire, Strait, STEVE WARINER, and Wynonna are among the country stars who have scored #1 hits with recordings he produced.

As a child Brown traveled in his family's singing group, appearing at churches of every denomination. In his early teens he began playing piano onstage, and after high school he worked with the renowned gospel Stamps Quartet, led by J. D. Sumner, and later with the OAK RIDGE BOYS. Around the time the Oaks made the transition from gospel to country music, Brown left to join Voice, a gospel group placed on call to sing for and accompany ELVIS PRESLEY. From Voice, Brown graduated to a spot in the band backing the Sweet Inspirations, an opening act for Presley. When Glen D. Hardin left the main Presley band in 1975, Brown took another step up the ladder, joining Presley's "A-team," where he stayed until Presley's death in 1977.

Forced to look for another job, Brown parlayed a referral from pianist DAVID BRIGGS into a spot with EMMYLOU HARRIS's highly regarded Hot Band. In doing so he again replaced the departing Hardin. Brown's potential as a record company staffer began to show at about this time. In 1978 he took a post with Free Flight Records, an RCA pop venture. The label closed two years later, and Brown transferred to RCA's Nashville division, where he stayed long enough to sign super group ALABAMA. He then answered a highway call to join the Cherry Bombs, the touring band behind progressive country singer-songwriters Rodney Crowell and ROSANNE CASH.

In 1983 Brown returned to Nashville and RCA, this time adding friend and former bandmate Vince Gill to the company's roster. Brown's gospel credentials landed him a job as producer of three albums for Shirley Caesar, including *Sailin'*, a Grammy winner in 1985.

When record company iconoclast JIMMY BOWEN recruited Brown to join him at MCA as vice president of A&R in 1984, he jumped at the dream job and immediately expanded his production opportunities. Brown learned from Bowen, but he also followed his own instincts in signing creative, artistically ambitious talents such as STEVE EARLE and NANCI GRIFFITH. He made a name for himself as a progressive force in country music.

Following Bowen's departure from MCA, Brown renegotiated his contract with the company and assumed the title of president, in partnership with another Bowen colleague, chairman BRUCE HINTON. The label has prospered, ranked first among country imprints by both *Billboard* and *Radio & Records*. Brown has been *Billboard*'s top country producer for four years. Among the other artists he has signed to MCA's roster are Byrd, MARK CHESNUTT, JOE ELY, Patty Loveless, the MAVERICKS, DAVID LEE MURPHY, Todd Snider, MARTY STUART, and TRISHA YEARWOOD. Brown produced Grammy-winning albums by LYLE LOVETT and Vince Gill, as well as COUNTRY MUSIC ASSOCIATION award-winning albums and singles by Gill and George Strait.   —*Jay Orr*

Brown Radio Productions
established in Nashville, Tennessee, ca. 1945; ended ca. 1953

Brown Radio Productions and its companion firm, Monogram Radio Productions, constituted one of the earliest commercial recording studios in Nashville. Charles Brown and his brother Bill organized it in about 1945. Located on Fourth Avenue North, the Brown company first made its mark by handling midday shows starring ERNEST TUBB and EDDY ARNOLD. They were produced from a downtown Nashville theater and fed to the Mutual radio network via Nashville station WSM. Charles, a veteran of both the prominent Gardner Agency in St. Louis and a Nashville advertising firm, was aggressive in securing accounts, and the brothers were soon busy producing syndicated soap operas and musicals using locally based radio talent such as Eddy Arnold, the DUKE OF PADUCAH, and others.

In about 1950 the Brown studio (a small affair located on the second floor of an office building) also began to host sessions held by RCA RECORDS. Over the next few years, major RCA country acts such as HANK SNOW, JOHNNIE & JACK, and Eddy Arnold recorded hits there, including "I'm Moving On," "Poison Love," and "Lovebug Itch," respectively.

By 1953, however, the Nashville company faded, and the Browns sold their equipment to engineer Cliff Thomas, who began to hold RCA sessions in a building on Thirteenth Avenue South. Charles Brown eventually moved to Springfield, Missouri, then a rising radio syndication and TV production center, where he and his brother had started a branch office in 1950. There Charles wrote and produced *The Eddy Arnold Show* for Springfield's Crossroads TV Productions and ABC-TV. In 1956 Charles made the move from broadcasting to politics, eventually representing his district in the U.S. House of Representatives. —*John Rumble*

Jann Browne

b. Anderson, Indiana, March 14, 1954

A petite vocal powerhouse, Jann Browne fittingly cites BRENDA LEE ("Little Miss Dynamite") as an early influence. The granddaughter of professional square dancers (the Kentucky Briarhoppers), Browne grew up with Ramona and GRANDPA JONES as family friends. However, it was her 1976 exposure to EMMYLOU HARRIS's *Elite Hotel* (1975) that converted her to country. Intimidated by Nashville, Browne instead moved to Southern California in 1978, where she became a familiar voice in Orange County country bars. An impromptu performance with ASLEEP AT THE WHEEL in 1981 led to a two-year road stint with the band; Browne left in 1983 to concentrate on songwriting. In the mid-eighties she became one of the leading women in the young country scene that blossomed in DWIGHT YOAKAM's wake in Los Angeles. Her song "Louisville," co-written with Pat Gallagher, appeared on PETE ANDERSON's anthology of L.A. country talent, *A Town South of Bakersfield, Volume II* (Enigma, 1988). Her debut album, *Tell Me Why,* was also the first major production effort of steel guitarist Steve Fishell of Emmylou Harris's Hot Band; Fishell has since moved on to become a successful Nashville producer and A&R executive. *Tell Me Why* yielded two Top Twenty hits, the title song, and "You Ain't Down Home"; but the follow-up album, *It Only Hurts When I Laugh,* enjoyed little chart success. Dropped by Curb in 1992, Browne continued to co-write songs (with Gallagher and guitarist Matthew Barnes) and developed a following in Europe, where her third album, *Count Me In,* was released on the Swiss label Red Moon in 1994. —*Mark Humphrey*

REPRESENTATIVE RECORDINGS

Tell Me Why (Curb, 1990); *It Only Hurts When I Laugh* (Curb, 1991)

The Browns

Ella Maxine Brown b. Campti, Louisiana, April 27, 1931
James Edward Brown b. Sparkman, Arkansas, April 1, 1934
Bonnie Marie Brown Ring b. Sparkman, Arkansas, July 31, 1937

Jim Ed, Maxine, and Bonnie, known professionally as the Browns, were perhaps the most important vocal group of the NASHVILLE SOUND era. The Browns' smooth three-part harmonies, which have influenced acts ranging from the WHITES to the Beatles, centered around Jim Ed's rich baritone. Maxine's alto voice and Bonnie's breathy soprano added the spice.

The Brown siblings grew up in southwestern Arkansas, where they sang at church socials and school functions while still in their teens. Their first career break came in 1952, when Maxine entered Jim Ed in a talent contest staged at Dutch O'Neal's *Barnyard Frolic* on KLRA in Little Rock, Arkansas. Although Brown lost to a harmonica whiz, he was invited to join the cast. Maxine soon joined Jim Ed onstage to sing, and their career was launched.

By 1954 the duo was a featured act on the *LOUISIANA HAYRIDE*. On March 15, 1954, they recorded "Looking Back to See" in the KWKH–Shreveport, Louisiana, studios. Written by Maxine—with a little help from Jim Ed—the song was released on the FABOR label. Three months later, the song debuted on the *Billboard* charts, topping out at #8. From Shreveport the duo moved to KWTO's *OZARK JUBILEE* in Springfield, Missouri.

In 1955 Bonnie joined the act, and the group's recording of "Here Today and Gone Tomorrow" climbed the charts to #7. In that same year the trio signed with RCA RECORDS. Over the next four years they managed to produce some sizable hits, including "I Take the Chance" and "I Heard the Bluebirds Sing." In 1959 the Browns recorded their signature song, "The Three Bells," at RCA's Studio B in Nashville.

At the time they recorded "Bells," the Browns had grown disillusioned with the music business and were considering quitting. As their swan song, they had asked producer CHET ATKINS to let them try the song, earlier recorded by French pop star Edith Piaf. Within a month of its chart debut, the record sold more than half a million copies. Network television appearances on *The Ed Sullivan Show* and *American Bandstand* followed. Follow-up songs such as "Scarlet Ribbons" and "The Old Lamplighter" placed on both the country and pop charts. In 1963 the group joined the cast of the GRAND OLE OPRY.

In 1967 the Browns disbanded: Maxine and Bonnie retired to Arkansas to raise their young families, while Jim Ed stayed on in Nashville, pursued a solo career with RCA, and hosted a string of syndicated TV shows.

In the 1990s the Browns made a limited number of personal appearances, including guest spots at the Grand Ole Opry that brought standing ovations. —*Chris Skinker*

REPRESENTATIVE RECORDINGS

The Three Bells (Bear Family, 1994), 4 discs; *The Essential Jim Ed Brown and the Browns* (RCA, 1997)

The Browns: (from left) Bonnie, Jim Ed, and (below) Maxine

Brown's Ferry Four

Emerging in the 1940s, Brown's Ferry Four was, along with the CHUCK WAGON GANG, one of the first really successful country gospel quartets. While formal gospel quartet music had been popular since the World War I era, most of the time it was sung a cappella or with a piano, such as in the case of the STAMPS-BAXTER Quartet or the Vaughan Quartet. But Brown's Ferry Four featured a guitar accompaniment, and singers who were trained as mainstream country singers.

Brown's Ferry Four began as a radio group playing over WLW-Cincinnati, in 1943. A mainstay of the station, the Drifting Pioneers, was so decimated by the draft that they had to break up. The Pioneers had always added gospel songs to their programs, and the program director, George Biggar, began searching for a replacement. By coincidence, the WLW roster at that time included a young MERLE TRAVIS (who had been a member of the Pioneers), GRANDPA JONES, and the DELMORE BROTHERS. When Alton Delmore heard a new band was needed, he became interested; as a boy in Alabama he had learned to sing shape notes from the old paperback gospel songbooks. He talked the other three into forming an impromptu quartet (they literally rehearsed in the studio hallway), promising to teach them enough of the shape notes to get by. They were accepted, and Alton named them after Brown's Ferry, near their home in northern Alabama (and after his bawdy hit song "Brown's Ferry Blues").

The group found itself doing a thirty-minute show each day, drawing material from the old Stamps-Baxter songbooks as well as old used black gospel records they hunted up in local used-records shops. As Grandpa Jones recalled, "We were amazed at the response we started getting from farmers and factory workers." Soon both Travis and Alton Delmore had to leave for service, but the station—which owned the name of the quartet—kept the broadcasts going with local singers such as Rome Johnson, Roy Lanham, and even Dollie Good. The original group did not get back together until 1946, when SYD NATHAN recorded them for KING RECORDS; their first single, "Just a Little Talk with Jesus" and "Will the Circle Be Unbroken," was wildly successful, and a long series of similar sides followed—some forty-four in all between 1946 and 1952.

Travis soon had to drop from the group, and both Grandpa and the Delmores left WLW; the recordings continued, though, with a stellar cast of replacements: RED FOLEY, Red & Lige Turner, CLYDE MOODY, and LOUIS INNIS. Often Grandpa and the Delmores were also present on the recordings. WLW continued to have a radio version of the quartet on the air through the 1950s.

In later years it was Grandpa Jones who kept the memory of Brown's Ferry Four alive. He did a fine album with Travis re-creating the sound for MONUMENT in the 1960s, and instigated the *Hee Haw* Gospel Quartet on the popular TV show in 1975. Like the original Brown's Ferry, the *Hee Haw* Quartet, also composed of mainstream country singers, delighted audiences throughout the country.

—*Charles Wolfe*

Ed Bruce

b. Keiser, Arkansas, December 29, 1940

A multitalented performer, William Edwin Bruce Jr. has scored as a hit recording artist, songwriter, actor, and singer of commercials.

Bruce was raised in Memphis, where he recorded for SUN RECORDS in 1957–58. In the early 1960s he recorded on the Wand/Scepter label, and in 1966 he quit his job as a Memphis car salesman and moved to Nashville. His first *Billboard* chart record came in 1967 with "Walker's Woods" on RCA. He later recorded for MONUMENT; United Artists; EPIC; MCA; and then, beginning in 1984, for RCA again. He had a #1 record for MCA in 1981 with "You're the Best Break This Old Heart Ever Had."

As a songwriter, Bruce won his first BMI award for country airplay with "See the Big Man Cry," a 1965 Top Ten for CHARLIE LOUVIN. Bruce also wrote or co-wrote such hits as "The Man That Turned My Mama On" and "Texas (When I Die)," recorded by TANYA TUCKER, and the 1978 #1 standard for WAYLON JENNINGS and WILLIE NELSON, "Mammas Don't Let Your Babies Grow Up to Be Cowboys."

Bruce's distinctive voice has graced nationally broadcast commercials for such clients as John Deere; McDonald's; AC/Delco; and, most recently, Ford Trucks. As an actor he has appeared in the CBS-TV miniseries *The Chisholms,* with James Garner in the *Maverick* TV series, and in such made-for-TV movies as *The Last Days of Frank and Jesse James* and *Separated by Murder.* Bruce has also hosted THE NASHVILLE NETWORK's shows *American Sports Cavalcade* and *Truckin' USA.* —*Gerry Wood*

REPRESENTATIVE RECORDING
The Best of Ed Bruce (Varese Sarabande, 1995)

Albert E. Brumley

b. LeFlore County, Oklahoma, October 29, 1905; d. November 15, 1977

Even the most casual students of country and gospel music recognize the name and the songs of Albert Edward Brumley. Working from his base in the tiny town of Powell, Missouri, Brumley produced an amazingly potent body of work that made him the single most influential songwriter in gospel music. His masterpiece "I'll Fly Away" has been recorded more than five hundred times by artists in every field of music, and dozens of his other songs have become standards.

Brumley's star began to rise in the late 1920s, when he left his eastern Oklahoma farm to study at the Hartford Music Company in nearby Hartford, Arkansas. This was a "convention" book publisher, in the mold of James D. Vaughan and Stamps-Baxter, which published new gospel songs in seven-shape notation systems. After studying with several of Hartford's veteran writers, Brumley began to create his own songs. Between 1932 and 1945 he published— often in Hartford books—his best-known works. These included "I'll Fly Away" (1932), "Jesus Hold My Hand" (1933), "I'd Rather Be an Old-Time Christian" (1934), "I'll Meet You in the Morning' (1936), "Camping in Canaan's Land" (1937), "There's a Little Pine Log Cabin" (1937), "Turn Your Radio On" (1938), "Did You Ever Go Sailing" (1938), "I've Found a Hiding Place" (1939), "Rank Stranger to Me" (1942), and "If We Never Meet Again" (1945). Though gospel quartets turned these into standards, they were also featured on radio and records by groups such as BILL MONROE & the Blue Grass Quartet, the CHUCK WAGON GANG, BROWN'S FERRY FOUR, RED FOLEY, and the STANLEY BROTHERS.

Brumley also began to publish his own songbooks to circulate his songs even further; by 1937, *Albert E. Brumley's Book of Radio Favorites* had appeared. He purchased the

Hartford Music Company in the late 1940s, primarily to regain copyright control of many of his classic songs, and began to publish books at his own headquarters in Powell (where he also served as postmaster). Though Brumley died in 1977, his family still runs his publishing company. His son Tom, a respected steel guitarist in country circles, manages a show at Branson, and the organization sponsors an annual homecoming festival in Powell. —*Charles Wolfe*

Cliff Bruner

b. Texas City, Texas, April 25, 1915

One of the most individual, hard-driving fiddlers in country music, Cliff Bruner enjoyed significant influence and popularity as both a musician and bandleader during the 1930s and 1940s.

By age fourteen Bruner was hopping freights in search of musical challenges. Although an instinctive, rurally reared musician, he was never enamored of country fiddling and became essentially a jazz player. Bruner was already a seasoned veteran when he joined MILTON BROWN's pioneering western swing band, the Musical Brownies, in Fort Worth in 1935. Teaming with the classically trained CECIL BROWER to form the genre's classic twin fiddle duo, Bruner recorded forty-nine sides with Brown in March 1936.

Brown died soon after, and Bruner formed his Texas Wanderers in Houston in the summer of 1936. He moved on to Beaumont, broadcasting on KDFM and gaining an enthusiastic following in the region, influencing Cajun as well as country dance music with a lineup that eventually included electric steel pioneer BOB DUNN, pianist MOON MULLICAN, electric mandolinist Leo Raley, and smooth vocalist DICKIE MCBRIDE. Bruner signed with DECCA in 1937 and by decade's end had waxed such seminal classics as FLOYD TILLMAN's "It Makes No Difference Now"; TED DAFFAN's "Truck Driver's Blues"; and his signature tune, an old Mexican polka, "Jessie."

In about 1939, Bruner experienced a religious conversion and temporarily gave up bandleading, working for Texas governor W. LEE O'DANIEL and with JIMMIE DAVIS in Louisiana. Bruner led a band in Chicago during 1942 before returning to the Beaumont–Port Arthur area. Often teamed with Moon Mullican and calling his band the Showboys, Bruner was one of the most popular bandleaders on the Texas–Louisiana Gulf Coast in the mid-forties, recording for MERCURY and Houston's Ayo label after his association with Decca ended. A family man, Bruner refused to tour far beyond his home base, which may account for his failure to hit nationally. After 1950, following his wife's death and the drowning of singer and right-hand man Buddy Duhon, Bruner played only part-time. In the late seventies his musical activities increased and he has remained active into the mid-nineties. —*Kevin Coffey*

REPRESENTATIVE RECORDINGS

Milton Brown & His Brownies: Pioneer Western Swing Band (1935–36) (MCA, 1982); *Cliff Bruner's Texas Wanderers* (Texas Rose, 1983); *Cliff Bruner and His Texas Wanderers* (Bear Family, 1997), 5 CDs

Brunswick Records

established in Dubuque, Iowa, 1919; ended 1970s

A subsidiary of the piano and bowling equipment manufacturer Brunswick-Balke-Collender, Brunswick Records debuted in 1919 and made its first foray into country music in November 1924 with recordings by Bill Chitwood & Bud Landress. A month later, BRUNSWICK acquired Vocalion Records, which included mid-1924 country product by UNCLE DAVE MACON, among others. In 1927 Vocalion's 5000 series for country material was launched, followed a year later by Brunswick's 100 country series. Following the lead of other major labels, Brunswick/Vocalion conducted field recording trips in the South from 1928 to 1930 as a means of capturing the region's vast array of ethnic sounds.

Consolidated Film Industries, parent of the AMERICAN RECORD CORPORATION, acquired Brunswick/Vocalion in December 1931 and later secured COLUMBIA/OKEH in August 1934. The entire record complex was subsequently bought by the Columbia Broadcasting System in February 1938, thus becoming the CBS subsidiary COLUMBIA RECORDING CORPORATION. Rights to pre-1932 recordings by Brunswick/Vocalion were not included, though, and were later acquired by DECCA, which also gained rights to the Brunswick label name. The Vocalion label name remained Columbia's until mid-1940, and it, too, became a Decca property in 1941, only to remain dormant until its revival in 1949. Meanwhile, Decca debuted a Brunswick 80000 reissue series in 1943 (which existed for more than a decade) and began the 54000 (LP) and 55000 (singles) series for newer product. The latter two Brunswick series ran from the late 1950s into the mid-1970s. —*Bob Pinson*

Felice and Boudleaux Bryant

Felice (Scaduto) Bryant b. Milwaukee, Wisconsin, August 7, 1925
Diadorius Boudleaux Bryant b. Shellman, Georgia, February 13, 1920; d. June 25, 1987

Husband and wife Felice and Boudleaux Bryant were among the first in Nashville to make a full-time career of songwriting. More importantly, they wrote some of the most enduring songs of the 1950s and 1960s, including many of the EVERLY BROTHERS' best-known hits.

Diadorius Boudleaux Bryant grew up in Moultrie, Georgia, the son of a small-town lawyer and his wife. The name Boudleaux came from the elder Bryant, who named his son after a Frenchman who saved his life during World War I. A classical violin student from age six through seventeen, Boudleaux spent the 1937–38 season with the Atlanta Philharmonic. Afterward he made the leap to hillbilly fiddling when he joined HANK PENNY's Radio Cowboys, then performing at WSB in Atlanta. Boudleaux remained with Penny into 1940, long enough to appear on a few of Penny's records. He later worked with Gene Steele & His Sunny Southerners in Memphis over WMC before moving on to a touring jazz group. In the summer of 1945, while Boudleaux was performing at Milwaukee's Schroeder Hotel, he met Felice Scaduto, then working at the hotel as an elevator operator. After a whirlwind courtship, they married in Newport, Kentucky, on September 5, 1945.

In contrast to Boudleaux, Felice wasn't a musician, though she had sung on radio as a child and later did some volunteer entertaining during World War II with a Milwaukee USO show. Her real passion was poetry. During the couple's first year together, they began putting his melodies together with her verses, and a songwriting team was born. Their break came in late 1948, when singer Rome Johnson passed their song "Country Boy" along to

Felice & Boudleaux Bryant

FRED ROSE of ACUFF-ROSE PUBLICATIONS in Nashville. Rose got the song to LITTLE JIMMY DICKENS, who scored a #7 hit with it on *Billboard*'s Best-Selling Retail Folk Records chart in the spring of 1949. The following year, Rose persuaded the Bryants to move to Nashville, where they concentrated on songwriting full time, with Dickens and CARL SMITH being their most dependable clients early on. Among the many tailor-made Bryant songs Dickens recorded are "I'm Little but I'm Loud," "Take Me As I Am," "Out Behind the Barn," and "Hole in My Pocket." Carl Smith had big hits with "Hey, Joe," "Back Up, Buddy," and "It's a Lovely, Lovely World." Meanwhile, between 1951 and 1953, the prolific couple recorded four singles for MGM, the last three billing them as "Bud & Betty Bryant."

In 1957 the Bryants connected with their biggest outlet for their songs—the Everly Brothers. The Bryants supplied the Everlys' first hit, "Bye, Bye Love," and continued to be the Everlys' main source of material through the early sixties (a relationship that was helped by their publisher WESLEY ROSE, who was also the Everlys' manager). All told, the Bryants wrote twenty-nine songs for the Everly Brothers, twelve of them hits, including "Wake Up, Little Susie," "All I Have to Do Is Dream," "Take a Message to Mary," and "Sleepless Nights."

The diversity and quantity of the Bryants' total output are staggering. Among their hits for others are RED FOLEY's "Midnight" (co-written with Chet Atkins), EDDY ARNOLD's "How's the World Treating You" (also with Atkins), JIM REEVES's "Blue Boy," BOB LUMAN's "Let's Think About Living," and ROY ORBISON's "Love Hurts." One of the Bryants' best-known songs is "Rocky Top." First popularized by the OSBORNE BROTHERS in 1968, "Rocky Top" is now known as an official Tennessee state song and the fight song for the University of Tennessee's athletic teams.

All told, the Bryants had some 1,500 songs recorded by more than 400 artists, amounting to sales of more than 250 million records. Along the way, they raised two sons, Dane and Del Bryant. Dane now works in Nashville real estate; Del is an executive with BMI. Boudleaux died of cancer in 1987. In 1991 the Bryants were elected to the COUNTRY MUSIC HALL OF FAME. —*Paul Kingsbury*

REPRESENTATIVE RECORDINGS

The Everly Brothers: Harmonies & Heartaches (Rhino, 1994), 4 CDs; *The Everly Brothers: Cadence Classics* (Rhino, 1989);

Carl Smith: The Essential Carl Smith, 1950–1956 (Columbia/Legacy, 1991)

Jimmy Bryant (*see* Speedy West & Jimmy Bryant)

Slim Bryant
b. Atlanta, Georgia, December 7, 1908

Perhaps best known as the writer of the JIMMIE RODGERS song "Mother, the Queen of My Heart," Thomas Hoyt Bryant had a long career as a country music performer. Beginning in his native Atlanta, after a brief stint as an electrician, he worked on radio stations in Cincinnati, Chicago (where he served two brief separate stints as a member of the *NATIONAL BARN DANCE*), Louisville, Richmond, and Pittsburgh. In the latter city he appeared on radio and later, television, for two decades, 1940–60. During 1950 he had his own *Slim Bryant Show* on NBC Radio, and in 1959–60 he performed on WTRF-TV in Wheeling, West Virginia.

From 1939 until the end of his performing career he led a band called the Georgia Wildcats (after a brief time Georgia was dropped from their name). The group consisted of Bryant, guitar; his brother "Loppy," bass; Jerry Wallace, banjo; and Kenny Newton, fiddle. First organized in Richmond, Virginia, as Clayton McMichen's Georgia Wildcats, the five-man unit became a quartet when the famous fiddler left in 1939 for Louisville, where he formed a new band.

One of the highlights of Bryant's career was playing with Jimmie Rodgers on two recording sessions, one of them being the first recording of "Mother, the Queen of My Heart." He later recorded for Majestic, MGM, DECCA, and Lion, frequently waxing his own compositions. Of his more than 200 original songs, the biggest hit was "Eeny Meeny Dixie Deeny." The Wildcats' recording of it made it to *Billboard*'s 1947 list of Top Ten country records. His most enduring success, however, was the Rodgers song.

Bryant supplemented his income with various enterprises, including a gift shop and a guitar studio, but probably his most lucrative activity has been the writing of radio theme songs and commercial jingles for Westinghouse, Chevrolet, U.S. Steel, Alcoa Aluminum, and other concerns. In the 1980s he appeared at a few festivals, but in the 1990s his musical work has been confined to teaching guitar at the South Hills Music Center in Pittsburgh.
—*W. K. McNeil*

Buck dancing; buck and wing (*see* Square Dancing)

Steve Buckingham
b. Richmond, Virginia, February 24, 1949

Steve Buckingham is one of the most versatile producers in Nashville, having produced twenty-seven #1 singles on seven different charts, including pop, r&b, Hispanic, and dance. Since his producing career began with the 1978 Alicia Bridges disco hit "I Love the Night Life," he has gone on to earn nine platinum and seventeen gold albums with such acts as DOLLY PARTON, RICKY VAN SHELTON, MARY CHAPIN CARPENTER, RICKY SKAGGS, and TAMMY WYNETTE. In 1994 Buckingham formed Blue Eye Records with Parton and became its president.

Buckingham started out as a guitarist in Virginia bands that toured the mid-Atlantic seaboard. He soon established himself as a session player, working with such acts as

BOBBY BARE, JOE SOUTH, and Johnny Nash. He and George Massenburg, who later produced LINDA RONSTADT, learned to make records on the weekends.

In 1973 Buckingham moved to Atlanta, where he continued to play on sessions. The first record he produced was "I Love the Night Life," which sold 2 million copies and earned a Grammy nomination. That success captured the attention of Clive Davis, president of the ARISTA label, who asked Buckingham to produce records by Melissa Manchester and Dionne Warwick.

In 1980 Buckingham moved to Nashville so he wouldn't have to continue to travel to New York or Los Angeles to record. Drawn to country, he soon began recording almost exclusively country acts. In 1986 he was named vice president of A&R for CBS Records (later renamed Sony), where he remained for nine years.

During his CBS/Sony tenure, Buckingham played an integral part in the careers of Ricky Van Shelton, Mary Chapin Carpenter, RICK TREVINO, and SWEETHEARTS OF THE RODEO. He produced Trevino's #1 hits "Learning as You Go" and "Running out of Reasons to Run," as well as the Dolly Parton–VINCE GILL duet "I Will Always Love You," which won CMA Vocal Event of the Year in 1996.

—*Beverly Keel*

Buddy Lee Attractions (*see* Buddy Lee)

Bug Music
established in Los Angeles, March 1975

Though never exclusively a country-oriented song firm, Bug Music, an independent publishing administration company, has helped foster the careers of many of country's more maverick songwriters and artists, including JOHN PRINE (since 1985), NANCI GRIFFITH (1986–90), and ROSANNE CASH (since 1987).

Bug was founded in Los Angeles in March 1975 when music-industry veteran Dan Bourgoise, a close friend and then manager of pop star Del Shannon, tracked down a decade's worth of back royalties owed Shannon for such hits as "Runaway." A portion of those royalties funded the creation of Bug, which Bourgoise has helmed ever since. Fred Bourgoise, Dan's brother, joined the company shortly after its creation and later signed such trend-setting L.A. bands as the Blasters and Los Lobos.

The Bourgoises had a long-standing interest in country music (Dan Bourgoise signed ASLEEP AT THE WHEEL to their first record deal), and by the early 1980s Bug had established a presence in Nashville. A permanent Nashville office was opened in 1985, with Garry Velletri as the head. In the years since, Bug in Nashville has grown into a thriving Music Row enterprise, a place where country producers and singers often look to find interesting, less mainstream material. A London office was opened in 1992, and in 1997 a New York office was opened with Velletri relocating there to run it. Dave Durocher, previously director of creative services, was promoted to general manager on Velletri's departure.

—*Daniel Cooper*

Jim Bulleit
b. Corydon, Indiana, November 4, 1908; d. December 12, 1988

Jim Bulleit was one of the pioneers of the record industry in Nashville, although he left music almost before the country music business had centered itself on the city.

He attended Illinois Wesleyan College in Bloomington and worked in radio in San Francisco before moving to Nashville in late 1943 to join the announcing staff at WSM. He cofounded BULLET RECORDS in 1946 and stayed until 1949. After he left he started Delta Records and bought and sold masters and copyrights in country and r&b.

At some point in 1950, Bulleit acquired part ownership of four LEFTY FRIZZELL copyrights, including "If You've Got the Money, I've Got the Time" and "I Love You a Thousand Ways," and, as a result, was embroiled in a publishing power struggle; ultimately he sold these copyrights to the Peer-Southern publishing firm. Early in 1951 he joined KWKH in Shreveport to start a booking service for the *LOUISIANA HAYRIDE,* but he left in August 1951 and tried unsuccessfully to start his own jamboree in Spruce Pine, North Carolina. Back in Nashville, he launched J-B Records, and owned a share of SUN RECORDS in 1953–54, which he sold prematurely for $1,200, well before the label's successes with ELVIS PRESLEY, JOHNNY CASH, and JERRY LEE LEWIS. Bulleit then left the music business and worked in several different occupations. In his retirement he started a candy brokerage business, which he operated until his death.

—*Colin Escott*

Bullet Records
established in Nashville, Tennessee, April 1946; ended 1956

Bullet Records was quite possibly the first independent label in Nashville and certainly the first to achieve any kind of national profile. Considering its location, it is ironic that its chief claim to fame rests with the overwhelming success of Francis Craig's "Near You," the best-selling pop record of 1947.

The Bullet Recording and Transcription Company was incorporated in April 1946. The principals were JIM BULLEIT, an announcer at WSM; banker Orville Zickler; and C. V. Hitchcock, owner of the Hermitage Music Store and (as of April 1946) Volunteer Music Sales. Hitchcock couldn't get enough country records for his jukebox accounts and tried to solve the problem by cutting his own. The first recordings were made during the 1945 Christmas season, and the first record ("Zeb's Mountain Boogie" by "Brad Brady," a pseudonym for OWEN BRADLEY, and ZEB TURNER) was issued the following May. Bradley was the *de facto* musical director.

Bullet recorded an eclectic mix of artists. PEE WEE KING, SHEB WOOLEY, MINNIE PEARL, CHET ATKINS, and RAY PRICE made their first recordings for the label, as did B. B. King. LEON PAYNE also cut the original version of "Lost Highway" for Bullet. Bulleit recorded r&b records by Wynonie Harris, Red Miller, and Cecil Gant that sold well, but everything was eclipsed by "Near You." Its success enabled Bullet to incorporate Bullet Plastics in 1949, Nashville's first record-pressing plant, located near Berry Field airport. Bulleit himself was forced out that year as the company tried to become a major label, signing big-name acts such as Milton Berle and Bob Crosby. It limped into the 1950s under Hitchcock's ownership, continuing until 1956. In the early 1960s the imprint was revived by Red Wortham for a dozen or so releases.

—*Colin Escott*

Samantha Bumgarner
b. North Carolina ca.1880; d. December 24, 1960

Samantha Bumgarner was a link between Appalachian folk tradition and the commercial country music industry. The daughter of mountain fiddler Has Biddix, she began playing fiddle and banjo in public in 1895. After achieving local renown winning old-time fiddle competitions, she traveled from Silva, North Carolina, to New York with fiddler Eva Davis to record for COLUMBIA in 1924. She was one of the first five-string banjo players ever recorded.

Bumgarner appeared at the 1927 Georgia Old-Time Fiddlers Convention in Atlanta. Back in North Carolina, she became a yearly headliner at Bascom Lamar Lunsford's Mountain Dance and Folk Festival in Asheville, 1928–59.

Folk enthusiasts of the 1950s "rediscovered" her as "Aunt Samanthy," and she was recorded for the 1955 Riverside LP *Banjo Songs of the Southern Mountains*. ROUNDER RECORDS included one of her 1920s recordings on its *Banjo Pickin' Girl* reissue LP of 1979.   —*Robert K. Oermann*

Sonny Burgess

b. Newport, Arkansas, May 28, 1931

Sonny Burgess belongs to a small group of artists who embodied the energetic spirit of rockabilly music created for SAM PHILLIPS's SUN RECORDS. Born fewer than one hundred miles from Memphis, Albert Burgess heard country music on Nashville's GRAND OLE OPRY but found himself more attracted to blues and r&b. After an earlier unsuccessful audition for Phillips, Burgess returned to Memphis on May 2, 1956, with an expanded band called the Pacers. Phillips recorded them the same afternoon, creating the frenzied, raw rockabilly classics "We Wanna Boogie" and "Red Headed Woman."

Later singles "Ain't Got a Thing" and "My Bucket's Got a Hole in It" continued the promise, but Burgess and the Pacers never achieved huge commercial success. So Burgess played for a short stretch in CONWAY TWITTY's road band and eventually pursued a career as a traveling sales representative. With the Sun Rhythm Section—first-generation rock & roll musicians from the Memphis area—Burgess became active again in the mid-1980s. In 1992 he released *Tennessee Border*, produced by ex-Blaster Dave Alvin. Later, in 1996, he recorded a self-titled album with producer Garry Tallent, the bassist of Bruce Springsteen's E Street Band. Springsteen contributed an original song, "Tiger Rose," to the album.   —*Jay Orr*

REPRESENTATIVE RECORDINGS

We Wanna Boogie (Rounder, 1990); *Sonny Burgess* (Rounder, 1996)

Johnny Burnette & the Rock 'n' Roll Trio

Johnny Burnette b. Memphis, Tennessee, March 25, 1934;
d. August 1, 1964
Dorsey Burnette b. Memphis, Tennessee, December 28, 1932;
d. August 19, 1979
Paul Burlison b. Brownsville, Tennessee, February 4, 1929

Between May 1956 and March 1957 Johnny Burnette & the Rock 'n' Roll Trio entered a recording studio a mere three times. In that period they recorded seventeen tracks, pioneered the use of distortion, and achieved a reputation as the wildest rockabilly band of all.

Lead guitarist Burlison moved to Memphis from Brownsville, Tennessee, at age seven. He met pedal steel player Dorsey and guitarist-singer Johnny Burnette in 1949

The Rock 'n' Roll Trio: (from left) Johnny Burnette, Dorsey Burnette, and Paul Burlison

at a boxing tournament that featured Dorsey. At the time Burlison was playing in a country band led by Shelby Follin. When the Follin band broke up, Burlison and Johnny Burnette joined a pop-country band led by pianist Doc McQueen, while Dorsey Burnette enjoyed steady work in a band with Scotty Moore and Bill Black (who later backed ELVIS PRESLEY). Dorsey eventually joined the McQueen band, switching from pedal steel to bass, receiving his initial tutelage on this new instrument from Burlison. Beginning in 1953, the Burnette brothers and Burlison performed regularly as a trio between sets by the McQueen band. The trio started out playing straight country music but soon found that the wilder they got, the more the audience reacted. In late 1953 they recorded a country single on the Mississippi-based Von label.

In early 1956 Burlison and Dorsey Burnette found themselves out of work as electricians in Memphis and, together with Johnny, journeyed to New York in search of day jobs. A couple of weeks after establishing themselves in New York, the threesome decided to audition for the *Ted Mack Amateur Hour* network television show. The trio went on to win three weeks in a row and were subsequently offered a recording contract with DECCA subsidiary Coral Records.

Their first session was scheduled for May 1956 at the Pythian Temple in New York. Their remaining two sessions, conducted in July 1956 and March 1957, were held in Nashville at OWEN BRADLEY's famed studio. CARL PERKINS's cousin, drummer Tony Austin, joined the trio shortly after the first session (session ace BUDDY HARMAN played drums on the band's second session). The Rock 'n' Roll Trio enjoyed two regional hits, the original "Tear It

Up" and a cover of r&b artist Tiny Bradshaw's "The Train Kept A-Rollin'," and had an eponymously titled album issued in December 1956. Although the trio's recordings were revered by later generations of rockabilly collectors and had a large influence on rockabilly revival artists such as the Stray Cats and Robert Gordon, in the 1950s they were unable to chart nationally, and their touring for the most part was confined to the Northeast.

After their third and final recording session, Dorsey Burnette quit, upset at the group's new billing as Johnny Burnette & the Rock 'n' Roll Trio. He was replaced by Johnny Black, brother of Elvis Presley bass player Bill Black. It was this version of the band that appeared in the 1957 film *Rock, Rock, Rock,* which also featured Chuck Berry, LaVern Baker, and Frankie Lymon & the Teenagers.

In 1957 the band broke up. Johnny and Dorsey resolved their differences, moved to California, and formed a songwriting partnership, achieving initial success through RICKY NELSON's recording of two of their songs. As artists, Dorsey hit the pop charts twice in 1960 before enjoying an extended run on the country charts between 1972 and 1977. Johnny was more successful initially, landing five chart records in 1960 and 1961, four of them reaching the Top Twenty. His biggest hit, "You're Sixteen," peaked at #8 in December 1960. Johnny died in a boating accident in 1964, while Dorsey succumbed to a heart attack in 1979. Johnny's son, Rocky Burnette, had a Top Ten hit in 1980 while Dorsey's son, Billy Burnette, achieved limited success as an artist in the rock and country fields.

After the breakup of the Rock 'n' Roll Trio, Paul Burlison settled in Memphis, building a successful construction business. In the 1990s he continued to perform occasionally at festivals in the Memphis area, and beginning in the mid-1980s he gigged semiregularly, fronting a band of SUN RECORDS alumni dubbed the Sun Rhythm Section and recording one album for Flying Fish Records.

—*Rob Bowman*

REPRESENTATIVE RECORDINGS

Johnny Burnette and the Rock 'n' Roll Trio (Bear Family, 1989); *Johnny Burnette: Best of: You're Sixteen* (Capitol, 1992); *Dorsey Burnette: Best of: The Era Years* (Era, 1994)

Smiley Burnette
b. Summum, Illinois, March 18, 1911; d. February 17, 1967

He had a vast and adoring country audience for more than thirty years, brought down the house whenever he guested on the GRAND OLE OPRY, and composed hundreds of songs, some still performed today, but Lester Alvin "Smiley" Burnette's highly successful work on film overshadowed his recorded music.

The son of two ordained ministers, Burnette was singing and playing piano, accordion, guitar, and two dozen more instruments at WDZ in Tuscola, Illinois, when promoter J. L. FRANK urged GENE AUTRY to hire Burnette in December 1933. Six months later, Burnette and Autry went to Hollywood, where they made movies (together and apart) for the next twenty years.

A natural and often inspired comedian, Burnette became singing cowboy Autry's sidekick "Frog Millhouse" at Republic Pictures, and also composed most of the songs used in their early films. By the late 1930s his screen popularity was on a par with Autry's, and he became the first sidekick to be listed among the Top Ten western stars. In 1943 he became the only cowboy comic to receive top billing in a series of his own.

After 150 movies and two syndicated radio series, Burnette became jovial railroad engineer Charley Pratt on CBS-TV's *Petticoat Junction* in 1963. His classic compositions include "Ridin' Down the Canyon," "It's My Lazy Day," "Hominy Grits," and "Catfish, Take a Look at That Worm."

—*Jonathan Guyot Smith*

REPRESENTATIVE RECORDING

Ole Frog (Starday, 1962)

James Burton
b. Dubberly, Louisiana, August 21, 1939

At age fourteen, James Burton was the youngest staff musician on the Shreveport-based *LOUISIANA HAYRIDE*. Within a few years—thanks to accomplishments that included playing on Dale Hawkins's 1957 rock & roll classic "Susie-Q," and on a lengthy string of hit singles by RICKY NELSON—Burton was among the most influential guitarists in the world. For many years a highly sought session player noted for the distinctive, steely tone he got from his 1953 Fender Telecaster, Burton also toured with Elvis Presley, and played a lead role in popularizing a Telecaster-based electric guitar sound that remains a part of country music to this day.

"I was just trying to create my own identity, mixing blues and country together," Burton later explained, commenting on his famous tone, and on his technique of using fingerpicks with a flatpick instead of the more conventional thumbpick.

In addition to his work on the weekly *Hayride,* Burton played in local bands, including those led by Hawkins (with whom he co-wrote and recorded "Susie-Q" at fifteen), JOHNNY HORTON, and BOB LUMAN. Luman took Burton to Los Angeles to record, and it wasn't long before the young guitarist came to the attention of Ricky Nelson. Nelson invited Burton and Luman's bassist, James Kirkland, to meet his parents, and soon thereafter the two were hired to play on the Nelson family TV show, *The Adventures of Ozzie & Harriet.*

With Nelson, Burton started playing second guitar to JOE MAPHIS's lead on singles including "Waitin' in School" and "Stood Up" (both 1957); his first session as lead guitarist included "Believe What You Say" (1958). Burton didn't do many sessions with other artists while working for Nelson, but he did record with Dorsey Burnette shortly before leaving Nelson in 1964. Then business picked up considerably, and during the 1960s he recorded with such varied acts as MERLE HAGGARD, BUCK OWENS, Sammy Davis Jr., Sandy Nelson, Frank Sinatra, the Supremes, and with Johnny Rivers on the 1966 pop hit "Poor Side of Town."

For a year Burton appeared as a member of the house band on ABC-TV's *Shindig* and also played on numerous television and film soundtracks, including ELVIS PRESLEY's *Viva Las Vegas.* Later, Presley hired Burton to put together a backup band for his August 1969 debut performance at the International Hotel in Las Vegas; Burton remained with Presley's touring band until the singer's death in 1977.

Burton continued his extensive studio work when not on tour with Presley. He played on GRAM PARSONS's solo albums, and after Parsons's death, he joined EMMYLOU HAR-

RIS's first Hot Band, eventually leaving it when he found it too difficult to juggle working with both Harris and Presley. Burton also recorded and toured for several years with JOHN DENVER and has frequently played with JERRY LEE LEWIS. Today he maintains residences in Nashville and in Shreveport, Louisiana, and remains in demand as a session guitarist.

Burton has recorded two albums under his own name: *Corn Pickin' and Slick Slidin'* (with steel guitarist and frequent session partner Ralph Mooney) for Capitol in 1967, and *James Burton*, recorded during Presley session downtime and released on A&M in 1971. —*Todd Everett*

Judge Bob Burton
b. New York, New York, September 21, 1914; d. March 29, 1965

Judge Robert J. "Bob" Burton, a visionary BMI executive, was an early and potent voice on behalf of Nashville and country music. He was instrumental in formulating a key system of tracking performances of music that encompassed the many rural and small urban radio stations programming country. Previously these stations had not been included in any surveys on which royalty payments were based.

Close to many country artists, songwriters, and publishers, Burton was one of the founders of the COUNTRY MUSIC ASSOCIATION and a member of its first board of directors. He played a major role in raising money for building the COUNTRY MUSIC HALL OF FAME. His belief in the importance and future of country music was further evidenced by the part he played in opening a BMI office in Nashville in 1958, years before most other major New York and Los Angeles companies did so.

Raised in Larchmont, New York, Burton was educated in Larchmont public schools and at the Château de Beurs, a private school in France. He graduated from Columbia University in 1935, Columbia Law School in 1937, and joined BMI in January 1941.

In the foreground as BMI grew, Burton advanced rapidly and became the organization's president in 1964. Unfortunately, *Billboard*'s Country Man of the Year for 1964 didn't live long enough to witness the full impact of what he had done for Nashville and country music—indeed, for all forms of popular music—as he died in 1965 in a hotel fire in Vancouver, British Columbia.

—*Burt Korall*

Buzz Busby
b. Eros, Louisiana, September 6, 1933

An energetic, eccentric singer and mandolinist, Buzz Busby (real name Bernarr Graham Busbice) pioneered the supercharged style that defined the early Baltimore-Washington bluegrass scene: taut vocals with edgy, dissonant harmonies; and swooping, unconventional instrumental breaks driven by exaggerated guitar runs.

Busby learned both guitar and mandolin while growing up near Monroe, Louisiana; BILL MONROE was an early influence. In 1951 Busby moved to Washington to work for the Federal Bureau of Investigation; he formed a band featuring Scotty Stoneman on fiddle, JACK CLEMENT on guitar, and ROY CLARK on banjo. In 1953 Busby left the FBI to pursue a career in music. After a brief stint with MAC WISEMAN, he and Clement formed a comedy duo, Ham and Scram,

which toured with the HAWKSHAW HAWKINS show (Pete Pike later replaced Clement). In 1954 Busby organized the Bayou Boys, whose members included such bluegrass notables as BILL HARRELL, Don Stover, Charlie Waller, Bill Emerson, and Carl Nelson.

In the fall of 1955, the Bayou Boys headed west for a nine-month stint on the *LOUISIANA HAYRIDE* in Shreveport. After returning to Washington, Busby recorded five STARDAY singles that many consider to be among the most intense bluegrass records ever released. Escalating personal and legal problems unraveled Busby's career during the early 1960s. He recorded sporadically for various labels into the mid-1980s, but with largely indifferent results.

His brother Wayne Busbice (b. Chatham, Louisiana, March 28, 1929) recorded country and ROCKABILLY music under the names Wayne Busby and Red McCoy.

—*Dave Samuelson*

Johnny Bush
b. Houston, Texas, February 17, 1935

With his early musical associations with both WILLIE NELSON and RAY PRICE, singer-songwriter John Bush Shin III was a minor but significant figure in 1960s and 1970s Texas honky-tonk. Bush's most enduring claim to fame is the song "Whiskey River," which he wrote and had a Top Twenty country hit with in 1972.

With a vocal style hauntingly—perhaps damningly—reminiscent of Ray Price, Bush enjoyed minor chart success between 1969 and 1981 on Stop Records and RCA RECORDS, as well as various independent labels. But his career was more than once hampered by a severe neurological condition that affected his voice. His highest entry in the *Billboard* charts came in 1969, when he reached #7 with his spirited rendition of "You Gave Me a Mountain," a MARTY ROBBINS original that was also a minor pop hit for Frankie Laine in 1969.

The real impact of "Whiskey River" came when Bush's friend Willie Nelson recorded it and eventually made it his theme song. Though Nelson's single release of "Whiskey River" only reached #12 in 1978, Nelson has included it on several of his best-selling albums and has featured the song prominently in his live shows for years.

Bush began his professional career in San Antonio area clubs in the early 1950s. One of the early Texas bands he joined (as a drummer) also included Nelson, then still an aspiring recording artist himself. In the 1960s Bush became a member of the Record Men, one of Nelson's early road bands. Bush soon moved on to join Ray Price's band, the Cherokee Cowboy, for three years. In 1968 Bush recorded his own first Top Ten single, "Undo the Right," on the Stop label. His "You Gave Me a Mountain" reached #7 in 1969.

He has continued to perform and to release albums, including a collection of duets with DARRELL MCCALL, *Hot Texas Country* (Step One, 1986), and *Time Changes Everything* (TCE, 1994), featuring guest artists HANK THOMPSON and Willie Nelson. In 1998 Bush released the new album *Talk to My Heart*, which includes JIMMY DAY on pedal-steel guitar and Floyd Domino on piano. —*Bob Allen*

REPRESENTATIVE RECORDINGS

Greatest Hits (Stop, 1972); *Greatest Hits* (RCA, 1994), 2 CDs; *Talk to My Heart* (Watermelon, 1998)

Sam Bush

b. Bowling Green, Kentucky, April 13, 1952

Since the 1970s, fiddler-mandolinist Charles Samuel Bush has been one of the most influential acoustic musicians of his time. Known for fusing bluegrass, rock, blues, and jazz styles, he was a founding member of the groundbreaking NEW GRASS REVIVAL, and musical director of EMMYLOU HARRIS's Nash Ramblers. He has also been for many years an in-demand session player.

Bush began playing mandolin at age eleven and fiddle at thirteen. He won the National Junior Fiddle Championships in Weiser, Idaho, three years in a row (1967–69), and in 1969 he recorded the album *Poor Richard's Almanac* with banjoist Alan Munde and guitarist Wayne Stewart.

Bush joined the Louisville-based BLUEGRASS ALLIANCE as mandolin player in 1970; banjo player Courtney Johnson joined shortly thereafter. Bush, Johnson, and bassist Harry "Ebo Walker" Shelor formed New Grass Revival in 1971 with guitarist Curtis Burch. When New Grass Revival broke up at the close of 1989, Bush was the only original member still with the group.

Bush joined Emmylou Harris's band in time for the 1991 recording of her *At the Ryman* CD, and he remained with her until 1995. Since then, Bush has remained in demand as a solo performer and session musician. A survivor of cancer in 1982, he serves as a role model for young people with the disease. In 1996 he released *Glamour and Grits* on Sugar Hill. —*Frank and Marty Godbey*

REPRESENTATIVE RECORDINGS

Late As Usual (Rounder, 1985); *Emmylou Harris & the Nash Ramblers: At the Ryman* (Reprise, 1992)

Allen Butler

b. Clarksville, Tennessee, January 10, 1951

As president of Sony Music Nashville, Allen Butler has been directly involved in the careers of such acts as MARY CHAPIN CARPENTER, JOE DIFFIE, PATTY LOVELESS, COLLIN RAYE, and WADE HAYES. Known for his expertise in radio promotion, Butler had previously helped ARISTA NASHVILLE achieve major success in just its first three years of business before he joined Sony in December 1993.

Butler graduated with dual degrees in marketing and management from Memphis State University and Christian Brothers University in Memphis, having played in local bands along the way to pay the bills. He decided to pursue a career in the industry's business side, and after spending five years in marketing at MCA RECORDS, he spent more than a decade at RCA, including four years as regional country promotion manager in Dallas. This led to a friendship with TIM DUBOIS, manager of RESTLESS HEART, who was to become the head of Arista Nashville. DuBois convinced Butler to join his infant Arista team as national director of promotion.

Butler's success at Arista caught the attention of Sony executives, who lured him away as part of a restructuring of their executive ranks. Initially part of a leadership triumvirate that also included PAUL WORLEY and Scott Siman, Butler has since emerged as sole head of Sony's Nashville office. In 1997 he supervised the launching of the Lucky Dog label and a reactivated MONUMENT, both Sony subsidiaries. —*Beverly Keel*

Carl & Pearl Butler

Carl & Pearl Butler

Carl Roberts Butler b. Knoxville, Tennessee, June 2, 1927; d. September 4, 1992

Pearl Dee Jones b. Nashville, Tennessee, September 20, 1927; d. March 1, 1989

Carl & Pearl Butler's first charted duet became their greatest success; "Don't Let Me Cross Over," which spent eleven weeks at #1 on the country charts in 1962 and 1963. On the strength of that success Pearl joined her husband on the GRAND OLE OPRY, where he had been a regular since 1958.

Carl Butler had been playing guitar in public since age twelve, when he entertained between square dance sets. Later he was featured on WROL and WNOX in Knoxville and WPTF in Raleigh, North Carolina. While in Knoxville he began amassing credits as a tunesmith with such songs as "My Tears Don't Show," "If Teardrops Were Pennies," "Guilty Conscience," "Hold Back the Dawn," and "Cryin' My Heart Out Over You." The songs were recorded through the years by ROY ACUFF, CARL SMITH, BILL MONROE, Rosemary Clooney, FLATT & SCRUGGS, and RICKY SKAGGS. Pearl Jones co-wrote "Kisses Don't Lie," a Carl Smith hit.

Carl Butler kicked off his solo recording career in 1951 with CAPITOL RECORDS, switching to COLUMBIA in 1953. His early recordings included "River of Tears" and "That's What It's Like to Be Lonesome," but "Honkytonkitis" became his first record to hit the country charts (#25, 1961).

Although Pearl often sang with her husband at shows, she resisted recording until "Don't Let Me Cross Over." In 1964 the couple had another *Billboard* Top Ten hit, "Too Late to Try Again" (#9), and a few months later scored again with "I'm Hanging Up the Phone" (#14). Their last chart entry, "We'll Sweep Out the Ashes in the Morning" (#63, 1969), was later recorded as a duet by GRAM PARSONS and EMMYLOU HARRIS.

In Knoxville the Butlers took in child performer DOLLY PARTON when she performed for Cas Walker's local TV show and later helped arrange for Parton's first appearance on the Opry in 1959.

The Butlers appeared in the film *Second Fiddle to a Steel Guitar* (1967).   —*Walt Trott*

REPRESENTATIVE RECORDING

Crying My Heart Out Over You (Bear Family, 1993)

Larry Butler

b. Pensacola, Florida, March 26, 1942

A multitalented music industry veteran, Larry Lee Butler has been the only Nashville producer to win the coveted Grammy for Producer of the Year (Non-Classical), beating the competition from all genres of popular music for 1979.

A child prodigy, Butler began playing piano at age four. Two years later he performed with the Harry James Orchestra, and at age ten he sang with RED FOLEY. As a preteen Butler hosted his own local radio show and co-hosted a TV show. After joining a Florida band he made a trip to Nashville, where he met publisher-producer BUDDY KILLEN of Tree Publishing.

Encouraged by Killen, Butler moved to Nashville in 1963. There he became one of the city's top session players, through the years providing piano work on such hits as BOBBY GOLDSBORO's "Honey" and CONWAY TWITTY's "Hello Darlin'."

Butler moved to Memphis in the late 1960s and worked with producer CHIPS MOMAN. Butler recorded as a member of the pop group the Gentrys and as a solo artist, and he became Goldsboro's musical director and pianist.

After returning to Nashville, Butler produced for CAPITOL RECORDS, then for CBS, where he worked closely with JOHNNY CASH, later becoming Cash's pianist, producer, studio manager, and musical director. Butler joined United Artists Records in 1973 as head of the Nashville division and brought in such acts as DOTTIE WEST and CRYSTAL GAYLE. His biggest success came at United Artists when he produced such hits of KENNY ROGERS's as "Lucille" and "The Gambler."

Leaving United Artists in 1983, Butler formed Larry Butler Productions and worked with such acts as MAC DAVIS, CHARLIE RICH, Debby Boone, Don McLean, JOHN DENVER, and BILLIE JO SPEARS.

As a songwriter, Butler co-wrote with Moman "(Hey Won't You Play) Another Somebody Done Somebody Wrong Song," a #1 country and pop hit for B. J. THOMAS and a 1975 Grammy winner as Song of the Year.

Butler's latest ventures include Nashville Music Consultants—an organization established to help those trying to break into the music business—and the production of two various-artists Christmas albums. Butler is chairman of the International Country Music Expo held annually in Nashville and founded the Nashville Academy of Songwriting.   —*Gerry Wood*

Billy Byrd

b. Nashville, Tennessee, February 17, 1920

William Lewis "Billy" Byrd is best known for having been ERNEST TUBB's longtime lead guitarist. A self-taught player enamored of jazz greats Stephane Grappelli and Django Reinhardt, Byrd gained his earliest professional experience in radio and club work with Nashville pop bands, but his earliest recordings were made with Herald Goodman's

GRAND OLE OPRY group in 1938. After military service, Byrd worked at the Opry for PAUL HOWARD's Arkansas Cotton Pickers and WALLY FOWLER's Oak Ridge Quartet before moving to Shreveport in 1948 to work with Fowler alumnus Curly Kinsey and later with CURLEY WILLIAMS. Upon returning to Nashville in about early 1949, Byrd backed Opry newcomers JIMMY DICKENS and GEORGE MORGAN and then joined ERNEST TUBB's Texas Troubadours in mid-1949. For the next ten years Tubb relied on his electric lead guitarist not only for dependable instrumental support but also as one of his limo and bus drivers. Meanwhile, on hit after hit, Tubb immortalized Byrd with his oft-repeated aside of "Aw, Billy Byrd now," which introduced the guitarist's succinct, melodic solos. In 1955 Byrd and HANK GARLAND collaborated to design the Byrdland semi-hollow-body electric guitar for the Gibson company.

In 1959 Byrd made his first instrumental recordings (two albums) for WARNER BROS. RECORDS. After leaving Tubb that year, Byrd worked briefly in California for Gordon Terry, then returned to Nashville for club work, TV shows, and more recording. Byrd briefly rejoined Ernest Tubb's band, not once but twice—1969–70 and 1973–74. After driving a cab for many years, he retired in Nashville.   —*Ronnie Pugh*

REPRESENTATIVE RECORDINGS

I Love a Guitar (Warner Bros., 1960, out of print); *Ernest Tubb: Country Music Hall of Fame Series* (MCA, 1991)

Jerry Byrd

b. Lima, Ohio, March 29, 1920

Gerald Lester Byrd ranks as one of country music's most influential steel guitar stylists. By the time he finished high school, he had started playing steel guitar on local radio programs, having been inspired by a Hawaiian troupe he saw in a traveling tent show. He had also begun to work Saturday nights with the *RENFRO VALLEY BARN DANCE*, temporarily originating from Dayton, Ohio, and airing over Cincinnati's WLW. This led to a full-time job with the barn dance, which moved to Renfro Valley, Kentucky, late in 1939. There Byrd backed stars such as RED FOLEY and Ernie Lee, blending Hawaiian sounds into a variety of country material. By this time he had begun to experiment with slanted-bar left-hand techniques and alternate tunings, such as his trademark C6 tuning.

A bout with pneumonia temporarily sidelined him, but Byrd returned to the Renfro Valley stage briefly during World War II before moving to Detroit's WJR with Lee. After the war Byrd went to Nashville to play onstage and in the studio with ERNEST TUBB, and then with Foley, both GRAND OLE OPRY stars at the time. Byrd's popularity as a studio musician increased steadily through his years at WLW's *MIDWESTERN HAYRIDE* in Cincinnati (1948–51), when he also supplied steel parts for sessions at the nearby HERZOG STUDIO and the KING RECORDS studio, both for locally based talent and for visiting country and pop stars such as JIMMY WAKELY, Patti Page, and HANK WILLIAMS.

Byrd returned to Nashville to play in GEORGE MORGAN's band for three years, all the while continuing to work sessions. After signing with MERCURY RECORDS in 1949, Byrd recorded "Steelin' the Blues" and other original hits for that label before moving on to make well-received albums for DECCA, RCA, and MONUMENT during the 1950s and 1960s. During these same years he could be seen on nu-

Jerry Byrd

merous Nashville-originated TV programs, including *Country Junction*, the *Bobby Lord Show*, and syndicated shows using Opry talent.

Despite the rise of the pedal steel guitar in the mid-1950s, Byrd stuck by his original nonpedal style, and his session work dwindled. In 1972 he moved to Hawaii and found acceptance in resort hotels, sometimes recording for small labels as well. Even after retiring, in the 1980s, he has continued to teach young Hawaiian players their own native instrument. "It's gone full circle," he said, "in that I'm putting it back where I got it from."   —*John Rumble*

REPRESENTATIVE RECORDINGS

Steel Guitar Favorites (Mercury, 1958, out of print); *Guitar Player Presents Legends of Country Guitar, Volume 2* (Rhino, 1991)

Tracy Byrd
b. Vidor, Texas, December 18, 1966

Tracy Lynn Byrd earned his musical spurs on the southeastern Texas "Golden Triangle" nightclub circuit that has nurtured country vocal greats from LEFTY FRIZZELL and GEORGE JONES to MARK CHESNUTT. Byrd grew up in Vidor, fifteen miles up the road from Beaumont. His brown eyes and smooth features indicate his French heritage, although he says he's not a true Cajun: "There's no telling what else I've got in me."

Byrd made his recording debut in a booth at a Beaumont shopping mall. He paid $7.95 to sing HANK WILLIAMS's "Your Cheatin' Heart" over a prerecorded track. Byrd's pure country vocal impressed the sales clerk, who invited him to sing at a monthly amateur show, where he

received a standing ovation. Byrd says he decided right then and there that his future would be in music. When his bass fishing buddy Mark Chesnutt left on his first national tour in 1990, Byrd inherited the latter's gig at Cutter's Nightclub, a Beaumont dance hall. He was signed to MCA Records by producer-executive TONY BROWN, who'd previously roped in such Texas talents as STEVE EARLE and Chesnutt. Byrd's self-titled 1993 debut album revealed an easy command of classic Lone Star country traditions, from western swing and outlaw honky-tonk to lonesome barstool ballads. The album spawned a #1 hit in "Holdin' Heaven."

But it was the follow-up album, *No Ordinary Man*, that established Byrd as a contemporary country star. Although some critics complained that the album was too heavily weighted toward novelty numbers such as "Watermelon Crawl" and "Lifestyles of the Not So Rich and Famous," radio programmers loved it. The ballad "The Keeper of the Stars" became a popular selection at wedding ceremonies. Byrd's third album, *Love Lessons*, balanced the staunch traditionalism of his debut with the radio-friendly approach of his second album.

Byrd—who cites BOB WILLS, MERLE HAGGARD, and GEORGE STRAIT as his biggest influences—seems intent on retaining a Texas feeling in his music. "I'm a big Bob Wills fan," he said. "I used to listen to my dad's 78s when I was a kid. There's a line connecting Wills and Haggard and Strait. That's the line I'd like to be in."   —*Rick Mitchell*

REPRESENTATIVE RECORDINGS

Tracy Byrd (MCA, 1993); *No Ordinary Man* (MCA, 1994); *Love Lessons* (MCA, 1995); *Big Love* (MCA, 1996)

The Byrds
Harold Eugene Clark b. Tipton, Missouri, November 17, 1944; d. May 24, 1991

Michael Clarke (Michael Dick) b. New York, New York, June 3, 1946; d. December 19, 1993

David Van Cortlandt Crosby b. Los Angeles, California, August 14, 1941

Chris Hillman b. Los Angeles, California, December 4, 1944

Roger McGuinn (James Joseph McGuinn III) b. Chicago, Illinois, July 13, 1942

The Byrds were among the first successful purveyors of folk-rock in the mid-1960s and one of the 1960s rock acts most heavily influenced by country music. The original members came mostly from folk music backgrounds (CHRIS HILLMAN was steeped in bluegrass as well), but co-founder Roger McGuinn had an eclectic vision for the Byrds that enveloped his own folk roots, the harmonic rock & roll of the Beatles, and American rock, along with any music that reflected the times.

Not long after BOB DYLAN's "Mr. Tambourine Man" gave the Los Angeles–based band their first hit record in 1965, they began to reveal their interest in country. On their second album, *Turn! Turn! Turn!*, they recorded the country standard "Satisfied Mind" at Hillman's suggestion. And on their 1967 release *Younger Than Yesterday*, the song "Time Between" featured the acclaimed bluegrass guitarist CLARENCE WHITE of the Kentucky Colonels (along with VERN GOSDIN on rhythm guitar).

But it was GRAM PARSONS who pointed the Byrds toward

Nashville. Parsons and Hillman had struck up a friendship late in 1967. A few months later, when the Byrds needed to replace David Crosby, who had left the band, Hillman suggested Parsons. He joined the Byrds along with drummer Kevin Kelley, who replaced Michael Clarke. (Gene Clark had earlier departed the Byrds, though he returned briefly after Crosby's departure.)

McGuinn recalled Parsons as a forceful personality with a musical plan "to blend the Beatles and country; to really do something revolutionary. Gram thought we could win over the country audience. He figured, once they dig you, they never let go." The Byrds went country all the way. After deciding to cut their next record in Nashville, they got outfitted at NUDIE's and, with help from COLUMBIA RECORDS, got booked onto the GRAND OLE OPRY. With several Nashville musicians on board, they recorded several tracks in Music City, including Parsons's evocative "Hickory Wind," then played the Opry on March 15, 1968. The long-haired California boys drew a few hoots and suggestions that they get haircuts. The Byrds quieted the crowd with a straightforward rendition of MERLE HAGGARD's "Sing Me Back Home." Then, instead of performing an expected second Haggard song, Parsons pulled a switch and led the shocked band into "Hickory Wind," upsetting Opry producers.

Back in Los Angeles, the band finished the album, titled *Sweetheart of the Rodeo*. Though now considered a landmark in the meshing of country traditions with rock & roll sensibilities, *Sweetheart of the Rodeo* received mixed notices upon release and was the poorest-selling of the Byrds' albums to that point. Disgruntled over a proposed South African tour, Parsons left not long after, to be replaced by Clarence White. Hillman also soon left, as did Kelley, and Hillman and Parsons went on to form the Flying Burrito Brothers. Other musicians who joined the Byrds for varying lengths of time included Skip Battin, Gene Parsons, and John York. In all their numerous permutations, the Byrds continued to include country as part of their wide-ranging repertoire. McGuinn finally disbanded the group in early 1973.
— *Ben Fong-Torres*

REPRESENTATIVE RECORDINGS

Sweetheart of the Rodeo (Columbia, 1968); *The Ballad of Easy Rider* (Columbia, 1970); *The Byrds* (Columbia/Legacy, 1990), 4 discs

Cackle Sisters (*see* the DeZurick Sisters)

The Cactus Brothers

Paul David Kirby b. Albuquerque, New Mexico, July 26, 1972

Michael Halpin "Tramp" Lawing b. Marion, North Carolina, March 15, 1965

William James "Will" Goleman b. Shreveport, Louisiana, November 16, 1963

John Robert Goleman b. Shreveport, Louisiana, July 18, 1962

James N. "Jim" Fungaroli b. Harrisonburg, Pennsylvania, February 28, 1958

Johnny M. Tulucci b. Miami, Florida, February 25, 1959

The Cactus Brothers formed from a sideline project begun in 1986 by Nashville roots-rock band Walk the West—Paul Kirby, Tramp Lawing, and Will and John Goleman—and noted dulcimer whiz David Schnaufer, who left the band in 1994. Their mixture of rock, bluegrass, country, and Celtic styles, in addition to their popularity as a high-energy live act, gained the group a contract with Nashville-based country label LIBERTY RECORDS. Their 1994 release *The Cactus Brothers* was produced by GARTH BROOKS's producer, ALLEN REYNOLDS. It featured tunes mainly penned by Kirby and pushed along with frenzied speed by steel guitar and an occasional dulcimer or harmonica. While the album captured the band's spirit, it and a second album, *Twenty-four Hours, Seven Days a Week*, didn't garner play over country radio. Although they enjoyed great success touring Europe and appeared in the film *Pure Country*, the band ultimately gave up, dissolving in January 1996. Walk the West played a final gig in February 1996, and its members parted for good after a ten-year partnership.

—*Clark Parsons*

REPRESENTATIVE RECORDINGS

The Cactus Brothers (Capitol Nashville, 1994); *Twenty-four Hours, Seven Days a Week* (Capitol Nashville, 1995)

Cajun Music

Cajun music is the music of the French-speaking Cajun people of Louisiana and southeastern Texas. Originally descended from French Canadians who had been forced by the English to leave their homeland of Acadia (now Nova Scotia) in the mid-1700s, many Acadians settled in Louisiana, where there was already a sizable French-speaking population. There the Cajuns, as they came to be known, freely intermarried with French and Spanish colonials, African slaves, and Native Americans. Their music came to reflect their diverse heritage, as well as a lingering melancholy rooted in their forced exile from their homeland. The related music developed by the region's black Creoles came to be known as Zydeco.

As the music developed, the Cajuns added new songs reflecting their lives in the bayous and prairies of Louisiana to the body of old French folk songs and tunes they had brought with them. By the late 1700s the Cajuns were developing a distinctive style of twin fiddling based on their old dance tunes and incorporating elements of Anglo-American fiddling. In the mid-1800s German settlers introduced the diatonic accordion, which became a key ingredient of the Cajun sound. By 1900 a typical Cajun band included an accordion, a fiddle, maybe a triangle, and later a guitar.

The first commercial recordings of Cajun music were made in 1928, when the COLUMBIA RECORD COMPANY recorded accordionist JOE FALCON and his wife, Cleoma. Other companies, notably VICTOR and BRUNSWICK, were not far behind. Quickly realizing the regional sales potential for French music in Cajun country, they recorded artists such as DENNIS MCGEE, Amedee Ardoin, LEO SOILEAU, and the Walker Brothers.

During the period prior to World War II, significant changes took place in Cajun music. As radio and records became popular, Cajun musicians were influenced by country music and WESTERN SWING. As bands such as the HACKBERRY RAMBLERS and the Rayne-Bo Ramblers incorporated those sounds into their music, the accordion passed out of style, replaced by fiddles and steel guitars. After the war the accordion enjoyed a resurgence, thanks primarily to the playing of accordion masters such as IRY LEJEUNE, LAWRENCE WALKER, and NATHAN ABSHIRE.

During the 1950s and the 1960s Cajun music continued to be influenced by other forms of popular music, from HONKY-TONK to r&b. HANK WILLIAMS, in particular, had a profound impact on performers such as D. L. MENARD, Aldus Roger, and Vin Bruce.

Cajun music remained essentially a regional music, although musicians such as HARRY CHOATES, JIMMY C. NEWMAN, and DOUG KERSHAW enjoyed successes on the mainstream country charts. The 1960s saw a revival of traditional Cajun music, as the folk music boom brought performers such as the Balfa Brothers to the attention of audiences at venues such as the Newport Folk Festival and renewed interest in the older forms among younger Cajun musicians. MARC SAVOY, MICHAEL DOUCET, JO-EL SONNIER, Zachary Richard, Wayne Toups, Paul Daigle, Bruce Daigrepont, and Steve Riley were among the younger performers inspired to play Cajun music ranging from the very traditional to the commercial and contemporary. Cajun musicians were regularly invited to perform at folk festivals around the country, and the Cajun music scene was also energized by the general Cajun cultural and linguistic revival of the 1970s and 1980s.

Cajun and Zydeco music have evolved and changed greatly since the 1800s; they have been repeatedly modified by the introduction of new instruments—from the accordion to the electric guitar—and by popular musical influences from country to rock & roll and reggae. Still, Cajun music remains a popular and vital tradition, reflecting, as it always has, the culture, lives, and times of contemporary Cajuns. —*Charlie Seemann*

REPRESENTATIVE RECORDINGS

Le Gran Mamou: A Cajun Music Anthology: The Historic Victor Bluebird Sessions: 1928–1941: Volume 1 (Country Music Foundation, 1990); *Raise Your Window: A Cajun Music Anthology: The Historic Victor Bluebird Sessions: 1928–1941: Volume 2* (Country Music Foundation, 1993); *Gran Prairie: A Cajun Music Anthology: The Historic Victor Bluebird Sessions: 1935–1940: Volume 3* (Country Music Foundation, 1993)

W. R. Calaway

b. Boone, North Carolina, date unknown; d. 1949

From 1928 to 1938 William Ronald "Bill" Calaway was active as an A&R man connected with various country and blues artists' recording careers, including those of ROY ACUFF, the CALLAHAN BROTHERS, the CARLISLE BROTHERS, David Miller, JOHN MCGHEE & FRANK WELLING, Charley Patton, and Walter Roland, to name a few.

Working with GENNETT RECORDS (1928–30) and AMERICAN RECORD CORPORATION (1930–38), Calaway served as a recruiter-auditioner-producer of talent, often benefiting on the side by acquiring full or part ownership of publishing rights and writer's copyrights of certain songs. Thus he frequently received writer's credit on songs that his artists recorded. From 1930 to 1938, from addresses in Huntington, West Virginia (1930), New Richmond, Ohio (1931–32), New York City (1931), and Orlando, Florida (1935 on), Calaway registered approximately 180 song copyrights in which he shared. Among these songs are Cliff Carlisle's "Don't Marry the Wrong Woman," Ramblin' Red Lowery's "Take Me Back to Tennessee," the Callahan Brothers' "She's My Curly Headed Baby," and Roy Acuff's "Steel Guitar Blues."

He reportedly died in an automobile accident in 1949. —*Bob Pinson*

The Callahan Brothers

Walter Tommie "Joe" Callahan b. Madison County, North Carolina, January 27, 1910; d. September 10, 1971
Homer C. "Bill" Callahan b. Madison County, North Carolina, March 27, 1912

During the thirties the Callahan Brothers ranked as one of the leading brother harmony duos and the main one represented on AMERICAN RECORD CORPORATION labels. Natives of Asheville, North Carolina, in the Appalachian highlands, Homer and Walter—sometimes known as Bill and Joe—may have been a little less skilled than some of their competition on BLUEBIRD, but they displayed more blues influence as well as a knack for duet yodeling that distinguished them from their rivals.

The brothers began their professional careers at WWNC-Asheville, in 1933 and had their initial recording session in 1934. By 1935 their discs had received sufficient attention to take them to WHAS-Louisville, and then to radio jobs in Wheeling, Cincinnati, Tulsa, and Springfield, Missouri. Their repertory ranged from blues numbers such as "Gonna Quit My Rowdy Ways" and sentimental mountain songs such as "Little Poplar Log House" to sacred numbers and even risqué tidbits typified by "She Came Rollin' Down the Mountain." "She's My Curly Headed Baby" was probably their best-known song.

By 1941 the Callahans had moved to Texas, where they spent their remaining show business years alternating between KWFT–Wichita Falls, and KRLD-Dallas. In that same year they switched to DECCA RECORDS for one session and also cut numerous Sellers Transcriptions. In 1945 they were featured in the film *Springtime in Texas,* which starred JIMMY WAKELY. Their final recordings in 1951 with COLUMBIA reflected a more modern sound. In later years Walter Callahan returned to North Carolina, where he died in 1971. Homer Callahan played bass and performed comedy in the Dallas area for many years on a part-time basis while earning his livelihood as a photographer. At last report he was still semiactive in that Texas metropolis. —*Ivan M. Tribe*

REPRESENTATIVE RECORDINGS

The Callahan Brothers 1934–1941 (Old Homestead, 1975); *A Lighter Shade of Blue* (Columbia, 1993) (various-artists set containing three numbers by the Callahans)

Camel Caravan

began June 1941; ended December 1942

The WSM Camel Caravan played a significant role in spreading and popularizing country music. In 1941, with World War II raging in Europe and the draft under way in the United States, the R. J. Reynolds Tobacco Company decided to sponsor troupes of entertainers to tour U.S. military bases, mostly in the States. Named for Camel Cigarettes, one of R. J. Reynolds's most popular brands, the Camel Caravan shows were intended to boost R. J. Reynolds's sales as well as troop morale. (Presumably, distributing free cigarettes, sometimes shot into audiences with slingshots, would stimulate demand for the Camels.)

The most important Camel Caravan unit was assembled by Nashville-based promoter J. L. FRANK, who put together a team embracing WSM country and pop talent. Central to this group were PEE WEE KING's Golden West Cowboys, then including EDDY ARNOLD as lead vocalist, and MINNIE PEARL as a featured attraction as well. Also in King's band were fiddler REDD STEWART, singer San Antonio Rose, and bassist JOE ZINKAN. Kay Carlisle, a young pop vocalist; a trio of female pop singers (Mary Dinwiddie, Evelyn Wilson, and Alcyone Bate Beasley, daughter of Opry pioneer DR. HUMPHREY BATE); dancer Dollie Dearman; and four dancers called the Camelettes were also on board, while the GRAND OLE OPRY's Ford Rush served as master of ceremonies. The tour began in the summer of 1941 and concluded in December 1942. Although the group made oc-

casional rest stops back in Nashville, most of this period was spent on the road at U.S. military installations, especially in the South. The 75,000-mile itinerary included shows in thirty-two states, the Canal Zone, Panama, and Guatemala.
— *John Rumble*

Shawn Camp

b. Little Rock, Arkansas, August 29, 1966

With his soulful vocals and expertise on both fiddle and guitar, Shawn Camp brought youthful energy to country's classic traditions on his debut album, *Shawn Camp*, released in 1993.

When Camp was a child growing up in Perryville, Arkansas, one of his earliest aspirations was to appear on the GRAND OLE OPRY. By his teenage years he was much in demand as a touring musician, playing VFW and American Legion halls around his native state with a group called the Grand Prairie Boys.

In the mid-1980s, already known for his prowess as a fiddle player, Camp went to work for the Oklahoma-based Signal Mountain Boys. He moved to Nashville in January 1987. Hearing that the OSBORNE BROTHERS needed a fiddle player, Camp auditioned and began working with them on the Opry a month later. Following a six-month stint with the famed bluegrass veterans, Camp subsequently worked with JERRY REED, ALAN JACKSON, SHELBY LYNNE, SUZY BOGGUSS, and TRISHA YEARWOOD.

Camp also began honing his songwriting skills, working with music publisher Pat Higdon at Patrick Joseph Music and collaborating with writers such as John Scott Sherrill, Jim Rushing, and Dean Miller. In 1992 Higdon set up an industry showcase for the talented newcomer, who was signed by Reprise Records shortly thereafter. *Shawn Camp* did not fare well commercially, however, as two singles off the album, "Fallin' Never Felt So Good" and "Confessin' My Love," barely reached the Top Forty.

In 1995 Camp signed a publishing deal with Forerunner Music Group.
— *Janet E. Williams*

REPRESENTATIVE RECORDING

Shawn Camp (Reprise, 1993)

Camp Creek Boys

The Camp Creek Boys were a loose aggregation of old-time musicians from the Round Peak area of North Carolina, a region famous for its hard-driving local style of traditional mountain fiddle and banjo music and its wealth of great musicians. The group was started by banjo player Kyle Creed in the early 1960s and included a number of area musicians as personnel changed over the years. The original band included Creed on banjo, Paul Sutphin on guitar, Ronald Collins on guitar, Vernon Clifton on mandolin, and Fred Cockerham and Earnest East on fiddles. Eventually, fiddler Benton Flippen would play with the group, as would guitarist Larry Flippen and mandolin player Hoyle Jones. A later incarnation of the group included the bluegrass banjo of Bobby Patterson, with Pete Lissman on guitar and Dave Freeman on mandolin.
— *Charlie Seemann*

REPRESENTATIVE RECORDING

Camp Creek Boys (County, 1967)

Archie Campbell

Archie Campbell

b. Bulls Gap, Tennessee, November 7, 1914; d. August 29, 1987

Archie James Campbell was a popular country comedian before he joined *HEE HAW* in 1969, but that popular TV show made him a household name.

After two years at Mars Hill College, Campbell traveled the South as a musician and sign painter before he landed a job at Knoxville's WNOX in 1936. There he sang on a daily show, the *MIDDAY MERRY-GO-ROUND*, with ROY ACUFF & His Crazy Tennesseans. In 1936 announcer Lowell Blanchard came to WNOX to put more emphasis on country music, and he saw a need for comedy. Under his tutelage Campbell developed a character called Grandpappy, who was a hit with listeners.

Campbell later had his own shows at Bristol's WOPI and at Chattanooga's WDOD before spending two years in the navy in World War II. He then rejoined WNOX's *Midday Merry-Go-Round*. In 1949, however, he went to WNOX's rival station WROL for a show called *Country Playhouse*, which became the city's first country music television show.

In 1958 Campbell won a spot on the GRAND OLE OPRY as a comedian on the "Prince Albert Show," the Opry's NBC network segment, replacing the recently deceased ROD BRASFIELD. There Campbell shed his Grandpappy character and worked in everyday clothes. In addition to radio, Campbell played road shows and made comedy records for RCA (1959–62), including "Trouble in the Amen Corner";"The Cockfight"; and "Rinderceller," a spoonerism version of the fairy tale Cinderella. Spoonerisms, transpositions of word sounds, became his trademark. In 1962 he signed with STARDAY RECORDS (1962–65) and then returned to RCA in 1966, where he had modest hits showing off his singing abilities in duets with Lorene Mann: "Dark

End of the Street" (1968), "Tell It Like It Is" (1968), and "My Special Prayer" (1969). In 1976, he had an album released by ELEKTRA RECORDS.

In 1969 Campbell was hired as a writer-comedian for *HEE HAW*, which first aired in June of that year, and he won a CMA award as Comedian of the Year that fall. The routines and characters he developed—such as the lecherous country doctor who ogled Nurse Goodbody—had been inspired by earlier skits he and Lowell Blanchard had created in Knoxville. In 1987 Campbell died of heart problems in Knoxville following a heart attack.

—*Loyal Jones*

REPRESENTATIVE RECORDING

An Evening with Archie and Phil Campbell (CRAC, 1987)

Cecil Campbell
b. Danbury, North Carolina, March 22, 1911; d. June 18, 1989

Steel guitar pioneer Cecil Robert Campbell was born into a farming family. After working in local musical groups, he turned professional at twenty-one at WSJS, Winston-Salem, and performed over a number of radio stations during the thirties, mostly in the South but also ranging into Pennsylvania and New York. An excellent showman with quick wit, he soon became known for his rapid-fire comedy as well as his musicianship. With the primary exception of a 1938–39 stint at WSB in Atlanta, he was based at WBT in Charlotte from the mid-1930s into the 1950s, working on the station's popular *Briarhopper Time* programs as well as on the *Dixie Jamboree, Carolina Hayride,* and *Carolina Calling,* broadcast over regional CBS networks.

During the mid-1930s Campbell was a key member of Dick Hartman's Tennessee Ramblers, recording with that group for BLUEBIRD. Later Campbell took over the group name and recorded as the Tennessee Ramblers and under his own name for Bluebird, Super Disc, and RCA VICTOR between 1939 and 1951. He later recorded for MGM (1960) and STARDAY (1965). Other credits include several musical performances in films with GENE AUTRY, TEX RITTER, ROY ACUFF, and Charles Starrett during the late thirties and early forties. Like many steel players, Campbell made the switch from the acoustic dobro to the electric steel guitar and composed numerous instrumentals, his two biggest hits being "Hawaiian Skies" and "Beaty Steel Blues." Following TV work in Charlotte during the late 1950s, Campbell went into real estate in 1958 and remained active in this field into the 1970s, all the while keeping a hand in recording and publishing with his own Winston Records firm (not to be confused with SLIM WILLET's label of the same name). —*John Rumble*

Glen Campbell
b. Delight, Arkansas, April 22, 1936

A gifted singer and accomplished guitarist, Glen Travis Campbell is best known for his string of pop and country hits released in the 1960s and 1970s—"Gentle on My Mind" (1967), "By the Time I Get to Phoenix" (1967), "Wichita Lineman" (1968), "Dreams of the Everyday Housewife" (1968), "Galveston" (1969), "Rhinestone Cowboy" (1975), and "Southern Nights" (1977), to cite only a few.

At the height of his popularity, Campbell hosted *The Glen Campbell Goodtime Hour,* a CBS-TV musical variety

Glen Campbell

show, from 1968 to 1972. He also starred in several feature films, including *True Grit* (1969) with John Wayne.

The seventh son in a sharecropper's family of twelve children, Campbell was born into hard times. From an early age he set himself apart with his proficiency on guitar. By the time he was a teenager, he was playing in his uncle's western swing band and in other local groups.

By his early twenties, Campbell had moved to the West Coast. From October 1960 to May 1961 he toured as lead guitarist for the Champs, two years after their hit with "Tequila." His first entry into the pop charts came in 1961 with "Turn Around, Look at Me" on Crest Records. In 1962 he played guitar and sang on "Kentucky Means Paradise," a single by a group called the Green River Boys. It was the first of Campbell's efforts to hit the country charts, though he remained an unknown. The group released only one album, *Big Bluegrass Special.*

In 1962 he signed with CAPITOL RECORDS, but for several years he recorded without commercial success. Indeed, between 1962 and 1967 Campbell was in much more demand as a session guitarist and vocalist than as an artist. During the 1960s he worked with such notables as RICKY NELSON, Frank Sinatra, Bobby Darin, Dean Martin, MERLE HAGGARD, the Mamas & Papas, and the Beach Boys. In 1964 he also toured briefly with the Beach Boys as Brian Wilson's replacement. During these early years Campbell also poured his instrumental prowess into his own records. He recorded several guitar-dominated albums, including two with TUT TAYLOR and THE DILLARDS, in an ensemble billed as the Folkswingers.

Campbell's breakthrough came with JOHN HARTFORD's modern hobo song "Gentle on My Mind" in 1967. Though it hit only #30 on the country charts and #26 on the pop charts, the song struck a chord with listeners. In 1990, in a testament to its copious radio airplay, BMI named the song its fourth-most-played song of all time.

In 1968 Campbell scored his first Top Five pop hit with "Wichita Lineman." His first entry into the country Top Five came in 1967 with "By the Time I Get to Phoenix." Between 1967 and 1980 Campbell effortlessly straddled the country and pop fields, racking up forty-eight country hits and thirty-four pop hits on the charts.

During the 1980s Campbell recorded for WARNER BROS. and ATLANTIC RECORDS and continued to have occasional Top Ten country hits. He lost ground, however, due to alcohol and cocaine problems, three divorces, and a much-publicized, tempestuous engagement to TANYA TUCKER in 1980.

In 1987 Campbell was signed to MCA's country division by his old friend, producer JIMMY BOWEN, with whom he'd worked extensively on the West Coast in the 1960s. At MCA Campbell saw Top Ten action with single releases such as "The Hand That Rocks the Cradle" (with STEVE WARINER), "Still Within the Sound of My Voice," and "She's Gone, Gone, Gone." In about 1990 he returned to CAPITOL, but he has yet to place more hits on the charts.

As of the late 1990s Campbell has fully retired from his wild ways of yore and is now a devout Christian. He continues to perform and record, and he often delves into gospel music. In 1994 Villard Books published his memoirs, *Rhinestone Cowboy: An Autobiography*, coauthored with Tom Carter. —*Bob Allen*

REPRESENTATIVE RECORDINGS

The Folkswingers: 12 String Guitar (World Pacific, 1963); *The Astounding 12 String Guitar of Glen Campbell* (Capitol, 1964); *Gentle on My Mind: The Collection* (Razor & Tie, 1997), 2 discs; *Still Within the Sound of My Voice* (MCA, 1987)

Stacy Dean Campbell
b. Carlsbad, New Mexico, July 27, 1967

Stacy Dean Campbell arrived in Nashville in 1990, coming from the desert Southwest, and two years later he released the critically acclaimed album *Lonesome Wins Again,* on CO-LUMBIA RECORDS. The young singer was admittedly a fan of the "old school" sound, particularly invoking stylists such as BUCK OWENS and MARTY ROBBINS. He also cast a James Dean sort of image, projecting a sullen, moody figure in his music videos for the early singles "Rosalee" and "Poor Man's Rose," both released in 1992. That intriguing combination caught on with purists but failed to get in the mainstream. The two debut singles received only meager chart play and activity. His second album for Columbia, *Hurt City,* released in 1995, fell victim to a similar fate. Critics loved Campbell's first (and only) single from the album, "Eight Feet High," a superb re-creation of Owens's BAKERSFIELD sound, along with the remake of the JIM ED BROWN standard "Pop A Top." *Hurt City* successfully echoed the past with its rockabilly flavor, yet maintained a contemporary, edgy feel. But even with a highly stylized music video for "Eight Feet High," directed by actor (and fan) Kiefer Sutherland, Campbell again could not catch fire with the general listening audience. His attempts at blending the classic with the contemporary gave Campbell a certain cult status, which he maintains. —*Bob Paxman*

REPRESENTATIVE RECORDING

Lonesome Wins Again (Columbia, 1992)

Judy Canova
b. Jacksonville, Florida, November 20, 1916; d. August 5, 1983

For a number of years, Juliette "Judy" Canova was the nation's preeminent hillbilly comedienne. With her brother Leon and sister Diane, she had begun professionally as part of a family group called "Anne, Judy, and Zeke, the Three Georgia Crackers." Judy had sung on radio at age twelve, and after their father's death, their mother had encouraged the children's theatrical ambitions. They hit New York City in the early 1930s with an act that included hillbilly dress, comedy, dance routines, songs, yodels, and hog calls. They began a Broadway career in 1934 in *Calling All Stars*, and in 1939 they became one of country's first acts to broadcast on television. On radio and records the Canovas' songs were merry and cornball, with titles such as "Me and My Still."

Scatterbrain (1940) was Judy's first in a fifteen-year string of feature films that showcased her characters' guileless country simplicity triumphing over sophisticated urban corruption. Other titles included *Joan of Ozark* (1942) and *Singin' in the Corn* (1946). She became the Republic studio's top moneymaking female, surpassed at the box office only by cowboy stars such as ROY ROGERS.

During the 1940s Canova's national Top Ten radio show pulled in an estimated 18 million listeners, and she formed her own production company to gain further financial control of the profits from her work. Her fine recordings during these years captured her gifted singing, a unique blend of jazz phrasing, country yodeling, and gymnastic leaps.

A millionaire by 1955, Canova retired, thereafter making only occasional television appearances until her death from cancer at age sixty-six. —*Mary A. Bufwack*

Capitol Records
established in Hollywood, California, April 8, 1942

When Capitol Records was formed by pop lyricist-singer Johnny Mercer, music store owner Glenn Wallichs, and Paramount Pictures executive and songwriter George "Buddy" DeSylva, three major record companies dominated popular music (including country): COLUMBIA, RCA, and DECCA. In less than a decade, Capitol had also became a major label to reckon with. From the 1940s through the 1960s, Capitol recorded nearly all of the West Coast country artists of note, and the label played a major role in popularizing the BAKERSFIELD sound.

Initially named Liberty at its April 1942 formation, the label was renamed Capitol on June 4, 1942, to avoid a conflict with Liberty Music Shops in New York. After scoring two quick pop Top Ten hits with Johnny Mercer's "Strip Polka" and Freddie Slack's "Cow Cow Boogie" by September 1942, Capitol soon signed an impressive array of pop artists, including Nat King Cole, Peggy Lee, LES PAUL & MARY FORD, and (in 1954) Frank Sinatra. In the early 1940s Capitol became the first record company ever to service radio stations with free records to encourage airplay. In 1949 Capitol became the first label to release records in all three speeds: 78, 33 1/3, and 45 rpm.

Initially located above Wallichs's Music City store at Hollywood's Sunset & Vine, Capitol had a West Coast orientation from the very beginning that proved a boon to California country music. Starting with the signing of TEX RITTER in 1942, Capitol proved astute in assessing country talent. Under the direction of A&R man LEE GILLETTE and assistant CLIFFIE STONE, the label signed MERLE TRAVIS, TEX WILLIAMS, HANK THOMPSON, JIMMY WAKELY, and TENNESSEE ERNIE FORD.

When KEN NELSON took over as country A&R man in 1951, he ushered in such talents as FARON YOUNG, FERLIN HUSKY, JEAN SHEPARD, SONNY JAMES, WANDA JACKSON, THE LOUVIN BROTHERS, Gene Vincent, and ROSE MADDOX. Nelson proved particularly adept at mining the talent pool of Bakersfield, signing TOMMY COLLINS, BUCK OWENS, MERLE HAGGARD, and WYNN STEWART.

Meanwhile, behind the scenes, corporate changes had taken place. On January 1, 1955, British conglomerate EMI announced its purchase of a controlling interest in Capitol for $8.5 million; Capitol president Glenn Wallichs became a director of EMI. On April 6, 1956, the company's famous cylindrical office building, Capitol Towers, opened in Hollywood.

Following Nelson's retirement in 1976, Capitol's country division increasingly developed a Nashville orientation. Kelso Herston ran the office in the mid- to late 1960s. FRANK JONES was the Nashville chief from 1973 to 1978. Owing to the departures of Merle Haggard and Buck Owens in the 1970s, Capitol's country division was no longer the industry leader it had been. Still, the label continued to sign commercial acts in the 1970s such as ANNE MURRAY, FREDDIE HART, GENE WATSON, and MEL McDANIEL. In the 1980s, under the leadership of JIM FOGLESONG (1984–89), the label's talents included T. GRAHAM BROWN, SAWYER BROWN, and TANYA TUCKER. In 1989, under Fogelsong's command, Capitol scored its biggest country coup of all in signing GARTH BROOKS, who has since become the biggest-selling record artist of the modern era.

JIMMY BOWEN took over the Nashville division in late 1989 and helped maximize Brooks's commercial potential through canny marketing, spearheaded by marketing specialist Joe Mansfield. From 1992 to 1995, during Bowen's tenure, the Nashville division was known as LIBERTY RECORDS. Following Bowen's departure in the spring of 1995, record producer and engineer SCOTT HENDRICKS took over the division and had the name changed back to Capitol Nashville; the most commercially successful new artists to emerge during Hendricks's tenure were DEANA CARTER (signed and initially produced by Bowen) and TRACE ADKINS. In November 1997, reportedly at the insistence of Garth Brooks, Hendricks was replaced as the Nashville division head by Patrick Quigley, a transfer from EMI's New York office whose previous principal experience consisted of marketing beer. —*Paul Kingsbury*

Captain Stubby & the Buccaneers
Captain Stubby b. near Galveston, Indiana, November 24, 1918

Captain Stubby & the Buccaneers are best remembered for their eleven-year stint (1949–60) on Chicago's WLS, where their eclectic mix of novelty, gospel, and uptown country music was a feature of the *NATIONAL BARN DANCE*. They had previously worked at WDAN in Danville, Illinois, and WLW in Cincinnati. When the group joined WLS, it consisted of Tom C. Fouts (a.k.a. Captain Stubby), washboard and other novelty instruments; Dwight "Tiny" Stokes, string bass; Jerry Richards, clarinet; Sonny Fleming, guitar; and Tony Walberg, accordion. Pete Kaye joined the group as accordionist following the death of Tony Walberg. Ralph "Rusty" Gill later replaced Sonny Fleming after Fleming's

death. The group recorded for DECCA, MERCURY, Majestic, and COLUMBIA.
—*Wayne W. Daniel*

Henson Cargill
b. Oklahoma City, Oklahoma, February 5, 1941

Ex-deputy sheriff Henson Cargill was a fitting choice for "Skip a Rope" (#1, 1968), a near million-seller. The song is interesting not only for its provocative message but also for a successful fusion of country and pop music elements.

The son of a trial lawyer and grandson of an Oklahoma City mayor, Cargill attended Colorado State University. He had long nurtured an interest in music, playing guitar from an early age. After college he joined the Kimberleys, touring the Pacific Northwest, and later performed on the Las Vegas nightclub circuit. In 1966 he met producer DON LAW in Nashville. Law got Cargill signed to MONUMENT RECORDS and produced "Skip a Rope," his first and only #1 country hit. He scored only two more: "Row, Row, Row" (#11, 1968) and "None of My Business" (#8, 1969), both for Monument. Between 1971 and 1972 he recorded for Mega Records and then signed with ATLANTIC RECORDS in 1973 but was left in the lurch when Atlantic closed its Nashville doors. He did, however, chart with two more songs, "Silence on the Line" (1979) and "Have a Good Day" (1980) on the Copper Mountain label. Now he commutes between Nashville and Oklahoma, doing only occasional shows.
—*Walt Trott*

REPRESENTATIVE RECORDING
Henson Cargill: Welcome to My World (CBS/Harmony, 1972)

The Carlisles
Clifford Raymond Carlisle b. Mount Eden, Kentucky, March 6, 1904; d. April 2, 1983
William Carlisle b. Wakefield, Kentucky, December 19, 1908

As individuals and as a brother duet, the Carlisles have enjoyed distinguished careers in the field of country music. Born into a musical family in Kentucky, Bill and Cliff began singing and playing instruments as children. While Cliff would one day help popularize the dobro as a hillbilly instrument, Bill chose the straight guitar to accompany his singing. In 1929 the brothers began performing on a Louisville, Kentucky, radio station as members of the Carlisle Family Saturday Night Barn Dance, a show that featured their father and other members of the family.

In the early 1930s Cliff struck out on his own and achieved success as a JIMMIE RODGERS imitator on radio and records before developing his own style. In the mid-1930s Cliff asked Bill to become his musical partner, and for the next decade and a half they were one of the more popular of the country music brother duets heard widely on records and radio. Their work on several southeastern radio stations included an approximately thirteen-year stint at Knoxville's WNOX, where they were stars of the famous daily *MIDDAY MERRY-GO-ROUND* and the Saturday night *Tennessee Barn Dance*.

Cliff's early solo recorded material appeared on GENNETT and the many subsidiary labels of ARC. He later recorded for VICTOR, DECCA, KING, and MERCURY. Through the years, Bill also recorded for a variety of labels, including BLUEBIRD, RCA VICTOR, MERCURY, KING, and HICKORY. The Carlisle Brothers' largest recorded output as a duet

The Carlisles: (from left) Tommy Bishop, Bill Carlisle, Tillman Franks (manager), and Betty Amos

was for Decca, for whom they recorded from 1938 to 1940. However, perhaps their biggest hit, "Rainbow at Midnight" (1946), appeared on King.

In the late 1940s Cliff and Bill again embarked on separate careers. Thereafter, Cliff's profile as an entertainer shrank in proportion to the expansion of Bill's. With a newly formed group called the Carlisles, Bill achieved his greatest success as a recording artist with such signature novelty hits as "Too Old to Cut the Mustard," "No Help Wanted," "Is Zat You Myrtle," and "Knothole." (Early in his career, Bill had created a comic alter ego named Hotshot Elmer, whose antics paved the way for fans' acceptance of Bill's later novelties.) After stints at WNOX, the *WSB Barn Dance* in Atlanta, and the *LOUISIANA HAYRIDE,* Bill's career took him to the GRAND OLE OPRY, which he joined in 1953, and on which he would continue to perform well into the 1990s.

In addition to the novelty songs recorded by Bill after 1950, he and Cliff penned some of country music's most enduring songs. These include Cliff's "I Believe I'm Entitled to You" and "Shanghai Rooster," and Bill's "Rattlesnake Daddy."
—*Wayne W. Daniel*

REPRESENTATIVE RECORDINGS

The Carlisles, *Busy Body Boogie* (Bear Family, 1985); Cliff Carlisle, *Blues Yodeler & Steel Guitar Wizard* (Arhoolie/Folk Lyric, 1996)

Paulette Carlson (*see* Highway 101)

Carnegie Hall

Country music was first heard in New York City's Carnegie Hall (opened 1892) when DENVER DARLING performed country songs as one of several artists during a 1945 concert. Nevertheless, it was the September 18–19, 1947, two-night appearance by a full troupe of country performers led by ERNEST TUBB that has come to be known as country music's breakthrough at that venue. Tubb headlined a GRAND OLE OPRY show that included MINNIE PEARL, Radio

Dot & Smoky Swann, ROSALIE ALLEN, and MC GEORGE D. HAY. Though press reaction was scanty and mixed, both shows were well attended.

T. TEXAS TYLER appeared at Carnegie on April 25, 1948, on the strength of his hit "Deck of Cards," and the SONS OF THE PIONEERS played there in June 1951. On December 29, 1961, the Grand Ole Opry presented a Carnegie show to benefit the Musicians Aid Society. A sellout crowd of 2,700 was on hand to see PATSY CLINE, GRANDPA JONES, JIM REEVES, BILL MONROE, FARON YOUNG, MARTY ROBBINS, the JORDANAIRES, and Minnie Pearl. A year later, on December 8, 1962, FLATT & SCRUGGS, along with MERLE TRAVIS, enjoyed another full house, as did BUCK OWENS for his March 25, 1966, appearance; both of these shows were recorded for live concert albums. Since then, country music has continued to hold successful concerts at Carnegie Hall with such artists as JOHNNY CASH, DOTTIE WEST, and REBA MCENTIRE.
—*Don Roy*

Carolina Cotton
b. Cash, Arkansas, October 20, 1926; d. June 10, 1997

From 1944 to 1954, Carolina Cotton came to symbolize both the yodeling cowgirl and the spirit of rural youth in B-westerns and country music movies. Born Helen Hagstrom in the tiny community of Cash, Arkansas, the youngster moved in early childhood to California with her family. The Hagstroms enrolled their daughter in dancing classes, and she began working on radio in San Francisco with Dude Martin, who gave her the southern-sounding name of Carolina Cotton. In 1944 she landed a small role in the Republic film *Sing Neighbor Sing* with ROY ACUFF. From there, Cotton appeared in a string of movies, mostly at Columbia Studios, with Ken Curtis, Charles Starrett, EDDY ARNOLD, GENE AUTRY, and others. She had record sessions with KING, Crystal, Mastertone, and MGM, some of the latter with backing by BOB WILLS & His Texas Playboys. An excellent yodeler, her signature song became "Three Miles South of Cash in Arkansas."

Through much of the fifties she had the program *Carolina Calls* on the Armed Forces Radio Network and became a favorite with GIs, touring extensively in Korea and elsewhere. Later she opted for a teaching career and spent her last years teaching elementary school in Bakersfield, California. Recent appearances at western film festivals found her a continued favorite with fans, until curtailed by her fatal bout with cancer.
—*Ivan M. Tribe*

REPRESENTATIVE RECORDING

Bob Wills: Papa's Jumpin' (Bear Family, 1985) (Boxed set containing Cotton's recordings with Wills)

Carolina Tarheels
Doctor Coble "Dock" Walsh b. Wilkes County, North Carolina, July 23, 1901; d. May 1967
Garley Foster b. Wilkes County, North Carolina, January 10, 1905; d. October 1968
Clarence Earl McCurry ("Tom Ashley") b. Bristol, Tennessee, September 29, 1895; d. June 2, 1967

The Carolina Tarheels were among the best old-time southern stringbands of the 1920s and 1930s. While the personnel of the band varied, the central figure was Dock

Walsh, a banjo player who made his first solo recordings in 1925. Walsh teamed up briefly with guitarist and harmonica player Gwen Foster, with whom he formed a short-lived quartet that recorded for Victor in 1927. Walsh then formed a lasting partnership with Garley Foster (no relation to Gwen), who played guitar and harmonica and was a talented whistler often billed as "the human bird." In 1929 they were joined for some recording sessions by guitarist and banjo player TOM ASHLEY. In 1962 Walsh and Foster were "rediscovered" and recorded an LP for Folk Legacy.

—*Charlie Seemann*

REPRESENTATIVE RECORDINGS

The Carolina Tarheels (Folk Legacy, 1962); *The Carolina Tarheels* (GHP, 1969)

Mary Chapin Carpenter
b. Princeton, New Jersey, February 21, 1958

A long parade of folkie singer-songwriters came to Nashville in the 1980s, believing they could translate their quirky, personal songs into country stardom, but Mary Chapin Carpenter was the only one who succeeded. She did it by mixing catchy country-rock dance numbers with confessional ballads and story songs. The result: five platinum albums, two trophies as CMA Female Vocalist of the Year (1992 and 1993), and five Grammy Awards.

She had a most atypical background for a country star. The daughter of a *Life* magazine executive, she grew up in Princeton, spent two years in Tokyo, and graduated from Brown University with a degree in American Civilization. (Known to friends and family as Chapin, she eventually hyphenated her name to Mary-Chapin Carpenter in 1990, to discourage people from calling her Mary, but she dropped the hyphen in 1994 after becoming a household name.)

She wound up in Washington, D.C., strumming an acoustic guitar and singing her songs at local coffeehouses. Local guitarist John Jennings invited her to record those songs in his basement studio, a tape she later sold at local shows. Carpenter was ready to sign a deal with the independent folk label ROUNDER RECORDS when COLUMBIA RECORDS in Nashville asked to hear her tape.

Columbia signed Carpenter and released the homemade tape as the album *Hometown Girl* in 1987. It received enthusiastic reviews but failed to penetrate country radio. She had more luck with the 1989 follow-up, *State of the Heart,* which established the pattern of including a few catchy, uptempo singles (Top Twenty country hits "How Do" and "Never Had It So Good") amid the more reflective album cuts.

The breakthrough, though, came in 1991 with the single "Down at the Twist & Shout" from the album *Shooting Straight in the Dark.* Carpenter wrote about the joy of dancing to BEAUSOLEIL at the Twist & Shout (a nightclub in Bethesda, Maryland) and convinced the Cajun band to play on her recording of the song. The result was a #2 country hit and a Grammy Award.

She took that success to a new level with her 1992 album *Come On Come On,* which sold 3 million copies and yielded an astonishing seven Top Twenty country singles. Among the hits were "I Feel Lucky" (co-written by Carpenter and Music Row veteran DON SCHLITZ), "Passionate Kisses" (penned by Lucinda Williams), and "Not Too Much to Ask" (a duet with JOE DIFFIE).

She accomplished all this by resisting the usual Nash-

Mary Chapin Carpenter

ville formulas. She continued to record in the D.C. area with her original producer, John Jennings, and largely with local musicians. She continued to avoid the expensive hairdos and costumes favored by most country divas and kept the low-key collegiate look she had always had. She remained outspokenly liberal, spearheading the Country Music AIDS Awareness Campaign Nashville and allying herself with Earth Day and Voters for Choice.

"Stones in the Road," a Carpenter composition which had earlier been recorded by her hero Joan Baez, became the title track for Carpenter's 1994 album. That album held the #1 position on the country album charts for five weeks, marking Carpenter as the second woman to achieve that feat. (The first woman, WYNONNA JUDD, had enjoyed a big hit with the Carpenter composition "Girls with Guitars.") "Shut Up and Kiss Me," the only boisterous cut on *Stones in the Road,* became Carpenter's first #1 single.

—*Geoffrey Himes*

REPRESENTATIVE RECORDINGS

Hometown Girl (Columbia, 1987); *State of the Heart* (Columbia, 1989); *Shooting Straight in the Dark* (Columbia, 1990); *Come On Come On* (Columbia, 1992); *Stones in the Road* (Columbia, 1994)

Johnny Carroll
b. Cleburne, Texas, October 23, 1937; d. February 18, 1995

John Lewis Carroll was best known as a rockabilly performer and for appearing in the 1956 rock & roll cult film *Rock, Baby Rock It.* His group, the Moonlighters, later renamed the Hot Rocks, appeared on KCLE–Cleburne, Texas, as early as 1952. Three commercially unsuccessful but musically significant 1956 DECCA singles—"Hot Rock," "Wild, Wild Woman," and "Rock & Roll Ruby"—established his reputation and are considered rockabilly classics. Subsequent recordings on Phillips International, WARNER BROS., and other labels were less successful. Carroll joined with Judy Lindsey in the early seventies to form the Judy & Johnny Band, performing in the North Texas area. He commands a faithful following in Europe and appeared there to enthusiastic audiences in later years.

—*William P. Davis*

Fiddlin' John Carson
b. Fannin County, Georgia, March 23, ca. 1868; d. December 11, 1949

A pioneering country performer on record and radio in the genre's commercial infancy, John William Carson was the first folk-based southern artist to sell a large number of records, spurring record companies and performers both to record hillbilly music.

Carson spent his early life at several different places in northern Georgia and at several jobs—farming, railroad work, horse jockeying, and moonshining. At an early age he distinguished himself as a fiddler and became acquainted with Bob Taylor, fiddler and three-time governor of Tennessee. Carson played in the campaigns of many politicians, including Senator Tom Watson and Georgia governors Eugene and Herman Talmadge.

In 1900 he moved to Atlanta to work in a cotton mill, but a 1913 strike caused him to turn more to fiddling and singing on the streets. Carson became well known in Atlanta, partly through performing to the crowds gathered in connection with the case of Leo Frank, who was accused of the murder of Mary Phagan, a young girl Carson knew personally and about whom he composed at least four songs, one dealing with Frank's lynching.

Carson was the most written about of the fiddlers who participated in a series of Georgia fiddlers' contests beginning in 1913. His defeat by Lowe Stokes in one of these competitions inspired Stephen Vincent Benét's poem "The Mountain Whippoorwill." Beginning on September 9, 1922, Carson was a featured performer on station WSB; he was one of the earliest country artists on radio. On June

14, 1923, he made his first recordings in Atlanta for the A&R man RALPH PEER of the OKEH label, marking Carson as one of the first acts to be commercially recorded in the South. His first released sides—the minstrel song "The Little Old Log Cabin in the Lane" and a fiddle instrumental called "The Old Hen Cackled and the Rooster's Going to Crow"—did not immediately impress Peer. But when OKeh's first pressing of 500 copies (released without an assigned issue number) quickly sold out a month later, Peer and other record label executives recognized that the hillbilly music of Carson and his peers could reach an untapped market of rural record buyers. Thus country music was launched as a commercial genre.

Through the 1920s he continued to record for OKeh—solo, with his daughter Rosa Lee, and with a band called the Virginia Reelers. Some recordings mixed "moonshiner comedy" with music, and in these Rosa Lee played the role of Moonshine Kate. Carson recorded 123 different songs and fiddle tunes, many of them more than once, and these recordings provide early texts of major folksongs. After a break in his recording, largely caused by the Depression, he had a final session for RCA VICTOR'S BLUEBIRD label in 1934. His primitive style was already out of favor by then, and thereafter Carson received little attention outside Georgia. In Georgia he remained a well-known showman, comedian, and political campaigner, winning a sinecure as elevator operator in the capitol. —*Gene Wiggins*

REPRESENTATIVE RECORDINGS
The Old Hen Cackled and the Rooster's Going to Crow (Rounder, 1973); cassette accompanying the Carson biography *Fiddling Georgia Crazy* by Gene Wiggins (University of Illinois Press, 1986)

Jenny Lou Carson
b. Decatur, Illinois, January 13, 1915; d. December 16, 1978

From career origins in the 1930s as a member of the THREE LITTLE MAIDS, a prominent sister act on Chicago's WLS, Lucille Overstake went on to individual fame as singing-songwriting cowgirl Jenny Lou Carson.

As teens, the Three Little Maids became regulars at WLS. Evelyn Overstake's was the distinctive low voice on their records, but Lucille's guitar was their only accompaniment. Under the pseudonym Lucille Lee, she also recorded suggestive records with jazzy swinging instrumentation provided by the PRAIRIE RAMBLERS, identified on disc as the Sweet Violet Boys. Her vocals from these sessions on titles such as "I Love My Fruit" are among her finest.

Adopting the name Jenny Lou Carson in the 1940s, she continued to record, but it's really her songs that are memorable. Her songwriting credits include such classics as "Jealous Heart," a #2 hit for TEX RITTER in 1944. Most famous is "Let Me Go Lover," a #1 hit for HANK SNOW in 1954 and later recorded by Teresa Brewer and Patti Page. EDDY ARNOLD recorded many of Carson's songs, and her patriotic tunes to support the World War II effort were also numerous. —*Mary A. Bufwack*

Martha Carson
b. Neon, Kentucky, May 19, 1921

Martha Carson, born Irene Ethel Amburgey, rose to prominence in the late 1940s and early 1950s as a powerful

Fiddlin' John Carson and daughter Moonshine Kate

Martha Carson

singer of uptempo country gospel songs. Born in the coal-mining country of eastern Kentucky, she was the middle sister of a trio who first sang on WLAP–Lexington, Kentucky, as the Sunshine Sisters in 1938. Renfro Valley's JOHN LAIR invited Irene and sisters Bertha and Opal (later known as JEAN CHAPEL) to join WSB-Atlanta's *Barn Dance* as the Hoot Owl Holler Girls—inspired by his COON CREEK GIRLS (in which the Amburgeys substituted briefly). Lair also gave the Amburgeys quaint stage names as Hoot Owl Holler Girls: Minnie (Bertha), Marthie (Irene), and Mattie (Opal).

When her sisters married and departed, Marthie began blending her big, rawboned alto in harmony with James Roberts, son of FIDDLIN' DOC ROBERTS. She played guitar, and he mandolin, and together Martha and James recorded country gospel for CAPITOL RECORDS (as James & Martha Carson) and were known at WSB as the Barn Dance Sweethearts. They were married on June 8, 1939. After moving to WNOX in Knoxville, however, the couple's personal problems ended their marriage and their act in 1951. In the early 1950s Martha Carson reunited with her sisters to record for Capitol (as the Amber Sisters) and KING RECORDS.

While with WNOX's *MIDDAY MERRY-GO-ROUND* (where she toured and recorded for a time with the CARLISLES), Carson recorded what would become her signature song, "Satisfied," for Capitol on November 5, 1951. Although the rousing gospel number was not a chart hit, it proved immensely popular and became her springboard to the GRAND OLE OPRY, which she joined April 26, 1952. In Nashville she met and wed promoter XAVIER COSSE (1953). He encouraged her to leave Capitol and sign with RCA, while he attempted to glamorize the statuesque redhead and steer her music toward big-band pop gospel, which she recorded with some success in the pop market. At about this time the couple moved to New York, and Carson increasingly played the northeastern supper-club circuit and

appeared on the TV shows of Steve Allen, TENNESSEE ERNIE FORD, and Arthur Godfrey. She also recorded some proto–rock & roll material as well. After a few years playing Las Vegas supper clubs and California's TOWN HALL PARTY TV show, and a brief move to the New York area, Carson opted for semiretirement and released only a few more records on the DECCA, Cadence, and Sims labels.

A gifted writer, she composed "I Can't Wait," a #5, 1953 single for FARON YOUNG; "I'm Gonna Walk and Talk with My Lord," a hit by pop stylist Johnnie Ray; and "I Can't Stand Up Alone," a successful cut for r&b's Clyde McPhatter. Carson's dynamic performing style influenced ELVIS PRESLEY, BRENDA LEE, and CONNIE SMITH.   —*Walt Trott*

REPRESENTATIVE RECORDINGS

Satisfied (Capitol, 1960, rereleased on Longhorn, 1989); *Martha Carson Explodes!* (Bear Family, 1987)

Carlene Carter

b. Madison, Tennessee, September 26, 1955

She's the daughter of CARL SMITH and JUNE CARTER; her stepfather is JOHNNY CASH; her stepmother is GOLDIE HILL. Still, Rebecca Carlene Smith, better known as Carlene Carter, didn't take the path to a country career that one might have predicted for her. She studied piano as a child; didn't pick up a guitar until she was ten; had her own rock band, the Yellow Submarines, at twelve; studied music theory at Belmont College in Nashville (dropping out to record her first album); and cites a 1969 performance by LINDA RONSTADT at the Troubadour in Los Angeles as one of her earliest motivations to become a professional performer.

While growing up, Carter hadn't totally ignored country music, however. She took guitar lessons from her great-aunt Maybelle Carter and would step onstage as a child to perform during Cash's sets. She married aspiring country singer Jack Routh in 1974, and her recording debut was as a guest performer (billed as "Carlene Routh") on a version of Routh's "Friendly Gates" that appeared on Cash's 1974

Carlene Carter

Deana Carter

album *The Junkie and the Juicehead Minus Me.* She also included country songs on her own earliest albums.

Her debut album, *Carlene Carter* (WARNER BROS., 1977), was recorded in England with instrumental accompaniment by Graham Parker's group, the Rumour, and had a decided rock flavor. But it was her third album, *Musical Shapes,* that could be considered her artistic breakthrough. Produced by her third husband, English musician Nick Lowe, the album (like its two predecessors) combined Carter originals with canny outside choices; the backing was by Rockpile, a band led by Lowe and Dave Edmunds.

In 1988 Carlene met Howie Epstein, bassist for Tom Petty and the Heartbreakers, and the two began a professional and personal relationship that led to his producing several of her subsequent albums. She recorded for GIANT RECORDS beginning in 1993; in 1996 the label released *Hindsight—20/20,* a sixteen-track career retrospective.

Though Carter's records have been consistently smart and interesting and her writing above average, her singles have not always done well on the charts. "I Fell in Love" and "Come on Back" (both 1990) and "Every Little Thing" (1993) fared best, all reaching the Top Five on *Billboard's* country chart.

In 1995 Carter and her father, Carl Smith, recorded a duet remake of Smith's 1954 hit "Loose Talk" for her *Little Acts of Treason* album. In 1996 she toured with fellow country star progeny LORRIE MORGAN and PAM TILLIS.

—*Todd Everett*

REPRESENTATIVE RECORDINGS

Musical Shapes (Warner Bros., 1980); *Hindsight—20/20* (Giant, 1996)

Deana Carter

b. Nashville, Tennessee, January 4, 1966

Deana Carter's 1996 debut album, the breezy *Did I Shave My Legs for This?*, was propelled to multiplatinum status by her #1 debut single, "Strawberry Wine." Written by MATRACA BERG and Gary Harrison, the steamy yet sweetly nostalgic song, with its mature theme of lost innocence, echoed 1970's pop teen anthems such as Bob Seger's "Night Moves" and was a bit risky for country radio but proved wildly successful. Carter's follow-up single "We Danced Anyway" also went to #1.

A self-professed fan of adult contemporary pop music by the likes of Kenny Loggins, Bread, and Elton John, Carter was also influenced by her father, famed session gui-

tarist Fred Carter Jr., who played on records ranging from MARTY ROBBINS's "El Paso" to Simon & Garfunkel's "The Boxer." A Nashville native and Goodlettsville High School cheerleader, Deana studied rehabilitation therapy at the University of Tennessee at Knoxville and worked for a time as a physical therapist. In 1994, after taking the waitress/struggling songwriter route in Nashville, Carter recorded an album produced by JIMMY BOWEN and titled *Did I Shave My Legs for This?* for LIBERTY RECORDS that was released in Europe though not in the United States.

When SCOTT HENDRICKS took over Liberty upon the departure of Bowen in the spring of 1995, he brought in producer Chris Farren to remake the album. When it was finally released under the same title for CAPITOL RECORDS in September 1996, only two tunes produced by Bowen remained. "Strawberry Wine," rerecorded from the original album, won the CMA's Single of the Year and Song of the Year awards in 1997. Carter sang the haunting "Once Upon A December" in the 1997 animated film *Anastasia.* "Did I Shave My Legs for This" earned Carter two Grammy nominations in 1997 for the Best Female Country Performance and Best Country Song. —*Stephen L. Betts*

REPRESENTATIVE RECORDING

Did I Shave My Legs for This? (Capitol, 1996)

Wilf Carter

b. Guysboro, Nova Scotia, Canada, December 18, 1904;
d. December 5, 1996

Wilf Carter, known to American fans as Montana Slim, is a legend in Canada, where his popularity rivals that of fellow Canadian HANK SNOW.

Carter's father, a Baptist minister, was not exactly thrilled that his son wanted to be a singer, but as Wilf put it, he "couldn't stop me even though he wore out more than a dozen slippers on the seat of my pants." Carter left his Nova Scotia home at an early age to seek adventure in Alberta and the Canadian West, where he became a cow-

Wilf Carter

boy and rodeo performer. There he was also able to pursue his career as a musician and singer, broadcasting on radio station CFCN in Calgary, Alberta, in the early 1930s. He simultaneously launched a recording career with RCA VICTOR, a relationship that would last more than fifty years. Shortly thereafter he adopted the name Montana Slim for his U.S. performances while performing on CBS Radio in New York. Like many aspiring performers of his day, Carter was inspired by JIMMIE RODGERS, and became one of the most accomplished yodelers in the cowboy genre, incorporating a strong Swiss influence, as heard in "Little Old Log Shack I Can Always Call My Home," "My Little Yoho Lady," and "Streamlined Yodel Song." He created what he called "the three-in-one-yodel," which can be heard in songs such as "My Swiss Moonlight Lullaby."

Carter's repertoire included many cowboy songs, such as "Pete Knight's Last Ride," "Old Alberta Plains," and "The Fate of Old Strawberry Roan." He wrote more than 500 songs and has enjoyed one of the longest careers in the business. In addition, he was an important figure in the evolution from traditional cowboy songs to the composed, romanticized songs of the popular SINGING COWBOYS.

—*Charlie Seemann*

REPRESENTATIVE RECORDING

A Prairie Legend (Bear Family, 1996)

Carter Family

A. P. Carter b. Maces Spring, Virginia, December 15, 1891;
d. November 7, 1960
Sara Dougherty Carter b. Flat Woods, Virginia, July 21, 1899;
d. January 8, 1979
Maybelle Addington Carter b. Nickelsville, Virginia, May 10, 1909;
d. October 23, 1978

To call the Carter Family "the first family of country music," as many do, is a historical truth. Not only were they key players at the famed BRISTOL sessions—the "big bang" that put country music on the map—but they also dominated the music during its first two decades of popularity. They essentially invented the type of harmony singing used for years in country music.

Maybelle Carter crafted the "Carter lick" on the guitar and watched it become the best-known picking style in the genre; the group popularized dozens of songs that became country standards; they served as a platform for the two most creative and talented women in the music, Sara and her cousin Maybelle; they produced an amazing number of hit records during their recording days, from 1927 to 1941; they explored a wide variety of song genres, from blues to gospel, from old ballads to nineteenth-century parlor songs; and in A. P. they had one of the greatest creative song doctors in country music history. In spite of all this, however, the Carters never had spectacular financial success like that of JIMMIE RODGERS or GENE AUTRY. They never really "crossed over" to the huge popular audiences of network radio, Hollywood films, and big-time vaudeville. They kept returning to their beloved Clinch Valley, disgusted or puzzled by the show business world.

Alvin Pleasant Delaney Carter (A. P.) grew up in hilly Scott County, Virginia, just a few miles from the Virginia-Tennessee border. His family farmed, but his father was a well-respected banjo player and his mother sang old folk ballads. An uncle, Flanders Bays, taught singing schools

The Carter Family: (from left) Maybelle, A. P., and Sara

for local churches and taught him to read the old shape note songbooks (many of which provided gospel songs for the Carter repertoire). By 1915, after traveling around the country, A. P. returned home to start selling fruit trees; at about this time he met Sara Dougherty. (According to family legend she was sitting under a tree, playing her autoharp, and singing "Engine 143.") After a courtship, the pair were married on June 18, 1915. For the next several years the young couple entertained informally in the neighborhood, often at churches. Unlike many of the older mountain singers, who often sang unaccompanied, the Carters backed their singing with their guitar and autoharp; occasionally A. P. even played the fiddle. In early 1927 the pair auditioned for the BRUNSWICK RECORD COMPANY in nearby Norton; the company wanted to develop A. P. as a fiddler, but he felt his real talent was in singing, and so he passed on the offer.

Also in that year of 1927, Sara and A. P. were joined by Sara's younger cousin Maybelle Addington. As a girl of twelve, Maybelle had begun playing the guitar, then a new instrument in the mountains. "There weren't many guitar pickers around," she said. Addington came up with her own style of picking the melody on the bass strings while the fingers kept rhythm by downstroking the higher ones—the "thumb brush" technique. In March 1926 Maybelle married A. P.'s brother Ezra and later joined the group as a guitarist and part-time singer. In late July 1927 they traveled to Bristol to make their first records for VICTOR producer RALPH PEER.

Their very first recording was "Bury Me Under the Weeping Willow" (Victor 21074), an old folk lyric that had been reworked by A. P. It would be the first of numerous songs they would record for the company over the next eight years, including best-sellers such as "The Storms Are on the Ocean" (1927), "Keep on the Sunny Side" (1928) (their theme song), "Wildwood Flower" (1928), "John Hardy Was a Desperate Little Man" (1928), "I'm Thinking Tonight of My Blue Eyes" (1929), "Wabash Cannonball" (1929), "Anchored in Love" (1928), and "Worried Man Blues" (1930). Their sparse but elegant arrangements helped make these songs country standards and led them to record more than 300 songs on Victor and subsequent labels such as the AMERICAN RECORD COMPANY, the Sears custom label CONQUEROR, and DECCA. On many of these recordings Sara and Maybelle did most of the singing and picking, with A. P. occasionally joining in on harmony. A. P. took most of the responsibility in finding their songs, arranging them, and booking the group's performances.

During the height of their popularity, the Carters were often separated for various reasons. In 1931 Maybelle and her husband were living as far away as Washington, D.C., where Ezra's work took them; for a time A. P. was in Detroit working at auto factories. In early 1932 Sara left A. P., returning only for record sessions or serious concerts.

In 1939 Sara remarried, to another of A. P.'s cousins. By the mid-1930s the Carters landed decent radio contracts, and by the latter part of the decade they found a lucrative job at the Texas border station XERA, Del Rio; this station would broadcast from across the Mexican border, using a more powerful signal than U.S. stations were allowed to use. The station helped spread the Carter sound farther than any previous radio station. By now the family involved its children: Sara's daughter Janette and Maybelle's girls Helen, June, and Anita. When World War II had broken out, the family was working over Charlotte radio.

In 1943 the group broke up for good even though A. P., Sara, and Maybelle were still at the peak of their performing careers. A. P. returned to Maces Spring to open a country store, and Sara moved to California with her husband. Maybelle started her own career featuring her daughters and herself; they eventually settled in Nashville.

In 1952 A. P. and Sara briefly reunited and made a series of records on the independent label Acme. In 1967 Sara and Maybelle got together for a reunion LP on COLUMBIA. —*Charles Wolfe*

REPRESENTATIVE RECORDINGS

Country Music Hall of Fame (MCA, 1991); Rounder series: complete recordings 1927–33 (Rounder, 1993–1997)

Carter Sisters

Helen Myrl Carter b. Maces Spring, Virginia, September 12, 1927; d. June 2, 1998
Valerie June Carter b. Maces Spring, Virginia, June 23, 1929
Ina Anita Carter b. Maces Spring, Virginia, March 31, 1933

Helen, June, and Anita Carter were born to Maybelle Addington Carter and Ezra Carter. As a member of the famous CARTER FAMILY, Maybelle brought her children into the group (as did parents in many family acts), thus beginning the sisters' long, influential careers as both members of country music's "first family" and as individual performers.

In 1938, while the Carter Family was broadcasting on BORDER RADIO in Texas, Anita became the first sister to join the group; ten-year-old June and twelve-year-old Helen followed in 1939. The trio of girls also recorded their own border radio shows.

After Sara resigned from the Carter Family in 1943, Maybelle retired briefly, but she was soon back on the airwaves, in Richmond, Virginia, with her teenage girls as full-time musicians. Maybelle played guitar; Helen, the most capable instrumentalist, played accordion; June, the best comedienne and performer, was on autoharp; and Anita, the soprano and best singer, handled the bass (sometimes standing on her head to play). Their material was a combination of Carter Family songs and popular tunes of the day. By 1947 they were top stars at the *Old Dominion Barn Dance* in Richmond and soon moved to the *Tennessee Barn Dance* on WNOX in Knoxville. CHET ATKINS joined the band there in 1949, later moving with them to the *Ozark Jubilee* in Springfield, Missouri.

Mother Maybelle & the Carter Sisters took up permanent residence at the GRAND OLE OPRY in 1950. Though they maintained an old-fashioned image, in 1956 and 1957 they opened for ELVIS PRESLEY, and in 1961 they joined the JOHNNY CASH road show. Maybelle and her daughters found a new audience in the 1960s with the folk revival. Anita also performed as a solo act, and her mid-1960s albums of folk songs were the equal of those by Joan Baez. (In 1951 Anita and HANK SNOW had enjoyed a duet hit record with "Bluebird Island" b/w "Down the Trail of Achin' Hearts.")

The Carters became regulars on Johnny Cash's network TV series in 1969. June, the comic, had studied at the Actors' Studio in New York and had appeared on television in the 1950s. She and HOMER & JETHRO had a Top Ten hit with "Baby It's Cold Outside" in 1949, and June and MERLE KILGORE had penned Cash's 1963 #1 tune "Ring of Fire." June's most notable recording success came with Cash on a series of strong folk-country hit duets that included "It Ain't Me Babe" (1964), "Jackson" (1967), and "If I Were a Carpenter" (1970). Cash and June Carter married in 1968, and in 1975, at age forty-six, June released her mountain-flavored LP *Appalachian Pride,* produced by Cash.

The Carter Sisters continued to perform together, and in 1988, with June's daughter CARLENE CARTER, the sisters recorded *Wildwood Flower* for Mercury. June has also been a touching and philosophical writer; her autobiography, *Among My Klediments,* appeared in 1979, and she published a memoir, *From the Heart,* in 1987. —*Mary A. Bufwack*

Lionel Cartwright

b. Gallipolis, Ohio, February 10, 1960

Lionel Cartwright's single "Leap of Faith" landed him at the top of the country charts in 1991 after years of preparation. As a child, Cartwright was performing country music at local social events in Milton, West Virginia. He worked on a radio show in his hometown while still in high school. Later he became a featured singer and musician on *Country Cavalcade,* broadcast by WMNI–Columbus, Ohio, before a stint as a performer and musical director for the WWVA-Wheeling, *Jamboree* in West Virginia.

He made the transition to television on TNN's *I-40 Paradise* and *Pickin' At the Paradise;* he wrote the theme songs for both programs. In addition to "Leap of Faith," Cartwright scored three other Top Ten singles on MCA: "Give Me His Last Chance" (1989), "I Watched It All (On My Radio)" (1990), and "My Heart Is Set on You" (1990). Subsequent singles failed to parallel his earlier successes, and Cartwright was dropped from the label in 1993.

Since then, Cartwright has concentrated on his songwriting. One of his notable compositions, "If That's What You Call Love," appears on KATHY MATTEA's 1997 album *Love Travels.* —*Calvin Gilbert*

Claude Casey

b. Enoree, South Carolina, September 13, 1912

Singer and bandleader Jesse Claude Casey rose to regional prominence in the Southeast from the mid-1930s to the mid-1950s. During the late 1930s he fronted the Pine State

Playboys onstage and in the recording studio. His specialty was romantic love songs, for which announcers would tag him the Lady Killer or the Boy with the Golden Voice. Casey made three sessions for RCA's BLUEBIRD label with this group between 1938 and 1941 and then three sessions under his own name for the RCA VICTOR label during 1945–46.

In 1941 Casey began a twelve-year stint on Charlotte, North Carolina's, 50,000-watt WBT. In addition to regular daytime shows such as the popular *Briarhopper Time,* Casey appeared on regional network originations like *Carolina Hayride* and *The Dixie Jamboree,* both weekly barn dances. For the latter, he also served as writer and master of ceremonies. Between 1946 and 1953 he had three recording sessions for MGM and continued to write tunes on his own or with ACUFF-ROSE PUBLICATIONS songwriter and promotion man Mel Foree. Casey also had minor musical roles in several films, among them *Swing Your Partner* (1943), *Square Dance Jubilee* (1949), and *Buster and Billie* (1973).

Following his WBT years Casey moved on to radio and TV work in the Carolinas and Georgia, both in sales and on camera. In 1961 he began his own successful radio operation, WJES, in Johnston, South Carolina, where he now lives in semiretirement. —*John Rumble*

Johnny Cash
b. Kingsland, Arkansas, February 26, 1932

Beginning with his mid-1950s recordings for SUN RECORDS, John R. "Johnny" Cash has established an international profile as an ambassador of American roots music. He overcame personal demons to reach superstar status in the late 1960s and has continued to hew his own path musically through the 1980s and 1990s. With extensive hit recordings on the country and pop charts—both singles and albums—he has extended the scope of country music and helped broaden its audience through his exploration of many themes and types of songs. A prolific songwriter and an astute selector of songs from the pens of others, he has reached out to folk and rock sources for his enormous repertory, and his music has consistently appealed to both rock and country audiences. Cash has been honored for his commanding position in music history through election to the COUNTRY MUSIC HALL OF FAME (1980), the Rock and Roll Hall of Fame (1992), and as a recipient of the Grammy Legend Award (1990).

Cash grew up at the Dyess government resettlement colony in northeastern Arkansas, where he worked in the cotton fields with his family and absorbed country and gospel music. The tragic death of his older brother Jack at age fourteen had a dramatic effect on his life and would also have a lasting impact on the tone of his music.

Listening to a battery-run radio, Cash heard local country shows from Memphis, the CARTER FAMILY on BORDER RADIO, and the newest hits of singers such as HANK SNOW. He sang on radio KLCN in Blytheville, Arkansas, and after working briefly in Pontiac, Michigan, enlisted in the air force and served in Germany for four years, during which time he wrote the future Sun Records classics "Folsom Prison Blues" and "Hey Porter." Cash returned home in 1954, settled in Memphis, married, and became an appliance salesman. Wanting to build a career in music, he got together with Luther Perkins (electric guitar) and Marshall Grant (upright bass) to perform gospel songs on a local radio station.

Johnny Cash

In the wake of ELVIS PRESLEY's 1954 breakthrough at Sun, Cash and his minimalist band auditioned for Sun owner-producer SAM PHILLIPS. Beginning with the June 21, 1955, release of "Cry! Cry! Cry!" and "Hey Porter," Cash became one of the most promising young artists on the label. Country hits such as "I Walk the Line," "Ballad of a Teenage Queen," and "Guess Things Happen That Way" crossed over to the pop charts and made Cash one of the dominant new country singers of 1956–58. He joined the GRAND OLE OPRY cast on July 7, 1956 (though in 1958 he left for California to pursue a career in movies—without much success initially). The style Cash set in those early days—his deep baritone voice in front of a basic rhythmic background—has changed little over the years, though it was enlarged in 1960 by the addition of his longtime drummer W. S. Holland.

Cash left Sun and signed with COLUMBIA in mid-1958. Hit singles such as "Don't Take Your Guns to Town" (1959) and "Ring of Fire" (1963) followed, but Cash turned his attention increasingly to recording concept albums such as *Ride This Train* (1960), *Blood Sweat and Tears* (1962), *Bitter Tears: Ballads of the American Indian* (1964), and *Ballads of the True West* (1965). Producer DON LAW encouraged Cash to venture out in new directions to connect with the burgeoning folk music revival of the times. This direction seems to have been natural for Cash as he explored cowboy songs, gospel and traditional spirituals, songs of social conscience and protest, and adaptations of folk material. Appearing at the 1964 Newport Folk Festival and connecting with BOB DYLAN, Cash continued to broaden his appeal and deepen his creative sources. His new directions did not always find favor with country's old guard, however. In 1964, when his recording of "The Ballad of Ira Hayes" (about the tragic end suffered by a Native American hero of World War II) received an initially lukewarm reception at radio, Cash took out a full-page ad in *Billboard* demanding of programmers, "Where are your guts?"

The late 1960s witnessed Cash suffering from addiction to pills while his first marriage failed. In 1965 he was arrested for carrying a large quantity of pills across the Mexican border at El Paso. But with the help of June Carter (of the CARTER SISTERS), with whom he recorded several hit duets, and whom he married on March 1, 1968, Cash was able to overcome his addiction.

On January 13, 1968, Cash recorded his masterly live album at Folsom Prison, from which came a new #1 hit version of "Folsom Prison Blues." This album and the follow-up 1969 live recording at San Quentin pushed his career to new heights. Taken from the San Quentin album, "A Boy Named Sue" (#1 country, #2 pop) became his biggest-selling single and the CMA Single of the Year (1969). Cash was also voted the CMA's Entertainer of the Year for 1969.

From 1969 through 1971 Cash hosted a prime-time network television variety show that showcased his status as a national icon while featuring an eclectic mix of guest performers. A live cut from this show, "Sunday Morning Coming Down" (written by KRIS KRISTOFFERSON), was a #1 country hit. Increasingly, Cash recorded and featured on his television show the work of new songwriters drawn to country from folk and rock music backgrounds. His younger brother Tommy (b. 1940) had also established a successful singing career around this time and scored several hits, including "Six White Horses" (1969) and "Rise and Shine" (1970).

From the late 1960s, and into the 1970s and 1980s, Cash continued to tour with his powerful road troupe—which included at various times Mother Maybelle Carter, the Carter Sisters (Helen, June, and Anita), and the STATLER BROTHERS. He also broadened the range of his pursuits to include acting. Outstanding among his credits have been the feature film *A Gunfight* (1971) with Kirk Douglas, the made-for-TV movies *Thaddeus Rose and Eddie* (1978, with June) and *The Pride of Jesse Hallam* (1981), and a guest-star appearance in an episode of *Columbo*.

As the 1970s progressed, Cash's hit records grew more infrequent. By the early 1980s his daughter ROSANNE CASH was having more success as a recording artist than he was. But with his old friends WAYLON JENNINGS, WILLIE NELSON, and Kris Kristofferson, Cash had a #1 hit with the title cut of the *Highwayman* album in 1985. The foursome did a series of special limited concert tours and recorded two more albums: *Highwayman 2* (1990), and *Highwayman: The Road Goes on Forever* (1995).

After Cash left Columbia Records in 1986, he recorded for Mercury until 1992, though again with minimal commercial success. But signed subsequently to the American label, he released the widely acclaimed *American Recordings* (1994), an album consisting of Cash's voice accompanied only by an acoustic guitar. The thirteen songs—some his own, some adaptations of folk pieces, and some from songwriters such as Tom Waits, Nick Lowe, and Loudon Wainwright—are often searing explorations of loss and sorrow. His 1996 American album *Unchained* featured a similarly eclectic mix of material, but with Cash backed by Tom Petty & the Heartbreakers and other guest performers. This album gained Cash a 1997 Grammy nomination in the category of Best Male Country Performance for the song "The Cage." In 1998 *Unchained* was awarded a Grammy Award as the Best Country Album of the Year.

—*Fred Danker*

REPRESENTATIVE RECORDINGS

Ride This Train (Columbia, 1960); *Johnny Cash at Folsom Prison* (Columbia, 1968); *Highwayman* (Columbia, 1985); *The Essential Johnny Cash, 1955–1983* (Columbia, 1992), 3 CDs; *American Recordings* (American, 1994); *Unchained* (American, 1996)

Rosanne Cash

b. Memphis, Tennessee, May 24, 1955

The daughter of American music icon JOHNNY CASH, singer-songwriter Rosanne Cash faced the unenviable challenge of forging an artistic identity in the shadow of her larger-than-life father. The fact that she has done so with candor, grace, and commercial success—including eleven #1 country singles—makes her musical legacy all the more impressive.

Cash's parents divorced while she was still a young girl; her mother, Vivian Liberto, raised her in Southern California. Upon graduation from high school, Cash moved to Nashville and began working with her father's show—primarily in the wardrobe department but occasionally performing as well. She moved to London in 1976 but soon returned to the United States to study acting before recording her self-titled debut album for the German Ariola label. Although the album was never released in the United States, it generated enough interest to secure Cash a recording contract with COLUMBIA. This was also the point at which she embarked on a long-term musical and romantic partnership with RODNEY CROWELL, whom she married in 1979.

Produced by Crowell, Cash's debut Columbia album, *Right or Wrong*, featured three Top Forty singles. But it was her second Columbia album, *Seven Year Ache*, that broke through commercially, yielding the #1 singles "Seven Year Ache" (1981), "My Baby Thinks He's a Train" (1981), and "Blue Moon with Heartache" (1981–82). After hastily

Rosanne Cash

recording *Somewhere in the Stars* during her first pregnancy, Cash followed with the new-wave-influenced *Rhythm & Romance,* which earned her two more #1 hits and a 1985 Grammy award for Best Country Vocal Performance, Female. She then returned to her country roots with *King's Record Shop,* which charted four more #1 hits, among them covers of JOHN HIATT's "The Way We Make a Broken Heart" (1987) and her father's "Tennessee Flat Top Box" (1987–88).

After being named *Billboard*'s Top Singles Artist in 1988, Cash released a collection of her Columbia hits that included two new songs, one of which, a cover of the Beatles' "I Don't Want to Spoil the Party," would also rise to #1. At that point Cash's music and personal life took a dramatic turn, with the dark, introspective *Interiors* (1990), chronicling her painful split from Crowell (they divorced in 1992). Although *Interiors* sold poorly compared with Cash's previous records, the album is arguably the most affecting and ambitious of her career. Cash's next two records—along with *Bodies of Water,* a collection of short stories published in 1996—added to an uncompromising creative output that ranks with the finest of any country performer to emerge since the late 1970s.

—*Bill Friskics-Warren*

REPRESENTATIVE RECORDINGS

King's Record Shop (Columbia, 1987); *Interiors* (Columbia, 1990)

Pete Cassell
b. Cobb County, near Atlanta, Georgia, August 27, 1917;
d. July 29, 1954

A popular radio performer of the 1940s and early 1950s, Peter Webster Cassell delivered soulful interpretations of songs such as "Where the Old Red River Flows," "Freight Train Blues," and "One Step More." As a result of his smooth, expressive voice, critics have compared Cassell favorably with the likes of Jim Reeves, George Morgan, Red Foley, and Eddy Arnold.

When he was three days old, Cassell was robbed of his sight when a physician erred in the application of medicine to his infant eyes. As a result of this misfortune he obtained his education in special schools, including the Georgia Academy for the Blind in Macon. Cassell showed an early interest in music, especially country and gospel. By the time he entered high school he had learned to play the piano and guitar. Except for some lessons taken at the Academy for the Blind, he was a self-taught musician.

In 1937 Cassell made his professional debut on radio station WDOD in Chattanooga, Tennessee. He soon returned home to Atlanta to work at WAGA and WSB, where he reigned as one of the most popular artists on the *WSB Barn Dance* during the 1940s. He later worked on WWVA in Wheeling, West Virginia (where he hosted his own show as well as appearing on the *WWVA Jamboree*); on WARL in Arlington, Virginia; and on CONNIE B. GAY's *Town & Country Time* radio and TV programs.

Cassell recorded some twenty-five sides on the DECCA, Majestic, and MERCURY labels. —*Wayne W. Daniel*

REPRESENTATIVE RECORDING

Pete Cassell: Blind Minstrel, Volume 1 (Old Homestead, 1993)

Castle Recording Studio
established 1946; ended 1956

As Nashville's first professional recording service, the Castle Recording Studio was crucial to Nashville's growth as a recording center during the decade after World War II. The operation was organized shortly after war's end by three WSM radio engineers: Aaron Shelton, Carl Jenkins, and George Reynolds. Although Castle took its name from the WSM logo "Air Castle of the South," WSM executives tolerated rather than encouraged the enterprise.

At first the three entrepreneurs used a WSM studio in the old National Life Building at Seventh Avenue North and Union Street, with signals transferred via telephone line to their lathe at WSM's backup transmitter site at Fifteenth Avenue South and Weston. As their workload increased, the Castle engineers moved the operation to the former dining room of the Tulane Hotel on Church Street between Seventh and Eighth Avenue North. Equipment eventually included a mixing board the engineers designed themselves, an up-to-date Scully lathe, and an Ampex tape recorder.

Castle cut master discs for all major labels except RCA RECORDS, which had an exclusive contract with the National Association of Broadcast Employees and Technicians (NABET) to provide engineers. Independent labels using Castle's services included Cincinnati's KING RECORDS and Nashville's own DOT and BULLET labels. In addition, Castle recorded radio shows for regional networks (some issued on its own Castle Recording Laboratories label) and local advertising jingles. Castle-recorded hits such as RED FOLEY's "Chattanoogie Shoeshine Boy" and HANK WILLIAMS's "You Win Again" helped put Nashville on the map as *the* place to record country music. From a technical standpoint, Castle engineers were also charting new territory by putting more "level" on their recordings (i.e., cutting grooves more deeply) than New York or Chicago engineers, thus giving the resulting commercial discs a hotter, more exciting sound.

By 1956, when the Tulane Hotel was razed, Castle had closed because of a WSM policy change that forced employees to choose between various sideline enterprises and continuing employment with WSM. The Castle engineers had established twenty-five-year service records and elected to stay with WSM's radio and television operations, but by then they had helped earn Nashville the moniker "MUSIC CITY U.S.A." in the music trade press.

—*John Rumble*

Cedarwood Publishing Company
established in Nashville, Tennessee, 1953

Cedarwood Publishing Company was a top country music publisher of its day, and one of the first music publishers to locate on Music Row. GRAND OLE OPRY artists service manager JIM DENNY and country artist WEBB PIERCE each put up $200 to start Cedarwood in 1953. Pierce was then one of country music's hottest recording artists, and Cedarwood got off to a quick start on the strength of his hits.

Cedarwood soon became the focus of controversy. Denny was promoting his own shows on the side, and it was rumored that as WSM artists service boss he favored Opry acts who recorded Cedarwood songs. When WSM, owner of the Opry, asked Denny and other WSM staffers to drop their involvement in outside businesses, Denny left WSM in September 1956.

Denny immediately formed the Jim Denny Artist Bureau and secured agreements to book many of the acts he had represented at the Opry. During his years at the Opry, Denny had built solid ties with performers, TV shows, DJs, and record label A&R men, and those connections paid off. Both Cedarwood and the Denny Artist Bureau flourished.

The publishing company's success was fed by Denny's strong ties to talent. His bureau's contract to provide acts for the PHILIP MORRIS COUNTRY MUSIC SHOW (1957–58) attracted even more country performers to Denny. The relationship was mutually beneficial: Denny offered TV and concert exposure as well as strong record label ties; in return, acts often recorded songs Denny published. Stars who recorded many Cedarwood tunes included WEBB PIERCE, CARL SMITH (who also owned a piece of Cedarwood), KITTY WELLS, HANK SNOW, and dozens of others.

Through the years Cedarwood staff writers MEL TILLIS, CARL PERKINS, WAYNE WALKER, DANNY DILL, MARIJOHN WILKIN, JOHN D. LOUDERMILK, and others wrote such hits as "Detroit City," "Ruby, Don't Take Your Love to Town," "The Long Black Veil," "Tobacco Road," "Teddy Bear," "I Ain't Never," "Waterloo," "Are You Sincere," "Daddy Sang Bass," and many others.

At the time of Denny's death in August 1963, Cedarwood boasted a catalogue of more than 2,200 songs and a staff of approximately a dozen songwriters. Denny's sons Bill and John subsequently managed Cedarwood until the company was purchased by Mel Tillis in 1983 for nearly $3 million. Tillis later sold the song catalogue to PolyGram Music.   —Al Cunniff

Central Songs
established ca. 1946; sold to Capitol Records, 1969

An important country publishing firm, Central Songs was active from the late 1940s into the mid-1960s. The company was formed as Century Songs in Chicago in about 1946, organized by LEE GILLETTE, KEN NELSON, and CLIFFIE STONE. Gillette, who had played in pop bands with Nelson, was then head of country recording for CAPITOL RECORDS, while Stone played bass on the label's West Coast sessions and helped produce rising Capitol talent such as MERLE TRAVIS. Nelson assumed Gillette's role in 1951 when Gillette took over Capitol's transcription department, and by this point Central shifted headquarters to Los Angeles and changed its name to "Central" to avoid conflict with other "Century" music firms.

While Nelson handled accounting behind the scenes, Stone served as president, signing writers and placing songs with record producers, including Nelson, of course. Central's first country chartmakers were "The Gods Were Angry with Me" (1948–49), penned by "Foreman" Bill and Ruth "Roma" Mackintosh, and several 1949–50 hits written and recorded by CAPITOL powerhouse TENNESSEE ERNIE FORD with assistance from Stone. During the 1950s the company published hits written by TOMMY COLLINS ("You Better Not Do That"), Jack Rhodes ("Conscience I'm Guilty"), Audrey and JOE ALLISON ("He'll Have to Go"), and Hazel Houser ("My Baby's Gone"). By 1959 Central also was publishing songs composed by Capitol star BUCK OWENS, who wrote and recorded such hits as "Under Your Spell Again" (with Rhodes) and "Foolin' Around" (with

HARLAN HOWARD) over the next few years. During Central's early 1960s heyday, achieved under Joe Allison's leadership, singer-songwriter NED MILLER, among others, supplied additional hit tunes.

Gradually, however, the proliferation of new publishers eroded Central's position; many of these—including Owens's Blue Book Music—were artist-owned, making it increasingly difficult to secure recordings and thus attract writers. What's more, Gillette and Nelson were ready to retire, while Stone had attractive—and ultimately successful—options in publishing. In 1969 the partners sold Central to CAPITOL RECORDS. Through this corporate connection, the catalogue today resides with the international conglomerate EMI.   —John Rumble

Curly Chalker
b. Enterprise, Alabama, October 22, 1931; d. April 30, 1998

The sophisticated chordal steel guitar style of Curly Chalker enhanced many classic country records of the 1950s, 1960s, and 1970s, and added a touch of class to the bucolic set of *HEE HAW* in the 1970s. The youngest of ten children, Harold Lee Chalker was raised on an Alabama farm where, he recalled, a guitar was always around. Starting with an Electromuse lap steel, he began emulating the steel stylings of a variety of notable players of the 1940s: JERRY BYRD, ROY WIGGINS, NOEL BOGGS, and JOAQUIN MURPHEY.

He struck out for Cincinnati at age thirteen and started working in clubs. By 1950 Chalker was in Paris, Texas, where he began touring with LEFTY FRIZZELL the following year. Chalker's recording debut was Frizzell's "Always Late (With Your Kisses)" (1951), followed by further recordings with Frizzell and Hank Thompson, whose "Wild Side of Life" (1952) featured Chalker.

Following an army hitch in 1952, Chalker rejoined Thompson's Brazos Valley Boys for a while before settling into the Las Vegas club circuit. In 1967 Chalker moved to Nashville and distinguished himself on sessions with DON GIBSON, Sue Thompson, CARL SMITH, WEBB PIERCE, and RAY PRICE, for whom he played on "For the Good Times" (1970). In 1973 Chalker became the staff pedal player with *Hee Haw*.

Chalker's fast and fluid chordal runs sometimes surprised even the artists he was accompanying. Once, while entertaining at a truck drivers' convention, DICK CURLESS missed his cue to sing after a jaw-dropping Chalker solo. Curless stopped the song and announced: "Folks, I'm really sorry, but Curly Chalker just played such a hell of a solo I plumb forgot what I was doing."   —Mark Humphrey

REPRESENTATIVE RECORDING

Big Hits on Big Steel (Columbia, 1967)

Challenge Records
established Los Angeles, California, March 1957; ended 1976

Challenge Records enjoyed substantial success from the late 1950s into the early 1970s. The independent label was founded in Los Angeles in March 1957 by GENE AUTRY and Joe Johnson, a recording entrepreneur and music publisher who was then managing Golden West Melodies and Western Music, Autry's principal publishing firms. Difficulties with major labels in securing recordings of their copyrights led the two men to establish their own record operation, although profits from pop star Johnnie Ray's COLUMBIA rendition of "Just Walking in the Rain" did provide the capital to start Challenge.

Originally, Autry and Johnson had called their organization "Champion," after the name of Autry's horse appearing in his movies, but DECCA already owned the title. Johnson said, therefore, that he named the company "Challenge," issuing a challenge to those who denied the partners permission to use their first choice. He also said that he called Challenge's country label Jackpot because country sales had been declining and he claimed that a great-selling country hit would be akin to hitting the jackpot.

Early on, Challenge's country artists included WYNN STEWART (chart years: 1959–64) and JAN HOWARD (1960). JEANNIE SEELY, JUSTIN TUBB, BOBBY BARE, Johnny and Jonie Mosby, and Bobby Austin recorded briefly for the label but did not chart. Challenge also leased AL DOWNING's "Down on the Farm," now a rockabilly cult classic, from a small Texas label. In the beginning, though, Challenge made a bigger mark with pop acts such as the Champs and Jerry Wallace.

Early on, Autry sold his 56 percent controlling interest in Challenge to Johnson and sales manager John Thompson. Johnson moved Challenge's headquarters to Nashville in 1972. By this time, Johnson had secured major-label distribution—with Challenge product appearing on the DECCA or MCA labels—and soon turned out chartmaking recordings with artists such as JERRY WALLACE (now primarily a country act), Marie Owens, GEORGE MORGAN, CARL BELEW, and BONNIE GUITAR. By 1976, however, personal financial problems plagued Johnson, and he eventually struck an administration deal with TREE MUSIC (now Sony/ATV Tree), which today leases Challenge masters to various labels. —*John Rumble*

Lightnin' Chance

b. Como, Mississippi, December 21, 1925

Onetime GRAND OLE OPRY staff musician Floyd Taylor Chance was a stand-up acoustic bass player on the road and in the recording studio for artists ranging from MARTHA CARSON to MARTY ROBBINS. His specialty was providing a foundation for harmony while adding tonal color. "I played with tone as much as possible," Chance said. "Back then there were no electrified amplifiers [for basses], but you could achieve varied effects, offering a greater variety of tones. . . . It's all in the wrist movement really."

Chance's father, Jody, a Dixieland banjoist, first gave him a four-string Martin guitar. In school Chance played clarinet, saxophone, and bass horn. While making touchdowns on the football field he earned the nickname "Lightnin'."

During World War II, the U.S. Naval Conservatory provided Chance with advanced musical training while he served with the Fourth Fleet Band, entertaining the troops in battle zones such as North Africa. Discharged, Chance moved to Memphis, playing in EDDIE HILL's band (1947–51) and performing on WMPS radio and WMC-TV. Chance's first recordings were in SAM PHILLIPS's Memphis studio, which later housed SUN RECORDS.

In Nashville, Chance played on HANK WILLIAMS's last session (September 23, 1952), which yielded three #1 records of 1953: "Your Cheatin' Heart," "Kaw-Liga," and "Take These Chains from My Heart." Other million sellers

boasting Chance's bass include CONWAY TWITTY's "It's Only Make Believe," FARON YOUNG's "Hello Walls," and the EVERLY BROTHERS' rockabilly classics "Bye Bye Love" and "Bird Dog."

Noting the JORDANAIRES' vocal chart relating to the tones of the diatonic scale, Chance adapted it so studio instrumentalists who did not read music might follow along. It became the Nashville Numbering System.

In 1952 Chance joined an Opry touring contingent that played New York City's Astor Hotel. During the 1960s he opened the Nashville office for Chappell Music publishing and worked on Nashville's WLAC-TV. He later played RALPH EMERY's early-morning WSM-TV program (until 1988, when Chance retired). —*Walt Trott*

Jean Chapel

b. Neon, Kentucky, March 6, 1925; d. August 12, 1995

During her long, colorful career, Opal Jean "Jean Chapel" Amburgey performed in a variety of styles under several billings. She left a significant songwriting legacy.

With sisters Bertha and Irene, Chapel performed on Kentucky and West Virginia radio as the Sunshine Sisters beginning in 1938. In 1940 they joined the COON CREEK GIRLS at Kentucky's *RENFRO VALLEY BARN DANCE*. Chapel played banjo, fiddle, bass, and guitar.

At Atlanta's WSB *Barn Dance* in the 1940s they were dubbed the Hoot Owl Holler Girls—"Mattie" (Jean), "Marthie" (Irene), and "Minnie" (Bertha). "Marthie" married James Roberts and they became "James & MARTHA CARSON."

Jean married Floyd "Salty" Holmes. They were billed as "Salty and Mattie" on MGM, and on WLW's televised *MIDWESTERN HAYRIDE* in Cincinnati, WLS's *NATIONAL BARN DANCE* in Chicago, and the *GRAND OLE OPRY*'s earliest syndicated TV programs. During this period she wrote and sang "Don't Sell Daddy Any More Whiskey" (1950), best known via Molly O'Day's recording of it. By 1954 she had written more than 300 songs, for artists such as Rosemary Clooney, Milton Berle, and WILMA LEE COOPER.

In the early 1950s the sister trio reunited to record for CAPITOL (as the Amber Sisters) and KING. As a solo, Chapel was "Opal Jean" on HICKORY. She became "Jean Chapel" when she signed with SUN in Memphis to sing rockabilly in 1956. Next on RCA, she toured in Alan Freed's famed rock & roll road show.

In the 1960s Chapel recorded for Smash, London, and CHALLENGE, and continued songwriting. Among those who recorded her songs were GEORGE JONES, HANK SNOW, PATSY CLINE, RED FOLEY, and SONNY JAMES. EDDY ARNOLD hit #1 with Chapel's "Lonely Again" in 1967, the same year "Lay Some Happiness on Me" became a pop hit for Dean Martin. "To Get to You," recorded by JERRY WALLACE, was nominated for 1972 CMA Song of the Year.

In the 1970s and 1980s Chapel entertained as "Opal Jean Cologne." Daughter Lana Chapel also became a Nashville singer-songwriter, as did younger brother Don Chapel, TAMMY WYNETTE's second husband. —*Robert K. Oermann*

Leon Chappelear

b. Tyler, Texas, August 1, 1909; d. October 22, 1962

An associate of JIMMIE DAVIS for many years, guitarist-vocalist-bandleader Horace Leon Chappelear began a varied two-decade recording career in 1932 as a soloist of country and cowboy fare for Starr Piano's Champion label. Along with the SHELTON BROTHERS, Chappelear was part of the Lone Star Cowboys, a Texas string trio that recorded the classics "Just Because" and "Deep Elm Blues" for VICTOR in 1933. He supplied memorable blues guitar backings for several Davis recordings that year as well.

After Davis established himself as a star at DECCA in the mid-thirties, he brought Chappelear to the label. Calling his band Leon's Lone Star Cowboys, Chappelear recorded several dozen western swing sides from 1935 through 1937. After the war, Davis also helped secure Chappelear a CAPITOL contract. Under the name Leon Chappel, Chappelear recorded several memorable honky-tonkers for the label such as "True Blue Poppa," later revived by fellow Texan FRANKIE MILLER on STARDAY. In 1962 Chappelear ended his own life by gunshot. —*Kevin Coffey*

REPRESENTATIVE RECORDING

Nite Spot Blues (Krazy Kat, 1998) (British various-artists western swing anthology containing two recordings by Leon's Lone Star Cowboys)

Ray Charles

b. Albany, Georgia, September 23, 1930

Best known for his gospel-driven r&b classics such as "What'd I Say" and "Georgia on My Mind," and highly respected for a series of jazz piano recordings, Ray Charles Robinson has also had a major impact on country music. His 1962 album *Modern Sounds in Country and Western Music* was a landmark recording, bringing untold numbers of new fans to country, and he has repeatedly worked country in with the unique mix of r&b, gospel, and jazz stylings that have made him one of the most important figures in the annals of popular music.

Completely blind since age seven, Charles first heard country as a child in Greensville, Florida, by way of broadcasts of the GRAND OLE OPRY. "I felt it was the closest music, really, to the blues—they'd make them steel guitars cry and whine, and it really attracted me," he later recalled. Early in his performing career he played piano in a country band, and among the now legendary r&b recordings he made for the ATLANTIC label during the 1950s was a version of HANK SNOW's "I'm Movin' On" (1959).

After he left Atlantic to accept a lucrative offer from ABC-Paramount, Charles struck gold. In 1960, "Georgia on My Mind" became his first #1 pop hit; then, after a couple more jazz outings, he released the pivotal *Modern Sounds in Country and Western Music.* The album melded his swinging, big-band r&b sound with classic country tunes such as "You Win Again," "Half as Much," and "Hey, Good-Lookin'" (all associated with HANK WILLIAMS), and DON GIBSON's "I Can't Stop Loving You."

Although Charles thought of *Modern Sounds* as a concept album and didn't intend it to produce any singles, his hand was forced when the actor Tab Hunter covered "I Can't Stop Loving You." Charles agreed to release the song as a single, and it rocketed to #1 on the pop charts, eventually becoming a million seller. After pulling another hit ("You Don't Know Me") from the album, Charles cut *Modern Sounds in Country and Western Music, Volume Two,* which included the Top Ten hits "You Are My Sunshine" and "Take These Chains from My Heart."

Although he'd proven his point—that good music is

Ray Charles

good music, and that country music need not be confined to country audiences—Charles didn't quit recording country material; later hits included "Crying Time" in 1966 and "Don't Change on Me," from the album *Love Country Style,* in 1971.

Through much of the 1980s Charles recorded country for the Columbia label, including *Friendship* (1984), an album of duets with such stars as HANK WILLIAMS JR., MERLE HAGGARD, and WILLIE NELSON. His duet with Nelson on "Seven Spanish Angels" hit #1 on the country charts. —*Ben Fong-Torres*

REPRESENTATIVE RECORDINGS

Modern Sounds in Country and Western Music (ABC-Paramount, 1962); *Modern Sounds in Country and Western Music, Volume Two* (ABC-Paramount, 1962); *Friendship* (Columbia, 1984)

Hugh Cherry

b. Louisville, Kentucky, October 7, 1922

One of Nashville's first postwar hillbilly disc jockeys, Hugh Cherry perfected a smooth, straight presentation and mood-driven programming style that made him a key force in country music. As a child he saw performances by both JIMMIE RODGERS and the CARTER FAMILY; as a soldier, he was among the forces who liberated Dachau. In 1946 Cherry began broadcasting at tiny WKAY in Glasgow, Kentucky, then moved to WKLO in Louisville. PEE WEE KING befriended and mentored him, offering advice and access to a cache of country music clippings and songbooks.

Arriving at Nashville's WKDA in 1949, the restless, intense Cherry developed an urbane style that established him as a popular airwaves personality who showcased artists such as HANK WILLIAMS, UNCLE DAVE MACON, and GRANDPA JONES. Broadcasting over Memphis's WMPS in

1950–51, he won fervent listeners, including JOHNNY CASH, CARL PERKINS, and ELVIS PRESLEY. Returning to Nashville in 1951, Cherry broadcast over WMAK. In Nashville he played an important role in getting FARON YOUNG hired by the GRAND OLE OPRY and was instrumental in getting Pat Boone his first recording contract. During 1955–57 Cherry worked at Cincinnati superstation WLW.

Discouraged by rock & roll's impact, Cherry turned to television news at Nashville's WSIX and found himself covering the Civil Rights movement—starting at Little Rock—for the next four years. Relocating to California in 1959, Cherry soon had a nightly radio show on KFOX, airing rarely broadcast folk and hillbilly recordings that influenced listeners such as GRAM PARSONS and David Crosby. Cherry, now retired, also wrote liner notes for numerous country music albums and scripted and narrated numerous radio and television country music documentaries.

—*Jonny Whiteside*

Mark Chesnutt

b. Beaumont, Texas, September 6, 1963

Mark Nelson Chesnutt might be the most underrated singer to emerge from country's second wave of NEW TRADITIONALISTS in the late 1980s and early 1990s. He's arguably the strongest pure-country voice to come out of southeastern Texas since GEORGE JONES. Chesnutt's music reflects the mix of sounds he heard growing up along the Texas-Louisiana border: HONKY-TONK, OUTLAW-country, CAJUN and zydeco, rhythm & blues, and a touch of WESTERN SWING. In addition to Jones—his biggest influence—Chesnutt cites MERLE HAGGARD, HANK WILLIAMS, HANK WILLIAMS JR., and ELVIS PRESLEY among his favorites.

The son of a musician, the late Bobby Chesnutt, Chesnutt dropped out of high school to play drums in a rock band. By the time he released his first album (on the independent Axbar label) at twenty-six, he'd already logged ten years playing in clubs. He was signed to MCA RECORDS after regional promotion rep Roger Ramsey Corkill heard the single "Too Cold at Home," which Chesnutt had recorded for the independent Cherry label in Houston. The song, a mournful barstool ballad, became the title track to his debut album. An instant classic, "Too Cold at Home" held the #3 spot on the country chart for three weeks in October 1990, during which time the #1 position was held by GARTH BROOKS's "Friends in Low Places." (Ironically, Chesnutt had planned to release his own version of "Friends in Low Places" as a single, but Brooks beat him to the punch.)

While ballads are Chesnutt's forte, like Jones, he's also adept at uptempo ditties such as "Blame It on Texas," "Old Flames Have New Names," and "Bubba Shot the Jukebox." His knowledge of country music history is indicated by his choice of vintage covers such as RAY PRICE's "Uptown Downtown (Misery's All the Same)," CHARLIE RICH's "Who Will the Next Fool Be," and DON GIBSON's "Woman, Sensuous Woman." Chesnutt's second album, *Longnecks & Short Stories,* featured a duet with his hero George Jones on "Talkin' to Hank." The later hits "It Sure Is Monday" and "Gonna Get a Life" indicated his flair for Cajun-flavored country.

By the time Chesnutt released his fourth album (and first for the revived DECCA label), *What a Way to Live,* in 1994, he'd landed four #1 hits. Although he won the CMA's 1993 Horizon Award, Chesnutt remained something of a secret outside the hard-core country radio audi-

Mark Chesnutt

ence. "I don't feel I'm like what they call these country hunks," he said. "I feel like my career is based mainly on the music, and I'm comfortable with that. I'm not out there swinging on ropes or doing somersaults or anything I won't be able to do in twenty years, if I'm still out there."

Chesnutt's fifth album, *Wings,* might be his best. A honky-tonk concept album, it bucked the commercial trend toward throwaway novelty tunes and lightweight country-pop. His 1997 album, *Thank God for Believers,* features Chesnutt's own songwriting skills and those of frequent collaborator Roger Springer.   —*Rick Mitchell*

REPRESENTATIVE RECORDINGS

Too Cold at Home (MCA, 1990); *Longnecks & Short Stories* (MCA, 1992); *Wings* (Decca, 1995); *Thank God for Believers* (Decca, 1997)

Lew Childre

b. Opp, Alabama, November 1, 1901; d. December 3, 1961

"Doctor Lew" Childre, as he is fondly remembered by generations, was one of the great one-man shows in country music. He was one of the last country stars to come up through the old-time medicine show and vaudeville circuit, and he was a master of the classic nineteenth-century and early twentieth-century skills. He could buck-dance, sing, play the old-fashioned Hawaiian steel guitar, do hundreds of vintage jokes and comedy routines, ad-lib commercials, recite poetry, and improvise dialogue. Though many fans remember him for his days on the GRAND OLE OPRY in the late 1940s and 1950s (when he often teamed with a young STRINGBEAN), he had had a long and influential career before then. He did comedy for many of the greats, including Wiley Walker, FLOYD TILLMAN, CURLY FOX, BILL MONROE, and BILL BOYD.

Growing up in Opp, just a few miles from the Florida

line, young Childre embarrassed his father, a local judge, by buck-dancing on street corners for nickels. He actually finished college, in 1923, but couldn't resist the lure of show business and so joined the Milt Tolbert tent show as a singer of pop songs. A little later Childre formed his own group, a jazz band called the Alabama Cotton Pickers. Though he preferred to work in traveling tent shows in the 1930s, he did manage to record a couple of times—first for GENNETT in 1930, and again for ARC in 1934. His three big recorded hits were "Fishing Blues," "Hang Out the Front Door Key," and "Riding on the Elevated Railway."

Soon Childre managed to translate his tent circuit showmanship to radio, having popular shows over WWL (New Orleans), XERA (Del Rio), WWVA (Wheeling), and WAGA (Atlanta). He came to the Opry in 1945 but continued to do several series of his own shows on transcriptions. In later years he invented a number of fishing lures that won impressive royalties. He died in 1961, shortly after completing an album for the STARDAY label.

—*Charles Wolfe*

REPRESENTATIVE RECORDINGS

Old Time Get Together with Lew Childre (Starday, 1961); *On the Air* (Old Homestead, 1983)

Harry Choates
b. Rayne, Louisiana, December 26, 1922; d. July 17, 1951

In his brief life, fiddler Harry Henry Choates immortalized the traditional Cajun song "Jolie Blonde (Pretty Blonde)" with his best-selling 1946 Gold Star recording titled "Jole Blon." Unfortunately, a longtime battle with alcoholism took this talented musician's life before he reached age thirty.

Choates's childhood was rocky. When he was nine years old, his father died, leaving him to fend for himself. As a boy, he moved from home to home, living off kindly friends and relatives and tips he made playing his fiddle in bars. A natural musician, he not only mastered the fiddle but also the guitar, mandolin, and accordion. Much of his life was spent in Texas, and though he adopted Cajun music he was proficient in jazz and western swing as well. French was not his native language; he learned just enough of it to sing the Cajun songs he loved so well. By his early teenage years he not only had become a professional musician but also a hard drinker.

After his father's death, Choates spent a lot of time in Basile, Louisiana, where he played guitar in fiddlemaster LEO SOILEAU's band in the late 1930s. A great innovator in Cajun music, Soileau served as mentor to Choates, who learned many of Soileau's stage tricks and songs, including "Jolie Blonde." Choates also played in other popular bands of the time, including those of HAPPY FATS (whom he joined in December 1939) and SHELLY LEE ALLEY (joined in summer 1940). Never a dependable band member, Choates eventually formed his own band, the Rhythm Boys, consisting of bassist B. D. Williams, banjoist-vocalist Joe Manuel, guitarist Ed Pursley, steel guitarist "Papa Cairo" Lamperez, and pianist Johnnie Mae Smirle. The band worked for Basile music mogul Quincy Davis, who had a habit of taking in musicians, feeding them, and hiring them seven nights a week plus radio shows and matinees for the meager fee of $10 a week. The musicians rarely complained, since for most of them it was better than picking cotton in hot fields.

In April 1946 Choates made his epochal recording of "Jole Blon" backed with "Basile Waltz" for Gold Star Records in Houston; in January 1947 it registered on *Billboard*'s national country charts, peaking at #4. So popular was the tune that MOON MULLICAN, ROY ACUFF, and others rushed in with cover versions. Between 1946 and 1950 Choates toured extensively throughout Texas and Louisiana, and recorded several more sessions for Gold Star before moving to Macy Lela Henry's Macy's Records label in early 1950.

The brilliant young musician had a sad end. A 1945 marriage to Helen Daenen ended in divorce, but not before the Choateses had a son in 1946 and a daughter in 1947. On July 14, 1951, Choates was arrested in Austin, Texas, for chronic failure to pay child support. Deprived of alcohol in jail, he suffered withdrawal symptoms and went into delirium tremens. When he died three days later, the official cause of death was cirrhosis of the liver, though rumors of a jailhouse beating persist to this day. In just six years, twenty-nine-year-old Harry Choates had taken Cajun music to national popularity, recorded its biggest hit ever, and left behind beautiful recordings of songs such as "Allons à Lafayette," "Lawtell Waltz," "Poor Hobo," and "Opelousas Waltz" that still live today.   —*Ann Allen Savoy*

REPRESENTATIVE RECORDING

Harry Choates—The Fiddle King of Cajun Swing (Arhoolie)

Chuck Wagon Gang
David Parker "Dad" Carter b. Milltown, Kentucky, September 28, 1889; d. April 28, 1963
Effie Juanita "Anna" Carter b. Shannon, Texas, February 15, 1917
Rosa Lola Lee "Rose" Carter b. Snyder, Oklahoma, December 31, 1914; d. May 13, 1997
Ernest Ray "Jim" Carter b. Tioga, Texas, August 10, 1910; d. 1971

Of all the gospel groups flourishing during the Depression and early war years, the Chuck Wagon Gang had the closest relationship to country music in both style and choice of songs. The original group, composed of Dad Carter and three of his children—Anna, Rose, and Jim—began singing in Lubbock, Texas, in 1935, and by 1936 had inaugurated their popular radio show on WBAP-KGKO in Fort Worth. There they assumed the name of a cowboy act, the Chuck Wagon Gang, which had already been on local radio, as well as the sponsorship of a local flour concern, Bewley Mills. Their first recordings for ARC in 1936 included both secular and religious material; they did not turn to the exclusive recording of gospel songs until April 1940.

The Chuck Wagon Gang became a radio institution in the Southwest, singing songs that came directly from the shape-note hymnals, and using a vocal style strongly influenced by the gospel publishing house quartets. Generally accompanied only by a chorded guitar (played at first by Jim), the group produced a style of four-part harmony that was cherished by their many fans because of its warmth and predictability. Rose's high soprano lead and Anna's rich alto harmony were supported by the basic vocal underpinnings of Dad's baritone and Jim's bass.

Greater national exposure came in the 1950s, when radio evangelist J. Bazzel Mull began featuring and selling their records on his widely syndicated radio show, *Mull's Singing Convention*, and after 1966, when the group moved to Nashville. Although the Chuck Wagon Gang has experi-

The Chuck Wagon Gang

enced numerous personnel changes—beginning with Jim's retirement in 1951, Dad's departure in 1955, and, most significantly, Rose's retirement in 1966—the Chuck Wagon Gang style has remained intact, and the Chuck Wagon Gang has enjoyed one of the longest-enduring careers in American entertainment. While remaining one of the most popular gospel groups in America, the Chuck Wagon Gang also introduced many of ALBERT E. BRUMLEY's gospel compositions to a wide public, and, with the release of *Favorite Country Hymns* (Columbia, 1950), the Chuck Wagon Gang became the first gospel group to have an album of songs issued. The group broke up in December 1995.

—*Bill C. Malone*

REPRESENTATIVE RECORDINGS

Greatest Hits, Volume 1 (Arrival, 1991); *Old Time Hymns, Volume 2* (Arrival, 1991)

Guy Clark
b. Monahans, Texas, November 6, 1941

One of Nashville's most influential and respected songwriters of the past two decades, Guy Clark began his career in the 1960s as a guitar-picking folksinger, playing clubs in Houston and Austin alongside such fellow artists as TOWNES VAN ZANDT, K. T. OSLIN, and JERRY JEFF WALKER. In the late 1960s, Clark moved to San Francisco, then back to Houston, and then to Southern California, where he built Dobros at the Dopyera Brothers' guitar factory in Long Beach. After eight months in Los Angeles, where he signed a songwriting contract with RCA's Sunbury Music, Clark moved to Nashville in late 1971 with his wife, Susanna, who is an artist and also an accomplished songwriter ("Easy from Now On," among others).

The son of an attorney, Clark grew up in Monahans, in West Texas, and in Rockport, near the Texas Gulf Coast.

These two locales have been featured prominently in Clark's work, providing memories and inspiration for such songs as "Desperados Waitin' for a Train" (Jerry Jeff Walker, 1973), "Texas 1947" (JOHNNY CASH, 1975), and "Blowin' Like a Bandit" (ASLEEP AT THE WHEEL, 1987).

Clark's own recording career began in 1975 with his classic collection *Old No. 1* and most recently resulted in the 1997 SUGAR HILL album *Keepers—a Live Recording.* While these and other albums have earned him extensive critical praise, Clark has enjoyed more commercial success with songs covered by other artists. His first songwriting success came in 1973 with Jerry Jeff Walker's recording of "L.A. Freeway," a song written by Clark during his months in Los Angeles. He hit #1 in 1982 via RICKY SKAGGS's recording of "Heartbroke," and in 1988 with RODNEY CROWELL's "She's Crazy for Leavin'," which Clark and Crowell co-wrote. Clark's other hits as a songwriter have included "New Cut Road" (BOBBY BARE, 1982), "Oklahoma Borderline" (VINCE GILL, 1985), "The Carpenter" (JOHN CONLEE, 1986), and "Baby I'm Yours" (STEVE WARINER, 1988).

—*Jack Bernhardt*

REPRESENTATIVE RECORDINGS

Old No. 1 (RCA, 1975); *Boats to Build* (Asylum, 1992)

Roy Clark
b. Meherrin, Virginia, April 15, 1933

His country music credentials range from touring with GRANDPA JONES as a teenager, to hosting *HEE HAW* for the show's entire twenty-five-year run, to pioneering in the development of BRANSON, MISSOURI, as a prime country music tourist destination. Yet Roy Linwood Clark, in a career managed for many years by JIM HALSEY, positioned himself as an all-around entertainer who could host *The Tonight Show* (which he did, several times) and win crowds in Las

Roy Clark

Vegas showrooms as easily as he could perform on the GRAND OLE OPRY. A singer, instrumentalist, actor, and comic, Clark was also one of the first country musicians to perform with a symphony orchestra, to tour in the Soviet Union, and to appear at Carnegie Hall and Madison Square Garden.

Clark's father, Hester, moved the family around (Virginia, West Virginia, the District of Columbia, even New York City) as he worked at several jobs during the Depression and World War II. Hester Clark was also a semiprofessional musician, playing guitar, fiddle, and banjo, instruments that Roy also would master. Roy's mother, Lillian, played piano, and his brother and sister played mandolin and guitar. By 1949 Roy had made his television debut (on the Dumont Network's District of Columbia affiliate), toured with Grandpa Jones, and played for two weeks on a bill headed by HANK WILLIAMS. Clark eventually signed on with singer JIMMY DEAN, who was then hosting daily television and radio programs in the Washington, D.C., area.

In 1957, Clark—who had been fired by Dean for chronic lateness—appeared on Arthur Godfrey's nationally televised *Talent Scouts* program. Before long, Dean's manager, CONNIE B. GAY, arranged a regular spot on a CBS radio series headlined by another client, George Hamilton IV.

Clark continued working in the D.C. area until 1960, when he was recruited by WANDA JACKSON to front her band. Clark joined her at the Golden Nugget Hotel in Las Vegas, performing a twenty-minute opening set and then joining her backing group as guitarist. Jackson's manager, Jim Halsey, brought Clark to CAPITOL RECORDS. His first Capitol album, *The Lightning Fingers of Roy Clark,* was released in 1962, and his first hit single—a version of BILL ANDERSON's "The Tips of My Fingers"—was released the same year, reaching #10 on *Billboard*'s country chart and #45 pop. Clark never duplicated that success while on Capitol, though the label allowed him to record in a number of environments, including a jazz album with guitarist Barney Kessel and saxophonist Plas Johnson.

In 1967 Roy moved to the DOT label, which resulted in a string of hits, including "Yesterday When I Was Young" (1969), "I Never Picked Cotton" (1970), "Come Live with Me" (1973), and "If I Had to Do It All Over Again" (1976). He also recorded albums, including duet efforts with his banjo player, Buck Trent, and blues artist Clarence "Gatemouth" Brown. Leaving Dot (by 1974 it had been absorbed by ABC), Roy charted throughout the 1980s on the MCA, Churchill, Songbird, Silver Dollar, and Hallmark labels, but largely concentrated on live performances and his *Hee Haw* hosting, begun in 1969.

In 1983 Roy opened The Roy Clark Celebrity Theater in Branson, which has since become his base of operations. He joined the Grand Ole Opry as a member on August 22, 1987. —*Todd Everett*

REPRESENTATIVE RECORDINGS

Greatest Hits (Varese Sarabande, 1995); *Roy Clark and Joe Pass Play Hank Williams* (Ranwood, 1995); *Greatest Hits, Volume 2* (Varese Vintage, 1997)

Terri Clark
b. Montréal, Québec, August 5, 1968

....

One of 1995's most critically acclaimed country newcomers, TERRI CLARK (born Terri Sauson) cites her maternal

Terri Clark

grandparents, who opened for Nashville's stars in Canadian nightclubs during the 1950s, as early musical influences.

Raised in Calgary, Alberta, the daughter of a truck driver and a secretary, Clark moved to Nashville after graduating from high school, earning the money needed to relocate by working in a Chinese restaurant. After making the 1,800-mile trek with $2,000 to her name, Clark quickly landed a gig at the famed TOOTSIE'S ORCHID LOUNGE by asking to sing a song. "The place was empty," she told the *Chicago Tribune*. "They had the door open so people could hear the music out on the street. And people started coming in. They asked me if I would sing there. I thought I had arrived."

Four hours a day, Clark performed at Tootsie's for $15 plus tips. After finding management, she began writing with some of Nashville's best tunesmiths. A four-song demo brought her to the attention of singer-songwriter-producer KEITH STEGALL, who eventually signed her to MERCURY NASHVILLE.

Clark's debut single, "Better Things to Do," captured the public's attention. Follow-up hits included "When Boy Meets Girl," "Suddenly Single," and "If I Were You." The four tunes resulted in the gold certification of her first album, *Terri Clark*. Her traditional sound allowed her to forge a distinctive persona, and she quickly found herself opening for GEORGE STRAIT, one of her influences. She was named Best New Female Artist by the ACADEMY OF COUNTRY MUSIC in May 1996, and she was also nominated for the prestigious Horizon Award by the COUNTRY MUSIC ASSOCIATION.

Released in late 1996, Clark's second album, *Just the Same,* featured a cover of "Poor Poor Pitiful Me," a country-rock favorite popularized by LINDA RONSTADT in 1978. —*Janet Williams*

REPRESENTATIVE RECORDINGS

Terri Clark (Mercury Nashville, 1995); *Just the Same* (Mercury Nashville, 1996)

Al Clauser

b. Manitoa, Illinois, February 23, 1911; d. March 3, 1989

As the leader of Al Clauser & His Oklahoma Outlaws, Henry Alfred Clauser became a popular WESTERN SWING bandleader-guitarist-songwriter in the 1930s. He started his musical career in Illinois, where he claimed to have used the actual term "western swing" as early as 1928. His band broadcast their radio show from WHO, Des Moines, Iowa, and by 1938 the program was carried by 272 Mutual network stations. In 1937 GENE AUTRY used Clauser's band in the movie *Rootin' Tootin' Rhythm,* and that year they also recorded twelve sides for ARC.

In 1942 Clauser moved the band to Tulsa, Oklahoma, where it grew to nine members and competed with JOHNNIE LEE WILLS and LEON MCAULIFFE for dance crowds. Broadcasting daily over station KTUL, the Clauser outfit introduced twelve-year-old Clara Ann Fowler, who became known professionally as Patti Page; she made her first recording with them (as Al Clauser & the Oklahomans) in Tulsa for the Okla label. Clauser disbanded the group in the 1950s and worked for KTUL Television, Tulsa.

—*Guy Logsdon*

Joe Clay

b. Harvey, Louisiana, September 9, 1938

Never a best-selling artist, Joe Clay enjoys high regard among rockabilly enthusiasts for recording some of the finest examples of the style ever waxed. The Cajun raver's reputation rests on nine songs he cut in just over a month. Claiborne Joseph Cheramie was living in Harvey, Louisiana, when he was discovered by a New Orleans–based disc jockey, who knew that the RCA subsidiary Vik Records was looking for talent. Clay landed a recording session for the company on the strength of a demo tape he made at a local radio station. He recorded on April 24, 1956, at Bill Quinn's Gold Star studio in Houston. Two songs, "Duck Tail" and "Sixteen Chicks," were released by Vik and helped Clay gain bookings on the *LOUISIANA HAYRIDE* in Shreveport.

In May Clay went to New York for a guest spot on *The Ed Sullivan Show*—several months before ELVIS PRESLEY appeared on the television show—and to record with a band that included fiery guitarist Mickey Baker and two drummers. Again Vik released two songs, "Get on the Right Track" and "Cracker Jack," but neither established Clay as a star.

Forty years later, the singer and guitarist still ranks among the best practitioners of the rockabilly style. His early recordings have been reissued on compact disc. He works as a bus driver and leaves his home in Gretna, Louisiana, occasionally to tour the United States and Europe.

—*Jay Orr*

REPRESENTATIVE RECORDING

Get Hot or Go Home: Vintage RCA Rockabilly '56–'59 (Country Music Foundation Records, 1989)

"Cowboy" Jack Clement

b. Whitehaven, Tennessee, April 5, 1931

Born and raised in suburban Memphis, Jack Henderson Clement went on to become one of the most highly re-

Jack Clement

garded—and colorful—producers, songwriters, and entrepreneurs in the history of country music. Following a four-year hitch in the marines that ended in 1952, Clement—along with BUZZ BUSBY and Scotty Stoneman—played bluegrass up and down the eastern seaboard in a band called Buzz and Jack and the Bayou Boys. In 1954 Clement returned to Memphis, where he soon became the first hired staff producer-engineer at SUN RECORDS; from 1956 to 1959 he was at the mixing board for recording sessions of ROY ORBISON, CARL PERKINS, JOHNNY CASH, CHARLIE RICH, and JERRY LEE LEWIS. An accomplished songwriter, Clement penned "It'll Be Me" for Lewis, "Guess Things Happen That Way" and "Ballad of a Teenage Queen" for Cash, and numerous hits for other performers.

Fired in 1959 by Sun owner SAM PHILLIPS over what Clement described as a misunderstanding, Clement moved to Nashville in 1960 to work as a songwriter and producer for Chet Atkins at RCA. Several months later, lured away by friend and fellow producer Bill Hall, Clement relocated to Beaumont, Texas, where he and Hall opened Gulf Coast Recording Studios together. It was there that Clement met GEORGE JONES and suggested that Jones cut DICKEY LEE's "She Thinks I Still Care," a move that paid off when the song became Jones's first #1 for United Artists, in 1962. Not long afterward Clement offered Jones one of his own compositions, "A Girl I Used to Know," a song that hit #3 on the country charts for Jones that same year.

In 1965 Clement moved back to Nashville and began his lengthy association with singer CHARLEY PRIDE. Convinced that Pride could be a big success, Clement financed a demo session and passed the tape along to Atkins, who decided to sign Pride to RCA. Clement produced or coproduced Pride's first thirteen albums for RCA.

During the early 1970s Clement established the JMI label, expanded his publishing company, and opened three Nashville recording studios. He produced the 1975 Outlaw classic *Dreaming My Dreams* for WAYLON JENNINGS, and hosted recording sessions for MERLE HAGGARD, Ivory Joe Hunter, RAY STEVENS, WANDA JACKSON, MICKEY NEWBURY, and DON WILLIAMS. Williams was a member of Clement's songwriting stable, as were BOB MCDILL ("Amanda") and ALLEN REYNOLDS ("Dreaming My Dreams with You"). During this time, artists ranging from TAMMY WYNETTE, to Eric Clapton, to Perry Como, to ELVIS PRESLEY recorded material from Clement's vast publishing catalogue.

Clement didn't record an album under his own name until age forty-six, though he had cut several sides for Sun in the late 1950s. His full-length debut, *All I Want to Do in Life* (1978), charted two singles—the title cut, and "When I Dream" b/w "We Must Believe in Magic." During the 1980s Clement produced records for Johnny Cash, as well as portions of U2's 1988 tribute album to American roots music, *Rattle and Hum.*   —*Bill Friskics-Warren*

REPRESENTATIVE RECORDING

All I Want to Do in Life (Elektra, 1978)

Vassar Clements

b. Kinard, South Carolina April 25, 1928

Vassar Carlton Clements is widely acknowledged to be one of the country's foremost fiddle virtuosos. His ability to play almost any kind of music—from BLUEGRASS and country to rock and jazz—has brought him five Grammy nominations.

Clements grew up in Kissimmee, Florida, in a family of musicians, and he was playing his stepfather's fiddle by the time he was five. He was strongly influenced by the legendary Florida bluegrass fiddler CHUBBY WISE, who was a family friend. In 1949, at age fourteen, Clements became a member of BILL MONROE's Bluegrass Boys, and he continued to perform with Monroe on and off until 1956. From 1958 to 1961 he worked with JIM AND JESSE McReynolds, recording for STARDAY.

Clements more or less dropped out of the music business for several years until 1967, when he resumed performing full-time with bluegrass pioneer JIMMY MARTIN and country singer FARON YOUNG. In 1971 Clements began working with JOHN HARTFORD, forming an association that has continued to the present. Clements's career received a major boost in 1972 when he appeared on the NITTY GRITTY DIRT BAND's landmark *Will the Circle Be Unbroken* album. As Clements continued to broaden his musical horizons, experimenting with new musical fusions, he worked for a while with the progressive EARL SCRUGGS Revue and became one of Nashville's most in-demand session musicians. In 1974 he collaborated with guitarist David Bromberg on the classic *Hillbilly Jazz* double album.

Clements has continued to tour and work as a Nashville session picker. In 1991 ROUNDER RECORDS convinced him to return to his bluegrass roots to record the highly acclaimed *Grass Routes,* which showcases Clements at the top of his bluegrass form.   —*Charlie Seemann*

REPRESENTATIVE RECORDINGS

Hillbilly Jazz (Flying Fish, 1974); *Grass Routes* (Rounder, 1991)

Zeke Clements

b. Warrior, Alabama, September 6, 1911; d. June 4, 1994

One of the most versatile yet unheralded figures in country music, Zeke Clements was a major star on radio and films in the 1930s and 1940s and composed some of the best-known songs of that era. A native of northern Alabama, he came from a family that included other early recording artists such as Stanley Clements. Though he was fond of fiddle music and Sacred Harp singing, Zeke began his career by specializing in yodeling and cowboy songs, billing himself as the Alabama Cowboy and the Dixie Yodeler. He started his career over WLS in Chicago in 1929, then moved to Philadelphia. He eventually arrived in Nashville, where he joined WSM as a member of Ken Hackney's Bronco Busters, the first western act on the station. For a time he also worked with Texas Ruby Owens, moving on to WHAS in Louisville and WHO in Des Moines.

While working on the *Hollywood Barn Dance* in 1937, Clements answered an ad from the Walt Disney studio for a cowboy singer who could both read musical scores and yodel. The job was for the soundtrack to *Snow White and the Seven Dwarf*s, and Clements became the voice for the cartoon character Bashful in that classic. This led to his appearing in B-grade westerns, often as the sidekick for Charles Starrett. By 1939, after his professional breakup with Texas Ruby, Clements returned to WSM, where he became a leading GRAND OLE OPRY soloist and a successful songwriter. His "Smoke on the Water," a strong World War II song, was featured by ROY ACUFF and became a major hit for RED FOLEY in 1944. EDDY ARNOLD had hits with Clements's "Just a Little Lovin'" (1948), "Why Should I Cry?" (1950), and "Somebody's Been Beating My Time" (1950). During this time, Clements also founded his own record company, Liberty, on which he recorded such acts as Paul Howard, the John Daniel Quartet, and himself. By the 1950s he was a seasoned veteran, headlining TV variety shows in New Orleans, Birmingham, Atlanta, and Nashville. He died in Nashville.   —*Charles Wolfe*

Bill Clifton

b. Riverwood, Maryland, April 5, 1931

Singer-guitarist Bill Clifton played a major role in popularizing bluegrass abroad and in highlighting the traditional roots of the music. He was born William August Marburg in Maryland's rural Baltimore County and raised on a farm owned by his wealthy family. Records and radio introduced him to country music, which he played with a part-time band (the Dixie Mountain Boys) while pursuing a graduate business degree at the University of Virginia in Charlottesville. He changed his last name to counter family objections to his association with the music world. The band, with Bill Wiltshire (fiddle), Curly Lambert (mandolin), Johnny Clark (banjo), and Jack Cassidy (bass), made its first records for the Blue Ridge label at the university in 1954. "Flower Blooming in the Wildwood" became a regional hit and led to a second session in 1955 while Clifton was in the marine corps, just before Blue Ridge folded.

Clifton's 1955 songbook *150 Old-Time Folk and Gospel Songs* included many traditional songs taken from early country records that Clifton himself favored. It was the first song collection directed to bluegrass performers, and it enjoyed a major influence. When he was discharged from the marines in 1956, he resumed performing and recorded a number of successful titles for MERCURY, including "Gathering Flowers from the Hillside," "Little Whitewashed Chimney," and "Mary Dear."

Clifton organized the first bluegrass festival at Oak Leaf Park in Luray, Virginia, on July 4, 1961, bringing JIM &

JESSE, the STANLEY BROTHERS, BILL MONROE, the COUNTRY GENTLEMEN, and himself together for an all-day show that (along with the NEWPORT FOLK FESTIVALS) provided a model for CARLTON HANEY's seminal Roanoke bluegrass festival in 1965. Clifton moved to England in 1963 and spent much of the 1960s and 1970s overseas. In recent years he has made occasional appearances and records for his own Elf label.   —*Dick Spottswood*

REPRESENTATIVE RECORDINGS

Bill Clifton: The Early Years (Rounder, 1992); *Mountain Folk Songs* (Starday, 1959, out of print)

Patsy Cline
b. Winchester, Virginia, September 8, 1932; d. March 5, 1963

The most popular female country singer in recording history, PATSY CLINE has achieved icon status since her tragic early death at age thirty in 1963. Cline is invariably invoked as a standard for female vocalists, and she has inspired scores of singers, including K. D. LANG, LORETTA LYNN, LINDA RONSTADT, TRISHA YEARWOOD, and WYNONNA JUDD. Cline's brief career produced the #1 jukebox hit of all time, WILLIE NELSON's "Crazy" (written by Willie Nelson), and her unique, crying style and vocal impeccability have established her reputation as the quintessential torch singer.

Cline's short life reads like the heart-torn lyrics of many of the ballads she recorded. Born Virginia Patterson Hensley in Winchester, Virginia, in the midst of the Depression, she demonstrated musical proclivity at an early age—a talent inherited from her father, an accomplished amateur singer, whom Cline later confessed sexually abused her as a child. The family moved nineteen times around the state of Virginia before "Ginny," as she was known in her youth, reached fifteen. A perpetual outsider, Cline dropped out of school at age fifteen to support her family after her father deserted them. They settled in Winchester, the Shenandoah Valley town with which she would grow to have a love-hate relationship.

Haunted by her early experiences, the teenage Cline directed herself toward a career as a singer with unbending single-mindedness. She sang in juke joints in the Winchester area and did a nightclub cabaret act à la Helen Morgan, the tear-stained pop chanteuse of the 1920s said to be one of Cline's primary influences (along with Kay Starr, Kate Smith, and CHARLINE ARTHUR). She also appeared in amateur musicals, talent shows, and on local radio station WINC.

By age twenty Cline connected with local country bandleader Bill Peer, an association that nurtured her desire to become a country music star. She adopted the name Patsy after her middle name, Patterson, and possibly in a nod to singer Patsy Montana, whose feisty cowgirl persona anticipated both Cline's spunk and early stage costuming. She married her first husband, staid Gerald Cline, on March 7, 1953, but she found the relationship unfulfilling and they divorced four years later.

During this period Cline made inroads into the thriving Washington, D.C., country music scene masterminded by country music's "media magician," CONNIE B. GAY. Beginning in the fall of 1954, Gay spotlighted Cline as a featured soloist on his *Town & Country* regional TV broadcasts, which included JIMMY DEAN as host, along with ROY CLARK, GEORGE HAMILTON IV, BILLY GRAMMER, Dale Turner, and

Mary Klick. Through her web of Washington contacts Cline landed her first recording contract in September 1954, with BILL MCCALL's Pasadena, California–based FOUR STAR RECORDS, an association that lasted six years and was to become the single greatest hindrance to her career. Cline alleged that McCall swindled her out of record earnings and gave her substandard material to record.

Cline's debut single, the country weeper "A Church, a Courtroom and Then Goodbye," sold poorly when released in July 1955 on the DECCA label's Coral subsidiary (by lease arrangement between McCall and Decca A&R man PAUL COHEN). Cohen turned production over to his protégé and eventual successor, OWEN BRADLEY, who became Cline's guiding light for the duration of her recording career.

Cline's first four singles flopped, but the "hillbilly with oomph" act she developed on TV and in personal appearances earned her regional fame. Her recording stalemate ended when she made her national TV debut on Arthur Godfrey's *Talent Scouts* show on January 21, 1957, singing "Walkin' After Midnight," which hit #2 country and #12 pop. Cline rode high on the hit for the next year, doing personal appearances and performing regularly on Godfrey's weekly CBS broadcast *Arthur Godfrey and Friends* and on ABC's *Country Music Jubilee,* but there were no follow-up hits. Her September 1957 marriage to second husband Charlie Dick resulted in a tumultuous relationship glamorized in *Sweet Dreams,* the 1985 film of Cline's life, starring Jessica Lange. By the end of 1957 Cline had retreated into semiretirement.

After giving birth to a daughter (Julia) in August 1958, Cline moved to Nashville and signed with manager RANDY HUGHES, who attempted to revive her stone-cold career by

Patsy Cline

booking one-nighters across the country and helping her ride out her Four Star contract. Back to working $50 gigs, she was at the nadir of her career when the GRAND OLE OPRY belatedly made her a member on January 9, 1960. That summer she signed with Decca, and Bradley began to direct her toward becoming a leading exponent of the emergent NASHVILLE SOUND, beginning with her recording of the HARLAN HOWARD–HANK COCHRAN tune "I Fall to Pieces." Cline initially fought Bradley's lush arrangements, which featured backings by the JORDANAIRES.

Cline gave birth to a son (Randy) in January 1961 and survived a near-fatal car accident in June as "Pieces" slowly started its climb up the charts, reaching #1 country in August and #12 pop eight months after its release. Cline maintained her chart momentum with the Top Ten hits "Crazy" and "She's Got You" and with albums such as *Patsy Cline Showcase* and *Sentimentally Yours*. Other highlights included appearances at Carnegie Hall and the Hollywood Bowl, and on Dick Clark's *American Bandstand*. Cline joined "The Johnny Cash Show" as the touring group's star female vocalist in January 1962, and over the next fourteen months she played numerous dates with Cash's "family," which included DON GIBSON, GEORGE JONES, CARL PERKINS, JUNE CARTER, BARBARA MANDRELL, GORDON TERRY, and Johnny Western.

Cline related premonitions of her death to close friends LORETTA LYNN, DOTTIE WEST, and JUNE CARTER as early as September 1962. Her last public performance was a benefit in Kansas City, March 3, 1963. Returning home, she was killed in a plane crash that also took the lives of pilot Randy Hughes and fellow Opry stars COWBOY COPAS and HAWKSHAW HAWKINS. Ironically in death as in life, Cline's posthumously released singles "Leavin' on Your Mind" and "Sweet Dreams" both charted Top Ten. Numerous new recordings have appeared since her death, and she has remained one of the MCA label's most consistent sellers. The subject of both *Sweet Dreams* and the hit 1990s play *Always . . . Patsy Cline*, she was voted into the Country Music Hall of Fame in 1973.
—*Margaret Jones*

REPRESENTATIVE RECORDINGS

The Patsy Cline Collection, MCA (1991); *Walkin' Dreams: Her First Recordings, Volume 1*, (Rhino, 1989); *Hungry for Love: Her First Recordings, Volume 2* (Rhino, 1989); *The Rockin' Side: Her First Recordings, Volume 3* (Rhino, 1989); *Live at the Opry* (MCA, 1988)

Clogging

Clogging is a form of percussive rhythmic dance performed on toes and heels, to music with duple or 6/8 time. The elemental clogging step (called a "basic") consists of a double toe (two-tap movement) followed by a transfer of weight to the opposite foot. Although sometimes referred to as "square dance in overdrive" and often performed to similar music, clogging did not descend directly from square dancing, but rather from several kinds of individual European step-dancing.

English clogging (rendered by industrial workers in their wooden-soled clogs, and eventually perfected in North England music halls) and jig-influenced Irish step-dancing, or "shoe music," immigrated to North America during the eighteenth and nineteenth centuries. This melded dance form, which eventually incorporated sliding movements from Cherokee ceremonial dances and synco-

pation from African-descended slave dances, became a popular feature in vaudeville and traveling minstrel shows and later at folk music festivals.

According to clogging authority Ira Bernstein, the American dance now known as clogging got its name in 1939, when Sam Queen's Soco Gap Dancers were asked to perform at the White House for President Franklin D. Roosevelt and the queen of England, who likened the distinctive performance to the clog dancing performed in her own country.

In the 1940s and 1950s American clogging benefited from the growing popularity of square dances, where showing off clogging steps became a popular diversion during breaks between dance sets. In 1968 the National Clogging and Hoe-Down Council organized to standardize steps. Other institutions and activities followed, including the U.S. National Clogging Competition, the National Clogging Hall of Fame, the National Cloggers Association, and numerous conventions, workshops, and championships offering trophies and cash prizes. Currently there are more than 600 clogging dance groups in the United States and abroad. Clogging is performed to country, bluegrass, and even rock & roll music—anything with a steady beat—often with directions called out by a "cuer." Cloggers wear leather shoes with two metal taps sandwiched together, called "jingle taps." In performance (called "precision clogging"), dancers usually form a line, and although encouraged to improvise, they follow certain choreographed formation steps.

Although many consider "buck dancing" a subgenre of contemporary clogging, there are distinctive differences. According to traditional dance expert Jackie Christian, clogging (which evolved primarily in the southern Appalachians) has English and Scots-Irish roots, and is danced with an erect upper body, on the toes, with an emphasis on "down" rhythms. Buck dancing, on the other hand, has African-based roots, and is performed flat-footed, lower to the floor than clogging, with more fluid body movements and an emphasis on the "up" rhythms (the sixteenth notes between eighth notes).
—*Patricia Hall*

Jerry Clower
b. Liberty, Mississippi, September 28, 1926

One of the most successful country comedians ever and a mainstay on TNN shows, Clower got into show business at age nine, he says, when he joined a 4-H club to get out of a class. Four years later, at thirteen, he won a 4-H district competition, but it was a long time before he became a professional entertainer. While in the navy he was asked to tell some of his stories, and later, after becoming a fertilizer field representative with Mississippi Chemical Company, he used country stories as part of his sales technique. Clower became so well known for his routines that a friend suggested he record an album of them. This LP, *Jerry Clower from Yazoo City Mississippi Talkin'*, was released on the Lemon label and advertised only by word of mouth. It sold more than 8,000 copies in a relatively short time and brought Clower to the attention of MCA. The company signed him to a contract in 1971. His album eventually made it on the *Billboard* charts for a long stay. This was followed by several other strong-selling LPs, including *Clower Power* and *From the Mouth of Mississippi*, which led to Clower joining the GRAND OLE OPRY in 1973.

In addition to performing live comic routines, Clower has hosted the nationally syndicated radio show *Country Crossroads* and the TV show *Nashville on the Road*. Clower is also the subject of a documentary film, *Ain't God Good*.

Clower's routines are based on people he knew growing up in Amite County, Mississippi. He has written three books based on this material, the most recent being *Stories from Home* (1992). In addition to his comedy, Clower is very serious about his religious beliefs, being a Baptist deacon and an active member of the Gideon Bible Society. He says Christianity is the single greatest influence on his life. He is also a passionate advocate of education, family life, and racial equality and integration. —*W. K. McNeil*

CMA

established in Nashville, Tennessee, November 1958

The Country Music Association was organized in 1958 amid the rise of rock & roll, which temporarily cut into country record sales, road show receipts, and radio exposure. Country publishers, disc jockeys, recording executives, artists, songwriters, managers, and promoters banded together to boost public awareness of country music and gain more radio and TV exposure by convincing broadcasters and advertisers of the music's selling power.

A move to reform the five-year-old Country Music Disc Jockeys Association (CMDJA) led to the creation of a new, more active, and more comprehensive organization. In the summer of 1958 CMDJA dissolved itself, and a caretaker CMA committee took charge pending formal organization of CMA at the annual DJ CONVENTION in Nashville the following November. The founding president was broadcasting mogul CONNIE B. GAY; the founding board chairman was music publisher WESLEY ROSE. Veteran broadcaster HARRY STONE was named the CMA's first executive director, but in November 1959 he relinquished his position. In 1962 the CMA board appointed secretary JO WALKER-MEADOR as executive director; she held the CMA's top post until ED BENSON took over in 1992.

The CMA set about increasing the number of full-time country radio stations (a mere eighty-one in 1961) through demographic research, sales kits, and special presentations to broadcasters' and advertisers' conventions. These efforts, combined with a national trend toward radio market segmentation along stylistic lines, helped push the ranks of country stations past the 600 mark in 1969.

In 1961 CMA created the COUNTRY MUSIC HALL OF FAME. Plaques were displayed at the Tennessee State Museum in downtown Nashville until the opening of the COUNTRY MUSIC HALL OF FAME and Museum on April 1, 1967. CMA had spearheaded the campaign to erect this building, partly financed by a special telemarketed album of performances by numerous artists—one of the first such projects in music marketing history.

In that same year, CMA held its first awards show, in Nashville, and in 1968, largely through the efforts of WSM's IRVING WAUGH and publisher JACK STAPP, the program was televised for the first time, as part of the NBC *Kraft Music Hall* series. Since then, the number of full-time country stations in the United States has surpassed 2,000, membership has climbed to 7,000, and CMA opened an office in the United Kingdom in 1982. —*John Rumble*

CMF

established in Nashville, Tennessee, 1964

The Country Music Foundation (CMF), a tax-exempt educational and charitable organization headquartered in Nashville, operates the COUNTRY MUSIC HALL OF FAME and Museum and is the world's largest and most active popular music research center. Early in the 1960s, as CMA's campaign to publicize country music was shifting into high gear, CMA leaders determined that a new organization was needed to carry out research and educational activities beyond the scope of the CMA trade organization. Therefore, the CMF was chartered by the state of Tennessee in 1964 to collect, preserve, and publicize information and artifacts relating to the history of country music. The new entity existed largely on paper until the Country Music Hall of Fame and Museum opened on April 1, 1967. Located on Music Row, the museum was erected on the site of a small Nashville city park. At this point, museum artifacts began to be displayed and a small library was begun in a loft above the museum.

Early in the 1970s the basement of the Hall of Fame building was partially completed and library expansion began, embracing not only recordings but also books and periodicals, sheet music and songbooks, photographs, business documents, and other materials. CMA and CMF boards of directors have continued to overlap (both consist of leading country music executives and entertainers), but at this point CMF acquired its own small staff, which has steadily increased to about thirty-five full-time professionals.

Building expansions took place in 1974, 1977, and 1984. An education department was created to conduct ongoing programs with Middle Tennessee schools, an oral history program was begun, and a publications department was launched to handle books as well as the foundation's *Journal of Country Music*. CMF also began to reissue historic recordings on its own label and to provide consulting services for other labels as well. Its Hall of Fame and Museum offers more than 20,000 square feet of exhibits displaying costumes, films, historic cars, and a large collection of instruments. In addition, the foundation owns and operates Studio B—RCA RECORDS' Nashville recording studio from 1957 to 1977—as a historic site and operational studio, as well as HATCH SHOW PRINT, a historic show-business letterpress printing firm opened in 1879. —*John Rumble*

CMT

established in Nashville, Tennessee, March 6, 1983

Airing country music videos twenty-four hours a day, Country Music Television (CMT) has become the most powerful vehicle for breaking new acts and establishing artist identities. The all-video channel was launched as CMTV on March 6, 1983, from the facilities of Video World International in Hendersonville, Tennessee. GAYLORD ENTERTAINMENT COMPANY and Group W Satellite Communications acquired the network, now called CMT, in January 1991. From that time, CMT has operated at 2806 Opryland Drive in Nashville.

Strictly a video channel, CMT provides instant exposure for new country music acts and often is the first outlet for new single releases, as the accompanying video generally precedes the single's radio debut by two to three weeks. CMT's importance has been recognized throughout the record industry. Such artists as BILLY RAY CYRUS and TRAVIS TRITT have pointed to the role of CMT in starting their careers. In an interview with the trade magazine *Gavin Report,* DWIGHT YOAKAM stated that "the biggest change in country music has to do with CMT's impact on the marketing of country music and its artists."

In the 1990s CMT began expanding to overseas markets. On October 19, 1992, CMT International was launched in Europe; on October 4, 1994, in the Asia-Pacific region; and on April 1, 1995, in Latin America.

In February 1997 Gaylord Entertainment announced the impending sale of its domestic interests in CMT and The Nashville Network (TNN) to Westinghouse for $1.55 billion in stock, retaining only CMT's international division. In 1998 CMT International announced a shift in focus from Europe to the Latin American and Australian markets. —*Bob Paxman*

Cy Coben
b. Jersey City, New Jersey, April 4, 1919

Cyrus Coben's songwriting brought a twist of urban wit to country music during the 1950s and 1960s.

He attended Jersey City's Lincoln High School and New York's Clinton School of Music. He went on to play trumpet in local bands and with the Jersey City Symphony. Coben began writing pop songs in the early 1940s and scored his first hit for Benny Goodman in 1942. World War II interrupted his career with a stint in the navy. Later, joining ASCAP in 1947, he became one of the earliest members to be heavily involved in country music.

Coben first wrote for country artists after a chance meeting with Charles Grean, STEVE SHOLES's assistant in RCA VICTOR's country division. Coben's uncomplicated, often humorous stories appropriately landed with RCA's EDDY ARNOLD, who, in the early 1950s, was experimenting with the simplistic, lyrical themes of the day. He posted hits with Coben's "There's Been a Change in Me" (1951), "I Wanna Play House with You" (1951), "Older and Bolder" (1952), and "Hep Cat Baby" (1954).

STEVE SHOLES, and later his successor CHET ATKINS, frequently tapped Coben for material. Coben responded prolifically with hits for RCA artists such as "Lady's Man" (HANK SNOW, 1952), "Beware of 'It'" (JOHNNIE & JACK, 1954), "I'm Hurtin' Inside" (JIM REEVES, 1955), "The Great El Tigre (The Tiger)" (STU PHILLIPS, 1966), and "Johnny's Cash and Charley's Pride" (MAC WISEMAN, 1969).

Although most of Coben's songs incorporated novelty, his writing could exhibit sensitivity, as in "Burning a Hole in My Mind" (CONNIE SMITH, 1967) and "A Good Woman's Love" (BILL MONROE, 1957). Coben stopped writing in the 1980s, and today oversees his vast song catalogue. —*Michael Streissguth*

Eddie Cochran
b. Oklahoma City, Oklahoma, October 3, 1938; d. April 17, 1960

Though he died tragically at an early age, rock & roll singer and guitarist Eddie Cochran assured his place in pop music history when he co-wrote the classic "Summertime Blues" with partner Jerry Capehart.

Raised in Albert Lea, Minnesota, Edward Ray Cochran was living in the Bell Gardens suburb of Los Angeles by the time he reached his teens. In 1954 he performed and recorded as one of a country duo, the Cochran Brothers, with future songwriting great HANK COCHRAN (not related).

Eddie Cochran made his national chart debut with a remake of "Sittin' in the Balcony," originally recorded by Johnny Dee (songwriter JOHN D. LOUDERMILK). Cochran's breakthrough came in late 1958, when his recording of "Summertime Blues" became a Top Ten pop hit. Cochran appeared in several rock & roll–oriented films but had only modest success on the pop charts after "Summertime Blues." While in England, where he enjoyed great popularity and was touring for a second time with fellow rock & roller Gene Vincent, Cochran died in a car crash on April 17, 1960, near Chippenham, Wiltshire.

Rock groups Blue Cheer and the Who had hits with "Summertime Blues" in 1968 and 1970, respectively, and ALAN JACKSON's version of the song, with accompanying water ski video, was a #1 country hit in 1994. Cochran was inducted into the Rock and Roll Hall of Fame in 1987. —*Jay Orr*

REPRESENTATIVE RECORDINGS
Legendary Masters Series, Volume 1 (EMI, 1990); *Singin' to My Baby & Never to Be Forgotten* (EMI, 1993)

Hank Cochran
b. Isola, Mississippi, August 2, 1935

Along with such figures as HARLAN HOWARD, JOHN D. LOUDERMILK, BILL ANDERSON, and DALLAS FRAZIER, Hank Cochran defined country songwriting in the 1960s, and he has continued to be a major creative force in Nashville into the 1990s.

Garland Perry "Hank" Cochran spent part of his childhood in a Memphis orphanage. He dropped out of school and eventually moved to California. Future rockabilly star EDDIE COCHRAN (no relation) became his partner in the

Hank Cochran

Cochran Brothers. They appeared on TV's *Town Hall Party* and briefly backed LEFTY FRIZZELL.

After having songs published by PAMPER MUSIC while he was in California, Cochran moved to Nashville in 1959, where he was signed by Pamper at $50 a week to write and plug songs. SKEETS MCDONALD recorded his "Where You Go I'll Follow" in November 1959, and other stars followed suit in the 1960s: PATSY CLINE ("She's Got You," "I Fall to Pieces"), ERNEST TUBB ("Through That Door"), EDDY ARNOLD ("Make the World Go Away," "I Want to Go with You"), GEORGE JONES ("You Comb Her Hair"), BURL IVES ("A Little Bitty Tear"), JIM REEVES ("I'd Fight the World"), and RAY PRICE ("Don't You Ever Get Tired of Hurting Me," "A Way to Survive") among them. Most of his big hits were written solo, but at times Cochran has co-written with such notables as HARLAN HOWARD; WILLIE NELSON; and, since the 1980s, DEAN DILLON.

In 1962 Ives's recording of Cochran's "Funny Way of Laughing" won a Grammy Award, and in 1966 JEANNIE SEELY's version of his "Don't Touch Me" did, too. Cochran and Seely were married from 1969 to 1979; she saluted him with the 1967 LP *Thanks Hank*.

Over the years, Cochran has made several records himself. In addition to Cochran Brothers efforts on Ekko, he has recorded for LIBERTY, RCA, Gaylord, MONUMENT, CAPITOL, and ELEKTRA. Cochran's biggest hit as a singer was 1962's "Sally Was a Good Old Girl." He sometimes harmonized with good friend Nelson, who nicknamed him "Hanktum" and featured him in the 1980 film *Honeysuckle Rose*.

Cochran's 1970s successes included "It's Not Love (But It's Not Bad)" for MERLE HAGGARD and "Why Can't He Be You" for LORETTA LYNN. His 1980s credits included MICKEY GILLEY's "That's All That Matters to Me," VERN GOSDIN's "What Would Your Memories Do," and GEORGE STRAIT's "The Chair" and "Ocean Front Property."

In the 1990s LORRIE MORGAN and Etta James both revived "Don't Touch Me." Cochran entered the Nashville Songwriters Hall of Fame in 1974. Currently the head of Co-Heart Music Group, a publishing firm, he recorded a 1996 duet album with Billy Don Burns. —*Robert K. Oermann*

David Allan Coe

b. Akron, Ohio, September 6, 1939

A genuine country music eccentric, David Allan Coe is an accomplished singer-songwriter, gifted mimic, and often brilliant performance artist whose personal excesses often obscured his many talents and subverted his career.

Coe arrived in Nashville in 1967 after almost a lifetime of incarceration, including a stint at the Ohio State Penitentiary. His claims to have spent time on Death Row for killing another inmate have been questioned as dubious, and were the first of many "image" ploys that would backfire on the fledgling musician.

Though he had recorded for SHELBY SINGLETON's Plantation label, Coe first achieved recognition as a songwriter, providing a #1 hit for TANYA TUCKER in 1973 with "Would You Lay with Me (In a Field of Stone)." By the time he signed with the COLUMBIA label in 1973, he had adopted the stage persona of the Mysterious Rhinestone Cowboy (complete with mask) and attached himself to the burgeoning progressive country, later known as music of the OUTLAW movement. Despite significant success as a recording artist—"You Never Even Called Me By My Name" (1975, written by Steve Goodman), "Longhaired Redneck"

(1976), and "Willie, Waylon and Me" (1976)—Coe's career stalled in the late 1970s.

The popularity of GLEN CAMPBELL's 1976 hit "Like a Rhinestone Cowboy" effectively undermined Coe's image, and his popularity suffered from his own penchant for peppering his live performances with obscenities and graphic sexual allusions. After providing JOHNNY PAYCHECK with a #1 hit song, "Take This Job and Shove It" (1977), Coe rarely surfaced on the charts as either a singer or a songwriter.

Country audiences, it seemed, tired of Coe's outlaw posturing—his sporting of 365 tattoos, his claims of polygamy with as many as seven women (allegedly the product of a conversion to Mormonism), his affiliation with a motorcycle gang (appropriately named the Outlaws)—and it wasn't until 1983 that he gained another Top Ten hit with "The Ride" (written by Gary Gentry). Coe's final successes to date came in 1984 with the COLUMBIA release of one of his finest compositions, "Mona Lisa Lost Her Smile," which reached #2, and then "She Used to Love Me a Lot," #11. Neither Coe's recording of at least six sexually explicit albums nor the publication of two books (an autobiography and a pornographic novel, *The Psychopath*) garnered much more than cult notoriety for the once-promising artist.

Images aside, Coe's recorded legacy is substantial, revealing a songwriter of lyrical sensitivity ("Jody Like a Melody") and a singer of masculine bravado ("Jack Daniels if You Please"). —*Stephen R. Tucker*

REPRESENTATIVE RECORDINGS

The Mysterious Rhinestone Cowboy (Columbia, 1974); *Super Hits* (Columbia, 1993)

Paul Cohen

b. Chicago, Illinois, November 10, 1908; d. April 1, 1970

Chicago-born Paul E. Cohen, longtime DECCA RECORDS executive, was one of the men chiefly responsible for Nashville's emergence as country music's recording capital.

Cohen first entered the record business with COLUMBIA in the late 1920s, but in 1934 he joined DECCA's newly formed American operation, organized by the brothers JACK and DAVE KAPP—old Chicago friends of Cohen's. Cohen moved to Cincinnati to become Decca's midwestern branch manager in 1935; in this role he was responsible for scouting and signing new talent in addition to marketing records. During World War II he gradually took over Decca's hillbilly production work from Dave Kapp, and in the mid-1940s moved to New York to head that branch of the company.

With two of Decca's main country stars at Nashville's GRAND OLE OPRY—ERNEST TUBB and RED FOLEY—Cohen, in August 1947, began regular recording of his country roster in CASTLE RECORDING's new studios. They were located in the Tulane Hotel at Eighth Avenue North and Church Street in Nashville. Musicians Beasley Smith and OWEN BRADLEY helped Cohen schedule his intense, two- to three-week Nashville visits by lining up stars, musicians, and arrangements (many of them created on the spot). Cohen is remembered for an energetic production style—as much cheerleader as executive—and a knack for spotting new artists and matching them with songs, often published by his own companies. KITTY WELLS, WEBB PIERCE, BRENDA LEE, PATSY CLINE, and BOBBY HELMS were among the new acts signed to Decca during Cohen's tenure, while Tubb,

Paul Cohen

Foley, JIMMIE DAVIS, and others continued to have success with the label.

Cohen left Decca's country department early in 1958 (replaced by Owen Bradley some weeks later), first to do pop production for Decca's Coral subsidiary. Soon Cohen launched his own company, Todd Records, and besides signing such country acts as PEE WEE KING and Dub Dickerson, the label enjoyed a pop hit, Joe Henderson's "Snap Your Fingers." In 1964 Cohen rejoined his old boss Dave Kapp as head of Kapp Records' country division in Nashville. In four years at Kapp, Cohen signed and produced Hugh X. Lewis, CAL SMITH, Billy Edd Wheeler, and MEL TILLIS, among others. Cohen's last major executive position was as head of ABC's Nashville office (1968–69), a position he left after being diagnosed with cancer.

As president of the CMA, Cohen was on board when the COUNTRY MUSIC HALL OF FAME opened in 1967. He died in Bryan, Texas, on April 1, 1970, and was buried in nearby College Station. In an unprecedented gesture, Nashville's Music Row offices closed for a memorial service a week later (April 7), but a lasting testimony to his memory and importance came with his posthumous election to the COUNTRY MUSIC HALL OF FAME in 1976.   —*Ronnie Pugh*

Nudie Cohn (*see* Nudie the Rodeo Tailor)

Ben Colder (*see* Sheb Wooley)

M. M. Cole (*see* M. M. Cole Music, under *M*)

Biff Collie
b. Little Rock, Arkansas, November 25, 1926; d. February 19, 1992

Hiram Abiff "Biff" Collie was a pioneer country disc jockey, show promoter, and trade reporter. Born in Little Rock, Collie was raised in San Antonio and first worked in radio there at KMAC, in 1943. After military service, he returned to Texas radio work and in 1948 became Houston's first and most popular country disc jockey at KNUZ, later promoting big shows at Cook's Hoedown Club. He made his first recordings for Houston's Macy's Records and later recorded for COLUMBIA, Specialty, and STARDAY (early 1950s), but his only charted record came in 1972 as "Billy Bob Bowman" for United Artists. At Columbia he recorded with "Little Marge" Tillman, wife of FLOYD TILLMAN, who in

1953 became Collie's first wife. (After a divorce, Collie married Shirley Caddell.)

Collie emceed the PHILIP MORRIS COUNTRY MUSIC SHOW (1957–58), then moved to Southern California, ultimately becoming one of the many top DJs on KFOX in Long Beach, where he stayed until 1969. Just as he had taken one songwriter's wife, so another songwriter—WILLIE NELSON—took his wife in 1962, when second wife Shirley Collie became the second Mrs. Nelson. By this time Biff Collie had found an auxiliary career as trade paper reporter; later he started a radio reporting service. During the 1970s and 1980s he produced and hosted several network or syndicated radio programs.

Elected to the Country DJ Hall of Fame in 1978, Collie was a guiding force behind ROPE, and briefly operated his own station, Brentwood, Tennessee's, WWCR (1985–86).
      —*Ronnie Pugh*

Mark Collie
b. Waynesboro, Tennessee, January 18, 1956

At a time when most of Nashville's new male country acts were duplicating the GEORGE STRAIT–inspired hat-and-boot look and new traditionalist sound, Mark Collie has remained an individualist. His high-energy, rock-tinged country music is electric, and it offers hints of rockabilly and r&b.

Born in Waynesboro, between Nashville and Memphis, George Mark Collie grew up listening to country music, and he began playing in bands at age twelve. As a young adult he continued to tour the Southeast playing music, and after a stint in Hawaii, he attempted to join the armed forces but was refused because of his diabetes. Collie moved to Nashville in 1982 with his wife, Anne, but his dreams of becoming a staff songwriter didn't pan out. He began writing songs for himself and eventually playing a regular gig at the city's Douglas Corner Cafe.

As his popularity grew, Collie arranged a showcase in 1989: He was heard by MCA's producer and creative director TONY BROWN and signed the next day. His first album, *Hardin County Line* (1990), yielded three singles but no hits, and it wasn't until his second album, *Born and Raised in Black and White,* that Collie found a toehold in the country scene—"She's Never Comin' Back" reached #28 in 1991. Then 1993's *Mark Collie* produced the hits "Even the Man in the Moon is Crying" (#5, 1992) and "Born to Love You" (#6, 1993), and Collie was well on his way.

Although he ultimately released four albums for MCA—his fourth album, *Unleashed,* yielded a #13 hit, "Hard Lovin' Woman," in 1994—Collie didn't break into the upper echelon of country superstars. Collie's live show remained strong, though; when he joined GIANT RECORDS, producer JAMES STROUD and Collie pursued an aggressive, live sound for his fifth album, *Tennessee Plates.* Drawing from material written by the likes of JOHN HIATT and TONY JOE WHITE, it features seven tunes written by Collie himself. The album's "Three Words, Two Hearts, One Night" reached #25 in 1995.

Collie remains visible through his charity work with the annual Celebrity Race for Diabetes Cure. This event calls on the participation of NASCAR legend drivers and country music celebrities in a car race to help raise money for diabetes research.   —*Clark Parsons*

REPRESENTATIVE RECORDINGS
Mark Collie (MCA, 1993); *Tennessee Plates* (Giant, 1995)

Tom Collins

b. Lenoir City, Tennessee, May 30, 1942

One of Nashville's most awarded and acclaimed producers and publishers, Bernie Tom Collins has received seven Grammy Award nominations and three CMA awards as Producer of the Year. Some of those honors came from his production work with such artists as BARBARA MANDRELL, RONNIE MILSAP, SYLVIA, STEVE WARINER, MARIE OSMOND, and flutist James Galway.

Collins grew up in Lenoir City, Tennessee, and attended the University of Tennessee at Knoxville, receiving a bachelor of science degree with majors in psychology, zoology, and political science. An interest in dentistry was outweighed by his fascination with music. He moved to Nashville in 1970 when he was hired by Jack D. Johnson and CHARLEY PRIDE at Pi-Gem Music.

In 1982 Collins established his own publishing company, Tom Collins Music, which soon received the Robert J. Burton Award from BMI for the Most Performed Song of the Year: "Nobody," recorded by RCA artist Sylvia and written by Dennis Morgan and Kye Fleming. In the years since, Collins's various publishing operations have continued to grow, making him one of Nashville's most successful independent publishers. In 1991 Tom Collins Music acquired the valuable catalogue of hit songwriter TOM T. HALL.

—*Gerry Wood*

Tommy Collins

b. near Oklahoma City, Oklahoma, September 28, 1930

Immortalized by his friend MERLE HAGGARD's 1980 song "Leonard," Leonard Raymond Sipes, better known as Tommy Collins, was one of the first recording artists to set the standard for country music's BAKERSFIELD Sound in the early 1950s. In addition, Collins's intellectual and humorous songwriting style has strongly influenced such songwriters as Haggard and ROGER MILLER (who once told Tommy "I got my *attitude* for songwriting from you").

While attending college near Oklahoma City, Leonard Sipes worked as a DJ and performer on local radio station KLPR and, in 1951, recorded four sides with the small Morgan label out of Fresno, California. He arrived in Bakersfield in 1952, having traveled there with WANDA JACKSON and her family on their vacation, and was immediately befriended by a young recording artist–disc jockey named Terry Preston (whose given name was FERLIN HUSKY). It was Husky who renamed Sipes "Tommy Collins" when, during a recording session, one of the musicians ordered a Tom Collins drink.

By 1953, Collins was writing songs for CLIFFIE STONE's CENTRAL SONGS firm and recording for CAPITOL RECORDS. Husky played guitar on Collins's first session; beginning with the second session and on into 1957, BUCK OWENS replaced Husky on lead guitar. Collins's Top Ten country hits from these years, including "You Better Not Do That," "Whatcha Gonna Do Now," "Untied," and "It Tickles," significantly influenced the guitar-driven, live sound that came to be associated with Bakersfield.

Everything changed for Collins in 1956, though, when he felt the call to enter the ministry and the following year enrolled at the Golden Gate Theological Seminary at Berkeley, California. A few years later, however, he began to miss songwriting and recording. After hearing Merle Haggard's 1963–64 hit "Sing a Sad Song" on the radio,

Tommy Collins

Collins sought out Haggard. The two became friends while fishing together on the Kern River and participating in each other's sessions. In 1964 Merle recorded Collins's "Sam Hill" and throughout the next two decades recorded many more of Collins's compositions, including "Carolyn" and "The Roots of My Raising."

In 1966 Collins began recording for COLUMBIA RECORDS, turning out such hits as "If You Can't Bite, Don't Growl." He recorded a 1972 album for STARDAY RECORDS and moved to Nashville in 1976.

Beginning with Ferlin Husky and FARON YOUNG in the early fifties, Collins's songs have been recorded and rerecorded by country music's greatest stars. Young's 1954 hit of "If You Ain't Lovin' (You Ain't Livin')," a Collins composition, was also a #1 song for GEORGE STRAIT in 1988.

—*Dale Vinicur*

REPRESENTATIVE RECORDINGS

The Dynamic Tommy Collins (Columbia, 1966, out of print); *Tommy Collins Calling* (Starday, 1972); *Leonard* (Bear Family, 1992), 5 discs

Collins Kids

Lawrence "Larry" Albert Collins b. Tulsa, Oklahoma, October 4, 1944
Lawrencine "Lorrie" May Collins b. Tulsa, Oklahoma, May 7, 1942

The brother-sister team of Lorrie Collins and Larry Collins are premier examples of California's rockabilly sound. They signed in 1955 to COLUMBIA RECORDS, but their fifties and early sixties releases, greatly admired today, failed to enter the charts.

At age eight Lorrie won a talent contest in Tulsa hosted by LEON MCAULIFFE, who encouraged her parents to take her to California for greater professional exposure. After the family moved to Southern California, Lorrie appeared on several local programs, and Larry won a talent contest on a local country radio program, the *Squeakin' Deacon Show.* A successful audition led to a regular position on the

TOWN HALL PARTY TV program beginning in February 1954. The pair were noted for colorful costumes and more colorful performances. Larry was an outstanding double-neck guitarist, trained by JOE MAPHIS, while Lorrie handled the lead vocals. Appearances on several major radio and television programs, including the *OZARK JUBILEE*, the *Steve Allen Show*, and the GRAND OLE OPRY extended their influence. In 1958 she began dating RICKY NELSON, but the relationship proved to be short-lived.

The Collins Kids toured with JOHNNY CASH's road show, where Lorrie met Cash's manager, Stu Carnall, whom she married in late 1959. Lorrie and Larry dissolved their act in 1961 after the birth of Lorrie's first child. Larry continued to record as a solo act, although without chart success. He is as an accomplished songwriter, however, with such country hits to his credit as "Delta Dawn" and "You're the Reason God Made Oklahoma." Several reissue LPs have appeared in the United States and Europe, and the two reunite for occasional appearances.   —*William P. Davis*

REPRESENTATIVE RECORDING

Introducing Larry and Lorrie . . . The Collins Kids (Sony Music, 1983)

Jessi Colter
b. Phoenix, Arizona, May 25, 1943

With her religious upbringing and refined manner, singer-songwriter Jessi Colter seemed to be an unlikely participant in the Outlaw movement that transformed country music in the 1970s. Yet the hazel-eyed beauty's tremulous voice disguised the fact that she was no more obedient to Music Row convention than the rowdy "Willie, Waylon, and the boys."

Profoundly influenced by her mother—an ordained Pentecostal minister—Jessi joined the church choir at age six and became its pianist five years later. She was discovered in Phoenix by celebrated rock & roll guitarist Duane Eddy, who produced her first recording on the Jamie label. Released under Colter's real name of Mirriam Johnson in 1961, the single "Lonesome Road" revealed a style aptly described on the picture sleeve as a mixture of "church music with western music . . . and overtones of the blues." In 1962 the singer married Eddy, and they eventually settled in California.

After the marriage ended in divorce in 1968, she returned to Phoenix and took the stage name from her great-great uncle Jesse Colter, a member of the notorious James Gang. It was there that she met rising star WAYLON JENNINGS, who would not only become her second husband the following year but also would be instrumental in nurturing her career in Nashville.

A Country Star Is Born (RCA, 1970), the debut LP co-produced by Jennings, proved to be mistitled, as Colter's vocal and songwriting talents came to fruition five years later at CAPITOL RECORDS. Spearheaded by "I'm Not Lisa," a #1 crossover lament that netted two Grammy nominations, *I'm Jessi Colter* was certified gold. It was followed into the pop album charts by *Jessi* (1976), and Colter scored hit singles with two other original compositions: "What's Happened to Blue Eyes" (#5, 1975) and "It's Morning" (#11, 1976).

Colter has not revisited the Top Forty as a solo artist since 1976. Nevertheless, her presence on RCA's platinum *Wanted: The Outlaws* collection from that year, as well as

Waylon & Jessi duets such as the self-penned "Storms Never Last" (#17, 1981), maintained her profile in country circles through the early 1980s.   —*Pete Loesch*

REPRESENTATIVE RECORDINGS

I'm Jessi Colter (Capitol, 1975); *Jessi Colter Collection* (Liberty, 1995)

Columbia Records
established in Washington, D.C., 1889

Columbia Records began as a distributor for Edison phonographs and supplies. In the early 1890s the company began to produce its own machines and cylinder records. It entered the disc record market in 1902 and gradually abandoned cylinder production over the next decade. Columbia's first "race" records (aimed toward the African-American market) came out in 1921. In September 1924 the company brought the blind minstrel ERNEST THOMPSON, the North Carolina fiddle and banjo team of SAMANTHA BUMGARNER & Eva Davis, and North Georgia's GID TANNER and RILEY PUCKETT to New York to make the company's first country records.

In 1923 Columbia introduced the 14000-D catalogue series exclusively for African-American music. Early in 1925 the 15000-D series was added for white country music. Its prominent artists included Gid Tanner's Skillet Lickers (with Puckett), CHARLIE POOLE, SMITH'S SACRED SINGERS, VERNON DALHART, and DARBY & TARLTON.

In 1926 Columbia acquired the General Phonograph Corporation and its OKEH label, which continued to operate independently of Columbia. OKeh country artists included FIDDLIN' JOHN CARSON, NARMOUR & SMITH, and FRANK HUTCHISON. The label went into eclipse in 1932.

Columbia's 15000-D series lasted through 1932; the company was sold, resold, and eventually purchased in 1934 by the BRUNSWICK (later American) Record Corporation (ARC), which gradually limited Columbia label releases to classical and ethnic material. ARC released country and "race" items on a series of low-priced labels, including Banner, Melotone, Oriole, Perfect, Romeo, Vocalion, and CONQUEROR, a Sears, Roebuck label. The series' major country artists included ROY ACUFF, GENE AUTRY, BOB WILLS, the PRAIRIE RAMBLERS (with PATSY MONTANA), and BILL & CLIFF CARLISLE.

When the Columbia Broadcasting System (CBS) purchased ARC in 1938, only the Vocalion and Conqueror labels remained. (ART SATHERLEY, an ARC employee at the time of the purchase, continued as the head of A&R for hillbilly and race divisions of Columbia until 1952.) In 1940 Vocalion was discontinued as the old OKeh label was revived. Conqueror was dropped in 1942; OKeh was dropped again in 1945 as country music began to appear once again on Columbia, for the first time since 1932.

In 1945 the Columbia roster still included Autry, Acuff, and Wills. New additions in the postwar years included BILL MONROE, MOLLY O'DAY, and the BAILES BROTHERS. By the early 1950s Columbia's impressive stable included CARL SMITH, LEFTY FRIZZELL, the STANLEY BROTHERS, MARTY ROBBINS, RAY PRICE, WILMA LEE & STONEY COOPER, LITTLE JIMMY DICKENS, FLATT & SCRUGGS, and GEORGE MORGAN.

In June 1948 Columbia introduced the modern long-play (LP) record, primarily to present uninterrupted versions of classical and other longer works. When 12-inch LPs began to dominate the market in the mid-1950s, Columbia produced albums by all its major country artists, as it continues to do in the compact disc era.

DON LAW headed the country division of Columbia from 1952 to 1967 and was followed in that role by FRANK JONES until 1973 (with BOB JOHNSTON as head of A&R), Ron Bledsoe into the late 1970s (with BILLY SHERRILL as head of A&R), RICK BLACKBURN in the 1980s, ROY WUNSCH from the late 1980s to the mid-1990s, and then Allen Butler in the late 1990s. These executives presided over a leading label that enjoyed the successes of such best-selling artists from the 1960s through the 1990s as JOHNNY CASH, WILLIE NELSON, JANIE FRICKE, ROSANNE CASH, RODNEY CROWELL, and MARY CHAPIN CARPENTER.

In November 1987 the Japanese electronics giant Sony Music acquired the Columbia label and all its subsidiary labels, including EPIC.   —*Dick Spottswood*

Combine Music Publishing

established in Baltimore, Maryland, 1958; ended 1986

Founded by FRED FOSTER, in conjunction with his creation of MONUMENT RECORDS, Combine Music became a leading Nashville publishing house and a prototype of what today is called a "boutique" publisher. Foster, a frustrated record salesman working around Baltimore, established Monument first in 1958, then Combine, hoping to capture some stray copyrights.

Foster moved his companies to MUSIC CITY in 1960, locating just north of town in suburban Hendersonville. Despite Monument's success with ROY ORBISON, the early 1960s were lean years for Combine until BOB BECKHAM was hired in 1964. With Beckham running Combine, the firm nurtured such talents as DOLLY PARTON, KRIS KRISTOFFERSON, LARRY GATLIN, RAY STEVENS, JERRY REED, Dennis Linde, TONY JOE WHITE, Bob Morrison, John Scott Sherrill, Johnny MacRae, Bob DiPiero, and others.

Combine peaked in the early 1970s via Kristofferson songs such as "Me and Bobby McGee" (co-written with Foster), "Help Me Make It Through the Night," and "Sunday Morning Coming Down," and Elvis Presley's version of Linde's "Burning Love," all smashes that became pop-country standards.

Cash flow and legal problems surrounding Monument's bankruptcy led to Combine's sale to the SBK publishing operation of New York City in 1986; today the Combine copyrights belong to EMI Music.
                                                    —*John Lomax III*

Comedy

From its beginnings as a commercial art form in the 1920s, country comedy has been a part of country performance. Humor was already the centerpiece of vaudeville and minstrel shows, from which country entertainers drew heavily. Successful country comedians such as Whitey Ford (the DUKE OF PADUCAH) and James "Goober" Buchanan, as well as others, were veterans of vaudeville. MEDICINE SHOWS that visited even the most remote rural areas offered comedy along with music to lure people who sought entertainment as eagerly as they did cures for their ailments. Numerous early country musicians worked in these shows, including ROY ACUFF, who began his career in a medicine show playing both blackface and unsophisticated "rube" characters.

Radio barn dance shows and road shows required variety, and comedy became essential. JOHN LAIR, at Chicago's WLS beginning in 1928, and Lowell Blanchard, at Knox-

ville's WNOX from 1936, began writing comedy scripts that borrowed from minstrel, vaudeville, and medicine show routines as well as from traditional folk humor. These scripts were performed by entertainers such as LULU BELLE & SCOTTY and the COON CREEK GIRLS at WLS and ARCHIE CAMPBELL (as Grandpappy), BILL CARLISLE (as Hotshot Elmer), and HOMER & JETHRO at WNOX. JAMUP & HONEY, whose WSM heyday spanned the 1940s, was the best-known blackface act of its day. They followed the format and content of early minstrel and vaudeville shows, usually with a straight man and one or more comedians.

Most early traveling country bands had a comedian, usually the bass player. Such performers were often thrown into the role by necessity, as in the cases of Dave Sutherland and Chick Stripling, who did comedy with several bluegrass bands. They usually worked in street clothing until comedy time, and then dressed up in funny costumes and makeup to assume their comedic roles. However, some entertainers, such as SNUFFY JENKINS, GRANDPA JONES, and Old Joe Clark, dressed in character throughout their shows. Some comedians—Lazy Jim Day with his "singing news," Homer & Jethro, and LONZO & OSCAR—were known for their comic songs.

Several star comedians soon emerged: MINNIE PEARL, ROD BRASFIELD, and Whitey Ford (The Duke of Paducah) at the GRAND OLE OPRY; Pat Buttram, SMILEY BURNETTE, and GEORGE GOBEL at the *NATIONAL BARN DANCE;* Archie Campbell, Bill Carlisle, and Homer & Jethro at the *MIDDAY MERRY-GO-ROUND;* and Crazy Elmer and Lazy Jim Day at the *WWVA JAMBOREE.* The Opry's UNCLE DAVE MACON represented in one man what most entertainment shows wanted to present: musical artistry, comedy, sentiment, and religion, all delivered with great humor and showmanship.

Country humor reached its peak with the syndicated show *HEE HAW,* produced for twenty-three years beginning in 1969. The show was simple, rural, and corny, characteristics that would seem to guarantee failure in the modern age, but audiences loved it. *Hee Haw* helped to make household celebrities of hosts BUCK OWENS and ROY CLARK, and a cast that included such veteran comedians as Grandpa Jones, Minnie Pearl, Archie Campbell, Roni Stoneman, JUNIOR SAMPLES, George "Goober" Lindsey, STRINGBEAN, and Lulu Roman.

With the recent deaths of Archie Campbell and Minnie Pearl, few genuine stars of country comedy remain, but JERRY CLOWER and the versatile RAY STEVENS are among them. Even though comedy generally has waned, Grandpa Jones, JOHNNY RUSSELL, and MIKE SNIDER have continued to tell jokes as a part of their acts at the Grand Ole Opry, and many bluegrass bands do comedy, too. The *RENFRO VALLEY BARN DANCE* still features comedians as it always has, including Pete Stamper, Betty Lou York, Bun Wilson, and Old Joe Clark, until his death in 1998. TNN and comedy clubs offer new venues for stand-up comics, and some of them—James Gregory, JEFF FOXWORTHY, Cledus T. Judd, and Chonda Pierce, as examples—perform country-oriented routines.

The decline in country comedy has been blamed on the increasing sophistication of country's audience. Though they value the music, they may be uneasy with the old rural-oriented humor. Nevertheless, many country entertainers continue to inject humor into their shows because they enjoy making people laugh, and they know that humor makes us forget our daily problems, fears, and disappointments and gives us a joyful feeling, if only for a little while.   —*Loyal Jones*

Confederate Railroad

Danny Shirley b. Chattanooga, Tennessee, August 12, 1956

Chris McDaniel b. Rock Springs, Georgia, February 4, 1965

Wayne Secrest b. Alton, Illinois, April 29, 1950

Gates Nichols b. New York City, New York, May 26, 1944

Mark DuFresne b. Green Bay, Wisconsin, August 6, 1953

Jimmy Dormire b. Ann Arbor, Michigan, March 8, 1960

Covering the same turf as HANK WILLIAMS JR. and TRAVIS TRITT, Confederate Railroad pulls its audience from people who favor both country and southern rock. ATLANTIC RECORDS originally signed singer Danny Shirley as a solo artist. Shirley had released a series of singles on independent Amor Records (1984–88), and the Danny Shirley Band was well known in the Chattanooga-Atlanta region; they had backed JOHNNY PAYCHECK and DAVID ALLAN COE as well as played on their own. But after noting the increase in successful new male singers in the early 1990s, Shirley and Atlantic changed the group's name to Confederate Railroad and billed Shirley's album as a band effort.

Confederate Railroad's first single, "She Took It Like a Man," reached #37 in *Billboard;* the second, "Jesus and Mama," gave them their first Top Five hit. "Queen of Memphis," from the same album, reached #2 in *Billboard.* The group's sense of campy redneck humor brought them more attention: The video for the Chris Wall–penned "Trashy Women" featured band members in drag.

The group's eponymous debut album sold more than 2 million copies; its follow-up, *Notorious* (1994), also sold more than 1 million on the strength of such singles as "Daddy Never Was the Cadillac Kind" and "Elvis & Andy," a homage to Elvis Presley and Andy Griffith. The band won the ACM's Best New Vocal Group award for 1992 and toured with Lynyrd Skynyrd and the MARSHALL TUCKER BAND in 1993. Guitarist Jimmy Dormire replaced Michael Lamb in January 1995, shortly before the release of the group's third album, *Where and When.*   —*Brian Mansfield*

REPRESENTATIVE RECORDINGS

Confederate Railroad (Atlantic, 1992); *Notorious* (Atlantic, 1994)

Conjunto Music

Conjunto, the button accordion–based music of South Texas, emerged as the popular music of the Texas-Mexican working class in the late nineteenth and early twentieth centuries. As such it represented the interests and aspirations of the *gente pobre*—the poorest people in Texas-Mexican society. Throughout its history, *conjunto* has been alternately despised as "low-class" or treasured as an expression of Texas-Mexican art.

Conjunto history may be divided into three periods—from the late nineteenth century to 1935, from 1935 to the end of World War II, and from the end of World War II to the present.

In the first period, *conjunto* was born when German and Czech immigrants brought the diatonic accordion to Mexico and Texas. The earliest music consisted of polkas along with other popular salon dances—schottisches, mazurkas, waltzes, redowas. The Mexican *corrido* was also prominent. The accordion was played solo or with other instruments on an ad hoc basis.

In the second period, more emphasis was placed on Mexican and Latin-American song forms such as the *huapango,* bolero, and *ranchera* (country song), and the twelve-string guitarlike bajo sexto became the standard accompaniment to the accordion.

Following World War II the *conjunto* ensemble took its current form—three-row diatonic button accordion, bajo sexto, electric bass, and drum kit. The Colombian *cumbia* was introduced along with the tango, chachacha, rock, blues, and country-western music.

While *conjunto* is considered simple, happy, dance music whose lyrics focus on love and romance, there are many songs of political and social oppression, of discrimination and racism, of longing for a former homeland, of back-breaking labor.

Major early figures in *conjunto* include accordionist Narciso Martinez, "El Huracán del Valle" (the Hurricane of the Valley), who was born in 1911. Martinez and his musical partner Santiago Almeida established the accordion and bajo sexto as the basic constituents in the *conjunto* style. Almeida was the first to play the bajo sexto as a solo, melody-line instrument. Martinez concentrated on the right-hand lead of the accordion, disregarding the bass chord accompaniment and thus moving the music away from its "Germanic" roots.

Other important early figures in *conjunto* music are Pedro Ayala, "El Monarca del Acordeón" (the Monarch of the Accordion); Santiago Jimenez Sr., "El Flaco" (the Skinny One); and Bruno Villareal, "El Azote del Valle" (the Scourge of the Valley).

Born in 1912 and almost completely blind since birth, Villareal said in a 1986 interview: "It's not been so beautiful our life—more a life of suffering, but, oh, well—I never saw anything else I could do but be a musician. I couldn't do ordinary work because of my blindness. My entire life was suffering. Like people say, only he who carries the burden knows its weight."

Major *conjunto* figures in the years following World War II include Valerio Longoria and Tony de la Rosa. Both are widely known for their inclusion of the drum kit, for the replacement of the acoustic upright bass (the tololoche) with the electric bass, for the use of amplification and PA systems, and for more vocal music. Longoria introduced the bolero to *conjunto,* while de la Rosa slowed the basic tempo of *conjunto* polkas, which allowed for more emphasis on the melody, more complex fingering techniques, and a smoother, gliding dance form, *el tacuachito,* which replaced the European-influenced *baile de brinquito* (the hopping dance).

Many contemporary *conjunto* players perform hybrid music. Such players include Nick Villareal, Esteban Jordan, and FLACO JIMENEZ. Santiago Jimenez Jr. is a contemporary player who strives to maintain the *conjunto* style of the past, basing his playing largely on his father's style.

Conjunto, always a regional music, has in recent years begun to have a national and international following and is now crossing over into other Texas music forms (*orquesta, tejana, la onda chicana*) and into other national forms (rock, and country western).   —*David Romtvedt*

REPRESENTATIVE RECORDINGS

There are thousands of *conjunto* recordings, including reissues of recordings made in the first forty years of the twentieth century. The early recordings appeared on many labels, including national ones such as OKEH, Vocalion, and BLUEBIRD, as well as Texas labels such as Ideal and Falcon. Current Texas labels include Joey, Zarape, and Hacienda.

Larger companies promoting *conjunto* recently are ROUN-DER and Arhoolie, which has issued a useful multivolume history of Texas–Mexican border music.

John Conlee
b. Versailles, Kentucky, August 11, 1946

John Conlee achieved star status with a high-in-the-throat delivery and songs that gave voice to the everyday concerns of aging "baby boomers." Stylistically, he drifted from neo-honky-tonk in his early years to a more pop-oriented country sound.

John Wayne Conlee came by his country credentials honestly, growing up on a farm near Versailles, Kentucky, a short distance from Lexington. After high school he earned a mortician's license and serviced the recently deceased for six years before putting his gift for gab to good use as a radio announcer. That line of work brought him to Nashville in 1971, where he worked as an announcer at WLAC-FM.

By 1976 Conlee had a recording contract with ABC/DOT. An early release of "Backside of Thirty" failed to chart, but the bittersweet honky-tonk charm of "Rose Colored Glasses," co-written by Conlee and touched up by Bud Logan's lush production, gave the singer a #5 hit in 1978.

His first #1, "Lady Lay Down," topped the charts early in 1979, and a rereleased "Backside of Thirty" soon matched the feat. Conlee's hottest streak came during 1983–84 when he scored four consecutive #1s: "Common Man," "I'm Only in It for the Love," "In My Eyes," and "As Long as I'm Rockin' with You." Listeners identified with his "regular Joe" looks, comforting voice, and his songs about ordinary people in everyday situations. When Conlee pledged enduring faithfulness in "As Long as I'm Rockin' with You," "Old School," or "In My Eyes," he gained the credibility of a teddy bear.

A GRAND OLE OPRY cast member since 1981, Conlee continues to make appearances on the show. True to his agrarian roots, he has served as honorary chairman of the Family Farm Defense Fund and on the board of Farm Aid. He lives now on a Nashville-area farm. —*Jay Orr*

REPRESENTATIVE RECORDINGS

20 Greatest Hits (MCA, 1988); *Best of John Conlee* (Curb, 1991)

Earl Thomas Conley
b. Portsmouth, Ohio, October 17, 1941

Merging a hard country sound with rock & roll energy, Earl Thomas Conley gained four #1 singles off one album and a series of hit records that made him a dominant force in country music in the 1980s.

When Conley's father lost his railroad job, the family, with eight children, dipped to the poverty level in their small town of Portsmouth, which is across the Ohio River from Kentucky in a valley among hills referred to as the "Little Smokies." Conley's hometown later inspired his song "Smokey Mountain Memories" (co-written with Dick Heard), a #13 hit for Mel Street in 1975.

Conley credits his schoolteacher John Brandel as a motivational influence who encouraged students to follow their dreams. Following a tour of duty in the army, Conley settled in Xenia, Ohio, where he worked for the Pennsylvania Railroad. He also toiled in a steel mill in Portsmouth

before moving, in 1971, to Huntsville, Alabama, where he had met local studio owner Nelson Larkin. Conley played clubs by night and gained valuable studio experience.

Conley moved from Huntsville to Nashville in 1973. Two years later he hit the charts as an artist on GRT Records. In 1976 CONWAY TWITTY took Conley's composition "This Time I've Hurt Her More Than She Loves Me" to #1.

After a brief stay at WARNER BROS., Conley moved to Sunbird Records, where he enjoyed his first #1 hit as a singer, "Fire and Smoke," in 1981. RCA RECORDS promptly signed the hot singer, and he accumulated seventeen *Billboard* #1 singles over the next eight years, such as "Holding Her and Loving You," "Once in a Blue Moon," and "Nobody Falls Like a Fool." Included in his Top Ten songs were duets with Anita Pointer, EMMYLOU HARRIS, and KEITH WHITLEY. Conley co-produced his albums with Larkin, who also had moved to Nashville from Huntsville.

Conley is also an accomplished artist and designer.
—*Gerry Wood*

REPRESENTATIVE RECORDINGS

Fire and Smoke (RCA, 1981); *Earl Thomas Conley Greatest Hits* (RCA, 1985); *The Essential Earl Thomas Conley* (RCA, 1996)

Conqueror Records
established in Chicago, Illinois, 1928; ended 1942

The Conqueror label was in evidence from 1928 to 1942, and releases numbered almost 3000. As a Sears, Roebuck–owned, Chicago-based label (along with Challenge, Silvertone, and Supertone), Conqueror and its sister labels leased all of their material from other labels for mail-order catalogue sales and were not in the recording business per se.

The Plaza group of labels, headed by Banner, provided initial product for Conqueror releases before becoming part of the evolving AMERICAN RECORD CORPORATION (ARC). In turn, ARC was bought by COLUMBIA in 1938. ARC/Columbia continued the leasing process with Conqueror thereafter. Thus, except for a minute block of GENNETT RECORDS matrices, rights to Conqueror-released material by ROY ACUFF, the CARTER FAMILY, BOB WILLS, and others reside today with Sony Music, which purchased Columbia in November 1987. —*Bob Pinson*

Don Cook
b. San Antonio, Texas, May 25, 1949

A renowned producer, songwriter, and publishing executive, DON COOK currently serves as Chief Creative Officer of Sony/ATV Tree, Nashville's most profitable music publishing firm, and as president of DKC Records, a joint-venture label with Sony Music. He is also half of the production force and a big part of the songwriting success behind BROOKS & DUNN, country's most recognizable award-winning, multiplatinum-selling duo since the JUDDS.

Since 1976 Cook has been a staff songwriter with Tree, his name gracing titles such as "Who's Lonely Now" (HIGHWAY 101), "Lady Lay Down" (JOHN CONLEE), "Somebody's Gonna Love You" (LEE GREENWOOD), and the Brooks & Dunn #1s "Brand New Man," "My Next Broken Heart," and "That Ain't No Way to Go." Since 1990 much of his creative attention has centered on producing. Besides Brooks & Dunn, Cook has produced or currently produces the MAV-

ERICKS, SHENANDOAH, CONWAY TWITTY, MARTY STUART, MARK COLLIE, JAMES HOUSE, and WADE HAYES.

Growing up in a desolate area south of San Antonio, Texas, Cook found little else to do but dream and write. His taste was formed by his father's love for big-band music, his mother's love for country, and his own affinity for rock & roll. At age fourteen he went to Houston and recorded an original song. He stuck around Texas long enough to graduate from the University of Texas with a degree in English and then moved to MUSIC CITY, where he started writing commercial jingles and performing at Opryland. He toured the Soviet Union with the Opryland Country Music USA Tour in 1974. Soon after, Don Gant of ACUFF-ROSE PUBLICATIONS offered Cook his first writing deal. He switched to TREE International, where he produced many of his own song demos and earned a reputation as a top-notch song-and-sound man. —*Michael Hight*

Spade Cooley
b. Grand, Oklahoma, December 17, 1910; d. November 23, 1969

The fiddler-bandleader who first popularized the phrase "western swing" and revolutionized country music presentation with natty, uniform-clad band and lush, melodic sound, Donnell Clyde "Spade" Cooley was one of the major forces in World War II–era West Coast country.

An accomplished fiddler by his teens, he cut his teeth working with Oklahoma dance bands until hard times blew the Cooley family west, first to Oregon and then to Modesto, California, in 1931. Several years later, "with nothing but my fiddle and three cents in my pocket," as he put it, Cooley jumped a freight train to Los Angeles and was hired as a film set stand-in by ROY ROGERS. Cooley also picked up local musical jobs with Rogers, STUART HAMBLEN, Cal Shrum, and, later, JIMMY WAKELY.

When promoter FOREMAN PHILLIPS plucked the fiddler away from Wakely in 1942 and made him a bandleader at

Spade Cooley

the Venice Pier Ballroom, Cooley's popularity soared. Throughout 1942–44 Cooley's large swing outfit (featuring players such as singer-guitarist SMOKEY ROGERS, steel guitarists JOAQUIN MURPHEY or NOEL BOGGS, and vocalists TEX WILLIAMS and Deuce Spriggins) regularly drew tens of thousands of dancers and stirred up a good-natured publicity feud between Cooley and BOB WILLS, who had just moved to the San Fernando Valley. Cooley's band definitely swung, but their sound was full and rich, with an almost orchestral approach far more refined than Wills's hot fiddle band style; Tex Williams's urbane croon added even more elegance. It was a formula for success, and Cooley continued to pack the Pier, the RIVERSIDE RANCHO, and the Santa Monica Ballroom.

Signed to OKEH, a subsidiary of COLUMBIA, Cooley's band first recorded in December 1944 and immediately scored a double-sided hit with "Shame on You" (which spent nine weeks at #1) and "A Pair of Broken Hearts" (which entered the Top Ten). With his recordings shifted to the Columbia red label, Cooley scored more hits during 1946–47 ("Detour," "Crazy 'Cause I Love You") and, despite the departure of Tex Williams, remained one of the Coast's top acts. When Cooley broke away from Columbia and signed with RCA in 1947, he also began to appear regularly on Phillips's top-rated *Hoffman Hayride* KTLA television show as well as in a series of B-grade western movies.

Moving to DECCA in 1951, Cooley's and western swing's popularity began to subside, and the hot-tempered, hard-drinking fiddler began a gradual psychological nosedive that culminated in the tragic, vicious April 1961 torture-murder of his wife, Ella Mae, at his Kern County ranch. In one of country music's most high-profile scandals ever, he testified that "rockets ran through my brain when Ella Mae told me of her desire to join a 'free love cult.'" Convicted on first-degree murder charges in August, largely on the gruesome eyewitness account of his fourteen-year-old daughter Melody (whom Cooley branded "a liar"), he was sentenced to life in Vacaville Prison. In November 1969, on a seventy-two-hour furlough, Cooley performed three songs at a police benefit in Oakland, California. After the nearly 3,000-strong audience gave him a standing ovation, he strolled offstage, suffered a massive heart attack, and died on the spot, ending one of the most dramatic and tragic sagas in popular music history. —*Jonny Whiteside*

REPRESENTATIVE RECORDING

Spadella! The Essential Spade Cooley (Columbia/Legacy, 1994)

Coon Creek Girls
Lily May Ledford b. Powell County, Kentucky, March 17, 1917; d. July 14, 1985
Charlotte "Rosie" Ledford b. Powell County, Kentucky, August 16, 1915; d. July 24, 1976
Esther "Violet" Koehler b. Wilton, Wisconsin, February 6, 1916; d. October 4, 1973
Evelyn "Daisy" Lange b. St. Henry, Ohio, July 7, 1919
Minnie "Susie" Ledford b. Powell County, Kentucky, October 10, 1923; d. July 22, 1987

The first all-woman stringband, the Coon Creek Girls, was organized and named by JOHN LAIR in 1937 in Cincinnati around the talents of Lily May Ledford, a regular on his previous shows at WLS in Chicago. The Coon Creek Girls were enthusiastically received over WLW and WCKY in the Cincinnati area, as part of Lair's *RENFRO VALLEY BARN DANCE*. Playing off Lily's name, the other band members all received stage names from flowers: Her older sister Charlotte became "Rosie," Esther Koehler became "Violet," and Evelyn Lange became "Daisy."

An old-time band with fiddle and banjo (Lily), guitar (Rosie), mandolin (Violet), and bass (Daisy), the Coon Creek Girls harmonized in vocal duets, trios, and quartets, playing folksongs and other numbers learned from Lair and fellow performers. In 1938 the group recorded nine numbers for Vocalion. In 1939, at the invitation of Eleanor Roosevelt, they performed their old-time music and comedy routines at the White House for the Roosevelts and the king and queen of England.

When Lair's show was moved to Renfro Valley, Kentucky, in 1939, Koehler and Lange went with the CALLAHAN BROTHERS to KVOO in Tulsa and then to KRLD in Dallas. As a result, younger sister Minnie Ledford, who became "Black-Eyed Susie," joined sisters Lily and Daisy in the band, and the three Ledfords recorded several sides for the *Renfro Valley* label during their tenure with that barn dance. From Renfro Valley, the Coon Creek Girls went to the *OLD DOMINION BARN DANCE* in Richmond, Virginia, and were part of SUNSHINE SUE's New York Broadway show. By 1957, the Coon Creek Girls ended the act so that they could raise families, but in 1968 RALPH RINZLER persuaded them to play at the NEWPORT FOLK FESTIVAL and the Smithsonian's American Folklife Festival in 1972. In the 1970s Mike Seeger persuaded Lily May to revive her career at college concerts and folk festivals. In 1983 she recorded an LP, *Banjo Picking Girl*, for the Greenhays label.

—*Loyal Jones*

REPRESENTATIVE RECORDINGS

Coon Creek Girls (County, 1969); *Coon Creek Girls—Early Radio Favorites* (Old Homestead, 1982)

George Cooper Jr.

b. Nashville, Tennessee, December 20, 1897; d. July 17, 1974

Local 257 of the AMERICAN FEDERATION OF MUSICIANS was almost inactive and penniless when George Wesley Cooper Jr. became its president in 1937. The chapter had been founded in Nashville in 1902, but had fallen on lean times during the Depression and had declined in membership to a total of seventy-five.

Many believe that Nashville's music business growth would have been impossible without Cooper's leadership in the AFM during the next thirty-six years. He led the fight against musical exams for union membership, thus allowing hillbilly, blues, and rock musicians who couldn't read music to enter the AFM. He also pioneered "demo rates," recording studio payments to musicians for demo sessions that were lower than the union scale rates for master sessions. Demo rates permitted song publishing companies to thrive and encouraged experimentation. He raised scale at the GRAND OLE OPRY and for master sessions, but encouraged cooperation rather than confrontation at recording dates.

Cooper was a horn player and bassist who joined the AFM in 1918 when he was performing in a traveling circus band. He returned to Nashville to play for silent pictures and vaudeville, and then joined the radio band at WSM.

His early tenure at the union was marked by the national musicians' strike of 1942–44, which eventually resulted in sidemen receiving profits based upon the number of records they performed on, the "special payments fund."

Cooper retired in 1973. He was succeeded by Johnny DeGeorge (1973–86), Jay Collins (1986–91), and HAROLD BRADLEY (since 1991).

—*Robert K. Oermann*

Wilma Lee & Stoney Cooper

Wilma Leigh Leary Cooper b. Valley Head, West Virginia, February 7, 1921

Dale Troy "Stoney" Cooper b. Harman, West Virginia, October 16, 1918; d. March 22, 1977

The duo of Wilma Lee & Stoney Cooper ranked as one of country music's premier husband-and-wife teams for some three decades. Their career evolved out of the Leary Family Singers, for whom young Stoney had worked as a fiddler prior to his marriage to one of the group's members, Wilma Leigh Leary, on June 9, 1941. The Coopers worked at WMMN radio in Fairmont, West Virginia, and in other radio locales extending from Arkansas and Nebraska to Illinois and North Carolina, before they settled in for ten years at WWVA and the *Wheeling Jamboree* in 1947.

After a brief stint with RICH-R-TONE RECORDS in 1947, Wilma Lee & Stoney signed with COLUMBIA. They recorded most of their trademark numbers on that label, including "Thirty Pieces of Silver," "Legend of the Dogwood Tree," "Sunny Side of the Mountain," and "Walking My Lord up Calvary Hill." Like ROY ACUFF's Smoky Mountain Boys, the Cooper support group, the Clinch Mountain Clan, favored an acoustical sound highlighted by dobro, fiddle, and mandolin. In 1955 the pair switched to HICKORY RECORDS, where they registered their biggest chartmakers, including "Cheated Too," "Come Walk with Me," "Big Midnight Special," and "There's a Big Wheel." The first of these helped bring them to the GRAND OLE OPRY in 1957, where they

Wilma Lee & Stoney Cooper with daughter Carol Lee

were regulars for some twenty years. The Coopers vanished from the *Billboard* chart listings after 1961, but continued as a force for traditionalism in country music. Their later recordings appeared on DECCA, Skylite, Power Pak, STAR-DAY, and ROUNDER.

Ill health plagued Stoney's last years, and after his death Wilma Lee Cooper continued at the Opry as a solo act, veering somewhat more in the direction of BLUEGRASS. Her recordings have been released on Rounder and Rebel. Daughter Carol Lee Cooper (b. March 21, 1942), formerly married to the Rev. Jimmie Snow (the son of HANK SNOW), has forged an independent career at the Grand Ole Opry since 1975 with a vocal support quartet known as the Carol Lee Singers, formed in 1973. —*Ivan M. Tribe*

REPRESENTATIVE RECORDINGS

Walking My Lord Up Calvary Hill (Power Pak, 1973; reissued on Highland, 1992); *Early Recordings* (County, 1979)

Cowboy Copas
b. Blue Creek, Ohio, July 15, 1913; d. March 5, 1963

Loyd Estel "Cowboy" Copas possessed a strong tenor voice, distinctive phrasing, and flat-top guitar picking that gave his recordings a unique sound in an era dominated by instantly identifiable performers. One of six children of Marion and Lola Mae (Ramsey) Copas, he began performing at fairs and talent contests with his brother, Marion, when both were teenagers. He was still a teenager when he teamed with local fiddler Lester Vernon Storer, known professionally as Natchee the Indian, and acquired the alliterative stage name Cowboy. His brother later recalled that Copas was advised by a college professor to say he was born on a ranch in Oklahoma, a locale deemed more colorful that the family corn and tobacco farm at Blue Creek. Copas never professed to be a cowboy singer, however, and recorded virtually nothing with a western motif. His overall style might be described as occupying a middle ground between honky-tonk and the crossover approach of smooth vocalists such as EDDY ARNOLD and GEORGE MORGAN.

In the early 1940s Copas worked at WLW in Cincinnati and became affiliated there with KING RECORDS. He made his first record for the label, "Filipino Baby," during his first sessions for the label in 1944. When it was finally released nearly two years later, in the summer of 1946, it became a #4 hit that helped put King on the map and propelled Copas to the GRAND OLE OPRY. In 1946 he joined PEE WEE KING's Golden West Cowboys, with whom he worked briefly as a guitarist and featured vocalist. "Tragic Romance," "Signed, Sealed and Delivered," "Tennessee Waltz," "Kentucky Waltz," "Breeze," "The Strange Little Girl," and "Copy Cat" (a duet with his sixteen-year-old daughter, Kathy) were among his hits. Copas's tenor voice seemed best suited to lilting and melodious love songs, resulting in announcer GRANT TURNER's dubbing him Waltz King of the Grand Ole Opry.

Like many country artists, his career was temporarily muffled by the rock revolution, but Copas enjoyed a renaissance after signing with STARDAY in 1959. The album *Unforgettable* was made, with one cut serving to showcase his Martin guitar, which he played with a thumb pick. Consisting of verses found in several lyrical folksongs, "Alabam" was the highlight of the LP and, when released as a single in 1960, became a #1 hit. Thereafter, Copas was consistently on the charts and recorded prolifically until, return-

Cowboy Copas

ing from a Kansas City benefit show in a plane piloted by Copas's son-in-law RANDY HUGHES, Copas, PATSY CLINE, and HAWKSHAW HAWKINS were killed in a crash near Camden, Tennessee. The final Copas single, with the too-prophetic title "Goodbye Kisses" (coauthored by Copas and LEFTY FRIZZELL a few week before the accident), was a posthumous hit. —*Jonathan Guyot Smith*

REPRESENTATIVE RECORDINGS

Opry Star Spotlight (Starday, 1961); *24 Greatest Hits* (Deluxe, 1987)

Helen Cornelius (*see* Jim Ed Brown)

X. Cosse
b. New Orleans, Louisiana, September 19, 1917; d. November 18, 1990

Xavier B. "X." Cosse is best remembered as the husband and manager of MARTHA CARSON, whom he married in 1953. A graduate of St. Aloysius College in New Orleans and the Army Medical School in Washington, D.C., Cosse gained experience managing shows for the army in Panama and for USO tours in Europe. This led to his tenure as entertainment director for the U.S. Armed Forces. Subsequently, for nineteen years, Cosse managed and promoted the Festival of Music tour, headlined by CHET ATKINS, FLOYD CRAMER, and BOOTS RANDOLPH. —*Don Cusic*

Country Blues

In country music as with pop music, the term "blues" today is used rather casually to describe a number of songs that have little in common with the classic, well-defined African-American blues styles of the 1920s and 1930s. There was a time, however, in prewar country music, when white country singers created a number of subgenres based on legitimate forms of blues. Some of these singers, including major figures such as JIMMIE RODGERS (q.v.), influenced later singers and songwriters, both in singing style and song form.

Country's fascination with blues dates to 1924, when OKEH issued the first country record bearing the name "blues," HENRY WHITTER's "Lonesome Road Blues," with its famous verse "I'm going down the road feeling bad." A few months later, UNCLE DAVE MACON, who had learned much of his music from blacks around rural middle Tennessee, recorded a reworking of W. C. Handy's "Hesitation Blues" that he called "Hill Billie Blues."

Few of these early blues sides actually sounded much like the distinctive delta blues or Texas blues of singers Charley Patton or Blind Lemon Jefferson, respectively. But in 1926 FRANK HUTCHISON, a West Virginia singer, began recording with a slide guitar, crafting pieces such as "Worried Blues" and "The Train That Carried the Girl from Town." The following year the team of Darby and Tarlton, who had listened very closely to black singers in Georgia and South Carolina, recorded the two-sided hit "Columbus Stockade Blues" and "Birmingham Jail." They, too, featured a slide guitar, and sounded very close to authentic black country blues singers of the day. A third act, that of Reece Fleming and Respers Townsend, from West Tennessee, incorporated the Memphis blues style into a long series of records for VICTOR and ARC.

Appalachian coal miners and factory workers created a different type of "mountain blues," based on eerie modal chord patterns (sometimes on the banjo) and a high, lonesome keening style. Foremost among these singers was Dock Boggs, from Norton, Virginia, and the Kentuckian B.F. Shelton; the Shepherd Family, miners from the Appalachia, Virginia area, adapted the style to string band music, though they recorded far too little.

A third style involved the famous "blue yodel" of Jimmie Rodgers, first defined in his November 1927 recording "Blue Yodel #1 (T for Texas)." Though Rodgers often used the classic three-line blues stanza in his songs, his regular, almost bouncy tempo and fluid falsetto had rather little in common with black styles. Two of Rodgers's emulators were CLIFF CARLISLE and the young GENE AUTRY, both of whom achieved great fame in the 1930s and who eventually moved into more mainstream styles. Carlisle and his brother Bill also developed a form of off-color "hokum blues" of the sort popularized by Georgia Tom (Dorsey) and others. This style also had an impact on the young BOB WILLS, who borrowed pieces such as "Eagle Riding Papa" from Dorsey. In the 1930s groups such as MILTON BROWN's Musical Brownies adapted even more blues (and even early jazz) to the early western swing sound.

—*Charles Wolfe*

The Country Gazette

Byron Berline b. Caldwell, Kansas, July 6, 1944
Kenny Wertz b. Washington, D.C., February 4, 1942
Roger Bush b. Hollywood, California, September 16, 1940
Alan Munde b. Norman, Oklahoma, November 4, 1946
Roland White b. Madawaska, Maine, April 23, 1938
Herb Pedersen b. Berkeley, California, April 27, 1944

The Los Angeles–based Country Gazette evolved from the Doug Dillard Expedition. Touring as members of the FLY-ING BURRITO BROTHERS, fiddler Byron Berline, singer-guitarist Kenny Wertz, and bassist Roger Bush would perform a short bluegrass set at each show. After the dissolution of the Burritos in early 1972, this core group decided to stay together. Calling themselves the Country Gazette, they added Oklahoman and former Sunny Mountain Boy banjo player Alan Munde. The group soon landed a record deal with United Artists. Bringing singer and multi-instrumentalist Herb Pedersen on board, the group released *A Traitor in Our Midst,* produced by Jim Dickson, who had enjoyed earlier success with the BYRDS, the DILLARDS, and the Flying Burrito Brothers.

In 1973 mandolin player Roland White joined the Gazette, and Berline moved on to work sessions with musicians such as Elton John and Rod Stewart. Berline is currently working with the West Coast–based group California, which also includes guitarist Dan Crary and banjoist John Hickman.

White and Munde became the foundation of the Gazette as other members would come and go. They made several trips to Europe and were voted the Top Country Band at the British CMA Awards. The group disbanded briefly in 1982 after releasing *America's Bluegrass Band* for Flying Fish. They regrouped in 1983 but permanently called it a day four years later. ROLAND WHITE joined forces with one of Bluegrass's premier groups, the NASHVILLE BLUEGRASS BAND. In recent years Munde has developed a series on instructional materials and encouraged musicians to develop their bluegrass skills. —*Chris Skinker*

The Country Gentlemen

Organized in Arlington, Virginia, the Country Gentlemen played their first official date on July 4, 1957. Although such musicians as Bill Emerson, Pete Kuykendall, ED FERRIS, Jimmy Gaudreau, Jerry Douglas, DOYLE LAWSON, Bill Yates, and RICKY SKAGGS have played with the group during its forty-year history, the performers most closely identified with it—the "Classic country Gentlemen" who were elected to the International Bluegrass Music Association's Hall of Honor in 1996—are Charlie Waller, the late John Duffey, Eddie Adcock, and Tom Gray.

The Country Gentlemen were one of several bands in the late fifties who helped give "bluegrass" its name and reputation through their adoption and popularization of sounds borrowed from BILL MONROE and other pioneers of the genre. On one hand, the Country Gentlemen were hyperbluegrass in that they accentuated the stylistic trademarks first introduced by Monroe and his musicians. Charlie Waller repeatedly played dynamic guitar runs; John Duffey and Eddie Adcock played pyrotechnical instrumental breaks on the mandolin and banjo; and Duffey soared into high, sometimes strident harmonies that competed favorably with those of Bill Monroe.

Although they were respectful of tradition, the Country Gentlemen were also one of the most important early innovative bands in bluegrass, taking the genre into new arenas of repertoire and stylistic performance while steadfastly using acoustic instruments. The Gentlemen could play hard-driving bluegrass reminiscent of Monroe or the STANLEY BROTHERS, but they were also at home with blues and jazz, or with the soft lyricism of a 1920s pop song such as "Heartaches" or a movie soundtrack melody such as *Theme from Exodus.* On songs such as these, Eddie Adcock's banjo improvisations forecast the "newgrass" departures of the 1970s.

The Country Gentlemen were strongly influenced by the folk revival, and their Folkways albums introduced them to an audience who had not earlier patronized the bluegrass style. Songs such as "Handsome Molly" and "Poor Ellen Smith" exhibited their knowledge of early recorded country music, but these choices seemed most calculated to appeal to the emerging folk audience. The Country Gentlemen, in turn, influenced the folk community's acceptance and perception of bluegrass, and they became one of the earliest bluegrass bands to bridge the gap between the folk and bluegrass audiences.

The Country Gentlemen's modern, eclectic repertoire—encompassing pop, folk, rock, country, vintage bluegrass, BOB DYLAN songs, and, of course, newly composed songs—earned them one of the broadest constituencies that any bluegrass band has ever enjoyed. While partisans of traditional bluegrass generally remained loyal to them, the band built an even larger following among middle-class professionals, a body of fans who have remained one of the core elements of the bluegrass community.

The Country Gentlemen's appeal went well beyond musicianship. They were also first-class entertainers. Comedy sometimes meant little more than madcap antics onstage, playing their instruments behind their backs, or Waller's imitations of HANK SNOW or MAC WISEMAN; but their humor often seemed spontaneous, especially when Duffey directed his barbs at fans who bought no records but instead taped their shows.

Despite numerous personnel changes, the Country Gentlemen survive, with guitarist and lead singer Charlie Waller as the remaining link to the early years, and a new lineup as of November 1996: Greg Corbett on banjo, Ronnie Davis on bass, Matthew Allred on mandolin, and Brian Blaylock on resonator guitar. The group constantly refreshes its repertoire but will always be identified with such songs as "Two Little Boys," "Bringing Mary Home," "New Freedom Bell," "Legend of the Rebel Soldier," "This Morning at Nine," and other "classic" songs they introduced to the bluegrass field.　　　　　　　—Bill C. Malone

REPRESENTATIVE RECORDINGS

Country Songs—Old and New (Folkways, 1963); *John Duffey, Charley Waller, & the Country Gentlemen Sing and Play Folk Songs and Bluegrass* (Folkways, 1961); *On the Road* (Folkways, 1962); *Bluegrass at Carnegie Hall* (Starday, 1962; reissued Gusto, 1988); *Award-Winning Country Gentlemen* (Rebel, 1972); *Twenty-fifth Anniversary* (Rebel, 1982)

Country Music Association (*see* CMA)

Country Music Disc Jockeys Association (*see* DJ Convention)

Country Music Foundation (*see* CMF)

The Country Music Hall of Fame
established in Nashville, Tennessee, 1961

Membership in the Country Music Hall of Fame is an honor extended to performers, songwriters, broadcasters, and executives in recognition of their contributions to the development of country music. The Country Music Hall of Fame honor was created in 1961 by the CMA; the first inductees were HANK WILLIAMS, JIMMIE RODGERS, and FRED ROSE. ROY ACUFF, the first living artist to join the Hall of Fame, was elected in 1962.

Over the Hall of Fame's four-decade history, the number of new members inducted each year has varied from one to four (no nominee was inducted in 1963, no candidate having received sufficient votes). The election procedure is as follows: Slates of nominees created by a small committee are narrowed to recipients through a two-stage balloting process. The larger select committee, which votes on Hall of Fame membership, is composed of CMA members who have participated in the country music industry for at least ten years. New Hall of Fame members receive special recognition on the CMA Awards telecast each fall.

Bas-relief portraits cast in bronze honoring each Hall of Fame member were originally displayed at the Tennessee State Museum in downtown Nashville until the Country Music Hall of Fame opened its own building in April 1967, a barn-roofed facility at the head of MUSIC ROW. Today the Hall of Fame is also an institution—a museum, library, and research center owned and operated by the COUNTRY MUSIC FOUNDATION and located in Nashville, Tennessee.

Since its inception, nearly 10 million visitors have toured this vast repository of country music memorabilia. In 2000 the Country Music Hall of Fame will be relocated to a new building in downtown Nashville.　　　—Bill Ivey

Country Music Television (*see* CMT)

Country-Rock

The term *country-rock* generally refers to a blend of country and rock music that came to the fore in the late 1960s. Country-rock has been a source of controversy, the main debate being whether the introduction of rock into country and country into rock was diluting or strengthening either music. With hindsight the Beatles can be seen to have performed country-rock many times with original material such as "I Don't Want to Spoil the Party" (1964), the groundbreaking *Rubber Soul* (1965) album, and a cover of BUCK OWENS's "Act Naturally" (1965). Certainly Lennon and McCartney's harmonies echo those of the EVERLY BROTHERS, and George Harrison's guitar hero was CHET ATKINS as much as Chuck Berry.

Where the Beatles went, others followed. The BYRDS, even before their lineup embraced GRAM PARSONS, were performing country material, with bassist CHRIS HILLMAN leading the way on a cover of the country standard "A Satisfied Mind" (1965). When Parsons did join, in early 1968 after leaving his pioneering International Submarine Band, the Byrds recorded *the* seminal country-rock album, *Sweetheart of the Rodeo*.

In the early 1970s, country-rock proliferated. Bands such as POCO, RICK NELSON's Stone Canyon Band, and the players behind LINDA RONSTADT all finally embraced country instrumentation such as pedal steel and banjo. Ex-Byrds once again led the way, with Gene Clark utilizing Doug Dillard's banjo to punctuate Dillard & Clark, and Gram Parsons and Chris Hillman relying on Sneaky Pete Kleinow's distorted pedal steel in their FLYING BURRITO BROTHERS band.

The 1960s–1970s trends began to affect mainstream country, as WAYLON JENNINGS, in particular, grew his hair long and shaggy and rebelled against his record label and staid GRAND OLE OPRY thinking—Waylon insisted on using his road band, and not session musicians, as well as a full drum kit on his recordings. Allied alongside him were WILLIE NELSON and TOMPALL GLASER; their efforts at injecting some drive into country kickstarted the OUTLAW movement.

By the mid-1970s, the EAGLES' smooth hybrid of rock & roll and country was garnering them platinum album after platinum album, making them country-rock's greatest commercial success and opening the door for country-rock bands in mainstream country, beginning with ALABAMA, in 1980. In the early 1980s, young punk rock–influenced bands such as Green on Red, the Long Ryders, JASON & THE SCORCHERS, and RANK & FILE leaned in the opposite direction of Alabama, wedding the energy of New Wave rock with country licks and harmonies, spawning a brief musical movement dubbed cowpunk.

In recent years, country-rock has continued in many guises, ranging from the West Texas rave-ups of JOE ELY to the loose groove of the TRACTORS to the rock adventures of STEVE EARLE. In the mid-1990s, the alternative country movement that coalesced around the band UNCLE TUPELO and its spin-off bands Wilco and Son-Volt further extended the possible combinations of country and rock, and inspired a small but far-flung subculture on the Internet who carried on passionate exchanges about country-rock music through the "No Depression" online folder and, subsequently, a magazine of the same name. —*Sid Griffin*

County Records
established in New York, New York, 1963

County Records was an outgrowth of collector Dave Freeman's love of OLD-TIME country music and traditional BLUEGRASS. In the early 1960s he compiled several LP sets of reissue anthologies, beginning with *A Collection of Mountain Fiddle Music* (County 501) and *A Collection of Mountain Ballads* (County 502). These were followed by County's first live recordings in 1964–65. County Sales, Freeman's mail-order record service, began in 1965 as a means of making his own and similar releases broadly available. Freeman issued a regular newsletter that reviewed new recordings, offering positive and negative observations as each warranted. County Sales is still a thriving business.

In 1978, Dave Freeman and Barry Poss founded the SUGAR HILL label, which focused on contemporary bluegrass. Later, Poss bought out Freeman's share of Sugar Hill and continues the label today. In 1979 Freeman acquired REBEL RECORDS from its founder, Dick Freeland. Rebel's primary artists, the SELDOM SCENE, RALPH STANLEY, and the COUNTRY GENTLEMEN, continued to record for the label. When Gary Reid came to work for County/Rebel in 1983, he and Freeman focused on promising young bluegrass bands and developed an impressive catalogue, with groups such as Lost & Found, the Virginia Squires, and IIIrd Tyme Out. —*Dick Spottswood*

Farris Coursey
b. Mt. Pleasant, Tennessee, May 28, 1911; d. January 13, 1968

Farris H. Coursey worked as a Nashville session musician and WSM staff drummer for thirty years. As a young man, he performed in OWEN BRADLEY's big band. He joined WSM radio as a staff drummer in 1937 and later worked in WSM-TV's Waking Crew staff band.

During a historic November 7, 1949, CASTLE studio session with RED FOLEY for "Chattanoogie Shoe Shine Boy," producer PAUL COHEN and arranger Bradley wondered how to re-create the sound of a rhythmic shoeshiner's rag when Coursey started slapping his thigh, creating a catchy solution. Others benefiting from Coursey's creativity include HANK WILLIAMS in his last studio effort (September 23, 1952) for "Kaw-Liga"; and newcomer BOBBY HELMS, whose "Fräulein" (recorded November 15, 1956) charted fifty-two weeks. Coursey died of a heart attack.—*Walt Trott*

Cousin Emmy
b. Lamb, Kentucky, 1903; d. April 11, 1980

Cousin Emmy was a boisterous, loudmouthed, dynamic entertainer best known for her banjo frailing, her jokes, and her platinum blond hair; during the 1930s and 1940s she became one of the best-loved and most popular figures on the radio. In later years she became known as the person who taught GRANDPA JONES how to frail the banjo and as a figure on the folk revival circuit linking the modern commercial industry and the older traditional folk music of rural Kentucky. The fact that she made relatively few phonograph records in her career has caused many modern fans to underestimate her influence and importance.

Coming from a family of tobacco sharecroppers in the southern Kentucky barrens, Cynthia May Carver taught herself to read by looking at Sears catalogues and then joined two of her cousins, Noble "Bozo" Carver and Warner Carver, who had organized a local string band that recorded for Paramount in the 1920s. Soon she was performing with them over WHB–Kansas City, and by 1935 had returned to WHAS in nearby Lousiville. During the following decade she organized her own troupe—becoming one of the first women performers to do so—and swept through radio stations from West Virginia (where she met Grandpa Jones) to St. Louis. During the late 1940s, folklorist Alan Lomax heard her and got her a record deal with DECCA, where she cut what would become her most famous song, "Ruby," later to become repopularized by the OSBORNE BROTHERS.

As live radio went into decline in the 1950s, Cousin Emmy took her showmanship and talent to the West Coast, where she appeared for a time at Disneyland, and appeared in the 1955 film *The Second Greatest Sex*. In the 1960s she was discovered by a young stringband then riding the crest of the folk revival, the NEW LOST CITY RAMBLERS, and she toured with them, making her only LP with them for Folkways in 1968. She also appeared with the STANLEY BROTHERS on an episode of Pete Seeger's TV series *Rainbow Quest*, which has become popular on home video. —*Charles Wolfe*

Cousin Wilbur Wesbrooks
b. Gibson County, Tennessee, March 5, 1911; d. August 13, 1984

Bill E. "Cousin Wilbur" Wesbrooks was a comedian and bass player who played an important role in a number of country careers, and whose own work ranged from rural TENT SHOWS to television. He began his performing career as a singer on radio at WTJS in Jackson, Tennessee, and by 1936 he had organized a band that included a young EDDY ARNOLD and fiddler Speedy McNatt.

Coming to Nashville in 1940, he got a job as a bass player with BILL MONROE's band and played on the first Blue Grass Boys recording session (for RCA VICTOR

RECORDS) later that year. By 1945 he had his own GRAND OLE OPRY troupe, Cousin Wilbur & the Tennessee Mountain Boys, which traveled widely. In 1947 he married fellow entertainer Blondie Brooks, who became his performing partner. The 1950s saw them working on the *WWVA JAMBOREE* and on their own television show in Asheville. In later years they often toured military bases and were active in various country reunion efforts. In 1979 Wesbrooks penned a fascinating and underappreciated autobiography, *Everybody's Cousin.*   —*Stacey Wolfe*

Cowboy Music

There are two types of cowboy music—traditional cowboy songs and the western songs of Hollywood and New York's Tin Pan Alley. Traditional cowboy music can be loosely described as any music working cowboys sing or play; but, more precisely, traditional cowboy music has used the cowboy as a basic theme, with setting, action, plot, and terminology based on the working cowboys' experiences and attitudes. In contrast, the popular western song is usually a romanticized vision of the West that does not accurately reflect the working cowboy's life or language.

The American preoccupation with the cowboy image grew out of the trail drive days after the Civil War (1865–90), when millions of Texas longhorn cattle were herded north to market. Soon after the trail drives started, journalists and dime novelists started romanticizing the men who worked with horses and cattle. Although some cowboys may have sung to cattle while night herding, generally cowboys sang, hummed, or whistled more as a distraction from nighttime fears than to let cattle know a human was nearby. Cowboy music, as was poetry and storytelling, was really for entertainment in the cow camp or bunkhouse.

In the nineteenth century, the fiddle was the most popular instrument in the cow camps, followed by the old-time banjo. The guitar and the harmonica were instruments imposed on the singing cowboy image by Hollywood.

Our popular conception of the cowboy came from those cowboys who trail-herded cattle north out of Texas. It is their songs that are generally considered to be the traditional cowboy songs, even though Hispanics, Hawaiians, and Native Americans also had their own cowboy songs. The quintessential cowboys were mostly southerners who migrated to Texas seeking a new life and carrying strong English-Scottish traditions, and the first traditional cowboy songs were merely folk reconstructions of the songs they brought with them.

The oldest cowboy-themed song is generally considered to be "The Old Chisholm Trail," a variant of an English folksong, "A Dainty Duck," which dates back to 1640. Another popular traditional cowboy song, possibly the best known, is "Bury Me Not on the Lone Prairie"; it is a cowboy folk recomposition of Edwin Hubbell Chapin's poem "The Ocean-Buried," written in 1839. "Streets of Laredo" (also known as "The Cowboy's Lament") is a recomposition of the British broadside "The Unfortunate Rake," which dates back at least to 1790. While many have claimed to have written such reconstructed songs, most of the identities of the cowboy balladeers have been lost.

New Mexico cowboy N. Howard "Jack" Thorp was the first known collector of cowboy songs. In 1889 he traveled on horseback from New Mexico to Texas and into Indian Territory swapping songs as he rode from cow camp to cow camp, and in 1908 he paid the News Print Shop in Estancia, New Mexico, to print a small paperbound book titled *Songs of the Cowboys* (twenty-three songs with no music). Thorp included songs he had written such as "Little Joe, the Wrangler," composed in 1898 while he was trailherding cattle from New Mexico to Texas.

The most popular and influential book of cowboy songs was published two years later—*Cowboy Songs and Other Frontier Ballads,* collected by a noncowboy Texan, John A. Lomax. The Lomax collection was expanded and reissued in 1916 and 1938, with numerous reprintings issued between each new edition, and it remains in print.

The image of the cowboy changed radically, as did the music, when Hollywood created its own version of the cowboy. Even during the days of silent movies, Hollywood depicted cowboys as singers, posting song lyrics onscreen to assist the audience in singing along with the silent actors. During the same period, Tin Pan Alley songwriters started writing songs about cowboys and the West. When talking movies were introduced in 1927, the two business communities—Hollywood and Tin Pan Alley—combined their creative talents and introduced romanticized cowboy images and songs that real working cowboys scorned. The public loved the movie cowboys, however, and the 1930s became the decade for the greatest popularity of the singing cowboy.

It is impossible to state who the first cowboy or western recording artist was, for documentation of cylinder recordings is scarce, but as the 78-rpm disc became popular, more discographic information was preserved. The first hit cowboy song was CARL T. SPRAGUE's version of "When the Work's All Done This Fall," recorded August 5, 1925; reportedly it sold 900,000 copies. First recorded by FIDDLIN' JOHN CARSON under the title Dixie Cowboy in August 1924, the song had been recorded by at least twenty-nine additional artists by 1941, making it the most recorded traditional cowboy song during that time span. Performers who recorded cowboy songs in the 1920s and 1930s were numerous, including VERNON DALHART, JULES VERNE ALLEN, GEORGE RENEAU, ERNEST V. STONEMAN, OTTO GRAY, Harry "HAYWIRE MAC" McClintock, MARC WILLIAMS, BRADLEY KINCAID, CARSON ROBISON, PATSY MONTANA, and many more.

Commercial radio broadcasting, starting in 1920, played a major role in cowboy music. By the 1930s there were hundreds of small stations across the nation, and each had local talent providing music—often the singer claimed to be a cowboy singer. From the 1930s through the 1950s, numerous Mexican BORDER RADIO stations broadcasted hillbilly (country) and cowboy singers, such as Jules Verne Allen, COWBOY SLIM RINEHART, and Dallas "Nevada Slim" Turner, but it was the WLS *NATIONAL BARN DANCE* that had the greatest impact on cowboy music.

One of its early stars, GENE AUTRY, set the pattern for Hollywood's singing cowboys. In 1934 he and his sidekick, LESTER "SMILEY" BURNETTE, traveled to Hollywood to appear in the Ken Maynard movie *In Old Santa Fe.* The following year the concept of a musical cowboy movie genre was realized, with Autry starring in the Republic Pictures production of *Tumbling Tumbleweeds.* Though Ken Maynard is considered to be the first cowboy star to sing in a sound movie, Gene Autry was the first singing cowboy *star,* followed in short order by Dick Foran, TEX RITTER, ROY ROGERS, and a host of others.

The 1930s also saw the proliferation of cowboy songbooks by publishers who paid songwriters to fill file drawers with songs about cowboys and the West, such publishing firms as M. M. COLE, BOB MILLER, American Music, Joe

Davis, Southern Music, Peer International, and others. When a recording artist, movie star, or radio personality gained fame, a publisher would pay the individual to use his or her name and photographs, and the publisher would pull enough songs from the file drawers to fill a songbook. Often the songs had never been sung by anyone—and still are not being sung. It was not unusual for cowboy movie stars who could not sing to have a songbook published and their name added as a songwriter (e.g., *Tom Mix Western Songs,* published by M. M. Cole, 1935). Such was the commercial allure of the cowboy.

In 1949, with the *Hopalong Cassidy* series leading the way, television introduced the 1950s generation to westerns but had a limited impact on cowboy music, even though Gene Autry and Roy Rogers & DALE EVANS had their own TV series. Some theme songs of TV westerns, such as Johnny Western's "Paladin," did enjoy popularity, but Roy and Dale's closing song, "Happy Trails," is the only one to endure as a western standard.

As rock & roll music gained in popularity and entertainment tastes changed, traditional cowboy music became limited to a small number of hard-core fans. The word *western* was removed from the *country & western* rubric; the music became simply *country,* although many of its stars' costumes were designed in the western style, accented with cowboy hats and boots. However, western songs remained in the repertoire and writing interests of a few country stars; MARTY ROBBINS, for example, wrote and recorded many western songs, and his "El Paso" won the first Grammy to be awarded to a genuinely country song. In the late 1970s the RIDERS IN THE SKY played an important role in reacquainting country fans with western songs.

Starting in 1985 with the annual Cowboy Poetry Gathering in Elko, Nevada, a resurgence in the popularity of traditional cowboy music occurred, and similar gatherings throughout the West continue to create an audience for cowboy music. The greatest impact came through the efforts of MICHAEL MARTIN MURPHEY. He persuaded WARNER BROS. RECORDS to create a western division, Warner Western, with his collection *Cowboy Songs* as the imprint's first release. Cowboy or western singers such as RED STEAGALL, DON EDWARDS, the SONS OF THE SAN JOAQUIN, and Herb Jeffries, along with cowboy poet Waddie Mitchell, were signed by Warner Western, and western songs previously recorded by other stars were reissued. Murphey also has attracted new fans to cowboy music through his WestFests, particularly the annual show at Copper Mountain, Colorado. Today numerous self-produced cassettes and compact discs of genuine working cowboys and cowgirls singing both traditional and contemporary songs are available, along with noncowboy singers who enjoy singing about the West. —*Guy Logsdon*

Bill Cox

b. Kanawha County, West Virginia, August 4, 1897; d. December 10, 1968

A prolific recording artist for GENNETT (1929–31) and AMERICAN RECORD CORPORATION/COLUMBIA (1933–40), William Jennings Cox was musically influenced by his harmonica-playing, ballad-singing mother and as an adult by recordings of VERNON DALHART, RILEY PUCKETT, JIMMIE RODGERS, and others. Cox learned to play harmonica and guitar during his youth and at age sixteen did some rudimentary songwriting.

While working periodically at an ax factory and a hotel, Cox began to eye music as a career and hired out for performances at parties, picnics, and church functions. Walter Fredericks, owner of radio station WOBU (later WCHS), became aware of Cox's music, hired him in 1928 to perform daily, and instigated his first recording session.

Nicknamed the Dixie Songbird, Cox was noted for several topical/social commentary songs: "NRA Blues" (1933), "Trial of Bruno Richard Hauptman" (1935), and "Franklin D. Roosevelt's Back Again" (1936), among others. In duet with Cliff Hobbs, he made the first known recordings of "Sally Let Your Bangs Hang Down" (1936), "Oozlin' Daddy Blues" (1936), "Sparkling Brown Eyes" (1937, Cox's most successful composition), "Filipino Baby" (1937), and "Don't Make Me Go to Bed (And I'll Be Good)" (1937).

In 1965, a folklorist found a poverty-stricken Cox living in a Charleston slum. This led to one last recording effort—an LP of seventeen songs released in 1966 on Kanawha Records. —*Bob Pinson*

The Cox Family

Willard Lawrence Cox b. Cotton Valley, Louisiana, June 9, 1937
Evelyn Marie Cox Hobbs b. Springhill, Louisiana, June 20, 1959
Sidney Lawrence Cox b. Homer, Louisiana, July 21, 1965
Marla Suzanne Cox Ratcliff b. Springhill, Louisiana, June 5, 1967

The Cox Family has combined kindred harmonies and original songs to emerge as one of the leading bluegrass groups of the 1990s. In 1972 oil refinery worker Willard Cox formed a family singing group with his children. From an early age, each Cox child learned an instrument: eldest sister Lynn took up the bass; Evelyn the guitar; Suzanne the mandolin; and Sidney the dobro, banjo, and guitar. Together they developed their much-admired vocal harmonies. In the early days, the group included Lynn, and mother Marie traveled along as well.

"Broken Engagement" was their first, do-it-yourself record in 1974, recorded on their own label at a run of about 1,000 copies (it appears in its original form on their 1995 album *Beyond the City,* along with an updated version). At a Perrin, Texas, music festival in 1988 they met ALISON KRAUSS. Mutual admiration led Krauss to record several of Sidney's songs, including "I've Got That Old Feeling," which appeared on her 1990 album of the same name. (In interviews, Krauss has repeatedly cited Suzanne Cox as one of her chief vocal influences.) At Krauss's urging, ROUNDER RECORDS signed the Coxes in 1993, and Krauss produced their debut, *Everybody's Reaching Out for Someone,* and its two follow-ups, *Beyond the City* and *Just When We're Thinking It's Over;* the latter was the group's first album for ASYLUM RECORDS. In addition, Krauss produced and collaborated vocally with the Coxes on a jointly released Grammy-winning bluegrass gospel album, *I Know Who Holds Tomorrow.* A fixture at bluegrass festivals nationwide, the Cox Family has received widespread acclaim for their blend of bluegrass, gospel, country, and pop music, which runs the gamut from traditional songs such as "I'll Be All Smiles Tonight" and "Little Birdie" to bluegrass remakes of pop hits such as "Runaway," "Blue Bayou," and "That's the Way Love Is." Suzanne Cox has become one of the most sought-after harmony vocalists in Nashville, backing DOLLY PARTON, RANDY TRAVIS, and many others. —*Stephen L. Betts*

Everybody's Reaching Out for Someone (Rounder, 1993);
I Know Who Holds Tomorrow (Rounder, 1994) with Alison
Krauss; *Beyond the City* (Rounder, 1995); *Just When We're
Thinking It's Over* (Asylum, 1996)

Billy "Crash" Craddock

b. Greensboro, North Carolina, June 16, 1939

William Wayne "Crash" Craddock (the nickname came
from his exploits as a high school running back) was one
of country music's most consistent hitmakers of the 1970s.
Early in his career, the mid-1950s, he began by emulating
ELVIS PRESLEY, and released a few unsuccessful singles on
minor regional labels and Colonial Records; he played
with his brother Ronald in a rock band called the Four
Rebels. After a decade on the periphery of show business,
he recorded a country cover of pop trio Dawn's #1 hit
"Knock Three Times," for the Cartwheel label. The record
reached #3 on the country charts in 1971, and from there
he went on to achieve more than a dozen Top Ten releases, including #1 songs "Rub It In" and "Ruby, Baby,"
both released on the ABC label in 1974. He regularly released hits for the Cartwheel, ABC/Dot, and CAPITOL labels throughout the 1970s—on ABC/Dot Craddock
earned #2 country hit "Easy as Pie" in 1975 and #1 "Broken
Down in Pieces" in 1976—but his career declined in the
early 1980s as subsequent affiliations with CeeCee (a self-
owned company) and Atlantic yielded no significant
recordings.

Craddock's career personified the shifting tastes of contemporary audiences. He was only marginally a country
artist (like his model, Elvis), yet he was far too old-fashioned to appeal to rock audiences of the post-Woodstock
era. Thus his Elvis-derived style—replete with spangled
jumpsuits, copious displays of chest hair, masculine ath-
leticism, and a Vegas-inspired version of rockabilly music—made him at first a highly popular performer, until
tastes changed and neotraditionalists such as RICKY SKAGGS,
RANDY TRAVIS, and GEORGE STRAIT emerged. Still, Craddock continues to perform, and in 1996 Razor & Tie Music
released a compilation CD of his hits, *Crash's Smashes*.

—*Stephen R. Tucker*

"Crash" (ABC/Dot, 1976); *Greatest Hits—"Crash" Craddock*
(Capitol, 1983)

Paul Craft

b. Memphis, Tennessee, August 12, 1938

One of Nashville's most understated and wry songwriters,
Paul Charles Craft has composed a number of songs that
have been pivotal in the success of country artists.

Born in Memphis, with a formative period in his youth
spent in Richmond, Virginia (where he listened to the *OLD
DOMINION BARN DANCE* and saw the show in person), Craft's
life has mostly been spent in Memphis and Nashville. He
owned a music store in Memphis for four years (1966–70)
before he notched his first songwriting success—when
JACK GREENE cut his song "Making Up Your Mind" in 1971.
A warm, mellow-voiced singer, Craft was signed as a vocalist with Truth Records in 1974; among the records he cut
there was an early version of his humorous song "It's Me

Again, Margaret," covered by RAY STEVENS in 1985. Craft
moved to Nashville in 1976 and signed with RCA RECORDS.
The label released four Craft singles, including "Lean on
Jesus Before He Leans on You" (#55, 1977) and "Brother
Jukebox" (1978). The latter became a #1 hit for MARK
CHESNUTT in 1991.

Songwriting success began to mount through the seventies, with "Keep Me from Blowing Away" (LINDA RONSTADT,
1974), "Hank Williams, You Wrote My Life" (MOE BANDY,
1975) and "Dropkick Me, Jesus (Through the Goal Posts of
Life)" (BOBBY BARE, 1976). His long list of compositions
also includes "Blue Heartache" (OSBORNE BROTHERS, 1973,
and GAIL DAVIES, 1979) and "Come As You Were" (JERRY
LEE LEWIS, 1983, and T. GRAHAM BROWN, 1988).

In addition, Craft is a successful music publisher. His
Writers Night Music firm published DON SCHLITZ's first hit,
"The Gambler."

—*Don Rhodes*

Floyd Cramer

b. Campti, Louisiana, October 27, 1933; d. December 31, 1997

When the piano became an integral part of Nashville
arrangements in the early 1960s, the pianist who shoul-
dered the load was Floyd Cramer. He popularized the
"slip-note" technique but deserves to be just as famous for
his unerring taste and his understanding of what *not* to
play.

Cramer grew up in the small sawmill town of Huttig,
Arkansas. He learned piano by ear, and, after graduation
from high school in 1951, he moved to Shreveport and
found a job on the *LOUISIANA HAYRIDE*. He arrived just as
LEFTY FRIZZELL's records were popularizing what Cramer
termed "a plinking honky-tonk-type piano." He played in

Floyd Cramer

that style on JIM REEVES's "Mexican Joe" and made his first record for ABBOTT RECORDS in 1953.

Aside from OWEN BRADLEY, there were virtually no studio pianists in Nashville when Cramer first went there in 1952 with T. TOMMY CUTRER. After a year or two of commuting, he talked to CHET ATKINS about becoming a session pianist and left Shreveport in January 1955. "By 1956 and '57, I was in day and night doing sessions," he said. One of the few records on which he played something other than piano was JIMMY DEAN's "Big Bad John" (he created the pickax sound effects by hanging an iron doorstop on a coat hanger and hitting the doorstop with a hammer).

In 1958 Atkins signed Cramer to RCA as an instrumental artist; his fourth single "Last Date," was his first chart hit and featured the slip-note style. Earlier, Cramer had worked on the HANK LOCKLIN session that had produced "Please Help Me, I'm Falling"; the composer, DON ROBERTSON, had sent a demo on which he played piano, sliding up into a note from the one beneath, and that was the technique Cramer incorporated into his style and made his signature.

"It's been done for a long time on the guitar by people like MAYBELLE CARTER," Cramer said, "and by lots of people on the steel guitar. Half-tones are very common, but the style I use mainly is a whole-tone slur which gives more of a lonesome, cowboy sound."

It was at Atkins's suggestion that Cramer wrote "Last Date" to showcase the slip-note style. It was a bigger pop than country hit, climbing to #2; the only record keeping it from #1 was Elvis Presley's "Are You Lonesome Tonight," another record Cramer had played on. By the mid-1960s, Cramer was established as an album act, recording prolifically for RCA. He continued to do occasional concerts and recorded television-marketed albums until sidelined by cancer, which eventually took his life.   —*Colin Escott*

REPRESENTATIVE RECORDINGS

The Best of Floyd Cramer (RCA, 1964); *The Essential Floyd Cramer* (RCA, 1995)

Crazy Water Crystals

A popular Depression-era nostrum that relieved conditions "caused or made worse by a sluggish system," Crazy Water Crystals sponsored country radio performers in several regions of the United States and Canada.

Produced in Mineral Wells, Texas, the crystals were obtained by evaporation of the town's famed "Crazy" water, named for an alleged cure of two insane ladies in the early 1880s. Company owner Carr P. Collins, a political adviser to W. LEE "PAPPY" O'DANIEL, made the product familiar with radio listeners in the 1930s. When WSM's GRAND OLE OPRY was first divided into fifteen-minute segments, in 1934, and sold to sponsors, the first company to sign up was Crazy Water Crystals.

The Crazy Water Barn Dance on WBT in Charlotte, North Carolina, advertised the crystals in the Southeast, along with shows on thirteen other stations in the Carolinas and Georgia. The Crazy Hickory Nuts, the Crazy Mountaineers, and other groups adopted the "Crazy" theme. Bluegrass pioneer BILL MONROE played for Crazy Crystals-sponsored programs, as did J. E. MAINER, WADE MAINER, LEW CHILDRE, and Zeke Morris. Earl and Bill Bolick (the BLUE SKY BOYS), and Homer "Pappy" Sherrill performed for the company as the Crazy Blue Ridge Hillbillies.

In 1935 HANK SNOW made $10 a week singing cowboy songs for a Crazy Water Crystals show on CHNS in Halifax, Nova Scotia. Colonel Jack and Shorty's Hillbillies recorded transcriptions for the company in New York, performing their theme "Hot Time in the Old Town Tonight," along with tunes such as "Pop Goes the Weasel" and "Hand Me Down My Walking Cane."

In its home state, the company broadcast from the lobby of Mineral Wells's Crazy Hotel. Picked up by NBC in 1932, the Crazy Water Crystal shows were reportedly the first regular commercial broadcast of the NBC network originating outside the NBC studio. These Texas shows featured big band sounds as well as country musicians and comedians. Bassist Jim Boyd, who later joined the LIGHT CRUST DOUGHBOYS, played with the Crazy Gang.

A typical regional Crazy broadcast in its home area, the *Saturday Night Stampede* of 1936, aired live from Ranger Junior College on Fort Worth's WBAP. Western song scholar and performer JULES VERNE ALLEN appeared on the *Stampede*, singing "Cowboy's Lament" and "Santa Fe Trail." Ranger's American Legion Tickville Band favored Crazy fans with lively renditions of "Washington and Lee" and "Smile, Darn You, Smile."

Changing health care trends—along with the Federal Drug Administration's anti-Crazy campaign and the product's high price—caused sales to decline dramatically in the 1940s, and the company's sponsorship of radio shows faded accordingly.   —*Gene Fowler*

Crockett Mountaineers (Crockett's Kentucky Mountaineers; Crockett Family)

The Crockett Mountaineers, led by John "Dad" Crockett (b. April 28, 1877, West Virginia; d. January 1972) and including his five sons, was one of the earliest groups to professionally perform old-time stringband music on the West Coast. Originally from West Virginia, the Crocketts eventually moved to California in 1919. In the band, Dad played fiddle or banjo, John H. "Johnny" Jr. the banjo and guitar, Alan the harmony fiddle, George the fiddle, Clarence the guitar and harmonica, and Albert Tenor the guitar and bass fiddle. Dad, Johnny, and Clarence did most of the singing. They performed on a number of California radio stations in the 1920s and 1930s, including KNJ, KMJ, and KHJ. They traveled nationally as well as on the West Coast, eventually recording for BRUNSWICK and Crown and publishing two song folios. Alan left in fall 1938 to join the Prairie Ramblers, and the group disbanded after Clarence's death in the 1940s.   —*Charlie Seemann*

Crook & Chase

Lorianne Crook b. Wichita, Kansas, February 19, 1957
Charlie Chase b. Rogersville, Tennessee, October 19, 1952

Since 1983, Lorianne Lynee Crook has become one of the most identifiable broadcast personalities in country music. In that year, television producer Jim Owens asked her to cohost the nationally syndicated *This Week in Country Music* with Charlie Chase, which ran through 1990. Her past experience had included stints as a news reporter for KAUZ in Wichita Falls, Texas, in 1980, and the host of *PM Magazine* at Nashville's WKRN in 1981. From 1986 to 1993 Lorianne teamed with Chase for TNN's popular *Crook & Chase*, a weeknight series combining entertainment, news, and

Lorianne Crook & Charlie Chase

celebrity interviews. Crook shared executive producer duties on the show with her husband, Jim Owens, whom she married in January 1985. *Weekend with Crook & Chase,* a thirty-minute weekly entertainment series, aired in syndication from 1987 to 1992. During the years 1988–93 Crook produced and hosted *Celebrities Offstage* for TNN, an ongoing series of one-on-one interview specials. From October 18, 1993, through December 1995, Crook and Chase hosted TNN's prime-time weeknight show, *Music City Tonight,* which replaced Ralph Emery's ten-year-old *Nashville Now* show. Crook also cohosts, with Chase, *The Nashville Record Review,* a four-hour weekly radio program. Crook has a bachelor's degree (1978) from Vanderbilt University in Nashville, with degrees in Russian and Chinese. She is a partner in the Jim Owens Companies, which produces her television series and specials.

Charles Wayne Chase's trademark deep voice has been familiar to country music listeners for more than two decades. His career started in radio when, at age thirteen, he received an on-air assignment in his hometown of Rogersville. Chase then worked at stations in Kingsport and Knoxville, Tennessee, before moving to Nashville in the early 1970s. From 1974 to 1983 Chase was a popular DJ and radio personality for WSM in Nashville. At this time WSM also owned the local NBC-TV affiliate and produced a live daytime show, *Channel 4 Magazine,* which Chase hosted in 1982–83. Beginning in 1983 Chase has shared hosting duties with Lorianne Crook for *This Week in Country Music, Crook & Chase, Weekend with Crook & Chase,* and *Music City Tonight,* all produced by the Jim Owens Companies. He also served as host and producer of *Funny Business with Charlie Chase,* a show devoted to playing practical jokes on country music headliners, which aired on TNN from 1989 to 1993. His radio work continues with *The Nashville Record Review,* a countdown of the week's Top Forty country hits. He and Lorianne Crook have cohosted this program since 1988. Chase had his own album released, *My Wife . . . My Life* (Epic, 1993), though it was not a hit.

Their joint autobiography (written with Mickey Herskowitz), *Crook and Chase: Our Lives, the Music, and the Stars,* was published in 1995. In January 1996 Crook & Chase began a new syndicated TV series produced in Hollywood. Owens moved the operation back to Nashville, and *Crook & Chase* returned to TNN in September 1997.

—*Bob Paxman*

The Crook Brothers
Matthew Crook b. Scottsboro, Tennessee, 1896; d. unknown

Herman Crook b. Scottsboro, Tennessee, December 2, 1898;
d. June 10, 1988

Lewis Crook b. Castalian Springs, Tennessee, May 30, 1909;
d. April 12, 1997

On July 24, 1926, the Crook Brothers Band began the most remarkable marathon in the history of country music when they appeared on WSM's *Barn Dance,* an eight-month-old radio program on Nashville's WSM that would later become celebrated as the GRAND OLE OPRY. Various incarnations of this outstanding stringband would perform nearly every Saturday night on the Opry for the next sixty-two years.

The original group featured the twin harmonicas of brothers Matthew and Herman Crook, who hailed from the hill country south of Nashville that has produced many outstanding mouth organists. The brothers performed at local functions and house parties as youngsters; in late 1925 they played regularly on Nashville's first station, WDAD, though they continued to make their living by day as "twist rollers" with the American Tobacco Company. Soon after, they began appearing at WSM and WLAC as well. In 1928 the band—consisting of Herman and Matthew on harmonicas, Tom J. Givans on banjo, George Miles on guitar, and Hick Burnett on guitar—recorded four instrumentals in Nashville for RALPH PEER of the Victor company. Those would be the last recordings the group would make until a joint album with SAM & KIRK McGEE, which was released in 1962 on STARDAY.

In 1929, at a fiddlers' contest at Walter Hill High School, DR. HUMPHREY BATE introduced the Crooks to another musical Crook, banjo-playing Lewis Crook (no relation), who joined the band in the fall of 1929. Though Matthew Crook left music to join the police force in 1930, the band continued under the same name without him, with Herman and Lewis remaining the only constant members. In the late 1950s the Crook Brothers were combined with remaining members of Dr. Humphrey Bate's Possum Hunters and accompanied square dancers on the Opry broadcasts. Herman Crook would occasionally play a harmonica solo on the show as well. The group's long run ended in 1988 with the death of this quiet, courtly mouth organist, who had lived the entire history of country music's preeminent showcase. —*Kim Field*

REPRESENTATIVE RECORDING
Opry Old Timers: Sam & Kirk McGee and the Crook Brothers (Starday, 1962)

J. D. Crowe
b. Lexington, Kentucky, August 27, 1937

Although a "second generation" bluegrass performer, banjo guru James Dee Crowe has credentials that begin in the 1950s, when bluegrass music was in its infancy. Captivated by Earl Scruggs's banjo artistry, Crowe studied FLATT & SCRUGGS' frequent performances in Crowe's hometown.

While in his teens, Crowe performed part-time in bands headed by Esco Hankins, Curley Parker & Pee Wee Lambert, MAC WISEMAN, and JIMMY MARTIN. Full-time employment with Martin in 1956 included work on the LOUISIANA HAYRIDE and recording twenty-four sides for DECCA RECORDS. Leaving Martin in 1960, Crowe returned in 1963 to record four more titles, and in 1966 for five instrumentals.

Experience with Martin taught Crowe musicianship at a professional level and the inner workings of the music business, knowledge he utilized in building his own bands and passed along to musicians who worked for him. Eventually a road-weary Crowe based his Kentucky Mountain Boys near home. By 1969 he had attracted Red Allen (guitar), DOYLE LAWSON (mandolin), and Bobby Slone (fiddle and bass) to the band. A lengthy Holiday Inn engagement drew listeners from great distances and created a demand for appearances on the emerging bluegrass festival circuit.

In 1970 Lawson switched to guitar when Larry Rice came to play mandolin; Rice's brother, guitarist TONY RICE, of the BLUEGRASS ALLIANCE, joined in September 1971, when Lawson went to the COUNTRY GENTLEMEN. The band's mixture, already leaning away from bluegrass tradition, developed a more contemporary flavor, with material drawn from country-rock pioneer GRAM PARSONS and folk balladeer Gordon Lightfoot. With the band's new sound came a new name—the New South.

Mandolinist RICKY SKAGGS replaced Larry Rice in 1974, and the release of the The New South album on ROUNDER RECORDS in 1975 was a watershed event. Characterized by smooth vocal harmonies and meticulous instrumentation, the influential 1975 New South only lasted through the summer when Rice, Skaggs, and dobro player JERRY DOUGLAS, who had joined for the summer, all left.

Through the remainder of the decade, the New South was a magnet for young musicians. Gene Johnson (later of DIAMOND RIO), Jimmy Gaudreau, and the late KEITH WHITLEY passed through the band, which made several stylistic changes during this period.

Crowe retreated from the music business somewhat in the late 1980s, limiting himself to reunion concerts and selected recording opportunities, including five Bluegrass Album Band recordings produced by Tony Rice.

In 1992 Crowe formed a new band, striving for the sound of his forward-looking 1975 band, and re-entered the mainstream of bluegrass music. In 1994 he won the Instrumental Performer, Banjo Award from the International Bluegrass Music Association (IBMA).

—*Frank and Marty Godbey*

REPRESENTATIVE RECORDINGS

The New South (Rounder, 1975); *Flashback* (Rounder, 1994)

Rodney Crowell

b. Houston, Texas, August 7, 1950

When Rodney Crowell arrived in Nashville in 1972, he brought with him a musical background that stretched from the classic honky-tonk he learned as drummer in his father's band to the influence of the Beatles and other pop acts familiar to his generation. With a circle of friends that

Rodney Crowell

included progressive Texas songwriters GUY CLARK and TOWNES VAN ZANDT, Crowell parlayed his eclecticism into an endearing songwriting and performing style that blended honky-tonk poetics with rock & roll spunk, earning him the respect of his Nashville peers and a reputation as one of country music's most versatile artists.

In 1975 Crowell joined EMMYLOU HARRIS's Hot Band as guitarist, songwriter, and arranger, often drawing comparisons to Harris's late mentor, GRAM PARSONS. During this time, Crowell began to develop production skills, and he also contributed songs to Harris's repertoire, including "'Til I Gain Control Again" and "Bluebird Wine."

In 1977 Crowell left Harris and began working on his first album, *I Ain't Livin' Long Like This*. He also assembled his legendary road band, the Cherry Bombs, which included a young VINCE GILL and future producers RICHARD BENNETT, EMORY GORDY JR., and TONY BROWN. Released the following year, the LP achieved only modest sales, but it enhanced Crowell's reputation as a songwriter when three of its songs became hits for other artists: the title track for WAYLON JENNINGS, "Leaving Louisiana in the Broad Daylight" for the OAK RIDGE BOYS, and "An American Dream" for the NITTY GRITTY DIRT BAND.

Throughout the 1980s Crowell enjoyed success as a songwriter with hits for such artists as rocker Bob Seger, who took his "Shame on the Moon" to #2 on the pop chart in 1983. Crowell also produced albums for ROSANNE CASH, to whom he was married from 1979 to 1992. His own recordings enjoyed only modest success until 1988's benchmark LP *Diamonds and Dirt*. Produced by Crowell and Tony Brown, the album made history as the first country music album to yield five #1 singles: "It's Such a Small World," "She's Crazy for Leavin'," "I Couldn't Leave You if I Tried," "Above and Beyond," and "After All This Time," which also won Crowell a 1989 Grammy for Best Country Song.

In the 1990s, Crowell has continued to record, earning Top Ten singles with "Lovin' All Night" and "What Kind of Love," both in 1992. He's also extended his reach as a producer, guiding albums by Guy Clark, LARI WHITE, and JIM LAUDERDALE, among others. In 1997 Crowell joined

STEUART SMITH, MICHAEL RHODES, and Vince Santoro in the country-rock band the Cicadas. —*Jack Bernhardt*

REPRESENTATIVE RECORDINGS

Ain't Livin' Long Like This (Warner Bros., 1978); *Diamonds and Dirt* (Columbia, 1988); *The Cicadas* (Warner Bros., 1997)

Simon Crum (*see* Ferlin Husky)

Jerry Crutchfield
b. Paducah, Kentucky, August 10, 1934

Since his arrival in Nashville in the late 1950s, Jerry Crutchfield has distinguished himself as a performer, studio singer and musician, songwriter, record producer, music publisher, and corporate executive.

While still a student at Murray State University in his native Kentucky, Crutchfield made his first foray to Music City as part of a group called the Country Gentlemen. Renamed the Escorts, the group was signed by RCA RECORDS. Shortly thereafter, sparked by the interest of EDDY ARNOLD, ERNEST TUBB, and other country stars in his material, Crutchfield decided he should concentrate on songwriting rather than singing.

Crutchfield returned to Kentucky to finish school and began managing a small radio station. Nashville's TREE PUBLISHING, then a fledgling music publisher, agreed to handle his songs and ultimately convinced him to work for the company. He stayed with Tree for more than a year, learning the business side of music publishing. He also found songwriting success, as artists such as TAMMY WYNETTE, ELVIS PRESLEY, BRENDA LEE, and numerous others recorded his tunes.

Crutchfield joined the staff of DECCA RECORDS' publishing arm, which subsequently merged with MCA MUSIC. In 1971 Crutchfield got his first producing assignment for a major label, supervising the studio fortunes of Columbia's BARBARA FAIRCHILD, with whom he had already been working before she signed with Columbia. Within a year she topped the charts with "Teddy Bear," then followed with one of Crutchfield's own compositions, "Kid Stuff," which soared to #2.

Crutchfield found pop success with singer-songwriter Dave Loggins. His production of Loggins's 1974 classic "Please Come to Boston" led to his reputation as one of Nashville's most effective producers. He has since produced numerous gold and platinum albums for a stellar list of country entertainers, including LEE GREENWOOD, TRACY BYRD, ANNE MURRAY, TAMMY WYNETTE, DOTTIE WEST, LARRY GATLIN, GLEN CAMPBELL, and TANYA TUCKER, in whose career he has played an especially prominent role.

Crutchfiel held the position of executive vice president general manager with CAPITOL/LIBERTY RECORDS from 1989 to 1992. He briefly returned to MCA RECORDS as president and is currently active with his own publishing companies, Glitterfish Music, Inc. and Crutchfield Music. Glitterfish staff writer Mark Nesler co-wrote the TIM MCGRAW smash "Just to See You Smile" (#1 for six weeks, 1998). Crutchfield produced Nesler's ASYLUM RECORDS debut album, with a planned June 1998 release.

Crutchfield's brother Jan is also a respected songwriter; his credits include the country standard "Statue of a Fool." —*Janet E. Williams*

Manuel Cuevas (*see* Manuel)

Cumberland Ridge Runners
Hugh Ballard Cross b. Oliver Springs, Tennessee, October 19, 1904; d. mid-1960s
Karl Victor Davis b. Mt. Vernon, Kentucky, December 17, 1905; d. May 30, 1979
Clyde Julian "Red" Foley b. Berea, Kentucky, June 17, 1910; d. September 19, 1968
Doctor Howard "Doc" Hopkins b. Harlan County, Kentucky, January 26, 1899; d. January 3, 1988
John Lee Lair b. Renfro Valley, Kentucky, July 1, 1894; d. November 12, 1985
Homer Edgar "Slim" Miller b. Lizton, Indiana, March 8, 1898; d. August 27, 1962
Linda Parker b. Covington, Kentucky, January 18, 1912; d. August 12, 1935
Hartford Connecticut "Harty" Taylor b. Mt. Vernon, Kentucky, April 11, 1905; d. October 18, 1963

In 1930 John Lair put the Cumberland Ridge Runners on the radio at WLS in Chicago, where they appeared on the WLS *NATIONAL BARN DANCE* on Saturday nights and were the featured act on weekday programs bearing such titles as *Home Folks* and *Coon Creek Social*. According to WLS publicity, the group's programs were like a "chapter out of the past, suggesting the days of the long rifles and coonskin caps of pioneer Kentucky. Many of their songs have come straight out of the hills." The Ridge Runners offered their listeners a variety of instrumentals as well as vocal solos, duets, and trios on such numbers as "Chicken Reel," "Treasures Untold," and "River of Jordan." The original members of the group were JOHN LAIR (jug, group manager), Harty Taylor (vocals, guitar), Gene Ruppe (fiddle), DOC HOPKINS (vocals, banjo), and Karl Davis (vocals, mandolin). Hugh Cross, RED FOLEY, and Slim Miller later replaced Ruppe and Hopkins. Karl Davis and Harty Taylor formed their own act, KARL & HARTY, in the BROTHER DUET style. LINDA PARKER, known as the Sunbonnet Girl, added to the act's variety with her unaffected renditions of sentimental old-time songs such as "Bury Me Beneath the Weeping Willow," "Give My Love to Nell," and "I'll Be All Smiles Tonight."

In 1935 Linda Parker died unexpectedly, while other members of the troupe eventually went separate ways, thereby closing the book on the Cumberland Ridge Runners. —*Wayne W. Daniel*

Curb Records
established in Los Angeles, 1964

Through more than three decades of success in the music business, songwriter and record producer Mike Curb built his company into one of the most important independent country record labels of the 1990s. Curb's roster includes one of the decade's biggest-selling country artists, TIM MC-GRAW, along with two female acts who seem destined for continued success: LEANN RIMES and JO DEE MESSINA.

Curb was just twenty years old when he founded his empire in Los Angeles in 1964. Initially he called it Sidewalk Records but changed the name to Curb Records a few years later. The company's early releases were primarily motion picture soundtracks that he composed for major film studios. During the same period, Curb launched his own musical group, the Mike Curb Congregation, which found international success with a series of albums, including *Burning Bridges* and *Put Your Hand in the Hand.* Through the group, he found early country success with "All for the Love of Sunshine," a #1 for HANK WILLIAMS JR. that Curb wrote.

In 1969 Curb merged his company with MGM RECORDS and was named president of the company. Curb is credited with turning MGM's fortunes around by producing a series of hits, including "One Bad Apple" (the Osmonds), "The Candy Man" (Sammy Davis Jr.), and "I'm Leaving It All Up to You" (Donny & MARIE OSMOND).

After MGM was sold in 1974, Curb continued to build the Curb Music Company and the Curb/WARNER label. Through the 1970s and 1980 Curb was involved in several co-ventures with other labels, including RCA and MCA. The co-ventures permitted Curb to build his own label by concentrating on the music, while allowing the other companies to handle distribution, marketing, and radio promotion.

Over the years, Curb Records evolved into a fully self-contained record company. Curb had maintained a Nashville office, but in 1993 he decided to move his headquarters to Tennessee and left the L.A. operation as a satellite office. By 1996 the Curb Group of companies was operating no less than three labels: Curb, MCG/Curb, and Curb/Universal. In addition to McGraw, Rimes, and Messina, the company roster includes WYNONNA, HAL KETCHUM, MERLE HAGGARD, LYLE LOVETT, Hank Williams Jr., David Kersh, Burnin' Daylight, JUNIOR BROWN, EDDY ARNOLD, and SAWYER BROWN.

One of the industry's most astute businessmen, Mike Curb structured his co-ventures to ensure that he would maintain control of the master recordings from all projects. In addition to contemporary releases, Curb's catalogue of reissues and compilations now total more than 500 albums, including titles by ROY ACUFF, Eddy Arnold, and KENNY ROGERS.
—*Calvin Gilbert*

Dick Curless
b. Fort Fairfield, Maine, March 17, 1932; d. May 25, 1995

Richard William Curless, nicknamed the Baron of Country Music after his 1966 hit "The Baron," was a regional favorite in the Northeast for his wide-ranging repertoire and his smooth, sonorous baritone. Curless's family moved to Massachusetts from Maine when he was eight, he grew up in Gilbertville, and in 1948 he landed his own fifteen-minute radio slot as the Tumbleweed Kid in Ware, Massachusetts. In 1952 he was drafted and shipped out to Korea, where he served as Rice Paddy Ranger, a GI-DJ for the Armed Forces Network, through 1954; his own record "China Nights" became a hit in Far Eastern theater.

Back home in 1957, he won an Arthur Godfrey *Talent Scouts* contest singing "Nine Pound Hammer." In 1965 Curless released the driving "A Tombstone Every Mile" on his own Allagash label; the trucker's song eventually became a #5 hit after being picked up by CAPITOL's Tower subsidiary label. He followed that success with twenty-one more country chart hits, including "Six Times a Day" (#12, 1965) and "Big Wheel Cannonball" (#27, 1970). In the

1960s he toured with BUCK OWENS's All-American Show, and in 1968 he was heard on the *Killers Three* movie soundtrack. He died shortly after recording his final album, *Traveling Through.*
—*Walt Trott*

REPRESENTATIVE RECORDINGS
Long, Lonesome Road (Stetson, 1986); *Traveling Through* (Rounder, 1995)

Ken Curtis
Curtis Wain Gates b. Lamar, Colorado, July 2, 1916; d. April 28, 1991

Curtis Wain Gates, who was to gain worldwide fame as Festus Haggen on the TV series *Gunsmoke,* was born on a homestead in southeastern Colorado. Influenced by his musical pioneer family, a deep and abiding interest in music surfaced at an early age and was further stimulated by his participation in college musicals. In 1938 Curtis was signed by NBC Radio in Hollywood. Then, seeking a replacement for his vocalist Frank Sinatra, Tommy Dorsey signed Curtis in 1941 and gave him the professional name Ken Curtis. Upon the return of Sinatra, Curtis was loaned out to the Shep Fields Orchestra shortly before he joined the army in 1942.

Returning to civilian life, Curtis was signed by Columbia Pictures for a series of musical westerns. In 1949 the SONS OF THE PIONEERS hired him to fill the spot created by the departure of their longtime lead singer, Tim Spencer. Although Curtis officially left the Sons of the Pioneers in 1953, he recorded with the group on RCA through 1957 and is the featured vocalist on such Sons of the Pioneers recordings as "Room Full of Roses," "This Ain't the Same Ol' Range," "Little White Cross," "Roses," "Wedding Dolls," and "Crazy Heart."

His role as "Monk" in the *Have Gun, Will Travel* television series led to his big break in television when he was signed for the Festus Haggen role in the *Gunsmoke* episodes that ran from 1964 to 1975.
—*Ken Griffis*

Sonny Curtis
b. Meadow, Texas, May 9, 1937

Throughout his career as a songwriter, singer, and musician, Sonny Curtis has helped shape the sound of American music. Citing bluegrass as his earliest musical influence, he began his performing career at age fourteen, playing with numerous young singers and musicians in the Lubbock, Texas, area. Among them were WAYLON JENNINGS and BUDDY HOLLY. Curtis played on Holly's first commercial recordings and wrote his "Rock Around with Ollie Vee."

After Curtis graduated from high school, his song "Someday" was recorded by WEBB PIERCE, whose version reached #12 on the charts in 1957. Curtis joined SLIM WHITMAN's band in 1956, and his first recordings as a solo artist were released on DOT RECORDS in 1958. As a member of the Crickets (post-Holly), he backed the EVERLY BROTHERS on a tour of England. Drafted into the army in 1960, he wrote the Everlys' "Walk Right Back" during basic training.

Curtis's other hit songs through the years have included Bobby Fuller's "I Fought the Law" and Keith Whitley's "I'm No Stranger to the Rain." He also wrote and performed the now-classic TV theme "Love Is All Around" for *The*

Mary Tyler Moore Show. After recording for a variety of record labels through the 1960s and 1970s, he released three LPs for ELEKTRA RECORDS in the early 1980s and scored a Top Twenty hit with "Good Ol' Girls."

In addition to his songwriting, Curtis has continued to tour internationally. He was featured in 1994 along with Eric Clapton, Mark Knopfler, and Keith Richards in a television special celebrating the fortieth anniversary of the Fender Stratocaster guitar.

Curtis participated in the 1996 Decca album *Not Fade Away (Remembering Buddy Holly)* as a member of the Crickets. —*Janet E. Williams*

T. Tommy Cutrer
b. Osyka, Mississippi, June 29, 1924

Thomas Clinton Cutrer was one of country radio's best-known personalities—and one of its busiest. Cutrer (pronounced *Cut-trair*) announced both national (ABC-TV's *Johnny Cash Show*) and regional broadcasts (*Nashville Scene, Music City USA*); tried his hand as a recording artist (MERCURY, DOT, RCA); and worked as a promoter and restaurateur (Kentucky Fried Chicken franchises). In a bid for Congress in 1976, he lost to Albert Gore Jr. Cutrer was later elected in 1978 to the Tennessee State Senate, serving as Transportation Committee chairman, which indirectly led to work on behalf of the national AFL/CIO.

Cutrer was eighteen when hired by WSKB, McComb, Mississippi. He moved on to jobs at WDSU–New Orleans; WJDX–Jackson, Mississippi; KARK–LittleRock; WMC–Memphis; and WREC–Memphis, where Cutrer worked with studio engineer SAM PHILLIPS, who later founded the SUN RECORDS label. After stints at WSLI in Jackson, Mississippi, and KWYZ and KNUZ in Houston, Cutrer landed at KCIJ in Shreveport. A drummer, Cutrer performed in honky-tonks and inherited WEBB PIERCE's band (including Jimmy Day, FLOYD CRAMER, and Lloyd Ellis) when Pierce left Shreveport for the GRAND OLE OPRY in 1952. Cutrer's own drumming halted when he lost a leg in a 1953 car crash; at the time he was making the move to Nashville to work for WSM. During his ten years at WSM, Cutrer announced at the GRAND OLE OPRY and handled the all-night show *Opry Star Spotlight*. He augmented his pay doing commercials. In 1964 Cutrer left WSM to buy his own station, WJQS, in Jackson, Mississippi. In 1980 he was inducted into the Country Disc Jockey Hall of Fame.
—*Walt Trott*

Billy Ray Cyrus
b. Flatwoods, Kentucky, August 25, 1961

Pegged as a one-hit wonder for his debut smash "Achy Breaky Heart," Billy Ray Cyrus has gone on to display staying power in country music and a commitment to doing music his way, as demonstrated by his reliance on his road band in the recording studio.

Cyrus burst upon the Nashville scene like a shooting star in June 1992 when his debut album, *Some Gave All,* topped the *Billboard* Hot 200 pop album chart within two weeks of its May 30 release, propelled there by its catchy, guitar-driven #1 country single (#4 pop), "Achy Breaky Heart." The album's swift rise to #1 was the fastest in the history of the *Billboard* Hot 200. (The album also hit #1 on

Billy Ray Cyrus

the country charts.) By the end of year the single went on to sell more than 1 million copies, while the album topped 5 million.

Although Cyrus seemed an overnight success, the thirty-year-old singer had been working a full decade for his shot at stardom. At age twenty he dropped out of Kentucky's Georgetown College and began playing in nightclubs around his hometown of Flatwoods. In 1984 he moved to Los Angeles, trying to break into the town's rock recording scene. After two years of rejection, during which he was reduced to working by turns as an exotic dancer and a used-car salesman, he returned to Flatwoods and formed the band Sly Dog. Alternating regular gigs at a Huntington, West Virginia, nightclub called the Ragtime Lounge with regular trips to Nashville, he gradually made inroads in the country music business.

In July 1989 prominent manager JACK MCFADDEN agreed to handle Cyrus. In 1990 HAROLD SHEDD signed Cyrus to MERCURY RECORDS, and in February 1991 Cyrus and Sly Dog began recording *Some Gave All,* which he completed in July. (Sly Dog backed Cyrus on his first four releases.) The album's release was delayed nearly a year as Mercury executives determined how best to market the rock-influenced record to country fans. Ultimately they offered the album's debut single, "Achy Breaky Heart," initially only to country dance clubs, along with a dance contest and instructional dance video. Next, the song's music video premiered in March 1992 on TNN and CMT, where Cyrus's good looks and dancing ability helped to sell the song. By the time the album *Some Gave All* was finally released, demand was skyrocketing.

Although Cyrus's white-hot popularity cooled off considerably since 1992, he continued to place hits in the country Top Ten through 1993 with "Could've Been Me" (#2, 1992), "She's Not Cryin' Anymore" (#6, 1992), "In the Heart of a Woman" (#3, 1993), and "Somebody New" (#9,

1993). As of late 1997 his highest-charting single since then has been "It's All the Same to Me," which reached #19 in September 1997. Similarly, after the multiplatinum success of *Some Gave All,* Cyrus has seen only *It Won't Be the Last* certified platinum and *Storm in the Heartland* certified gold.

His fourth album, *Trail of Tears* (Mercury, 1996), earned considerable critical acclaim for its tasteful blend of acoustic and electric textures as well as for Cyrus's maturing taste in songs. That album also was the first that he and Sly Dog lead guitarist Terry Shelton produced themselves after three productions by Joe Scaife and Jim Cotton. At the 1997 TNN/*Music City News* awards, fans voted his "Trail of Tears" the Single of the Year. —*Paul Kingsbury*

REPRESENTATIVE RECORDINGS

Some Gave All (Mercury, 1992); *It Won't Be the Last* (Mercury, 1993); *Storm in the Heartland* (Mercury, 1994); *Trail of Tears* (Mercury, 1996); *The Best of Billy Ray Cyrus: Cover to Cover* (Mercury, 1997)

The Look of Country:
The Colorful History of Country Music Costuming

Holly George-Warren

Perhaps more than any other form of American music, country music has been closely identified with a certain visual style. From the music's earliest popular entertainers—JIM-MIE RODGERS and the CARTER FAMILY—to contemporary superstars such as GARTH BROOKS and SHANIA TWAIN, fashion has played a key role in defining the public personas of country artists. During the first decade or so of commercial country music, a link was forged between the performer's music and his or her geographical and cultural roots in the rural Southeast. Entertainers' typical attire ranged from work clothes such as overalls to Sunday-go-to-meeting best. By the late 1930s, with the greater dissemination of American popular culture via movies, radio, and recordings, the heroic look of the cowboy—reinforced and popularized by B-western and singing cowboy idols—became *de rigueur* among country artists and remains a major component of the country image today.

Back in the 1920s and 1930s, the Carter Family dressed as their audiences would for church. This was only fitting, since many of the Carters' early performances took place in church halls and schoolhouses in rural Virginia and Tennessee. The Singing Brakeman, Jimmie Rodgers, also typically gussied himself up in crisp white linen suits with matching boaters but also drew on his background as a railroad worker to forge a look (railroad cap and canvas railman garb) that gave credence to his moniker. For one publicity shot, Rodgers dressed like a cowboy, down to his chaps, neckerchief, and Stetson—a signpost of what was to come. Popular at about this time were traveling vaudeville and minstrel shows, which usually featured a backwoods rube character or family dressed similarly to denizens of Dogpatch in the *Li'l Abner* comic strip. Patched britches and gingham dresses, worn-out straw hats, pigtails and protruding front teeth, corncob pipes—these exaggerated clichés defined hayseed style, the look that predominated during the early years of the WLS *NATIONAL BARN DANCE*, the GRAND OLE OPRY, and other barn dance programs. Like his counterparts at WLS, Opry founder and first MC GEORGE D. HAY required his performers to forgo their Sunday best for this hillbilly look.

Things began to change, though, in the late 1930s, when western-attired singers such as GENE AUTRY and PATSY MONTANA, stars of the *National Barn Dance,* and L.A.-based SONS OF THE PIONEERS began making hits with buckaroo-themed songs such as Autry's "Back in the Saddle Again" and Montana's "I Want to Be a Cowboy's Sweetheart." Building on the precedents established earlier by OTTO GRAY and a handful of others, these stars pushed the trend toward heroic-looking western wear, which helped country performers overcome negative hillbilly stereotypes. After all, who wouldn't prefer the garb of a dashing buckaroo to that of a backwoods clodhopper? Autry, who grew up on a small ranch in Texas before moving to Oklahoma, was a natural in his wide-brimmed Stetson, western shirt with neckerchief, and cowboy boots. Likewise, Montana's cowgirl outfits, which included a cowboy hat, bolero vest, neck scarf, and fringed split skirt, influenced generations of female country performers, as did her contemporaries the GIRLS OF THE GOLDEN WEST and LOUISE MASSEY & THE WESTERNERS.

Early in his career, Autry dressed in a casual, workaday western style like that of cattle-punching cowpokes. This practical clothing style can be traced back to the mid-1800s, when cowboys developed functional garb to cope with the necessities of life on the range. The prototypical denim jeans, Levi's, were "invented" in 1849 when Levi Strauss, of a New York tailoring family, joined the California Gold Rush, intended to finance his trip by selling bolts of canvas to make into tents. Instead, he found customers needing britches, so he fashioned the durable fabric into trousers, and by 1860 his indigo-dyed pants with copper rivets were a smashing success among miners and cowboys alike.

Cowboy boots and Stetson hats—a roughrider's essential accoutrements—also date from these years. Derived from British cavalry boots in the 1860s cowboy boots with high heels, high tops, and stitching on the toe gradually evolved over forty years. Designed to fit easily into stirrups without sliding out, cowboy boots with tall leather tops protected the legs and feet from such hazards as snakebite and stinging nettles. By 1920, with rodeos and dude ranches commonplace out West and with westerns popular on the silver screen, fancier boot styles, with colorful inlaid designs, a variation of toe styles, and intricate stitching, began appearing. When he became a sensation, Autry ordered custom boots by Lucchese, Olsen-Seltzer, and other specialty leathercraft companies that created one-of-a-kind handmade boots in a variety of shades with elaborate detailing, featuring intricate hand tooling and inlay of arrows, bald eagles, flowers, butterflies, suits of cards, and other designs on the boot fronts.

Cowboy hats similarly evolved from a prototype designed by John B. Stetson, a Philadelphia milliner who ventured to Colorado during the Gold Rush in 1865. Fashioning a broad-brimmed, high-crowned creation from beaver and rabbit hide that he boiled and turned into felt, Stetson developed a waterproof derivative of the sombreros that Mexican vaqueros had been wearing for years. After selling his sample to an eager cowpoke for five bucks, Stetson rushed back to Philadelphia and began sending his "Boss of the Plains" headgear out west for sales. Dimensions for crown height and brim width varied, evolving into the popular ten-gallon hat (so called for its high crown and volume), as stars of screen, recording, and rodeos chose individual looks with which they became identified. (As a rule, the bigger the star, the higher and broader the hat.) The first hats came in taupe or beige, but by the time of B-western talkies, white and black hats—which came to signify good and evil—were in great demand. Cowboy hats and boots graced the Grand Ole Opry stage at least as early as western singer ZEKE CLEMENTS's 1934–36 stint with the long-running radio show. In 1937 PEE WEE KING's flashy Golden West Cowboys joined the show and took stylish western wear to new heights at the Opry.

Cowboy shirts and western suits assumed greater fashion importance beginning in the 1930s. By this time, casual western clothes had already been catching on among country artists and, of course, the singing cowboys of Hollywood movies. Moreover, the western shirt also had distinctive styling developed for practical reasons for the working cowboy and rodeo rider. The front and back yokes and bibfront, for example, provided extra warmth and padding; snaps (which first appeared in the 1930s) substituted for buttons to prevent rodeo injuries: "If your shirt got snagged on the pommel of your saddle, the snaps would pop open and not hang you there like buttons would," explained Jack Weil, who founded Rockmount, one of the first western-wear companies, in 1936. H-Bar-C is another mass-market western clothing firm dating from the 1930s that is still in business today. Both companies were among those with mail-order western catalogues, which first began appearing in the 1920s.

Other design elements found in the West made their way into cowboy clothes: fringe and buckskin (inspired by the garments of various Indian tribes) worn by mountain men, fancy embroidery on Mexican vaqueros' jackets, and intricate beadwork found on Plains Indians' attire. In Buffalo Bill's Wild West shows of the 1880s, these dazzling, eye-catching details became more and more popular, as they were depicted in all their glory in books and magazines.

Eventually the opulent merged with the ordinary in the work of a few tailors who specialized in western wear. One of the first, Philadelphia-based Ben the Rodeo Tailor (or Rodeo Ben, for short), found a batch of clients among B-western, rodeo, and singing cowboy stars who wanted unique, customized looks. Born in 1894, Rodeo Ben opened his first shop, billed "the East's most western store," in 1930. With a retail business in front and custom tailoring in back, Ben attracted Tom Mix and Gene Autry, among others, with his kaleidoscopic fabrics (including gabardine, flannel, and twill), fine embroidery (from Indian heads to bluebirds), and high-quality designs. When ROY ROGERS became his client a few years after Autry (Rogers's Republic Films predecessor), Rodeo Ben vowed never to design similar outfits for the two. Rodeo Ben is credited with being the first to put metal glove snaps instead of buttons on cowboy shirts, in 1933, for his rodeo customers; he began using mother-of-pearl snaps for Autry and Rogers's shirts. Also on the East Coast, catering to rodeo stars who performed at Madison Square Garden, was New York City–based Fay Ward.

Just outside Los Angeles, amid the San Fernando Valley's ranches and western movie sets, was the Turk of Hollywood shop, opened by Polish-born tailor NATHAN TURK in 1923. By the 1930s, Turk's Sherman Oaks operation had begun catering to rodeo riders as well as to the film industry. Soon Turk won Autry and Rogers's business. Turk specialized in ornate costumes for Pasadena's annual Rose Bowl parade, and his designs became more and more spectacular. West Coast–based artists the MADDOX BROTHERS & ROSE and western swing bandleader SPADE COOLEY had discovered Turk's beautifully embroidered and vividly fringed garments by the 1940s. By then, themes and sounds were overlapping more than ever before, coinciding with not only a change in nomenclature (from hillbilly to country & western) but also the spread of the western look throughout country music. As vintage-clothing collector MARTY STUART has remarked, "Western wear and country music—there was a marriage there and it made perfect sense."

Perhaps more responsible than anyone else for country's embrace of fancy cowboy clothes was the loquacious, North Hollywood–based tailor NUDIE. Born in Russia and raised in Brooklyn, Nudie Cohn landed in Los Angeles in 1940, and after reportedly apprenticing with Turk, began creating custom western wear. Nudie's first client, "Smoke! Smoke! Smoke!" hitmaker TEX WILLIAMS, outfitted his band in Nudie's custom-made western suits. Though legend has it that Nudie's measurements were way off, Tex loved the suits anyway and began spreading the word. To meet the demand, the tailor opened Nudie's of Hollywood in 1947, where he tried to top each outfit with the next, embellishing the cowboy look with detailed embroidered designs, fringe, and, by late 1951, rhinestones. "My impression of an entertainer is that he should wear a flashy outfit," Nudie once said, "to be fair to the public." Of course, Autry and Rogers began commissioning Nudie to design spectacular outfits for their public appearances; Rogers's canine pal Bullet the Wonder Dog was handstitched on the back of one of Roy's shirts. Said Rogers of his sparkly Nudie suits, "When I came through the gates and the lights hit me, I lit up like a Christmas tree."

In 1951, LEFTY FRIZZELL became the first country artist to wear a rhinestone-studded Nudie shirt. Soon after, western wear became so popular in Nashville that Audrey and Hank Williams, both satisfied Nudie customers, opened Hank and Audrey's Corral there in 1951; Hank's trademark white suit dotted with black musical notes was a Nudie. By the late 1950s, rhinestones had become synonymous with country music. "Back in those days," says Marty Stuart, "they wore rhinestones as if they were badges on a uniform." Nudie's specialty lay in designing ensembles featuring an artist's own unique trademark, such as PORTER WAGONER's wagon wheel–covered costumes, and embroidered details from hit songs such as WEBB PIERCE's "In the Jailhouse Now" and GEORGE JONES's "White Lightnin'." Appearing next to their shimmering cowboy-suited counterparts, female country artists dressed up in rhinestone-studded or appliquéd-and-fringed cowgirl suits (Audrey Williams's, DALE EVANS's, and the young PATSY CLINE's favorite look), or colorful tiered-and-trimmed gauze frocks inspired by Mexican fiesta dresses and Navajo Indian skirts (favored by Mother Maybelle and the Carter Sisters).

Beginning in the mid-sixties, Nudie employed English-born embroidery artisan Rose Clements (b. Rose Grossman in London, August 13, 1919), who brought special machines with her when she moved from Britain to California. Her intricate and original designs required a great amount of skill and encompassed Swiss, chain, and satin stitches. Nudie also hired expert leatherworkers who created fancy, custom cowboy boots that often matched the outfits.

To meet the demand, Nudie eventually employed twenty-one tailors, one of whom, MANUEL Cuevas, soon became a star in his own right. Born in about 1933 in Mexico, the deliberately mysterious Manuel (who, like his mentor, goes by his first name alone) learned tailoring from his older brothers before moving to Los Angeles. He joined Nudie in the 1950s, just in time for western wear's flashy peak, when the clientele included the aforementioned artists plus HANK SNOW (bullfrogs and lily pads on one suit), ERNEST TUBB, FARON YOUNG, COWBOY COPAS, MERLE TRAVIS, RAY PRICE, JOHNNY CASH (black, of course), and JIMMY C. NEWMAN (a Cajun motif).

"That's when I discovered what I wanted to do with my life," Manuel has said. "I dressed artists in rhinestones, fringe, and embroidery, and brought all this craftsmanship into clothing for entertainers. It was a wonderful time." Manuel, who was married to and divorced from Nudie's daughter and eventually branched out on his own in the 1970s, became the link to the next generation of flashy western wearers.

By the late 1960s, country's look had become more sophisticated as its music became sweetened via the NASHVILLE SOUND. Cocktail dresses and tuxedos, like those worn by singers in New York cabarets, became the norm. Gradually, gleaming cowboy clothes fell out of favor in Nashville, though BAKERSFIELD-based BUCK OWENS began wearing his own distinctive Nudie suits featuring short bolero jackets studded with luminous rhinestones and twinkling metallic embroidery.

In the early 1970s, the Outlaw movement spearheaded by WAYLON JENNINGS and WILLIE NELSON ushered in the down-home-meets-counterculture style, with bandannas worn on the head rather than around the neck. Scuffed cowboy boots—or tennis shoes—peeked out from under faded, patched jeans, and simple cowboy shirts were most often made of denim. A segment of the long-haired audience who became the Outlaws' fans stuck with the flash and sparkle, however. Beginning in the late 1960s, members of the Rolling Stones and BYRDS began buying from Nudie, culminating in the spectacular suits designed by Manuel for GRAM PARSONS and his FLYING BURRITO BROTHERS. The embodiment of Parsons's musical goals—taking traditional country to the rock & roll audience—his most famous suit featured white flared hiphugger pants, and a short fitted jacket embroidered with naked women, marijuana leaves, pills, and a large cross on the jacket's back. Other country-rock artists who embraced the western look included NEW RIDERS OF THE PURPLE SAGE, Commander Cody, and western swing practitioners ASLEEP AT THE WHEEL. Into the 1980s, cowpunks—artists playing country-tinged, high-energy music outside the mainstream of both rock & roll and country—wore western, including RANK & FILE; Lone Justice; and, before she evolved into a pop diva, K. D. LANG.

It wasn't until the late 1970s and early 1980s that the decorative cowboy look began coming back in a big way to country music. Two quite different trends in country music—Urban Cowboy and New Traditionalist—ushered in western wear's resurgence. The former tended toward the polyester, mass-market, cheaply made look popularized by the 1980 film URBAN COWBOY, starring John Travolta. The clean-cut New Traditionalist look, brought into vogue largely by GEORGE STRAIT in the early 1980s, called for top-quality cowboy boots and hats, along with freshly pressed jeans and western shirts. That clothing style has remained the dominant look in country music through the 1990s and is worn by nearly every best-selling young male star and even a few females, such as TERRI CLARK. From this everyman western look, Garth Brooks developed his trademark style—oversized hat; snug, crisp jeans; and busy-print cowboy shirt with oversized yoke—which remains prevalent among the boot-scooting set. BROOKS & DUNN parlayed their flamboyant look into their own retail line of ready-to-western-wear manufactured by Panhandle Slim.

By the late 1970s, the dominant look for female country stars was high-glitz, a style ushered in by DOLLY PARTON. As she evolved from Porter Wagoner's duet partner, a country-lass bombshell busting out of gingham and denim, to solo superstar, her look rivaled that of a Las Vegas showgirl, with sparkly and sheer fabrics that clung to every curve. Other stars followed suit, with LORETTA LYNN and TAMMY WYNETTE abandoning demure lace gowns and down-homey denim and polyester pantsuits for glitzy tulle and sequin-studded Bob Mackie knockoffs. In the late 1980s, former rodeo cowgirl Reba McEntire also began indulging in a lavish, Hollywood-style wardrobe for concert appearances—changing into and out of as many as ten different outfits in a single concert.

As country became more like rock music, so did its dress code. By the mid-nineties, the hottest new country queens were almost indistinguishable from their pop-diva sisters, in both their vocal styles and their stage looks. Shania Twain made a splash with sexy midriff-baring tops, minis, hot pants, and skin-tight catsuits; likewise, MINDY MCCREADY sported torso-baring getups, showing off her gleaming navel ring. In short, both dressed as if they were rock stars—or rock stars' supermodel girlfriends. Of course, TANYA TUCKER had blazed the country-coquette-meets-rock-star trail back in the early seventies with her second-skin leather jumpsuits, modeled after those of ELVIS PRESLEY.

Concurrently, however, the New Traditionalist style embraced the golden years of western wear as its model. CARLENE CARTER, daughter of June and granddaughter of Maybelle, began wearing western-detailed jackets with her miniskirts and cowboy boots. In the mid-eighties, L.A.-based DWIGHT YOAKAM made his own contribution to the revival of classic western styling when he sought out Manuel. "I asked him about what I used to call the Buck Owens jacket," said Yoakam. "Manuel said, 'Oh, yes, the bolero. I did so many of them in the fifties and sixties.' I said, 'Yeah, I wanna try one of those,' and he started making them for me." Yoakam and Manuel began a creative partnership that resulted in the singer's signature western style: low-slung cowboy hat, with fancy embroidered bolero or suede-fringed jacket over skin-tight, concho-studded jeans (sometimes adorned with suede chaps) or leather pants, and cowboy boots. "Manuel makes reality from ideas I have in my head," Yoakam has said.

In Nashville, where Manuel moved his shop in October 1989, his foremost client is Marty Stuart, who, in the late 1980s, began collecting classic designs by Manuel, Nudie, and Turk after borrowing a classic western jacket from veteran singer CARL SMITH. "I thought, 'If I got some of those and put them on a band, it might make our videos jump a little better and give us an identity," Stuart has recalled. "Nashville never wore them anymore, so I called everyone who ever wore rhinestones" to inquire about buying their old show clothes.

Stuart acquired his first Manuel designs when he was a twelve-year-old mandolin player touring with LESTER FLATT. Manuel and Stuart have since collaborated on an array of resplendent pieces, many featuring Stuart's trademark horseshoes and hearts; to go with his dazzling duds, Stuart commissions the fanciest boots since the days of Gene Autry and Roy Rogers from Nashville custom bootmaker Bo Riddle. Stuart also frequents Ranch Dressing, the Nashville shop owned by designer Katy K (née Kattelman), who first began making imaginatively embroidered cowboy shirts and jackets in New York in the 1980s. Encouraged by Manuel, Katy K moved her distinctive line of western wear, along with her collection of vintage pieces by Turk, Nudie, and Rodeo Ben, to Music City and opened her Ranch Dressing shop in November 1994. She has since begun outfitting Nashville's hippest honky-tonk artists, including BR5-49, whose repertoire of classic country mirrors the golden age of western style.

Hanging in Marty Stuart's Nashville office is an elaborately detailed, exquisitely embroidered wall hanging. He commissioned it from Rose Clements, the English artist responsible for many of Nudie's and Manuel's most intricate embroidery designs. Asked about the origin of his obsession with western wear and its accoutrements, Stuart says, "I thought about those old suits people used to wear when I was a kid, when country was colorful, happy, and carefree. I think that's what those clothes represent. A tremendous amount of integrity and labor goes into their art. They are truly pieces of art."

D·D·D·D · D·D·D·D

D Records

established in Houston, Texas, 1958

Formed by HAROLD "PAPPY" DAILY after he and DON PIERCE, his partner in STARDAY RECORDS, parted in 1958, D Records has continued in some form into the 1990s, still operated by the Daily family.

Pierce kept the Starday name, but Daily managed, at least initially, to hold on to some of its roster, including ED-DIE NOACK, James O'Gwynn, and Glenn Barber. Intended originally as an experimental label—material was issued in hope that it would hit and be leased to a major label, as proved the case with the BIG BOPPER's "Chantilly Lace"—D issued a varied, uneven flow of material, from country classics like Noack's "Have Blues Will Travel" to custom issues of questionable quality. Between 1976 and 1979 GEORGE STRAIT and the Ace in the Hole Band had three singles released on D Records. An example of a recent D release is "A Day with Remington," an excellent instrumental album featuring steel guitar legends HERB REMINGTON and JIMMY DAY.

— *Kevin Coffey*

REPRESENTATIVE RECORDING

"D" Records, Volume One (Bear Family, 1995), 4 CD set of 1958–59 recordings

Da Costa Woltz's Southern Broadcasters

This remarkable stringband consisted of fiddler Ben Jarrell (father of TOMMY JARRELL) and banjo players Da Costa Woltz and Frank Jenkins, whose homes were in the Mount Airy–Round Peak area of western North Carolina. The group seems to have existed only for purposes of an extended session for GENNETT RECORDS in Richmond, Indiana, where they journeyed for the session in April 1927.

Leader Woltz had visions of radio work (hence the band's name) and other public appearances for the band, but these never materialized. A fourth member, Price Goodson, was only twelve and was featured on only a few solos. Jenkins performed solos on fiddle and banjo; the remainder of the eighteen sides consisted of old songs and breakdowns by the band, forcefully led by Jarrell's singing and fiddling.

Gennett issued the records on its own imprint as well as a variety of inexpensive, poorly distributed labels, including Champion, CHALLENGE, and Herwin. Good copies of these are rare today, though an LP collecting some of the band's 1927 recordings was issued in 1972.

—*Dick Spottswood*

REPRESENTATIVE RECORDING

Da Costa Woltz's Southern Broadcasters (County, 1972)

Ted Daffan

b. Beauregard Parish, Louisiana, September 21, 1912; d. October 6, 1996

One of the great songwriters in country music, who helped usher in the modern era of country songwriting, Theron Eugene Daffan was also one of the best-selling bandleaders of the 1940s.

Uninterested in a music career until he fell in love with HAWAIIAN MUSIC at age twenty, Daffan quickly began learning the steel guitar. By the following year he was not only

Ted Daffan

teaching guitar but also leading his Blue Islanders on Houston radio. His introduction to country music came via the Blue Ridge Playboys, a fledgling local western swing band that included fiddler LEON SELPH and guitarist FLOYD TILLMAN, in 1934. Daffan joined the group until sidelined by ill health. In 1936 he teamed with vocalist JERRY IRBY and made his recording debut the following year with SHELLY LEE ALLEY, recording his first composition, "I'm Still in Love with You." Soon he joined the popular BAR X COW-BOYS, but concentrated on songwriting in hopes of getting his own recording contract.

Daffan's big break came when CLIFF BRUNER recorded a number of his songs at his 1939 DECCA sessions, including the seminal trucker's song, "Truck Driver's Blues," which sold more than 100,000 copies. The song led to a COLUM-BIA recording contract for Daffan, who began recording in 1940, though he remained with the Bar X Cowboys until mid-1941. Daffan's band, the Texans, featured the lead guitar of Buddy Buller and the accordion of Harry Sorensen and Freddy Courtney. His emphasis on these instruments proved distinctive and influential. Daffan immediately produced major hits "Worried Mind" and "I'm a Fool to Care." He was already one of Columbia's top acts when he followed these with the classic two-sided million seller "Born to Lose," backed with "No Letter Today," recorded in Hollywood in 1942. The songs established Daffan as a major star, and he worked the competitive West Coast dance circuit from 1944 to 1946. Although he returned to Texas after that, the hits kept coming, from "Heading Down the Wrong Highway" to "I've Got Five Dollars and It's Saturday Night." By the early fifties, his career was in eclipse, and he returned to Houston and disbanded the Texans. In 1955 Daffan started his own label, Daffan Records, which he revived intermittently until 1971, but his main source of income became new hit versions of his classic songs, such as Joe Barry's 1961 revival of "I'm a Fool to Care," and especially Ray Charles's early sixties covers of "Born to Lose," "No Letter Today," and "Worried Mind."

—*Kevin Coffey*

REPRESENTATIVE RECORDING

Hillbilly Fever, Volume Two: Honky-Tonk (Rhino, 1995) (various-artists reissue containing Daffan's original recording of "Born to Lose")

Pappy Daily
b. Yoakum, Texas, February 8, 1902; d. December 5, 1987

Almost a caricature of an old-time record man, Harold Westcott Daily was blunt, cigar-chomping, and very much a hands-on operator who knew every facet of the business but made a point of emphasizing his lack of musical knowledge. Based in Houston, he was able to tap into a pool of talent that most labels ignored. He made the first commercial recordings by GEORGE JONES, WEBB PIERCE, HANK LOCKLIN, ROGER MILLER, the BIG BOPPER, and WILLIE NELSON. Even GEORGE STRAIT made early recordings for his D RECORDS label.

After serving in the marines during World War I, Daily joined the Southern Pacific Railroad as a bookkeeper and stayed until 1932. Then he started the South Coast Amusement Company, selling and servicing amusement machines. South Coast branched into jukeboxes and then records. In 1949 Daily began recording local acts, selling the masters to FOUR STAR RECORDS, a label he distributed.

Pappy Daily (standing) with George Jones

Among the artists he uncovered in this way were Webb Pierce and Hank Locklin (the latter bestowing the affectionate nickname "Pappy"). Seeing little return from the Four Star arrangement, Daily started STARDAY RECORDS with Jack Starnes Jr. in June 1953.

Daily's distribution companies, H. W. Daily, Inc., and Big State, dominated record wholesaling in Texas, although he sold them to his sons in 1957 shortly after Starday entered into a pact with MERCURY RECORDS. After Mercury and Starday split, Daily started D Records, which is still in business. He shunted virtually all the promising artists he uncovered to major labels, forging a particularly close alliance with Art Talmadge, who was first at Mercury, then United Artists, and then Musicor.

Daily will also be remembered as George Jones's producer from 1953 until 1971. Their relationship ended acrimoniously when Jones bought his way out of his Musicor contract to join TAMMY WYNETTE at EPIC RECORDS.

—*Colin Escott*

Vernon Dalhart
b. Jefferson, Texas, April 6, 1883; d. September 15, 1948

Vernon Dalhart was one of the most productive and versatile figures of the early recording industry, who by chance slipped into the role of a singer of hillbilly songs and became by far the most prolific recorder of such material in the 1920s. Born Marion Try Slaughter, he derived his professional name from a couple of Texas towns where he worked as a cattle puncher in his teens before studying voice at the Dallas Conservatory of Music. By 1910 he was pursuing his career in New York, where he filled roles in opera and operetta productions. His first recording, "Can't You Heah Me Callin', Caroline?" (EDISON, 1917), revealed his skill with dialect songs, and for some years he

Vernon Dalhart

was busy making records for Edison, COLUMBIA, and other labels, a journeyman studio artist handling every kind of repertoire required by the popular disc market, from "coon song" to Hawaiian.

His 1924 Victor recording of "The Wreck of the Old '97" coupled with "The Prisoner's Song" became country music's first million seller and redirected the course of his career. Over the next nine years he devoted himself primarily to hillbilly songs, of which he recorded several hundred, routinely cutting the same material for half a dozen or more different companies. Since many of these recordings would then be released on subsidiary labels, a collection of all his distinct issues would run into thousands, though this near-domination of the hillbilly disc market was somewhat masked by an extensive use of pseudonyms such as Al Craver (Columbia), Tobe Little (OKEH), and Jeff Fuller (Vocalion).

A typical Dalhart recording featured a studio violinist, his own harmonica and sometimes Jew's harp, and the guitar of CARSON ROBISON, Dalhart's regular partner from 1924 to 1928, who also frequently sang a tenor part and wrote much of his material. They were joined in trio performances by the singer and violinist Adelyne Hood. Though Dalhart drew on minstrel-stage repertoire such as "Golden Slippers" and cowboy songs such as "Bury Me Not on the Lone Prairie," which he had learned in his youth in Texas, his richest vein of song was topical compositions such as "The Death of Floyd Collins," "The John T. Scopes Trial" (about the Dayton, Tennessee, court case over the teaching of evolution), "Little Marian Parker," "Farm Relief Song," and other pieces inspired by news stories of the day.

Although Dalhart is regarded by most scholars as peripheral to the stylistic development of country music, his recordings undoubtedly circulated widely in the South and disseminated songs that were taken up by both profes-

sional and amateur country performers. He is perhaps more important, however, for conveying a flavor of southern song to audiences unaccustomed to it, without the distractions of bucolic humor or impenetrable accent. As the veteran producer RALPH PEER wrote in *Variety* in 1955, "Dalhart had the peculiar ability to adapt hillbilly music to suit the taste of the non-hillbilly population. . . . He was a professional substitute for a real hillbilly." In this respect Dalhart may be seen as a kind of role model for BRADLEY KINCAID as well as for more obviously dependent figures such as FRANK LUTHER.

Dalhart's recording career virtually ended with the Depression—after 1933 there was just one final session for BLUEBIRD, in 1939—and by 1942 he was reduced to working as a factory night watchman. For a few years he offered his services as a voice teacher, though the thousands of recordings that could have furnished his credentials had long passed out of circulation, and the musical idiom to which he had made so singular a contribution had left him far behind.
—*Tony Russell*

REPRESENTATIVE RECORDINGS

The First Singing Cowboy (Mark 56, 1978, out of print); *Vernon Dalhart, Volumes I–IV* (Old Homestead, 1988, out of print)

Lacy J. Dalton
b. Bloomsburg, Pennsylvania, October 13, 1946

Lacy J. Dalton (Jill Byrem) arrived on the country scene in late 1979 with a promising self-titled album that spawned the Top Twenty hits "Crazy Blue Eyes" and "Losing Kind of Love." Different from most female country music singers of her generation in her gritty attitude and sensuous barroom voice, Dalton was named Best New Female Vocalist by the ACM in 1979. Unfortunately, her career predated country music's 1990s era of strong, independent women, and she never realized the commercial success she deserved.

Influenced by the folk music of BOB DYLAN and Joan Baez, Dalton abandoned her art studies at Brigham Young University to play folk and, later, after moving to California, rock music. Recording under the name Jill Croston, she released an album in 1978 that was sent by a lawyer friend to COLUMBIA RECORDS. BILLY SHERRILL signed her to Columbia and urged her to change her name; she adopted the name Lacy J. Dalton. Sherrill produced most of her hits for Columbia, including "Hard Times" (#7, 1980); "Takin' It Easy" (#2, 1981); "Everybody Makes Mistakes" (#5, 1981); and her signature song, "16th Avenue" (#7, 1982).

Dalton is also an excellent songwriter who often writes firsthand about working-class trials and triumphs. In 1971 her husband was paralyzed in a swimming pool accident. A week later, Dalton discovered she was pregnant. She supported her family on food stamps and part-time jobs, including waitressing, until her husband died in 1974.

The last of Dalton's seven studio albums for Columbia, *Highway Diner*, was released in 1986. A contract dispute and personal struggles with alcoholism kept her from recording again until 1988 when she was signed as the flagship artist for JIMMY BOWEN's Universal label. Her Universal debut, 1989's *Survivor,* arguably the best album of her career, featured KRIS KRISTOFFERSON's "The Heart" (#13, 1989) and the self-penned "Walking Wounded" and "Hard Luck

Ace." She next recorded *Lacy J.* for CAPITOL and scored a minor hit with "Black Coffee" (#15, 1990), but was not able to regain the momentum she enjoyed in the early 1980s.

—*Jack Bernhardt*

REPRESENTATIVE RECORDINGS

Lacy J. Dalton (Columbia, 1980); *Survivor* (Universal, 1989)

Dance (*see* Line Dancing, Square Dancing, and Clogging)

Charlie Daniels

b. Wilmington, North Carolina, October 28, 1936

The son of a Tarheel State lumberman, Charles Edward Daniels taught himself to play guitar by age fifteen and began learning the rudiments of bluegrass, rock, jazz, and country music that would become the foundation of his career. After playing in rock bands for several years, he enjoyed some success as a songwriter when ELVIS PRESLEY recorded his "It Hurts Me" in 1964. But the turning point came when, at the urging of BOB DYLAN's producer BOB JOHNSTON, Daniels moved to Nashville in 1967 and began to work as a session guitarist. He contributed to Dylan's *Nashville Skyline* and to albums by Ringo Starr, Leonard Cohen, MARTY ROBBINS, and others.

Daniels released his self-titled first album in 1970 on CAPITOL RECORDS, and the next year he assembled the Charlie Daniels Band, with Tom Crain (guitar), Joe "Taz" DeGregorio (keyboards), Charles Hayward (bass), and James Marshall (drums). *Te John, Grease & Wolfman* (1972), named for the band members' nicknames, was the first of five Daniels albums on the independent Kama Sutra label.

Charlie Daniels

By this time Daniels had been influenced by the Allman Brothers, and *Te John, Grease & Wolfman* exemplifies the style that Daniels would develop as one of the main exponents of southern rock.

Honey in the Rock, released the following year, contained the talking blues number "Uneasy Rider," a tale of confrontation between a long-haired, peace-loving hippie and a bar full of antagonistic honky-tonkers. The song became a Top Ten pop hit, and it began Daniels's tradition of recording successful songs—often novelty numbers—with topical content. He later revised the song as "Uneasy Rider '88," changing the scene of action from a honky-tonk to a gay bar.

Fire on the Mountain, released on Kama Sutra in 1974 and reissued by EPIC RECORDS in 1980, is perhaps Daniels's best album, featuring several concert favorites, including the redneck anthems "Long Haired Country Boy" and "The South's Gonna Do It," along with a hard-driving cover of the CHUBBY WISE bluegrass classic "Orange Blossom Special."

Daniels's greatest success came with the release in 1979 of *Million Mile Reflections.* Although musically similar to his earlier work, it featured "The Devil Went Down to Georgia," a rousing fiddle story-song based on the South's fiddle contest tradition and a Mephistopheles tale of gambling one's soul. Daniels's only song to hit #1 on the country chart, it also became a #3 pop hit and earned Daniels a Grammy and a CMA award for Single of the Year. Both the single and album sold 1 million copies. Riding the wave of success, the Charlie Daniels Band was named the CMA's Top Instrumental Group for 1979 and 1980.

Daniels continued to record and tour throughout the 1980s and 1990s. He also continued writing topical songs from a conservative political slant, such as "In America" (#13, 1980), "American Farmer" (#54, 1985), "Simple Man" (#12, 1989–90), and "America, I Believe in You" (#73, 1993), which dealt scathingly with such issues as crime, farm foreclosures, homelessness, and immigration. His 1994 release *The Door* was honored with a Dove Award for Best Gospel Album.

Daniels lives on his ranch in Mount Juliet, Tennessee. He continues to record and tour, and to host the "Volunteer Jam" charity concert he initiated in 1974.

—*Jack Bernhardt*

REPRESENTATIVE RECORDINGS

Te John, Grease & Wolfman (Buddah/Kama Sutra, 1972); *Fire on the Mountain* (Buddah/Kama Sutra, 1974); *Million Mile Reflections* (Epic, 1979); *Simple Man* (Epic, 1989)

Darby & Tarlton

Tom Darby b. Columbus, Georgia, 1890; d. ca. 1971
Jimmie Tarlton b. Cheraw, South Carolina, May 8, 1892; d. 1979

The team of Tom Darby and Jimmie Tarlton was the first country act to seriously incorporate the blues into their music. With Darby's soulful singing and Tarlton's remarkable work on what was then called the Hawaiian guitar, they produced an impressive series of records in the late 1920s and early 1930s, including several that became standards in the country repertoire. Their repertoire was one of the most eclectic in old-time music, ranging from genuine traditional ballads to vaudeville pieces, and from parlor songs to blues. Their loose, improvisational style, vastly different from the quiet precision of later duet acts such as the BLUE SKY BOYS, linked them more to authentic African-American country blues than other old-time styles.

The son of sharecroppers in Orange County, South Carolina, Tarlton was learning to play slide guitar from local blacks by the time he was twelve. At seventeen he left home and began busking—playing in bars and on street corners for spare change—and in 1922 met the famed Hawaiian guitarist Frank Ferrara, who taught him how to better use his slide. Returning to Georgia, in 1927 Tarlton met another skilled guitarist, Tom Darby. A cousin of RILEY PUCKETT, a nephew of a full-blooded Cherokee, Darby was a solid blues musician. The pair teamed up, and by late that year had attracted the notice of COLUMBIA talent scout FRANK WALKER.

Their second Columbia session, in November 1927, produced their career record—a two-sided hit of "Columbus Stockade Blues" and "Birmingham Jail." Sales of more than 200,000 made it one of the all-time Columbia bestsellers in those days and helped both songs become country music standards. Both songs had genuine folk roots, but had been reworked by the singers; in later years, Tarlton would claim he had written "Birmingham Jail" in 1925 when he really was incarcerated there; the song, in fact, helped win him a pardon.

During the next seven years (1927–33), Darby and Tarlton recorded some sixty songs for three major labels, but they never quite duplicated the success of their first hit. By 1935 both had pretty much retired from the professional circuit. During the 1960s, historians and folk music buffs rediscovered both men, and Tarlton, at least, made a comeback of sorts, doing several major festivals and recording a new solo LP. —*Charles Wolfe*

REPRESENTATIVE RECORDING

Darby and Tarlton: Complete Recordings (Bear Family, 1995)

Denver Darling
b. Whopock, Illinois, April 6, 1909; d. April 27, 1981

Although he is now remembered mainly as a songwriter, Denver Darling was one of country music's brightest and most prolific recording artists in the 1940s. Essentially a self-taught musician, he learned how to play three chords on the guitar from a neighbor in Jewett, Illinois (where the family moved after World War I). Within a couple of years he was singing and playing guitar at various places around his home area of Cumberland County. In 1929 he landed his first professional job as a performer on WBOW in Terre Haute, Indiana. Throughout the 1930s Darling spent time at several radio stations, mostly in the Midwest. For a brief time he was on the *NATIONAL BARN DANCE*, appearing in a trio with George "Shug" Fisher and Hugh Cross. Darling didn't gain widespread popularity, however, until he moved to New York City in September 1937.

Darling initially went to New York to appear on WOR and at a famous Greenwich Village nightspot, the VILLAGE BARN. He soon got his own radio show on WNEW and in 1941 made the first of several recording sessions for DECCA. He later recorded also for Deluxe and MGM. (Most of the Deluxe sides were issued under the pseudonym of Tex Grande.) Two weeks after the bombing of Pearl Harbor, Darling recorded "Cowards over Pearl Harbor," the first of several similar topical songs with which he had success during World War II. In 1945 he recorded "Juke Joint Mama," a song often believed to be the primary source of Jerry

Lieber and Mike Stoller's 1952 "Kansas City." On this and several other recordings he was backed by jazz cornetist Wild Bill Davison. At about the same time Darling wrote, in collaboration with Vaughn Horton and Milton Gabler, his most famous song: "Choo Choo Ch' Boogie." Although Darling never recorded the song, several others did. And in 1945 Louis Jordan & his Tympany Five had the biggest hit with the number; BILL HALEY resurrected "Choo Choo Ch' Boogie" again in 1950. ASLEEP AT THE WHEEL even revived the song in the 1970s.

Darling appeared at the First Annual Clef Award Presentation in CARNEGIE HALL, thereby becoming in 1945 the first country artist to perform in the prestigious hall. Unfortunately, within two years Denver had quit performing. Throat problems that plagued him for some time and a desire to raise his family somewhere other than New York City led to his retiring and moving to Jewett, Illinois, where he lived the life of a gentleman farmer. He remained a songwriter but never again achieved the level of popularity he attained during the 1940s, when he was headquartered in New York City and leading his bands, the Trail Blazers, the Texas Cowhands, and the Georgie Porgie Boys.
—*W. K. McNeil*

Johnny Darrell
b. Hopewell, Alabama, July 23, 1940; d. October 7, 1997

During his heyday, Johnny Darrell practically made a career of releasing lyrically adventurous country singles that then became standards through other singers' versions. Among the landmark tunes he helped introduce were CURLY PUTMAN's "Green Green Grass of Home" (1965), MEL TILLIS's "Ruby, Don't Take Your Love to Town" (1967), and DALLAS FRAZIER's "The Son of Hickory Holler's Tramp" (1967). Given his history, Darrell once described his career as "big, but unfortunately not many ever realized it."

Born in Alabama, Darrell grew up in Marietta, Georgia, a suburb of Atlanta. When he was thirteen he bought a guitar, though he didn't dream of a career in music. In the army he sang in the base clubs, but as the self-deprecating singer put it, "If I remember correctly, they threw me out every time I sang."

In 1964 Darrell moved to Nashville, where he managed the Holiday Inn near Music Row. There he got to know producer Kelso Herston of United Artists, whose office was next door to the motel. Herston heard Darrell sing and signed him. "Green Green Grass of Home" was Darrell's first UA single, and "Ruby, Don't Take Your Love to Town," which encountered radio resistance, nevertheless became his first Top Ten hit. Darrell's biggest hit was "With Pen in Hand," which went to #3 in 1968.

During the 1970s Darrell became associated with the OUTLAW movement, but by then his career was in decline. After a period of inactivity and poor health, the determined singer returned to recording and songwriting in the late 1980s.
—*Daniel Cooper*

Dave & Sugar
Dave Rowland b. Sanger, California, January 26, 1942
Vicki Hackeman b. Louisville, Kentucky, August 4, 1950
Jackie Frantz b. Sidney, Ohio, October 8, 1950

The pop-country vocal group Dave & Sugar had a string of hit records in the 1970s, beginning with "Queen of the

Silver Dollar" (1975) and including the #1s "The Door Is Always Open" (1976), "Tear Time" (1978), and "Golden Tears" (1979). Between 1976 and 1979 they had ten consecutive Top Ten songs with their smooth, tight harmonies and mellow pop sound.

The group was formed in 1975 by Dave Rowland, and the original members included Vicki Hackeman and Jackie Frantz. In 1977 Frantz left and was replaced by Sue Powell; in 1979 Vicki Hackeman (who had married CHARLEY PRIDE's guitar player, Ronnie Baker) left. Afterward a series of Sugars performed with the group, including Melissa Dean, Lisa Alvey, Jamie Kaye, and Cindy Smith.

Rowland's musical background included stints as trumpeter in the 75th Army band, as a member of the Stamps Quartet gospel singers while they toured with Elvis, and as a member of the FOUR GUYS. Rowland formed a group to work as Charley Pride's back-up singers; Pride liked the sound of the group and got them a recording contract with his label, RCA.

The group lived in Nashville, then Dallas, and then Rowland moved to Los Angeles to pursue an acting career. After their contract with RCA expired in 1983, Rowland signed with Elektra where he released a solo album, *Sugar Free*, and then performed as Dave Rowland & Sugar.

—*Don Cusic*

REPRESENTATIVE RECORDING

Dave and Sugar (RCA, 1976)

Gail Davies
b. Broken Bow, Oklahoma, June 5, 1948

Versatile singer-songwriter Patricia Gail Dickerson is an unjustly overlooked figure among the West Coast transplants who counteracted Nashville's crossover excesses in the early eighties "Urban Cowboy" era. Both as a bandleader and the first woman in country music to produce and arrange her own recordings, Davies has exerted an in-

Gail Davies

fluence well beyond the popularity she enjoyed during that period. Oddly, while most of her hits were written by others, it was Gail's pen that propelled Ava Barber ("Bucket to the South," 1978) and Jann Browne ("Tell Me Why," 1989) to their loftiest chart positions.

Davies drew her earliest musical inspiration from her father, a guitar player who favored such country pioneers as WEBB PIERCE, CARL SMITH, and JOHNNIE & JACK. At age five, when her parents separated, she moved from Oklahoma to the Seattle area with her mother (who would remarry to Darby Alan Davies) and two brothers. In high school, Gail "left country music for the Beatles." After graduating in 1966, she headed for Los Angeles and spent most of the next nine years on the road with a rock band. The cumulative toll on her voice prompted a return to her roots.

In about 1976, on the advice of her song publisher, Davies relocated to Nashville. Her self-titled debut LP appeared on CBS/Lifesong Records two years later. Spiced with three revivals of country oldies remembered from her childhood, the album featured such enduring originals as the autobiographical "Grandma's Song" and "Someone Is Looking For Someone Like You"—her first significant hit. Though not a strong seller, *Gail Davies* earned the artist a new deal with Warner Bros. and total control in the studio. Her four albums for the label (1980–83) yielded a flurry of Top Ten singles that deftly explored bluegrass ("Blue Heartache"); traditional country ("I'll Be There" and "It's a Lovely, Lovely World"); soul ("Round the Clock Lovin'"); and even jazz ("Singin' The Blues").

Then, despite Davies's consistently excellent output for RCA, MCA, and Capitol, she encountered stubborn resistance—perhaps attributable to antifeminism on Music Row, and a turbulent personal life marked by two divorces and an out-of-wedlock birth. A more plausible explanation, however, is that her increasingly rock-oriented work on RCA (including a 1986 LP under the name of her experimental band Wild Choir) alienated the notoriously conservative gatekeepers of country radio. In any event, the recent release of the entirely self-composed *Eclectic* on Davies's own label reveals no diminution of her vocal and creative powers.

—*Pete Loesch*

REPRESENTATIVE RECORDINGS

The Best of Gail Davies (Capitol, 1991); *Eclectic* (Little Chickadee, 1995)

Danny Davis
b. Dorchester, Massachusetts, May 29, 1925

A trumpet player with a big band background, Danny Davis (born George Nowlan) arrived in Nashville in the mid-1960s to become executive A&R producer and production assistant to CHET ATKINS at RCA. Davis soon formed a band called the Nashville Brass, which blended swing music with country.

A soloist with the Massachusetts All State Symphony Orchestra when he was only fourteen, Davis later accepted a job to go on the road with Gene Krupa. Davis subsequently played in the brass sections of big bands led by Art Mooney, Freddy Martin, and Bob Crosby, respectively.

Davis worked as a producer in New York City but at times had used Nashville studios to record Connie Francis for MGM RECORDS during 1962–65. In addition, his big band experience and the 1960s success of Herb Alpert & the Tijuana Brass gave him the idea for the Nashville Brass, which he formed in 1968. The group's first RCA album, *The Nashville Brass Play the Nashville Sound*, was released in 1969; the group won a Grammy that year for Best Country Instrumental Performance, beating out Atkins, FLOYD CRAMER, BOB DYLAN, and Tommy Allsup.

Davis and his band won the CMA's Instrumental Group of the Year honors from 1969 through 1974. The Nashville Brass became a popular touring attraction and appeared on such TV shows as *The Red Skelton Show* and *The Ed Sullivan Show*.

Today Davis continues to lead the Nashvile Brass on one-night shows. —*Gerry Wood*

REPRESENTATIVE RECORDING

Nashville Brass Turns to Gold (RCA)

Jimmie Davis

b. Beech Springs (near Quitman), Louisiana, September 11, 1899

Jimmie Davis rose to prominence in the 1930s with a smooth vocal style that helped popularize country music far beyond its original rural southern audience. In many ways, his music was a harbinger of EDDY ARNOLD's broadly accessible style. Davis's best-selling songs—particularly "Nobody's Darling but Mine" and "You Are My Sunshine"—not only made him a wealthy and well-known singer but also carried him to the governorship of Louisiana.

One of eleven children born to a sharecropping couple in Beech Springs, Louisiana, James Houston Davis began his singing career in the Glee Club of Louisiana College in Pineville. At the same time he was a member of a local quartet, the Wildcat Four, singing lead tenor. As a graduate student at Louisiana State University in Baton Rouge, he sang in the Glee Club as a tenor in a quartet, the Tiger Four. After his musical activities in college days, which included street-singing, he began to sing regularly at KWKH in Shreveport.

In about September 1927, Davis accepted a teaching position at Dodd College, a Baptist junior college for women. Davis resigned after one year and began working as a clerk at the Shreveport Criminal Court, a job that lasted until 1938 and that helped usher him into a career in Louisiana politics.

Davis's recording career developed noticeably during this ten-year period. After recording a couple of piano-accompanied records for KWKH in 1928, he recorded sixty-eight sides for VICTOR RECORDS from 1929 to 1933, proving himself an able JIMMIE RODGERS imitator and an enthusiastic singer of risqué blues such as "Organ Grinder's Blues" and "Tom Cat and Pussy Blues." In 1934 he began recording for the newly formed DECCA RECORDS. His first release, "Nobody's Darling but Mine," became his first substantial hit. Although a risqué element remained in his repertoire for a while, Davis soon focused on western swing, recording briefly with MILTON BROWN's Brownies.

From 1938 to 1942 Davis served as the public safety commissioner of Shreveport. In these years he established a hugely successful campaign style in which he followed a brief speech with songs backed by a hillbilly band. During this period as commissioner, Davis put many of his musicians on the payroll as Shreveport policemen, including Charles Mitchell, MOON MULLICAN, CLIFF BRUNER, and BUDDY JONES.

Between 1942 and 1947 Davis appeared in five Holly-

Jimmie Davis

wood motion pictures: *Strictly in the Groove* (1942); *Riding Through Nevada* (1943); *Frontier Fury* (1943); *Cyclone Prairie Ramblers* (1944); and his own life story, *Louisiana* (1947).

In 1942 Davis was elected as the northern public service commissioner of Louisiana and, in 1944, as Democratic governor of Louisiana. On both occasions he exploited his reputed authorship of "You Are My Sunshine," which had become nationally known in 1941 through recordings by GENE AUTRY and Bing Crosby. (Davis's own Decca recording was released in 1940; prior to his purchase of the song, it was credited to Paul Rice of the RICE BROTHERS, who previously may have purchased the copyright himself.) After his term as governor, Davis began singing full time for the first time and tended toward a gospel style, as represented by "Suppertime," a hit in the early 1950s. Since serving as Louisiana's governor for a second term, from 1960 to 1964 (elected largely on a segregationist platform), he recorded for Decca and afterward for a handful of small labels.

After the death of his first wife, Alvern, in 1967, he married Anna Carter Gordon, a member of the CHUCK WAGON GANG gospel group, in 1969. Davis was elected to the COUNTRY MUSIC HALL OF FAME in 1972, the year after he lost the election for his third-term governorship. Even in his nineties, Davis was continuously involved in performing. In the spring of 1992 he appeared on CBS-TV's special celebrating the Country Music Hall of Fame's twenty-fifth anniversary. —*Toru Mitsui*

REPRESENTATIVE RECORDINGS

Rockin' Blues (Bear Family, 1983); *Barnyard Stomp* (Bear Family, 19880; *Jimmie Davis* (MCA, 1991)

Linda Davis

b. Dodson, Texas, November 26, 1962

The overnight success story of Linda Davis belies years of drudgery. Davis began her singing career in the late 1970s on the local country circuit around Panola County, Texas. She moved to Nashville in 1982, where she and Skip Eaton (as Skip & Linda) recorded three obscure singles for MDJ Records. The experience left Davis frustrated, but she began recording demos and performing at Nashville's Music City Sheraton Hotel.

There, Davis caught the attention of producer BOB MONTGOMERY at EPIC RECORDS, which signed her in 1987. Epic released three singles by Davis to no avail; undaunted, she switched to LIBERTY RECORDS and recorded two now out-of-print albums, *In a Different Light* (whose title track eked into the charts in 1989) and *Linda Davis* (1991).

During that time, however, Davis met REBA MCENTIRE and her manager and husband, Narvel Blackstock, who became Davis's manager in 1989. When Davis's husband, guitarist Lang Scott, joined McEntire's touring band in 1993, she signed on as a background vocalist. On the strength of Davis's voice, McEntire asked her to record a duet, "Does He Love You"—which rocketed to #1 and netted Davis a 1993 Grammy and a 1994 CMA Award for Vocal Event of the Year. The song's success brought Davis to ARISTA RECORDS, which released *Shoot for the Moon* in 1994 and *Some Things Are Meant to Be* in 1996. Although these albums didn't match the success of "Does He Love You," Linda Davis has rebounded from the canvas too often to be counted out.   —*Jim Ridley*

REPRESENTATIVE RECORDINGS

Shoot for the Moon (Arista, 1994); "Does He Love You," *Reba McEntire's Greatest Hits, Volume 2* (MCA, 1993)

Mac Davis
b. Lubbock, Texas, January 21, 1942

A major pop-country crossover star during the 1970s and 1980s, Mac Davis initially made his mark as a songwriter. Some of his most notable contributions as a writer have been ELVIS PRESLEY's "In the Ghetto," "Memories," and "Don't Cry Daddy"; BOBBY GOLDSBORO's "Watching Scotty Grow"; the oft-recorded "I Believe in Music"; and Davis's own 1972 hit "Baby Don't Get Hooked on Me."

Scott "Mac" Davis spent most of his early years in Atlanta; he played in a rock & roll band and worked for a couple of record labels as a regional manager. After his songwriting success with Presley and other artists during 1968–69, Davis signed with COLUMBIA RECORDS. His first chart single, "Whoever Finds This, I Love You," appeared in 1970, but his recording career didn't take off until two years later, when "Baby Don't Get Hooked on Me" went to #1 pop and sold 1 million copies.

Though most of Davis's pop hits received country airplay, he didn't make major inroads in country radio until "It's Hard to Be Humble," recorded for the Casablanca label, broke into the country Top Ten in 1980. Subsequent hits included "Texas in My Rear View Mirror" (#9, 1980) and "Hooked on Music" (#2, 1981), but his country career waned shortly thereafter. Davis recorded briefly for MCA, and he co-wrote and recorded the duet "Wait 'Til I Get You Home" with DOLLY PARTON for her 1989 *White Limozeen* album, the title cut of which Davis and Parton also cowrote.

Davis parlayed his success in music into careers in television (he hosted his own variety show from 1974 to 1976) and film. His first movie role was as the quarterback who seemed to be based on Don Meredith of the Dallas Cowboys in the 1979 movie *North Dallas Forty*. Davis has also appeared on Broadway in the title role of *The Will Rogers Follies*. He was the ACM Entertainer of the Year in 1974.
                                              —*Chet Flippo*

REPRESENTATIVE RECORDINGS

Greatest Hits (Columbia, 1979); *Very Best & More* (Casablanca, 1984)

Oscar Davis
b. Providence, Rhode Island, May 20, 1902; d. April 5, 1975

Oscar William Davis, the Baron of the Box Office, was one of the greatest of the early country music promoters, who also managed several famous country artists during a long-lived career.

A veteran of World War I, Davis studied law at the American University in Paris and later at Boston University, but he eventually followed his father into the theater business. Though he was an actor, a singer, and a violinist as a young man, Davis also showed a flair for promoting dance marathons; walkathons; and, after about 1937, hillbilly music. He worked at first with Birmingham promoter-performer "Happy" Hal Burns. Davis plugged his own shows, which he booked via saturation radio ads—many of which he announced in a rapid-fire delivery, marked by his tag line, "Don't you dare miss it!" He also bought bold newspaper ads and hyped the shows through such gimmicks as yodeling and fiddling contests and onstage weddings.

By the early 1940s his National Hillbilly Jamborees, held in such southern cities as Little Rock, Dallas, Memphis, and Atlanta, were drawing large crowds and six-figure box office receipts over the course of a summer. Most of these cities broadcast Burns's Garrett Snuff Varieties acts; therefore, the large shows featured Burns along with big-name regional favorites such as ROY ACUFF, ERNEST TUBB, LULU BELLE AND SCOTTY, and the HOOSIER HOT SHOTS.

A promotional genius, Davis later expanded his endeavors and managed such artists as CURLY FOX, Ernest Tubb, MINNIE PEARL, HANK WILLIAMS, GEORGE MORGAN, and RAY PRICE—many of whom enjoyed their peak years under Davis's tutelage. Although most eventually complained that Davis spent too much money on promotion, none denied that he helped to draw huge crowds.

A stroke slowed his activity in the 1960s, but Davis remained in the business until his death, working at different times for talent booking agents JIM DENNY, CONNIE B. GAY, and BUDDY LEE.   —*Ronnie Pugh*

Skeeter Davis
b. Dry Ridge, Kentucky, December 30, 1931

Few artists have traversed the perilous line between country and pop as disarmingly as Mary Frances Penick—a product, fittingly, of the border state of Kentucky. Under the aegis of NASHVILLE SOUND mastermind CHET ATKINS, she amassed a sizable following in both camps during her sixties heyday. Yet the musical legacy of the outspoken singer has undoubtedly been obscured by a series of personal tragedies and controversies.

Born at the onset of the Depression, Skeeter (a nickname bestowed by her grandfather) learned at an early age to harmonize with the singers she heard on the GRAND OLE OPRY. In high school, she and her best friend, Betty Jack Davis (no relation), formed a vocal duo called the Davis Sisters. Radio and television exposure eventually landed them a recording opportunity on RCA in 1952. But as their smashing debut for the label ("I Forgot More Than You'll Ever Know") began what would be a six-month stay on the

Skeeter Davis

country charts the following year, Skeeter and Betty Jack were involved in a car accident that fatally injured the latter.

Devastated by the loss, Skeeter nonetheless persevered in her career. Although she and Betty Jack's sister Georgia were unable to duplicate the original Davis Sisters' success, Skeeter ultimately established herself as a solo act with such Top Ten hits as "Set Him Free" (1959), the "answer" song "(I Can't Help You) I'm Falling Too" (1960), and "My Last Date (With You)" (1961). On these as well as most of Skeeter's early-sixties releases, producer Atkins "double-tracked" the artist's plaintive voice to re-create the feel of her Davis Sisters work. The subsequent addition of uptown embellishments resulted in a string of crossover hits highlighted by the million-selling "The End of the World" and the Gerry Goffin/Carole King composition "I Can't Stay Mad at You" (1963).

Meanwhile, Skeeter became a member of the Opry in 1959, and wed Nashville media celebrity Ralph Emery one year later. Alas, as would be chronicled in their respective autobiographies, the stormy relationship lasted only until 1964—not much longer than her earlier marriage to the anonymous Kenneth Depew. Later, in 1973, the deeply religious singer became embroiled in a well-publicized dispute with Opry management over her broadcast support for some "Jesus people" who had been arrested at a local shopping mall. She was suspended for more than a year.

Though hitless since the early seventies, the seemingly ageless Davis continues to perform regularly, and her wide-ranging album catalogue remains of considerable in-

terest to collectors. *She Sings, They Play* (1985), a charming collaboration with the revered rock band NRBQ, led to her third marriage, in 1987—to the group's bassist, Joey Spampinato. —*Pete Loesch*

REPRESENTATIVE RECORDINGS

She Sings, They Play (Rounder, 1985) with NRBQ; *The Essential Skeeter Davis* (RCA, 1995)

Jimmy Day
b. Tuscaloosa, Alabama, January 9, 1934

James Clayton Day, a true pedal steel guitar innovator specializing in hardcore honky-tonk and western swing, idolized SHOT JACKSON, LITTLE ROY WIGGINS, and JERRY BYRD as well as West Coast pedal steel pioneer SPEEDY WEST and western swing master HERB REMINGTON. Playing (non-pedal) steel as a teenager, he landed a job on Shreveport's *LOUISIANA HAYRIDE*, remaining there into the 1950s. He backed many Hayride performers who became fifties megastars, including HANK WILLIAMS, FARON YOUNG, JOHNNY HORTON, ELVIS PRESLEY, and JIM REEVES.

Day, who eventually became a regular member of Reeves's mid-1950s touring band, changed to a pedal steel. When Reeves moved to Nashville, Day came along in late December 1955. In January 1956 RAY PRICE asked him to join his Cherokee Cowboys. Day remained with them, except for two brief absences, until 1962. He quickly placed his imprint on Price's sound, beginning with solos and fills on Price's 1956 smash "Crazy Arms." Day's sensitive way of modulating from one chord to another also created rich, stunning tonal colors on Price's "Heartaches by the Number," "City Lights," "Invitation to the Blues," and on CHARLIE WALKER's 1958 hit "Pick Me Up on Your Way Down."

In 1962, Day left Price to work with former Cherokee Cowboy WILLIE NELSON, whose hit recording of "Touch Me" had launched a solo career. Day also made two solo LPs for Philips in 1962 and 1963. In the mid-1960s, Day worked on his own with both Price and Nelson. Day continued working with Nelson when the singer moved to Austin, Texas; Day can be heard on Nelson's 1973 *Shotgun Willie* LP. In addition, Day recorded a solo LP for DeWitt Scott's Mid-Land label.

Day was inducted into the International Steel Guitar Hall of Fame in 1982, and continues to perform around Texas. He also plays selected dates with Price.
—*Rich Kienzle*

De Luxe Records
established in Linden, New Jersey, 1944

The small, independent De Luxe label was founded by the Braun family in Linden, New Jersey. SYD NATHAN, owner of KING RECORDS, purchased a portion of De Luxe in 1947. From 1947 until 1949, the Brauns operated the label under Nathan's control, then left to start a new label. King revived the label in the fifties. Country artists signed to De Luxe included the Rouse Brothers, BUDDY STARCHER, the SHELTON BROTHERS, DENVER DARLING, Lost John Miller, LOUIS INNIS, ARTHUR Q. SMITH, and Tex Atchison. The masters are currently owned by IMG, which purchased the STARDAY-KING catalogue in the mid-seventies.

—*Don Roy*

Dead Reckoning Records
established in Nashville, Tennessee, late 1994

Having already established themselves as accomplished and critically touted artists-songwriters, Kieran Kane (of 1980s country duo the O'KANES), KEVIN WELCH, Mike Henderson, Harry Stinson, and Tammy Rogers formed Dead Reckoning Records in 1994, allowing the five partners to release their own solo records and group projects. Kane helps run the independent label out of his Nashville home, and his *Dead Rekoning* album (spelled slightly different from the label name) was the company's first release, in March 1995.

The Dead Reckoning concept began to take shape when pals Kane and Welch realized they had strong fan bases overseas, Norway in particular, even after they had been dropped by major Nashville labels (Atlantic and Warner Bros., respectively). Kane then decided to make a simple, acoustic record for the Norway market. The venture snowballed, and within two years of its initial release the co-operative had seven records available in the marketplace, with national distribution through ROUNDER RECORDS. Country singer-songwriters Kane and Welch each had put out solo records. Guitarist-vocalist Henderson released a pair of blues projects, one solo and one fronting the Bluebloods. Fiddle ace Rogers also had two efforts to her credit, a self-titled release predominantly featuring her vocals, and a largely instrumental collaboration with former Lone Justice drummer Don Heffington. And the five artist-owners, plus multi-instrumentalist Fats Kaplin and bassist Alison Prestwood, released a group project as the Dead Reckoners. The album was patterned after the group's "A Night of Reckoning" shows, where the artists performed all together onstage, taking turns up front and backing each other during the collection of tunes. Stinson produced, played drums, and provided backing vocals on most of the Dead Reckoning projects.

"We're just trying to prove to ourselves that we've been here long enough that we can take matters into our own hands, and we can shepherd our own music through the recording process and straight into the hands of human beings who want to listen to it and not be controlled by a system we have no control over," Welch told the *Nashville Banner* in July 1995. —*Michael Gray*

Billy Dean
b. Quincy, Florida, April 2, 1962

Billy Dean was playing guitar in his father's band, the Country Rocks, at age eight. The experience gave him an early education in classic country (HANK WILLIAMS and CHARLEY PRIDE) and early rock (Chuck Berry and ELVIS PRESLEY). In his spare time, Dean was listening to a radio station that specialized in soul and r&b.

After gaining his own following in Florida, Dean was nineteen when he made his first Nashville appearance in the national finals of the Wrangler Star Search talent competition. Later he moved to Nashville and quickly found work as a jingle singer and background vocalist. Continuing to work on his writing, his songs were recorded by the OAK RIDGE BOYS, Shelly West, Les Taylor, and others. In 1989 RANDY TRAVIS recorded "Somewhere in My Broken Heart," a song that Dean co-wrote with Richard Leigh.

Following the release of his 1990 debut album, *Young Man,* Dean's first single, "Only Here For a Little While,"

went to #3. Since Travis never released "Somewhere in My Broken Heart," Dean made it his second single (#3). Dean's achievements did not go unnoticed by the industry. In 1992 the ACADEMY OF COUNTRY MUSIC named him Top New Male Vocalist, and "Somewhere In My Broken Heart" won Song of the Year honors. Dean also garnered a Grammy nomination for Best Male Country Performance.

Dean's self-titled second album, released in 1991, included another hit single, "Billy the Kid" (#4). In 1992, *Fire in the Dark* revealed even stronger pop sensibilities, including a remake of Dave Mason's 1977 hit, "We Just Disagree."

In 1994, Dean decided that the rigors of the road were taking a toll on his career and personal life. He took a hiatus to concentrate on songwriting and to gain a life focus before working on his fourth album, *It's What I Do.* —*Calvin Gilbert*

REPRESENTATIVE RECORDINGS
Billy Dean (Liberty, 1991); *It's What I Do* (Capitol, 1996)

Eddie Dean
b. Posey, Texas, July 9, 1907

Although Eddie Dean didn't gain quite the notoriety that other singing cowboys did, he is remembered for having one of the finest voices of any of the screen's western stars. Texas-born Edgar Glosup changed his last name to Dean and journeyed to Chicago in 1926, seeking a career as a singer. From there he moved to Shenandoah, Iowa, in 1927 and then Yankton, South Dakota, in 1929. Dean and his brother Jimmy (not the Jimmy Dean of "Big Bad John" fame) spent 1930–32 singing on radio station WIBW in Topeka, Kansas, before returning to Chicago, where they were featured on the WLS NATIONAL BARN DANCE for three years and recorded for ARC and later for DECCA.

Late in 1937 Dean moved to Los Angeles, where he gradually began to land small roles in films starring ROY ROGERS, GENE AUTRY, Don "Red" Barry, and William Boyd (Hopalong Cassidy). Dean's roles ranged from villain to vocalist. Beginning in 1944, he starred in his own western TV series, including *Harmony Trail* and *Song of Old Wyoming.* Over the next four years he also starred in twenty western films.

Dean had written many of his film songs, including his trademark "On the Banks of the Sunny San Juan," which he recorded for DECCA. In 1948 he wrote "One Has My Name (The Other Has My Heart)," which became a hit for him and an even bigger hit for his friend JIMMY WAKELY (JERRY LEE LEWIS revived the song in 1969). In 1955 Dean wrote and recorded his hit "I Dreamed of a Hillbilly Heaven." TEX RITTER's 1961 recording of that song became a major hit in the country and pop fields.

Throughout the years Eddie Dean toured steadily and appeared frequently on radio and on television. He was featured on the network radio show *Judy Canova* and also *TOWN HALL PARTY,* in the 1950s. More recently he has performed primarily in nightclubs, where his repertoire is equally balanced between country music and the western songs for which he is best known. In 1993 he was inducted into the Cowboy Hall of Fame. —*Laurence Zwisohn*

REPRESENTATIVE RECORDINGS
Eddie Dean Sings a Tribute to Hank Williams (Design, 1958); *A Cowboy Sings Country* (Shasta, 1974); *Dean of the West* (WFC, 1976)

Jimmy Dean

b. Plainview, Texas, August 10, 1928

Dean's cornflake charm and fresh-faced good looks epitomized the country TV star of the 1950s. Though Dean was able to parlay his specialty, the dramatic recitative, into a string of hit records in the 1960s, his biggest success was as a television personality.

Born Jimmy Ray Dean in a poor, rural West Texas family, Dean first tried his hand at entertaining as a serviceman while stationed at Bolling Air Force Base near Washington, D.C. Upon his discharge in 1948 he formed his group, the Texas Wildcats, and under the tutelage of Washington, D.C., country music impresario CONNIE B. GAY Dean honed his act as an all-around entertainer via live appearances on WARL radio and WMAL-TV, as well as in the then-thriving D.C. country music club scene. Dean's only chart hit of the fifties, "Bummin' Around," on the FOUR STAR RECORDS label, made it to #5 on the country charts in 1953, but his celebrity burgeoned as a TV personality. Dean hosted the regionally syndicated TV show *Town & Country Jamboree*, which included PATSY CLINE, ROY CLARK, and GEORGE HAMILTON IV as regulars. In 1957 the show incarnated for a brief six months on the CBS network as *The Jimmy Dean Show*, a distant forerunner of Roy Clark's *HEE HAW*.

Dean found a recording niche as a reciter of dramatic narrative with his pop hit in 1961, the self-penned "Big Bad John," for COLUMBIA RECORDS (on which a 1988 motion picture was based, starring Dean, Ned Beatty, and Bo Hopkins). With its hammer sound effects and lean production, the song, a #1 hit on both pop and country charts, exemplified the best of the creative early NASHVILLE SOUND era. Dean followed with five more Top Thirty crossover hits in 1962, three of them spoken narratives: "Dear Ivan," "The Cajun Queen" and "To a Sleeping Beauty," "Little Black Book," and "PT 109," which rode the wave of popularity of President John F. Kennedy, about Kennedy's wartime exploits.

Dean's string of hits and proven TV charisma brought him back into network television from 1963 to 1966 on ABC with a new version of *The Jimmy Dean Show*. In 1965 he reached #1 with "The First Thing Every Morning," and in 1966 Dean switched labels to RCA. There he met with limited success apart from a duo with DOTTIE WEST, "Slowly," which hit Top Thirty in 1971. However, Dean's TV career continued to grow. He branched out into dramatic roles, with regular appearances on Fess Parker's *Daniel Boone* series on NBC from 1967 to 1970, playing Boone's best friend, Josh Clements. Dean appeared in various Movies of the Week opposite Lee Majors, Dennis Weaver, and Mark Hamill, and he made his feature film debut in the 1971 James Bond film *Diamonds Are Forever*, starring Sean Connery. Dean was also a popular guest host for Johnny Carson, Merv Griffin, Mike Douglas, Dinah Shore, and Joey Bishop. Dean joined the Casino label in 1976 and rebounded briefly with another recitation, "I.O.U.," which charted #9 country and #35 pop. More recently Dean is better known as the Sausage King, serving as spokesperson for his namesake company, Jimmy Dean Meat Company, which he founded in 1968. —*Margaret Jones*

REPRESENTATIVE RECORDINGS

The Jimmy Dean Show (RCA, 1968); *Jimmy Dean: American Originals* (Columbia, 1989); *Big Bad John* (Bear Family, 1993)

Jimmy Dean

Decca Records

established in New York, New York, July 1934

Decca Records has been one of the most influential labels in the history of country music. In 1934, with initial capital from English stockbroker Edward Lewis (who owned the British corporation Decca Records, founded in 1929), BRUNSWICK RECORDS executive JACK KAPP established Decca Records. His younger brother DAVE KAPP joined the firm that same year as A&R director for the hillbilly music division. Although Decca used its own recording studios in New York and Chicago, Dave Kapp began undertaking expeditions across America to seek out potential artists and make field recordings. During that year and following, Dave signed a wealth of talent to the label, including STUART HAMBLEN (the first Decca country artist to record: August 3, 1934), JIMMIE DAVIS, the SONS OF THE PIONEERS, MILTON BROWN & HIS MUSICAL BROWNIES, REX GRIFFIN, the CARTER FAMILY, ERNEST TUBB, and RED FOLEY.

In the late 1940s, at the urging of such artists as Tubb and Foley, the hillbilly division was renamed country & western. By this time, Dave Kapp had turned the country A&R duties over to PAUL COHEN, a Cincinnati branch manager for the label. Cohen was the first producer to regularly record country artists in Nashville, beginning in 1947.

During Cohen's tenure as head of country A&R, many changes took place: Jack Kapp died in 1949, and in 1952 Decca gained controlling interest in Universal Pictures. Cohen was responsible for signing and producing many new acts, including BILL MONROE, WEBB PIERCE, KITTY WELLS, BOBBY HELMS, and BRENDA LEE, and for making a distribution deal with FOUR STAR RECORDS to release recordings by PATSY CLINE (1955–60).

In 1958 Paul Cohen became head of Coral Records (a division of Decca) and relinquished his position to OWEN BRADLEY, a bandleader and arranger who had been working with Cohen since 1949. Bradley's recently built Quonset hut studio and the adjoining remodeled house became Decca's Nashville office. With Bradley's keen ear for music and talent, he was able to steer country music into a more pop-oriented style known as the NASHVILLE SOUND. His formula was most successful for Patsy Cline (signed to Decca in 1960) and Brenda Lee. Though Bradley, along with his assistant Harry Silverstein, made good use of the existing label roster, he was also responsible for signing BILL ANDERSON, LORETTA LYNN, the OSBORNE BROTHERS, and CONWAY TWITTY.

In June 1962 Music Corporation of American (MCA) purchased 81 percent of Decca's public stock, and Decca officially became a division of MCA on January 1, 1966. On March 1, 1973, Decca (and other labels that MCA had acquired) ceased to exist, and the MCA Records label was launched. In 1994, MCA reactivated Decca solely as a country music label featuring Dawn Sears, and adding artists such as MARK CHESNUTT, RHETT AKINS, Helen Darling, Lee Ann Womack, Chris Knight, and the Frazier River Band. The Decca legacy has been honored with two A&R men being inducted into the COUNTRY MUSIC HALL OF FAME—OWEN BRADLEY (1974) and PAUL COHEN (1976)—along with twelve of their artists.   —*Don Roy*

Delmore Brothers

Alton Delmore b. Elkmont, Alabama, December 25, 1908;
d. June 8, 1964
Rabon Delmore b. Elkmont, Alabama, December 3, 1916;
d. December 4, 1952

One of the first of the great brother duos of the 1930s, the Delmore Brothers were perhaps the most the musically sophisticated, most creative, and most technically proficient of all the duo acts. Their soft, pliant harmony, dazzling guitar work, love of blues, and well-crafted songs endeared them to generations of fans. And though their hit songs such as "Brown's Ferry Blues," "Gonna Lay Down My Old Guitar," and "Blues Stay Away from Me" became country standards that are still heard today, the Delmores never seemed able to win fame and fortune.

Hailing from the red clay hills of northern Alabama, the brothers grew up in a gospel music tradition of shaped note songbooks and singing schools; their mother, Mollie, was a composer of such songs, and some of Alton's first efforts were gospel songs co-written with her. The brothers soon developed a style based around the new microphone and radio technology (where their soft voices could be heard), and won their reputation by singing at local fiddling contests. After an early record for COLUMBIA in 1931 ("Got the Kansas City Blues"), they won a job on the GRAND OLE OPRY in 1933. In that same year they began a long-term relationship with Victor's new budget label, BLUEBIRD, and Alton began to seriously write new songs. They soon began attracting buckets of fan mail, and by 1936 the Opry reported they were the most popular act on the show.

For several years they toured and recorded with fellow Opry star UNCLE DAVE MACON, and in 1936 they teamed with FIDDLIN' ARTHUR SMITH. With Smith they recorded classic tunes such as "There's More Pretty Girls Than One" and "Beautiful Brown Eyes." On their own, they recorded pieces such as "Southern Moon" and "When It's Time for the Whippoorwill to Sing."

Disagreements with the Opry management over bookings led the brothers to leave the show in 1938; it proved to be a mistake, and while their records continued to do well (they switched to DECCA in 1940), they had a hard time finding a new radio base. The next few years saw them moving restlessly to several cities from Raleigh, North Carolina, to Birmingham, until finally landing at WLW, the powerhouse station in Cincinnati.

Here they resurrected their career. In 1943 Alton organized the gospel quartet BROWN'S FERRY FOUR with MERLE TRAVIS and GRANDPA JONES; it became one of country's first really successful gospel quartets, excelling both on the radio and on records. They signed with the local independent label KING RECORDS and began mixing blues and boogie with their songs. Often working with harmonica ace WAYNE RANEY, they produced pieces such as "Hillbilly Boogie," "Freight Train Boogie," and "Blues Stay Away from Me." Here, too, though, they seemed unable to capitalize on their new hit records. During the late 1940s they were on the move again: to Memphis; then to Chattanooga; to Jackson, Mississippi; to Athens, Alabama; then to Covington, Kentucky; to Fort Smith; to Del Rio, Texas; and finally to Houston. Here they broke up the act. Alton wanted to try his hand at full-time songwriting (he had been responsible for most of the original songs they did), and Rabon found he had lung cancer. An operation was of little help, and in 1952 Rabon died.

Alton continued to record with independent labels, but eventually dropped out of music, bitter and disillusioned. He got some satisfaction out of seeing some of the 1,000 songs he wrote recorded by a wide variety of modern artists, and he was able to complete most of a remarkable autobiography that was published posthumously as *Truth Is Stranger Than Publicity.*   —*Charles Wolfe*

REPRESENTATIVE RECORDING

Brown's Ferry Blues (County, 1995)

Iris DeMent

b. Paragould, Arkansas, January 5, 1961

Singer-songwriter Iris Luella DeMent has enjoyed critical if not massive commercial success, combining a spare folk and old-time country musical style with incisive, heartfelt, largely autobiographical lyrics. The youngest of fourteen children in a home filled with music, DeMent sang along with her mother, Flora Mae, who played LORETTA LYNN and

The Delmore Brothers

JOHNNY CASH gospel records while doing housework, a memory DeMent recalled in her song "Mama's Opry" on her debut record. When she was three, her family moved to California, where father Pat DeMent, formerly a farmer, took a job as a janitor at the Movieland Wax Museum. Iris struck out on her own at seventeen. She worked as a waitress in a Lake Tahoe casino, where a performance by EMMYLOU HARRIS inspired her to begin a career in music. After taking up songwriting, DeMent moved to Kansas City and began performing at local writers nights. She moved to Nashville in 1990, finding work as a back-up singer on records by JANN BROWNE and EMMYLOU HARRIS. In 1992 she signed with Philo Records, a division of ROUNDER, and released her critically acclaimed debut, *Infamous Angel,* produced by JIM ROONEY.

When WARNER BROS. signed DeMent in 1993, the label rereleased the album, followed by *My Life* in 1994. Both feature original, predominantly acoustic material, alongside faithful remakes of songs from the CARTER FAMILY and LEFTY FRIZZELL. In 1994 DeMent contributed the track "Big City" to the MERLE HAGGARD tribute album *Tulare Dust.* Impressed, Haggard asked her to perform with him on occasion; the two began working on songwriting together; and Haggard recorded DeMent's "No Time to Cry" from her second album for his album *1996.* Rock singers Natalie Merchant and David Byrne performed DeMent's "Let the Mystery Be" as a duet on *MTV Unplugged;* their recording was subsequently released as a single. DeMent's original version can be heard on her debut album and on the soundtrack to Bernardo Bertolucci's film *Little Buddha.* The 1996 album *The Way I Should* was somewhat of a departure for DeMent and featured songs with a more political edge. "Trouble," a rollicking duet with DELBERT MCCLINTON, closes the album.   — *Stephen L. Betts*

REPRESENTATIVE RECORDINGS

Infamous Angel (Philo, 1992, re-released by Warner Bros., 1993); *My Life* (Warner Bros., 1994); *The Way I Should* (Warner Bros., 1996)

Jim Denny
b. Buffalo Valley, Tennessee, February 28, 1911; d. August 27, 1963

James Rae Denny (he changed his last name to Denny) was a longtime manager of the GRAND OLE OPRY Artists Service who went on to become one of the most successful talent agents and song publishers in country music history. His skill as a promoter and developer of talent played a vital role in the growth of country music in the 1950s and early 1960s.

Born in the poor Buffalo Valley region of Tennessee, Denny moved to Nashville and found work at age sixteen as a mailroom clerk for the National Life and Accident Insurance Company, owner of WSM Radio and the Grand Ole Opry. While rising through the ranks of the insurance company's accounting division, Denny found himself increasingly drawn to sidejobs backstage at the Opry. When the opportunities presented themselves in the late 1940s he eventually took over as director of WSM's Artists Service, or booking department, while also serving as house manager for the Opry.

During his tenure at the Opry, Denny dealt with dozens of major country music acts, record label executives, and top show promoters such as A. V. BAMFORD, Dub Albritten, JIM HALSEY, OSCAR DAVIS, X. COSSE, and others.

Jim Denny

Denny formed CEDARWOOD PUBLISHING COMPANY early in 1953 with WEBB PIERCE (CARL SMITH later acquired an interest as well). Over the next decade his staff of writers churned out hit after hit, including "Detroit City," "Tobacco Road," and others. In 1955 Denny was voted Country and Western Man of the Year by *Billboard* magazine. But when he was fired from the Opry in September 1956, amid allegations of conflict of interest stemming from his involvement in booking and publishing, Denny formed the Jim Denny Artist Bureau and signed most of the Opry's top acts. Three months later, in what was then called the largest individual package sale in country music history, he signed an agreement with Philip Morris Tobacco Company to provide the talent for the PHILIP MORRIS COUNTRY MUSIC SHOW. This show simultaneously made a fortune for Denny's talent agency and helped boost the popularity of country music across America. Denny's company booked most of the top country acts of the day, including Pierce, Smith, MINNIE PEARL, RED SOVINE, HANK SNOW, GOLDIE HILL, the DUKE OF PADUCAH, MOON MULLICAN, and many more. By 1963 the Denny Artist Bureau was booking nearly 4,000 country shows annually.

Denny was a hard-nosed businessman whose charismatic personality and devotion to his acts and songs earned him respect and devotion—sometimes tinged with fear—from artists, writers, and others with whom he did business. He and Pierce, who quit the Opry a few months after Denny was fired, prospered from their investment in Cedarwood, and branched out to acquire several radio stations.

At the time of Denny's death, Cedarwood and the Jim Denny Artist Bureau were outstanding in their respective fields. LUCKY MOELLER quickly took over the artist bureau, but without Denny's guiding force it withered away within a few years. Denny's sons Bill and John managed Cedarwood until its sale to Mel Tillis in 1983. Jim Denny was elected to the COUNTRY MUSIC HALL OF FAME in 1966.

—*Al Cunniff*

John Denver
b. Roswell, New Mexico, December 31, 1943; d. October 12, 1997

John Denver became a country star in the 1970s by accident, just as most of his career came together by seeming happenstance. John Henry Deutschendorf Jr. was the child of an air force family that moved constantly throughout the United States. His grandmother's gift of an acoustic guitar became a constant in his nomadic life, and he began studying the folk music of the late 1950s and early 1960s. He began performing and got a breakthrough at Leadbetter's in Los Angeles. The club was owned by Randy Sparks, the founder of the folk music group the New Christy Minstrels, who hired him as a regular at the club. After performing in a Sparks road band called the Back Porch Majority, Denver got word that the popular Chad Mitchell Trio was auditioning for a replacement for Mitchell on the road. Denver got the job and was well received, especially when he began performing his own original material. His composition "Leaving on a Jet Plane" got to Peter, Paul & Mary, who made it a hit in 1969.

After leaving the Chad Mitchell Trio, Denver settled in Aspen, Colorado, where he serenaded the ski crowd. On a tour stop in Washington, D.C., Denver attracted the attention of influential manager Jerry Weintraub, who took Denver to broader audiences than he had known. Denver signed with RCA, and in 1971 his "Take Me Home, Country Roads" became a #2 pop hit and a million seller.

Though "Country Roads" received some country air-play, Denver became introduced to the country music audience primarily though such 1974–75 crossover hits as "Annie's Song," "Back Home Again," and "Thank God I'm a Country Boy." Country music observers find it difficult in retrospect to explain why Denver suddenly became a country favorite and just as suddenly fell out of favor. In any case, the CMA's selection of Denver as the 1975 Entertainer of the Year was highly controversial, as many in Nashville did not consider him to be a true country artist. During the nationally televised awards ceremony that year, after announcing Denver as the winner, performer CHARLIE RICH took out his cigarette lighter and ignited the envelope.

Denver never repeated his mid-1970s successes as a recording artist, though he did have a Top Ten country hit in 1981 with "Some Days Are Diamonds (Some Days Are Stone)." Among his other activities, he starred with George Burns in the 1977 movie *Oh, God* and throughout his career was well known for his work in behalf of the environment and various humanitarian causes. Denver's last years were also marked by personal problems, however, as he was twice arrested for drunken driving. He was killed at age fifty-three when the home-built, single-engine plane he was piloting crashed into California's Monterey Bay. A pilot for more than twenty years, Denver was said to have been testing the Long EZ model on a planned one-hour flight when its engine quit. —*Chet Flippo*

REPRESENTATIVE RECORDING
The Country Roads Collection (RCA, 1997), 4 discs

Desert Rose Band
Chris Hillman b. Los Angeles, California, December 4, 1944
Herb Pedersen b. Berkeley, California, April 27, 1944
John Jorgenson b. Madison, Wisconsin, July 6, 1956

One of the prime exponents of the West Coast country sound in the 1980s was the Desert Rose Band. The group was the commercial culmination of CHRIS HILLMAN's decades around the fringes of country, beginning with California BLUEGRASS groups in the early 1960s (Scottsville Squirrel Barkers, the Hillmen) and extending into pioneering country-rock bands (the BYRDS, FLYING BURRITO BROTHERS) in the late 1960s and early 1970s. By 1984 Hillman, who had played bass with the Byrds and writes his songs on guitar, was again playing bluegrass mandolin and singing country classics on a solo album, *Desert Rose* (Sugar Hill, 1984). On it he was accompanied by (among others) veteran session vocalist and picker (guitar, banjo) Herb Pedersen. Hillman and Pedersen accompanied Dan Fogelberg on his *High Country Snows* album (1985) and, joined by veteran bassist Bill Bryson and young guitar wizard John Jorgenson, opened for Fogelberg on his tour later that year. This was the nucleus of the Desert Rose Band, filled out by pedal steel ace Jay Dee Maness (formerly of BUCK OWENS's Buckaroos) and drummer Steve Duncan (long-time house drummer at North Hollywood's Palomino Club).

Building their sound around the tight vocal harmonies of Hillman and Pedersen, the twangy guitar hooks of Jorgenson, and Hillman's songs, the Desert Rose Band was, in Hillman's words, "a highly evolved Burrito Brothers." Signed to CURB RECORDS, the Desert Rose Band enjoyed eight Top Ten hits from September 1987 through September 1990, including two #1s in 1988, "He's Back and

John Denver

I'm Blue" and "I Still Believe in You." A six-month hiatus by Hillman (1990–91) to write songs may have signaled the beginning of the end for the group, which never regained its momentum afterward and soon lost Maness (in 1990), Duncan (1992), and founding member Jorgenson (1992). Outflanked by younger, hungrier bands by the early 1990s, Desert Rose quietly faded in 1994 after its belated validation of Chris Hillman's commitment to country music.

—Mark Humphrey

REPRESENTATIVE RECORDINGS

The Desert Rose Band (Curb, 1987); *A Dozen Roses: Greatest Hits* (Curb, 1991)

Ott Devine

b. Gadsden, Alabama, May 1, 1910; d. January 30, 1994

Ottis Edward Devine was a prominent radio executive at WSM in Nashville from the 1940s through the 1960s. After high school in Anniston, Alabama, he worked as announcer at WJBY in Gadsden, Alabama; WRGA in Rome, Georgia; and WDOD in Chattanooga before signing on as a WSM staff announcer in 1935. He shifted into the program department in 1942 and, along with program director JACK STAPP, supervised WSM-originated programs such as *Sunday Down South* and *Wormwood Forest,* fed to the NBC, CBS, and Mutual radio networks. By the late 1950s Devine replaced Stapp as program director and took on the additional role of GRAND OLE OPRY manager when D KILPATRICK stepped down from this position in 1959. Overseeing both the Friday night and Saturday night Opry shows, Devine signed many new acts during the 1960s, including LORETTA LYNN, ROY DRUSKY, BILL ANDERSON, JAN HOWARD, BOBBY BARE, JIM & JESSE McREYNOLDS, CONNIE SMITH, DOTTIE WEST, and JACK GREENE. Devine retired from WSM in 1968.

—John Rumble

Al Dexter

b. Troup, Texas, May 4, 1905; d. January 28, 1984

Clarence Albert Poindexter, better known as Al Dexter, was one of country music's biggest stars of the 1940s. He released a string of huge hits, beginning in 1943 with the million seller "Pistol Packin' Mama," which also became one of the first important country crossovers when Bing Crosby made it a pop hit. Hard to categorize, falling somewhere along an indistinct line between western swing and honky-tonk, Dexter's reputation has, as Nick Tosches pointed out, likely suffered as a result.

Stardom came relatively late to Dexter, who was almost forty by the time "Pistol Packin' Mama" was issued. He began playing music as a youth, graduating from banjo and harmonica to mandolin and guitar, but it is unclear when he began pursuing music as a career. He was playing and running his own Round-Up club in Longview, Texas, by the mid-1930s. It was in New Orleans, however, that he was signed to an ARC contract by DON LAW in 1936. Supposedly unable to convince any local country dance musicians to take him very seriously, Dexter, who at one point led an all-black band for similar reasons, was forced to pick up a trio of San Antonio musicians to back him on his first recordings. The Nite Owls would also record under their own name record for Vocalion and work on Dexter's sessions through 1938. Early electric guitarist Bob Symons was a band member.

Al Dexter

Dexter's first release was the seminal "Honky-Tonk Blues," and his recordings for the rest of the decade retained an often hard-edged, proto-honky-tonk approach. Dexter began playing lead guitar and mandolin in 1939 and started calling his band, which featured novelty musician Aubrey Gass (of postwar "Dear John" fame), the Troopers. By the early forties Dexter's music was becoming decidedly smoother as well. His watershed 1942 sessions for COLUMBIA in Hollywood featured studio musicians such as accordionist Paul Sells and trumpeter Holly Hollinger and arrangements that, on paper, seemed ill suited for material such as "Pistol Packin' Mama." It all worked wonderfully in the studio, however, and more hits followed: "Too Late to Worry, Too Blue to Cry" and "So Long Pal" (1944), "I'm Losing My Mind Over You" (1945), and "Guitar Polka" (1946). By the end of the forties, Dexter's star began to fade; he relocated to Texas, opening his own club in Dallas. By the 1960s, Dexter—who also recorded for KING, DECCA, CAPITOL, Ekko, and Aldex—had essentially retired from music.

—Kevin Coffey

REPRESENTATIVE RECORDINGS

Columbia Country Classics, Volume One: The Golden Era (Columbia, 1990) (various-artists reissue containing "Pistol Packin' Mama"); *Hillbilly Fever, Volume Two: Honky-Tonk* (Rhino, 1995) (various-artists reissue containing "Honky-Tonk Blues")

DeZurik Sisters

Mary Jane DeZurik b. Royalton, Minnesota, February 1, 1917; d. September 3, 1981

Caroline DeZurik b. Royalton, Minnesota, December 24, 1918

A popular singing duo, sisters Caroline and Mary DeZurik combined European Swiss-style yodeling with African-

American–influenced JIMMIE RODGERS vocal runs. Warbling, tweeting, and whistling their way through multiple octaves, often imitating animal sounds and bird calls, the DeZurik Sisters eventually earned spots on both the WLS *NATIONAL BARN DANCE* and WSM's *GRAND OLE OPRY*. They were among the first female performers to become known on country music's most popular radio shows.

Born in Royalton, Minnesota, to a Dutch dairy farming family, Mary Jane and Caroline were two of seven siblings. With Caroline playing guitar, the sisters were hired in 1936 by the Chicago-based WLS *National Barn Dance,* which billed the fresh-faced duo as trick yodelers. In 1941 Caroline and Mary Jane (by this time, married to fellow *Barn Dance* performers Rusty Gill and Augie Klein, respectively) appeared on the *MIDWESTERN HAYRIDE.* By 1944 the DeZurik Sisters were amazing millions with their distinctive chicken yodel as part of the Ralston Purina–sponsored portion of the GRAND OLE OPRY, where they became known as the Cackle Sisters.

After years of shuttling between Nashville and Chicago to perform on WLS and WSM, Mary Jane DeZurik retired in 1948, and younger sister Lorraine took her place for a time. (Sister Eva DeZurik would also occasionally stand in if one sister could not appear.) The Cackle Sisters continued performing on the Opry into the early 1950s, their precision yodeling style becoming even more intricate.

Despite a near twenty-year career, the DeZurik sisters recorded only six commercial 78-rpm sides (all in 1938) for the AMERICAN RECORD CORPORATION. However, many of their live performances are preserved on radio transcriptions of Ralston Purina's *Checkerboard Square* program. The sisters' inventive vocalizing, spirited performance style, and willingness to experiment were inspirations to later female country yodelers. —*Patricia Hall*

REPRESENTATIVE RECORDING

"Arizona Yodeler," *The Women* (Time-Life Records, 1981)

Diamond Rio

Gene Johnson b. Jamestown, New York, August 10, 1949
Jimmy Olander b. Minneapolis, Minnesota, August 26, 1961
Brian Prout b. Troy, New York, December 4, 1955
Marty Roe b. Lebanon, Ohio, December 28, 1960
Dan Truman b. St. George, Utah, August 29, 1956
Dana Williams b. Dayton, Ohio, May 22, 1961

In a town where the concept of the "group" has often derived from the southern gospel model of vocal harmonizers fronting anonymous musicians, Diamond Rio is something of an anomaly: a legitimate band of six musicians who play on their albums as well as on the road, and who perform with the proficiency of Nashville's best session musicians.

Diamond Rio's notion of the group comes from bluegrass. The band evolved from the Tennessee River Boys, a bluegrass group at Nashville's OPRYLAND USA theme park that also once featured TY HERNDON. Marty Roe sang lead vocals, and both guitarist Jimmy Olander and keyboardist Dan Truman played in the band. Drummer Brian Prout previously played in Heartbreak Mountain (which also included SHENANDOAH's Marty Raybon); the other members of Diamond Rio are bassist-vocalist Dana Williams, and Gene Johnson, who plays fiddle and mandolin and sings backing vocals. The group changed its name to Diamond Rio after signing with ARISTA RECORDS.

Released in 1991, the group's first single, "Meet in the Middle," was a charming tale of young, rural love that hit #1—the first debut by a country group to do so—and Diamond Rio, with its combination of musical talent and accessible songs, quickly became one of country's premier groups. The band won the ACM's Top Vocal Group award in 1991 and 1992; the CMA named Diamond Rio its Vocal Group of the Year from 1992 to 1994. The band's first album, *Diamond Rio,* was certified platinum; the next two, *Close to the Edge* and *Love a Little Stronger,* both were certified gold. Diamond Rio single hits include "Norma Jean Riley," "In a Week or Two," and "Love a Little Stronger." In 1997 the group scored a #1 *Billboard* hit with "How Your Love Makes Me Feel" and once again captured the CMA Vocal Group of the Year Award.

Diamond Rio's music is characterized by facile picking, old-fashioned virtues (in such hits as "Love a Little Stronger" and "Mama Don't Forget to Pray for Me"), and bad puns ("This Romeo Ain't Got Julie Yet," "Bubba Hyde"). While the group's main source of inspiration re-

Diamond Rio: (from left) Brian Prout, Jimmy Olander, Dan Truman, Marty Roe, Dana Williams, and Gene Johnson

mains bluegrass, the band's members draw on all sorts of music, from pop to jazz to traditional country.

—*Brian Mansfield*

REPRESENTATIVE RECORDINGS

Diamond Rio (Arista, 1991); *Love a Little Stronger* (Arista, 1994); *Greatest Hits* (Arista, 1997)

Hazel Dickens

b. Mercer County, West Virginia, June 1, 1935

The eighth in a family of eleven children, Hazel Jane Dickens spent her childhood in poverty. Her family rarely had enough to eat, and there weren't even sufficient pencils and paper to do schoolwork. One of their few possessions was a radio, on which Hazel listened to such country music acts as UNCLE DAVE MACON, the CARTER FAMILY, and WILMA LEE & STONEY COOPER.

In 1954 Hazel moved to Baltimore, Maryland, where she worked in a variety of jobs. More importantly, she began to attend "pickin' parties" where old-time country and bluegrass music was played. It was at these venues that she first sang publicly. Through her brother, Robert, she met Mike Seeger, and began playing music with him, at first casually and then in a band (including her brothers Robert and Arnold) that performed in bars and small clubs. Next, she spent a period of time playing bass and singing with several bands, including the Pike County Boys and the GREENBRIAR BOYS, a popular urban bluegrass revival band. Then she stopped performing for a brief period.

In the early 1960s Dickens met Alice Gerrard, a classically trained singer enthusiastic about traditional forms of country music, and the two began singing and writing together. They built up an extensive repertoire consisting of original material and songs learned from Library of Congress files and old-time musicians the duo taped at several folk festivals. They then embarked on a tour of festivals in the South, and between 1965 and 1976 they recorded four albums, which distinctively featured both women singing the lead parts in a duet fashion usually associated with men. Although they acquired a devoted following, the act broke up in 1976.

After parting with Gerrard, Dickens gained acclaim for her songwriting, particularly after four of her songs were included on the soundtrack of the documentary *Harlan County, U.S.A.* In 1981 her first solo album, *Hard Hitting Songs for Hard Hit People,* appeared on ROUNDER; subsequent albums followed in 1983 and 1987. Her original songs were anthologized on several albums, and she became a popular figure at folk festivals in the United States and on worldwide tours. In 1994 Dickens became the first female recipient of IBMA's Merit Award, given for her contributions to bluegrass.

—*W. K. McNeil*

REPRESENTATIVE RECORDINGS

Hazel Dickens and Alice Gerrard (Rounder, 1976); *Hard Hitting Songs for Hard Hit People* (Rounder, 1981)

Little Jimmy Dickens

b. Bolt, West Virginia, December 19, 1920

James Cecil Dickens burst onto the country scene at the end of the 1940s with a string of humorous novelty songs typified by "Take an Old Cold 'Tater (And Wait)" (1949),

"I'm Little But I'm Loud" (1950), "Country Boy" (1949), and "Sleepin' at the Foot of the Bed" (1950). His small physical stature (four feet, eleven inches), big voice, and brassy style made him a longtime favorite with country fans.

Born into a large West Virginia family, Dickens got his early radio experience on local radio station WJLS with performers such as Mel Steele, MOLLY O'DAY, and Johnnie Bailes. Through the 1940s he had his own radio programs in such spots as Fairmont, West Virginia; Indianapolis; Cincinnati; Topeka; and Saginaw, Michigan. ROY ACUFF heard him for the first time in Cincinnati in 1947 and brought him to the attention of both GRAND OLE OPRY officials and ART SATHERLEY at COLUMBIA RECORDS. After guest appearances he signed with Columbia on September 25, 1948, and joined the Opry in November 1948. Dickens became an instant success for both, beginning in early 1949.

At the Opry, HANK WILLIAMS gave Dickens the nickname Tater, from the Dickens hit "Take an Old Cold 'Tater (And Wait)." Shortly after joining the show, Dickens took over Paul Howard's band, which included crack guitarists R. M. "Jabbo" Arrington and Grady Martin (later Jimmy "Spider" Wilson and Howard Rhoton), and bassist BOB MOORE. Named the Country Boys, Dickens's band became known for its topflight musicianship and for its pioneering twin lead guitar sound. Later Dickens hired young steel guitarist BUDDY EMMONS and guitarist Thumbs Carllile.

In the late 1950s he recorded some rockabilly numbers—including "Salty Boogie," "Blackeyed Joes," and "I Got a Hole in My Pocket" (later a hit for RICKY VAN SHELTON). Other well-known Dickens novelty numbers include "Hillbilly Fever," "Bessie the Heifer," "Hot Diggity Dog,"

Little Jimmy Dickens

and "Cold Feet." He also performed romantic ballads, such as "I've Just Got to See You Once More" and "My Heart's Bouquet," but his novelty hits overshadowed them.

Following his #9 hit with BOUDLEAUX AND FELICE BRYANT's "Out Behind the Barn" in 1954, Dickens failed to place another song on the country chart until "The Violet and a Rose" in 1962. In 1957 he left the Opry to tour with the PHILIP MORRIS COUNTRY MUSIC SHOW, but he returned in 1975. His biggest hit came in 1965 with a new novelty song, "May the Bird of Paradise Fly Up Your Nose," which peaked at #1 and went on to #15 on the pop listings. Thereafter, Dickens placed singles for Columbia regularly on the charts until 1972. He moved to DECCA RECORDS in 1967 and United Artists in 1971. Of his later songs, "Country Music Lover" in 1967 had the highest chart ranking, but the sentimental recitation "Raggedy Ann" has probably retained the longest popularity with his fans.

At the Opry, Dickens continues to be an enduring favorite. An inductee into the COUNTRY MUSIC HALL OF FAME in 1983, Dickens often jokes about his size, referring to himself as "Mighty Mouse in his pajamas," but his stature in country history is great.   —*Ivan M. Tribe*

REPRESENTATIVE RECORDINGS

Columbia Historic Edition (Columbia 1984); *Straight . . . From the Heart (1949–1955)* (CSP/Rounder, 1989); *I'm Little But I'm Loud: The Little Jimmy Dickens Collection* (Razor & Tie, 1996); *Country Boy* (Bear Family, 1997, CD boxed set); *Out Behind the Barn* (Bear Family, 1998, CD boxed set)

Diesel Only Records
established in Brooklyn, New York, January 1990

Diesel Only Records is an anomaly among record labels: It favors the 45-rpm single and eschews radio airplay, instead releasing records that range from muscular truck-driving anthems to rocked-up honky-tonk. Founded by Jeremy Tepper, Jay Sherman-Godfrey, and Albert Caiati, the Brooklyn-based label formed with the goal of putting out 45s by young country and rock bands from New York City and distributing them to jukeboxes nationwide. By the close of its third year, the label had more than thirty releases, from artists across the country, that managed to reach truck drivers and urban hipsters alike. Notable was Mark Brine's "New Blue Yodel," an update of JIMMIE RODGERS's Blue Yodels that earned the singer an invitation from HANK SNOW to perform on the GRAND OLE OPRY.

Diesel Only soon began working in tandem with other labels that were able to reach a wider audience. The *Rig Rock Jukebox* CD compilation, which received considerable critical acclaim, was put out jointly with First Warning Records in 1992 and featured such label mainstays as the World Famous Blue Jays and Courtney & Western. Other collaborative projects included a follow-up compilation CD, *Rig Rock Truckstop* in 1993.

The label's most recent full-length release, *Rig Rock Deluxe,* came out in 1996 on the ROUNDER RECORDS subsidiary Upstart. The compilation paired 1960s country legends with current alternative-country artists, resulting in such inspired match-ups as Kay Adams and BR5-49, Red Simpson and Junior Brown, and Del Reeves and Jim Lauderdale. Although the vinyl format has become largely outmoded, the label remains committed to releasing 45s.   —*Jonathan Marx*

Joe Diffie

Joe Diffie
b. Tulsa, Oklahoma, December 28, 1958

His voice is so admired by his peers that before he ever had a recording contract, Joe Logan Diffie was one of the most in-demand demo singers in Nashville. As an artist he established himself as a viable flag-waver for traditional country music, but with his third album, he became a major proponent of the high-energy "turbo tonk" sound that mixed country with a heavy dose of rock music in the mid-1990s.

Diffie's traditional bent came naturally. His father listened to the likes of GEORGE JONES, MERLE HAGGARD, JOHNNY CASH, and LEFTY FRIZZELL, and the family frequently sang country and gospel songs while riding in the family pickup. Diffie could sing harmony at age three, and five years later, his father taught him to play the guitar.

Diffie gave some thought to work as a chiropractor, but he found himself married and working in a foundry in Oklahoma while performing at nightclubs on weekends. Originally he sang with a gospel quartet; Diffie then moved to a bluegrass band before developing his own solo act.

In 1986, with the oil business in a serious funk, Diffie lost his job. With nothing to lose, he followed the advice of some admirers and moved to Nashville, where he went to work for Gibson Guitars. He also began singing on songwriters' demos. Diffie's voice is the one RICKY VAN SHELTON heard when he first ran across "I've Cried My Last Tear for You." Songs that were demoed by Diffie also landed on albums by KEITH WHITLEY, GEORGE STRAIT, and DOUG STONE.

Signed to EPIC RECORDS by BOB MONTGOMERY, Diffie's 1990 debut single, "Home," became the first debut ever to reach #1 on the *Billboard, Radio & Records,* and *Gavin* industry charts. Diffie at times embodied George Jones or BUCK OWENS in some of his early singles: interpretive ballads such as "Is It Cold in Here" and "Ships That Don't Come In," and the honky-tonk efforts "If the Devil Danced

(In Empty Pockets)" and "New Way (To Light Up an Old Flame)."

But with 1993's *Honky Tonk Attitude* album, Diffie shifted into overdrive, piecing together a string of borderline-novelty records that melded heavy rock guitar overtones with honky-tonk elements. "Prop Me Up Beside the Jukebox (If I Die)," "John Deere Green," "Bigger Than the Beatles," "Pickup Man" (four weeks at #1, 1994), and "Third Rock from the Sun" received mixed critical reaction, but they contributed to the most commercially successful period in Diffie's career. Subsequent albums *Life's So Funny* (1995) and *Twice Upon a Time* (1997) yielded disappointing results; Diffie dropped longtime Epic manager and producer Johnny Slate. Recording new sides with producer Don Cook, Diffie released a greatest hits package in 1998.

—*Tom Roland*

REPRESENTATIVE RECORDINGS

A Thousand Winding Roads (Epic, 1990); *Third Rock from the Sun* (Epic, 1994)

Annie Lou & Danny Dill

Annie Lou Stockard Dill b. Skull Bone, Tennessee, July 27, 1925;
d. January 4, 1982

Horace Eldred "Danny" Dill b. Dollar Hill, Tennessee,
September 19, 1924

"The Sweethearts of Country Music," Annie Lou & Danny were a duet act on the GRAND OLE OPRY between 1946 and the mid-1950s. After their joint career, Danny Dill became one of the CEDARWOOD publishing company's best songwriters.

Annie Lou Stockard was singing with her twin sisters on radio in Jackson, Tennessee, where she met and in 1945 married another radio singer, Horace Dill—later dubbed Danny by one of his first touring partners, the DUKE OF PADUCAH. Their music was much in the style of LULU BELLE & SCOTTY, and they joined the Grand Ole Opry in January 1946, first recording for BULLET in 1949. Besides their Nashville radio work, they toured with the DUKE OF PADUCAH, EDDY ARNOLD, ERNEST TUBB, GEORGE MORGAN, and other Opry stars until their act and marriage broke up in the 1960s.

Danny Dill recorded solo for ABC and Cub, and turned to songwriting, his first hit being "If You Saw Her Through My Eyes" for CARL SMITH (1954). Best known of his later song hits were "Long Black Veil" (co-written with MARIJOHN WILKIN, 1959) for LEFTY FRIZZELL and "Detroit City" (co-written with MEL TILLIS, 1963) for BOBBY BARE.

Annie Lou never remarried and died at Bradford, Tennessee, in her fifty-seventh year. Danny still performs on songwriter showcases and played the part of an old man in STEVE WARINER's 1992 video *The Tips of My Fingers*.

—*Ronnie Pugh*

The Dillards

Douglas Flint Dillard b. East St. Louis, Illinois, March 6, 1937
Rodney Adean Dillard b. East St. Louis, Illinois, May 18, 1942
Mitchell Jayne b. Hammond, Indiana, July 5, 1930
Roy Dean Webb b. Independence, Missouri, March 28, 1937

The Dillards rose to national prominence in the 1960s through their appearances on CBS television's THE ANDY GRIFFITH SHOW. Playing the part of the Darling Family, Briscoe T. Darling's four boys never uttered a word on their appearances but played like the dickens. Through these network appearances, sales of their ELEKTRA albums skyrocketed, and they were one of the most in-demand groups on the folk and bluegrass circuit.

Reared in Salem, Missouri, the Dillards—brothers Rodney and Doug—began their musical training early, as both their father, Homer, and older brother Homer Jr. played music in the family's front room. In 1962 the group, which now included Mitch Jayne on bass and mandolin player Dean Webb, packed up a station wagon and headed for Los Angeles, seeking fame and fortune. While performing a gig at the legendary Ash Grove, a haven for bluegrass and folk musicians in the L.A. area, record producer Jim Dickson heard them, and within a week they were signed to Elektra Records. Shortly thereafter they landed their first spot on the Griffith show. Their first album, *Back Porch Bluegrass* (1963), was given a boost through these appearances. Two original songs, "The Old Home Place" and "Dooley," have since become bluegrass standards. In 1964 they appeared on a Judy Garland special and released their second album, *Live . . . Almost*, recorded at the folk club Mecca. The album showcases the group's homespun comedy routines in addition to their tight picking. It contains a mix of material, ranging from the original "There Is a Time" to traditional numbers such as "Pretty Polly." It also includes a cover of BOB DYLAN's "Walking Down the Line," and appears to be the first cover of a Dylan song by a bluegrass outfit. *Pickin' and Fiddlin'* (1965) was also a popular album for the group. For that project the Dillards teamed up with fiddler and future Blue Grass Boy Byron Berline.

Influenced by West Coast rock musicians, the Dillards began experimenting in the recording studio. The group waited three years before releasing their fourth album, *Wheatstraw Suite*. It featured some high-tech vocals by Herb Pedersen, who replaced Doug Dillard on banjo. The vocal parts were doubled and tripled in some instances to give the recordings a fuller sound. The album also included orchestral arrangements, drums, and pedal steel. It didn't overwhelm the traditionalists but did find favor with the younger crowd.

The Dillards released one final album for Elektra before moving on to a series of smaller labels, including Anthem, Poppy, and Flying Fish. Today, Rodney Dillard, Jayne, and Webb continue to perform together as the Dillards, with Steve Cooley handling the banjo chores. Doug Dillard heads his own outfit and is based out of Nashville.

—*Chris Skinker*

REPRESENTATIVE RECORDINGS

There Is a Time (Vanguard, 1991); *Take Me Along for the Ride* (Vanguard, 1992)

Dean Dillon

b. Lake City, Tennessee, March 26, 1955

During the 1980s, Dean Dillon became one of the more prominent songwriters in country music, thanks in great part to his relationship with GEORGE STRAIT. Strait's first hit single, "Unwound" (#6, 1981), was co-written by Dillon and Frank Dycus. With its simple chord progressions and slight twists of phrases, the song suited Strait's affinity for traditional country. Since then, Dillon has provided Strait with numerous other songs, including "Marina Del Rey,"

"The Chair," "Nobody in His Right Mind Would've Left Her," "It Ain't Cool to Be Crazy About You," "Ocean Front Property," "Easy Come, Easy Go," "If I Know Me," and "I've Come to Expect It From You," among others.

Dillon originally moved to Nashville to become a singer. Given the name Rutherford when he was adopted in 1967, he had never liked the moniker and wrote only one hit under it: Jim Ed Brown & Helen Cornelius's 1979 release "Lying in Love with You." Subsequently signed as a recording artist by RCA Records, he worked with division head Jerry Bradley to come up with his stage name out of the phone book.

Dillon's songwriting credits also include Steve Wariner's "By Now," George Jones's "Tennessee Whiskey," Vern Gosdin's "Set 'Em Up Joe," Hank Williams Jr.'s "Leave Them Boys Alone," Keith Whitley's "Homecoming '63," and Pam Tillis's "All the Good Ones Are Gone." As an artist, Dillon's hard-edged style has earned him a fair amount of critical acclaim, though stints with RCA, Capitol, and Atlantic never brought him a single that charted higher than #25.
—*Tom Roland*

Disc Jockey Convention (*see* DJ Convention)

The Dixon Brothers
Dorsey Murdock Dixon b. Darlington, South Carolina, October 14, 1897; d. April 17, 1968
Howard Briten Dixon b. Darlington, South Carolina, June 19, 1903; d. March 24, 1961

Although the Dixon Brothers built influential careers as country musicians, and introduced songs that have been valued by both country music fans and academic folklorists, they never made music their full-time profession. Instead, they remained cotton mill workers until death ended Howard's labors in 1961 and until retirement finally took Dorsey out of the mills. The Dixons sang in a rough but affecting style that suggested country-gospel singing, and Dorsey played finger-style guitar while Howard played Hawaiian-style steel guitar (inspired by seeing Jimmie Tarlton of Darby & Tarlton play the instrument). They introduced a wide variety of songs, mostly written or arranged by Dorsey, that span most of the themes stressed in country music. These include humorous songs such as "The Intoxicated Rat"; religious numbers such as "I'm Not Turning Backward"; moralistic songs such as "Wreck on the Highway" (made famous by Roy Acuff); topical songs such as "Down with the Old Canoe" (about the sinking of the *Titanic*); and social comments that graphically document or recall their experiences as cotton mill workers, such as "Weave Room Blues" and "Spinning Room Blues." They recorded these songs (and a total of fifty-five released sides) for Bluebird from 1936 to 1938. Fortunately for modern fans of old-time country music, Dorsey Dixon made a few concert appearances in the 1960s and was recorded (with his sister Nancy) in 1962 by Eugene Earle and Archie Green for an album that appeared on the independent Testament label.
—*Bill C. Malone*

REPRESENTATIVE RECORDINGS
Babies in the Mill (Testament, 1965); *Are You From Dixie? Great Country Brother Teams of the 1930s* (RCA, 1988) (various-artists release containing three 1930s tracks by the Dixon Brothers)

DJ Convention
began November 22, 1952

Since 1952 the annual fall festival once known as the DJ Convention has honored the Grand Ole Opry while consolidating Nashville's role in the country music industry. Now popularly called Country Music Week, the event originally commemorated the Grand Ole Opry Birthday Celebration and was first organized by radio station WSM, using Acuff-Rose Publications' DJ list.

The first event took place on November 22, 1952, and involved some 100 DJs who were welcomed to WSM and treated to a Grand Ole Opry show. The 1953 celebration extended over two days, with record companies and publishers hosting receptions and BMI giving its first country music awards for radio airplay. In addition, DJs organized the Country Music Disc Jockeys Association (CMDJA), precursor to CMA. By 1958 attendance had grown to 2,000 DJs; entertainers were making special appearances; and several trade magazines were bestowing awards. In addition to formal and informal parties, there were now panels on industry issues such as record labels' service to disc jockeys, programming, and merchandising.

In that year, CMDJA disbanded, and CMA was organized at the fall DJ Convention. Since then, CMA has made the event an ongoing project. In 1963 the CMA began a successful push to have state governors proclaim October as Country Music Month, and the festival was shifted from November to October to avoid winter weather. By then attendance had reached 3,500, and ASCAP held its first country awards ceremony. (SESAC followed suit in 1964, and the NSAI in 1970.)

In 1969 the first Country Radio Broadcasters (CRB) seminar was held, and CRB soon established its own board of directors. This event is now held each year in February, the distinction symbolizing the rise of tightly formatted radio and declining power of once-freewheeling DJs vis-à-vis station program directors and radio consultants. In 1972 CMA organized the first Fan Fair to relieve the congestion of Country Music Week and to give artists and fans a special spring event at which to meet each other. Fan Fair attendance now approaches 25,000 annually, while some 4,000 attend the fall festivities.
—*John Rumble*

Dobro

Properly called a resophonic guitar, "dobro" was originally a brand name for an instrument with metal resonating chambers. Generally played Hawaiian-style (positioned with strings facing up, tuned to an open chord, and noted using a metal slide), the dobro is valued for its bluesy, insinuating sound, its versatility in producing sustained slides or crisp arpeggios, and as an acoustic alternative to the electrified pedal steel.

John and Rudy Dopyera perfected resophonic instruments in 1926 while attempting to mechanically amplify guitars in the days before electric instruments and multi-microphone sound systems. Built into their guitars' tops were one large or three small metal resonators similar in shape to record player speaker cones. Many variations followed, including metal and wood-bodied instruments, and cones of various designs and manufacture. In 1927 the Dopyeras joined with three partners to found the National Guitar Company. Of Czechoslovakian descent, the Dopyera brothers (five in all) called their creation the Dobro, using a Slavic word for "good" that also referenced their name and relation.

In 1929 the Dopyeras left National and formed the Dobro Company. (The two entities eventually merged, and in 1987 the Gibson Guitar Company acquired rights to the Dobro brand name.) The Dopyeras built resophonic mandolins, banjos, and ukuleles as well. Resophonic guitars became popular with blues musicians (who played them slide-style or by standard finger fretting) and Hawaiian music bands.

By the late 1920s the dobro had begun to affect country music. CLIFF CARLISLE played on JIMMIE RODGERS sessions in the late 1920s and early 1930s, while ROY ACUFF featured dobroists in his band—notably Beecher "BASHFUL BROTHER OSWALD" Kirby, whose GRAND OLE OPRY appearances maintained interest in the dobro after electric guitars virtually supplanted resophonic instruments. George Edward "Speedy" Krise performed with MOLLY O'DAY in the late 1940s, and Ray Atkins and HAROLD "SHOT" JACKSON worked with JOHNNIE & JACK in the 1950s.

The dobro experienced a renaissance in the late 1950s thanks to BURKETT "UNCLE JOSH" GRAVES. Hired by LESTER FLATT & EARL SCRUGGS to play bass, Graves was quickly switched to the dobro. His brilliant vocabulary of lead and back-up lines and his dynamic three-finger picking inspired a new generation of bluegrass and acoustic country musicians, notably Mike Auldridge, known for his work with the SELDOM SCENE, and JERRY DOUGLAS, who became Nashville's most active dobro session player. Other respected contemporary dobroists include TUT TAYLOR (with his trademark single-plectrum picking style), Rob Ickles, Phil Leadbetter, Sally Van Meter, and Gene Wooten.

—*Richard D. Smith*

Jimmie Dolan
b. Gardena, California, October 29, 1916; d. July 31, 1994

Jimmie Lee Dolan, best known as Ramblin' Jimmie Dolan, was a California recording artist, club singer, and disc jockey, most active between 1945 and 1955. Dolan learned guitar playing at fourteen through mail-order instruction, and first sang on radio at KWK in St. Louis. After service as a naval radio operator in World War II, Dolan returned to California and started a recording career with West Coast independents Colonial, Modern, and Crystal Records. He joined CAPITOL in 1949; Dolan's best-remembered releases, during his six-year tenure there, were his 1950 covers of MOON MULLICAN's "I'll Sail My Ship Alone" and Arkie Shibley's "Hot Rod Race."

As his nickname suggests, good-timing, fun-loving songs were his specialty, such as 1952's "Rack Up the Balls, Boys" and "Playin' Dominoes and Shootin' Dice" of 1953. He was also a popular country disc jockey on California stations in the 1950s, mostly in Southern California, except for a time when he worked at KYA in San Francisco. However, Dolan sank into obscurity with the coming of rock & roll, though he was cited as an active freelance musician and member of the Los Angeles Local 47 of the AMERICAN FEDERATION OF MUSICIANS in his obituaries nearly forty years later.

—*Ronnie Pugh*

Dot Records
established in Gallatin, Tennessee, 1950

Dot Records was an independent label that released pop music for the most part but eventually evolved into a major presence in country music. Randy Wood, owner of Randy's Record Shop in Gallatin, Tennessee, started Dot Records to add to his growing mail-order business. The label's first release was "Boogie Beat Rag" (1950) by the Tennessee Drifters, a teenage band from Nashville's East High School. The label's biggest-selling artist by far was clean-cut pop singer Pat Boone. His cover of the r&b hit "Two Hearts" in 1955 became first of his fifty-nine chart hits for the label.

MAC WISEMAN (on the label from 1951 to 1961) was one of Dot's first country acts. During the fifties he had several Top Ten country hits on the charts, including "Ballad of Davy Crockett" (#10, 1955) and "Jimmy Brown the Newsboy" (#5, 1959). In the late fifties Wiseman served as Dot's A&R country director. Other artists during the fifties included fiddler TOMMY JACKSON (1952–55), JIMMY C. NEWMAN (1954–57), COWBOY COPAS (1957), and LEROY VAN DYKE (1956–58).

Wood moved the company to Hollywood in 1957 and later sold it to Paramount Pictures. ABC Records merged their country roster with Dot's in 1974 to create ABC/DOT. Among those recording during the seventies were ROY CLARK (1968–77), BARBARA MANDRELL (1975–77), DON WILLIAMS (1974–77), JOE STAMPLEY (1971–75), Tommy Overstreet (1969–78), and DONNA FARGO (1972–76). In 1977 MCA RECORDS purchased ABC/Dot, and except for a brief period in the late eighties, retired the Dot name.

—*Don Roy*

Michael Doucet & BeauSoleil
Michael Doucet b. Scott, Louisiana, February 14, 1951

Since 1975, BeauSoleil has expanded the parameters of Cajun music while honoring the genre's roots and reviving old-time material. Led by fiddler, vocalist, and songwriter Michael Doucet, BeauSoleil combines traditional Cajun and zydeco songs with such diverse modern elements as rock, blues, and jazz. Played with passion and expertise, this danceable mixture has led to global renown and six Grammy nominations.

Michael Doucet was raised in Scott, Louisiana, at a time when Cajun music and culture were often scorned. By the mid-1970s, however, such tradition began to be appreciated, and Doucet emerged as both a pioneer in its new acceptance, and an accomplished, adventurous fiddler. In 1974 he formed the regionally oriented Bayou Drifter Band with singer/accordionist Zachary Richard. While Richard went on to blend Cajun music with rock, Doucet explored traditional sounds through informal apprenticeships with such venerable Cajun/Creole fiddlers as Dennis McGee, Luderin Darbone, and Canray Fontenot. Other important influences on Doucet's fiddling include Will and DEWEY BALFA, and HARRY CHOATES. BeauSoleil often records songs by these and other Louisiana music masters.

Michael Doucet formed BeauSoleil in 1975 to honor this legacy, while expressing his modernism in a popular rock band called Coteau, also known as the Cajun Grateful Dead. When Coteau disbanded in 1977, Doucet channeled both approaches into BeauSoleil. The band's rise to prominence was spurred by appearances on radio's *A Prairie Home Companion,* and inclusion on the soundtracks of such films as *The Big Easy.* BeauSoleil also features David Doucet (born July 6, 1957), whose unique guitar sound blends Cajun and country styles.

Besides BeauSoleil, Michael Doucet has recorded with such diverse artists as the Savoy-Doucet Band, Keith Richard, Richard Thompson, Mark Knopfler, Thomas Dolby, Wayne Toups, zydeco accordionist Nathan Williams, the HACKBERRY RAMBLERS, and MARY CHAPIN CARPENTER—whose work with the group won her a Grammy in 1992. In addition, Doucet has recorded several solo releases, and a children's album with his wife, Sharon.

BeauSoleil's prolific recordings reflect Michael Doucet's eclectic vision, ranging from acoustic, all-Cajun albums such as *Parlez-nous à boire* to the rock-influenced productions *Bayou Boogie* and *Cajun Conja,* which also feature guest guitarist Sonny Landreth. On the brink of its third decade, BeauSoleil continues to flourish, and can be credited as leaders in the ongoing resurgence of Cajun and Creole music, both old and new. After six nominations, Michael Doucet & BeauSoleil garnered a Grammy Award, in Traditional Folk, for the 1997 release *L'amour ou la Folie.*
—*Ben Sandmel*

REPRESENTATIVE RECORDINGS

L'Echo (Rhino/Forward, 1995); *The Hoogie Boogie* (children's album with Sharon Arms Doucet) (Rounder, 1992); *L'amour ou la Folie* (Rhino/Forward, 1997)

Jerry Douglas
b. Warren, Ohio, May 28, 1956

The dobro, associated primarily with BLUEGRASS via JOSH GRAVES, suddenly became a fixture of mainstream country in the 1980s after Jerry Douglas made it a prominent part of hits by RICKY SKAGGS ("Don't Get Above Your Raising," 1981) and the WHITES ("Hangin' Around," 1982). Douglas's flashy, aggressive style proved that the anachronistic dobro had a voice in a country scene that honored the past even as it eagerly absorbed rock influences.

The son of a steelworker who played bluegrass on the side, Gerald Calvin Douglas was eight when he first heard both BASHFUL BROTHER OSWALD and Josh Graves in a FLATT & SCRUGGS concert. Smitten by their sound, Douglas acquired his first dobro in 1966 and began playing with his father's band, the West Virginia Travelers. He joined the COUNTRY GENTLEMEN in 1973, playing in a style imitative of Mike Auldridge, and in 1974 joined J. D. CROWE's New South. Ricky Skaggs was also in Crowe's band at the time, and in 1976 Douglas and Skaggs formed Boone Creek. Two years later Douglas rejoined the Gentlemen and was working on his first solo album, *Fluxology* (Rounder, 1979), a title taken from his nickname, "Flux."

In 1979 Douglas joined Buck White & the Down Home Folks while the Whites were touring as the opening act for EMMYLOU HARRIS. Douglas played on Harris's largely acoustic *Roses in the Snow* (1980) and became a recognized player in commercial country's emerging traditionalist vanguard via recordings with Harris, Skaggs, and the Whites. Douglas retired from the Whites' road band in 1985 and concentrated on Nashville session work, appearing on recordings by JOHNNY CASH, GAIL DAVIES, and RAY CHARLES, among others. He fronted two albums in MCA's Masters Series (*Under the Wire,* 1986; *Plant Early,* 1989), works exploring newgrass and Nashville New Age. Since 1989 Douglas has performed and recorded with Strength in Numbers, an irregular ensemble that has included violinist MARK O'CONNOR, mandolinist SAM BUSH, banjoist BÉLA FLECK, and bassist Edgar Meyer.   —*Mark Humphrey*

REPRESENTATIVE RECORDING

Under the Wire (MCA, 1986; reissued by Sugar Hill, 1995)

Big Al Downing
b. Centralia, Oklahoma, January 9, 1940

Al Downing's career reflects the diverse musical influences he heard growing up in Lenapah, Oklahoma. One of country music's largest-selling African-American artists, Downing eschews classifying his music, also recording rock & roll, r&b, even venturing into disco, but always returning to country.

Early influences included ERNEST TUBB, HANK WILLIAMS, the OSBORNE BROTHERS, and PORTER WAGONER heard on WSM's GRAND OLE OPRY and the 5 Blind Boys, Fats Domino, and New Orleans r&b artists heard over WLAC in Nashville. Downing's first piano, missing several keys, was found on a junk pile one day when he was returning from cutting hay.

A 1956 trip to Coffeyville, Kansas, to appear on a talent contest at WTTP-AM led to his professional career. Downing played "Blueberry Hill" and won the contest. Bobby Poe heard him on radio, and together they formed an early biracial band, the Poe Kats, named because, as Downing observes, "That's what we were." Downing's 1958 ROCK-ABILLY release "Down on the Farm," on White Rock, was picked up by CHALLENGE and barely missed the charts, but it became a rock & roll classic.

In that same year, WANDA JACKSON invited the band to join her. Downing appeared on several Jackson recordings, including her biggest hit, "Let's Have a Party." On the road with Jackson, they opened for MARTY ROBBINS, BOBBY BARE, RED SOVINE, DON GIBSON, and others.

Following the Jackson tour, the band moved to Washington, D.C., for several years and then to the Boston area, where Downing recorded on several labels in a Fats Domino–influenced style. His band, the Chartbusters, charted with two rock releases in 1964. A soul duet with Little Esther Phillips charted in 1963, and a disco record charted in 1975.

A 1978 move to WARNER BROS. brought him back to his country roots. A release of "Mr. Jones" that year, followed by "Touch Me (I'll Be Your Fool Once More)," led to a string of fifteen country chart records over the next decade. In recent years Downing has concentrated on performing in Europe, where he has a strong fan base.
—*William P. Davis*

REPRESENTATIVE RECORDING

Rockin' & Rollin' (Tug Boat International, 1996)

Pete Drake
b. Augusta, Georgia, October 8, 1932; d. July 29, 1988

As a producer, musician, and publisher of music from traditional country to rock, and as an innovator with his "talking" steel guitar sound (built on techniques pioneered by Alvino Rey), Roddis Franklin "Pete" Drake blazed a solid pathway through the creative canyons of the Nashville music industry.

Drake's father was a Pentecostal preacher, and his brothers Jack and Bill performed as the Drake Brothers. Jack Drake later spent twenty-four years as the bass player for ERNEST TUBB and His Texas Troubadours.

When eighteen-year-old Pete drove to Nashville to visit his brothers, he heard steel guitar maestro JERRY BYRD playing on the GRAND OLE OPRY. The sliding steel sound in-

Pete Drake

spired Drake to buy a steel guitar for $38 at a pawnshop in Atlanta.

Drake organized a band in Atlanta in the 1950s that included future stars JACK GREENE, JERRY REED, ROGER MILLER, JOE SOUTH, and DOUG KERSHAW. Drake moved to Nashville in 1959 and later worked on the road with stars such as DON GIBSON and MARTY ROBBINS. While playing on the Opry with CARL & PEARL BUTLER, Drake tried his innovative steel solos. Opry star ROY DRUSKY booked him for a session that resulted in the hit single "Anymore" (#3, 1960).

As word spread about the new steel player in town, Drake was booked for twenty-four studio sessions the next month, igniting a career of one of the most prolific and commercial studio musicians in country music history. At one time Drake was believed to be the steel guitarist on fifty-nine of the recordings listed in *Billboard*'s country singles chart. During the mid-1960s he began utilizing his "talking" steel guitar technique, which involved (in simplified terms) his forming and amplifying words via a tube running from his mouth to the instrument.

Drake's influences and success go far beyond the realms of country music. As a producer he worked with Ringo Starr, the first Beatle to record in the United States, and also produced such acts as B. J. THOMAS, the Four Freshmen, Bobby Vinton, LEON RUSSELL, Tracy Nelson, Ernest Tubb, SLIM WHITMAN, BOXCAR WILLIE, the OAK RIDGE BOYS, and BILLIE JO SPEARS. Drake's steel guitar stylings have graced the hit records of such artists as BOB DYLAN, Joan Baez, George Harrison, and ELVIS PRESLEY, as well as his own recordings made for the Smash label. Five Presley movie tracks also featured Drake's "talking" steel guitar. As a music publisher Drake prodded such talents as ED BRUCE, DAVID ALLAN COE, and DOTTIE WEST to new heights. His la-

bel Stop Records released recordings by JOHNNY BUSH and others during the 1960s and early 1970s.

The Nashville Entertainment Association presented Pete Drake with its coveted Masters Award on May 7, 1987. In that year he was also inducted into the International Steel Guitar Hall of Fame. In 1989 Drake was elected to the Atlanta Music Hall of Fame.

First Generation Records, started by Drake and since run by his widow, Rose Drake, has released an album of Drake's recordings, as well as albums by Tubb and other Grand Ole Opry stars.   —*Gerry Wood*

REPRESENTATIVE RECORDINGS

Forever (Smash, 1962); *Talking Steel Guitar* (Smash, 1964)

Rusty Draper

b. Kirksville, Missouri, January 25, ca. 1920s

Farrell "Rusty" Draper began his singing career at age twelve in Tulsa, Oklahoma, with sojourns in Des Moines, Iowa, and Quincy, Illinois, before age eighteen. A 1942 move to California led to becoming MC at the Mel Hertz Club in San Francisco and then several years at Hermie King's Rumpus Room. "Gambler's Guitar," a 1953 MERCURY release, was a million seller, hitting the #6 spot on both the pop and country charts. Subsequent releases, including the 1955 pop hit "Shifting, Whispering Sands," were frequently pop renditions of country songs. In 1963 he signed with MONUMENT RECORDS. Draper did not reach the country charts again until 1967. His last country chart record was a 1980 release of the pop standard "Harbor Lights."   —*William P. Davis*

The Drifting Cowboys

Although there were several bands called Drifting Cowboys, the name is indelibly associated with HANK WILLIAMS. He appears to have used it from the time he assembled his first bands in Montgomery, Alabama, in 1937 or 1938. It highlighted his fascination with western music, a fascination barely reflected in his recorded work. Over a fifteen-year period there were literally hundreds of Drifting Cowboys.

During the 1930s, most Drifting Cowboys played no more than a few shows with Williams, who was not then considered a plum employer. Two of the most famous Drifting Cowboys, Don Helms and Sammy Pruett, first joined Williams as early as 1944. Helms played steel guitar, and Pruett played lead guitar. They left within a year, and by the time Williams signed with Sterling Records in 1946, his band comprised R. D. Norred on steel guitar, Joe Pennington (born Penney) on guitar, Lum York on bass, and Winston "Red" Todd on guitar. It's worth noting that Williams's Cowboys seldom recorded with him until 1950; session musicians were used, although the Drifting Cowboys were label-credited.

Several months after Williams went to Shreveport in August 1948, to join the LOUISIANA HAYRIDE, he formed another band that comprised York, guitarist Bob McNett, Tony Francini on fiddle, steel guitarist Felton Pruett, and guitarist Clent Holmes. He left them in Shreveport after being offered a place on the GRAND OLE OPRY in June 1949, although McNett was brought into the Nashville group. Helms also returned, and the group was rounded out by fiddle player Jerry Rivers and bassist Hillous Butrum.

McNett left in 1950 to be replaced by Sammy Pruett, and Butrum left that year to be replaced by Howard Watts, a.k.a. Cedric Rainwater. Williams disbanded the group shortly before he underwent an operation in December 1951 and worked with pickup bands thereafter. Various Drifting Cowboys, almost always under the leadership of Helms and Rivers, have re-formed at times to work independently and with legitimate or illegitimate Williams offspring.

—*Colin Escott*

Jimmy Driftwood

b. near Mountain View, Arkansas, June 20, 1907

Mostly known as a songwriter, James Corbett Morris was born into a family locally noted as musicians and singers, so it was natural that Driftwood would have some connection with music. However, Morris's first professional experience was in education; he worked as a teacher, principal, and school superintendent. Toward this end, he had studied at John Brown University, Arkansas College, State Teachers College at Conway, Arkansas, and the University of Southern Mississippi. At the same time, he wrote songs, frequently setting original lyrics to traditional melodies. He also tried for several years to become a country recording artist, but he didn't meet with success until the folksong revival of the late 1950s.

While trying to break into the folksinger market, he adopted the name "Driftwood." (This was either a deliberate substitution by recording studio personnel or a simple misunderstanding of the word "Richwood," the last name Jimmy himself had been using, a name borrowed from a community in his native Stone County, Arkansas.) He also started playing a primitive-looking guitar made during the late 1940s by two craftsmen in Mountain View, Arkansas.

For a brief period, beginning in the late 1950s, Driftwood was a member of the GRAND OLE OPRY cast, but he is better known as a songwriter. His most successful songs have been "Battle of New Orleans" and "Tennessee Stud." Although he recorded both numbers, the most successful recordings of his songs were made by JOHNNY HORTON ("Battle of New Orleans," *Billboard*'s #1 country & western song in 1959) and EDDY ARNOLD ("Tennessee Stud"). In the late 1960s and early 1970s, Driftwood worked for the Ozark Folk Center, a complex that was the brainchild of John Opitz, a representative of the Arkansas Office of Economic Opportunity. The center opened in 1973 and recently completed its twenty-fifth season. —*W. K. McNeil*

REPRESENTATIVE RECORDING

Americana (Bear Family), 3 CDs

Roy Drusky

b. Atlanta, Georgia, June 22, 1930

Country music has always had its crooners, whose smooth voices are devoid of any twang. With his full, mellow baritone, Roy Frank Drusky Jr. is one of the best examples. According to Drusky, music did not enter his mind until he joined the navy and met some fellow sailors who enjoyed performing. His interest piqued, Drusky purchased a guitar and taught himself to play. After his service stint he enrolled at Emory University in his hometown of Atlanta to study veterinary medicine. To make extra money he formed the Southern Ranch Boys, began to perform

around the area, and soon had his own fifteen-minute radio show on WEAS in Decatur, Georgia.

Choosing music over animal husbandry, Drusky began a recording career with STARDAY RECORDS in 1953 and moved to the COLUMBIA label in 1956. Failing to hit the charts on either label, Drusky took a disc jockey position at KEVE in Minneapolis. During that tenure, his songwriting ability began to be noticed. FARON YOUNG recorded the Drusky composition "Alone with You," and the ballad spent thirteen weeks at #1 on the country charts. Young had two more notable hits with Drusky songs: "That's the Way It's Gotta Be" (#11, 1959) and "Country Girl" (#1, 1959).

In the fall of 1958, OWEN BRADLEY signed him to DECCA RECORDS, and Drusky joined the cast of the GRAND OLE OPRY in June 1959. He co-wrote his first two hits, "Another" (#2, 1960) and "Anymore" (#3, 1960). After three years of hits with Decca, Drusky moved to MERCURY RECORDS, where he stepped out of character and recorded the novelty tune "Peel Me a Nanner" (#8, 1963). In 1965 "Yes Mr. Peters," a cheating-song duet with Priscilla Mitchell (JERRY REED's wife), became his only #1 hit. Drusky continued to place records on the charts well through 1977, racking up a total of forty-two charts hits over a seventeen-year period.

—*Don Roy*

REPRESENTATIVE RECORDINGS

Anymore (Decca, 1961, reissued by Stetson, 1990); *Songs of Love and Life* (Mercury, 1995)

Tim DuBois

b. Grove, Oklahoma, May 4, 1948

Though he holds a master's degree from Oklahoma State University and is a licensed accountant, Tim DuBois feels his most valuable assets as head of ARISTA RECORDS' Nashville office are his "musical instincts" and his "ability to lead people." As the first and only president of the Nashville division, founded in 1989, DuBois built his roster from scratch, beginning with ALAN JACKSON and quickly adding BROOKS & DUNN. Under DuBois's guidance, the label's roster has grown to include DIAMOND RIO, LEE ROY PARNELL, PAM TILLIS, and BLACKHAWK, among others. In

Tim DuBois

the first seven years of operation, Arista Nashville sold more than 55 million albums.

After finishing his master's degree, DuBois moved from Oklahoma to Texas, where he worked as a staff auditor for Arthur Anderson & Co., then as a senior financial analyst at the Federal Reserve Bank of Dallas. After briefly teaching accounting at Tulsa University and then his alma mater, DuBois moved to Nashville in 1977 to further his songwriting career. By 1982 he had written three #1 hits, including ALABAMA's "Love in the First Degree" and JERRY REED's "She Got the Goldmine (I Got the Shaft)." He convinced Los Angeles–based management firm Fitzgerald-Hartley to open a Nashville office, then in 1985 became a partner with the firm, personally managing RESTLESS HEART, a group he helped assemble and later produced.

When VINCE GILL joined the Fitzgerald-Hartley roster, DuBois and Gill became occasional writing partners. Their songwriting collaboration produced "When I Call Your Name," a #1 hit for Gill and Song of the Year for both the CMA and the ACM in 1992.

Arista tapped DuBois, who had never worked at a record company, to start its Nashville division in 1989. His new post forced him to cut back on producing and songwriting, but DuBois continued to do both, overseeing albums for EXILE, Diamond Rio, STEVE WARINER, and Black-Hawk. In 1991 DuBois encouraged singer-songwriters Kix Brooks and Ronnie Dunn to try writing and recording together, then offered them a record deal on the strength of the result. Brooks & Dunn went on to sell more than 14 million records by 1998 and become the CMA's 1996 Entertainer of the Year. DuBois also urged Henry Paul, Dave Robbins, and Van Stephenson to form a group. As Black-Hawk the trio has recorded two successful albums, the first co-produced by DuBois.

DuBois has taken some chances in the name of expanding the horizons of his company and of country music. He signed aging fellow Oklahomans the TRACTORS, who rode a catchy video hit, "Baby Likes to Rock It," to a million-selling debut album. And retro-country group BR5-49 caught his attention when they built a grassroots following at a honky-tonk bar in downtown Nashville. In 1993 DuBois expanded Arista Nashville's reach by founding the Austin, Texas–based offshoot Arista Texas, with the goal of tapping the indigenous music of the Lone Star State. He founded a second Arista country label, Career Records, in 1995, and moved Lee Roy Parnell over to it as flagship artist. DuBois shifted the structure of Arista Texas in 1997, signing singer-songwriters ROBERT EARL KEEN, Jeff Black, Abra Moore, and alternative rock act Sister 7 to the renamed Arista Austin division and grouping Spanish-speaking artists in sister Arista Latin.

Entertainment Weekly named DuBois in its annual list of the 101 most powerful people in the entertainment business in 1994 and 1995. In 1996 he was elected president of the CMA. —*Jay Orr*

George Ducas
b. Texas City, Texas, August 1, 1966

After working one unfulfilling year as a banker in Atlanta, George Ducas returned to Nashville in 1990, where he had attended Vanderbilt University, to become a country artist. His gamble paid off. Ducas spent several years playing gigs as a solo artist in small bars and rib joints, befriending other songwriters, and building a following with a reper-

toire of originals along with rock and country standards. A&R man John Allen of LIBERTY RECORDS (now Capitol Nashville) became a fan and eventually brought Ducas to the attention of the label's then president, JIMMY BOWEN, who signed the young singer.

Ducas co-wrote RADNEY FOSTER's 1992 hit "Just Call Me Lonesome," and his material features similar jangly pop sensibilities tempered by dirt-floor shuffles and other standard country elements. His debut album, *George Ducas,* yielded the Top Ten single "Lipstick Promises," and his follow-up album, *Where I Stand,* yielded the Beatlesque "Every Time She Passes By." Both albums were produced by RICHARD BENNETT and harbor a warm guitar sound similar to that found on albums by the Bennett-produced artist KIM RICHEY. Like Richey, Ducas has yet to create a major stir in the marketplace, but his ability as both an artist and a songwriter suggests that his best work may still be ahead of him. —*Clark Parsons*

REPRESENTATIVE RECORDINGS
George Ducas (Liberty, 1994); *Where I Stand* (Capitol, 1996)

Dave Dudley
b. Spencer, Wisconsin, May 3, 1928

Dave Dudley spearheaded the trucking song phenomenon. Between 1963 and 1980 he hit the *Billboard* charts consistently with such songs, including "Truck Drivin' Son-of-a-Gun" (#3, 1965), "There Ain't No Easy Run" (#10, 1968), and "Me and Old C.B." (#12, 1976). Born David Darwin Pedruska, Dudley learned guitar as a child growing up in Wisconsin. However, his real love was baseball, and after graduating from high school, Dudley played on semi-pro teams. But an arm injury retired him from baseball and turned his attention toward music. Impressing a DJ friend, Dudley landed his own radio show and band.

Just as his career was gaining momentum, Dudley was struck by a car after a performance in Minneapolis in 1960. After a six-month recovery, he returned to the music scene, hitting the charts in 1961 with "Maybe I Do" on Vee Records. In 1963 he recorded the truckers' anthem "Six Days on the Road," a song passed along to him by JIMMY C. NEWMAN and written by Earl Greene and Earl "Peanut" Montgomery. Released on the independent Golden Wing label, it took the country by storm, reaching #2 on the country charts and #32 in the pop field. MERCURY RECORDS signed him later that year, and he continued his string of songs for the workingman, such as "Last Day in the Mines" (#7, 1964), "Viet Nam Blues" (#12, 1966), "The Pool Shark" (#1, 1970), and "If It Feels Good Do It" (#14, 1971). In 1980, the last year he appeared on the charts, a German pop group called Truck Stop recorded a tribute to Dudley ("I Want to Hear More Dave Dudley"). Since then he's had an active career in several European countries. —*Don Roy*

Arlie Duff
b. Jack's Branch, Texas, March 28, 1924; d. July 4, 1996

If there ever was a country music anthem, it would have to be "You All Come," written by Arleigh "Arlie" Elton Duff. (Although later recorded as "Y'all Come" by other artists, STARDAY originally released the record as "You All Come.") Duff grew up in the southeastern part of Texas known as the Big Thicket. He was teaching school in 1953, when after hearing LEFTY FRIZZELL on the radio, he wondered if he could write a country song. Inspired by an elderly family friend who kept repeating "Y'all come" seventeen times as she was leaving their house, Duff wrote the song in twenty minutes. He met JACK STARNES of Starday Records, who shortly thereafter recorded and released Duff's version. "You All Come" reached #7 on the country charts in 1954. Much to Duff's surprise, Bing Crosby also recorded the song, and his version reached #20 in the pop field, earning Duff a BMI award.

Known as the Singing School Teacher, Duff toured nationally, appeared on the GRAND OLE OPRY and the LOUISIANA HAYRIDE, and briefly joined the OZARK JUBILEE ABC-TV show. He recorded for DECCA RECORDS in the mid-fifties without chart success and then left the road to raise a family and settle down as a radio announcer in Colorado Springs. In 1963 he returned to Texas and worked on radio in Austin for several years. In 1983 Eakin Press of Austin published his autobiography. He moved to Woodbury, Connecticut, in June 1985 and passed away while playing golf in Waterbury, Connecticut, on July 4, 1996.

—Don Roy

The Duke of Paducah
b. DeSoto, Missouri, May 12, 1901; d. June 20, 1986

Benjamin Francis "Whitey" Ford was a leading country comedian from the late 1930s to the mid-1950s. He had only a third-grade education and was fond of calling himself a graduate of the "University of Hard Knocks." Following four years in the navy (1918–22), he joined a Dixieland jazz group as a banjoist, working in Arkansas and Missouri. Based in Chicago, beginning around 1929, Ford performed on WLS and eventually toured with GENE AUTRY.

In the mid-1930s, while based at the St. Louis station KWK, Ford acquired his Duke of Paducah stage moniker, earlier invented by humorist Irvin S. Cobb. (Ford's nickname "Whitey" came from his blond hair.) By then he had

Whitey Ford, a.k.a. The Duke of Paducah

developed his comic rube character, begun to compile an enormous library of jokes, and adopted his famous tag line, "I'm goin' back to the wagon, boys, these shoes are killin' me!" In 1937 Ford teamed with RED FOLEY and JOHN LAIR to organize the RENFRO VALLEY BARN DANCE.

During the late thirties and early 1940s Ford starred with LOUISE MASSEY & THE WESTERNERS on the NBC network radio show *Plantation Party* out of Cincinnati and Chicago before moving in 1942 to star on the the GRAND OLE OPRY's NBC network segment, a role he would maintain until replaced in 1947 by ROD BRASFIELD, whom he helped to recruit. Subsequently Ford made several series of popular radio shows, some of them recorded and syndicated widely throughout the United States and others fed to CBS.

Ford kept working at the Opry and touring, even heading a troupe billed as the Rock and Roll Revue during the mid-1950s. Beginning in 1958 he hosted *Country Junction*, a Nashville television show that aired on WLAC-TV for a number of years. Eventually many of his jokes found their way to *HEE HAW*, whose producers bought his joke library. The remainder of his substantial collection of American humor was acquired by Emory University shortly before his death. Four months after his passing, he was elected to the COUNTRY MUSIC HALL OF FAME.

—John Rumble

Glen Duncan
b. Columbus, Indiana, May 5, 1955

Glen Carlton Duncan, bluegrass fiddle player-tenor singer since 1975 and busy session-player since moving to Nashville in 1983, worked on the road with major bluegrass acts BILL MONROE, JIM & JESSE, and the OSBORNE BROTHERS, and toured with country stars REBA MCENTIRE, BARBARA MANDRELL, and the KENDALLS.

Duncan's style incorporates bluesy elements from bluegrass fiddle stylists BENNY MARTIN and Bobby Hicks, as well as melodic and swing-oriented influences of mainstream country musicians. His adaptability and technique make him a valuable session musician whose work has appeared on recordings by artists as diverse as BILL MONROE, DOLLY PARTON, ROY ROGERS, and JOHNNY RODRIGUEZ.

In September 1995 Duncan and songwriter Larry Cordle disbanded their bluegrass group Lonesome Standard Time when the successful band began to interfere with Duncan's recording sessions and Cordle's songwriting.

—Frank and Marty Godbey

Johnny Duncan
b. Dublin, Texas, October 5, 1938

Johnny Duncan's slow-building country career saw him gain his first of three #1 singles, "Thinkin' of a Rendezvous," in 1976. A cousin of DAN SEALS and Jim Seals (of Seals & Crofts), John Richard Duncan grew up on a Texas farm near Stephenville, where his mother taught him how to play guitar.

Influenced by MERLE TRAVIS, LES PAUL, and CHET ATKINS, Duncan wanted to become a professional guitarist. He began considering a singing career when he was a teenager and kept that ambition alive while attending Texas Christian University. He moved to Clovis, New Mexico, in 1959, teaming with producer Norman Petty for three years. Following a brief stint as a DJ in the Southwest, Duncan decided to move to Nashville in 1964.

While trying to break into the country music business, Duncan worked as a DJ at WAGG in Franklin, Tennessee, and at a series of other jobs. Performing on WSM-TV shows emceed by RALPH EMERY and BOBBY LORD, he gained the attention of COLUMBIA RECORDS executive DON LAW, who signed him to the label in 1966. The following year Duncan scored his first chart single, "Hard Luck Joe." He gained songwriting success when Chet Atkins recorded his "Summer Sunday."

The traditional-sounding singer also hit the top of the charts with "It Couldn't Have Been Any Better" (1977) and "She Can Put Her Shoes Under My Bed (Anytime)" (1978). JANIE FRICKE provided harmony vocals on three of his hits and joined Duncan for two duets—"Come a Little Bit Closer" and "He's Out of My Life."

Following a divorce, Duncan left the music business in the early 1980s to return to Texas and raise his three daughters. He returned to the recording studio in 1997 in hopes of making a career comeback.   —Gerry Wood

REPRESENTATIVE RECORDINGS

Sweet Country Woman (Columbia, 1973); *The Best of Johnny Duncan* (Columbia, 1976)

Tommy Duncan
b. Hillsboro, Texas, January 11, 1911; d. July 23, 1967

Although he had a notable career as a solo artist, Tommy Duncan's name remains inseparable from that of BOB WILLS. Duncan's warm, bluesy vocal style was one of the keys to Wills's success and a cornerstone of the Texas Playboys' sound. Duncan was also an underrated songwriter who wrote or co-wrote some of the most enduring songs in the Wills repertoire, including "Time Changes Everything," "Bubbles in My Beer," and "Misery."

Tommy Duncan

One of the most influential singers in country music, Thomas Elmer Duncan began—as did so many of his contemporaries—as a devotee of JIMMIE RODGERS. Duncan was singing Rodgers songs at a Fort Worth root beer stand before replacing MILTON BROWN in the LIGHT CRUST DOUGHBOYS in 1932. Although Duncan quickly adapted to the Doughboys' varied repertoire, he remained in obvious thrall to Rodgers and jazzy minstrel/yodeler EMMETT MILLER.

Duncan left the Doughboys with Wills in 1933, and over the next fifteen years, in Tulsa and on the West Coast, with two years lost to war service, Duncan became Wills's chief vocalist and right-hand man, maturing into an instantly recognizable WESTERN SWING crooner. Classic vocals include "Right or Wrong" (1936), "The Waltz You Saved for Me" (1938), "New San Antonio Rose" (1940), "Roly Poly" (1945), and many others. A star in his own right, Duncan parted with Wills in 1948 to form his Western All-Stars. He scored with Rodgers's "Gambling Polka Dot Blues" for CAPITOL in 1949 and went on to record excellent sessions for Intro, Coral, and other labels. His career in western swing faded, however, until he reteamed with Wills in 1960. "Heart to Heart Talk" proved a best-seller that year, and the three albums the pair cut for LIBERTY remained in print for years. Duncan and Wills split again in 1962, and Duncan continued to perform as a solo act until his death from a heart attack at fifty-six.   —Kevin Coffey

REPRESENTATIVE RECORDINGS

Texas Moon (Bear Family, 1996); *Beneath a Neon Star in a Honky Tonk* (Bear Family, 1996)

Bob Dunn
b. Fort Gibson (or Braggs), Oklahoma, February 8, 1908; d. May 27, 1971

Robert Lee Dunn's electric amplification of his steel guitar, upon joining MILTON BROWN's Musical Brownies in Fort Worth in late 1934, signaled an important change in the course of country music. His January 1935 recordings with Brown were the first in country music with an electric string instrument, and the impact was immediate and irrevocable. Dunn, who also played trombone, aspired to be a jazz musician, and he approached the steel like a jazz horn—blaring jagged yet sophisticated, swinging phrases. His playing style helped define western swing, especially in the Southwest, in the thirties and early forties.

Dunn's first love was HAWAIIAN MUSIC, but he quickly moved beyond it. He was playing professionally by 1927, and before joining Brown had played in a variety of vaudeville, jazz, and string bands. He made more than ninety recordings with the Brownies before Milton Brown's death in April 1936, including his classic signature tune, "Taking Off" (1935), and then resumed a nomadic lifestyle. He played and recorded with such acts as ROY NEWMAN & His Boys (1937), the SHELTON BROTHERS (1939), and extensively—and influentially—with former Brownie CLIFF BRUNER's Texas Wanderers (intermittently from 1937 to 1940), cutting such classics as "It Makes No Difference Now" and "I'll Keep On Loving You," on which he took a searing solo. He also formed his own band, the Vagabonds, and completed several jazz-filled sessions for DECCA.

Dunn served in the navy during World War II and then settled in Houston and opened a music store in 1950. He taught music there extensively, but—with the exception of the occasional local gig—his playing career basically ended by the early fifties. He retired in 1970 and died of lung cancer within weeks of selling his store. His influence, however, reverberates into the 1990s in the sounds of countless steel players. —*Kevin Coffey*

REPRESENTATIVE RECORDINGS

Milton Brown (Texas Rose, 1996), 5 CD boxed set; *Cliff Bruner's Complete Recordings* (Bear Family, 1997)

Holly Dunn
b. San Antonio, Texas, August 22, 1957

Singer-songwriter Holly Suzette Dunn emerged in the mid-1980s and is known for her clear soprano vocals and folk-tinged country.

Born the daughter of a Church of Christ preacher and a landscape painter, Dunn got her musical start in the 1970s with the Freedom Folk Singers. She graduated from Abilene Christian College in 1979 with a degree in advertising and public relations, then moved to Nashville, where her brother, Chris Waters, was already established as a professional songwriter and record producer. For six years she worked as a receptionist, demo singer, and staff writer, penning LOUISE MANDRELL's 1984 Top Ten single "I'm Not Through Loving You Yet" as well as other chart hits.

In 1984 Dunn signed with MTM RECORDS, earning her first Top Ten single in 1986 with "Daddy's Hands," a song she wrote as a Father's Day gift. When MTM folded in 1989, Dunn signed with WARNER BROS. RECORDS, recording four albums, including her two-volume greatest-hits package, *Milestones*, which included the #1 "You Really Had Me Going" (1990).

In 1995 Dunn moved to River North's Nashville division, releasing two albums before accepting a one-year position as morning drive show cohost at WWWW-FM radio in Detroit. In 1998 she returned to Nashville to concentrate on songwriting.

Dunn's honors include the Academy of Country Music's 1986 Top New Female Vocalist award, the COUNTRY MUSIC ASSOCIATION's 1987 Horizon Award, and BMI's 1988 Country Songwriter of the Year award. She became a cast member of the GRAND OLE OPRY on October 14, 1989. —*Marjie McGraw*

REPRESENTATIVE RECORDINGS

Across the Rio Grande (MTM, 1988); *Milestones* (Warner Bros., 1991)

Hal Durham
b. McMinnville, Tennessee, August 5, 1931

Through thirty years as announcer, radio station executive, and general manager of the GRAND OLE OPRY, Hal Durham helped bring the Opry forward from its AM radio days into the modern age of satellite TV—at the same time taking care to preserve the traditions and integrity of the show.

Durham started in radio at WROL in Knoxville while attending the University of Tennessee. He graduated in 1956 with a degree in journalism, intending to be a sportswriter, but found work as an announcer at WSB in Atlanta, then program director for a small station in McMinnville

in 1960. He started at WSM in 1964 and over the next decade progressed from Opry announcer to chief announcer to program director of WSM-AM.

In January 1974 Opry general manager E. W. "BUD" WENDELL appointed Durham manager of the Opry, and at that point Durham stopped announcing. He succeeded Wendell as general manager in 1978.

Durham made constant adjustments to keep the Opry relevant to current country music. He allowed a full set of drums on the stage at the new Grand Ole Opry House (previously drummers had been limited to a snare and a cymbal). He relaxed the required number of Saturday night appearances for Opry cast members, and as a result was able to sign such superstars as GARTH BROOKS, REBA MCENTIRE, VINCE GILL, and ALAN JACKSON to Opry membership. When he brought the Opry to television audiences, first through specials on the Public Broadcasting System and later with a *Grand Ole Opry Live* segment on THE NASHVILLE NETWORK (TNN), he insisted on an as-is, "look-in" format with no changes in the Opry program.

In 1993 Durham turned over Opry management to BOB WHITTAKER and became president of the Grand Ole Opry group, which includes the Opry, OPRYLAND Productions, and the RYMAN AUDITORIUM. He retired in 1996. —*Walter Carter*

Bob Dylan's Nashville Recording Sessions

When Bob Dylan (b. Robert Allen Zimmerman, Duluth, Minnesota, May 24, 1941) recorded *Blonde on Blonde* in Nashville in 1966, he not only made one of the great rock albums, but also opened MUSIC CITY's doors wider for rock musicians who followed him. Nashville had already recorded many rock artists in its studios in the 1950s and 1960s. But those artists—the EVERLY BROTHERS, ELVIS PRESLEY, ROY ORBISON, and BRENDA LEE—all had very strong country music ties. Dylan paved the way in Nashville for rockers of all stripes.

Bob Dylan

Blonde on Blonde was recorded at Columbia's studio in the heart of Music Row. Work had originally begun on the project at the company's New York studios, with an exhaustive number of hours being spent and precious little to show for the effort. Bob Johnston, who was by then producing Dylan, suggested that the star consider a change of scenery. Since his base of operations was in Nashville, Johnston convinced Dylan to try a new approach and utilize Nashville's stable of session musicians.

From February to March 1966, Johnston assembled more than a half dozen of the Row's top studio professionals: Hargus "Pig" Robbins, Charlie McCoy, Jerry Kennedy, Henry Strzelecki, Kenny Buttrey, Bill Aikens, Joe South, Wayne Moss, and (uncredited on the album) Mac Gayden. Robbie Robertson of the Band and keyboardist Al Kooper also played on the sessions. They logged more than forty hours in the studio, an enormously long period by Nashville recording standards in 1966. But the record's artistic and commercial success more than justified the studio expense: Dylan's double record climbed to #9 on *Billboard*'s LP charts and yielded three chart singles: "I Want You," "Just Like a Woman," and "Rainy Day Women #12 & 35." Shortly after completing the album, Dylan crashed his motorcycle in Woodstock, New York. For nearly two years he avoided the limelight.

Dylan's second Nashville album, *John Wesley Harding*, starkly contrasted his previous efforts, and Dylan made a sharp turn back to his earthier days. Gone were Dylan's usual accompaniment by a heavy Hammond B-3 organ and such odd touches as Salvation Army–styled horns. In fall 1967 Dylan and Johnston brought McCoy, Buttrey, and Drake to Nashville's Columbia studio. They cut a scaled-back, acoustically dominated album, which charted at #2. Among the songs cut and mixed during the six-hour session were "All Along the Watchtower," "The Ballad of Frankie Lee and Judas Priest," and "I'll Be Your Baby Tonight."

Dylan began working on his next Nashville project, *Nashville Skyline*, in February 1968. It was his goal to record what he thought was a straight country record. Session personnel were beefed up with the addition of Bob Wilson and multi-instrumentalists Charlie Daniels and Norman Blake. Friend and Columbia Records labelmate Johnny Cash sang a duet with Dylan on the *Nashville Skyline* song "Girl from the North Country." (Cash, incidentally, won a Grammy for the album's liner notes.) Reported to have only four songs ready for the sessions, Dylan is said to have written the remaining seven in his Nashville hotel room. "Lay Lady Lay" reached #7 on the pop single charts, but Dylan failed to place any singles on the country charts.

Money couldn't buy Music Row the publicity Dylan's Nashville trilogy garnered, and soon numerous rock artists followed his path to Nashville.

—*Chris Skinker*

The Eagles

Bernie Leadon b. Minneapolis, Minnesota, July 19, 1947

Glenn Frey b. Detroit, Michigan, November 6, 1948

Randy Meisner b. Scottsbluff, Nebraska, March 8, 1946

Don Henley b. Gilmer, Texas, July 22, 1947

Don Felder b. Gainesville, Florida, September 21, 1947

Joe Walsh b. Wichita, Kansas, November 20, 1947

Timothy B. Schmit b. Sacramento, California, October 30, 1947

The Eagles capitalized on the groundwork laid by others with their easy-listening country-rock style. They formed in 1971 to back singer LINDA RONSTADT on tour. Glenn Frey sang backup on Bob Seger's "Ramblin' Gamblin' Man"; Bernie Leadon had been in country-rock pioneers Hearts & Flowers, Dillard & Clark, and the FLYING BURRITO BROTHERS; Don Henley had been in Shiloh; and Randy Meisner had been in POCO and RICK NELSON's Stone Canyon Band and the aptly named L.A. combo the Poor.

The Eagles became one of the most popular rock acts of all time and the most successful country-rock act ever. They enjoyed many hit singles, and each of their albums has gone platinum. Their self-titled first album from June 1972 was launched with three Top Forty pop singles: "Take It Easy," "Witchy Woman," and "Peaceful Easy Feelin'." These three smoothly harmonized singles defined the band's style for some time. Their second album, *Desperado*, was a thematically linked story of the demise of the Old West, and while it has stood the test of time better than other Eagle releases, it sold less well than the debut. Director Sam Peckinpah had plans to turn the album into a film, but no footage was ever shot.

Producer Bill Szymczyk was brought in for their third album, *On the Border*, as was slide guitarist Don Felder, to give the group more of a rock sound. They then enjoyed their first #1 with the acoustic ballad "The Best of My Love." The same team made *One of These Nights* in 1975, a #1 pop album for five weeks. The new rocking direction proved too much for bluegrass fan Bernie Leadon, however, and he left at the end of that year, replaced by hard-rock lead guitarist Joe Walsh.

Now a more r&b–influenced act, the Eagles hit their commercial stride with 1977's *Hotel California* album. Singles "New Kid in Town" and the title track both reached #1 on the pop charts. Randy Meisner left in late 1977, replaced by Poco's Timothy B. Schmit, Schmit having previously replaced Meisner in Poco.

The Eagles' final studio album was *The Long Run* (1979), which reached #1 and remained there for nine weeks. *Eagles Live* followed in 1980, and the band dissolved, having been inactive in 1980. Henley and Frey, in particular, enjoyed strong solo success.

In 1993 a country tribute album to the Eagles, *Common*

The Eagles

Thread: The Songs of the Eagles, became a smash success, underscoring the strong influence of the band on 1990s country. The Eagles reunited for a hugely profitable tour in 1994, something they had long said they would never do, and released a reunion album of live tracks and studio material, *Hell Freezes Over.* —*Sid Griffin*

REPRESENTATIVE RECORDINGS

The Eagles (Asylum, 1972); *Desperado* (Asylum, 1973); *On the Border* (Asylum, 1974); *One of These Nights* (Asylum, 1975); *Hotel California* (Asylum, 1977)

Jim Eanes

b. Mountain Valley, Virginia, December 6, 1923; d. November 21, 1995

Although he frequently recorded in a modern country setting, Homer Robert Eanes Jr. (a.k.a. Jim Eanes) is better known as one of bluegrass music's great baritone leads.

After a prewar apprenticeship with Roy Hall and His Blue Ridge Entertainers, Eanes worked with the Blue Mountain Boys, Lester Flatt & Earl Scruggs, and Bill Monroe before launching a solo career in 1949. Settling in Martinsville, Virginia, in February 1951, Eanes organized the Shenandoah Valley Boys for appearances on the WWVA Jamboree. Regional bluegrass hits on Rich-R-Tone and Blue Ridge records led to a Decca contract in January 1952. Decca issued fourteen singles during the next four years; many were country sides using Nashville session musicians, but several were bluegrass and featured Hubert Davis on banjo, such as "Plunkin' Rag," "Possum Hollow," and "Ridin' the Waves."

Disbanding his group in 1955, Eanes became a disc jockey on WHEE, Martinsville, Virginia; he remained with the station for eleven years. When Starday Records offered him a contract in 1956, Eanes assembled a new Shenandoah Valley Boys with banjo player Allen Shelton, fiddler Roy Russell, and bassist Arnold Terry. Considered one of bluegrass music's classic bands, this group continued into 1964 with minor personnel changes.

In 1967 Eanes briefly fronted the Shenandoah Cut-Ups on the WWVA *Jamboree.* He continued recording bluegrass and country music for various labels into the early 1990s.

His compositions include "Baby Blue Eyes," "Your Old Standby," "Wiggle Worm Wiggle," and "I Wouldn't Change You If I Could." —*Dave Samuelson*

Steve Earle

b. Fort Monroe, Virginia, January 17, 1955

Steve Earle became an international star in the mid-1980s with a smart, gritty, new traditionalist brand of country-rock that crossed over to pop radio and gave Nashville's hipper artists hope that their least formulaic urges might be satisfied. With sharply observed songs such as "Guitar Town," "Someday," and "Good Ol' Boy (Gettin' Tough)," he raised the artistic stakes in Nashville. But Earle foundered into the gray area between pop and country and then into a gray period in his personal life. He went to prison on a drug charge, only to reemerge in 1995 clean, sober, and artistically reborn.

Stephen F. Earle was born with a cup of Texas dirt under the delivery room table. Raised outside San Antonio, he dropped out of high school in 1973, and with guitar in

Steve Earle

hand he began working the coffeehouse circuit, emulating idols Townes Van Zandt and Guy Clark.

He arrived in Nashville in the mid-1970s and within a few years was earning a living as a briefcase songwriter, churning out songs for other artists. He put out some rockabilly-tinged singles on an independent label and then signed with Epic, which released several singles but declined to release an album at the time. Dropped by Epic, Earle soon signed with MCA and in 1986 became a critical darling and cultural phenomenon with *Guitar Town,* routinely chosen by critics as one of the ten best albums of the 1980s.

But after a second less successful album, 1987's *Exit O,* Earle veered toward rock with *Copperhead Road* in 1989. He became an MCA pop artist, handled from the label's L.A. office, and disappeared from country radio. On his next two albums, *The Hard Way* and the live *Shut Up and Die Like an Aviator,* Earle completed his transition to a loud, metallic brand of arena rock. MCA dropped him in 1991, releasing a greatest-hits album called *The Essential Steve Earle* that ignored his last two albums.

Earle's always turbulent personal life caught up with him after his label deal ended. After numerous arrests in Nashville for cocaine and heroin possession, he was finally incarcerated in the fall of 1994. And after a short stay behind bars, he transferred to a drug rehabilitation center. Meanwhile, Music Row, which had been turned off by Earle's irascible personality and hard-to-categorize music, rediscovered one of its most original artists. His publishing company Warner/Chappell Music issued an industry-only disc called *Uncut Gems,* in hopes that country stars might cover some of the tunes that Earle had penned during his briefcase days.

Post-rehab, Earle launched a comeback. He recorded an album for the independent label Winter Harvest. The folksy *Train A Comin'* finds Earle returning to his troubadour roots, finally recording songs he wrote back in the 1970s as well as dark, ominous songs he wrote while strung out and trying to get a new record deal in Nashville. By

1998 he had formed his own label, released two rock records, *I Feel Alright* and *El Corazon,* and contributed a song to the soundtrack of the film *Dead Man Walking.* Drug-free, heavier, older, and busy cutting his own songs and producing other acts, Earle really does seem, for now, to feel all right.

—*Mark Schone*

REPRESENTATIVE RECORDINGS

Guitar Town (MCA, 1986); *The Essential Steve Earle* (MCA, 1991); *Train A Comin'* (Winter Harvest, 1995); *I Feel Alright* (E-Squared, 1996); *El Corazon* (E-Squared, 1997)

East Texas Serenaders

This influential stringband comprised a variety of musicians who came from the area around Mineola, Lindale, and Garden Valley, Texas. Its core cadre of performers included the left-handed fiddler Daniel Huggins Williams (b. September 13, 1900; d. June 1974), guitarist Cloet Hammons (b. May 4, 1899; d. July 1982), cello player Henry Bogan, and banjoist D. P. Munnerlyn. The group evolved from an earlier fiddle band headed by Will Hammons (Cloet's father), which played at house parties and other social functions after 1910. The Serenaders, who actually did go from house to house giving unexpected performances at night, stayed close to home and never played any farther than Dallas, about a hundred miles away. In fact, their only regular gig, at the Ashby Cafe in Tyler, lasted only a few months.

Although they made a number of prized recordings, from 1927 to 1930 and in 1937, they never gave up their day jobs, and instead lived out their lives as farmers and craftsmen. Nevertheless, their influence has extended far beyond East Texas and beyond their own time because of their superb recordings for BRUNSWICK (1928) and DECCA (1934). Williams was a much-admired fiddler whose influence extended to musicians such as Buddy Brady, Red Hayes, and JOHNNY GIMBLE, who learned technique and tunes from him. Because of their wide-ranging repertoire, which included ragtime, blues, waltzes, and breakdowns, they pointed the way toward western swing.

—*Bill C. Malone*

Ray Edenton
b. Mineral, Virginia, November 3, 1926

Ray Quarles Edenton was one of those Nashville studio musicians whose rhythm section work seldom stood out on records but whose subtle skills made him an essential contributor to scores of hit records, from the 1950s through the 1970s—his most active years. As a boy he began playing around his home area, both before World War II and after returning in 1946 from his service in the army. Edenton then worked with JOE MAPHIS as bassist in Maphis's Korn Krackers at the WRVA OLD DOMINION BARN DANCE in Richmond. In 1949 Edenton began working at WNOX in Knoxville.

After a two-year convalescence from tuberculosis, Edenton moved to Nashville in 1952 and started playing acoustic rhythm guitar on the GRAND OLE OPRY. His first session work came in 1953. Since few Nashville artists were using drums on records, Edenton's acoustic rhythm style, emulating a snare drum, impressed many producers. One of the first hits on which he played was the KITTY WELLS–RED FOLEY hit duet "One By One." Though he

rarely soloed, Edenton did play the memorable electric guitar lead on MARTY ROBBINS's 1956 hit "Singin' the Blues."

The arrival of rock & roll briefly reduced Edenton's recording work for a time. However, he became an integral part of the EVERLY BROTHERS' recorded sound along with CHET ATKINS and HANK GARLAND. Along with Don Everly, Edenton played the hard-strummed acoustic rhythm guitar on hits such as "Wake Up Little Susie" and "Bye Bye Love." His work on the Everly records enhanced his session work, and after Garland's disabling 1961 accident, Edenton became part of the triumvirate of Nashville guitar session players who worked countless sessions together. Garland had specialized in jazz leads, a role that HAROLD BRADLEY resumed after Garland's accident. GRADY MARTIN played funkier solos, and Edenton moved into Bradley's former spot handling rhythm guitar chores. Edenton's rhythm playing, subtle though it was, graced dozens of hits. He continued to be active into the 1980s.

—*Rich Kienzle*

REPRESENTATIVE RECORDING

Ray Edenton Plays Uptown Country (Columbia, 1962)

Edison Records
established in West Orange, New Jersey, April 24, 1878; ended November 1, 1929

Although initially established as the Edison Speaking Phonograph Company in 1878, the Edison company began in earnest in 1888, when inventor Thomas Alva Edison belatedly began to exploit his 1877 creation in partnership with businessman Jesse Lippincott and his North American Phonograph Company.

The earliest phonographs, aimed at the business community, could both record and reproduce sound. In 1889 and 1890, German manufacturers made tiny machines for talking dolls; U.S. companies built larger phonographs for amusement arcades and public exhibitions. The 1890s saw a slowly developing market for home phonograph entertainment, which ultimately proved to be the primary direction the industry would take.

Edison preferred the cylinder medium, even as disc records became dominant after 1900. He continued to manufacture cylinders until leaving the business in 1929, two years before his death. He did make disc records and phonographs in 1912 and thereafter, but they were of an unconventional design that was incompatible with competing media.

Edison made some country records in the 1920s. He encountered some fiddlers (Allen Sisson, Jasper Bisbee, and John Baltzell) through his friendship with Henry Ford, who sponsored a number of fiddle contests. VERNON DALHART's influential "Wreck of the Old 97" was first recorded for Edison, though it was his re-recording for Victor that became a best-seller. ERNEST STONEMAN and fellow Galax musicians recorded frequently for Edison between 1926 and 1928.

—*Dick Spottswood*

Don Edwards
b. Boonton, New Jersey, March 20, 1939

Singer-songwriter Don Edwards, whose voice is often compared to that of MARTY ROBBINS, is one of the most popular contemporary performers of COWBOY and WESTERN SWING music. As a boy growing up in New Jersey, he was attracted by the cowboy mystique, and in 1958 he moved to Texas, where he worked as a cowboy singer at Six Flags Over Texas from 1960 to 1964, and made his first recording, a 45-rpm single, "The Young Ranger." He became a well-known performer in the Houston area, eventually releasing several albums on his own SevenShoux label, one of which, *Chant of the Wanderer*, won a Western Heritage Wrangler Award from the Cowboy Hall of Fame in 1991. A talented songwriter, Edwards has also penned a number of fine western songs, including "The Chant of the Night Songs" (1986) and "Horses" (1986).

Edwards was one of the first artists signed to the Warner Western label, which has released three of his albums through 1997. He has appeared on television shows, such as *Austin City Limits* and *Nashville Now*, and has become a mainstay of the cowboy poetry and music scene, appearing at gatherings and festivals throughout the West.

—*Charlie Seemann*

REPRESENTATIVE RECORDINGS

Songs of the Trail (Warner Western, 1992); *Goin' Back to Texas* (Warner Western, 1993); *West of Yesterday* (Warner Western, 1996)

John Edwards
b. Sydney, Australia, July 22, 1932; d. December 24, 1960

Although he never set foot outside Australia, John Kenneth Fielder Edwards assembled one of the world's finest collections of early country and folk music. In so doing, he contributed significantly to the preservation and presentation of American vernacular music, particularly to that branch he designated as "Golden Age hillbilly recordings."

Raised in an educated professional family, Edwards moved against the grain of musical taste expected in Australian formal society. At age thirteen he heard CARTER FAMILY songs on a New South Wales radio station. A year later he began playing the guitar as well as seeking old-time songs and stringband instrumentals from the American South, then available on the Australian Regal Zonophone label. In 1948 Edwards started work in Sydney's Transport Department as a tram roster officer. Unmarried, he amassed an enormous 78-rpm disc library, initially by purchase in Australia and later by indefatigable correspondence with collectors and performers in the United States. Enthralled by Appalachian song lore rooted 10,000 miles from his home, he transcended global barriers by writing regularly for discographical journals in New Zealand, England, and America. Essentially he took country music seriously, although he found it difficult to accept Nashville's growth from bedrock tradition to pop-media success. Listening to his beloved music, Edwards sensed its links to other facets of expressive culture: JIMMIE RODGERS to Geoffrey Chaucer, BUELL KAZEE to John Donne, DORSEY DIXON to Herman Melville.

In a note written in late 1958, Edwards left instructions that in the event of his death his collection of more than 2,000 discs, reel-to-reel tapes, song folios, photographs, and letters was to be sent to his American friend Eugene Earle "to be used for the furtherance of serious study, recognition, appreciation, and preservation of genuine country and hillbilly music." After Edwards's death in an auto accident, Eugene Earle, Ed Kahn, Archie Green, and friends formed the John Edwards Memorial Foundation (now Forum) to preserve his vast collection of recordings and related materials. Since 1986 those materials have been housed within the Southern Folklife Collection of the University of North Carolina at Chapel Hill.

—*Archie Green*

Stoney Edwards
b. near Seminole, Oklahoma, December 24, 1929; d. April 5, 1997

During the 1970s, Frenchy "Stoney" Edwards was second only to CHARLEY PRIDE in commercial prominence as an African-American star in country music. Born into a large, dysfunctional family in rural Depression-era Oklahoma, Edwards was forced into the role of caretaker for three younger siblings after his parents abandoned their children; he never attended school and never learned to read or write. Because of his mixed-race background (African-American, Irish, and Native American), Edwards experienced constant discrimination. Yet he found he could gain a measure of social acceptance by performing country music. His first exposure to country music involved witnessing his bootlegger uncles' stringband music; on radio he listened to BOB WILLS out of Tulsa ("every day at twelve o'-clock") and the GRAND OLE OPRY from Nashville. Edwards not only began to perform country music for those who would listen but also began to compose his own country songs.

In the early 1950s Edwards moved to Richmond, California, where he married and began a long stint as a manual laborer, performing music only occasionally. In the late 1960s, unable to continue as a laborer because of a near-fatal work-related accident, Edwards turned to music. He composed new songs and began to perform again. In 1970, while appearing at a benefit concert for Bob Wills, who had suffered a recent stroke, Edwards was discovered by a local lawyer, who encouraged Edwards to make a demo. CAPITOL RECORDS, recognizing his singing and song-

Stoney Edwards

writing talents and no doubt noting Charley Pride's emergence as a country music star, signed Edwards to a recording contract. Five albums and a dozen chart singles for Capitol ensued, including "She's My Rock" (1972), later a #1 hit for GEORGE JONES, and "Hank and Lefty Raised My Country Soul" (1973), a tribute to country greats HANK WILLIAMS and LEFTY FRIZZELL. After his run with Capitol ended in 1977, Edwards went on to record for JMI, Music America, and Boot.

—*Ted Olson*

REPRESENTATIVE RECORDINGS

From Where I Stand: The Black Experience in Country Music (Warner Bros., 1998; various-artists 3 CD boxed set); *The Best of Stoney Edwards: Poor Folks Stick Together* (Razor & Tie, 1998)

Elektra Records
established in New York, New York, 1950

An eclectic folk and rock label founded by Jac Holzman in 1950, Elektra opened a Nashville office in 1973. The company's success with Judy Collins, Love, the Doors, Bread, and Carly Simon's debut album in the pop market helped fund the Music City office; after several years of instability at the top, JIMMY BOWEN took charge of the Nashville office late in 1978.

At that point the label had already established a track record in country. In 1976 EDDIE RABBITT launched his string of eighteen Top Tens, including three pop smashes, the biggest being 1981's "I Love a Rainy Night." In 1982 HANK WILLIAMS JR. made his big breakthrough with "Family Tradition," produced by Bowen. MEL TILLIS, signed in 1979, contributed ten Top Tens, most notably "Southern Rains." CONWAY TWITTY came aboard in 1982, racking up three #1s, the biggest being "Slow Hand," a cover of the Pointer Sisters' pop hit. Those four artists contributed 72 percent of Elektra's country Top Tens and all but two of the label's twenty-one #1 country hits.

VERN GOSDIN made a comeback at Elektra between 1976 and 1979, presaging later success on COLUMBIA, while JERRY LEE LEWIS delivered his last major hits, highlighted by 1981's "Thirty Nine and Holding." Elektra also issued MELBA MONTGOMERY's classic #1 hit "No Charge," Rabbitt and CRYSTAL GAYLE's pop crossover duet hit "You and I," and enjoyed moderate success with EDDY RAVEN, TOMPALL & THE GLASER BROTHERS, the WHITES, and Stella Parton.

Elektra was folded into WARNER BROS. Nashville operation in 1983, with Bowen taking over; many acts were dropped, although not Hank Williams Jr. or Conway Twitty.

—*John Lomax III*

Joe Ely
b. Amarillo, Texas, February 9, 1947

Earle R. "Joe" Ely is the uncrowned king of Texas roadhouse rock & roll. He might not be a household name nationally, but he's known as the Lord of the Highway in his home state. Ely's career is proof that it's possible to maintain a regional musical identity despite the homogenization of the mass media. "In the last ten or fifteen years, there's been a lot of focus on Texas music, all the way from the Outlaw country music to the blues stuff," Ely said in 1993. "It's a lot more diverse than it used to be. But there's still a thing among Texas players that I find unique. I think that mystique will always be there."

Joe Ely

Ely says he knew what he wanted to do with his life since age seven, when he saw JERRY LEE LEWIS playing on the back of a flatbed truck in Amarillo. At age twelve Ely's family moved to Lubbock. He hit the road before he finished high school, though, jumping trains and retracing the routes of his literary and musical heroes, Jack Kerouac and WOODY GUTHRIE. After finding himself stranded in New York and touring Europe with a rock & roll theatrical production, he came back to Lubbock in the early 1970s and ended up living with two old friends. He joined these fellow singer-songwriters, JIMMIE DALE GILMORE and BUTCH HANCOCK, to form the FLATLANDERS, a country-folk group that has been described as fifty years behind or fifteen years ahead of its time. After gaining local recognition, the Flatlanders recorded one album for SHELBY SINGLETON's Plantation label in Nashville during 1972. (The album was later released on Rounder Records in 1990.) The band dissolved, though, and Ely spent some time wandering, at one time entertaining standers-by in the subways of New York City.

Ely returned to Lubbock in 1974 and formed his own band combining the talents of lead guitarist Jesse Taylor, a blues fanatic and at one time an occasional Flatlander, along with pedal steel guitarist Lloyd Maines, who was a country traditionalist. The band, signed by MCA Nashville, brought a distinctively Texas approach to country-rock and opened tours for everyone from MERLE HAGGARD to the Clash. Their 1977 LP, *Joe Ely*, was a critical success. Ely's 1978 album *Honky Tonk Masquerade*, which featured songs by Hancock and Gilmore as well as Ely's originals, was listed by *Rolling Stone* magazine among the best albums of the 1970s.

Ely was dropped by MCA Records in 1984 after the critical and commercial failure of *Hi-Res,* an ill-advised venture into techno-pop. But the legend continued to grow, especially after Ely added Austin guitar-slinger David Grissom to his band. Ely continued to record between 1984 and 1990, including one album, *Lord of the Highway* (High-Tone, 1987), which featured "Me and Billy the Kid." By the late 1980s, the charismatic front man led one of the tightest, most exciting rock & roll bands in the nation.

In 1990 he re-signed with MCA Nashville. MCA vice president TONY BROWN said he signed him so Ely could make "real" rock & roll recordings without the pressure to cut a pop hit. *Love and Danger* featured two instant classics by fellow Texan ROBERT EARL KEEN: "Whenever Kindness Fails" and "The Road Goes On Forever." *Letter to Laredo* in 1995 was an ambitious acoustic affair in which flamenco guitar meets dobro and accordion to create unique gypsy-cowboy border music. The album was widely hailed as a career statement, although it produced no hits and failed to introduce Ely to mainstream country or rock radio audiences. —*Rick Mitchell*

REPRESENTATIVE RECORDINGS

Honky Tonk Masquerade (MCA, 1978); *Love and Danger* (MCA, 1992); *Letter to Laredo* (MCA, 1995)

Ralph Emery
b. McEwen, Tennessee, March 10, 1933

The most famous TV and radio personality in country music, Walter Ralph Emery was for years a fixture on Nashville's WSM radio and television stations. From 1972 to 1991 he hosted the live, early-morning weekday *Ralph Emery Show,* broadcast over WSM-TV to Nashville-area audiences. For a decade (from 1983 until 1993) he also hosted the popular TNN prime-time talk show *NASHVILLE NOW.* Through the years he has also done other stints as a TV host—for *Pop Goes the Country* (1974–80) and a brief early 1980s run with *Nashville Alive,* which aired on WTBS, the cable TV superstation. Emery also worked for while as an announcer on the GRAND OLE OPRY.

Once dubbed "the Johnny Carson of Cable" by *Cable* magazine, Emery displayed a low-key informality that his audience and guests warmed to. Also, as a longtime member of Nashville's country music community and a personal friend of many of the stars, he was a comfortable and reassuring presence for country fans in the heartland.

For all his poise and confidence, Emery had a troubled early life. After his parents divorced, he worked at various odd jobs and briefly attended Belmont College in Nashville before landing a string of small-town broadcasting jobs, including WAGG in Paris, Tennessee. Emery worked at Nashville's radio WSIX before landing a graveyard slot—10 P.M. to 3 A.M., Monday through Thursday—on Music City's powerful WSM, the clear-channel flagship station of the Grand Ole Opry. Where other DJs dreaded the all-night shift, Emery, who began at WSM in 1957, at age twenty-four, turned it into an art form with his open-house policy. Recording artists—both stars and novices—would often drop by Emery's *Opry Star Spotlight* show in the middle of the night to shoot the breeze, drink coffee, and play their latest records, all in a relaxed, informal atmosphere.

Along the way, Emery has had a few brief forays of his own into recordmaking, though he has always been the first to admit his singing talents are limited. In the early

Ralph Emery

1960s he recorded "Hello Fool," a sequel of sorts to the FARON YOUNG hit "Hello Walls." Released by LIBERTY RECORDS in 1961, "Hello Fool" was a #4 country hit. In the 1960s Emery also appeared in several B-movies with country music themes, including *The Road to Nashville, Country Music on Broadway,* and *The Girl from Tobacco Road.* In 1991 Emery's autobiography (co-written with Tom Carter), *Memories,* surprised nearly everyone by making the national best-seller lists. Its runaway success prompted him to write a second memoir, *More Memories,* in 1993.

Though an admitted workaholic whose four marriages include a brief period with singer SKEETER DAVIS (1960–64), Emery has scaled back in recent years, limiting his workload to occasional radio appearances and producing and hosting occasional specials for TNN through his own production company. —*Bob Allen*

Emilio
b. San Antonio, Texas, August 23, 1963

The man who does "The Emilio Shuffle" was the standard-bearer for country's march into the Hispanic market in the 1990s. Emilio Navaira III grew up in San Antonio. He began playing guitar at age five, practicing on the songs of WILLIE NELSON.

He majored in music in college, but quit to become the lead singer for bandleader David Lee Garza in 1983. He formed his own Grupo Rio in 1989. Seven top-selling Spanish-language albums made him a major Hispanic star. Billed under his full name, he performed both Tejano and country material. (Tejano is a style of Spanish-language music that's laced with heartache ballads and lively dance tunes.) Emilio was chosen six times as Male Entertainer of the Year at the Tejano Music Awards, and he is a two-time Grammy nominee.

Having achieved stardom in Spanish, Emilio reached out to Anglo audiences. Billed under his first name only, he issued his debut country CD, *Life Is Good,* in 1995. The single "It's Not the End of the World" reached #27. The follow-up, "Even If I Tried," had a video that showcased the Emilio Shuffle. The dance was invented by his 280-pound younger brother, Raul; the two demonstrated it onstage and in the clip. Raul is Emilio's harmony singer, comedic foil, and the major writer of his Tejano hits.

CMT promoted Emilio's videos heavily as part of its expansion into Latin America.　　　—*Robert K. Oermann*

REPRESENTATIVE RECORDING

Life Is Good (Capitol, 1995)

Buddy Emmons
b. Mishawaka, Indiana, January 27, 1937

Ever since LITTLE JIMMY DICKENS brought him to Nashville in 1955, Buddy Gene Emmons has proven to be among the most in-demand and influential steel guitarists in the history of country music. He has played on countless records and has worked in the road bands of such acclaimed acts as Dickens; ERNEST TUBB; RAY PRICE; ROGER MILLER; and, most recently, the EVERLY BROTHERS. A musical pioneer, he was one of the first session men to play pedal steel guitar, and he was also one of the first to design his own signature model, the popular Emmons Guitar.

Raised in South Bend, Indiana, Emmons was introduced to the steel guitar when he and his father listened to the GRAND OLE OPRY one night. HANK WILLIAMS was on the program, so the first steel guitar Emmons heard was that of Williams's sideman Don Helms. Emmons's parents bought him a steel not long thereafter, and by the time he was fourteen he was getting work locally. At sixteen he headed to Calumet City, Illinois, where he worked honky-tonks and strip joints. He moved to Kennett, Missouri, and was heard there by CARL SMITH, who recommended him to WEBB PIERCE. When a job with Pierce didn't materialize, Emmons moved to Detroit. There he sat in with Little Jimmy Dickens for a night, and when Dickens offered him a job, Emmons moved to Nashville.

As a session player Emmons contributed significantly to such landmark records as FARON YOUNG's "Sweet Dreams" and Ray Price's "Night Life." Emmon's long-standing love of jazz led to his fine *Steel Guitar Jazz* album, which he recorded in New York in 1963 with a group of respected jazz players. All the while Emmons was experimenting with pedal steel design, having collaborated with SHOT JACKSON in a venture called Sho-Bud Guitars that was initially run out of Jackson's garage, and that preceded Emmons's marketing of his own namesake model.

A tireless talent, Emmons was still recording and still working the road with the Everlys as of 1998.

　　　—*Daniel Cooper*

REPRESENTATIVE RECORDINGS

Steel Guitar Jazz (Mercury, 1963); *Amazing Steel Guitar: The Buddy Emmons Collection* (Razor & Tie, 1997); Buddy Emmons, Ray Pennington, and the Swing Shift Band *Swing and Other Things* (Step One, 1988)

Melvin Endsley
b. Drasco, Arkansas, January 30, 1934

Melvin Endsley was one of the most commercially astute songwriters of the 1950s for the way he blended country and pop themes with simple, catchy melodies. His biggest hit was "Singing the Blues," although he wrote several other hits and was a recording artist, albeit an unsuccessful one, for twenty years.

Endsley contracted polio when he was three, which left him with a withered right arm and confined to a wheelchair for life. He became interested in music in the Memphis Crippled Childrens' Hospital (inspired by local broadcasts by WAYNE RANEY and the DELMORE BROTHERS), and began writing songs after he returned to Arkansas. He wrote "Singing the Blues" in 1954, and in July 1955 he took it to Nashville. Backstage at the Opry, he pitched the song to MARTY ROBBINS. After its success the following year, Endsley became a greatly in-demand songwriter. "Love Me to Pieces" was recorded by Jill Corey and JANIS MARTIN; Robbins and Guy Mitchell had hits with "Knee Deep in the Blues"; Andy Williams covered "I Like Your Kind of Love," and the BROWNS covered "I'd Just Be Fool Enough," the latter two first recorded by Endsley himself for RCA during his two-year stint (1957–58) with the label.

Endsley also recorded for MGM (1959), HICKORY (1960–61), and intermittently for his own Mel-Ark label. His last major hit was STONEWALL JACKSON's "Why I'm Walkin'" (1960).　　　—*Colin Escott*

REPRESENTATIVE RECORDINGS

I Like Your Kind of Love (Bear Family, 1992); *Getting Used to the Blues* (Melark, ca. 1993)

Epic Records
established in New York, New York, 1954; Nashville office established in 1963

Formed in 1954 as a COLUMBIA subsidiary, Epic Records established a Nashville beachhead in 1963. Always a "weak sister" to Columbia, the label has never had a distinct identity on Music Row. And although executives such as BILLY SHERRILL, George Richey, and BOB MONTGOMERY have been associated with Epic, it never had a truly independent staff. Nevertheless, Epic has made important contributions to Nashville and country music generally.

The earliest Epic country act of note was DAVID HOUSTON (1963–76), who achieved virtually all his success with the company. JIM & JESSE (1964–70) recorded some of their finest bluegrass work for the label. CHARLIE WALKER scored several notable hits during his tenure (1964–71), but Epic didn't hit its stride until the late 1960s, when CHARLIE RICH (1968–61), Tommy Cash (1969–73), and TAMMY WYNETTE (1966–93) joined Houston and Walker in giving the label a consistent chart presence.

Epic's strong sellers of the 1970s were GEORGE JONES (1971–90), JOHNNY PAYCHECK (1970–83), JODY MILLER (1970–1979), BOB LUMAN (1970–77), and JOE STAMPLEY (1975–86). The label also tried to engineer country-crossover hits for pop acts Bobby Vinton, Tom Jones, and Engelbert Humperdinck.

During the late 1970s and 1980s, Epic's stars were MICKEY GILLEY (1978–87), CHARLY McCLAIN (1976–88), RONNIE McDOWELL (1979–86), JOHNNY RODRIGUEZ (1978–86) and, especially, the million-selling CHARLIE

DANIELS BAND, an act signed out of New York, not Nashville.

Other Epic hitmakers of the 1980s were MERLE HAGGARD (1981–90), EXILE (1983–89), and RICKY SKAGGS (1981–92). But the company missed as often as it hit, failing commercially with STEVE EARLE (1983–85), Pam Rose (1980), Russell Smith (1989), ASLEEP AT THE WHEEL (1987–88), LINDA DAVIS (1988–89), JIM LAUDERDALE (1988), and SHELBY LYNNE (1988–1992). Honky-tonk master GENE WATSON (1985–87) fared only moderately well. Veterans BILLY SWAN (1981–83), WAYLON JENNINGS (1990–91), and CONNIE SMITH (1985) stayed only briefly.

In the 1990s Epic found star power with acts such as PATTY LOVELESS, JOE DIFFIE, DOUG STONE, and COLLIN RAYE.

—*Robert K. Oermann*

Esmereldy
b. Middleton, Tennessee, June 1, 1920

Known as "The Streamlined Hillbilly," blond Esmereldy became a country headliner of the 1940s as a radio, disc, and film personality.

Born Verna Sherrill, she was raised in Memphis, where she began her radio career at age eight on WMC. She moved to New York, married pop singer Harry Boersma, and sang with Zeke Manners, Elton Britt, and Jones & Hare (the Happiness Boys). In 1941 and 1944 Esmereldy became one of the earliest country acts to make "soundies," film shorts that were the precursors of music videos.

She was instrumental in popularizing country in New York, becoming a pioneering female country disc jockey when she hosted her own show on WNBC during World War II. She was also a regular on NBC's *Mirth & Madness* program and an early country act on New York TV.

Esmereldy's first records appeared in the Musicraft label's "Authentic Hillbilly Ballads" series in 1947. She scored a Top Ten hit with 1948's comedic "Slap 'Er Down Agin', Paw," billed as "Esmereldy and Her Novelty Band." She also recorded for MGM.

In the 1950s she returned to Memphis to appear on WHBQ's daily *Tennessee Jamboree* (carried on the Mutual Network) and her own DJ show.

Daughter Amy Holland became a pop recording artist in the 1980s. —*Robert K. Oermann*

Milton Estes
b. Arthur, Tennessee, May 9, 1914; d. August 23, 1963

Milton Esco Estes came to the GRAND OLE OPRY in 1937 as a featured performer with PEE WEE KING's Golden West Cowboys. An accomplished musician (guitar, bass, mandolin, piano) and superb master of ceremonies, he left King in 1941 to lead STAMPS-BAXTER's Lone Star Quartet at radio stations throughout the South. By 1946 Estes had returned to WSM and the Opry as the Old Flour Peddler and formed a band called the Musical Millers to promote MARTHA WHITE FLOUR. Band members included front man Jimmy Selph and sidemen Oral "Curly" Rhodes, TOMMY JACKSON, Clell "Cousin Jody" Summey, and DALE POTTER. Estes also did ten live WSM radio shows weekly, including the weekday *Noontime Neighbors* with OWEN BRADLEY's orchestra. Estes also appeared on the Opry's NBC radio segment and became a familiar voice, calling square dances on the Opry.

Some of the recordings Estes made for DECCA between 1947 and 1950 were "Whoa Sailor"/"Too Many Women," "New Filipino Baby"/"Answer to Drivin' Nails in My Coffin," and "House of Gold"/"Thirty Pieces of Silver."

Estes left country music in 1951, but the Martha White jingle "How Many Biscuits Can You Eat This Mornin'" and the company slogan "Goodness, Gracious, It's Good," begun by Estes and still used today, may be his most memorable contributions to the music's history.

—*Dennis M. Estes and Micki Estes*

Dale Evans
b. Uvalde, Texas, October 31, 1912

The most popular woman to ever appear in western films was Dale Evans. She also wrote her husband ROY ROGERS's theme song "Happy Trails," a song that has become an icon of American culture. Still proud of being known as the Queen of the West, the singer, actress, songwriter, and author was one of the first women to bring national attention to western music.

Texas-born Frances Octavia Smith (Dale's given name) grew up in Osceola, Arkansas. While Evans was in high school her family moved to Memphis, Tennessee, where she worked as a secretary. One day her boss overheard her singing at her desk and arranged for her to appear on a radio program the company sponsored. Before long she was employed full time as a vocalist on radio in Memphis. A few years later, station WHAS in Louisville, Kentucky, hired her and changed her name to Dale Evans.

In 1938 she moved to Chicago and soon became the vocalist with Anson Weeks's orchestra. After touring with his band for a year, Evans returned to Chicago, where she sang on WBBM, the CBS radio affiliate, for three years. At this point in her career she wasn't singing western songs. In-

Dale Evans

stead, she was singing pop music and jazz on radio and in some of the finer supper clubs in Chicago.

An offer of a Hollywood screen test resulted in a short contract with Twentieth Century-Fox. After leaving Fox, Dale became the vocalist on radio's top-rated Edgar Bergen and Charlie McCarthy program during the 1942 season. Republic Pictures began starring her in musicals before casting her as Roy Rogers's leading lady in his 1944 film *The Cowboy and the Señorita.*

The unique chemistry between the two led to Evans's being featured in Rogers's next nineteen films. In December 1947, a little more than a year after the death of his first wife, Rogers and Evans were married. Starting with Evans's son from a teenage marriage and Rogers's three children from his first marriage, the couple began building a large family. Their daughter Robin suffered from Down's syndrome and died just before her second birthday. Evans expressed the impact Robin's life had on her family in her best-selling book, *Angel Unaware.* She has since written more than twenty books about her religious faith. Following Robin's death, Rogers and Evans added to their family by adopting four children from a variety of backgrounds; they became the parents of nine children.

Moving from films to television, the couple starred in *The Roy Rogers Show* on NBC for seven years. The series became a Sunday night family viewing tradition. Each episode ended with Rogers and Evans singing "Happy Trails," which Evans had written especially for Rogers. Among the other songs Evans has written are "Aha San Antone" and "The Bible Tells Me So."

—*Laurence Zwisohn*

REPRESENTATIVE RECORDINGS

Sweet Hour of Prayer (RCA Victor, 1957); *How Great Thou Art* (Capitol, 1961); *Get to Know the Lord* (Capitol, 1969); *Country Dale* (Word, 1976)

The Everly Brothers
Isaac Donald Everly b. Brownie, Kentucky, February 1, 1937
Philip Everly b. Chicago, Illinois, January 19, 1939

In purely commercial terms, the Everly Brothers were one of the most successful acts in popular music between 1957 and 1962. Only ELVIS PRESLEY, Pat Boone, and possibly RICK NELSON outsold them. In a sense, though, they were more important to Nashville. They were the first consistently successful rock & roll act to come from there. Their management and their songs came from Nashville, and they recorded there with local session men. In other words, they extended Nashville's sense of what was commercially possible.

In artistic terms, the Everlys took the country BROTHER DUET one step farther. They added Bo Diddley riffs, teenage anxieties, and sharkskin suits, but—for all that—the core of their sound remained country brother harmony. That link was underscored on their album *Songs Our Daddy Taught Us.*

The Everlys' father, Ike, was an accomplished finger-style guitarist, a contemporary of MERLE TRAVIS, who went to Chicago trying to sustain a career in country radio and ended up in the Midwest. He brought his family to Nashville in 1955, possibly hoping that his boys could find the success that had eluded him. Don found some success as a songwriter ("Thou Shalt Not Steal" for KITTY WELLS,

The Everly Brothers

two songs for JUSTIN TUBB, and another for ANITA CARTER), but a contract with COLUMBIA RECORDS' Nashville division in 1955 yielded just one undistinguished single.

By the time the brothers signed with Cadence Records in March 1957 (a deal midwifed by WESLEY ROSE of ACUFF-ROSE), they were singing teenage playlets crafted by BOUDLEAUX AND FELICE BRYANT overlaid with r&b rhythm patterns. The Everlys scored a string of hits, including "Bye, Bye Love," "Wake Up, Little Susie," "All I Have to Do Is Dream," "Bird Dog," and others. When they switched to WARNER BROS. RECORDS in 1960, they were, at first, even more successful. "Cathy's Clown," "Ebony Eyes," "Walk Right Back," and "So Sad" were among their hits. Their records were among the most immaculately crafted and innovative of the era, a testimony to the brothers' musical vision and to the skill of the Nashville session men who proved themselves adept at executing more than they were often given credit for.

The responsibility for the downward slide in their career is usually laid at the door of the Beatles, but the brothers' appeal was beginning to wane a year or more before the Beatles appeared. They broke with Wesley Rose in 1961, moved to California, and began making singles that were probably too experimental for the time. A slowdown in their touring schedule brought on by a joint enlistment in the marines, the loss of access to the Bryants' songs owing to the split with ACUFF-ROSE, and Don's subsequent overreliance upon prescription drugs probably figured in their decline, too.

In 1968 they issued *Roots,* a daring country-rock record that failed to find them a new market. In 1970 they switched to RCA, but they split angrily from each other in July 1973. Don returned to Nashville; Phil stayed in

Los Angeles. They reunited in September 1983 and still tour. —*Colin Escott*

REPRESENTATIVE RECORDINGS

Heartaches and Harmonies (Rhino, 1994), 4-CD set; *Cadence Classics* (Rhino, 1989); *Songs Our Daddy Taught Us* (Cadence, 1958; Rhino, 1989); *Walk Right Back* (Warner Bros., 1993); *Roots* (Warner Bros., 1968, 1996)

Skip Ewing

b. Redlands, California, March 6, 1964

Donald Ralph Ewing has earned a reputation as an in-demand songwriter while also issuing several albums as a singer. The son of a serviceman, Ewing relocated often in his formative years. He found the guitar to be a faithful companion and began writing tunes in his teens. He moved to Nashville after high school, landed a performing job at OPRYLAND USA, and signed with Nashville music publishing company ACUFF-ROSE. GEORGE JONES was the first artist to record a Skip Ewing song, titled "One Hell of a Song."

In 1988 Ewing emerged as a hit artist on the MCA label with the Top Ten hits "The Gospel According to Luke," "I Don't Have Far to Fall," and "Burnin' a Hole in My Heart," all from his debut release, *The Coast of Colorado*. When his recording career quieted in the 1990s, Ewing's prowess as a writer brought him continued recognition for such hits as "Love, Me" (COLLIN RAYE, 1992), "If I Didn't Have You" (RANDY TRAVIS, 1993), and "Little Houses" (DOUG STONE, 1995). BRYAN WHITE, in particular, has had success with Ewing's compositions, such as the #1 hits "Someone Else's Star," "Rebecca Lynn," and "I'm Not Supposed to Love You Anymore."

After ending his stint with MCA in 1990, Ewing recorded for CAPITOL/LIBERTY from 1991 to 1993. By 1997 he had signed with the GAYLORD ENTERTAINMENT, Christian music label Word Nashville. —*Michael Hight*

REPRESENTATIVE RECORDINGS

The Coast of Colorado (MCA, 1988); *The Will to Love* (MCA, 1989); *Until I Found You* (Word Nashville, 1997)

Exile

J. P. Pennington b. Berea, Kentucky, January 22, 1949
Steve Goetzman b. Louisville, Kentucky, September 1, 1950
Marlon Hargis b. Somerset, Kentucky, May 13, 1949
Les Taylor b. Oneida, Kentucky, December 27, 1948
Sonny LeMaire b. Fort Lee, Virginia, September 16, 1946
Paul Martin b. Winchester, Kentucky, December 22, 1962
Lee Carroll b. Glasgow, Kentucky, January 27, 1953
Mark Jones b. Harlan, Kentucky, July 18, 1954

After a 1978 worldwide pop hit "Kiss You All Over," the group Exile seemed to live up to its name, fading quickly into obscurity. They returned with a different sound, adapting rhythmic elements of pop and r&b into an engaging, hook-oriented style of country music. From 1983 to 1992 they had ten #1 country hits.

J. P. Pennington, son of Lily May Ledford of the original COON CREEK GIRLS, formed the Exiles in high school in Richmond, Kentucky, in 1963 (they became Exile in 1973). In 1967 they toured with Dick Clark's Caravan of Stars. In 1978, after several albums for independent labels, they released "Kiss You All Over" on the Warner/Curb label; it stayed at #1 on the pop charts for four weeks and sold more than 5 million copies worldwide. In 1980 MARK GRAY (keyboards) joined for a two-year stint.

Unable to follow up their hit, they quit touring, but the success of two Pennington-Gray tunes, "The Closer You Get" and "Take Me Down"—both hits for ALABAMA—inspired them to try country music. In 1983 their second single on Epic, "Woke Up in Love," became their first #1. The lineup during their 1980s run on the country charts comprised Pennington (lead vocals, lead guitar), Les Taylor (guitar, vocals), Sonny LeMaire (bass, vocals), Marlon Hargis (keyboards), and Steve Goetzman (drums). Lee Carroll replaced Hargis on keyboards in 1985. Paul Martin replaced Pennington on lead vocals, and Mark Jones joined the band on acoustic guitar and vocals in 1989.

By the end of the eighties, three members had departed, and the new lineup had to audition again for a record deal. They signed with ARISTA RECORDS and hit with "Keep It in the Middle of the Road" (#17, 1989), featuring Paul Martin on lead vocals. They eventually returned to #1 on the country charts with "Yet," featuring LeMaire on lead vocals. At the end of 1993, after thirty years and twenty-one group members, Exile disbanded. LeMaire, Goetzman, Martin, Jones, and Carroll reunited for a 1995 album, *Latest and Greatest*. After disbanding again, Exile regrouped once more in December 1995, with a new lineup led by J. P. Pennington and Les Taylor. —*Walter Carter*

REPRESENTATIVE RECORDING

Greatest Hits (Epic, 1986)

F·F·F·F ·F·F·F·F

Fabor Records

established in Malibu, California, October 1953; ended 1965

In August 1953, after Jim Reeves's success with "Mexican Joe" on ABBOTT RECORDS, FABOR ROBISON bought out all other interests in that label, and, in October, launched his eponymous Fabor Records from his house/studio complex in Malibu, California.

Fabor Records went through several quiescent periods when Robison was out of the music business. In 1957 he concluded a deal that gave DOT RECORDS first refusal on all Fabor masters. Dot acquired BONNIE GUITAR's "Dark Moon" and NED MILLER's "From a Jack to a King" in this way. In about 1959 Robison sold off his music publishing and some masters to Jamie/Guyden Records, and when "From a Jack to a King" was reissued successfully on Fabor in 1962, it was via Jamie. Robison exited the business completely in 1965 and sold all remaining masters to the SHELBY SINGLETON Corporation. —*Colin Escott*

Barbara Fairchild

b. Lafe, Arkansas, November 12, 1950

Barbara Fairchild, best known for her 1972 chart-topping hit "Teddy Bear Song," has achieved success as a songwriter and singer in the genres of country and gospel music.

Fairchild first took the stage at age five as a contestant in an Arkansas talent show. When she was thirteen her parents moved to St. Louis, where she appeared on local TV and radio. At age fifteen she made her first record, "A Brand New Bed of Roses," which received local airplay. She also honed her songwriting skills and made her first trip to Nashville when she was seventeen. She encountered producer-publisher JERRY CRUTCHFIELD in the DECCA RECORDS parking lot and convinced him to listen to her tape. Crutchfield saw potential in one of her songs and encouraged her to go back home and write seven more with that quality before returning. Fairchild returned with fifteen songs; Crutchfield became her producer and manager and signed her to MCA Music as a songwriter.

Two singles were released on Kapp Records but failed to chart. Crutchfield took the young singer to COLUMBIA RECORDS executive and producer BILLY SHERRILL, who signed her to a contract. She first charted in 1969 with "Love Is a Gentle Thing," but her career broke wide open three years later with the Grammy-nominated "Teddy Bear Song," which was followed by two more derivative Top Ten hits: "Kid Stuff" and "Baby Doll."

Besides co-writing several of her own hits (though not "Teddy Bear Song"), Fairchild wrote songs recorded by such acts as LORETTA LYNN and LIZ ANDERSON. She left Columbia in 1978, and in 1981, after two unsuccessful marriages, she married Milton Carroll, an evangelical singer and minister. In 1990 Fairchild joined and recorded with a gospel group, Heirloom, and two years later she opened her Barbara Fairchild Theater in BRANSON, MISSOURI. —*Gerry Wood*

REPRESENTATIVE RECORDINGS

A Sweeter Love (Columbia, 1972); *Standing in Your Line* (Columbia, 1974)

Joseph Falcon

b. Rayne, Louisiana, September 28, 1900; d. November 29, 1965

Accordion player Joseph Falcon and his wife, Cleoma Breaux, made the first commercial Cajun recordings in 1928, when they cut "Allons à Lafayette" and "The Waltz That Carried Me to My Grave" for COLUMBIA. The regional popularity of the recordings led record companies to pursue the recording of other Cajun musicians. Falcon began to learn the accordion at age seven, playing and singing traditional Cajun songs. Backed by Cleoma on guitar, he was in demand for local dances well before recording for Columbia. Joseph and Cleoma were often joined by Falcon's cousin Ulysses on fiddle. Cleoma, herself from a well-known musical family, recorded for Columbia with her brothers Amidie and Ophy Breaux in late 1928. After recording for Columbia, the Falcons recorded for DECCA and for BLUEBIRD.

Falcon's career suffered with the decline of the popularity of the accordion, and he refused to record again, although he continued to play for dances with his Silver Bell Band. In 1963 a live performance was privately recorded at the Triangle Dance Hall in Scott, Louisiana, for Arhoolie Records. He died two years later in Crowley, Louisiana. —*Charlie Seemann*

REPRESENTATIVE RECORDING

Joseph Falcon: Louisiana Cajun Music (Arhoolie, 1968)

Fan Fair
established in Nashville, Tennessee, April 1972

The International Country Music Fan Fair, held annually since 1972, is arguably the most renowned gathering of country music entertainers and fans worldwide. Co-sponsored by the CMA and the GRAND OLE OPRY, Fan Fair attracts more than 24,000 ardent country music fans each year.

The event was created to relieve some of the excessive congestion during the annual country music DJ CONVENTION in Nashville, which took place in October. Because of the large number of artists attending the convention, fans converged on Music City to catch a glimpse of their favorite stars. Spurred by then CMA board member and WSM president IRVING WAUGH, executives representing the CMA and the Opry concluded that if a festival was created especially for fans at a different time during the year, it would no doubt be well attended.

The first Fan Fair was held in April 1972 at Nashville's Municipal Auditorium and attracted 5,000 fans. Attendance doubled in 1973, when the event was moved to June, and continued to grow in subsequent years, creating the need for a larger venue. In 1982 Fan Fair moved to the Tennessee State Fairgrounds, where ticket sales are capped at approximately 24,000.

Fans line up for autographs at nearly two hundred exhibit booths, where they meet some of their favorite stars. In addition, live concerts are held on the Fan Fair stage each day of the five-day event. In 1995 twenty record labels sponsored talent on the grandstand stage. Fan Fair also includes the annual Grand Masters Fiddling Championship, held at OPRYLAND USA. —*Janet E. Williams*

Donna Fargo
b. Mount Airy, North Carolina, November 10, 1940

An important country-pop crossover artist in the early 1970s, Donna Fargo began her string of hits with her self-penned signature tune "Happiest Girl in the Whole U.S.A.," followed by "Funny Face" and "Superman." Raised on her father's rural North Carolina tobacco farm, Yvonne Vaughn was the youngest of four children. She attended High Point College in North Carolina, moving to Southern California upon graduation and teaching ninth- and twelfth-grade English in the Los Angeles suburb of Covina. She met local record producer Stan Silver (whom she married in 1969); he taught her to play guitar, and she began to write songs.

Through publisher Don Sessions and disc jockey BIFF COLLIE, she was introduced to Floyd Ramsey, owner of Phoenix-based Ramco Records, for whom she recorded her first single, "Would You Believe," using the stage name Donna Fargo. After a second Ramco single ("Who's Been Sleeping on My Side of the Bed?"), she moved to Los Angeles–based CHALLENGE RECORDS for "Daddy." The Silvers saved their money and financed the Nashville session (produced by Silver) that generated "Happiest Girl." Picked up by DOT RECORDS, it won a Grammy and became the CMA's Single of the Year. It was also the first of thirty-eight Fargo singles to hit *Billboard*'s country chart on the Dot, ABC/Dot, WARNER BROS., RCA, COLUMBIA, and Cleveland International labels between 1972 and 1991. Six of the singles landed at #1. (She also recorded, briefly, for MERCURY, with no chart success.)

Fargo composed and published most of her hit material, including all of the above-mentioned songs. The syndicated *Donna Fargo Show* television variety series aired during the 1978–79 season. Fargo was stricken with multiple sclerosis in 1979, and while the disease is currently in remission, it caused a serious setback in her performing and recording career. —*Todd Everett*

REPRESENTATIVE RECORDING
The Best of Donna Fargo (Varese Sarabande, 1995)

Charlie Feathers
b. Holly Springs, Mississippi, June 12, 1932

Charlie Feathers is an acknowledged pioneer of the SUN RECORDS Memphis rockabilly sound that was popularized by ELVIS PRESLEY in the mid-1950s. The extent and significance of Feather's contributions are a matter of some debate, though; Feathers sees himself as Presley's mentor and main vocal coach but is considered a more peripheral figure by his peers and most historians. It is a matter of fact that Feathers co-wrote (with Stan Kesler) the 1955 Presley hit "I Forgot to Remember to Forget," and had a hand in writing some 200 other songs, mainly in the rockabilly vein. Although commercial success eluded Feathers, he still performs, writes, and records rockabilly material with passion. His fierce dedication and eccentric vocal style have made him a cult hero among rockabilly fans and music journalists. He is also an accomplished country singer with an unvarnished rural style.

Feathers was raised as a sharecropper in rural northwestern Mississippi, where he was strongly influenced by both country music radio and the blues performers of the local black community. After several years on the road as an oil field laborer, Feathers settled in Memphis at age eighteen. He claims to have been a creative force at SAM PHILLIPS's Sun studio since the early 1950s, although this assertion is unsubstantiated. Phillips did record Feathers on his Flip label, however, releasing a country 45—"I've Been Deceived," backed with "Peepin' Eyes"—in 1955. After other sessions for Phillips with minimal results, Feathers went to a rival Memphis label, Meteor, and cut the rockabilly cult classics "Tongue Tied Jill" and "Get With It," in 1956. His next records of note, "Bottle for the Baby" and "One Hand Loose," appeared on Cincinnati's KING label. None of these or his many ensuing records were major hits, but they established Feathers's reputation as a rockabilly hero. Undaunted, Charlie Feathers has continued to pursue his vision. —*Ben Sandmel*

REPRESENTATIVE RECORDINGS
Charlie Feathers (Elektra/Nonesuch, 1991); *Uh Huh Honey* (Norton, 1992); *Get With It: Essential Recordings, 1954–69* (Revenant, 1998)

Freddy Fender
b. San Benito, Texas, June 4, 1937

Baldemar G. Huerta adopted the stage name of Freddy Fender in the late 1950s as he made the transition from Spanish-speaking CONJUNTO MUSIC to rockabilly-tinged rock & roll. He had first used his birth name when recording on the Mission label (Spain). Thereafter billed as El Bebop Kid, the former migrant worker and marine achieved early success with the regional hit "Holy One"

(1959) and followed it with the even more popular, self-penned "Wasted Days and Wasted Nights" (1959). The latter recording received national exposure when it was transferred from the San Antonio–based Duncan label to Imperial Records of Los Angeles in 1960.

Just as Fender's career was ascending he was convicted of marijuana possession and sentenced to five years at the Louisiana State Penitentiary in Angola. While in prison, he cut recordings for Goldband. He gained early release in 1963 (due in part to the efforts of Governor JIMMIE DAVIS, himself a country music star) and moved to New Orleans, where he eventually became a regular performer at the Bourbon Street nightclub Papa Joe's. While in Louisiana he also absorbed the emerging sound of "swamp-pop" music, an amalgam of Cajun-inflected country and rhythm-and-blues, and made the acquaintance of Cajun record promoter and music entrepreneur Huey P. Meaux.

After spending five unproductive years back in Texas, Fender became reacquainted with Meaux, who had moved to Houston. Meaux persuaded a reluctant Fender to record a ballad titled "Before the Next Teardrop Falls," which became one of the surprise hits of the 1970s. Released on Meaux's Crazy Cajun label in late 1974 and picked up for national distribution by ABC/Dot Records in 1975, "Teardrop" reached the top of both the country and pop charts and was awarded CMA's Single of the Year (1975). Not the least of "Teardrop"'s virtues was Fender's insertion of a verse in Spanish. From 1975 to 1976 Fender enjoyed several hits: a re-released "Wasted Days," #1 country and #8 pop; a version of Doris Day's pop standard "Secret Love"; and his rendition of Ivory Joe Hunter's "Since I Met You Baby," among others. To each song, Fender brought an emotional power and exotic ethnic connotations that attracted a mass audience. He also gained numerous nominations and awards and made dozens of television appearances during this period.

Subsequently, Fender's career declined rapidly, due in part to marital, drug, and alcohol problems. Later affiliations with Meaux's Starflite label and WARNER BROS. yielded no commercial success. Only in the late 1980s and early 1990s did an association with the Tex-Mex country all-star band the Texas Tornadoes (including Doug Sahm, Angie Myers, and FLACO JIMENEZ) bring Fender back into the limelight. He still possessed the same dramatic vocal style as he had in the 1970s, when he added a much-needed dose of vitality and ethnic variety to country. In 1994 Fender signed on as a single artist with ARISTA/Texas.   —*Stephen R. Tucker*

REPRESENTATIVE RECORDINGS

Rock 'N' Country (ABC/Dot, 1976); *The Best of Freddy Fender* (ABC/Dot, 1977)

Bob Ferguson
b. Willow Springs, Missouri, December 30, 1927

As a staff producer for RCA in Nashville during the 1960s and early 1970s, Robert B. Ferguson played a prominent role in building the careers of such RCA artists as CONNIE SMITH, PORTER WAGONER, and DOLLY PARTON. A successful songwriter as well, he wrote Wagoner's "The Carroll County Accident," and, most significantly, FERLIN HUSKY's million-selling 1960 smash "Wings of a Dove."

A lifelong scholar, Ferguson attended Southwest Missouri State University and Washington State University in Pullman, Washington. At Washington State Ferguson worked as an announcer for the college station, KWSC, and put together a country band called the KWSC Ramblers. In 1955 he landed a job producing movies for the Tennessee Game & Fish Commission, a position he held until 1960. With the success of "Wings of a Dove," his music career was made, and Ferguson himself recorded a few long-forgotten numbers under the stage name Eli Possumtrot.

As an RCA producer, Ferguson was noteworthy for his relatively light touch on such landmark records as Connie Smith's "Once a Day." Though he often did record his artists with lush NASHVILLE SOUND string and chorus arrangements, he also knew when to back away from them. Smith, Wagoner, and especially Parton all benefited from Ferguson's sensitive approach, as is evident on Dolly's spare and remarkably undated early RCA sides.

—*Daniel Cooper*

Fiddle

The fiddle has always been one of the principal instruments in country music. Recorded country music began when Texas fiddler A. C. "ECK" ROBERTSON recorded for VICTOR in New York in 1922. Beginning in 1923, sales of recordings by another fiddler, JOHN CARSON of Atlanta, led to the active exploitation of white southern rural music by the phonograph industry. Fiddlers such as CLARK KESSINGER from West Virginia, CLAYTON McMICHEN from Georgia, Charlie Bowman and ARTHUR SMITH from Tennessee, and DOC ROBERTS from Kentucky recorded extensively during country music's first two decades and influenced many fiddlers in succeeding generations.

The fiddle lies at the heart of many country music styles. BOB WILLS and MILTON BROWN built the western swing sound around the fiddle. Although fiddlers were rare in mainstream jazz, many young fiddlers in Texas and Oklahoma in the 1930s and 1940s eagerly listened to and took musical ideas from jazz violinists Joe Venuti, Stuff Smith, and Stephane Grappelli. CECIL BROWER, J. R. Chatwell, Hugh Farr (SONS OF THE PIONEERS), CLIFF BRUNER, Joe Holley, JOHNNY GIMBLE, and many others learned how to make traditional fiddle tunes swing, and to take hot choruses on new songs such as "Stay All Night, Stay a Little Longer," "Take Me Back to Tulsa," "Fat Boy Rag," and "San Antonio Rose."

BILL MONROE likewise put the fiddle at the center of the bluegrass sound. Monroe was greatly influenced by the music of his uncle, Pendleton Vandiver, who was a master old-time fiddler from Kentucky. Monroe not only recorded many tunes that he learned from his Uncle Pen but also wrote dozens of new tunes in the fiddle tune mold. Many Monroe compositions, such as "Jerusalem Ridge," "Big Mon," "Wheel Hoss," and "Brown County Breakdown," have become staples of the current bluegrass fiddler's repertoire. Most of the musicians who defined bluegrass fiddle style, including CHUBBY WISE, TOMMY MAGNESS, Bobby Hicks, Merle "Red" Taylor, BENNY MARTIN, Richard Greene, VASSAR CLEMENTS, and KENNY BAKER, have toured or recorded as members of Monroe's Blue Grass Boys. Other fiddlers, such as Paul Warren, Clarence "Tater" Tate, Jimmy Buchanan, Scott Stoneman, Stuart Duncan, and Blaine Sprouse, have also made an impact on bluegrass music.

Mainstream country artists such as HANK WILLIAMS, ROY ACUFF, HANK SNOW, RAY PRICE, BUCK OWENS, PORTER WAG-

ONER, MERLE HAGGARD, EMMYLOU HARRIS, and RICKY SKAGGS (an expert fiddler himself) have featured fiddlers prominently in their touring bands and on their recordings. Fiddlers such as DALE POTTER, TOMMY JACKSON, Tommy Vaden, HOWDY FORRESTER, and Tommy Williams played on the road and in recording sessions with a variety of country singers. MARK O'CONNOR, a prodigiously talented multi-instrumentalist who is best known as a fiddler, has dominated the CMA's Instrumentalist of the Year award competition throughout the 1990s.

Fiddling had existed in the United States for nearly three centuries prior to the beginning of country music as a commercial popular music genre, and has its roots in European dance music traditions. The word "fiddle," in several variant spellings, has been used to designate various bowed stringed instruments since the twelfth century, and when the violin emerged in the middle of the sixteenth century, it acquired the name "fiddle" as an informal appellation. In its early years the violin was used primarily as a dance instrument, and it has maintained this function in a wide range of folk music traditions throughout Europe and North America. Early violinists playing for dancers probably performed a preexisting body of dance music; the "modern" fiddle tune repertoire is rooted in the body of tunes and tune types that crystallized throughout the British Isles and Ireland, and in places settled by people from these areas, in the mid- to late eighteenth century. However, only a minority of the tunes current among American fiddlers can be traced directly to Old World antecedents, and it is probably incorrect to view American fiddling in terms of an imported tradition that developed its own characteristics in the New World. Rather, independent development of local styles seems to have occurred more or less simultaneously in many different parts of the English-speaking world, including various regions of the United States.

Fiddle tunes typically consist of two distinct melodic sections, each of which is played twice in an AABB pattern for one complete execution of the tune. The tune is then repeated several times in a performance, sometimes with variations. In the context of a bluegrass or western swing band, players of other instruments will also take turns at playing the melody, or in improvising solos based on it.

Country fiddling reflects a considerable amount of cultural synthesis. For example, the sliding into and out of notes—one of the distinguishing features of southern fiddling—is generally thought to be a stylistic trait derived from African-American music. Popular fiddlers such as Arthur Smith and Chubby Wise brought this bluesy trait to commercial country music. The CAJUN music of French Louisiana has long had a tangential, but persistent, relationship to mainstream country music, with fiddling being perhaps the most distinctive Cajun music element that has influenced country. Aspects of repertoire and style of the German, Czech, and Hispanic communities in the Southwest have been incorporated into the fiddling of that region and, by extension, into regional commercial country styles.
—*Paul F. Wells*

Field Recording

In the first two decades of country music's commercial history, field recording was one of the basic methods used to find new talent and to record other musicians of proven merit. Recording company talent scouts (generally known as artists and repertoire or A&R men), accompanied by engineers who transported and operated the recording equipment, traveled to various cities in the South such as Atlanta, New Orleans, Memphis, and San Antonio, and recorded entertainers on location. The A&R men sometimes ran newspaper ads searching for potential talent, but they also acted on tips provided by other musicians or by local informants. Recording sessions were held in hotel rooms, radio stations, warehouses, or other rented spaces.

Country music's first field session came in June 1923 when RALPH PEER, talent scout for the OKEH company, discovered and recorded FIDDLIN' JOHN CARSON in Atlanta. Much more significant, though, were the recordings made by Peer for VICTOR in July and August 1927 in BRISTOL, TENNESSEE, where such historic figures as the CARTER FAMILY, JIMMIE RODGERS, and Alfred Karnes were first recorded. In the years that followed, men such as FRANK WALKER, ARTHUR SATHERLEY, ELI OBERSTEIN, and DAVE KAPP conducted similar recording sessions that brought comparable talent to country music.

As important as these country music field sessions have been, they were not the first on-site explorations of American folk music. Field recording actually began with the private expeditions of collectors who looked for folk music in the southern Appalachians and other rural areas in the early years of the twentieth century. These first collections, however, were generally made with pen and paper, and they concentrated on songs and not the singers. The most significant field recordings were conducted by John Lomax, whose findings were published in 1910 as *Cowboy Songs and Other Frontier Ballads,* and Cecil Sharp, whose collection of mountain ballads was first published in 1917 as *English Folk Songs from the Southern Appalachians.* In the 1920s Robert Winslow Gordon, who in 1928 became the first curator of the Archive of Folk Song in the Library of Congress, began collecting ballads and songs with a primitive wire recorder.
—*Bill C. Malone*

REPRESENTATIVE RECORDING

The Bristol Sessions (Country Music Foundation, 1987)

Steve Fishell

b. Oak Harbor, Washington, September 18, 1953

Raised in Southern California, Steve H. Fishell took up the steel guitar and dobro the year he turned eighteen. By 1978 he had become proficient enough to tour with eclectic country-rock artist Commander Cody (George Frayne). In 1980 Fishell joined EMMYLOU HARRIS's Hot Band, replacing Hank DeVito in the edition of that renowned group that included RICKY SKAGGS. As sideman to Harris, Fishell appeared on six of her albums and on the 1987 *Trio* album ("Those Memories of You") by Harris, DOLLY PARTON, and LINDA RONSTADT.

Fishell started producing records in 1986. His clients have included former ASLEEP AT THE WHEEL vocalist JANN BROWNE (*Tell Me Why*), MCBRIDE & THE RIDE (*Burning Up the Road*), the MAVERICKS (*From Hell to Paradise*), RADNEY FOSTER, and PAM TILLIS (the million-selling *Sweetheart's Dance*). Foster's *Del Rio, Texas 1959* yielded the hits "Just Call Me Lonesome" and "Nobody Wins," while Tillis's *Sweetheart's Dance*, with the hits "When You Walk in the Room" and "Mi Vida Loca," helped earn her the COUNTRY MUSIC ASSOCIATION's award for Female Vocalist of the Year in 1994. Fishell also has produced BOB WOODRUFF and Canadian artists Charlie Major (*The Other Side*, winner of the 1994

Canadian Country Music Award for album of the year) and Prairie Oyster.

In addition to production work, Fishell played in studio sessions with Marshall Crenshaw, Leon Redbone, and Sheena Easton. He moved to Nashville in 1988 with wife and music industry executive Tracy Gershon. He joined (now defunct) Rising Tide Nashville in 1996 as director of A&R. "The studio can be a very alien place," Fishell says. "You have to make people comfortable, to remove the pressure—and then make sure you're ready when the magic and the chemistry come together." —*Jay Orr*

The Flatlanders

As indicated by the title of their one and only album, the Flatlanders were *More A Legend Than a Band.* The group was formed in 1970, when childhood friends BUTCH HANCOCK, JIMMIE DALE GILMORE, and JOE ELY found themselves back in their hometown of Lubbock, Texas. Flatlanders' lead singer Gilmore had played in the Austin band Hub City Movers; Hancock had been in San Francisco; and Ely had traveled in Europe. The three singer-songwriters then roomed together on Fourteenth Street in Lubbock, and they shared an affection for traditional country and blues as well contemporary folk and rock. Other key members of the group included Steve Wesson, who played the musical saw and autoharp, and fiddler Tommy Hancock (no relation to Butch), who also ran a bar. In addition, bassist Sylvester Rice, mandolinist Tony Pearson, Jesse Taylor (who later played in Ely's band), and others came and went during the band's lifetime.

In 1972 the Flatlanders traveled from Lubbock to Nashville to record with producer Royce Clark for SHELBY SINGLETON's Plantation label. The record deal resulted from a meeting between Clark and Gilmore's manager Lou Driver. The band's music had little in common with the bland, overproduced Nashville country-pop sound, or with the laid-back, country-rock style developing in Los Angeles. The Flatlanders combined a hillbilly musical sensibility taken from JIMMIE RODGERS and HANK WILLIAMS with the lyrical sophistication of BOB DYLAN. The saw added an eerie, lonesome, feeling like the sound of the West Texas wind blowing out of a big open sky. Singleton released a single version of "Dallas" (later rerecorded separately by Ely and Gilmore) to radio with minimal response. When the album eventually came out, it was released only in the 8-track tape configuration. (It was finally reissued in the United States on compact disc by ROUNDER RECORDS in 1990.)

The Flatlanders played a few gigs together and then went their separate ways. Gilmore and Tommy ended up living in Denver, but Gilmore moved back to Austin and later recorded for HighTone; Ely eventually formed another band in Lubbock with Taylor and Lloyd Maines and was signed by MCA Nashville; and Hancock moved to Clarendon, where he recorded albums on his own Rainlight label. Although Gilmore, Ely, and Hancock have remained close friends and professional associates over the years, it took twenty years for the Flatlanders to reunite onstage at Austin's Broken Spoke Saloon. By this time the main members had established their individual reputations and influenced successive generations of Texas singer-songwriters. —*Rick Mitchell*

REPRESENTATIVE RECORDING

More a Legend Than a Band (Rounder, 1990)

Lester Flatt & the Nashville Grass

After dissolving his partnership with Earl Scruggs in late February 1969, Lester Flatt remained on the GRAND OLE OPRY featuring the traditional bluegrass sound with which he felt most comfortable. Retaining longtime Foggy Mountain Boys BURKETT "JOSH" GRAVES, E. P. "JAKE" TULLOCK, and Paul Warren, he recruited banjo player Vic Jordan and mandolinist ROLAND WHITE from BILL MONROE's Blue Grass Boys. Critics and fans hailed Flatt's early recordings on Nugget and RCA VICTOR—particularly three duet albums with MAC WISEMAN—as a return to form.

Because Flatt was contractually prevented from using the Foggy Mountain Boys name, the advertising agency handling the MARTHA WHITE Foods account promoted a "name the band" contest. The Nashville Grass was selected from more than 20,000 entries. Flatt initially disliked the name, a punning reference on DANNY DAVIS's Nashville Brass. However, his resistance faded when it proved popular among fans; other bluegrass bands adopted similar "grass" monikers.

The Nashville Grass roster began turning over in 1972, but Flatt carefully maintained his trademark sound. MARTY STUART—not yet fourteen years old—joined as lead guitarist in September. When White left the band in March 1973, Flatt persuaded his retired tenor singer Curly Seckler to replace him; Seckler played gutar, and Stuart switched to mandolin.

Troubled by lingering problems from a 1967 heart attack, Flatt underwent open heart surgery in June 1975. Although his health continued to deteriorate, Flatt kept the band on the road until shortly before his death on May 11, 1979. Seckler helmed the Nashville Grass through the 1980s, primarily in partnership with Flatt sound-alike Willis Spears. —*Dave Samuelson*

REPRESENTATIVE RECORDINGS

Lester Flatt at His Best (Hollywood, 1996); *Lester Raymond Flatt* (Flying Fish, 1976)

Flatt & Scruggs and the Foggy Mountain Boys
Lester Raymond Flatt b. Duncan's Chapel, Tennessee, June 14, 1914; d. May 11, 1979
Earl Eugene Scruggs b. Flint Hill, North Carolina, January 6, 1924

Flatt and Scruggs and the Foggy Mountain Boys did much to popularize bluegrass music. Their sound became widely recognized in the 1960s through their recording of "The Ballad of Jed Clampett," the theme for the network television show THE BEVERLY HILLBILLIES.

Both Flatt and Scruggs grew up in rural farm homes rich with musical traditions. Both worked in textile mills before becoming full-time musicians. Flatt, who left school at age twelve and married at seventeen, began his radio career in 1939 and worked in several bands, including that of CHARLIE MONROE and his Kentucky Partners, with whom, in 1943, he sang tenor and played guitar and mandolin. In 1945 Flatt was hired as guitarist and lead singer in BILL MONROE's Blue Grass Boys.

Scruggs, who remained close to home through the war years to help his widowed mother, was recognized from an early age as a banjo prodigy. By the time he was a teen, he had developed a distinctive banjo style that enabled him to play a broad variety of music with speed and clarity.

The two met in 1945 when Scruggs joined Monroe's

Flatt & Scruggs with the Foggy Mountain Boys: (from left) Earl Scruggs, Paul Warren, Burkett "Uncle Josh" Graves, E. P. "Cousin Jake" Tulloch, and Lester Flatt

Blue Grass Boys, and both became part of what proved to be Monroe's most influential lineup. Along with fiddler CHUBBY WISE and bassist Cedric Rainwater, Flatt and Scruggs played a crucial role in the development of the sound that later came to be known as "bluegrass"—a name taken from the band's. In addition to Monroe's high-tenor vocals and fiery mandolin playing, this sound featured Flatt's warm lead singing and solid rhythm guitar. Scruggs used the banjo as a lead instrument, like a fiddle or a guitar, particularly on faster pieces and instrumentals. This novel sound attracted considerable attention to their GRAND OLE OPRY performances and COLUMBIA recordings.

Early in 1948, Flatt and Scruggs left Monroe's band. Later that spring they formed their own band, the Foggy Mountain Boys. Early band members included guitarist/vocalists JIM EANES and MAC WISEMAN, along with fiddler Jim Shumate and bassist Rainwater. By the end of the year they were playing at WCYB in BRISTOL, TENNESSEE, and recording for MERCURY. Afterward they worked at a number of other radio stations in the Southeast. In 1950 they signed with Columbia, the label they would be with for the rest of their career together.

In 1949 mandolinist/tenor singer Curley Seckler joined the band. He remained for most years until 1962, although for several periods he was replaced by others, most notably EVERETT LILLY. A number of outstanding fiddlers also played with the band in its early years; in 1954 master fiddler Paul Warren joined and remained with the band for the rest of its history. Several bassists worked with the band before 1953, when English P. "Cousin Jake" Lambert joined. He, too, remained until the end. However, the Flatt & Scruggs sound took its definitive form in 1955 with the addition of the DOBRO resonator guitar of BUCK "UNCLE JOSH" GRAVES. With this instrument they departed significantly from Bill Monroe's sound, although, like him, they maintained a purely acoustic sound.

In 1953 MARTHA WHITE FLOUR began sponsoring Flatt & Scruggs's daily early morning radio shows over WSM-Nashville and continued to support them for the rest of their career. Two years later they became members of the GRAND OLE OPRY. During the late fifties and early sixties their syndicated television shows were seen by millions of viewers in the Southeast. Their recordings, including gospel songs such as "Cabin on the Hill," began hitting the country charts. Meanwhile, their banjo-sparked acoustic sound found favor with young listeners in the folk music revival. Appearances at the NEWPORT FOLK FESTIVAL and on TV brought them national acclaim (*New York Times* music critic Robert Shelton compared Scruggs to Paganini), paving the way for a series of folk-oriented albums. An appearance at the Hollywood folk club The Ash Grove caught the ear of the producer of *The Beverly Hillbillies* and led to the recording of "The Ballad of Jed Clampett," their only single to reach #1 on the country charts.

The early sixties was a time of great popularity for the group. And while later in the decade there were health problems for both men, particularly Lester, they continued to tour and broadcast widely. Highlights from these years included sensational appearances in Japan and at San Francisco's Avalon Ballroom, during the peak of its hippie light-show years, and another sound track success when their 1949 recording of "Foggy Mountain Breakdown" was used in the 1967 movie *Bonnie and Clyde*.

Musical and business differences brought the act to an end early in 1969. Both men continued to perform, Scruggs with his sons in the EARL SCRUGGS REVUE, and Flatt with his NASHVILLE GRASS. In 1985 the duo of Flatt & Scruggs was elected to the COUNTRY MUSIC HALL OF FAME.
—*Neil V. Rosenberg*

REPRESENTATIVE RECORDINGS

Flatt & Scruggs 1948-1959 (Bear Family, 1991), 4 CDs ; *The Essential Flatt & Scruggs* (Columbia, 1997), 2 CDs; *Don't Get Above Your Raisin'* (Rounder, 1992); *Golden Era* (Rounder, 1992); *Blue Ridge Cabin Home* (County, 1990)

Béla Fleck
b. New York, New York, July 10, 1959

Named after composer Béla Bartok, banjo virtuoso Béla Anton Leos Fleck picked up his primary instrument at fifteen upon hearing FLATT & SCRUGGS's theme song to *THE BEVERLY HILLBILLIES*. Like his hero Earl Scruggs, Fleck would go on to expand the language of the banjo, rewriting the rules and assumptions for the instrument as a solo artist, a member of NEW GRASS REVIVAL, and as the leader of the Flecktones.

Two years after his grandfather gave him his first banjo, the teenage musician witnessed keyboardist Chick Corea in concert at New York's Beacon Theater with the jazz supergroup Return to Forever. Fleck, who had mostly played bluegrass and folk up to that point, has cited that evening as a musical milestone on numerous occasions; he said that it was the night that changed his entire approach to playing the banjo. "When they soloed they were over every inch of their instrument necks," Fleck recalled, referring to Return to Forever guitarist Al DiMeola and bassist Stanley Clarke. "Just from a purely technical standpoint, I sat there in the audience, loving every minute of it and going, 'All of those notes they're playing have got to be on the banjo somewhere. I just have to find them.' " Fleck would go on to master a single-note style on the banjo.

Fleck launched his recording career in the late 1970s, contributing to a pair of releases as a member of the Boston-based Tasty Licks. He moved to Kentucky and then became a member of Spectrum, with whom he recorded two albums on ROUNDER RECORDS. After putting out one solo effort, 1979's *Crossing the Tracks,* he accepted an invitation to join the New Grass Revival in 1981 and moved to Nashville the same year. Throughout the 1980s he continued to make solo albums and he worked with New Grass Revival until 1989, the year he formed his present group, the jazz-based, highly improvisational Flecktones, with bassist Victor Wooten, Wooten's brother Roy "Future Man" Wooten, and Howard Levy, who left the band in 1993. (Future Man is the inventor of the synth-ax drumitar, a guitar-shaped electronic instrument on which percussive sounds are created via pressure-sensitive finger pads.)

Fleck went on to win Grammy awards. In 1995 he won with ASLEEP AT THE WHEEL an award for Best Country Instrumental Performance ("Hightower"). And in 1996 Béla Fleck & the Flecktones won a Grammy: Best Pop Instrumental for their song "Sinister Minister." —*Michael Gray*

REPRESENTATIVE RECORDINGS

Béla Fleck & the Flecktones: *Live Art* (Warner Bros., 1996); Béla Fleck: *Daybreak* (Rounder Records, 1987)

Fleming & Townsend

Guitarist Reece Fleming and multi-instrumentalist Respers Townsend recorded seventy-six sides for VICTOR, AMERICAN RECORD CORPORATION, and DECCA from 1930 to 1937. Biographically, however, little is known about them beyond their Memphis, Tennessee, residency in 1930 when they cut their first songs.

Influential as a harmony-singing duet, Fleming & Townsend also pioneered the art of duet yodeling. This vocal technique and their co-writing on songs such as "I'm Blue and Lonesome," "She's Always on My Mind," "Just One Little Kiss," "She's Just That Kind," and others reveal a most direct influence on the repertoire and vocal style of the CALLAHAN BROTHERS, a very successful recording duo from 1934 to 1951. —*Bob Pinson*

Rosie Flores

b. San Antonio, Texas, September 10, 1956

Rosalie Durango Flores has been a key figure in the alternative country movement that began on the West Coast in the mid-1980s and picked up steam in Austin in the 1990s. Her recording career began at age seven, when her father taped her singing at home with her brothers and sisters. When she was twelve, her family moved to San Diego, California. A few years later, Flores formed her first band, Penelope's Children, an all-female group that reflected her influences from rockabilly and surf guitars to country-rock and blues. By 1978 her next band, Rosie and the Screamers (who were all men), was a fixture on the Southern California club scene. After moving to Los Angeles, she joined the Screaming Sirens, an all-female punk band. She returned to her hard country roots on her self-titled 1987 debut album, which was produced by PETE ANDERSON. But the album proved at once too edgy and too traditional for country radio, and she was dropped by her Nashville label, WARNER BROS. (Her Warner Bros. sides have since been released on ROUNDER RECORDS.) In recent years, Flores has migrated between Texas and California, following a pattern established long ago by BOB WILLS. Between 1992 and 1995 she recorded three albums for West Coast indie HIGHTONE RECORDS. The last, *Rockabilly Filly,* is notable for Flores's duets with the original rockabilly queens, WANDA JACKSON and JANIS MARTIN. Flores also has continued to develop as a guitarist. In 1994 she toured as a lead player with BUTCH HANCOCK's band. —*Rick Mitchell*

REPRESENTATIVE RECORDINGS

A Honky-Tonk Reprise (Rounder, 1996); *Rockabilly Filly* (HighTone, 1995)

The Flying Burrito Brothers *(see* Gram Parsons*)*

Jim Foglesong

b. Lundale, West Virginia, July 26, 1922

As a producer and record label executive, James Staton Foglesong helped propel the careers of many major country artists. A professional singer, and a graduate of the Eastman School of Music in Rochester, New York, he moved in 1951 to New York City, where COLUMBIA RECORDS hired him as a musical assistant. He later toured with Fred Waring's Pennsylvanians, then returned to Columbia and helped form EPIC RECORDS.

As a producer for Columbia and, starting in 1963, for RCA RECORDS, Foglesong worked with such acts as Julie Andrews, Ed Ames, and Robert Goulet and was among the out-of-town pop producers who cut records in Nashville. He moved from New York to Nashville as the A&R chief at DOT RECORDS. With the success of such acts as DONNA FARGO and ROY CLARK, Foglesong became president of Dot in 1973; then, in succession, he served as president of ABC Records and ABC-Dot, president of MCA's Nashville operation, and then president of CAPITOL Nashville. His work as executive, producer, and mentor benefited the careers of such artists as GARTH BROOKS, the OAK RIDGE BOYS, JOHN CONLEE, BARBARA MANDRELL, GEORGE STRAIT, REBA MCENTIRE, and TANYA TUCKER.

Honored by the Nashville Entertainment Association with its Master Award, Foglesong, former chairman and board member of the CMA, has remained active as a consultant, independent producer, and as a board member of the COUNTRY MUSIC FOUNDATION.

—*Gerry Wood*

Red Foley

b. Blue Lick, Kentucky, June 17, 1910; d. September 19, 1968

Clyde Julian "Red" Foley contributed greatly to the rise of the country music industry following World War II. Emerging as a star in Chicago, he later played major roles in the expansion of Nashville and Springfield, Missouri, as country music centers. Over the course of his career he recorded some of the most durable performances in the field, including both sacred and secular material.

Nicknamed for his red hair, Foley grew up around Berea, Kentucky. At his father's general store he learned to play harmonica and guitar while soaking in songs and styles from his father and other local musicians, black and white. Voice lessons also improved his native singing talent. After high school he briefly attended Kentucky's Georgetown College, where he continued his formal musical studies.

In 1931, however, Chicago's WLS recruited him with a salary offer of $60 a week, and soon he was winning crowds at the WLS *Barn Dance*, renamed the NATIONAL BARN DANCE when NBC began picking up a segment of the show in 1933. He played bass and guitar and sang in JOHN LAIR'S CUMBERLAND RIDGE RUNNERS, performed in duets with LULU BELLE (Wiseman) Stamey, and ultimately took solo spots as well.

Next, Foley joined forces with Lair, the DUKE OF PADUCAH, and Chicago advertising executive Freeman Keyes to launch the RENFRO VALLEY BARN DANCE, broadcasting from Cincinnati over WLW before shifting to Renfro Valley, Kentucky, and eventually airing over Louisville's WHAS. Foley didn't stay long, though, and went on to work network radio shows such as *Avalon Time* and *Plantation Party*

at WLW before returning to the *National Barn Dance* in 1940.

During the thirties Foley had recorded for the AMERICAN RECORD CORPORATION with the Cumberland Ridge Runners, but his recording career took off when DECCA signed him in 1941. Soon he hit with "Old Shep," a song he had written years earlier about his own German shepherd, Hoover, and which he had recorded earlier for ARC.

Other hits followed, and Foley was a hot property when he came to Nashville early in 1946 to headline the *Prince Albert Show*, the GRAND OLE OPRY's network segment, in the process replacing ROY ACUFF, who temporarily left the Opry in a salary dispute. The change personified the rise of smooth-voiced, solo country vocalists and the waning of the stringband era.

Along with HANK WILLIAMS and other artists, Foley became a natural focus of Nashville's nascent recording industry, and in 1947 Decca executive Paul Cohen began making frequent trips to record Foley and other country talent there. Among the many hits Foley cut in Nashville are the boogie tune "Tennessee Saturday Night"; "Sugarfoot Rag"; the inspiring gospel song "Peace in the Valley"; and the monster crossover hit "Chattanoogie Shoe Shine Boy," which reached #1 on both country and pop charts in 1950.

In 1953 Foley quit his MC role on the *Prince Albert Show*, although he continued to tour as an Opry act for a time. In Springfield, Missouri (1954), executive SI SIMAN persuaded him to move west and become headliner for KWTO's *Ozark Jubilee* on ABC radio. Early in 1955 he became the host for *Ozark Jubilee USA*, an ABC network TV show that ran until 1960 and was later renamed *Jubilee USA*.

After working on the 1962–63 ABC television show *Mr. Smith Goes to Washington,* starring Fess Parker as Eugene Smith and featuring Foley as Eugene's Uncle Cooter, a homespun philosopher, Foley moved back to Nashville and continued to tour until his death. Foley had already lived to enjoy election to the COUNTRY MUSIC HALL OF FAME, in 1967.

—*John Rumble*

REPRESENTATIVE RECORDING

Country Music Hall of Fame: Red Foley (MCA, 1991)

Tennessee Ernie Ford

b. Bristol, Tennessee, February 13, 1919; d. Reston, Virginia, October 17, 1991

Ernest Jennings "Tennessee Ernie" Ford, a resonant-voiced baritone and master of good-natured corn, rose to great popularity during the 1950s and 1960s and is best remembered for his exuberant 1955 cover of MERLE TRAVIS's "Sixteen Tons."

As a child, Ford was musically inclined, singing in school choirs and playing trombone in the school band. By 1937, working as an announcer at Bristol's WOAI, he went on to study at the Cincinnati Conservatory of Music before joining the air force. Discharged in 1946, and living in San Bernardino, California, Ford soon landed an announcer's job with Pasadena's KXLA. His comical Tennessee Ernie character ("bless your pea-pickin' little heart . . . ") caught the ear of disc jockey–TV host CLIFFIE STONE, who made Ford a regular cast member of Los Angeles's *Hometown Jamboree* country music television and radio shows.

Signed to CAPITOL RECORDS in 1948 by LEE GILLETTE, Ford began cutting typically hot California country-boogie

Red Foley

Tennessee Ernie Ford

and novelty records that were driven as much by his big, warm voice as by the guitar stylings of Merle Travis and the idiosyncratic steel wizardry of SPEEDY WEST. Most of Ford's early releases made the Top Ten. He first guested on the GRAND OLE OPRY in 1950, and in 1953 he became the first country singer to appear at London's prestigious Palladium. Soon NBC hired him to MC the television game show the *Kollege of Musical Knowledge*, and also to host his own weekday program.

But it was "Sixteen Tons," with sales totaling 4 million copies, that cemented Ford's place as one of America's top entertainers. Due partly to this hit, Ford Motor Company recruited Ford to host a prime-time NBC variety program, *The Ford Show* (1956–61), and the *Tennessee Ernie Ford Show* (1961–65). He also made numerous guest appearances on *I Love Lucy* and other TV shows and became a fixture on television for the next decade (moving to daytime television by 1961).

Ford's first spiritual album, *Hymns*, was certified gold in 1959; by 1963 it was the biggest-selling album in Capitol's catalogue. Ford ultimately recorded eighty-one sacred LPs.

Ford remained active through the 1970s with numerous television specials and guest appearances. He participated in a 1973 *Hometown Jamboree* reunion at Los Angeles's Palladium and recorded for Capitol until 1977. Inducted into the COUNTRY MUSIC HALL OF FAME in 1990, Ford was hospitalized after falling at a White House dinner in September 1991 and remained hospitalized until his death from liver disease the following month. —*Jonny Whiteside*

REPRESENTATIVE RECORDINGS

Hymns (Capitol, 1956); *Sixteen Tons of Boogie* (Rhino, 1990); *Masters, 1949–1976* (Liberty, 1994), 4 discs

Forester Sisters
Kathy Forester Adkins b. Fort Oglethorpe, Georgia, January 4, 1955
Karen June Forester b. Fort Oglethorpe, Georgia, September 22, 1956
Kimatha ("Kim") Joy Forester b. Fort Oglethorpe, Georgia, November 4, 1960
Christy Forester Smith b. Fort Oglethorpe, Georgia, December 21, 1962

From the moment their debut single, "(That's What You Do) When You're in Love," hit the Top Ten in 1985, the Forester Sisters were off and running toward one of the more successful country careers of the decade. After "I Fell in Love Again Last Night," "Just in Case," and "Mama's Never Seen Those Eyes"—all from their self-titled debut album—reached #1 that year, the Foresters were chosen the ACM's Vocal Group of the Year. By the end of 1991 they had released nine studio albums with a total yield of fifteen Top Ten singles, five of which hit #1.

The Forester Sisters—Kathy, June, Kim, and Christy—were born in Fort Oglethorpe, on Georgia's Lookout Mountain, to a farmer father and a mother who worked in a rug fiber mill. The sisters grew up on church singing, which greatly influenced the harmonies they brought to country music. While they were singing in clubs around Chattanooga, Tennessee, a demo tape they had recorded in Muscle Shoals, Alabama, ended up at WARNER BROS., and the Foresters were invited to Nashville for a showcase performance. Shortly afterward they signed a recording contract, and their career was launched.

The Foresters owe their success to tightly crafted and naturally blended harmonies that complement the lead singing of Kathy and Kim, and to a spunky attitude that imparts a female perspective of strength to such songs as "Lyin' in His Arms Again" (#5, 1987), "Leave It Alone" (#7, 1989), and "Don't You" (#9, 1989). In an ironic twist, the sassy track "Men" (#8, 1991), from their *Talkin' 'Bout Men* album, was chosen by conservative talk show host Rush Limbaugh as the theme song for a segment of his show featuring unsympathetic critiques of women's issues.

The Forester Sisters most recently signed with Warner/Alliance, with a gospel album scheduled for release in 1998. —*Jack Bernhardt*

REPRESENTATIVE RECORDINGS

The Forester Sisters (Warner Bros., 1985); *Talkin' 'Bout Men* (Warner Bros., 1991)

Howdy Forrester
b. Vernon, Tennessee, March 31, 1922; d. August 1, 1987

Howard Wilson "Howdy" Forrester was central to developing the modern Texas fiddle style, a tradition carried on today by fiddlers such as MARK O'CONNOR and BYRON BERLINE. He came by his talent naturally: His father and a grandfather both fiddled, and his Uncle Bob Forrester was a champion contest fiddler. At age eleven Howdy contracted rheumatic fever, and during an extended convalescence he taught himself to play tunes on his father's fiddle by listening to his mother sing. (His father had been killed in an auto crash six years earlier.) In 1935 Howdy's family moved to Nashville, where he graduated from Isaac Litton High School.

After working local square dances with his brothers, Forrester graduated to professional entertainment with the Curt Poulton's VAGABONDS on the GRAND OLE OPRY in 1938 and 1939. Next he moved to Tulsa, Oklahoma, station KVOO in 1939 to join the Tennessee Valley Boys, a band led by former Vagabond Herald Goodman, founder of KVOO's *Saddle Mountain Roundup* barn dance show. In 1940 Forrester switched to Dallas station KRLD, then returned to Nashville during the years 1941–42 for a stint with BILL MONROE's Blue Grass Boys. (Howdy's wife, Wilene "Sally Ann" Russell, whom he had met in Tulsa, played accordion for Monroe while Howdy served in the Navy during World War II.)

His military hitch over, Howdy went back to KRLD from 1946 to 1949, teaming with Robert "Georgia Slim" Rutland. There they joined Benny Thomasson, Red Franklin, and others in perfecting what came to be called the Texas fiddle style, an intricate, exciting style emphasizing continuous melodic variations through long bow strokes, double stops, and varied accents. After playing briefly with Opry star COWBOY COPAS in 1950, Forrester joined ROY ACUFF's Smoky Mountain Boys in 1951 and remained a mainstay of that group until 1964, when he joined the Acuff-Rose Artists Corporation (ARAC), which at the time was the booking operation of the ACUFF-ROSE PUBLICATIONS empire. In 1965 he became ARAC's president, a position he held until his death, while still making occasional tours and working the Opry with Acuff.

Over the years, Forrester made most of his recordings with Roy Acuff's band but also made a few sides for MERCURY with Georgia Slim in the late 1940s and later made solo albums for MGM (1957), United Artists (1963), Stoneway (1970s), and COUNTY (1983). In 1987 he received the prestigious Fiddler Trophy at the Grand Masters Fiddle Contest held at Opryland in Nashville, an award honoring his lifetime influence and achievements.

—*John Rumble*

Fred Foster

b. Rutherford County, North Carolina, July 26, 1931

As owner of MONUMENT RECORDS and COMBINE MUSIC, Fred Luther Foster played a pivotal role in the careers of ROY ORBISON, DOLLY PARTON, and KRIS KRISTOFFERSON, among many other singular talents. All of Orbison's classic hits of the early 1960s were produced by Foster and released on Monument; Parton was signed to both Monument and Combine before joining PORTER WAGONER; and Kristofferson was with Combine when he wrote some of his most well-known tunes (including "Me and Bobby McGee," on which Foster has co-writer's credit). In addition, Foster bankrolled many of Nashville's independent pop and r&b enterprises of the 1960s and 1970s, ultimately generating one of MUSIC CITY's most complex and interesting legacies.

The youngest of eight children, Foster started writing songs while working in the food service industry in Washington, D.C. There he met JIMMY DEAN, whose career he helped push. Foster later worked for MERCURY RECORDS, ABC-Paramount, and for an independent pop record distributor in Baltimore. In early 1958, with virtually no capital, Foster started Monument Records, which he named for the Washington Monument. Later that year, BILLY GRAMMER's "Gotta Travel On," recorded in Nashville, became Monument's first hit.

In 1960, with songwriter BOUDLEAUX BRYANT's help, Foster moved to Nashville. Orbison's first Monument smash, "Only the Lonely (Know How I Feel)," was released that year. In 1963 Foster started Sound Stage 7, Nashville's most prominent soul music–oriented label of the 1960s, and two years later he signed Parton, in whom he presciently saw enormous pop-country crossover potential. Foster's enterprises thrived into the early 1970s, but by March 1983 his finances were in such a state that he filed for Chapter 11 bankruptcy. Combine was sold in 1986, and the Monument masters were bought by CBS Special Projects a year later. Among those who had made a bid for both companies was Parton, who, in 1981, had summed up the feelings of many who worked with Foster when she said, "Fred believed in me when nobody else did."

—*Daniel Cooper*

Radney Foster

b. Del Rio, Texas, July 20, 1959

Radney Foster came from a family of Texas lawyers, so he was naturally expected to head in that direction as well. He did graduate from the University of the South in Sewanee, Tennessee, but decided to pursue his first loves: singing and songwriting. In Nashville, Foster made headway first as a writer for HOLLY DUNN and other artists. He and Dunn co-wrote her hit "Love Someone Like Me," and Foster later wrote a successful song for T. GRAHAM BROWN and TANYA TUCKER, "Don't Go Out With Him." He became a staff writer for MTM in 1985 and then hooked up with fellow writer Bill Lloyd, in 1987, to form the duo FOSTER & LLOYD. The act has often been credited for helping assign rock influences to country, and released two popular albums in the late 1980s. In 1992 Foster signed a solo recording deal with ARISTA RECORDS. His debut album, *Del Rio, Texas, 1959*, was released in 1992, spawning two hit singles, "Just Call Me Lonesome" and "Nobody Wins," which peaked at #2 on the *Billboard* charts. Both featured an edgy rock musical sound, though Foster's voice resonated with a considerably more country feel. In the mid-1990s Foster would occasionally return to his rock roots, writing and performing with rock act Hootie & the Blowfish. —*Bob Paxman*

REPRESENTATIVE RECORDING

Del Rio, Texas, 1959 (Arista, 1992)

Stephen Foster

b. Lawrenceville, Pennsylvania, July 4, 1826; d. January 13, 1864

Stephen Collins Foster, one of America's first great songsmiths, left an enduring impact on country music. The son of a local politician, Foster followed his brothers into business when he was twenty, but he had already evinced a strong interest in music, which eventually became his principal pursuit. He wrote 189 songs in the last eighteen years of his short life. For many he was poorly paid; some (including "Old Folks at Home") he allowed to be published without his name for fear they would stigmatize his more serious efforts. An unhappy marriage and poor health plagued him until he died, penniless, from the consequences of excessive drinking. Many of his sentimental ballads ("Jeanie with the Light Brown Hair," "Beautiful Dreamer") endure; but his deepest mark was on the minstrel stage, which he enriched with such favorites as "Oh! Susanna," "Camptown Races," "Old Folks at Home," "My

Old Kentucky Home, Good Night," "Old Black Joe," and "Massa's in de Cold Ground." All of the latter were recorded by country music's first generation of recording artists (1924–30), a fact that attests to Foster's impact on the music of rural America long after his death. Still in print are recordings of Foster compositions by MARTY ROBBINS, ROY ORBISON ("Beautiful Dreamer"), the BYRDS, PETER ROWAN ("Susanna"), the NITTY GRITTY DIRT BAND ("Sewanee"), and other country musicians. —*Norm Cohen*

Foster & Lloyd

Radney Foster b. Del Rio, Texas, July 20, 1959
John William "Bill" Lloyd III b. Fort Hood, Texas, December 6, 1955

Foster & Lloyd brought their rock influences to country. Both had been rock & roll buffs growing up in Texas, with Lloyd especially influenced by the Beatles. Consequently, their music featured a heavy rock beat, jangly guitars, and an uptempo attitude.

Radney Foster and Bill Lloyd met in 1985, and began writing songs and recording demos together at MTM. In 1987 RCA signed them as a duo, and they released their debut album, *Foster & Lloyd*, that same year. Their first single, "Crazy Over You," which had elements of rockabilly and the EVERLY BROTHERS, peaked at #4 on the *Billboard* country chart. "Sure Thing," also released in 1987, went to #8. Foster & Lloyd released a second album, *Faster & Llouder,* in 1989, continuing to blend rock with country.

They were a band, however, split down the middle: They were more appreciated by critics and younger fans than traditional country listeners, and Lloyd was captivated by alternative rock while Foster leaned toward country. The duo broke up in February 1991, and the next year Foster earned a solo recording contract with ARISTA RECORDS. Foster & Lloyd will always be remembered for ushering in a fresh, youthful style to country and winning over a great many crossover fans. —*Bob Paxman*

REPRESENTATIVE RECORDINGS

Faster & Llouder (RCA, 1989); *The Essential Foster & Lloyd* (RCA, 1996)

The Four Guys

"Harold" Brent Burkett b. Steubenville, Ohio, July 28, 1939
Laddie Cain b. Houston, Texas, November 22, 1951
John Frost b. Eagleville, Tennessee, December 3, 1949
Samuel Wellington b. Steubenville, Ohio, March 20, 1939

The Four Guys, a harmony quartet, has been a fixture on the GRAND OLE OPRY since 1967. The group formed in the late 1950s with an original lineup comprising bass singer Sam Wellington, baritone Brent Burkett, Berl Lyons (all from Steubenville), and Richard Garratt of McKeesport, Pennsylvania. Later they landed a vocal back-up spot on WWVA's WHEELING JAMBOREE in West Virginia. On New Year's Day 1967 the Four Guys arrived in Nashville. "We were very lucky that first year. Songwriter Bill Brock took an interest and asked OTT DEVINE [then the Opry's manager] to listen to us . . . and we became the first [modern] group to join the Opry without a hit record," said group co-founder Sam Wellington. The group joined the Opry cast on April 22, 1967. Through the years the group's lineup changed. Ex-gospel singer Gary Buck, a tenor, came

aboard when Lyons left. After Buck and Garratt departed, baritone John Frost and tenor Laddie Cain joined.

Although the Four Guys recorded at various times for the MERCURY, RCA, Collage, and JNB labels, the group to date has logged only three records at the lower end of the charts. ("We never made any money to speak of from record sales. We just didn't get the promotion," noted Wellington.) The group owned and operated the Harmony House dinner theater in Nashville between 1975 and 1984. —*Walt Trott*

Four Star Records

established in 1945

Founded in 1945 by Dick Nelson as a sister label to his successful r&b imprint Gilt Edge, Four Star initially developed a scattershot roster ranging from pop singer Ted Fio Rito to country performer T TEXAS TYLER. The label, a combination office/pressing plant located at 467 Larchmont Avenue in Pasadena, California, was on the brink of receivership when Bill McCall, a hard-nosed entrepreneur with no music business background, invested $5,000 and gained controlling interest in the company. DON PIERCE, another industry novice, also joined the operation, and shortly thereafter Tyler's recordings of "Remember Me," "Filipino Baby," and "Deck of Cards" became the label's first substantive successes and led the company to concentrate on hillbilly releases.

Among Four Star's early acts were MADDOX BROTHERS & ROSE (ca. 1947–52), FERLIN HUSKY (1949–51), WEBB PIERCE (1950), and SLIM WILLET (1952). PATSY CLINE was signed to Four Star from 1954 to 1960 (though her recordings appeared on Coral and DECCA as the result of a licensing agreement), and Four Star singer-songwriter CARL BELEW (1955) introduced the standards "Lonely Street," "Stop the World and Let Me Off," and "Am I That Easy to Forget?"

While Four Star's stable of talent was impressive, most acts left the label as soon as possible because, as Webb Pierce said, "he [McCall] thought it was a sin to pay anybody." Notorious for exploiting the acts on his roster, McCall made it a regular practice not to pay or release from contractual obligation any Four Star artist—unless he was compelled to do so by circumstance (such as Union intervention or threats of physical harm). McCall's contractual stipulation that Cline record only songs from the Four Star publishing catalogue is generally perceived as having hobbled the singer's career early on.

In 1948 Four Star pioneered the use of semiflexible vinylite, squeezing songs from several artists onto ten-inch discs and making them available for broadcast—one of the earliest forerunners of the LP. Don Pierce sold his interest in Four Star in 1953 to become a principal in Starday Records; shortly thereafter McCall himself relocated to Nashville to concentrate on publishing. GENE AUTRY and Joe Johnson bought Four Star Records in 1961 and subsequently leased the masters to Pickwick for several years. Current ownership is unclear. —*Jonny Whiteside*

Wally Fowler

b. near Adairsville, Georgia, February 15, 1917; d. June 3, 1994

John Wallace "Wally" Fowler was a GRAND OLE OPRY star in the mid-1940s and founder of the group that became the OAK RIDGE BOYS. As the originator of the monthly "All

Night Sing" gospel show at the RYMAN AUDITORIUM, he is one of the most important figures in gospel music history.

Fowler joined the John Daniel Quartet in 1935 as baritone singer and comedian, and the Daniel group joined the Opry in 1940. Fowler left the Daniel group in 1943 for a solo spot on WNOX's *MIDDAY MERRY-GO-ROUND* in Knoxville, Tennessee. At about this time he began to have some success as a songwriter, supplying EDDY ARNOLD with his first single, "Mommy, Please Stay Home with Me" (1944) and JIMMY WAKELY with the #2 hit "I'm Sending You Red Roses" (1944). With his group, the Georgia Clodhoppers, Fowler recorded two of his own tunes for CAPITOL RECORDS in 1945: "Propaganda Papa" and "Mother's Prayer" (Capitol #190). CHET ATKINS, Fowler's fellow WNOX cast member, made his recording debut as lead guitarist on the session.

Fowler joined the Opry on September 15, 1945. He recorded again for Capitol in 1946 and made the cover of *Billboard* (September 14, 1946) dressed in cowboy garb. He also opened his own song publishing company, Wallace Fowler Publications. By 1947, however, his Oak Ridge Quartet (a gospel unit made up of the Clodhoppers) had gained such a following that he turned all his attention to promoting gospel music. On Friday, November 5, 1948, he booked several gospel acts into the Ryman Auditorium for the first of many "all-night singing" programs. Broadcast in part over WSM, they were to gospel music what the Opry was to country. Fowler became one of the biggest gospel promoters of the 1950s, but as his son-in-law, gospel musician Larry McCoy, observed, "Wally was a visionary, but not a very adept businessman." He sold his interest in the Oak Ridge Quartet (twice—he was legally enjoined from using the group name in 1965) and put together several country groups (one of them still an attraction in BRANSON, MISSOURI).

Fowler drowned accidentally while fishing on Dale Hollow Lake near Nashville, apparently slipping off the bank. His fall may have been precipitated by a heart attack, but his family did not request an autopsy.   —*Walter Carter*

Curly Fox & Texas Ruby

Arnim LeRoy Fox b. Graysville, Tennessee, November 9, 1910; d. November 10, 1995

Ruby Agnes Owens b. Decatur, Texas, June 4, 1909; d. March 29, 1963

Curly Fox & Texas Ruby were a popular husband-and-wife team at the *Boone County Jamboree* and the GRAND OLE OPRY. A flamboyant showman on the fiddle, Fox influenced many younger players onstage and on record, while Texas Ruby had a husky contralto voice that probably influenced PATSY CLINE.

Curly Fox's father played fiddle, and Fox was also influenced by area musicians Tom Douglas and Ab Ferguson, as well as black railroad workers nearby. His friend Jimmy Brown played the harp and buck danced, and they and Bob Douglas answered a *Billboard* ad to join White Owl's Medicine Show.

Fox made his first recordings in 1929 with the Roane County Ramblers, and in 1932 he left that group to play at WSB in Atlanta as Curly Fox & the Tennessee Firecrackers. He also recorded with the SHELTON BROTHERS for DECCA RECORDS. CLAYTON MCMICHEN got him into a fiddle contest circuit sponsored by promoter Larry Sunbrock that took

Curly Fox & Texas Ruby

him to Fort Worth, Texas, where he met and teamed up with Ruby Owens, the younger sister of TEX OWENS and an established performer in her own right. (She had worked with ZEKE CLEMENTS at the Grand Ole Opry and at WHO in Des Moines, Iowa.) By 1936 the duo joined the Opry, where they remained until 1938, moving on to the *Boone County Jamboree* at WLW in Cincinnati from 1940 to 1944, and then returned to the Opry from 1944 to 1948. They were married in Marion, Arkansas, on July 1, 1939.

In 1945 and 1946 they recorded for COLUMBIA RECORDS, with Ruby singing on numbers such as "Blue Love" and "Don't Let That Man Get You Down." Fox's instrumental recordings of the classic fiddle tunes "Fire on the Mountain," "Listen to the Mockingbird," and "Black Mountain Rag" were genuine hits of the 78-rpm era, although record charts did not reflect their popularity. Fox's version of the "Black Mountain Rag," recorded in November 1947 for KING RECORDS and released in June 1948, played a major role in popularizing the tune.

Stylishly attired and crisp in performance, Curly Fox & Texas Ruby commanded a wide following. In the 1940s they toured with the #1 WSM tent show, played Constitution and Carnegie Halls, and the *LOUISIANA HAYRIDE*. By 1948 the William Morris Agency signed them to WNBC-TV in New York, followed by seven years for KPRC-TV in Houston, Texas. In August 1962 they returned to the Opry.

Texas Ruby died on March 29, 1963, in a trailer fire while Curly was playing the Friday Night Frolics at WSM. Fox moved back to Graysville, Tennessee, in 1975, but retired from music in 1991 and lived with his sister, Helen Cofer. He died at the Rhea County Medical Center and is buried on a hill overlooking the town of his birth.
          —*Tom Morgan*

Jeff Foxworthy

b. Hapeville, Georgia, September 6, 1958

After years as one of the biggest draws on the U.S. comedy club circuit, Jeff Foxworthy became a household name with the six-word setup, "You might be a redneck if . . ." Those words also provided the title for a 1994 WARNER BROS. album that sold more that 2 million copies, becoming the best-selling country comedy recording ever.

Foxworthy grew up in an Atlanta suburb, graduated from Georgia Tech in 1979, and landed a job as a computer engineer for IBM. In 1984 he embarked on a career as a professional stand-up comic, eventually performing as many as 500 shows annually. In 1990 he made Los Angeles his home base and continued to tour nationally while attempting to break into the television business. Foxworthy used the redneck questionnaire as the basis for seven books that sold a combined total of more than 2 million copies.

In 1995 his next album *Games Rednecks Play* was released. The year also marked another dream come true when *The Jeff Foxworthy Show* premiered on ABC-TV. It lasted one season on the network. Before the show had finished the year, a competing network offered him a home, and *The Jeff Foxworthy Show* returned during the 1996 fall season on NBC-TV for another brief run. He joined the ranks of other well-known sitcom comedians when Hyperion Press paid him a reported $1.75 million to write an autobiography.

—*Calvin Gilbert*

REPRESENTATIVE RECORDINGS

You Might Be a Redneck If . . . (Warner Bros., 1994); *Games Rednecks Play* (Warner Bros., 1995)

Cleve Francis

b. Jennings, Louisiana, April 22, 1945

Cleveland Francis Jr. sought acceptance as a typical country artist, but the media never overlooked the fact that he was a black cardiologist. He had graduated from Southern University in Baton Rouge, Louisiana, obtained a master's degree in biology from the College of William and Mary in 1967, and eventually earned his medical degree from the Medical College of Virginia in 1973. Francis walked away from his successful medical practice in Alexandria, Virginia, to seek success as a country singer. When LIBERTY

Cleve Francis

RECORDS president JIMMY BOWEN signed him to a recording contract, Francis became the first black to join a major label's country roster in many a year.

Born to Louisiana sharecroppers as their oldest of six—all of whom graduated from college and became professionals—Francis grew up listening to gospel, country, and CAJUN music. His influences included Mahalia Jackson, HANK WILLIAMS, Sam Cooke, GLEN CAMPBELL, and Brook Benton. He played a guitar made from a cigar box and window screen wire until his mother bought him a Sears, Roebuck Silvertone model. Francis performed in his church choir and at school, social gatherings, and clubs. He even made some independent albums along the way. Eventually he was signed to Miami's Playback Records, long after he began his cardiology practice. He had made contact with Playback through one of his heart patients.

To promote his 1990 Playback single, "Love Light," Francis spent $25,000 of his own money to produce his first music video, which was featured prominently on CMT. The video and the pop sound of his smooth, somewhat breathy vocals caught Bowen's attention: Francis rerecorded the song for his 1991 LIBERTY album *Tourist In Paradise.* "Love Light" and the album's next two singles, "You Do My Heart Good" and "How Can I Hold You," resulted in modest chart success. After the meager sales of *Tourist In Paradise* and the follow-up albums *Walkin'* (1993) and *You've Got Me Now* (1994), the label declined to renew his contract in 1995. He has resumed his cardiology practice, but made his GRAND OLE OPRY debut in 1996 and continues to perform throughout the United States and the world.

—*Calvin Gilbert*

REPRESENTATIVE RECORDINGS

Tourist In Paradise (Liberty, 1991); *Walkin'* (Liberty, 1993); *From Where I Stand: The Black Experience in Country Music* (Warner Bros., 1998) (various-artists 3 CD boxed set)

J. L. Frank

b. Limestone County, Alabama, April 15, 1900; d. May 4, 1952

Known as the "Flo Ziegfeld of Country Music," Joseph Lee "J. L." Frank was the first major promoter and manager on the Nashville country music scene. He grew up in Giles County, Tennessee, near the Alabama border, and worked in Birmingham steel mills as a young man before moving to the coal mines of Illinois. At twenty-three, Frank headed for Chicago, where he eventually became a booking agent for radio stars Fibber McGee & Molly, GENE AUTRY, and other entertainers.

During the mid-1930s Frank centered his operations in Louisville, Kentucky, for a time, promoting Autry briefly before Autry's move to Hollywood. Other acts then under Frank's wing were fiddler CLAYTON McMICHEN and Frankie More & His Log Cabin Boys, then including Frank's son-in-law and future GRAND OLE OPRY star PEE WEE KING. In mid-decade King struck out on his own, and Frank helped promote him around the Knoxville area. In 1937 Frank helped land King & His Golden West Cowboys a berth on the Opry. By this time Frank had met ROY ACUFF around Knoxville and helped him follow King's example in 1938. It was Frank who suggested that Acuff change his band's name from Crazy Tennesseans to the nobler-sounding Smoky Mountain Boys.

Determined in his efforts, with a professional sense of show business flair, Frank was instrumental in boosting

Opry acts from small-town theaters and schools to big-city auditoriums. Frank's behind-the-scenes activities were just as significant as the sellout PACKAGE SHOWS he organized. He helped boost the early careers of both EDDY ARNOLD and MINNIE PEARL. Generous to a fault, he lent a helping hand to many young musicians, not only in business matters but also in personal ones. Opry veteran Alton Delmore of the DELMORE BROTHERS described Frank as "a clean-cut, neat fellow, handsome, with a little mustache and a big Texas hat. . . . He always had his heart in his work, and he always had a good word for the down-and-out musician. . . . He was an excellent promoter and he knew just what he wanted and he always got it." Thus, Frank's death, at the peak of his career, was widely regarded as a great loss to the industry. Frank was elected to the COUNTRY MUSIC HALL OF FAME in 1967.

—John Rumble

Paul Franklin
b. Detroit, Michigan, May 31, 1954

Steel guitarist Paul V. Franklin has been one of the top session musicians in Nashville during the late 1980s and 1990s, appearing on albums by such country stars as GEORGE STRAIT, ALAN JACKSON, GEORGE JONES, and SHANIA TWAIN as well as rock acts such as Dire Straits, Peter Cetera, Sting, Billy Joel, and Megadeth. He has won a number of musician awards, including *Guitar Player* magazine's reader's poll award for pedal steel in 1992 and 1993, and he was voted the ACM's best steel guitarist in 1994, 1995, and 1996.

Franklin started playing pedal steel guitar when he was nine years old. His major influences were steel players PETE DRAKE and LLOYD GREEN. His studio career began in 1970, when he played the steel solo on Gallery's pop hit "It's So Nice to Be With You." In 1972 Franklin graduated from high school, moved to Nashville, and started playing in BARBARA MANDRELL's road band. He later played steel on the road for DOTTIE WEST, LYNN ANDERSON, JERRY REED, and MEL TILLIS. In 1986 he returned to being primarily a session player, with a hiatus in 1992 when he played a world tour with Dire Straits.

—Jonita Aadland

Tillman Franks
b. Stamps, Arkansas, September 29, 1920

Tillman Franks moved up from sideman to manager during his many years with Shreveport's *LOUISIANA HAYRIDE*. Franks came to Shreveport as a young man and worked on the police force while ingratiating himself with the city's growing country music community of the late 1940s. Franks was soon playing bass for several acts on KWKH's Louisiana Hayride. He wrote "How Far Is Heaven" for KITTY WELLS (1949) and brought Elmer Laird's "Poison Love" to JOHNNIE & JACK (1950).

Later Franks toured with the entourage of one of the show's newer acts, WEBB PIERCE, in which he was part of a band that included FLOYD CRAMER, FARON YOUNG, JIMMY DAY, and the WILBURN BROTHERS. Professional management was needed for the Hayride's growing number of country stars, and Franks successfully stepped in to manage Pierce, the CARLISLES, CLAUDE KING, SLIM WHITMAN, and JOHNNY HORTON, for whom he co-wrote the classics "Honky Tonk Man," "When It's Springtime in Alaska," and

"Sink the Bismarck." He operated the Louisiana Hayride Artist Bureau between September 1957 and August 1960. Franks was injured in the Texas car crash that took Horton's life in November 1960.

A group Franks dubbed the Tillman Franks Singers hit the charts in the mid-1960s with two STARDAY records, at about the time he began a long managerial association with Shreveport area native DAVID HOUSTON. Franks continues to work from a Shreveport office.

—Ronnie Pugh

Dallas Frazier
b. Spiro, Oklahoma, October 27, 1939

One of the most successful, prolific, and influential songwriters ever to hit Nashville, Dallas J. Frazier began his entertainment career at age twelve by winning a singing contest hosted by FERLIN HUSKY in BAKERSFIELD, California. By age fourteen Frazier had published and recorded his first song, "Ain't You Had No Bringin' Up at All" on CAPITOL RECORDS. (He was signed to Capitol by KEN NELSON.) During the years 1954–58, Frazier appeared as a regular performer on CLIFFIE STONE's *HOMETOWN JAMBOREE* TV show in Los Angeles, and when the Hollywood Argyles' 1960 recording of Frazier's "Alley Oop" hit #1 on the pop charts in just four short weeks, the young songwriter was on his way to a long and distinguished career.

Frazier arrived in Nashville on September 5, 1963, as a staff writer for Ferlin Husky's Husky Music Company. Then in 1965, while writing for JIM REEVES Enterprises' Acclaim Music, he penned "Mohair Sam" for CHARLIE RICH. Following former Reeves songplugger Ray Baker to Blue Crest Music, Frazier began to reel off hit after hit, including JACK GREENE's classic "There Goes My Everything," which won 1967 CMA Song of the Year honors. In the late 1960s Frazier, frequently writing with A. L. "DOODLE" OWENS, had songs recorded by CONNIE SMITH ("Ain't Had No Lovin'," 1966), CHARLEY PRIDE ("I'm So Afraid of Losing You Again," 1969), BRENDA LEE ("Johnny One Time," 1969), GEORGE JONES ("If My Heart Had Windows," 1967), and JOHNNY DARRELL and O. C. SMITH ("The Son of Hickory Holler's Tramp," 1968). George Jones paid homage to Frazier's songwriting skill with his *Sings the Songs of Dallas Frazier* album on the Musicor label in 1968. Frazier also had the honor of writing the first #1 hit for TANYA TUCKER, "What's Your Mama's Name" (1973). This tremendous run of success earned Frazier induction into the Nashville Songwriters Association International's Hall of Fame in 1976. Hits continued to flow from the Frazier pen and catalogue. "Fourteen Carat Mind" was a smash for GENE WATSON in 1981. "Elvira," originally written and recorded by Frazier in 1966, was cut by RODNEY CROWELL in 1978 and then covered by the OAK RIDGE BOYS; their million-selling version earned CMA's Single of the Year Award in 1981.

—Kent Henderson

Freakwater
Catherine Ann Irwin b. New Haven, Connecticut, March 4, 1962
Janet Beveridge Bean b. Bartow, Florida, February 10, 1964

Freakwater's Catherine Irwin and Janet Bean grew up together in Louisville, Kentucky, where they developed a deep affection for the close harmony singing of the CARTER FAMILY and LOUVIN BROTHERS. Often pegged as part of the alt-country movement of the 1990s, Irwin and

Bean—both of whom sing and play acoustic guitar—began performing as a duo in 1982, years before many in the 1990s wave of alternative-country bands started incorporating mountain harmonies and instrumentation into their music. Rounding out the current Freakwater lineup are Dave Gay on upright bass and Max Johnston (late of the alternative country-rock band Wilco) on fiddle, banjo, dobro, and mandolin.

An earlier incarnation of the group recorded appealingly rustic LPs for the independent Amoeba label in 1989 and 1991. However Freakwater didn't come into its own until the release of its third album, *Feels Like the Third Time* (Thrill Jockey, 1993), when Irwin emerged as a songwriter able to relate rural fatalism and resiliency to contemporary social and political issues. Her wry feminist reading of CONWAY TWITTY's "You've Never Been This Far Before" also displayed a subversive sense of humor.

The group's subsequent releases on Thrill Jockey, *Old Paint* in 1995 and *Springtime* in 1998, were equally worthy.
—*Bill Friskics-Warren*

REPRESENTATIVE RECORDINGS

Feels Like the Third Time (Thrill Jockey, 1993); *Old Paint* (Thrill Jockey, 1995); *Springtime* (Thrill Jockey, 1998)

Porky Freeman
b. Vera Cruz, Missouri, June 29, 1916

Quilla Hugh "Porky" Freeman has claimed to have been the first artist to play the eight-beats-to-the-bar, boogie woogie style of music on the guitar. "Back in 1935," Freeman recalled to this author, "I got the idea of playing boogie woogie on the guitar. It amazed everybody, so we included it whenever we played the blues. I didn't realize at the time that this style of music was to become the standard of rock music as we know it today." In 1943 "Porky's Boogie Woogie on the Strings" was recorded on the Morris Lee label and again as "Boogie Woogie on the Strings," issued in the spring of 1944 on the ARA label. It proved to be an extremely popular recording.

Freeman had his earliest brush with professional music in the Springfield, Missouri, area where he worked staff at radio station KWTO and the Slim Wilson radio show at KGBX before becoming a member of the WEAVER BROTHERS & ELVIRY troupe. A move to Fort Worth, Texas, brought about an association with the ROY NEWMAN and BILL BOYD bands. Upon his arrival in Hollywood, Freeman worked throughout the Southern California area, finally settling down with Red Murrell's band at one of western music's favorite watering holes, the Four Aces Club in Los Angeles. At that time the Murrell band included JACK GUTHRIE, MERLE TRAVIS, Red Egner, BILLY HUGHES, JIMMIE DOLAN, and Bill "Slumber" Nichols.

In the late 1940s and on into the 1950s, Freeman appeared with numerous groups in the Los Angeles area, the most notable of which was that of TEXAS JIM LEWIS. During that period Freeman recorded for the FOUR STAR label while providing solos and background fills on a number of hit recordings—"Oklahoma Hills" (JACK GUTHRIE), "Remember Me" (T. TEXAS TYLER), and "Love Song in 32 Bars" (JOHNNY BOND), as well as guitar backing on recordings by MERLE TRAVIS, Curt Massey, STUART HAMBLEN, SHEB WOOLEY, and JESSE ASHLOCK, to name but a few. Freeman is the holder of three guitar patents.
—*Ken Griffis*

Janie Fricke

Janie Fricke
b. South Whitney, Indiana, December 19, 1947

Janie Fricke emerged from the shadows of a career as a background and jingle singer to become a successful solo artist, first charting in 1977 and remaining on the country charts throughout the 1980s. She had nine #1 country singles (two were duets), and she was the CMA's Female Vocalist of the Year in 1982 and 1983.

Fricke grew up on a 400-acre farm. Her mother taught piano and played the organ while her father played guitar. Fricke began singing in church, and while in high school she earned pocket money singing at local shows. She continued performing while she attended the University of Indiana in the mid-1960s, her style influenced by such artists as Joan Baez, Judy Collins, and Neil Diamond. Between her sophomore and junior years she went to Memphis, where she sang radio station call letter jingles.

After postgraduation stays in Dallas, Los Angeles, and again in Memphis, Fricke moved to Nashville in 1975. She became one of the town's most requested background and jingle singers, contributing vocals to national ad campaigns by Coors Beer, McDonald's, Ford, Pizza Hut, United Airlines, and Red Lobster. She sang backup with such artists as ELVIS PRESLEY, DOLLY PARTON, TANYA TUCKER, CHARLEY PRIDE, and RONNIE MILSAP. Her work with JOHNNY DUNCAN brought her to the attention of BILLY SHERRILL, Duncan's producer at COLUMBIA RECORDS. Signed to Columbia in 1977, Fricke recorded hit duets with Duncan and Charlie Rich and had her first solo #1 record in 1982 with "Don't Worry 'Bout Me Baby." That was followed by a second consecutive #1 hit, "It Ain't Easy Bein' Easy."

Fricke dabbled with a name change in mid-career. While her surname is pronounced as two syllables, with a long "e," it was often mispronounced "Frick." She experimented with spelling her name "Frickie," but that only seemed to confuse the recognition issue more. She eventually returned to the original, correct spelling.

Fricke performed at Camp David at the invitation of President Ronald Reagan in 1981. She appeared on TV in her own 1983 special and performed as a regular on *The Statler Brothers Show* on TNN.　　　　　　*—Gerry Wood*

REPRESENTATIVE RECORDINGS

It Ain't Easy (Columbia, 1982); *The Very Best of Janie Fricke* (Columbia, 1985)

Kinky Friedman
b. Chicago, Illinois, October 31, 1944

Richard F. "Kinky" Friedman may be the most original, but is undoubtedly the most acerbic and iconoclastic performer in country music history. He was born in Chicago and reared in Austin, where his father was on the faculty of the University of Texas. Upon graduation from the university with a psychology degree, Friedman joined the Peace Corps for three years and served in Borneo.

He formed a country-rock band, the Texas Jewboys, in 1971 and, after being rebuffed by record companies in Los Angeles, Friedman relocated to Nashville. There he recorded his first album under the production of Chuck Glaser of the GLASER BROTHERS for the New York–based, folk-oriented Vanguard label. *Sold American* generated instant notoriety with its mix of caustic but somber ballads, such as the title song "Ride 'Em Jewboy," and satirical bombshells such as "The Ballad of Charles Whitman" and "Get Your Biscuits in the Oven (and Your Buns in the Bed)." It was a critical success but a commercial failure due in part to Vanguard's weak marketing and distribution capacities.

In 1974 Friedman moved to ABC Records and released *Kinky Friedman* with similar critical and commercial results, yet predictably, with less notoriety and controversy. After touring with BOB DYLAN's Rolling Thunder Revue in 1975-76, Friedman's third album, *Lasso From El Paso*, appeared, this time on the EPIC label. In each case he demonstrated an unrivaled talent for ribald social commentary and a mocking ethnocentrism, as well as a capacity for writing songs of remarkable melodic and emotional delicacy. Among the former were "They Ain't Making Jews Like Jesus Anymore," "Homo Erectus," and "Men's Room, L.A." The latter included "Popeye the Sailor," "Dear Abbie," "The Wild Man from Borneo," and "Rapid City, South Dakota."

In 1983 Friedman released *Under the Double Ego*, his most eloquent and subtle work, which included the memorable "Marilyn and Joe" and "People Who Read People Magazine."

Friedman has published a series of mystery novels featuring a wisecracking Jewish former country music star from Texas known as the "Kinkster," along with assorted friends and ex-bandmates. He also ran unsuccessfully as a Republican for the office of justice of the peace in Kerr County, Texas, in 1986 (under his given name, Richard).

Friedman remains country music's answer to Lenny Bruce, whose occasional personal appearances reinforce his stature as a brilliant wit and inventive songwriter unlike anyone else in country music.　　　*—Stephen R. Tucker*

REPRESENTATIVE RECORDINGS

Sold American (Vanguard, 1973); *Kinky Friedman* (ABC, 1974)

PUBLISHED NOVELS

Greenwich Killing Time (1986); *A Case of Lone Star* (1987); *When the Cat's Away* (1988); *Frequent Flyer* (1989); *Musical Chairs* (1991); *Elvis, Jesus and Coca-Cola* (1993); *Armadillos and Old Lace* (1994); *God Bless John Wayne* (1995); *The Love Song of J. Edgar Hoover* (1996); *Roadkill* (1997)

David Frizzell
b. El Dorado, Arkansas, September 26, 1941

Lewey David Frizzell, a younger brother of LEFTY FRIZZELL, first topped the charts in 1981 with "You're the Reason God Made Oklahoma," a duet he recorded with SHELLY WEST, DOTTIE WEST's daughter. At the time, Frizzell and West appeared to be fast-rising young stars of the *URBAN COWBOY* era. But in Frizzell's case, his triumphs were the result of more than twenty years' worth of hard work and career perseverance.

Like his brother Lefty, David Frizzell grew up around the oil fields of the Southwest. But in 1956 his family moved to California, near where Lefty, already a star, was living, and Lefty soon started taking his adolescent brother out on the road. David made his first full-fledged tour with Lefty as "Little David (Rock & Roll Sensation)," and in 1959 he recorded a couple of singles for COLUMBIA RECORDS, Lefty's label.

David's rock & roll career got sidetracked when he joined the air force in 1960, but after his discharge he made a go of it in the West Coast country music scene. He eventually re-signed with Columbia, and in 1970 he recorded a version of "L. A. International Airport" that preceded Susan Raye's hit version. Soon thereafter BUCK OWENS made Frizzell a member of his road troupe, featuring him on his syndicated TV show and bringing him to CAPITOL RECORDS in 1973. But it wasn't until "You're the Reason God Made Oklahoma" was picked up by WARNER BROS. and featured in the movie *Any Which Way You Can* that David Frizzell's career took off. A string of duets with West ensued, as did "I'm Gonna Hire a Wino to Decorate Our Home," a #1 solo hit for Frizzell in 1982. His last Top Forty hit was in 1984, though he has continued to be involved in the country music business into the 1990s.
　　　　　　　　　　　　　　　　　—Daniel Cooper

REPRESENTATIVE RECORDINGS

Carryin' On the Family Names with Shelly West (Warner Brothers/Viva, 1981); *The Family's Fine, But This One's All Mine!* (Warner Bros./Viva, 1982)

Lefty Frizzell
b. Corsicana, Texas, March 31, 1928; d. July 19, 1975

Described by MERLE HAGGARD as "the most unique thing that ever happened to country music," William Orville "Lefty" Frizzell was certainly one of the most influential performers in country music history. A supreme vocal stylist, he introduced an intimate, vowel-bending style of singing that has been internalized by countless younger stars in the years since Frizzell burst to stardom in 1950. Besides Haggard, such major acts as GEORGE JONES, ROY ORBISON, GEORGE STRAIT, KEITH WHITLEY, and RANDY TRAVIS have all paid him homage.

The son of an oil field worker, Frizzell grew up in and around the oil towns of Arkansas, East Texas, and Lou-

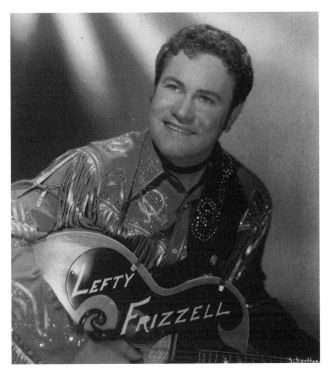

Lefty Frizzell

isiana. Captivated by the yodel of JIMMIE RODGERS, he decided by the time he was twelve years old that he, too, wanted to be a professional singer. His first public performance was during a school program, and it was also at school that he picked up the lifelong nickname of Lefty by decking a schoolmate with his left hand.

Living in Greenville, Texas, during the war years, Frizzell performed on KPLT in nearby Paris. During that time he met Alice Harper, whom he married in March 1945. After moving to Roswell, New Mexico, in 1946, Frizzell made regular appearances on Roswell's KGFL and with the house band at the Cactus Garden. But disaster struck in July 1947 when Frizzell was charged with statutory rape. Convicted the following month, he served six months in the county jail, during which time he wrote numerous songs to his wife, including "I Love You a Thousand Ways."

Several months after his release in 1948, Frizzell traveled to Shreveport, Louisiana, for a failed audition with the LOUISIANA HAYRIDE. After a time in El Dorado, Arkansas, he returned to southeastern New Mexico, and from there moved to Big Spring, Texas, where he sang at the Ace of Clubs.

In early 1950, while working in Big Spring, Frizzell made a trip to Dallas to "audition" at JIM BECK's recording studio. Beck showed little interest in Frizzell as a singer but was impressed with one of Frizzell's original songs, "If You've Got the Money I've Got the Time," which was only half written when Frizzell arrived in Dallas. Beck recorded Frizzell singing a demo of the lively honky-tonk number and took it to Nashville, hoping to interest COLUMBIA executive DON LAW in the song as a vehicle for LITTLE JIMMY DICKENS. Instead, Law took an immediate interest in Frizzell's voice. In June 1950 Frizzell signed with Columbia, and his first session for the label was held at the Beck studio the following month. The two songs chosen for the first single were "If You've Got the Money I've Got the

Time" and "I Love You a Thousand Ways." Released near the end of that summer, both sides of the record eventually hit #1 on the charts.

From that point forward, Frizzell's star rose with phenomenal speed. The year 1951 saw the release of several of his most memorable records, including the double-sided sensation "Always Late (With Your Kisses)" b/w "Mom and Dad's Waltz." Kicked off by Curly Chalker's ascending steel guitar intro, which leads into Frizzell's multisyllabic delivery of the words "always late," the former hit remains perhaps the definitive example of Frizzell's revolutionary vocal technique. It spent twelve weeks at #1, and in October 1951 it was one of four songs that Frizzell placed in the *Billboard* Top Ten simultaneously. In April that year he toured for a week with HANK WILLIAMS, and in July he became a member of the GRAND OLE OPRY.

However, Frizzell's life had been in turmoil throughout this period. He drank heavily, and in August 1951 he was arrested backstage at the Opry and charged with contributory delinquency; the charge stemmed from a liaison in Arkansas during his tour with Williams. (Frizzell was never prosecuted.) Frizzell also signed a succession of ill-considered, conflicting contracts, including one in January 1951 that designated JACK STARNES JR. as his manager. That contract led to a major lawsuit filed by Starnes against Frizzell in June 1952. It was settled out of court a year later.

Frizzell's extended stay at the top of the charts (thirteen Top Ten hits in roughly two years' time) was over by 1953, but he remained a popular star on the road. In 1954 he embarked on a grueling three-month tour backed by musicians from the *Louisiana Hayride*. The tour bankrolled a Frizzell family relocation to Southern California, and they ultimately settled in Northridge. While in California, Frizzell became a regular on the television program TOWN HALL PARTY (he had previously made a succession of sellout appearances on HOMETOWN JAMBOREE), starred in the first country concert ever held at the Hollywood Bowl (August 6, 1955), and was given a star in the Hollywood Walk of Fame. But without full-time managerial care, Frizzell's career went into decline. From early 1955 to late 1958 he failed to score a chart hit of any kind. (The rock & roll crisis that so affected the country industry during these years had less to do with Frizzell's troubles than did his basic lack of career direction.) But as the decade neared a close, Frizzell scored a pair of back-to-back hits with "Cigarettes and Coffee Blues" and his original, classic version of "The Long Black Veil."

In 1962 the Frizzells moved to Nashville, eventually settling north of the city, in Hendersonville. The following year Frizzell recorded the last #1 record of his career, "Saginaw, Michigan." It topped the charts early in 1964 and was nominated for a Grammy. Then Frizzell's career again went into decline. His main advocate, producer Don Law, retired from Columbia in 1967, and in 1972 Frizzell was dropped from the label. He was quickly signed by ABC Records, however, and in December of that year he recorded the first of his ABC sessions.

By that time Frizzell had befriended songwriter SANGER D. "WHITEY" SHAFER, with whom he began co-writing. Their collaborations included "That's the Way Love Goes" and "I Never Go Around Mirrors," two of the most well-known songs in Frizzell's catalogue. (The former was a #1 hit for JOHNNY RODRIGUEZ in 1973–74 and for Merle Haggard in 1984.) Frizzell's own versions of the two songs appeared on his 1973 ABC album *The Legendary Lefty Frizzell*, which was followed a year later by *The Classic Style of Lefty Frizzell*.

Though applauded by critics in the years since, the two albums went largely unnoticed when released.

By early 1975 Frizzell was telling friends and family that he wanted to get off the road and concentrate on songwriting. His pet project was a gospel album for which he and his songwriter friends would write new material. The project never came to pass.

A heavy drinker all his adult life, Frizzell also suffered from high blood pressure. In the early hours of July 19, 1975, he was felled by a stroke. He died that night. In 1982, Frizzell's memory and achievements were honored when he was elected to the COUNTRY MUSIC HALL OF FAME.

—*Daniel Cooper*

REPRESENTATIVE RECORDINGS

Saginaw, Michigan (Columbia, 1964); *The Sad Side of Love* (Columbia, 1965); *The Best of Lefty Frizzell* (Rhino, 1991); *That's the Way Love Goes, the Final Recordings of Lefty Frizzell* (Varese Sarabande, 1996); *Lefty Frizzell: Look What Thoughts Will Do* (Columbia/Legacy, 1997)

Fruit Jar Drinkers

GRAND OLE OPRY founder GEORGE D. HAY called the Fruit Jar Drinkers one of the show's original hoedown bands, but they were also one of the most influential and dynamic bands on the program. During the 1930s, as the Opry was consolidating its position in the country music world, the Fruit Jar Drinkers were often chosen to sign off the radio broadcasts, and they were one of the first Opry groups to try any touring beyond the Nashville area.

The leader and founder of the band was George Wilkerson (b. Stevenson, Alabama, July 8, 1895; d. March 5, 1954), a fiddler who had lived in Nashville since he was thirteen, and who as an adult worked in a West Nashville lumber yard. By late 1927 he had formed a stringband with mandolin player Tommy Leffew (b. June 3, 1905; d. July 1, 1971), banjoist Claude Lampley (b. Bon Aqua, Tennessee, February 10, 1896; d. May 30, 1975), and guitarist Howard Ragsdale (b. Lyles, Tennessee, February 9, 1908; d. December 1966). All the band members lived and worked in West Nashville.

Though the Fruit Jar Drinkers soon became regulars on the Opry, they were the only one of the regular hoedown bands that did not record in their prime. (A studio band formed by UNCLE DAVE MACON recorded for Vocalion under the name Fruit Jar Drinkers, but it had no connection to Wilkerson's band.) A handful of home recordings dating from the mid-1930s, as well as air checks from the 1940s, show the band as a fast, driving ensemble propelled by Wilkerson's fine fiddling and Ragsdale's tenorlike banjo.

Throughout the 1930s and 1940s the Fruit Jar Drinkers continued to play the old-time stringband style; even after Wilkerson's death in 1953, the group, with varying personnel, kept going, often playing for Opry square dancers through the mid-1970s.   —*Charles Wolfe*

Robbie Fulks
b. York, Pennsylvania, March, 25, 1963

Robert William Fulks III spent his childhood years in Pennsylvania, Virginia, and North Carolina before joining the New York–based Special Consensus Bluegrass Band as vocalist and guitarist in the early 1980s. After that he moved

to Chicago and began teaching guitar at the Old Town School of Folk Music. As a solo artist, Fulks first received national attention when two of his singles appeared on compilations of alternative country music released on the Chicago-based Bloodshot label. Fulks's debut album, *Country Love Songs* (1996), also on Bloodshot, included one of those singles, "She Took a Lot of Pills (and Died)," and immediately established him as one of the finest, if iconoclastic, traditionalists working in alternative country circles.

Fulks is at his best when evoking the BAKERSFIELD style of BUCK OWENS, as on the Owens tribute "The Buck Stops Here," and "Rock Bottom, Pop. 1," both of which boast the steel guitar playing of original Buckaroo Tom Brumley. Backed by Missouri bar band the Skeletons, Fulks also assays tortured 1950s honky-tonk à la WEBB PIERCE and GEORGE JONES, but always with a distinctly contemporary edge. In 1997 Fulks signed a major label deal with Geffen Records.   —*Bill Friskics-Warren*

REPRESENTATIVE RECORDINGS

Country Love Songs (Bloodshot, 1996); *South Mouth* (Bloodshot, 1997)

Garth Fundis
b. Lawrence, Kansas, September 20, 1949

Respected for the integrity of his work with DON WILLIAMS, KEITH WHITLEY, and TRISHA YEARWOOD, among others, Garth M. Fundis worked his way up from second engineer to producer, studio owner, RCA A&R executive, and, finally, to record label chief.

He began his Nashville career in 1971 at Sound Emporium, the Belmont Boulevard studio that Fundis now owns, as a gofer and second engineer to the legendary JACK CLEMENT. He then became a staff engineer at Sound Emporium before moving on to build and operate Jack's Tracks Recording Studios. He engineered and sang harmony on Don Williams's records until 1978, when Williams invited Fundis to become his co-producer. They collaborated on a long string of Williams's laid-back country hits, including "Tulsa Time," "I Believe in You" (and the COUNTRY MUSIC ASSOCIATION's 1981 Album of the Year by the same name), "Good Ole Boys Like Me," "Lord I Hope This Day Is Good," and "Old Coyote Town."

Fundis succeeded Blake Mevis as Keith Whitley's Nashville producer and helped the young traditional singer break through to stardom in 1988, beginning with the hits "Don't Close Your Eyes," "When You Say Nothing at All," "I'm No Stranger to the Rain" (the CMA's Single of the Year for 1989), and the posthumous "I Wonder Do You Think of Me." In 1991 Fundis pulled together some unreleased material for Whitley's album *Kentucky Bluebird*.

In the meantime, in early 1990, Fundis had heard demo singer Trisha Yearwood perform at a Nashville nightclub, introduced himself, and began a collaboration that yielded a string of quality albums and such hits as "She's in Love with the Boy," "Walkaway Joe," "The Song Remembers When," "Thinkin' About You," and "Believe Me Baby (I Lied)."

Fundis joined the RCA Label Group-Nashville in 1993 as vice president of A&R. He signed Jon Randall, a veteran of EMMYLOU HARRIS's Nash Ramblers, and former GARTH BROOKS guitarist Ty England before leaving the label in April 1995. At the invitation of legendary industry veterans

Herb Alpert and Jerry Moss, Fundis opened the Nashville office of their new label, Almo Sounds. His first signing was young singer Paul Jefferson, and by February 1997 he had enlisted Fleetwood Mac member Billy Burnette, son of rockabilly original DORSEY BURNETTE, and Bekka Bramlett, daughter of Delaney and Bonnie Bramlett, as a duo act, Bekka & Billy.

In all, Fundis has been associated with more than fifty Top Five country singles, including twenty-five that have gone to #1. —*Jay Orr*

J. B. Fusilier
b. Oberlin, Louisiana, April 17, 1901; d. August 1976

Jean Batiste Fusilier was, from the mid-1930s to the mid-1960s, a leading fiddle pioneer of the Cajun genre. The height of his success was in the Cajun stringband era, from 1935 to 1942. He is attributed with writing the popular Cajun hit "Chère Te Te," and he recorded early stylized versions for many later fiddle standards, such as "Lake Arthur Stomp" and "Lake Arthur Waltz." His greatest Cajun hit was "Ma Cher Bassett," written for one of his wives, Regina Fontenot. Initially he was the fiddler in the band Miller's Merrymakers, led by Beethoven Miller. But Fusilier's talent quickly had him leading the band, and when Beethoven Miller left the group, the band name changed to J. B. Fusilier & His Merrymakers.

Live radio broadcasts had much to do with Fusilier's huge success. His early band, comprising J. B. Fusilier on fiddle, Preston Manual on guitar, Beethoven Miller on drums, and Atlas Frugé on steel, would play live radio shows during the day (10:30 A.M.) then play dances at night. After World War II the band was composed of J. B. on accordion, Preston Manuel on guitar, Norris T-Boy Courville on drums, and Elius Soileau on fiddle.

Fusilier suffered a setback in 1955 when he was hit by a car while changing a tire in the fog on Highway 190 in Eunice, Louisiana. The legendary accordionist IRY LEJEUNE, with him at the time of the accident, was killed by the same car.

Fusilier lived to be seventy-five years old, dying in 1976. He had been a musician most of his life, putting music before everything. —*Ann Allen Savoy*

REPRESENTATIVE RECORDINGS
Gran Prairie: A Cajun Music Anthology, 1935–1940 (CMF, 1993); *Cajun String Bands—The 1930s* (Arhoolie, 1997)

The Folk and Popular Roots of Country Music

Norm Cohen

The Folk Roots

Just as there are many substyles of country music, so, too, the precursors to the music are many. Today's commercial country music did not simply evolve from a single strain of rural folk music but was in fact a melding of a number of earlier musical types, including folk music, minstrel songs, jazz, ragtime, and the sentimental songs of Tin Pan Alley. The most well-known component of early country music, of course, was the folk music of the largely rural southern United States, much of which can be traced back to the folk music of the British Isles.

Because a handful of folklorists were first among the few scholars to pay serious attention to country music, the strong link between early country (i.e., hillbilly) music and traditional folk music was long ago established. (In this article I use the term "hillbilly" nonpejoratively to refer to recorded country music of the period 1924–41. It is a term that was widely used in the industry at the time, though with varying degrees of deprecation.) John and Alan Lomax, in brochure notes to early LP reissues of 78-rpm recordings from the 1920s and 1930s, and D. K. Wilgus, Archie Green, Ed Kahn, and other folklorists, in the pages of the *Journal of American Folklore, Western Folklore,* and other scholarly publications, argued persuasively that early hillbilly recording acts in the years 1923–26 were folk musicians who learned their music orally from family and friends, just as do any traditional folk artists. These scholars further argued that these performers' repertoires were rich in Anglo-American folk ballads, songs, and fiddle tunes of the nineteenth century—even including a small but significant handful of yet older material of Anglo-Celtic origin. In support of their thesis, they pointed to early recordings of British ballads (e. g., "Barbara Allen" by VERNON DALHART, "Pretty Polly" by DOCK BOGGS, and "Knoxville Girl" by MAC & BOB), English or Irish fiddle tunes (numerous recordings of "Soldier's Joy," "Leather Breeches," or "Devil's Dream"), and traditional American ballads from the nineteenth century ("Omie Wise" by G. B. Grayson & HENRY WHITTER, "When the Work's All Done This Fall" by CARL T. SPRAGUE, and "John Henry" by almost everyone). Wilgus, Green, and other scholars following their example expended considerable efforts in the 1950s, 1960s, and 1970s locating the hillbilly artists who had made the recordings of the 1920s and 1930s to document their careers and establish how traditional folk music became the basis for a commercially successful idiom.

In a very general way, two standard patterns emerged, though many musicians fell between these two idealized extremes. On the one hand, early A&R men ("artists and repertoire" men, the early term for producers), sought out well-known (and, incidentally, older) regional artists who, while not professional musicians, had nevertheless established local reputations as popular performers at fiddlers' conventions, political rallies, and other social events. These entertainers—FIDDLIN' JOHN CARSON, GID TANNER, Uncle Am Stuart, and Uncle Bunt Stephens among them—were happy to entertain on records as they did in person, but in most cases did not give up their day jobs. At the other extreme were a younger generation of artists—JIMMIE RODGERS, the CARTER FAMILY, CLAYTON MCMICHEN, BOB WILLS, and others—who cherished fervent aspirations of becoming full-time professional musicians. These were the musicians who provided the impetus for the changes in the styles of country music between the 1920s and 1940s. And, as the industry developed, the contributions of the "part-time" musicians diminished and their places were taken by those who would make music their careers. In barest outline, this synopsis accounts for the emergence of a professional country music industry out of the casual efforts of semiprofessional folk artists—a transformation that took place in the late 1920s and early 1930s.

The Less-Well-Known Wellsprings of Country

In addition to traditional British-American folk music, other important strains of American popular music had some bearing on the music we have come to know as country—namely, the American commercial musical traditions of the late nineteenth and early twentieth centuries, such as minstrel shows, vaudeville, ragtime, blues, jazz, Tin Pan Alley sentimental balladry, and hymnody and gospel music, both African-American and Anglo-American. These tributary streams are evident not only in the recordings by early hillbilly musicians (which are our most extensive, most durable, and certainly most tangible documentation) but also in the fragmentary gleanings from reports of live concerts, radio broadcasts, fiddlers' conventions, and other public events featuring country music. (It is ironic that phonograph records, which are our primary sources of information, were often regarded by early hillbilly musicians as only of second- or third-rate importance in terms of income potential.)

The Minstrel Stage

If we ignore the problem of the origins of minstrel music—a problem that in the past engendered some mean-spirited (if not outright racist) denigrations of the contributions of African-American entertainers to the genre—the fact remains that the minstrel stage was the first important commercial entertainment medium in the United States to have demonstrable influence on our folk culture. The influence of BLACKFACE MINSTRELSY has been in both form and content, in areas musical and nonmusical.

Musically, the influence is most visible in the songs and tunes created for the minstrel stage that long outlived that form of presentation: songs by STEPHEN FOSTER ("My Old Kentucky Home," "Old Black Joe"), Daniel D. Emmett ("Old Dan Tucker," "De Blue Tail Fly," "Jawbone," and possibly "Dixie," whose authorship has recently been strongly contested), B. R. Hanby ("Darling Nellie Gray"), Sam DeVere ("Carve Dat Possum"), and others. In the twentieth century these titles came to be associated with country music entertainers such as UNCLE DAVE MACON, the McGEE BROTHERS, GRANDPA JONES, and STRINGBEAN; some of them are still current in repertoires of bluegrass musicians. Some of the most racially offensive songs have mercifully been stripped of their lyrics, surviving in hillbilly/country music only as instrumental pieces (e. g., "Turkey in the Straw," published in 1834 as "Zip Coon").

Nonmusically, the minstrel influence was in terms of performance style. The three stock minstrel show figures—Mr. Interlocutor, the pompous master of ceremonies who played the straight man, and Mr. Tambo and Mr. Bones, the tambourine- and castanet-playing virtuosi who excelled at humorous repartee—have influenced the comedy routines of innumerable country and bluegrass acts. (ARCHIE CAMPBELL's longtime favorite routine, "That's Good, That's Bad," was a minstrel show standard.) The very essence of the minstrel show—namely, the interspersion of musical with nonmusical entertainment—became part and parcel of live country music shows for much of the twentieth century. A recent manifestation of the minstrel show format was in the widely popular *HEE HAW*, a nationally syndicated television series that combined country music with humor. Furthermore, a case has been made (though it is not indisputable) for the role of the minstrel stage in making the banjo and certain styles of banjo playing traditional in the southern mountains.

Finally, the defining minstrel technique of blacking one's face with burnt cork to emulate—nay, caricature—the facial features of African-American slaves became so taken for granted (even African-American minstrel entertainers after the Reconstruction were obliged to use burnt cork!) that performers such as Al Jolson and Eddie Cantor continued the practice onstage well into the twentieth century. In more rural settings, "blacking up" survived in traveling musical troupes such as tent shows and medicine shows—entertainment media in which many early country music stars (JIMMIE RODGERS, GENE AUTRY, BOB WILLS, and ROY ACUFF among them) gained early experience.

Tin Pan Alley

In the late 1880s, the sheet music publishing business became centralized on New York's Twenty-eighth Street. Out of this cluster of publishers, dubbed "Tin Pan Alley" by a newspaper reporter, came most of America's popular music for more than four decades. Since a major product of this pop music industry during the 1880s and 1890s was the sentimental ballad, it has sometimes been convenient to use the terms "Tin Pan Alley music" and "sentimental songs" interchangeably, notwithstanding the lack of perfect congruity between these rubrics. Among the titles that were long current in hillbilly repertoires and also were frequently encountered by folksong collectors "in the field" were "When You and I Were Young, Maggie" (written by Johnson and Butterfield, 1866; recorded, for example, by Fiddlin' John Carson), "Little Rosewood Casket" (Goullaud and White, 1870; Bradley Kincaid), "Little Old Log Cabin in the Lane" (WILL HAYS, 1871; Carson), "Silver Threads Among the Gold" (Rexford and Danks, 1873; RILEY PUCK-ETT), "In the Baggage Coach Ahead" (Davis, 1896; GEORGE RENEAU), "The Letter Edged in Black" (Nevada, 1897; Vernon Dalhart), "Lightning Express" (Helf and Moran, 1898; BLUE SKY BOYS), and "Down By the Old Mill Stream" (Taylor, 1910; CLIFF CARLISLE). (Only one recording artist has been noted for each of these songs; many others could also be cited.) Many of these compositions actually predate the geographic "Tin Pan Alley," but they came from the same urbane professional songwriting tradition. Also important in this period were novelty songs—in particular the "coon songs," which were compositions in pseudo-Negro dialect. Most of these portrayed the African American in a deprecatory light, though a few (e.g., "Golden Slippers") were fairly neutral.

The principal media of dissemination of Tin Pan Alley's products were at first the song sheet and the stage show. The successor to the minstrel show (though it began in the 1860s) was "variety," renamed in 1871 with the French term "vaudeville." Tony Pastor (not to be confused with the 1920s–50s orchestra leader of the same name) is generally credited with launching variety/vaudeville on the stage, and he vigorously laundered his shows to make them acceptable to women and children. Pastor also was the first to send vaudeville shows on tour. In the 1920s, vaudeville shows in many southern and midwestern cities, such as Nashville, Cincinnati, or Birmingham, occasionally included hillbilly acts on their bill, thus increasing the opportunity for popular and folk repertoires to borrow from one another.

Ragtime

As the dance craze of the early 1900s seized the nation's attention, instrumental and dance music began to supplement the sentimental ballads and songs of the Victorian era. The term "ragtime" is used in two different senses. Some writers apply it narrowly to the very formal creations of classically oriented composers such as Scott Joplin, James Scott, and Joseph Lamb; others use it more broadly to encompass a much larger body of popular compositions, instrumental or vocal, with certain kinds of syncopation. In any case, it now seems clear that there was an earlier style of syncopated or ragtime music that existed on a folk level, which professional composers drew on and formalized. Very few formal rags entered hillbilly tradition—"Dill Pickles" (recorded by the KESSINGER BROTHERS), "Black and White Rag" (BILL BOYD's Cowboy Ramblers), "St. Louis Tickle" (Lowe Stokes & Riley Puckett), and a few cakewalks were the principal ones. It seems, rather, that the ragtime influence entered folk/country music via the older African-American folk ragtime tradition and expressed itself in raggy pieces such as "Beaumont Rag" (Bob Wills, Bill Boyd), "East Tennessee Blues" (Al Hopkins & His Bucklebusters), or "Ragtime Annie" (W. LEE O'DANIEL & His LIGHT CRUST DOUGHBOYS). Other sheet music standards with ragtime elements or precursors that entered hillbilly tradition included Kerry Mills's "At a Georgia Camp Meeting" (recorded by the Leake County Revelers) and Irving Berlin's "Alexander's Ragtime Band" (McMichen's Georgia Wildcats).

Jazz

While its roots are older, jazz emerged in the 1910s as a style with major exposure and impact, to a large extent replacing ragtime as the most popular music in America. Many hillbilly musicians of the 1920s—notably younger ones such as Clayton McMichen, Lowe Stokes, and Hoke Rice, all of North Georgia—were fascinated by jazz and persevered in incorporating it into their recorded repertoires, though with mixed success. Important early examples include "Farewell Blues," "House of David Blues," "Take Me to the Land of Jazz," "Tiger Rag," and "Twelfth Street Rag." In the Southwest, this association was even stronger, with western swing pioneers MILTON BROWN and Bob Wills regularly listening to, and borrowing from, jazz and blues hits of the day.

Blues

Commercial recordings of country blues began in 1924. There is ample evidence that early hillbilly performers listened to the records of such black musicians as Blind Lemon Jefferson (e.g., listen to Larry Hensley's remarkable 1934 recording "Match Box Blues," reissued on CD in 1993), Blind Blake, the Mississippi Sheiks, and others. Still earlier were recordings of pop blues compositions by such writers as W. C. Handy, who created a formal style of blues out of a folk tradition, much as did Scott Joplin with ragtime. Several of Handy's compositions subsequently became hillbilly and/or early western swing standards ("Hesitating Blues" and "Beale Street Blues" were both recorded by CHARLIE POOLE & THE NORTH CAROLINA RAMBLERS; "St. Louis Blues" by Milton Brown and Bob Wills), as did other blues of the 1920s, including "Corrine" (recorded by Wills and Milton Brown, probably learned from Cab Calloway), "Sittin' on Top of the World" (by Wills, Brown, BILL MONROE, and others, learned from the Mississippi Sheiks), and "(Steel) Guitar Rag" (originated by bluesman Sylvester Weaver and later popularized by Bob Wills's band).

Gospel Music and Hymnody

While seventy-five years of recorded country music have witnessed the steady erosion of the barriers between it and pop music in both musical style and lyrical content, one persistent difference is the extent to which country musicians still incorporate religious songs into their performances and recordings. Though the distinction between a folk tradition and a more formal one is often difficult to discern in the sphere of religious music, there are many standard pieces in the early hillbilly repertoire that are unmistakably identified with sheet music or early concert-type recordings. Among them are "The Old Rugged Cross" (recorded by the Light Crust Doughboys, Mac & Bob, and others), "Shall We Gather at the River" (Uncle Dave Macon), "Sweet Bye and Bye" (SID HARKREADER & Grady Moore), and "Church in the Wildwood" (Carter Family, CHUCK WAGON GANG).

The Early Influence of Popular Recordings

Because hillbilly music was largely (though not exclusively) an aural/oral tradition, it is not surprising that recordings influenced pioneering hillbilly musicians far more than sheet music did. Wind-up cylinder and disc-playing machines found their way into the homes of many people in the southern mountains early in the twentieth century. We also have the word of several artists that they bought and listened to early records. Charlie Poole was captivated by the banjo playing of the oft-recorded turn-of-the-century virtuosi Fred Van Eps and Vess L. Ossman; Clayton McMichen doted on classical violinist Fritz Kreisler; Jimmie Rodgers learned "Bill Bailey" from an early pop recording, and DORSEY DIXON learned "Preacher and the Bear" in the same manner. Nonprofessional singers, too, were influenced by the early records they played on their wind-up machines.

On the other hand, pianos and sheet music were not unfamiliar in rural southern homes. So the mere occurrence of a hillbilly recording of a song that had been recorded previously by popular entertainers does not necessarily indicate that the song was learned from the early recording, if sheet music was also available. But in some cases, particularly if the vocal nuances of the hillbilly recording are strikingly reminiscent of the earlier pop recording, we can confidently assert a direct aural influence. Examples would be "Moving Day" (compare Arthur Collins's version with the later Charlie Poole recording); "Ticklish Reuben," written and popularized by Cal Stewart ("Uncle Josh") and recorded by many hillbilly singers; or "Sleep, Baby, Sleep" (recorded by Jimmie

Rodgers at his first session), with its ubiquitous yodel on both the hillbilly recordings and the earlier pop ones. The numerous pop recordings of "Listen to the Mocking Bird" (ARTHUR SMITH, CURLY FOX, and others) must have left their mark, since there is nothing in the sheet music to suggest the elaborate bird imitations that have become a standard part of the piece.

In some cases, we can reasonably assume an influence by phonograph recording simply on the grounds that the recording was much more popular and widespread than the sheet music. This would seem to be the case for Uncle Josh's "Monkey on a String" (covered by Charlie Poole) and "I'm Old but Awfully Tough" (the latter has been recorded by traditional folk artists but not commercially by hillbilly musicians), "Whistling Rufus," and various "laughing" and "crying" novelty records. On the other hand, while numerous pop recordings of the dialogue "Arkansas Traveler" may have prompted hillbilly artists such as Gid Tanner & Riley Puckett, Earl Johnson & His Clodhoppers, J. W. Day, Clayton McMichen & Dan Hornsby, or the Tennessee Ramblers to record this humorous sketch, the textual variations suggest that the piece was known from other sources—probably oral tradition. With pre–World War I pieces such as "Casey Jones" or "The Bully" that were equally popular in sheet music and on record, it is difficult to assert the priority of disc influence. But by the 1920s, the influence of records had, in general, come to outweigh that of sheet music so preponderantly that an aural source can in most instances be assumed. WENDELL HALL's "It Ain't Gonna Rain No Mo'" is a case in point: It must have been his recordings rather than the sheet music that inspired so many early folk and hillbilly singers (including Gid Tanner, the TUNE WRANGLERS, and HANK PENNY) to cover it.

As we have seen, then, along with the folk-derived "Barbara Allen"'s and "John Henry"'s and "Devil's Dream"'s, there are many "Letter Edged in Black"'s and "Old Kentucky Home"'s in the early country/hillbilly musicians' repertoires—songs whose paternities have indisputable genetic markers that still smell of the printer's ink, or the turntable's wax. As country music became a commercially viable product, songs and ballads of regional interest gave way to lyrics with national appeal; local dialects and accents lost favor to a more homogeneous singing style; and rustic instruments (banjo, mandolin, dulcimer, even fiddle) were supplemented if not replaced by various guitars, basses, pianos, and percussion back ups. As the 1930s wore on, most hillbilly artists who strove to make professional careers out of their musical skills exhausted their supply of old standards learned in childhood, from friends and relatives, or from early 78s and cylinders on the family wind-up phonographs and gramophones. Naturally, they then turned to composing their own material or to using songs written by professional songwriters. In the decades after World War II, such newly minted songs have become predominant in country music, and the trend toward separating the roles of professional composer/writer and performer has steadily increased.

G·G·G·G · G·G·G·G

Joe Galante
b. Queens, New York, December 18, 1949

Long associated with RCA RECORDS, Joe Galante is one of the most successful and influential record executives in the history of country music. Under his leadership, RCA became *Billboard*'s Country Label of the Year for more than a decade on the strength of acts such as ALABAMA, the JUDDS, CLINT BLACK, KEITH WHITLEY, and K. T. OSLIN.

After graduating from Fordham University with a finance and marketing degree in 1971, Galante joined RCA in New York as a budget analyst. He soon moved into product management and was transferred to Nashville in 1973 to become manager of administration. The New Yorker soon adapted to the southern style and learned about country music from RCA executives CHET ATKINS and JERRY BRADLEY.

In 1977 Galante was named director of Nashville operations, then vice president of promotion, then vice president of marketing. In 1982 he succeeded Bradley as head of RCA Nashville, becoming the youngest man to lead a major Nashville label and one of the first to rise primarily through marketing instead of via the traditional A&R role. RCA became the top country label during the 1980s, securing the #1 spot for an unprecedented eleven years. During Galante's 1980s administration, RCA sold more than 750 million units.

Galante established a reputation in the areas of marketing, merchandising, and finance, but he was instrumental in signing and developing artists as well. After hearing the group Alabama during a Country Radio Seminar showcase, he recommended them to Bradley, who signed them. To date Alabama has sold 57 million units.

In 1983 Galante signed the mother-daughter duo the Judds, and a year later he signed Keith Whitley, who would emerge as one of the most influential country singers of that decade. In 1988 Galante signed Whitley's wife, LORRIE MORGAN, and he defied country music's conventional wisdom by signing K. T. Oslin, a mature singer-songwriter who went on to win a Grammy. Galante also signed CLINT BLACK, EARL THOMAS CONLEY, and RESTLESS HEART. Other artists on Galante's RCA roster have included RONNIE MILSAP, KENNY ROGERS, JOHN ANDERSON, AARON TIPPIN, and JUICE NEWTON.

In 1990 Galante was named president of RCA Records Label U.S. and moved to New York, where he remained for four years. In this role he signed such acts as the Dave Matthews Band and the hip-hop group Wu-Tang. In late 1994 Galante returned to Nashville and was named chairman of RCA Label Group/Nashville. During his absence, RCA's country division had lost its dominance to MCA and ARISTA, but Galante quickly moved to regain RCA's momentum with such acts as MINDY MCCREADY, Kenny Chesney, and MARTINA MCBRIDE.   — *Beverly Keel*

Galax, Virginia

On the second weekend every August, thousands of old-time music and BLUEGRASS enthusiasts make the pilgrimage to Galax, a small textile town in the Blue Ridge Mountains, for the annual Old Fiddlers' Convention. Nestled between Carroll and Grayson Counties in southwestern Virginia, the Galax area was home to such early country music stalwarts as HENRY WHITTER and ERNEST "POP" STONEMAN, and it boasts a rich heritage of stringband music that goes back centuries.

The earliest known FIDDLE contest in the United States took place near Richmond in 1736, and the tradition re-

Joe Galante

mained strong in Appalachian Mountain communities. The first Galax convention was held in 1935 to raise money for local Moose Lodge #733; the winning fiddle tune was a rendition of "The Old Hen Cackled," and Galax's own Bog Trotters took honors as Most Entertaining Band. Through the years, contestants have included Stoneman; claw-hammer banjoist Wade Ward; medicine-show performer and banjoist CLARENCE "UNCLE TOM" ASHLEY; fiddler Benton Flippen; and bluegrass multi-instrumentalist JIMMY ARNOLD. One of the largest on the old-time festival circuit, the four-day event now features more than a dozen competitive categories, thousands of dollars in prizes, and musicians from around the world. However, the basic rules remain as if etched in stone: Only nonelectrified string instruments are allowed, and contestants must perform only folk and mountain songs in the public domain.

—*Eddie Dean*

Al Gallico
b. Brooklyn, New York, June 5, 1919

Al Gallico was one of country music's foremost independent publishers during the 1960s and 1970s; his firms handled such famous copyrights as "Almost Persuaded," "Stand By Your Man," and "The Most Beautiful Girl." Gallico also co-published "The Happiest Girl (In the Whole U.S.A.)," written and recorded by DONNA FARGO.

After working as an errand boy at G. Schirmer in New York in 1938, Gallico landed a job in 1939 at Leeds Music, and in 1953 he became general manager of pop publisher Shapiro-Bernstein. In 1961 he set up Shapiro-Bernstein's Painted Desert Music in Nashville, commuting monthly while singer-songwriter MERLE KILGORE oversaw the Nashville operation. A huge hit with Kilgore's "Wolverton Mountain" (recorded by CLAUDE KING) prompted Gallico to establish Al Gallico Music in 1963. Kilgore signed as a writer and ran the Nashville office. Affiliated companies eventually included Algee (a partnership with BILLY SHERRILL, whose songwriting and producing careers Gallico helped to launch), Altam (jointly owned by Gallico, Sherrill, and TAMMY WYNETTE), Flagship, Galleon, Starship, L & G, and Easy Listening.

In addition to Kilgore and Sherrill, other writers whose songs Gallico published over the years included Glenn Sutton, NORRO WILSON, George Richey, and Earl Montgomery, among others. Gallico's connections with producers such as Sherrill helped Gallico get songs recorded, as did his working to secure recording contracts for singer-songwriters such as DAVID HOUSTON, JOE STAMPLEY (whom Gallico managed), JOHN ANDERSON, BECKY HOBBS, and BIG AL DOWNING.

In 1986 Gallico sold Al Gallico Music, Algee, and Easy Listening to Columbia Pictures; these interests now reside with EMI. He later sold Galleon and Altam to MCA, while retaining L & G and Mainstay, which includes several standards by the rock group the Zombies.

—*Beverly Keel and John Rumble*

Al Gannaway
b. April 3, 1920

Albert C. Gannaway was the first TV/movie producer to capture on film the live performances of scores of the top country music acts of the mid-1950s. Gannaway worked as a TV and motion picture writer and producer in the 1940s and 1950s. In 1954, when country music's popularity was mounting, his Flamingo Films company secured the cooperation of the GRAND OLE OPRY to make 16-mm black-and-white films of ROY ACUFF, ERNEST TUBB, CARL SMITH and LITTLE JIMMY DICKENS performing onstage, sometimes at Vanderbilt University's auditorium. The shows, offered for TV syndication in thirty-minute packages as *Stars of the Grand Ole Opry*, were sponsored by the Pillsbury flour company in many areas of the country. The success of the Gannaway-Opry pairing led to an additional ninety-two half-hour shows, featuring more than 1,000 performances by Opry stars shot in 35-mm Technicolor, many times at the RYMAN AUDITORIUM. Half-hour shows were packaged for TV syndication, and full-length two-hour movie versions were marketed under the names *Country Music Caravan*, *Country Music Jubilee*, and *Country Music Jamboree*. Gannaway worked with Opry manager JIM DENNY, WSM's JACK STAPP, record engineer/producer OWEN BRADLEY, and talent agent HUBERT LONG in coordinating the filming, which also took place at Bradley's Music Row recording and film studio. Gannaway went on to direct a dozen or so budget feature films, including *Buffalo Gun*, *Hidden Guns*, and *Daniel Boone, Trailblazer*. Casts featured MARTY ROBBINS, WEBB PIERCE, FARON YOUNG, CARL SMITH, and other country stars. His TV shows are now widely packaged for the home video market.

—*Al Cunniff*

Clarence Ganus
b. Searles, Alabama, July 13, 1910

Clarence Powell Ganus was the third of four musically active sons born to gospel composer Walter Powell Ganus and his wife, Ada. As a country music act, Clarence recorded both solo and in duet with his oldest brother, Claude Patton Ganus. Clarence and Claude also joined with brothers Clyde Patterson and Cecil Palmer (the youngest of the four) as the gospel-singing Ganus Brothers Quartet. Altogether the Ganuses recorded twenty-eight country/gospel sides for Columbia and Brunswick/Vocalion, from October 1928 to November 1930.

Clarence Ganus wrote and recorded "Take a 'Tater and Wait" in 1929, preceding LITTLE JIMMY DICKENS's hit version by twenty years. Interestingly, Ganus also wrote and recorded another well-known Dickens title the same year, "Sleeping at the Foot of the Bed," but this song is different from Dickens's.

After their recording years, the Ganuses operated various Alabama musical enterprises, such as W. P. Ganus & Sons Music Co., Ganus Brothers Extension Conservatory, and Ganus Brothers Sweetertone Instruments.

—*Bob Pinson*

Hank Garland
b. Cowpens, South Carolina, November 11, 1930

Of Nashville's "A-Team" of studio guitarists in the 1950s, few could match Hank Garland's versatility. At home on country, pop, or ROCKABILLY recordings, he was earning acclaim for his jazz skills when a near-fatal auto accident ended his musical career.

Walter Louis Garland, influenced as a child by the guitar playing of MAYBELLE CARTER, became a guitar prodigy by age fifteen, playing with bands around Spartanburg. In

Hank Garland

1945, GRAND OLE OPRY artist PAUL HOWARD, leader of the western swing–oriented Arkansas Cotton Pickers, heard Garland while touring South Carolina, invited him to the Opry, and hired him. Child labor laws forced Garland to quit the Cotton Pickers and rejoin in 1946 at age sixteen, but he soon left Howard to become COWBOY COPAS's lead guitarist. Nashville guitarists BILLY BYRD and HAROLD BRADLEY taught him the rudiments of jazz. In 1949 PAUL COHEN signed Garland to DECCA. Though his vocal records weren't successful, he recorded instrumentals including "Sugarfoot Rag." With lyrics by Vaughn Horton, RED FOLEY recorded a hit version of this song in 1950, and Garland soloed behind him. Garland also worked in EDDY ARNOLD's touring band.

By the early 1950s Garland had become a fixture in Nashville studios, and in 1954 he and Byrd designed the Byrdland electric guitar for GIBSON. Garland also recorded with everyone from the EVERLY BROTHERS to Patti Page. He created the memorable opening guitar figures on PATSY CLINE's *I Fall to Pieces* and the leads on ELVIS PRESLEY's "A Fool Such As I" and "Little Sister." After Presley's discharge from the army, Garland appeared with the singer at his 1961 Honolulu "Farewell Concert."

While Nashville saw Garland as a brilliant country player, his jazz skills were growing. He and other like-minded session players frequently played jazz in jam sessions at Nashville's Carousel Club. In 1960 Garland recorded *Jazz Winds From a New Direction* for COLUMBIA RECORDS in Nashville while continuing his session work. Then a September 1961 auto accident near Nashville left him comatose. Though he regained consciousness, his physical and motor skills were impaired. He struggled to regain his abilities but could never resume an active role in music. Even so, he appeared at an Opry old-timers show in 1975.

—*Rich Kienzle*

REPRESENTATIVE RECORDINGS

Jazz Winds From a New Direction (Columbia, 1960); *The Unforgettable Hank Garland* (Columbia, 1962); *Hank Garland & His Sugarfooters* (Bear Family, 1992)

Sonny Garrish

b. Fairplay, Maryland, May 14, 1943

For thirty years, Bruce Franklin "Sonny" Garrish has been contributing pedal steel guitar to Nashville recordings. He started in Nashville as a member of BILL ANDERSON's touring and TV show band of the mid-1960s and early 1970s and eventually turned to studio sessions exclusively. Over the years Garrish has put his touch on recordings by DON WILLIAMS, REBA MCENTIRE, the JUDDS, Dean Martin, B. B. King, and, more recently, TIM MCGRAW, TRACY LAWRENCE, TOBY KEITH, and many others.

As a child of performing parents, Garrish absorbed country music early on, getting the chance to sing and play at age seven. Through Hawaiian lap guitar lessons he learned the basics, and when the pedal steel became prominent in the late 1950s, he bought records to learn the licks. He played in a western swing band called the String Dusters at the Hunter's Lodge in Fairfax, Virginia, which hosted Nashville acts and offered the youngster the opportunity to jam with the bands of RAY PRICE, FARON YOUNG, JOHNNY PAYCHECK, and others. The Bill Anderson offer convinced him to move to Music City in 1966.

He was part of the band that backed CONWAY TWITTY, LORETTA LYNN, and TOM T. HALL when they played for Jimmy Carter at the White House and was also part of the 1990 ROY ACUFF tribute at the Kennedy Center.

—*Michael Hight*

The Gatlin Brothers

Larry Gatlin b. Seminole, Texas, May 2, 1948
Steve Gatlin b. Olney, Texas, April 4, 1951
Rudy Gatlin b. Olney, Texas, August 20, 1952

The words "blood harmony" come to mind when discussing the tight-knit vocal efforts of lead singer Larry Wayne Gatlin and his harmonizing brothers Steve Daryl Gatlin and Rudy Michael Gatlin. With Larry's soaring vocals and the solid background singing of Steve and Rudy, the brothers have enjoyed a career that has brought them #1 records, a Grammy Award, and three awards from the ACM.

Raised in a musical family, the Gatlin Brothers were joined by their sister LaDonna, who sang on several Gatlin albums through 1976. The boys and their sister grew up on the gospel harmonies of the Blackwood Brothers and the Statesmen Quartet. The brothers first performed in public at the 1954 Cavalcade of Talent at Hardin-Simmons University when Larry was six, Steve was four, and Rudy was two. They later sang on Abilene radio and had an Abilene TV series.

Larry won a football scholarship to the University of Houston, where he majored in English and studied law. He later worked various jobs and sang with the gospel group the Imperials. While touring with the Imperials in 1972, he met DOTTIE WEST in Las Vegas. After he later sent her a tape containing eight original songs, West sent him an airplane ticket to Nashville. A few months later he moved to Nashville permanently. In 1973 Larry and Rita

The Gatlin Brothers: (from left) Steve, Larry, and Rudy

Coolidge provided backing vocals for KRIS KRISTOFFERSON's #1 record "Why Me." In the same year Larry charted for the first time with his MONUMENT RECORDS single "Sweet Becky Walker."

Before joining Larry, Steve and Rudy were members of Young Country (as were LaDonna and her husband, Tim Johnson), a group that provided background vocals for TAMMY WYNETTE. Larry's career with his brothers featured smooth country stylings and went through several name incarnations (Larry Gatlin; Larry Gatlin with Family and Friends; Larry Gatlin & the Gatlin Brothers, etc.). They won a Grammy in 1976 for "Broken Lady" and reached #1 in 1977 with "I Just Wish You Were Someone I Love." After switching from Monument to COLUMBIA, they again hit #1 with "All the Gold in California" (1979) and "Houston (Means I'm One Day Closer to You)" (1983).

In 1989 the Gatlins moved from Columbia to JIMMY BOWEN's new Universal Records, then to CAPITOL RECORDS when Bowen took over the helm of that label.

Besides writing his own hits, Larry's songs have been cut by such artists as ELVIS PRESLEY, HANK SNOW, Dottie West, Barbra Streisand, CHARLIE RICH, Johnny Mathis, the Carpenters, Judy Collins, Tom Jones, ANNE MURRAY, and JOHNNY CASH.

Drug addiction led Larry to a California treatment center, where he made a recovery in 1984; he has since lectured on the dangers of alcohol and drug abuse.

The Gatlin Brothers have performed at events at the invitations of Presidents Jimmy Carter, Ronald Reagan, and George Bush. —*Gerry Wood*

REPRESENTATIVE RECORDINGS

The Pilgrim (Monument, 1974); *Larry Gatlin with Family and Friends* (Monument, 1976); *Straight Ahead* (Monument, 1978)

Connie B. Gay
b. Lizard Lick, North Carolina, August 22, 1914; d. December 4, 1989

Dubbed country music's Media Magician, Connie Barriot Gay was one of country's leading entrepreneurs of the 1950s, playing a seminal role in transforming what was still called "hillbilly" music into a modern entertainment industry in just one decade from his base in the Washington, D.C.–Virginia area. Gay was one of the first to coin the term *country music,* in place of the less flattering hillbilly music. Gay got his start in radio broadcasting on the Farm Security Administration's *National Farm and Home Hour.* Later, at WARL, Gay introduced country music to Washington, D.C., where he nurtured a vibrant, profitable music scene beginning in 1946 through the 1950s. His activities spanned TV and radio, as well as live stage shows in the blockbuster mode, using the all-purpose moniker *Town & Country.* His early stable of talent included the Wheeler Brothers, Clyde Moody, and the Radio Ranchmen, with guitarist BILLY GRAMMER, GRANDPA AND RAMONA JONES, HANK PENNY, and a then unknown JIMMY DEAN. Gay took over the management of Dean, whom he developed into a TV star and host of the regionally popular *Town & Country Jamboree* show and the short-lived CBS effort *The Jimmy Dean Show* (1957–59), until Dean and Gay split in 1959. In his heyday Gay's steady roster of talent included, besides Dean, PATSY CLINE (who made her TV debut on Gay's *Town & Country* TV shows), ROY CLARK, and GEORGE HAMILTON IV. In 1958 Gay became the founding president of the COUNTRY MUSIC ASSOCIATION, and several years later he helped launch the COUNTRY MUSIC FOUNDATION. He was elected to the COUNTRY MUSIC HALL OF FAME in 1980.

—*Margaret Jones*

Crystal Gayle
b. Paintsville, Kentucky, January 9, 1951

LORETTA LYNN's youngest sister bears no vocal and little physical resemblance to Lynn, but Crystal Gayle—the CMA's Female Vocalist of the Year for 1977 and 1978—was encouraged in her career by big sister Loretta, who even suggested the stage name "Crystal" after the Krystal hamburger chain.

Born Brenda Gail Webb, the youngest of the Webb children, she grew up in Wabash, Indiana, after the family moved there; as opposed to Lynn's childhood in Butcher Hollow, Kentucky. Gayle began touring with big sister Lynn after high school graduation and even signed with the same record label, DECCA RECORDS. Gayle's first record-

Crystal Gayle

ing was a Lynn composition titled "I've Cried the Blue Right Out of My Eyes." The song charted in the Top Thirty in 1970 but did no better than that. Gayle felt that she was being treated as a superstar's little sister and she eventually signed with United Artists Records. There she teamed up with producer ALLEN REYNOLDS, who guided her to a more pop-country approach, and she began having such hits as "I'll Get Over You." Gayle consciously sang with a diction-perfect, almost operettaish populist approach to country.

In 1977 Gayle's single "Don't It Make My Brown Eyes Blue" (from the album *We Must Believe in Magic*) was a country (#1) and pop (#2) hit, and she won awards from both the CMA and the ACM. Her 1978 album *When I Dream* yielded the hits "Talking in Your Sleep" and "Why Have You Left the One You Left Me For," and she repeated as the CMA's Female Vocalist of the Year. She switched labels to COLUMBIA in 1979 and had hits with "Half the Way" and "It's Like We Never Said Goodbye." Gayle became a television and touring star, especially in such glitzy locations as Las Vegas and Atlantic City. Her trademark ankle-length hair became nearly as famous as her hit songs.

—*Chet Flippo*

REPRESENTATIVE RECORDINGS

Classic Crystal (EMI Manhattan, 1979); *Greatest Hits* (Columbia, 1983)

Gaylord Entertainment Company
established in Nashville, Tennessee, October 24, 1991

Gaylord Entertainment Company (GEC) has participated significantly in the growth of country music through its various entertainment divisions. Gaylord owns and operates the Opryland Hotel; the Wildhorse Saloon in Nashville; Nashville's radio station WSM; the home of the Grand Ole Opry since 1925; the RYMAN AUDITORIUM; and Opryland Music Group. For most of the 1980s and 1990s Gaylord also owned and operated THE NASHVILLE NETWORK (TNN) and COUNTRY MUSIC TELEVISION (CMT) and, until its closing in 1997, the OPRYLAND USA theme park.

The company's first milestone occurred in July 1983, when Gaylord Broadcasting Company purchased the Opryland properties from American General Corporation. The sale resulted in the creation of Opryland USA, Inc. On July 15, 1984, Gaylord Syndicom was launched as a division of Opryland USA to develop television shows for broadcast syndication. Gaylord Entertainment Company was officially created on October 24, 1991, when the new corporation offered its stock to the general public. Opryland USA, Inc., became the cornerstone of GEC, ably guided by E. W. "BUD" WENDELL until his retirement in 1997. Current officers are Edward L. Gaylord, chairman, and Terry London, president and chief executive officer.

In 1997 Gaylord sold CMT and TNN to CBS-Westinghouse and closed Opryland USA for redevelopment into a shopping and entertainment complex. —*Bob Paxman*

The Geezinslaws
Samuel Morris Allred b. Austin, Texas, May 5, 1938
Raymond Dewayne Smith b. Bertram, Texas, September 19, 1946

The Geezinslaws have taken the art of country parody and made it uniquely their own. In reality the act represents the alteregos of Sammy Allred and Dewayne Smith (also

known as Son), who are not related but who have performed together since Smith was in high school. Their irreverent humor often involves putting a twist on well-known songs. Examples of their song parodies include "Help I'm White and I Can't Get Down," co-written by CLINTON GREGORY and Roger Ball, and "Play It Backwards." While never enjoying huge record sales, the Geezinslaws became cult favorites through television and video. They were regular performers on TNN's *Nashville Now* and other TNN programs. Their video for "Help, I'm White and I Can't Get Down," nominated for several awards, was a long-running clip on CMT. From 1990 to 1993 they received nominations for Comedian of the Year from the TNN/Music City News Country Awards. The act won the National Association of Record Merchandisers (NARM) Independent Country Album of the Year in 1993, for *Feelin' Good, Gittin' Up, Gittin' Down.* —*Bob Paxman*

REPRESENTATIVE RECORDINGS

The Geezinslaws World Tour (Step One, 1990); *Feelin' Good, Gittin' Up, Gittin' Down* (Step One, 1993); *Blah Blah Blah* (Step One, 1996)

Gennett Records
established in Richmond, Indiana, 1919; ended 1934

Gennett Records was formed as a subsidiary of the Starr Piano Company of Richmond, Indiana, which had marketed vertically cut Starr records as early as 1915. When the Gennett label (named after the family who owned Starr) appeared on some lateral-cut releases in 1919, the Victor Talking Machine Company sued, contending that the Gennett product was in violation of jointly owned Victor/COLUMBIA patents. A decision in Starr's favor made it possible for Gennett, OKEH, BRUNSWICK, and a host of smaller labels to compete for customers with conventionally produced discs.

Gennett's earliest records were made in New York. Studios in its Richmond factory went into operation in 1921. A few fiddlers, notably the Tweedy Brothers and William Houchens, recorded some early versions of traditional dance tunes there. When Gennett contracted with the Sears, Roebuck chain to produce records for its budget CHALLENGE and Silvertone labels, the company took a serious interest in country music, which Sears marketed via catalogue sales to its rural customers. In 1928 Supertone replaced Sears's Silvertone label; in 1929 Sears issued some Gennett masters on CONQUEROR.

All were low-priced labels, which usually disguised performer identities with pseudonyms. Together with Champion, Gennett's own discount label, these labels were responsible for hundreds of country releases in the late 1920s. Artists such as BRADLEY KINCAID, ARKIE THE ARKANSAS WOODCHOPPER, and others associated with Sears's radio station WLS in Chicago were prominently featured, but Gennett also sought out regional performers from nearby rural Kentucky, such as FIDDLIN' DOC ROBERTS, Asa Martin, and Taylor's Kentucky Boys. Other contacts brought performers such as the Red Fox Chasers (North Carolina), Fiddlin' Sam Long (Arkansas), and DA COSTA WOLTZ'S SOUTHERN BROADCASTERS (North Carolina) from farther away.

In 1930 the Sears agreement was terminated, as was the Gennett label itself, except for a profitable sound-effects series. However, the company kept Champion and a new Superior label active, recording CLIFF CARLISLE, GENE

AUTRY, the Tobacco Tags, LEW CHILDRE, and a host of stringbands before closing down commercial record production in 1934.

DECCA purchased the Champion name and selected masters in 1935, mixing items from the original catalogue with new releases for a few months. The label was permanently retired early in 1936. The Gennett name was revived briefly by producer Joe Davis during World War II, when he made temporary use of the Richmond factory for pressing. The Starr Piano Company finally closed in 1952.

—Dick Spottswood

Bobbie Gentry
b. Chickasaw County, Mississippi, July 27, 1944

Best known as writer and performer of the 1967 country-pop smash "Ode to Billie Joe," Bobbie Gentry began writing songs at age seven. She was born Roberta Streeter and taught herself to play piano on her grandmother's upright. Her family moved to California when Gentry was thirteen, and she went on to study philosophy at UCLA and music at the Los Angeles Conservatory.

Working as a secretary, nightclub singer, and Las Vegas dancer, Gentry was finally able to cut "Ode to Billie Joe" as her first recording with CAPITOL. The record had a sparse and haunting sound, with Gentry's bluesy voice and guitar accompanied by strings. It topped the pop charts for four weeks and also made the country Top Twenty. Gentry won three Grammy awards, the ACM named her its Top New Female Vocalist of 1967, and the CMA chose her to co-host its first awards show, also in 1967. Gentry subsequently recorded several successful duets with GLEN CAMPBELL, including "Let It Be Me" (1969).

A prolific writer, Gentry's material typically displayed her characteristic drawling phrasing, delta-tinged melodies, and vivid southern imagery. She further explored the seamy side of life in songs such as "Fancy" (1969–70), also a 1991 hit for REBA MCENTIRE.

Having produced many of her own records, Gentry went on to produce a Las Vegas nightclub revue. Television tried to tap her talent, but her 1974 program the *Bobbie Gentry Show* (also known as as *Bobbie Gentry's Happiness*) on CBS aired only four episodes. "Ode to Billie Joe" inspired a TV movie by the same title in 1976.

Gentry's marriage to JIM STAFFORD in 1978 lasted eleven months.

—Mary A. Bufwack

REPRESENTATIVE RECORDING
Bobbie Gentry's Greatest Hits (Capitol, 1969)

The Georgia Yellow Hammers
George Oscar "Uncle Bud" Landress b. Gwinnett County, Georgia, May 2, 1881; d. May 14, 1966
William Hewlett "Bill" Chitwood b. Resaca, Georgia, June 30, 1888; d. March 3, 1961
Charles Ernest "C. E." Moody b. Calhoun County, Georgia, October 8, 1891; d. June 1977
Phil Reeve b. 1896; d. 1949

The Georgia Yellow Hammers were an old-time stringband active in Calhoun County in rural North Georgia during the mid- and late 1920s. They were distinguished from other similar groups by their strong singing and original songs. Their primary personnel included Uncle Bud Landress (banjo, fiddle, vocals), Bill Chitwood (fiddle, vocals), Phil Reeve (guitar, vocal), and C. E. Moody (ukulele, banjo, guitar, vocals). Moody was a particularly gifted songwriter who earlier had composed "Kneel at the Cross," "Drifting Too Far from the Shore," and other gospel songs. In addition to original songs, the Georgia Yellow Hammers also recorded comedy skits, gospel quartets, sentimental songs, blues, pop songs, and fiddle breakdowns. Their most successful recording was "Picture on the Wall"/"My Carolina Girl," which sold in excess of 100,000 copies. Primarily a studio group, they recorded in various combinations from 1924 to 1929 for several companies, using a number of different names. Among these were Bill Chitwood & His Georgia Mountaineers and the Turkey Mountain Singers. Occasional personnel on their sessions included Andrew Baxter (fiddle), Clyde Evans (guitar, vocal), Melvin Dupree (guitar), and Elias Meadows (vocals).

—John Lilly

REPRESENTATIVE RECORDING
The Moonshine Hollow Band (Rounder, 1979)

Giant Records
established 1989; Nashville office established 1991

Small company, big presence. That was JAMES STROUD's goal when he took the job as president of Giant Records' then new Nashville operation in the fall of 1991. A successful independent producer, Stroud came into the employ of Irving Azoff (best known as the manager of the EAGLES), who founded the label in 1989.

Giant's first country release came on April 1, 1992, when the company shipped Dennis Robbins's "Home Sweet Home," but it wasn't until the following year that Giant hit the big time. CARLENE CARTER's "Every Little Thing" became the label's first bona fide hit record, rising to #3, while CLAY WALKER's "What's It to You," produced by Stroud, became Giant's first #1 single. Meanwhile, the label found success with *Common Thread: The Songs of the Eagles* (1993), a 3-million-selling tribute album that featured EAGLES remakes recorded by the likes of ALAN JACKSON, LORRIE MORGAN, and DIAMOND RIO, among others.

From the beginning, Stroud adopted something of a "boutique" approach, articulating a desire to keep the roster small but manageable. Giant has concentrated primarily on acts that can test the boundaries of the country format—MARK COLLIE, DEBORAH ALLEN, Daron Norwood, Carter—with decent results, though the label has not attained the stature its name might imply. In 1997 Doug Johnson replaced Stroud, who had moved to Dreamworks SKG.

—Tom Roland

Terri Gibbs
b. Miami, Florida, June 15, 1954

In 1981 Terri Gibbs became the first artist ever to win the COUNTRY MUSIC ASSOCIATION's Horizon Award for up-and-coming performers (later won by the JUDDS, RANDY TRAVIS, and GARTH BROOKS). The previous year she had won the ACADEMY OF COUNTRY MUSIC's Best New Female Vocalist Award.

Born Teresa Fay Gibbs, she lost her sight as a newborn in an incubator accident. After graduation in 1972 from

Butler High School in Augusta, Georgia, the bluesy-timbred alto vocalist and keyboard player began to make local, independently produced records and to appear on Augusta-area country music shows. Her early group, the Terri Gibbs Trio, included guitarist Warren Gowers, who later recorded with many country stars and toured as a sideman with RONNIE MILSAP.

In about 1979, Nashville songwriter–record producer Ed Penney heard one of Gibbs's demonstration tapes and eventually tracked her to a Steak and Ale restaurant in Augusta, where she had a regular lounge gig. Penney talked MCA's Nashville chief JIM FOGLESONG into hearing Gibbs at the Augusta restaurant and signing her to the label. That led to Penney producing Gibbs's breakthrough 1980 single "Somebody's Knockin'" (coauthored by Penney and Jerry Gillespie) as well as the 1981 album by the same title. That first single hit #8 on the *Billboard* charts and became her biggest hit to date.

Gibbs recorded three more albums for MCA—*I'm a Lady* (1981), *Some Days It Rains All Night Long* (1982), and *Over Easy* (1983)—which yielded eight more hits for the country charts. Gibbs left MCA and made one album, *Old Friends* (1985), and three more chart hits for WARNER BROS. RECORDS before switching to gospel music and recording two albums for Canaan Records, *Turnaround* (1987) and *Comfort the People* (1988), and one for the Morning Gate label, *What a Great Day* (1990). *Turnaround* was nominated for a Grammy Award in 1988. Married on April 28, 1988, to Grovetown, Georgia, city councilman David Daughtry, Gibbs still tours nationally, performing gospel music.

—*Don Rhodes*

REPRESENTATIVE RECORDING

The Best of Terri Gibbs (MCA, 1985)

Don Gibson

b. Shelby, North Carolina, April 3, 1928

Don Gibson might or might not have been thinking of himself when he wrote his 1960 song "(I'd Be) A Legend in My Time," but the title is an apt description of his own career. He has been responsible for writing at least three of the most famous songs in country music history, for helping to define the sound and studio style of modern country music, and for releasing more than seventy charted records between 1956 and 1980. "I consider myself a songwriter who sings rather than a singer who writes songs," Gibson has said, and as late as 1986 he estimated he had as many as 150 to 175 "working songs"—songs that were still performed enough to earn him regular royalties. In addition, as a singer, between 1949 and 1985 he had recorded 513 titles on a range of labels that included MERCURY, COLUMBIA, RCA VICTOR, HICKORY, MGM, and K-Tel. When all the data are in, historians may be hard pressed on just how to catalogue this remarkable talent.

Born Donald Eugene Gibson in Shelby, North Carolina, Gibson got his start with a local band called the Sons of the Soil on Shelby station WHOS. In 1949 he made his first recording with them, a Mercury side called "Automatic Mama." By 1952 he had gotten a job at Knoxville's WNOX and was recording for Columbia. His recordings for this label were not commercially successful, but he was discovering he had a knack for songwriting. By 1955 Gibson had written his first masterpiece, "Sweet Dreams," later to be a hit for Gibson, FARON YOUNG, and PATSY CLINE. It

Don Gibson

won him a songwriter's contract with ACUFF-ROSE PUBLICATIONS and a recording deal with MGM. Then, in 1957, while living in a trailer park north of Knoxville, he wrote his other two career songs on the same day: "Oh Lonesome Me" and "I Can't Stop Loving You." (The latter would eventually be recorded more than 700 times by singers in many music genres and sell more than 30 million records worldwide.)

In 1957 Gibson traveled back to Nashville to record "Oh Lonesome Me" for RCA. He and producer CHET ATKINS decided to abandon the traditional steel guitar and fiddle and use a new sound featuring only guitars, a piano, a drummer, upright bass, and background singers. It became one of the first examples of what would be called the NASHVILLE SOUND and won Gibson a #1 hit; it also set the pattern for a long series of other RCA hits, including "Blue Blue Day" (1958), "Who Cares" (1959), "Sea of Heartbreak" (1961), and "Rings of Gold" (1969). These accomplishments were even more remarkable because Gibson achieved them while suffering from personal problems and drug abuse. By 1967 he had married Bobbi Patterson and was making a fresh start with Hickory Records, moved to Nashville, and once again began to concentrate on his first love, songwriting. He was inducted into the Nashville Songwriters Hall of Fame in 1973 and has repeatedly been nominated for the COUNTRY MUSIC HALL OF FAME.

—*Stacey Wolfe*

REPRESENTATIVE RECORDINGS

All-Time Greatest Hits (RCA, 1990); *18 Greatest Hits* (Curb, 1990); *The Singer, The Songwriter, 1949–1960* (Bear Family), 6 discs

Steve Gibson

b. Peoria, Illinois, July 31, 1952

During his more than twenty-five years in Nashville, session guitarist–producer Steven D. Gibson has played on nearly 12,000 recording sessions. More recently he has spent most of his time producing records for MICHAEL JOHNSON, AARON TIPPIN, MCBRIDE & THE RIDE, Pearl River, Kim Carnes, MICHAEL MARTIN MURPHEY, and others.

Gibson's parents, Chet and Grace Gibson, owned Golden Voice Recording Studio in Pekin, Illinois, and from an early age Steve was encouraged to develop his own talents in the studio. By age twelve he was being paid to play guitar, and at fourteen he recorded his first record. Gibson gained steady session and production work in Peoria before moving to Nashville in 1972. After landing early work on jingles, his first big break came playing guitar on friend Dave Loggins's 1974 pop hit "Please Come to Boston"; soon after came work with Nashville-recorded pop acts such as Dr. Hook and England Dan & John Ford Coley. Since then Gibson has played on records for RANDY TRAVIS, ALABAMA, GEORGE STRAIT, KENNY ROGERS, GEORGE JONES, CLINT BLACK, REBA MCENTIRE, WYNONNA, LORRIE MORGAN, RONNIE MILSAP, TAMMY WYNETTE, ROY ORBISON, ELVIS PRESLEY, JOHN MICHAEL MONTGOMERY, and many, many others. On the basis of how many country hits he had played on, *Music Row* magazine named Gibson the Top Session Guitarist from 1989 to 1992.   —*Michael Hight*

The Gibson/Miller Band

Dave Lowell Gibson b. El Dorado, Arkansas, October 1, 1956

Blue Miller (born William Mueller) b. Detroit, Michigan, July 15, 1952

Mike Daly b. Cleveland, Ohio, June 11, 1955

Steve Grossman b. West Ipswich, New York, April 3, 1962

Bryan Grassmeyer b. Nebraska, June 6, 1954

Doug Kahan b. Detroit, Michigan, January 30, 1956

The Gibson/Miller Band combined songwriter Dave Gibson's country vocals with the classic rock guitar of former Bob Seger guitarist Blue Miller. After being introduced in 1989 by EPIC RECORDS executive Doug Johnson, the two assembled a band that included veteran road musicians Mike Daly (steel guitar), Steve Grossman (drums), and Bryan Grassmeyer (bass). Gibson's songwriting credits include "Ships That Don't Come In" (JOE DIFFIE), "Jukebox in My Mind" (ALABAMA), "If It Don't Come Easy" (TANYA TUCKER), "Queen of Memphis" and "Daddy Never Was the Cadillac Kind" (CONFEDERATE RAILROAD), and "Do You Know Where Your Man Is" (PAM TILLIS). In addition to his work with Seger and rhythm & blues legend Isaac Hayes, Miller has worked on numerous national commercial jingles.

With an aggressive sound, "Big Heart"—the first single from the 1992 debut album, *Where There's Smoke*—received a mixed reception in radio, with many programmers perceiving the band as leaning too far toward rock. Although the "Big Heart" reached the Top Forty on *Billboard*'s country chart, the band fared slightly better with the more restrained "High Rollin'," "A Small Price," and "Texas Tattoo."

Grassmeyer left the band in 1992, to be replaced by Doug Kahan. A second album, *Red, White, and Blue Collar*, was released in 1993. Although the band was named the ACADEMY OF COUNTRY MUSIC's Best New Group or Duo in 1994, Gibson quit the band later that year, expressing a desire to take a more traditional country route as a solo artist. After Gibson's departure, Epic dropped the act from its roster. Miller continued to work as a songwriter, producer, and session musician. Following the band's breakup, the other members quickly found work on the road and in the studio with top country acts.   —*Calvin Gilbert*

REPRESENTATIVE RECORDINGS

Where There's Smoke (Epic, 1992); *Red, White, and Blue Collar* (Epic, 1993)

Vince Gill

b. Norman, Oklahoma, April 12, 1957

With an aching tenor, award-winning songwriting skills, and virtuoso guitar chops that rival those of any ace Nashville session player, Vince Gill is one of today's biggest country superstars. His easygoing demeanor, accessibility, and penchant for charitable causes have also made him one of MUSIC CITY's most well-liked insiders. Gill, however, was no overnight success, having spent a number of years paying dues before he found solo stardom. Ever since his 1989 breakthrough album *When I Call Your Name*, he has reigned as a major commercial and critical force. As evidence of his industry stature, he's racked up a room full of awards, including eleven Grammys and seventeen awards from the COUNTRY MUSIC ASSOCIATION (two of which were for Entertainer of the Year).

Vincent Grant Gill was born and raised in Norman, Oklahoma. Through his federal appellate court judge father, Gill received his introduction to what would become the two greatest passions of his life—music and golf. A talented athlete who at one time considered a career as a professional golfer, Gill also proved a precocious bluegrass student. He learned BANJO from his dad and soon became proficient on a number of stringed instruments, including GUITAR. In high school he played with Mountain Smoke, an outfit that went on to play an ill-fated opening gig for the theatrical rock band KISS.

Vince Gill

Playing a progressive form of BLUEGRASS known as "new grass," Gill began to perform in a series of bands. After high school he joined the BLUEGRASS ALLIANCE and briefly relocated to Kentucky in 1975. While there he also played in the band Boone Creek with future country/bluegrass star RICKY SKAGGS.

In 1976 Gill moved to Los Angeles, where he played with bluegrass fiddler BYRON BERLINE in Sundance. After several years he joined the country-pop act PURE PRAIRIE LEAGUE and recorded three albums with the group. His stint with the outfit led to Gill singing lead on the band's 1980 pop hit "Let Me Love You Tonight."

Gill married Janis Oliver on April 12, 1980, and their only child, Jenifer, was born May 5, 1982. In the mid-1980s Janis and her sister Kristine formed the duo SWEETHEARTS OF THE RODEO, and for a time Janis's commercial success outshone that of her husband.

After leaving Pure Prairie League, Gill hooked up with then-married singer-songwriters ROSANNE CASH and RODNEY CROWELL, two musicians on the leading edge of progressive country. Gill became a respected guitarist in Crowell's backing band the Cherry Bombs, an outfit that included, at different times, future powerhouse country producers EMORY GORDY JR. and RICHARD BENNETT. Playing extensive live dates with the band, Gill also began to refine his songwriting skills.

In the Cherry Bombs, Gill also played with TONY BROWN, the man who would later become the key figure in Gill's eventual solo breakthrough. (A keyboardist who played with, among others, ELVIS PRESLEY, Brown has subsequently become a major figure in Nashville as both producer and record label honcho, and is currently the president of MCA NASHVILLE.) In 1983 Brown had become, for the second time, an A&R man at RCA; he signed Gill. Shortly thereafter, Brown left the label to work at MCA.

At RCA, Gill recorded three releases. His six-song debut LP *Turn Me Loose* (1984) was followed by *The Things That Matter* (1985) and *The Way Back Home* (1987). During his tenure at RCA Gill managed to chart several singles, including the Top Ten 1985 entries "Oklahoma Borderline" and a duet with Rosanne Cash, "If It Weren't for Him." Despite this occasional chart action, Gill continued to languish as a solo artist, unable to break big enough to establish himself as a bona fide star.

Gill also logged a long tour of duty as a session player, recording with the likes of REBA MCENTIRE, EMMYLOU HARRIS, Rosanne Cash, and Bonnie Raitt. He also recorded with the English rock band Dire Straits, and was invited by singer-guitarist Mark Knopfler to join the band. Gill declined and continued to pursue a solo career.

After leaving RCA, Gill signed on with his old pal Brown at MCA. The music, chemistry, and timing coincided at last. With Brown as producer, Gill's MCA debut album *When I Call Your Name* (1989) eventually sold 1 million copies. The title track, a wistful steel guitar and piano ballad with plaintive harmonies from singer PATTY LOVELESS, spotlighted Gill's wistful tenor and rocketed him to solo stardom.

Gill's hit album streak continued, making him a top concert draw. He followed his MCA debut with *Pocket Full of Gold* (1991), which yielded hit singles such as the country-rocking "Liza Jane" and the tender love ballad "Look at Us." His next album, *I Still Believe in You* (1992), continued to prominently feature the winning Gill formula—ballads that highlighted his sensitive vocal side, and sprightly country-pop rockers, such as "One More Last Chance,"

that showcased his impressive guitar skills. His 1994 album *When Love Finds You* produced six singles, including "Go Rest High on That Mountain." *Tennessean* music columnist Jay Orr reported that Gill composed this inspiring song reflecting over the deaths of singer KEITH WHITLEY and Gill's halfbrother Bob Cohen, who had died about two years prior. "Go Rest High on That Mountain" eventually earned Gill a 1996 CMA Award for Song of the Year.

Although Gill's mix of pop, country, and rock influences are evident on all of his recordings, the release *High Lonesome Sound* (1996) included some older influences. While many of the tracks have been recorded in the contemporary adult country-pop vein, the title track featured a return to his new grass roots (with harmony vocals by bluegrass-country star ALISON KRAUSS). Also in 1996, Gill's wife Janis filed for divorce.

Gill seems to have taken the career lows and highs all in his laid-back stride. A photo of the man is just as likely to show him with a golfclub in his hand as a guitar. But don't let the mellow demeanor fool you; Gill gets a lot done. On the personal front, he has long been an active participant in charitable causes, activities that earned him the Kiwanis Club's 1994 Outstanding Nashvillian award.

On the career side of the equation, he's a star who can fill arenas, a singer who can effectively croon a love ballad, a picker overshadowed by few, and a songwriter with talent. He's also a several-times CMA awards show host who never gets flustered. On those nights, Gill never breaks a sweat pulling double duty—both handing out statuettes and receiving them.
—*Chris Dickinson*

REPRESENTATIVE RECORDINGS

When I Call Your Name (MCA, 1989); *Pocket Full of Gold* (MCA, 1991); *I Still Believe in You* (MCA, 1992); *When Love Finds You* (MCA, 1994); *The Essential Vince Gill* (RCA, 1995); *High Lonesome Sound* (MCA, 1996)

Lee Gillette
b. Indianapolis, Indiana, October 30, 1912; d. August 20, 1981

Aside from co-founder Johnny Mercer, Lee Gillette was CAPITOL RECORDS' first A&R man. His pioneering work with the label in both country and pop music established the label's musical identity for the first twenty years of its existence.

Leland James Gillette grew up working on the Chicago pop music scene, singing and playing drums. He often worked with teenage friend KEN NELSON, who had already gained experience in song publishing during the 1920s and 1930s. Gillette, working as a drummer, had visited Hollywood and met record store owner Glenn Wallichs. In 1944 Wallichs, by then co-founder of the two-year-old Capitol label, hired Gillette as head of country A&R. Gillette signed some of Capitol's greatest postwar country acts—among them were JACK GUTHRIE, MERLE TRAVIS, JIMMY WAKELY, TEX WILLIAMS, and TENNESSEE ERNIE FORD—and produced hits with all of them until he moved to pop A&R in 1950. Ken Nelson took over country. Ford was the only country artist Gillette continued to produce. As co-owner of the CENTRAL SONGS publishing company with CLIFFIE STONE and Ken Nelson, Gillette helped to organize the National Academy of Recording Arts and Sciences (NARAS).

After Nat King Cole's 1965 death, Gillette was devastated over the loss of his friend and took early retirement from Capitol to travel and occasionally produce independently. He died three weeks after suffering a serious fall at his California home in August 1981.   —*Rich Kienzle*

Mickey Gilley
b. Natchez, Mississippi, March 9, 1936

Mickey Leroy Gilley comes from a famous family. His first cousin Jimmy Lee Swaggart became an infamous TV evangelist, and another first cousin, JERRY LEE LEWIS, became a rock & roll music pioneer and later a country star. Gilley made his mark remaking old country and pop ballads and as co-owner of GILLEY'S, his 48,000-square foot nightclub in Pasadena, Texas.

In 1970, a millionaire ex-welder named Sherwood Cryer talked Gilley into becoming business partners in a nightclub they named Gilley's. Up to that point, Gilley had recorded briefly for DOT RECORDS and had lived in Louisiana and Mississippi before moving to Pasadena. In 1974 Gilley recorded a single on his own Astro label, pairing the 1964 PATSY CLINE hit "She Called Me Baby (All Night Long)" for the A-side and the 1949 GEORGE MORGAN hit "Room Full of Roses" for the flip side. When the B-side started getting airplay, Hugh Hefner's Playboy Records rereleased the disc, and "Room Full of Roses" became Gilley's first #1 country hit in 1974.

Sixteen more #1 hits followed for Playboy and later for EPIC RECORDS, including "I Overlooked an Orchid (While Searching for a Rose)" (1974), "Don't the Girls All Get Prettier at Closing Time" (1976), "True Love Ways," "Stand by Me," and "That's All That Matters to Me" (all in 1980), and a duet with CHARLY MCCLAIN, "Paradise Tonight" (1983).

After winning the ACM's Top New Male Vocalist award in 1974, Gilley experienced his biggest year of accolades in 1976, winning the Most Promising Male Artist award from *Music City News* in 1976 and four awards from the ACM: Entertainer of the Year, Top Male Vocalist, Single of the Year ("Bring It on Home"), and Album of the Year (*Gilley's Smoking*).

Gilley parted acrimoniously from Cryer in the late

1980s; a Houston court awarded Gilley $17 million in damages from Cryer in July 1988. Two years later, Gilley was back in the country building business—this time opening the Mickey Gilley Theater in BRANSON, Missouri, on April 27, 1990. The success of that showplace resulted in the adjacent Gilley's Texas Cafe opening in 1992 and another Gilley's Texas Cafe opening in 1995 in Myrtle Beach, South Carolina.

In his spare time Gilley has acted on the TV series *Murder, She Wrote, Fantasy Island, CHIPS, Fall Guy*, and *Dukes of Hazzard.*   —*Don Rhodes*

REPRESENTATIVE RECORDINGS

Mickey Gilley—Ten Years of Hits (Epic, 1984); *Fool for Your Love* (Epic, 1983)

Gilley's
established in Pasadena, Texas, 1971; closed 1989

In its late seventies to early eighties heyday, Gilley's nightclub was a symbol of country music's growing popularity and potential for mass appeal. Singer MICKEY GILLEY and manager Sherwood Cryer opened Gilley's in 1971 on the site of a former nightclub known as Shelley's. Catering to the young, well-paid, and restless workers in the desolate, east-of-Houston oil refinery suburb of Pasadena, Gilley's started out as a local bar and dance hall with a capacity of 750 people. Extensive expansion followed, and for a while, prior to the opening of Billy Bob's in Fort Worth, Gilley's was the world's largest honky-tonk, encompassing more than 48,000 square feet and accommodating crowds of up to 5,000 people on its parquet dance floor. Attractions included not only Mickey Gilley himself and other country stars, but also a shooting gallery, pool tables, a sledgehammer strength test, and a mechanical bull ($2 a ride).

Gilley's was introduced as a cultural phenomenon to the noncountry populace through Aaron Latham's article in *Esquire* magazine (September 12, 1978). A successful movie *(Urban Cowboy)*, filmed largely in and around Gilley's, and starring John Travolta and Debra Winger, followed in 1980.

The club, its mechanical bull, and the whole romantic Hollywood version of the country music milieu rose to fantastic, if short-lived popularity. Modeled on more practical scales after this idealized Gilley's, cowboy-themed nightclubs with wooden dance floors opened in such disparate places as New York City and Washington, D.C., during the country craze. When the *Urban Cowboy* fad predictably ended by the mid-eighties, the business failed, Gilley's closed (in 1989), acrimonious lawsuits followed, and the building mysteriously burned down.   —*Bob Millard*

Jimmie Dale Gilmore
b. Amarillo, Texas, May 6, 1945

Jimmie Dale Gilmore is one of contemporary country's most original and affecting stylists. Gilmore is a uniquely ethereal yet twangy singer, and his songwriting reflects the blend of traditional country and eastern philosophy he's pursued since the late sixties—a seemingly unlikely combination that's cohesive, articulate, and quite popular.

Gilmore was raised in Tulia, Texas; early musical influences included HANK WILLIAMS, LEFTY FRIZZELL, the MAD-

Mickey Gilley

DOX BROTHERS & ROSE, and his father's HONKY-TONK band. "The radio was playing a lot when I was growing up in the late forties, early fifties," Gilmore once explained. "I was a fluke in that I didn't come to country music because of BOB DYLAN and the whole folk movement. . . . I am a traditionalist, but the tradition that I come out of is country and rock radio."

Moving to Lubbock, Gilmore took violin and trombone lessons, learned guitar at sixteen, and began performing mainstream country. He became strongly influenced by such noncommercial, country-tinged songwriters as TOWNES VAN ZANDT and Lubbock artist Terry Allen. Soon Gilmore was writing as well, penning such signature numbers as "Treat Me Like a Saturday Night," "Tonight I Think I'm Gonna Go Downtown," and "Dallas." In 1970 he formed the FLATLANDERS with Tony Pearson, Steve Wesson, and fellow singing-songwriters JOE ELY and BUTCH HANCOCK. This visionary group from Lubbock combined roots-revival instrumentation (including a musical saw) with substantial, creative lyrics. The Flatlanders recorded a fine album in 1972 that was hopelessly at odds with current trends, and then disbanded; they now play occasional reunion concerts in Austin, and a new album is planned.

Gilmore spent the next fifteen years away from the music industry, pursuing such as interests as Buddhism, meditation, and Hindu cosmology. Joe Ely's renditions of his songs kept Gilmore's name in circulation, however, and in 1988 and 1989 Gilmore recorded two progressive-country albums for HIGHTONE. In 1991 Gilmore's *After Awhile,* which focused on his own compositions, established Gilmore as a major artist whose appeal has a distinctly spiritual component; it also inspired the term "sagebrush soul" to describe his style.

Gilmore's subsequent albums, *Spinning 'Round the Sun* and *Braver Newer World,* were both nominated for Grammy Awards in Contemporary Folk. He has also recorded with such diverse artists as WILLIE NELSON, the HACKBERRY RAMBLERS, and Mudhoney. Recently Gilmore has branched into cinema, appearing in feature films such as *The Big Lebowski* and contributing to the soundtrack *Traveler.*

—Ben Sandmel

REPRESENTATIVE RECORDINGS

Fair & Square (HighTone, 1988); *Jimmie Dale Gilmore* (HighTone, 1989); *After Awhile* (Elektra/Nonesuch, 1991); *Spinning 'Round the Sun* (Elektra, 1993); *Braver New World* (Elektra/Asylum, 1996)

Johnny Gimble

b. Tyler, Texas, May 30, 1926

Five-time winner of the CMA Instrumentalist of the Year award, Johnny Gimble is one of country music's best-known sidemen, having appeared on countless recordings from 1948 to the present. He is most recognized as a western swing fiddler and electric mandolinist and has recorded in almost every style and context.

Precociously talented, John Paul Gimble was playing fiddle around Tyler, Texas, alongside his brothers in the Rose City Swingsters by 1940. Inspired by western swing fiddle legends CLIFF BRUNER and J. R. Chatwell, Gimble would become a vastly influential stylist in his own right. By 1944 he was playing banjo in JIMMIE DAVIS's gubernatorial campaign band. After the war Gimble worked with Jesse

Johnny Gimble

James in Austin and formed the Blues Rustlers with his brothers in Goose Creek, Texas, before joining Buck Roberts's Rhythmairs in 1948. Gimble made his recording debut with Roberts, introducing a Gimble trademark: scat singing in unison with his fiddle. Gimble attracted the attention of BOB WILLS and joined the Texas Playboys in California in early 1949.

Gimble worked with Wills until 1951, often playing intricate duets with fellow mandolinist TINY MOORE. Afterward, he worked in Dallas with AL DEXTER and Dewey Groom, waxing numerous sessions as a sideman at JIM BECK's recording studios with MARTY ROBBINS, RAY PRICE, and others. Gimble moved to Waco in 1955, appearing on local TV, with fiddler Jimmy Thomason and others, and barbering for a living. He moved back to Tyler in 1958. Although he worked some on RED FOLEY's *Jubilee, U.S.A* in Springfield, Gimble's career did not really take off until he moved to Nashville in the late sixties. He quickly became an almost ubiquitous session sideman, appearing on thousands of recordings. He also recorded under his own name with his Bosque Bandits, which included son Dick Gimble on bass. Johnny Gimble returned to Texas in the eighties, touring and recording with WILLIE NELSON; he appeared in the Nelson film *Honeysuckle Rose* (1980) and as Bob Wills in Clint Eastwood's *Honky Tonk Man* (1982). He has since proven his place among tireless champions of Texas swing, such as his idols Bruner and Chatwell, and currently co-leads the Wills-revival group Playboys II with steel guitarist HERB REMINGTON. As of this writing Gimble has won CMA's Musician of the Year Award five times.

—Kevin Coffey

REPRESENTATIVE RECORDINGS

Bob Wills: Papa's Jumpin (Bear Family, 1985); *Johnny Gimble: The Texas Fiddle Collection* (CMH, 1981); *Johnny Gimble & the Texas Swing Pioneers: Still Swingin'* (CMH, 1980)

The Girls of the Golden West

Mildred Fern Goad ("Millie Good") b. Mount Carmel, Illinois,
April 11, 1913; d. May 2, 1993
Dorothy Lavern Goad ("Dollie Good") b. Mount Carmel, Illinois,
December 11, 1915; d. November 12, 1967

Probably the only country music duo named after a grand opera (Puccini, 1910), the Girls of the Golden West were also the first nationally successful all-woman act in country. To say they were a female version of the BLUE SKY BOYS is accurate but incomplete; they did indeed sing a lot of sentimental songs in incredibly close harmony, but they also specialized in western songs and perfected the trick of doing yodeling and falsetto in harmony. Though they set the stage for later groups such as SWEETHEARTS OF THE RODEO and the JUDDS, there has been nothing quite like them before or since.

For decades the WLS publicity machine made much of the fact that Millie and Dollie were from Muleshoe, Texas, and that their last name was Good, misnomers that still find their way into sloppy reference books today. Good was actually a stage name, and the sisters, in fact, were born in Illinois and grew up around the St. Louis area and in downstate Illinois. Though their mother was a singer of old ballads, the sisters found their harmony by accident; Millie explained, "When I hear a note, I automatically hear the harmony to it." Soon they found work over St. Louis radio stations, and then border station XER. By the time they came to WLS in 1933, they had found their new name and had had their mother sew for them the first in a series of stylish "cowgirl" costumes.

In 1933 they began recording for BLUEBIRD, having hits such as "Old Chisholm Trail," "Cowboy Jack," and "My Love Is a Rider." Eventually their biggest hit would be a 1938 ARC side, "There's a Silver Moon on the Golden Gate." Needing material that was from a female perspective, they began writing their own songs, and getting others from fellow WLS mates PATSY MONTANA and Lucille Overstake. Fans watched the sisters grow up on the air, and showered them with gifts when both married in the late 1930s: Dollie to PRAIRIE RAMBLERS fiddler Tex Atchison and Millie to announcer-promoter Bill McCluskey. By 1945 the Girls had relocated to WLW in Cincinnati, and they retired in about 1949. In 1963 they reunited for a series of albums on the Bluebonnet label. Dollie passed away in 1967, and Millie followed in 1993.   —*Charles Wolfe*

REPRESENTATIVE RECORDING

Girls of the Golden West (Sonyatone, 1977)

The Glaser Brothers

Thomas Paul Glaser b. Spalding, Nebraska, September 3, 1933
James William Glaser b. Spalding, Nebraska, December 16, 1937
Charles Glaser b. Spalding, Nebraska, February 27, 1936

Best known to country audiences today for Tompall Glaser's music having been part of RCA's epochal *Wanted: The Outlaws* album (1976), the Glaser Brothers were prominent country performers of the 1960s and 1970s. After appearing on Arthur Godfrey's popular television show in the late 1950s, they moved to Nashville, where success initially eluded them. They worked as session players, were recorded as a folk music act for DECCA RECORDS (with OWEN BRADLEY as producer), toured with MARTY ROBBINS

and with JOHNNY CASH, played the GRAND OLE OPRY, and eventually signed with MGM RECORDS in 1966. On that label they had modest chart hits with producer JACK CLEMENT and were named the CMA's Vocal Group of the Year in 1970. In 1971, "Rings" became their first single to hit the Top Ten.

The brothers eventually made more of a mark in Nashville with their publishing company (John Hartford's "Gentle on My Mind" was an early signing), songwriting (Jim Glaser co-wrote the Gary Puckett pop smash "Woman, Woman"), management careers, and historic recording studio. That studio, at 916 Nineteenth Avenue South, became known as "Hillbilly Central," and it was there that the Outlaw country movement was headquartered. It served as clubhouse for Tompall, who began recording as a solo act, WAYLON JENNINGS, BOBBY BARE, KRIS KRISTOFFERSON, KINKY FRIEDMAN & His Texas Jewboys (who were managed by Chuck Glaser), BILLY JOE SHAVER, and any number of self-proclaimed outlaws.

As a performing group, the Glaser Brothers (sometimes billed as "Tompall & The Glaser Brothers") broke up in 1973, were reunited in 1980, scored a #2 hit with Kristofferson's "Lovin' Her Was Easier (Than Anything I'll Ever Do Again)" in 1981, and finally retired in 1982. Chuck Glaser was sidelined by a stroke in 1975 but recovered within two years. Jim Glaser, who had recorded as a solo act in the 1960s and 1970s with little success, enjoyed a brief run of hits during the 1980s, including the 1984 chart-topper "You're Gettin' to Me Again."   —*Chet Flippo*

REPRESENTATIVE RECORDINGS

This Land—Folk Songs by Tompall and the Glaser Brothers (Decca, 1960); *The Wonderful World of the Glaser Brothers* (MGM, 1968); Tompall Glaser, *Charlie* (MGM, 1973); *After All These Years* (Elektra, 1982)

Lonnie Glosson

b. Judsonia, Arkansas, February 14, 1908

A talented harmonica player, guitarist, singer, and songwriter, Lonnie Glosson was one of the most popular country music disc jockeys during the late 1940s.

Taught the rudiments of the harmonica by his mother, Glosson hoboed throughout the South and Midwest before beginning his musical career in 1925 with KMOX in St. Louis. He later moved to Chicago to join the cast of WLS's *NATIONAL BARN DANCE* and afterward was featured on the *Suppertime Frolic* program on Chicago's WJJD. His first recordings were issued in 1932 on Paramount's Broadway label. Glosson's 1936 recording of "Arkansas Hard Luck Blues" for ARC was an early example of the "talking blues" style later adopted by WOODY GUTHRIE and BOB DYLAN.

Glosson moved to California in 1934 to work for a Los Angeles radio station but soon returned to the Midwest as the MC for the *RENFRO VALLEY BARN DANCE*. In 1936 Glosson and WAYNE RANEY began a long musical partnership, fueled by the younger Raney's longstanding admiration for Glosson's harmonica style; in 1938 the two harmonica players teamed up briefly for a regular program at KARK in Little Rock. During the late 1940s the pair had a nationally syndicated radio program broadcast from WCKY in Cincinnati, and they also backed the DELMORE BROTHERS on several recordings for KING RECORDS, including "Blues Stay Away from Me." Glosson recorded for DECCA and MERCURY during this period. In 1949 he became one of the first country performers to work in Atlanta television when he hosted a program for WSB.

After parting company with Raney in 1960, Glosson remained active as a solo performer in the United States and Europe.

—*Kim Field*

REPRESENTATIVE RECORDING

The Living Legend (Old Homestead, 1982)

Henry Glover

b. Hot Springs, Arkansas, May 21, 1921; d. April 7, 1991

Henry Bernard Glover was country music's first major African-American executive, whose work helped pave the way for the rise of rock & roll in the mid-1950s. He received extensive formal musical education during high school in Hot Springs and at Alabama A&M in Huntsville, where he graduated in 1943. For a time he pursued a master's program in political science at Wayne State University in Detroit, but dropped out to work with bands led by Buddy Johnson, Tiny Bradshaw, and Lucky Millinder. While with Millinder, in about 1945, he began to produce Bull Moose Jackson, Millinder's vocalist at the time, as a separate act for Cincinnati-based KING RECORDS.

Glover wrote and produced several hits for Jackson, including "I Love You, Yes I Do" in 1947, and King owner SYD NATHAN signed Glover as a producer and songwriter in 1948. Soon Nathan and Glover organized a publishing company, Jay & Cee. In addition to r&b acts such as Bill Doggett and Little Willie John, Glover produced sessions with King's country roster, then including GRANDPA JONES, HAWKSHAW HAWKINS, JIMMIE OSBORNE, and COWBOY COPAS. With the DELMORE BROTHERS Glover wrote and produced the 1949 hit "Blues Stay Away from Me" (based on Glover's "Boardinghouse Blues"). In blending country and r&b sounds, however, Glover found his most consistent success with country star MOON MULLICAN, with whom Glover co-wrote "I'll Sail My Ship Alone," "Rocket to the Moon," "Southern Hospitality," and other songs, many of them derived from r&b hits of the day.

Glover left King in about 1959 and eventually moved to Roulette Records, where he worked with Joey Dee ("Peppermint Twist"), Sarah Vaughn, and other artists. He rejoined the STARDAY-KING organization in about 1968 and managed the New York office of Lin Broadcasting's music division after Lin purchased Starday. When Lin divested itself of its music holdings early in the 1970s, Glover took up independent production. In this regard, his credits include *The Muddy Waters Woodstock Album*, winner of a 1975 Grammy; Paul Butterfield's album *Put It in Your Ear* (1975); and the soundtrack for the Martin Scorsese film *The Last Waltz* (1978), documenting a 1976 concert by The Band. In 1986 Glover was placed on the National Academy of Recording Arts and Sciences (NARAS) Honor Roll of A&R Producers.

—*John Rumble*

George Gobel

b. Chicago, Illinois, May 20, 1919; d. February 24, 1991

George Leslie Gobel was a child star of the WLS NATIONAL BARN DANCE who grew up to become a popular TV comedian. While in grade school, young George began singing in his church choir, and, because of his exceptional voice, he frequently was assigned solo parts.

In 1932, when he was thirteen, Gobel was hired to sing on the WLS *Barn Dance* and other WLS programs. Billed as

the Little Cowboy, he sang a variety of popular songs, including the latest hits from the cowboy genre. Except for brief stints at radio stations WMAQ-Chicago (where he filled the juvenile role on the Tom Mix serial); WDOD–Chattanooga, Tennessee; and KMOX–St. Louis, he was a fixture at WLS for ten years. In 1933 he recorded four sides for ARC, all released on the CONQUEROR label.

In the fall of 1942 Gobel was inducted into the U.S. Army's Flying Cadets in a ceremony that took place on the stage of the *National Barn Dance*. After fulfilling his World War II military duties, he returned to Chicago, where he worked as a stand-up comedian. In the 1950s, while living in Los Angeles, Gobel became one of the most popular comedians on television, appearing on such programs as *The Colgate Comedy Hour, The Spike Jones Show*, and *Who Said That?* From 1957 to 1959 he had his own TV program, called *The George Gobel Show*. His signature expression, "Well, I'll be a dirty bird," entered the popular language of the era. The latter years of Gobel's career found him making guest appearances on television shows, performing in several movies, and entertaining in supper clubs across the country.

—*Wayne W. Daniel*

Bobby Goldsboro

b. Marianna, Florida, January 18, 1941

Successfully bridging the gap between pop and country audiences, Bobby Goldsboro first hit the pop Top Ten in 1964 with "See the Funny Little Clown," then exploded to the #1 spot on both the pop and country charts in 1968 with "Honey."

During a two-year stint at Auburn University, Goldsboro and his group the Webs played at parties. In 1962 they received an offer to go on the road with ROY ORBISON, who later collaborated with Goldsboro on a number of songs. Signed to United Artists, Goldsboro charted with "See the Funny Little Clown" and other self-penned songs, including "Little Things" and "Voodoo Woman" (both 1965). He toured with the Beatles in England and with the Rolling Stones on the group's first American tour.

Goldsboro's career milestone came with "Honey." Written by Bobby Russell, the song spent five weeks atop the pop chart and three at #1 on the country chart. "Watching Scotty Grow" (1970–71), a wistful song of parenting, became another pop-country crossover hit. The singer-songwriter appeared often on network TV shows and starred in his own syndicated TV show from 1972 to 1975, *The Bobby Goldsboro Show*.

A shrewd businessman as well as entertainer, Goldsboro founded House of Gold Music, Inc., which, among other successes, published "Behind Closed Doors," the CHARLIE RICH hit written by Kenny O'Dell that won Song of the Year honors from the CMA in 1973. Among those recording Goldsboro-written songs have been Al Hirt, Vikki Carr, and DOLLY PARTON. More than seventy artists have recorded his song "With Pen in Hand."

—*Gerry Wood*

REPRESENTATIVE RECORDING

The Best of Bobby Goldsboro (Collectables, 1996)

Emory Gordy Jr.

b. Atlanta, Georgia, December 25, 1944

Emory Gordy Jr. has been a highly sought-after musician and record producer for more than three decades. After playing bass on recordings for such acts as ELVIS PRESLEY, Tom Petty, Neil Diamond, and Billy Joel, Gordy ventured to the other side of the glass to produce such acts as STEVE EARLE; ALABAMA; AARON TIPPIN; BILL MONROE; JIMMIE DALE GILMORE; and Gordy's wife, PATTY LOVELESS.

Gordy began playing the bass at age eighteen and received his big break in 1964, when he was asked to be in the rhythm section for Tommy Roe, who was accompanied by JOE SOUTH. About one week later, South asked Gordy to play on a session. Gordy subsequently recorded with acts such as BILLY JOE ROYAL, MAC DAVIS, and the Tams. Gordy also co-wrote the Classics IV's 1969 hit "Traces." While in Atlanta he frequently worked for music publisher Bill Lowery.

Gordy moved to Los Angeles in 1970 and joined Neil Diamond's band in 1971. He played nine instruments on Diamond's *Hot August Night,* which established Gordy's reputation as a musician. He played the prominent bass line on Presley's "Burning Love" as well as parts on GRAM PARSONS's *Grievous Angel.* Gordy also produced records by Debbie Reynolds and Liberace. In 1975 Gordy became a charter member of EMMYLOU HARRIS's Hot Band while continuing to record with Diamond, Tom Petty, and the BELLAMY BROTHERS. Gordy played with JOHN DENVER and became a member of RODNEY CROWELL's back-up band the Cherry Bombs, a band that also included VINCE GILL, TONY BROWN, and RICHARD BENNETT.

In 1984 Brown convinced Gordy to work with him in the A&R department at MCA RECORDS in Nashville. It was at MCA that Gordy met Patty Loveless, whom he married on February 6, 1989. During his three years at MCA, he co-produced Steve Earle's *Guitar Town* and *Exit 0,* and he also produced the Grammy-winning Bill Monroe album *Southern Flavor.* He joined Rising Tide as senior vice president of A&R in 1996 and guided the recording careers of DELBERT MCCLINTON, the NITTY GRITTY DIRT BAND, and MATRACA BERG, among others. Rising Tide ceased operations in March 1998.

—*Beverly Keel*

Vern Gosdin
b. Woodland, Alabama, August 5, 1934

....

After an early career in bluegrass and a tangential involvement in the birth of country-rock, Vernon Gosdin finally found his proper role as one of the finest honky-tonk singers of his generation. He has been described as a "neo-traditionalist," but there was nothing "neo" about him because he came from the same generation and influences as GEORGE JONES and MERLE HAGGARD. TAMMY WYNETTE once called him "the only other singer who can hold a candle to George Jones."

Growing up in rural Alabama, Gosdin learned mandolin and formed a fraternal-harmony duo with his brother Rex in the style of their heroes, the BLUE SKY BOYS. Both boys also sang in the Gosdin Brothers quartet with their brother Ray and fiddle champion Chuck Reeves. After detours through Chicago and Atlanta, Vern and Rex reunited in Los Angeles in 1970, where they joined a bluegrass band called the Golden State Boys. The group was renamed the Hillmen after its mandolinist, CHRIS HILLMAN, who later co-founded the FLYING BURRITO BROTHERS and the DESERT ROSE BAND.

More immediately, though, Hillman joined the BYRDS, who launched both the folk-rock and country-rock movements. The Gosdin Brothers shared a manager, Eddie

Vern Gosdin

Tickner, with the Byrds and EMMYLOU HARRIS, so they stayed close to the scene. In 1967, when founder Gene Clark left the Byrds, his first solo album was titled *Gene Clark with the Gosdin Brothers.* That same year the Gosdin Brothers by themselves scored a Top Forty country single, "Hangin' On," on the Bakersfield International Records label. In 1972 Vern and Rex hung up the guitars and took day jobs in Atlanta. Vern, though, decided to give music one more try, in 1976, and convinced his old pal Emmylou Harris to fly to Nashville for a demo session.

That session included a remake of "Hangin' On" and a new song, "Yesterday's Gone." They were good enough to convince ELEKTRA to sign Gosdin as a solo artist, and the songs became country hits. He also had a hit with "Till the End," featuring a then-unknown session singer named JANIE FRICKE. These Elektra years were later reissued on the CD *Warning: Contains Country Music (The Great Ballads of Vern Gosdin).* From Elektra he moved to Ovation Records, then to AMI, where he had a Top Ten hit with "Today My World Slipped Away," and then on to Compleat.

There he began a long-running songwriting partnership with MAX D. BARNES that yielded the Top Ten hits "If You're Gonna Do Me Wrong (Do It Right)" and "Slow Burnin' Memory." The Compleat years also included the Top Five hit "Way Down Deep" and Gosdin's first #1, 1984's "I Can Tell by the Way You Dance." For his 1984 album *There Is a Season,* Vern reunited with the Byrds' Roger McGuinn, who contributed twelve-string electric guitar and harmonies to Gosdin's country remake of the Byrds' "Turn, Turn, Turn." All these Compleat releases have now been reissued on CD as *The Truly Great Hits of Vern Gosdin.*

After Compleat went bankrupt, Gosdin signed with COLUMBIA in 1987. He had success right off the bat with two Gosdin-Barnes compositions, "Do You Believe Me Now" and "Chiseled in Stone." The latter was voted the 1989 CMA Song of the Year. Gosdin also started co-writing with

HANK COCHRAN, and that team authored such Gosdin hits as "Is It Raining at Your House," "Right in the Wrong Direction," "This Ain't My First Rodeo," and the #1 hit "Set 'Em Up Joe." Gosdin also topped the charts with "I'm Still Crazy" from *Alone,* his 1989 autobiographical album about his divorce. Those singles are now available on CD as *Super Hits.* —*Geoffrey Himes*

REPRESENTATIVE RECORDINGS

The Truly Great Hits of Vern Gosdin (American Harvest, 1996); *Super Hits* (Columbia, 1993)

Gospel Music

Several of the many subgenres of gospel music have made a major impact on country music. The classic folk hymns that originated in England or the American frontier (such as "Amazing Grace" or "Rock of Ages") have entered many country repertoires, and have been featured in albums such as TENNESSEE ERNIE FORD's 1956 *Hymns.*

The great revival movements of the nineteenth century generated the so-called gospel hymns, such as "Farther Along" and "Leaning on the Everlasting Arms," common in many country and bluegrass repertoires since the 1930s. African-American sacred composers such as Thomas Dorsey loaned to the genre standards such as RED FOLEY's hit "Peace in the Valley," and the a cappella black quartet movement has heavily influenced bluegrass groups such as BILL MONROE's Blue Grass Quartet, DOYLE LAWSON & QUICKSILVER, and the NASHVILLE BLUEGRASS BAND.

However, the most potent influence on country music was the type of gospel usually referred to as southern gospel, the gospel quartet tradition, or southern singing convention songs. This tradition dates from 1866, when the Ruebush-Kieffer publishing company was founded in Virginia's Shenandoah Valley. This firm issued songbooks, usually full of new compositions, in a seven-shape notation system of buckwheat notes in which the shape of note determined its pitch. The organization also started the South's first Normal Singing School, where people were taught this singing system, and sent traveling teachers around the South. By the turn of the century, graduates of Ruebush-Kieffer had started their own companies and teacher training "normal" schools in Georgia (A. J. Showalter), Texas (Trio, Showalter-Patton), Arkansas (Eureka), and Tennessee (JAMES D. VAUGHAN). Of these, it was Vaughan who soon came to dominate the market; after settling in Lawrenceburg, Tennessee, in 1903, he began publishing songbooks that by 1912 were selling 85,000 copies a year. His songs were picked up by dozens of early country stars, including the Monroe Brothers, the DELMORE BROTHERS, and the CARTER FAMILY; other singers, such as KIRK MCGEE, attended Vaughan normal schools as teenagers. It was also Vaughan who virtually invented the gospel quartet by having employees travel the country singing songs from his latest books to demonstrate them; church congregations and fans soon began enjoying the quartets themselves as much as the songbooks they promoted.

By the late 1920s, quartets were popular enough to go out on their own, giving up the direct sponsorship of their parent companies. The John Daniel Quartet and the Old Hickory Singers are among the groups who started out as Vaughan quartets and eventually won spots on stations such as WSM-Nashville. Probably the first fully independent gospel group was the McDonald Brothers from southern Missouri, who recorded extensively in the 1920s and 1930s. Even more successful was the CHUCK WAGON GANG, the Texas family group who began recording for ARC/COLUMBIA in 1936.

By the 1930s the Vaughan company found itself with a number of new rivals, including STAMPS-BAXTER (Dallas) and Hartford (Arkansas); the latter featured the works of ALBERT E. BRUMLEY, whose works such as "I'll Fly Away" and "I'll Meet You in the Morning" were especially popular with country acts. At about this time, many of the companies began to systematically pitch their songs to radio singers; the firms employed professional song pluggers and even issued special collections of radio favorites. Many of their efforts bore fruit, and soon every country radio show had its "hymn time" where the cast gathered around the microphone to sing a sacred favorite.

By the 1940s some country groups were relying heavily on gospel songs, including the BAILES BROTHERS, the Masters Family, the BROWN's FERRY FOUR, James and MARTHA CARSON, and bluegrass musician CARL STORY. The movement was boosted in the early 1950s with the national fad for what *Billboard* called religioso songs—songs rendered in a pop style but based on religious themes. These included huge best-sellers such as STUART HAMBLEN's "This Ole House" and "It Is No Secret" and Martha Carson's "Satisfied." During the 1950s and 1960s almost every major country singer felt obliged to do at least one all-gospel album, and bluegrass groups, following Bill Monroe's lead, were especially receptive to gospel influences. Gospel quartets such as the Statesmen (from Georgia) and the Blackwood Brothers (from Mississippi) won a national audience, often did shows and albums with Opry stars, and strongly influenced a young ELVIS PRESLEY. By the 1970s country acts were seldom seeing many gospel songs on the actual charts, but by then the music had become entrenched as part of the general core repertoire of many country singers. —*Charles Wolfe*

Billy Grammer

b. Benton, Illinois, August 28, 1925

"Gotta Travel On" put singer Billy Wayne Grammer on the musical map. Adapted from a 150-year-old British folk tune, that October 1958 release landed him on a trio of charts: country (#5), pop (#4), and r&b (#14). In addition, the million-selling record was the first hit for MONUMENT RECORDS and its founder, record producer FRED FOSTER. A 1961 release, "Bonaparte's Retreat" b/w "The Kissing Tree," is estimated to have sold 500,000 units.

The eldest of thirteen children, Grammer began playing guitar at five and from an early age played locally with fiddler father Arch Grammer. Billy Grammer made his radio debut on WJPF–Herrin, Illinois, in 1940. After military service in World War II he worked for CONNIE B. GAY at WARL–Arlington, Virginia. There Grammer performed on JIMMY DEAN's CBS-TV show (1957–58). Grammer joined the GRAND OLE OPRY in 1959, remaining until he lost his eyesight.

He designed the Grammer Flat Top Guitar, donating his first model to the COUNTRY MUSIC HALL OF FAME in 1969. The agile guitarist's sophisticated licks garnered numerous studio sessions with artists such as EDDY ARNOLD, Louis Armstrong, and Patti Page, and inspired other guitarists, such as ROY CLARK. In 1965 Grammer had his own syndicated TV series.

Deeply religious, Grammer delivered the invocation for the Grand Ole Opry House opening on March 16, 1974.

—*Walt Trott*

REPRESENTATIVE RECORDINGS

Sunday Guitar (Epic, 1967); *Billy Grammer Back Home* (Circle, 1986)

Grand Ole Opry

established in Nashville, Tennessee, November 28, 1925

The longest-lived radio show in the United States, the Grand Ole Opry is also one of the single most important radio programs in the history of broadcasting. Its popularity as the leading country music radio show in America from 1945 through 1965 made possible Nashville's rise to power as the undisputed commercial center of the country music industry. Throughout the course of its storied history, the Opry has featured the performances of a host of notable country performers.

The Grand Ole Opry's history is very much intertwined with that of its parent station, Nashville's WSM. Within weeks of WSM's inaugural broadcast, on October 5, 1925, the station hired star radio announcer GEORGE D. HAY away from WLS-Chicago. Joining WSM as "radio director" on November 9, Hay quickly began introducing local folk music performers into the station's programming. The epiphany that sparked the Grand Ole Opry came on the Saturday evening of November 28, 1925, when seventy-seven-year-old UNCLE JIMMY THOMPSON performed his fiddle tunes on the air. The live performance prompted a flood of favorable mail, telegrams, and telephone calls for such programming, and Hay moved to make the Saturday-night show a fixture in the station's lineup.

Initially the program featured a rather informal aggregation of local, mostly amateur performers. Among the most popular regulars were Uncle Jimmy Thompson, UNCLE DAVE MACON, DeFORD BAILEY, and DR. HUMPHREY BATE. The show also featured a number of stringbands (colorfully named by Hay), including the GULLY JUMPERS, the FRUIT JAR DRINKERS, and the BINKLEY BROTHERS' DIXIE CLODHOPPERS.

In its first years, the *WSM Barn Dance,* as it was known in those days, was broadcast from WSM's Studio A on the fifth floor of the National Life and Accident Insurance building in downtown Nashville. As audiences for the Opry expanded, the show moved to more spacious accommodations. In about 1928 the Opry moved to newly built, larger Studio B, which accommodated a studio audience of about 200. These were the first of several moves the show would make in the ensuing years.

In 1928 HARRY STONE joined WSM as a staff announcer. Within a very short time Stone proved himself so capable that he assumed supervisory duties. In 1930 Stone was promoted into Hay's position as program director and Hay was relegated to announcing the Opry, writing the show's press releases, and briefly helping to run WSM's Artist Service, which was created in 1933 to book Opry acts for per-

Ad for the Purina segment of the Grand Ole Opry

sonal appearances around the country. Under Stone's direction, stage manager VITO PELLETTIERI divided the show into distinct, sponsored segments in 1934, an arrangement the show retains to this day.

Stone, with the help of his brother, DAVID STONE, moved the direction of the show away from the hoedown stringbands and fiddlers that Hay preferred and increasingly cultivated a "star system" (much as had been successfully done with movies made in Hollywood) that focused attention on individual, professional performers. During Harry Stone's tenure with the Opry (1930–50), he ushered in such key figures as the DELMORE BROTHERS, PEE WEE KING, ROY ACUFF, BILL MONROE, MINNIE PEARL, EDDY ARNOLD, ERNEST TUBB, HANK WILLIAMS, and HANK SNOW. During Stone's years, the Opry moved to Studio C in February 1934, the Hillsboro Theater in October 1934, the Dixie Tabernacle on Fatherland Street in East Nashville in June 1936, the War Memorial Auditorium in downtown Nashville in July 1939, and the RYMAN AUDITORIUM in June 1943.

Through the efforts of WSM program director JACK STAPP, the Opry became a featured half hour on the NBC radio network beginning in October 1939. Sponsored by Prince Albert Smoking Tobacco, the segment became known as the *Prince Albert Show*. With its network affiliation, the Opry became the nation's most listened-to country radio program, soon outdistancing WLS's *NATIONAL BARN DANCE*, which lost its network connection in 1946. In 1940 the Opry became the subject of a Republic Pictures movie titled *Grand Ole Opry* and featuring cast members Roy Acuff, Uncle Dave Macon, and Judge Hay.

In 1948 the Opry began a Friday night show, initially broadcast from Studio C in the National Life Building and called the Friday Night Frolics. In 1963 this Friday program moved to the Ryman and became known as the Friday Night Opry, a broadcast virtually identical to the Saturday night show.

Through the early 1950s the Opry solidified its position as America's most popular country radio show, weathering the 1950 departure of Harry Stone and the 1952 dismissal and subsequent death of star attraction Hank Williams. Other executive changes included the departures of JIM DENNY, WSM Artist Service chief and de facto Opry manager (1951–56), and of Jack Stapp in 1957.

In the late 1950s the Opry was buffeted by two major forces it failed to accommodate: television and rock & roll. Though Opry shows aired briefly on a regular basis on ABC-TV in 1955 and 1956, that was all the regular television exposure the show had for decades. Meanwhile, despite inviting ELVIS PRESLEY to appear on the show in October 1954, Opry officials failed to sign him to the cast, and he was allowed to slip away to the *LOUISIANA HAYRIDE*. Afterward the Opry made only token efforts in signing a few rock & roll performers, such as the EVERLY BROTHERS. As a result of such shortsightedness, the Opry's attendance plummeted in the late 1950s. The show suffered further in the early 1960s when some of its biggest stars, including PATSY CLINE and JIM REEVES, died in travel accidents. In December 1964 the show dismissed twelve cast members for making too few required appearances on the show; only half of these eventually returned. During the 1960s and through the 1970s, fewer and fewer stars of real consequence joined the cast because of the show's low wages and the diminishing power of the live radio show to build careers. The Opry's managers during these years were D. KILPATRICK (1956–59), OTT DEVINE (1959–68), and BUD WENDELL (1968–74).

The show's attendance rebounded for a time with its March 1974 move from the Ryman Auditorium to the opulent new Grand Ole Opry House at OPRYLAND. The March 16 opening ceremonies included an appearance by President Richard Nixon.

During HAL DURHAM's tenure as Opry manager (1974–93), he relaxed the required number of appearances for Opry cast members. This in turn allowed an infusion of young, in-demand talent when RANDY TRAVIS, REBA MCENTIRE, CLINT BLACK, ALAN JACKSON, GARTH BROOKS, and VINCE GILL joined the cast. Unfortunately for the Opry and its audiences, most of these dynamic performers rarely make more than a half dozen apppearances a year because the Opry pays performers at musicians' union scale, which amounts to less than 1 percent of what these artists earn for a single concert on the road.

In 1983 the Opry was purchased as part of the Opryland properties by the GAYLORD company. In 1985 TNN began televising a half-hour segment of the Opry—the show's first regular television exposure in thirty years.

In 1993 BOB WHITTAKER became the Opry's manager, and from time to time he arranged special multiperformer events at the Opry, involving venerable stars of yesterday with younger artists. Despite the occasional star-studded half-hour segment, overall the Opry has left the widely held impression that it has become a home for aging acts who no longer have hit records. And yet somehow the Opry has endured, still broadcast every Friday and Saturday night over WSM at 650 on the AM dial and still entertaining audiences in-house and around the country with folksy, family-oriented music and comedy. For all its recent failings as a business enterprise, the Opry remains, for artists and fans alike, one of country music's most cherished institutions.
—*Paul Kingsbury*

Uncle Josh Graves
b. Tellico Plains, Tennessee, September 27, 1928

When Burkett H. "Uncle Josh" Graves joined FLATT & SCRUGGS in 1955, his bluesy DOBRO style added a new dimension to their music. Graves began his professional career in 1942, when he was hired on as bass player for the Pierce Brothers, based in Gatlinburg. A year later he joined ROY ACUFF imitator Esco Hankins in Knoxville. In the late 1940s Graves made his professional recording debut with Hankins on the KING label.

Graves worked with MAC WISEMAN and WILMA LEE & STONEY COOPER's band before signing on with Flatt & Scruggs. After one month as their bass player, Graves switched over to dobro. Graves incorporated the guitar styles of CLIFF CARLISLE and blues artist Blind Boy Fuller with Scruggs's three-finger banjo roll. Graves also shared comedic duties with Cousin Jake Tullock. Although Tullock eventually left, Graves stayed on with Flatt & Scruggs, recording hundreds of sides with the duo for COLUMBIA RECORDS. After the group disbanded in 1969, Graves worked with Flatt's Nashville Grass from 1971 through 1974 before joining the EARL SCRUGGS REVUE.

Graves recorded two albums with KENNY BAKER for the Puritan label, *Buck Time* and *Something Different,* in the 1970s. Today Graves tours and records with Baker. In 1989 he and Baker, along with banjo player Eddie Adcock and mandolinist Jesse McReynolds, recorded and toured as the Masters. In 1992 Graves received an Award of Merit from IBMA and in 1995 was acknowledged for his participation in "The Great Dobro Sessions," which won that organization's Recorded Event of the Year Award. Few dobro players today fail to cite Graves as a major influence.

—*Chris Skinker*

REPRESENTATIVE RECORDINGS

The Great Dobro Sessions (Sugar Hill, 1994); *The Puritan Sessions* (Rebel, 1989)

Claude Gray

b. Henderson, Texas, January 25, 1932

Born just a few miles from JIM REEVES in rural East Texas, Claude N. Gray refined a style that was somewhat similar to Reeves's. Gray was on the smoother side of country music and scored several sizable hits in the early 1960s.

Gray left the navy in 1954; attended college in Longview, Texas; and worked as a field rep for a haulage company before joining the on-air staff at KOCA–Kilgore, Texas, in 1958. He moved to WDAI–Meridian, Mississippi, in 1959. Gray first recorded for Minor Records in 1958, and then for D RECORDS in 1959 and 1960. His second D release was WILLIE NELSON's song "Family Bible." It became Nelson's and Gray's first hit; Nelson had sold the song to Gray, session musician Paul Buskirk, and Gray's manager, Walt Breeland. In August 1960 Gray signed with MERCURY RECORDS and immediately scored two Top Five hits, "I'll Just Have a Cup of Coffee (Then I'll Go)" and ROGER MILLER's composition "My Ears Should Burn (When Fools Are Talked About)."

Gray left Mercury in 1967 and recorded for DECCA until 1971. From that point he recorded for several smaller companies and last scored a hit in 1986 with Neil Diamond's "Sweet Caroline" on the Country International label. Based in Longview, Texas, he still tours occasionally.

—*Colin Escott*

REPRESENTATIVE RECORDING

Songs of Broken Love Affairs (Mercury, 1962, out of print)

Mark Gray

b. Vicksburg, Mississippi, October 24, 1952

An accomplished songwriter, Mark Gray recorded for COLUMBIA RECORDS during the 1980s with modest success.

Gray began his professional career as the leader, vocalist, and piano player of a gospel group, the Revelations, in his native Mississippi in the early 1970s. He was spotted by members of the OAK RIDGE BOYS and ended up in Nashville working in the group's office and opening shows for them.

In the early 1980s Gray became a member of the popular country-rock band EXILE. He also began to make a mark as a songwriter. He and fellow Exile member J. P. Pennington co-wrote "Take Me Down" and "The Closer You Get"—both #1 hits for ALABAMA. Gray also wrote "It Ain't Easy Being Easy," a #1 for JANIE FRICKE.

Gray's expansive, energetic country-pop piano sound seemed tailor-made for the early 1980s when pop-country singers such as KENNY ROGERS were major forces in country's mainstream. Thus, when Columbia signed Gray in the early 1980s, it was with high hopes of making him a country-to-pop crossover star. Yet despite the label's huge promotional budget, the highest chart position Gray attained

came with his glossy duet with TAMMY WYNETTE on a remake of the Dan Hill pop hit "Sometimes When We Touch." Released in 1985, it reached #6.

Though he recorded briefly for the independent 615 label after leaving Columbia, little has been heard from Gray in the music business since the late 1980s.

—*Bob Allen*

REPRESENTATIVE RECORDINGS

Magic (Columbia, 1984); *This Ol' Piano* (Columbia, 1984)

Otto Gray

b. South Dakota, March 2, 1884 ; d. November 8, 1967

Otto Gray & His Oklahoma Cowboy Band were the most popular western stage act in the nation in the late 1920s and early 1930s, touring on the Loew's, RKO, and Fox theater circuits. They were equally as popular as radio and recording artists. NBC fed the band's radio shows to 150 stations, and the group recorded for OKEH, GENNETT, Vocalion, and BRUNSWICK's Melotone label. They were possibly the first touring group to use large, custom-made Cadillacs for transportation. The band started as the Billy McGinty Cowboy Band in Ripley, Oklahoma (1921). As their popularity and engagements grew, McGinty withdrew, turning the leadership to Gray, who changed the name and expanded the band's membership. Their radio appearances started in 1925 over KFRU (now KVOO in Tulsa, Oklahoma). Their stage program included cowboy, folk, and popular songs, and novelty acts such as trick roping, whip popping, dog tricks, and trick musical instrument playing. Whitey Ford (the DUKE OF PADUCAH) was a member of the band before joining the GRAND OLE OPRY, and Otto Gray was the first western artist featured on the cover of *Billboard*. In 1929, Gray's band appeared in the movie short *Otto Gray and His Oklahoma Cowboys*. The group disbanded by 1936.

—*Guy Logsdon*

Grayson, G. B. *(see* Henry Whitter)

Grayson & Whitter *(see* Henry Whitter)

Charles Grean

b. New York, New York, October 1, 1913

As an assistant to A&R representative STEVE SHOLES, Charles Randolph Grean was an integral component of Sholes's effort to bring RCA VICTOR to the forefront of recorded country music in the late 1940s. Grean collected repertoire, played bass on sessions, wrote arrangements for country recordings, and produced WILF CARTER, the SONS OF THE PIONEERS, ELTON BRITT, JOHNNIE & JACK, TEXAS JIM ROBERTSON, ROY ROGERS, and others. In 1947 he and Sholes co-produced three EDDY ARNOLD sessions that spawned six Top Ten hits, including four chart-toppers.

Before joining Sholes in 1946, Grean led New York society bands and worked as bandleader Glenn Miller's copyist. In 1950 Grean rose to head RCA's pop department. Grean co-wrote several Eddy Arnold hits with CY COBEN, and, alone, penned the pop novelty for Phil Harris "The Thing" and the answer to JIM REEVES's "He'll Have to Go"—"He'll Have to Stay" for Jeanne Black in 1960.

After leaving RCA in 1952, and for the next forty years, Grean maintained a periodic association with Eddy Arnold. Grean was a partner in the management group that directed Arnold's career after the star split with manager TOM PARKER in 1953, and, as late as 1978, Grean produced Arnold's minor hit "I'm the South." Grean occasionally conducted Arnold's road band from the 1970s into the 1990s. —*Michael Streissguth*

Great Plains

Often compared stylistically to the EAGLES, Great Plains is a band comprising Nashville studio and touring musicians Jack Sundrud (guitar, vocals), Denny Dadmun-Bixby (bass, vocals), and Lex Browning (guitar, mandolin, fiddle).

The members of Great Plains worked together and separately for the decade prior to their signing with artists such as VINCE GILL, MICHAEL JOHNSON, GEORGE JONES, GAIL DAVIES, MARY CHAPIN CARPENTER, KATHY MATTEA, Mark Knopfler, and others.

When original drummer Michael Young was commissioned to build an antique car for producer BRENT MAHER, he gave Maher a tape of the band. Maher hired them for demos and ended up producing them with DON POTTER, getting Columbia interested in 1990. The band's highest charting *Billboard* single on Columbia was "Faster Gun," (#41, 1991) and, though Sundrud and Dadmun-Bixby (Portland, Oregon) continued as a duo, Columbia went through staff changes and dropped them.

When Brent Maher cofounded Magnatone Entertainment in 1995, he signed and produced a new album for Great Plains, which now includes Lex Browning.

—*Michael Hight*

REPRESENTATIVE RECORDINGS

Great Plains (Columbia, 1991); *Homeland* (Magnatone, 1996)

Lloyd Green
b. Mobile, Alabama, October 4, 1937

Along with BUD ISAACS, BUDDY EMMONS, JIMMY DAY, and a few others, Lloyd Lamar Green was among the steel guitarists who revolutionized the instrument in the 1950s by utilizing pedals. Though he arrived at the pedal technique somewhat later than his aforementioned peers, by the mid-1960s Green was the steel man of choice for any number of Nashville stars and producers. He also played on the BYRDS' landmark *Sweetheart of the Rodeo* LP in 1968, thereby influencing generations of nonmainstream country pickers.

The precocious Green first started playing Hawaiian steel guitar when he was seven years old, and by age ten he was playing professionally around Mobile. Initially, his repertoire favored pop standards such as "Star Dust." But when he was sixteen, Bud Isaacs's seminal pedal steel work on WEBB PIERCE's "Slowly" captivated Green and for him changed the instrument "from a moth to a butterfly," as he told interviewer Douglas B. Green. The young picker immediately modified his own steel guitar, attaching a Model T gas pedal.

In 1956, after attending the University of Southern Mississippi, Green arrived in Nashville, where his first job was with HAWKSHAW HAWKINS. Green then joined FARON YOUNG's band and later worked with FERLIN HUSKY. After a brief departure from the music business, Green settled in

Lloyd Green

Nashville for good in 1963. When the LITTLE DARLIN' label was formed in 1966, Green served as in-house arranger. He recorded several Little Darlin' records under his own name and provided the "left field" licks that helped make JOHNNY PAYCHECK's Little Darlin' sides among the most interesting country records of their era. "People still ask me how to play those things," Green said in 1991.

In 1973, recording for MONUMENT RECORDS, Green scored a Top Forty hit with an instrumental version of "I Can See Clearly Now," but since the 1970s he has been less and less active in the studio. His influence is still strong, however: Hotshot picker JUNIOR BROWN, for one, has singled Green out as an idol. —*Daniel Cooper*

REPRESENTATIVE RECORDINGS

Day for Decision (Little Darlin', 1966); *Shades of Steel* (CBS/Monument, 1973)

The Greenbriar Boys
John Herald (John Whittier Sirabian) b. New York, New York, September 6, 1939
Ralph Rinzler b. Passaic, New Jersey, July 20, 1934; d. July 2, 1994
Frank Wakefield b. Emory Gap, Tennessee, June 26, 1934
Bob Yellin b. New York, New York, June 10, 1936

One of the first professional bluegrass bands to emerge from the northern folk music revival, the Greenbriar Boys coalesced from lower Manhattan picking sessions in 1958. The original band included guitarist/lead vocalist John Herald, banjo player/tenor Bob Yellin, and mandolinist/baritone Eric Weissberg. When Weissberg joined the Tarriers in fall 1959, RALPH RINZLER replaced him, playing mandolin from 1959 to 1964.

In 1960 and 1961 the group won the old-time band competition in Union Grove, North Carolina. A fall 1961 tour with folksinger Joan Baez led to a Vanguard recording contract. The band's first full-length album was released in June 1962; Rinzler's detailed notes explained bluegrass music to first-time listeners.

The Greenbriar Boys primarily performed at urban folk music venues, featuring an eclectic repertoire considerably broader than its southern counterparts. When Rinzler left in early 1964, Herald and Yellin replaced him with Frank Wakefield, an established mandolinist with unorthodox ideas. With Wakefield playing mandolin from 1964 to 1968, the group often took extended instrumental solos that prefigured modern rock. "Different Drum," a Michael Nesmith song from the band's only album with Wakefield, was successfully covered by LINDA RONSTADT and the Stone Poneys.

The Greenbriar Boys basically disbanded in 1966, although Wakefield continued using the name for two more years. During the late 1990s Herald, Yellin, and Weissberg occasionally reunited for festival appearances.

—Dave Samuelson

REPRESENTATIVE RECORDING

The Best of John Herald and the Greenbriar Boys (Vanguard, 1972)

Jack Greene

b. Maryville, Tennessee, January 7, 1930

Jack Henry Greene graduated from ERNEST TUBB's Texas Troubadours to become the CMA's first single-year multiple award winner and a popular singing star.

Starting in radio at WGAP in Maryville (1947), Greene was initially a singer-guitarist who played bass and drums in various groups, both in his native East Tennessee and in Georgia with the Peachtree Cowboys. For a time he owned a downtown Atlanta club, the Covered Wagon, while working a day job for a glassmaker. He was working the *Dixie Jubilee* in East Point (an Atlanta suburb) when Ernest Tubb came through in late 1961, saw Greene play, and hired him six months later. For the next five years Greene was the band's "big-eared singing drummer," as Tubb liked to call him.

Greene's version of "The Last Letter," released on the first Texas Troubadours album, was popular enough for DECCA RECORDS to issue it as a single and offer Greene his own recording contract in 1964. Greene's 1966 release of the DALLAS FRAZIER song "There Goes My Everything" made him a star. The record topped *Billboard*'s chart for seven weeks, and Ernest Tubb persuaded Greene to leave the band and build his own career in May 1967.

Between then and 1969 Greene was at his best, scoring seven more Top Five country hits, including "All the Time," "You Are My Treasure," "What Locks the Door," and the majestic "Statue of a Fool." At the first CMA Awards event (1967), Greene won Single of the Year (for "There Goes My Everything") and Male Vocalist of the Year. From 1969 through the mid-1970s Decca Records paired Greene with JEANNIE SEELY on a series of successful duets, the first and most popular of which was "Wish I Didn't Have to Miss You." Greene joined the GRAND OLE OPRY in 1967 and remains in the cast, where today (a devout Christian) he often sings "There Goes My Everything" adapted with a newer gospel slant, "He Is My Everything."

—Ronnie Pugh

REPRESENTATIVE RECORDING

Greatest Hits (Gusto, 1986)

Lee Greenwood

Lee Greenwood

b. Southgate, California, October 27, 1942

Raised in Sacramento, California, Melvin Lee Greenwood started playing a saxophone at age ten. The road to Nashville would one day lead him to #1 hits, a 1984 Grammy award, and CMA honors as male vocalist of the year in 1983 and 1984. It would also lead to visits with U.S. presidents, thanks in large part to his patriotic anthem "God Bless the USA."

While in high school Greenwood formed his first band, the Moonbeams, and toured as a performer before graduating. He turned down a music scholarship at the College of the Pacific and skipped his high school graduation ceremony when starting a job in Reno, Nevada, with another band, the Apollos.

Over time, Greenwood established a long career on the Nevada casino lounge circuit as a bandleader, performer, arranger, and songwriter. There were periods when he worked as a blackjack dealer by day and performed as a sax and piano player in the lounges at night. His early music career was not without disappointments, however. At one point, a band he was traveling with broke up in New York City, sending Greenwood back to Las Vegas; his bandmates subsequently re-formed the group into the hit-making Young Rascals. Greenwood organized another band, the Lee Greenwood Affair, that was signed to a record contract. But the record company was sold and the project was shelved. Greenwood was not released from his contract, and he ended up working in a fast-food chicken restaurant.

Greenwood later returned to the steady work offered by

the casino circuit he terms "the green felt jungle." In 1978 he moved to Reno, where Larry McFaden, bass player for MEL TILLIS, heard him sing. Impressed, McFaden became Greenwood's manager and arranged for the singer to journey to Nashville to record demos. Producer JERRY CRUTCHFIELD, then head of MCA Music Publishing, produced a demo session that resulted in his first MCA RECORDS chart song, "It Turns Me Inside Out" (1981). While the song began its twenty-two-week run on the charts, Greenwood was back in Las Vegas, working in the piano bar of the Tropicana Hotel.

A polished contemporary country performer, Greenwood soon began touring on the strength of a string of Top Ten hits that ran from 1982 to 1988 and that included his first #1, "Somebody's Gonna Love You" (1983), and "God Bless the USA," which earned the CMA's 1985 Song of the Year award. His first three albums, along with his *Greatest Hits* package, were certified gold. Meanwhile, "God Bless the USA" was used during the presidential campaigns of both Ronald Reagan and George Bush. When the Lee Greenwood Theater opened in Sevierville, Tennessee, in 1996, the audience included former president Bush and former first lady Barbara Bush. —*Gerry Wood*

Greatest Hits (MCA, 1985); *If There's Any Justice* (MCA, 1987); *Holdin' a Good Hand* (Capitol, 1990)

Ricky Lynn Gregg
b. Longview, Texas, August 22, 1961

As country music in the 1990s began drawing listeners who had grown up on rock, Nashville labels looked for singers with a foot in both genres; one such act was Ricky Lynn Gregg. Gregg had grown up playing the music of both JOHNNY CASH and the 1970s rock group Foghat; by the mid-1980s he was a regular on the Texas club circuit. (He had also spent time fronting the hard-rock band Head East, which had earlier had brief album-rock success.) Though he didn't play it up, Gregg was one of country's few singers of Native American descent: his great-grandmother was Cherokee, and he called his band Cherokee Thunder.

Gregg had a passion for traditional country—he covered MEL STREET's 1978 hit "If I Had a Cheatin' Heart" for his first single (#36, 1993)—but his music contained enough rock influences that it found its greatest popularity in country dance clubs. His second album, *Get a Little Closer*, opened with a souped-up cover of CONWAY TWITTY and LORETTA LYNN's "After the Fire Is Gone" and ended with a MERLE HAGGARD song, "Silver Wings." Other singles included "Can You Feel It" (1993) and "Get a Little Closer" (1994). —*Brian Mansfield*

Ricky Lynn Gregg (Liberty, 1993); *Get a Little Closer* (Liberty, 1994)

Clinton Gregory
b. Martinsville, Virginia, March 1, 1966

Clinton Gregory's success on the country charts is even more remarkable because he achieved it without the benefit of a major record label. With "(If It Weren't For Coun-try Music) I'd Go Crazy" (1991) peaking at #26, Gregory and the independent STEP ONE RECORDS set the stage for two other Top Thirty hits, "Who Needs It" (1991) and "Play, Ruby, Play" (1992).

Although Gregory is a singer and multi-instrumentalist, he's most closely identified with the fiddle, the instrument he's played since age four. The son of a bluegrass fiddler, Gregory later won more than seventy fiddle championships. He worked as a stuntman at a North Carolina western theme park before moving to Nashville in 1987. Gregory's fiddling skills earned him tenures in the road bands of SUZY BOGGUSS and the McCARTERS. He later worked as a singer and instrumentalist in a Nashville club band before signing his contract with Step One. After five albums for the independent label, Gregory signed with Polydor Nashville. A self-titled album was released in 1994, but Polydor had limited success with most of its artists, and Gregory was dropped from the label a year later. He continued to perform and also worked on an album with songwriter HANK COCHRAN. At the time of this writing Gregory was considering his future options.
—*Calvin Gilbert*

If It Weren't For Country Music (I'd Go Crazy) (Step One, 1991); *Freeborn Man* (Step One, 1992)

Rex Griffin
b. Gadsden, Alabama, August 12, 1912; d. October 7, 1958

Though he is little remembered today, in his day Alsie "Rex" Griffin was a popular and influential singer and songwriter who left a strong impression on HANK WILLIAMS, ERNEST TUBB, and HANK PENNY. Himself a fan of JIMMIE RODGERS, Griffin performed much in the blue yodeling style of Rodgers, first around Gadsden in 1930. While Griffin was performing in a Birmingham group, the Smokey Mountaineers, a WAPI announcer first called him Rex since fan mail usually misspelled Alsie. Rex later became his legal name. Griffin made thirty-six recordings for DECCA between 1935 and 1939, the most popular of which were "Everybody's Tryin' to Be My Baby" (later adapted, and adopted, by CARL PERKINS), "My Hillbilly Baby," and the immortal "The Last Letter." At his final Decca recording session (September 25, 1939) he cut "Lovesick Blues." Hank Williams's huge hit version ten years later was a close copy. In the late 1930s Griffin wrote but never recorded (though many others did) the popular "Won't You Ride in My Little Red Wagon."

In 1941 Griffin moved to KRLD in Dallas, Texas, to star on Gus Foster's *Texas Roundup* program. When Foster left the show, Griffin became its leader. After World War II Griffin worked Chicago nightclubs, then opened his own with Johnny Barfield in the Columbus, Georgia, area. In 1946 Griffin made eight recordings for SYD NATHAN's KING, DE LUXE, and Federal labels.

Griffin continued to write songs until his death, though his performing was curtailed by diabetes, alcoholism, and even tuberculosis. The most well known of Griffin's later songs was 1955's "Just Call Me Lonesome," a big hit for EDDY ARNOLD. Drifting between Gadsden (where a sister lived) and New Orleans for most of his later life, Griffin died in a New Orleans charity hospital October 7, 1958, and was buried three days later in Gadsden. In 1970 Griffin was elected to the Hall of Fame of the Nashville Songwriters Association, recognition of the power of his greatest songs. —*Ronnie Pugh*

REPRESENTATIVE RECORDING

The Last Letter (Bear Family, 1996)

Nanci Griffith

b. Seguin, Texas, July 16, 1954

With influences ranging from folksinger Carolyn Hester to novelist Carson McCullers, and greater acceptance at clubs and colleges than at country radio, Nanci Griffith proved to be alternative country when alt-country wasn't cool. In the mid-1980s neither labels nor radio knew what to make of her high, breathy voice and hard-to-classify songs. Since then, however, Griffith has emerged as a role model in the burgeoning roots-music movement of the 1990s, both as a performer and as a champion of other artists.

Griffith grew up in Austin, Texas, the child of parents who divorced when she was six. Fans of everything from WOODY GUTHRIE to Sinatra, her parents encouraged her interest in music, literature, and theater; by age fourteen she was singing in local coffeehouses. She majored in education at the University of Texas, and after graduation she maintained a day gig teaching kindergarten. She quit in 1977 to become a full-time musician. By 1982 she had recorded two obscure LPs.

In 1985 Griffith arrived in Nashville, where she cut her groundbreaking third album, *Once in a Very Blue Moon,* with producer JIM ROONEY for the Philo label. The record did two things: It showcased her gift for evocative, novelettish detail, and it gave many listeners their first exposure to songs by LYLE LOVETT and ROBERT EARL KEEN JR., among others. As her audience grew, MCA Nashville signed her in 1986 to a roster that included offbeat singer-songwriters Lovett and STEVE EARLE.

Nanci Griffith

Like those Texas troubadours, though, Griffith drew mostly blank stares from mainstream country programmers, despite the strength of her material. In 1986 KATHY MATTEA rode Griffith's signature song "Love at the Five and Dime" to the Top Five—a mixed triumph, since Griffith's own version never appeared on the charts—while a few years later Bette Midler scored a blockbuster hit off Julie Gold's "From a Distance," a song Griffith introduced without chart success.

In frustration, after three good-to-excellent albums that fared poorly at radio, MCA shuffled her to its L.A. pop division. The label promptly paired her with producers like Glyn Johns, best known for his work with rock bands such as the Who and the Clash. The records that resulted, especially 1989's *Storms,* sounded uncomfortable.

Griffith signed to ELEKTRA in 1992 and rebounded in 1993 with *Other Voices, Other Rooms,* an album of covers by favorite songwriters, including JOHN PRINE and TOWNES VAN ZANDT. Her 1995 LP *Flyer* found her collaborating with members of U2, R.E.M., and other college-radio favorites. The record's startlingly personal tone is a departure—Griffith seems more at ease with story-songs than with confessional balladry—but its spirit and passion place it among her best work. *Blue Roses from the Moon,* released in 1997, showcases past and present members of her band the Blue Moon Orchestra as well as guests Darius Rucker, of Hootie & the Blowfish, and the Crickets. Griffith's music is featured in a collaboration with the Nashville Ballet and the Nashville Symphony in a modern ballet titled *This Heart.* Griffith currently lives in Franklin, Tennessee.
—*Jim Ridley*

REPRESENTATIVE RECORDINGS

Once in a Very Blue Moon (Philo/Rounder, 1985); *Other Voices, Other Rooms* (Elektra, 1993)

David Grisman

b. Hackensack, New Jersey, March 23, 1945

Mandolinist, composer, and producer David Jay Grisman was part of an early wave of talented New York City–area bluegrassers and later became a pioneer of the jazz- and bluegrass-influenced genre known as "new acoustic" music. Introduced to the mandolin in 1960 by folklorist-musician RALPH RINZLER, Grisman was heavily influenced by the playing of BILL MONROE and Frank Wakefield. He performed in the New York Ramblers (bluegrass contest winners at the 1964 Union Grove, North Carolina, fiddlers convention) and the Even Dozen Jug Band (with such future folk-pop stars as Maria Muldaur and John Sebastian). In 1963 he produced his first album, a record by bluegrass veterans RED ALLEN, Frank Wakefield, and the Kentuckians for Folkways. Grisman and friend Jerry Garcia (the Grateful Dead rock singer-guitarist who also played banjo) attracted new fans to bluegrass in 1973 as members of the band Old And In The Way.

Grisman later melded jazz, swing, Latin, and Jewish klezmer sounds with bluegrass to create the distinctive new acoustic style referred to as "dawg music" (after the canine nickname given him by Garcia). He formed the David Grisman Quintet in 1976 and founded the Acoustic Disc label in 1990. Grisman's eclectic tastes have led to collaborations with a broad range of talents, including fiddlers Stephane Grapelli, Swend Asmussen, Vassar Clements,

Richard Greene, and MARK O'CONNOR, mandolinists Jethro Burns and Andy Statman, and guitarists Jerry Garcia, John Carlini, TONY RICE, and Martin Taylor. But his frequent returns to traditional bluegrass and his widely admired mandolin playing, noted for its inventiveness, bright tone, and jaunty syncopations, have maintained his specific influence within country music.   —*Richard D. Smith*

REPRESENTATIVE RECORDINGS

Home Is Where the Heart Is (Rounder, 1988); *The David Grisman Quintet: DGQ-20* (Acoustic Disc, 1996)

Bonnie Guitar
b. Seattle, Washington, March 25, 1923

Chiefly known for the haunting, melancholic original of the 1957 Top Ten pop crossover hit "Dark Moon," Bonnie Guitar (born Buckingham) should be better remembered as one of the first women in the studio and production scene.

After performing in and around Seattle, she moved to Los Angeles to work as a guitarist for FABOR ROBISON on mid-fifties sessions for his FABOR and ABBOTT labels, and as a Fabor artist. She sang the demo of NED MILLER's "Dark Moon" (and played the lead guitar) and persuaded Robison to issue her version by foregoing royalties. Robison had an agreement with DOT RECORDS, and Dot not only picked up Bonnie's original but covered her with pop singer Gale Storm. Both were hits.

Leaving Robison, Bonnie went back to Seattle, and started the Dolphin label (soon renamed Dolton) in partnership with a refrigerator salesman, Bob Reisdorf, and a local record distributor, Lou Lavinthal. They scored pop hits with the Fleetwoods ("Come Softly to Me," "Mr. Blue") and the Ventures; Bonnie herself had a minor pop hit on the label in 1959 with "Candy Apple Red." Dolton was later sold to LIBERTY, now owned by EMI. Following a brief recording stint with RCA (1961–1962) Bonnie re-signed with Dot in 1965 and consistently hit the country charts through the late 1960s; among the songs was a minor hit in 1969 recorded with BUDDY KILLEN (as Bonnie & Buddy), "A Truer Love You'll Never Find Than Mine." During the late sixties, she also handled A&R work on the West Coast for Dot and ABC-Paramount. She later recorded for several other labels, including ABC-Paramount, COLUMBIA, MCA, FOUR STAR, and Playback.   —*Colin Escott*

REPRESENTATIVE RECORDING

Dark Moon (Bear Family, 1991)

Guitar

After delta blues, country music was the first style of popular music based around the guitar, and the prominent guitar lines in the recordings of JIMMIE RODGERS and the CARTER FAMILY helped bring the guitar forward in the early thirties to become the dominant stringed instrument of the twentieth century.

The guitar had evolved in Europe by 1800 from a lute-like instrument, with paired strings, into its present form with six single strings. It was refined in America into two major styles: the flat-top, perfected by 1850 by C. F. Martin of Nazareth, Pennsylvania; and the "arched-top" (with a top carved in the manner of a violin), invented by Orville Gibson of Kalamazoo, Michigan, in the 1890s.

Prior to the 1920s the guitar had been a refined parlor instrument that was overshadowed in American popular music by (chronologically) the lute, minstrel banjo, mandolin, and tenor banjo. By the end of the 1920s, however, players were finding the guitar to be more versatile and better suited for the new music than the banjo. Used as either a solo instrument or as part of an ensemble, the guitar could be strummed; its individual strings could be "fingerpicked" in a variety of patterns; or single strings could be picked with a plectrum for solos and instrumental fills. In addition to Jimmie Rodgers (who played a Martin) and the Carter Family (with Maybelle Carter on a Gibson), pop artist Nick Lucas and jazz players Eddie Lang and Lonnie Johnson helped bring the guitar into prominence.

The first viable electric guitar was introduced by the Rickenbacker company in 1932, giving guitarists the volume necessary to compete with other instruments in a big band setting. In 1950 Leo Fender of Fullerton, California, introduced an electric guitar with a body of solid wood that produced greater sustain and a sharper tone than the traditional arched-top design. The brilliant, piercing Fender sound was adopted by West Coast country guitarists, including Jimmy Bryant, Bill Carson (with HANK THOMPSON), Eldon Shamblin (with BOB WILLS), and Don Rich (with BUCK OWENS). For several decades Nashville session players such as CHET ATKINS, HANK GARLAND, and HAROLD BRADLEY preferred the warm tones of the Gibson and Gretsch arch-top electrics, but the "hot" Fender style—as played by such notables as JAMES BURTON, ALBERT LEE, Ray Flacke, and VINCE GILL—eventually prevailed as the signature guitar sound of country.   —*Walter Carter*

Gully Jumpers
Paul Warmack b. Whites Creek, Tennessee, August 16, 1889; d. July 2, 1954
C. B. Arrington b. Cheatham County, Tennessee, 1893; d. unknown
William Roy Hardison b. Maury County, Tennessee, July 19, 1896; d. February 1966
Burt Hutcherson b. Bethel, Tennessee, 1893; d. July 10, 1980

One of the original "hoedown bands" that formed the cornerstone of the early Grand Ole Opry, the Gully Jumpers began on the show in 1927 and continued in various forms until the 1970s. The members all came from rural communities around Nashville; Warmack himself (bandleader, mandolinist, guitarist, and vocalist) hailed from Goodlettsville, and was a mechanic by trade. Fiddler Charlie Arrington, described by GRAND OLE OPRY founder GEORGE D. HAY as "an Irishman with quick wit," had a farm north of Nashville, in Joelton. (In the late 1930s Arrington played and recorded with UNCLE DAVE MACON.) Banjoist William Hardison was also a mechanic, and guitarist Bert Hutcherson was a woodworker.

In 1928 the Gully Jumpers appeared on the Opry more than any other stringband, and Warmack and Hutcherson had a separate duo show in the mornings on WSM, where they called themselves the Early Birds. The band recorded for Victor at that company's first Nashville session in 1928, leaving behind masterpieces such as "Stone Rag," "Robertson County," and "The Little Red Caboose Behind the Train."   —*Charles Wolfe*

Hardrock Gunter

b. Birmingham, Alabama, February 27, 1925

A singer, songwriter, guitarist, booking agent, artist manager, DJ, and ultimately insurance agent, Sidney Louie "Hardrock" Gunter Jr. is perhaps best known as the author of "Birmingham Bounce." Released by Gunter on the tiny Bama label in 1950, the song was covered by RED FOLEY on DECCA and became a crossover smash. Though Gunter's records—some of which fell into the pre-Elvis transitional mode between country swing and rockabilly—went largely unnoticed when released, they have attracted considerable interest among rock & roll historians and collectors in decades since.

Born and raised in Birmingham, Gunter early on fell under the spell of local swing hero HANK PENNY. Gunter formed the Hoodal Ramblers when he was thirteen, then joined Happy Wilson in the Golden River Boys, who had a radio show on WAPI in Birmingham. Several band members, including Gunter, served in the army during the war years, but the Golden River Boys re-formed after the war and recorded for the Vulcan label in 1948. Gunter eventually broke away from the band, becoming an active booking agent and appearing on local television station WABT in 1949.

With the success of "Birmingham Bounce," Gunter was signed to Decca in January 1951. But that same month he was called back into the army. Discharged in late 1952, he spent most of the remainder of the decade with the *WWVA JAMBOREE* in Wheeling, West Virginia. He continued to record his idiosyncratic records, two of which appeared on the SUN label. In 1963 he quit the *Jamboree* and relocated to Golden, Colorado, where he established himself in the insurance business. He still made an occasional record, the last of any note being a 1972 tribute album to HANK WILLIAMS, whom Gunter had known while both were coming up in the music business. —*Daniel Cooper*

Jack Guthrie

b. Olive, Oklahoma, November 13, 1915; d. January 15, 1948

In his short career, Leon Jerry Guthrie developed his own distinctive style of singing and yodeling based on that of his idol, JIMMIE RODGERS. From his love of horses and his days as a rodeo rough stock rider, Guthrie developed a western persona. Though a talented singer-songwriter who played fiddle, guitar, bass, and other instruments, he was undisciplined as a youth and as an entertainer.

In 1937 his cousin and good friend WOODY GUTHRIE moved to Los Angeles, where Jack was living. Even with different musical styles, the two became a musical team, landing the *Oke & Woody Show* on KFVD, Hollywood. During the fall of 1937 Woody wrote "Oklahoma Hills," which they performed during their shows. Each cousin had different ambitions, and they soon went their separate ways.

In 1944 CAPITOL RECORDS recorded Jack Guthrie singing "Oklahoma Hills." Released in 1945, it quickly became a #1 country hit. When Woody heard "Oklahoma Hills" on a jukebox, he called Capitol and claimed it as his song. Jack's position was that had he not recorded it, the song would have remained dormant among Woody's many songs. Furthermore, Jack maintained he had made modifications that improved the song. Eventually they decided to share the copyright.

Guthrie served a short stint in military service in 1945–46, and when discharged he resumed playing western dances up and down the West Coast, and recording for Capitol hits such as "Oakie Boogie." Although diagnosed with tuberculosis in 1946, he continued making personal appearances. In 1947 his friend ERNEST TUBB arranged for Guthrie to appear in the movie *Hollywood Barn Dance.* His last recording session was similar to the last Jimmie Rodgers session, for a cot had to be set up in the studio on which Guthrie could rest. He died a few weeks later at a V.A. hospital in Livermore. —*Guy Logsdon*

REPRESENTATIVE RECORDING

Jack Guthrie: Oklahoma Hills (Bear Family, 1991)

Woody Guthrie

b. Okemah, Oklahoma, July 14, 1912; d. October 3, 1967

Folksinger, artist, novelist, and prolific songwriter Woodrow Wilson Guthrie was a major influence in the urban folk revival during the 1950s and 1960s. Through his early influence on BOB DYLAN, Guthrie became a legendary figure in urban folk music. During the 1930s and 1940s Guthrie wrote more than 1,000 songs, including such enduring standards as "Oklahoma Hills," "Philadelphia Lawyer," "So Long, It's Been Good to Know You," and "This Land Is Your Land." Believing that songs could change social conditions, he produced a diverse catalogue of work, including children's songs, love songs, cowboy and hobo songs, Dust Bowl songs, and social protest songs about peace and war, unions and bosses, and the problems of migrant agricultural workers.

Guthrie's parents were prosperous until Huntington's disease altered his mother's behavior and tore the family apart. When he was fourteen, she was committed to an insane asylum, and his father was taken to Pampa, Texas, to recuperate from severe burns. In his autobiographical novel *Bound for Glory,* Woody Guthrie recounts how those tribulations taught him compassion and shaped his constant desire to travel.

In 1929 he joined his father in Pampa, and there experienced the privations of the Dust Bowl. In 1937 he moved to California, where driven by a desire to become a country singer, he teamed with his cousin JACK GUTHRIE as radio entertainers on KFVD-Hollywood. When Jack left the

Woody Guthrie

show, Maxine "Lefty Lou" Crissman became his partner on the *Woody and Lefty Lou* show.

Guthrie became acquainted with socialist sympathizers, and in late 1939 he moved to New York City and became involved in the social protest song movement. He recorded for the Library of Congress and for RCA VICTOR, but his greatest number of recordings was for Folkways Records. His album *Dust Bowl Ballads*, issued by RCA Victor Records in 1940, has sold consistently through the years in various reissue formats, and his Library of Congress recordings issued by ELEKTRA RECORDS in 1964 played a major role in influencing the urban folksong revival.

Guthrie was hospitalized with Huntington's disease for the last fifteen years of his life. In 1966 the U. S. Department of the Interior honored him for his "Bonneville Power/Columbia River" songs by naming a substation after him. On October 9, 1977, he was posthumously inducted into the Nashville Songwriters Association Hall of Fame, and in 1988, he was posthumously inducted into the Rock & Roll Hall of Fame. His influence continues to grow among songwriters and singers in folk, country, and rock & roll music. His son is the folk-rock artist Arlo Guthrie.

—*Guy Logsdon*

REPRESENTATIVE RECORDINGS

Woody Guthrie: Library of Congress Recordings (Rounder, 1988); *Woody Guthrie: Dust Bowl Ballads* (Rounder, 1988); *Woody Guthrie Sings Folk Songs* (Smithsonian/Folkways, 1989)

The Gospel Truth:
Christianity and Country Music

Bill C. Malone

Country music is the product of a society permeated with the culture of evangelical Protestant Christianity. The "Christ-haunted" South, as novelist Flannery O'Connor described it, consequently produced a style of rural music that was distinctively different from that of the North, and that style has endured as one of the central components of commercial country music.

Religion has inspired much of the lyric content of country music, while also contributing directly to the shaping of its performance style. Many songs speak explicitly about God and spiritual matters, while others exhibit the shaping force of religion through their concern with guilt, shame, and retribution, or through their advocacy of a tradition-based, religion-centered morality. Religious inspiration, though, has extended far beyond lyric content; it has also influenced the way country entertainers sing. Folklorist Alan Lomax may be correct in arguing that the repressive doctrine of southern Calvinism inhibited the free expression of emotionalism and consequently encouraged a tight or pinched-throat style of singing. But we should not forget that southern white folk also learned vocal mannerisms from their black neighbors, and that both of these groups were encouraged to sing in a freewheeling, open-throated manner by the Pentecostal evangelists who swept through the South in the decades around the turn of the twentieth century.

Before the dawn of country music's commercial history in the 1920s, the public performance of vocal music in the rural South was most often done in a religious setting. Plain working folk did occasionally have "musicals" in their homes where they joined their neighbors in the singing of old ballads or hymns, but more often, they sang at the outdoor camp meetings that began in the upper South in the early 1800s. They continued to do so as part of the congregations of the evangelical churches, or as participants in singing conventions—monthly religious sessions generally described as "all-day singings with dinner on the grounds." Not only did people receive community-sanctioned encouragement to sing, they also learned harmony and other vocal techniques by listening to each other, or by practicing the rudiments of singing found in most of the "shape-note" songbooks that circulated widely in country churches or at the conventions.

Using symbols to indicate the pitch of musical notes, the shape-note system flourished in the rural South after 1800, when itinerant music teachers popularized the method at their ten-day singing schools. After the Civil War, the shape-note method became the basis of a flourishing music publishing business in the South, led most notably by the Ruebush-Kiefer Company in Singer's Glen, Virginia, and by A. J. Showalter's company in Dalton, Georgia. While sending their books and music teachers throughout the South, these companies also circulated hundreds of original songs along with the new "gospel" songs that emerged after 1875 in the wake of the great revivalistic campaigns that toured the United States. Although originating for the most part in the northern United States, these revivals, ironically, were the sources of many of the songs, such as "Softly and Tenderly," "The Uncloudy Day," and "The Old Rugged Cross," that became greatly beloved by both the southern people and by commercial country entertainers.

Gospel music was already a pervasive force, then, when country music began its commercial evolution in the 1920s. Working from his base in Lawrenceburg, Tennessee, music publisher JAMES D. VAUGHAN was in fact already sending his quartets far and wide before country entertainers began making public appearances or giving radio performances. Vaughan viewed gospel music through the lens of an evangelistic missionary (he was a devout member of the Church of the Nazarene), but as an astute businessman, he also knew that his published songs could gain new audiences through the new media of radio and phonograph recordings. His pioneering fusion of gospel music and commerce was followed by other publishing houses, such as STAMPS-BAXTER, Hartford, and Trio, each of which employed traveling quartets as salesmen for their paperback gospel songbooks. Although gospel and country musicians professed to have dramatically different goals, their respective arts evolved commercially in a parallel interrelationship. Gospel and country have never ceased to influence each other.

Songs from the paperback hymnals, or from the performances of the gospel quartets, or from the older tradition of nineteenth-century hymnody began to appear on country recordings or radio broadcasts virtually from the beginning of commercialization. Most singers, such as UNCLE DAVE MACON, BRADLEY KINCAID, or the CARTER FAMILY, usually performed older songs, but a few, such as BLIND ALFRED REED, ANDREW JENKINS, and Charles E. Moody (of the GEORGIA YELLOW HAMMERS), inaugurated a tradition that still endures in country music: the writing of religious songs or pieces that have strong moralistic content. Jenkins's "God Put a Rainbow in the Clouds" and Moody's "Drifting Too Far from the Shore," for example, became standard inclusions in the repertories of both country and gospel singers.

Probably the most important link between the shape-note gospel tradition and country music was a family of singers from Texas known as the CHUCK WAGON GANG. Ernest "Dad" Carter and his three children (Anna, Rose, and Jim) sang all kinds of old-time music when they began their career in Lubbock in 1935, and did not find their niche as gospel singers until after 1936, when they moved to Fort Worth and acquired the name of the Chuck Wagon Gang. Despite their performing title, the Carters were not cowboy singers. They had a decidedly rural sound and performed usually with only guitar accompaniment, but their style came directly from shape-note and gospel quartet sources. Appearing each weekday on a Fort Worth radio station, and recording for the COLUMBIA label, the Chuck Wagon Gang became household words in working-class homes throughout the Southwest. Unlike many of the gospel quartets of their day, they were never employed by a shape-note publishing house. Nevertheless, the Chuck Wagon Gang probably circulated the songs of Stamps-Baxter and other publishers more widely than did any other singing group, and were instrumental in introducing the songs of ALBERT E. BRUMLEY to the country audience. Brumley claimed that he never explicitly wrote a "country" song, but such items as "I'll Fly Away," "I'll Meet You in the Morning," and "If We Never Meet Again" became standards in country repertoires largely through the performances of the Chuck Wagon Gang. Still other Brumley songs, such as "Rank Strangers to Me," "By the Side of the Road," and "Did You Ever Go Sailing," eventually became perennial favorites among bluegrass entertainers.

Religious songs appeared so prominently in the repertoires of pre–World War II country singers that some of these numbers became permanently identified with certain acts. The Carter Family, for instance, used "Keep on the Sunny Side" as the theme for their broadcasts on the Mexican BORDER RADIO station XERF. The MONROE BROTHERS (Charlie and Bill) sang a wide variety of songs, but were most closely identified with "What Would You Give in Exchange For Your Soul?" ROY ACUFF similarly performed a broad spectrum of country items, but was hired by WSM and the GRAND OLE OPRY on the strength of one song, his version of a rather mysterious religious number called "The Great Speckled Bird."

Despite the prominence of religious songs in the earlier country repertoires, the peak of such performance came after World War II, during the late forties and early fifties. In a sense, the popularity of such material suggests the efforts made by transplanted rural people to preserve elements of their older culture in a newly emerging urban-industrial society while also using the old-time religion to explain and cope with new and sometimes frightening problems. Southern fundamentalism has never been more prominently displayed than in the music of entertainers such as the BAILES BROTHERS and the LOUVIN BROTHERS. The Louvin Brothers, preeminently, employed their clear and searing tenor harmonies and the fine writing of Ira Louvin on such songs as "The Family Who Prays," "Born Again," and "Insured Beyond the Grave," which describe a world of declining values and moral collapse that could only be redeemed by the spiritual new birth. Other songs, such as the Bailes Brothers' "Dust on the Bible" and "When Heaven Comes

Down," the Louvins' "The Great Atomic Power," WILMA LEE & STONEY COOPER's "That's What's the Matter With This World," Roy Acuff's "This World Can't Stand Long," and MOLLY O'DAY's "Matthew 24," saw prophetic meaning in the societal instability and political events of the day, and spoke of the imminent Second Coming of Christ. The recordings of this period even included a handful of powerful and rare performances made by Rev. Claude Ely, "the Gospel Ranger," at a Pentecostal revival in eastern Kentucky. Country music has never since been so close to its folk roots, nor as clearly linked to its southern origins.

Other country religious songs of the era were not nearly as explicit in their doctrinal evocations, but were probably appealing because of the heightened American religiosity that accompanied our postwar affluence and the nation's ideological conflict with the avowedly atheistic dictates of the Soviet Union. Recordings such as STUART HAMBLEN's "It Is No Secret," RED FOLEY's "Peace in the Valley" and "Just a Closer Walk with Thee," MARTHA CARSON's "Satisfied," JIMMIE DAVIS's "Someone to Care," and HANK WILLIAMS's "I Saw the Light" promised spiritual satisfaction without apocalyptic portent and denominational identification.

To be sure, ELVIS PRESLEY loved gospel music and identified with such entertainers as the Blackwood Brothers and the Stamps Quartet. Yet in general the performance of religious material in mainstream country music has declined significantly since the sixties. The STATLER BROTHERS and the OAK RIDGE BOYS did come to country music from backgrounds in the gospel field, but their immense popularity came after they veered sharply away from full-time gospel performance. The decline of religious music among country performers has been a consequence perhaps of the country industry's growing affluence and middle-class pretensions, and a mark of its efforts to embrace a larger and nonregional constituency. Gospel songs, however, have never disappeared completely, as any observer of a WILLIE NELSON concert would readily know. Periodically, such songs have made their way to the charts, as did FERLIN HUSKY's version of "Wings of a Dove" in 1959, JOHNNY CASH's rendition of "Daddy Sang Bass" in 1968, and KRIS KRISTOFFERSON's "Why Me?" in 1972. Albums devoted solely to gospel songs, such as MERLE HAGGARD's *Land of Many Churches* and EMMYLOU HARRIS's *Angel Band,* also appear occasionally but without the frequency that was once common in country music.

Although the performance of religious music has declined in mainstream country music, the fan of spiritually oriented material need not despair. Bluegrass musicians still perform gospel songs that reflect the traditional roots of country music, while a newly defined genre of "positive country" singers perform material that combines the style of contemporary country-pop music with Christian themes. Some bluegrass groups, such as the LEWIS FAMILY, TAMMY AND JERRY SULLIVAN, and the Forbes Family, sing religious songs exclusively, while other bluegrass performers, such as the venerable RALPH STANLEY or the youthful LYNN MORRIS, always showcase religious material along with their secular numbers. Stanley made the bluegrass world conscious of the a cappella performance of gospel hymns, many of them drawn from the repertoires of Old Regular Baptists in his corner of Appalachia, while his younger colleagues, the NASHVILLE BLUEGRASS BAND and DOYLE LAWSON, dipped into the African-American songbag to do their versions of songs earlier identified with performers like Sister Rosetta Tharpe and the Fairfield Four. PAUL OVERSTREET, RICKY SKAGGS, RICKY VAN SHELTON, and other "positive country singers" (so called because they claim to be resisting the seamy and defeatist themes of mainstream country) generally perform very modern styles of religious music and aim their performances at the listeners who tune in the broadcasts of contemporary Christian radio stations.

Religious music may be less important today in the country field than it was, say, thirty years ago, but the profession of religious faith remains a defining trait of country entertainers. Some country singers, such as Molly O'Day, have totally abandoned mainstream country songs after their conversions, but most, such as MARTY STUART, Ricky Skaggs, and GLEN CAMPBELL, have chosen to "witness for Christ" while maintaining their usual performing schedules. Stuart Hamblen's conversion in a Billy Graham crusade in Los Angeles in the early fifties may have been the first well-publicized example of a country singer's acceptance of Christ, but it has been emulated many times since. Johnny Cash, for instance, has become closely identified with Graham and is a familiar participant in the famous evangelist's revivals. Cash, and many of his country colleagues—such as CONNIE SMITH, BILLY GRAMMER, BILLY WALKER, and Kris Kristofferson—made public avowals of religious commitment in the sixties when Pentecostal evangelist Jimmie Rodgers Snow (the son of country singer HANK SNOW) began his ministry among country musicians in Nashville. The religious confessional, issued often in the form of an autobiography, has become a familiar element of country music's compendium of self-definition, and a form of moral legitimization demanded by many country fans. It is tempting to interpret this kind of religious posturing as little more than an attempt to assert country music's moral superiority, but it is also the lingering evidence of the music's origins, and of its enduring linkage to a Protestant evangelical tradition.

H·H·H·H SKIDROW (Merle Haggard) TALLY BAKERSFIELD CALIFORNIA MERLE HAGGARD T-152-B H·H·H·H

The Hackberry Ramblers

Since 1933 the Hackberry Ramblers have been filling dance floors with a distinctive blend of CAJUN MUSIC and WESTERN SWING. The group has remained active well into the nineties, featuring cofounders Luderin Darbone (born in Evangeline, Louisiana, January 14, 1913) on fiddle and multi-instrumentalist Edwin Duhon (born near Lafayette, Louisiana, June 11, 1910) on accordion.

Live radio broadcasts, beginning in 1933 from Lake Charles, Louisiana, established the band in local dance halls. To boost their acoustic stringband sound, Darbone bought a recently invented PA system and powered it with his idling 1931 Ford at clubs that lacked electricity. Amplification encouraged soloing and expanded the band's musical scope. The Ramblers' innovative Cajun-country synthesis influenced such seminal Cajun musicians as HARRY CHOATES and MICHAEL DOUCET.

In 1935 the Hackberry Ramblers signed with RCA's BLUEBIRD subsidiary. Their diverse, prolific repertoire included the first recording of "Jolie Blonde" (Lennis Sonnier, vocal) in 1936, the blues standard "Sitting on Top of the World" (Floyd Rainwater, vocal) in 1935, and the country hit "Wondering" (Joe Werner, vocal) in 1936. From 1936 to 1939 Bluebird issued the group's recordings sung in English under the pseudonym Riverside Ramblers, while continuing to issue the Cajun French recordings as the Hackberry Ramblers.

In the forties the Hackberry Ramblers' stringband format evolved into a western swing ensemble, complete with horns, and played a regular Saturday gig at the Silver Star Club in Lake Charles from 1946 to 1956. A sixties slump prompted thoughts of retirement, but the Ramblers stayed together with support from Chris Strachwitz, who recorded them for his Arhoolie label. The addition of electric guitarist Glen Croker again changed the Ramblers' sound to the postwar honky-tonk style played today; the other current members are bassist Johnny Faulk, rhythm guitarist Johnny Farque, and this writer as drummer-producer. After more than sixty years, the Hackberry Ramblers continue to tour and record. The band's *Deep Water* album, featuring guest appearances by Marcia Ball, RODNEY CROWELL, Michael Doucet, and JIMMIE DALE GILMORE, was nominated for a Grammy Award in the Traditional Folk category. —*Ben Sandmel*

REPRESENTATIVE RECORDINGS

Le Gran Mamou (CMF, 1990); *Jolie Blonde* (Arhoolie, 1993); *Cajun Boogie* (Flying Fish, 1993); *Deep Water* (Hot Biscuits, 1997)

Hadacol Caravan

The Hadacol Caravan was the last great medicine show. Hadacol was a foul-tasting patent medicine developed in 1945 by a Louisiana politician, Dudley J. LeBlanc. He believed in music as a promotional tool and, in 1950, decided to promote Hadacol using a troupe of entertainers. He toured the South, giving free admission to anyone with a Hadacol box top. The stars of the first caravan were ROY ACUFF, Connee Boswell, George Burns & Gracie Allen, Chico Marx, and Mickey Rooney.

In 1951 LeBlanc became more ambitious—partly out of natural grandiosity, partly out of a desire to use the show as a platform for his bid for the Louisiana governorship, and partly to create a smoke screen around Hadacol's financial picture in order to sell the company. He hired HANK WILLIAMS as the principal act backed by MINNIE PEARL, Candy Candido, and Cesar Romero. There were guests on some dates such as Bob Hope, Milton Berle, Jack Benny, and Jimmy Durante. The Caravan began in LeBlanc's hometown of Lafayette, Louisiana, on August 14, and was scheduled to end on October 2, but it closed down in Dallas on September 17 when LeBlanc sold the corporation to the Tobey Maltz Company. The shows were hugely successful, and financially were probably the high-water mark of Hank Williams's career. —*Colin Escott*

Merle Haggard
b. Bakersfield, California, April 6, 1937

Though for the last decade, his new recordings have received almost no airplay—in the innocently cruel Nashville taxonomy, he is classified as a living legend—Merle Ronald Haggard remains, with the arguable exception of HANK WILLIAMS, the single most influential singer-songwriter in country music history. Haggard is certainly one of the genre's most versatile artists. His repertory ranges wide: aching ballads ("Today I Started Loving You Again" and "Silver Wings"); sly, frisky narratives ("Old Man from the Mountain," "It's Been a Great Afternoon"); semi-autobiographical reflections ("Mama Tried," "Hungry Eyes"); political commentaries ("Under the Bridge," "Rainbow Stew"); proletarian homages ("Workin' Man Blues," "White Line Fever"); as well as drinking songs that are jukebox, cover-band, and closing-time standards ("Swinging Doors," "The Bottle Let Me Down," "I Think I'll Just Stay Here and Drink"). His acolytes are legion and include many of country music's brightest and lesser lights, as well as thousands of nightclub musicians. As fid-

Merle Haggard

dler Jimmy Belken, a longtime member of the Strangers, Haggard's exemplary touring band, once told *The New Yorker,* "If someone out there workin' music doesn't bow deep to Merle, don't trust him about much anything else."

Haggard was born poor, though not desperately so, in Depression-era Bakersfield to Jim and Flossie Haggard, migrants from Oklahoma. Jim, a railroad carpenter, died of a stroke in 1946, forcing Flossie to find work as a bookkeeper.

Flossie was a fundamentalist Christian and a stern, somewhat overprotective mother. Not surprisingly, Merle grew quickly from rambunctious to rake-hell. By his twenty-first birthday he had run away regularly from home, been placed in two separate reform schools (from which he in turn escaped a half dozen times), worked as a laborer, played guitar and sung informally, begun a family, and performed sporadically at Southern California clubs and, for three weeks, on the *Smilin' Jack Tyree Radio Show* in Springfield, Missouri. He also spent time in local jails for theft and bad checks.

His woebegone criminal career culminated in 1957 when, drunk and confused, he was caught burglarizing a Bakersfield roadhouse. After an attempted escape from county jail, he was sent to San Quentin. There, in a final burst of antisocial activity, he got drunk on prison home brew, landing himself briefly in solitary confinement. He was paroled in 1960 and, after a fitful series of odd jobs, got a regular gig playing bass for WYNN STEWART in Las Vegas.

Another Bakersfield mainstay, FUZZY OWEN, signed Haggard to his tiny Tally Records in 1962. After recording five singles there—the release "Skid Row" b/w "Singin' My Heart Out" sold few copies; the fourth, "(My Friends Are Gonna Be) Strangers," entered *Billboard*'s Top Ten (1965)—Haggard signed with CAPITOL. He moved to MCA in 1976, to EPIC in 1981, and in 1990 to CURB.

He released his first album, *Strangers,* in 1965. Nearly seventy feature albums have followed. Counting repackagings, reissues, compilations, promotional and moviesoundtrack albums, as well as albums in which Haggard has participated—with the likes of WILLIE NELSON, PORTER WAGONER, JOHNNY PAYCHECK, BOB WILLS, Dean Martin, RAY CHARLES, and Clint Eastwood—the number of albums rises close to the 150 mark.

Haggard has recorded more than 600 songs, about 250

of them his own compositions. (He often shares writing credits as gestures of financial and personal largess.) He has had thirty-eight #1 songs, and his "Today I Started Loving You Again" (Capitol, 1968) has been recorded by nearly 400 other artists. In addition, Haggard is an accomplished instrumentalist, playing a commendable fiddle and a to-be-reckoned-with lead guitar. He and the Strangers played for Richard Nixon at the White House in 1973, at a barbecue on the Reagan ranch in 1982, at Washington's Kennedy Center, and 60,000 miles from earth—courtesy of astronaut Charles Duke, who brought a tape aboard *Apollo 16* in 1972. Haggard has won numerous CMA and ACM Awards, including both organizations' 1970 Entertainer of the Year awards, been nominated for scores of others, was elected to the Songwriters' Hall of Fame in 1977, and won COUNTRY MUSIC HALL OF FAME membership in 1994. In 1984 he won a Grammy in the Best Country Vocal Performance, Male category for "That's the Way Love Goes." Even so, he has remained famously independent (he once walked out on an imminent appearance on the *Ed Sullivan* television show), and he has kept himself at arm's length from musical Nashville's sociopolitical vortex. He currently lives near Redding, in northern California, well away from music industry power centers.

There is no such thing as a typical Merle Haggard concert. He prides himself on riding the winds of whim and cussedness and, on any given night, might divert from chart and fan favorites and give himself over to a long set of songs by JIMMIE RODGERS, LEFTY FRIZZELL, or BOB WILLS. The three men constitute Haggard's most lasting musical influences. Additionally, he takes great pride in the Strangers' musicianship, and their importance transcends that of mere sidemen. The band has ranged in number from three to ten over the years, incorporates such atypical country instruments as trombones, trumpets, and saxophones, and has included long-respected players such as ROY NICHOLS, Norm Hamlet, Biff Adam, and Clint Strong. The Strangers themselves have garnered eight ACM Touring Band of the Year Awards.

Ironically, Haggard is inextricably linked with a casual ditty that shifted attention from his soaring musicianship to his politics. "Okie from Muskogee" (Capitol, 1969), a #1 song for four weeks and the 1970 Single of the Year for both the ACM and CMA, is a seemingly belligerent and defensive screen of traditional American-heartland values that appeared at the height of the fractious decade of the Vietnam War. Haggard's retellings of the song's intent are manifold and contradictory. In 1974 he told a Michigan newspaper reporter, "Son, the only place I *don't* smoke is Muskogee." A dozen years later, however, he told the *Birmingham Post-Herald* that "Okie" was "a patriotic song that went to the top of the charts at a time when patriotism wasn't really that popular." Although he has frequently bemoaned the public's perception of him as a political animal, he followed "Okie" with the truly angry "The Fightin' Side of Me" (Capitol, 1970) and, in 1988, a sentimental reaction to flag burning, "Me and Crippled Soldiers."

Nor has Haggard's personal life been without drama. His business acumen is notoriously erratic, and he has been married five times. At the time that this was written, he had five children, four by his first wife, Leona Hobbs, and one by his present wife, Theresa Lane. From 1965 to 1978 Haggard was married to singer BONNIE OWENS, with whom he recorded a duet album, *Just Between the Two of Us* (Capitol, 1966) and who is a regular member of Haggard's musical company. He was also married for a time to singer

Leona Williams, who wrote his #1 hits "You Take Me for Granted" and "Someday When Things are Good" (co-written with Haggard). —*Bryan Di Salvatore*

Down Every Road (Capitol, 1996), 4 discs; *A Tribute to the Best Damn Fiddle Player in the World* (Capitol, 1970); *1996* (Curb, 1996); *Chill Factor* (Epic, 1987); *Rainbow Stew (Live at Anaheim Stadium)* (MCA, 1981)

Rob Hajacos

b. Richmond, Virginia, December 20, 1956

Even though Robert Hajacos played second fiddle to top session man MARK O'CONNOR through much of the eighties, Hajacos has become one of Nashville's busiest fiddle players of late. On the basis of how many country hits he had played on, Hajacos was judged *Music Row* magazine's top session fiddle player in 1992, 1993, 1994 (tied), and 1996. His recent credits include albums by GARTH BROOKS, REBA MCENTIRE, Neil Diamond, PAM TILLIS, ALAN JACKSON, MARK CHESNUTT, and many, many others.

Hajacos's dad was a professional fiddle player who had a regular spot on the *OLD DOMINION BARN DANCE*, where Rob often hung out backstage. He didn't take his instrument seriously until junior high, when he joined the school orchestra and began classical training. Hajacos also played country music with his dad through high school, but moved to Nashville in 1976 with a dream of playing alongside MEL TILLIS. Hajacos had a road gig with LITTLE JIMMY DICKENS, investigated studio work, and realized his dream when he got a spot touring with Tillis from 1982 to 1983. Since then he has focused on sessions (about 5,000) and has performed in regular backing groups on such TNN series as *Nashville Music* and *New Country*. —*Michael Hight*

Bill Haley

b. Highland Park, Michigan, July 6, 1925; d. February 9, 1981

Rock & roll history has tended to emphasize ELVIS PRESLEY at the expense of William Clifton Haley, but the fact remains that Haley was scoring hits with what was identifiably rock & roll before Presley first set foot in a studio.

Before Haley developed his brand of rock & roll he, like Presley, was a country musician. Raised in Wilmington, Delaware, Haley played in accordion-led East Coast country bands and was a yodeling champion. He first recorded with the Down Homers for VOGUE in 1944; the first group he led, the Four Aces of Western Swing (based in Chester, Pennsylvania), recorded in 1948. Haley began introducing r&b into his music, experimenting constantly between 1951 and the first big hit, "Crazy, Man, Crazy," for Essex Records, in 1953.

Switching to DECCA RECORDS in 1954, Haley spearheaded the as yet unnamed music with a series of classic recordings, such as "(We're Gonna) Rock Around the Clock," "Shake, Rattle, and Roll," and "See You Later, Alligator." It was "Rock Around the Clock" that established Haley as a star. Cut in April 1954, the record languished until it appeared on the soundtrack of the 1955 teen rebellion film *Blackboard Jungle*. On June 19, 1955, it topped the pop charts, and at year's end *Billboard* named it the best-selling single of 1955.

His downfall was swift; it was exacerbated by Presley's rise but was as much due to Haley's own lapse into self-parody and his tendency to draw too many substandard songs from his own publishing companies. Though he continued to place songs on the pop charts through the fifties, the hits never broke the Top Twenty after 1956. His last hit (until the 1974 reissue of "Rock Around the Clock") was "Skokiaan" in 1960. Even though Haley's star quickly set in the United States, he remained a revered figure in Britain and Europe and a big draw overseas until his death. —*Colin Escott*

Greatest Hits (MCA, 1975); *From the Original Master Tapes* (MCA, 1984)

Roy Hall & His Blue Ridge Entertainers

Roy Davis Hall b. Waynesville, North Carolina, January 6, 1907; d. May 16, 1943

Roy Hall & His Blue Ridge Entertainers helped set the stage for bluegrass with their uptempo brand of string-band music. A product of the Carolina textile mills, Hall initially recorded for BLUEBIRD with sibling Jay Hugh as the Hall Brothers in 1937 and 1938. In the fall of 1938, Roy formed the Blue Ridge Entertainers and played daily radio shows at WAIR in Winston-Salem, and then at WDBJ in Roanoke, where his career peaked. Fiddler TOMMY MAGNESS and steel guitarist Bill Brown dominated the group's instrumental sound. After an eight-side session for Vocalion in 1938, Hall returned to Bluebird in 1940 and 1941. He died in an automobile crash. —*Ivan M. Tribe*

Roy Hall & His Blue Ridge Entertainers (County, 1979)

Tom T. Hall

b. Olive Hill, Kentucky, May 25, 1936

In the late 1960s and early 1970s, Tom T. Hall, along with a handful of other songwriters, such as KRIS KRISTOFFERSON, BILLY JOE SHAVER, and JAMES TALLEY, succeeded in imbuing country music with a new level of lyric and thematic sophistication and social consciousness without violating the music's inherent rusticity and simplicity of form.

Hall also flourished as a recording artist for MERCURY RECORDS in the late 1960s through the early 1980s with his poignant, often sardonic self-written musical slices of life. "Ballad of Forty Dollars" (1968), "Homecoming" (1969), "A Week in a County Jail" (1969), "The Year That Clayton Delaney Died" (1971), "(Old Dogs, Children and) Watermelon Wine" (1972), "I Love" (1973), and "Faster Horses" (1976) were all Top Five country hits.

Hall was born into near poverty in rural Kentucky. He worked as a DJ, headed a bluegrass band, served in the army in Germany, and briefly attended college on the GI Bill before breaking in as a songwriter in the early 1960s. The song that really put him over the top was "Harper Valley PTA." Recorded by JEANNIE C. RILEY, it became a million seller in 1968.

As Hall's success grew, he seemed to turn more and more back to his hardscrabble country roots for creative inspiration—even long after his royalties had made him a millionaire and he was ensconced in Fox Hollow, his elegant Franklin, Tennessee, estate.

Hall has published six books: *How I Write Songs, Why You Can* (1976), *The Storyteller's Nashville* (1979), *The Laughing*

Tom T. Hall

Man of Woodmont Coves (1982), *The Acts of Life* (1986), *Spring Hill, Tennessee* (1990), and *What a Book!* (1996). His love of American literature has inspired him to befriend noted American literary figures like William Styron and Kurt Vonnegut.

For several years in the early 1980s, Hall also hosted *Pop Goes the Country*, a Nashville-produced syndicated TV show, and he has been involved in numerous TNN programs and productions. In 1996, after a long absence from recording, he released a new set of wry, laid-back recordings, *Songs from Sopchoppy*, for Mercury Records. In that same year he hit as a songwriter with "Little Bitty," which scored a #1 spot for ALAN JACKSON. —*Bob Allen*

REPRESENTATIVE RECORDINGS

In Search of a Song (Mercury, 1971); *The Rhymer & Other Five and Dimers* (Mercury, 1973); *The Storyteller & The Banjo Man* (with Earl Scruggs) (Columbia, 1982); *Storyteller, Poet, Philosopher* (Mercury, 1995), 2 discs; *Songs from Sopchoppy* (Mercury, 1996)

Wendell Hall
b. St. George, Kansas, August 23, 1896; d. April 2, 1969

Wendell Woods Hall's professional career began in vaudeville as a singing xylophonist, but his most enduring contribution to America's music was his first recording, "It Ain't Gonna Rain No Mo'," recorded for the GENNETT, VICTOR, and EDISON labels within weeks in October 1923. At one time, the song's country flavor led some writers to claim it as the first commercial hillbilly recording. Though copyrighted by Hall, parts of the song were traditional well before 1923, and Hall probably based his composition on fragments heard in his youth. Very likely he was aware of the folk roots of the piece, because in 1926 he wrote to Robert W. Gordon, a leading authority on American folk music, suggesting that they collaborate to produce commercialized hit songs out of material Gordon had collected.

The song enjoyed great popularity, reportedly selling sheet music in the millions. This and some of his other recordings also helped popularize the ukulele. Its success on wax prompted several sequels: "It Ain't Gonna Rain No Mo'—2nd Installation," "It Ain't Gonna Rain No Mo'—Part 2," and others. "It Ain't Gonna Rain No Mo'" was among the early recordings of both FIDDLIN' JOHN CARSON and GID TANNER and has often been collected from both white and black folksingers. Between 1923 and 1933 Hall, known as the "Red Headed Music Maker," made close to eighty recordings. He continued to write songs into the 1960s, even as he moved from a career in radio to one as an advertising executive. —*Norm Cohen*

REPRESENTATIVE RECORDING

Minstrels & Tunesmiths: The Commercial Roots of Early Country Music (JEMF, 1981); includes Hall's "It Ain't Gonna Rain No Mo'"

Jim Halsey
b. Independence, Kansas, October 7, 1930

James Albert Halsey has been one of country music's most influential business figures as a manager to stars including ROY CLARK, HANK THOMPSON, and the OAK RIDGE BOYS, and as a promoter and booker of major concerts in the United States and internationally. Halsey also pioneered the placement of country acts on television, an emphasis that continued throughout his long career.

Beginning his career as a promoter while a teenager at Independence Junior College in his hometown, Halsey had founded his agency by 1951, the year he started representing western swing star Hank Thompson. A farsighted businessman who likes to plan for the long term, Halsey achieved such milestones as booking some of the earliest country acts as headliners in Las Vegas in 1956–57; booking Roy Clark in 1963 as the first country-music guest host on *The Tonight Show;* and arranging the first country music headliners tour of the Soviet Union, with Clark and the Oak Ridge Boys in 1976. MERLE TRAVIS once joked that the circumspect and low-keyed Halsey would "use a pencil to write out a bomb threat," but he has made an enormous impact with his highly professional management and booking work for some of the biggest names in country music, including the JUDDS, MERLE HAGGARD, MEL TILLIS, LEE GREENWOOD, MINNIE PEARL, TAMMY WYNETTE, DWIGHT YOAKAM, CLINT BLACK, and many others.

On February 1, 1990, the Jim Halsey Company merged with the long-established William Morris Agency. Halsey continued as consultant to the new firm and also heads the music business program at Oklahoma City University. In addition, he has lectured nationally and internationally on music business issues. —*Thomas Goldsmith*

Stuart Hamblen
b. Kellyville, Texas, October 20, 1908; d. March 8, 1989

Singer-songwriter Carl Stuart Hamblen left a lasting impression on country music and popular music in general by composing such songs as "Texas Plains," "This Ole House," "It Is No Secret," "My Mary," and "Remember Me (I'm the One Who Loves You)."

He was born to an itinerant preacher, James Henry

Stuart Hamblen

Hamblen, and his wife, Ernestine. Preparing to enter the teaching profession, Hamblen graduated from McMurray Teachers College in Abilene, but he chose a life in music instead. Hamblen first appeared on radio in 1925. RCA VICTOR RECORDS recorded him in June 1929, releasing "The Boy in Blue," "Drifting Back to Dixie," "When the Moon Shines Down on the Mountain," and "The Big Rock Candy Mountains #2," all Hamblen compositions.

In late 1929 Stuart appeared on Los Angeles radio station KFI as Cowboy Joe, possibly the earliest cowboy act on Los Angeles radio. Hamblen soon became a member of a very popular radio group, the BEVERLY HILL BILLIES, joining them in 1930. Remaining only briefly with the Hill Billies, he assembled his own band, a group that included PATSY MONTANA. In 1932 he began his *Lucky Stars* program over KFWB–Los Angeles, and for the next twenty years he was probably the most popular western performer on Los Angeles radio. He was the first West Coast artist to be signed, in 1934, by DECCA RECORDS, a move that resulted in the August 1934 and February 1935 recording sessions with Hamblen's newly named band, Covered Wagon Jubilee. After a ten-year hiatus Hamblen's recording career began anew for the West Coast–based ARA label. This led to lengthier contracts with COLUMBIA (1949–53; 1960–62), RCA (1954–57), and Coral (1958–59).

In addition to his popularity as a radio personality and his strong, expressive singing style, Hamblen made a name for himself as a prolific composer of love ballads, religious, western, country, patriotic, and children's songs. A devout Christian following a conversion by the Rev. Billy Graham, Hamblen ran unsuccessfully for the U.S. presidency in 1952 on the independent Prohibition Party ticket. After departing from radio in 1952, he syndicated the very popular *Cowboy Church of the Air* series of programs, which were heard over selected radio stations until the late 1970s.

In 1972 the Academy of Country Music (ACM) recognized Hamblen as "the first western singer on Los Angeles radio." For his many accomplishments in radio and the recording industry, the Hollywood Chamber of Commerce honored Hamblen in 1976 by placing his star in their Hollywood Walk of Fame.   —*Ken Griffis*

George Hamilton IV

b. Winston-Salem, North Carolina, July 19, 1937

Although George Hege Hamilton IV began his career as a teen idol with the pop hit "A Rose and a Baby Ruth," he was one of the first pop singers to switch to country music, and he broadened country's appeal with his recordings of American and Canadian folk music.

In 1956, as a freshman at the University of North Carolina, Hamilton recorded "A Rose and a Baby Ruth" (written by JOHN D. LOUDERMILK) for local newspaperman Orville Campbell's small Colonial label. ABC-Paramount Records bought the master, and it became the label's first million-selling record, thrusting Hamilton into tours with leading pop music stars, such as BUDDY HOLLY and the EVERLY BROTHERS, and national TV appearances.

In the late 1950s, Hamilton was a regular on CONNIE B. GAY's *Town & Country* radio and television shows in Washington, D.C., starring JIMMY DEAN and featuring PATSY CLINE. He also had a TV show of his own in the late fifties with many of the *Town & Country* regulars.

Hamilton moved to Nashville and began recording country music for RCA RECORDS in 1960. The following year, he joined the cast of the GRAND OLE OPRY. "Abilene" was a #1 country (and Top Twenty pop) hit for him in 1963. In the mid-1960s Hamilton met singer-songwriter Gordon Lightfoot and was introduced into the Canadian folk music circles, recording such hits as Lightfoot's "Early Morning Rain."

Since the mid-1970s, Hamilton has recorded a number of folk/country/gospel albums, including two with his son, George Hamilton V. Also in the seventies, George IV hosted long-running country music television variety shows in both Canada and the United Kingdom, and made a pioneering tour behind the Iron Curtain.

Hamilton's continuing popularity overseas has earned him the title of International Ambassador of Country Music. Most recently, he has spent six months out of each year since 1993 touring with the UK production *Patsy Cline— The Musical.*   —*Dale Vinicur*

REPRESENTATIVE RECORDINGS

To You and Yours, From Me and Mine (Bear Family, 1995), 5 discs; *Steel Rail Blues* (RCA, 1966, out of print); *Canadian Country Gold* (Broadland International, 1995)

Butch Hancock

b. Lubbock, Texas, July 12, 1945

George Norman "Butch" Hancock is a West Texas singer-songwriter steeped in the tradition of WOODY GUTHRIE and BOB DYLAN. Hancock's songs have been popularized by boyhood buddies JOE ELY and JIMMIE DALE GILMORE—with whom he teamed in an early seventies band called the FLATLANDERS—as well as by other artists, including EMMYLOU HARRIS and JERRY JEFF WALKER. Among the best known of Hancock's hundreds of songs are the oft-recorded "If

THE SOUND SEEN

Country Album Cover Art

Almost from its very beginnings, commercial country music has been as concerned with its look as with its sound. In the 1920s, for example, Grand Ole Opry founder George D. Hay instructed performers on the program to dress in down-home work clothes rather than their Sunday best to make the music seem more authentically rural. Likewise, Jimmie Rodgers appeared in publicity photos dressed alter-

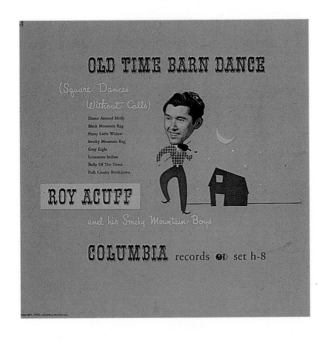

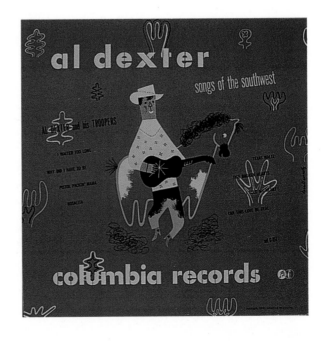

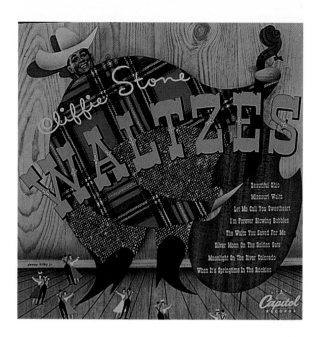

nately in cowboy gear and railroad man's clothes to underscore the adventurous nature of his music. This natural preoccupation with the appearances behind the music has extended to country music's recordings with dazzling results.

On the following pages we have assembled 75 photographs of colorful and rare album jackets from the

Country Music Foundation Library's record collections, which encompass more than 250,000 recordings.

Country album covers are fascinating to pore over because they offer a window into how national record companies perceived country music and its audience. Because we have assembled these more or less chronologically, we can see how country album cover art has

reflected the times. In the early era of country album-

making, the 1940s, when 78-rpm albums (three or four

sleeved 10-inch records in a stamp album-like book—

hence the name "album") appeared on the scene,

album art was in its infancy, and cartoon illustrations,

often combined with photos, were employed to suggest

country music's essential simplicity, gaiety, and high

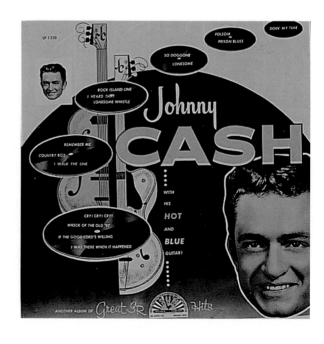

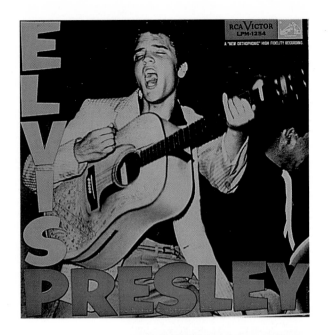

spirits. (The first ten covers displayed are of 78-rpm albums.)

As country music moved through the 1950s to the 1960s and gained increasing mainstream acceptance, its album art began to rely more on classy color portrait photography to convey the essence of the performer. Usually this resulted in a more dignified depiction of

country music, although often the record companies made sure to include rural imagery or colorful country costumes to underscore that the music was country. Sometimes the opposite was true as well. For instance, to convey the sophistication of Jim Reeves's music, the cover for *A Touch of Velvet* showed Reeves in a smart red dinner jacket.

When illustrations were employed, they were

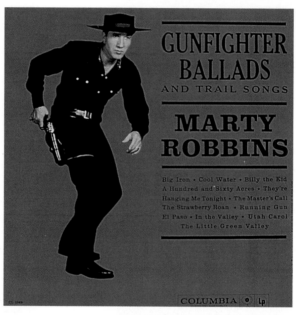

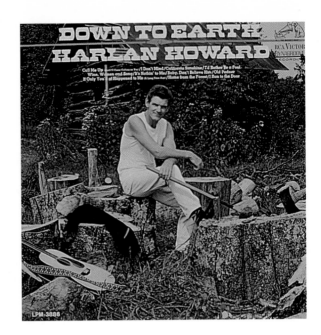

more sophisticated than they had been just a decade or two before. In the early 1960s, for instance, Columbia Records hired Tom Allen to paint a series of album covers for their star bluegrass act, Flatt & Scruggs, after Allen depicted the duo in an illustration accompanying Alan Lomax's famous profile of Flatt & Scruggs in *Esquire* in October 1959. On the opposite side of the coin, Smash Records chose to convey the essential

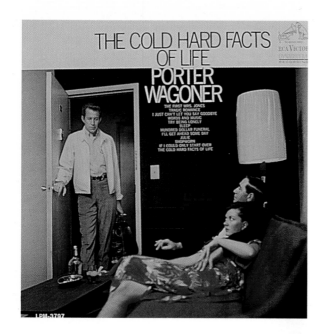

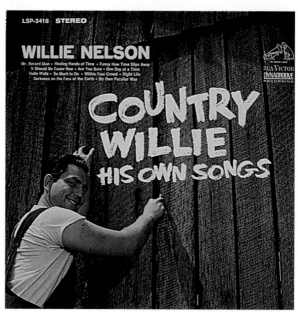

wackiness of Roger Miller's songs with a head-rolling cartoon worthy of Monty Python on Miller's breakthrough *Roger and Out* album in 1964.

In the 1960s and 1970s record companies saw profits from their country divisions rise, and they committed more money to album art as a result. Country music performers got more say-so about the art in the process. One of the results of this artist empowerment

was that country album art began to reflect more accurately the performer's vision. Porter Wagoner used his artistic clout to arrange a striking series of album cover tableaus, including that for *The Cold Hard Facts of Life* and the Grammy-winning cover for *Confessions of a Broken Man*, that left no doubt as to the seriousness of the albums' content. In a similar vein is Moe Bandy's *I Just Started Hatin' Cheatin' Songs Today*, where he sits for-

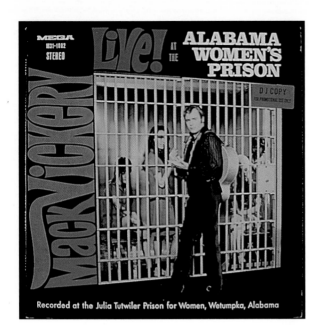

lornly in a bar brandishing a broken bottle. Sometimes this tableau approach could go too far, as when Mack Vickery posed in front of a jail cell full of fetching women in his *Live! at the Alabama Women's Prison* album.

As country moved from the 1970s through the 1980s, record companies became more sophisticated at zeroing in on the persona of the artist they wanted to convey. Thus, Tanya Tucker was frequently depicted as

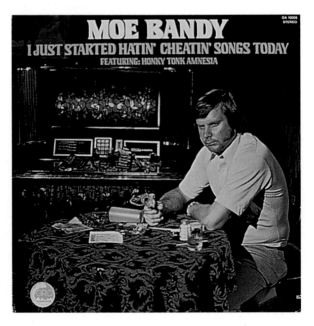

a sexy nymphet, Hank Williams Jr. and Mickey Gilley as good-timin' hell-raisers, the Outlaws Waylon and Willie as genuine desperadoes, Conway Twitty as a debonair man about town (with a pre-stardom Naomi Judd in one album cover), the glamorous mother-and-daughter duo the Judds as virtual twins, and so on. To convey such subtleties as a leaning towards traditional, hard-country music, Randy Travis was posed in front of

an old general store for his debut album, and Reba McEntire was dressed in her rodeo belt and placed in front of the wide-open vista of the Colorado Rocky Mountains, with an American flag waving proudly in the background. In contrast, for edgier artists it was almost expected that the album cover would be a little out of the ordinary. In the late 1980s, to sell such out-

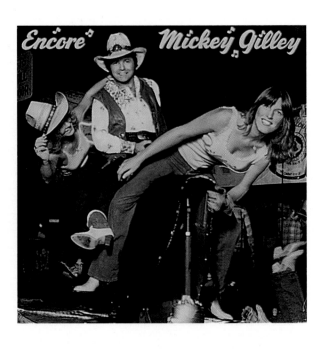

side-the-mainstream talents as Lyle Lovett and Mary Chapin Carpenter, record companies employed photographer Peter Nash to shoot black and white, slightly out-of-focus images. Columbia Records art director Bill Johnson won a 1987 Grammy for Rosanne Cash's *King's Record Shop,* showing Cash in front of an actual, rather antique-looking record shop in Louisville,

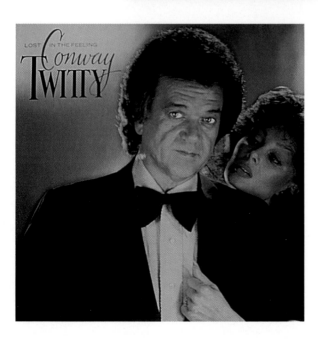

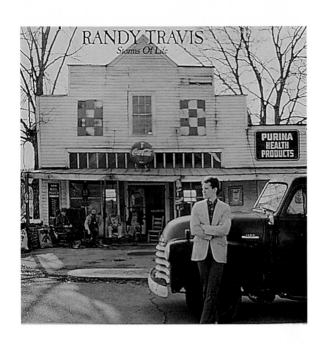

Kentucky (owned coincidentally by Pee Wee King's brother Gene), with no mention of Cash's name on the album's front cover.

In the 1990s, country album art became every bit as attractive and carefully executed as anything from the realm of rock & roll. The key costume and rural motifs have remained elements of most country album

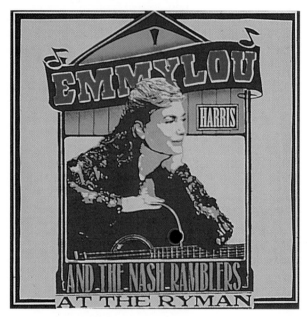

art (note the hats, boots, and outdoors), but they are employed with a much subtler touch than they had been fifty years earlier. By the 1990s country album art usually maintained a delicate equipoise between rusticity and elegance, so as to attract the widest possible audience without alienating hard-core country fans.

Regardless of what these commercial artworks tell

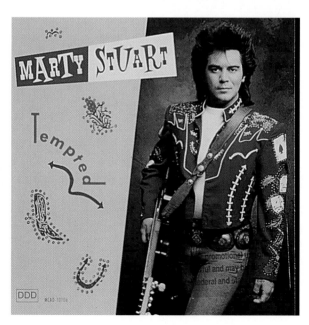

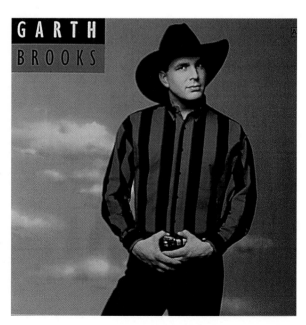

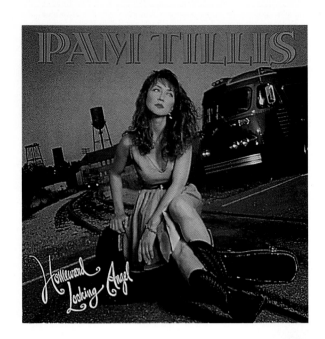

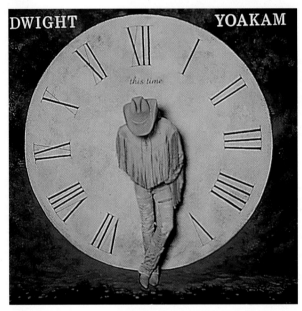

us about record companies' views of the country audience over the years, one truth stands clear: Country recordings are as much a feast for the eye as they are for the ear. —*Paul Kingsbury*

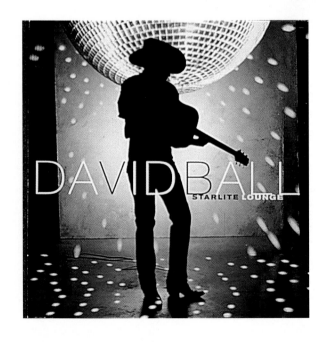

You Were a Bluebird," "West Texas Waltz," and "My Mind's Got a Mind of Its Own."

A free-spirited photographer and architect in addition to his musical pursuits, Hancock long confined his own recording to self-released albums and cassettes. Selections were subsequently compiled for a pair of CDs on SUGAR HILL, *Own & Own* and *Own the Way Over Here*. His prolific songwriting is additionally documented through the *No 2 Alike* fourteen-cassette subscription series, a 1990 recording of a week's engagement at the Cactus Cafe in AUSTIN, Texas, during which Hancock never repeated a song.

In contrast to the slapdash spontaneity of so many of his solo live recordings, Hancock teamed with producer-guitarist Gurf Morlix for a polished studio collection titled *Eats Away the Night*, released by Sugar Hill in 1995.

—*Don McLeese*

REPRESENTATIVE RECORDINGS

Own & Own (Sugar Hill, 1991); *Own the Way Over Here* (Sugar Hill, 1993); *Eats Away the Night* (Sugar Hill, 1995); *You Coulda Walked Around the World* (Rainlight, 1997)

Wayne Hancock
b. Dallas, Texas, May 1, 1965

Thomas Wayne "The Train" Hancock is among the most musically uncompromising neo-hillbilly singers to emerge during the 1990s. A military brat who spent his childhood years moving from town to town, Hancock grew up listening to a wide range of music, including big band jazz, classic honky-tonk, and Broadway soundtracks. During his late teenage years, he played the juke joints and roadhouses of East Texas before serving a six-year hitch in the marines, where, stationed in Hawaii, he continued to write songs and perform, mainly for tips. Hancock then returned to Texas and, within a year, had several major record labels interested in signing him, until they decided that he was "too country" for commercial country radio.

In 1994 Hancock appeared with JOE ELY, BUTCH HANCOCK, Jo Carol Pierce, and ROBERT EARL KEEN JR. in the theatrical production of *Chippy* and contributed two performances to the show's soundtrack album. In 1995 he released *Thunderstorms and Neon Signs* (Dejadisc), a first-rate collection of hard-driving, drummerless hillbilly blues. Hancock's major label debut, *That's What Daddy Wants*, was released on EMI/ARK 21 in the fall of 1997.

—*Bill Friskics-Warren*

REPRESENTATIVE RECORDING

Thunderstorms and Neon Signs (Dejadisc, 1995)

Carlton L. Haney
b. Rockingham County, North Carolina, September 19, 1928

Carlton Haney was a major figure in the growth of country and bluegrass music from the 1950s to the 1980s. Best known as a founder of bluegrass music festivals, Haney also promoted country music package shows and helped to build careers of artists ranging from BILL MONROE, RENO & SMILEY, and the OSBORNE BROTHERS to PORTER WAGONER, LORETTA LYNN, MERLE HAGGARD, and CONWAY TWITTY.

Haney began his country music career as a booking agent for Bill Monroe in 1953. For a decade, starting in 1955, Haney managed Reno & Smiley and the *Old Dominion Barn Dance* in Virginia. In 1964 Haney rented a coliseum in Winston-Salem, North Carolina, and began to promote country music package shows, featuring artists such as RAY PRICE, Porter Wagoner, NORMA JEAN, and KITTY WELLS. This led to an eight-year series of Country Shindig shows in thirty-seven southeastern and northeastern cities.

In 1965, Haney and RALPH RINZLER, a member of the GREENBRIAR BOYS and, earlier, Bill Monroe's manager, conceived plans for a multiday outdoor bluegrass festival, modeled on the NEWPORT FOLK FESTIVAL and centered on the musicians who had apprenticed with Monroe. Originally produced by Haney at Fincastle, Virginia, during Labor Day weekend (1965), the festival drew about 1,000 diehard fans. Haney served as MC. When moved to Berryville, Virginia, and later Camp Springs, North Carolina, the festival grew and became the prototype for at least 300 such events now held throughout the United States.

—*Fred Bartenstein*

Happy Fats
b. Rayne, Louisiana, January 15, 1915; d. February 23, 1988

Leroy LeBlanc, better known as Happy Fats, led one of the most interesting and prolific Cajun dance bands from the 1930s into the 1950s. Happy Fats & His Rayne-Bo Ramblers showed, perhaps better than any other group, the deep effect that western swing had on Cajun musicians.

The Rayne-Bo Ramblers began recording as a traditional Cajun fiddle band in 1935, but as the decade progressed LeBlanc added instruments such as steel guitar and piano, played in the manner of western swing bands. Of particular importance was the impact of CLIFF BRUNER's Texas Wanderers, based across the border in Texas but touring in Louisiana and blasting their broadcast signal eastward. By 1940, when he was broadcasting on KVOL, LeBlanc's BLUEBIRD sessions were as weighted toward western swing as they were Cajun music, and his band included the soon-to-be-legendary fiddler HARRY CHOATES, then obviously under Bruner's spell. After the war, LeBlanc continued in this dual Cajun/western swing mode. By the end of the forties he had joined forces with fiddler Doc Guidry, recording for J. D. MILLER's Feature label as Happy, Doc & all the Boys and for De Luxe. LeBlanc continued to be active in later years, gaining some unfortunate notoriety for his segregationist recordings on Miller's Rebel Records in the 1960s.

—*Kevin Coffey*

REPRESENTATIVE RECORDINGS

Gran Prairie: A Cajun Music Anthology, 1935–1940 (Country Music Foundation, 1993) (various-artists reissue containing several sides by Happy Fats)

Linda Hargrove
b. Tallahassee, Florida, February 3, 1949

Singer-songwriter-guitarist Linda Hargrove created some of the most memorable, personal music to come out of Nashville during the 1970s. Perhaps the only woman of the era who not only wrote hit songs, but also worked consistently as a session musician, Hargrove presaged a later generation of country music women who controlled their own musical destinies.

Hargrove moved to Nashville from Florida in 1970 and endured hard times before coming under the tutelage of famed session steel guitarist PETE DRAKE, who helped her find session work and gave her an "in-depth education in country music," she said. Her first record, *Music Is Your Mistress*, issued on ELEKTRA in 1973, resulted from of a chance encounter with former Monkee Mike Nesmith, who introduced her to Elektra chief Russ Miller. Her 1974 release *Blue Jean Country Queen* defined Hargrove's image as an eclectic, imaginative songwriter and singer who fused country, rock, soul, and western swing in an independent-minded mix. She never rose higher on the singles charts than #39, with "Love Was (Once Around the Dance Floor)" from the 1975 LP *Love, You're the Teacher*, but she toured successfully and achieved songwriting peaks with "Let It Shine" (OLIVIA NEWTON-JOHN), "Just Get Up and Close the Door" (JOHNNY RODRIGUEZ), and the plaintive "I've Never Loved Anyone More" (LYNN ANDERSON), written with Nesmith.

Albums for CAPITOL and RCA failed to catch fire, and a "burned out" Hargrove left Nashville and the music business in 1980. Marriage to businessman Charlie Bartholomew that year brought stability, and she released Christian LPs as Linda Bartholomew in 1982 and 1988. A return to Nashville in 1985 was followed by the devastating news that Hargrove had a type of blood cancer that was almost invariably fatal. A draining battle against the disease culminated in a risky but ultimately successful bone marrow transplant. The mid-nineties found Hargrove cancer free, writing and singing at peak form. Hargrove is the subject of a chapter in a 1997 book that examined the Nashville music business, Laurence Leamer's *Three Chords and the Truth*. —*Thomas Goldsmith*

REPRESENTATIVE RECORDINGS

Music Is Your Mistress (Elektra, 1973, out of print); *Blue Jean Country Queen* (Elektra, 1974, out of print); *Love, You're the Teacher* (Capitol, 1975, out of print)

Sid Harkreader

b. Gladeville, Tennessee, February 26, 1898; d. March 19, 1988

Best known today as the first partner of UNCLE DAVE MACON, Sidney J. Harkreader was a distinctive fiddler and guitarist who had a long and varied career on and off the GRAND OLE OPRY. A native of the great Cedar Glades east of Nashville, Harkreader determined as a young man to try to make a full-time living with his music—a daring plan for a country musician in the 1920s. In about 1923 he began performing with Uncle Dave Macon, sometimes being billed as his "son." Harkreader backed Macon on many of his early 1924–25 recordings, as well as on several later ones. By 1926 he was out on his own, heading up a troupe of Charleston dancers for the Loew's vaudeville circuit; he also began recording on his own for the Paramount (and Broadway) labels, first with guitarist Grady Moore and then with singer-guitarist Blythe Poteet.

By 1935 Harkreader was back on the Opry—this time with a full stringband, Sid Harkreader and Company, that included luminaries such as mandolinist Mack McGar and the one-armed banjo player Emory Martin. By now Sid was known for two signature pieces: "Mocking Bird Breakdown" and "Old Joe." Trying to keep current, he organized his Round-Up Gang, a western band, but by 1940 he had decided to retire from music and open a restaurant in downtown Nashville. In later years he would return to the Opry, though, appearing with several of the hoedown bands such as the GULLY JUMPERS. —*Charles Wolfe*

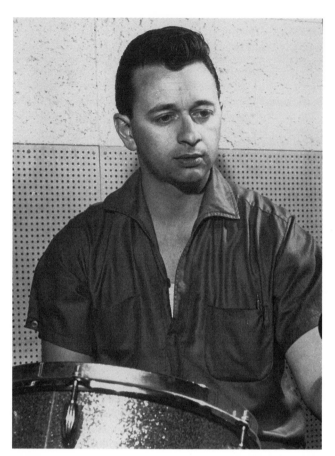

Buddy Harman

Buddy Harman

b. Nashville, Tennessee, December 23, 1928

Nashville's first full-time studio session drummer, Murrey M. Harman has played on an estimated 15,000 sessions during his career, backing stars ranging from PATSY CLINE, BRENDA LEE, ROY ORBISON, and the EVERLY BROTHERS to DOLLY PARTON, WAYLON JENNINGS, Simon & Garfunkel, and Perry Como.

Harman's parents had their own part-time band in Nashville, with his mother on drums, and jazz drummers Gene Krupa and Buddy Rich inspired the young musician to become a professional drummer. After playing in high school and navy bands, he dropped out of college to study for three years at Chicago's Roy Knapp School of Percussion. In 1952 he returned to Nashville to play with area groups.

Gradually, Harman worked his way into Nashville's emerging recording scene and took up full-time studio work about 1955. Initially some country producers were reluctant to allow him much leeway, but his solid, tasteful playing on sessions with artists such as MOON MULLICAN, MARTHA CARSON, the Everlys, and RAY PRICE helped to expand the role of drums in country music. By the mid-1960s, Harman was working some 600 sessions a year. This number declined by the late seventies, as the influx of new pickers from other cities and Nashville's growing recording activity reduced the dominance he had once enjoyed. Harman remained active in the studio, however, and toured as a member of the Nashville Superpickers early in the eighties. Today, he plays sessions and serves part-time as a business agent for the Nashville local of the the AMERICAN FEDERATION OF MUSICIANS. —*John Rumble*

REPRESENTATIVE RECORDINGS

Walk Right Back: The Everly Brothers on Warner Brothers, 1960-1969 (Warner Bros., 1993); *The All Time Greatest Hits of Roy Orbison* (CBS, 1989)

Harmonica

The harmonica is based on the principle of the *free reed,* an Asian invention that dates back 3,000 years in which a tongue made of metal or wood is attached at one end over a close-fitting opening through which the free end vibrates when air passes over it. In 1821 a German named Christian Buschmann patented an instrument called the *aura* that had steel reeds placed in small channels. In 1825 Richter devised a mouth organ with reed plates mounted on either side of a wooden comb that enabled both draw and blow notes. It was Richter's design and diatonic tuning scheme that became the basis for the harmonica as we know it today.

The mouth organ proved immediately popular. The German harmonica manufacturer Matthias Hohner was the first to adopt mass-production techniques and to import mouth organs to the United States, successes that enabled his firm to attain a worldwide monopoly. By the middle of the nineteenth century the inexpensive and portable harmonica was commonly displayed on the shelves of general stores throughout America, especially in the South, where it was commonly known as the "French harp." Several regions settled largely by German immigrants—notably Texas, Illinois, and the Carolinas—became known for the high caliber of their harmonicists. The mouth organ's uncanny ability for mimicry led virtuosos in rural America to perfect "talking" harmonica showpieces and startlingly realistic re-creations of fox chases and speeding locomotives. DEFORD BAILEY ("The Harmonica Wizard"), who performed on the GRAND OLE OPRY from 1926 until 1941, excelled at such showpieces.

Although the harmonica has been used successfully in every form of music, it is usually identified with the blues and with country music. HENRY WHITTER recorded several harmonica solos in 1923 that rank as some of the earliest recordings of country music. The Tennessee hill country around Nashville produced many first-rate harmonica players, including DR. HUMPHREY BATE, Herman Crook of the CROOK BROTHERS, and DeFord Bailey. LONNIE GLOSSON and WAYNE RANEY reportedly sold more than 5 million harmonicas through the mail during the 1940s and 1950s, when they hosted a nationally syndicated radio program. Jimmie Riddle and ONIE WHEELER were also prominent hillbilly mouth harpists.

By the mid-1960s the harmonica was rarely heard in country music, but all that changed with the arrival in Nashville of CHARLIE MCCOY, a phenomenal player whose harmonica has been heard on thousands of recordings. The mouth organ work of Don Brooks and Mickey Raphael, members of the bands of WAYLON JENNINGS and WILLIE NELSON, respectively, built on McCoy's accomplishments, and the fine playing of younger harmonicists such as Terry McMillan and Kirk "Jellyroll" Johnson is ensuring the instrument a prominent role in country music for the foreseeable future. —*Kim Field*

Bill Harrell
b. Marion, Virginia, September 14, 1934

Bluegrass guitarist-singer William Harrell became active in the Washington, D.C., area in the late 1950s. Bill Harrell & the Virginians' recordings were included on STARDAY RECORDs singles and anthologies, and United Artists Records issued their first album in 1963. Appearing semi-regularly on *The Jimmy Dean Show* on ABC-TV in the early 1960s as Buck Ryan & Smitty Irvin, the band recorded an album for MONUMENT RECORDS in 1965.

Harrell and banjo great Don Reno (RENO & SMILEY) formed a partnership in 1966, with prolific recordings (eventually for CMH Records) and performances in the style Reno had established with his former partner, Red Smiley. In 1978 Harrell reactivated the Virginians band and returned to performing in his own style.
—*Frank and Marty Godbey*

REPRESENTATIVE RECORDINGS
Blue Virginia Blue (Rebel, 1986); *A Song for Everyone* (Rebel, 1987)

Kelly Harrell
b. Wythe County, Virginia, September 13, 1889; d. July 9, 1942

Like country music pioneers CHARLIE POOLE, Dave McCarn, HENRY WHITTER, and the DIXON BROTHERS, Crockett Kelly Harrell left a job in the textile mills to try his luck in commercial country music. Unlike some of the other singers, Harrell eventually failed in his attempt to make a living in music, but along the way he made more than forty excellent records, including several definitive interpretations of traditional songs and several that became country standards. Ironically, he never recorded his most famous song, "Away Out on the Mountain"; JIMMIE RODGERS made it a hit, with Harrell receiving thousands of dollars in royalties. As a result, Harrell was probably one of the first country songwriters to make a considerable profit from song royalties.

As a young man, Harrell worked in textile mills around Fries, Virginia, where he met old-time fiddler Henry Whitter. Whitter had gone north and talked record companies into recording him, and Harrell was inspired to follow suit—in spite of the fact that he was just a singer and could not even play the guitar or banjo. In January 1925 he made it to New York to record four songs for VICTOR RECORDS, including versions of "New River Train" and the old murder ballad "The Butcher's Boy." These sold well enough that a year later Victor asked him to rerecord them using the new electrical recording process. Soon Harrell had organized his own back-up band, the Virginia String Band; this consisted of Posey Rorer on fiddle, R. D. Hundley on banjo, and Alfred Steagel on guitar. Over the next three years they recorded songs such as "My Name Is John Johanna," "Charles Guiteau," and "Row Us over the Tide." Some of these stayed in print through the 1950s, when they were included in Harry Smith's famous 1952 *Anthology of American Folk Music.*

Harrell's record royalties were impressive by standards of the day, but when the Depression curtailed record sales, and record companies began to pressure him to learn an instrument, he lost interest and returned to the mills. Plagued by asthma, he collapsed at work one day in 1942 and died on his way to the hospital. —*Stacey Wolfe*

Emmylou Harris

Emmylou Harris
b. Birmingham, Alabama, April 2, 1947

A country singer by way of a high school marching band (she played alto sax), folk music, and country-rock, Emmylou Harris has produced a tall stack of albums, on any one of which listeners will find her exploring beyond the conventional parameters of country, bluegrass, and rockabilly and paying heartfelt tributes to pop, rock, folk, gospel, and blues—all while remaining country at the core. Long before artists were being called NEW TRADITIONALISTS, Harris was already stretching boundaries—and succeeding on her own terms, introducing traditional country to a wider audience while helping to redefine country music itself.

Harris has had seven #1 and twenty other Top Ten country hits. Eight of her twenty-four albums have been certified gold, and *Trio,* her 1987 album with DOLLY PARTON and LINDA RONSTADT, has sold more than 1 million copies. Harris has received seven Grammys, been named Female Vocalist of the Year by the CMA, serves on the board of the COUNTRY MUSIC FOUNDATION, and was inducted into the GRAND OLE OPRY in 1992.

Born in Birmingham, Alabama, and raised in Woodbridge, Virginia, Harris was considered an "oddball" in high school, she said, "because she kept her nose buried in her books." Wanting acceptance, she sang at parties, won a local beauty contest, and tried out to be a majorette. She ended up in the marching band.

At the University of North Carolina in Greensboro, she studied drama but soon turned to music, singing in a folk duo at a local club. Her first love, she said, was folk and country blues, because of their "intense emphasis on lyrics." She transferred briefly to Boston University, then moved to New York, where she sang in Greenwich Village and developed an appreciation for country music through fellow performers JERRY JEFF WALKER and David Bromberg.

Harris made a record (a disaster) for the Jubilee label, was married for a short time, and had a daughter. In Nashville, with her marriage ended, she worked odd jobs, including a stint as a singing waitress. Barely able to pay her rent, Harris moved with her baby to Maryland in 1970 to live with her parents. There she began singing again, mostly at folk clubs in and around nearby Washington, D.C.

While performing in the back room of Clyde's, a singles bar in Georgetown, Harris was discovered by two members of the Flying Burrito Brothers, who for a time thought of adding her as a Burrito Sister. That didn't happen, but CHRIS HILLMAN of the Burritos told GRAM PARSONS—who had just left the band—about Harris.

Harris and Parsons clicked instantly. Possessed of a silvery, high-lonesome voice, Harris was also an instinctive duet singer, and she soared with Parsons on two albums, helping him realize his dreams of a fusion of country and rock & roll. In later years, Harris would also record moving duets with such artists as ROY ORBISON ("That Lovin' You Feelin' Again," 1980) and DON WILLIAMS ("If I Needed You," 1981), among others.

Parsons died in 1973, and in 1975 Harris released her first major label solo album, *Pieces of the Sky,* on WARNER BROS./Reprise. It included a version of the LOUVIN BROTHERS' "If I Could Only Win Your Love" that became her first Top Ten country hit. Harris's first #1 hit, "Together Again" (from *Elite Hotel,* 1976), came from the pen of BUCK OWENS. But throughout, Harris made it a point to perform songs by Parsons and to talk about his legacy. "I wanted to carry on with what I thought he would have wanted me to do," she said, "bringing certain elements of folk music, with its emphasis on the lyric, trying eclectic things, but always coming back to that electric country blues."

A musicologist at heart, Harris found and employed a succession of excellent writers and musicians who brought new sounds and sensibilities to country music. These included RODNEY CROWELL (who wrote some of her material and anchored the initial version of her famous Hot Band), RICKY SKAGGS (who reflected Harris's devotion to bluegrass, most notably in *Roses in the Snow,* 1980), VINCE GILL (who appeared on three albums, including *The Ballad of Sally Rose,* 1985), and EMORY GORDY JR. Others who gained exposure through Harris included the WHITES and steel guitarist Hank DeVito. Producer and A&R executive TONY BROWN, who joined as pianist in the late 1970s, credits her for widening his own understanding of country music.

Harris's producers have included Brian Ahern, who worked on her early Warner Bros. albums, and whom she married in 1977 (they divorced in 1984), and songwriter Paul Kennerley, who became her producer in 1985. She and Kennerley were married from 1985 to 1993.

Through the years, the constant in Harris's career has been adventurousness, whether it's to tackle a Chuck Berry or a Bruce Springsteen composition, to record her acoustic live *At the RYMAN* album (1992), or to venture into the alternative arena with producer Daniel Lanois, as she did for her acclaimed 1995 album *Wrecking Ball.* As Harris herself has said, she's "always tried to fight against categories." —*Ben Fong-Torres*

REPRESENTATIVE RECORDINGS

Pieces of the Sky (Reprise, 1975); *Profile: The Best of Emmylou Harris* (Warner Bros., 1978); *Roses in the Snow* (Warner Bros. 1980); *Profile: The Best of Emmylou Harris, Volume II* (Warner Bros., 1984); *Duets* (Reprise, 1990); *Wrecking Ball* (Asylum, 1995)

Freddie Hart
b. Lochapoka, Alabama, December 21, 1926

Freddie Hart's recording of "Easy Loving" was voted the CMA's Song of the Year in 1971 and 1972. This recording was the highlight of Hart's career, and he never achieved the stardom such an honor might bestow, although he had several more successful recordings.

Born Frederick Segrest in a family of fifteen children, Hart had a troubled childhood, running away from home at seven, then being sent to a Civilian Conservation Corps camp at twelve. He joined the Marine Corps in 1942 when he was only fifteen and served in the Pacific Theater (Iwo Jima, Okinawa, and Guam). He entertained at a number of NCO clubs and after his discharge worked in Texas and Hempstead, New York, as a laborer. In 1949 he came to Nashville, where he met HANK WILLIAMS. Hart had his first song recorded in 1952, when GEORGE MORGAN did "Every Little Thing Rolled into One." Hart moved to Phoenix and met LEFTY FRIZZELL and toured with him until 1953; Hart then became a regular on TOWN HALL PARTY in Los Angeles until 1956.

His first recording contract was with CAPITOL RECORDS, then COLUMBIA RECORDS and Kapp Records before returning to Capitol in 1970. His early 1954 release of his song "Loose Talk" caught the attention of CARL SMITH, who covered it and had a #1 hit later that year. Another songwriting success for Hart was "Skid Row Joe," which hit #3 for PORTER WAGONER in 1966. Although Hart had a number of chart singles, none was a major hit until "Easy Loving" in 1971. This was followed by a five-year period when he had a number of hit singles, including "My Hang-Up Is You," "Bless Your Heart," "Got the All Overs for You (All Over Me)," "Super Kind of Woman," "Trip to Heaven," "Hang in There Girl," and "The First Time," all on Capitol. He continued releasing singles throughout the seventies; in 1980 he moved to Sunbird, then to El Dorado and Fifth St. and, although he had chart records, he could not repeat his success from the early 1970s. —*Don Cusic*

REPRESENTATIVE RECORDING

Freddie Hart's Greatest Hits (Capitol, 1975)

John Hartford
b. New York, New York, December 30, 1937

After making his mark in Nashville and Los Angeles as an innovative singer-songwriter, lanky banjo player John Cowan Harford (Chet Atkins added a *t* to John's last name when he signed to RCA VICTOR) reversed his progressive musical direction to pursue the acoustic music he preferred.

Raised in St. Louis, Hartford was fascinated by the music he heard on country radio, particularly LESTER FLATT & EARL SCRUGGS. Learning banjo, guitar, fiddle, and mandolin, he played with various central Missouri and Illinois bluegrass bands during the early 1960s. In 1965 he moved to Nashville to work as a late-night disc jockey on WSIX. After hearing Hartford's songs, Chuck Glazer of the GLASER BROTHERS signed him to a publishing contract and arranged an RCA VICTOR recording contract. Hartford's 1966 album debut, *John Hartford Looks at Life*, revealed a highly original talent; his introspective lyrics would influence a generation of Nashville songwriters. "Gentle on My Mind," a love song from Hartford's second album, became a modest hit in 1967, and GLEN CAMPBELL's lush version of it landed on both pop and country charts. Over the years this song has become one of the most recorded and broadcast songs in country music history.

Moving to California in 1968, Hartford became a writer-performer on CBS-TV's *The Smothers Brothers Comedy Hour*

and *The Glen Campbell Goodtime Hour*. But within two years Hartford became dissatisfied with both Los Angeles and his commercial direction. Returning to Nashville, he recruited veteran bluegrass musicians VASSAR CLEMENTS, TUT TAYLOR, and Norman Blake to record *Aereo Plain*, an acoustic album, for WARNER BROTHERS. Released in 1971, it found an immediate audience among sharp, young bluegrass musicians who best appreciated Hartford's unorthodox lyrics and rhythmic ideas.

After 1975 Hartford largely worked club, concert, and festival dates without a band; his first unaccompanied album, *Mark Twang* (Flying Fish, 1976), won a Grammy for Best Ethnic or Traditional Recording. When not performing, Hartford pursued a second vocation as a riverboat pilot. He also did voice-overs for film and television documentaries, most notably Ken Burns's acclaimed *The Civil War* series for PBS. —*Dave Samuelson*

REPRESENTATIVE RECORDINGS

Aereo Plain (Warner Brothers, 1971; Rounder, 1997); *Me Oh My, How the Time Does Fly: A John Hartford Collection* (Flying Fish, 1988)

Hatch Show Print
established 1879 in Nashville, Tennessee

Located at 316 Broadway in downtown Nashville, Hatch Show Print is believed to be the oldest active poster print shop in America. For years its most famous client was the GRAND OLE OPRY, and to this day the shop's evocative, archaic handiwork is favored by music industry art directors and others seeking the visual warmth of woodblock print. Through the years, everyone from the prewar blues queen Bessie Smith, to ERNEST TUBB, to EMMYLOU HARRIS (the cover of her 1992 *At the Ryman* album) have seen their music advertised in the bold, minimalist Hatch Show Print style.

Hatch was founded in 1879 by the brothers Charles R. and Herbert H. Hatch of Wisconsin. Their first shop opened at the corner of what are now Fifth and Deaderick Streets in Nashville, and their first known job was a six-by-nine-inch "dodger" advertising an April 1879 appearance by the Rev. Henry Ward Beecher at the Grand Opera House. As the shop's fame grew, all manner of clients came its way—from circuses to minstrel shows to Negro League baseball promoters. Charles's son William took over the business in 1921 and moved it three years later to 116 Fourth Avenue North. By 1938 Hatch was routinely printing the Opry's posters, which, along with those of Hatch's other clients, could be seen on barns and storefronts all over the South. The business went into decline, however, when Will Hatch died in 1952. After various ownership changes, Hatch Show Print was successfully revived in 1987 by the COUNTRY MUSIC FOUNDATION, which moved it to its current location in 1992. —*Daniel Cooper*

Hawaiian Music

Musicians from the Hawaiian Islands toured the United States before World War I. The Hawaiian steel guitar was not in evidence until exotic dancer Toots Paka's troupe brought guitarist Joseph Kekuku to New York in 1909, where he and the group made several EDISON cylinders. Popular accounts have it that Kekuku "invented" the instrument when a comb fell from his pocket and slid along his guitar neck.

Other early Hawaiian recordings show no further evidence of the steel guitar until Walter Kolomoku's appearance with the Hawaiian Quintette at New York's Winter Garden in a play that ran through the 1912–13 season. The Quintette recorded extensively for VICTOR in April 1913, and these recordings established Hawaiian music as a major genre on the mainland. Polynesian artists and their American counterparts recorded prolifically through World War I and beyond.

In those years, Hawaiian guitar style merged to an extent with African-American blues slide guitar style. In 1921 one Sam Moore recorded his "Laughing Rag" on his octochorda (presumably an eight-string Hawaiian guitar). Louisville, Kentucky, blues guitarist Sylvester Weaver's 1923 "Guitar Rag" was even more influential—thirteen years later it became LEON MCAULIFFE's signature piece "Steel Guitar Rag," and his boss BOB WILLS's first major hit.

In the 1920s Hawaiian (or slide) guitars found a place in recorded country music. RILEY PUCKETT recorded a solo called "Darkey's Wail" in 1926. Jimmie Tarlton featured the instrument in duets with his partner TOM DARBY, and even Maybelle Carter featured the instrument on CARTER FAMILY records from 1928 to 1930.

The amplified steel guitar was first recorded in 1933 by Noelani's Hawaiian Orchestra. By 1934, influential guitarists Sol Hoopii and Sam Koki were playing amplified instruments. Late that year, BOB DUNN brought one to MILTON BROWN's Brownies; their January 1935 records with Dunn's aggressive solos redefined the sound of western swing, especially after Leon McAuliffe followed Dunn's example and introduced the electric steel guitar with Bob Wills's Texas Playboys a few months later.

Back east, ROY ACUFF adopted the string bass and steel from western swing for his own music, though he almost always used a nonamplified steel guitar (or dobro). Acuff's 1937 "Steel Guitar Chimes" featured Clell (Cousin Jody) Summey, playing his version of the Hawaiian standard "Maui Chimes."

The postwar era witnessed technological development of the steel guitar, and players such as BUD ISAACS, PETE DRAKE, Johnny Sibert, HERB REMINGTON, and others who developed modern styles far removed from the Hawaiian sound.
—*Dick Spottswood*

Hawkshaw Hawkins
b. Huntington, West Virginia, December 22, 1921; d. March 5, 1963

Honky-tonk singer Hawkshaw Hawkins was billed as "eleven and an half yards of personality." As a youth, Harold Franklin Hawkins traded five trapped rabbits for his first guitar, and a short time later, at age fifteen, he entered and won a talent show on radio station WSAZ in Huntington, West Virginia. In addition to the fifteen-dollar prize, Hawkins got his first job working at the station. He later moved to WCHS in Charleston, West Virginia, and occasionally teamed as a duo with Clarence "Sherlock" Jack. In 1941 Hawkins briefly worked in a traveling show for a Lawrence, Massachusetts, radio station and in a Baltimore shipyard before entering the military, where he spent the war years in the Pacific. While in the Philippines, he performed on Manila radio station WJUM.

Upon returning to civilian life, Hawkins joined WWVA *JAMBOREE* and remained there until 1954; during this time

Hawkshaw Hawkins

he also had a CBS radio program. He developed a large following due not only to recordings featuring his rich, smooth, honky-tonk vocals, but also to his showmanship. Especially popular were his colorful summer shows, which included trained horse acts and rope and Australian bullwhip tricks.

Hawkins's first record successes were "Pan American" and "Doghouse Boogie" in 1948. The following year, 1949, he scored with "I Wasted a Nickel." In 1951 he had two Top Ten hits, "I Love You a Thousand Ways" and "I'm Waiting Just for You." His version of "Slow Poke" in 1952 reached both the country and pop charts.

On the strength of his record successes, Hawkins joined the GRAND OLE OPRY in 1955. It was not until four years later, though, that he made another hit, his 1959 "Soldier's Joy"—a pseudo–Revolutionary War song set to the melody of a traditional fiddle tune and that reached #15 on *Billboard* charts. The following year, on November 26, 1960, he married country singer JEAN SHEPARD; the ceremony was conducted on an auditorium stage in Wichita, Kansas. Late in 1962 he recorded a JUSTIN TUBB song, "Lonesome 7-7203," that turned out to be Hawkins's all-time biggest hit. Unfortunately, he never lived to see it reach #1.

In 1963, Hawkins, along with PATSY CLINE, COWBOY COPAS, and pilot Randy Hughes, who was also Copas's son-in-law and Cline's personal manager, were flying to Nashville from Kansas City. They had performed in a concert benefiting the family of a DJ who had lost his life in a car wreck. Their plane came down in a blinding thunderstorm and crashed in the hills near Camden, Tennessee, killing all aboard. Ironically, Hawkins feared flying and seldom traveled by air. It was a particularly sad ending to the life of a man who was one of country's finest honky-tonk singers.
—*W. K. McNeil*

REPRESENTATIVE RECORDINGS
Hawk (Bear Family, 1991); *Hawkshaw Hawkins Sings Hawkshaw Hawkins* (Stetson, 1992)

George D. Hay
b. Attica, Indiana, November 9, 1895; d. May 8, 1968

Rightfully given credit as the founder of WSM's GRAND OLE OPRY, George Dewey Hay was a remarkable visionary and colorful romantic who played a vital role in the commercializing and promotion of country music.

Following service in the army, the Indiana native made his way to Memphis, where he worked as a reporter for the *Commercial Appeal.* One of his assignments was to cover the city court beat, from which he developed a popular humorous column called "Howdy, Judge," based on the dialogue between the judge and those charged with petty crimes. The success of these columns (which were collected in book form in 1925) won him the sobriquet "The Solemn Ole Judge," though he was only in his twenties and had no legal training. When the newspaper established its own radio station, WMC, in January 1923, Hay was soon prevailed upon to serve as late-night station announcer and radio editor.

Hay found he had a flair for this kind of work and brought a sense of showmanship and style to it. He chanted the call letters, scripted his shows, and blew an imitation steamboat whistle (dubbed "Hushpuckena") to announce the start of the evening's shows. (All of these he would later bring with him to WSM.) His popularity grew so fast that in May 1924 he was hired to work at WLS in Chicago, where, among other duties, he announced for the show that would eventually become the *NATIONAL BARN DANCE.*

In the fall of 1924 Hay won the *Radio Digest* poll as the most popular announcer in the country. This led to his being offered the job as "radio director" for the newly opened WSM in Nashville; he accepted and on November 9, 1925, began work at the station. Hay told a friend shortly after arriving that he wanted to re-create the kind of barn dance he had worked on at WLS. He was happy to see that performers such as DR. HUMPHREY BATE and UNCLE DAVE MACON had already made occasional appearances on WSM.

George D. Hay

In late November 1925 Hay invited a seventy-eight-year-old fiddler from Laguardo, Tennessee, UNCLE JIMMY THOMPSON, to come up and play at his microphones. Hay later wrote that he was astounded at the calls and telegrams that poured in. Hay announced in late December 1925 that due to the audience interest, WSM would feature "an hour or two" of old-time tunes every Saturday night.

Hay bombarded the local newspapers with a steady stream of press releases in which he trumpeted the values of this kind of down-to-earth "folk music." He soon began to augment this image by coming up with colorful names for his bands (Dr. Bate's Augmented String Orchestra became the Possum Hunters, for instance), and by encouraging the musicians to dress in overalls and straw hats. He also helped set up a booking agency, and by 1933 some of the bands were so well known across the country that they were able to tour theaters as far away as Iowa. It was Hay, too, who redubbed the program the GRAND OLE OPRY in 1927.

Though Hay was the show's figurehead, publicist, and announcer, he began to lose power with the station in the 1930s. Hay lacked managerial skills, and the station's owners began to bring in a series of professional managers who took over many of Hay's duties. To compound problems, Hay suffered a nervous breakdown in the late 1930s, causing him to take sick leaves as long as eighteen months. (During part of this time he worked with a magazine called *Rural Radio,* one of the first periodicals covering country music.) By the spring of 1938, however, he was back at work and playing important roles in two key Opry events, the show's half-hour contribution to the NBC network, beginning in 1939, and the 1940 Hollywood film *Grand Ole Opry* with Hay, ROY ACUFF, and UNCLE DAVE MACON.

Throughout the 1940s Hay remained as a major announcer with the show, often touring with Opry troupes around the country. In September 1947 he made one of his last appearances with an Opry show group, at New York City's CARNEGIE HALL. In 1945 he wrote a fascinating little book called *A Story of the Grand Ole Opry,* and in 1953 he became an editor of an important early country music newspaper, *Pickin' and Singin' News.* In the 1960s he attempted two syndicated radio shows that were devoted to reminiscing about the Opry. Upset at the direction of the Opry, and its virtual neglect of him, he had actually left Nashville by the end of the 1950s and settled in Virginia Beach, Virginia, where he died in 1968 and where he is buried.
—*Charles Wolfe*

Kendall Hayes
b. Perryville, Kentucky, October 6, 1935; d. February 10, 1995

A successful songwriter of the 1960s, Kendall Hayes was thrust into the media limelight in 1994 when *Billboard* ranked LEROY VAN DYKE's "Walk on By," which Hayes wrote, as the #1 country hit of all time. "Walk on By" earned the ranking by having spent nineteen weeks at #1 in 1961 and 1962. Adding immeasurable poignancy to the saga of the song was that Hayes learned of the *Billboard* honor at almost literally the same time he learned he had terminal cancer.

Raised on a farm outside Perryville, Hayes learned to sing and play piano but didn't write songs until he joined the air force. Stationed in Sacramento, he met with a representative of CAPITOL RECORDS who suggested he write his own material. After his discharge, Hayes worked in Kentucky and then in Florida. In 1959, while driving north to Kentucky, he said to his wife, "Doris, I got a '52 Chevy, a fourteen-dollar guitar—Sears, Roebuck guitar—and fourteen songs. I'm goin' to Nashville."

One of country's classic cheating songs, "Walk on By" was Hayes's first recorded song and the most important of his career. Besides Van Dyke, such diverse artists as CONWAY TWITTY, Dean Martin, Patti Page, HANK WILLIAMS JR. and Connie Francis, Robert Gordon, DONNA FARGO, and ASLEEP AT THE WHEEL have recorded it.   —*Daniel Cooper*

Wade Hayes

b. Bethel Acres, Oklahoma, April 20, 1969

One of the promising traditional talents to emerge in the mid-1990s, Tony Wade Hayes has the ability to sing stone-country ballads and high-energy songs that don't lean heavily toward rock & roll. His voice is an impressive instrument—he's one of country's few singers to claim a legitimate bass range—but he's also a capable writer and guitarist. (Before getting his record deal, he briefly played lead guitar for Johnny Lee.)

The first two singles from Hayes's gold-selling debut, "Old Enough to Know Better" and "I'm Still Dancin' With You," both climbed high on the charts; other hits were "Don't Stop," "What I Meant to Say," and "On a Good Night." He cut "Kentucky Bluebird," previously sung by KEITH WHITLEY, on his first album, and his second disc contained songs by BILL ANDERSON and WILLIE NELSON. Hayes's third album, *When the Wrong One Loves You Right,* produced by DON COOK, features the hit single, "The Day that She Left Tulsa (In a Chevy)."

Hayes has been influenced primarily by the OUTLAW and BAKERSFIELD movements—the Telecaster he plays onstage boasts three signatures: MERLE HAGGARD, Willie Nelson, and WAYLON JENNINGS.   —*Brian Mansfield*

Wade Hayes

Old Enough to Know Better (Columbia /DKC, 1994); *On a Good Night* (Columbia /DKC, 1996); *When the Wrong One Loves You Right* (Columbia/DKC, 1998)

Will Hays

b. Louisville, Kentucky, July 19, 1837; d. July 23, 1907

William Shakespeare Hays was the most popular songwriter of the late nineteenth century. Although he wrote some 350 songs, and at least as many poems, some of which were set to music, he never made music his full-time profession. He was a riverboat pilot on the Ohio and Mississippi Rivers at various periods of his life (at least two steamboats were named for him), and was the river editor for the *Louisville Courier-Journal* from 1868 to 1898.

His songs were immensely popular in his own day, but Hays could not have anticipated the longevity of some of them. Several of his songs—often mistakenly identified and collected as folksongs by scholars in the early twentieth century—moved into the hinterlands to become the possession of plain people. Thus they became part of country music's repertoire when the first recordings and radio broadcasts were made in the 1920s. His "Little Old Log Cabin in the Lane" was on one side of FIDDLIN' JOHN CARSON's seminal recording in 1923, and other songs, such as "We Parted by the River Side," "You've Been a Friend to Me," "I'll Remember You, Love, in My Prayers," and "Nobody's Darling on Earth," found their way to country recordings. His "Jimmie Brown the Paper Boy," adapted by the CARTER FAMILY as "Jimmie Brown the Newsboy" and prominently recorded by FLATT & SCRUGGS, has become a bluegrass standard and Hays's most recorded song. His biggest hit song, "Molly Darling," was a Top Ten country record for EDDY ARNOLD in 1948.   —*Bill C. Malone*

Haywire Mac

b. Knoxville, Tennessee, October 8, 1882; d. April 24, 1957

Alternately employed as cowboy, railroader, union organizer, songwriter, seaman, recording artist, and radio performer, Harry Kirby "Haywire Mac" McClintock was one of the most colorful personalities in American music. He left home for the life of a hobo at age fourteen, an experience that later contributed to his writing of the classic hobo song "Hallelujah, I'm a Bum." After two years rambling around the country, he shipped out to the Philippines, where he worked as a mule packer for American troops, and then to China, where he assisted journalists covering the Boxer Rebellion. Later travel and trades took him to Australia, Africa, South America, and finally to the West Coast of the United States.

Throughout his checkered career, McClintock learned and sang songs. He was also a songwriter, and his compositions included "Big Rock Candy Mountain" and numerous union songs written and performed while a member of the Industrial Workers of the World. In 1925 he had his own radio show on San Francisco station KFRC, performing solo as well as with his Haywire Orchestry. Three years later he began his recording career, eventually turning out forty-one sides for Victor and several sides for other labels. He is most well known for his recordings of cowboy, railroad, and hobo songs. McClintock continued to write and perform until his retirement in 1955. He died in San Francisco in 1957.   —*Charlie Seemann*

Hee Haw *cast*

Jimmy Heap

b. Taylor, Texas, March 3, 1922; d. December 4, 1977

James Arthur Heap was a guitarist, songwriter, and honky-tonk bandleader (the Melody Masters), best known for making early recordings of songs later immortalized by others.

Jimmy Heap's recorded output was large: thirty-two released sides with IMPERIAL RECORDS (1948–52), including the original version of "The Wild Side of Life," co-written by Heap's pianist, Arlie Carter. On CAPITOL (1951–55), Heap released thirty sides. Among these were the first big version of EDDIE MILLER's "Release Me" (1953) and an early cut of "Conscience I'm Guilty" (1955), later a HANK SNOW hit. Heap later recorded for the Big Band, Fame, and Winston labels.

When "Release Me" hit, Heap was booked on national tours, though normally he stayed close to his hometown of Taylor. At age fifty-five Heap was killed in a boating accident. Seven months later, ERNEST TUBB, for whom young Jimmy Heap Jr. was then drumming, made the speech inducting Jimmy Heap Sr. into the CMF's Walkway of Stars (June 1978).　—*Ronnie Pugh*

Bobby Hebb

b. Nashville, Tennessee, July 26, 1938

One of the most intriguing examples of African-American participation in country music is that of Bobby Hebb, who performed on the GRAND OLE OPRY in the 1950s and then went on to greater fame as the author and singer of the 1966 soul-pop smash "Sunny."

Hebb grew up near the Nashville neighborhood that became Music Row. His parents, both blind, were musicians, and Hebb absorbed heavy doses of gospel, classical, jazz, blues, and country. "It was very important that one

understood more than one culture of music," he said. He also learned to tap-dance and play spoons, and while still a child he found work in nightclubs, fraternity houses, and at black-tie parties. Then, "the year that television came to Nashville," as Hebb put it, he landed a spot on a WSM variety show hosted by OWEN BRADLEY. ROY ACUFF saw Hebb on TV and hired him.

Hebb worked on the Opry with Acuff from roughly 1950 to 1955, and in 1960 recorded his own version of the Acuff hit "Night Train to Memphis." From there, Hebb's career moved more toward r&b, but after "Sunny" made him an international star, he deliberately followed with a soul version of the country chestnut "A Satisfied Mind" in 1966. The song had multiple meanings for Hebb, but among them was his wish to tell his friends from the old days on the Opry, "Thanks, fellas." As of 1998, Hebb was still performing, most often in the Boston region.
　—*Daniel Cooper*

Hee Haw

established 1969; ended 1994

Hee Haw is generally considered the most successful country TV show of all time. It is also the longest-lasting syndicated television program in history.

Created by Frank Peppiatt and John Aylesworth and produced by Sam Lovullo, all of whom had previously worked together on *The Jonathan Winters Show*, *Hee Haw* originated in 1969 as a country imitation of the comedy series *Laugh-In*, aping the earlier show's "black out" sketches and one-liners with hick/cornball versions. Stock "rube" vaudeville characters and hillbilly stereotypes from *Li'l Abner* and *Tobacco Road* were cast, as well as animated barnyard animals.

Hee Haw was in the Top Twenty of the television ratings when it was dropped by CBS in 1971 in a move to decountrify the network's programming. *Hee Haw* went immediately into syndication and thrived for nearly twenty-five years. More than six hundred episodes were produced in all.

The initial hosts were BUCK OWENS and ROY CLARK. Owens left in 1986 and was not replaced. Key to the show's success were such regulars as ARCHIE CAMPBELL (who also wrote gags), GRANDPA JONES, Roni Stoneman, KENNY PRICE, STRINGBEAN, MINNIE PEARL, Gordie Tapp, and George Lindsey (who played "Goober" on THE ANDY GRIFFITH SHOW), all of whom had established careers when the series began.

But *Hee Haw* originated a number of equally talented and memorable characters who were less well known, including Lulu Roman, Gailard Sartain, JUNIOR SAMPLES (whose used-car-salesman phone number later titled the country band BR5-49), Don Harron, Grady Nutt, the Hager Twins, and Mike Snyder.

Among the show's female cast, some of whom came to be known as the "Hee Haw Honeys," were Cathy Baker, Gunilla Hutton, Lisa Todd, Marianne Gordon Rogers, Misty Rowe, Linda Thompson, Irlene Mandrell, and Mackenzie Colt. Barbi Benton was a regular for five years. *Hee Haw Honeys* aired as a spin-off series in syndication, 1978–79.

Production values were first-rate, and the music segments were particularly well done. George Richey, and then CHARLIE MCCOY, led the house band, which featured the Nashville Edition singers. Virtually every legendary country star of the era guested at one time or another.

Controversy erupted in 1991 when the show was redesigned and many of the regulars were fired. A more modern *Hee Haw* broadcast on TNN bombed. The show died during the 1993–94 season, and TNN aired vintage *Hee Haw* programs thereafter.

Several former cast members reunited for a "Hee Haw Live" stage production at OPRYLAND and on the road in 1994–95.   —*Robert K. Oermann*

Bobby Helms
b. Bloomington, Indiana, August 15, 1933; d. June 19, 1997

Rock & roll opened the door for country singers who could adapt to the exigencies of teenage music. Bobby Lee Helms was one of the first to show the way, with a series of hits that were neither pop nor country but drew from both. The productions, all from Nashville, revealed that the country music industry adapted very well to the new music.

Helms grew up with country music (his father hosted the *Monroe County Jamboree* in Bloomington). He made his first recordings for the Nashville-based Speed Records in 1955 and was brought to Nashville by ERNEST TUBB the following year. Helms's voice worked the same tenor range as WEBB PIERCE's, and Helms's style was, in some regards, an update of Pierce's sound. Signed to DECCA RECORDS, Helms recorded "Fraulein," a song written by LAWTON WILLIAMS for Tubb eight years earlier, during his second session, in November 1956. It was a #1 country hit in September 1957, broke into the pop Top Forty, and spent a total of fifty-two weeks on the country charts. He followed it with "My Special Angel," a country #1 in December 1957 as well as a pop Top Ten. He finished 1957 with "Jingle Bell Rock," soon to be a pop and country seasonal classic and an eventual million seller. The latter two hits made Helms's connection to pop music explicit. After leaving Decca in 1962, he continued to record for a plethora of labels but with diminishing chart impact and regularity, his

last chart record coming in at #19 for Certron Records. His fame is wedded forever to his three 1957 hits.
                                                    —*Colin Escott*

Fräulein (Bear Family, 1992), 2 CD set

Mike Henderson
b. Independence, Missouri, January 16, 1954

A solo artist, group leader, singer, and in-demand session guitarist, Mike Henderson has one foot in honky-tonk and the other in blues. He began playing harmonica at age five, graduating to guitar before hitting his teens. Born just outside Kansas City, Michael J. Henderson played in bluegrass and blues bands, letting his feel for those styles mature before deciding it was time to show Nashville in 1985 what he could do with a six-string and a slide.

He broke into the Nashville scene right away, playing with the Roosters and then the Kingsnakes, the latter who released an album. As a songwriter, his career got a boost when the Fabulous Thunderbirds scored a modest hit with Henderson's co-written "Powerful Stuff" in 1988.

He also landed cuts with a number of country acts, including PATTY LOVELESS, RANDY TRAVIS, and NEAL MCCOY. He played electric slide guitar, harmonica, dobro, mandolin, and fiddle, and his studio work includes a roster of EMMYLOU HARRIS, JOHN HIATT, Joy Lynn White, Kelly Willis, HANK WILLIAMS JR., SUZY BOGGUSS, GUY CLARK, and DELBERT MCCLINTON.

His debut solo album, RCA's *Country Music Made Me Do It*, was released in 1994 and featured "Hillbilly Jitters," a modest hit on the line dance circuit. His second solo album, *Edge of Night*, was released in 1996 on DEAD RECKONING RECORDS, an independent label he co-owns with Kieran Kane, KEVIN WELCH, Tammy Rogers, and Harry Stinson. Later that year the label put out the bluesy *First Blood* by the Henderson-fronted Bluebloods.   —*Michael Gray*

Edge of Night (Dead Reckoning, 1996); *First Blood* (Dead Reckoning, 1996)

Fisher Hendley
b. North Carolina, ca. mid-1880s; d. mid-1960s

A winner in some thirty-two southern championship contests during the 1920s–1930s for prowess with his dropthumb, frailing, picking style on the five-string banjo, Fisher Hendley began his professional career in New York City. A Trinity College (now Duke University) graduate, Hendley moved to New York and, according to former 1940s Hendley band member and writer, Al Wall, was doing "a hillbilly music-comedy act on the nightclub circuit," plus "engagements on NBC radio variety shows" by the early 1920s.

On a brief return south to North Carolina in August 1925, Hendley launched his recording career by singing and playing his banjo on two songs at an OKEH RECORDS session in Asheville. Sales for his first disc were sparse, and Hendley had other unsuccessful recording efforts for VICTOR RECORDS (Memphis, 1930) and for ARC (New York, 1933) before resettling to the Carolinas in the mid-1930s, at first making a brief stay in Charlotte.

In the mid-1930s, Greenville, South Carolina, witnessed

Hendley's formation of his Aristocratic Pigs, a band name adapted from a meat-packing plant sponsor on WFBC. Sporting theater makeup and decked out in custom-made tuxedos, the band's attention-grabbing image contributed strongly to its regional success. A new recording contract ensued with Vocalion Records for whom two dozen songs were waxed in Columbia, South Carolina (1938), where Hendley and his band were popular on WIS from the late 1930s to the mid-1940s.   —*Bob Pinson*

Scott Hendricks
b. Clinton, Oklahoma, July 26, 1956

Scott Hendricks has been one of the most successful producers of the 1990s, having worked with such acts as ALAN JACKSON, BROOKS & DUNN, JOHN MICHAEL MONTGOMERY, TRACE ADKINS, and RESTLESS HEART. Hendricks, who served as president and chief executive officer of CAPITOL Nashville Records in 1995–97, has produced or co-produced more than thirty #1 hits on the *Billboard* country charts, including "I'll Still Be Loving You," "I Swear," "That Rock Won't Roll," "Don't Rock the Jukebox," and "Neon Moon." He has been a producer on nine multiplatinum albums, and the combined U.S. sales of all the records he has produced surpasses 40 million copies.

Hendricks attended Oklahoma State University, where he met TIM DUBOIS, now president of ARISTA Nashville, and Greg Jennings, who became part of the group Restless Heart. After graduation they all moved to Nashville. Hendricks arrived in 1978 and began working as an engineer at the GLASER BROTHERS studio and Bullet Recording before going independent in 1985. He then worked with such producers as JIM ED NORMAN, BARRY BECKETT, and JERRY CRUTCHFIELD, learning various production techniques.

Hendricks made the move to the producer's chair in 1985, when he and DuBois recorded Restless Heart. The result was three gold records and six #1 hits. Hendricks quickly established himself as one of Nashville's top independent producers, having as many as seven #1 hits in a year. Since 1991 he has produced songs on three albums each of Alan Jackson, Brooks & Dunn, and LEE ROY PARNELL, as well as two albums each by FAITH HILL, JOHN MICHAEL MONTGOMERY, STEVE WARINER, Trace Adkins, and SUZY BOGGUSS.

In 1995 Hendricks decided to stop producing outside acts to focus on his work at Capitol. He produced Trace Adkins's debut album, *Dreamin' Out Loud*, which was certified gold in 1997, and he oversaw the release of DEANA CARTER's debut release, which to date has sold more than 2 million copies. In 1997 Hendricks exited Capitol Nashville and is now awaiting the finalization of an offer to head Virgin Records' Nashville office.   —*Beverly Keel*

Don Henry
b. San Jose, California, December 30, 1959

DON HENRY shot to national prominence in 1990 as the award-winning co-writer (with Jon Vezner) of KATHY MATTEA's chart-topping hit "Where've You Been," which was named Song of the Year by the CMA, ACM, the Grammys, and the Nashville Songwriters Association International. Henry also picked up a Writer of the Year Award from his music publisher, Sony Tree.

Henry moved to Nashville from California in 1979, landing a job as tape librarian at TREE INTERNATIONAL, where he refined his craft by working alongside songwriting legends such as HARLAN HOWARD, BOBBY BRADDOCK, CURLY PUTMAN, WILLIE NELSON, and HANK COCHRAN, among others. Henry's own tunes have been recorded by numerous artists, including JOHN CONLEE, RAY CHARLES, THE OAK RIDGE BOYS, HIGHWAY 101, and more.

Released in 1991, Henry's album *Wild in the Backyard* was compared favorably to the work of singer-songwriter Randy Newman. The album, referred to as an acoustic alternative rock project, allowed Henry to sing stories about people in all stages of life, while demonstrating his wry sense of humor by lampooning cultural targets and human relationships.   —*Janet E. Williams*

REPRESENTATIVE RECORDING
Wild in the Backyard (Epic, 1991)

Ty Herndon
b. Butler, Alabama, May 2, 1962

A highly publicized run-in with the law threatened Boyd Ty Herndon's career at its outset and put many of country music's long-held notions to the test. Shortly after his debut single, "What Mattered Most," hit #1 on the country charts, Herndon was charged with indecent exposure after allegedly masturbating in front of a male police officer in Fort Worth's Gateway Park, June 13, 1995. While he was being booked, 2.49 grams of a powdered narcotic were found in his wallet.

Herndon pleaded guilty to the drug charge, and the indecency charge was dropped. But the incident raised sexuality questions that had rarely been addressed in the genre. Herndon's associates insisted he was not gay, and the event became merely a difficult hitch in the early going of a promising career. Subsequent singles fared well on the charts, and his first two albums were both certified gold, indicating that country music's audience is apparently more tolerant than had previously been believed. In 1996 Herndon won the TNN *Music City News* Male Star of Tomorrow Award, an honor determined by fan voting.

Able to play piano at age five, Herndon left his Alabama home at seventeen for a job at Nashville's OPRYLAND theme park. He performed at Opryland off and on for ten years, beginning in 1979. He attended Belmont University on scholarship, and in 1983 he was a prize winner on the syndicated television program *Star Search*. Herndon was featured on *Nashville Now*, sang jingles for Dodge and Pepsi, and became a model. But when record labels ignored him, he moved to Dallas, where he got something of a honky-tonk education playing in the clubs.

Eventually signed to EPIC RECORDS, Herndon began recording his first album, *What Mattered Most*, in 1994 with producer Doug Johnson; it was released the following year. The title cut of his 1996 follow-up, *Living in a Moment*, also became a #1 hit for Herndon.   —*Tom Roland*

REPRESENTATIVE RECORDINGS
What Mattered Most (Epic, 1995); *Living in a Moment* (Epic, 1996)

E. T. Herzog Recording Studio
established in Cincinnati, Ohio, 1945; ended 1951

The E. T. Herzog Recording Studio, located at 811 Race Street in Cincinnati, Ohio, was one of the first commercial studios to record country music. Opened in 1945 by Earl T. Herzog (b. January 26, 1908; d. December 6, 1986), a moonlighting engineer from radio station WLW, the studio was used to record some of the earliest releases on KING RECORDS. Because of the availability of talented musicians working on Cincinnati radio station WLW, as well as Herzog's cooperative attitude and technical expertise, the studio also attracted artists from Nashville, including HANK WILLIAMS, who cut eight songs there in two sessions (1948–49). Though the Race Street studio closed in 1951, Herzog remained active, working in various other studios until his death.

—Jon Hartley Fox

The Hi Flyers

Cary Ginell has written that the Hi Flyers "best reflected the transition Texas string bands went through during the turbulent 1930s"—from a traditional stringband to a jazzy dance band in the course of a few years.

Not the first Texas stringband to feature jazz improvisation, as has been claimed, the group was formed by Fort Worth radio personality Zack Hurt at KFJZ in 1929 as the High Fliers. The original group included Kentucky fiddler Clifford Gross and featured mainly breakdowns, waltzes, and pop tunes. By 1932, guitarist Elmer Scarborough had taken over the band, its name now streamlined to Hi Flyers. Inspired by MILTON BROWN's forays into string jazz, Scarborough and band members such as fiddler Pat Trotter and guitarist Willie Wells began to change the group's orientation. Several key band members left to form the Sons of the West in Amarillo in 1936, but by the time of the band's first sessions for Vocalion in 1937 it could boast a lineup that included hot steel guitarist Billy Briggs, versatile fiddler Darrell Kirkpatrick, and jazz pianist Landon Beaver.

Relocated to Eagle Pass for a time in 1937–38, the band broke up briefly before Scarborough revived it at Oklahoma City's KOMA in 1939. Featuring the vocals of Buster Ferguson and the forward-looking electric guitar of Sheldon Bennett, with former pianist Beaver returning for recordings, the band's recordings from 1939 to 1941 show it pointing not only toward the smoother sound of postwar western swing but also toward the lyrical themes of postwar, beer-joint honky-tonk. Scarborough disbanded the Hi Flyers as World War II dawned and re-formed it in Fort Worth in 1945, but by the end of 1946 the Hi Flyers were history.

—Kevin Coffey

REPRESENTATIVE RECORDING

The Hi–Flyers, 1937–41 (Texas Rose, 1982)

John Hiatt

b. Indianapolis, Indiana, August 20, 1952

Raised in Indianapolis, John Hiatt moved in 1970 to Nashville, where he first made his mark as a young songwriter at TREE PUBLISHING. Hiatt's acerbic original songs have since appeared on records by artists as diverse as EARL THOMAS CONLEY, the Neville Brothers, and Iggy Pop. ROSANNE CASH topped the country charts with Hiatt's "The Way We Make a Broken Heart" (1987), and Bonnie Raitt reached the #1 spot on *Billboard's* Hot 100 Singles Chart with Hiatt's "Thing Called Love" (1989). Hiatt nonetheless achieved only marginal success as a performer until 1987,

when *Bring the Family* brought him critical and popular acclaim, including Best Male Vocalist honors in *Rolling Stone's* 1987 Critics Poll.

After a pair of mid-1970s albums he made for EPIC failed to generate much interest or sales, Hiatt moved to Los Angeles and made two albums for MCA; both drew comparisons to records made by fellow angry young men Graham Parker and Elvis Costello. Hiatt then recorded three albums for Geffen, including 1983's excellent *Riding with the King*, before his wife's suicide and his own alcoholism nearly became his undoing.

After remarrying and getting his life back on track, Hiatt enlisted Ry Cooder, Jim Keltner, and Nick Lowe to help him make *Bring the Family*, a record that effortlessly fused his country, rock, and r&b influences and brimmed with newfound affirmation and insight. He also reestablished himself in Nashville, and except for 1992's uninspired *Little Village*, a project that reunited the cast of *Bring the Family*, Hiatt has continued to make gritty, soulful records, even though none has had more than a modest commercial impact. As testimony to his songwriting talent, in 1993 Rhino Records released a collection of Hiatt originals recorded by other artists called *Love Gets Strange: The Songs of John Hiatt*. Hiatt's 1997 release on CAPITOL, *Little Head*, reflected his continuing blend of rock & roll and country influences.

—Bill Friskics-Warren

REPRESENTATIVE RECORDINGS

Slug Line (MCA, 1979); *Riding with the King* (Geffen, 1983); *Bring the Family* (A&M, 1987); *Little Head* (Capitol, 1997)

Hickory Records

established 1953; ended 1985

Hickory Records, a subsidiary of ACUFF-ROSE PUBLICATIONS, was created as a partnership among Acuff-Rose principals ROY ACUFF, FRED ROSE, and Rose's son WESLEY ROSE. Beginning shipments early in 1954, Hickory immediately provided a recording outlet for Acuff-Rose copyrights while allowing Fred Rose—also an aggressive talent scout—to record artists he felt the majors had neglected.

Hickory scored its first country chart hit, "Good Deal, Lucille," early in 1954 with AL TERRY. The label remained fairly active during the sixties but tapered off in the seventies, when its product was distributed by the larger ABC organization for a time. It was virtually defunct by the time the GAYLORD organization bought the Acuff-Rose publishing and recording properties in 1985 and merged Acuff-Rose into the Opryland Music Group. Other Hickory or ABC-Hickory artists, noted here with years of chart activity, include Rusty and DOUG KERSHAW (1955–1961), WILMA LEE & STONEY COOPER (1956–61), ERNIE ASHWORTH (1960–70), Roy Acuff (1958–59, 1965, 1974), DON GIBSON (1969–79), DON EVERLY (1976–77), and MICKEY NEWBURY (1977–80).

—John Rumble

HighTone Records

established 1983

Founded by record industry veterans Bruce Bromberg and Larry Sloven, the Oakland, California–based independent label HighTone Records takes its name from the HANK WILLIAMS song "Mind Your Own Business," which includes the line "Mindin' other people's business seems to be hightone." The company made its mark first with Seattle bluesman Robert Cray. In 1987, after selling Cray's contract to Polygram, Bromberg and Sloven ventured into country music with releases by Austin, Texas–based singer-songwriter JOE ELY and Bakersfield, California–based country mainstay Bobby Durham.

In the years since, despite only modest success in getting records played on country radio, HighTone has continued to release albums by country artists such as JIMMIE DALE GILMORE, GARY STEWART (including a reissue of the classic Stewart album *Out of Hand*), Heather Myles, ROSIE FLORES, Chris Gaffney, DALE WATSON, BUDDY MILLER, Big Sandy & His Fly-Rite Boys, and MARTY BROWN.

HighTone's *Tulare Dust: A Songwriters' Tribute to Merle Haggard* (1994) featured DWIGHT YOAKAM, Lucinda Williams, Tom Russell, Dave Alvin, and others performing Haggard compositions. IRIS DEMENT's contribution to this album attracted Haggard's attention, and she began touring and playing with him occasionally. Haggard recorded DeMent's song "No Time to Cry" for his *1996* album.

"We've tried to make records that have something to say in a unique and compelling way," Bromberg told one writer, and his catalogue suggests the company frequently succeeds.
— *Jay Orr*

Highway 101

Paulette Carlson b. Northfield, Minnesota, October 11, 1953
Scott "Cactus" Moser b. Montrose, Colorado, May 3, 1957
Curtis Stone b. North Hollywood, California, April 3, 1950
Jack Daniels b. Choctaw, Oklahoma, October 27, 1949
Nikki Nelson b. San Diego, California, January 3, 1969

In the late 1980s, Highway 101 brought to country a distinctive contemporary sound and style that blended California with Nashville and that owed much to the husky vocals of the group's original lead singer, Paulette Carlson.

Often described as the "Stevie Nicks of Country," Carlson played in country bar bands in Minnesota before moving to Nashville in 1978 and finding work as a staff songwriter for the OAK RIDGE BOYS' publishing company (Silverline/Goldline), and as a backup singer for GAIL DAVIES. When an RCA recording contract (1983–84) did not result in commercial success for Carlson, she left Nashville.

NITTY GRITTY DIRT BAND manager Chuck Morris built Highway 101 around Carlson, enlisting California country-rockers Cactus Moser, Curtis Stone, and Jack Daniels. Moser played drums and sang; bassist-vocalist Stone—the son of COUNTRY MUSIC HALL OF FAME member CLIFFIE STONE—had been a country performer most of his life; guitarist Daniels had been performing since age sixteen, and, with Stone, had toured with the pop group Guess Who.

The casual-flash look of the band blended roots music and show business sensibilities. Carlson dressed in prairie skirts, boots, buckskin, and hats; the band wore western shirts and embroidered jackets and jeans. Their WARNER BROS. debut single, "The Bed You Made for Me" (written by Carlson), was an instant success, entering the Top Five early in 1987. Their third single, "Somewhere Tonight," went to #1. Highway 101 was chosen CMA Vocal Group of the Year in 1988 and 1989.

After a run of Top Ten singles, Carlson left Highway 101 in 1991. She gave birth to a daughter and pursued a solo career, co-producing a very personal album, *Love Goes On,* for which she wrote seven of the ten songs.

Nikki Nelson was recruited to Highway 101 to replace Carlson. Nelson had performed in her father's Nevada band since age fourteen; she came to Nashville at eighteen. Twenty-two when she joined Highway 101, she continued to perform the straight-ahead, assertive material typical of the band, adding her own strong interpretations of ballads. "Bing Bang Boom" and several minor hits followed, but Jack Daniels also left the group. After leaving Warner Bros. and joining LIBERTY, Highway 101 recorded a 1993 album, *The New Frontier,* in an unsuccessful attempt to establish a strong new identity and regain the success they had experienced in the late 1980s.

In 1996 Carlson, Stone, and Daniels returned for *Highway 101 and Paulette Carlson Reunited,* a Willow Tree Records project.
— *Mary A. Bufwack*

REPRESENTATIVE RECORDINGS

Highway 101 (Warner Bros., 1987); *Highway 101 2* (Warner Bros., 1988)

The Highwaymen (*see* separate entries for Johnny Cash, Waylon Jennings, Kris Kristofferson, and Willie Nelson)

Eddie Hill

b. Delano, Tennessee, July 21, 1921; d. January 18, 1994

Singer, songwriter, musician, television host and DJ, Smilin' Eddie Hill was a jack-of-all-trades who performed with JOHNNIE & JACK and the LOUVIN BROTHERS, and for many years was a mainstay as a radio announcer at WSM-Nashville. Hosting the all-night truckers' show helped him win numerous DJ polls. In 1975 he and GRANT TURNER were the first living inductees into the Country Disc Jockey Hall of Fame.

At an early age, James Edward Hill was inspired by a banjo-picking granddad and fiddling father. At seventeen Hill won a talent contest in Chattanooga, leading to his first major radio stint: WROL-Knoxville. Switching to WNOX, he performed on the popular *MIDDAY MERRY-GO-ROUND* with Buster Moore and Claude Boone, before moving to WKRC-Cincinnati.

In 1943 he teamed with Johnnie Wright after his partner Jack Anglin was drafted into the army. When Anglin mustered out in 1946, the trio worked briefly together at WPTF-Raleigh. Hill next moved to WMPS-Memphis, hooking up with a new duo, the Louvin Brothers.

He shared a session in 1947 with Johnnie & Jack at Apollo Records, a New York r&b label. He also recorded for MERCURY, DECCA, and RCA with minimal impact. During a March 1950 RCA session, however, he and bass player ERNIE NEWTON hit on a Latin rhythm for "Poison Love" that propelled Johnnie & Jack to stardom. Hill's guitar and baritone enhanced other Johnnie & Jack sessions. He also sang trios with them on the GRAND OLE OPRY and played rhythm guitar on numerous Decca song sessions for KITTY WELLS. His song "Someday You'll Call My Name" was a Top Ten single for JIMMY WAKELY (1949). From the mid-1950s, Hill served as a popular host on WLAC-TV in Nashville. In 1968 he suffered a stroke that left him partially paralyzed.
— *Walt Trott*

Faith Hill

Faith Hill

b. Jackson, Mississippi, September 21, 1967

With her 1993 debut single, "Wild One," Faith Hill (Audrey Faith Perry) gave notice to country fans that her voice would be one they would hear for some time to come. The tune stayed at #1 in *Billboard* for four weeks and propelled the talented newcomer's album, *Take Me As I Am,* to million-selling success.

Adopted less than one week after her birth, Hill grew up in the tiny community of Star, Mississippi. She made her first public appearance singing in church at age three. Moving to Nashville at nineteen in 1987, she landed a job selling T-shirts at FAN FAIR. A stint as receptionist for GARY MORRIS's music publishing company followed, leading to work as a demo singer. Top tunesmith Gary Burr fell in love with Hill's voice and asked her to sing with him during a performance at the BLUEBIRD CAFE. She was signed to WARNER BROS. almost immediately.

Hill's follow-up singles, "Piece of My Heart" and "Take Me As I Am," also reached the top of the charts, but her voice was stilled temporarily due to vocal cord surgery. More than 150 concert dates with REBA MCENTIRE and BROOKS & DUNN had taken their toll on her voice, but Hill enjoyed a complete recovery following the February 1995 procedure and released *It Matters to Me* later that year. In 1996, while on tour together, she and fellow star TIM MCGRAW became involved romantically; they married on October 6 of that year.

In 1997 Hill and McGraw teamed up vocally for the chart-topping "It's Your Love." The recording earned them CMA's Vocal Event of the Year Award. They also celebrated the birth of their daughter, Gracie, in May of that year.   —*Janet E. Williams*

REPRESENTATIVE RECORDINGS

Take Me As I Am (Warner Bros., 1993); *It Matters to Me* (Warner Bros., 1995); *Faith* (Warner Bros., 1998)

Goldie Hill

b. Coy City, Karnes County, Texas, January 11, 1933

Known as "The Golden Hillbilly," Argolda Voncile "Goldie" Hill was country music's glamor girl of the 1950s and a popular DECCA recording artist of that era.

The baby sister of musical brothers who practically raised her in San Antonio's hillbilly venues, "Golda" Hill began singing in her teens, and with brother TOMMY HILL joined WEBB PIERCE's band at Shreveport's *LOUISIANA HAYRIDE* in about April 1952. On a Pierce recording trip to Nashville in July 1952, Goldie auditioned for Decca's PAUL COHEN and signed a contract on the spot, cutting "Why Talk to My Heart" (an answer to RAY PRICE's "Talk to Your Heart") and three other songs. Answer songs would always be her forte—"I Let the Stars Get in My Eyes" (1952), "I'm Yvonne" (1953), and "I'm Yesterday's Girl" (1953) were among her musical ripostes.

Convinced by manager Norm Riley to move to Nashville in September 1953, Hill worked the GRAND OLE OPRY and co-starred briefly in a radio series, *Country Tune Parade,* with ERNEST TUBB (1954). In 1954–55 she recorded two popular duets with JUSTIN TUBB, "Looking Back to See" and "Sure Fire Kisses," and one with RED SOVINE, "Are You Mine."

Hill joined the traveling PHILIP MORRIS COUNTRY MUSIC SHOW at the beginning of 1957, but left the show to marry its star, CARL SMITH, on September 19 of that year. She did no further touring, staying home to raise three children on their Tennessee farm, although she recorded for DECCA until 1964 and for EPIC briefly after that.   —*Ronnie Pugh*

Tommy Hill

b. near Coy City, Texas, April 27, 1929

John Thomas Hill has been the consummate journeyman in the country music business. He has been a songwriter, featured artist, session musician, engineer, record label owner, and A&R man. He has played on and produced hundreds of sessions and written hundreds of songs, two of them classics: "Slowly" and "Teddy Bear."

Hill grew up very close to JIMMIE RODGERS's Blue Yodeler's Paradise in Kerrville, Texas, and it was Rodgers who inspired him to enter the music business. He worked with BIG BILL LISTER around San Antonio, and then he and his brother Ken joined SMILEY BURNETTE in California. Returning to Texas, Tommy joined WEBB PIERCE's band in Shreveport and gave him "Slowly," which spent seventeen weeks at #1 in 1954. He also wrote "I Let the Stars Get in My Eyes" for his sister, GOLDIE HILL, and he followed her to Nashville in 1954.

Hill worked as a front man for JIM REEVES and as a featured act on the PHILIP MORRIS COUNTRY MUSIC SHOW, but he couldn't get his career as a performer off the ground. In October 1959, after cutting a single for STARDAY RECORDS, Hill joined Don Pierce's maverick enterprise and later built a studio for him, which opened in 1960. Hill stayed until Starday was sold in 1968, then joined a short-lived MGM RECORDS subsidiary, Blue Valley Records. He then formed Stop Records with PETE DRAKE, one of the more successful Nashville independents.

Hill took some of the Stop assets and started Gusto Records in 1972. He brought in Moe Lytle as a partner two years later, and Lytle later bought Starday-KING RECORDS. Hill continued to produce for Starday and gave the label its biggest ever hit, RED SOVINE's "Teddy Bear," in 1976. After selling his interest in the company, Hill continued to work for Gusto until 1982. He retained the old Starday Studio and has since worked on King and Starday tape restoration for Gusto. —*Colin Escott*

REPRESENTATIVE RECORDING

Get Ready Baby (Bear Family, 1993)

Hill and Range Songs, Inc.

established in New York, New York, December 9, 1944; sold to Chappell & Co., 1975

Between 1945 and 1955, a single corporation and its many affiliated companies published most of the new country hits—Hill and Range Songs, Inc., the empire of the brothers Aberbach.

Joachim Jean Aberbach (known as "Jean," b. Vienna, Austria, August 12, 1910; d. May 24, 1992) and brother Julian J. (b. Vienna, Austria, February 8, 1909) had worked for various Berlin and Paris publishing offices before Jean moved to New York City in 1936 and joined the music publishing firm of Chappell & Co. Julian followed his brother and moved to New York three years later. They found the field of hillbilly publishing relatively wide open, and eventually bought out the remaining 50 percent share of Biltmore Music, a company they had co-owned with a Chicago transcription firm. By 1945 they had renamed the company Hill and Range Songs, Inc., with Julian running the company offices from Hollywood. Jean had remained with Chappell Music until 1948, when he was fired for not bringing his employer "Bouquet of Roses," a Hill and Range hit. Thereafter, both brothers devoted all their time to growing the Hill and Range empire.

Operating mostly with advance monies from BMI for their first two big hits, "Shame On You" and "Detour," they settled on an astoundingly successful modus operandi—luring singing stars into their fold with generous bonuses and advance money in order to set up subsidiary companies. Stars would co-own their own companies with Hill and Range, which would handle their song hits. One by one many major country singers fell into line—BOB WILLS, ERNEST TUBB, EDDY ARNOLD, RED FOLEY, and later LEFTY FRIZZELL, HANK SNOW, JENNY LOU CARSON, LEON PAYNE, and JOHNNY CASH. Hill and Range employed several talented staff writers as well, such as CY COBEN, Jack Rollins, Steve and Ed Nelson, and Ben Weisman.

Not surprisingly, the list of Hill and Range hits became massive and includes "Bouquet of Roses," "Candy Kisses," "Letters Have No Arms," "Faded Love," "I'm Movin' On," "There Stands the Glass," "I Really Don't Want to Know," "Mexican Joe," "These Hands," and "I Walk the Line," just to name a select few. They swelled their country catalogue by buying older companies as well, but the Aberbachs never limited themselves to country music, particularly broadening their repertoire after they moved offices to New York City's Brill Building in 1953. From the thirty-plus publishers in the Aberbach Group came gospel classics ("Peace in the Valley"), pop standards ("Spanish Harlem"), and kiddie favorites ("Frosty the Snow Man," "Peter Cottontail," "Suzy Snowflake"). Signing ELVIS PRES-

LEY in 1955 was ultimately their biggest coup. In exchange for an unspecified amount of cash and services, which helped convince RCA RECORDS to buy Presley's contract, Hill and Range took control of his publishing; thereafter, most of what Presley recorded came from Hill and Range demos.

Demands of the Presley career and the growth of Nashville-based publishers cut into Hill and Range's country dominance after the 1950s. In 1975 the brothers sold Hill and Range to Chappell, Jean's early employer, though they retained a 25 percent share. —*Ronnie Pugh*

The Hill Billies

Albert Green Hopkins b. Gap Creek, North Carolina, June 5, 1889; d. October 21, 1932
Alonzo Elvis "Tony" Alderman b. River Hill, Virginia, September 10, 1900; d. October 25, 1983
John Rector birthplace and birth date unknown; d. August 28, 1985
Joe Hopkins birthplace, birth date, and death date unknown
later: Charlie Bowman b. Gray Station, Tennessee, July 30, 1889; d. May 20, 1962

The first band to use the name Hill Billies on phonograph records—thereby contributing to the rapid acceptance of the term for the new commercial genre—was organized at GALAX, Virginia, in the spring of 1924. The band made its first successful recordings in January 1925, in New York, for the OKEH label. After the group recorded six selections, A&R man RALPH PEER asked the quartet their name, and bandleader Al Hopkins replied, "We're nothing but a bunch of hillbillies from North Carolina and Virginia. Call us anything." Peer at once dubbed them the Hill Billies—an appellation not all band members felt comfortable with initially, because of the frequent pejorative connotation the term had. The band left OKeh later in 1925 to record for the jointly owned BRUNSWICK and Vocalion labels, using simultaneously the names of Hill Billies and Buckle Busters. The band's repertoire consisted largely of old-time fiddle tunes (often played on twin fiddles by Tony Alderman and Charlie Bowman) with relatively little jazz and blues influence. Although Al Hopkins's piano playing was not unique in country music at that time, it was certainly not common, and it contributed to the band's distinctive sound, which was fleshed out by the banjo of John Rector and the guitar of Joe Hopkins. In addition to their recordings, the band appeared frequently at fiddle conventions, county fairs, and on radio. The band's promising career was abruptly terminated when Al Hopkins, their able leader and promoter, died in an automobile accident. —*Norm Cohen*

REPRESENTATIVE RECORDING

The Hillbillies (County, 1974)

Donna Hilley

b. Birmingham, Alabama, June 30, 1946

As president and chief executive officer of Sony/ATV Tree, the largest country music publisher, Donna Hilley is one of the most successful and prominent women in the country music industry. In addition to guiding Sony/ATV Tree to its frequent position as *Billboard*'s country music publisher of the year, Hilley has also expanded the company into such areas as film, television, Broadway, and commercials. She has negotiated the company's acquisition of more than sixty songwriting catalogues, including those of CONWAY TWITTY, MERLE HAGGARD, JIM REEVES, and BUCK OWENS. She has worked with such copyrights as "He Stopped Loving Her Today," "Heartbreak Hotel," and "Crazy," and with such acts as ROGER MILLER, BROOKS & DUNN, and TRAVIS TRITT.

After moving to Nashville, Hilley accepted a job at WKDA, which was run by JACK STAPP, who also founded TREE PUBLISHING. After eight years at WKDA, she spent another eight years with a public relations firm before joining Tree in 1973. She was named vice president and chief operating officer in 1978, and she negotiated the sale of Tree to CBS (now Sony Music) in 1989. Hilley was named president and chief executive officer in 1994, the same year she was also appointed to the boards of ASCAP and the National Music Publishers Association. —*Beverly Keel*

Chris Hillman

b. Los Angeles, California, December 4, 1944

Best known as a member of three popular and influential groups—the BYRDS, the FLYING BURRITO BROTHERS, and the DESERT ROSE BAND—Chris Hillman is a pioneer of what has come to be called California country-rock. He is a singer and songwriter, and a musician adept at guitar, bass, and his main instrument, the mandolin. "I started to play guitar in high school," Hillman has recalled, "and then, in the ninth or tenth grade, I heard the mandolin and loved it. . . . I learned to play from listening to records."

Attending high school in North San Diego County, strongly influenced by the music of LEFTY FRIZZELL and BILL MONROE, Hillman met banjoist Kenny Wertz, who introduced him to guitarist-singer and songwriter Larry Murray. As the Scottsville Squirrel Barkers, they cut an album in one frantic, three-hour, early 1960s session. Not long after, Hillman joined the Golden State Boys, a band that included VERN GOSDIN, Rex Gosdin, and banjoist Don Parmley; they changed their name to the Hillmen and recorded one album before breaking up. Jim Dickson, who had produced the Hillmen sessions, was also producing the Byrds and hired Hillman as their bass player. "[Byrds member] David Crosby didn't want to sing and play bass at the same time," Hillman explained.

Hillman's best-known compositions for the Byrds were "Time Between" and "So You Want to Be a Rock and Roll Star," the latter co-written with band member Roger McGuinn as "sort of a funny song about the Monkees." It was Hillman who started the Byrds along the path to country, he says, before CLARENCE WHITE and GRAM PARSONS joined the group. Later, with Parsons, Hillman formed the Flying Burrito Brothers; Hillman played guitar, and he and Parsons co-wrote such songs as "Sin City," "Wheels," and "Devil in Disguise (Christine's Tune)."

Subsequent bands that Hillman recorded with included Manassas (with Stephen Stills, ATLANTIC, 1972–73); the Souther, Hillman, Furay Band (with John David Souther and Richie Furay, ASYLUM, 1974–75); and McGuinn, Clark and Hillman (with Roger McGuinn and Gene Clark, CAPITOL, 1979–80). Hillman also recorded two solo albums for Asylum (*Slippin' Away*, 1976; and *Clear Sailin'*, 1977).

In 1982 Hillman recorded the bluegrass-flavored *Desert Rose* album for SUGAR HILL RECORDS, which led to the formation of the Desert Rose Band and his post-Desert Rose

Band solo albums for Sugar Hill, including 1996's *Bakersfield Bound* with HERB PEDERSEN.   —*Todd Everett*

REPRESENTATIVE RECORDINGS

The Hillmen (Together, 1969; reissued Sugar Hill, 1981); Flying Burrito Brothers, *Gilded Palace of Sin* (A&M, 1969); *Desert Rose* (Sugar Hill, 1982)

Tish Hinojosa

b. San Antonio, Texas, February 6, 1955

Leticia "Tish" Hinojosa is a politically astute, bilingual folk singer who writes deeply spiritual songs that reflect her Latina heritage. The youngest of thirteen children born to immigrant Mexican-American parents, Hinojosa cut her teeth on a panoply of musical styles, from cumbia and conjunto to folk, rock, and country. Hinojosa began singing and playing guitar as a teenager, but didn't pursue music full-time until she moved to Nashville in 1983. After two long years in MUSIC CITY, disillusioned, she returned to New Mexico, where she previously lived, and in 1987 released her cassette-only debut, *Taos to Tennessee*. On the strength of that record, Hinojosa signed with A&M and promptly released *Homeland* (1989), a record of dulcet beauty and incisive social commentary—especially on the border trilogy of "Joaquin," "West Side of Town," and "Donde Voy"—that established her as a visionary artist and performer.

More success followed as *Culture Swing*, Hinojosa's debut for ROUNDER (1992, produced by Booker T. Jones), garnered Folk Album of the Year honors from the National Association of Independent Record Distributors (NAIRD). Throughout the 1990s Hinojosa has continued to make artful, passionate records that span musical and cultural boundaries and embody the border sensibility that has shaped the life of her people.   —*Bill Friskics-Warren*

REPRESENTATIVE RECORDINGS

Homeland (A&M, 1989); *Culture Swing* (Rounder, 1992)

Bruce Hinton

b. Tell City, Indiana, November 17, 1936

After moving from Los Angeles to Nashville in 1984, Bruce Hinton quietly built the administrative foundation for the rise to dominance of MCA's country music division, with an artist roster that would come to include REBA MCENTIRE, VINCE GILL, GEORGE STRAIT, WYNONNA, and GEORGE JONES, among others.

Hinton's first record company job, in 1960, put him in the warehouse of WARNER BROS. RECORDS' New York operation. He became national promotion manager for WARNER/REPRISE before jumping to COLUMBIA RECORDS in 1965, where he assumed duties as western promotion manager and then director of custom label distribution in New York.

The soft-spoken Hinton set the course for his move to Nashville in 1967 when he joined JIMMY BOWEN, a former colleague at Warner Bros., in Amos Productions. The company's clients included pop singer-actor KENNY ROGERS the act First Edition, Kim Carnes, and Mason Williams. Hinton later formed L.A.–based Hinton/Svendsen Promotions, which was evidently the first national independent promotion company in country music. The million-selling *URBAN COWBOY* soundtrack (1980) was among the company's successful productions. TAMMY WYNETTE, CONWAY TWITTY, MICKEY GILLEY, and ANNE MURRAY eventually joined the Hinton/Svendsen client roster.

At the same time, Hinton also founded Hin/Jen Productions with producer JIM ED NORMAN. In 1980 Hinton promoted two Norman-produced singles, by Mickey Gilley, which hit the Top Five within the same week of July 1980: "True Love Ways" and "Stand By Me."

Hinton moved to Nashville in 1984 to join Bowen again, this time as senior vice president and general manager at MCA. When Bowen left the company for CAPITOL NASHVILLE in 1989, Hinton stepped in as president. Working with TONY BROWN, executive vice president and head of A&R, Hinton trimmed the MCA roster from forty-six to twenty. The move allowed the company to undertake a more focused approach to marketing, promotion, and publicity for each new release. Hinton assumed the title of chairman in 1993, when Brown became MCA's president. Since then he has sustained MCA's status as a first-rate label in the country market. —*Jay Orr*

Becky Hobbs
b. Bartlesville, Oklahoma, January 24, 1950

Despite her undeniable prowess as a musician and entertainer, singer-songwriter Rebecca Ann Hobbs has experienced a frustrating recording career marked by changes of style and label affiliation.

The piano-pounding blonde led several all-girl groups during her teenage years. In 1973, following a two-year stint with the band Swamp Fox in Baton Rouge, Hobbs moved to Los Angeles. After three pop-oriented LPs were largely ignored in the mid-seventies, she rediscovered country music and signed with MERCURY's Nashville division. "I Can't Say Goodbye to You," a single released in 1979, had been a prize winner at the American Song Festival the previous year. The emotional ballad met resistance at the upper levels of the charts, a fate that befell virtually all of Hobbs's equally impressive honky-tonk, rockabilly, and western swing originals over the next decade. Only "Let's Get Over Them Together," a 1983 duet with MOE BANDY, managed to penetrate the Top Ten. It was not until 1988, in the wake of the strong-selling "Jones on the Jukebox," that her first country album appeared—on MTM RECORDS, a label that folded soon thereafter.

Though not a technically imposing vocalist, the well-traveled "Beckaroo" benefits from a heartland drawl that is instantly recognizable. Among her most successful compositions are "I Want to Know You Before We Make Love" (recorded by CONWAY TWITTY) and, more recently, "Angels Among Us" (ALABAMA). — *Pete Loesch*

REPRESENTATIVE RECORDINGS
All Keyed Up (MTM, 1988); *The Boots I Came To Town In* (Intersound, 1994)

Adolph Hofner
b. Moulton, Texas, June 8, 1916

Of German-Czech heritage and reared in musically, ethnically diverse central Texas, bandleader-vocalist-guitarist Adolph Hofner began his career playing HAWAIIAN MUSIC with brother Emil ("Bash," b. 1918), a steel guitarist, in San Antonio in the early 1930s. The Hofners were soon converted by the western swing of MILTON BROWN & HIS MUSICAL BROWNIES. Adolph chose Brown and Bing Crosby as his vocal models, while Bash chose Brown's steel guitarist BOB DUNN. One of the Hofners' early musical cohorts was future songwriting legend FLOYD TILLMAN.

By 1935 the Hofners had joined with JIMMIE REVARD to form the Oklahoma Playboys, a prolific, popular group that signed with BLUEBIRD in 1936. Adolph was recording as a solo act for Bluebird by April 1938. His first sessions were ad hoc affairs, a mix of swing numbers and Crosbyesque ballads. Adolph also worked with Tom Dickey's Show Boys, with whom he cut a hit version of Tillman's "It Makes No Difference Now" in October 1938. In 1939 Hofner formed his first working band, establishing from the beginning a distinctive split emphasis between swing and Czech music. Hofner had a sizable hit with "Maria Elina" (*sic*) for Bluebird in 1940, and by 1941 he was recording for OKEH with a band that boasted the influential swing fiddler J. R. Chatwell.

Hofner made California his base of operations at the close of World War II and went by the name of Dub Hofner because his first name was deemed too close to Hitler's; he returned to San Antonio in 1946. He traveled central Texas for the next half century with his Pearl Wranglers, recording for IMPERIAL, COLUMBIA, and DECCA before beginning a two-decade association with Sarg Records. Ill health has recently stalled his six-decade career. —*Kevin Coffey*

REPRESENTATIVE RECORDING
Adolph Hofner: South Texas Swing (Arhoolie-Folklyric, 1994)

Buddy Holly
b. Lubbock, Texas, September 7, 1936; d. February 3, 1959

For all that he accomplished in life, Charles Hardin Holley is chiefly famous for dying. The manner of his death and its untimeliness became a metaphor for the toll of the rock & roll lifestyle, and the timing of his death is often seen as marking the symbolic end of 1950s rock & roll. These views, enshrined in Don McLean's "American Pie," have tended to obscure both Holly's origins in country music and his career.

Buddy Holly

Holly and a high-school friend, BOB MONTGOMERY, performed around their hometown of Lubbock, Texas, from about 1950 and were on KDAV from 1953. They were introducing elements of r&b into their work before ELVIS PRESLEY, but it was Presley's influence in particular that galvanized Holly. Working as a solo act, he appeared as a local added attraction on several country package shows, and Eddie Crandall, then MARTY ROBBINS's manager, helped him develop an affiliation with prominent booker and publisher JIM DENNY. Denny placed him with DECCA. The first session was held in January 1956. Holly was one of many rockabillies sucked in and spat out by Decca during this period, and, after two releases, he was dropped.

Holly had more success with Norman Petty, who ran a maverick studio-music publishing operation in Clovis, New Mexico. A successful lounge act, Petty nevertheless saw the uniqueness in Holly and started recording him in February 1957. The first record, "That'll Be the Day," was offered around as recorded by "the Crickets" to sidestep the fact that Holly had previously recorded it for Decca, although Petty and music publisher Murray Deutch eventually signed the Crickets to Decca's BRUNSWICK subsidiary, and Holly (renamed from Holley) to Decca's Coral subsidiary as a solo act.

The records that Holly made for Coral/Brunswick were among the most innovative from the early days of rock & roll. Early on, he got out from under his debt to Presley and was a triple threat in that he wrote the songs, sang them, and played lead guitar. "That'll Be the Day" went to #1 on the pop charts. There were another seven hits before Holly died; they ran the gamut from ballads such as "True Love Ways" to flat-out rockers such as "Oh, Boy!" Holly was, in many respects, the most accomplished all-around performer in early rock & roll.

In August 1958 he married Maria Elena Santiago and moved to New York. In that year he split with Petty and the Crickets. His career was on a downswing when he agreed to go on the Winter Dance Party Tour and subsequently lost his life in an airplane crash near Mason City, Iowa. Also killed were singers Ritchie Valens and the BIG BOPPER, who, at the last minute, took the seat on the plane given up by Holly's bass player on this tour, WAYLON JENNINGS.

—*Colin Escott*

REPRESENTATIVE RECORDINGS

From the Original Master Tapes (MCA, 1985); *The Buddy Holly Collection* (MCA, 1993), 2 CDs

Hollywood Barndance Radio Program
established in Los Angeles, California, ca. 1932

One of the earliest regularly scheduled live remote broadcasts of hillbilly and folk programming (as opposed to studio-originated shows), the *Hollywood Barndance* was a weekly showcase for the aspiring western and country performers who crowded the Southern California airwaves. Originally located adjacent to Grauman's Chinese Theatre in a dance hall at the corner of Hollywood Boulevard and Orange Avenue, the *Barndance*, with its live audience, served as a forerunner for postwar shows such as CLIFFIE STONE's *HOMETOWN JAMBOREE* and Bill Wagnon's *TOWN HALL PARTY* (both of which began on radio before graduating to television).

Featuring the likes of EDDIE DEAN and JIMMY WAKELY, the *Barndance*, by the mid-1940s, had relocated to CBS's Fairfax Avenue studio; there, Foy Willing & the Riders of the Purple Sage (who joined the *Barndance* cast in 1942) served as official hosts of the network broadcast show.

Though important as both a Tinsel Town focal point for country music and as a showcase for up-and-coming talent, the *Barndance*—faced with intense competition from *Hometown Jamboree* and *Town Hall Party*—was unable to make the switch to the small screen.

—*Jonny Whiteside*

Homer & Jethro
Henry Doyle "Homer" Haynes b. Knoxville, Tennessee, July 27, 1920; d. August 7, 1971
Kenneth C. "Jethro" Burns b. Conasauga, Tennessee, March 10, 1920; d. February 4, 1989

Best known for their song satires, dry comic delivery, and instrumental virtuosity, Homer & Jethro became one of the most successful comedy acts in country music history. The team leaped beyond the conventional country music venues of rural schoolhouses, tent shows, package tours, and county fairs to take high-visibility bookings on network television variety shows and in Las Vegas showrooms and swank urban nightclubs.

Guitarist Homer "Junior" Haynes and mandolinist Kenneth "Dude" Burns met in 1932, when radio impresario Lowell Blanchard pulled the youngsters from two separate bands auditioning for his *MIDDAY MERRY-GO-ROUND* on WNOX-Knoxville. As the String Dusters, Haynes and Burns handled country tunes, hoedowns, and contemporary pop tunes with ease. For comic relief, Junior & Dude satirized the deadly serious close-harmony duets of the era by wailing hillbilly versions of sophisticated pop standards. When Blanchard forgot their nicknames during a 1936 broadcast, he introduced the team as Homer & Jethro. The amused teenagers quickly adopted the names they would use for the rest of their careers.

Homer & Jethro

When the String Dusters disbanded in 1938, Haynes and Burns continued as a duet, eventually joining the REN-FRO VALLEY BARN DANCE. After serving in World War II, they resumed their act with a Saturday morning show on WLW-Cincinnati. Their musicianship impressed KING RECORDS owner SYD NATHAN, who recruited them for the label's house band in early 1946. After playing on numerous sessions for others, Homer & Jethro recorded a hillbilly version of Frank Sinatra's chart-topping "Five Minutes More" for KING. The record's regional success prompted similar releases.

Veteran producer STEVE SHOLES signed the team to an RCA VICTOR contract in spring 1949. Recognizing the limited potential of their act, Sholes encouraged them to write song parodies. Their first two attempts—"Baby, It's Cold Outside" and "Tennessee Border No. 2"—became best-sellers.

In 1950, Haynes and Burns joined WLS in Chicago; they frequently appeared on the NATIONAL BARN DANCE and Don McNeill's *Breakfast Club*. Their 1953 parody "(How Much Is) That Hound Dog in the Window" was an enormous hit, rising to #2 on *Billboard*'s country charts. Their most successful record was "The Battle of Kookamonga," which transformed JIMMIE DRIFTWOOD's lyrical account of the Battle of New Orleans into a rowdy saga about Boy Scouts raiding a nearby Girl Scout camp. Landing on both country and pop charts, it won a 1959 Grammy in the Best Comedy Performance, Musical category.

Following the success of their classic 1960 live album *Homer & Jethro at the Country Club*, the team largely abandoned single releases to concentrate on albums. Their professional profile soared as on-air spokesmen for two highly successful Kellogg's Corn Flakes ad campaigns; they also made frequent guest shots on network television variety shows.

When Haynes died suddenly while preparing for an August 1971 fair date, Burns's career took a different turn. Gifted young bluegrass mandolinists sought him out for ideas, techniques, and inspiration, and Burns began playing folk clubs and festivals as a jazz instrumentalist. He briefly revived his comedy act with multi-instrumentalist Ken Eidson, then toured for five years with Chicago singer-songwriter Steve Goodman. Despite a lengthy battle with prostate cancer, Burns continued to perform until his death.
—*Dave Samuelson*

REPRESENTATIVE RECORDINGS

America's Song Butchers: The Weird World of Homer and Jethro (Razor & Tie, 1997); *The Country All-Stars: Jazz from the Hills* (Bear Family, 1993)

Hometown Jamboree

established in El Monte, California, December 18, 1949; ended September 12, 1959

Hometown Jamboree was a popular TV variety show in Southern California that was broadcast from the American Legion Stadium, 11151 Valley Boulevard, El Monte, California. It was produced by CLIFFIE STONE, in association with promoter STEVE STEBBINS, under the umbrella of their newly formed Americana Corporation.

In effect, the *Jamboree* was a continuation of Stone's *Dinner Bell Roundup* radio program, which was heard in the mid- to late 1940s over station KXLA in Pasadena. *Dinner Bell Roundup* featured a cast of West Coast performers who included MERLE TRAVIS, BILLY LIEBERT, TENNESSEE ERNIE FORD, Eddie Kirk, WESLEY TUTTLE, Harold Hensley, Herman the Hermit (CLIFFIE STONE's father, comedian Herman Snyder), Judy Hayden, and Tex Atchison.

In 1949 Cliffie Stone took most of the *Dinner Bell Roundup* cast to inaugurate *Hometown Jamboree*, which was televised over KLAC-TV (now KCOP-TV) in Los Angeles each Saturday night, from 7:00 P.M. to 8:00 P.M. A dance followed from 9:00 P.M. until 1:00 A.M., the 10:00 P.M. to 11:00 P.M. portion broadcast locally over KXLA. In 1953 the TV broadcast moved to KTLA-TV.

To augment the cast for *Hometown Jamboree*, several new members were added—vocalists Molly Bee, Bucky Tibbs, FERLIN HUSKY, Gene O'Quin, DALLAS FRAZIER, Jonie O'Brien, Harry Rodcay, and Jonell & Glennell McQuaid. Staff musicians included, at various times, pianists Les Taylor, Vic Davis, and MERRILL MOORE; drummers Johnny Powers and Roy Harte; guitarists Billy Strange, "Talkin'" Charlie Aldrich, and Jimmy Bryant; steel guitarist SPEEDY WEST; and bassist Al Williams. Among the visiting artists to appear on the *Jamboree* were EDDY ARNOLD, LEFTY FRIZZELL, JOHNNY HORTON, JIM REEVES, BOB WILLS, the EVERLY BROTHERS, GRANDPA JONES, the MADDOX BROTHERS & ROSE, PEE WEE KING, PATSY MONTANA, RED FOLEY, and T. TEXAS TYLER.

In 1954 the *Jamboree* moved for one year to the Valley Gardens Arena in Sun Valley, California, before returning to El Monte. In 1957 the show moved to the Valley Garden Arena in North Hollywood and finally to KTLA's studios before signing off for the last time on September 12, 1959.
—*Ken Griffis*

Honky-Tonk Music

"Honky-tonk" is a term that is now used to describe a style of country music whose beat, rhythm, and mood evoke the ambience and flavor of the working-class beer and dancing clubs where the style was born. Neither the origin nor the precise meaning of the term "honky-tonk" have been sufficiently determined, although singer and folklorist Oscar Brand has speculated that it may have referred to clubs where Tonk pianos were used (a brand made and merchandised in the late nineteenth century by a New York firm, William Tonk and Sons). The term was being used to describe black dives by the 1890s, but does not seem to have been widely applied to white clubs until the 1930s.

A similar imprecision clouds our understanding of exactly what a honky-tonk is, because the name has been applied to giant dance halls such as Billy Bob's in Fort Worth and the now defunct GILLEY's club in Pasadena, Texas, as well as to small clubs that scarcely have room for a dance floor. The large institutions typically now have numerous pinball machines, pool tables, mechanical bulls, and other diversions (Billy Bob's even has a small rodeo arena), while the little clubs might have only a bar, a few tables, and a jukebox.

Whatever the size or style of the club, the linkage between the honky-tonk and country music appears to have begun in Texas in the years immediately following the repeal of prohibition. Country musicians began playing in the numerous beer joints that opened up in "wet" counties in the state, particularly in the rough oil field towns of East Texas where money was available to Depression-starved patrons. One veteran of the East Texas dance hall scene, AL DEXTER, recorded in 1936 the first song in country music to bear "honky-tonk" in its title: "Honky Tonk Blues" (not the one later recorded by HANK WILLIAMS). The honky-tonk environment encouraged louder music, the electrification of instruments, strong dance beats, and lyrics that reflected honky-tonk life itself and the changing lives of country people. In this social milieu, where musicians learned to adapt to new conditions and a not always receptive audience, country music lost much of the rustic or pastoral tone that had defined it during its early commercial existence. In 1943 Al Dexter recalled the rough environment from which honky-tonk music emerged in his wartime hit "Pistol Packin' Mama," a song inspired by an incident he had observed in an East Texas dance hall during the mid-1930s. Honky-tonks were not always rough and dangerous, but enough violence occurred in them, or immediately outside their walls, that many musicians recalled them not too fondly as "skull orchards."

By World War II the honky-tonk had become an escapist haven for many transplanted rural southerners, whose lives were being transformed by the new experiences of city life and industrial labor and who sought emotional release and camaraderie through drinking and dancing (and sometimes fighting). They sought also a style of music that would preserve their older scheme of values and social relationships while addressing the newer realities that were transforming their lives. Although "honky-tonking" became a Saturday night diversion for working people all over the South, and was a pastime that was often enjoyed by wives as well as husbands, the honky-tonk was essentially a masculine retreat—a respite from the pressures of work and the responsibilities of home, or simply a place to aggressively assert one's manhood. The woman who went there alone generally was not respected, even if her affections were sought. Women, however, were central preoccupations of honky-tonk song lyrics, either as "honky-tonk angels" or as the person whose affections were being sought or lost.

Honky-tonk songs have dealt with virtually every theme or issue found in country music, although religion, if treated at all, generally serves as an explanation or antidote for guilt. Rollicking or happy-go-lucky songs have abounded in the honky-tonk repertory, and are often used as nothing more than backdrops for dancing. The songs have spoken often about drinking, cheating, marital instability, and divorce, but such lyrics are not uniformly somber, as songs such as "Divorce Me C-O-D" and "If You've Got the Money, I've Got the Time" would attest. Nevertheless, the "cry in your beer" theme has been a powerful ingredient of this repertory, and although observers might differ about the effects of such material—whether it is psychologically damaging or merely cathartic—emotionally wrenching items such as GEORGE JONES's "The Grand Tour" or GARY STEWART's "Drinking Thing" probably come closer than any other kind of songs to embodying the essence of honky-tonk music.

The vocal and instrumental styles of honky-tonk music have also varied widely. Worlds of difference, for example, separate the laid-back, understated vocal style of Leon Seago's 1940 version of "Born to Lose" (performed with TED DAFFAN's Texans), the tenor wail of WEBB PIERCE's 1953 performance of "There Stands the Glass," and the soaring passion conveyed by GENE WATSON's 1979 rendition of "Farewell Party." The singers who popularized styles heard most often today on honky-tonk recordings—LEFTY FRIZZELL, HANK WILLIAMS, and George Jones—also projected dissimilar sounds, although, each could interpret the message of a song in a very personal way. The instrumental sound of honky-tonk music has also changed dramatically since the late 1930s, when ERNEST TUBB, one of the genre's founding fathers, was performing with only an acoustic rhythm guitar. The adoption of drums, the introduction of the bass guitar, the development of the pedal steel guitar (first widely heard on Webb Pierce's recordings in the early 1950s), and the embracing of electrical amplification all resulted in the full-bodied ensemble sound that now defines honky-tonk instrumentation. Many musicians contributed to the evolution of the honky-tonk sound, but RAY PRICE's Cherokee Cowboys made crucial and enduring innovations in the 1950s with their heavily bowed, electrified fiddles, walking electric bass, and shuffle dance beat, while the sidemen associated with BUCK OWENS, WYNN STEWART, MERLE HAGGARD, and other California stylists popularized an even more aggressive electric sound in the 1960s, which combined the beat and themes of honky-tonk with the energy of rockabilly.

The honky-tonk sound still appears in the music of such entertainers as ALAN JACKSON, JOE DIFFIE, DAVID BALL, and BROOKS & DUNN, but it continues to be reflective of the social and musical context in which it exists. Modern honky-tonkers pay homage to and draw inspiration from the veterans of the genre, but they also borrow ideas from today's jazz, rock, blues, and forms that have won currency in modern America. This ability to be simultaneously eclectic and distinctive suggests that honky-tonk music is an organic reflection of a similarly dichotomous working-class culture, while its lyrics about everyday problems and dreams indicate that it is a more honest representation of the changing lives of working people than any other form of country music.

—*Bill C. Malone*

Hoosier Hot Shots

Frank Delaney Kettering b. Monmouth, Illinois, January 1, 1909; d. June 1973
Kenny "Rudy" Trietsch b. Arcadia, Indiana, September 13, 1903; d. September 17, 1987
Paul "Hezzie" Trietsch b. Arcadia, Indiana, April 11, 1905; d. April 27, 1980
Charles Otto "Gabe" Ward b. Knightstown, Indiana, November 26, 1904; d. January 14, 1992

The Hoosier Hot Shots' specialty was comic novelty songs—"I Like Bananas (Because They Have No Bones)," "From the Indies to the Andes in His Undies," and "When There's Tears in the Eyes of a Potato"—accompanied by a conglomeration of unorthodox instruments such as the washboard and the tin whistle. They made their name on the WLS *NATIONAL BARN DANCE*, which they joined in 1933.

Prior to their affiliation with WLS, the nucleus of the group, Kenny Trietsch, his brother Hezzie, and Gabe Ward had spent twelve years on the vaudeville circuit and two years in radio at WOWO in Fort Wayne, Indiana. Much of their repertoire appeared on records, of which they made more than a hundred for the ARC labels, Vocalion, OKEH, and DECCA. The band reached the record charts with "She Broke My Heart in Three Places" (#3 country, #21 pop, 1944), "Someday You'll Want Me to Want You" (#3 country, #12 pop, 1946), and "Sioux City Sue" (#2 country, 1946). Onstage, on disc, and on the air, the Hot Shots introduced most of their numbers with the question

"Are you ready, Hezzie?" The question became part of the American vernacular during the 1930s and 1940s.

The band—including Gil Taylor, the replacement for Frank Kettering who left the group in 1944—departed WLS and the *National Barn Dance* in the mid-1940s and settled on the West Coast, where they appeared in more than twenty movies and worked the Nevada nightclub circuit. With some personnel changes (Nate Harrison and Gil Hartman on bass and Keith Milheim on drums) the group continued to record, making an LP for DOT in 1963 and an album for Tops and Golden Tone, also in the 1960s. They went on to play a FAN FAIR Reunion Show in June 1975.

Of the original members, Gabe Ward stayed active the longest, touring in the 1970s as a solo act and in a foursome with Hartman, Emil Staub, and Roy Wade.

—*Wayne W. Daniel*

REPRESENTATIVE RECORDING

Rural Rhythm, 1935-1942 (Columbia/Legacy, 1992)

Doc Hopkins
b. Harlan County, Kentucky, January 26, 1899; d. January 3, 1988

A fixture on Chicago radio during the 1930s and 1940s, Howard "Doc" Hopkins was a smooth-voiced balladeer with a storehouse of traditional material.

Raised on a farm near Mount Vernon, Kentucky, Hopkins learned to play guitar, banjo, and mandolin in his early youth. Hopkins served in France with the American Expeditionary Forces during World War I; he also served in the U.S. Marine Corps after the war. Outside of a brief tour with a Kentucky medicine show, Hopkins did not perform professionally until 1929, when he formed the Krazy Kats with Mount Vernon natives Karl Davis and Harty Taylor. After a year on WHAS-Louisville, the band moved to Chicago to become the core of the CUMBERLAND RIDGE RUNNERS on WLS's *NATIONAL BARN DANCE.*

Hopkins soon left to pursue a solo career, and he made his first records for Paramount in December 1931. By 1935 he was featured on WJJD's *SUPPERTIME FROLIC;* he recorded for AMERICAN RECORD CORP. in 1936 and for DECCA in 1941. In 1942 Hopkins returned to WLS, where he had a morning wake-up show in addition to regular *National Barn Dance* appearances and numerous radio transcription recordings for M. M. COLE.

Retiring from show business in 1949, Hopkins worked as a machinist, first in Chicago and later in Los Angeles. He returned to Chicago in 1968. During the 1960s and 1970s Hopkins appeared at various folk festivals and also recorded an album for David Wylie's Birch label.

—*Dave Samuelson*

Hal Horton
b. Montclair, New Jersey, 1893; d. November 28, 1948

Hal Horton, popular Dallas disc jockey and show promoter, first acted onstage with his parents at age ten. He worked as a sideshow barker all over the country and entered broadcasting in Davenport, Iowa. From Mexican border stations he came to Dallas in 1936, where an auto dealer sponsored Horton's first hillbilly record programs on WRR.

In the early 1940s Horton launched the KRLD *Hillbilly Hit Parade,* a 10:30 P.M. program on which he played and ranked records and interviewed the many country stars he brought to Dallas. Later he added the *Cornbread Matinee* and announced Mutual's *Checkerboard Jamboree* with EDDY ARNOLD. Horton co-founded Metro Music, which published HANK THOMPSON's earliest songs and Tommy Dilbeck's biggest hits for Eddy Arnold.

Horton made two records for Sonora in 1946. He was plagued by a heart ailment in the last years of his life, and he did his final broadcast from a back porch home studio two weeks before he died. —*Ronnie Pugh*

Johnny Horton
b. Los Angeles, California, April 30, 1925; d. November 5, 1960

There were two hallmarks of Johnny Horton's style. The first was his amiability, which, by all accounts, reflected his sanguine nature; the second was his malleability, reflecting the fact that Horton was not a musician with a commanding vision of how his music should sound.

Born in Los Angeles to parents who shuttled between East Texas and California, John Gale Horton flirted with several lines of work before he won a talent contest in 1950 and decided to try singing for a living. He entered talent contests in California and was signed to a management contract by FABOR ROBISON, who placed him with Cormac Records in 1951. Cormac folded later that year, and Robison started ABBOTT RECORDS to record Horton. Early in 1952, shortly after his first marriage, to Donna Cook, Horton moved to Shreveport, Louisiana, to become a regular on the *LOUISIANA HAYRIDE.* In June, Robison sold Horton's recording contract to MERCURY RECORDS.

Horton's Mercury recordings made little impact. After a divorce, his first wife returned to Los Angeles, and on September 26, 1953, he married the widow of HANK WILLIAMS, Billie Jean Jones. Horton and Robison subsequently parted company, and Horton probably quit the

Johnny Horton

music business for a while. Early in 1955, his management was taken over by TILLMAN FRANKS, and Horton re-oriented himself toward rockabilly music. He quit Mercury Records, and signed with COLUMBIA RECORDS in Nashville. At his first Columbia session, he recorded the seminal "Honky Tonk Man."

For a short period Horton found success with rockabilly music, but his career soon went cold again. He rebounded in late 1958 with the pseudo-folky "When It's Springtime in Alaska," which peaked at #1 in the country charts. The follow-up, "The Battle of New Orleans," topped both the pop and the country charts. Subsequent records in a similar vein, such as "Johnny Reb," "Sink the Bismarck," and "Johnny Freedom," all achieved varying degrees of success and gave Horton a reputation for saga songs. His last hit during his lifetime was "North to Alaska," the theme song to a John Wayne movie.

A firm believer in spiritualism, Horton had strong premonitions that he would die prematurely. Paradoxically, he accepted his fate but tried to avoid it. He apparently tried to cancel what became his last show in AUSTIN, TEXAS, on November 4, 1960. While driving back to Shreveport, he was killed in a head-on collision on a bridge near Milano, Texas. —*Colin Escott*

REPRESENTATIVE RECORDINGS

Rockin' Rollin' (Bear Family, 1990); *Honky Tonk Man: The Essential Johnny Horton, 1956–1960* (Columbia/Legacy, 1996)

Roy Horton

b. near Broad Top, Pennsylvania, November 5, 1914

One of eleven children, Roy Horton grew up in the Allegheny Mountains of western Pennsylvania, where he was born near Broad Top. He and older brother Vaughn (George Vaughn Horton, b. Broad Top, Pennsylvania, June 6, 1911) turned from coal mining, their father's occupation, to making music—first on radio in Pennsylvania and later in New York City, with club work all along the East Coast. Roy played bass behind RED RIVER DAVE McEnery at the 1939 New York World's Fair. Roy also did a good many New York recording sessions for different artists, some of which were secured for him by Vaughn in his capacity as r&b-specialty producer for New York companies (Continental, National, Majestic, MGM, London, and Varsity, among others).

With three other men plus the Beaver Valley Sweethearts, or Trudy and Gloria Martin, the Hortons formed the band Pinetoppers, which popularized on Coral Records one of Vaughn's biggest songwriting hits—"Mockin' Bird Hill," in 1951. Vaughn hit it big with his country songwriting: he wrote "Hillbilly Fever," "'Til the End of the World," "Address Unknown," and "Sugarfoot Rag." Roy's talents, on the other hand, turned toward music publishing.

In the 1940s Roy began his long association with Peer-Southern Music, where he worked for more than forty years, promoting the classic repertoires of such artists as JIMMIE RODGERS, the CARTER FAMILY, FLOYD TILLMAN, TED DAFFAN, JIMMIE DAVIS, and BILL MONROE. Though based in New York, Roy has served the COUNTRY MUSIC ASSOCIATION and COUNTRY MUSIC FOUNDATION since their inceptions: in fact, he was CMA board chairman in March 1967, and participated in the ribbon-cutting for the Country Music Hall of Fame and Museum building. He was elected to the COUNTRY MUSIC HALL OF FAME in 1982.

Vaughn Horton died February 29, 1988; Roy currently lives in Woodside, New York. —*Ronnie Pugh*

Hot Rize

Peter Wernick b. New York, New York, February 25, 1946
Tim O'Brien b. Wheeling, West Virginia, March 16, 1954
Nick Forster b. Beirut, Lebanon, May 16, 1955
Charles Sawtelle b. Austin, Texas, September 20, 1946

From the time they organized in 1978 until 1990, Hot Rize remained one of the most popular acts in bluegrass. Their forte was the performance of classic traditional songs from a pre-1955 era mixed with originals that various band members put together. Their name was derived from the special "Hot Rize" ingredient in Martha White Flour, a longtime sponsor of FLATT & SCRUGGS on the GRAND OLE OPRY.

The base of operations for Hot Rize was Colorado. The ensemble evolved from the interaction of regional Colorado musicians Pete Wernick, Charles Sawtelle, and TIM O'BRIEN. A fourth member, Nick Forster, completed the lineup. Their initial engagements were mainly in Colorado, but their impressive showmanship soon earned them national touring status.

Quality original material was a big plus for the group. Tim O'Brien's "Walk the Way the Wind Blows," which was recorded by Hot Rize, was a major hit for KATHY MATTEA in 1986. Even bluegrass patriarch RALPH STANLEY recorded the O'Brien-Forster ballad "Footsteps So Near."

Eagerly anticipated at each Hot Rize performance was the appearance of the band's alter-ego persona, the traditional country band Red Knuckles & the Trailblazers. The group mixed genuine respect for country music with a lighthearted spoof to arrive at a thoroughly entertaining package. The band consisted of Red Knuckles (Tim O'Brien) on lead vocals and flat top guitar, Waldo Otto (Pete Wernick) on steel guitar, Wendell Mercantile (Nick Forster) on electric guitar, and Slade (Charles Sawtelle) on electric bass.

Including recordings made as Red Knuckles & the Trailblazers, Hot Rize released a total of nine recorded projects, including one French release. Their domestic releases were evenly split between the Flying Fish label of Chicago and the Durham, North Carolina–based SUGAR HILL RECORDS. For both quality of content and production, *Untold Stories* and *Take It Home* remain as favorites with their fans.

Ironically, in 1990, after Hot Rize disbanded, they received IBMA's Entertainer of the Year Award. The following year, the song "Colleen Malone," from their final Sugar Hill album, won IBMA's Song of the Year award. Hot Rize ceased performing as a unit so that individual members could pursue personal career goals. Pete Wernick conducts music camps for aspiring banjo players and is the president of IBMA. Tim O'Brien maintains a high profile as an acoustic/quasi-bluegrass personality. Nick Forster hosts and performs on the nationally syndicated radio show *E-Town*, and Charles Sawtelle operates a recording studio. —*Gary B. Reid*

REPRESENTATIVE RECORDINGS

In Concert (Flying Fish, 1984); *Untold Stories* (Sugar Hill, 1987)

Gerry House

b. Covington, Kentucky, March 28, 1948

Gerry House has successfully blended a career as one of the nation's top country disc jockeys with an impressive string of hits as a country songwriter. House has spent much of his time on the morning shift at WSIX in Nashville, where his humor has propelled the station to a perennial spot at the top of the ratings and has earned him numerous awards from *Billboard*, the ACM, and the CMA.

After graduating from Eastern Kentucky University in 1970, House worked for an Ithaca, New York, radio station for one year before moving to a DJ position in Tallahassee, Florida, for one year. This was followed by more than two years at a Jacksonville, Florida, station. House joined WSIX-AM in 1975 and switched to the station's FM broadcast in 1981.

House joined KZLA in Los Angeles in 1986 but returned to WSIX after two years. In the early 1990s he hosted two syndicated radio programs, *Saturday Night House Party* and *America's Number Ones*. He also released two comedy albums on MCA, *Cheater's Telethon* in 1990 and *Bull* in 1991.

House began writing songs while living in Florida and had his first cut, "Old Time Lovin'" by the OAK RIDGE BOYS, in 1977. He co-wrote such hits as REBA McENTIRE's "Little Rock," GEORGE STRAIT's "The Big One," MARK COLLIE's "Three Words, Two Hearts, One Night," and PAM TILLIS's "The River and the Highway." Frequent collaborators include Collie, DON SCHLITZ, and Bob DiPiero.

—*Beverly Keel*

David Houston

b. Bossier City, Louisiana, December 9, 1938; d. November 30, 1993

David Houston had one of the widest vocal ranges of any country performer. His ability to slide from a warm baritone to a lofty tenor garnered him sixty charted singles during the sixties and seventies. Growing up in Bossier City, outside Shreveport, Houston claimed ancestry from both Robert E. Lee and Sam Houston. Music had always been an integral part of his life, as he was playing guitar by age five. Encouraged by his godfather Gene Austin, who had been a popular singer during the 1920s and 1930s ("Ramona," "My Blue Heaven"), Houston learned to sing and perform. While still in his teens, he became a regular on the *LOUISIANA HAYRIDE* and recorded for RCA VICTOR RECORDS.

However, it wasn't until 1963 that Houston began to taste real success. He signed with EPIC RECORDS and had a #2 country hit with "Mountain of Love." Then, in 1966, he recorded the #1 hit "Almost Persuaded," which remained at the top of the charts for nine weeks and earned Houston a 1966 Grammy Award for Best Country Male Vocal Performance. Other hits followed in rapid succession: "A Loser's Cathedral" (#3, 1967), "You Mean the World to Me" (#1, 1967) and "Have a Little Faith" (#1, 1968).

Recording for Epic gave Houston the chance to record duets with two top female talents. He and TAMMY WYNETTE recorded "My Elusive Dreams" (#1, 1967) and "It's All Over" (#11, 1968). Two years later, he began a string of hits with BARBARA MANDRELL, including "After Closing Time" (#6, 1970) and "I Love You, I Love You" (#6, 1973).

In 1972 Houston joined the Grand Ole Opry, where he remained a member until his death, and in later years, he

recorded for various record labels, including Gusto-STAR-DAY, ELEKTRA, and Derrick.

—*Don Roy*

American Originals (Columbia, 1989)

Harlan Howard

b. Detroit, Michigan, September 8, 1927

Since arriving in Nashville in June 1960, Harlan Perry Howard has come to represent the archetype of the professional MUSIC CITY songwriter. Among the thousands of songs he has written or co-written are such country standards as "Pick Me Up on Your Way Down," "Heartaches by the Number," "I Fall to Pieces," and "I've Got a Tiger by the Tail." Howard has continued to pen hits into the 1990s, scoring with such songs as PATTY LOVELESS's "Blame It on Your Heart." Also a popular raconteur, Howard is routinely described as the "dean" of country songwriters.

Though Howard's family roots are in Kentucky, he is a native of Detroit. His first music idol was ERNEST TUBB, whose songwriting inspired Howard as much as his singing did. Howard spent four years in the service, worked a variety of mostly factory jobs, and moved to Los Angeles in 1955. Determined to make it as a country songwriter, he held down a day job driving a forklift while spending his free time pitching his tunes to Hollywood song publishers. "Looking back, I was probably just a country bumpkin running up and down with a guitar and a handful of lyrics," he said.

Nevertheless, Howard befriended such fellow West Coast up-and-comers as BOBBY BARE, WYNN STEWART, and BUCK OWENS. He also met singer Lula Grace Smith [*née* Johnson], whom he married on May 11, 1957, and who would later attain country stardom as JAN HOWARD. (The two would divorce in August 1967.) His prolific writing and relentless song plugging began to pay off as singers such as SKEETS McDONALD ("You Oughta See Grandma Rock," 1956) recorded Howard's material. Howard's big break came when CHARLIE WALKER, at RAY PRICE's sugges-

Harlan Howard

tion, recorded Howard's "Pick Me Up on Your Way Down," a #2 country smash in 1958. Price himself soon followed with Howard's "Heartaches by the Number," likewise a #2 hit. When Guy Mitchell covered "Heartaches" for the pop market and took it to #1, Howard felt confident enough to pull up stakes and move to Nashville.

In Nashville Howard initially wrote for PAMPER MUSIC, which was partly owned by Ray Price and which was also the songwriting home of WILLIE NELSON and HANK COCHRAN. In 1961 Howard and Cochran hit as the co-writers of PATSY CLINE's "I Fall to Pieces." Besides succeeding in the country field, Howard's songs proved readily adaptable to r&b. RAY CHARLES had a #4 pop hit in 1963 with Howard's "Busted," and in 1969 soul singer Joe Simon sold 1 million copies of Howard's "The Chokin' Kind." Howard cut a handful of albums himself during the 1960s, for labels such as CAPITOL, MONUMENT, and RCA, but he has never seriously pursued a career as an artist.

In 1974 MELBA MONTGOMERY hit #1 with Howard's "No Charge." The song has since become a gospel standard, and Howard has often cited it as possibly his favorite among all the songs he has written. But shortly thereafter, Howard took a seven-year hiatus from songwriting. Returning to the field in the early 1980s, he continued to add to his incomparable record with such hits as CONWAY TWITTY's "I Don't Know a Thing About Love (The Moon Song)" and the JUDDS' "Why Not Me?" He formed his own publishing company, Harlan Howard Songs, in 1990 (he had dabbled as a publisher in the mid-1960s with a firm called Wilderness Music, which he eventually sold to TREE INTERNATIONAL). Though health problems have slowed him down, he has remained a major force in MUSIC CITY, and in 1997 he was elected to the COUNTRY MUSIC HALL OF FAME.

—*Daniel Cooper*

Jan Howard

b. West Plains, Missouri, March 13, 1930

GRAND OLE OPRY star Jan Howard is best known for her hit duets with BILL ANDERSON and as the former wife of songwriter HARLAN HOWARD.

Born Lula Grace Johnson, she married for the first time at age sixteen, was the mother of three at age twenty-one, and was divorced at twenty-four. After moving to Los Angeles in 1953, she met singer WYNN STEWART, who in turn introduced her to his friend Harlan Howard. Then twice divorced, Lula Smith Johnson married Howard in a civil ceremony in Las Vegas on May 10, 1957, and Howard quickly recruited her to sing demos intended for female stars. One of these demos, "Mommy for a Day," co-written with BUCK OWENS, was targeted for KITTY WELLS. When a record executive heard her demo, he signed her to CHALLENGE RECORDS. Her first release for the label was "Yankee Go Home" (1959), a duet with WYNN STEWART; it was also her first appearance as Jan Howard. Her first record to make the charts was a solo effort, "The One You Slip Around With" (#13, 1960), which earned Howard the Jukebox Operators of America's Most Promising Country Female honor.

In 1964 Howard signed with DECCA RECORDS, and the following year she began working with Bill Anderson on his syndicated television show and on the road. Between 1967 and 1971 Anderson and Howard placed four duets in the country Top Five, including the #1 hit "For Loving You" (1967). Earlier, the auburn-haired vocalist scored two solo hits: "Evil on Your Mind" (#5, 1966) and "Bad Seed" (#10, 1966).

Following a divorce from Harlan Howard, Jan began writing songs, including "Love Is a Sometimes Thing" (collaborating with Anderson). Ironically, she cut a mother's tribute tune, "My Son" (#15, 1968), weeks before son Jim died in Vietnam. (Tragically, son David committed suicide four years later.) In 1971 Howard was invited to join the GRAND OLE OPRY. She has since cut back on performing, except to play the Opry. Her autobiography, *Sunshine & Shadow,* was published by Richardson & Steirman in 1989.

—*Walt Trott*

REPRESENTATIVE RECORDINGS
Jan Howard (First Generation, 1981); *Jan Howard* (Dot, 1985)

Paul Howard

b. Midland, Arkansas, July 10, 1908; d. June 18, 1984

In some ways a forgotten pioneer, Paul Jack Howard is little remembered as the man who brought WESTERN SWING to the GRAND OLE OPRY and to the Southeast. He drifted in and out of music until 1940, when he joined the Opry as a solo singer. He was entranced by the BOB WILLS sound coming out of Texas, however, and began building a swing band that grew, at times, to nine or ten pieces. (Alumni of his band include guitarist HANK GARLAND and GRADY MARTIN.) One of the first to use drums on the Opry, he had previously skirted the longtime Opry ban on drums by using two basses to provide the dance-oriented rhythm. Paul Howard & His Arkansas Cotton Pickers recorded for COLUMBIA RECORDS and KING RECORDS in the band's heyday, although none of Howard's music is currently available on reissue.

Howard eventually lost heart with the lack of attention western swing got in the Southeast and left the Opry in 1949 to work steadily in Texas, Louisiana, and Arkansas. He is credited for penning the Wesley Tuttle hit "With Tears in My Eyes," but after the rock era relegated western swing to the age of the dinosaur, he continued working on a smaller scale, performing steadily and leading a band out of Shreveport well into his sixties. He spent his last years in Little Rock, occasionally performing gospel and bluegrass.

—*Douglas B. Green*

Leon Huff

b. Whitesboro, Texas, November 3, 1912; d. May 8, 1952

Nicknamed "The Texas Songbird," the honey-voiced Leon Huff lived up to the billing. Perhaps even more than MILTON BROWN or TOMMY DUNCAN, whom he replaced in the LIGHT CRUST DOUGHBOYS, Huff embodied the smoothness and versatility associated with WESTERN SWING's great vocalists.

Like Duncan, Huff venerated JIMMIE RODGERS and featured his songs often, displaying a distinct feel for blues. With the Doughboys from 1933 to 1935, Huff rendered classic vocals on Vocalion sides such as "My Mary" and "Prairie Lullaby." When boss W. LEE O'DANIEL was fired by the Burrus Mill company (makers of Light Crust Flour) in 1935 and started his own flour mill and band, Huff left with him. Huff worked with O'Daniel for the next five years, dominating the Hillbilly Boys' on-record personality, excelling on Rodgers-like numbers such as "Dirty Hangover Blues." When O'Daniel won the Texas governorship, Huff followed him to Austin, but the two parted angrily during O'Daniel's 1940 re-election bid. Huff sang for O'Daniel's opponent, then led his own band over San Antonio's WOAI. He guested on steel guitarist Charles Mitchell's 1941 BLUEBIRD classic "If It's Wrong to Love You," then joined BOB WILLS after Tommy Duncan enlisted in the army in 1942. Huff recorded with Wills later that year, including the classic "Ten Years," and, when Duncan returned, joined JOHNNIE LEE WILLS & His Boys. Huff would sing with the younger Wills for the rest of his life, recording for DECCA, BULLET, and VICTOR. Huff sang Wills's 1951 hit "Peter Cottontail" and remained in top form until his untimely death.   —*Kevin Coffey*

REPRESENTATIVE RECORDINGS

W. Lee O'Daniel & His Hillbilly Boys, 1935–38 (Texas Rose, 1982); *Johnnie Lee Wills: The Band's A-Rockin'* (Krazy Kat, 1997)

Billy Hughes
b. Sallisaw, Oklahoma, September 14, 1908; d. May 6, 1995

Everette Ishmael "Billy" Hughes, although a fine fiddler heard on many record sessions, was foremost a songwriter. He wrote hundreds of songs throughout his life. Many were placed with HILL & RANGE, including "Tennessee Saturday Night," a #1 hit for RED FOLEY in 1948–49. Others using his compositions included ROSALIE ALLEN, EDDY ARNOLD, SPADE COOLEY, and TEX WILLIAMS. Hughes later wrote songs for ERNEST TUBB. Hughes first came to prominence in Oklahoma City in the band of "Pop" Moore. There he played and sang with JOHNNY BOND. In about 1938 Hughes moved to Southern California, finding success at a club called Murphy's in Los Angeles. His band, the Pals of the Pecos, included stellar musicians such as steel guitarist Curly Cochran and singer Johnny Tyler. Hughes started the Fargo Records label to record this band. His own records on FOUR STAR, KING, Mutual, and others show off his exceptional western swing and blues vocals. His compositions on these recordings, such as "Rose of the Alamo," "Take Your Hands Off of It," "Atomic Sermon," and "Stop That Stuff," ranged from ballad to novelty. Billy Hughes played fiddle and wrote for JACK GUTHRIE and sang on some of LUKE WILLS's recordings.   —*Steve Hathaway*

Marvin Hughes
b. Nashville, Tennessee, June 15, 1911; d. December 2, 1986

Marvin Hammond Hughes was a pianist who played a number of behind-the-scenes roles in Nashville from the 1940s through the 1960s. Hughes's first professional gig came in 1928 for Forrest Sanders's big band in Tennessee. Hughes subsequently worked in New York and Chicago clubs as a single, playing blues. He toured with the bands of Slatz Randall, Bob Crosby, and Ben Pollack, and worked with Snooky Lanson of *Your Hit Parade*. Back in Nashville, he performed with radio station WLAC before joining WSM's staff band. In 1958 Hughes succeeded OWEN BRADLEY as WSM's music director, a position he held until 1964. During his tenure with WSM he played keyboards at the GRAND OLE OPRY and frequently moonlighted as a session musician in recording studios, playing piano on

MARTHA CARSON's signature song "Satisfied" (1951) and the LOUVIN BROTHERS' "When I Stop Dreaming" (1955), and vibes on JIM REEVES's "He'll Have to Go" (1959).

After leaving WSM he served briefly as A&R chief for CAPITOL RECORDS in Nashville. The World War II veteran also produced air force recruiting programs for radio (*Country Music Time*) and was president of Larrick Music, a music publishing firm. In addition, he had been a member of the Nashville Symphony. He is also credited with helping to introduce the revolutionary Nashville number system of chord charts to Music City. In 1963 he became the second husband of Kathy Copas Hughes, widow of RANDY HUGHES and daughter of COWBOY COPAS.   —*Walt Trott*

REPRESENTATIVE RECORDING

Sing the Top C&W Hits (Capitol, 1966)

Randy Hughes
b. Gum, Tennessee, September 11, 1928; d. March 5, 1963

Ramsey Dorris Hughes is best remembered as PATSY CLINE's manager and pilot of the plane that took their lives in a crash near Camden, Tennessee. But Hughes was much more than a manager—he was also an entrepreneur. An adequate rhythm guitarist, he had begun working on the GRAND OLE OPRY as a sideman when he was fifteen. He was also constantly on the road with such stars as MOON MULLICAN, MARTHA CARSON, and GEORGE MORGAN. In 1951 and 1952 Hughes was the featured artist on a string of sexually suggestive records on the TENNESSEE label, including "Birthday Cake," "Tattooed Lady," and "Not Big Enough" b/w "Tappin' That Thing." In 1952, while he was fronting COWBOY COPAS's band, Hughes met and married Copas's daughter Kathaloma (Kathy). By the late fifties he was working with FERLIN HUSKY, who introduced him to HUBERT LONG, the owner of a successful artist-management company. Under Long's tutelage Hughes learned about management and became acquainted with Patsy Cline, whom he began managing in late 1959. At the time, Cline's career was at a standstill, both professionally and financially. Hughes believed he could change things for the better and increase both their earnings. He succeeded on both counts and still found time to start a music publishing company, work as a stockbroker for Jack M. Bass & Sons, run his own small insurance firm, play guitar on most of Cline's recording sessions after 1959, and obtain his pilot's license.   —*Don Roy*

Junior Huskey
b. Knoxville, Tennessee, July 21, 1928; d. September 8, 1971

Roy Madison Huskey Jr., known as Junior Huskey, was one of Nashville's early "first team" session bassists. He performed with CHET ATKINS as a teenager and went on to play with other greats such as DON GIBSON, the EVERLY BROTHERS, and CARL SMITH. Huskey appeared weekly on the GRAND OLE OPRY and can be seen on the Albert Gannaway *Stars of the Grand Ole Opry* shows that were filmed during the 1950s and that have been reissued and syndicated for television. He can be heard on many albums of the 1950s and 1960s, including those of LORETTA LYNN, GEORGE JONES, and TAMMY WYNETTE. In August 1971 he appeared on the Nitty Gritty Dirt Band's *Will the Circle Be Unbroken* album. When he died of a heart attack a month later, the album was dedicated to his memory and earned him his first and only gold album. His son, ROY HUSKEY JR., followed in his footsteps as a noted country music bass player.

—*Jonita Aadland*

Roy Huskey Jr.

b. Nashville, Tennessee, December 17, 1956; d. September 6, 1997

Roy Milton Huskey, known as Roy Huskey Jr., specialized in playing the upright, acoustic bass and for most of his career was widely acknowledged as the best in Nashville on his chosen instrument. The son of one of Nashville's early "first team" session bassists, JUNIOR HUSKEY, Roy Jr. started playing at age twelve and did his first professional gig at age fourteen on the GRAND OLE OPRY with DEL WOOD. His first job on the road was with ROY ACUFF at age sixteen. A regular on recording sessions in Nashville beginning in the 1980s, he was also a member of EMMYLOU HARRIS's Nash Ramblers during the early 1990s. His is the thumping bass heard on Harris's Grammy-winning *At the Ryman* release, and he can be heard on recordings ranging from the likes of STEVE EARLE, NANCI GRIFFITH, and GILLIAN WELCH to those of ALAN JACKSON, GARTH BROOKS, and BILLY RAY CYRUS. He died following a long bout with cancer in 1997.

—*Michael Hight and Jonita Aadland*

Ferlin Husky

b. Flat River, Missouri, December 3, 1927

Ferlin Husky was a mainstay on the country charts for more than two decades. As one of the pioneers of the BAKERSFIELD Sound, he helped establish the West Coast country music scene.

Raised in rural Flat River, Missouri (about fifty miles south of St. Louis), Husky began performing in his teens at various social functions around town. After serving for five years in the Merchant Marines during World War II, he wound up in Bakersfield, California, working as a DJ. In 1949 Husky signed a contract with FOUR STAR RECORDS, recording under the name Terry Preston because he felt his real name sounded "too made up."

In 1951 Husky hooked up with CLIFFIE STONE after replacing TENNESSEE ERNIE FORD on the *HOMETOWN JAMBOREE* TV show. In 1952 Stone helped him get a recording deal with CAPITOL RECORDS, recording five singles under the name Terry Preston before using his own name. Husky developed a reputation for lending a helping hand to the new artists, such as TOMMY COLLINS and DALLAS FRAZIER. Collins credits Husky as showing him the music business and even coining Collins's stage name. Husky's first chart success was "A Dear John letter" (#1 country, #4 pop, 1953), a duet with JEAN SHEPARD (though he was not credited on the original label). They followed up their success the same year with the answer song "Forgive Me, John" (#4 country, #24 pop). Beginning in 1955, Husky recorded under his given name, as well as his as in the guise of a comic alter ego, Simon Crum. As Crum he had his first Top Five solo hit with "Cuzz You're So Sweet" (1955), and was even more successful with the second Crum single "Country Music Is Here to Stay" (#2, 1959).

As a singer, Husky made a major breakthrough when he recorded "Gone" in November 1956. His second crack at the song (he had previously recorded it without success in 1952) was produced by KEN NELSON and featured the powerful chorus vocals of the JORDANAIRES and soprano Millie

Ferlin Husky

Kirkham. Buoyed by the fresh, airy sound, the single hit #1 on the country charts and crossed over to #4 on the pop charts in early 1957. Historians now point to the record as possibly the earliest hit record of the NASHVILLE SOUND production style.

As Husky's popularity grew, Hollywood beckoned and he was soon appearing in films and on television. Unfortunately, his first starring role was in the slapdash 1958 movie *Country Music Holiday* with Zsa Zsa Gabor and FARON YOUNG, and a movie career did not blossom for Husky. Nevertheless, he continued to rack up country hits in the 1960s with such songs as the enduring gospel number "Wings of a Dove," his biggest hit, (#1, 1960), "Timber I'm Fallin'" (#13, 1964), "Once" (#4, 1967), and "Just For You" (#4, 1968). He moved to ABC Records in 1972. Between 1953 and 1975 Husky placed forty-nine singles on the country charts.

—*Don Roy*

REPRESENTATIVE RECORDINGS

Greatest Hits (Curb, 1990); *Ferlin Husky: Vintage Collection* (Capitol, 1996)

Frank Hutchison

b. Raleigh County, West Virginia, March 20, 1897; d. November 9, 1945

Frank Hutchison displayed some of the most pronounced African-American musical influences among white country artists of the twenties, both in the bluesy quality of his bottleneck-style guitar playing and in his choice of traditional folk-blues material. Reared in the coal camps of Logan County, West Virginia, he spent much of his youth absorbing the guitar styles of black railroaders and other workers, and learning to play slide guitar using a pocket knife as a slide. At twenty he married, had two daughters, and subsequently toiled in the mines and at other laboring jobs to support his family. For several years from the mid-twenties, Hutchison made his living as a musician, primarily in West Virginia and neighboring states.

In 1926 Frank began a three-year stint with OKEH RECORDS, recording thirty-two masters, including such significant songs as "Coney Isle" (later known as "Alabam"), "The Train That Carried My Girl from Town," "Stackalee," and "Worried Blues." Hutchison also waxed such guitar tunes as "Cannon Ball Blues" and "Logan County Blues." At his last session, in September 1929, Hutchison appeared on six sides in the "OKeh Medicine Show" series that also featured FIDDLIN' JOHN CARSON, NARMOUR & SMITH, and EMMETT MILLER.

The Great Depression ended Frank Hutchison's recording career and curtailed his show business activity. At various later times he resided in Chesapeake, Ohio, where he did a little work as a showboat entertainer, and in Lake, West Virginia, where he ran a general store and post office. After his store was destroyed in a fire in 1942, he moved first to Columbus, Ohio, and then Dayton, where he died of cancer. —*Ivan M. Tribe*

REPRESENTATIVE RECORDINGS

The Train That Carried My Girl from Town (Rounder, 1973); *White Country Blues, 1926–1938: A Lighter Shade of Blue* (Columbia/Legacy, 1993), 2 CD set containing four cuts by Frank Hutchison; *Complete Recorded Works in Chronological Order, Volume One, 1926–1929* (Document, 1997)

IFCO (International Fan Club Organization)
established in Wild Horse, Colorado, 1965

Most country music fan clubs didn't come into being until the 1960s. The proliferation of these clubs and the success of the annual FAN FAIR convention in Nashville can be attributed in large part to the International Fan Club Organization created and run by three sisters: Loudilla Maxine Johnson (b. Forgan, Oklahoma, September 16, 1938), Loretta Irene Johnson (b. Forgan, Oklahoma, November 29, 1941) and Velma Kay Johnson (b. Alamosa, California, June 26, 1944).

In 1963 the Johnsons started the Loretta Lynn Fan Club at their family ranch in Wild Horse, Colorado, following a two-year correspondence between Loretta Johnson and Loretta Lynn. As word spread about Loretta Lynn's growing career and her fan club, fans of other singers began asking Lynn how to start fan clubs for their favorite artist. "Loretta suggested we form an organization to deal with the other fan clubs, and that's how IFCO was started," Loudilla recalled. IFCO, which began with seventy-five fan clubs its first year, 1965, now unites and advises more than 375 fan clubs of country entertainers, ranging from virtual unknowns to superstars. Throughout the years the Johnson sisters have served as co-presidents of both the Loretta Lynn Fan Club (until Loretta disbanded it in 1996) and IFCO.

In 1968 IFCO staged its first showcase concert to spotlight entertainers in Nashville during the Country Music DISC JOCKEY CONVENTION, four years before Fan Fair began in April 1972. After years of having their annual IFCO concert take place at the Nashville Fairgrounds during Fan Fair, the event was moved in 1995 to the recently restored RYMAN AUDITORIUM.

Today IFCO has its own online Web site, which in 1997 averaged 500 hits a day. "A fan club is the best promotional tool an artist can have," Loudilla Johnson said. "It provides a kind of support an artist cannot buy. All fan club members ask for is a thank you here and there. They don't ask for much, and they give a lot in return." Address: IFCO, P.O. Box 40328, Nashville, TN 37204.

—*Don Rhodes*

Imperial Records
established in Los Angeles, California, January 1946

Business entrepreneur Lew Chudd started Imperial Records and issued mostly ethnic (primarily Mexican) records until 1947. Instead of recording, he tended to release masters that artists sent him. Various country acts had their songs released on Imperial, including JIMMY HEAP (1949–51), CHARLINE ARTHUR (1950), ZEKE CLEMENTS (1950), SLIM WHITMAN (1951–70), MITCHELL TOROK (1953), MERLE KILGORE (1954–56), BOB LUMAN (1957), and FREDDY FENDER (1960). By the time RICK NELSON (1957–62) was signed, the label was in full swing. Imperial was absorbed by LIBERTY in 1963, and the name was retired in 1970. The masters are currently owned by CAPITOL-EMI.

—*Don Roy*

Imprint Records (*see* Roy Wunsch)

Red Ingle
b. Toledo, Ohio, November 7, 1906; d. September 7, 1965

A former big band sideman and Spike Jones comedian, Ernest Jansen "Red" Ingle successfully fused country music with outrageous satire. His first CAPITOL record, "Tim-Tayshun," became a unexpected #1 pop and #2 country hit during summer 1947 and inspired a brief flurry of ersatz hillbilly records by Jo Stafford, Johnny Mercer, DOROTHY SHAY, Arthur Godfrey, and other pop artists.

A violin prodigy as a child, Ingle took up the saxophone as a youth and landed jobs with dance bands around Toledo, Ohio. In spring 1927 he served two brief stints with the Jean Goldkette Orchestra, which then included jazz greats Bix Beiderbecke and Frankie Trumbauer. From 1931 to 1941 Ingle sang and played alto sax with Ted Weems.

In April 1943 former Weems bandmate Joseph "Country" Washburne recruited him for Spike Jones and his City Slickers. Ingle spent more than three years as the novelty band's principal comedian; his showcase number "Chloe" gave Jones a Top Five pop hit in April 1945.

Signing a Capitol contract in March 1947, Ingle cut two sides as leader of "The Natural Seven," a recording band organized by Washburne and featuring NOEL BOGGS, Herman (the Hermit) Snyder, Art Wenzel, and City Slickers alumni. The band's unorthodox hillbilly arrangement of the pop standard "Temptation" featured vocals by Ingle and Cinderella G. Stump, a pseudonym for pop singer Jo Stafford. The record's popularity led Ingle to assemble a road troupe, with Karen Tedder replacing Stafford. Other successful novelties followed, most notably "Them Durn Fool Things," "Nowhere," and "Cigareetes, Whuskey and Wild, Wild Women." Ingle showcases his violin skill on "Pagan Ninny's Keep 'Er Goin' Stomp," which turns a classical virtuoso piece into a fiddle breakdown. A 1948 union recording ban prevented Ingle from appearing on his final hit, "Serutan Yob," a satire of Nat King Cole's "Nature Boy.''

After disbanding his group in 1952, Ingle toured with orchestra leaders Ted Weems and Eddy Howard before retiring from music. —*Dave Samuelson*

REPRESENTATIVE RECORDING

Tim-Tayshun (Bear Family, 1997)

Louis Innis

b. Seymour, Indiana, January 21, 1919; d. August 20, 1982

Louis Todd Innis was a much-recorded singer-songwriter between 1947 and 1955. However, he is best remembered as rhythm guitarist for a quality group of Cincinnati-based musicians known as the String Dusters, whose instrumentalists all became legends in their own right—steel guitarist JERRY BYRD, fiddler TOMMY JACKSON, and the Grishaw brothers, better known as guitarists ZEKE & ZEB TURNER. Innis was then as well known as any of them. Besides his MERCURY and KING recordings, he hosted radio shows at Cincinnati's WLW, in addition to weekday TV shows across Ohio (Cincinnati, Columbus, and Dayton).

The Indiana native turned pro in his teens, working fair dates at first. He broke into radio in Chattanooga in the mid-1930s and worked on Atlanta's WSB barn dance in the 1940s. In the mid-1940s he joined HANK PENNY's Radio Cowboys on WLW and began playing sessions for King. Chosen by GRAND OLE OPRY network host RED FOLEY for his new band, the Cumberland Valley Boys, in 1946, Innis moved to Nashville and worked for Foley into 1948. In 1947 Innis made his own first feature recordings for Sterling (the same label then introducing HANK WILLIAMS), and worked early Nashville sessions behind Foley, Williams, and others. Innis joined Mercury about the time that he, Jackson, Byrd, and the Turners left Nashville for Cincinnati to perform on WLW's *Midwestern Hayride* as well as numerous other radio and TV programs.

There, Byrd led the String Dusters on their Mercury instrumental recordings; Innis was featured on vocal recordings, almost all of which were his own compositions. While none really became hits, Innis's "Good Night, Cincinnati, Good Morning, Tennessee" (cut by himself and also by COWBOY COPAS) is probably the best remembered. His studio abilities brought him plenty of session work—including Hank Williams's breakthrough hit "Lovesick Blues"—and for a time the Cincinnati-based independent KING RECORDS hired Innis as an A&R man.

As his own A&R man, Innis's fondness for novelty material probably hurt him in the long run. His sixteen released Mercury sides (1949–52) and twenty-plus King-DELUXE sides (1953–55) have never been reissued in album format.

Although Innis would return to King intermittently in succeeding years, he moved to Nashville by 1957, when he signed with TREE PUBLISHING. There his duties evidently included producing demo sessions. Later he performed similar functions for Craymart, a publishing company owned by guitarist extraordinaire GRADY MARTIN and piano great FLOYD CRAMER. By the mid-1970s Innis was also working for DOLLY PARTON's Owepar publishing firm, but his principal role was coordinator of album product for STARDAY-KING, where he was employed by 1969. Until his death he continued in this position with Starday-King's successors: Lin

Broadcasting, the Freddie Bienstock publishing group, and Gusto Records. —*Ronnie Pugh*

International Fan Club Organization (*see* IFCO)

Jerry Irby

b. New Braunfels, Texas, October 20, 1917; d. December 1983

A singer-songwriter who straddled the fence between WESTERN SWING and HONKY-TONK in a career that spanned more than forty-five years, Gerald F. Irby never quite attained the stardom he seemed poised for in the late forties.

Irby arrived in Houston, guitar in hand, in 1933, teaming briefly with songwriter/steel guitarist TED DAFFAN in 1936. Irby's first band, the Serenaders, was not successful. He subsequently recorded with the Texas Wanderers (1939) and Bill Mounce (1941) before joining the BAR X COWBOYS in 1941. He recorded as the group's vocalist—and with the MODERN MOUNTAINEERS—for BLUEBIRD in October 1941.

Irby remained with the Cowboys until 1947, but began waxing under his own name in 1945, scoring a considerable hit with his "[Driving] Nails in My Coffin" for the Gulf label. He subsequently recorded for Globe, MERCURY, Cireco, and IMPERIAL and formed his Texas Ranchers in mid-1947. He signed with MGM late that year and quickly had a sizable hit, "Roses Have Thorns." His songs were also hits for others, notably "Driving Nails in My Coffin" (FLOYD TILLMAN, ERNEST TUBB, 1946) and "Keeper of My Heart" (BOB WILLS, 1947). Irby opened his Texas Corral nightclub in 1948.

Irby's career was in a tailspin by the early fifties. Several comeback attempts failed, although he did have a local hit when he teamed with Daffan to record "Tangled Mind" in 1956. In the 1970s Irby switched to gospel music, reworking his old songs and recording several albums before his death. —*Kevin Coffey*

REPRESENTATIVE RECORDINGS

Jerry Irby: Boppin' Hillbilly Series (Collector, 1993); *The Daffan Records Story* (Bear Family, 1995)

Bud Isaacs

b. Bedford, Indiana, March 26, 1928

Although explored on the West Coast by SPADE COOLEY's JOAQUIN MURPHEY and SPEEDY WEST as early as 1947, the pedal steel guitar didn't become a fixture of Nashville-produced country until after Bud Isaacs played it on WEBB PIERCE's 1954 hit "Slowly." Isaacs's effort was a watershed that suddenly made pedals de rigueur for country steel guitarists. Rarely has a single performance by a sideman resulted in such a sweeping stylistic overhaul.

Isaacs grew up hearing JERRY BYRD on Cincinnati radio station WLW and learning six-string Hawaiian guitar. Isaacs debuted on radio at WIBC in Indianapolis, and by age sixteen he was playing the short-lived but pioneering four-pedal Gibson Electraharp. He used it at radio station WOAI in San Antonio, Texas, where he got his first professional break in 1944. For most of the next decade Isaacs followed the peripatetic sideman's life across America from Arizona to Lansing, Michigan, where LITTLE JIMMY DICKENS hired him. Isaacs's association with Dickens would lead to staff work on the GRAND OLE OPRY (1950–54), a regular spot in RED FOLEY's band at the *OZARK JUBILEE*

Bud Isaacs

(1954–57), and a return to Opry staff band work in the late 1950s and early 1960s.

"I began to realize how important it was to have a sound of your own," Isaacs told John Haggard in a 1976 *Guitar Player* interview. "Everybody in Nashville was trying to create his own thing; get tagged for it." Isaacs was tagged when Webb Pierce used him on his November 1953 recording of "Slowly," a song Pierce had previously recorded twice but shelved because he was dissatisfied with the performances.

The issued version became the nation's top country hit for seventeen weeks early in 1954. Isaacs's "moving tone," played on a double-neck, dual pedal steel with a knee lever built by West Coast innovator Paul Bigsby, was prominent on the hit and elicited "laundry bags stuffed with mail," Isaacs recalled, from fans and fellow players inquiring about his unique sound. Webb Pierce, then at the peak of his popularity, made Isaacs's sound a feature of many subsequent hits, despite the fact that Isaacs only worked the one session with him. (Pierce's regular steel player, Basil "Sonny" Burnette, once admitted: "My job was to copy what Bud Isaacs had done.")

In addition to extensive sideman chores in the 1950s, Isaacs enjoyed a solo career on RCA (1954–60), which issued such instrumentals as "Hot Mocking Bird" and the steel guitar standard "Bud's Bounce." He later recorded for the Jabs and Midland labels. In 1956 Isaacs worked with Gibson in designing their Multiharp pedal steel, which debuted in 1957. With his wife, singer Geri Mapes, Isaacs still performs as the Golden West Singers.

—*Mark Humphrey*

REPRESENTATIVE RECORDINGS

Session with Chet (RCA, 1954, out of print); *The Legendary Bud Isaacs* (Midland, 1973, out of print)

Burl Ives
b. Hunt, Illinois, June 14, 1909; d. April 14, 1995

Burl Icle Ivanhoe Ives was the best-known folksinger of the 1940s and 1950s. The son of struggling Illinois tenant farmers, he showed interest and talent in singing and acting during his school years and considered both as careers. In 1929 he left college to hobo around the country, playing banjo and later guitar, learning songs everywhere. He made his way to New York in 1933, where he struggled for years to make a living until success came with his radio program on CBS, *The Wayfaring Stranger* (1940–42). His recording career began in 1941 with an album of folksongs for COLUMBIA (though he had auditioned in 1929 for the GENNETT label). In the mid-1940s a series of folksong albums on the DECCA and Asch labels made his name almost synonymous with "folksinger"; he popularized such songs as "Foggy Foggy Dew," "The Erie Canal," "Blue-Tail Fly," and "Big Rock Candy Mountain," sung simply to unadorned guitar accompaniment—performances that came to define folk music for many in the late 1940s. He continued to record folk and country music through the 1950s to the 1970s for Decca (mostly in Nashville between 1952 and 1972), putting several songs in *Billboard*'s country music Top Ten ("Wild Side of Life," "A Little Bitty Tear," "Funny Way of Laughin'," "Call Me Mr. In-Between"), but gradually the focus of his career shifted to stage, screen, and television. Today he is perhaps better remembered as the narrator and singer of the annual holiday TV staple *Rudolph the Red-Nosed Reindeer* and as Big Daddy in the 1958 film version of *Cat on a Hot Tin Roof*, a role he originated on Broadway.

—*Norm Cohen*

REPRESENTATIVE RECORDINGS

Burl Ives' Greatest Hits (MCA, 1967, out of print); *The Best of Burl Ives* (MCA, 1961, out of print)

Bill Ivey
b. Detroit, Michigan, September 6, 1944

William James Ivey became the director of the Country Music Foundation (CMF) in 1971. Educated at the University of Michigan and Indiana University, he earned degrees in history, folklore, and ethnomusicology. Initially appointed to the CMF as librarian, Ivey was promoted within months to the directorship. During his tenure as director, the CMF increased fourfold in budget and staff, and by the 1980s it had emerged as the premier popular music research organization in the United States.

The founding editor of the *Journal of Country Music* (1972–75), Ivey has written for numerous books and magazines on the subjects of country, folk, and popular music. In addition, he has been writer, producer, or executive producer for several country music television programs. Ivey is a past national president of the National Academy of Recording Arts and Sciences (NARAS) and past national chairman of the NARAS Board of Trustees. For several years, Ivey served as a consultant to the National Endowment for the Arts. In August 1994 President Bill Clinton appointed Ivey to the President's Committee on the Arts and the Humanities. In December 1997 President Clinton selected Ivey to be chairman of the National Endowment for the Arts, based in Washington, D.C.

—*Paul Kingsbury*

J·J·J·J ·  · J·J·J·J

Alan Jackson

b. Newnan, Georgia, October 17, 1958

A member of country music's vaunted "class of '89," Alan Eugene Jackson has risen to modern country superstardom by holding fast to country tradition—for the most part eschewing the pop-rock-country hybrid sounds that have made stars of GARTH BROOKS and others of his generation. Though Jackson adheres to a no-frills concert style as well, the lanky Georgia native's relaxed, casual performances have only enhanced his popularity; in 1995 the CMA voted him Entertainer of the Year.

Raised in a close-knit family whose members all loved gospel music and sang in church, Jackson nevertheless didn't aspire to a musical career until he reached age twenty. Cars held his early interest. Encouraged by his father, a mechanic, the younger Jackson spent a year rebuilding a vintage Thunderbird when he was fifteen, and after leaving school he went into the used-car business.

Jackson met his future wife, Denise, when he was seventeen. Three years later, and married by then, he began sitting in with local country bands, playing cover tunes. A fan of GEORGE JONES, MERLE HAGGARD, and HANK WILLIAMS, Jackson began writing songs of his own. In 1985 he decided to move to Nashville to pursue music as a career. Denise Jackson, a flight attendant at the time, ran into singer GLEN CAMPBELL at an airport and asked him for advice for her husband. Campbell gave her a card with his office address in Nashville, where Jackson later received some tips on how to break into the business.

Jackson's first music industry job was in the mailroom at TNN. Gradually he began singing on songwriters' demos while still concentrating on his own writing. His dedication paid off when he landed a songwriting deal with Glen Campbell's KayTeeKay Music publishing firm.

After recording demos of his own with producer KEITH STEGALL, Jackson became the first artist signed to the country division of ARISTA RECORDS, inking his recording contract on June 26, 1989. His debut album, *Here in the Real World*, was co-produced by Stegall and SCOTT HENDRICKS. Despite a poor showing by the first single, "Blue Blooded Woman" (it failed to make the Top Forty), *Billboard* and various radio professionals predicted major success for Jackson. Their judgments were proven correct when the singer's next single, "Here in the Real World" (which Jackson co-wrote with Mark Irwin), hit #3 on the charts. Three other singles from Jackson's debut album hit the Top Ten: "Wanted" (#3), "Chasin' That Neon Rainbow" (#2), and "I'd Love You All Over Again" (#1). In 1990 Jackson gar-

nered the first of his many industry awards, taking honors as Top New Male Vocalist from the ACM.

Jackson's success continued with his second album, *Don't Rock the Jukebox*, thanks in large part to the popular title track. But his 1993 smash "Chattahoochee," from his album *A Lot About Livin' (And a Little 'Bout Love)*, raised Jackson's profile to superstar levels. Supported by a couple of televised Jackson performances of the infectious song—and by the release of its equally infectious video—"Chattahoochee" helped quadruple the average weekly sales of *A Lot About Livin' (And a Little 'Bout Love)*.

Other Jackson hits have included "She's Got the Rhythm (And I Got the Blues)," "Mercury Blues," and the somewhat controversial (at least in music industry circles, where its pointed barbs were aimed) "Gone Country." Jackson's albums have garnered numerous multiplatinum certifications, and even his holiday collection *Honky Tonk Christmas* was certified platinum. To date, Jackson's Arista releases have combined to sell more than 21 million copies.

In addition to success as an artist, Jackson has scored as a songwriter for other singers. RANDY TRAVIS, whom Jackson befriended before either was a star, recorded four Jackson tunes (three of which Travis co-wrote), including the singles "Forever Together" and "Better Class of Losers." CLAY WALKER scored a #1 with Jackson's "If I Could Make a Livin'," and FAITH HILL later did well with Jackson's "I Can't Do That Anymore." Underscoring the perceived

Alan Jackson

commercial value of Jackson's songwriting, in December 1994 the publishing firm Warner Chappell announced that, for a reported $13 million, it had acquired the publishing rights to Jackson's catalogue and had made arrangements to copublish all future Jackson songs.

Jackson has also participated on numerous collaborative projects throughout his career. Among them he teamed with longtime idol GEORGE JONES for "A Good Year for the Roses" on *George Jones: The Bradley Barn Sessions,* and he paid homage to MERLE HAGGARD with his contribution of "Trying Not to Love You" for the Haggard tribute album *Mama's Hungry Eyes.*

In early 1997 Ford Motor Company enlisted Jackson as a commercial spokesman. His first nationally televised commercial for the company, for which he adapted his hit "Mercury Blues," debuted on Super Bowl Sunday.

—*Janet Williams*

REPRESENTATIVE RECORDINGS

Here in the Real World (Arista, 1990); *Don't Rock the Jukebox* (Arista, 1991); *A Lot About Livin' (And a Little 'Bout Love)* (Arista, 1992)*; Who I Am* (Arista 1994)*; Everything I Love* (Arista 1996)

Carl Jackson
b. Louisville, Mississippi, September 18, 1953

One of the most respected banjo players in the bluegrass and country fields, Mississippi native Carl Jackson developed his tasteful, chromatic style by imitating the licks of Earl Scruggs as he listened to many a FLATT & SCRUGGS recording. Also proficient on the guitar, mandolin, dobro, and fiddle, Jackson was performing with his father, Lethal Jackson, and uncle's bluegrass band by age eleven.

Playing with JIM & JESSE, Jackson first appeared on the GRAND OLE OPRY at fourteen. In addition to being a member of Jim & Jesse's Virginia Boys for five years, Jackson backed numerous other Opry performers before joining the Sullivan Family Gospel group. In 1972, after less than a year with the Sullivan Family, Jackson became a member of GLEN CAMPBELL's band. Jackson played with Campbell for twelve years, 1972–84.

Jackson has been recording his own albums since 1971. They include *Banjo Player* (1973) and *Old Friends* (1978) for CAPITOL; *Banjo Man—A Tribute to Earl Scruggs* (1980), *Song of the South* (1982), and *Banjo Hits* (1983), and (with John Starling) *Spring Training* (1991) for SUGAR HILL. The latter received a Grammy for Best Bluegrass Recording. COLUMBIA RECORDS released four singles by Jackson during the mid-1980s.

As a songwriter his hits include PAM TILLIS's "Put Yourself in My Place" (1991) and VINCE GILL's "No Future in the Past" (1993). RICKY SKAGGS's recording of "Little Mountain Church House" for the NITTY GRITTY DIRT BAND's *Will the Circle Be Unbroken, Volume II* album earned Jackson and co-writer Jim Rushing the International Bluegrass Music Association's 1990 Song of the Year Award. Other artists who have recorded Jackson's songs include GARTH BROOKS, PATTY LOVELESS, DIAMOND RIO, TRISHA YEARWOOD, and MEL TILLIS.

Jackson is also an in-demand session musician and vocalist. Credits include albums by ALABAMA, Garth Brooks, JOE DIFFIE, VINCE GILL, STEVE WARINER, STEVE EARLE, and ROGER MILLER. Jackson played along with Vince Gill and EMORY GORDY JR. on EMMYLOU HARRIS's 1986 album *Angel*

Band. Also, Jackson produced Bobbie Cryner's 1993 critically acclaimed EPIC RECORDS debut. Jackson continues to write, record, and produce; his recent projects include collaborations with frequent co-writers Jim Rushing, Larry Cordle, and Jerry Salley, as well as coordinating and producing a multi-artist tribute to GRAM PARSONS.

—*Kent Henderson*

Shot Jackson
b. Wilmington, North Carolina, September 4, 1920; d. January 24, 1991

Sideman and session player Harold Bradley Jackson worked for both the king and queen of country music: ROY ACUFF and KITTY WELLS. He made many recordings on his own, but he was celebrated for his innovative instrument designs, notably the Sho-Bud steel guitar, created in collaboration with BUDDY EMMONS, and the Sho-Bro, Jackson's seven-stringed DOBRO.

Jackson's stage name was a shortening of Buckshot, a family nickname. He first played Spanish guitar but within a few years mastered dobro and steel. In 1937 he joined George Smith's Rhythm Ramblers on WMBA–Jacksonville, Florida.

COUSIN WILBUR (Bill Wesbrooks) hired Jackson in 1944 to join the GRAND OLE OPRY. During 1945–46 Jackson served in the navy. Returning, he played electric steel for the BAILES BROTHERS, recording with them in 1946 for KING RECORDS and in 1947 for COLUMBIA RECORDS and backing them as headliners of the first *LOUISIANA HAYRIDE* broadcast on April 3, 1948.

At KWKH Jackson met Johnnie Wright and Jack Anglin (JOHNNIE & JACK), and in 1949 went to Atlanta with them (and KITTY WELLS) to record for RCA RECORDS. Jackson's steel guitar touches were heard on the first #1 records for both Wells ("It Wasn't God Who Made Honky Tonk Angels," 1952) and Johnnie & Jack ("Oh Baby Mine," 1954).

Shot Jackson

During 1950 Jackson also recorded with WEBB PIERCE and on his own for Pacemaker Records.

After playing a landmark country show in New York City's Palace Theatre with Wells and Acuff in November 1955, Jackson joined Acuff's Smoky Mountain Boys. In 1962 he left to manage, tour, and record with MELBA MONTGOMERY. Briefly reunited with Acuff, he was sidelined for many months recuperating from a near-fatal car crash suffered by Acuff's band in July 1965. In that year he opened a shop in downtown Nashville to repair and build instruments, continuing until 1983, when ill health prompted retirement. A member of the Steel Guitar Players Hall of Fame (inducted 1986), Jackson died in 1991.

—*Walt Trott*

REPRESENTATIVE RECORDINGS

Singin' Strings of Steel Guitar & Dobro (Starday, 1962); *Steel Guitar & Dobro Sound with Buddy Emmons* (Nashville, 1965)

Stonewall Jackson
b. Emerson, North Carolina, November 6, 1932

Stonewall Jackson is known as a longtime star of the GRAND OLE OPRY and as a staunchly hard country singer. Jackson's father, Waymond, claiming to be a descendant, had planned to name his third son after Confederate general Thomas "Stonewall" Jackson. The elder Jackson, a railroad engineer, became injured in a work-related accident and died shortly before the birth of young Stonewall. Nearly destitute, his mother took her family and hitchhiked to Georgia to work on a brother-in-law's farm. After she remarried, Stonewall suffered years of physical abuse at the hands of his stepfather. At fifteen Jackson ran away to enlist in the army, lying about his age. The truth surfaced and he was discharged. At seventeen he enlisted in the navy for four years. In 1954 he returned to Georgia to work as a sharecropper, saving some $350 of his pay to finance a move to Nashville.

His career got off to a storybook start. Two days after his twenty-fourth birthday, Jackson drove his gray 1955 Chevrolet pickup into Nashville and walked uninvited that day into the offices of ACUFF-ROSE PUBLICATIONS. His singing and songwriting impressed WESLEY ROSE enough that Rose helped Jackson gain an audition the following day for the Opry's GEORGE D. HAY and W. D. KILPATRICK, who gave him a contract without benefit of a label or hit record. On his third day in Nashville, November 10, 1956, he appeared on the Opry's *Friday Night Frolics* program and became a member of the cast.

ERNEST TUBB, who met Jackson onstage at that first Friday night broadcast, took the young singer under his wing, buying his first stage clothes, giving him the opening berth on his road show, and steering him to COLUMBIA RECORDS. His first hit came in 1958–59 with "Life to Go," written by GEORGE JONES, with whom he was then touring. His next hit, "Waterloo," was a #1 country hit for five weeks in the summer of 1959 and crossed over into the *Billboard* pop charts (#4), generating bookings on such pop TV programs as Dick Clark's *American Bandstand*.

Hot on the heels of his successes "Life to Go" and "Waterloo," Stonewall Jackson was named Most Promising Country Male Star by *Cash Box*. Other Top Ten hits in the sixties include "A Wound Time Can't Erase" (#3, 1962), "B. J. the DJ" (#1, 1964), "Don't Be Angry" (#4), and "I Washed My Hands in Muddy Water" (#8, 1965). He's also

Stonewall Jackson

known for his pro–Vietnam War hit "The Minute Men (Are Turning in Their Graves)." He left Columbia in 1973 for MGM RECORDS, where he logged his final chart hit, "Herman Schwartz," that year. Jackson and his Minutemen band (including son Turp on drums) occasionally tour and still keep their weekend Opry dates. His autobiography, *From the Bottom Up*, was published by L. C. Parsons in 1991.

—*Walt Trott*

REPRESENTATIVE RECORDINGS

The Dynamic Stonewall Jackson (Columbia, 1959; Sony, 1993); *Stonewall Jackson, American Original* (Columbia, 1989)

Tommy Jackson
b. Birmingham, Alabama, March 31, 1926; d. December 9, 1979

Tommy Jackson is generally considered to be one of the two or three greatest commercial country fiddle players of all time. He did for country fiddle playing what EARL SCRUGGS did for the banjo in bluegrass: He set a precedent. Stylistically, on the recordings of artists such as HANK WILLIAMS and WEBB PIERCE, Jackson popularized the playing of simple double-stop (playing two strings at once in harmony) restatements of the melody. In addition, he developed an influential single-string style that he introduced on RAY PRICE's massive 1956 hit "Crazy Arms." The first regular Nashville session fiddler, he played on thousands of recordings and ranged from bluegrass to western swing in fiddle styles.

Born Thomas Lee Jackson Jr. in Birmingham, Alabama, on March 31, 1926, he and his family moved to Nashville when he was about a year old. As a youngster, he played in bars and on street corners for tips. In the early 1940s he gained experience with the GRAND OLE OPRY bands of CURLEY WILLIAMS and then PAUL HOWARD. Following service with the Army Air Corps in the Pacific Theater in World War II, he returned to civilian life in April 1946. After touring briefly with the DUKE OF PADUCAH, ANNIE LOU & DANNY DILL, and the YORK BROTHERS, he moved up to the bands of MILTON ESTES and then RED FOLEY. While with Foley, he fell into session work with Foley's band, the Cumberland Valley Boys, an outfit that included JERRY BYRD, LOUIS INNIS, and ZEKE TURNER. When Foley fired the band, they became

Wanda Jackson

full-time session players known as the Pleasant Valley Boys. For his part, Jackson was happy with the change, having discovered that he didn't like traveling and preferred to be a full-time session player. From the late 1940s through the 1960s he was probably Nashville's most in-demand session fiddler. He also amassed a very large catalogue of traditional hoedowns on record (twelve sides for MERCURY, twelve for DECCA, and nearly one hundred for DOT), which serve as definitive versions of some of these titles.

Aside from his large catalogue of fiddle tunes, which are sought-after collector's items, some of Jackson's best solo and backup work can be heard on virtually every Ray Price recording from 1955 to 1966. —*Eddie Stubbs*

Wanda Jackson
b. Maud, Oklahoma, October 20, 1937

There were several women singers, such as BRENDA LEE and even Patti Page, who crossed easily between country and pop, but none did so with quite the eruptive quality of Wanda Lavonne Jackson. Her unbridled sensuality ran contrary to common expectations for female country singers, but it shouldn't distract one from her talent as both a singer and a songwriter.

Jackson began performing on KLPR–Oklahoma City, in 1953, and sang with TOMMY COLLINS before working on and off with HANK THOMPSON in 1954. She made her first recordings for DECCA in March that year in a deal abetted by Thompson. A duet with Thompson sideman Billy Gray, "You Can't Have My Love," cracked the country Top Ten. After high school graduation in June 1955, she joined the *OZARK JUBILEE* and worked road shows with ELVIS PRESLEY, whom she dated.

In June 1956 she switched to CAPITOL RECORDS. On her second session, she cut the original version of "Silver Threads and Golden Needles" and the rockabilly classic "Hot Dog (That Made Him Mad)," underscoring the way

in which her recordings veered precipitously between country and rock & roll. Her bands were legendarily hot. She employed a mixed-race rock band with Bobby Poe, BIG AL DOWNING, and Vernon Sandusky; after she took up residency in Las Vegas in 1960, she hired ROY CLARK, then playing bars in the D.C. area, to be her guitarist and opening act.

Jackson scored a surprise hit in Japan in 1958 with "Fujiyama Mama," and, in 1960, had a late-blooming rock & roll hit in the United States with "Let's Have a Party," an album cut from two years earlier and a cover of a 1957 Elvis track. Shortly before, she had decided to revert to country music and scored Top Ten country hits in 1961 with "Right or Wrong" and "In the Middle of a Heartache." There were twenty-five other country hits spread over the next thirteen years. She also wrote BUCK OWENS's Top Ten country hit "(Let's Stop) Kickin' Our Hearts Around."

Jackson began recording in Nashville in 1960 but decided not to move there. In 1973 she became a born-again Christian, and today she plays religious and secular shows in the United States and tours overseas with a rockabilly show. —*Colin Escott*

REPRESENTATIVE RECORDINGS

Right or Wrong (Bear Family, 1992), 4 CDs; *Rockin' the Country* (Rhino, 1990)

Sonny James
b. Hackleburg, Alabama, May 1, 1929

Sonny James has had one of the most successful careers in country music. He holds the distinguished record of having the most consecutive #1 hits in country music during the 1960s and 1970s. Known as the Southern Gentleman for his congenial personality, James has had his greatest success singing romantic ballads about the joys and trials of love.

James Hugh Loden was born into a family of professional entertainers. By the time he was four, Sonny (a family nickname) was performing with the Loden Family, which included his parents and four sisters. Within a few years, the group had their own radio show in Birmingham. By the time James was a teenager, he had mastered both the guitar and the fiddle (winning several fiddle championships) and later gained additional performing experience with appearances on such shows as the LOUISIANA HAYRIDE and the BIG D JAMBOREE.

After serving in the Korean War, James hooked up with CHET ATKINS, who introduced him to CAPITOL RECORDS' producer KEN NELSON. Nelson signed James to the label in 1952 and suggested James Loden use his nickname and first name to create the stage name Sonny James (to keep it simple for the DJs and record-buying public). James had several singles make the charts during the early 1950s, but 1956 was the year he recorded the breakthrough song that brought him worldwide attention. "Young Love," written by Ric Cartey and Carole Joyner, became one of the top songs of 1957, reaching #1 on both the country and pop charts.

After his initial success, James spent several years searching for another hit with various record labels: NRC (1960), RCA (1961–62), and DOT (1962). After re-signing with Capitol in 1963, he bounced back with "The Minute You're Gone" (#9), making him a fixture on the country charts for the next decade. Between 1967 and 1972 James had sixteen consecutive #1 hits, including "Need You" (1967), "Heaven Says Hello" (1968), "Running Bear" (1969), and "Here Comes Honey Again" (1972). He received numerous awards, including being named #1 Country Male Artist of the Decade by *Record World* and #1 Artist by *Billboard* (1969).

In the 1970s he switched over to COLUMBIA RECORDS and continued his chart success with seven Top Ten hits. In

1973 his production skills yielded MARIE OSMOND's first hit single and million seller, "Paper Roses." He left Columbia in 1979 for MONUMENT RECORDS and in 1981 moved on to Dimension Records, for whom he scored his last chart hit in 1983 with "A Free Roamin' Mind." —*Don Roy*

REPRESENTATIVE RECORDINGS

Greatest Hits (Curb, 1990); *Sonny James: Capitol Collector's Series* (Capitol, 1990); *Sonny James: American Originals* (Columbia, 1989)

Jamup and Honey (Lasses and Honey)

Lee Roy "Lasses" White b. Wills Point, Texas, August 28, 1888; d. December 16, 1949

Lee Davis "Honey" Wilds b. Betton, Texas, August 23, 1902; d. March 29, 1982

The origin of this famed GRAND OLE OPRY blackface comedy team dates from 1932, when WSM hired veteran comedian Lee Roy "Lasses" White to start a Friday night minstrel show. He came to Nashville with a partner, Lee Davis "Honey" Wilds, who had worked with him for a number of years.

Lasses White was one of the last avatars of an old vaudeville tradition of blackface comedy. Born on a farm in Wills Point, Texas, in the late nineteenth century, he was a protégé of the legendary George "Honeyboy" Evans and soon became known for a hit 1912 song called "Nigger Blues." By 1920 White had his own troupe and was recording sketches for COLUMBIA records. Opry founder GEORGE D. HAY was fond of this troupe and the tradition it represented, and hired White to reproduce it on WSM. *Amos and Andy* dialogue as well as Lasses and Honey's song parodies made the act immensely popular, and by 1934 the team was also performing regularly on the Opry.

In the mid-1930s White moved to Hollywood, where he worked as a character actor in cowboy films. In about 1939 Wilds left the Opry for a time to tour as part of an act called Honey and Alexander, but late that year he returned to WSM. There he continued the blackface tradition with an act called Jamup and Honey, which included a series of other partners such as Tom Woods and Bunny Biggs. In 1940 Wilds became one of the first Opry acts to take a TENT SHOW on the road. —*Charles Wolfe*

Tommy Jarrell

b. Round Peak, North Carolina, March 1, 1901; d. January 28, 1985

Though he made his living as a moonshiner and a road grader operator, Thomas Jefferson Jarrell made a name for himself as a quintessential old-time fiddler. Born in the Piedmont foothills of the Blue Ridge Mountains, he was one of eleven children of Ben Jarrell, who was the fiddler for DA COSTA WOLTZ & His Southern Broadcasters, a string-band that recorded 78-rpm records for GENNETT in 1927. At age fourteen Tommy bought his first FIDDLE with money he won from gambling. Following his father's example, Jarrell mastered the Round Peak bowing style—an intricate wrist-and-elbow technique more frenzied than the long, smooth strokes favored by modern fiddlers.

Jarrell performed at local house frolics and informal gatherings for most of his life. It wasn't until the mid-1960s, after retiring from his job at the North Carolina Highway Department, that he attended his first music fes-

Sonny James

tival. During the next two decades Jarrell became a beloved figure on the old-time circuit and nurtured an entire generation of young musicians, including JIMMY ARNOLD. A recipient of the 1982 National Heritage Fellowship Award, Jarrell was also the subject of Les Blank's documentary film *Sprout Wings and Fly,* which took its title from lyrics of his signature tune, "Drunken Hiccups."

—*Eddie Dean*

REPRESENTATIVE RECORDING

Tommy & Fred: Best Fiddle Banjo Duets Played by Tommy Jarrell & Fred Cockerham (County, 1992)

John Barlow Jarvis
b. Pasadena, California, January 2, 1954

Regarded as a top Nashville session keyboard player, John Barlow Jarvis is also a hit songwriter. He collaborated with VINCE GILL on "I Still Believe in You," a composition that earned the pair a Grammy for Best Country Song in 1992, along with top song honors at the CMA and ACM Awards in 1993. Other writing successes include three songs on the JUDDS' *River of Time* album and cuts by the HIGHWAYMEN, OLIVIA NEWTON-JOHN, and STEVE WARINER.

Jarvis's virtuosity on the piano and related keyboards is chronicled in MCA RECORDS' Master Series, a late 1980s collection of recordings by Nashville musicians. Jarvis made four albums in the series, one of which, *Whatever Works,* was picked by *Time* magazine as one of the ten best pop records of 1988. In 1989 James Taylor picked Jarvis to be a member of his fall touring group. By 1990 Jarvis was doing sessions steadily, and in 1993 *Music Row* magazine named him top keyboard player for his work on albums by Vince Gill, BROOKS & DUNN, MARY CHAPIN CARPENTER, REBA MCENTIRE, DOLLY PARTON, GEORGE STRAIT, WYNONNA, and AARON TIPPIN.

—*Michael Hight*

REPRESENTATIVE RECORDINGS

So Far So Good (MCA Master Series, 1986); *Something Constructive* (MCA Master Series, 1987); *Whatever Works* (MCA Master Series, 1988); *Pure Contours* (MCA Master Series, 1990)

Jason & the Scorchers
Jason Ringenberg b. Kewanee, Illinois, November 22, 1958
Warner Hodges b. Wurzburg, Germany, June 4, 1959
Jeff Johnson b. Nashville, Tennessee, December 31, 1959
Kenny Ames b. Pittsburgh, Pennsylvania, June 8, 1967
Perry Baggs b. Nashville, Tennessee, March 22, 1962

Looking to wed his love of traditional country music with the confrontational energy and attitude of punk rock, Jason Ringenberg, transplanted son of an Illinois pig farmer, in 1981 formed a pioneering rock & roll band—Jason & the Nashville Scorchers, with guitarist Warner Hodges, bassist Jeff Johnson, and drummer Perry Baggs. After winning a following as one of the most dynamic live bands in Nashville, the Scorchers recorded a four-song EP, *Reckless Country Soul,* within three hours' studio time during December 1981. The disc boosted the band's rising profile as noncompromising rock & rollers with hillbilly hearts. Another EP, 1983's *Fervor,* on which the group recorded "Absolutely Sweet Marie" and "Hot Nights in Georgia," drew passionate critical acclaim and landed the

band (now known simply as Jason & the Scorchers) a record deal with EMI.

In 1985 the Scorchers released their first full-length album, *Lost & Found.* Commercial success never matched critical accolades, however, and after two more albums and some personnel changes, the band dissolved in 1989. Ringenberg courted the country mainstream on a solo album, *One Foot in the Honky Tonk,* in 1991, for LIBERTY RECORDS, but country radio did not embrace his raw and rowdy vocal style.

At the urging of bassist Johnson, the Scorchers' original lineup reunited and began touring again in mid-1993. A record deal followed, with *A Blazing Grace* released in 1995, followed by a reissue of *Reckless Country Soul* (including six rediscovered tracks), and another studio album, *Clear Impetuous Morning,* in 1996. A new wave of country-rock acts indebted to the Scorchers and inspired by a similar mix of country and punk sensibilities emerged in the mid-1990s. Showing no signs of quitting, the Scorchers—with bassist Kenny Ames replacing the departed Johnson—again impressed critics, fans, and music business insiders with a frenzied performance at the 1997 South by Southwest music conference in AUSTIN, TEXAS.

—*Jay Orr*

REPRESENTATIVE RECORDINGS

Essential Jason & the Scorchers, Volume 1 (EMI, 1992); *Reckless Country Soul* (Mammoth/Praxis, 1996)

JEMF (John Edwards Memorial Foundation, now Forum)
established in Los Angeles, California, 1961

Following JOHN EDWARDS's death on Christmas Eve 1960, in Australia, his mother, Irene, carried out her son's wishes by transferring his massive collection of 78-rpm discs, reel-to-reel tapes, photographs, letters, and ephemera to Eugene Earle in New Jersey. Long aware of John's affection for old-time music, Earle and colleagues (Archie Green, Ed Kahn, Fred Hoeptner, and D. K. Wilgus) chartered the John Edwards Memorial Foundation in California in 1961. An educational nonprofit corporation, it pioneered the preservation and presentation of folk and vernacular American music in its varied manifestations. From its inception, the JEMF brought together record collectors, ballad scholars, and country music artists and executives. From 1969 to 1985, Norm Cohen edited the influential *JEMF Quarterly* (seventy-eight issues); in these years he set superb analytic and aesthetic standards for treating sound recordings in their complex cultural roles. In JEMF endeavors, enthusiastic volunteers and occasional staff members such as Ken Griffis, JOHN HARTFORD, Barry Hansen, Chris Strachwitz, Paul Wells, and Peter Tamony joined hands in housekeeping, fundraising, LP album issues, radio programs, and archive-building. From 1964 to 1983 UCLA's Folklore Center housed the JEMF. In 1986 the University of North Carolina's Southern Folklife Collection (Wilson Library, Chapel Hill) absorbed the JEMF's holdings.

—*Archie Green*

Rev. Andrew Jenkins
b. Jenkinsburg, Georgia, November 26, 1885; d. April 25, 1957

Andrew Jenkins was a blind preacher, musician, and the writer of approximately 800 songs, including the gospel standard "God Put a Rainbow in the Cloud." During the

1920s and 1930s Jenkins was best known for his event songs, which include "The Death of Floyd Collins," "The Wreck of the Royal Palm," "The Fate of Frank Dupree," and "Ben Dewberry's Final Run."

Blind most of his life, Jenkins pretended to be a preacher as a child, delivering sermons to his playmates from tree stumps and front porches. He also discovered at an early age that he could play any musical instrument he wanted to. The adult Jenkins became a real-life evangelist and parlayed his musical talents into a parallel career as a radio, stage, and recording artist.

On August 14, 1922, Rev. Jenkins and his two step-daughters, Mary Lee Eskew and Irene Eskew Spain, made their debut on Atlanta's new radio station WSB in a program of sacred songs and secular ballads that included original compositions by Rev. Jenkins. The Jenkins Family was heard regularly on WSB during the ensuing decade. Radio exposure brought them to the attention of recording company executives, and from 1925 until 1934 the Jenkins Family, under various artist credits, recorded some one hundred sides for the OKEH and BLUEBIRD labels.

—*Wayne W. Daniel*

Snuffy Jenkins

b. Harris, North Carolina, October 27, 1908; d. April 30, 1990

Known primarily throughout South Carolina through his long musical partnership with fiddler Homer "Pappy" Sherrill, DeWitt "Snuffy" Jenkins is often credited as a major influence upon such first-generation bluegrass banjo players as EARL SCRUGGS, DON RENO, and RALPH STANLEY.

As a youth in Harris, North Carolina, Jenkins learned banjo from pioneering three-finger stylists Rex Brooks and Smith Hammett. Forming a stringband with his brother Verl, he began his radio career in 1934 over WBT, Charlotte. In 1937 Jenkins worked with J. E. MAINER's Mountaineers on WIS–Columbia, South Carolina. When Mainer left, announcer Byron Parker fronted the renamed WIS Hillbillies; Sherrill joined the group in 1939. As a self-contained showband, the WIS Hillbillies—later called the Hired Hands—entertained South Carolinians with medicine show skits, blackface comedy, and outstanding musicianship. Jenkins contributed broad, baggy-pants gags, as well as banjo, guitar, and washboard specialties.

In 1956 Jenkins recorded several banjo instrumentals for old-time music enthusiast Mike Seeger; four appeared on Folkways' *American Banjo Scruggs Style*, the first album devoted to bluegrass music. Sherrill and Jenkins made relatively few recordings during their prime, but later albums on Folk Lyric and ROUNDER fortunately preserve much of their repertoire.

—*Dave Samuelson*

John Jennings (*see* Mary Chapin Carpenter)

Waylon Jennings

b. Littlefield, Texas, June 15, 1937

Waylon Arnold Jennings's 1996 autobiography, *Waylon* (Warner Books), is perhaps as frank a country autobiography as has been written, and it graphically traces Jennings's career from hardscrabble poverty in West Texas to teenage bassist for BUDDY HOLLY to Nashville rebel to OUTLAW star to cocaine addict to redemption.

That journey has been a theme of Jennings's music and life since he escaped what he considered the futureless

Waylon Jennings

world of Littlefield, Texas, by working in radio in Lubbock and by picking up the guitar. His big break came when he was tapped by Holly to play bass in Holly's new band on a tour through the Midwest in late 1958 and early 1959. In an oft-told tale, Jennings gave up his airplane seat to the BIG BOPPER, J. P. Richardson, for an ill-fated flight that would claim the lives of Holly, the Bopper, and singer Ritchie Valens. After the plane crashed, Jennings's musical world crashed around him. Holly had been his mentor, producing his first record ("Jole Blon," BRUNSWICK, 1958), and Jennings felt responsible, because his last words to Holly had been the joking refrain, "I hope your ole plane crashes" (in response to Holly's "I hope your damned bus freezes up again").

It took Jennings years to regain some career equilibrium. He first went back to radio in West Texas, then began performing again, ending up at a bar in Phoenix, Arizona, called J. D.'s. Jennings became a local celebrity there, and when Nashville performer BOBBY BARE passed through Phoenix and heard Jennings, Bare headed for a pay phone to tell his producer, CHET ATKINS at RCA in Nashville, about this raw young talent out in Arizona.

Jennings had already cut some songs in a country-folk vein for then fledgling A&M Records in Los Angeles, but A&M demurred to Atkins, who signed Jennings to RCA. The singer's first session for RCA was held March 16, 1965.

Jennings moved to Nashville and, by sheer chance, became roommates with JOHNNY CASH; their legends as hell-raisers soon became cemented. Jennings starred in the 1966 movie *Nashville Rebel*, scored Top Ten hits with songs such as "The Chokin' Kind" (#8, 1967) and "Only Daddy That'll Walk the Line" (#2, 1968), and his 1969 collaboration with the Kimberlys on "MacArthur Park" won a Grammy Award. But Jennings chafed under RCA's tight rein, and at one point he also took a dramatic stand against the status quo: When Chet Atkins turned him over to staff producer DANNY DAVIS, Jennings pulled out a pistol in the studio to protest Davis's practice of what Jennings felt was studio bullying.

By the early 1970s Jennings was getting frozen out of country's mainstream. He retaliated by hiring jazz musician Miles Davis's maverick manager from New York City, who put him into such high-profile venues as the rock-retro Max's Kansas City in New York. Gradually Jennings began to win his war in the studio. He stayed true to his musical instincts and recorded a gallery of landmark recordings, most notably the 1973 albums *Lonesome, On'ry and Mean* and *Honky Tonk Heroes*. He also staged an alternative show at the 1973 DISC JOCKEY CONVENTION in Nashville, with WILLIE NELSON, SAMMI SMITH, and Troy Seals joining him in an Outlaw program.

Jennings was dubbed an Outlaw in Nashville for demanding and eventually getting what rock groups had been used to having for years—namely, the right to record what material he wanted, in what studio he wanted, and with what musicians he wanted to use. (His friend Willie Nelson won his own independence by moving back to Texas and recording there.) It was, as Jennings later said, a simple matter of artistic freedom.

Jennings won CMA's Male Vocalist of the Year Award in 1975, but what finally won the battle for Jennings and the Outlaws was the ultimate weapon in corporate wars: sales. *Wanted: The Outlaws*, an RCA package of songs by Jennings, Nelson, Jennings's wife JESSI COLTER, and TOMPALL GLASER, was released in January 1976, with only Jennings's name credited on the album spine (since he was the only one of the four artists still under contract to RCA). The album flew out of record stores and soon became the first album in country music history to be certified platinum. The Jennings-Nelson duet "Good Hearted Woman" became a major crossover hit in 1976, as did Jennings's "Luckenbach, Texas (Back to the Basics of Love)" the following year. Jennings and Nelson won a 1978 Grammy (Best Country Vocal Performance by a Duo or Group) for their hit "Mamas Don't Let Your Babies Grow Up to be Cowboys." They (forever linked as "Waylon and Willie") began selling records in numbers previously associated with rock album sales, and the Nashville system gradually moved away from a producer-dominated order to one in which the artist shares power.

Sadly, for the short term at least, Jennings's excesses also paralleled those of the rock world. He was soon spending $1,500 a day on a cocaine habit that eroded his career. He eventually faced his addiction, beat it, and returned to a career much scaled down through stints on MCA and Epic through the late 1980s and early 1990s. He also became a bit of a role model by going back to earn his GED, or high school equivalency diploma. Jennings had dropped out of school in the tenth grade and felt he owed it to his young son to prove his resolution about the importance of education by finishing high school himself. At the time of this writing, Jennings was still making concert appearances that attracted loyal fans. RCA reissued the historic *Outlaws* album on CD in 1996.   —*Chet Flippo*

REPRESENTATIVE RECORDINGS

Honky Tonk Heroes (RCA, 1973); *Wanted: The Outlaws* (RCA, 1976); *Only Daddy That'll Walk the Line: The RCA Years* (RCA, 1993); *The Essential Waylon Jennings* (RCA, 1996)

Jesse James & All the Boys

William Howard "Jesse" James b. Mississippi, December 5, 1916; d. April 16, 1972

Long before AUSTIN became the center for anti-Nashville progressive country in the 1970s, the Texas capital had a vibrant country music scene. The area's dominant band

from the mid-1940s through mid-1950s was the slick western swing group Jesse James & All the Boys.

Airing over KTBC radio (and later on TV) and recording for Bluebonnet and FOUR STAR RECORDS, the band included a slew of accomplished musicians such as classically trained violinists Joe Castle and the manic Roddy Bristol (who had come to Texas with PAUL HOWARD), steel guitarists Lefty Nason and Jimmy Grabowske, clarinetist-vocalist Hub Sutter, and others. The band's recorded output was of uniformly high quality, but it never gained more than regional reputation. In addition to its own recordings, the band backed comedian Cactus Pryor on his many Four Star releases. James disbanded the group in the mid-1950s.   —*Kevin Coffey*

Jim & Jesse

James Monroe McReynolds b. Carfax, Virginia, February 13, 1927
Jesse Lester McReynolds b. Carfax, Virginia, July 9, 1929

Brothers Jim and Jesse McReynolds are bluegrass performers known for stretching their musical boundaries while never forgetting their traditional roots. They have recorded and sung everything from old-time and contemporary country music to gospel, folk, train songs, and rock & roll by Chuck Berry.

The brothers' vocal harmonies, punctuated by Jim's soaring tenor, together with Jesse's innovative cross-picking and split-string mandolin techniques, have earned them a respected place in bluegrass history. Devoted to a high level of musicianship, their band, the Virginia Boys, has consistently featured some of bluegrass's finest pickers, such as VASSAR CLEMENTS, Allen Shelton, Jim Buchanan, and Jim Brock.

Born and raised in the hill country of Appalachian Virginia, Jim & Jesse's father and grandfather were fiddlers, and music was a way of life. The brothers began performing locally as the McReynolds Brothers, moving around to various radio stations throughout the Southeast and Midwest. They first recorded as the Virginia Trio for Kentucky Records in 1951.

By the time of their first sessions for CAPITOL RECORDS in 1952, Jesse was already experimenting with his cross-picking style, which he describes as "a backwards roll, like the technique used in banjo playing." At this time, they began calling themselves Jim & Jesse and their band the Virginia Boys.

In the 1950s Jim & Jesse appeared on a number of radio barn dances, including the *WDVA Barn Dance* in Danville, Virginia, the *MIDDAY MERRY-GO-ROUND* on WNOX in Knoxville, the *WWVA JAMBOREE* in Wheeling, West Virginia, and the *Suwanee River Jamboree* on WNER in Live Oak, Florida. Beginning in the mid-1950s they also had their own local television shows in Florida, Georgia, and Alabama, which were picked up by sponsor MARTHA WHITE in 1960 and expanded to include other markets as well.

In late 1960 Jim & Jesse began to record for EPIC RECORDS, and their first two albums, *Bluegrass Special* and *Bluegrass Classics*, with Allen Shelton on banjo, Don McHan on guitar and harmony vocals, and David Sutherland on bass, are considered to be the most definitive of their style and talents.

In 1964, the year they joined the GRAND OLE OPRY, "Cotton Mill Man" became Jim & Jesse's first record on the country charts, and "Diesel on My Tail," their most commercially successful single, reached the country Top

Jim (left) & Jesse McReynolds

Twenty in 1967. In 1965 they recorded their bluegrass tribute to Chuck Berry, *Berry Pickin' in the Country,* for Epic. Most of their recordings from the seventies onward have been on their own Double J label. From the mid-1960s into the 1970s Jim & Jesse had a popular, syndicated TV program; on it their music included electric guitars and steel guitars instead of traditional acoustic bluegrass instrumentation. —*Dale Vinicur*

REPRESENTATIVE RECORDINGS

The Epic Bluegrass Hits (Rounder, 1986); *Jim & Jesse: Bluegrass and More* (Bear Family, 1993), 5 discs

Jim Owens Productions (*see* Crook & Chase)

Flaco Jimenez
b. San Antonio, Texas, March 11, 1939

Leonardo "Flaco" Jimenez is a member of what has been called the First Family of Texas Conjunto Music. Flaco's father, Santiago "El Flaco" Jimenez Sr., who left his first son, Leonardo, his nickname (which means "The Skinny One"), was a conjunto accordion pioneer. Flaco's brother, Santiago Jimenez Jr., is a traditionalist who performs in his father's style.

Known for his fast, flashy, and hard-driving playing, no other conjunto accordionist has done as much to disseminate conjunto music outside of its traditional audience than Flaco Jimenez. He has performed with musicians such as Ry Cooder, TISH HINOJOSA, LINDA RONSTADT, EMMYLOU HARRIS, DWIGHT YOAKAM, and BUCK OWENS. By touring North America, Europe, and Japan, Flaco has brought conjunto to the world. With the Texas Tornados (formed in 1990), Flaco has created a music that combines conjunto's

Hispanic roots with Anglo-American country music and rock & roll.

In 1990 the Texas Tornados and Flaco received a Grammy for their single "Soy de San Luis," written by Flaco's father. Flaco also received a Grammy in 1986 for his album *Ay, Te Dejo en San Antonio.* When asked about the changes occurring in Tex-Mex music, Flaco said, "Conjunto is here to stay. Of course, *con acordeón!*" —*David Romtvedt*

REPRESENTATIVE RECORDINGS

Ay, Te Dejo en San Antonio y Mas (Arhoolie, 1987) ; *Arriba el Norte* (Rounder, 1989); *Texas Tornados* (Warner Bros., 1990)

John Edwards Memorial Foundation (*see* JEMF)

Johnnie & Jack
Johnnie Robert Wright b. Mount Juliet, Tennessee, May 13, 1914
Jack Anglin b. Franklin, Tennessee, May 13, 1916; d. March 7, 1963

Johnnie & Jack helped carry the BROTHER DUET style into the 1940s and 1950s, though they were not brothers but brothers-in-law. They also pioneered the use of Latin rhythms in country music and played a crucial role in the career of KITTY WELLS.

Prior to teaming with Wright, Jack Anglin performed with brothers Jim Anglin (b. March 23, 1913; d. January 21, 1987) and Van Buren "Red" Anglin (b. April 20, 1910; d. August 23, 1975); the trio first recorded in 1937 for ARC as the Anglin Twins & Red.

Johnnie Wright first worked with Jack Anglin in 1938 as fundraising entertainment for flood victims. In June 1938 Jack Anglin married Wright's sister Louise, then singing with Johnnie and his wife, Muriel (a.k.a. Kitty Wells) as Johnnie Wright & the Harmony Girls on WSIX-Nashville. Johnnie and Muriel wed October 30, 1937. An unseen partner in the Johnnie & Jack act was Jack's elder brother Jim, a gifted songwriter responsible for penning "Beneath That Lonely Mound of Clay" and "Stuck Up Blues" (both sold to ROY ACUFF), "One by One," and "Ashes of Love."

With their Tennessee Hillbillies band (featuring Muriel), Johnnie & Jack moved from station to station, engaging sponsors, and doing shows for crowds of radio listeners. Temporary home bases included WBIG-Greens-

Johnnie & Jack: Johnnie Wright (left) and Jack Anglin

boro, WCHS-Charleston, and WNOX-Knoxville. World War II gasoline rationing prompted a touring halt. Anglin was drafted and sent overseas. EDDIE HILL convinced Wright to regroup in 1943. While at WNOX they briefly hired young fiddler CHET ATKINS, who later became much better known as a guitarist. Discharged in February 1946, Anglin reunited with Wright at WPTF–Raleigh, North Carolina.

In 1947 Johnnie & Jack first recorded for the KING and Apollo labels. That year WSM offered Johnnie & Jack a regular spot on the GRAND OLE OPRY, contingent on dropping "hillbillies" from their band name, so the band was renamed the Tennessee Mountain Boys. They left WSM for KWKH-Shreveport, on New Year's Day 1948, and on April 3, 1948, they were in the cast of the first LOUISIANA HAYRIDE broadcast.

In 1949 the duo signed with RCA and went on to enjoy their greatest success in the 1950s. The duo first injected a Latin beat into country via their breakthrough single "Poison Love" (#4, 1951), followed by "Cryin' Heart Blues" (#5), which boasted a distinctive calypso rhythm. Next, they adapted r&b to a country beat with covers of the Four Knights' pop million seller "Oh, Baby Mine (I Get So Lonely)" (#1, 1954) and the Spaniels' "Goodnight, Sweetheart, Goodnight" (#3, 1954).

After "Poison Love" hit, the group was invited back to the Opry. When chart numbers dipped after 1958's #7 hit "Stop the World (And Let Me Off)," the act moved to DECCA in 1961. Their first chart record for the label, "Slow Poison" (#17, 1962), was issued as Johnny & Jack. Wright took the misprint as a sign and afterward continued to bill himself Johnny Wright.

Tragedy struck in 1963. Anglin died in a one-car crash on the day of services for plane-wreck victims PATSY CLINE, HAWKSHAW HAWKINS, COWBOY COPAS, and RANDY HUGHES. Afterward Wright continued as a solo recording act and scored a #1 single in 1965 with "Hello Vietnam." On the road he has continued to tour with the Kitty Wells Family Show, which includes son Bobby Wright. —*Walt Trott*

REPRESENTATIVE RECORDINGS

Johnnie & Jack & The Tennessee Mountain Boys (Bear Family, 1992), 6 discs; *Johnnie & Jack (with Kitty Wells)—Live at KWKH* (Bear Family, 1994)

Earl Johnson
b. Gwinnet County, Georgia, August 24, l886; d. May 24, 1965

Earl Johnson was in many ways the quintessential North Georgia fiddler, playing in a supercharged breakneck style that excited fans and record buyers alike. Beginning his career in a family band, Johnson won his initial fame as a second fiddler for JOHN CARSON's Virginia Reelers, who recorded widely for OKEH in the late 1920s. Earl soon had his own contract with OKeh, recording with his own band, the Clodhoppers, a series of popular sides that included "Ain't Nobody's Business," "Shortening Bread," and "Bully of the Town." The Clodhoppers generally included the fine guitarist Byrd Moore, as well as banjoist Emmett Bankston and guitarist Lee Henderson. In the 1930s Johnson re-created some of his best sides for Victor. After his recording days, he continued to be active in local fiddling contests, and became one of the first in his region to master the new bluegrass banjo styles of EARL SCRUGGS.
—*Charles Wolfe*

Michael Johnson
b. Alamosa, Colorado, August 8, 1944

This talented singer, guitarist, and songwriter had a long track record in folk and pop when he started making country records in 1985. Michael J. Johnson brought a high level of musicianship and an appealingly literary approach to songs when country was emerging out of doldrums to scale new heights.

"Coming out of folk music, my love has always been for songs," Johnson said of Nashville's attraction for him. Much earlier, the influences that were to make Johnson a guitarist of some note included Chuck Berry, Charlie Byrd, and the classical styles he learned during a year spent in Barcelona studying with Gracian Tarrago. In his early twenties, Johnson performed for a year with the folksy Chad Mitchell Trio, spent time as an actor, and by 1971 was in the studio with producers Peter Yarrow and Phil Ramone working on his Atlantic debut disc *There Is a Breeze*. Two albums for the independent Sanskrit Records followed. In 1978, Johnson had his first encounter with Nashville studios, beginning a partnership with producers STEVE GIBSON and BRENT MAHER that resulted in the tuneful pop hits "Bluer Than Blue" (1978) and "This Night Won't Last Forever" (1979), both on EMI America. It was to Maher and guitarist DON POTTER, both part of the JUDDS' hit sound, that Johnson turned to when he came back to Music City in the mid-1980s. Now on RCA, his first foray into country produced "I Love You by Heart," a Top Ten duet with SYLVIA. His country debut album, *Wings*, featured an attractive, acoustic-based sound and netted two #1 records, "Give Me Wings," written by DON SCHLITZ and Rhonda Fleming, and "The Moon Is Still Over Her Shoulder," by Hugh Prestwood. A 1988 follow-up disc, *That's That*, produced the Top Ten hits "Crying Shame," "I Will Whisper Your Name," and "That's That." Johnson elected to leave RCA, was temporarily sidelined by a skin disorder, but returned to disc for Atlantic in 1992 with a fine self-titled effort that failed to dent the charts. "It kind of leaked out, pretty much at the apex of the post-Garth stuff," he said. Johnson has continued to tour and record, entering the studio again in 1995 to record an Americana-styled disc for Vanguard Records and a career retrospective for Intersound Records in 1997. —*Thomas Goldsmith*

REPRESENTATIVE RECORDINGS

Wings (RCA, 1987); *That's That* (RCA, 1988); *Then & Now* (Intersound, 1997)

Johnson Mountain Boys
Dudley Dale Connell b. Olney, Maryland, February 18, 1956
Edward Lawrence Stubbs b. Bethesda, Maryland, November 25, 1961
David Wallace McLaughlin b. Washington, D.C., February 13, 1958
Richard Dean Underwood b. Washington, D.C., July 14, 1956
Larry Palmer Robbins b. Dickerson, Maryland, April 25, 1945
Richard Thomas Adams Jr. b. Gettysburg, Pennsylvania, November 17, 1958
Marshall Wilborn b. Austin, Texas, March 12, 1952
Hugh Clark "Earl" Yager b. Gordonsville, Virginia, November 2, 1953

In the late 1970s and early 1980s the Johnson Mountain Boys spearheaded a resurgence of interest in and respect for traditional bluegrass music. Formed in 1975 as a traditionally oriented duet, the act quickly grew into a five piece ensemble. One of the most popular incarnations of the band featured guitarist and lead and tenor vocalist Dudley Connell, fiddler Eddie Stubbs, banjoist Richard Underwood, mandolinist David McLaughlin, and bassist Larry Robbins. (In 1986 Marshall Wilborn took over for Robbins, and Tom Adams replaced Underwood; Earl Yager joined on bass in 1989.) The band's debut release for ROUNDER RECORDS in 1981, simply titled *The Johnson Mountain Boys,* met with critical acclaim and helped to establish the band on the bluegrass circuit.

Career highlights include performances at the White House, Madison Square Garden, the Kennedy Center, the GRAND OLE OPRY, and two appearances at CARNEGIE HALL, as well as appearances in England and a tour of Africa.

In 1988, after nearly thirteen years in the business and status as one of the genre's top bands, the group bade an emotional and much-publicized farewell to music, citing a grueling schedule and marginal economic gains as the chief reasons. The hiatus proved temporary, and in 1989 the band returned to making festival and concert appearances on an abbreviated schedule. Their *At the Old Schoolhouse* (1989) and *Blue Diamond* (1993) Rounder releases were nominated for Grammys in the field of Best Bluegrass Recording.

Since the spring of 1995 fiddler Eddie Stubbs in Washington, worked for a period with KITTY WELLS and then joined WSM in Nashville as a radio show host and Grand Ole Opry announcer. After the breakup of the Johnson Mountain Boys, Dudley Connell joined the SELDOM SCENE in 1996.

—*Gary B. Reid*

REPRESENTATIVE RECORDINGS

Let the Whole World Talk (Rounder, 1987); *At the Old Schoolhouse* (Rounder, 1989)

Bob Johnston
b. Hillsboro, Texas, May 14, 1932

For a brief period during the late 1960s, producer Don William "Bob" Johnston ran the Nashville division of CO-LUMBIA RECORDS. Though his executive tenure was relatively short, his impact on Music City's creative direction was huge. He produced BOB DYLAN's 1960s Nashville recordings, as well as JOHNNY CASH's *Live at Folsom Prison* and *Live at San Quentin* LPs. His success with these and other artists proved instrumental in bringing pop acts such as Simon & Garfunkel to Nashville to record.

Johnston was born in Hillsboro, Texas, but was raised in Fort Worth. His grandmother was a songwriter, as was his mother, Diane Johnston, whose credits include ASLEEP AT THE WHEEL's "Miles and Miles of Texas." By the late 1950s Johnston himself was writing songs, working for publishing companies, recording as a solo artist, and producing such acts as the Jaguars, a rock & roll band that included CHARLIE DANIELS. Johnston often traveled to Nashville to produce song demos, which eventually led to his being hired to do A&R work for Kapp Records in New York. From Kapp, Johnston moved to Columbia's New York office, where in 1965 he scored his first major A&R success producing Patti Page's "Hush, Hush, Sweet Charlotte"—for which the tracks (but not the strings or vocal, according to Johnston) were recorded in Nashville.

In 1965 Johnston produced most of Bob Dylan's *Highway 61 Revisited*. On the cut "Desolation Row" from that al-

bum, Nashville session pro CHARLIE MCCOY played acoustic guitar. After this initial experience working with Johnston and McCoy, Dylan elected to record his next album, *Blonde on Blonde* (1966), in Nashville itself. Johnston produced the record, as he would Dylan's *John Wesley Harding, Nashville Skyline,* and *Self Portrait,* all of which were cut in Music City (*Self Portrait* partially).

In early 1967 Columbia chose Johnston to take over their Nashville office from DON LAW, who had reached mandatory retirement age. Among his first moves, Johnston gave Johnny Cash the green light to record live at Folsom Prison. He also worked with FLATT & SCRUGGS, producing, for instance, their album *Changin' Times.*

In early 1968 BILLY SHERRILL replaced Johnston as the head of Columbia's Nashville operations. Johnston retained the title of executive producer at large and continued to produce some of Columbia's star country acts. Among these was MARTY ROBBINS, whose 1970 hit "My Woman, My Woman, My Wife" Johnston produced.

By the mid-1970s Johnston's profile was in decline, though he continued to play a behind-the-scenes role in such projects as Cheryl Lynn's 1979 disco smash "Got to Be Real" and WILLIE NELSON's *Who'll Buy My Memories,* better known as the IRS Tapes. More active in recent years, Johnston was heavily involved in the production of CARL PERKINS's 1996 album *Go Cat Go.*

—*Daniel Cooper*

Ann Jones
b. Hutchinson, Kansas, ca. 1920

Billed as the "Kate Smith of the West," husky Ann Jones recorded prolifically for the CAPITOL and KING labels during the post–World War II years and achieved prominence as a radio broadcaster, songwriter, and bandleader.

Jones was born Ann Matthews in Kansas but moved westward as a child. Initially part of a duo with sister Frances in Enid, Oklahoma, and Anaheim, California, she married in 1937 and temporarily retired. Jones starred on an all-girl softball team during the war years and then returned to music in 1947 on the West Coast. She scored her biggest hit in 1949 with "Give Me a Hundred Reasons" on Capitol. Much of her material was self-penned, making her one of country's trailblazing female composers.

Jones hosted her own *Ranch Roundup* TV show on KTTV in Hollywood and worked radio shows elsewhere in California, North Carolina, and West Virginia as well. By 1952 Jones was active on KVAN in Vancouver, Washington. In about 1955 she formed the all-female swing band the Western Sweethearts in the Pacific Northwest. Billed as "the queens of western swing," the group toured internationally and remained together for twenty years.

Jones was also an active participant in the early DISC JOCKEY CONVENTIONS in Nashville, when women in radio were still quite rare. She remained a touring attraction well into the 1970s.

—*Robert K. Oermann*

Buddy Jones
b. Asheville, North Carolina, December 25, 1906; d. October 20, 1956

Oscar Bergan Riley, better known as Buddy Jones, is best remembered for recording raucous, off-color tales of wild women and beer joints throughout most of his career, but the prurience of those recordings has often obscured the fact that he was one of the progenitors of honky-tonk. His grafting of WESTERN SWING tendencies and a roadhouse mentality onto a JIMMIE RODGERS–inspired blues and ballad tradition helped pave the way for postwar honky-tonkers.

Taught guitar by his stepfather, Joe Jones, around Port Arthur, Texas, Jones also absorbed a feel for Gulf Coast blues that gave his music a tougher edge than most Rodgers devotees, an edge Jones retained as he developed his own style. He settled in Shreveport in the late twenties, joining the Pelican Wildcats, a trio that would record for COLUMBIA in 1931. He also traveled to Chicago with up-and-coming JIMMIE DAVIS to provide backing at a VICTOR recording session. Davis and Jones were close and, as Davis began to tone down his own material as his fame increased, he secured a DECCA contract for Jones to record the same racy mix from which he was shying.

Initially Jones sang duets with Davis, such as the fine "Red River Blues" (1935), but soon was recording on his own, easing from talking blues to Rodgers remakes before emerging with a largely original repertoire beginning by the end of the thirties. Usually accompanied by brother Buster on steel, who also wrote or co-wrote much of his material, Jones began producing JUKEBOX hits such as "She's Selling What She Used to Give Away" and "The Roughest Gal in Town." His recordings began to lean toward western swing, featuring musicians such as MOON MULLICAN, CLIFF BRUNER, and Leo Raley, but retained a decidedly country feel. His last sessions, in 1941, were more mainstream than before but hardly tame. A Shreveport traffic cop from the mid-thirties until his death, Jones chose not to pursue his music career after World War II.   —*Kevin Coffey*

REPRESENTATIVE RECORDING

Buddy Jones: Louisiana's Honky-Tonk Man (Texas Rose, 1984)

Frank Jones
b. Toronto, Ontario, Canada, March 4, 1928

Music executive Frank Jones has served in leadership positions ranging from record and publishing companies to civic organizations. He grew up in the Canadian province of Ontario, where he was performing in his own band by age fifteen. By 1949 he had careers in both radio broadcasting and talent booking. During the 1950s Jones began working for COLUMBIA RECORDS' Canadian counterpart in sales, promotions, and eventually as head of A&R. DON LAW, executive producer of Columbia's U.S. country music division, requested that Jones join Nashville's A&R staff in 1961. During Jones's tenure at the label, he and Law were responsible for producing such artists as JOHNNY CASH, MARTY ROBBINS, and RAY PRICE. Jones later served as marketing director for all Columbia's Nashville record releases before leaving the label in 1973. During the following years, Jones presided over the Nashville operations of several labels: CAPITOL (1973–78), Inergi (1979), WARNER BROTHERS (1980–83), and MERCURY (1983–85).

Jones has served as a board member of the CMA as well as president and chairman of the CMF board. Jones has been the recipient of many honors, including the 1970 CMA President's Award for Outstanding Contribution and *Billboard*'s 1972 Record Executive of the Year Award.   —*Don Roy*

George Jones

George Jones
b. Saratoga, Texas, September 12, 1931

Many attempts have been made to capture in words the immense, singular vocal gifts that have made George Glenn Jones one of the most influential singers in country music history. He is the undisputed successor of earlier primitive geniuses such as HANK WILLIAMS and LEFTY FRIZZELL—singers who, in turn, so heavily influenced him in his formative years.

Jones launched his recording career in East Texas in the early 1950s, and as of the late 1990s he was still going strong. Yet it is more than sheer longevity, or the almost religious purity of his hard-core country instincts, that has made him such a towering, influential figure. In many ways Jones is one of country music's last vital links to its own rural past—a relic from a long-gone time and place before cable TV and FM rock radio and shopping malls, an era when life still revolved around the primitive Baptist Church, the honky-tonk down the road, and Saturday nights listening to the GRAND OLE OPRY on the radio. The fact that Jones himself has changed little over the years, and at times seems to be genuinely bewildered by the immensity of his own talent and the acclaim it has brought him, have merely enhanced his credibility.

Like Hank Williams before him, Jones has emerged—quite unintentionally—as an archetype of an era that most likely will never come around again. He is a singer who has earned his stature the hard way: by living his songs. His humble origins, his painful divorces, his legendary drinking and drugging, and his myriad financial, legal, and emotional problems have, over the years, merely confirmed his sincerity and enhanced his mystique, earning him a cachet that, in country music circles, approaches canonization.

Born in a log cabin in an oil patch settlement in a remote East Texas region known as the Big Thicket, Jones found early refuge in music from the rages of an alcoholic father. As a child George sang for tips in the streets of Beaumont, Texas, where, at an early age, he moved with his parents into a government-subsidized housing project. ROY ACUFF, Hank Williams, and Lefty Frizzell (whom he most resembles as a vocalist) comprised Jones's youthful triumvirate of influences.

In the late 1940s Jones made his radio debut singing with a friend on radio KTXJ in Jasper, Texas. A year or so later he began backing husband-and-wife team Eddie & Pearl. Performing with them on Beaumont's KRIC, he met for the one and only time his idol Hank Williams, who dropped by to sing a song and promote a local show date.

In 1950 Jones was married for the first of four times. But he and Dorothy Bonvillion, his first wife, divorced slightly more than a year later. In her petition Bonvillion cited her ex-husband's "violent temper" and asserted he was "addicted to the drinking of alcoholic beverages." These twin motifs would resurface again and again to wreak havoc in Jones's later life. After several incarcerations for nonpayment of support (he and Dorothy had a daughter in the course of their brief marriage) Jones sought refuge in the Marine Corps.

In January 1954, back in Houston, Texas, and back in civilian clothes, Jones cut his first record, a prophetically titled original called "No Money in This Deal." The session took place in the crude home studio of JACK STARNES, one of the original owners of STARDAY, a regional label that released Jones's earliest records. Starnes's partner, local jukebox operator HAROLD W. "PAPPY" DAILY, assumed the roles of Jones's producer and manager, roles he would continue to play until 1970.

"Why, Baby, Why," Jones's first Top Five hit, which he co-wrote, was released on STARDAY in 1955. When he moved on to MERCURY RECORDS and began recording in Nashville shortly thereafter, the hits kept coming: "Color of the Blues," "White Lightning" (his first #1, 1959), "Who Shot Sam," "The Window Up Above" (also written by Jones), and "Tender Years" are some of early classic titles from Jones's vast recorded catalogue.

In 1954 Jones married his second wife, Shirley Ann Corley, after a two-week courtship. They divorced in 1968.

In the 1960s Jones recorded for the United Artists and Musicor labels and the hits continued, though his style had begun to mellow and season somewhat from the jittery honky-tonk of "Why, Baby, Why" and the handful of rockabilly sides that Jones reluctantly cut in 1956, under the pseudonym Thumper Jones. High points of this era were hits such as "She Thinks I Still Care," "The Race Is On," "Love Bug," "Walk Through This World with Me," and "A Good Year for the Roses."

At about the turn of the decade, two significant things happened to Jones. In 1969 he married singer TAMMY WYNETTE, who had already become a star in her own right. Over the next decade (even long after they divorced in 1975) they would record classic duet hits such as "The Ceremony," "We're Gonna Hold On," "Golden Ring," "Near You," and "Two Story House."

In 1971 Jones signed with EPIC RECORDS and began working with producer BILLY SHERRILL, who was already producing Wynette and who produced most of the aforementioned Jones and Wynette duets. Sherrill would also, in the next decade or so, coax out of the temperamental, often hard-drinking singer some of his all-time best vocal performances. "A Picture of Me Without You," "The Grand Tour," "The Door," and "Bartender's Blues" are just a few commercial and aesthetic high points of the Jones-Sherrill collaboration.

The 1970s and early 1980s were, in the wake of his divorce from Tammy Wynette, dark times for Jones. Due to alcohol and cocaine addiction, he was arrested and hospitalized numerous times. He missed dozens of performances (thus earning the nickname No Show Jones) and was ensnared in a myriad of legal and financial problems. His health grew precarious, and his weight plummeted to ninety-seven pounds.

Yet in the midst of this adversity he recorded "He Stopped Loving Her Today," a mournful ballad that hit #1 in 1980, became his first million seller, and contributed toward his winning of the CMA's Male Vocalist of the Year Awards in 1980 and 1981.

In 1983 Jones married his fourth wife, Nancy Sepulvado, and it marked the beginning of his gradual rehabilitation. In 1990 he signed with MCA and has since recorded a string of critically lauded recordings on that label. Jones was inducted into the COUNTRY MUSIC HALL OF FAME in 1992. Ironically, the clean and sober George Jones of the late eighties and early nineties, though still recording credible music, has all but been banished from the country charts. Yet he has emerged as one of country music's most revered and cherished figures. Jones's autobiography, *I Lived to Tell It All* (Villard Books, 1996), was a hardcover best-seller. —*Bob Allen*

REPRESENTATIVE RECORDINGS

Cup of Loneliness: The Mercury Years (Mercury, 1994); *She Thinks I Still Care: The George Jones Collection* (Razor & Tie, 1997); *The Best of George Jones* (Rhino, 1991); *The Spirit of Country: The Essential George Jones* (Epic, 1995); *I Lived to Tell It All* (MCA, 1996)

Grandpa Jones
b. Niagara, Kentucky, October 20, 1913; d. February 19, 1998

Best known to the general public for his exuberant banjo playing, for his singing of novelty songs such as "Rattler" and "Mountain Dew," and for his infectious verbal comedy on shows such as *HEE HAW*, Grandpa Jones also has been one of country music's most dedicated champions of old-time music. Not only did he keep banjo playing alive during times when it had fallen into disfavor with most professional musicians, but he also helped to keep alive the songs of pioneers such as JIMMIE RODGERS, BRADLEY KINCAID, LULU BELLE & SCOTTY, and the DELMORE BROTHERS. A serious fan of southern gospel music, Jones also helped maintain the old gospel quartet tradition in groups such as BROWN'S FERRY FOUR and the Hee Haw Gospel Quartet. Though not an acoustic purist in the strict sense—he has always used an electric guitar in his act and on his records—his devotion to "keeping it country" has won him fans nationwide for seven decades, as well as a longtime tenure on the GRAND OLE OPRY and membership in the COUNTRY MUSIC HALL OF FAME in 1978.

The youngest of eight boys and two girls born to a tobacco farmer, Louis Marshall Jones grew up in northwestern Kentucky, just a few miles from the Ohio River. By the time he was in high school, the family was living in Akron,

Grandpa Jones

Ohio, and young Marshall (as he was called by his folks) was copying Jimmie Rodgers songs and was appearing on local station WJW as "The Young Singer of Old Songs." After a stint on the popular *Lum and Abner* radio show (as part of the show's stringband), he and friend Joe Troyan ("Harmonica Joe") met a man who was to have an immense impact on Jones's career—singer Bradley Kincaid. In 1935 they were working with Kincaid over WBZ in Boston, when Kincaid gave him the nickname Grandpa because he sounded old and grouchy on the early morning show. Kincaid had him outfitted with a vaudeville costume—including a fake mustache—and at age twenty-two Marshall Jones became Grandpa Jones.

By 1937 Jones struck out on his own, playing stations in West Virginia and Cincinnati; along the way he met boisterous entertainer COUSIN EMMY, who taught him how to play clawhammer banjo—which he soon incorporated into his act. At WLW he joined forces with the Delmore Brothers and MERLE TRAVIS to form Brown's Ferry Four, one of country's first and most popular gospel quartets. In the fall of 1943 he and Travis made their first records, for a new, locally based label to be called KING RECORDS; their disc, released under the pseudonym the Shepherd Brothers, was the first King release. Throughout the rest of the 1940s Jones recorded regularly for King, racking up hits such as "It's Raining Here This Morning," "Eight More Miles to Louisville," and "Mountain Dew."

In October 1946 Jones married Ramona Riggins, a talented fiddler and singer he had met at WLW, and the two moved to Nashville, where Jones joined the Grand Ole Opry. Throughout the 1950s the pair entertained troops in Korea; made brief stays at Arlington and Richmond, Virginia, and Washington, D.C.; and recorded for RCA and DECCA. By 1959 they had settled permanently on the Opry, and a few years later started a family that would include Mark, Alisa, and Marsha (a fourth child, Eloise, came from Jones's earlier marriage in West Virginia). In the early 1960s Jones began recording for FRED FOSTER's new MONUMENT label, producing a series of albums that Jones considers the best work he has done. They also produced two of his biggest hits, a version of Jimmie Rodgers's "T for Texas" (1963) and the seasonal narration "The Christmas Guest" (1969).

In 1969 Jones joined the cast of *Hee Haw*, where he perfected his comedy with routines such as "What's for Supper," and where he worked with greats such as MINNIE PEARL and his close friend STRINGBEAN. Jones and his wife started in 1976 a series of albums for CMH that included remakes of many of his early hits and that gave their talented children a chance to perform with their parents. In 1984 he wrote (with Charles Wolfe) a detailed autobiography, *Everybody's Grandpa,* and was still going strong when the Opry management helped him celebrate his fiftieth anniversary on the show in 1997. Jones had a severe stroke moments after his second show Opry performance on January 3, 1998, and he died February 19.   —*Charles Wolfe*

REPRESENTATIVE RECORDING

Country Music Hall of Fame (MCA, 1992)

Jordanaires

Hugh Gordon Stoker b. Gleason, Tennessee, August 3, 1924
Culley Holt b. McAlester, Oklahoma, July 2, 1925; d. June 26, 1980
Neal Matthews Jr. b. Nashville, Tennessee, October 26, 1929
Hoyt Hawkins b. Paducah, Kentucky, March 31, 1927; d. October 23, 1982
Hugh Jarrett b. Nashville, Tennessee, October 11, 1929
Bill Matthews b. LaFollette, Tennessee, September 19, 1923
Monty Matthews b. Pulaski, Kentucky, August 25, 1927
Bob Money b. Mount Vernon, Missouri, May 4, 1929
Bob Hubbard b. Chaffee, Missouri, July 3, 1928
Ray Walker b. Centerville, Mississippi, March 6, 1934
Duane West b. Salisbury, Maryland, April 29, 1941

Best known today as Nashville's premier background vocal group and as key architects of the NASHVILLE SOUND, the Jordanaires had established themselves as one of the nation's leading gospel quartets long before they won

The Jordanaires

fame for background and studio work. When young ELVIS PRESLEY asked the group to back him on his recording of "Hound Dog" in 1956, he knew them as a leading gospel quartet, and asked them to back him because he wanted the best. With the Jordanaires, he was getting it.

The group began in Springfield, Missouri, in 1948, formed by two young evangelists, brothers named Bill and Monty Matthews. Other original members include the remarkable bass singer Culley Holt and baritone Bob Hubbard. A year later, Gordon Stoker joined as pianist, fresh from a stint as pianist with WSM's John Daniel Quartet. He soon graduated to singing lead, and when the Matthews Brothers left to return to Missouri, he recruited a different (unrelated) Matthews, Neal, to sing; baritone Hoyt Hawkins also joined, giving the group stable personnel by 1955.

In the meantime, the group had signed with DECCA and in 1951 transferred to RCA-VICTOR. Here they soon won a reputation for specializing in what the trade press of the time called spirituals—white versions of black gospel songs. These included pieces such as "Noah" (from the Golden Gates), "My Rock," and "Dry Bones." They continued this style in a series of records for CAPITOL starting in December 1953. Meanwhile, they began singing background on records by mainstream country artists, including sides by RED FOLEY ("Just a Closer Walk with Thee") in 1950, and by HANK SNOW starting in 1951. Since 1949 the group had been regulars on the Opry, and had won more fame by appearances on EDDY ARNOLD's 1953 TV show.

Nonetheless, as Neal Matthews has recalled, the Elvis recording "opened the doors for us." During the golden age of rock & roll, the quartet was busy almost constantly; in one year alone—1957—they sang on hits that collectively sold more than 33 million copies. Often they did four sessions a day, six days a week; when Elvis asked them to rejoin him for his 1969 "comeback," they had to refuse: they had too much studio work in Nashville.

By 1958 Ray Walker had joined as bass singer, and when Hoyt Hawkins developed health problems in 1968, Duane West stepped into his shoes. The group also did dozens of commercials, first as staff members of WSM, later for national products. Though they continued to work primarily in the studios, British trade magazines have voted them the fourth biggest vocal group in the world, behind the Beatles, the Rolling Stones, and the Beach Boys.

—*Charles Wolfe*

John Jorgenson
b. Madison, Wisconsin, July 6, 1956

Best known as a guitarist and musical director, John Jorgenson was a member of the popular country-rock act the DESERT ROSE BAND and has played on recordings by such country artists as PAM TILLIS, HANK WILLIAMS JR., MARTY STUART, and LEE ROY PARNELL, among others. But Jorgenson is proficient on a variety of instruments and comfortable in a variety of styles. He's toured Europe playing oboe in a classical chamber group, and for a while he played in both Dixieland and bluegrass bands at Disneyland (on clarinet and mandolin, respectively) while moonlighting as a guitarist in punk and rockabilly groups.

Jorgenson's father was an orchestral conductor and teacher at the University of Redlands (California); his mother taught piano. John's first instrument was piano, which he began learning at age five, adding clarinet, ukulele, and guitar by the time he was twelve years old. His

first professional engagement was playing bassoon in a church performance of Handel's "Messiah"; he subsequently played in symphonies and all-state orchestras in Southern California's "Inland Empire."

While performing at the Aspen (Colorado) Music Festival, Jorgenson became interested in bluegrass and soon landed the two Disneyland jobs. In 1982, guitarist Jeff Ross "coaxed" him, as Jorgenson put it, into the rockabilly scene then developing in Southern California. Jorgenson was soon playing guitar and saxophone with transplanted young English rockabilly singer Levi Dexter.

Through his bluegrass connections, Jorgenson met ROSE MADDOX, with whom he wound up working for several years, and Bill Bryson, who introduced Jorgenson to CHRIS HILLMAN, an introduction that led to the formation of the Desert Rose Band. In the meantime, Jorgenson had a band called the Cheatin' Hearts with former FLYING BURRITO BROTHERS steel guitarist Sneaky Pete Kleinow, future Desert Rose Band drummer Bryson, and a female singer known as Kitra.

In 1988 Jorgenson began intensive studio work, eventually recording with Bonnie Raitt, CARLENE CARTER, Roger McGuinn, JOHN PRINE, and others. In 1990 guitarists Jorgenson, Will Ray, and Jerry Donahue formed the Hellecasters. Their first album, released on Mike Nesmith's Pacific Arts label in 1993, won *Guitar Player* magazine's Album of the Year Award; a second album was released on the independent Pharaoh label in 1995. Jorgenson won the ACM's Guitarist of the Year Award three times and was musical director of the *Hot Country Nights* television series (November 1991–March 1992) and Delta Burke's ABC sitcom *Delta* (1992–93). In the mid-1990s Jorgenson joined Elton John's band for concerts and recording; a job Jorgenson alternated with his continuing session work.

—*Todd Everett*

REPRESENTATIVE RECORDING
After You're Gone (Curb, 1988)

Cledus "T." Judd
b. Crowe Springs, Georgia, December 18, 1964

A former hairdresser whose accomplishments in that field include cutting the hair of former PTL secretary Jessica Hahn, Barry Poole, a.k.a. Cledus "T." Judd (the "T.," he says, stands for "Trouble," not "Tubby"), gained a reputation in country music in the 1990s as a parodist whose humor lies somewhere between that of RAY STEVENS and "Weird" Al Yankovic. Beginning his musical career by entering an amateur contest at the Buckboard nightclub in Atlanta, Judd performed his own "Farm Boy Rap" and won first prize. He moved to Nashville and tuned in to the radio, mining popular country hits as targets for his parodies. The first, a takeoff on TIM MCGRAW's "Indian Outlaw," was "Indian In-Laws," followed in quick succession by "Gone Funky" and "Stinkin' Problem," spoofing ALAN JACKSON and DAVID BALL, respectively. Ball and other artists appeared in Judd's music videos, which aired regularly on CMT. Following his debut Judd opened shows for BILLY RAY CYRUS. His second album included "Cledus Went Down to Florida" and "If Shania Was Mine." Both albums also feature a few original tunes as well, and his debut includes the pop parodies "Motel Californie" and "We Own the World." Judd wanted to title his 1998 release *Fourteens* because, he said, "it's twice gooder than Garth Brooks'

Sevens," an album released a few months earlier. He settled on a DEANA CARTER takeoff, *Did I Shave My Back For This?*
—*Stephen L. Betts*

REPRESENTATIVE RECORDINGS

Cledus "T." Judd (Laughing Hyena, 1995); *I Stoled This Record* (Razor and Tie, 1996); *Did I Shave My Back For This?* (Razor and Tie, 1998)

Wynonna Judd

b. Ashland, Kentucky, May 30, 1964

Wynonna Judd, frequently known by her first name alone, is one of the most recognizable female singers in contemporary country music. After her parents filed for divorce in 1972, Christina Claire Ciminella was raised in circumstances of adventurous transience, as her mother and former musical partner, Naomi, rambled between California and eastern Kentucky in search of herself and an opportunity to achieve celebrity. By age thirteen Wynonna was attempting her first recording sessions in California; by seventeen, following Naomi's brilliant and insistent musical direction, she and her mother were signed as the JUDDS to a record contract with RCA, and stardom soon followed.

A solo career was thrust on Wynonna in the early 1990s when illness forced Naomi to quit the group. Wynonna regrouped emotionally and woodshedded her music for a year after the December 1991 concert finale of the group before emerging on a new label, Curb/MCA, with a sound that pulled more toward the blues and West Coast country of her Bonnie Raitt and Lowell George influences that she had been able to evince during her duo days. Though the intense farewell Judds tour almost wore out her concert audience, damping early Wynonna shows ticket sales, her daring redefinition of herself musically paid off as she returned in 1992 to the top of the charts for the first time since 1989 with the quirky genius of Dave Loggins contributing her "debut" hit, "She Is His Only Need."

Wynonna's success, while built on prior recognition, has been her own. Record sales for the duo had begun lagging, despite the hype surrounding Naomi's farewell, but Wynonna has come back as a platinum seller in her own right, with such exemplary singles as "I Saw the Light," "No One Else on Earth," and "A Bad Goodbye," the latter a duet with CLINT BLACK.

The Judds, with their occasional infighting and Naomi's flamboyant hillbilly style and eventual illness, had long been of interest to the tattling tabloids. Wynonna kept herself in the newsprint soap opera columns by formally announcing an unintended pregnancy and giving birth out of wedlock to a son, Elijah, in 1994, and by grim confession in the summer of 1995 that she was not, as their Cinderella-style publicity biography had always asserted, the biological daughter of Mike Ciminella, her mother's first husband.

Despite fiery confrontations with her domineering mother all through the Judds epoch, Wynonna has leaned heavily on Naomi's guidance in business matters since going solo.
—*Bob Millard*

REPRESENTATIVE RECORDINGS

Wynonna (Curb/MCA, 1992); *Tell Me Why* (Curb/MCA, 1993)

The Judds

The Judds

Naomi Judd (Diana Ellen Judd) b. Ashland, Kentucky, January 11, 1946

Wynonna Judd (Christina Claire Ciminella) b. Ashland, Kentucky, May 30, 1964

With preternatural harmonies and Wynonna Judd's belting vocal power, this mother-daughter duo rose to become the top country vocal duet in a matter of months in 1983–84. They retained that position, virtually unassailable, until the act dissolved at the end of 1991. Their success helped to give a fresh, new, more acoustic and folk-tinged direction to the country music industry.

The Judds' story would be a classic American tabloid melodrama even if it weren't for Naomi's penchant for amplifying that slant. Born the daughter of Ashland, Kentucky's, biggest Ashland Oil service station owner, Diana Ellen Judd was an imaginative child, with an active and dramatic fantasy life. Among her fantasies— which developed later in Los Angeles, when Diana was the wife of a rising marketing executive and the mother of two daughters, Christina and Ashley—was to become a star. When her husband discovered he was not the biological father of Christina, the marriage began to fall apart. After divorce papers were filed in 1972, Diana rebounded to a gypsy life in the wealthy New Age community of Marin County, California, which fit her personality better. While there, she and her elder daughter changed their names to Naomi and Wynonna, respectively.

After bouncing around the country and in and out of nursing schools, Naomi finished her R.N. in 1977 while living again in Hollywood. Her classically restored 1957 Chevy was rented for the movie *More American Graffiti,* which Naomi parlayed into jobs as crowd scene extras for herself and Wynonna, plus a secretarial slot for herself on the production staff. As later acting efforts proved, screen acting was not Naomi's forte, but the film stint earned enough money to propel the threesome to Nashville.

With a nurse's salary to support her girls, and Wynonna already developing into an astounding vocal talent, Naomi moved her family to Franklin, Tennessee, and haunted Nashville's Music Row, bucking for a chance to prove the unique vocal and thematic concept she had developed for the mother-daughter duo. While few on the Row who heard them grasped the mother-daughter harmonies, the pair became semiregulars on RALPH EMERY's early morning Nashville television show, becoming known as the Soap Sisters because Emery couldn't remember their names.

Fate intervened when Naomi gave a homemade Judds demo tape to a patient in the hospital where she was working, the daughter of producer Brent Maher, who paired them with talented guitarist/arranger DON POTTER to create a fresh, acoustic country sound that led to the Judds being "discovered." Dick Whitehouse at CURB RECORDS in Los Angeles heard the potential of the striking sound and hooked the girls up for a "live" audition that floored RCA RECORDS executives in Nashville. The "live" audition was unusual and became a big part of the Judds' self-described Cinderella story. The Judds were signed to RCA, and their first release, "Had a Dream (For the Heart)," charted just before Christmas 1983, reached #17 on *Billboard* singles charts, and startled country radio with its freshness. Their second single, "Mama He's Crazy," established the mother-daughter dialogue that would cement their image and became the first of eight straight #1 singles, including CMA Single of the Year "Why Not Me," "Have Mercy," and "Grandpa (Tell Me 'Bout the Good Old Days)."

Altogether, the Judds scored twenty Top Ten singles, fourteen of which were #1s, and dominated the CMA Awards for the Vocal Group and Vocal Duo of the year consecutively from 1985 through 1991, when mother Naomi retired from the act due to a chronic hepatitis infection. The retirement, in characteristic flair, was announced on a rainy day in a tearful, impromptu press conference at the old RCA building. It was followed by a grueling 124-show farewell tour built around the *Love Can Build a Bridge* album, which interestingly was the only Judds album not to yield a #1 single, though it earned two Grammys.

Following her "retirement," Naomi worked with a writer to dictate her autobiography, *Love Can Build a Bridge*, published in 1993. Naomi could not stay "out of the business" after her retirement, and tried her hand at acting again, with a prominent speaking role opposite REBA MCENTIRE and KENNY ROGERS in one of the last *Gambler* made-for-TV movies. The Judds eventually staged an acrimoniously public firing of longtime manager Ken Stilts, and Naomi became the functional director of Wynonna's solo career, which got going about a year after the duo's splitup with a televised, pay-per-view concert in Murfreesboro, Tennessee. Naomi has also since begun working as an inspirational speaker.
—*Bob Millard*

REPRESENTATIVE RECORDINGS

Why Not Me (Curb/RCA, 1984); *Rockin' with the Rhythm* (Curb/RCA, 1985); *Greatest Hits* (RCA, 1988); *The Judds Collection, 1983–1990* (RCA, 1992), 3 discs

Jug Bands

Jug bands have their roots in African-American music. The earliest known were from Louisville, where they were a popular feature during each Kentucky Derby season, at both Churchill Downs and private parties. A Louisville jug band performed in New York and Chicago in 1914–16. Other jug bands made records under various names from 1924 to 1927 and in 1931, including "My Good Gal's Gone Blues" with JIMMIE RODGERS.

The Louisville model was taken up in the 1920s in Memphis, where guitarist Will Shade's loose-knit, rural-sounding Memphis Jug Band recorded extensively for VICTOR from 1927 to 1930 with varying personnel. Gus Cannon's Jug Stompers did likewise from 1928 to 1930. Each was an important part of the Memphis blues legacy.

Jugs and washboards became popular with country bands as they performed stage and radio comedy in the 1930s. The SHELTON BROTHERS' popular 1933 recording (as the Lone Star Cowboys) of the "Crawdad Song" used a jug. The Prairie Ramblers' 1935 "Jug Rag" reflected the group's Kentucky origins and earlier familiarity with Louisville jug music. ROY ACUFF's band often did comedy jug routines onstage. In 1953 the Acuff jug band made its only recording, Johnnie Masters' uproarious "Sixteen Chickens and a Tambourine."
—*Dick Spottswood*

Jukeboxes

"Jukebox" is the name applied colloquially to the coin-operated record-playing machines that were once omnipresent in dance halls, cafés, honky-tonks, bowling alleys, skating rinks, and other places of recreation in the United States. Coin-operated music machines, of course, date from the turn of the century, but they were not called "jukeboxes" until the late 1920s and early 1930s, when they became identified with juke joints in Florida and Georgia. Juke joints were small black clubs where drinking and dancing were common, and the word "juke" itself may have been a term of African extraction that survived in the coastal South (whether it referred to dancing or sexual intercourse is unclear).

Jukeboxes appeared frequently in speakeasies during Prohibition because those illegal establishments needed music but could not always afford bands. The repeal of Prohibition in 1933, though, inspired even greater numbers of jukeboxes as dance halls and honky-tonks proliferated. In 1934 the Rudolph Wurlitzer Manufacturing Company, which had been a major manufacturer of all kinds of music machines since the nineteenth century, introduced its first jukebox, the P-10. Although it met with intense competition from other companies, such as Mills, Seeburg, and Rock-ola, Wurlitzer continued to be the predominant jukebox distributor until about 1950. In the early 1950s Seeburg made giant strides in the industry, first through the introduction of a machine that could play 45-rpm records, and by 1955 with a model that played 200 selections. All of these brand names, of course, played major roles in the burgeoning of country music and the emergence of rock & roll.

Jukeboxes did more than play music. They also served as centerpieces for social diversion, and as symbols of America's dramatic capitalistic exuberance during the 1930s, 1940s, and 1950s—a celebration of our technological ingenuity. The new models introduced each year by the jukebox industry, particularly after 1946, when the Wurlitzer 1015 hit the market, not only played greater numbers of records; they also became increasingly sophisticated in design. Dominating their physical environment, jukeboxes became visual as well auditory items of entertainment. Led by the innovative designer Paul Fuller, the Wurlitzer company specialized in beautifully styled jukeboxes with Art Deco designs, brightly colored chrome-and-plastic exteriors, fluorescent illumination, and openly displayed record-changing mechanisms. The jukebox became not only a central focus for musical and social experience but also a ready reminder to displaced country folk of American capitalistic ingenuity and success in the postwar era.

Jukeboxes have a special historic relationship to country music because they made crucial contributions to the music's popularity and expansion, especially during the years of World War II, when uprooted military personnel and lonely civilians sought diversion through playing records. Close to 400,000 of these machines were in operation by 1941. Their massive proliferation did not simply symbolize country music's growth; it was also a key component of that growth. Jukebox distribution, along with the volume of records that were supplied to the operators, charted country music's growing popularity as it moved north and west during and after the war. The earliest popularity charts found in *Billboard* magazine, for example, were essentially compilations of the most popular songs heard on jukeboxes. The jukebox business became such an important gauge of country music's widening popularity during the 1940s and 1950s that some distributors, such as SYD NATHAN in Cincinnati and PAPPY DAILY in Houston, became sufficiently inspired to begin their own important music businesses, launched initially with used recordings but soon centered around their own newly produced material. Jukeboxes have been so intimately intertwined with the history of country music since the late 1930s that it is no wonder that country singers have often referred to them in their songs. When ALAN JACKSON sings "Don't Rock the Jukebox," he pays a simultaneous tribute to country music and to the marvelous machine that did so much to introduce the music to a receptive world. —*Bill C. Malone*

Kieran Kane (*see* O'Kanes and Dead Reckoning Records)

Dave Kapp

b. Chicago, Illinois, August 7, 1904; d. March 1, 1976

The man most responsible for building DECCA RECORDS' early hillbilly catalogue was David Kapp, younger brother of label founder JACK KAPP. Together the two owned and ran a Chicago music store from 1921 to 1931. Joining Decca in 1935 (its second year), Dave Kapp and a company engineer traveled several times per year into the South to find and record hillbilly talent. Under Kapp's supervision, MILTON BROWN, CLIFF BRUNER, REX GRIFFIN, ERNEST TUBB, and others made their most important recordings.

Kapp left Decca in 1951 and headed RCA VICTOR's pop department for two years, then in 1954 founded Kapp Records. Years later the label added a country roster—BOB WILLS, MEL TILLIS, and CAL SMITH became the label's best-known artists.

Also a writer ("160 Acres") and publisher (Garland Music), Kapp was RIAA president in 1966–67. He sold Kapp Records to MCA in 1967. —*Ronnie Pugh*

Jack Kapp

b. Chicago, Illinois, 1901; d. March 25, 1949

Jacob "Jack" Kapp, cofounder of American DECCA RECORDS, helped revitalize the U.S. popular record industry in the depths of the Depression with Decca's thirty-five-cent 78-rpm records at a time when most companies retailed their records for seventy-five cents.

Kapp worked in his hometown of Chicago as a mail clerk for COLUMBIA RECORDS, later taking a production job for BRUNSWICK. A proven talent and song scout, Kapp left Brunswick in 1934 to co-found Decca Records in partnership with Edward R. Lewis and his English branch of Decca (founded in 1929), taking some of Brunswick's top pop talent with him, including Bing Crosby, Guy Lombardo, and the Mills Brothers.

Decca corporate policy, as dictated by Kapp, stressed clear pronunciation of lyrics, simple melodies, and repetitive use of a song's title on records. Kapp's genius for teaming up his talent in various duet combinations also became a Decca trademark. Its cheaper records (discounted further to jukebox operators) helped Decca corner 36 percent of the U.S. market by 1940.

In its March 7, 1949, issue, a laudatory *Life* magazine ed-

itorial, read into the *Congressional Record,* called Kapp "living proof that no man in America is destined by circumstances to spend his life behind a large and immovable eight ball." Only weeks later, Kapp died of a cerebral hemorrhage at forty-seven. —*Ronnie Pugh*

Karl & Harty

Karl Victor Davis b. Mount Vernon, Kentucky, December 17, 1905; d. May 30, 1979

Hartford Connecticut "Harty" Taylor b. Mount Vernon, Kentucky, April 11, 1905; d. October 18, 1963

Popular figures on Chicago country music radio during the 1930s and 1940s, Karl Davis and Harty Taylor probably are better known today through Davis's compositions than their own recordings. Modeling themselves after Lester McFarland and Robert Gardner (MAC & BOB), they favored sentimental material with gentle, understated harmonies. Taylor strummed guitar and sang lead, while Davis played mandolin and harmonized.

In 1929 DOC HOPKINS recruited Davis and Taylor for the Krazy Kats, a stringband that mixed folk songs with current pop tunes. After a year on WHAS-Louisville, the band moved to Chicago to become the core of the CUMBERLAND RIDGE RUNNERS on WLS's *NATIONAL BARN DANCE.* Davis and Taylor originally were billed as the Renfro Valley Boys; they recorded under that name for Paramount in February 1932. However, radio listeners best knew them as Karl & Harty. In March 1934 the duo began recording for the AMERICAN RECORD CORPORATION labels. "I'm Just Here to Get My Baby out of Jail" was their first hit; later successes included "The Prisoner's Dream" and Davis's most enduring song, "Kentucky," recorded by the EVERLY BROTHERS and the OSBORNE BROTHERS, among others.

Karl & Harty joined WJJD-Chicago's popular *SUPPERTIME FROLIC* in 1937; but they returned to WLS in December 1947. At odds with the honky-tonk sound that predominated postwar country music, they amiably dissolved their partnership in 1951. Davis continued writing songs: "The Country Hall of Fame" was a Top Ten hit for HANK LOCKLIN in 1967. —*Dave Samuelson*

Buell Kazee

b. Magoffin County, Kentucky, August 29, 1900; d. August 31, 1976

Buell Kazee was a singer of traditional ballads who made his mark in the late 1920s and then again during the folk revival in the 1960s. Reared in the mountains of eastern

Kentucky, in a community where almost everybody sang ballads or hymns and where banjo players were plentiful, he started to play banjo when he was five years old but decided in his teens to become a Baptist preacher.

Kazee's interest in formal folksinging began during his studies at Georgetown College in Kentucky, when he realized that the ballads he was reading in English literature classes were still being sung in his native Kentucky. Between 1927 and 1929 he made nearly sixty recordings for the BRUNSWICK label, of which one of the most memorable (certainly the most often reissued) was an old British ballad, "Lady Gay," a version of the British folksong "The Wife of Usher's Well." Kazee's formal musical training put an overlay of polish and professionalism on his native folksinging style, resulting in a clear, high tenor and exceptionally careful diction. Years later he recalled that Brunswick's producers would not let him sing in his "good" (concert) voice but preferred his "bad" (hillbilly) voice. His banjo playing was in the "frailing" style characteristic of eastern Kentucky—but with a few unusual features, such as occasionally brushing upward across the strings with his thumb. In the 1960s and 1970s Kazee enjoyed a second round of musical exposure on college campuses and at folk festivals across the country. Few of his recordings from the 1920s have been reissued; two ("The Wagoner's Lad" and "The Butcher Boy") are on the Folkways album cited below. —*Norm Cohen*

REPRESENTATIVE RECORDINGS

Buell Kazee (June Appal, 1978); *Anthology of American Folk Music, Volume 1* (Folkways, 1952, 1997)

Robert Earl Keen
b. Houston, Texas, January 11, 1956

Robert Earl Keen Jr. is carving his own niche as a link between western underground cowboy music and alternative country. Keen is one in the Lone Star line of singing storytellers that extends back to the cowboy poets and balladeers of the late nineteenth century. "I listened to MARTY ROBBINS's *Gunfighter* album over and over when I was about four years old," he says. "The thing that's appealing to me is that there's always a real story going on in those songs, like "Little Joe the Wrangler" or the one about tying the knot in the devil's tail. Being as how I'm not much of a singer, I always try to tell the best story I can."

Keen has recorded five albums for the independent SUGAR HILL label and one for Philo/ROUNDER. His song "The Road Goes On Forever" was covered by JOE ELY and the Highwaymen, who used it as the title track of their third album. Sometimes it seems there are two Robert Earl Keens. There's the fun-loving performer who leads audiences in drunken sing-alongs about the joys of eating barbecue. And there's the serious songwriter who sets his little short stories to music. Keen has an almost frightening ability to empathize with the losers, boozers, and psychopaths who populate his songs. He clearly identifies with the drunken oil rig worker in "Corpus Christi Bay," the itchy-fingered gunslinger in "Whenever Kindness Fails," and the dysfunctional relatives in the hilarious happy-holiday snapshot "Merry Christmas from the Family."

The son of a West Texas oilman and a Houston attorney, Keen grew up listening to his parents' collection of folk and country records. He skipped his high school prom to see WILLIE NELSON play at a club in Pasadena, near Hous-

ton. But it wasn't until he went off to college at Texas A&M University that he got the idea to set the poems he had been writing to music. He was sometimes joined in his early songwriting efforts by a college buddy, LYLE LOVETT. The two arrived in Nashville at about the same time in the 1980s. Lovett was signed by MCA RECORDS; except for a 1984 album with Philo (*No Kinda Dancer*), Keen mostly languished in a series of dead-end day jobs.

Taking a cue from his old hero Willie Nelson, Keen came home to Texas to find success as a performer. His band worked an estimated 200 dates in 1993, most west of the Mississippi. His following in California and the mountain states rivals that in his home state. In 1996 he signed with ARISTA Texas. —*Rick Mitchell*

REPRESENTATIVE RECORDINGS

A Bigger Piece of Sky (Sugar Hill, 1993); *Gringo Honeymoon* (Sugar Hill, 1994); *Picnic* (Arista Texas, 1997)

Garrison Keillor (*see* Prairie Home Companion)

Bill Keith
b. Boston, Massachusetts, December 20, 1939

Banjo player William Bradford Keith became fascinated with bluegrass music in the late 1950s, influenced by Appalachian musicians Don Stover and the LILLY BROTHERS, who played at Boston's Hillbilly Ranch.

In the early 1960s Keith joined his Amherst College roommate, JIM ROONEY, to play folk and bluegrass shows, often with Joe Val, Herb Hooven, and Herb Applin. Keith eventually developed a banjo style that enabled him to play fiddle tunes in a melodic, note-for-note fashion, an outgrowth of a "bluegrass roll" in the EARL SCRUGGS style. The first recorded examples of Keith's playing in this style appeared on Keith & Rooney's Prestige/Folklore album, *Livin' On The Mountain*, in 1962.

Keith recorded and performed with RED ALLEN and Frank Wakefield prior to briefly joining BILL MONROE's Blue Grass Boys (where Monroe dubbed him Brad Keith; there was already a Bill in the band) in the spring of 1963. With the release of the Allen & Wakefield album *Bluegrass* on Folkways Records, and Monroe's performances and recordings featuring Keith's banjo, his style spread rapidly.

Keith is known today for his effective instructional workshops and his ability to communicate music theory, in terms of the five-string banjo, to students at all levels. Owner of the Beacon Banjo Company, manufacturer of Keith Tuners (devices that permit rapid, accurate pitch changes while playing), Keith continues to perform music that ranges from traditional to innovative. —*Frank and Marty Godbey*

REPRESENTATIVE RECORDINGS

Beating Around the Bush (Green Linnet, 1993); *The Grass Is Greener* (with Richard Greene, Rounder, 1995)

Toby Keith
b. Clinton, Oklahoma, July 8, 1961

Considering his height of six-foot-four, it's not hard to imagine Toby Keith's previous life as an oil field worker, rodeo hand, or defensive end for the Oklahoma City Drillers semipro football team. Influenced by country (ALABAMA, MERLE HAGGARD), folk (JOHN PRINE, Steve Goodman), and pop (Elton John, Lionel Richie), Keith brings a varied perspective to commercial country music.

As lead singer for the Oklahoma City–based club act Easy Money, Keith spent 1984–1988 touring throughout the Southwest. The work led to recording for independent labels while seeking his big break in Nashville. After flying to Oklahoma to witness a live performance, MERCURY RECORDS/Nashville President HAROLD SHEDD signed Keith to his first major label contract.

To support the 1993 release of his self-titled debut album, Keith became a part of the "Triple Play Tour," a Mercury promotion that placed him with Jon Brannen and a then unknown SHANIA TWAIN. Keith became the prime beneficiary of the tour, with his debut single "Should've Been a Cowboy" topping the country charts. The platinum album contained other follow-ups, including "He Ain't Worth Missing," "A Little Less Talk and a Lot More Action," and "Wish I Didn't Know Now."

When Shedd left Mercury to head its new sister label, Polydor, Keith followed him to become the new label's flagship artist. His second album, 1994's *Boomtown*, centered largely around working-class themes and contained the hits "Who's That Man," "Upstairs Downtown," "You Ain't Much Fun," and "Big Ol' Truck."

By the time he released his third album, *Blue Moon*, Polydor had switched logos to become A&M Records/Nashville. The 1996 project went for a more romantic approach, netting the #1 hit "Does That Blue Moon Ever Shine on You." After A&M closed its Nashville division in 1996, Keith returned to Mercury. His 1997 album *Dream Walkin'* features the hit "We Were In Love" and the Grammy-nominated collaboration with Sting, "I'm So Happy I Can't Stop Crying." —*Calvin Gilbert*

REPRESENTATIVE RECORDINGS

Toby Keith (Mercury, 1993); *Blue Moon* (A&M, 1996); *Dream Walkin'* (Mercury, 1997)

The Kendalls

Royce Kuykendall b. St. Louis, Missouri, September 25, 1934;
d. May 22, 1998
Jeannie Kuykendall b. St. Louis, Missouri, November 30, 1954

Just when it appeared close harmony singing was nearing extinction in country music, the father-daughter duo of Royce and Jeannie Kendall put it back on the charts. Placing thirty-seven singles on *Billboard's* charts from 1970 through 1989, they usually dealt with the theme of adultery. The idea of a father and daughter singing such suggestive lyrics to one another was a little too much for many new industry sophisticates to bear, but fans loved their hard-country, unabashed singing.

After releases for the Stop and DOT labels in the early 1970s, they signed on with Chicago-based Ovation Records and enjoyed their greatest chart success. Jeannie's high-pitched vocals drove uptempo songs such as 1977's "Heaven's Just a Sin Away" and 1978's "Sweet Desire" to the #1 spot on the charts. Her delivery on ballads such as "Pittsburgh Stealers" and "Just Like Real People" could wring tears from a stone. Daddy Royce's rich baritone was the grounding rod for Jeannie's electric performances. All told, the duo managed to crack *Billboard's* Top Ten eleven times. In 1981 they released their first single for MERCURY RECORDS, "Teach Me to Cheat," which made it to the #7 spot. Consistently on the charts throughout the early

The Kendalls, Jeannie & Royce

1980s, their 1984 release "Thank God for the Radio" spent twenty-three weeks on the charts, going all the way to #1.

Beginning in the latter half of the 1980s, the hits began to dwindle. Switching from Mercury to MCA/CURB, EPIC, and then STEP ONE, they had few hits. After recording for Lonesome Dove in Tulsa (1994–95) and for American Harvest (1996), the duo signed with Rounder Records. They were touring in 1998 when Royce had a stroke May 20. He died two days later. —*Chris Skinker*

Jerry Kennedy

b. Shreveport, Louisiana, August 10, 1940

Jerry Glenn Kennedy produced a number of top country acts, including ROGER MILLER, the STATLER BROTHERS, TOM T. HALL, JOHNNY RODRIGUEZ, and REBA MCENTIRE; played guitar on a number of sessions (including the dobro lead on "Harper Valley P.T.A." for JEANNIE C. RILEY); and was head of the country music division of MERCURY RECORDS from 1969 to 1984.

Jerry Kennedy

Kennedy learned guitar from TILLMAN FRANKS, then became a guitar player for FARON YOUNG and JOHNNY HORTON, and performed on the LOUISIANA HAYRIDE in Shreveport. Kennedy moved to Nashville in 1961 and in 1963 began work as SHELBY SINGLETON's assistant at Mercury Records. In 1965 Kennedy was promoted to A&R manager at the label and in 1969 became a Mercury vice president in charge of country music, which entailed overseeing the label's Nashville operation. Kennedy also worked as a session guitarist for a number of acts, including TAMMY WYNETTE, Patti Page, ROY ROGERS, KRIS KRISTOFFERSON, JERRY LEE LEWIS, GLEN CAMPBELL, BRENDA LEE, Perry Como, Faron Young, and Clint Eastwood. Kennedy played on BOB DYLAN's *Nashville Skyline* and ROY ORBISON's "Oh, Pretty Woman."

In 1984 Kennedy left Mercury and established his own independent firm, JK Productions, which produces the STATLER BROTHERS and others. —*Don Cusic*

Kentucky Colonels (*see* Roland and Clarence White)

The Kentucky HeadHunters
Richard Young b. Glasgow, Kentucky, January 27, 1955
Fred Young b. Glasgow, Kentucky, July 8, 1958
Greg Martin b. Louisville, Kentucky, March 31, 1954
Doug Phelps b. Leachville, Arkansas, February 16, 1960
Ricky Lee Phelps b. Paragould, Arkansas, October 8, 1953
Mark Orr b. Charlotte, Michigan, November 16, 1949
Anthony Kenney b. Glasgow Kentucky, October 8, 1953

This Edmonton, Kentucky–based country-rock band had fleeting commercial success and wielded considerable influence in the late 1980s and early 1990s. The group—to many people's surprise—was the winner of the CMA's Vocal Group of the Year Award in both 1990 and 1991, and also won a 1990 Grammy Award for Best Country Performance by a Duo or Group with Vocal.

The HeadHunters' ragged, hard-driving style was a sharp contrast to the more conventional sound of country bands such as ALABAMA and EXILE, which had flourished in the country charts in the 1980s. The irony of the HeadHunters' making it big in the country field after scuffling around the southern rock scene in various incarnations for years was not lost on the members themselves.

"We're a blues band that grew up on southern rock and somehow ended up as the country band of the year," said rhythm guitarist and founding member Richard Young. "I don't know how it happened. I'm just sure as hell glad it did."

The HeadHunters' original members were brothers Richard Young (rhythm guitarist) and Fred Young (drums); the Youngs' first cousin Greg Martin (lead guitar); and two Arkansas-born brothers, unrelated to the rest: Doug Phelps (bass) and Ricky Lee Phelps (vocals).

The HeadHunters evolved out of an earlier southern rock band called Itchy Brother, which enjoyed regional popularity from 1968 until the early 1970s. In late 1980 three Itchy Brother survivors, the Young brothers and Martin, joined with the Phelps brothers to form the Kentucky HeadHunters. In the summer of 1989 they recorded an eight-song cassette that landed them a contract with MERCURY RECORDS. Mercury Nashville's head of A&R, HAROLD SHEDD (the man who had been Alabama's producer for many years), liked their tape so much that Mercury re-

leased its eight recordings as-is, with two new tracks added for their debut album, *Pickin' on Nashville*. The record included their only Top Ten country hit to date, a cover of DON GIBSON's "Oh Lonesome Me."

In 1992 the Phelpses left the band and began recording on their own as BROTHER PHELPS. They were replaced in the HeadHunters by two other Itchy Brother alumni: the Youngs' cousin Anthony Kenney (bass) and Mark Orr (lead vocals). In 1994 the band recorded *That'll Work,* a blues album with former Chuck Berry pianist Johnnie Johnson. In 1996, with the breakup of Brother Phelps, Doug Phelps rejoined the band as lead vocalist, replacing Orr. Though the HeadHunters had ceased to be a presence on the country scene by the mid-1990s, they are still active on the touring circuit and have continued to record, most recently releasing an album *Stompin' Grounds* in 1997 for BNA Records. —*Bob Allen*

REPRESENTATIVE RECORDINGS

Pickin' on Nashville (Mercury, 1989); *Electric Barnyard* (Mercury, 1991); *Best of the Kentucky HeadHunters: Still Pickin'* (Mercury, 1994)

Anita Kerr/Anita Kerr Singers
Anita Kerr b. Memphis, Tennessee, October 31, 1927
Dottie Dillard b. Springfield, Missouri, August 3, 1923
Louis Nunley b. Sikeston, Missouri, October 15, 1931
Gil Wright b. Nashville, Tennessee, July 3, 1929

Anita Kerr was one of the most influential vocal and instrumental arrangers in the early evolution of the NASHVILLE SOUND. Her group, the Anita Kerr Singers, became a staple on countless recordings, helping to considerably broaden country music's market in the wake of the commercial threat posed by rock & roll.

Born Anita Jean Grilli to an Italian family who ran a Memphis grocery store, Kerr started taking piano lessons at age four. Later she played pipe organ and prepared vocal arrangements for the St. Thomas Church choir in Memphis. By age fourteen she was leading the Grilli Sisters vocal group. They performed on her mother's radio show, and Kerr herself became a singer, pianist, and organist on Memphis station WREC.

In 1948 Kerr moved to Nashville and started a singing group on WSM's *Sunday Down South* radio show. Her big break was adding backup to RED FOLEY's pop hit "Our Lady of Fatima" (#16, 1950). She became a regular on the GRAND OLE OPRY's *Prince Albert Show* and led an eight-voice group, the Anita Kerr Singers, for DECCA RECORDS recording sessions. In June 1956 the group was invited to appear on *Arthur Godfrey's Talent Scouts* show (CBS-TV), necessarily shrinking down to what was sometimes called the Anita Kerr Quartet: Kerr, Dottie Dillard, Louis Nunley, and Gil Wright.

By the late 1950s Kerr was working for many labels. She assisted on hits such as Decca artist BOBBY HELMS's "My Special Angel" (#1 country; #7 pop, 1957) and RCA star JIM REEVES's "He'll Have to Go" (#1 country; #2 pop, 1959).

Starting in 1961, Kerr became CHET ATKINS's recording assistant at RCA sessions, working as vocal group leader, arranger, and occasional producer for EDDY ARNOLD, HANK SNOW, WILLIE NELSON, FLOYD CRAMER, and others on the RCA roster. She also recorded sides of her own as Anita & th' So-And-So's.

The Anita Kerr Singers: (from left) Gil Wright, Kerr, Dottie Dillard, and Louis Nunley

Having tired of technical record-producing tasks—for which she received scant credit—Kerr resigned in 1963. Her later, noncountry career was launched by a move to California, where she wrote soundtracks for Rod McKuen's poetry readings and cut albums with her group. In about 1970 Kerr and her husband, Alex Grob, moved to his native Switzerland, where they opened their own recording studio in 1975. There Kerr continued to compose, arrange, and write musical scores for feature films.

—*Steve Eng*

Doug Kershaw
b. Tiel Ridge, Louisiana, January 24, 1936

Cajun fiddler Doug Kershaw, along with HARRY CHOATES, JIMMY C. NEWMAN, and JO-EL SONNIER, is one of a handful of Cajun musicians who enjoyed success in mainstream country music. Douglas James Kershaw began his career as a child, performing with his mother, Mama Rita, a fiddler, guitarist, and singer. In 1948 he formed the Continental Playboys with his brothers Russell Lee ("Rusty") and Nelson ("Pee Wee"), and performed for a while on station KPLC–Lake Charles, in 1953. Doug and Rusty then began performing as a duo, and soon hooked up with Crowley, Louisiana, record producer J. D. Miller's Feature label. As Rusty & Doug they recorded a number of country songs for Feature before making the pilgrimage to Nashville, where they inaugurated their recording career for the HICKORY label with the release of Doug's composition "So Lovely Baby."

Performing in the close vocal harmony style popularized by the EVERLY BROTHERS, the Kershaws' career began to flower. In 1955 they appeared on the *LOUISIANA HAYRIDE*

before moving on to the *WWVA JAMBOREE* in Wheeling, West Virginia. In September 1957 their song "Love Me to Pieces" rose to #14, while "Hey Sheryl" went to #22. That November they joined the GRAND OLE OPRY. In 1958 they enjoyed some chart success with their recording of BOUDLEAUX BRYANT's "Hey Sheriff" before their career was short-circuited when they were both drafted.

After finishing their stints in the military, Rusty and Doug returned to the recording studio to cut some hard-hitting Cajun-flavored songs, including "Louisiana Man," which went to #10 on the country charts, and "Diggy Diggy Lo," which went to #14. The brothers split up after 1964, and Doug went on to win fame as the "Cajun Hippie," whose outrageous stage antics and driving performance style made him a favorite of the musical counter-culture during the 1970s, recording for MERCURY, MGM, and WARNER BROTHERS. The late 1990s found him still touring, sometimes playing dates with fellow Louisianan EDDY RAVEN.

—*Charlie Seemann*

REPRESENTATIVE RECORDINGS

Rusty & Doug Kershaw (Bear Family, 1979); *The Best of Doug Kershaw* (Warner Bros., 1989)

Sammy Kershaw
b. Kaplan, Louisiana, February 24, 1958

While working with Louisiana musician J. B. Perry in the early 1980s, Sammy Kershaw would open for many of established country stars, including his idol, GEORGE JONES. Jones would have a profound influence on Kershaw's early music. Kershaw's first album for MERCURY RECORDS, 1991's *Don't Go Near the Water,* was full of Jones-styled vocal licks, with most of the material dealing with heartache and sorrow.

The old style came naturally to the Louisiana native, a cousin of legendary CAJUN fiddler DOUG KERSHAW. He had

Sammy Kershaw

seen his share of hard times, losing his father as a young man and being raised by the family's hardworking mother. In the late 1980s, burned out from traveling and chasing his dream, Kershaw developed alcohol and drug abuse problems. He had made up his mind to quit the business, taking a job as a remodeling supervisor for Wal-Mart. In 1990 Kershaw returned to music, and a demo tape and photo convinced Mercury to give him a private showcase. He signed with the label later that year.

His first album produced an immediate hit, "Cadillac Style," in 1991, which went to #3. The single led to a series of regional commercials for the Cadillac division of General Motors, a rare accomplishment for a new artist. *Don't Go Near the Water* reached gold status, but it was imperative that Kershaw become less of a Jones imitator and more of an individual stylist. The follow-up album for Mercury, *Haunted Heart,* was recorded with that in mind. *Haunted Heart* proved more contemporary with its southern-rock feel and was also certified gold. Kershaw gained his first career #1 single from that album, "She Don't Know She's Beautiful."

Feelin' Good Train, released in 1994 for Mercury, was an additional attempt to distance himself from the Jones comparisons. Kershaw did record a duet with Jones, "Never Bit a Bullet Like this Before," and also covered the Jones classic "A Good Year for the Roses" with LORRIE MORGAN. The remainder of the album confirmed Kershaw's stature as a strong interpreter of the country-rock hybrid, particularly with his version of the AMAZING RHYTHM ACES' "Third Rate Romance."

Sammy Kershaw still plays the music of Jones, CAL SMITH, MEL STREET, and his other influences at live shows, but he no longer hews so closely to the Jones style. Kershaw has become a master of what he calls "southern-fried rock & roll," or traditional country with a decidedly youthful edge.

—*Bob Paxman*

REPRESENTATIVE RECORDINGS

Don't Go Near the Water (Mercury, 1991); *Politics, Religion and Her* (Mercury, 1996); *Labor of Love* (Mercury, 1997)

Stan Kesler
b. Abbeville, Mississippi, August 11, 1928

Stan Kesler enjoyed a rich and varied career in Memphis as a songwriter, session musician, engineer, and producer. He is probably best known as the author of five songs recorded by ELVIS PRESLEY and as an integral member of the house band for country sessions recorded at SUN RECORDS in the 1950s.

Growing up the youngest of nine children, Kesler initially played both mandolin and guitar, picking up the pedal steel in 1945 while serving time in the Marine Corps. Shortly after being discharged in the fall of 1947, Kesler moved to Memphis, where he played both radio and club gigs with a number of western swing and country bands, including the Carradine Boys, Al Rogers's group, and Clyde Leoppard & the Snearly Ranch Boys. The latter ensemble auditioned successfully for SAM PHILLIPS's Sun Records in September 1954, initially recording "Lonely Sweetheart" and "Split Personality." Inspired by the work of HANK WILLIAMS, Kesler had penned both sides of the Leoppard 78. Phillips was impressed, and over the next several years

recorded a number of Kesler's songs on a variety of Sun artists, including Smokey Joe Baugh, Warren Smith, Barbara Pittman, the Miller Sisters, and Elvis Presley. The best known of Kesler's compositions, "I'm Left, You're Right, She's Gone" and "I Forgot to Remember to Forget," were cut by Presley in 1954 and 1955.

By late 1954 a Sun house country band had been informally constituted consisting of Kesler on pedal steel, Quinton Claunch on guitar, Bill Cantrell on fiddle, Wayne Deal or Marcus Van Storey on bass, and Clyde Leoppard or Johnny Bernero on drums. In late 1956 Kesler began playing bass as well as pedal steel, the bass eventually becoming his primary instrument. A year later Kesler founded his first label, Crystal Records. Over the years Crystal would be followed by Penn and XL. On the latter label, Kesler produced nine pop hits for Sam the Sham & the Pharaohs, the most famous being "Wooly Bully," as well as seminal blues recordings by the likes of Willie Cobb and the Binghampton Blues Boys.

In 1983 Kesler, Paul Burlison, D. J. Fontana, Smoochy Smith, and Marcus Van Storey formed the Sun Rhythm Section, performing regularly on the road and recording one album for Flying Fish Records. As of 1995 he continued to engineer at Phillips recording studio in Memphis.

—*Rob Bowman*

REPRESENTATIVE RECORDINGS

Various Artists: The Sun Country Years, 1950–1959 (Bear Family, 1986), 10 LPs; *Sam the Sham & the Pharaohs: The Best of* (Polygram, 1986); *The Sun Rhythm Section* (Flying Fish, 1987)

The Kessinger Brothers
Clark W. Kessinger b. South Hills, West Virginia, July 27, 1896; d. June 4, 1975
Luches Kessinger b. Kanawha County, West Virginia, August 21, 1906; d. May 6, 1944

Legendary West Virginia fiddler Clark Kessinger was playing the fiddle in a local saloon, making ten to fifteen dollars a night, when he was only seven years old. By the time he was ten, he was playing for nearby country dances. Kessinger's great-grandfather and great-uncle were both old-time fiddlers, and he was influenced by other Charleston, West Virginia, area fiddlers, such as Ed Haley, George Dillon, and Bob and Abe Glenn.

After serving in the navy during World War I he began playing in 1919 with his cousin, Luches "Luke" Kessinger, who accompanied him on guitar. In February 1928 they began recording for the BRUNSWICK label as the Kessinger Brothers, eventually waxing more than seventy sides for the company through September 1930. They also performed on radio station WCHS. After Luches's death, Clark played little until he was rediscovered in 1964, when he recorded for Ken Davidson's Folk Promotions (later Kanawha) label and began appearing at fiddle contests and folk festivals. Kessinger suffered a stroke in 1971 that effectively ended his fiddling career, and he died in 1975.

—*Charlie Seemann*

REPRESENTATIVE RECORDINGS

The Kessinger Brothers (County, 1975); *The Legend of Clark Kessinger* (Folk Promotion, 1964; reissued by County,

1971); *Complete Recorded Works in Chronological Order, Volume Three, 1929–1930* (Document, 1997)

Hal Ketchum
b. Greenwich, New York, April 9, 1953

Hal Michael Ketchum blew onto the country scene in 1991 with his first single, "Small Town Saturday Night," and he's maintained a viable career ever since. Ketchum is about as country as Times Square, however. A thoughtful song-writer with a literary eye for detail and the good sense to keep everything simple, he's a male version of MARY CHAPIN CARPENTER: folk-tinged, intellectual, and honest. These characteristics, combined with the sex appeal of his long salt-and-pepper mane and massive eyebrows, have drawn fans.

Raised near Vermont, Hal Michael Ketchum had a banjo-playing father. He was a young fan of BUCK OWENS— even a fan-club member—and played drums in an r&b band at age fifteen. His family moved to Florida when he was seventeen, and his interest in music continued. Ketchum picked up the trade of carpentry along the way, and it became the trade that sustained him. In later years Ketchum moved into a Texas home near a dance hall, which became his proving ground as a songwriter and per-former. In 1986 he moved to Nashville and concentrated on his songwriting. He released an independent collection of ten of his songs, *Threadbare Alibis*, on the independent la-bel Watermelon Records in 1989.

The CD helped Ketchum land a publishing deal and ul-timately a contract with CURB RECORDS. Instantly embraced by fans and country radio, Ketchum followed up his smash single "Small Town Saturday Night" (#2, 1991) with a half decade of signature singles such as "I Know Where Love Lives" (#13, 1991), "Sure Love" (#3, 1992), "Past the Point of Rescue" (#2, 1992) from the album with that name, "Hearts Are Gonna Roll" (#2, 1993), and "Mama Knows the Highway" (#8, 1993).

Ketchum's albums have been marked by his ability to write and find catchy ditties and place them alongside more artistically revealing songs. In 1994 he joined the GRAND OLE OPRY. —*Clark Parsons*

REPRESENTATIVE RECORDINGS

Past The Point of Rescue (Curb, 1991); *Sure Love* (Curb, 1992); *Every Little Word* (Curb, 1994); *The Hits* (Curb, 1996)

Merle Kilgore
b. Chickasha, Oklahoma, August 9, 1934

As a teenager in Shreveport, Louisiana, Wyatt Merle Kil-gore carried HANK WILLIAMS's guitar up the staircase to the KWKH studios. Later he became HANK WILLIAMS JR.'s opening act and then vice president of Hank Williams Jr. Enterprises. In between he has been a songwriter, song-plugger, performer, DJ, and program director. He worked with almost every major country act of the 1950s and 1960s, and has become a raconteur of note.

Kilgore grew up in Shreveport, and hung around the KWKH studio and the *LOUISIANA HAYRIDE*. His first job as a DJ was with KENT-Shreveport, in 1950. After leaving Louisiana Tech in 1953, he moved to Monroe, Louisiana, to work for American Optical. He worked as a DJ, sang at

Merle Kilgore

various stations in and around Monroe, and starred on KFAZ-TV as "The Tall Texan." WEBB PIERCE, originally from Monroe, spotted him on one of his trips home, landed Kilgore a contract with the Los Angeles–based IM-PERIAL RECORDS, and covered Kilgore's "More and More," taking it to #1 on the country charts.

Recording for Imperial for the next five years, Kilgore lagged just behind every trend, from rockabilly to folk. He even cut a teenage pop session in New Orleans with Fats Domino's producer, Dave Bartholomew. For most of that time, Kilgore worked at KCIJ-Shreveport. In 1959 Kilgore recorded for Jim Branch's Jim Records, and one of the songs, "Dear Mama," was leased to STARDAY and became a hit. It was followed by "Love Has Made You Beautiful," Kil-gore's only Top Ten hit as a performer. At the same time he scored a hit as the writer of JOHNNY HORTON's "Johnny Reb."

Kilgore moved to Nashville on December 31, 1961, to work for AL GALLICO at Shapiro-Bernstein Music and later for Gallico's own publishing firm, Al Gallico Publishing. Kilgore placed one of his own songs, "Wolverton Moun-tain," with CLAUDE KING, and later he and JUNE CARTER wrote "Love's Burning Ring of Fire," first recorded by Anita Carter and later potently revived by JOHNNY CASH as "Ring of Fire." Kilgore continued to record for a variety of labels and scored minor hits for COLUMBIA, ELEKTRA, and WARNER BROS. RECORDS between 1967 and 1985. He made several forays into movie work (*Nevada Smith, Country Mu-sic on Broadway,* and *Five Card Stud*), and for twenty-one years he was the opening act for Hank Williams Jr. He later managed Hank Jr. from an office in Paris, Tennessee, com-muting between there and Nashville. —*Colin Escott*

REPRESENTATIVE RECORDING

Teenager's Holiday (Bear Family, 1991)

Buddy Killen

b. Lexington, Alabama, November 13, 1932

Buddy Killen was affiliated with TREE PUBLISHING COMPANY for more than thirty-six years, first as an employee, then as part owner, and finally as sole owner of the publishing giant. He also served as a musician, songwriter, and producer through these years.

William D. "Buddy" Killen grew up in Florence, Alabama, where his family had a restaurant. He moved to Nashville in 1950, just after his high school graduation, at the invitation of country singer Autry Inman. In Nashville Killen joined the blackface comedy group JAMUP & HONEY as a bass player.

In 1953 Killen played bass for the comedy group Cousin Jody, Mart & Bart on the *WWVA JAMBOREE* in Wheeling, West Virginia. Three months later the group split, and Killen moved back to Nashville, where he was hired by JACK STAPP to handle the day-to-day activities of signing songs and songwriters and pitching songs to artists for recordings for Tree Publishing at $35 a week.

In 1957 Stapp bought out two of the original owners of Tree and gave Killen 30 percent of the company and the title of vice president. Killen continued to write songs, penning the pop hit "Forever," and to produce records for soul singer Joe Tex, RONNIE MCDOWELL, EXILE, and others. In 1974 Buddy Killen was named president and chief operating officer of Tree, though in theory he still reported to Stapp, who was chairman of the board and chief executive officer.

In 1980 Jack Stapp died and Killen purchased Tree. In 1989 he sold the company to Sony Music for $40 million. In 1994 Killen's autobiography, *By the Seat of My Pants*, written with Tom Carter, was published by Simon & Schuster.

—*Don Cusic*

Buddy Killen

D Kilpatrick

b. Charlotte, North Carolina, July 18, 1919

Walter David "D" Kilpatrick was a notable music executive from the late 1940s to the late 1960s. After high school, service with the marine corps, and sales experience in the auto parts field, he broke into the record business as a salesman with CAPITOL RECORDS' Charlotte, North Carolina, distributorship, servicing retailers and jukebox operators in parts of North Carolina and South Carolina. This prepared him for three years as Atlanta branch manager, beginning by early 1948. While there, he recruited and produced James and MARTHA CARSON and the Statesmen for the label. In 1950 Kilpatrick became the first salaried country producer to be based in Nashville. In this role he recorded numerous acts at various studios around the nation, including HANK THOMPSON, CARL BUTLER, JIMMIE SKINNER, TEX RITTER, and BOB ATCHER.

In 1951 Kilpatrick shifted to MERCURY RECORDS' country A&R slot. Although he remained heavily involved in southeastern sales and promotion, he concentrated on recording JERRY BYRD, JOHNNY HORTON, JIMMY DEAN, BENNY MARTIN, Ernie Lee, CARL STORY, and Bill Carlisle and the CARLISLES. In 1956 Kilpatrick became manager of WSM's GRAND OLE OPRY and its associated booking operation and brought in new blood such as Rusty and DOUG KERSHAW, WILMA LEE & STONEY COOPER, PORTER WAGONER, and the EVERLY BROTHERS. In 1958 Kilpatrick helped found the Country Music Association (CMA). In mid-1959 Kilpatrick left the Opry to form Acuff-Rose Artists Corporation (ARAC)—a booking agency—with ROY ACUFF and WESLEY ROSE. A companion firm to ACUFF-ROSE PUBLICATIONS and HICKORY RECORDS, ARAC promoted not only Opry acts but also pop stars such as ROY ORBISON and Mark Dinning. Next, Kilpatrick moved on to serve as southern district regional sales manager for WARNER BROS. RECORDS (1962–64), South and Southwest distribution and promotion manager for Philips Records (1964-65), and national sales and promotion chief for Mercury Records (1965–66). A number of smaller musical ventures followed, until Kilpatrick essentially left the music industry to run a custom drapery and fabrics business. He now lives in retirement in Nashville.

—*John Rumble*

Bradley Kincaid

b. Point Leavell, Kentucky, July 13, 1895; d. September 23, 1989

Bradley Kincaid was the first big country radio star, on Chicago's WLS and the *NATIONAL BARN DANCE,* and he built a bridge from folk music to commercial country on radio and on records.

After his first performance of "Barbara Allen" and other such folksongs, he received bushels of mail, and fans sent the Kentucky Mountain Boy 300,000 letters during his tenure at WLS (1926–29). His warm tenor voice, the old songs, and his simple guitar accompaniment (on his "Hound Dog Guitar," as he called it) appealed to rural-oriented audiences. He was the first country radio star to publish a SONGBOOK, *Favorite Mountain Ballads and Old Time Songs* (1928), selling 110,000 copies on the air and at performances for 50 cents each through six printings. He made trips through the Appalachians to collect songs but also included popular sentimental compositions in twelve

Bradley Kincaid

additional songbooks. There is no record of total sales, but they probably amounted to about 500,000.

In 1929 Kincaid went to WLW-Cincinnati and during his first month received 50,000 letters. In 1931 he moved to KDKA in Pittsburgh, and over the next ten years he moved from station to station, staying for a year or so at each, doing programs and personal appearances: WGY-Schenectady, New York; WEAF–New York City, and the NBC Red Network; WBZ-Boston; WTIC-Hartford; back to WGY-Schenectady; and then WHAM-Rochester. During most of these years in the East, Kincaid teamed with GRANDPA JONES and "Harmonica" Joe Troyan. Kincaid worked at WLW (and WKRC) in Cincinnati from 1941 to 1944, then went to WSM and the GRAND OLE OPRY, where he remained until 1950. After retiring from the Opry he bought into radio station WWSO in Springfield, Ohio, and operated a music store.

He recorded more than a hundred songs in 78-rpm format released on more than thirty different labels, including GENNETT, BRUNSWICK, BULLET, BLUEBIRD, DECCA, and CAPITOL. Scotty Wiseman, DOC HOPKINS, MAC WISEMAN, EDDY ARNOLD, BILL MONROE, and Grandpa and Ramona Jones have acknowledged Kincaid's influence.

—*Loyal Jones*

REPRESENTATIVE RECORDINGS

Bradley Kincaid—Volume 2—Favorite Old Time Songs (Old Homestead, 1984); *Bradley Kincaid—Old-Time Songs & Hymns* (Old Homestead, 1984)

Claude King

b. near Keithville, Louisiana, February 5, 1923

Despite a career that spanned more than forty years, Claude King remains identified with just one song, "Wolverton Mountain," and, by implication, the early 1960s NASHVILLE SOUND it epitomized.

King worked semiprofessionally in music before World War II, and in 1947 moved to Little Rock to work with Buddy Attaway and TILLMAN FRANKS. They made their first

recording there for President Records. Back in Shreveport in 1948, King worked in construction, played occasionally on the *LOUISIANA HAYRIDE,* and recorded for Pacemaker, Specialty, and Dee-Jay.

King and JOHNNY HORTON were fellow hunters, and, after Horton's death, Tillman Franks, who had been the late singer's manager, groomed King as his replacement. King was signed to COLUMBIA RECORDS in Nashville, and after two Top Ten hits with songs based on movies, "Big River, Big Man" and "The Comancheros," King recorded "Wolverton Mountain," which peaked at #1 in country and #6 in pop.

Nothing ever eclipsed "Wolverton Mountain," although King charted another twenty-seven records over the next fifteen years. He stayed in Shreveport, recording for several small labels after Columbia, and slowly scaled back his touring to the point where he had virtually retired by the mid-1980s.

—*Colin Escott*

REPRESENTATIVE RECORDINGS

More Than Climbing That Mountain (Bear Family Records, 1994), 5 CDs; *Claude King: American Originals* (Columbia Records, 1990)

Nelson King

b. Portsmouth, Ohio, April 1, 1914; d. March 16, 1974

The role of the radio disc jockey within country music grew in dramatic fashion in the years after World War II, but few DJs would come to wield more power than Nelson King, who ruled the airwaves at WCKY in Cincinnati, Ohio, from 1946 until 1961. King was voted America's top country music DJ for eight consecutive years in nationwide polls conducted by *Billboard*, at a time when WCKY, a 50,000-watt giant, was considered one of the nation's premier country music stations.

King worked at a number of radio stations in West Virginia, Kentucky, and Ohio before the war, but his greatest fame came at WCKY, where he hosted the *Jamboree* program and was active in various commercial ventures (for a time serving as a producer for Cincinnati-based KING RECORDS). He is credited as a co-writer on several country songs, most notably HANK WILLIAMS's "There'll Be No Teardrops Tonight," but those arrangements were likely more about securing airplay than actual collaboration.

King also made at least two recordings as an artist, "Deck of Cards" (1947) and "The Story of Our Lady of Fatima" (1950), both released on King Records. King left WCKY in 1961 and, except for a brief comeback at WCLU (1968–70), worked outside the music business until his death.

—*Jon Hartley Fox*

Pee Wee King

b. Milwaukee, Wisconsin, February 18, 1914

Pee Wee King was an unlikely candidate for country music stardom. Yet as a songwriter, bandleader, recording artist, and television entertainer, he broke new ground in country music, and he helped to bring waltzes, polkas, and cowboy songs into mainstream country music during ten productive years at the GRAND OLE OPRY.

Born Julius Frank Anthony Kuczynski into a working-class Polish-German family, he grew up in the polka-and-waltz culture of Wisconsin. His musical debut occurred at

Pee Wee King

age fifteen, when he played the accordion in his father's polka band. He changed his name to King (after the then popular polka performer Wayne King) and formed his own high school band, Frankie King & the King's Jesters. In 1933 young Frankie King joined the *Badger State Barn Dance* and soon had his own radio show on WJRN in Racine.

King's lucky break came in the spring of 1934, when he met promoter J. L. FRANK. He moved with Frank to Louisville in 1934 to back up GENE AUTRY for a time, joined Frankie More's Log Cabin Boys as accordionist on WHAS radio, and in 1936 married Joe Frank's stepdaughter Lydia.

In 1936 King was in Knoxville performing on WNOX. In 1937 he formed the Golden West Cowboys and moved to Nashville to begin a ten-year run on the Grand Ole Opry. In 1941–42 he and his band were featured with the CAMEL CARAVAN, a touring company that presented some 175 shows at military installations in the United States and Central America. At various times his band included EDDY ARNOLD, REDD STEWART, ERNEST TUBB, COWBOY COPAS, and MINNIE PEARL.

After joining the Grand Ole Opry in June 1937, he helped introduce an array of new instruments and sounds to that program's stage, including the trumpet, drums, and the electric guitar. In addition, he dressed his band members in spiffy western outfits designed by the Hollywood tailor NUDIE. His nattily attired Golden West Cowboys generally produced a smooth and danceable sound during their heyday in the 1940s; in the 1950s they even branched out briefly into mild rockabilly.

He wrote or co-wrote more than 400 songs, including some of the most popular songs in American musical history, notably "Slow Poke" (a #1 pop hit for fourteen weeks in 1951) with Chilton Price and the hugely successful "Tennessee Waltz" with Redd Stewart. Patti Page's 1950 version of the latter song was #1 on the pop charts and within six months sold almost 5 million copies. It became

an official Tennessee state song in 1965. His own recording career includes more than twenty albums and 157 singles, most of them issued during his seventeen-year association with RCA VICTOR. With the release of his recording of "Slow Poke" in 1951 he became one of the first country musicians to cross over successfully into the pop field.

King became also a pioneer television performer when in 1947 he returned to Louisville to work on WAVE radio and television. In the fifties and sixties he had regional and national TV shows originating from Louisville, Cincinnati, Cleveland, and Chicago, including a six-year run of *The Pee Wee King Show* on ABC television.

He appeared in four movies: *Gold Mine in the Sky* with Gene Autry in 1938; *Flame of the West* with Johnny Mack Brown in 1945; and *Bidin' the Outlaw Trail* (1951) and *The Rough, Tough West* (1955) with Charles Starrett. In 1967 King released his own production, *Country-Western Hoedown,* an artistic and financial disaster.

In 1974 King became the twenty-third member of the COUNTRY MUSIC HALL OF FAME. —*Wade Hall*

REPRESENTATIVE RECORDING

Pee Wee King & His Golden West Cowboys (Bear Family, 1994), 4 discs

King Records

established in Cincinnati, Ohio, November 1943

Perhaps more than any other record label, King was shaped by its founder, SYDNEY NATHAN. Under his direction, it became a very vertical company, controlling as much as possible of the process that took music from composition to the consumer. At its peak, King had its own studio, printing press, design house, and plant, as well as a wholly owned sales and distribution network. With that infrastructure Nathan hoped to solve the problems endemic to independent labels.

King started in Cincinnati in November 1943 with two records by MERLE TRAVIS and GRANDPA JONES that were pressed in minimal quantities. It was relaunched a year later with $25,000 raised from family members. At first it was a country label. The *Boone County Jamboree* was on the doorstep at Cincinnati's WLW, and many rural Kentuckians and Tennesseans worked in local factories, giving Nathan a pool of talent and a ready-made market. King stayed exclusively in country music for two years and ultimately scored many major hits with COWBOY COPAS, MOON MULLICAN, the DELMORE BROTHERS, and others.

Nathan entered the r&b market to give his distribution company more to sell, then found the climate of this market better suited for independents. The country releases slowly atrophied, and by the 1960s there were only a few bluegrass acts on King. One of the few mainstream country artists was HAWKSHAW HAWKINS, who re-signed in 1962 and scored a hit with "Lonesome 7-7203." It's worth noting, though, that King advanced r&b's influence on country music through black producer HENRY GLOVER, who sometimes recorded Moon Mullican's r&b style discs using black musicians.

King began limping in the early sixties, and, when Nathan closed out his distribution system in 1965, the label was almost entirely dependent on James Brown. Nathan died in March 1968, and in October King was sold to STARDAY RECORDS just as Starday was about to be sold to Lin Broadcasting. In July 1971, shortly before Lin sold King-

Starday, it sold James Brown's contract and catalogue to Polydor. King-Starday then went to Tennessee Recording and Publishing, which retained the music publishing and, in 1975, sold the repertoire to its current owner, GML, Inc., of Nashville.   —*Colin Escott*

Beecher "Pete" Kirby (*see* Bashful Brother Oswald)

Fred Kirby
b. Charlotte, North Carolina, July 19, 1910; d. April 22, 1996

Frederick Austin Kirby was one of several prominent country singers who emerged on radio around Charlotte, North Carolina, in the 1930s. Kirby entered the professional radio world on WIS in Columbia, South Carolina, in 1931, but "really hit the big time," as he phrased it, when he switched to WBT-Charlotte, soon thereafter. During the thirties he teamed first with Bob Phillips, then CLIFF CARLISLE on *Briarhopper Time* and the *Crazy Barn Dance,* modeling his musical style on that of the late JIMMIE RODGERS and even claiming Rodgers's mantle as America's Blue Yodeler, although Kirby dressed in cowboy garb while Rodgers typically did not.

While with Phillips, Kirby traveled north for a time to work at stations WIP and WFIL in Philadelphia. During the late thirties and early forties Kirby joined forces with western singer Don White and moved north once more for appearances on WLW's *Boone County Jamboree* in Cincinnati and the WLS *NATIONAL BARN DANCE* in Chicago. After splitting with White early in the 1940s, Kirby moved on to St. Louis, where his success entertaining at World War II bond rallies earned him the name Victory Cowboy.

In mid-decade Kirby returned to WBT to work *Briarhopper Time*, the *Dixie Jamboree,* and *Carolina Hayride,* and hosted his own disc jockey programs between 1945 and 1950. By this time Kirby had recorded for BLUEBIRD (1936–37), DECCA (1938), Sonora (1946–47), MGM (1949), and COLUMBIA (1950), in addition to writing songs such as "Atomic Power," a 1946 chartmaker for the Buchanan Brothers. For more than two decades, running into the 1980s, Kirby was also a featured western entertainer at the Tweetsie Railroad in Blowing Rock, North Carolina, where he sang and helped reenact life in the Old West.   —*John Rumble*

Kostas
b. Salonika, Greece, 1949

Using just his first name, self-described "Greek hillbilly" Kostas has been one of country's most successful writers since "Timber, I'm Falling in Love" went to #1 for PATTY LOVELESS in 1989. Kostas Lazarides arrived in the United States at age seven and quickly began absorbing American pop culture. In his new home of Montana, that meant a heavy dose of classic RAY PRICE country, then equal portions of British Invasion pop and psychedelic rock. For twenty years, starting in the late sixties, Lazarides supported himself as a rock musician, touring the Northwest and the Rockies solo or with a band. His singing and guitar-playing won a regional following, but he just barely scraped by.

Nothing came of his aspirations for a career as a pop artist other than an album for an obscure Seattle independent in 1980. It took Nashville producer and record executive TONY BROWN to discover Lazarides and steer him into a career he never expected: country songwriter. Kostas has been most closely associated with the careers of Loveless and DWIGHT YOAKAM, two artists who share his affinity for an earlier, pre-EAGLES era of country, but Kostas has also had big hits with TRAVIS TRITT and MCBRIDE & THE RIDE, and co-wrote half the MAVERICKS' 1994 breakthrough album *What a Crying Shame.* Admirers are particularly impressed with Kostas's melodic sense, with some thinking his Greek roots have subtly spiced his often retro stylings. He was the 1990 Nashville Songwriters Association's Songwriter of the Year. In 1994 he won a Grammy for Yoakam's single "Ain't That Lonely Yet" and a BMI award for the most performed country song, another Loveless #1, "Blame It on Your Heart," co-written with songwriting legend HARLAN HOWARD. Kostas is now a Nashville homeowner, though he continues to spend as much time as possible in the wilds of Montana, where he draws inspiration and hosts frequent co-writers such as Raul Malo of the Mavericks and James House.

His own country debut, *XS in Moderation,* released in 1994 on LIBERTY RECORDS as part of a series saluting Nashville songwriters, sold fewer than 5,000 copies (according to SoundScan), though it showed that a man now known as a songwriter also possesses a remarkable high, quavery tenor.   —*Mark Schone*

Alison Krauss (& Union Station)
b. Decatur, Illinois, July 23, 1971

At age twelve, Alison Maria Krauss was named the most promising fiddler in the Midwest by the Society for the Preservation of Bluegrass Music in America. A diminutive sixth-grader with red curls and fast fingers, she was winning every junior fiddle contest she entered, and three

Alison Krauss

years later ROUNDER RECORDS signed her in hopes she would turn into another fiddle virtuoso along the lines of MARK O'CONNOR. She turned out to be something quite different.

Krauss was encouraged to sing on her debut album, 1987's *Too Late to Cry*, and out came a pure, aching soprano, so strong and moving that her vocals soon eclipsed her fiddling. Backed by her handpicked quartet of top young bluegrass pickers, Union Station, she started making albums that not only topped the bluegrass charts but also revolutionized the field by shifting the emphasis from mostly male pickers playing fast, flashy solos to female singers delivering personal, folkish lyrics in patient, pristine stringband arrangements. In the process she transformed bluegrass from a small, aging sideshow into a commercial and creative force once again.

Krauss grew up in the college town of Champaign, Illinois, and when she was twelve she joined a local folk-bluegrass band that included John Pennell and Nelson Mandrell; she has continued to sing their songs ever since. Her 1987 debut album, *Too Late to Cry*, was recorded with Nashville session players (but featured six compositions by Pennell and one by Mandrell); the follow-up, 1989's *Two Highways*, was credited to Alison Krauss & Union Station and defined the style that would become her signature. The subject matter of the songs reflected the brokenhearted subject matter of mainstream country but with lyrics that shared the personal detail and irony of modern folk music; likewise the melodies had the sweet accessibility of modern country-pop but were set in drummerless Appalachian string arrangements.

The first two albums had their fair share of hot-picking instrumentals, but 1990's *I've Got That Old Feeling* shifted the emphasis decisively to contemporary, personal songwriting, including four numbers by Sidney Cox. He was a member of Louisiana's COX FAMILY, a bluegrass gospel group Krauss admired so greatly that she eventually produced and arranged three albums for them. In 1992 Krauss released her fourth album, *Every Time We Say Goodbye*, with songwriting by Pennell, Cox, and Union Station members Ron Block and Dan Tyminski. The 1994 album *I Know Who Holds Tomorrow* was credited to Alison Krauss and the Cox Family.

On July 3, 1993, the twenty-one-year-old Krauss became the first bluegrass artist to be inducted as a member of the GRAND OLE OPRY in the twenty-nine years since the OSBORNE BROTHERS and JIM & JESSE had been inducted in 1964. In 1995 she summed up the first part of her career with *Now That I've Found You: A Collection*, an anthology that included three brand-new songs, one piece from her first five albums, and four guest appearances on other artists' albums. Although it was released on the small Boston folk label Rounder, it defied conventional wisdom and became a double-platinum, Top Twenty album.

In that same year Krauss won her fourth and fifth Grammy Awards and four CMA Awards, including Female Vocalist of the Year, the Horizon Award, Single of the Year (with Union Station, "When You Say Nothing at All"), and Vocal Event of the Year (with SHENANDOAH, "Somewhere in the Vicinity of the Heart"). The awards confirmed what insiders in the music business had been saying about Krauss almost from her recording career's start—that she possesses one of the most distinctive voices in popular music and that her skillful updating of bluegrass had revitalized the music immensely. At a young age she has become one of country's most respected musicians and sought-after harmony vocalists. *—Geoffrey Himes*

REPRESENTATIVE RECORDINGS

Too Late to Cry (Rounder, 1987); *I've Got That Old Feeling* (Rounder, 1990); *Every Time You Say Goodbye* (Rounder, 1992); *Now That I've Found You: A Collection* (Rounder, 1995); *So Wrong So Long* (Rounder, 1997)

Kris Kristofferson
b. Brownsville, Texas, June 22, 1936

Few singer-songwriters have exerted more influence on country music, or have been as successful within and beyond the limits of Music Row, as Kris Kristofferson. In a career that began in the 1960s, Kristofferson has excelled as a recording artist and Hollywood actor, and has helped set standards for country music songwriting that continue to guide and inspire tunesmiths in Nashville and around the world.

A Rhodes Scholar and son of a U.S. Air Force major general, Kristofferson served as an army captain and helicopter pilot before turning to music. In 1965, two weeks before he was scheduled to begin teaching English literature at West Point, he resigned his commission to take up songwriting in Nashville, signing first with Buckhorn Music and later with COMBINE. For years he paid his dues with part-time jobs, including a stint as janitor at the COLUMBIA studios while BOB DYLAN was recording *Blonde on Blonde*.

Inspired by the Romantic poets, Greenwich Village folk-poet troubadours, and songwriter friend MICKEY NEWBURY, Kristofferson developed a style of songwriting that not only reflected the sense of alienation and loss that characterized the 1960s, but also celebrated the decade's insistence on freedom, honesty, and sexual candor. Among his early successes, ROGER MILLER recorded his "Me and Bobby

Kris Kristofferson

McGee" (#12, 1969), and RAY PRICE scored a #1 hit and earned a Grammy award in 1970 with Kristofferson's "For the Good Times." In that same year, JOHNNY CASH hit #1 with Kristofferson's moody hangover anthem "Sunday Morning Coming Down," which was later named the CMA Song of the Year. SAMMI SMITH's recording of "Help Me Make It Through the Night," unusual for the times in its open embrace of a one-night stand, held the #1 slot for three weeks in 1971 and earned Kristofferson a Grammy, along with a trophy for CMA Single of the Year. Also in 1971, a version of "Me and Bobby McGee" recorded by rock singer Janis Joplin (with whom Kristofferson had been romantically involved) became a million-selling hit on pop radio.

Kristofferson's literary, sensuous approach to writing helped open the doors of the generally conservative Nashville establishment and made the city inviting to artists intent on expressing the issues and tensions of the times. "Hearing Kristofferson's 'Me and Bobby McGee' on the radio and knowing it came out of Nashville made Nashville seem a lot more accessible to me," said GUY CLARK, a celebrated songwriter who moved from Los Angeles to Nashville in 1971.

Kristofferson's own recording career has met with uneven success. While he's popular as a live performer, his gruff, gravelly voice has rarely been a hit with radio programmers. Still, he managed to earn #1 singles as a solo artist with the gospel-flavored "Why Me" (1973), and with "Highwayman" (1985), the signature song of the Highwaymen, a superstar quartet that also includes WAYLON JENNINGS, WILLIE NELSON, and Johnny Cash.

Kristofferson was married to pop singer Rita Coolidge from 1973 to 1980. They recorded several albums together and earned two Grammys for Best Country Vocal Performance by a Duo or Group: 1973's "From the Bottle to the Bottom," and "Lover Please," their 1975 cover of Clyde McPhatter's 1962 r&b hit written by BILLY SWAN, a member of Kristofferson's band the Borderlords.

Kristofferson has made more than twenty films, including *Pat Garrett and Billy the Kid* (1973), *A Star Is Born* (1976), *Convoy* (1978), *Welcome Home* (1989), and *Lone Star* (1996). Since the mid-1970s he has lived in Southern California, where he continues his multifaceted career of acting, songwriting, recording, photography, and occasionally touring as a solo act and as a member of the Highwaymen.

—Jack Bernhardt

REPRESENTATIVE RECORDINGS

Me and Bobby McGee (Monument, 1971); *The Silver Tongued Devil and I* (Monument, 1971)

Sleepy LaBeef

b. Smackover, Arkansas, July 20, 1935

A one-man melting pot of roots music styles, Sleepy LaBeef has been known for years as one of rock & roll's great live performers. Whether playing rockabilly, straight-ahead country, r&b, or gospel, this towering (six-foot, six-inch) singer-guitarist invests nearly every performance with rare conviction and soulfulness.

Born Thomas Paulsley LaBeff (from LaBoeuf), he grew up in Arkansas but moved to Houston as a young man. With a strong gospel music background, he performed on the *Houston Jamboree* and eventually hooked up with PAPPY DAILY, who recorded LaBeef for STARDAY in 1957. Other records appeared on such tiny labels as Wayside, Gulf, and Finn. Though none came close to being hits, they are generally revered by rockabilly fans and collectors.

Signed to Columbia in 1964, LaBeef moved to Nashville but again had no measurable success on the label (though he did play the monster in the low-budget film *The Monster and the Stripper*). By the 1970s he was recording for SHELBY SINGLETON's Plantation label, then later for Singleton's version of SUN RECORDS. A 1977 residency at Alan's Fifth Wheel Lounge in Amesbury, Massachusetts, resulted in laudatory articles about LaBeef (most notably by Peter Guralnick), while the late 1970s rockabilly revival heightened his profile further. In 1981 LaBeef's *It Ain't What You Eat (It's the Way You Chew It)* was released on ROUNDER RECORDS, the label for which he has recorded a series of critically heralded albums in years since. LaBeef continues to work the road as he always has, with each performance offering fresh takes on some of the 6,000-plus tunes he is said to have at his command.　　　　*—Daniel Cooper*

REPRESENTATIVE RECORDINGS

Strange Things Happening (Rounder, 1994); *Sleepy LaBeef— The Human Jukebox* (Sun Entertainment, 1995)

John Lair

b. Renfro Valley, Kentucky, July 1, 1894; d. November 12, 1985

Few individuals in country music have fulfilled as many roles as John Lee Lair, a composer, collector, talent scout, radio producer, and performer best known for founding Kentucky's RENFRO VALLEY BARN DANCE. Lair brought a wealth of experience to country radio, which he entered full-time in the late 1920s at Chicago's WLS. After graduating from high school in Mount Vernon, Kentucky, he

served as principal of Renfro Valley's high school, helped to write and produce the show *Atta Boy* in a special services unit during World War I, performed in a sketch from this show included in Broadway's Ziegfeld Follies, and wound up in Chicago as claims manager for an insurance company. There he began performing on the WLS *NATIONAL BARN DANCE,* recruiting fellow Kentuckians such as Karl Davis and Harty Taylor (KARL & HARTY) for the CUMBERLAND RIDGE RUNNERS stringband. Eventually Lair became WLS's music director and scoured the Midwest for folk and popular tunes, thus beginning what became one of the nation's largest private music libraries.

Lair feared the prevailing cowboy music trend of the 1930s was taking country music too far from its folk roots, and he decided to found his own, more tradition-oriented *Renfro Valley Barn Dance* in Cincinnati in 1937, using many former WLS performers. In 1939 he realized his dream of bringing his show back home by building a 1,000-seat barn to put on the show in Renfro Valley. Other programs Lair broadcasted from the site included the *Sunday Morning Gatherin'* (which, like the barn dance, still runs today) and Lair's remote-location broadcasts of coon hunts, country breakfasts, and fish fries from Renfro Valley, all examples of his commitment to authentic, folk-based broadcasts of community life and music.

By the mid-1950s Lair had lost his network outlet, though he continued to publish the *Renfro Valley Bugle* and operate his pioneer museum, general store, and other attractions. In 1968 he sold his operation to Nashville musical entrepreneur HAL SMITH, but with other partners bought it back again four years later. The show continues under new management, attracting thousands of visitors each year. Its theme song is still the one Lair wrote for it, "Take Me Back to Renfro Valley."　　　*—John Rumble*

Charlie Lamb

b. Knoxville, Tennessee, June 21, 1921

Charles Stacy Lamb has worked for years behind the scenes in Nashville as a journalist, publisher *(Music Reporter),* and all-around promoter of country music. He started his career in Knoxville as a carnival barker, a copyboy for the *Knoxville Journal,* and copywriter for WKGN radio. In 1949 he ran the artists bureau at WROL in Knoxville, booking MOLLY O'DAY and CARL STORY. In 1951 Lamb moved to Nashville to write a column and sell ads for *Cash Box.* After a stint as MERCURY RECORDS' sales representative, he formed his own agency, promoting notables such as KITTY WELLS and ELVIS PRESLEY.

Convinced Nashville's growth as a music center warranted a locally based trade journal, he founded *Country Music Reporter* in September 1956, which became simply *Music Reporter* in March 1957 and continued publication into 1964. His innovative touches in that trade magazine included expanding singles charts to fifty and one hundred listings, using a "bullet" to denote hot sales or radio activity, and introducing an album chart for country records.

As a manager his clients included ED BRUCE and CONNIE SMITH. In 1965 Lamb received a Grammy nomination for his liner notes to *Father & Son—Hank Williams Sr. & Jr.* (MGM). In the sixties Lamb turned performer and comic, entertaining audiences at music-industry banquets and other events with the gibberish of his nonsensical "double-talk" comedy routines. He guested on Allen Funt's *Candid Camera,* acted in commercials and films such as *Ernest Goes to Jail* (1990), and won an *America's Funniest People* TV competition (1992). A member of founding boards for the CMA and the Gospel Music Association, he was first president of NARAS's Nashville chapter. —*Walt Trott*

Cristy Lane
b. Peoria, Illinois, January 8, 1940

Cristy Lane made her reputation through television marketing, promoting her 1980 cornerstone performance "One Day at a Time." Her blend of religious, patriotic, and heartache music appealed to an audience that then followed her to BRANSON, MISSOURI, where she became a regular featured performer.

Born Eleanor Johnston, Lane was the shy child among twelve in her midwestern family. She married Lee Stoller in 1959 and had three children by 1964. Stoller changed her name to Cristy Lane and pressed her to perform in public. It was a trying time for Lane; she attempted suicide in 1968, yet by 1969 she was touring outposts in Vietnam. Another suicide attempt followed.

Stoller and Lane moved to Nashville in 1972 and started their own label, promoting and selling Lane's singles themselves. Her Top Ten hits in the late 1970s, including "Let Me Down Easy," resulted in her winning the ACM's Top New Female Vocalist award for 1979.

In 1980 Lane's recording of the MARIJOHN WILKIN–KRIS KRISTOFFERSON composition "One Day at a Time" became a #1 hit for United Artists. An album and autobiography, both likewise titled *One Day at a Time,* were sold through mail order and marketed on television and in supermarket tabloids. Lee Stoller's 1982 conviction under federal racketeering statutes did little to slow them down. After his release from prison he and Lane were at the forefront of the Nashville exodus to Branson, helping to establish the Missouri town as a country music tourist center. —*Mary A. Bufwack*

REPRESENTATIVE RECORDING
One Day at a Time (LS) 1986

Red Lane
b. Bogalusa, Louisiana, February 2, 1939

Red Lane, born Hollis Rudolph DeLaughter, is one of Music Row's most respected songwriters. After polishing his guitar skills while in the air force, Lane was introduced in 1964 to JUSTIN TUBB, who arranged for BUDDY KILLEN to hear Lane's songs. Killen signed Lane to TREE INTERNATIONAL as an exclusive songwriter and encouraged Tubb to hire him as a guitar player so Lane could move to Nashville. In short order Lane's songs were being recorded, beginning with "My Friend on the Right" (FARON YOUNG, 1964). Lane's list of hits grew to include "My Own Kind of Hat" (MERLE HAGGARD, 1979), "Miss Emily's Picture" (JOHN CONLEE, 1981), "New Looks from an Old Lover" (B. J. Thomas, 1983), and "'Til I Get It Right" (TAMMY WYNETTE, 1973).

Lane's guitar prowess led to his fronting DOTTIE WEST's road band, the Heartaches, and a stint in Merle Haggard's Strangers during the 1980s. Haggard recorded more than twenty of Lane's songs; on most of those recordings Lane played guitar. In the early seventies he released four chart singles on RCA. He was inducted into the Nashville Songwriters Hall of Fame in 1993. —*Kent Henderson*

REPRESENTATIVE RECORDING
The World Needs a Melody (RCA, 1971, out of print)

k. d. lang
b. Consort, Alberta, Canada, November 2, 1961

One of the most critically heralded country acts to arrive on the scene in the late 1980s, k. d. lang released a series of albums as distinctive as any produced during that artistically rich era, yet never saw her acclaim translate into mainstream country success.

Though she played a guitar at ten, Kathryn Dawn Lang was classically trained and already in college when she discovered country music. While attending Alberta's Red Deer College in 1982, she landed a role in a theater

k. d. lang

production based on PATSY CLINE. Hearing Cline's music changed her life.

lang and her band, the reclines, became a sensation in Canada with the release of their 1984 album *Truly Western Experience*. It had a homage to Cline, but most of the tunes were lang's own. The band's honky-tonk sound, and lang's powerful and expressive voice, were showcased in a stage show that featured lang dressed in square-dance dresses and western shirts, whirling about the stage.

Signed to Sire Records, lang recorded *Angel with a Lariat* (1987), which made her a popular favorite among the executives and artists in Nashville. But despite good sales, radio would not play her debut single, a remake of LYNN ANDERSON's "Rose Garden." lang's 1987 duet with ROY OR-BISON on "Crying" won a Grammy Award, yet didn't reach the Top Forty. For her 1988 album *Shadowland,* lang teamed with legendary producer OWEN BRADLEY, and KITTY WELLS, BRENDA LEE, and LORETTA LYNN joined her on the album's "Honky-Tonk Angels' Medley." *Shadowland* won a gold record, but again, little radio support; "I'm Down to My Last Cigarette" reached only #21 on the charts.

Her 1989 gold album *Absolute Torch and Twang* included original tunes and reinterpretations of country chestnuts. A popular and critical success, it won the 1989 Grammy for Best Female Country Performance.

In 1990 lang promoted vegetarianism and kindness to animals in a television ad that said: "If you knew how meat was made, you'd probably lose your lunch." The ad never aired, and stations that had never played her records to begin with said they would now ban them. This was followed in 1992 by the public revelation that lang was a lesbian. But far from generating controversy, the news was met by a collective "So what?" from fans and Nashville alike.

With her 1992 pop-cabaret album *Ingenue,* lang moved away from country, though not necessarily for good. In 1994 she wrote and scored the soundtrack for *Even Cowgirls Get the Blues,* dipping again into her country vocabulary. This was followed in 1995 by the dance-funk of *All You Can Eat,* further displaying her talent and eclectic interests.

—*Mary A. Bufwack*

REPRESENTATIVE RECORDINGS

Angel with a Lariat (Sire, 1987); *Shadowland* (Sire, 1988); *Absolute Torch and Twang* (Sire, 1989)

Jim Lauderdale
b. Troutman, North Carolina, April 11, 1957

In the past eight years, despite spending much of his time in Los Angeles, James Russell Lauderdale has made a name for himself as a Nashville songwriter. He's landed eight cuts with the reliably platinum GEORGE STRAIT and has also had his songs covered by VINCE GILL, PATTY LOVE-LESS, MANDY BARNETT, KATHY MATTEA, and KELLY WILLIS, among others. MARK CHESNUTT notched a #1 with "Gonna Get a Life," co-written by Lauderdale and his regular writing partner, Nashville veteran Frank Dycus, and Lauderdale's "Miss Me" garnered a Grammy nomination and a #1 for Patty Loveless.

He's had less success as a recording artist, though he's received a briefcaseful of press raves, and his soulful voice keeps him busy as a harmony singer. His literate style of country applies the progressive mind-set of GRAM PARSONS to the musical legacies of Memphis and BAKERSFIELD. A precocious minister's kid from Due West, South Carolina,

Lauderdale spent his teen years obsessed with BLUEGRASS. After college he stopped in New York and Nashville long enough to record a still-unreleased album with bluegrass great Roland White, then moved to L.A. He finally made it into record stores with a cut on the second *Town South of Bakersfield* compilation, an anthology of Southern California's alternative country scene.

Lauderdale recorded an unreleased, PETE ANDER-SON–produced album for COLUMBIA RECORDS in 1987. Since then Lauderdale's records have found their way into release if not into mass acceptance. They include a stunning RODNEY CROWELL–John Leventhal co-production called *Planet of Love* on Warner Bros. in 1991 and equally fine efforts for Atlantic in 1994 and 1995 (*Pretty Close to the Truth* and *Every Second Counts,* respectively) and Upstart in 1996 (*Persimmons*). Unfortunately, none of them sold more than 10,000 copies, according to SoundScan. In July 1996 Lauderdale signed with RCA RECORDS and later released a more mainstream country album called *Whisper.*

—*Mark Schone*

REPRESENTATIVE RECORDINGS

Planet of Love (Warner Bros., 1991); *Pretty Close to the Truth* (Atlantic, 1994); *Every Second Counts* (Atlantic, 1995); *Persimmons* (Upstart, 1996); *Whisper* (RCA, 1998)

Shorty Lavender
b. Old Fort, North Carolina, August 19, 1932; d. March 1, 1982

Grover C. "Shorty" Lavender was a fiddler with RAY PRICE's Cherokee Cowboys. Lavender joined the WILBURN BROTH-ERS for their TV series launched in 1963 and was a session player for artists such as WEBB PIERCE. HUBERT LONG hired Lavender as a talent agent, and he booked early dates for BILL ANDERSON and TAMMY WYNETTE. After Long's 1972 death, Lavender started a booking agency in partnership with Wynette (whom he managed) and GEORGE JONES. In 1975 Lavender merged with Dick Blake as Lavender/Blake, adding acts such as RONNIE MILSAP and the STATLERS. After 1978 Lavender ran his own agency. The Nashville Association of Talent Directors voted him 1981 Man of the Year.

—*Walt Trott*

Don Law
b. London, England, February 24, 1902; d. December 20, 1982

As the head of COLUMBIA RECORDS' country music division through most of the 1950s and 1960s, Don Law was one of the most important and successful producers in the annals of country music. Among the top-selling artists he worked with at Columbia were CARL SMITH, LEFTY FRIZZELL, RAY PRICE, JOHNNY HORTON, and JOHNNY CASH, to name but a few. Prior to that, as the protégé of record industry pioneer ART SATHERLEY, Law had been instrumental in bringing to Columbia and its affiliated labels such major pre–World War II talents as BOB WILLS and AL DEXTER (not to mention blues legend Robert Johnson, whose landmark recordings Law produced). Popular with most of his acts, Law was, as Price once put it, a producer who "let an artist be an artist."

An Englishman by birth, Law sang with the London Choral Society as a young man. After various jobs overseas, he immigrated to the United States in 1924, eventually landing in Dallas, Texas, where he worked as a bookkeeper for BRUNSWICK RECORDS. When the AMERICAN RECORD COR-PORATION bought Brunswick in 1931, Law met ARC execu-

Don Law

tive Satherley. When Columbia merged with ARC, both men wound up working for Columbia.

In 1942 Law was called to Columbia's New York office to oversee the children's music division, but his time in that position didn't last long. At some point after World War II (apparently in 1945, though the evidence is unclear), Columbia divided its country division in two, putting Law in charge of all territory east of El Paso and making Satherley responsible for everything west of it. "Right off the bat we got LITTLE JIMMY DICKENS, Carl Smith, and Lefty Frizzell," Law later remarked. He found Frizzell in 1950 through the JIM BECK studio in Dallas, where Law often recorded such artists as Frizzell, Price, BILLY WALKER, and MARTY ROBBINS. Though Law also utilized the Nashville studios, he always maintained close ties with Texas. It was only after Beck died, in 1956, that Law focused his attention on MUSIC CITY. By that point he was sole head of the country division at Columbia, Satherley having retired in 1952.

Along with CHET ATKINS at RCA, OWEN BRADLEY at Decca, and KEN NELSON at Capitol, Law was instrumental in re-establishing country's commercial viability during the so-called NASHVILLE SOUND era (ca. 1957–72). Like Atkins and Bradley, Law headed a country division that amassed numerous country-pop crossover hits during the late 1950s and early 1960s. But unlike those two, he and his frequent co-producer FRANK JONES (and the session leaders to whom Law sometimes delegated the hands-on production duties) did not rely so much on the strings and smooth vocals commonly associated with the Nashville Sound. Rather, Columbia churned out such musically diverse crossover hits as Marty Robbins's "El Paso" and "Don't Worry," Johnny Horton's "The Battle of New Orleans" and "North to Alaska," STONEWALL JACKSON's "Wa-

terloo," and JIMMY DEAN's "Big Bad John." In February 1962, in the wake of this success, Columbia bought OWEN BRADLEY's Nashville recording studio on Sixteenth Avenue South and opened a permanent office there.

As successful as he was, Law nevertheless fell victim to the changes sweeping through American music in the late 1960s. In March 1967 he was forced to take mandatory retirement from Columbia. Law's place at the helm of the Nashville office was taken by BOB JOHNSTON, who had produced BOB DYLAN's *Blonde on Blonde* sessions in Music City the year before. Some of the Columbia artists, notably Ray Price, were allowed to continue working with Law as an independent producer. Calling his company Don Law Productions, he also scored an immediate crossover hit as an independent with HENSON CARGILL's "Skip a Rope," released on MONUMENT. But by the 1970s Law's role in the business was rapidly diminishing, and by the end of the decade he was fully retired. He died in 1982 in a suburb of Galveston, Texas.   —*Daniel Cooper*

Tracy Lawrence

b. Atlanta, Texas, January 27, 1968

Since bursting onto the country music scene in 1991 with his debut single, "Sticks and Stones," Tracy Lawrence has established himself as one of the most popular country singers of the 1990s. In 1991 he was said to be the tenth most programmed artist on U.S. radio, across all formats.

But Lawrence's career—and his life—almost ended before his career began. Just as his album *Sticks and Stones* was completed, the singer was shot four times in a holdup in the parking lot of the Quality Inn Hall of Fame, adjacent to Nashville's famed Music Row. Fortunately, his wounds were not critical.

With "Sticks and Stones" Lawrence became the first artist on ATLANTIC's country roster to score a #1 hit. Subsequent singles—including "Today's Lonely Fool," "Runnin' Behind," and "Somebody Paints the Wall"—cemented his position as a newcomer to watch by the end of 1992. In 1993 he was named Top New Male Vocalist by the ACM.

In the midst of his success, in 1994, Lawrence experienced a brief run-in with the law when he fired a handgun during a dispute with some teenagers in Wilson County, Tennessee. Admitting to overreacting, Lawrence cited his earlier experience at gunpoint for prompting him to use a weapon. He was charged with reckless endangerment, pos-

Tracy Lawrence

session of a firearm. Lawrence was granted pretrial diversion (a form of probation) in December 1994, meaning that the charges would be suspended for a year, and if he had no further brushes with the law, the case would be dismissed and records expunged.

With his court battles behind him, Lawrence scored with fans and critics alike with songs including "Can't Break It to My Heart," "If the World Had a Front Porch," "Texas Tornado," "Time Marches On," and numerous others. He also took over his own career management, opened a music publishing company, and began producing records for other artists as well as co-producing his own albums.

Early in 1997, shortly after the release of his album *The Coast Is Clear,* Lawrence began production duties for newcomer Rich McCready. At the time, Lawrence was also co-producing ten of the twenty cuts for a soundtrack for a theatrical production, *The Civil War.* In January 1998 Lawrence was convicted of spousal abuse, for which he received a misdemeanor and fine. As a result, Atlantic has suspended him from recording with the label until, as Rick Blackburn stated officially, his "personal matters reach a resolve."
—*Janet E. Williams*

REPRESENTATIVE RECORDINGS

Stick and Stones (Atlantic, 1991); *Alibis* (Atlantic 1993); *Time Marches On* (Atlantic 1996); *The Coast Is Clear* (Atlantic, 1997)

Doyle Lawson & Quicksilver
b. Kingsport, Tennessee, April 20, 1944

Following successful stints with J. D.CROWE (1966–71) and the COUNTRY GENTLEMEN (1972–79), mandolinist Doyle Lawson put together his own band, Quicksilver, in 1979, recruiting veteran bluegrass performers Terry Baucom (banjo), Lou Reid Pirtle (bass), and Jimmy Haley (guitar). The band quickly established a reputation for precise harmony singing, hard-driving instrumental work, and vibrant new material, as well as a gospel singing style based on 1940s and 1950s quartet singing from both black and white southern gospel traditions. This a cappella portion of their program is a favorite with fans, and a significant part of their recorded output features religious material, sometimes with instrumental accompaniment.

As the band's success and influence spread in the 1980s, other groups began to emulate Lawson's approach to the extent that, when his entire band left in 1986, he was able to hire immediate replacements from another band. The membership stabilized in the late 1980s with Russell Moore (guitar), Scott Vestal (banjo), and Ray Deaton (electric bass). Each was an accomplished instrumentalist but, more important to the overall structure of Lawson's sound, also a highly skilled vocalist.

Eventually these musicians also went on to other ventures, but by the late 1980s Lawson's style was being copied on such a wide scale that finding replacements posed few problems. In fact, Lawson's influence as a mandolinist is so pervasive that legions of young instrumentalists cite his playing as elemental to their own styles, much the way others would have mentioned BILL MONROE three decades ago.

Lawson's career has, in the past decade, developed two distinct aspects: He not only remains in demand as a featured act on the bluegrass circuit, but also the group's

commitment to gospel music and Christian life has gained them access to that side of the music business as well.
—*Frank and Marty Godbey*

REPRESENTATIVE RECORDINGS

Rock My Soul (Sugar Hill, 1981); *I'll Wander Back Someday* (Sugar Hill, 1988)

Zora Layman
b. Hutchinson, Kansas, March 12, 1900; d. November 2, 1981

Zora Layman was one of the first female artists to earn substantial sales with a country record, and her husband (FRANK LUTHER) was among the most popular and prolific country singers on record in the early 1930s, but the major labels then viewed hillbilly music as a fad rather than an emerging industry, and Zora Layman was too busy and multifaceted to think of becoming a country star.

A classically trained violinist and vocalist, Layman recorded with her husband and Len Stokes as the Frank Luther Trio beginning in 1932, turning out an impressive number of hits. Composer BOB MILLER concocted a spunky answer to their hit "Seven Years with the Wrong Woman" for Zora to perform solo. Recorded in 1933, "Seven Years with the Wrong Man" delivered the woman's viewpoint in vivid terms, describing a bad marriage as "like living in hell" and advising women that they may "find more real friendship in owning a dog."

When Zora first delivered her plaintively sincere rendition of "Seven Years" on ETHEL PARK RICHARDSON's NBC series *Hillbilly Heart-Throbs,* switchboards were swamped with enthusiastic response, and the tall, quiet contralto had a major hit. Subsequent Layman recordings included "Answer to Twenty-one Years," "Hooray, I'm Single Again," and the moving "Cowboy's Best Friend," written by Frank Luther for Zora to sing on horseback at the rodeo in Madison Square Garden.
—*Jonathan Guyot Smith*

Kostas Lazarides (see Kostas)

Leake County Revelers
Will Gilmer b. Leake County, Mississippi, February 27, 1897; d. 1960
Oscar Mosley b. Mississippi, 1885; d. 1930s
Jim Wolverton b. Mississippi, April 19, 1895; d. December 1969
Dallas Jones b. December 17, 1889; d. January 1985

One of the best-selling country records of the 1920s was "Wednesday Night Waltz," a 1927 COLUMBIA release by the Leake County Revelers, a band from Sebastopol, Mississippi. Unlike the fast-paced Georgia stringbands, the Revelers preferred slower tempos and intricate waltzes of the rural nineteenth-century South. Powered by the smooth, flowing fiddle style of Will Gilmer, the band was discovered in 1926 by famed talent scout H. C. Spier and released some twenty-two records before their breakup in the early 1930s. Other favorites included "Monkey in a Dog Cart" and "Crow Black Chicken," with Oscar Mosley playing mandolin, Jim Wolverton on banjo, and Dallas Jones on guitar.
—*Charles Wolfe*

REPRESENTATIVE RECORDING

The Leake County Revelers (County, 1975)

Chris LeDoux

b. Biloxi, Mississippi, October 2, 1948

Chris LeDoux, the Singing Bronc Rider, was born in Mississippi, and learned about horses and riding on his grandfather's farm in Michigan. Eventually his family moved to Texas. He developed an interest in music as well as rodeo, and he participated in saddle bronc and bull riding, later specializing in bareback-bronc riding. In 1976 he was World Champion Bareback Bronc Rider. LeDoux established his own recording company, Lucky Man Music, in Mount Juliet, Tennessee, just outside Nashville, and spent almost twenty years recording and marketing his own records to fans in the rodeo and cowboy subculture. He released more than a score of these albums between 1973 and 1991, such as *Wild and Wooly, Rodeo Songs,* and *Old Cowboy Heroes,* when his career received a major boost. GARTH BROOKS, in the song "Much Too Young to Feel This Damned Old" from his 1989 debut album, referred to listening to "a worn-out tape of Chris LeDoux." This attracted the attention of CAPITOL RECORDS, where LeDoux was signed to a major contract. Capitol reissued almost all of LeDoux's Lucky Man catalogue on CD, and took him into the studio in 1991 to record *Western Underground,* his first album for the label.

On his second Capitol album, *Watcha Gonna Do With a Cowboy,* he is joined by his benefactor Garth Brooks for a duet of the title cut that produced a hit single. LeDoux is a prolific songwriter, and his repertoire ranges from old-time traditional cowboy songs to his own songs about rodeo life to contemporary cowboy and western songs by other writers. While most of LeDoux's material is performed in typical country style with his Saddle Boogie Band, his songs are an authentic window on the life of the modern-day rodeo cowboy. —*Charlie Seemann*

REPRESENTATIVE RECORDINGS

Rodeo Songs, Old and New (Liberty, 1973); *Best of Chris LeDoux* (Liberty, 1994)

Albert Lee

b. Herefordshire, England, December 21, 1943

The propulsive drive whipping through many country lead guitar solos of the 1980s and 1990s echoes the high-velocity sounds Albert Lee pioneered in EMMYLOU HARRIS's Hot Band in the mid-seventies. "Everyone rips Albert off," VINCE GILL observed in an article in *Country Guitar* magazine, "but nobody sounds like him. His phrasing is totally unique."

Lee's penchant for American country music was nurtured by the skiffle sounds of Lonnie Donegan and the first wave of rock & roll to wash ashore in England. His first guitar came in 1958, and he promptly learned all Cliff Gallup's solos note for note from Gene Vincent's records.

Lee first distinguished himself in the London-based r&b band Chris Farlowe & the Thunderbirds (1964–67). By 1968 he was backing visiting country stars (CONNIE SMITH, BOBBY BARE) in a band called Country Fever. In 1969 he began working with a group that evolved into Head, Hands & Feet. The band's self-titled 1971 Island label debut album featured the first appearance of Lee's theme song, "Country Boy" (1985 #1 *Billboard* hit for RICKY SKAGGS).

Following a 1973 tour with the Crickets, Lee moved to Los Angeles in 1974. He became known in the Los Angeles country-rock fraternity, first working with Don Everly and later replacing JAMES BURTON in Emmylou Harris's Hot Band in 1976. His initial stint on tour and in the studio with Harris (1976–78) yielded guitar-playing of breathtaking speed and discrimination on her *Luxury Liner, Quarter Moon in a Ten Cent Town,* and *Blue Kentucky Girl* albums. "My style came together when I played with Emmylou," Lee told *Country Guitar*'s Askold Buk. "I think I put an English rock edge to the country idiom."

Lee has also toured and done studio work with (among others) Eric Clapton and the EVERLY BROTHERS, for whom Lee has acted as musical director since 1983. Harris, who has called Lee's playing "hard and metallic but clear and lyrical," enlisted him again into her Hot Band for its 1995 twentieth anniversary tour. —*Mark Humphrey*

Brenda Lee

b. Atlanta, Georgia, December 11, 1944

Brenda Lee has proved to be one of the most versatile singers ever to record in Nashville, and her commercial success (as measured by cumulative record sales) is probably second only to ELVIS PRESLEY among artists who have recorded heavily in Nashville. A professional singer by age six and a recording artist by twelve, she has fashioned a career of uncommon durability that spans more than forty years. In so doing, she has transcended the musical boundaries of pop and country music to earn the awards and respect of fans and peers worldwide.

Born Brenda Mae Tarpley in Atlanta's Emory University Hospital, she grew up in the Atlanta area. Her musical talent blossomed early, as by age three she was able to sing songs after hearing them but twice. When she was five, her

Brenda Lee

older sister entered her in a school talent contest, where she won first prize for belting out "Take Me Out to the Ball Game." Amazed at the big sound coming from such a little girl, this performance led to regular stints on local radio and television shows.

When Lee was nine, her father died following an accident at a construction site where he was working. After her mother remarried, the family relocated first to Cincinnati and then to Augusta, Georgia. Soon Lee was a star on local television. During this time the show's producer decided the name Tarpley was too hard to remember, so he shortened it and christened her Brenda Lee.

With the help of a local DJ, Lee was introduced to RED FOLEY during February 1956. Foley was so impressed with Lee's talent that shortly thereafter, the family moved to Springfield, Missouri, so Lee could become a regular performer on Foley's OZARK JUBILEE TV show. This led to appearances on network TV shows hosted by Perry Como, Ed Sullivan, and Steve Allen. Dub Albritten, Foley's manager, became Lee's personal manager in 1956 and remained in that position throughout her formative years.

In May 1956, Lee signed with DECCA RECORDS and two months later had her first recording session, supervised by PAUL COHEN with the assistance of OWEN BRADLEY. It was her third single, the foot-stomping, hand-clapping "One Step at a Time," produced in New York by Milt Gabler, that became her first chart record (#15 country, #43 pop, 1957). This marked her only appearance on the country charts for the next eleven years.

Owen Bradley took over as Lee's sole producer in 1958 and produced all of her Nashville sessions through 1968. Except for the rock & roll number "Dynamite" (which gave her the enduring nickname Little Miss Dynamite), chart hits eluded her for the next couple of years. However, in the interim, Albritten discovered that her records were selling in Europe and took the opportunity to tour France in February 1959. This was the beginning of international stardom for Lee. Not only was her tour successful, but also the following years would find her performing in South America, Australia, Japan, and all through Europe. During the 1960s she recorded her hits in several European languages.

Lee started hitting the pop charts with regularity in 1959 with the release of the rocking "Sweet Nothin's" (#4 pop). Owen Bradley changed her course for her follow-up hit and recorded the heartache ballad "I'm Sorry" (#1 pop). The recording's introduction of strings to Nashville sessions not only bridged the gap between country and pop music but also became one of the hallmarks of Lee's sound through the 1960s.

Lee soon became one of the best-selling female singers of the sixties. She could rock with the best of them, but as her voice matured she concentrated on singing heartfelt standards and original ballads. Between 1960 and 1973 she had fifty singles on the pop charts, including "I Want to Be Wanted" (#1, 1960), "Fool #1" (#3, 1961), "Break It to Me Gently" (#4, 1962), "All Alone Am I" (#3, 1962), "Too Many Rivers" (#13, 1965), "Coming on Strong" (#11, 1966), and the Christmas classic "Rockin' Around the Christmas Tree" (#14, 1960).

During the 1970s Lee began experiencing health problems. Along with damaged vocal chords, she had several serious abdominal operations, requiring her to take time off from touring. Even so, Lee had four country chart hits between 1969 and 1972. After teaming up again with Owen Bradley, she broke into the country Top Ten in early 1973

with "Nobody Wins" (#5). She continued with a string of country hits for the next twelve years with "Big Four Poster Bed" (#4 1974), "He's My Rock" (#8, 1975), and "Broken Trust" (#9, 1980).

In the 1980s Lee served as a television host for WILLIE NELSON's Farm Aid benefit concert and as guest host on TNN's prime-time talk show NASHVILLE NOW. She starred in musical theater for three seasons at OPRYLAND USA and served on the board of directors for the CMA. In addition, she recorded for WARNER BROS. RECORDS in the early 1990s and has continued to maintain a regular touring schedule. Truly a legend in her time, Brenda Lee was inducted into the COUNTRY MUSIC HALL OF FAME in 1997.   —*Don Roy*

REPRESENTATIVE RECORDINGS

Anthology 1956–1980 (MCA, 1991), 2 discs; *Little Miss Dynamite* (Bear Family, 1995), 4 discs

Buddy Lee

b. Brooklyn, New York, October 7, 1932; d. February 13, 1998

Buddy "Buddy Lee" Lioce rose from humble beginnings to become the head of one of the most successful booking agencies in country music history: Buddy Lee Attractions. Since opening its doors in Nashville in 1964, the agency has booked such artists as EMMYLOU HARRIS, MARK CHESNUTT, TRISHA YEARWOOD, GARTH BROOKS, WILLIE NELSON, MARTINA MCBRIDE, TRACY LAWRENCE, and WAYLON JENNINGS.

Growing up in an Italian neighborhood in New York, Lee worked in a restaurant and even tended bar at the tender, and illegal, age of fourteen. He became interested in wrestling and at age eighteen, weighing 230 pounds, trained for the sport. As Lee told a reporter, his wrestling career added up to "fourteen years of education, learning the geography I couldn't grasp while in high school classrooms. I learned how to advertise and promote an event by listening and watching various wrestling promoters, so I owe the success I have today to my wrestling experience."

In 1955 Lee moved to Columbia, South Carolina, where for the next eight years he promoted and booked such acts as Fats Domino, Jackie Wilson, RAY CHARLES, and Little Stevie Wonder. Invited to see a country music show, he was impressed by FARON YOUNG, but not by the meager audience of 800 in a 3,285-seat venue. He began promoting country shows, however, and managed to sell out venues from the Carolinas to Maine. In 1963 he moved to Boston, where he promoted a show by HANK WILLIAMS JR. The following year, Audrey Williams, Hank Williams Jr.'s mother, asked Lee to move to Nashville to represent her son. "It's the best move I ever made," Lee remarked, noting that it led to the start of Aud-Lee Attractions, and, in 1964, Buddy Lee Attractions.

The current president of Buddy Lee Attractions, Tony Conway (b. August 3, 1953), is a former drummer who joined the firm in 1976. He had previously operated his own talent agency in Lexington, Kentucky. Lee served as the firm's CEO until his death in 1998.   —*Gerry Wood*

Dickey Lee

b. Memphis, Tennessee, September 21, 1936

Royden Dickey Lee, known professionally as Dickey Lee, kicked off his recording career in earnest in 1962, when he had his first big pop hit, "Patches," on Smash Records. After that, he had his major chart successes in the 1970s on

RCA RECORDS with ephemeral pop-flavored country hits, many of which were cover versions of songs that had already been hits on the pop charts. "Rocky" (a #1 in 1975), "9,999,999 Tears" (a RAZZY BAILEY composition), and "Never Ending Song of Love" (a Top Ten hit in 1971) are a few of his better-known country hits.

Memphis disc jockey Dewey Phillips discovered Lee, who had released one single, "Stay True Baby," on Tampa Records and introduced the young Memphian to SAM PHILLIPS and his local SUN RECORDS label. In 1957 Lee recorded for Sun and forged a friendship with engineer-producer-songwriter JACK CLEMENT, with whom he would often work in coming years. Lee and his friend ALLEN REYNOLDS followed Clement to Beaumont, Texas, where they became part of a recording studio crew that also included BOB MCDILL. After a solid run through most of the 1970s with RCA, Lee signed with MERCURY in 1979. But his several years on that label produced no hits.

Lee's greatest claim to fame may be as the writer of "She Thinks I Still Care," which has become a country classic. GEORGE JONES had a #1 hit with the song in 1962, and ANNE MURRAY took it to the top of the charts again in 1974 as "He Thinks I Still Care." —*Bob Allen*

Johnny Lee
b. Texas City, Texas, July 3, 1946

Johnny Lee rose to fame in 1980 with the success of the movie URBAN COWBOY. Reared on a dairy farm south of Houston and schooled in sixties rock bands, John Lee Hamm didn't have to travel far to join the house band at GILLEY's nightclub in the late seventies. The connection with singer–club owner MICKEY GILLEY swept Lee into a deal to package the soundtrack for *Urban Cowboy*. Though Lee had had a few chart records between 1975 and 1978, the movie shifted his career into high gear. Overnight the strapping, bearded singer became a star, launched by the movie's theme song, "Looking for Love," a #1 country hit and a #5 pop hit.

In the wake of that success, Lee toured incessantly as Gilley's opening act and scored a string of #1 and Top Ten hits through 1985, including "One in a Million"; "Pickin' Up Strangers"; "Prisoner of Hope"; "Bet Your Heart on Me"; "Cherokee Fiddle"; "Hey Bartender"; and a duet with Lane Brody, "The Yellow Rose."

Lee entered a widely publicized Hollywood marriage to Charlene Tilton, a petit blond actress who starred on TV's popular series *Dallas*. They married in 1982, and the tabloids had a field day with them for the next few years. They divorced in 1984, when Lee had his last #1 single, "You Could've Heard a Heart Break." His last chart hits came in 1989. —*Bob Millard*

REPRESENTATIVE RECORDING
Greatest Hits (Warner Bros., 1983)

Kyle Lehning
b. Cairo, Illinois, April 18, 1949

If he had done nothing else but produce the albums of RANDY TRAVIS, Kyle Lehning would merit a special place in country history. But he has been a guiding force in the studio for several best-selling acts.

After earning a B.A. in music at Milikin University in Decatur, Illinois, Lehning moved to Nashville in 1971, aspiring to be a session keyboard player. He gained his initial experience in sound engineering at the GLASER BROTHERS studio in Nashville. By 1975 he had worked on records for WAYLON JENNINGS, WILLIE NELSON, KENNY ROGERS, and SHEL SILVERSTEIN. In 1976 Lehning began producing the pop duo England Dan & John Ford Coley. Lehning's first single with them, "I'd Really Love to See You Tonight," sold more than 1 million copies, and he continued to produce the successful duo through 1979. Afterward half of the group, DAN SEALS, kept working with Lehning as producer. Together they racked up twenty-four country chart hits between 1983 and 1992.

Lehning began working with hard-country singer Randy Travis in 1985 for a series of singles that developed into Travis's first WARNER BROS. album, *Storms of Life*. That multimillion-selling album signaled a strong return for the hard-country sound in the late 1980s, and its commercial and artistic success led to a long and prosperous association between Lehning and Travis that continued through his Warner Bros. releases. Meanwhile, Lehning continued to produce other country artists, including RONNIE MILSAP, ANNE MURRAY, and GEORGE JONES.

In February 1992 Lehning became executive vice president and general manager of the Nashville branch of ASYLUM RECORDS; among the Asylum artists he has produced are MANDY BARNETT and BRYAN WHITE. In 1996 Lehning was joined at the helm of Asylum by marketing specialist Joe Mansfield, who was given the role of co-president/CEO. Lehning and Mansfield left Asylum in 1998.

Lehning is co-owner (with Tony Gottlieb) of Morningstar Recording Studio in Hendersonville, Tennessee. —*Paul Kingsbury*

Iry Lejeune
b. Point Noir, Church Point, Louisiana, October 28, 1928;
d. October 8, 1954

Ira "Iry" Lejeune is considered one of the finest traditional Cajun accordionists and singers and is known for his exceptional accordion playing and searing, heartfelt vocals. He grew up in a remote farming region that was an enclave of old-time Cajun music, and learned to play from his uncle Angelais Lejeune, also a popular musician who recorded for BRUNSWICK in 1929. Iry was also influenced by Amadie Ardoin and Amidie Breaux.

Iry was almost completely blind, and music seemed the only viable career choice for him. He made his first recordings for the Opera label in Houston in 1948, releasing *Love Bridge Waltz* and *Evangeline Special*. He later recorded for Folk-Star, but most of his recording was for Goldband. Among the most popular of his classic recordings were *Lacassine Special*, *Convict Waltz*, and *Grande Bosco*.

Lejeune's brief career came to a tragic end in 1954. He was traveling home from a dance with fellow musician J. B. FUSILIER when their car had a blowout. While fixing the flat tire, both men were struck by a passing car, killing Lejeune and seriously injuring Fusilier. —*Charlie Seemann*

Jerry Lee Lewis
b. Ferriday, Louisiana, September 29, 1935

Nicknamed the Killer, pianist and singer Jerry Lee Lewis may be the wildest performer in the history of country music, rock & roll, or any form of American popular music. His greatest gift may be his assimilation of sundry forms

Jerry Lee Lewis

into a unique mixture that respects and scrambles all the elements. Lewis's ferocious early recordings, such as "Whole Lotta Shakin' Going On" and "Great Balls of Fire," routinely became hits on the pop, country, and r&b charts simultaneously, so great was Lewis's reach and his ambition.

Lewis learned piano early in life; his public debut was at a 1949 Ford dealership opening. By 1950 he hosted a show on WNAT-Natchez, the same year that he enrolled in Southwestern Bible Institute in Waxahachie, Texas. Lewis was expelled within the year, in part because he slipped boogie-woogie riffs into hymns.

Just as Lewis refuses to differentiate among different styles of music, so he frequently lets the sacred and the profane elements of his music bump against one another. This mix was not lost on SUN RECORDS head SAM PHILLIPS, who signed Lewis in late 1956. Lewis moved to Memphis (he lived with his cousin J. W. Brown, also his bass player), accompanied CARL PERKINS, and soon cut records of his own. "Whole Lotta Shakin' Going On," recorded in February 1957 and released the following month, made the Killer a star. Lewis's pumping piano, and a frankly sexual arrogance in his singing, appealed to teenagers and led many parents to appeal for the banning of his music. Wild, televised performances on *American Bandstand* and the *Steve Allen Show* brought Lewis's music before millions, many of whom snatched up his next hit, "Great Balls of Fire," which was backed with HANK WILLIAMS's "You Win Again."

On December 12, 1957, ten days after the release of "Great Balls of Fire," Lewis secretly married Myra Gale Brown, the thirteen-year-old daughter of his cousin J. W. Brown. The marriage became public during a 1958 British tour, and the ensuing scandal caused the cancellation of the tour after only three dates. Much of his audience abandoned Lewis, and it would be another decade before he scored another Top Ten hit, pop or country.

Lewis moved from Sun to Smash, a MERCURY subsidiary, in 1963, but his records did not match his Sun peaks. Even

so, his live performances remain historic (*The Greatest Live Show on Earth*, a 1964 album released on Smash, lived up to its title). In 1968 Lewis and his producers chose to focus on hard-edged contemporary country, and with "Another Place, Another Time" (#4, 1968) the hits returned—initially on Smash, and from 1970 forward on Mercury. From 1968 to early 1972 Lewis enjoyed sixteen Top Ten singles, including four #1s, and such memorable performances as "What's Made Milwaukee Famous (Has Made a Loser Out of Me)" (#2, 1968). By mid-1972, however, this hard-country formula had run out of steam, and except for two rock & roll albums (*The Session* and *Southern Roots*, both recorded in 1973) and the 1977 hit single "Middle Age Crazy," the remainder of Lewis's tenure with Mercury was nearly devoid of inspiration.

In late 1978 Lewis signed with ELEKTRA and recorded several spirited records, including an especially strong eponymous set released in 1979. The Elektra singles "Over the Rainbow" (1980) and "Thirty Nine and Holding" (1981) returned Lewis to the country Top Ten. A brief stint with MCA followed, and then a long silence in the studio.

Lewis's life has been as bumpy as his career. Two teenage marriages proved short-lived. His marriage to Myra Gale Brown cost him his rock & roll career, and two more brief marriages, in the 1980s, ended tragically: one in a drowning, the other in a drug overdose. (A sixth marriage has lasted nearly a decade.)

In 1989 Lewis rerecorded his Sun hits for the soundtrack to the biographical film *Great Balls of Fire*, but a British tour to support the album was canceled. Lewis's "It Was the Whiskey Talkin'" was a highlight of the 1990 soundtrack to *Dick Tracy*. In 1995 he signed with Sire Records and recorded *Young Blood Onstage*. He remains unquenched.

—*Jimmy Guterman*

REPRESENTATIVE RECORDINGS

Original Sun Greatest Hits (Rhino, 1984); *Killer: The Mercury Years, Volume 1* (Mercury, 1989); *Rockin' My Life Away* (Warner Bros., 1991)

Laurie Lewis
b. Long Beach, California, September 28, 1950

Fiddler, singer, and songwriter Laurie Lewis has focused her extraordinary musical abilities within the field of bluegrass music. Introduced to the violin by her family at twelve, she heard the DILLARDS in 1965 and became a bluegrass convert. She performed as bass player in the group The Phantom of the Opry in 1973, and as fiddler in the Good Ol' Persons String Band from 1975 to 1977. She then formed the Grant Street String Band, with whom she has continued to perform.

Living in the Bay Area of California, Lewis worked as a side musician for many performers and ran a violin repair shop. Her first album with the Grant Street String Band appeared in 1983, and her first solo album followed in 1986; she recorded albums for Flying Fish in 1989 and 1990. Lewis's fiddle virtuosity and touching vocals brought critical raves and increased attention. KATHY MATTEA recorded her "Love Chooses You."

As a veteran, Lewis's leadership within the community of women bluegrass performers has been subtle and supportive. She participated in the 1988 all-female *Blue Rose* project, and she recorded 1991's *Together* with Kathy Kallick, her partner from the Good Ol' Persons. In addition to securing a stronger place for women in bluegrass, Lewis is among those revitalizing the form. Her 1993 ROUNDER release *True Stories* was an innovative combination of new and old acoustic music. Her smooth melodies and thoughtful songs combined with her premier fiddling to give new freedom to bluegrass, and Lewis was recognized in 1992 and 1994 as Female Vocalist of the Year by the International Bluegrass Music Association.

In 1995 Lewis recorded *The Oak and the Laurel* with mandolin player Tom Rozum, a colleague from the Grant Street String Band. —*Mary A. Bufwack*

REPRESENTATIVE RECORDINGS

True Stories (Rounder, 1993); *The Oak and the Laurel* (Rounder, 1995)

Texas Jim Lewis

b. Meigs, Georgia, October 15, 1909; d. January 23, 1990

Raised in a musical family environment, Texas Jim Lewis launched his lifelong and varied entertainment career in 1928 with a Texas medicine show. In 1929, radio work with a musical trio beckoned at WTAW in College Station, Texas. After a stint at KPRC in Houston, Lewis was at WJR in Detroit, by 1933. Here he formed his band of Lone Star Rangers, changed later to Lone Star Cowboys. Lewis's musical trail led to New York City's VILLAGE BARN (1935–37) and to Hollywood (1940s) after vaudeville tours took him coast-to-coast and to England. During his Hollywood tenure, Lewis and his band appeared in several well-known stars' B-western films such as GENE AUTRY's *Carolina Moon* (1940), Johnny Mack Brown's *Badman from Red Butte* (1940), EDDIE DEAN's *My Pal Ringeye* (1947), and Charles Starrett's *Stranger from Ponca City* (1947), among others. Seattle served as Lewis's headquarters from 1950 on. There he hosted a 1950s children's TV show, *Safety Junction,* which ran for seven years.

Lewis's commercial recordings on Vocalion, DECCA, Exclusive, Magnolia, and Coral (1937–52) focused on western and western swing sounds, often with novelty overtones from his "hootin' nanny," a homemade contraption capable of dozens of noises similar to those popularized by the HOOSIER HOT SHOTS. Co-writer of the 1946 JACK GUTHRIE hit "I'm Telling You," Lewis was also the first to record "The Covered Wagon Rolled Right Along" (1940) and "Squaws Along the Yukon" (1944), the latter a hit for HANK THOMPSON (1958). —*Bob Pinson*

The Lewis Family

Roy "Pop" Lewis Sr. b. Pickens, South Carolina, September 22, 1905
Roy "Little Roy" Lewis Jr. b. Lincoln County, Georgia, February 24, 1942
Wallace Lewis b. Lincoln County, Georgia, July 6, 1928
Omega "Miggie" Lewis b. Richmond County, Georgia, May 22, 1926
Polly Lewis Copsey b. Lincoln County, Georgia, January 23, 1937
Janis Lewis Phillips b. Lincoln County, Georgia, February 13, 1939
Travis Lewis b. Greenwood, South Carolina, December 26, 1958
Lewis Phillips b. Washington, Georgia, April 5, 1972

The Lewis Family of tiny Lincolnton, Georgia, has become known as the First Family of Bluegrass Gospel and one of the few groups to headline bluegrass and gospel shows alike. Their performances are characterized by crisp harmonies and a lively, humorous stage show led by Little Roy Lewis, whose comedic talents are surpassed only by his banjo and guitar playing. The act has been truly a family affair, featuring father "Pop" Lewis on bass; sons Little Roy (banjo, guitar) and Wallace (lead guitar); daughters Miggie, Polly (piano), and Janis (bass); Wallace's son Travis and Janis's son Lewis. Staffing the family's retail records table at festivals and traveling with them for the past forty years has been Pauline "Mom" Lewis.

Roy Lewis Sr. and Pauline Lewis started their musical family when they eloped and married on October 25, 1925. The family became serious about performing in the late forties and early fifties, when the act was then known as the Lewis Brothers, featuring Wallace, Little Roy, Talmadge, and Esley. The latter two dropped out eventually (Esley in the 1950s, Talmadge in 1972), and the Lewis daughters gradually joined the act, along with their father.

In about 1951, the family made their first recordings, two 78s on the Sullivan label. Next, they began working with record entrepreneur DON PIERCE, then living in California, and released some 45-rpm records on the Hollywood label. Shortly after Pierce started STARDAY RECORDS' Nashville operation in 1957, he collected the Lewis Family's 45-rpm recordings and released them on a sixteen-song Starday album, *Singing Time Down South.* A long list of Starday albums followed in the sixties, before the group signed with the Christian music label Canaan Records in 1970. After a long relationship with that label, the group moved to the River Song label in the mid-eighties and to Day Wind Records in 1995. The family estimates that their total recording output has been about sixty albums.

In the meantime, in 1954 the Lewis Family had started a weekly television show on WJBF in Augusta, Georgia, a year after the station went on the air. The show—which the family did live every week for the first ten years—continued until 1992, making it one of the longest-running country and gospel shows in television history. At one point the show was syndicated to several stations around the nation.

The Lewis Family Homecoming & Bluegrass Festival has been held annually in their hometown of Lincolnton, Georgia, since 1990. —*Don Rhodes*

REPRESENTATIVE RECORDINGS

16 Greatest Hits (Gusto/Starday, 1977); *In Concert* (Canaan, 1983); *Best of the Lewis Family* (Canaan, 1985)

Liberty Records

established in Los Angeles, 1955

Liberty Records has played an important part in country music through the label's forty-three-year evolution. The label originated in Los Angeles in 1955, founded by Simon "Si" Waronker, a musician contractor for the 20th Century-Fox music department. He soon added Al Bennett as vice president and head of A&R. Though Liberty released several country singles during the early years (KEN CURTIS, 1955, and WILLIE NELSON, 1958), it wasn't until 1959 that songwriter JOE ALLISON was called on to establish a country division.

One of the first artists signed by Allison was WARREN SMITH (1960–64), whose first release, "I Don't Believe I'll Fall in Love Today," reached #5 on the country charts in 1960. Other acts added that same year included BOB WILLS & HIS TEXAS PLAYBOYS (1960–63), Ray Sanders (1960–63), and FLOYD TILLMAN (1960–61). Though the earliest Liberty country records were made in Hollywood, Allison preferred recording in Nashville and would make periodic trips to do so.

By 1962 Liberty had aggressively expanded its country roster. Country disc jockey RALPH EMERY (1961–63) recorded "Hello Fool" (#4, 1961) as an answer song to FARON YOUNG's recording of "Hello Walls." Willie Nelson had his first successful record ("Touch Me," #7) released in 1962, and his first album . . . And Then I Wrote.

Throughout the sixties, a variety of artists passed through Liberty's doors: HANK COCHRAN (1962), Molly Bee (1962–63), Shirley Collie (1961–63), the CARTER SISTERS (1962–64), TEX WILLIAMS (1963–64), and JERRY WALLACE (1967–1970).

By the early seventies, Liberty had been purchased by United Artists Records and its name retired. EMI/Capitol Records purchased the UA catalogue in 1979 and reactivated the Liberty name between 1980 and 1984, primarily as a country label. The roster included KENNY ROGERS, DOTTIE WEST, MICHAEL MARTIN MURPHEY, and DAN SEALS. The most recent incarnation came in January 1992, when JIMMY BOWEN renamed CAPITOL's Nashville division Liberty. Shortly after SCOTT HENDRICKS succeeded Bowen as Liberty's new chief in May 1995, he announced that he had changed Liberty back to Capitol Nashville.   —Don Roy

Billy Liebert
b. Detroit, Michigan, April 18, 1925

Conductor, arranger, composer, and performing musician William E. Liebert was playing the accordion in bands appearing in the Greater Detroit area at age fourteen. At sixteen he was teaching the accordion. TEXAS JIM LEWIS, who had a long and colorful career in western music, took Liebert under his wing in early 1942, covering the eastern and midwestern states on a "four a day" theater tour. In late 1942 Liebert continued his association with the newly expanded Texas Jim Lewis western swing band, appearing at BERT "FOREMAN" PHILLIPS's numerous ballrooms in and around Los Angeles.

Shortly after his discharge from the navy in 1946, Liebert's first recording session was with TEX RITTER. Over the next thirty-five years he provided accordion and piano backing, as well as arrangements and musical direction for a great number of recording artists—JOHNNY CASH, MERLE HAGGARD, TENNESSEE ERNIE FORD, MERLE TRAVIS, Kay Starr, Mel Tormé, the SONS OF THE PIONEERS, and ROY ROGERS, to name but a few. Other credits earned include acting as a musical director and arranger for CBS radio and TV from 1954 to 1969, and as a musical director and performer on CLIFFIE STONE's HOMETOWN JAMBOREE. In 1966 and again in 1967 the ACM honored Liebert with their Best Country Piano Player Award. He was a member of the SONS OF THE PIONEERS from 1973 to 1981. In 1972 Liebert composed, arranged, and conducted the John Wayne album America, Why I Love Her, which won the Freedom Foundation's George Washington Award.   —Ken Griffis

Light Crust Doughboys

Although they may not have started western swing, the Light Crust Doughboys certainly advanced it and became one of its most important exponents. Their list of alumni

reads like a who's who of the genre, and the band has continued well into the 1990s, some sixty years after its inception.

The act originated in late 1930, when Burrus Mill & Elevator Company of Fort Worth, Texas, began sponsoring a stringband to promote its Light Crust Flour on radio. Comprising MILTON BROWN, BOB WILLS, Derwood Brown, and Herman Arnspiger, the Light Crust Doughboys' popularity soared when mill general manager W. LEE O'DANIEL moved them from tiny KFJZ to 50,000-watt WBAP and took over the band's announcing. The original band recorded as the Fort Worth Doughboys for VICTOR in 1932, but the Brown brothers left later that year, and Wills in 1933. Undaunted, O'Daniel secured a recording contract with Vocalion, hired such key replacements as vocalist LEON HUFF and fiddlers Clifford Gross and Kenneth Pitts, and wrote standards for the band such as "Beautiful Texas," a huge hit in 1934, as was Huff's rendering of "My Mary."

Although O'Daniel was fired in 1935, late that year the Doughboys received a shot in the arm when jazz-minded guitarist-vocalist DICK REINHART, bassist Bert Dodson, and tenor banjoist Marvin Montgomery came over from Dallas's Wanderers. Also arriving was pioneering electric guitarist Zeke Campbell. The Doughboys appeared in two films with GENE AUTRY in 1936, then hit a deep musical groove with the addition of jazz pianist Knocky Parker in 1937. Over the next few years, under announcer Parker Willson, the group produced some of the most sophisticated and forward-looking western swing of the era, classics such as "Gin Mill Blues" and Montgomery's notorious "Pussy, Pussy, Pussy" (1938). Important members in the late thirties included fiddlers Buck Buchanan and CECIL BROWER and vocalist-guitarist JIM BOYD. The Doughboys broke up with World War II's arrival, but they regrouped in 1946 and recorded for KING. Only Marvin (soon "Smokey") Montgomery, who would become the band's leader in 1948, remained from the prewar group, but the level of musicianship remained high. The Doughboys served pseudonymously as a house band for the BIG D JAMBOREE throughout the fifties and have continued in various incarnations to the present, though their official association with Burrus Mill has ended.   —Kevin Coffey

REPRESENTATIVE RECORDINGS

The Light Crust Doughboys, 1936–39 (Texas Rose, 1982); The Light Crust Doughboys: 1936 Western Swing Live (Jambalaya, 1990); Light Crust Doughboys: Yesterday and Today (Doughboy, 1994)

The Lilly Brothers
Mitchell Burt Lilly b. Clear Creek, West Virginia, December 15, 1921
Charles Everett Lilly b. Clear Creek, West Virginia, July 1, 1924

The Lilly Brothers are widely credited—together with Don Stover and Tex Logan—with introducing bluegrass music to New England. Natives of the West Virginia mountains, Everett and Burt (or B.) Lilly grew up performing in the harmony duet style with mandolin and guitar accompaniment. From 1940 onward, they plied their trade on local radio stations and in 1945 went to WNOX-Knoxville, with Lynn Davis and MOLLY O'DAY. In 1948 they worked on the WWVA JAMBOREE in Wheeling with Red Belcher and cut their first recordings on the tiny Page label. Then Everett spent a year and a half as sideman with FLATT & SCRUGGS.

In 1952 the brothers, along with Stover on banjo and Logan on fiddle, went to Boston, where they first worked on WCOP's *Hayloft Jamboree.*

The Lilly Brothers and Stover also made almost nightly appearances at a nightclub called Hillbilly Ranch, where they attained a following from the intellectual crowd as well as homesick country folk. The brothers initially recorded for Event and then for Folkways, Prestige, County, and the Japanese label Towa. They also introduced bluegrass at college concerts and folk festivals, helping its spread in the Northeast. In 1970 Everett lost a son in an automobile wreck and returned to West Virginia. Thereafter, the brothers played only a few concerts yearly. By the nineties, even these had dwindled to one or two a year.

—*Ivan M. Tribe*

REPRESENTATIVE RECORDINGS

Early Recordings (County LP/Rebel CD, 1970); *Bluegrass Breakdown* (Prestige and Rounder, 1964)

Line Dancing

Line dancing is a dance form in which rows of western-garbed dancers kick, stomp, bend, shuffle, dip, turn, strut, and swivel their way through choreographed routines. Similar to many folk and ethnic traditional dances, country line dancing has existed for decades as a style of dance requiring no partner. Fueled by the popularity of disco, and John Travolta's performances in *Saturday Night Fever* and *Urban Cowboy,* line dancing began coming into its own in the 1980s, riding the wave of a surge in country music's popularity. In 1992 Melanie Greenwood choreographed a music video for BILLY RAY CYRUS's recording "Achy Breaky Heart," and Americans caught line dance fever.

By 1993, nightspots across the United States had transformed themselves into country dance clubs where line dancing proliferated. Also quick to spring up were cable television shows, contests, workshops, trade and popular magazines, and instructional videos devoted to line dancing, which was even adopted by exercise instructors as a beneficial aerobics workout. According to country dance guru Christy Lane, line dancing combined "opportunities for individualization with the camaraderie of the community dance hall."

Line dances are choreographed with repeated sequences of patterned foot and body movements. Schottische, polka, and cha-cha-cha comprise some of the basic steps of standard and regional versions of line dances such as "Tush Push," "Slappin' Leather," "Cowboy Hustle," "Cowboy Boogie," "Electric Slide," "Tennessee Stroll," "Cowboy Hip Hop," "Elvira," and "Alley Cat." In some cases, single songs such as Cyrus's "Achy Breaky Heart" and "Boot Scootin' Boogie" by BROOKS & DUNN have inspired line dances of their own. Declared dance historian Fred Rapport, "It would be the line dances, that are designed specifically for hit country songs, that would solidify the popularity of country dance." —*Patricia Hall*

Big Bill Lister

b. Karnes County, Texas, January 5, 1923

Weldon E. Lister was a journeyman country performer who never had the one hit that might have earned him some ongoing attention. His latter-day recognition revolves around his role in the HANK WILLIAMS SR.–HANK WILLIAMS JR. duet on "There's a Tear in My Beer."

Lister grew up in the hill country around Brady, Texas, idolizing JIMMIE RODGERS. Lister began performing in 1938 and became a staple of San Antonio area radio for almost a decade. In 1950 he went to Nashville and got a contract with CAPITOL RECORDS and a place on Hank Williams's shows starting in February 1951. In early 1952 Lister returned to San Antonio, worked the *BIG D JAMBOREE* in Dallas for several years, then retired from the music business in the mid-1950s.

Williams wrote two songs for Lister; one of them was "There's a Tear in My Beer." Lister held on to the acetate demo, and, after his retirement, rediscovered it. He notified Hank Jr.'s management and in July 1988 gave the acetate to Jr. That September, Hank Jr. overdubbed himself onto the recording and released it with an accompanying video that featured father and son. Hank Jr. freely acknowledged Lister's role in the song's revival and introduced him on TNN's *NASHVILLE NOW* in August 1989.

—*Colin Escott*

Little Darlin' Records

established in New York, New York, 1966

During its brief existence, Little Darlin' Records produced some of the most exciting, distinctive country records of its era. The label's primary artist was JOHNNY PAYCHECK, but others affiliated with Little Darlin' included BOBBY HELMS and JEANNIE C. RILEY (pre-"Harper Valley P.T.A."). At a time when the major labels in Nashville were, for the most part, still immersed in the pop-styled NASHVILLE SOUND, the independent Little Darlin' fashioned a hard-country product that favored LLOYD GREEN's dynamic steel guitar over soft strings. As label chief Aubrey Mayhew described it, when a Little Darlin' record was put on the turntable it "would jump right out of the radio at you."

Little Darlin' was the brainchild of Paycheck and Mayhew, his manager-producer. In 1965 Paycheck had recorded for Hilltop, a subsidiary of New York's Pickwick label, for which Mayhew worked. But when Pickwick refused to promote Paycheck, Mayhew quit his job and he and Paycheck started their own label. Little Darlin' was established in New York, apparently in early 1966, but soon moved to Nashville. Paycheck's first Little Darlin' single, "The Lovin' Machine," became his first Top Ten hit.

Paycheck was the only Little Darlin' act to enjoy significant success on the label, and after he and Mayhew had a falling out, Mayhew dissolved the company in about 1969. He revived it briefly in 1979 and issued a few overdubbed items from Paycheck's catalogue, but since then Little Darlin' has been inactive. —*Daniel Cooper*

Little Texas

Del Anthony Gray b. Hamilton, Ohio, May 8, 1968
Porter Carleton Howell b. Longview, Texas, June 21, 1964
Dwayne Keith O'Brien b. Ada, Oklahoma, June 30, 1963
Duane Carlisle Propes b. Longview, Texas, December 17, 1966
Jeffrey Howard Huskins b. Arlington, Texas, April 26, 1966
Timothy Ray Rushlow b. Arlington, Texas, October 6, 1966
Former member: Brady Seals b. Hamilton, Ohio, March 29, 1969

When Little Texas burst on the scene in 1991 with the Top Ten country hit "Some Guys Have All the Love," its pop-rock brand of country music attracted young, formerly

Little Texas (1992): (from left) Porter Howell, Duane Propes, Tim Rushlow, Del Gray, Dwayne O'Brien, and Brady Seals.

noncountry listeners. Influenced by the music of RESTLESS HEART, EXILE, and the EAGLES, the photogenic band members had volumes of long hair, a heavy-metal appearance, and harmonies as tight as their jeans.

Bassist Duane Propes and lead guitarist Porter Howell, high school friends from Longview, Texas, were students at Nashville's Belmont University when they met lead vocalist Tim Rushlow and guitarist Dwayne O'Brien and formed a band. They met drummer Del Gray and keyboardist Brady Seals (a cousin of DAN SEALS and nephew of songwriter Troy Seals) on a fair date in Massachusetts. In 1988 WARNER BROS. RECORDS signed them to a development deal.

Little Texas didn't take the expressway to success, however. In 1988, after their first Warner Bros. recording project failed to produce the signature sound the six members were looking for, the label put them in a van and sent them on an extended cross-country tour so they could find their musical identity. Three years later, the six returned to the studio as a cohesive, self-contained band and recorded *First Time for Everything*, which yielded "Some Guys Have All the Love" and the 1992 Top Five hit "You and Forever and Me."

"What Might Have Been," from their second LP, *Big Time* (1993), established Little Texas as a hit band, as did their subsequent hits "God Blessed Texas" (1993) and "My Love" (1994). Little Texas was named the ACM's Vocal Group of the Year in 1994. Seals left the group in mid-1994 to pursue a solo career and was replaced by Jeff Huskins.

Hits continued with the albums *Kick a Little* and *Greatest Hits,* including "Kick a Little" (#5, 1994), "Amy's Back in Austin" (#4, 1995), and "Life Goes On" (#5, 1995), pushing the groups' cumulative album sales to more than 5 million units. Their self-titled fifth album was released in April 1997, but disappointing sales and chart activity led to the group's decision to dissolve their act. Little Texas performed their final show on December 31, 1997, at Cookeville, Tennessee.   —*Marjie McGraw*

REPRESENTATIVE RECORDINGS

Big Time (Warner Bros., 1993); *Kick a Little* (Warner Bros., 1994)

Hank Locklin
b. McLellan, Florida, February 15, 1918

Lawrence Hankins Locklin was a straightforward tenor singer who enjoyed big hits with songs such as "Send Me the Pillow You Dream On" and "Please Help Me, I'm Falling" in the Nashville Sound era.

Locklin recalled being paid two dollars for one of his first professional gigs in a Florida roadhouse, while his expenses totaled five dollars. He fared better in 1942, with a regular stint on station WCOA in Pensacola. Later he was also a regular on the *BIG D JAMBOREE* on KRLD-Dallas.

Hank Locklin

In 1949 he joined Shreveport's LOUISIANA HAYRIDE. In that year he also scored his first Top Ten single, "The Same Sweet Girl," for FOUR STAR RECORDS. "Let Me Be the One" (1953) became his first #1 country hit. After signing with RCA RECORDS, Locklin had quick success with "Why, Baby, Why" (#9, 1956), a cover of GEORGE JONES's record, followed by a pop-country crossover original, "Geisha Girl" (#4, 1957).

Locklin's self-penned "Send Me the Pillow You Dream On" (#5, 1958) was a substantial country hit and received pop airplay. (Dean Martin and Johnny Tillotson both later recorded his song.) Locklin's 1958 follow-up was "It's a Little More Like Heaven" (#3).

He scored his biggest success via his composition "Please Help Me, I'm Falling" (#1, 1960), which also hit #8 on the pop charts. Locklin joined the GRAND OLE OPRY in 1960. During nineteen years with RCA he cut tribute albums to EDDY ARNOLD, HANK WILLIAMS, and ROY ACUFF. In the 1970s he hosted TV shows in Houston and Dallas and was honorary mayor of McLellan, Florida, where he bought a ranch on property where he had picked cotton as a youth. When not entertaining Opry crowds with still-strong vocals, he can be found at his home in Brewton, Alabama.　　　　　　　　　　　　　　　*—Walt Trott*

REPRESENTATIVE RECORDINGS

Golden Hits of Hank Locklin (Plantation, 1977); *Send Me the Pillow You Dream On* (Camden, 1973); *Please Help Me I'm Falling* (Bear Family, 1995), 4 discs

Larrie Londin

b. Norfolk, Virginia, October 15, 1943; d. August 24, 1992

Drummer Larrie Londin spent the bulk of his career living in Nashville and playing on thousands of sessions and dozens of #1 hits and platinum albums. Through his twenty-three years in Music City, Londin pounded out the beat for top country artists such as CHET ATKINS, JERRY REED, DOLLY PARTON, HANK WILLIAMS JR., MERLE HAGGARD, WAYLON JENNINGS, and many others, as well as pop artists such as B. B. King, Johnny Mathis, LINDA RONSTADT, Journey, and many more.

Londin (born Ralph Gallant) grew up in Miami, Florida, where he had a passion for boxing. As an unofficial bodyguard for a drummer friend of his, Londin soon became interested in drums and, while still a minor, migrated to Detroit with a band called the Headliners. That band was hired by Motown Records to back groups such as the Supremes, the Temptations, and Marvin Gaye in the studio.

At the urging of fellow instrumental virtuoso Chet Atkins, Londin moved to Nashville in 1969, introducing a somewhat unorthodox and impressionable playing style to the normally tranquil country scene. Early country gigs included tours with Jerry Reed and GLEN CAMPBELL.

Londin snagged a house job at the Carousel Club in Printer's Alley and began the studio tenure that earned him the Nashville NARAS chapter's Most Valuable Player Award from 1978 to 1980. He also took to the road with ELVIS PRESLEY (1976–77), the EVERLY BROTHERS, and RODNEY CROWELL and ROSANNE CASH. Londin was no stranger to TV either—he played shows including *The Tonight Show, Ed Sullivan, Dinah Shore,* and *Merv Griffin.* Londin was honored as the ACM Drummer of the Year (1984 and 1986)

and as *Modern Drummer Magazine*'s Country Drummer (1985–86).

While conducting a drum clinic in Texas, in 1992, Larrie Londin collapsed into a diabetic coma, resulting in his death two months later.　　　　　　　　*—Michael Hight*

Lone Pine & Betty Cody

Lone Pine (Harold John Breau) b. Pea Cove, Maine, June 5, 1916; d. Maine, March 26, 1977

Betty Cody (Rita M. Coté Breau) b. Sherbrooke, Québec, Canada, August 17, 1921

Known professionally by the aforementioned names, the husband-wife team of Harold John and Rita M. Coté Breau enjoyed marked success during the 1950s as a duo and individually as well. Reportedly dubbed "Lone Pine" by Penobscot Indian playmates, Breau formed his Lone Pine Mountaineers band in the mid-1930s after winning several amateur contests in Bangor, Maine. By the late 1930s he was performing on Bangor radio station WABI. Almost concurrently, Rita Coté, now living in Auburn, Maine, had begun singing at age fifteen with a local country band on radio station WCOU in nearby Lewiston.

After meeting at a radio studio in 1938 and an ensuing courtship, Harold and Rita were married on June 29, 1940. As Lone Pine and Betty Cody, they became Maine radio stalwarts in the 1940s and achieved even greater success in the Canadian Maritime Provinces via their radio broadcasts on St. John, New Brunswick, station CFBC during the early 1950s. Their popularity led RCA RECORDS in Canada to sign them to record in the fall of 1950. The first recording, a solo by Lone Pine titled "Prince Edward Island Is Heaven to Me," sold well enough to warrant release by RCA in the United States a year later, in December 1951. Betty succeeded with "Tom-Tom Yodel" in early 1952, and they scored as a duet on "Trail of the Lonesome Pine" that spring. With all of their Canadian recordings also selling well in the United States, RCA's studios in New York became the focal points for their recording sessions from July 1952 to September 1954. Their July 1952 rendering of "I Heard the Bluebirds Sing" sold fairly well and preceded the BROWNS' hit by five years.

From their Canadian triumphs in 1950–52, the trail led to the *WWVA JAMBOREE* in Wheeling (1953–54) to Prince Edward Island, Schenectady, and Bangor (1955) and to Winnipeg, Manitoba, in the late 1950s, where their marriage unraveled. Betty and the younger children returned to Maine, while their oldest son, Lenny, remained with his father. Lenny Breau would grow to prominence in jazz guitar circles in the 1970s and 1980s before being murdered on August 12, 1984, in Los Angeles. Lone Pine returned to Maine during the 1960s, where he remained musically active and remarried. By the early 1970s Betty was singing again in Maine on a part-time basis. She remarried in 1979.　　　　　　　　　　　　　　　*—Bob Pinson*

Lone Star Playboys

The Lone Star Playboys were one of the most important western dance bands in Texas for several years after World War II. Best known perhaps as an early backing band for HANK THOMPSON, the Playboys also introduced the dance hall classic "Westphalia Waltz." Based in Waco, the Playboys first formed in 1937, disbanded with the United

States' entry into the war, and did not really hit stride until it re-formed in late 1943. In 1945 fiddler Cotton Collins replaced original member Ed Booker, and played with the band during 1945–48, 1949–50, and 1951–53. Collins brought with him an unnamed German waltz he'd picked up during the war. Christened "Westphalia Waltz," the song became an immediate hit when it became the second release on Herb Rippa's fledgling Dallas label, Bluebonnet Records, in 1947.

Spearheaded by tenor banjoist-leader Vince Incardona (in 1937–39 and 1943–51), the Playboys owned their central Texas circuit over the next few years. In 1947 steel guitarist Lefty Nason, later one of the architects of Hank Thompson's sound, joined. Nason's "Steel Guitar Bounce" (Bluebonnet) from 1949 stands as the highlight of the Playboys' recorded output. Swing legend JOHNNY GIMBLE joined the Playboys on mandolin and fiddle during 1948.

The Playboys' popularity declined (as did western swing's) upon their return from a 1949 West Coast tour with Thompson, but the band remained a popular Waco-area attraction into 1953. After Bluebonnet, the group recorded for Everstate and, under the name of bassist Charlie Adams (1947–51), for Imperial. Adams left the group in 1951 and enjoyed several years of moderate success as a solo, recording for DECCA and COLUMBIA, scoring a minor hit with "Hey Liberace!" in 1953.

Other members over the years included Sammy Incardona, bass (1937–41); Morris Booker, mandolin (1937–41, 1943–53); Hamlet Booker, guitar and vocals (1937–41, 1943–53); Pee Wee Truehitt, bass (1943–47); Billy Walker, guitar and vocals (ca. 1949); and Johnny Manson, fiddle (1949–50).

—Kevin Coffey

REPRESENTATIVE RECORDING

"Banjo Boogie," *Wanderers Swing* (Krazy Kat, 1994)

Lonesome Pine Fiddlers

Ezra Cline b. Baisden, West Virginia, January 13, 1907; d. July 11, 1984

Curly Ray Cline b. Gilbert, West Virginia, January 10, 1923; d. August 19, 1997

Charlie Cline b. Gilbert, West Virginia, June 6, 1931

Paul Williams b. Wytheville, Virginia, March 30, 1935

Melvin Ray Goins b. Bramwell, West Virginia, December 30, 1933

Ray Elwood Goins b. Bramwell, West Virginia, January 3, 1936

The Lonesome Pine Fiddlers are considered to be one of the classic bands from the early days of bluegrass. Headquartered for many years in West Virginia, the Fiddlers essentially comprised the Cline family band, with Ezra Cline on bass and nephews Curly Ray Cline and Charlie Cline on fiddle and banjo, respectively. The outfit was bolstered at times by banjoists Larry Richardson and Ray Goins, mandolin players BOBBY OSBORNE and Paul Williams, and guitarist and vocalist Melvin Goins. The group made their best recordings in the early 1950s for RCA VICTOR; these included "Dirty Dishes Blues" and "Brown Eyed Darling." They later recorded for STARDAY in the 1960s.

—Gary B. Reid

REPRESENTATIVE RECORDINGS

The Lonesome Pine Fiddlers (Starday, ca. 1961); *Windy Mountain* (Bear Family, 1992)

Lonestar

Dean Sams b. Garland, Texas, August 3, 1966

John Rich b. Amarillo, Texas, January 7, 1974

Richie McDonald b. Lubbock, Texas, February 6, 1962

Michael Britt b. Fort Worth, Texas, June 15, 1966

Keech Rainwater b. Plano, Texas, January 24, 1963

Lonestar had its origins in 1992, when keyboardist Dean Sams and vocalist Richie McDonald met at an audition in Dallas for the OPRYLAND theme park in Nashville. After moving to Nashville, the two invited vocalist John Rich and guitarist Michael Britt to join their band, and later added drummer Keech Rainwater at Britt's recommendation. (Britt and Rainwater had previously worked together in a 1980s country group, Canyon.)

With all members boasting Texas origins, Lonestar's music naturally bears hints of traditional country and dance-hall swing. But the band also incorporates folk-rock and easygoing ballads into its overall sound. The band's reputation has been built on its greatest strengths: solid group harmonies, danceable uptempo tunes, and expressive lyrics. *Lonestar,* their debut album for BNA Records in 1995, featured four original compositions by various members of the band. The album produced a hit single, "Tequila Talkin'," which reached the #4 slot on the country charts. The follow-up, "No News," became the band's most popular song, staying #1 for three consecutive weeks in 1996. "No News," along with the additional singles "Runnin' Away With My Heart," which entered the Top Ten, and "Heartbroke Every Day," vaulted the *Lonestar* album to gold status nearly a year after its release. In 1996 Lonestar won its first major award: the ACADEMY OF COUNTRY MUSIC's 1995 Best New Vocal Group or Duo. A second album for BNA, *Crazy Nights,* was released in June 1997.

—Bob Paxman

REPRESENTATIVE RECORDING

Lonestar (BNA, 1995)

Hubert Long

b. Poteet, Texas, December 3, 1923; d. September 7, 1972

Hubert Long was one of the most influential country music executives of his day. As a leader in the industry, and through his roles as talent promoter and music publisher, he helped to spread country music worldwide.

Long grew up in Freer, Texas, and later relocated to Corpus Christi, where he worked in the record department of a dime store. After boosting record sales, he moved on to San Antonio to work for DECCA RECORDS. When his Decca boss went to RCA VICTOR RECORDS, Long followed. While with RCA he met COLONEL TOM PARKER, who hired him to do publicity work for EDDY ARNOLD.

In the early 1950s Long staked out the *LOUISIANA HAYRIDE* and signed WEBB PIERCE and FARON YOUNG to management contracts. In 1952 he established the Hubert Long Agency to expand his talent bookings. And in 1955 Long set up one of Nashville's first independent talent agencies, Stable of Stars. Throughout the following years he became involved in all aspects of the industry, including advertising, music publishing, and real estate, while still continuing in artist management and booking.

Long was a founding board member of both the CMA

and the CMF. He received the country music industry's highest honor when he was elected posthumously to the COUNTRY MUSIC HALL OF FAME in 1979. —*Don Roy*

Lonzo & Oscar

Rollin Sullivan (Oscar) b. Edmonton, Kentucky, January 19, 1919

Lloyd Leslie George, a.k.a. Ken Marvin (Lonzo #1) b. Haleyville, Alabama, June 27, 1924; d. October 16, 1991

John Y. Sullivan (Lonzo #2) b. Edmonton, Kentucky, July 7, 1917; d. June 5, 1967

Dave Hooten (Lonzo #3) b. St. Claire, Missouri, February 4, 1935

The musical comedy duo of Lonzo & Oscar was for many years a fixture at the GRAND OLE OPRY. Over the act's history of almost fifty years, three different men in succession played the role of Lonzo, while Rollin Sullivan held down the role of Oscar.

The act's beginnings can be traced to the late 1930s, when Kentucky-born brothers Johnny and Rollin Sullivan toured as a duo and made their professional radio debut on WTJS in Jackson, Tennessee. In 1942 Rollin Sullivan joined PAUL HOWARD's Arkansas Cotton Pickers at WSM's GRAND OLE OPRY, playing electric mandolin. With World War II under way, John Sullivan went into the service.

In 1945 the Sullivan brothers and Lloyd George all worked as sidemen for EDDY ARNOLD at WSM and on record for the next two years. While with Arnold, Lloyd George and Rollin Sullivan provided comic relief with an act they called Cicero & Oscar. It was Arnold who changed George's moniker to Lonzo.

In late 1947 Lonzo & Oscar left Arnold to become a Grand Ole Opry act in their own right. The following year they scored their biggest hit with "I'm My Own Grandpa" for RCA VICTOR. In 1950, when Lloyd George left for a solo

Lonzo & Oscar: Ken "Lonzo" Marvin (left) and Rollin "Oscar" Sullivan

career under the name Ken Marvin, John Sullivan rejoined his brother, continuing the Lonzo & Oscar tradition of satirizing songs. The pair often performed with Cousin Jody (Clell Summey), a toothless hayseed alumnus of the PEE WEE KING and ROY ACUFF troupes. For the next seventeen years, the act held forth at the Opry with such bizarre originals as "If Texas Knew What Arkansaw," "Did You Have to Bring That Up (While I Was Eatin')," and "There's a Hole in the Bottom of the Sea." In 1961 the duo hit the charts again with their STARDAY recording "Country Music Time."

Following his brother John's death in 1967, Rollin Sullivan engaged another Lonzo, Dave Hooten, who stayed until the team left the Opry and retired in 1985. The act's last chart hit was with the noncomedic "Traces of Life" for the GRC label in 1974. Through the 1990s Rollin "Oscar" Sullivan still performed the occasional benefit. —*Walt Trott*

REPRESENTATIVE RECORDINGS

Traces of Life (GRC, 1975); *Lonzo & Oscar, Old & New Songs* (Brylen, 1982)

Bobby Lord

b. Sanford, Florida, January 6, 1934

Singer Bobby Lord's career began on television, and he continued to use the media effectively throughout the fifties and sixties. At age nineteen, while a freshman at the University of Tampa, he was offered his own local television program on WSUN, the *Bobby Lord Homefolks Show*. In 1955, following appearances on several network programs, he joined ABC-TV's OZARK JUBILEE, where he spent five years as a regular cast member and occasional fill-in MC for host RED FOLEY. In 1960, when the *Jubilee* ended, Lord moved to the GRAND OLE OPRY and stayed with the Nashville show until 1969. In 1963 he began his own country music TV program, *The Bobby Lord Show*, produced by WSM-TV and syndicated by 1965.

"Without Your Love," a 1956 COLUMBIA release, marked his chart debut. During the next fifteen years he charted an additional ten times, on either HICKORY or MERCURY. Lord now lives in Stuart, Florida, where he owns an insurance agency. —*William P. Davis*

John D. Loudermilk

b. Durham, North Carolina, March 31, 1934

Though he started his career as an entertainer on Durham, North Carolina, radio and television stations, John D. Loudermilk achieved his greatest fame as one of Nashville's most successful songwriters, supplying numerous hits to country and pop artists. Loudermilk's compositions have repeatedly found favor with the public, beginning with GEORGE HAMILTON IV's "A Rose and a Baby Ruth" in 1956 and continuing through NEAL MCCOY's 1996 country cover of "Then You Can Tell Me Goodbye" (a Top Ten pop hit in 1967 for the Casinos and a #1 country hit for EDDY ARNOLD in 1968).

Loudermilk's father was a carpenter, and country stars CHARLIE AND IRA LOUVIN (real name: Loudermilk) were his cousins. Loudermilk received his musical training in a Salvation Army Band, where he learned to play trumpet, flugel horn, saxophone, trombone, and bass drum. By age thirteen he had a daily, half-hour radio show on Durham's WTIK as Johnny Dee, and later, while working as an art di-

John D. Loudermilk

rector at Durham's first television station (WTVD), he played stand-up bass on the live *Noon Show*. During this time Loudermilk wrote "A Rose and a Baby Ruth," and the song first charted for Hamilton in late 1956. Loudermilk, as Johnny Dee, hit the pop charts himself early the following year with another original, "Sittin' in the Balcony." A week later, however, EDDIE COCHRAN's recording of the same song became the rock & roller's first pop hit, climbing to #18, while Loudermilk's stalled at #38.

STONEWALL JACKSON scored his first #1 country hit (and a # 4 pop hit) in 1959 with Loudermilk's "Waterloo" (co-written with MARIJOHN WILKIN), which featured a bass drum beat inspired by Loudermilk's Salvation Army Band years.

Signed to ACUFF-ROSE PUBLISHING as a writer after a stint writing for CEDARWOOD, Loudermilk continued to make records, registering modest pop hits in 1961 and 1962 for RCA, and then moved to the label's country division, from 1963 to 1967, where he worked briefly as assistant to CHET ATKINS. Loudermilk's only Grammy came in 1967, for the liner notes to his album *Suburban Attitudes in Country Verse*. In 1971 he recorded for WARNER BROS.

Loudermilk's songwriting success far outstripped his performing career, however. The EVERLY BROTHERS had a #8 pop hit in 1961 with "Ebony Eyes" (#25 country), the same year Sue Thompson went to #5 pop with "Sad Movies (Make Me Cry)," and Bobby Vee went to #33 pop with "Stayin' In."

George Hamilton IV scored again in 1963 with "Abilene," a #15 pop hit and a #1 country hit (to be recycled by SONNY JAMES, in 1977, as a country hit), while ERNIE ASHWORTH had his own country #1 with Loudermilk's "Talk Back Trembling Lips."

Early the following year, Johnny Tillotson's recording of "Talk Back Trembling Lips" climbed to #7 on the pop chart. Later in 1964, the Nashville Teens, a British rock group, found pop success with Loudermilk's dark rocker "Tobacco Road," and JOHNNY CASH landed a country #8 with the writer's "Bad News."

Once the rock era took hold in the mid-1960s, Loudermilk had more success as a country writer, though the Casinos' #6 pop smash "Then You Can Tell Me Goodbye" came in 1967. On the country side that year, Hamilton IV went to #6 with "Break My Mind" (a #13 country charter for VERN GOSDIN in 1978), and GLEN CAMPBELL went to #1 country with "I Wanna Live."

Paul Revere & the Raiders scored their only #1 pop hit—and their last Top Ten—in 1971, with Loudermilk's "Indian Reservation (The Lament of the Cherokee Indian)." Lines from the song would show up later (with Loudermilk's permission) in TIM MCGRAW's 1994 country hit "Indian Outlaw."

Loudermilk was inducted into the Nashville Songwriters Association International's Hall of Fame in 1976.

—*Jay Orr*

Louisiana Hayride
established 1948; ended early 1980s

The *Louisiana Hayride*, a popular and influential live country radio show, was broadcasted first from Shreveport's Municipal Auditorium over the 50,000-watt, clear-channel station KWKH on April 3, 1948. The original cast included Harmie Smith, Hoot & Curley, Pappy Covington, Tex Grimsley, JOHNNIE & JACK with KITTY WELLS, and the BAILES BROTHERS. Horace Logan served as producer and MC.

The *Hayride* was the product of the efforts of several men: KWKH commercial manager Dean Upson, who secured sponsors and recruited talent; Johnnie and Kyle Bailes, who worked as announcer and booking agent, respectively (as well as performing with a third brother, Homer); Logan, who had worked at KWKH before World War II; and station manager Henry Clay, the authority on all matters and especially the show's finances.

Beginning with the first appearance of HANK WILLIAMS in August 1948, the show garnered a reputation as a proving ground for future stars—so much so, in fact, that it acquired the nickname "Cradle of the Stars." Among those who followed Williams to Shreveport (and most of whom followed him from there to Nashville, some of them to the GRAND OLE OPRY) were RED SOVINE, SLIM WHITMAN, the WILBURN BROTHERS, WEBB PIERCE, FARON YOUNG, JOHNNY HORTON, JIM REEVES (who began as an announcer), SONNY JAMES, BILLY WALKER, Jim Ed & Maxine Brown, Claude King, GEORGE JONES, JIMMIE C. NEWMAN, Rusty & DOUG KERSHAW, DAVID HOUSTON, PATSY MONTANA, T. TEXAS TYLER, MERLE KILGORE, and the MADDOX BROTHERS & ROSE. The Maddoxes pointed the way toward rockabilly music, which the *Hayride* played a crucial role in developing, primarily as a result of ELVIS PRESLEY's tenure on the show from October to December 1954.

Following Elvis, such rockabilly luminaries as JOHNNY CASH, BOB LUMAN, and Dale Hawkins, among many others, appeared often on the program.

Though the show was creatively successful, it was never a major financial success for the station nor its parent company, the *Shreveport Times* newspaper (owned by the Ewing family). A regional network was established in 1950, and affiliation with the CBS radio network began in 1953. CBS broadcast the first thirty minutes of the program on every third Saturday through 1957, after which it switched to

The Louisiana Hayride *cast*

every fifth Saturday. CBS dropped the *Hayride* in 1958, however, signaling a steady decline in the show's fortunes. In 1960 Henry Clay decided to discontinue the *Hayride* as a live weekly broadcast. Taped replays and periodic package shows (featuring mostly non-Shreveport–based acts) continued into the early 1970s. Local businessman David Kent attempted to revive a relocated *Hayride* (in neighboring Bossier Parish) in 1973 and renamed the show *Hayride, USA*. Kent's program ended in the early 1980s.

The *Hayride*'s demise can be attributed to several reasons, most notably the competition from television and college football, rising production costs, and the hegemony of rock & roll. Still, the show's legacy is particularly rich and venerable. Besides major stars, the *Hayride* also nurtured offstage talent—music businessmen such as booking agent and recording executive JIM BULLEIT, promoter TILLMAN FRANKS (also a fine songwriter), record producer SHELBY SINGLETON, booking agent and publisher HUBERT LONG, and producer JERRY KENNEDY (who began as a teenage guitarist). Significant instrumentalists among *Hayride* alumni include pianist FLOYD CRAMER, drummer D. J. Fontana, steel guitarists SHOT JACKSON and JIMMY DAY, and guitarists JAMES BURTON, Fred Carter Jr., and Charlie Waller. Announcers Frank Page, Ray Bartlett, Norm Bale, and Jeff Dale, among others, also contributed to the success of the program. —*Stephen R. Tucker*

The Louvin Brothers

Ira Lonnie Loudermilk b. Section, Alabama, April 21, 1924; d. June 20, 1965

Charlie Elzer Loudermilk b. Section, Alabama, July 7, 1927

In country music's long tradition of brother duet singing, Ira and Charlie Louvin served as the link between the DELMORE BROTHERS and the EVERLY BROTHERS. More important, the Louvin Brothers' stratospheric vocal interplay made them probably the most influential harmony duet in country music history, touching everybody from EMMYLOU HARRIS to the cowpunk band RANK & FILE.

First cousins of singer-songwriter JOHN D. LOUDERMILK,

Ira and Charlie grew up in a poor farm family in northeastern Alabama, mostly in Henegar. Ira mastered the mandolin, and Charlie picked guitar. Ira and Charlie first performed as the Radio Twins in 1942, worked in Chattanooga with the Foggy Mountain Boys in 1943, and changed their name to the Louvin Brothers in 1947 while working at WROL in Knoxville, because they wanted a professional name that was easier to pronounce and spell. They spent considerable time in Memphis, and they debuted on the GRAND OLE OPRY in Nashville in 1955.

The Louvin Brothers: Ira (left) and Charlie

The Louvins recorded for Apollo in 1947, DECCA in 1949, and MGM in 1951 and 1952—their early recording dates were sporadic, in part because of Charlie's military service in Korea. They did not achieve great commercial success, however, until they began recording for CAPITOL on September 30, 1952, an affiliation that would continue until the Louvins broke up in August 1963. Although the duo's biggest hits for Capitol were released in 1955 and 1956, during the early days of rock & roll, their musical style was already defiantly anachronistic. Their high, lonesome harmonies, punctuated by Ira's stirring mandolin solos, were closer to country music of the 1930s than the honky-tonk or country-pop of the mid-1950s. As a sign of their traditionalism, their first three Top Ten singles, "When I Stop Dreaming," the chart-topping "I Don't Believe You've Met My Baby," and "Hoping That You're Hoping," didn't include drums. They mixed gospel and secular forms, often focusing on the traditional themes of family, love, and obligation that link the two.

In the late 1950s a changing market and Ira's erratic, tempestuous behavior contributed to the brothers' sinking commercial fortunes. Capitol producer KEN NELSON made several attempts to update the duo's sound, including an ill-fated series of recordings without Ira's trademark mandolin, but 1959's "My Baby's Gone" served as their last Top Ten hit. Increasing personal tensions led to the pair's 1963 breakup, after which each brother embarked on a separate career. Ira's 1964 album *The Unforgettable Ira Louvin*, which featured electric mandolin and electric guitar, turned out to be his only solo LP; he died in a Missouri car crash on June 20, 1965. Charlie's solo career began with two Top Ten hits ("I Don't Love You Anymore" and "See the Big Man Cry"), but through the 1970s and 1980s he became best known as a fixture on weekly Opry broadcasts.

Country-rocker GRAM PARSONS introduced the Louvins' songs to the rock world, in several instances as duets with Emmylou Harris. Harris, in turn, reintroduced the Louvins' material to country audiences when her 1975 version of their song "If I Could Only Win Your Love" became her first Top Ten country hit.

In 1996 Watermelon Records released Charlie's album *The Longest Train,* on which he was joined by guest performers such as BARRY AND HOLLY TASHIAN and JIM LAUDERDALE.
—*Jimmy Guterman*

REPRESENTATIVE RECORDINGS

Tragic Songs of Life (Capitol, 1956); *Songs That Tell a Story* (Rounder, 1978); *Radio Favorites* (Country Music Foundation Records, 1987); *Close Harmony* (Bear Family, 1992), 8 discs

Patty Loveless
b. Pikeville, Kentucky, January 4, 1957

Although her album and ticket sales have been dwarfed by REBA MCENTIRE's, Patty Loveless is very likely country's mostly admired female singer of the 1990s for her consistently sensitive choice of songs and for her skillful balance of modern and traditional country vocal stylings.

Like her distant cousin LORETTA LYNN, Patricia Ramey was born a coal miner's daughter, the sixth of John and Naomi Ramey's seven children, in the small Appalachian town of Pikeville, Kentucky. Her father was forced to leave mining at age forty-two because of black lung disease; he died in 1979. A shy youngster, Patty regularly listened

Patty Loveless

to the GRAND OLE OPRY and showed an early aptitude for singing in partnership with brother Roger Ramey. In 1971, at age fourteen, she and Roger showed Patty's songs to PORTER WAGONER, who was encouraging but who counseled Patty to finish her high school education. Two years later she joined the WILBURN BROTHERS' touring show as their featured girl singer and was signed to the brothers' publishing firm, Sure-Fire Music, as well.

In 1976 she married the Wilburns' drummer Terry Lovelace and moved with him to Kings Mountain, North Carolina, where they both played in rock bands in Charlotte-area clubs. In 1985, after recovering from a bout with alcoholism, she moved to Nashville to pursue a career in country music once more. Her marriage to Lovelace dissolved later that year, although she kept the name with a slight change of spelling. With the help of brother and manager Roger Ramey, Loveless landed a recording contract with A&R man TONY BROWN at MCA RECORDS. Although it began as a singles deal, she graduated to doing her first album in 1987. Her first Top Ten hit was a cover of GEORGE JONES's "If My Heart Had Windows" (1988), which suggested her long-standing affinity for hard country. She joined the Grand Ole Opry cast on June 11, 1988.

Loveless soon showed a knack for finding good material from offbeat sources. Among her subsequent Top Ten hits were songs from STEVE EARLE ("A Little Bit in Love," 1988), country-rock band Lone Justice ("Don't Toss Us Away," 1989), and KOSTAS ("Timber, I'm Falling in Love," 1989). "Timber" was the first hit for the transplanted Greek, who became a frequent contributor to Loveless's albums.

A series of momentous changes occurred in her life beginning with her February 1989 marriage to producer/bass player EMORY GORDY JR. In 1990 she ended her management contract with Roger Ramey. In 1992 she left MCA Records for Sony Music and its EPIC label. Late that fall she had laser surgery on her vocal cords, from which she experienced a full recovery.

Her first album for Epic, *Only What I Feel,* was produced by Emory Gordy (as have been all her subsequent Epic efforts) and was an immediate critical and popular success. It became her first platinum album, and its sales were duplicated by the follow-up, *When Fallen Angels Fly,* which won the CMA's Best Country Album award for 1995. The following year her *The Trouble with the Truth* album led to winning Female Vocalist of the Year awards from both the CMA and the ACM. Among her best-known hit singles are "Blame It on Your Heart" (1993), "How Can I Help You Say Goodbye" (1994), "You Can Feel Bad" (1995), and "Lonely Too Long" (1996). She has also frequently appeared on VINCE GILL's recordings ("When I Call Your Name") as a harmony singer, as he has for her.　　　*—Paul Kingsbury*

REPRESENTATIVE RECORDINGS

Greatest Hits (MCA, 1993); *Only What I Feel* (Epic, 1993); *When Fallen Angels Fly* (Epic, 1994); *The Trouble with the Truth* (Epic, 1996); *Long Stretch of Lonesome* (Epic, 1997)

Lyle Lovett
b. Klein, Texas, November 1, 1957

Lyle Pearce Lovett creates eclectic music that touches on folk, jazz, and pop, yet remains unmistakably country-rooted. Marked by dry wit, dark humor, and unforgettable characters, his lyrics are among the most vivid of the contemporary scene.

Lovett grew up in a town outside Houston that was founded by his great-great-grandfather, and he has continued to live on his ancestral property. As a young player he was influenced by the Texas singer-songwriters he heard in folk clubs. By the late 1970s he was beginning to compose songs and appear onstage.

After graduating from Texas A & M University, Lovett traveled to Phoenix to make a tape of his tunes with musician Billy Williams. Fellow Texan GUY CLARK was enthusiastic about the result and began playing the tape for friends in Nashville.

Lyle Lovett

MCA offered a recording contract. *Lyle Lovett* appeared in 1986 and spawned the Top Ten hit "Cowboy Man," plus successes such as "God Will," "Why I Don't Know," and "Farther Down the Line." Critics turned handsprings. Lovett was grouped with NANCI GRIFFITH, STEVE EARLE, K. D. LANG, and DWIGHT YOAKAM as "cutting edge" artists who were transforming the country idiom.

Pontiac, the second album, yielded "Give Back My Heart" and "She's No Lady" as Top Twenty chart hits. *Lyle Lovett & His Large Band* was half folk-country in approach and half devoted to his bluesy, brassy road combo. Lovett's version of Tammy Wynette's "Stand By Your Man" attracted particular attention, and the album won a 1989 Grammy.

Joshua Judges Ruth (1992) and *I Love Everybody* (1994) continued to delight fans, but by this time mainstream country radio had turned its back on Lovett. However, he attracted media attention via appearances in such films as *The Player* and *Prêt-à-Porter.* It was while working on the former in 1993 that Lovett met actress Julia Roberts. They married later that year, but divorced in 1996.

The Road to Ensenada, 1996 Grammy Country Album of the Year, marked a return to country and featured guests Jackson Browne, Shawn Colvin, Randy Newman, and CHRIS HILLMAN.　　　*—Robert K. Oermann*

REPRESENTATIVE RECORDINGS

Lyle Lovett (Curb/MCA, 1986); *Lyle Lovett & His Large Band* (Curb/MCA, 1989); *The Road to Ensenada* (Curb/MCA, 1996)

The Lowery Music Group
established in Atlanta, Georgia, 1952

The Lowery Group of Music Publishing Companies has been one of America's most significant music publishing houses outside Nashville, New York, and the West Coast. Beginning as a two-person operation in a small back office of an Atlanta radio station, the Lowery Group progressed through quarters in the basement of founder Bill Lowery's home and space in an abandoned school building to the spacious office and studio complex it now occupies in a suburban office park. From its first hit, the 1953 country gospel song "I Have But One Goal," the Lowery Group quickly diversified to encompass r&b, rock, and pop music. Today it boasts a catalogue of more than 6,000 songs.

Despite phenomenal success in other genres, the Lowery Group never turned its back on country music. Over the years the proportion of its catalogue devoted to country music has been as high as 60 percent. *Billboard* magazine once characterized the Lowery Group's contribution to the country industry as "one of the greatest of all times." Country hits published by the Lowery Group include SONNY JAMES's "Young Love" (written by Ric Cartey and Carole Joyner), PORTER WAGONER's "Misery Loves Company" (written by JERRY REED), LEROY VAN DYKE's "Walk On By" (written by KENDALL HAYES), JOHN CONLEE's "Common Man" (written by Sammy Johns), and CONWAY TWITTY's "Desperado Love" (written by Michael Garvin and Sammy Johns). During the late 1960s JOE SOUTH was responsible for a raft of pop and country hits for the firm, writing and recording such songs as "(I Never Promised You a) Rose Garden," "Games People Play," and "These Are Not My People." The former was a 1967 #1 country hit for LYNN ANDERSON, and the latter two were big country hits for FREDDY

WELLER. Boosted by the royalty revenues of Joe South in particular, the Lowery Group was ranked as the second-largest publishing firm in the United States in 1969, according to an article in *Billboard* magazine that year.

The driving force behind the Lowery Group of Music Publishing Companies is its founder, Bill Lowery, a native of Leesville, Louisiana. At age twenty-two, Lowery came to Atlanta in 1946 to manage a new radio station, WQXI. His previous experience had included management and announcing positions at radio stations around the country.

Three years after moving to Atlanta, Lowery took a job at WGST, where he became a country music disc jockey known to listeners as Uncle Eb Brown, a rube character who attracted a host of aspiring young country music performers who wanted to appear on the program. The congenial Lowery not only provided them with airtime but also began giving them advice, encouraging their writing talents, introducing them to recording executives, and otherwise guiding and promoting their careers. From these informal interactions the Lowery Music Group was born, and the world became acquainted with such Lowery protégés as Joe South, Jerry Reed, ROY DRUSKY, RAY STEVENS, BILL ANDERSON, EMORY GORDY JR., Gene Vincent, and MAC DAVIS, among many others. —*Wayne W. Daniel*

Lulu Belle & Scotty

Lulu Belle (Wiseman) Stamey b. Boone, North Carolina, December 24, 1913

Scott Greene Wiseman b. Ingalls, North Carolina, November 8, 1909; d. January 31, 1981

Known as the "Hayloft Sweethearts" and the "Sweethearts of Country Music," Lulu Belle and Scotty were for twenty-five years stars on the NATIONAL BARN DANCE, the seminal country music radio program broadcast weekly by the powerful Chicago station WLS from 1924 to 1960. With Scotty on banjo and Lulu Belle on guitar, the duo performed Ap-

Lulu Belle & Scotty

palachian folksongs, gospel tunes, novelty pieces, sentimental Tin Pan Alley favorites, and mainstream country and pop songs in close vocal harmonies, blending their music with folksy patter and cornball comedy routines. They eventually became the longest-lasting and perhaps best-loved husband-wife duet in country music.

"Lulu Belle" was the name given the eighteen-year-old Myrtle Eleanor Cooper in 1932 by JOHN LAIR, artistic director of the *National Barn Dance,* when she joined the ensemble, representing the Appalachian girlfriend of RED "Burrhead" FOLEY, a member of Lair's Cumberland Ridge Runners. Her rambunctious behavior, her honest renditions of folksongs that she had learned from her mother, and her comic duets with Foley endeared her to audiences, and she rapidly became one of the *National Barn Dance*'s most popular performers. In 1936 readers of *Radio Guide* magazine voted her "National Radio Queen," the most popular woman on radio.

Scott grew up in a Blue Ridge Mountain community that was rich in traditional culture. He spent his early years collecting folksongs from his family and neighbors, becoming proficient on banjo, guitar, and harmonica. His love for Appalachian folk music was strengthened further when he fell under the influence of BASCOM LAMAR LUNSFORD and BRADLEY KINCAID, who had become one of WLS's biggest artists in the late 1920s. Scott became a member of the WLS staff in 1933, modeling himself as much as possible on Kincaid. He performed as a solo act for a few months, singing folksongs as well as his own compositions that evoked his Appalachian nurture, but in 1934 he was paired with Lulu Belle, whom he married on December 13, 1934.

Scott was a prolific songwriter, with some of his songs becoming c&w classics: "Mountain Dew" (with Lunsford), "Brown Mountain Light," "Remember Me," and the immortal "Have I Told You Lately That I Love You?," which has been recorded by innumerable pop and country artists. Scott was elected into the Nashville Songwriters Hall of Fame in 1971.

While their record sales were never spectacular, Lulu Belle & Scotty's comic "battles of the sexes," elegant harmony singing, winning songs, and superb musicianship were disseminated from 1933 to 1958 through radio broadcasts, personal appearances, and seven Hollywood films, providing for them a secure position in the history of country music. —*William E. Lightfoot*

REPRESENTATIVE RECORDINGS

Lulu Belle and Scotty: Early and Great, Volume 1 (Old Homestead, 1985); *Tender Memories Recalled, Volume 1* (Mar-Lu, 1989)

Bob Luman

b. Nacogdoches, Texas, April 15, 1937; d. December 27, 1978

Bobby Glynn Luman grew up trying to decide whether to seek a baseball career or a country music career. But when ELVIS PRESLEY played Kilgore, Texas, one May 1955 evening, Luman made his decision: He wanted to play Presley's brand of rockabilly music. "That was the last time I ever tried to sing like LEFTY FRIZZELL," Luman told author Paul Hemphill.

Winning a Future Farmers of America Talent contest judged by JOHNNY HORTON paved the way for an invitation from the LOUISIANA HAYRIDE to replace a departing JOHNNY

CASH. An invitation to join the Pittsburgh Pirates at spring training arrived at about the same time. Luman chose music.

IMPERIAL RECORDS signed Luman in early 1957. His band, assembled in Shreveport, consisted of JAMES BURTON on guitar, James Kirkland on bass, and Bruce White on drum. The first session produced a rockabilly classic, "Red Cadillac and a Black Mustache." Luman next traveled to California to appear in the film *Carnival Rock*. While in California he became a regular on the *TOWN HALL PARTY* television program. RICKY NELSON heard Luman's crack band at this time and hired them away.

Luman left Imperial and, after a brief stint with CAPITOL RECORDS, signed with WARNER BROS., but he was disappointed at the lack of progress in his career. During a performance at the Showboat Hotel in Las Vegas, Luman announced that he intended to ask the Pirates for another tryout. In the audience that night were the EVERLY BROTHERS, also on Warner Bros., who suggested that Luman try recording a FELICE AND BOUDLEAUX BRYANT song they had turned down, "Let's Think About Living." It became Luman's top career single, charting #7 pop and #9 country in 1960. Luman soon entered the army, however, and was unable to follow up on his success.

A 1964 move to Nashville found him as the rockabilly member of the GRAND OLE OPRY in a long-lasting but not always comfortable association with the long-running program. Senior cast member ROY ACUFF once caustically remarked, "That boy can't decide if he's colored or white."

Between 1964 and his death in 1978, Luman placed thirty-eight singles on the country charts for the HICKORY, EPIC, and Polydor labels, but only four of them were Top Ten hits. The highest-charting of these was the 1972 hit "Lonely Women Make Good Lovers." —*William P. Davis*

REPRESENTATIVE RECORDING

Bob Luman: American Originals (Columbia, 1989)

Robert Lunn
b. Franklin, Tennessee, November 28, 1912; d. March 8, 1966

Robert Rainey Lunn was an early GRAND OLE OPRY comedian who built a career on variations of a genre called the talking blues. Growing up in Franklin, southwest of Nashville, he knew the McGEE BROTHERS, and as a youth he took his impersonations and left-handed guitar stylings to the vaudeville stage. After traveling widely, during which time he heard the kind of spoken songs pioneered by South Carolinian CHRIS BOUCHILLON, he moved his act to radio, appearing on WCHS in Charleston, West Virginia, and KWTO in Springfield, Missouri. Thrown out of work during the Depression, he returned to Middle Tennessee and finally found work as a bellboy at Nashville's Hermitage Hotel.

As a gimmick, the hotel had its own in-house radio station that piped music into guest rooms. Lunn began entertaining on this, and soon was invited to appear on the Opry on Saturday nights. GEORGE D. "JUDGE" HAY, the show's master of ceremonies, found his patter delightful and dubbed him the Original Talking Blues Man. Lunn began building on the original talking blues verses, often creating topical or personalized verses, until he finally had a repertoire of some one hundred verses. Sacks of fan mail poured in, and throughout the early 1940s Lunn traveled with Opry tent shows, especially those of ROY ACUFF.

Oddly, Lunn never got around to recording his "Talking Blues" until 1947, when he cut a never-before-released version for MERCURY. He retired from the Opry in 1958, shortly after cutting his first LP for STARDAY.
—*Charles Wolfe*

REPRESENTATIVE RECORDING

The Original Talking Blues Man (Starday, 1957)

Bascom Lamar Lunsford
b. Mars Hill, North Carolina, March 21, 1882; d. September 4, 1973

Bascom Lamar Lunsford is best known as the originator in 1928 of Asheville, North Carolina's, Mountain Dance and Folk Festival, the first folk festival of its kind. He was also a collector and performer, and his work was influential in the folk revival of the 1960s.

Reared in the Blue Ridge Mountains, Lunsford earned an undergraduate degree from Rutherford College in 1909 and studied law at Trinity College (now Duke University), passing the bar in 1913. In addition to setting up a law practice, he worked at various jobs, including teaching at Rutherford College, auctioneering, newspaper work, and a job with the U.S. Justice Department. But he was always most committed to preserving the music of his native region.

A fiddler, banjoist, and singer, he recorded more than 300 songs, tunes, dance calls, and tales for the archives of Columbia University and the Library of Congress from his "memory collection" of traditional lore he had learned over the years. With Lamar Stringfield, he published *30 and 1 Folk Songs from the Southern Mountains* (Carl Fischer, 1929). Commercially, he recorded twenty-two sides for OKEH, BRUNSWICK, and COLUMBIA and four LPs for the Library of Congress, Folkways, Riverside, and ROUNDER. His best-known composition is "Mountain Dew," which he recorded for Brunswick in 1928 and later sold for 25 dollars to Scott Wiseman of LULU BELLE & SCOTTY, who recorded the song in 1939 for Vocalion. (Wiseman repaid Lunsford by arranging for Lunsford to continue receiving a 50 percent royalty during his lifetime.) Lunsford assisted Sarah Gertrude Knott in establishing the National Folk Festival, and in addition to the Asheville festival he organized other folk festivals at the North Carolina State Fair, the Cherokee Indian Fair, and the University of North Carolina, as well as in Kentucky, Virginia, and South Carolina. In 1939, at the request of President and Mrs. Roosevelt, he took a group of musicians and dancers to the White House to entertain the king and queen of England. Lunsford continued to organize, manage, and perform at the Asheville Mountain Dance and Folk Festival until he suffered a stroke in 1965. Afterward he continued to attend the festival annually until his death. —*Loyal Jones*

REPRESENTATIVE RECORDINGS

Smoky Mountain Ballads Sung by Bascom Lamar Lunsford with Banjo (Folkways, 1953); *Bascom Lamar Lunsford: Ballad, Banjo Tunes, and Sacred Songs of Western North Carolina* (Folkways/Smithsonian, 1996)

Frank Luther
b. Lakin, Kansas, August 4, 1899; d. November 16, 1980

Frank Luther recorded prolifically with CARSON ROBISON and as a solo act during the early years of commercial country music before moving exclusively into the children's recording field after World War II.

Born Francis Luther Crow on a ranch near Lakin, he graduated from high school in BAKERSFIELD, California, and became involved in church work as a choir director, evangelistic singer, and minister. He performed first professionally with the De Rezske Singers and the Revelers Male Quartet. He started recording country music in June 1928, when he replaced VERNON DALHART as Carson Robison's recording partner. Probably their best-selling records were some of the one hundred sides they recorded for VICTOR as Bud & Joe Billings and Billings & Robison. Many of these had a small orchestra accompaniment. One of the best known of these was the popular novelty song "Barnacle Bill the Sailor," which they composed jointly. Two sequels followed as well as a related song that commented on events of World War II.

Luther was the lead singer and soloist for most of the Carson Robison Trio records. He also sang duets with Robison under such pseudonyms as the Black Brothers, Jimson Brothers, Jones Brothers, and Harper Brothers, and he recorded solos as Jimmie Black, Harry Black, Lazy Larry, Weary Willie, Jeff Calhoun, Frank & Francis Evans, Pete Wiggins, and Frank Tuttle, among other names.

Luther was an expert at varying his singing style, and he recorded more than 400 sides of vocal choruses with dance orchestras, 150 for Victor alone, at the same time he was doing the country numbers.

After parting professionally with Robison in April 1932, Luther continued recording for Victor for a time with his wife, ZORA LAYMAN, whom he had married in 1926, and with Leonard Stokes, as the Bud Billings Trio. They also recorded for the ARC labels as the Frank Luther Trio and the Buddy Spencer Trio. RAY WHITLEY later joined them, in January 1934.

During this time Luther also recorded more than 130 songs for electrical transcription, made several movie shorts, and was very active in radio. From 1933 to 1935 he was a regular guest on ETHEL PARK RICHARDSON's folk music radio programs on WOR and the NBC network. He was also a noted songwriter and wrote a book, *Americans and Their Songs* (1942).

In August 1934 Luther became one of the first performers to sign a contract with DECCA RECORDS. He had eight of the first ten records in their 5000 "hill billy" series. He continued with Decca throughout the remainder of his career. A majority of his later recordings were for the children's market, and he was one of the leaders in this field. He had started recording children's songs for ARC in 1932 on the Playtime label, and he released fifteen seven-inch Victors contained in five albums, first appearing in the 1934 catalogue. For a time after the war he produced his own children's record label, LUTHERecords. In the 1950s Luther became a Decca executive in charge of children's and educational records. He retired in the 1960s.

—*Bob Olson*

Loretta Lynn
b. Butcher Holler, Kentucky, April 14, 1935

Loretta Lynn's life story reads more like fiction than fact. It's the story of a poorly educated woman from the coal mining hills of Kentucky, married at age thirteen and a mother at fourteen, who rose to become the most popular singer in country music.

Loretta Lynn

Loretta Webb was born in a one-room log cabin and was the second of eight children. At thirteen she attended a pie social, bringing a pie she had baked using salt instead of sugar. The highest bidder not only won the pie but also got to meet the girl who had baked the pie. Mooney Lynn had just returned home after having served in the army. A month after they had first met, still three months short of her fourteenth birthday, Loretta and Mooney married.

A year later, Mooney decided they should move to Washington state, where he had heard job opportunities were better. The couple's trip west was the first time Loretta had ever been away from home. Mooney found work while Loretta, still a child herself, became pregnant with their first child. By the time she was eighteen, she had four children.

Loretta had grown up listening to country music and often sang around the house. Mooney encouraged her and bought her a guitar so she could play as she sang. Later he helped arrange a singing engagement at the Grange Hall by bragging that his wife could sing better than anyone other than KITTY WELLS. Soon Loretta was singing with a local band and a few months later formed a band of her own.

Lynn's singing came to the attention of Zero Records, a small record company in nearby Vancouver, Canada. The label signed her to a contract in February 1960 and sent her to Los Angeles to record four songs. After the session she and Mooney stayed until the records were pressed and then mailed them out to country music radio stations. Loretta and Mooney then drove cross-country, stopping at stations along the way to promote her recording of "I'm a Honky Tonk Girl." The record began getting airplay and managed to reach #14 on the country music charts in 1960. It was through the strength of this hit that Lynn earned a first appearance on the GRAND OLE OPRY, on September 17, 1960.

When they arrived in Nashville, Loretta made the rounds to publicize her record. One of her stops was at the office of the WILBURN BROTHERS. Teddy and Doyle Wilburn were the top country vocal group and had built their enterprises to include a publishing company, a booking agency, a syndicated television program, and a touring show. Doyle Wilburn recognized Lynn's talent, unpolished though it was. He made her a part of the Wilburns' road show and a regular on their television series. Doyle eventually secured Lynn's release from Zero Records and persuaded DECCA RECORDS, the label for which the Wilburns recorded, to sign her. (Eventually, Lynn's desire to be out on her own with full control of her career led to personal differences between Lynn and the Wilburns. A lawsuit settled matters, and a few years later they were able to resume their friendship.)

Two years after she recorded "I'm a Honky Tonk Girl," Lynn began scoring with records such as "Success," "Before I'm Over You," and "Blue Kentucky Girl." But it wasn't until her recordings of "You Ain't Woman Enough" and "Don't Come Home A Drinkin'," that Lynn's music took a new direction. Instead of using traditional country music themes she wrote songs that were more realistic and less compromising. The country girl from the hills of Kentucky, who was raising a family of six, spoke more boldly and forcefully than many would have expected. Still, songs such as "Fist City" and "Your Squaw Is On the Warpath" had such humor that Lynn did not alienate any of her audience members.

She won the CMA's Female Vocalist of the Year Award in 1967, 1972, and 1973. She also began to appear on television variety shows and talk programs that had rarely featured country music performers. By the end of the 1960s Lynn's brother Jay Lee Webb and her sisters Peggy Sue and CRYSTAL GAYLE had also become country music recording artists.

In 1970 Lynn's recording of her signature song, "Coal Miner's Daughter," became one of her biggest hits. She had recorded three albums of duets with ERNEST TUBB before recording her first song with CONWAY TWITTY in 1970. "After the Fire Is Gone" became a #1 record in 1971 and marked the beginning of one of the most successful duet pairings in country music history. Lynn and Twitty won the CMA Vocal Duo of the Year Award from 1972 through 1975. Among their many hits were "Lead Me On," "Louisiana Woman, Mississippi Man," and "As Soon as I Hang Up the Phone." When Lynn won the CMA's Entertainer of the Year Award in 1972, she became the first woman to achieve that honor.

In 1976 Lynn's autobiography, appropriately titled *Coal Miner's Daughter,* became a best seller and was made into a hit movie starring Sissy Spacek. Meanwhile, the singer continued to score with musical hits such as "Out of My Head and Back in My Bed," "I've Got a Picture of Us on My Mind," and the aptly titled "We've Come a Long Way, Baby."

In 1988 Lynn was elected to the COUNTRY MUSIC HALL OF FAME. The honor paid tribute to her career as well as to the influence she has had on many of the women in country music. She still works as often as she likes, and audiences continue to embrace her for her music and for her endearing personality. —*Laurence Zwisohn*

REPRESENTATIVE RECORDINGS

Loretta Lynn's Greatest Hits (MCA, 1968); *Coal Miner's Daughter* (MCA, 1970); *Loretta Lynn's Greatest Hits: Volume 2* (MCA, 1974); *The Very Best of Loretta and Conway* (with Conway Twitty) (MCA, 1979); *Making Believe* (with Conway Twitty) (MCA, 1988); *Loretta Lynn: Country Music Hall of Fame* (MCA, 1991); *Honky Tonk Angels* (with Tammy Wynette and Dolly Parton) (Columbia, 1993); *Honky Tonk Girl: The Loretta Lynn Collection* (MCA, 1994), 3 CDs

Shelby Lynne
b. Quantico, Virginia, October 22, 1968

Like LYLE LOVETT and K. D. LANG before her, Shelby Lynne seems destined to become famous as a great singer whose talent is too broad for the narrow confines of country music as dictated by the constraints of radio. Raised in Jackson, Alabama, Shelby Lynn Moorer had wanted to form a singing duo with her mother, but tragedy struck when Lynne was seventeen. Her father took the life of her mother and then took his own, leaving Lynne and her younger sister Allison to cope.

Lynne and her sister eventually moved to Nashville in 1990, and after a chance appearance singing on TNN's *NASHVILLE NOW,* Lynne found herself working with producer BILLY SHERRILL and singing a duet with GEORGE JONES. Signed to EPIC RECORDS, she released three albums—*Tough All Over, Sunrise,* and *Soft Talk*—whose singles usually stalled between the Top Sixty and the Top Thirty, except for "Things Are Tough All Over" (#23, 1990).

Her fourth album, *Temptation,* released on the Morgan Creek label in 1993, was a swing tribute to BOB WILLS and demonstrated Lynne's versatility. In 1995 she released a fifth album, *Restless,* on Nashville's most impacting independent label, Magnatone Records; she mixed country, bluegrass, big band, and blues into an electrifying gumbo. In 1997 Lynne made a deal to release a pop record on MERCURY's New York label. —*Clark Parsons*

REPRESENTATIVE RECORDINGS

Temptation (Morgan Creek, 1993); *Restless* (Magnatone, 1995)

Extra! Read All About It!
The Literature of Country Music

Nolan Porterfield

Country music fans aren't known for being particularly bookish. "I only read when I want to think," says a gravelly voice overheard in a dim Nashville bar, "and that ain't often." Reading what was written about country music for many years—well into the 1960s—didn't require (or provoke) much thought. For decades after "hillbilly" music emerged in the twenties, what got into print was mostly sarcasm in urban newspapers and popular magazines, fanzine puffery, and occasional three-paragraph artist "profiles" that filled space in song-lyric magazines such as *Country Song Roundup* and *Cowboy Songs*. Serious commentary and historical accuracy were conspicuously absent.

In 1935 Carrie Rodgers wrote the first "life story" of a country star, *My Husband, JIM-MIE RODGERS,* followed three years later by Ruth Sheldon's *Hubbin' It: The Life of BOB WILLS.* Both books were privately published, highly romanticized, and less than reliable, appealing not so much to a general audience as to those who were already committed fans of America's Blue Yodeler and the King of Western Swing. Their historical value, however, is such that they are still consulted by scholars and still available, sixty years later, in reprinted editions from the COUNTRY MUSIC FOUNDATION Press.

By the 1960s, country music was outgrowing its cornbread-and-coondog image and reaching a broader, more diverse audience. As the Denim Chic crowd, hip academics, and the national media began tuning in, serious writers and scholars turned their attention to pickers 'n' singers past and present, producing at first a small trickle of books and articles that in recent years has become a steady stream. A groundbreaking event was the 1965 "Hillbilly Issue" of the *Journal of American Folklore,* devoted entirely to the history and sources of country music, with articles by such pioneering scholars as Archie Green, Norman Cohen, L. Mayne Smith, Ed Kahn, and the late D. K. Wilgus. A year later came *The Country Music Story* by *New York Times* reporter Robert Shelton, the first of many illustrated histories. Now out of print, *The Country Music Story* was an important work, despite errors and omissions, and remains valuable for its many rare photographs.

The one book that every fan and student of country music should own appeared in 1968. Bill C. Malone's *Country Music U.S.A.* immediately established itself as the definitive history, well written, thoroughly researched, and exhaustively documented. (I get exhausted just reading through the ninety-odd pages of bibliographic essays at the back of the revised edition, realizing how much painstaking work went into it.) This is the book that took country music from the realm of mere popular culture and made it intellectually respectable; the publication of a revised and expanded edition in 1985 further confirmed it as the most comprehensive and authoritative work on the subject yet available.

Between the first and second editions of *Country Music U.S.A.* there appeared several other useful histories, such as *Country Roots* (1976) by Douglas B. Green ("Ranger Doug" of RIDERS IN THE SKY), and *The Illustrated History of Country Music* (1979), a product of *Country Music* magazine. Green's book is unfortunately no longer in print, but an updated edition of *The Illustrated History of Country Music* was published in 1995. The Country Music Foundation's whopping *Country: The Music and the Musicians* (595 pages in its original 1988 edition, covering the subject from its beginnings), is unrivaled for its wealth of photographs and incisive essays by the cream of country music writers and scholars. It's an excellent read as well as a valuable sourcebook.

With increasing scholarly interest in country music came the need for basic reference works—indexes, directories, encyclopedias, and the like. A pioneering effort was *A History and Encyclopedia of Country, Western and Gospel Music*, privately printed by Linnell Gentry in 1961 and updated in 1969. Unfortunately, Gentry's book is long out of print and available in very few libraries.

In pursuit of the Big Picture in the 1970s and 1980s there came a spate of Big Picture Books and would-be "encyclopedias," many of which were error-laden and more glitter than gold. Useful in their time but now dated were Stambler and Landon's *Encyclopedia of Folk, Country & Western Music* (1969, revised 1983) and *The Illustrated Encyclopedia of Country Music* (1977, 1986), by Fred Dellar, Roy Thompson, and Douglas B. Green, which now exists in a third edition as *The Harmony Illustrated Encyclopedia of Country Music* with a more thorough collection of pictures. Despite a determined effort, Barry McCloud's *Definitive Country: The Ultimate Encyclopedia of Country Music and Its Performers* falls short of the claims announced in its title, although it is up to date and more complete than *Country Music* magazine's *Comprehensive Country Music Encyclopedia* (which does have better pictures and is more reliable). The consensus of those who use such reference works regularly is that each is strong in certain areas and weak in others, and anyone in search of comprehensiveness and absolute accuracy would do well to consult them all.

The earliest periodicals dealing with country music were fan club newsletters and cheaply printed (sometimes mimeographed) little magazines, such as *Country and Western Spotlight* and *Disc Collector,* that circulated among record collectors mostly interested in old-time artists and obscure recording data. In 1965 the JOHN EDWARDS MEMORIAL FOUNDATION began issuing a newsletter that soon evolved into the more substantial *JEMF Quarterly,* an early forum for country music scholarship.

Inaugurated by the Country Music Foundation in 1971, the *Journal of County Music* grew, like *JEMF Quarterly,* from a rudimentary tract aimed primarily at scholars into a glossy, vigorous showcase, indispensable reading for anyone who follows the country music scene. The appearance of Tony Russell's *Old Time Music* in 1971 attested to the international appeal of American country music; although edited and published in England, the magazine was devoted almost entirely to vintage artists on this side of the Atlantic and drew on the work of American writers and researchers. Unfortunately, both *JEMF Quarterly* and *Old Time Music* have ceased publication, the former in 1985, the latter in 1989, but their back issues offer a rich reference treasure for those who kept subscription copies or have access to the few libraries that acquired them.

Country Music magazine was founded in New York by then publisher John Killion in 1972, the first newsstand slick published for a broad general audience of country music readers. Under the guidance of Russell Barnard, it survived corporate restructuring and a brief hiatus in the early 1980s to become the ranking fan magazine in its field. Between 1991 and 1997 its offshoot, *The Journal* (official title: *The Journal of the American Academy for the Preservation of Old-Time Country Music,* which was almost longer than the magazine itself), helped fill the void left by the disappearance of *JEMF Quarterly* and *Old Time Music,* publishing articles and pictures of historical interest. Its contributors have included some of the best journalists writing about country music today, among them Rich Kienzle and John Morthland, whose work also appears from time to time in the *Journal of Country Music.* In 1997, to save mailing costs, the publishers of *Country Music* incorporated the *Journal* into issues of the parent magazine, and it is no longer published separately.

It has been said that we live in the age of biography. Certainly the lives of country artists, old and new, have gotten their share of scrutiny in the past twenty years or so. By interesting coincidence, the subjects of the two earliest books back in the 1930s—Bob Wills and Jimmie Rodgers—were the first to get serious scholarly attention. Charles Townsend's 1976 biography of the King of Western Swing, *San Antonio Rose,* is a landmark work that at once solidified Wills's reputation and broke new ground in detailing his life and career. On the downside, Townsend's objectivity was sometimes clouded by his reverence for his subject, leading to distortions and exaggerations that later scholars have sought to correct. Nevertheless, *San Antonio Rose* remains an important work and ought to be in every country fan's library. It is still available in paperback. My own contribution to the genre, *Jimmie Rodgers: The Life and Times of America's Blue Yodeler* (1979), took considerable inspiration from Townsend's pioneering effort and was aimed at producing an accurate and detailed account for a general audience. Whether I succeeded is for the reader to decide, but that book also remains in print, in a slightly revised 1992 paperback edition.

At least three other country music "immortals"—HANK WILLIAMS, LEFTY FRIZZELL, and ERNEST TUBB—have been well served by their biographers. There are many books dealing with the tragedy and glory of Hank Williams, but the two that clearly stand out are *Sing a Sad Song* by Roger Williams (no relation) and Colin Escott's *Hank Williams: The Biography*. The Williams book established a solid reputation when it appeared back in the seventies, but the addition of an excellent discography by Bob Pinson in a 1981 reissue gave it a permanent place on any country music bookshelf. A decade later, Escott, whose work is always knowledgeable and interesting, undertook the unenviable task of digging up new material and reinvigorating the Hank Williams legend; *Hank Williams: The Biography* is a testament to his success. Lefty Frizzell's story waited a long time for a writer who would do it justice but finally found one in Daniel Cooper, whose *Lefty Frizzell* is among the most solid, interesting, and entertaining country biographies. Ronnie Pugh, a longtime expert on Ernest Tubb, has at last put all his research into definitive book form. Pugh's *Ernest Tubb: The Texas Troubadour* is a book every country fan should have.

Another important historical figure who finally got the attention he deserved is MILTON BROWN. In *Milton Brown and the Founding of Western Swing*, Cary Ginell chronicled Brown's role as the innovator whose jazzy style and repertoire, pre–Bob Wills, was the original force behind western swing. Ginell is obviously a partisan, but his case is well documented and his book a welcome corrective to the extravagant claims made for Wills. Also historically important to country music, if less influential, was the career of DEFORD BAILEY, for years a popular member of the GRAND OLE OPRY and the only prominent black professional in country music prior to CHARLEY PRIDE. His story is set down honestly and sympathetically in *DeFord Bailey: A Black Star in Early Country Music*, by David C. Morton, in collaboration with Charles Wolfe. Other useful, appealing biographies of historical figures include Elizabeth Schlappi's *ROY ACUFF* (one of the more evenhanded fan-written biographies, available in a new edition since 1992); Gene Wiggins's story of FIDDLIN' JOHN CARSON, *Fiddlin' Georgia Crazy;* and Ivan Tribe's *The Stonemans*, the history of one of country music's founding families.

Since the 1970s, biographies of contemporary stars—mostly glitzy rip-offs—have been pouring from the presses. Among the few worthy of attention are Margaret Jones's *Patsy: The Life and Times of PATSY CLINE*; Bob Allen's *GEORGE JONES: The Saga of a Country Singer*; Steve Eng's *A Satisfied Mind: The Country Music Life of PORTER WAGONER*; and Jonny Whiteside's *Ramblin' Rose: The Life and Career of ROSE MADDOX*. Although ELVIS PRESLEY belongs to rock & roll, every fan should know about his country roots. Books about the King would fill a small library, but there's only one that reaches the level of serious biography: Peter Guralnick's excellent *Last Train to Memphis*. Ben Fong-Torres's *Hickory Wind: The Life and Times of GRAM PARSONS*, is valuable both as a biography and as an illumination of the country-rock era.

Then there's Country Music Bizarro, the parallel literary universe where the stars of today write books about their own lives, or pretend to, and turn them into best sellers. To the casual reader, a biography and an autobiography are pretty much the same thing. Each is the story of someone's life, and who cares who tells it, right? But, as Mark Twain almost said, the difference between biography and autobiography is the difference between lightning and the lightning bug. When celebrities sit down to write about their troubled-life-and-times—or, more often, make a tape for an "as told to" co-author—the result is often an exercise in ego-tripping, self-justification, revenge on ex-spouses, and shallow pontificating on the Meaning of Life. But these are the country music books the public knows best—in recent decades bookstores and best-seller lists across the nation have been flooded with "as told to" autobiographies of wildly varying quality by the likes of HANK WILLIAMS JR., WILLIE NELSON, MERLE HAGGARD, Charley Pride, GENE AUTRY, REBA MCENTIRE, NAOMI JUDD, talk show hosts CROOK & CHASE, and a dozen others.

In many respects the first of them was the best—LORETTA LYNN's *Coal Miner's Daughter* (1976), a literary sleeper and source for the hit movie of the same name, one of the finest country music films yet made. Credit coauthor George Vecsey for much of the book's success, but he wisely preserved Lynn's artless candor and her feisty (if sometimes irritating) voice. *Coal Miner's Daughter* records a vital slice of country music history as well as capturing the inner life of its subject. Published more than twenty years ago, it has recently been reissued by Da Capo Press.

Equally valuable for many of the same reasons and also back in print is the autobiography of Alton Delmore of the DELMORE BROTHERS, *Truth Is Stranger Than Publicity*. As a relic of an earlier time, the Delmore book is less trendy than *Coal Miner's Daughter* and unlikely to spawn a movie of any kind, but it is both an honest, illuminating record of human experience and a rare source of information about the country music business in its first three decades. It includes notes, commentary, and discography by the ubiquitous country music scholar Charles Wolfe, who was largely responsible for unearthing Delmore's unpublished and forgotten manuscript. Wolfe was also a nurturing force behind GRANDPA JONES's lively and rewarding autobiography, *Everybody's Grandpa: Fifty Years Behind the Mike*, still in print more than a decade after it first appeared. *Reflections*, JOHNNY BOND's slender but rewarding little volume, has vanished into limbo, and the authentic voices and experiences of two other country music mainstays were preserved in *The HANK SNOW Story* and *MINNIE PEARL: An Autobiography*. The latter, written with—or by—collaborator Joan Dew, profited from Minnie's excellent memory for details and events but is now out of print.

A few country celebrities have had the talent and courage to go it alone and write about themselves without the crutch of a coauthor. In most cases their books are a cut above the rest; see, for example, TOM T. HALL's *A Storyteller's Nashville*, SKEETER DAVIS's *Bus Fare to Kentucky*, DOLLY PARTON's *Dolly*, BILL ANDERSON's *Whisperin' Bill*, and even JOHNNY CASH's book-length sermon *Man in Black* ("'God's Superstar' tells his own story in his own words"). *Cash: An Autobiography* (1997) covers some of the same ground but adds interesting new dimensions, never-before-published photos, and the graceful prose of coauthor Patrick Carr. Among "as told to" collaborators, the most prolific and probably the best is journalist Tom Carter, who has wielded the pen for Reba McEntire, George Jones, GLEN CAMPBELL, RONNIE MILSAP, and RALPH EMERY. (Emery's *Memories* is essential reading; forget the sequel, *More Memories*).

Country music books of a general nature aimed at a national audience can be traced back to journalist Paul Hemphill's *Nashville Sound*, a lively anecdotal account of the Music City scene in the late 1960s. It was reissued in paperback in 1975, but like Larry Wacholtz's *Inside Country Music* (1986), which looks at the nuts and bolts of the business through the eyes of music executives and artists, it is difficult to find. The most engrossing of all efforts to catch the scope and flavor of country music is Nick Tosches's eccentric, irreverent *Country: The Biggest Music in America* (1977), full of obscure detail, written with wit and great precision. Briefly available in a revised 1985 paperback, *Country* is now back in print in paperback, updated with a couple of appendices. Covering the general ground in another fashion, *The Country Reader* presents some of the best writing and photos that have appeared in the *Journal of Country Music*. Subject and author indexes to all twenty-five years of *JCM* are an added bonus. Like Tosches's book, it belongs in the library of anyone interested in country music.

Regional styles and subgenres are the subjects of several important books, such as Charles Wolfe's *Tennessee Strings*, *Kentucky Country*, and *The Devil's Box: Masters of Southern Fiddling*. Wolfe is country music's preeminent scholar and certainly the most prolific; any work with his name on it deserves serious attention. Likewise, Bill Malone's c&w bible, *Country Music U.S.A.*, is now part of the national culture. His *Southern Music, American Music*, which examines the role of the South as a source of musical styles, is a valuable treatise as well.

Barry Jean Ancelet's *Makers of Cajun Music* and Ann Allen Savoy's *Cajun Music: A Reflection of a People* are the essential works on that topic; two somewhat different but complementary books, they were both published in 1984 and are still in print. Also useful, particularly for its 247 transcribed songs, is *Yé Yaille, Chere!: Traditional Cajun Dance Music*, by Raymond François. Neil Rosenberg's *Bluegrass: A History* has just about everything one needs to know about the development of that rich and pervasive musical form; if deeper analysis interests you, go to *Bluegrass Breakdown* by Robert Cantwell, a subjective and more theoretical approach. Western swing is covered by the Townsend and Ginell books cited above, while another vital phenomenon of the Southwest's early music scene is chronicled in *BORDER RADIO*, by Gene Fowler and Bill Crawford. Until the focus shifted to Nashville, Atlanta could lay claim to being country music's capital; for an account of that city's key role in the early years, see Wayne W. Daniel's *Pickin' on Peachtree*.

The role—and plight—of women in country music is narrated at length by Mary Bufwack and Robert Oermann in *Finding Her Voice: The Saga of Women in Country Music*, the first (and so far only) comprehensive study of this much-neglected topic. Bulging with pages of biographical information and social commentary, *Finding Her Voice* is both exhaustive and exhausting, but it stands as an important reference work, with a large and valuable bibliography.

As the Mother Church of country music, the Grand Ole Opry has inspired a veritable horde of pseudohistories, picture books, and souvenir programs, but until recently few of them were of much lasting value, except as curiosities out of the past. Jack Hurst's 1975 *Nashville's Grand Ole Opry,* now out of print, was an elephantine picture book redeemed by its lucid prose and "official" photos from Opry files. Next came Chet Hagan's detailed but not very reliable popular account, *Grand Ole Opry* (1989), and, finally, *The Grand Ole Opry History of Country Music* (1995) by Paul Kingsbury, which is accurate, well written, and beautifully packaged, despite its considerable heft. You won't find much about the dark side of the Opry—personal or commercial—in any of these books, and, as with country music "encyclopedias," a serious reader may need them all. If I could have only one, it would be Kingsbury's. Anyone lucky enough to own a copy of Charles Wolfe's long-vanished *Grand Ole Opry: The Early Years, 1925–1935* should keep it under lock and key.

More recently, serious scholars have moved from history and genre to sociocultural issues in country music, producing highly evolved academic studies such as Cecelia Tichi's *High Lonesome: The American Culture of Country Music* and Curtis Ellison's *Country Music Culture: From Hard Times to Heaven.* Tichi traces various c&w themes and motifs through other American art forms—poetry, novels, paintings, et al.—to argue that country music is the force behind all our national music—even, indeed, the wellspring of our entire national culture. Although her conclusion is not radically different from ideas set forth in more restrained fashion by Malone in *Southern Music, American Music,* her analyses are provocative, sometimes even dazzling. Like Tichi, Ellison ranges far and wide through intellectual jungle and plain, using institutions, traditions, interviews, and song texts to explore the interplay between country music and a broad flow of social and cultural currents. *Country Music Culture* shows a firm grasp of the subject and is written with grace and authority.

Focusing more narrowly on c&w song texts, Dorothy Horstman's *Sing Your Heart Out, Country Boy* tells the stories behind hundreds of favorite country songs and how they were written. Addressed to a more popular audience than the Tichi and Ellison books, it has proved no less compelling to scholars over the years since it first appeared in 1975. Reissued in 1996 in a new, expanded edition, *Sing Your Heart Out, Country Boy* contains an extensive discography and bibliography.

Perhaps the most serious impediment to country music research and scholarship has been the lack of a truly comprehensive discography, on the order of Brian Rust's jazz and dance band discographies. Tony Russell, with support from the Country Music Foundation, has been working to fill that void for decades; now, after several premature announcements, it seems certain that the final results will soon be published.

When all else is said and done—picture books, artists' biographies, social studies, lyrical analyses—the songs themselves remain. Where does one go to find out how country songs ranked as hits through the years, and where to find them? Start with Joel Whitburn's *Top Country Singles* (1994), which has every song that reached *Billboard*'s country charts between 1944 and 1993, with separate listings for titles and artists and a bundle of fascinating statistical trivia. For the vinyl era, John Morthland's mammoth and authoritative guide, *The Best of Country Music* (1984), lists 750 albums, with detailed reviews and critiques and a chronological arrangement that mirrors the evolution of country music. (All the albums listed were in print when the book was published; the fact that neither they nor the book are readily available today scarcely diminishes its value as a reference.) Finally and most impressive of all is the Country Music Foundation's *Country on Compact Disc,* containing reviews and rankings for more than 2,000 CDs, arranged alphabetically by artists (with a special section on various-artists' compilations). In addition to separate listings of the highest ranked CDs ("Four-Star," "Four-and-One-Half-Star," and "Five Star") by artist, album title, and record company, there's an especially useful appendix of *Billboard*'s #1 country hits from 1944 to 1992, showing which songs are available on CD and the disc they're found on. The imposing list of contributors includes most of the people who've written seriously about country music in the past twenty years. This guide will be a standard reference work for a long time to come.

The Essential Country Music Bookshelf

Although many bad books have been written about country music, the number of good ones runs into the dozens. Almost every book about country music—even the trashiest—is interesting in one way or another and adds something to our knowledge of the subject. Nonetheless, distinctions have to be made. I have the presumption to offer the following list as a thorough yet manageable survey of the publications that anyone who follows country music, for fun, knowledge, or profit, should know about. The list is admittedly subjective and to some degree arbitrary. A few historically important works are conspicuously absent because they are no longer readily available; others, old and new, fell by the wayside only in the interests of some reasonable limit to the list. Finally, the inclusion of certain entries will no doubt be the source of lasting—but, one hopes, profitable—dispute.

General Works

Carr, Patrick, ed. *The Illustrated History of Country Music,* rev. ed. New York: Times Books, 1995.
Country Music Foundation. *Country: The Music and the Musicians from the Beginnings to the '90s,* rev. ed., ed. Paul Kingsbury and Alan Axelrod. New York: Abbeville Press, 1994.
Horstman, Dorothy. *Sing Your Heart Out, Country Boy,* 3rd ed. Nashville: Country Music Foundation Press, 1996.
Kingsbury, Paul, ed. *The Country Reader: Twenty-five Years of the Journal of Country Music.* Nashville: Country Music Foundation Press and Vanderbilt University Press, 1996.
Malone, Bill C. *Country Music U.S.A,* rev. ed. Austin: University of Texas Press, 1985.
Tosches, Nick. *Country: The Biggest Music in America,* 3rd ed. New York: Da Capo Press, 1996.

Encyclopedias

Country Music Magazine, eds. *The Comprehensive Country Music Encyclopedia.* New York: Times Books, 1994.
Dellar, Fred, Alan Cackett, and Roy Thompson, eds. *The Harmony Illustrated Encyclopedia of Country Music.* New York: Harmony Books, 1994.
McCloud, Barry, with Ivan M. Tribe and others. *Definitive Country: The Ultimate Encyclopedia of Country Music.* New York: Perigee, 1995.

Autobiography

Cash, Johnny, with Patrick Carr. *Cash: An Autobiography.* San Francisco: Harper, 1997.
Davis, Skeeter. *Bus Fare to Kentucky: The Autobiography of Skeeter Davis.* New York: Carol Publishing Group, 1993.
Delmore, Alton. *Truth Is Stranger Than Publicity,* 2nd ed. Nashville: Country Music Foundation Press, 1995.
Emery, Ralph, with Tom Carter. *Memories.* New York: Macmillan, 1991.
Lynn, Loretta, with George Vecsey. *Coal Miner's Daughter.* New York: Da Capo Press, 1996.
McEntire, Reba, with Tom Carter. *Reba: My Story.* New York: Bantam Books, 1994.
Parton, Dolly. *Dolly: My Life and Other Unfinished Business.* New York: HarperCollins, 1994.
Snow, Hank, with Jack Ownbey and Bob Burris. *The Hank Snow Story.* Champaign: University of Illinois Press, 1994.

Biography

Allen, Bob. *George Jones: The Life and Times of a Honky Tonk Legend.* New York: Birch Lane Press, 1994.
Cooper, Daniel. *Lefty Frizzell: The Honky Tonk Life of Country Music's Greatest Singer.* New York: Little, Brown, 1995.
Eng, Steve. *A Satisfied Mind: The Country Music Life of Porter Wagoner.* Nashville: Rutledge Hill Press, 1992.

Escott, Colin, with George Merritt and William MacEwen. *Hank Williams: The Biography.* New York: Little, Brown, 1995.

Ginell, Cary. *Milton Brown and the Founding of Western Swing.* Urbana: University of Illinois Press, 1994.

Jones, Louis M. "Grandpa," with Charles K. Wolfe. *Everybody's Grandpa: Fifty Years Behind the Mike.* Knoxville: University of Tennessee Press, 1984.

Jones, Margaret. *Patsy: The Life and Times of Patsy Cline.* New York: HarperCollins, 1994.

Porterfield, Nolan. *Jimmie Rodgers: The Life and Times of America's Blue Yodeler,* rev. ed. Urbana: University of Illinois Press, 1992.

Pugh, Ronnie. *Ernest Tubb: The Texas Troubadour.* Durham, N.C.: Duke University Press, 1996.

Rodgers, Carrie. *My Husband, Jimmie Rodgers.* Nashville: Country Music Foundation Press, 1995.

Schlappi, Elizabeth. *Roy Acuff: The Smoky Mountain Boy.* Gretna, La.: Pelican, 1992.

Sheldon, Ruth. *Bob Wills: Hubbin' It.* Nashville: Country Music Foundation Press, 1995.

Townsend, Charles R. *San Antonio Rose: The Life and Music of Bob Wills.* Urbana: University of Illinois Press, 1976.

Whiteside, Jonny. *Ramblin' Rose: The Life and Career of Rose Maddox.* Nashville: Country Music Foundation Press and Vanderbilt University Press, 1997.

Williams, Roger M. *Sing a Sad Song: The Life of Hank Williams.* Urbana: University of Illinois Press, 1981.

Regions, Types, and Special Studies

Ancelet, Barry Jean. *Makers of Cajun Music: Musiciens Cadiens et Creoles.* Austin: University of Texas Press, 1984.

Bufwack, Mary A., and Robert K. Oermann. *Finding Her Voice: The Saga of Women in Country Music.* New York: Crown, 1993.

Fowler, Gene, and Bill Crawford. *Border Radio.* Austin: Texas Monthly Press, 1987.

Kingsbury, Paul. *The Grand Ole Opry History of Country Music: Seventy Years of the Songs, the Stars, and the Stories.* New York: Villard, 1995.

Malone, Bill C. *Southern Music, American Music.* Lexington: University Press of Kentucky, 1979.

Rosenberg, Neil V. *Bluegrass: A History.* Urbana: University of Illinois Press, 1985.

Wolfe, Charles K. *The Devil's Box: Masters of Southern Fiddling.* Nashville: Country Music Foundation Press and Vanderbilt University Press, 1997.

————. *Kentucky Country: Folk and Country Music of Kentucky.* Lexington: University Press of Kentucky, 1982.

————. *Tennessee Strings: The Story of Country Music in Tennessee.* Knoxville: University of Tennessee Press, 1977.

Scholarly Analyses

Ellison, Curtis. *Country Music Culture: From Hard Times to Heaven.* Oxford: University Press of Mississippi, 1995.

Tichi, Cecelia. *High Lonesome: The American Culture of Country Music.* Chapel Hill: University of North Carolina Press, 1994.

Record Guides

Country Music Foundation. *Country on Compact Disc: The Essential Guide to the Music,* ed. Paul Kingsbury. New York: Grove Press, 1993.

Morthland, John. *The Best of Country Music: A Critical and Historical Guide to the 750 Greatest Albums.* Garden City, N.Y.: Dolphin/Doubleday, 1984.

Periodicals

Country Music
Journal of Country Music

M·M·M · M·M·M

M. M. Cole Publishing
established in Chicago, Illinois, February 1930

Born circa 1893, company founder Morris M. Cole was raised in New York City but moved to Chicago as a young man where he became a sundries salesman. Soon he invested with a brother-in-law in a near-bankrupt music store and afterward started his own wholesale firm, Illinois Music Jobber.

By February 1930 Cole had sold his jobbing business and formed M. M. Cole Publishing, the Chicago company that turned into his most successful endeavor and one to which he devoted his remaining years of life up to his death at age sixty-five on August 19, 1958.

M. M. Cole's product line, which benefited greatly from sales in major mail-order retailers' catalogues, ran the gamut from musical instruction publications to sheet music to songbook folios. The latter were often associated with country music personalities such as GENE AUTRY, CLIFF CARLISLE, and RED FOLEY, among others. Generic folios of folksongs were printed as well, such as *Play and Sing: America's Greatest Collection of Old Time Songs and Mountain Ballads* (1930), possibly Cole's first effort. The firm's music licensing agreements were with SESAC until 1940, when M. M. Cole, along with subsidiaries Calumet Music and others, became among the first song publishers to affiliate with the newly formed BMI.

As an accessory to the firm's publishing interests, the M. M. Cole transcription library was active in the 1940s. This service provided fresh Cole-recorded product for radio use via subscription, and its artists included such Chicago-based talent as REX ALLEN, Rusty Gill, and Judy Martin.

In January 1965 ABC-Paramount purchased the M. M. Cole catalogue of song copyrights, including such standards as "That Silver Haired Daddy of Mine," "Mexicali Rose," and "Old Shep." The copyrights at this writing are administered by Duchess Music Corp., a division of MCA, which acquired the bulk of the Cole catalogue through a purchase of ABC-Paramount in January 1979.—*Bob Pinson*

Mac & Bob
Lester "Mac" McFarland b. Gray, Kentucky, February 2, 1902; d. July 24, 1984
Robert A. Gardner b. Oliver Springs, Tennessee, December 16, 1897; d. September 30, 1978

Stylistically, Mac & Bob reflect country music's roots in nineteenth-century popular song. Their repertoire primarily featured sentimental and sacred songs; their vocals were precise and clearly enunciated, with none of the modality, syncopation, or blues inflections favored by many of their contemporaries. Not surprisingly, the duo was popular with older listeners who remembered hearing such music in the parlors of a bygone America.

Both blind from birth, Lester McFarland and Robert Gardner met in 1915 while attending the Kentucky School for the Blind in Louisville. A musical prodigy, McFarland played piano, mandolin, cornet, trombone, and other instruments; he taught Gardner how to play guitar. They formed their professional partnership in 1922; Gardner played guitar and sang lead, while McFarland played mandolin and sang tenor.

By 1925 they were appearing on WNOX-Knoxville; their popularity led to a Brunswick contract in 1926. "When the Roses Bloom Again" was a significant hit; later record successes included "Are You Tired of Me, My Darling," "I'm Tying the Leaves So They Won't Come Down," "Twenty-one Years," and "'Tis Sweet to Be Remembered." They also recorded gospel numbers for BRUNSWICK as members of the Smoky Mountain Sacred Singers and the Old Southern Sacred Singers.

In 1931 the duo moved to Chicago, where they were featured on WLS's *NATIONAL BARN DANCE* as Mac & Bob. In the late 1930s they worked on KDKA-Pittsburgh, and KMA–Shenandoah, Iowa; they returned to WLS in 1939. They dissolved their partnership in 1950, when Gardner decided to devote his time to a Chicago religious mission. McFarland continued at WLS, first with KARL & HARTY, then as a soloist. He left broadcasting in 1953 to work in Chicago State Hospital's recreation department. Mac and Bob reunited for special occasions, including a 1964 WGN-TV appearance honoring the *National Barn Dance*'s fortieth anniversary. —*Dave Samuelson*

Bill Mack
b. Shamrock, Texas, June 4, 1929

A country broadcaster since the late 1940s, Bill Mack, a.k.a. the Midnight Cowboy, also enjoyed success as a singer, songwriter, and producer. Early STARDAY recordings, especially "Kitty Cat" and "The Cat Just Got in Town," represent Texas ROCKABILLY at its best. Later country recordings for several labels, including Starday, HICKORY, MGM, and United Artists, garnered moderate attention. Mack has been more successful as a songwriter. His "Drinking Champagne" was a hit twice—for CAL SMITH in 1968 and for GEORGE STRAIT in 1990. LEANN RIMES's recording of

"Blue," originally written and recorded by Mack in 1959, was a 1996 sensation.

Today the *Bill Mack Trucking Show* (begun in 1969) provides some of country radio's most creative programming, including diverse play lists, wide varieties of guests, trucker call-ins, and nationwide information on weather and road conditions. Broadcast from midnight to 5 A.M. on WBAP-AM in Fort Worth, Texas, the show reaches more than half the continental United States. Mack also hosts the syndicated country music inspirational program *Country Crossroads* on some 900 stations. Television credits include hosting *The Buck Owens Show*, *The Bob Wills Show*, and *Cowtown Jamboree*. Mack was elected to the Country Music Disc Jockey Hall of Fame in 1982.   —*William P. Davis*

Warner Mack

b. Nashville, Tennessee, April 2, 1935

Country traditionalist singer-songwriter Warner McPherson appeared regularly on the charts through the sixties and early seventies. He became Warner Mack when his nickname was inadvertently used in place of his last name on a record label. He grew up in Vicksburg, Mississippi, and began performing while still in high school. After gaining experience in clubs and radio, he moved on to the *LOUISIANA HAYRIDE* and the *OZARK JUBILEE*. During this time he recorded one of his own compositions, "Is It Wrong (For Loving You)" for DECCA RECORDS. The pop-sounding release not only reached #9 in 1958 and remained on the country charts for nine months but also became a hit for two other artists: WEBB PIERCE (#11, 1960) and SONNY JAMES (#1, 1974). On November 29, 1964, Mack was involved in a serious car accident in a snowstorm near Princeton, Indiana. This accident set his career back months, if not years.

After a career lull of six years, Mack bounced back with "Sittin' in an All Nite Cafe" (#4, 1965) and followed it with his biggest hit, "The Bridge Washed Out" (#1, 1965). Mack continued to place hits on the charts through 1977, though with considerably diminished impact after 1970. He also wrote RICKY VAN SHELTON's 1995 Top Ten single "After the Lights Go Down."   —*Don Roy*

REPRESENTATIVE RECORDINGS

From the Vaults: Decca Country Classics, 1934–1973 (MCA, 1994), one recording on various artists anthology; *The Best of the Best of Warner Mack* (Gusto, 1978)

Uncle Dave Macon

b. Smart Station, Warren County, Tennessee, October 7, 1870; d. March 22, 1952

Nicknamed the Dixie Dewdrop by GRAND OLE OPRY founder GEORGE D. HAY, David Harrison Macon, with his chin whiskers, gold teeth, gates-ajar collar, and open-backed Gibson banjo, was the first substantial star of the Grand Ole Opry and one of the most colorful personalities in the history of the music. He was an influential bridge between the folk and vaudeville music of the nineteenth century and the more modern music of the phonograph record, the radio, and motion pictures. He was a supremely skilled banjo player (modern historians have identified at least nineteen different picking styles on his records), a strong and clear singer, a skilled songwriter, an outrageous comedian, and a dedicated preserver of old

Uncle Dave Macon

songs and styles. Most of all, though, he was a master showman, bringing to the newly emerging country music a professionalism and polish sorely needed to establish it as a viable commercial art form.

Born into a well-to-do family in Warren County, in hilly central Tennessee, Macon began learning folksongs of the area by the time he was nine. In 1884, following financial reversals after the Civil War, the Macon family moved to Nashville, where they ran a hotel on Broadway. By coincidence, the hotel was headquarters for many of the vaudeville performers who came through town, and the teenager Dave Macon watched them as they rehearsed in the basement. He was especially entranced with the various trick banjo players then in vogue, especially one called Joel Davidson. Soon he had talked his mother into buying him a banjo, and he began to absorb as much as he could from the vaudeville entertainers. This was all interrupted, however, when his father was stabbed and killed in front of the hotel, and the family broke up and returned to the country. Dave stayed with his mother, who ran a stagecoach rest stop at Readyville. In charge of watering the horses, young Macon built a stage over the barn and would also entertain the passengers with his banjo.

Growing up away from Nashville, Macon abandoned any hope he had for a professional career. He married a local girl, inherited a large farm, and opened a freight line between Murfreesboro and Woodbury, Tennessee. But in the 1920s, when a rival company began to compete with trucks, Macon abandoned his faithful mules and thought about retiring (he was over fifty). Then one day when Macon was performing for customers in a Nashville barber shop, he was spotted by a talent scout for the Loew's vaudeville chain. Vastly impressed, he offered Macon a job, and, accompanied by local fiddler SID HARKREADER, he opened in Birmingham and was a sensation. The tour soon extended as far north as Boston, and in a short time Macon had a national reputation. In July 1924 Macon went to New York to record for Vocalion. The results were several best-sellers, including "Keep My Skillet Good and Greasy" (a Macon favorite throughout his career), "Chewing Gum," and "Hill Billie Blues."

Macon joined the cast of the WSM *Barn Dance* in 1925—he was one of the first two members, along with UNCLE JIMMY THOMPSON—and became the only member of the cast with any kind of national reputation. Throughout the 1920s, though, he appeared only occasionally, finding more money in touring and making records.

From 1924 through 1938 he recorded more than 180 songs for almost every major label. He also recorded and performed often with SAM MCGEE, the remarkable flat-top guitarist, McGee's brother Kirk, and Macon's own son Dorris. In the 1930s Macon worked for a time with the DELMORE BROTHERS as well as with young ROY ACUFF and BILL MONROE. Macon was a highlight of the 1940 Republic film *Grand Ole Opry,* in which he sang and danced around his banjo to "Take Me Back to My Carolina Home." Other popular Macon favorites that he routinely performed or recorded include "Bully of the Town," "Late Last Night When Willie Came Home," "Rock About My Saro Jane" (which he had learned from black stevedores on the Cumberland River in the 1880s), "From Jerusalem to Jericho," "Buddy, Won't You Roll Down the Line," "Sail Away, Ladies," "When the Train Comes Along," and "Cumberland Mountain Deer Chase." His signature hymn was "How Beautiful Heaven Must Be," which was carved on his monument near Woodbury, Tennessee.

Though his banjo playing began to suffer in the 1940s, Macon's comedy and singing helped carry him through Opry shows and tours. He was still on the show when he was over eighty, in 1952, and became ill. He died in Rutherford County Hospital, and was buried near the Woodbury–Murfreesboro pike, where he had spent so many years hauling freight. —*Charles Wolfe*

REPRESENTATIVE RECORDING

Laugh Your Blues Away (Rounder, 1979)

Maddox Brothers & Rose

Clifton R. E. Maddox b. Boaz, Alabama, 1912; d. 1949
John Calvin Maddox b. Boaz, Alabama, November 3, 1915;
d. July 3, 1968
Fred Roscoe Maddox b. Boaz, Alabama, July 2, 1919; d. October 29, 1992
Kenneth Chalmer Maddox b. Boaz, Alabama, December 7, 1922
Roselea Arbana Maddox b. Boaz, Alabama, August 15, 1925;
d. April 15, 1998
Henry Ford Maddox b. Boaz, Alabama, March 19, 1928; d. June 1974

Touted as the Most Colorful Hillbilly Band in America, the California-based Maddox Brothers & Rose were one of the postwar era's most hard-charging, forward-looking country bands. A family of sharecroppers driven by hard times from their Alabama home in the spring of 1933, they spent three weeks hitchhiking and jumping boxcars to reach California. After four years of migrant farm labor, seventeen-year-old Fred Maddox decided to form a family band and persuaded a Modesto businessman to sponsor them on local station KTRB—agreeing to the stipulation that the band have a "girl singer."

The Maddox Brothers & Rose

In 1937, dubbed the Alabama Outlaws, and fronted by eleven-year-old Rose (and managed by their strict mother, Lula Maddox), the family hit the airwaves and quickly garnered thousands of fan letters. Renamed Maddox Brothers & Rose before the year was out, the band, with their mix of southern folk music, contemporary western song, and roguish, black-influenced boogie, built an avid following. In 1939 they took first place in a hillbilly band competition at the California State Fair, winning a two-year contract on the McClatchy Broadcasting network based in Sacramento and broadcast from KFBK.

After war broke out and the brothers shipped overseas, Rose, at Lula's behest, entered into a short-lived marriage that produced a son, Donnie, but that broke up before the child was born. In December 1945, the band (now working without firstborn Cliff, due to a mother/son rift) returned to the airwaves at Stockton's KGDM and soon were recording for FOUR STAR RECORDS. They also hired rodeo tailor NATHAN TURK (who supplied wardrobe for Western stars GENE AUTRY and ROY ROGERS) to create some of the most elaborate and striking costumes worn by a country music act to date. The Maddoxes' unorthodox, high-volume honky-tonk music was matched by their legendary show-and-dance presentation, a fast-paced blend of gags, magic tricks, jokes, and pantomime; each member had a special stage nickname ("Cal the Laughing Cowboy," "Friendly Henry, the Workin' Girl's Friend," etc.). Records such as "Alimony," "Single Girl," and "Hangover Blues" established Rose as an independent, almost protofeminist figure, and by the time the family guested on the GRAND OLE OPRY in February 1949, she was possibly the leading national female star in country music.

In 1950, disgusted with the abysmal financial arrangements at Four Star (the group was never once paid by owner Bill McCall), the Maddoxes were freed of their contract, through union intervention. They promptly answered UNCLE ART SATHERLEY's call to sign with COLUMBIA. Although Rose was so popular that by the mid-1950s Columbia held three separate contracts on her (one with her brothers, one as a single, and one as a short-lived duet act with her sister-in-law), Satherley's retirement (in 1952), succeeding producer DON LAW's desire to tone down their sound, and Rose's ambition to cut more pop-slanted records worked against the group. They split up in late 1956 after Rose, with Cal accompanying, made a spectacular return to the Grand Ole Opry in September, as a member. After changing into a risqué, bare-midriff cowgirl suit, Rose hid until her name was called, then appeared to a tumultuous reception to sing "Tall Men." The political tensions between California-based and Tennessee-based performers ultimately led to her dismissal (at ROY ACUFF's request) in March 1957.

By 1959 Rose had married clubowner Jim Brogdon and had landed a seven-year contract with CAPITOL that produced her biggest chart successes: "Sing a Little Song of Heartache" (#3, 1962–63) and, with BUCK OWENS, "Loose Talk" (#4, 1961). At BILL MONROE's request she also became the first woman to record a bluegrass LP (one of five Capitol albums). However, by 1965 Capitol had dropped her, and her marriage broke up. She cut an album (*Rosie*) at STARDAY in 1967 and continued to record for a variety of independents, but she never regained a high national profile. Nonetheless, Rose's work with her brothers defined California's freewheeling country music style, and she was one of country's most influential performers.

—*Jonny Whiteside*

REPRESENTATIVE RECORDINGS

Maddox Brothers & Rose: America's Most Colorful Hillbilly Band, Volume I (1995, Arhoolie); *Maddox Brothers & Rose: America's Most Colorful Hillbilly Band, Volume II* (1996, Arhoolie)

Tommy Magness
b. Mineral Bluff, Georgia, October 21, 1916; d. October 5, 1971

Thomas Magness fiddled with both the King of Country Music, ROY ACUFF, and the Father of Bluegrass, BILL MONROE. At age sixteen Magness played on WWNC–Asheville, North Carolina, later on WBT-Charlotte, and in 1938 joined ROY HALL on WDBJ–Roanoke, Virginia.

Magness composed the classic fiddle tune "Natural Bridge Blues." On October 7, 1940, Magness recorded "Mule Skinner Blues" with Monroe; and on January 28, 1947, he cut "Wabash Cannonball" with Acuff in Hollywood, where Magness also appeared in four Acuff films. On January 15, 1949, Magness recorded the fiddle tune "Black Mountain Rag" with Acuff's Smoky Mountain Boys. Although the tune is copyrighted under Magness's name with ACUFF-ROSE PUBLICATIONS, it had been recorded by others (including CURLY FOX) before Magness, and did not originate with Magness. Other acts Magness worked with include CLYDE MOODY and RENO & SMILEY. In addition, Magness appeared on the GRAND OLE OPRY and the *RENFRO VALLEY BARN DANCE*.

—*Walt Trott*

Brent Maher
b. Great Bend, Kansas, August 14, 1942

One of the top record producers of the 1980s, Brent Maher was responsible for producing the JUDDS and for con-

necting them with RCA RECORDS. In addition, he helped pen such hits for the duo as "Why Not Me," "Girls Night Out," "Rockin' with the Rhythm of the Rain," and "Born to Be Blue." His songs have been recorded through the years by such acts as DOTTIE WEST ("A Lesson in Leavin'"), TANYA TUCKER ("Some Kind of Trouble"), KENNY ROGERS, Tina Turner, the FORESTER SISTERS, MICHELLE WRIGHT, SHELBY LYNNE, and CARL PERKINS. Maher has also written music for television.

Maher started out in Nashville as a recording engineer and then worked on the West Coast, engineering the initial album for Sly & the Family Stone, as well as records for Ike & Tina Turner ("Proud Mary"), the Fifth Dimension ("Aquarius"), and Gladys Knight as well as one of Duke Ellington's last albums.

Maher moved back to Nashville in 1974 as chief engineer at Creative Workshop, where he engineered for albums by OLIVIA NEWTON-JOHN, LARRY GATLIN, LEON RUSSELL, and ELVIS PRESLEY. In 1978 Maher moved up to co-produce MICHAEL JOHNSON's big pop hit "Bluer Than Blue." It was Maher's daughter, treated in a Nashville-area hospital by nurse Naomi Judd, who introduced her father to the Judds' music via a homemade tape; Maher subsequently brought the act to the attention of JOE GALANTE at RCA Records. Since the dissolution of the Judds, Maher has produced albums for KATHY MATTEA and Shelby Lynne. Representative productions include the albums *The Judds* (mini-LP), *Why Not Me* (the Judds), *Heartland* (the Judds), *Lonesome Standard Time* (Kathy Mattea), and *Good News* (Kathy Mattea).

In 1995 Maher co-founded the Nashville-based label Magnatone Records and served as the label's president until 1996. He owns the Moraine Music Group publishing company.

—*Bob Millard*

J. E. Mainer
b. Buncombe County, North Carolina, July 20, 1898; d. June 12, 1971

J. E. Mainer's Mountaineers constituted the leading Appalachian stringband of the middle and late thirties. Joseph Emmett Mainer came from a western North Carolina mountain family and went to work in the cotton mills at an early age. In the early twenties he settled in Concord, North Carolina, where he organized a band built around his own fiddle for local entertainment. By 1932 this endeavor landed him work at Charlotte's WBT radio under the sponsorship of CRAZY WATER CRYSTALS. In 1935 the Mountaineers included his brother WADE MAINER on banjo, with Zeke Morris and John Love on guitars.

The original band soon split up, but Mainer hired new musicians, most notably SNUFFY JENKINS, George Morris, and Leonard Stokes. Mainer continued to record for BLUEBIRD until 1939 and worked at various southern radio stations. After World War II Mainer became an early artist with KING RECORDS. His prominence faded during the fifties, but the folk revival renewed interest in his music. He recorded again for KING, Arhoolie, Blue Jay, and the Rural Rhythm labels. J. E. Mainer continued playing festivals and concerts until his death.

—*Ivan M. Tribe*

REPRESENTATIVE RECORDINGS

J. E. Mainer's Crazy Mountaineers (Old Timey, 1967–68), 2 vols.; *Good Ole Mountain Music* (King, 1960); *Ragged but Right: Great Country String Bands of the 1930s* (RCA, 1988)

Wade Mainer

b. Buncombe County, North Carolina, April 21, 1907

Wade E. Mainer left his brother J. E.'s original Mainer's Mountaineers in 1936 to forge his own musical career. Wade's band, the Sons of the Mountaineers, worked on radio in Charlotte, Raleigh, Asheville, and Knoxville and turned out numerous BLUEBIRD recordings in a style that could best be labeled as protobluegrass. Mainer's own unique two-finger banjo style was supplemented by the work of other musicians, who included at various times Tiny Dodson, Jay Hugh Hall, Steve Ledford, CLYDE MOODY, Zeke Morris, Homer Sherrill, and Jack and Curly Shelton. Through 1941 the Sons of the Mountaineers had nearly ninety numbers released on disc and entertained at the Roosevelt White House.

Mainer revived his career after World War II, again working on radio and recording for KING. As his style became increasingly dated, he moved to Michigan in 1953 and went to work for General Motors in Flint. For some years thereafter he and his wife, Julie, sang only in churches. After retirement in 1973, Wade and Julie began performing at folk and bluegrass festivals and recorded several new albums for Old Homestead, a firm that also reissued many of his earlier sides. At eighty he won a National Heritage Fellowship and at eighty-four recorded a new album for June Appal. He remains semiactive in the late 1990s.
—*Ivan M. Tribe*

REPRESENTATIVE RECORDINGS

Early and Great (Old Homestead, 1983–93), 3 vols.; *In the Land of Melody* (June Appal, 1992); *Ragged But Right: Great Country String Bands of the 1930s* (RCA, 1988)

Mandolin

Derived from the ancient lutes of renaissance Italy, the mandolin came into its present form as a short-necked instrument with eight paired strings in early eighteenth-century Naples, and it has endured as an important instrument in Italian popular music. Minor composers of the time wrote music for the mandolin; later operatists such as Handel, Mozart, and Verdi scored occasional passages for the instrument when atmospheric touches were needed. Otherwise the mandolin was regarded as a minor-league instrument with limited possibilities.

In the United States, mandolin orchestras, with mandolas, mando-cellos, and even an occasional mando-bass, were a popular feature of community life in many areas early in the twentieth century. A few early recordings were made by soloists Valentine Abt and Samuel Siegel. Giovanni Vicari and Giovanni Gioviale recorded some virtuoso pieces for Italian catalogues in the 1920s. Russian-born Dave Apollon headed a crack mandolin ensemble that toured the vaudeville circuit and made two memorable records for BRUNSWICK in 1932.

Luthier Orville Gibson introduced the flat-backed, scroll-bodied mandolin in 1898. When designer Lloyd Loar introduced his improvement of this design, the Gibson F-series mandolin in 1923, the model's improved tone and greater volume enhanced the mandolin's appeal, as did BILL MONROE's distinctive use of the F-5 model in the 1940s and beyond.

Earlier, blind minstrels Lester McFarland and Robert Gardner (MAC & BOB) had formed a popular duo whose songs were spread via broadcasts from WLS in Chicago and their popular records. Their singing and mandolin/guitar accompaniments inspired a host of brother-style duets in the 1930s, notably the BLUE SKY BOYS and the MONROE BROTHERS.

Bill Monroe became the mandolin's first country-style virtuoso and brought the instrument into new prominence when he joined the GRAND OLE OPRY in 1939 and featured it on his records in 1940 and thereafter. His mandolin, combined with his group's instrumental and vocal blend, helped define the genre that later became known as BLUE-GRASS.

Some important stylists in the 1940s, such as Paul Buskirk, Ernest Ferguson, TINY MOORE, Jethro Burns (HOMER & JETHRO), and Red Rector, developed individual approaches of their own. By 1950, however, the Monroe bluegrass model dominated; even unique performers such as Jesse McReynolds (JIM & JESSE) and BUZZ BUSBY drew on Monroe's example, as have mandolinists such as BOB OSBORNE, John Duffey, DAVID GRISMAN, Butch Baldassari, and others.
—*Dick Spottswood*

Barbara Mandrell

b. Houston, Texas, December 25, 1948

An entertainment dynamo, Barbara Ann Mandrell took her soul-country style to the biggest showrooms of Las Vegas, ruled the country charts during the late 1970s and early 1980s, starred on network TV, and told her story in one of country's best-selling autobiographies. A multi-instrumentalist as well as a singer, she has proven herself skilled at steel guitar, banjo, saxophone, accordion, bass, and mandolin.

Barbara Mandrell

Mandrell is the daughter of country guitarist Irby Mandrell, who guided her early career. Raised in Southern California, the blue-eyed blonde was a child prodigy—hence the title "The Princess of the Steel." Guitarist JOE MAPHIS got her a spot on TV's TOWN HALL PARTY, landed her a Mosrite Records deal, and brought her into his Vegas show. By 1962 she was touring with PATSY CLINE and JOHNNY CASH. Named Miss Oceanside at age sixteen, Mandrell married drummer Ken Dudney, entertained in the Mandrell Family Band, and toured Vietnam by age twenty.

A visit to the GRAND OLE OPRY in 1968 inspired her move to Nashville, where her performances in Printers Alley led to immediate record company offers. She signed with COLUMBIA, and in 1969–72 she was on the charts with remakes of soul songs such as "I've Been Loving You Too Long," "Do Right Woman," "Treat Him Right," and "Show Me." Her first Top Ten hit was 1971's "Tonight My Baby's Coming Home." She also scored on EPIC in duets with DAVID HOUSTON. Mandrell joined the Opry cast in 1972.

Her 1973 hit "The Midnight Oil" is regarded as a female breakthrough because of the song's frank sexuality. A move to ABC/DOT in 1975 resulted in more smoldering performances, including such Top Ten tunes as "Standing Room Only" (1976), "Married but Not to Each Other" (1977), and "Tonight" (1978).

Between 1978 and 1984 Mandrell dominated the charts with seventeen Top Ten hits. GEORGE JONES put in a cameo appearance on "I Was Country When Country Wasn't Cool," a #1 hit for Mandrell in 1981. "Sleeping Single in a Double Bed" (1978) also topped the charts, as did her 1979 cover of the r&b hit "(If Loving You Is Wrong) I Don't Want to Be Right." Mandrell was named CMA Female Vocalist of the Year in 1979 and 1981, and Entertainer of the Year in 1980 and 1981.

With sisters Louise and Irlene, she achieved mainstream popularity on her 1980–82 NBC-TV series Barbara Mandrell & the Mandrell Sisters. She learned choreography for the show, and on it she displayed her instrumental skills, did comedy, and brought dozens of country acts wide exposure. But wearying of the weekly grind, she quit the successful variety series when it was attracting 40 million viewers per week.

Mandrell returned to Las Vegas in triumph with her 1983 stage extravaganza The Lady Is a Champ. In 1984 she taped her first network special, acted in a TV movie, and built her career museum in Nashville. But later that year she was injured severely in an automobile accident. In its wake, she published her best-selling 1990 autobiography Get to the Heart.

With DOLLY PARTON as her opening act, Mandrell returned to the stage at the Universal Amphitheatre in Los Angeles in 1986. She signed with CAPITOL/EMI in 1987 but failed to recapture her radio popularity. In the 1990s Mandrell has been an entertainer at corporate conventions and a guest star on such TV shows as Baywatch. On October 23, 1997, Mandrell staged a farewell concert dubbed "The Last Dance." She intends to focus on her acting career.

—Robert K. Oermann

REPRESENTATIVE RECORDINGS

The Best of Barbara Mandrell (Columbia, 1977); The Best of Barbara Mandrell (MCA, 1980); He Set My Life to Music (MCA, 1983); Greatest Hits (MCA, 1985)

Louise Mandrell
b. Corpus Christi, Texas, July 13, 1954

Louise Mandrell, a younger sister of country star BARBARA MANDRELL, was one of the original members of Barbara's band the Do-Rites when Louise was fifteen years old. Louise later went on to modest success as a solo artist, with several of her singles reaching the country Top Ten in the mid-1980s. During 1980–82 she was spotlighted as one of the sisters (along with Irlene Mandrell) in the NBC television show Barbara Mandrell and the Mandrell Sisters.

Noted for her showmanship, Louise Mandrell is proficient on many instruments, including bass, fiddle, piano, banjo, guitar, and horn. She is also a dancer as well as a singer. After performing in her sister's band, she began pursuing her own career in 1974, initially working as a backup vocalist for other acts. Signed by Epic in 1977, she had little success on the label, though a duet version of "Reunited" with her husband, R. C. Bannon, made the Top Twenty. She fared better on RCA, beginning in 1982, hitting the Top Ten with such songs as "Save Me" (1983) and "Maybe My Baby" (1985). —Mary A. Bufwack

REPRESENTATIVE RECORDING

Best of Louise Mandrell (BNA, 1992)

Manuel
b. Coalcoman, Michoacan, Mexico, April 23, 1938

Manuel Arturo Jose Cuevas Martinez has been designing clothes for country performers since the 1950s. Having apprenticed with the preeminent western couturiers NATHAN TURK and NUDIE, he is a living link to the rhinestone-cowboy tradition pioneered in the 1930s and 1940s. Manuel's eye-catching designs for contemporary stars such as MARTY STUART and DWIGHT YOAKAM have helped to popularize ornate western wear among a new generation of country artists and fans.

Growing up one of a family of eleven children, Manuel was making his own clothes by age eight, and began a tailoring apprenticeship and creating costumes for the local theater soon after. "My dream was to own my own shop where I made everything—from all the accessories to the clothing," he has said.

His dream took him to Los Angeles in about 1953, where, after briefly apprenticing with Nathan Turk, he found a steady job with celebrity tailor Sy Devore. There, Manuel fitted movie stars such as Dean Martin and Frank Sinatra for tuxedos and other formal wear. On a recommendation from embroidery artist Viola Grae, Nudie hired the young designer away from Devore. It wasn't long after joining Nudie in 1958 that Manuel moved from doing fittings to creating original designs. In 1960 Manuel became Nudie's son-in-law, marrying Barbara Cohn, with whom he had a daughter, Morelia.

In the mid-1960s Manuel designed costumes for movie westerns and TV shows such as Bonanza. At about this time he reportedly convinced JOHNNY CASH, one of numerous star clients, to dress only in black. Later in the decade Manuel collaborated with GRAM PARSONS in creating the Burrito Brother's outrageous white Nudie suit decorated with pills, naked ladies, and marijuana leaves. After Manuel's marriage ended in divorce in 1972, he opened a by-appointment-only shop on Lankershim in North Hollywood in 1974.

Inspired by Manuel's designs for BUCK OWENS in the 1950s and 1960s, DWIGHT YOAKAM became a client just as his career was taking off in 1985. When he wore Manuel's turquoise rhinestone-studded bolero jacket on the cover of his 1987 *Hillbilly Deluxe* album, WARNER BROS. RECORDS received a reported 3,000 requests for information on obtaining the garment. In the early 1990s Manuel and Yoakam created a line of similar jackets called DY Ranchwear. Another longtime Manuel client is MARTY STUART, who commissioned an extensive wardrobe from Manuel, including rhinestone-studded jackets lavishly embroidered with dice, hearts, and horseshoes.

In 1989 Manuel moved his shop from Los Angeles to Nashville's Broadway, near Music Row, where his star clients include ALAN JACKSON and WYNONNA. He has also nurtured the talent of young western-wear designers such as Katy K, whom he advised to move from New York to Nashville. In 1996 Manuel introduced a ready-to-wear line, the Manuel Collection, which includes western shirts, dresses, and jackets. Primarily, Manuel remains known for his personalized custom designs.   —*Holly George-Warren*

Rose Lee & Joe Maphis

Joe & Rose Lee Maphis

Otis Wilson "Joe" Maphis b. Suffolk, Virginia, May 12, 1921; d. June 27, 1986

Rose Lee (Schetrompf) Maphis b. Hagerstown, Maryland, December 29, 1922

The husband-and-wife team of Joe & Rose Lee Maphis enjoyed their greatest success as performers in the heyday of live country music programs on radio and television. Joe began radio work while still a teenager, moving from local stations in Virginia to the *Boone County Jamboree* on WLW in Cincinnati and the NATIONAL BARN DANCE on WLS in Chicago. After serving in the army in World War II, he became a charter member of the OLD DOMINION BARN DANCE over WRVA in Richmond, Virginia. Rose Lee followed a similar path, performing in St. Louis and in Blytheville, Arkansas, before moving to WRVA in 1948. It was there that she and Joe met. In 1951 Joe and Rose Lee relocated to Los Angeles to work in the then new medium of television, doing live broadcasts nearly four hours a day, six days a week. They were married in February 1952. The following year they joined the cast of TOWN HALL PARTY on KTTV.

Although his proficiency on a variety of instruments earned him the title King of the Strings, it was as a guitarist that Joe had the greatest impact. With his 1955 COLUMBIA recording of "Fire on the Strings" (a re-working of the fiddle tune "Fire on the Mountain"), he demonstrated that he was among the first to adapt fiddle tunes to the guitar. A leading session guitarist in Hollywood, he played on the soundtracks of the films *Thunder Road* and *God's Little Acre* as well as supplying background music for a number of 1950s and 1960s TV series. He also performed on pop and rock records by RICK NELSON, the Four Preps, WANDA JACKSON, and Tommy Sands; and his twangy sound was an influence on the surf guitar sound of the 1960s. Through his influence on CLARENCE WHITE, Joe also had an impact on the development of the guitar as a lead instrument in bluegrass.

Joe and Rose Lee also contributed as songwriters, with

"Dim Lights, Thick Smoke (And Loud, Loud Music)" (Joe & Rose Lee Maphis, 1953; VERN GOSDIN, 1985) and "Love Is the Look You're Looking For" (CONNIE SMITH, 1972) being their most successful compositions. The Maphises recorded both as a duo and as solo artists for the COLUMBIA, CAPITOL, STARDAY, Chart, and CMH labels. Joe's instrumental double LP *The Joe Maphis Flat-Picking Spectacular* was nominated for a Grammy.   —*Paul F. Wells*

REPRESENTATIVE RECORDINGS

Rose Lee and Joe Maphis (with the Blue Ridge Mountain Boys) (Capitol, 1962); *The Joe Maphis Flat-Picking Spectacular* (CMH, 1981)

Marshall Tucker Band

The Marshall Tucker Band combined elements of several southern musical styles (especially country, rock, blues, and soul) into an original musical blend that has strongly influenced several contemporary country musicians, such as HANK WILLIAMS JR. and TRAVIS TRITT.

Formed in 1970 by six friends from Spartanburg, South Carolina, and named after a Spartanburg piano tuner, the Marshall Tucker Band included Toy Caldwell (b. November 13, 1947, d. February 25, 1993), lead and steel guitarist, lead vocalist, and chief songwriter; his brother Tommy Caldwell (b. November 9, 1949, d. April 28, 1980), bassist and background vocalist; George McCorkle (b. October 11, 1946), rhythm guitarist; Doug Gray (b. May 22, 1948), lead and background vocalist and percussionist; Paul Riddle (b. ca. 1953), drummer; and Jerry Eubanks (b. March 19, 1950), flutist, saxophonist, and background vocalist. The Marshall Tucker Band gained a large national base of fans through constant touring and through the release of numerous commercially and artistically successful albums (especially fine were seven made for Macon, Georgia–based Capricorn Records between 1973 and 1978; the group's subsequent albums for WARNER BROS. RECORDS—five in all—had their moments).

The Marshall Tucker Band suffered a significant blow in 1980 when Tommy Caldwell died in an automobile accident; he was replaced by Franklin Wilkie. Although Toy Caldwell left in 1985, the group continued, signing with MERCURY RECORDS in 1987 and the Cabin Fever label in 1992. The Marshall Tucker Band's classic songs ("Can't You See," "Ramblin'," "Fire on the Mountain," and "Heard It in a Love Song") continue to receive airplay on both oldie and country music radio stations.   —*Ted Olson*

REPRESENTATIVE RECORDINGS

The Marshall Tucker Band (Capricorn, 1973); *The Best of the Marshall Tucker Band: The Capricorn Years* (Era, 1994), 2 discs

Linda Martell
b. Lexington County, South Carolina, June 4, 1941

The first black female vocalist to perform at the GRAND OLE OPRY was five-foot-four-inch South Carolina native Linda Martell, who was born Thelma Bynem.

She grew up around Leesville, South Carolina, as one of five children. Her father was a minister, and she started singing in a church choir at age five.

"I also grew up singing country," Martell said. "My father, Clarence Bynem, loved country music. My three brothers were all musicians. We started out doing gospel at St. Mark Baptist Church in Leesville. I also started singing with a pop band in Columbia, South Carolina, when I was twelve and worked with them all around the Columbia area until I was nineteen." While still a teenager, she began singing with a racially integrated r&b group called the Anglos, with whom she recorded singles on the Fire and Vee-Jay labels. She also sang backup at recording sessions in Atlanta and Muscle Shoals.

Nashville businessman Duke Rayner heard about Martell's outstanding voice and tracked her down. He talked her into flying to Nashville for a demo session and then took the tape to SHELBY SINGLETON, who signed her to Plantation Records. Martell made her first guest appearance on the Opry in August 1969, within a week after her Plantation Records single, "Color Him Father" (a country version of the Winstons' soul hit), was released. It went to #22 on the *Billboard* charts. Soon afterward she made TV appearances in 1970 on *The BILL ANDERSON Show* and *HEE HAW*. Her second single, "Before The Next Teardrop Falls" (made well before FREDDY FENDER's 1975 hit), went to #33. Martell also made one album, another charting single ("Bad Case of the Blues"), and eleven more Opry appearances.

Although her recording career ended in 1974, she continued to perform, based in Florida, Tennessee, California, and New York before moving back to Leesville in 1992. She still sings throughout South Carolina with a rhythm & blues band called Eazzy.   —*Don Rhodes*

REPRESENTATIVE RECORDING

Color Me Country (Plantation, 1971)

Martha White Flour
established 1899

One of the South's most recognized brand names, Martha White Flour is linked to country music through its longtime sponsorship of the GRAND OLE OPRY and fifteen-year association with bluegrass pioneers LESTER FLATT & EARL SCRUGGS.

Royal Flour Mill Co. launched Martha White Flour in 1899; the brand was named after the original owner's young daughter. In 1941 the Nashville-based mill, officially called Royal, Barry-Carter Mills, was purchased by Cohen E. Williams and his sons, Cohen T. and Joe Williams. The younger Cohen became president of the company, which he eventually renamed Martha White Foods after its flagship product. The firm started sponsoring an Opry segment in 1945, and in 1946 Williams started sponsoring an early-morning WSM show with a western-style ensemble featuring a female singer billed as "Martha White."

In June 1953 Williams recruited Flatt & Scruggs to helm the wake-up show, although WSM executives feared repercussions from the musicians' former employer, BILL MONROE. Listeners immediately responded to the Foggy Mountain Boys' driving music and Flatt's warm personality. After Flatt & Scruggs were firmly established as the flour's on-air spokesmen, Williams demanded that WSM allow the band on the Martha White portion of the Opry. He threatened to pull his advertising from the station, and Flatt & Scruggs became Opry members in 1955.

Martha White's association with the Opry and Flatt & Scruggs proved mutually beneficial. Williams publicly credited the band for helping build Martha White Foods into a multimillion-dollar business; at the same time, Flatt & Scruggs's corporate relationship with Martha White helped them become one of the best-known acts in country music. The band rarely played a concert without performing the catchy "Bake Right with Martha White" theme. In the late 1950s and early 1960s the company sponsored bluegrass acts in other parts of the South, most notably HYLO BROWN and JIM & JESSE.

Williams sold his company to Beatrice Foods in 1974, but remained as chairman until his retirement ten years later. He died May 29, 1988, at age eighty-one.
     —*Dave Samuelson*

Benny Martin
b. Sparta, Tennessee, May 8, 1928

Influential fiddler Benjamin Edward Martin worked as a sideman and session player for some of the greatest names in country music. As a teenager, Martin was featured with Big Jeff Bess & the Radio Playboys on station WLAC, Nashville, in 1944. He also performed with ROBERT LUNN, CURLY FOX, and MILTON ESTES & His Musical Millers on WSM's GRAND OLE OPRY. In 1946 Martin cut his first record, "Me and My Fiddle," for Pioneer Records.

Impressed, BILL MONROE made him a Blue Grass Boy in 1948. Martin next replaced TOMMY MAGNESS in ROY ACUFF's Smoky Mountain Boys in 1949 and also recorded with Acuff. FLATT & SCRUGGS engaged Martin to play with the Foggy Mountain Boys at WNOX-Knoxville, on the MIDDAY MERRY-GO-ROUND, and later on WSM's *Martha White Biscuit Time* show. His fiddling can be heard on thirteen early Flatt

& Scruggs sides. In addition, MGM RECORDS released two Benny Martin singles, including vocals in 1953.

In February 1954 Martin joined the KITTY WELLS–JOHNNIE & JACK troupe, remaining through fall of 1955. During that period MERCURY RECORDS released twenty-one Martin sides, including "Ice Cold Love" and "Coming Attractions." He also worked solo on the Opry.

On recording sessions, Martin restricted himself to providing fiddle, rhythm guitar, and back-up vocals, but he also plays autoharp, bass, banjo, mandolin, ukelele, and viola. Occasionally he furnished compositions, notably "I'm In Love With You" and "Each Day" for Wells, and "Weary Moments" for Johnnie & Jack.

RCA Records was the next label to record Martin, in 1957. A year later he cut tracks for DECCA RECORDS—and introduced his invention, an eight-string fiddle. In 1960 STARDAY RECORDS signed Martin, releasing his first album, titled *Benny Martin: Country Music's Sensational Entertainer,* the following year. He placed two singles on the country charts—"Rosebuds and You" (Starday, 1963) and "A Soldier's Prayer in Vietnam" (MONUMENT, 1966)—and was briefly managed by COLONEL TOM PARKER (prior to Parker's representing ELVIS PRESLEY).

Other musicians Martin recorded with include JOHN HARTFORD, BUCK GRAVES, JOE MAPHIS, and DON RENO.

—*Walt Trott*

REPRESENTATIVE RECORDINGS

Tennessee Jubilee (Flying Fish, 1975); *Big Daddy of the Fiddle & Bow* (CMH, 1979), 2 LPs

Grady Martin
b. Chapel Hill, Tennessee, January 17, 1929

Grady Martin is one of the true legends of Nashville's original "A-Team" of studio musicians; his greatest strength was his versatility. Whether playing the fiddle or guitar—electric, acoustic, or six-string electric bass—his creativity helped to make hits of many records from the 1950s through the 1970s.

Thomas Grady Martin was just fifteen when he joined Big Jeff & His Radio Playboys as their fiddler in 1944. In 1946 he joined PAUL HOWARD's western swing–oriented Arkansas Cotton Pickers as half of Howard's "twin guitar" ensemble along with Robert "Jabbo" Arrington. After Howard left the GRAND OLE OPRY, Opry newcomer LITTLE JIMMY DICKENS hired several former Cotton Pickers, including Martin, as his original Country Boys road band.

Off the road, Martin began working recording sessions. He led RED FOLEY's band on the ABC-TV show *OZARK JUBILEE.* Paying service to a strong business relationship with DECCA A&R man PAUL COHEN and his successor, OWEN BRADLEY, Martin began to record instrumental singles and LPs for Decca, including a country-jazz instrumental LP as part of Decca's *Country and Western Dance-O-Rama* series. Martin recorded many more Decca recordings as lead for the Nashville pop band the Slew Foot Five.

Martin's role as studio guitarist yielded numerous memorable moments. It was he who played the throbbing leads on JOHNNY HORTON's 1956 hit "Honky Tonk Man," the exquisite nylon string guitar on MARTY ROBBINS's 1959 crossover smash "El Paso," and LEFTY FRIZZELL's 1964 "Saginaw Michigan." One of the most famous sessions was an accidental malfunction in mid-take when Grady played

the distorted "fuzz" guitar solo on Robbins's 1960 hit "Don't Worry." Though studio musicians in those days rarely received credit for their work, Martin's efforts didn't go unnoticed. Producers often designated him "session leader," which meant he led the musicians and directed the impromptu arrangements that became a trademark of Nashville sessions. In other words he often became the de facto producer in the process.

Martin continued to play sessions through the 1970s, working extensively with CONWAY TWITTY and LORETTA LYNN, and produced the country-rock band Brush Arbor. His funky leads helped to make a hit of JEANNE PRUETT's 1973 "Satin Sheets." Martin eventually returned to performing, first with JERRY REED and then with WILLIE NELSON's band, with whom he worked from 1980 to 1994. Martin became the first recipient of Nashville Music Association's Masters Award in 1983. —*Rich Kienzle*

REPRESENTATIVE RECORDING

Country and Western Dance-O-Rama: Grady Martin and his Winging Strings (Decca, 1955)

Janis Martin
b. Sutherlin, Virginia, March 27, 1940

Combining a spunky, boisterous vocal style with bold stage moves that drew comparisons to ELVIS PRESLEY, Janice Darlene Martin became a recording artist at age fifteen and went on to become one of the most acclaimed female rockabilly artists of the late 1950s.

Martin was singing and playing guitar by age six. At eight she entered her first talent contest and won second place. In 1953 she joined the cast of the *OLD DOMINION BARN DANCE* in Richmond, Virginia. In 1956 Martin recorded a demo tape of a song called "Will You, Willyum," written by two staff announcers at WRVA. The tape reached the hands of STEVE SHOLES (who had recently signed Elvis Presley), and Sholes quickly signed Martin to an RCA recording contract, bringing her to Nashville to record under the direction of CHET ATKINS in March 1956.

Released as her first single, "Will You, Willyum," with "Drugstore Rock 'n' Roll" on the flip side, sold well, and Martin was soon in demand for appearances all over the United States. RCA obtained permission from Presley to bill her as the Female Elvis, and her profile was boosted by such catchy rockabilly recordings as "My Boy Elvis," "Love Me to Pieces," "Love and Kisses," and "Ooby Dooby." She appeared on the *Tonight Show, American Bandstand,* the *Today Show,* the *OZARK JUBILEE,* and the GRAND OLE OPRY. RCA kept the promotional work going by getting her a screen test for MGM Pictures and booked her on RCA's multi-artist European tour in 1957. Her career booming, Martin formed her own band, the Marteens, and toured widely in the United States and Canada.

But in 1958 Martin's success was cut short when she became a mother. She had secretly married her childhood sweetheart when she was fifteen, much to RCA's surprise. Her teen idol image tarnished, Martin was soon dropped from the label. In 1960 she recorded four sides for the small Palette label, but her career could not compete with family life, and she retired.

Over the years Martin has made attempts at revitalizing her career and is still a popular draw in Europe, where there is a large rockabilly following. In 1995 she appeared on ROSIE FLORES's *Rockabilly Filly* album for HIGHTONE.

—Jonita Aadland

REPRESENTATIVE RECORDINGS

Rock This Town: Rockabilly Hits, Volume 1 (Rhino, 1991); *Get Hot or Go Home: Vintage RCA Rockabilly, 1956–1959* (CMF, 1989)

Jimmy Martin
b. Sneedville, Tennessee, August 10, 1927

Certainly one of the most colorful characters in all of country and bluegrass music is James Henry Martin, known to his scores of fans as the King of Bluegrass, Martin's big professional break came in 1949, when he joined BILL MONROE's Blue Grass Boys. The first lead singer to record with Monroe on DECCA, their recordings of "Uncle Pen," "On and On," and "The Little Girl and the Dreadful Snake" have become classics. Few singers before or after Martin have complemented Monroe's voice so well. Martin worked local radio in Kingsport and Morristown, Tennessee, before joining with Monroe to play on and off with his band through 1955. During this time Martin pursued other projects as well. In 1951 he and Bobby Osborne recorded a handful of sides for Cincinnati's KING RECORDS. Martin and company made brief stops at WNOX's *MIDDAY MERRY GO-ROUND* and WCYB in Bristol before settling for a while in Detroit. In 1954 the OSBORNE BROTHERS and Martin recorded six sides for RCA, including "20/20 Vision" and "Save It! Save It!" Although they were a popular act in the Detroit area, Martin and the Osbornes parted ways about a year later. Jimmy landed a deal with DECCA and recorded 139 sides over the next eighteen years. "Rock Hearts," "Sophronie," "Hold Whatcha Got," "Widow

Jimmy Martin

Maker," and "The Sunny Side of the Mountain" are all bluegrass standards.

Martin's powerful vocals, rock-solid rhythm, and ability to communicate with his musicians yielded some powerful recordings. Countless musicians honed their musical skills under Martin's tutelage, including J. D. CROWE, Paul Williams, Alan Munde, Gloria Belle, and Bill Emerson. In the late 1950s and 1960s Martin was a featured act on both the *LOUISIANA HAYRIDE* and the *WWVA WHEELING JAMBOREE*. Semiretired, Martin now works about two dozen dates a year. In 1995 his contributions were formally recognized with his induction into the IBMA Hall of Honor.

—Chris Skinker

REPRESENTATIVE RECORDING

Jimmy Martin and the Sunny Mountain Boys (Bear Family, 1995)

Frankie and Johnny Marvin
Frank James Marvin b. Butler, Oklahoma, January 27, 1904;
d. January 1985
John Senator Marvin b. Butler, Oklahoma, July 11, 1897;
d. December 20, 1944

A side of GENE AUTRY not often recognized is his loyalty to old friends. A case in point is Frankie Marvin and his brother Johnny, who were popular vaudeville entertainers when young Gene, full of ambition but green as grass, showed up at their New York apartment in the late 1920s. They befriended the young Oklahoman, tutored him in the ways of show business, and sent him home for more seasoning. When he became a film star a few years later, Autry sent for both brothers, making them integral parts of his growing organization.

John Senator Marvin was born in Butler, Oklahoma, in 1897; Frank James Marvin, in 1904. Johnny pursued a successful musical career in New York, where he became well known as a songwriter and on radio as the Lonesome Singer of the Air; Frankie soon followed, working steadily as a steel guitarist, ukulele player, and comedian. Autry brought them to Hollywood when the Depression had slowed their careers, Johnny as a songwriter and producer for his *Melody Ranch* network radio series and Frankie as the steel guitarist in Autry's band, where his playing became one of the consistently recognizable components of the Autry sound.

—Douglas B. Green

Brent Mason
b. Vanwert, Ohio, July 13, 1959

Brent Mason was born into a guitar-playing family and taught himself the thumb- and finger-picking style of JERRY REED and CHET ATKINS as a youngster. Perhaps best known for his electric guitar work on ALAN JACKSON's records ("Chattahoochee"), Mason has also played on albums by scores of country acts, including BROOKS & DUNN, TRISHA YEARWOOD, and GEORGE STRAIT.

During and after high school, he made modest money playing lounges and bowling alleys before striking up correspondence with Nashville steel player PAUL FRANKLIN. Mason moved to Nashville in 1981 and quickly got a regular gig at the Stagecoach Lounge. Chet Atkins saw him there and invited him to play on his 1985 LP *Stay Tuned*, which featured George Benson, Earl Klugh, Larry Carlton, and other guitar virtuosos.

Since then, Mason has been a much in-demand session guitarist, working on at least an album a week for dozens of country artists. He has won recognition as the ACM's Top Guitarist for the years 1993–96 and as *Music Row* magazine's Top Guitarist for 1994, 1995, and 1997. He is also a recorded songwriter whose cuts include "Hurry Sundown" (MCBRIDE & THE RIDE) and "Who Needs It" (CLINTON GREGORY). MERCURY issued *Hot Wired,* his first solo album, in 1997, and in that same year he became the CMA's Musician of the Year.   *—Michael Hight*

REPRESENTATIVE RECORDING

Hot Wired (Mercury, 1997)

Louise Massey & the Westerners

Victoria Louise Massey b. Midland, Texas, August 10, 1902; d. June 20, 1983

D. Curtis Massey b. Midland, Texas, May 3, 1910; d. October 20, 1991

Allen Massey b. Texas, December 12, 1907; d. March 3, 1983

Milt Mabie b. birthplace unknown, June 27, 1900; d. September 1973

Larry Wellington b. birthplace and birth date unknown

A classy western ensemble, Louise Massey & the Westerners achieved pop-crossover success, recorded abundantly throughout the 1930s and 1940s, starred on national radio, and were accomplished in Mexican, polka, cowboy, ragtime, and swing genres.

Louise, Curt, and Allen Massey were children of old-time fiddler and rancher Henry Massey, who formed an amateur family band in New Mexico. Louise married bassist Milt Mabie in 1919, and the act went professional. They toured the United States on the Chautauqua circuit in 1928; then Henry retired.

Adding accordionist Larry Wellington, the Massey kids moved on. A five-year stint on KMBC in Kansas City—including CBS network exposure—led to fame on WLS's NA-TIONAL BARN DANCE in Chicago, beginning in 1933. Three years later the act hit New York, starring on NBC's *Log Cabin Dude Ranch* show and headlining at the Waldorf-Astoria, the Rainbow Room, and other midtown venues. The group also filmed several musical shorts and appeared in the 1938 Tex Ritter feature *Where the Buffalo Roam.* Returning to Chicago in 1939, the Massey band starred on NBC's *Plantation Party.*

The group recorded more than a hundred sides for ARC/Columbia from 1933 to 1942. Members doubled on several instruments. They also were bilingual, and so were among the first recording acts to popularize Latin American material in the United States. The instrumental "Beer and Skittles" and Curt's "The Honey Song," hits of the early 1940s, sold steadily for years. Louise's self-composed ballad "When the White Azaleas Start Blooming" became a big hit in 1934, and her 1947 smash "My Adobe Hacienda" was one of the first country-pop crossover successes.

Louise and Mabie eventually retired to Roswell, New Mexico. Curt settled in Hollywood and became the musical director/theme composer for the 1960s TV hits *The Beverly Hillbillies* and *Petticoat Junction.*   *—Robert K. Oermann*

Kathy Mattea

Kathy Mattea

b. Cross Lanes, West Virginia, June 21, 1959

A two-time Grammy winner and two-time CMA Female Vocalist of the Year, Kathy Mattea was reared on the folk-pop repertoires of Buffy St. Marie, Joni Mitchell, and James Taylor, and tempered by the genuineness of folk classics sung around Girl Scout campfires. She learned respect for her voice as an instrument through classical training and church singing. Her musical direction took an earthy twist when she began her brief college career at West Virginia University in the mid-1970s. There she joined a bluegrass band, fell in love with the bandleader, and quit school to move with him to Nashville in 1978.

When Mattea, then barely twenty years old, was abandoned by the bluegrass musician, she thought hard about her own ambitions for the first time and elected to stick it out in Nashville. Taking day jobs as a typesetter's apprentice and a tour guide at the COUNTRY MUSIC HALL OF FAME AND MUSEUM, she found roommates and began to find a home in the circle of unknown songwriters who haunted the run-down residential neighborhoods just south and west of Music Row. She became a rising star of the Music Row demo session scene while building her own unique club act from little-known folksongs, novelty tunes, and the best of her friends' compositions.

Mattea's best-known prestardom job was as a waitress at a Nashville T.G.I. Friday's, where she was known as the girl with the heart-shaped record in her hair until MERCURY RECORDS offered her a recording deal in 1983. Her second album teamed her up with ALLEN REYNOLDS in a creative alliance that lasted out the decade.

Mattea struggled until she cut a sweet yet earthy song written by contemporary folkie NANCI GRIFFITH, "Love at the Five and Dime," a #3 country hit in 1986. That song defined Mattea for radio. She followed it with a string of Top

Ten singles until her second #1, "Eighteen Wheels and a Dozen Roses," which took a 1989 CMA Award for Best Single. Confirming her stature in country music, Mattea won the CMA's Female Vocalist of the Year Award two years running, in 1989 and 1990.

While "Eighteen Wheels and a Dozen Roses" remains her biggest chart hit, she became closely identified with left-of-center releases and songs of conscience, such as the 1990 Grammy-winning "Where've You Been," penned by her husband, Jon Vezner, and DON HENRY. She won a 1993 Grammy for *Good News,* a Christmas album, as well. After a decade of records with producer Allen Reynolds, she worked with producer Josh Leo for *Walking Away a Winner* (1994) and then in 1996 co-produced *Love Travels* with Ben Wisch. She undoubtedly opened doors for folk-influenced artists such as MARY CHAPIN CARPENTER and LYLE LOVETT, who followed her in commercial country music.

—*Bob Millard*

REPRESENTATIVE RECORDINGS

Willow in the Wind (Mercury, 1989); *A Collection of Hits* (Mercury, 1990); *Time Passes By* (Mercury, 1991); *Walking Away a Winner* (Mercury, 1994); *Love Travels* (Mercury, 1996)

The Mavericks

Raul Malo b. Miami, Florida, August 7, 1965
Robert Earl Reynolds b. Kansas City, Missouri, April 30, 1962
Paul Wylie Deakin b. Miami, Florida, September 2, 1959
Nicholas James "Nick" Kane b. Jerusalem, Georgia, August 21, 1954

By combining rock & roll exuberance, pop songcraft, and honky-tonk panache, the Mavericks managed to corral jaded fans of many genres. In so doing, they suggested a future for country music that didn't involve either stern traditionalism or a rehash of 1970s country-rock.

The band has an eclectic sound; the group members play their own instruments and write their own songs. The Mavericks originated in the rock clubs of Miami, where bassist Robert Reynolds and drummer Paul Deakin had been friends since 1986. Reynolds, a collector of vintage country sides, had played ELVIS PRESLEY and HANK WILLIAMS covers since his first band; Deakin had been a session and touring drummer for various punk, new wave, and funk bands.

Reynolds introduced Deakin to hard country, and they discussed forming a band together for the first time. Reynolds wanted to play rhythm guitar, so he suggested a friend, Raul Malo—a lifelong Elvis fan who had never sung in a band before—as bassist. The three hit it off, and in 1990 they started playing Miami rock clubs. Reynolds switched to bass; Malo began singing; people started to notice.

In October 1990 the group released an independently produced thirteen-song LP. Copies filtered back to Music Row labels, along with reports of the band's incendiary live shows. A Nashville showcase was arranged for the group in May 1991, and MCA Nashville signed the band instantly. A new lead guitarist, David Lee Holt, was drafted from stints with CARLENE CARTER and JOE ELY, and the group went into a Miami studio with producer STEVE FISHELL.

The result was 1992's *From Hell to Paradise,* a mix of gently crooned ballads, revved-up standards, and five-minute protest songs of staggering ambition. (The astonishing title track detailed the flight of Malo's family from Castro's Cuba in 1959.) It was excellent, but the only charting single—a 90-mph cover of "Hey Good Lookin' " that left programmers scratching their heads—nose-dived after one week in the Top Seventy-five.

The band learned its lesson. By 1994 the group had a new lead guitarist—Nick Kane, a blues fanatic and former cabinetmaker whose parents were a professor and an opera singer—and a stripped-down style to match. Gone were the sprawling social anthems. In their place was an album's worth of tightly crafted three-minute singles, including four co-written by hit ensurer KOSTAS. The album, *What a Crying Shame,* took a few months to catch fire, but its lush retro sound (courtesy of producer DON COOK) and irresistible ROY ORBISON–styled melodies propelled it to the Top Forty. It sold steadily and eventually went platinum. In the same year, Reynolds and TRISHA YEARWOOD were married in a lavish ceremony at the RYMAN AUDITORIUM.

The Mavericks burnished their sound to a lounge-lizard gloss on 1995's *Music for All Occasions,* which drew the first mixed reviews of their career. Nevertheless, it yielded two hit singles, and their live show remained a top draw, fueled by the piano-pounding antics of Jerry Dale McFadden and

The Mavericks: (from left) Robert Reynolds, Nick Kane, Paul Deakin, and Raul Malo

a repertoire that ranged from "Guantanamera" to Bob Marley songs. —*Jim Ridley*

REPRESENTATIVE RECORDINGS

From Hell to Paradise (MCA, 1992); *What a Crying Shame* (MCA, 1994); *Trampoline* (MCA, 1998)

MCA Records

established in Universal City, California, March 1, 1973

MCA Records has long been a major force in country music and the recording industry in general. It has a rich heritage that has played an integral part in the entertainment field for more than sixty years. Music Corporation of America (MCA) was founded in 1925 in New York by Jules Stein as a talent booking agency. Through the years MCA expanded to include music publishing, film, television, distribution, theme parks, and concert facilities.

MCA's work in the recording industry began in 1962 with the purchase of DECCA RECORDS (which also included the Coral, BRUNSWICK, and Vocalion labels). In 1967 MCA formed the UNI label (which first introduced OLIVIA NEWTON-JOHN to American audiences in 1971) and also acquired Kapp Records (whose country roster included MEL TILLIS, CAL SMITH, BILLY EDD WHEELER, BOB WILLS, and LEROY VAN DYKE). However, it wasn't until 1973 that MCA retired these various record labels and gathered all artists under the newly launched MCA label, headquartered in Universal City, California. OWEN BRADLEY was left in charge of the Nashville offices (as he had been with Decca since 1958) and remained in that position into 1976.

During the seventies, while MCA's existing stars such as JEANNE PRUETT, CONWAY TWITTY, Cal Smith, and LORETTA LYNN met with continued success, MCA added TANYA TUCKER, Mel Tillis, and MERLE HAGGARD, and re-signed BRENDA LEE to its roster. Between 1976 and 1979 Chick Dougherty, Eddie Kilroy, and JIMMY BOWEN took turns presiding over the Nashville office. In 1979 MCA purchased the ABC/DOT RECORDS to beef up the country division, and in so doing acquired the contracts of BARBARA MANDRELL, DON WILLIAMS, JOHN CONLEE, the OAK RIDGE BOYS, and ROY CLARK. At the same time, ABC/Dot president JIM FOGLESONG became head of MCA's Nashville operations.

In 1984 BRUCE HINTON replaced Foglesong as senior vice president/general manager and Jimmy Bowen was named president of MCA Nashville. Artists signed during the 1980s included ED BRUCE, GENE WATSON, GEORGE STRAIT, LEE GREENWOOD, JOHN SCHNEIDER, REBA MCENTIRE, STEVE WARINER, PATTY LOVELESS, MARTY STUART, and VINCE GILL. In December 1988 Bowen left MCA to create Universal Records, Hinton was promoted to president, and producer TONY BROWN was named executive vice president and head of A&R.

On November 27, 1990, Matsushita Electric Industrial (Japan's largest electronics company) purchased MCA. Five years later, Matsushita sold 80 percent of MCA to Seagram, a Montreal-based distiller. However, it was business as usual at MCA Nashville except for the promotions of Hinton to chairman and Brown to president in 1993. The Decca label was reactivated the following year with MARK WRIGHT and Shelia Shipley in charge and with Dawn Sears as their first artist. In the 1990s MCA Nashville's signings included TRISHA YEARWOOD, MARK COLLIE, MARK CHESNUTT, GEORGE JONES, the MAVERICKS, and TRACY BYRD.

—*Don Roy*

Mac McAnally

b. Red Bay, Alabama, July 1, 1957

Lyman "Mac" McAnally Jr. hails from the same Memphis/Mobile/New Orleans triangle of the Deep South that has produced Jimmy Buffett, TONY JOE WHITE, Steve Forbert, and Jesse Winchester—singer-songwriters who employ country music, folk-rock, and rhythm & blues interchangeably to tell their stories. McAnally has had more luck selling his songs to other singers and hiring himself out as a session musician than he's had scoring hits with his own records. Nonetheless, industry insiders have long recognized him as one of the South's most gifted troubadours.

McAnally was raised in northern Mississippi on his mother's gospel piano playing. He was performing in bars by age thirteen and by nineteen had landed a gig as a session guitarist at the Muscle Shoals Recording Studios in Alabama. After hours at the studio, he recorded *Mac McAnally*, and the 1977 debut album yielded a Top Forty pop single, "It's a Crazy World."

He never again matched that teenage chart success, though, and soon began jumping from label to label, recording albums for Ariola (*No Problem Here*, 1978), RCA (*Cuttin' Corners*, 1980), Geffen (*Nothing But the Truth*, 1983, and *Finish Lines*, 1988), WARNER BROS. (*Simple Life*, 1990), and MCA (*Live and Learn*, 1992, and *Knots*, 1994). Despite their modest sales, these albums attracted a loyal following of critics and fellow musicians who appreciated McAnally's insinuating melodies and understated narratives.

Meanwhile, McAnally was building a successful career as a songwriter, picker, and producer. His compositions were recorded by Jimmy Buffett ("It's My Job"), ALABAMA ("Old Flame"), SHENANDOAH ("Two Dozen Roses"), RANDY TRAVIS ("Written in Stone"), SAWYER BROWN ("All These Years"), and more. He has played guitar on albums by GEORGE JONES, DOLLY PARTON, TRISHA YEARWOOD, LINDA RONSTADT, and others. He also produced RICKY SKAGGS's *My Father's Son* and Sawyer Brown's *Outskirts of Town*. In 1998 Dreamworks Records in Nashville signed McAnally.

—*Geoffrey Himes*

REPRESENTATIVE RECORDINGS

Cuttin' Corners (RCA, 1980); *Live and Learn* (MCA, 1992)

Leon McAuliffe

b. Houston, Texas, January 3, 1917; d. Tulsa, Oklahoma, August 20, 1988

William Leon McAuliffe was BOB WILLS's most famous steel guitarist and a popular WESTERN SWING bandleader in his own right. In 1933 he became the steel guitarist for the LIGHT CRUST DOUGHBOYS—only a month or two after Bob Wills had left the band. In March 1935 Leon made the most important move of his career, joining Bob Wills & His Texas Playboys, soon to become the most famous western dance band in the world. In 1936 McAuliffe recorded "Steel Guitar Rag" with the Wills band, and the instrumental number—adapted from a blues recording by Sylvester Weaver—is now seen as a seminal moment in the history of the steel guitar. In addition, the uninhibited manner in which Wills introduced the recording singled out McAuliffe for special attention. Wills hollered "Leon" and told him to "take it away." "Calling me by name on our recordings, as Bob did it, made me famous," McAuliffe maintained years later.

In 1942 McAuliffe left the Wills band and entered the U. S. Army Air Corps as a flight instructor, where he worked with Tex Beneke of Glenn Miller's orchestra. After the war McAuliffe formed his own western swing band, the Cimarron Boys, in Tulsa, where he also opened his own nightclub, the Cimarron Ballroom, in 1950. He handled vocals as well as steel for his band, and he was quite successful, recording numerous sides for Majestic, COLUMBIA, STARDAY, DOT, CAPITOL, and his own Cimarron label (sometimes spelling his name "McAuliff"). His biggest-selling recording was a 1949 steel guitar instrumental for Columbia, "Panhandle Rag."

McAuliffe broke up his band in the sixties and devoted his time to real-estate interests and his radio station in Rogers, Arkansas. In 1973 Bob Wills revived McAuliffe's musical career when the aging bandleader asked McAuliffe to perform in what proved to be Wills's final recording session. After Wills's death, Betty Wills permitted McAuliffe to lead a band called Bob Wills's Original Texas Playboys. The band made several albums and played concerts in the United States and Europe.

To the end of his life, Leon McAuliffe's name was always tied to that of Bob Wills, for it was while he was with Wills that he really left his most enduring mark on American music.

—*Charles R. Townsend*

REPRESENTATIVE RECORDINGS

Bob Wills: Anthology, 1935–1973 (Rhino, 1991); *"Take It Away Leon": Leon McAuliffe & the Cimarron Boys* (Stoneway, 1974); *Bob Wills & His Texas Playboys: For the Last Time* (United Artists, 1974)

Laura Lee & Dickie McBride

Dickie McBride b. New Baden, Texas, January 22, 1914; d. June 1971

Laura Lee Owens McBride b. Kansas City, Missouri, 1920; d. January 25, 1989

Although they worked as a duo from the mid-1940s, both Laura Lee and Dickie McBride are probably better known for their separate careers—Laura Lee for her stints with BOB WILLS's Texas Playboys and Dickie McBride for his days with CLIFF BRUNER's Texas Wanderers and with his own Village Boys.

The daughter of singer TEX OWENS and the niece of Texas Ruby, Laura Lee Owens began singing with her sister while still in her teens on Kansas City's *Brush Creek Follies*. After an early marriage to the Texas Rangers' guitarist Herb Kratoska and a stint with the Oklahoma Wranglers, Laura Lee joined Bob Wills's Texas Playboys at the end of 1943. She became Wills's first female vocalist and was best known for the yodeling on her signature tune, "Betcha My Heart." She married Wills's guitarist Cameron Hill, and when Hill entered the army in 1945, she relocated to Houston, Texas, where she would meet and later marry McBride.

Dickie McBride, who idolized western swing pioneer MILTON BROWN, joined the band of Brown alumnus Cliff Bruner—the Texas Wanderers—in Houston during 1936. McBride's smooth vocals were prominent on Bruner 1937–38 DECCA sides, including the FLOYD TILLMAN–penned, seminal honky-tonk hit "It Makes No Differ-

ence Now." When Bruner departed, McBride continued to record for Decca with both the Texas Wanderers and under his own name. McBride and fiddler Grady Hester formed the Village Boys in 1940; after Hester's departure, the band, again recording for Decca, became McBride's. The Village Boys disbanded in 1943; McBride picked up the pieces and formed his Music Macs.

Following their marriage, the McBrides worked mostly outside Houston; they toured some with Bob Wills and worked in California in 1948–49. Although they usually recorded as a team—for Decca, MGM, and several smaller labels—they continued to record separately on independent labels such as Daffan, Ayo, and Freedom. As popular radio, TV, and dance performers in Houston throughout the 1950s they performed and recorded sporadically until just before Dickie McBride's death in 1971, after which Laura Lee became more active. She performed and recorded through the 1980s until her death in 1989.

—*Kevin Coffey*

Martina McBride

b. Sharon, Kansas, July 29, 1966

A strong sophomore album, several defiantly woman-centered songs, and a haircut helped separate Martina Mariea Schiff McBride from the many long-haired brunette singers who flooded Nashville in the early 1990s. The daughter of Kansas farmer Daryl Schiff, McBride began singing country classics at age eight in a family band. After graduating from high school, she eventually moved to Wichita, where she temporarily damaged her voice belting hard-rock tunes in local bands. During this period she met sound technician John McBride, whom she married in 1988.

In 1990, after Martina's stint with a country act called the Fowler Brothers, the McBrides moved to Nashville. While John worked the board for GARTH BROOKS's 1991 tour, Martina ran his T-shirt booth and struggled to get her demos heard. Her tapes reached RCA RECORDS, which issued her promising 1992 debut, *The Time Has Come*. Although the title track reached the Top Thirty, a follow-up featuring Garth Brooks on backing vocals, "Cheap Whiskey," sputtered on the charts. The album's lukewarm reception—along with success as Brooks's opening act in 1992—convinced McBride to toughen up her sound, material, and look. The result was 1993's *The Way That I Am*, whose first single, "My Baby Loves Me," fought its way to #2 and spent twenty-one weeks on the charts. While women embraced its message of independence and self-worth, it was the album's third single, a Gretchen Peters anthem of triumph over domestic abuse titled "Independence Day," that really connected with female listeners. The award-winning video, the song, and the album that contained it placed McBride among mainstream country's most ambitious new performers.

On November 30, 1995, she joined the cast of the GRAND OLE OPRY. McBride charted consistently with the singles "Safe In the Arms of Love" (1995, #4), "Wild Angels" (1996, #1), and "A Broken Wing" (1997, #1).

—*Jim Ridley*

REPRESENTATIVE RECORDINGS

The Time Has Come (RCA, 1992); *The Way That I Am* (RCA, 1993); *Wild Angels* (RCA, 1995); *Evolution* (RCA, 1997)

Terry McBride & the Ride

Terry McBride b. Taylor, Texas, September 16, 1958
Ray Herndon b. Phoenix, Arizona, July 14, 1960
Billy Thomas b. Ft. Myers, Florida, October 24, 1953

McBride & the Ride began as a superpicker dream team but found success with a series of middle-of-the-road singles with tight harmonies. The original group consisted of singer-bassist Terry McBride, who had backed DELBERT MCCLINTON and LEE ROY PARNELL; guitarist Ray Herndon, who had played with LYLE LOVETT; and Billy Thomas, a session drummer who had recorded with VINCE GILL and EMMYLOU HARRIS, among others. The three got together at the suggestion of producer TONY BROWN.

The trio released its first chart single, "Can I Count on You," in March 1991. The next year, "Sacred Ground" started a string of Top Five hits that also included "Going Out of My Mind" (1992) and "Love on the Loose, Heart on the Run" (1993). Herndon and Thomas left the group at the end of 1993 to pursue individual careers.

McBride bought the rights to the name and renamed the act Terry McBride & the Ride. The new lineup downplayed the group concept in favor of McBride as a singer; in concert, he switched from bass to guitar. McBride's success as a songwriter includes the BROOKS & DUNN hits "I Am That Man" and "He's Got You."

McBride is the son of Dale McBride (1936–92), who recorded regional hits for Thunderbird and Con Brio Records (1971–79), reaching #26 with "Ordinary Man" (1977).　　　　　　　　　　　　　　*—Brian Mansfield*

REPRESENTATIVE RECORDINGS

Sacred Ground (MCA, 1992); *Terry McBride & the Ride* (MCA, 1994)

Bill McCall (*see* Four Star Records)

C. W. McCall

b. Audubon, Iowa, November 15, 1928

In 1975 the nation struggled with an energy crisis, the speed limit was set at 55 mph, citizens' band radio became a national craze, and C. W. McCall's "Convoy"—an ode to the defiant American trucker—enjoyed a six-week run at the top of the country chart and also hit #1 pop.

As an advertising executive, McCall (William Fries) did the voice-over for a fictitious bread truck driver named C. W. McCall, which in turn inspired his stage name. On his albums McCall alternated between the narrative style of "Convoy" and other trucking/highway songs, and lethargic ballad crooning reminiscent of Leonard Cohen. McCall had a #2 hit in 1977 with "Roses for Mama," but in 1978 he left the music business, returning to the studio only occasionally thereafter. An environmentalist, he served as mayor of Ouray, Colorado, during the 1980s.
　　　　　　　　　　　　　　—Jack Bernhardt

REPRESENTATIVE RECORDINGS

Wolf Creek Pass (MGM, 1975); *Black Bear Road* (MGM, 1975)

Darrell McCall

b. New Jasper, Ohio, April 30, 1940

Anyone who loves the traditional country shuffles and sounds of FARON YOUNG or RAY PRICE during the late 1950s and early 1960s will probably admire the music of Darrell McCall. His intense and soulful hard-core honky-tonk traditional style has amassed a very loyal and dedicated following in both the United States and Europe.

Darrell McCall came up through the ranks the way people used to in the country music business—by serving an apprenticeship as a front man and harmony vocalist for a major star. McCall did this very effectively for more than a dozen years in the employment of Faron Young, Ray Price, CARL SMITH, CHARLIE LOUVIN, and HANK WILLIAMS JR. Though McCall had been recording during much of this period for CAPITOL, STARDAY, Philips, and Wayside with some occasional chart success ("A Stranger Was Here" reached the Top Twenty in 1963), it wasn't until Hank Williams Jr. recorded McCall's "Eleven Roses" in 1972 (#1) that McCall was able to embark successfully into a solo career.

While with ATLANTIC RECORDS, McCall released "There's Still a Lot of Love in San Antone" (#48, 1974) before moving to COLUMBIA, where he had several chart records, including "Dreams of a Dreamer" and "Lily Dale," a duet with WILLIE NELSON.

Long based in Nashville, Darrell McCall is considered by many artists to be a singer's singer as well as a musician's singer: Both professional singers and musicians flock to hear him perform. McCall has been recording for Artap Records since 1992 and continues to work considerably in the Texas and Oklahoma dance hall circuit, where he has been extremely popular for years.　　　*—Eddie Stubbs*

REPRESENTATIVE RECORDINGS

A Way to Survive (Artap, 1995); *The Real McCall* (Bear Family, 1996), 5 discs; *Pictures Can't Talk Back* (Artap, 1997)

The McCarters

Jennifer Lorene b. Sevierville, Tennessee, March 1, 1964
Lisa Kaye b. Sevierville, Tennessee, November 11, 1966
Teresa Faye b. Sevierville, Tennessee, November 11, 1966

Siblings Jennifer, Lisa, and Teresa McCarter brought their sweet family harmonies to country music with their first single, "Timeless and True Love," in 1988. The tune signaled an impressive debut for the East Tennessee natives, peaking at #5 on the charts.

The sisters began their career by clog dancing on a local weekly TV show for four years. They next spent three years performing with ARCHIE CAMPBELL and STU PHILLIPS. Veteran performers by then, they realized that clogging, while providing an open door into the entertainment field, would take them only so far. Still in their teens, the girls started harmonizing. Meanwhile, Jennifer attended East Tennessee State University, where she played in the ETSU Bluegrass Band.

Eventually, producer KYLE LEHNING heard the McCarters sing, which led to their being signed to WARNER BROS. Their first album, *The Gift*, featured finger-picked acoustic guitars that set off the sisters' impeccable harmonies. The title song was a #4 hit. Their second album,

Better Be Home Soon, showcased their voices in a wider range of musical textures. The first single from the album, "Up and Gone," reached #9 in 1989, but subsequent releases failed to capture the public's attention. They concentrated on touring for a few years, and in 1995 the McCarters were re-signed to Warner Bros. —*Janet E. Williams*

REPRESENTATIVE RECORDINGS

The Gift (Warner Bros., 1988); *Better Be Home Soon* (Warner Bros., 1990)

Charly McClain
b. Jackson, Tennessee, March 26, 1956

Charlotte Denise McClain mixed her country heritage with a contemporary feel to become one of the stars of the UR-BAN COWBOY era. Raised in Memphis, she grew up with that city's rich mixture of rock, country, jazz, and blues, but has said she was most attracted to country.

When she was only nine years old, McClain made recordings of school songs to play for her father, who was hospitalized with tuberculosis, and sang with her brother's band. She performed as a regular on the Memphis country music showcase the *Mid-South Jamboree* from 1973 to 1975.

McClain was signed by EPIC RECORDS in 1976. Her first chart single, "Lay Down," and her debut album, *Here's Charly McClain,* appeared that year. Within two years she had hit the Top Ten, and in early 1981 "Who's Cheatin' Who" became her first #1. McClain's hit-making career peaked in 1985 with her #1 smash "Radio Heart" and a couple of Top Ten duets with her actor husband, Wayne Massey. She had earlier recorded duets with Mickey Gilley, including "Paradise Tonight," which topped the charts in 1983.

Besides her recording and touring career, McClain appeared on such television shows as *Austin City Limits, Solid Gold,* and the ABC-TV series *Hart to Hart.* —*Gerry Wood*

REPRESENTATIVE RECORDINGS

Let Me Be Your Baby (Epic, 1978); *Who's Cheatin' Who* (Epic, 1980)

Delbert McClinton
b. Lubbock, Texas, November 4, 1940

A roadhouse veteran who knows how to find the pocket of a groove, Delbert McClinton blurs the lines between country, blues, and r&b. For example, he won a Grammy for a rock duet with Bonnie Raitt, "Good Man, Good Woman" from her *Luck of the Draw* album, and EMMYLOU HARRIS scored a #1 country hit with his "Two More Bottles of Wine." In addition, his country duet with TANYA TUCKER, "Tell Me About It," drew a Grammy nomination.

McClinton made his performing debut at seventeen, singing "Crazy Arms" on the *Big V Jamboree* in Lubbock. In the late 1950s, with his band the Straitjackets, he backed blues legends including Lightnin' Hopkins, Howlin' Wolf, and Big Joe Turner, when they visited the famous Jack's Place nightclub in Fort Worth. His first single, in 1960, was a cover of Sonny Boy Williamson's "Wake Up Baby" and was the first record by a white artist to be played on Fort Worth's KNOK.

In a style he learned and adapted from Jimmy Reed, Mc-Clinton became an accomplished harmonica player, contributing distinctively to Bruce Channel's "Hey! Baby," a #1 pop hit in 1962. While on tour with Channel in the United Kingdom, McClinton shared his stylings with John Lennon, and his influence can be heard clearly on the Beatles' "Love Me Do."

In 1964 and 1965 McClinton teamed with Ronnie Kelly as the Ron-Dels. The duo registered briefly on the pop chart in 1965 with "If You Really Want Me To, I'll Go." (The Memphis-based Silver City Band released this song as a country tune in 1977, with equally unspectacular results, and WAYLON JENNINGS and BOB DYLAN later recorded it.) In the early 1970s McClinton teamed with fellow Texan Glen Clark, and they recorded two albums as Delbert and Glen. The Blues Brothers included the duo's "B Movie Box Car Blues" on their debut album.

McClinton signed as a solo artist with ABC Records in 1975, relocated briefly to Nashville, and won critical acclaim for *Victim of Life's Circumstances, Love Rustler,* and *Genuine Cowhide.* He moved on to Capricorn in 1978, but the label folded just as his second album for the company, *Keeper of the Flame,* began to sell. A first album for CAPITOL, *The Jealous Kind,* yielded his only major pop hit to date, "Giving It Up for Your Love." His 1989 release *Live from Austin* pulled his first Grammy nomination, and McClinton won his only Grammy, with Raitt, in 1991, though McClinton received a nomination for the Tucker collaboration in 1993.

McClinton moved back to Nashville in 1989, where he recorded critically acclaimed albums for CURB. Recently he recorded for the Rising Tide label and contributed to an album featuring guest appearances by Mavis Staples, LYLE LOVETT, JOHN PRINE, PATTY LOVELESS, VINCE GILL, PAM TILLIS, and LEE ROY PARNELL. Rising Tide's demise in March 1998 shifted McClinton to the DECCA label.—*Jay Orr*

REPRESENTATIVE RECORDING

One of the Fortunate Few (Rising Tide, 1997)

O. B. McClinton

The Del McCoury Band: (from left) Ronnie McCoury, Mike Bub, Del McCoury, Jason Carter, and Rob McCoury

O. B. McClinton
b. Senatobia, Mississippi, April 25, 1940; d. Sept. 23, 1987

Active as a country performer during the 1970s and 1980s, Obie Burnett McClinton was one of the few black artists to land multiple songs on the country charts. Earlier, during the 1960s, he had distinguished himself as a songwriter in Memphis.

McClinton grew up in the segregated South, working in the cotton fields. He enjoyed listening to the Grand Ole Opry, as well as to the blues and rockabilly records aired by WLAC in Nashville and WHBQ in Memphis, respectively. TENNESSEE ERNIE FORD's "Sixteen Tons" was also a favorite of his.

McClinton graduated from Rust College in Holly Springs, Mississippi, served in the air force, and worked as a DJ at WDIA in Memphis. As a songwriter he provided material for soul artists such as Otis Redding and James Carr.

Influenced by MERLE HAGGARD, HANK WILLIAMS, and CHARLEY PRIDE, McClinton was signed as a country artist to Stax Records (but placed on their affiliate label Enterprise) in 1971. His most successful singles were "Don't Let the Green Grass Fool You" (1972–73) and "My Whole World Is Falling Down" (1973), both of which broke into the lower reaches of the country Top Forty. He also recorded albums for Enterprise, including *O. B. McClinton: Country* and *Obie from Senatobie,* then later recorded for MERCURY, EPIC, and smaller labels. He died of cancer in 1987.

—*Gerry Wood*

REPRESENTATIVE RECORDING

Obie from Senatobie (Enterprise, 1972)

Del McCoury
b. Bakersville, North Carolina, February 1, 1939

After more than three decades playing and singing bluegrass music, Delano Floyd McCoury has finally received some recognition for his immense talent. As one of the few current bandleaders who worked at the side of BILL MONROE, McCoury and his top-flight band—including sons Ronnie and Rob on mandolin and banjo, respectively, Kentucky native Jason Carter on fiddle, and bassist Mike Bub—have earned nearly every award in bluegrass music. The group has taken home three Entertainer of the Year Awards from the International Bluegrass Music Association, and all of the band's members have been nominated for or won awards on their respective instruments.

The elder McCoury was the fourth of six children. In the early 1940s the family moved to southeastern Pennsylvania, where his father worked in the logging business. Mother Hazel often entertained her young family with her mountain-style vocals and guitar playing. Inspired by a FLATT & SCRUGGS recording his brother brought home, Del originally cast his sights on the banjo. He honed those skills in the Baltimore area working with Jack Cooke's Virginia Mountain Boys.

By 1963 McCoury was tapped to join BILL MONROE's Blue Grass Boys. Originally he was hired on as a banjo player but soon was moved to the lead singer–guitar player's spot. After a stint with Monroe, McCoury broke out on his own and moved to California in 1964. There he worked with the Golden State Boys before moving back to Pennsylvania and forming the Dixie Pals. In 1968 he released his first album, *Del McCoury Sings Bluegrass* for Arhoolie Records. *Del McCoury and the Dixie Pals, Take Me to the Mountains,* and *High on a Mountain* were released for a variety of independent labels. For the next two decades Del worked the festival circuit, amassing a loyal following of fans.

In 1981 eldest son Ronnie joined the band, and Rob followed suit in 1989. Del relocated from Pennsylvania to Nashville in 1992 and added Carter and Bub to the group.

—*Chris Skinker*

REPRESENTATIVE RECORDINGS

Classic Bluegrass (Rebel, 1991); *Blue Side of Town* (Rounder, 1992); *The Cold Hard Facts* (Rounder, 1996)

Charlie McCoy

b. Oak Hill, West Virginia, March 28, 1941

Undoubtedly the most recorded harmonica player in history, multi-instrumentalist Charles Ray McCoy is a bona fide Nashville studio legend.

McCoy came to Music City in 1960 and recorded several singles as a rock & roll singer and guitarist for Cadence and MONUMENT. His harmonica playing on a demo tape caught the ear of CHET ATKINS, who hired him to play on Ann-Margret's "I Just Don't Understand," which became a Top Twenty pop hit. A week later he contributed a bluesy harmonica track to ROY ORBISON's "Candy Man" and launched a career as a Nashville studio musician, specializing in harmonica but also contributing occasionly on guitar, bass, keyboards, vibes, trumpet, saxophone, tuba, and vocals. During the next fifteen years McCoy participated in more than 6,000 sessions in support of nearly every major country artist. (He ranks his playing on the GEORGE JONES classic "He Stopped Loving Her Today" as a personal favorite.) McCoy's trademark harmonica style, distinguished by its speed, precision, clarity, and unerring phrasing, was radically different from the down-home approach of his predecessors and reestablished the mouth organ as a voice in country music.

During the 1960s McCoy influenced the creation of the folk-rock movement through his contributions to BOB DYLAN's early rock albums and to recordings by Joan Baez, Simon & Garfunkel, and Ringo Starr. McCoy was a charter member of Area Code 615, a group of younger Nashville session players that released two outstanding instrumental albums that were some of the first attempts to blend rock and country music.

Beginning in 1970, McCoy recorded a series of solo harmonica albums for MONUMENT. In the decade that followed he scored two Top Twenty country hits and twice won the CMA's Instrumentalist of the Year Award. A twenty-year stint as music director for *HEE HAW* followed. Still a sought-after studio player, McCoy today enjoys considerable popularity in Europe, where he has toured regularly since 1987.
—*Kim Field*

REPRESENTATIVE RECORDINGS

Greatest Hits (Sony, 1976); *Out on a Limb* (Step One, 1991)

Neal McCoy

b. Jacksonville, Texas, July 30, 1958

Neal McCoy never claimed that his baritone matched the voices of country music's masters, but he has an undeniable knack for connecting with an audience, whether live or through recording. He is, above all, an entertainer whose energy and unassuming demeanor have fueled his popularity. The son of Irish and Filipino parents, he was born Hubert Neal McGauhey Jr. When he began singing in East Texas clubs, he changed his stage name to McGoy (the phonetic spelling of his surname) and later McCoy.

McCoy was influenced by country, gospel quartets, big bands, and rhythm & blues, and his first career break came in 1981, when JANIE FRICKE heard him sing at a Dallas talent show. The connection led to six years of opening shows for CHARLEY PRIDE.

In the late 1980s McCoy recorded as Neal McCoy for the independent 16th Avenue Records. In 1991 he signed with ATLANTIC RECORDS and released his debut album, *At*

Neal McCoy

This Moment, the title track a cover of an r&b-tinged pop hit by Billy Vera. The album and the follow-up, *Where Forever Begins* (1992), included several singles that resulted in moderate chart success.

McCoy's career took an upward spiral with the 1994 album *No Doubt About It,* which netted his first two #1 singles—the title track and "Wink." McCoy's stardom was further ensured with the title title track from his fourth album, *You Gotta Love That.* The project also included other hits, including "They're Playing Our Song." McCoy waited until 1996 to release a self-titled album that contained the hit "Then You Can Tell Me Goodbye," a JOHN D. LOUDERMILK song that was a 1960s pop hit for the Casinos. McCoy's hit single "The Shake" from his *Greatest Hits* album marked his first effort with producer KYLE LEHNING. *Be Good at It,* McCoy's 1998 Atlantic album, was also produced by Lehning.

As a measure of McCoy's success, two of his albums—*No Doubt About It* and *You Gotta Love That*—have achieved platinum status for sales of more than 1 million copies each.
—*Calvin Gilbert*

REPRESENTATIVE RECORDINGS

No Doubt About It (Atlantic, 1994); *You Gotta Love That* (Atlantic, 1995); *Greatest Hits* (Atlantic, 1997)

Frank and James McCravy

With almost 200 recorded sides from 1925 to 1935, Frank and James McCravy were quite successful recording a repertoire heavily anchored in gospel song, which mirrored their concurrent evangelistic work in the South and qualified them for promotion by record companies as an authentic country act despite their proclivity toward a rather refined, formal music style.

Natives of Laurens, South Carolina, the McCravys both attended Furman University and began establishing their baritone/tenor duet style at about this time. With good diction an important factor in their singing, it's not surprising that the McCravy Brothers preferred to trek north to record all of their material in a more formal way by using New York studios and musicians, although James would occasionally play guitar and, possibly, violin.

—*Bob Pinson*

Mindy McCready
b. Fort Myers, Florida, November 30, 1976

Malinda Gayle McCready catapulted onto the country charts in 1996 with a powerfully expressive voice, a cocky musical persona, a penchant for skin-tight clothes and bare midriffs, and a run of hits that included her Top Ten debut single, "Ten Thousand Angels," and her first #1 hit, "Guys Do It All the Time." McCready's humorous head-on approach to male chauvinism created for her an immediate fan base of women.

From the time three-year-old McCready performed her first church solo, she was determined to have a career in country music. She took seven years of private vocal lessons and attended summer school so she could graduate from high school at sixteen and pursue music full-time. For practice she sang in Fort Myers's karaoke bars.

In 1994 the eighteen-year-old took tapes of her karaoke vocals to Nashville and gave herself a one-year deadline to land a recording contract. When producer NORRO WILSON heard the tapes—renditions of Bonnie Raitt and TRISHA YEARWOOD hits—he and producer David Malloy took McCready into the studio. Just under her self-imposed deadline, exactly fifty-one weeks after her arrival in MUSIC CITY, McCready signed with BNA RECORDS. Her debut album, *Ten Thousand Angels,* was certified platinum within a few months of its release.

In 1997 McCready was named the Country Radio Seminar's Best New Artist and became the youngest country artist ever elected to the CMA's Board of Directors. That fall she announced her engagement to actor Dean Cain.

—*Marjie McGraw*

REPRESENTATIVE RECORDINGS
Ten Thousand Angels (BNA, 1996); *If I Don't Stay the Night* (BNA, 1997)

Brad McCuen
b. New York, New York, May 17, 1921

A respected music industry veteran, Brad McCuen worked for RCA in sales and production from 1948 until 1969, at which point he left and founded Mega Records. During his years with RCA he helped the careers of DON GIBSON and HANK SNOW, among others, and as a field man in the Southeast he was among the first to alert RCA to the impact ELVIS PRESLEY was having on the region in 1954. In the 1960s McCuen produced RCA's Vintage line, one of the industry's earliest, and best, record reissue series. As head of Mega, he oversaw, most notably, the release of SAMMI SMITH's "Help Me Make It Through the Night." A longtime member of the COUNTRY MUSIC FOUNDATION's Board of Trustees, McCuen sold his 30,000-piece record collection and business papers to Middle Tennessee State University's Center for Popular Music in the fall of 1997.

—*Daniel Cooper*

Mel McDaniel
b. Checotah, Oklahoma, September 6, 1942

Mel McDaniel is the quintessential journeyman honky-tonker, a burly purveyor of mainstream good-time music. He was inspired to a singing career as a painfully shy youngster by an early television appearance by ELVIS PRESLEY. Poor and scarred by his parents' divorce, McDaniel worked nightclubs in Oklahoma to help support his mother. Following two unsuccessful years in Nashville (1969–71), he migrated to his father's side in Alaska to sing for oil field workers during the pipeline construction boom of the early to mid-seventies.

CAPITOL RECORDS signed him to a recording contract in 1976 and stayed with him another five years until he scored his first Top Ten hit, "Louisiana Saturday Night." Despite his citation of seminal rockabilly and country artists of the fifties as his influences, McDaniel's records are primarily contemporary JUKEBOX picks for a keg party. Hits such as "Big Ole Brew," "Let It Roll (Let It Rock)," "Stand Up," and "Baby's Got Her Blue Jeans On" were lots of fun, and while McDaniel didn't leave us much to think about, he never stooped to smarmy romance or formulaic wordplay ditties. Most of his hits could be rolled into the title of his 1988 hit "Real Good Feel Good Song," ironically his last entry in the Top Ten.

McDaniel has written songs cut by a number of artists, including HOYT AXTON, CONWAY TWITTY, KENNY ROGERS, and JOHNNY RODRIGUEZ. Among McDaniel's best-known compositions is "The Grandest Lady of Them All," a tribute to the GRAND OLE OPRY, co-written with Bob Morrison. McDaniel joined the Opry cast on January 11, 1986.

—*Bob Millard*

Mindy McCready

REPRESENTATIVE RECORDINGS
Stand Up (Capitol, 1985); *Greatest Hits* (Capitol, 1987)

Bob McDill

b. Beaumont, Texas, April 5, 1944

With an artist's spirit and an eagle-eyed sense of observation, songwriter Robert Lee McDill has captured character, emotion, and circumstance in hit song after hit song.

First influenced by his mother's piano playing and family gospel singing, McDill obtained his first guitar at fourteen and began to play in bands and folk groups. While attending Lamar University (1962–66), McDill played in a folk group known as the Newcomers. It was as a member of the Newcomers that McDill first met ALLEN REYNOLDS, who—along with DICKEY LEE, JACK CLEMENT, and Bill Hall—was operating Beaumont's Gulf Coast Recording Studios. Impressed with McDill's talent and potential, Reynolds arranged for Perry Como to record McDill's "The Happy Man" (1967) during McDill's two-year stint as a boatswain's mate in the U.S. Navy. The following year Sam the Sham & the Pharaohs' recording of "Black Sheep" became McDill's second hit song.

Following discharge from the navy, McDill moved to Memphis. When Jack Clement purchased the local publishing company Il Gatto, he hired McDill, Reynolds, and Lee, and moved operations to Nashville in 1970. The Nashville move introduced McDill to DON WILLIAMS and GARTH FUNDIS. Writing for Clement's Jack Music, McDill began to focus on country music and, with the exceptions of the albums *Short Stories* (JMI, 1972) and *Signatures* (RCA, 1988), put his performance aspirations to rest.

Country success arrived for McDill with JOHNNY RUSSELL's 1973 recording of "Catfish John" (written with Reynolds). Also in 1973, Russell's hit "Rednecks, White Socks, and Blue Ribbon Beer" became a #1 *Cashbox* hit for McDill (a *Billboard* Top Five hit). He has since scored some thirty *Billboard* #1s, including Don Williams's "Good Ole Boys Like Me" (1980); RONNIE MILSAP's "Nobody Likes Sad Songs" (1979); WAYLON JENNINGS's "Amanda" (1979); MEL MCDANIEL's "Baby's Got Her Blue Jeans On" (1984); DAN SEALS's "Everything That Glitters (Is Not Gold)" (1986); KEITH WHITLEY's "Don't Close Your Eyes" (1988); and ALAN JACKSON's "Gone Country" (1994).

Impressive as it is, the list of #1s barely scratches the surface of McDill's catalogue. He has also had songs recorded by artists as diverse as RAY CHARLES, ANNE MURRAY, LEFTY FRIZZELL, and Joe Cocker. McDill's many awards include honors in 1976 and 1985 as the NSAI's Songwriter of the Year, 1985 induction into the Nashville Songwriters Hall of Fame, and a 1997 Grammy nomination in the Country Song of the Year category for the Pam Tillis hit "All the Good Ones are Gone." In 1989 he was named a distinguished alumnus of Lamar University. McDill continues to write for his longtime publisher, PolyGram Music Publishing Group.

—*Kent Henderson*

Skeets McDonald

b. Greenway, Arkansas, October 1, 1915; d. March 31, 1968

Enos William "Skeets" McDonald is best known for the #1 hit "Don't Let the Stars Get in Your Eyes" and his longtime tenure with *TOWN HALL PARTY*. He grew up in Rector, Arkansas, and got his nickname as a youngster after he was attacked by a swarm of mosquitoes. He worked in the auto plants around Detroit after school and in 1935 started playing in a country band called the Lonesome Cowboys on WEXL–Royal Oak. After active service in World War II he returned to Detroit and made his first recordings for Fortune Records in 1950, including the risqué "Tattooed Lady." He then recorded for London and MERCURY (as Skeets Saunders) before heading out to the West Coast in February 1951.

CLIFFIE STONE signed McDonald to appear on his *HOMETOWN JAMBOREE* television show on KXLA-Pasadena, and he joined CAPITOL RECORDS in April 1951. His only charted hit on Capitol was his cover of "Don't Let the Stars Get in Your Eyes" in late 1952, but he recorded prolifically for the company until 1958, and appeared regularly on *Town Hall Party*. He was slightly more successful on COLUMBIA, scoring three hits, including "Call Me Mr. Brown" in 1963, and was still recording for the label and touring when he died.

—*Colin Escott*

REPRESENTATIVE RECORDING

Rockin' Rollin' Volumes 1 & 2 (Bear Family, 1986)

Ronnie McDowell

b. Fountain Head, Tennessee, March 26, 1950

Ronald Dean McDowell took a giant step from near obscurity into the big time with his 1977 sound-alike tribute to ELVIS PRESLEY, "The King Is Gone."

"I think it touched home," McDowell said shortly after the Scorpion Records release, fueled by interest from millions of grieving Presley fans, started its climb to Top Twenty status on both the country and pop charts. McDowell, long a Presley fan himself, had had earlier releases on the Chart and Scorpion labels and some success as a songwriter, with cuts by ROY DRUSKY and BILLY WALKER. But "The King Is Gone," co-written with Lee Morgan, opened the door to a career that has produced eighteen Top Twenty hits and created a famously loyal fan following.

A smooth singer with a flair for rockabilly-flavored country pop, McDowell has often gravitated toward shallow commercial songs and novelty material through the years. He moved from Scorpion to EPIC in 1979, producing hits including the #2 "Wandering Eyes" and the #1s "Older Women" and "You're Going to Make Me Lose My Bad Reputation." Moving to CURB/MCA in 1986 and to Curb in 1987, McDowell recorded additional chart records, including most notably a rocked-out 1987 remake of CONWAY TWITTY's massive 1958 hit "It's Only Make Believe," with Twitty providing a guest vocal. A favorite of Priscilla Presley, McDowell has provided Elvis's singing voice for several TV movies on the star's life as well as for the 1990 ABC television series *Elvis*. In 1995 McDowell was back in the studio with his longtime producer BUDDY KILLEN. He also clung to his Elvis associations into the nineties, heading a 1993 touring package that included notable Presley sidemen such as Scotty Moore, D. J. Fontana, and the JORDANAIRES.

—*Thomas Goldsmith*

REPRESENTATIVE RECORDINGS

A Tribute to the King (Elvis) in Memory (Scorpion, 1979); *Greatest Hits* (Epic, 1982); *The Best of Ronnie McDowell* (1990)

Red River Dave McEnery (see Red River Dave)

Reba McEntire

Reba McEntire
b. Chockie, Oklahoma, March 28, 1954

Reba Nell McEntire has been the most successful female country performer of the 1980s and 1990s. With nearly twenty #1 *Billboard* hits at last count, she has sold more than 35 million records and has starred in a road show that requires thirteen trucks to cart. Her elaborate stage productions, and her emphasis on acting and videos, have redefined what it means to be a country star. She has also built Starstruck Entertainment, a conglomerate that contains her own booking, management, publishing, transportation, and recording services. The firm is housed in a luxurious, 29,000-square-foot office building on Music Row and includes a state-of-the-art music studio.

McEntire's drive and ambition have been visible throughout her life and career. She spent her early years on a 7,000-acre cattle ranch and with her family on the back roads of Oklahoma, visiting rodeos with her father, champion calf roper Clark McEntire. Her mother, Jackie, was a singer who influenced Reba and the other children. By the time Reba was in high school, the children had a group called the Singing McEntires. In 1971 they made a locally distributed tribute record to their grandfather, "The Ballad of John McEntire," and in 1974 Reba sang the national anthem at the National Rodeo finals in Oklahoma City. RED STEAGALL heard her and financed a recording session. MERCURY RECORDS offered her a contract in 1975. Married in June 1976 to Charlie Battles, a rodeo star ten years her senior, she continued to ride in rodeos and also finished college.

McEntire began her career with a PATSY CLINE heart-ache style and an emphasis on her cowgirl image and traditional country roots. Her first Mercury recording, in 1976, went nowhere. Other singles and a 1977 album also flopped. But in 1979 McEntire finally hit the Top Twenty with a remake of "Sweet Dreams," a song closely associated with Cline, and in 1980 McEntire entered the Top Ten with "(You Lift Me) Up to Heaven." A third LP followed, built around tributes to Cline and featuring McEntire's distinctive phrasing and accent.

Signing with MCA RECORDS in 1984, McEntire began to take more charge of her career. Her back-to-basics album *My Kind of Country* contained her #1 hits "How Blue" and "Somebody Should Leave." The COUNTRY MUSIC ASSOCIATION recognized her as Female Vocalist of the Year, and she went on to win the CMA Female Vocalist award three more years in succession. In 1986 she joined the Grand Ole Opry cast and won a Grammy; an upgraded stage show and several acting stints brought her the CMA's Entertainer of the Year award that same year.

McEntire's 1986 video of her hit "Whoever's in New England" began her interest in videos and acting. She has often been featured in roles that have story content, as in her portrayal of a waitress-wife-mother who goes back to school to get her degree in 1992's video of "Is There Life Out There" (a 1994 TV movie was also made from this concept). McEntire's movie career began in 1990 with *Tremors* and continued with roles in *Luck of the Draw. The Gambler Returns,* Rob Reiner's *North,* and *Buffalo Girls.* Her bestselling autobiography, *Reba,* was published by Bantam in 1994.

With her 1987 divorce from Charlie Battles, McEntire moved to Nashville from her Oklahoma ranch and began building her business enterprises. She married Narvel Blackstock, her former steel guitarist, who by then had become her road manager. McEntire's climb to success was marred in March 1991, however, when seven members of her band, her road manager (not Blackstock), and the pilot and co-pilot of a chartered private jet bringing them to Fort Wayne, Indiana, from a show in San Diego were killed when the plane hit a mountainside during takeoff. McEntire, Blackstock, and two other band members were booked on other flights.

McEntire has always claimed the female country audience as her first concern, addressing their lives and troubles. "I'm trying to sing songs for women, to say for them what they can't say for themselves," she told the *Chicago Tribune*'s Jack Hurst in 1984. "But I'm trying to do it for the eighties and nineties." In addition to her touring productions and videos that compare with the most elaborate of Broadway productions, she has also stepped out in musical style, adopting more pop sounds and songs into her repertoire and recordings.

McEntire celebrated her twentieth year in the music business with the 1995 album *Starting Over.* That was followed in 1996 by *What If It's You,* co-produced with John Guess. In 1997 she teamed with country superduo BROOKS & DUNN for an eighty-five-city tour. That year her Starstruck Films production company formed an alliance with Universal Studios in Los Angeles.

—*Mary A. Bufwack*

REPRESENTATIVE RECORDINGS

My Kind of Country (MCA, 1984); *Whoever's in New England* (MCA, 1986); *Greatest Hits* (MCA, 1987); *Greatest Hits Volume II* (MCA, 1993)

Jack McFadden
b. Sikeston, Missouri, January 9, 1927; d. June 16, 1998

Jack McFadden's career as manager of country music performers began with, and will forever be associated with, the career of BUCK OWENS. A former movie theater and radio station manager, McFadden got his start as a booking agent in California for the MADDOX BROTHERS & ROSE shortly after World War II. He went on to book and promote other artists on the West Coast, including HANK WILLIAMS and TOMMY COLLINS. In 1963 McFadden made a quantum leap in income and prestige when he was hired by Owens, just as Owens's career was hitting a peak that would last through that decade. In 1965, with Owens, Mc-Fadden formed the BAKERSFIELD-based OMAC firm (Owens-McFadden Artists Corporation), which booked live appearances for Owens and an entire stable of West Coast artists that included, at one time or another, MERLE HAGGARD, ROSE MADDOX, and WYNN STEWART. In that capacity McFadden was one of the most important figures in the country music scene in California, and he was one of the founding members of the ACADEMY OF COUNTRY MUSIC, the West Coast's version of the COUNTRY MUSIC ASSOCIATION. In 1983 he moved his operations to Nashville and established McFadden Artists Corporation as a major Music City management firm with its own office building on Eighteenth Avenue near Music Row. McFadden managed BILLY RAY CYRUS, Rhonda Vincent, STEVE WARINER, KEITH WHITLEY, and LORRIE MORGAN. He died from liver cirrhosis at age seventy-one. —*Mark Fenster*

Dennis McGee
b. Bayou Marron, Louisiana, January 26, 1893; d. October 3, 1989

Of all the great Cajun fiddlers, Dennis McGee recorded the largest body of early Cajun fiddle tunes between the years 1929 and 1930. Because of him, we have an insight into the early Acadian fiddle style and into the original versions of the tunes. His music offers a baseline by which we can measure how tunes are learned through aural traditions.

McGee's early life was that of a turn-of-the-century orphan in southwestern Louisiana, passed from home to home, mistreated and used as a servant by family members who took him in. Finally he found a happy home with his uncle Theodore McGee. It was this uncle who bought him a fiddle, giving the youngster an outlet for his musical talent.

McGee's early career was typical of a talented musician in Louisiana in the late 1920s. He performed at dances almost nightly, competed in local talent competitions, played with different area musicians, and finally recorded, chosen from among other competitors at a music contest in Opelousas.

McGee recorded fiddle duets (the preaccordion Cajun music) with two famed *segoneurs*, or second fiddle players. One was his brother-in-law, Sady Courville of Eunice; the second was Ernest Frugé from Grand Marais. Courville's style was more basic chording, whereas Frugé's style involved more complex noting and bow rocking. Both styles complemented McGee's fiddle work beautifully in recordings for Vocalion (1929) and BRUNSWICK (1930).

In addition to these early fiddle duet recordings, McGee played second fiddle on recordings by accordionists Angelas LeJeune and Amédé Ardoin. McGee's friendship with Ardoin, a legendary black Louisiana accordionist, produced eleven released sides for the COLUMBIA, Brunswick, and BLUEBIRD labels (1929–34). McGee's intense rocking second-fiddle style combined with Ardoin's syncopations and triplets to produce excellent examples of early Cajun accordion-fiddle duets.

Angelas LeJeune from Church Point, Louisiana, was another good friend of McGee's, and these two (joined by Ernest Frugé on fiddle) made six interesting sides for the Brunswick label, including "Perrodin Two-Step" and "Valse de Pointe Noire," in September 1929. McGee and LeJeune also performed together in accordion contests and traveled throughout southwestern Louisiana, playing in dance halls.

Two of McGee's most influential early tunes are "Madame Young donnez-moi votre plus jolie blonde" (later to become "Allons danser Colinda") and the haunting "Mon cher bébé creole"; both of these were recorded with Sady Courville for Vocalion in March 1929, at McGee's first recording session.

After several years McGee retired from the dance-hall scene and supported his family of twelve children through tenant farming, barbering, and various odd jobs. In later life he resumed his musical career, touring throughout the United States with his old friend Sady Courville. He died in 1989 at age ninety-six, in Eunice, Louisiana.
—*Ann Allen Savoy*

REPRESENTATIVE RECORDING

The Complete Early Recordings of Dennis McGee (Yazoo, 1994)

McGee Brothers
Sam Fleming McGee b. Williamson County, Tennessee, May 1, 1894; d. August 21, 1975
Kirk McGee b. Williamson County, Tennessee, November 4, 1899; d. October 24, 1983

Though folk music fans remember them primarily as the accompanists for UNCLE DAVE MACON, Sam and Kirk McGee had a career that extended from the very earliest days of the GRAND OLE OPRY to the show's movement from the RYMAN AUDITORIUM in 1974. In fact, it was one of their acoustic guitar duets that so impressed visiting journalist Garrison Keillor in 1974 that he was moved to start his radio show *A PRAIRIE HOME COMPANION*.

The music of the McGees was much more eclectic than that of early Opry denizens. Sam learned guitar tunings and slide techniques from black railroad workers near his family home; Kirk adapted the blues records of Papa Charley Jackson and others to the stringband style, and sported a singing style derived partly from his tenure at old-time singing schools; both liked old-time jazz, and Sam adapted ragtime piano rolls to the guitar.

It was Sam who first tested the waters, playing guitar and banjo for the already famed Uncle Dave Macon. While with Macon at a 1926 recording session, Sam made several guitar solos, including his famous "Buck Dancer's Choice," and "Franklin Blues." The discs were the first serious country guitar solos, initiating a tradition that would extend from RILEY PUCKETT to CHET ATKINS. In the early 1930s the brothers joined forces with Dickson County fiddler ARTHUR SMITH to form the Dixieliners, by most accounts the hottest string band the Opry ever had.

Unfortunately, the band never recorded in its prime

(the BLUEBIRD records under the same name featured Smith and the DELMORE BROTHERS).

As other of the classic Opry bands broke up, Sam and Kirk kept at it until the late 1950s, when they were discovered by folk revival fans. The McGees made a comeback of sorts, recording albums for Folkways and STARDAY and appearing at a number of festivals. Sam recorded several solo albums for Arhoolie and for MBA, a company he partly owned. In their later years, both Kirk and Sam hosted a procession of young instrumentalists anxious to learn from two masters.

Sam was killed in a farming accident in 1975; Kirk died in 1983. —*Charles Wolfe*

REPRESENTATIVE RECORDINGS

The McGee Brothers (Bear Family, 1974); *Grand Dad of the Country Guitar Pickers* (Arhoolie, 1963, 1997)

John McGhee & Frank Welling

John Leftridge McGhee b. Griffithsville, West Virginia, April 9, 1882; d. May 9, 1945

Benjamin Franklin Welling b. Lawrence County, Ohio, February 16, 1898; d. January 23, 1957

John McGhee & Frank Welling recorded more than 200 sides between 1927 and 1933. Their music appeared on such labels as BRUNSWICK, GENNETT, Melotone, Paramount, and subsidiaries. Sacred material featuring McGhee's strong bass vocal and harmonica, coupled with Welling's lead singing and steel guitar, comprised their main fare, augmented by some sentimental and humorous songs. Welling also performed some of the earliest recitations in recorded country music. Based in Huntington, West Virginia, in their duet days, Welling relocated to WCHS-Charleston in 1937 and spent the rest of his life as a radio announcer, creating the character of Uncle Si.

—*Ivan M. Tribe*

REPRESENTATIVE RECORDING

Sacred, Sentimental and Silly Songs (Old Homestead, 1987)

Tim McGraw

b. Delhi, Louisiana, May 1, 1967

Though he has publicly claimed KEITH WHITLEY as his musical role model, Tim McGraw's canny balancing of raucous rockers and tender ballads suggests he has learned much from observing GARTH BROOKS. Crossover hits such as the pounding "Indian Outlaw" (#15, pop) and the poignant ballad "Don't Take the Girl" (#17, pop) have boosted his cumulative album sales to more than 7 million and earned him the ACM's 1994 Top New Male Vocalist of the Year and Album of the Year Awards.

The out-of-wedlock offspring of a summer romance between his mother and star baseball pitcher Tug McGraw, Timothy Samuel McGraw grew up as Tim Smith, believing himself to be the son of a long-distance trucker. He didn't know his real father, who pitched for the New York Mets' and Philadelphia Phillies' championship teams, until he was twelve and didn't establish a relationship with him until he turned eighteen and needed financial assistance for college.

When a knee injury at Northeastern Louisiana University ended his dream of a professional sports career, Mc-

Tim McGraw

Graw bought a guitar and started performing at area clubs. In 1989 he moved to Nashville, arriving on May 9, the day Keith Whitley died.

In 1991 McGraw began circulating demo tapes, and on a whim sent one to Tug McGraw, who had a friend forward it to CURB RECORDS, where Mike Borchetta, Curb's vice president of promotion, reluctantly agreed to meet with the young singer. Three weeks later, McGraw had a recording contract.

His self-titled debut album yielded three chart singles, but it was not until his 1994 sophomore release, *Not a Moment Too Soon,* that he rocketed to stardom. The quintuple-platinum disc reached #1 on *Billboard*'s Top 200 pop album chart and was named *Billboard*'s best-selling country album of 1994.

In that year McGraw became the first country artist in a decade to achieve two gold singles in fewer than three months ("Indian Outlaw," "Don't Take the Girl") and saw the single "Not a Moment Too Soon" hit #1 and "Down on the Farm" reach #2 on *Billboard*'s country charts. In addition,"Don't Take the Girl" received the TNN/*Music City News* award for Best Song.

His 1995 multiplatinum LP *All I Want* yielded the #1 singles "I Like It, I Love It" and "Can't Be Really Gone." Tim McGraw married FAITH HILL on October 6, 1996. Their duet "It's Your Love" hit #1 on the country charts in July 1997 and was named the CMA's 1997 Vocal Event of the Year. Additional hits from this song's album, *Everywhere*, include the #1 title cut and "Just to See You Smile," which spent six weeks at the top in early 1998. —*Marjie McGraw*

REPRESENTATIVE RECORDINGS

Tim McGraw (Curb, 1993); *Not a Moment Too Soon* (Curb, 1994); *All I Want* (Curb, 1995); *Everywhere* (Curb, 1997)

Clayton McMichen

Clayton McMichen

b. Allatoona, Georgia, January 26, 1900; d. January 4, 1970

Clayton "Pappy" McMichen learned to fiddle at age eleven from uncles and from his father, a trained musician who played fiddle in North Georgia, providing tunes at local square dances and Viennese waltzes at uptown hotel society dances. In 1913 the family moved to Atlanta, and young Clayton became an automobile mechanic. Soon after, he entered his first fiddlers' contest and took third prize. In about 1918 he put together a band called the Hometown Boys, which made its radio debut on WSB in 1922 within weeks after the station's opening. In 1926 McMichen joined GID TANNER, RILEY PUCKETT, and Fate Norris to record for COLUMBIA RECORDS as the SKILLET LICKERS, but concurrently and subsequently McMichen organized a succession of other bands, best known of which was the Georgia Wildcats. While the Skillet Lickers' sound was dominated by Tanner and Puckett, and heavily oriented toward older traditional fiddle tunes, banjo songs, and ballads, McMichen, considerably younger than his cohorts in the Skillet Lickers and much more attuned to jazz and contemporary pop music, led his own bands in more modern directions.

Nevertheless, his skills as old-time breakdown fiddler were seldom matched, and, together with Lowe Stokes, McMichen provided dynamic lead fiddling on all the Skillet Lickers' recordings between 1926 and 1931. In 1945, after he stopped making records, McMichen's Wildcats became a Dixieland jazz band and played six days each week on radio stations in Louisville, Kentucky, for a decade. In the 1960s, the college revival in old-time music provided a new venue for McMichen on college campuses and at folk festivals. McMichen also penned a number of the pieces that his bands recorded, most successful of which was "Peach Pickin' Time in Georgia," subsequently recorded by JIMMIE RODGERS in 1932, with McMichen playing violin back up.

While most of country music's first generation of recording stars—Gid Tanner, ERNEST STONEMAN, UNCLE DAVE MACON, and FIDDLIN' JOHN CARSON—were farmers or tradesmen first and musicians second, McMichen stood out in his highly professional approach to his music. For years he had difficulty watching what he regarded as less musically gifted colleagues (such as Tanner and Carson) dominating the limelight, and he struggled to raise country music's image and standards by moving from the rural to the uptown. It was an embittered McMichen who stood before college crowds at Newport and mocked their enthusiasm for the older traditional music of the Skillet Lickers—a musical genre for which he still held considerable contempt. But, ironically, the music of the Skillet Lickers and their ilk is still widely accessible on LPs or CDs, while recordings by the Georgia Wildcats are practically unobtainable. —*Norm Cohen*

REPRESENTATIVE RECORDING

Gid Tanner and His Skillet Lickers—with Riley Puckett and Clayton McMichen (Rounder, 1973)

Medicine Shows

Early in the nineteenth century, rural Americans, often without a resident physician within easy traveling distance, patronized purveyors of various elixirs, ointments, herbs, and tonics. These medicinal salesmen traveled by wagon from town to town, urging people to purchase remedies for their ills. Without the watchful eye of today's governmental regulatory agencies, the potions often lacked any demonstrable efficacy; but the "doctor" was miles away by the time his disenchanted customers might have come to such a conclusion. To attract a large audience of potential buyers, the dispenser of remedies would host a free show featuring music, comedians, dancers, jugglers, acrobats, short dramatic performances, and testimonials from confederates before launching into his pitch. These medicine shows flourished through much of the nineteenth century and the early twentieth century, languishing by World War I as a result of both improved medical care and competing forms of entertainment. In the rural Southeast, traveling medicine shows were still common into the 1930s, rare by the 1950s, and extinct by the mid-1970s.

Many early country music performers (and African-American entertainers as well) spent time on the road with one or more medicine shows, and the music of the genre impacted their own musical styles and repertoires. Medicine show music was invariably secular and lighthearted, often comical or bawdy. Among the country musicians who worked medicine shows early in their careers were UNCLE DAVE MACON, CLARENCE "TOM" ASHLEY, DOC HOPKINS, LEW CHILDRE, JIMMIE RODGERS, ROY ACUFF, GENE AUTRY, and HANK WILLIAMS. In 1929 both COLUMBIA and OKEH issued rural comedy skits parodying the still-familiar medicine show (Columbia 15482-D: "Kickapoo Medicine Show"; OKeh 45380, 45391, and 45413: "The Medicine Show, Acts 1–6"). Microgroove recordings by veteran medicine show entertainers Harmonica Frank Floyd and Tom Ashley recreated typical medicine show musical humor, as did stage shows by Ramblin' Tommy Scott. —*Norm Cohen*

D. L. Menard
b. Erath, Louisiana, April 14, 1932

D. L. Menard, known as the Cajun Hank Williams, has given Cajun music some of its most beloved songs. His "Porte d'en arrière" ("The Back Door") has remained a top regional favorite ever since it was first released on the Swallow label in 1962.

Doris Leon Menard began his musical career as a teenage guitarist and vocalist in accordionist Elias Badeaux's band, Badeaux & the Louisiana Aces, in about 1949. It was with this group that the first recording of "The Back Door" was made, with Menard on guitar and vocals.

The major influence on Menard's music was songwriter HANK WILLIAMS. In a 1951 meeting in a Louisiana nightclub, Williams encouraged Menard to record his own songs, advising the aspiring Cajun songwriter that if music was truly one's own, it was valuable. In addition, Williams's profound insight—that keeping music simple made it possible for the common man to relate to it—affected all of Menard's writing.

Since then, Menard has written many beautiful songs, such as "Under the Green Oak Tree," "I Can't Forget You," "She Didn't Know I Was Married," and "Rebecca Ann." His music has attracted the attention of such country musicians as RICKY SKAGGS, Buck White, and JERRY DOUGLAS, all of whom appeared with him on his 1985 Rounder release *Cajun Saturday Night.*

When not traveling throughout the world playing music, Menard has made his living building chairs. There in his native town of Erath, living with some of his seven children, he runs a small, home-based chair factory, working with his wife, Louella, who puts the hemp seats on the ladderback frames. Grandchildren are usually present as Menard and wife work on chairs or cook huge pots of food in their rocking-chair-filled kitchen.

In 1994 Menard received the prestigious National Heritage Fellowship Award from the National Endowment for the Arts.
—*Ann Allen Savoy*

REPRESENTATIVE RECORDINGS

D. L. Menard Sings the Back Door and His Other Cajun Hits (Swallow, 1980); *Le Trio Cadien* (Rounder, 1992)

Mercury Records
established in Chicago, Illinois, 1945

Mercury Records celebrated its fiftieth year in the music industry in 1995. Over the years the company has not only proven that an independent label can successfully compete with the majors, but it has also introduced some of country music's biggest talents.

Mercury was founded by record-pressing plant owner Irving Green and artist manager Berle Adams. Though the first year saw their entry into the country market, Mercury's roster really began to grow in 1948, when MURRAY NASH took over as A&R representative. Operating out of Knoxville, Nash was responsible for signing local talent such as LESTER FLATT & EARL SCRUGGS, the CARLISLES, and CARL STORY. In 1951 Mercury pop singer Patti Page had a huge hit with "Tennessee Waltz," written by PEE WEE KING and REDD STEWART.

D. KILPATRICK served in the country A&R position from late 1951 through 1955 and was responsible for adding the talents of JOHNNY HORTON and the STANLEY BROTHERS. Mercury was struggling, however, to be a strong force in country music. To remedy the situation, STARDAY RECORDS, an independent country label out of Houston, was added to form Mercury/Starday in 1957. Though the merger lasted only a year and a half, it did bring Mercury several new artists, including GEORGE JONES.

In 1961 Mercury was purchased by the Dutch firm Philips Electronics, and the following year Philips expanded the record company into three labels: Mercury, Smash, and Philips. Mercury became a mainstay in country music during the 1960s after SHELBY SINGLETON was appointed A&R chief. With the aid of JERRY KENNEDY, he began producing hits by LEROY VAN DYKE, FARON YOUNG, ROY DRUSKY, and DAVE DUDLEY. Two of their top stars, ROGER MILLER and JERRY LEE LEWIS, were signed to Smash Records before they joined the parent label in 1970.

As the 1970s began, Jerry Kennedy had already taken over the country A&R and opened Mercury's Nashville studio. New talent during his tenure included TOM T. HALL, the STATLER BROTHERS, JOHNNY RODRIGUEZ, and REBA MCENTIRE. In 1971 Dutch conglomerate PolyGram took over the Mercury labels and would later acquire MGM and Polydor.

During the 1980s, under the direction of FRANK JONES (1983–85) and later Steve Popovich (1986–87), additions to the country roster included KATHY MATTEA and veteran performer JOHNNY CASH. With Paul Lucks (1987–93) and A&R chief HAROLD SHEDD (1988–94) supervising the Nashville office, Mercury headed into the 1990s with the KENTUCKY HEADHUNTERS, SAMMY KERSHAW, and BILLY RAY CYRUS. In 1992 Luke Lewis took charge of the Nashville office, with KEITH STEGALL soon becoming head of A&R. In the late 1990s Mercury Nashville has had continued success with SHANIA TWAIN and TERRI CLARK.   —*Don Roy*

Jo Dee Messina
b. Holliston, Massachusetts, August 25, 1970

Massachusetts native Jo Dee Messina grew up in a small farming community forty miles north of Boston. Making her first appearance at age thirteen when she sang TAMMY WYNETTE's "Stand By Your Man" at a Holiday Inn lounge, Messina formed her own country band three years later, adding songs by the JUDDS, REBA MCENTIRE, PATSY CLINE, and ROSANNE CASH to her repertoire.

Her band enjoyed regional success in New England, and at age twenty Messina began to consider her ultimate career goals. Abandoning plans to attend law school, Messina moved to Nashville in 1990, supporting herself as a computer operator while entering talent contests at night.

A friendship with producer Byron Gallimore led to her introduction to TIM MCGRAW. After a failed developmental deal with RCA, a 1994 showcase led to a contract with CURB RECORDS. Her 1996 self-titled debut album, co-produced by Gallimore and McGraw, netted the #1 hit "Heads Carolina, Tails California" and the follow-up "We're Not In Kansas Anymore." The lead single from Messina's second Curb album, "Bye Bye," had reached the Top Twenty as of early 1998.   —*Calvin Gilbert*

REPRESENTATIVE RECORDINGS

Jo Dee Messina (Curb, 1996); *I'm Alright* (Curb, 1998)

MGM Records

established in New York, New York, March 1947

Loew's, Inc., parent company of MGM film studios (Metro-Goldwyn-Mayer, established in 1924), decided in 1945 to start a record division to issue soundtracks from its musicals. In August that year, FRANK WALKER was hired to start MGM Records, and by the time of the launch in March 1947, it was a full-line record company headquartered in New York with a plant in New Jersey. Walker stayed until 1956.

Throughout its existence, the core of the business was soundtracks such as *Gone With the Wind*, *Brigadoon*, and *Gigi*. Walker signed pop acts including Jimmy Dorsey and Kate Smith, some r&b acts such as Billy Eckstine, and country artists such as HANK WILLIAMS and BOB WILLS, while his successor, Arnold Maxin, signed Connie Francis, the Animals, ROY ORBISON, Herman's Hermits, CONWAY TWITTY, and others. Even with those acquisitions, and the purchase of Verve Records in 1960, MGM never rose above quasi-major label status. It opened a Nashville office in 1965 under JIM VIENNEAU.

With wavering commitment from the parent corporation, there were several presidents after Maxin, including Mike Curb (then twenty-five years old) and JIMMY BOWEN. Polydor Records eventually bought the nonmovie repertoire of MGM Records in April 1972 and ceased using the MGM trademark in 1976.　　　　　　—*Colin Escott*

Midday Merry-Go-Round

established in Knoxville, Tennessee, 1936; ended 1962

From the mid-1930s and into the 1950s, WNOX, Tennessee's oldest station and number eight in age nationwide, came to be known as a stepping-stone to the GRAND OLE OPRY because of the many stars recruited for the Opry from WNOX stages. The popular noontime WNOX show the *Midday Merry-Go-Round* was the station's most prominent country music program.

The acquisition of WNOX by E. W. Scripps Co. (Scripps-Howard) in 1935 brought a new staff and increased the station's broadcasting power. Richard Westergaard became station manager and hired Lowell Blanchard (b. Palmer, Illinois, November 15, 1910; d. February 19, 1968), a young announcer just graduated from the University of Illinois.

Blanchard began his twenty-eight-year career at WNOX in late January 1936. He immediately implemented particular ideas about entertaining by polishing acts, creating new gimmicks and comic materials, and developing a professional cast.

The *Midday Merry-Go-Round*, launched soon after Blanchard arrived, was essentially a variety show with an experimental flavor. It catered to a largely rural audience, but the show did not exclusively contain folk or traditional music. Some of its headliners—the Stringdusters (HOMER & JETHRO) and Dixieland Swingsters, for example—played a mixture of country, Dixieland, swing, and jazz.

On the WNOX shows, comedy was king. Programs were laced with jokes, many masterminded by Blanchard himself. The station's country-comedy format helped to develop some of the most popular rural comedians (including Homer & Jethro and ARCHIE CAMPBELL) of the twentieth century.

An abbreviated list of performers at WNOX between 1936 and 1962 includes ROY ACUFF, Archie Campbell, the Tennessee Ramblers, PEE WEE KING, CHARLIE MONROE, JOHNNIE & JACK, EDDIE HILL, BILL CARLISLE, CHET ATKINS, BENNY MARTIN, ARTHUR Q. SMITH, the LILLY BROTHERS, JIMMY MARTIN, DON GIBSON, and Lost John Miller.

During the post–World War II years the WNOX country shows reached their peak in popularity. The Saturday night *Tennessee Barn Dance* and weekday *Midday Merry-Go-Round* attracted a constant stream of first-rate performers. The 1950s marked a turning point in WNOX history. WNOX, with its relatively small 10,000-watt transmitter, found that it could not compete with 50,000-watt giants such as WSM and WLW and with television.

A landmark decision in Knoxville country-music history was made in late 1954 when the Federal Communications Commission ruled that WNOX could not have a television affiliate. During the next five years, WNOX's *Midday Merry-Go-Round* and *Tennessee Barn Dance* gradually died out. If only a few things had been different, perhaps Knoxville could have rivaled Nashville for dominance as country music's number-one city. In 1962 the station changed its format to rock & roll.　　　　　　—*Willie Smyth*

Midnite Jamboree (*see* Ernest Tubb)

Midwestern Hayride

established in Cincinnati, 1938; ended 1972

The *Midwestern Hayride* was one of America's foremost and longest-running barn dance shows. After JOHN LAIR organized the RENFRO VALLEY BARN DANCE in Cincinnati in 1937 and broadcast over WLW, the station launched its own barn dance, the *Boone County Jamboree*, the following year. Executive George Biggar was imported from Chicago's WLS, and, together with booker-agent-manager Bill McCluskey, another WLS veteran, Biggar built the show around talent such as HANK PENNY, CURLY FOX AND TEXAS RUBY, HOMER AND JETHRO, BRADLEY KINCAID, and Hugh Cross. LULU BELLE AND SCOTTY, already a big-name act were brought from WLS for a time, and the GIRLS OF THE GOLDEN WEST came for a longer stay.

By 1945 the show became the *Midwestern Hayride*, a name more appropriate to the broad area covered by WLW's 50,000-watt signal. At this point station managers deliberately began to feature polished, pop-influenced country acts to widen the program's appeal, but 1940s talent remained diverse and included Ernie Lee, KENNY ROBERTS, the DeZURIK SISTERS, and BONNIE LOU (Sally Carson). During the late 1940s and early 1950s WLW singing talent and prominent instrumentalists such as LOUIS INNIS, TOMMY JACKSON, ZEKE AND ZEB TURNER, and JERRY BYRD helped sustain a local recording industry.

In 1948 WLW began telecasting the *Hayride*. From this point TV became the program's primary outlet, and the show's radio broadcasts became sporadic and ultimately ended. During the 1950s, network slots broadened the *Hayride*'s TV exposure. The program was a summer replacement show on NBC in 1950, 1951, 1952, 1954, 1955, and 1959, and an NBC fill-in during 1957 and 1958. The *Hayride* also gained network exposure during nonevening hours in the regular season. By 1966 it was syndicated on forty-one TV stations nationwide, plus five stations run by AVCO Broadcasting, then WLW's owner.

Through the 1950s and 1960s the *Hayride* remained a variety show with a country flavor, featuring typical barn dance sets with wagon wheels, fences, and front porches, and offering everything from solo and duet singing to comedy and square dancing. Performers, who featured both their own recordings and hits by bigger-name artists, included KENNY PRICE, Bonnie Lou, Bobby Bobo, and the Lucky Pennies.

The *Hayride* held on amid the rise of rock and the proliferation of alternative TV programming, but its popularity was waning by the late 1960s. A revamped show featuring more name guests, background voices, and electric bass, together with new host HENSON CARGILL (followed by KENNY PRICE), who replaced longtime MC Dean Richards, failed to rally the *Hayride*'s fortunes, and the show went off the air in 1972. —*John Rumble*

Bob Miller
b. Memphis, Tennessee, September 20, 1895; d. August 26, 1955

Bob Miller was one of the first full-time professional songwriters in country music. He had been immersed in music, however, for most of his life, and, as a native southerner, he was very conscious of southern grassroots musical traditions. He led a dance band for several years on the steamer *Idlewild* on the Mississippi River and had played often at the Dreamland nightclub in Memphis. He also established the Beale Street Music Shop in Memphis, where he wrote jazz and blues tunes. In 1922 he moved to New York as an arranger for the Irving Berlin Publishing Company but soon began trying his hand, very successfully, at writing country songs. In the years that followed he wrote such country standards as "Twenty One Years," "Seven Years with the Wrong Woman," "Eleven Cent Cotton and Forty Cent Meat," "When the White Azaleas Start Blooming," and "Rocking Alone in an Old Rocking Chair." He opened his own music publishing company in 1933, the same year he joined ASCAP. One of his many topical songs, which dealt with the death of Huey Long, was written a few years *before* the Louisiana politician died! Miller's greatest success, though, came during World War II, when he arranged and wrote the melody for ELTON BRITT's great patriotic hit "There's a Star Spangled Banner Waving Somewhere." Miller also worked as an A&R man for the COLUMBIA and OKEH labels, managing the hillbilly and race divisions, and recording many country artists, from the late 1920s until June 1, 1932. —*Bill C. Malone*

Eddie Miller
b. Camargo, Oklahoma, December 10, 1919; d. April 11, 1977

Eddie Miller will forever be known as writer of the country-pop standard "Release Me," though he was a prolific tunesmith whose credits include such Top Ten hits as "There She Goes" (CARL SMITH, 1955), "After Loving You" (EDDY ARNOLD, 1962), and "Thanks a Lot" (ERNEST TUBB, 1963). He also was a music industry activist, having founded the ACADEMY OF COUNTRY MUSIC and co-founded the Nashville Songwriters Association International.

Miller was born in southwestern Oklahoma and raised on WESTERN SWING. He formed his own swing outfit, Eddie Miller & His Oklahomans, but had to disband it temporarily during the war years, when he worked on the Katy Line railroad in Texas. He later re-formed the Oklahomans and recorded for the Dallas-based Bluebonnet label ca. 1947–48. At some point after the war he moved to Los Angeles and signed with FOUR STAR as both artist and songwriter. On a club date in San Francisco, reportedly in late 1946, Miller overheard a woman say to the man she was with, "If you would release me, we'd get along all right." He went home and wrote "Release Me," which he recorded for Four Star in 1949. The song went largely unnoticed, however, until Jimmy Heap recorded it for CAPITOL RECORDS in 1953. RAY PRICE and KITTY WELLS both covered it, and all three versions hit the Top Ten in 1954. By the 1970s, more than 200 versions of "Release Me" had been recorded, including the Top Ten pop renditions of Esther Phillips (1962) and Engelbert Humperdinck (1967). After turning to religion, Miller himself, by then living near Nashville, retooled the standard as "Please Release Me from My Sins."

Miller's wife Barbara also wrote songs, and his daughter Pam had a brief career as a singer. —*Daniel Cooper*

Emmett Miller
b. Macon, Georgia, February 2, 1900; d. March 29, 1962

For most of his career, Emmett Dewey Miller worked in minstrel shows and in vaudeville as a BLACKFACE comedian, specializing in Amos & Andy types of dialogue and in what the 1920s press described as "vocal contortions." While Miller himself never considered himself a country singer, his yodeling and falsetto singing had a major influence on a number of early country singers. The blue yodels of Jimmie Rodgers bear an uncanny resemblance to Miller's yodels, and there is circumstantial evidence that Rodgers heard Miller in his own early career. The CALLAHAN BROTHERS admitted that they learned the arrangement for their biggest hit, "St. Louis Blues," from Miller's rendition of the song. BOB WILLS was so fascinated with Miller that he kept a notebook in which he copied down most of Miller's recorded songs—and even skits—and recorded a Miller favorite, "I Ain't Got Nobody."

Miller's masterpiece, "Lovesick Blues," which he recorded in 1925 and again in 1928, was known by both REX GRIFFIN and HANK WILLIAMS. Miller was also the first to record country standards such as "Anytime" and "Right or Wrong." In later years artists as diverse as MERLE HAGGARD and Leon Redbone did tribute albums to Miller, paying homage to the way his style had permeated country music for fifty years.

Miller began his professional career in his late teens by joining Neil O'Brien's minstrels, which eventually evolved into the Dan Fitch Minstrels; here he did blackface comedy (he perfected a comic walk and dialect) and sang in the show's quartet, the Kings of Harmony. Here Miller got his schooling in classic minstrel stagecraft and showmanship. When the troupe hit New York, critics were ecstatic over Miller, and soon he was being given solo spots in which he did what he called "blues singing." After a stint in Asheville, North Carolina, as a soloist, he joined the grandaddy of touring minstrel shows, the Al G. Field show. Here he won fame throughout the eastern United States and found himself recording for the OKEH company in 1924, 1925, and in 1928–30, when he did the majority of his recorded work, for a total of some thirty issued sides.

Miller played nightclubs in the 1930s and 1940s; recorded an additional four sides for BLUEBIRD RECORDS in 1936; made a final minstrel tour, called "Dixieana," in 1949; and even appeared briefly in the 1951 film *Yes Sir, Mister Bones*. —*Charles Wolfe*

REPRESENTATIVE RECORDING
Minstrel Man from Georgia (Columbia Legacy, 1996)

Frankie Miller

b. Victoria, Texas, December 17, 1930

Best known for his 1959 smash "Blackland Farmer" and subsequent hits such as "Family Man" (1959) and "Baby Rocked Her Dolly" (1960), Frank Miller Jr. was hailed in those days as a throwback—a "pure country" singer when such seemed to be disappearing.

Miller had been recording for almost a decade before "Blackland Farmer" hit. Taught guitar by his brother Norman, he left Victoria College after his sophomore year to pursue a career in the clubs along his native Gulf Coast. A big break came in 1950, when he filled in for vacationing HANK LOCKLIN on Houston's KLEE; Locklin helped secure Miller a recording contract with the Gilt-Edge label, and Miller produced a series of excellent, mostly self-penned releases during 1951, such as "I'm Getting Rid of You" and "I Don't Know," but was drafted just as he seemed poised for greater success. Miller earned a Bronze Star in Korea and snared a COLUMBIA contract upon returning in 1954. His strong releases unfortunately coincided with the first wave of rock & roll and went nowhere, despite their occasional but undeniable rockabilly tinge. Miller toured constantly and appeared regularly on such shows as the LOUISIANA HAYRIDE and BIG D JAMBOREE before landing a contract with STARDAY on the strength of "Blackland Farmer" at the end of 1958. He spent the next few years turning out strong material for that label and United Artists, but grew tired of the touring grind and retired by the end of the 1960s. —*Kevin Coffey*

REPRESENTATIVE RECORDINGS

Rockin' Rollin' Frankie Miller (Bear Family, 1983); *Sugar Coated Baby* (Bear Family, 1996)

J. D. Miller

b. Iota, Louisiana, May 5, 1922; d. March 23, 1996

Beginning in 1946, producer-songwriter Joseph Delton "J. D." Miller (a.k.a. Jay Miller) operated an independent recording studio in Crowley, Louisiana, that exerted an influence far out of proportion to its size. He produced scores of Cajun, country, rockabilly, and blues artists, and his MTE studio was used for some recording on Paul Simon's *Graceland* LP. Yet for all Miller's achievements as a producer, his most famous contribution to country music may have been as a songwriter, for in 1952 it was Miller who wrote KITTY WELLS's first #1 hit, "It Wasn't God Who Made Honky Tonk Angels," which Miller had originally released on his Feature Records label on a recording by Alice "Al" Montgomery.

Initially drawn to the cowboy style of GENE AUTRY, Miller didn't pay attention to Cajun music until he moved to Crowley in 1937. Playing in a variety of bands, he was influenced most strongly by western swing star CLIFF BRUNER. Miller quit performing when he got married, however, and joined his father in the family music store, M&S Music (for Miller and son). In 1946 he set up shop as a record label, recording in a small studio behind the music store. He put Cajun acts such as HAPPY FATS and Doc Guidry on his Fais Do Do label and country acts on his Feature imprint; among artists who made their recording debut on Feature were DOUG KERSHAW and JIMMY C. NEWMAN (who co-wrote his first national hit, "Cry, Cry, Darling," with Miller). Miller also managed LEFTY FRIZZELL briefly in 1952, the

year "It Wasn't God Who Made Honky Tonk Angels" soared to #1. Miller then signed a writer's deal with ACUFF-ROSE PUBLICATIONS, but by the mid-1950s he was focusing on recording rockabilly and blues artists, most notably Slim Harpo. Miller died at Lourdes Hospital in Lafayette, Louisiana, following quadruple cardiac bypass surgery. —*Daniel Cooper*

Jody Miller

b. Phoenix, Arizona, November 29, 1941

Raised in the Southwest and the daughter of a fiddler, Jody Miller (Myrna Joy Brooks) was greatly influenced by the folk music currents of her time. Still, she is best known for her 1965 hit "Queen of the House," an answer song to ROGER MILLER's smash "King of the Road."

Miller learned the guitar at age fourteen and performed folk songs in a trio while still in high school. Her first recording with CAPITOL RECORDS, in 1963, came after a move to Los Angeles. She recorded a folk revival collection, *Wednesday's Child Is Full of Woe*, and became a regular on Tom Paxton's folk TV show.

"Queen of the House" was a Top Five hit on the country charts and reached #12 on the pop charts, earning Miller a Grammy for Best Female Country and Western Vocal Performance. Through the late 1960s and 1970s she attempted a fusion of pop and country. After a switch to EPIC, she had some success throughout the 1970s translating older pop songs into a country format. —*Mary A. Bufwack*

REPRESENTATIVE RECORDING

The Best of Jody Miller (Capitol, 1973)

Julie and Buddy Miller

Julie Anne Miller b. Dallas, Texas, July 12, 1956
Steven Paul "Buddy" Miller b. Fairborn, Ohio, September 6, 1952

A critically acclaimed husband-wife duo who perform both separately and together, Buddy and Julie Miller met in Austin, Texas, in 1976, when they both played in the local country-rock band Partners in Crime. They married in Waco in 1981. Throughout the 1980s, the Millers were active on the music scenes of New York and Los Angeles, Buddy playing lead guitar and singing with country singer-songwriter JIM LAUDERDALE, Julie releasing four albums of contemporary Christian music.

After moving to Nashville in 1993, Buddy built a studio in the couple's home, where he recorded his 1995 solo debut, *Your Love and Other Lies*, one of the finest hard-country records of the 1990s. Two of its tracks also landed on the mainstream country albums of BROOKS & DUNN and GEORGE DUCAS. Meanwhile, jazz singer Jimmy Scott and EMMYLOU HARRIS both cut Julie's "All My Tears (Be Washed Away)," Harris's version appearing on her influential *Wrecking Ball* album (1995). Julie subsequently recorded her secular debut, *Blue Pony*—a beguiling mix of folk, blues, Appalachian, and Celtic music set to a rock backbeat. Buddy, who currently plays guitar with Harris and STEVE EARLE released his second HIGHTONE album, *Poison Love*, in late 1997. —*Bill Friskics-Warren*

REPRESENTATIVE RECORDINGS

Buddy Miller: *Your Love and Other Lies* (HighTone, 1995); Julie Miller: *Blue Pony* (HighTone, 1997)

Ned Miller

b. Raines, Utah, April 12, 1925

Singer-songwriter Ned Miller wrote and/or recorded a handful of classic country music hits during a recording career spanning fewer than fourteen years. Henry Ned Miller grew up in Salt Lake City and began writing songs as a teen. In the mid-1950s, after working as a pipefitter, he decided to pursue his dreams and move to California. He sought out independent record producer FABOR ROBISON, who signed him to a recording contract in 1956. His first release on the FABOR label was a song he had written titled "From a Jack to a King," which did not chart. However, DOT RECORDS took another of Miller's songs, "Dark Moon," and gave BONNIE GUITAR her first hit (#14 country, #6 pop, 1957).

After several unsuccessful recordings for both CAPITOL and Jackpot, Miller's luck began to change when his original recording of "From a Jack to a King" was reissued to become one of 1963's big hits (#2 country, #6 pop). He followed with "Invisible Tears" (#13, 1964) and "Do What You Do Do Well" (#7 country). In that same year SONNY JAMES took Miller's "Behind the Tear" to the top of the charts. Miller continued to record until 1970 and then retired to Arizona. In 1989 RICKY VAN SHELTON's recording of "From a Jack to a King" reached #1.
—*Don Roy*

REPRESENTATIVE RECORDING

From a Jack to a King (Bear Family, 1991)

Roger Miller

b. Fort Worth, Texas, January 2, 1936; d. October 25, 1992

One of the most multifaceted talents country music has ever known, Roger Dean Miller left a musical legacy of astonishing depth and range. A struggling honky-tonk singer and songwriter when he first hit Nashville in 1957, he blossomed into a country-pop superstar in the 1960s with self-penned crossover hits such as "Dang Me" and "King of the Road." In 1965–66 he won eleven Grammys. Two decades later, he received a 1985 Tony Award for his score for *Big River*, a Broadway musical based on Mark Twain's *The Adventures of Huckleberry Finn*. In between such career triumphs, Miller kept friends and fans in constant stitches as his extemporaneous wit proved almost as famous as his music.

Born in Fort Worth, Texas, Miller was sent to live with an uncle in Erick, Oklahoma ("population 1,500, and that includes rakes and tractors," he liked to joke), when he was three years old. He grew up in Erick, working the family farm and dreaming of a different life. As a teenager enamored of BOB WILLS and HANK WILLIAMS, Miller would drift from town to town in Texas and Oklahoma, trying to land nightclub work as a country singer. Drafted during the Korean War, Miller was sent to Fort McPherson in Atlanta, where he played fiddle in a Special Services outfit called the Circle A Wranglers. While stationed there he met BILL ANDERSON, and the two young, would-be country stars embarked on a lifelong friendship.

After his discharge, Miller headed to Nashville. While working as a bellhop, he wormed his way into the local music community. He was first hired to play fiddle in MINNIE PEARL's road band; then, in about the spring of 1957, he struck up a friendship with GEORGE JONES. Impressed with Miller's songwriting, Jones introduced him to PAPPY DAILY

Roger Miller

and DON PIERCE of Mercury-Starday Records. Miller's first single, "My Pillow" b/w "Poor Little John," was released on STARDAY in the fall of 1957. In the meantime, Jones and Miller had co-written some songs, including "Tall, Tall Trees," which Jones released in 1957 to little response but which ALAN JACKSON would take to #1 nearly forty years later.

After a brief return to the Southwest, Miller was hired in 1958 to front RAY PRICE's Cherokee Cowboys. From that position he suggested that Price cover "Invitation to the Blues," a song Miller had written that was starting to take off in REX ALLEN's version. Released as the B-side of Price's 1958 smash "City Lights," "Invitation to the Blues" rose to #3 on the charts, giving Miller his first major success in the business.

Signed to TREE PUBLISHING as a staff writer in 1958, Miller began to see his tunes recorded by such stars as ERNEST TUBB, JIM REEVES, and FARON YOUNG. (Miller also served for a time as Young's drummer.) Though he had continued to record for Starday and then DECCA, he had no success as an artist until he signed with RCA in 1960. His first RCA single, "You Don't Want My Love," became his first Top Forty hit. It was followed a year later by his first Top Ten, "When Two Worlds Collide," which he had written with his friend Bill Anderson.

Miller's RCA career never quite panned out, though, and by 1963 he was ready to quit Nashville to pursue an acting career in Los Angeles. He had made guest appearances on the *Jimmy Dean Show* and the *Tonight Show*, and his humor had been well received. Late that year, when his RCA contract ran out, he was picked up by Smash Records, in part because a Smash executive had liked Miller's TV routine. An agreement was struck whereby Miller would cut a single and an additional album's worth of material for $100 per side, thereby raising the money he would need to finance his move. Not only did the recordings pay for the move, they also made Roger Miller a star, for out of those off-the-cuff 1964 sessions came "Dang Me."

A #1 smash on the country charts, "Dang Me" was also a Top Ten pop hit, as were four more of the singles he released during his first two years on Smash. The most famous was "King of the Road," a million seller. Miller's success was all the more astounding for having arrived during the British Invasion. With his exceptional wordplay and jazzlike delivery, he was able to compete with the Beatles and the Rolling Stones on the pop charts. While he is often remembered as a novelty specialist due to mid-1960s hits such as "Chug-a-Lug" and "Kansas City Star," he was capable of great soulfulness, as on the Top Five hit "Husbands and Wives."

By 1968, fearing his own songwriting well had run dry, Miller turned to the work of other imaginative young Nashville writers, such as KRIS KRISTOFFERSON, whose "Me and Bobby McGee" was recorded first by Miller. He continued to record into the 1970s, and in 1974 he provided soundtrack music for the Walt Disney movie *Robin Hood*. Still, Miller became less of a force on radio as the decade progressed. He apparently didn't mind, for he was content to live a quieter life with his third wife, Mary Arnold (formerly a singer with KENNY ROGERS and the First Edition), and their children. And so he would have done had he not been talked into writing the score for *Big River*.

Opening on Broadway in 1985, *Big River* was, in Miller's own eyes, the crowning achievement of his career. Rejuvenated by its success, he maintained an active career through the remainder of the decade. In 1991, though, he left the road when he learned he had cancer. He fought the disease for a year, but died on October 25, 1992. Three years later he was inducted posthumously into the COUNTRY MUSIC HALL OF FAME. —*Daniel Cooper*

REPRESENTATIVE RECORDINGS

Roger and Out, retitled *Roger Miller Featuring Dang Me (& the New Hit Chug-a-Lug)* (Smash, 1964); *The Return of Roger Miller* (Smash, 1965); *The 3rd Time Around* (Smash, 1965); *Roger Miller* (Smash, 1969); *King of the Road: The Genius of Roger Miller* (Mercury Nashville, 1995)

The Miller Brothers

One of the most enduring and popular western swing bands, the Miller Brothers (based in Wichita Falls, Texas) never scored any chart hits yet constantly finished high in trade polls of the 1950s, just behind the likes of HANK THOMPSON and BOB WILLS.

The group was originally formed in the late 1930s by the Gibbs brothers, Leon, Sam, and Nat, who adopted the pseudonym Miller to keep from getting fired from their day jobs. Fiddler Leon fronted the band, and it played over KWFT. The brothers were drafted during World War II, and after the war they formed a new Miller Brothers band in partnership with trumpeter Lee Cochran, who also adopted the Miller moniker. The group recorded for the local Delta record label, in 1947, a fascinating combination of straight country dance titles coupled on releases with pure big band music.

The Millers broadened their horizons and graduated from playing in the North Texas–Oklahoma area to playing across the western states by 1953. In that year the group toured and recorded with former Texas Playboys vocalist TOMMY DUNCAN; the association broadened the Millers' territory even further. In the 1950s the band recorded a varied mix of swing instrumentals and vocal features for FOUR STAR with singers such as Billy Thompson and Jimmy McGraw. The Millers soon toured as far away as Puerto Rico and Canada.

Sam Gibbs left the group in 1953 (Nat Gibbs had left earlier) to concentrate on his work in a booking agency, which, in addition to the Millers, would boast such clients as Bob Wills. The Millers' work with Four Star ended by the close of the decade; by that time both Leon Gibbs and Lee Cochran had quit the group and joined Sam in the booking agency.

In about 1959 the Miller Brothers' name was sold to fiddler Bobby Rhodes, steel guitarist Bill Jourdan, and bassist Jimmy McGraw, who kept the group going into the early 1960s. An interesting footnote: The Millers' longtime pianist Madge Suttee is perhaps best remembered for the distinctive playing she laid down on LEFTY FRIZZELL's early 1950s hits. —*Kevin Coffey*

REPRESENTATIVE RECORDING

Diggin': Hot, Small Label Texas Swing, 1946–55 (Krazy Kat, 1998)

Ronnie Milsap

b. Robbinsville, North Carolina, January 16, 1943

As much as any other country vocal star, singer-keyboardist Ronnie Milsap has mastered a broad range of musical styles—from Bach to rock. Milsap's command of country, country-pop, pop standards, rock & roll, rhythm & blues, funk, and classical has meant he's a formidable performer who sometimes has trouble falling into a music business niche. However, he's one of the most successful country artists ever, with six Grammy Awards; four CMA Awards, including the 1977 Entertainer of the Year crown; and some thirty-five #1 *Billboard* hits to his credit. An energetic performer and an exemplar of the sometimes overly bland late 1970s to early 1980s country-pop sound, Milsap continued to have hits into the youth-driven late 1980s to early 1990s country boom.

Born blind into an Appalachian family, their last name being Millsaps, Ronnie went to live with grandparents at

Ronnie Milsap

age one. According to his 1990 autobiography, *It Was Almost Like a Song,* Milsap's mother asked his father to take young Ronnie away, viewing him as a punishment from God because of his blindness. At age six, having already absorbed hillbilly music via radio and gospel music at church, Milsap was sent to the State School for the Blind in Raleigh, North Carolina. Despite some harsh treatment there, he blossomed musically; he later called the place "education heaven and disciplinary hell." He soaked in both the school's classical techniques and the many pop styles available on radio.

Graduating in 1962, Milsap continued to pursue music while attending Young Harris Junior College (he graduated in 1964), and he released his debut single, "Total Disaster," in 1963 on Atlanta's Princess Records. Law school was in the offing, but Milsap chose music and by 1965 was recording for New York's famed Scepter label. He recorded r&b-tinged pop with Scepter until a 1968 move to Memphis, enjoying a minor hit with 1965's "Never Had It So Good." In Memphis awaited CHIPS MOMAN's hot American Studio and a standing gig at "the jumping nightclub— T. J.'s." Milsap played piano and sang on ELVIS PRESLEY's "Kentucky Rain" (1970) and recorded briefly for Moman's Chips label, then cut LPs for WARNER BROTHERS and Reprise in 1971–72.

In late 1972 Milsap moved to Nashville, took up a standing gig at an industry hangout club, the King of the Road, and in 1973 began a long-term association with RCA RECORDS. Hooking up with publisher-producer TOM COLLINS, Milsap began charting with country fare including "I Hate You" and "That Girl Who Waits on Tables" (1973). Successes such as "Pure Love" (1974) and "Daydreams About Night Things" (1975) positioned Milsap as a purveyor of "uptempo love songs with a positive hook" even though his overall output was more varied. Top hits continued in 1976 (when Milsap also was inducted into the GRAND OLE OPRY) with "What Goes On When the Sun Goes Down" and "(I'm a) Stand By My Woman Man." The singer reached a career peak and cracked the pop charts in 1977-78 with the pop-laden "It Was Almost Like a Song," "What a Difference You've Made in My Life," "Only One Love in My Life," and "Let's Take the Long Way Around the World," all #1 hits. In 1977 Milsap capped off a series of CMA Awards for Male Vocalist of the Year (1974, 1976, and 1977) with the organization's Entertainer of the Year title (1977).

Milsap's winning ways continued through the 1980s, with numerous Top Tens between 1976 and 1991. A few of the biggest: "In No Time at All" (1979), "My Heart" (1980), "I Wouldn't Have Missed It for the World" (1981–82), and the Grammy-winning "There's No Getting Over Me" (1981), "Any Day Now" (1982), and "Don't You Know How Much I Love You" (1983). The 1985 "Lost in the Fifties Tonight (In the Still of the Night)" single and the similarly titled album—with its reinterpretation of the 1956 Five Satins hit—displayed Milsap's r&b roots and earned him a Grammy in 1986.

Milsap established his Ronnie Milsap Foundation for individuals with visual impairments in 1985 and maintained a grueling schedule of recording, television appearances, and touring. He built his own state-of-the-art studio and published songwriter Mike Reid and others in collaboration with longtime business associate Rob Galbraith. And the hits kept coming. In 1987 "Snap Your Fingers" reprised the 1962 Joe Henderson r&b hit, and a Milsap–KENNY ROGERS duet, "Make No Mistake, She's Mine," won a

Grammy for two champions of country-pop. But the winds of country were changing, and Milsap followed up the steaming dance-pop of "Button off My Shirt" (1988) with the hillbilly-hearted LP *Stranger Things Have Happened.* As country line-dance fodder came to dominate the radio, Milsap continued to gain hits through 1992, but ended nearly two decades with RCA in 1993 by signing with LIBERTY RECORDS. He released the LP "True Believer" with only moderate success. In 1995 the entertainer opened and appeared at his Ronnie Milsap Theatre in the East Coast country mecca of Myrtle Beach, South Carolina; he had previously opened a restaurant and tourist attraction in Gatlinburg, Tennessee. RCA compiled many of Milsap's hits in a 1995 reissue CD, *Essential Ronnie Milsap.*

—*Thomas Goldsmith*

REPRESENTATIVE RECORDINGS

Greatest Hits (RCA, 1980); *Essential Ronnie Milsap* (RCA, 1995)

Minstrel Shows (*see* Blackface Minstrelsy)

Billy Mize
b. Arkansas City, Kansas, April 29, 1929

A stylish and popular radio and television personality in L.A. and BAKERSFIELD in the 1950s and 1960s, William Robert Mize became best known as the MC of several of the West Coast's best-loved country music variety shows, including his own *Chuck Wagon Show* (with singing, recording, and songwriting partner Cliff Crawford), "Cousin" Herb Henson's *Trading Post Show,* and GENE AUTRY's *Melody Ranch.* Mize received the ACM's award for Top TV Personality of 1966. He also worked as a western swing steel guitarist and vocalist, appearing on Long Beach's TOWN HALL PARTY, and as a songwriter ("Who'll Buy the Wine").

—*Dale Vinicur*

REPRESENTATIVE RECORDINGS

This Time and Place (Imperial, 1969, out of print); *You're All Right with Me* (United Artists, 1971, out of print)

The Modern Mountaineers

The Modern Mountaineers formed in Houston in late 1936 as the Georgia Fliers, led by tenor banjoist Johnny Thames, with brother Roy Thames as manager. The band broadcasted over Houston's KTRH and featured the Fats Waller–inspired piano and vocals of Smokey Wood, the hot jazz fiddle of J. R. Chatwell, and the saxophone of Hal Hebert. Prior to a first recording session for BLUEBIRD in March 1937, the band changed its name to the Modern Mountaineers.

That jazzy session resulted in several jukebox hits, including the slyly obscene "Everybody's Truckin'." Wood was fired soon after and, by the band's September 1937 session, it had moved to Shreveport and added Waco fiddler Jimmy Thomason, fiddler-guitarist Buddy Ray, and several others. The struggling band limped back into Houston in late 1937 and disbanded.

By 1940, Johnny and Roy Thames had taken over the Texas Wanderers (following the departure of CLIFF BRUNER) and were contracted to DECCA. However, they revived the Modern Mountaineers name for Bluebird recording sessions in February 1940 and April 1941. Musicians included pianist MOON MULLICAN, who waxed the original version of his "Pipeliner's Blues" with the Mountaineers; fiddler Buddy Ray; and vocalist Buddy Duhon. The band's last session, in October 1941, was an ad hoc affair led by Johnny Thames and featuring BAR X COWBOY JERRY IRBY on vocals. Short-lived, the Mountaineers were nevertheless influential, prolific, and served as early training ground for several important musicians. —*Kevin Coffey*

REPRESENTATIVE RECORDINGS

Jitterbug Jive (Krazy Kat, 1997) (contains several 1940–41 recordings)

Lucky Moeller
b. Okarche, Oklahoma, February 12, 1912; d. June 15, 1992

Walter Ernest "Lucky" Moeller was a major name in the field of country music booking and promotion in the early 1960s, chiefly through his association with artist WEBB PIERCE and talent agent JIM DENNY. Moeller was a banker turned ballroom owner in Oklahoma in the mid-1940s when he began promoting concerts for BOB WILLS. Moeller moved to Nashville in 1954 to help manage Webb Pierce's career but three years later moved to Springfield, Missouri, to work for the *OZARK JUBILEE* and manage talent for the Top Talent Agency. He returned to Nashville in 1957 to work for the Jim Denny Artist Bureau, which represented most of the top country acts of the 1950s and early 1960s. After Denny's death in 1963 Moeller took over the agency, changing its name to Denny-Moeller Talent, then in 1965 to Moeller Talent. The agency remained based in Nashville until Moeller suffered a severe stroke in November 1974. Soon after, Moeller and the agency moved back to his hometown of Okarche; less than a year later, it closed. Son Larry Moeller, who had left his father's business in 1973, went on to form his own Nashville talent agency, at one time handling WAYLON JENNINGS, WILLIE NELSON, and SAMMI SMITH. Later he moved to Austin, handling Willie Nelson alone for many years. —*Al Cunniff*

Chips Moman
b. LaGrange, Georgia, ca. 1936

Lincoln Wayne Moman (called "Chips" for his skill as a poker player) rose to prominence as an r&b and pop record producer in Memphis during the 1960s. During the 1970s and 1980s he became a successful country producer as well.

While still in his teens, Moman worked as a road musician for Gene Vincent, WARREN SMITH, and JOHNNY AND DORSEY BURNETTE and then, with introductions from the Burnettes, as a session guitarist at the Gold Star studio in Los Angeles. At age twenty-one he began working with Jim Stewart and his newly founded Satellite Records label, soon to become better known as Stax Records. At Stax, Moman functioned as Stewart's right-hand man, in-house producer, and chief songwriter. In 1962 Moman had a falling out with Stewart and left Stax. With a $3,000 settlement from Stewart, he started American Studio in Memphis in 1964 while continuing to do session guitar work in Memphis and in Muscle Shoals, Alabama.

In 1965 Moman began producing hit pop records at American for such acts as the Gentrys, Sandy Posey, Merilee Rush ("Angel of the Morning"), B. J. THOMAS, and Neil Diamond. Between 1968 and 1970 Moman produced

more than seventy-five charting pop singles, with the help of the American Studio band he assembled: REGGIE YOUNG (guitar), Bobby Wood and Bobby Emmons (keyboards), Tommy Cogbill and Mike Leech (bass), and Gene Chrisman (drums). In January and February 1969 Moman produced comeback hits for ELVIS PRESLEY—"In the Ghetto," "Suspicious Minds," and "Kentucky Rain"—at American Studio.

Meanwhile, Moman also wrote hit r&b standards in the 1960s with Dan Penn ("Do Right Woman," "Dark End of the Street") and 1970s country hits as well: B. J. Thomas's "(Hey Won't You Play) Another Somebody Done Somebody Wrong Song" and WAYLON JENNINGS's "Luckenbach, Texas (Back to the Basics of Love)."

In 1972 Moman closed American Studio and moved to Atlanta. In 1975 he moved to Nashville. In the 1970s and 1980s he produced hit albums for Waylon Jennings (*Ol' Waylon*), WILLIE NELSON (*Always on My Mind*), Nelson and MERLE HAGGARD (*Pancho and Lefty*), and a pair of albums for the quartet of Jennings, Nelson, JOHNNY CASH, and KRIS KRISTOFFERSON (*Highwayman, Highwayman 2*). In 1985 Moman produced another all-star aggregation, the *Class of '55* album, featuring Cash, JERRY LEE LEWIS, ROY ORBISON, and CARL PERKINS. Between 1986 and 1990, Moman ran Three Alarm Studio in Memphis. Since moving to Nashville in 1990 and back to Georgia in 1994, Moman has kept a low profile in the music business. —*Paul Kingsbury*

Charlie Monk
b. Noma, Florida, October 29, 1938

A former disc jockey and ASCAP associate director, Charles Franklin Monk has spent the bulk of his career in music publishing. He headed CBS Songs in Nashville from 1977 to 1982, opened his own firm (Charlie Monk Music) shortly afterward, and worked for Opryland Music Group as creative services director from 1988 until 1993.

As a music publisher he has played key roles in advancing the careers of then unknowns RANDY TRAVIS, Kenny Chesney, and AARON TIPPIN. Within the country music industry Monk is widely known for more than two decades' worth of biting humor as host on the Country Radio Seminar's *New Faces Show*, which he still chairs. Monk originated the Country Radio Seminar with Tom McEntee. Monk's comments occasionally have brought a worthy little guy to notice but more often have roasted the great and near great, much to the delight of radio seminar attendees.

Monk currently heads Monk Family Music Group; has hosted a syndicated radio show (*Charlie Monk's Classic Country*) since 1997; and is father of Collin Wade Monk, a Nashville rock artist, and Chip Monk, a singer-songwriter based in Washington, D.C. —*Bob Millard*

Bill Monroe
b. Rosine, Kentucky, September 13, 1911; d. September 9, 1996

As singer, songwriter, bandleader, showman, and instrumentalist, no individual is so closely identified with an American musical style as Bill Monroe, the Father of Bluegrass Music. For more than half a century he shaped bluegrass with his forceful mandolin playing; high, lonesome singing; and mastery of his band, the Blue Grass Boys. In doing so he gave older country sounds new life; gave the mandolin a new role as a lead instrument in country, pop, and rock; and set standards for musicians as diverse as the

Bill Monroe

EVERLY BROTHERS, ELVIS PRESLEY, GEORGE JONES, and rock star Jerry Garcia.

William Smith Monroe was the youngest of eight children born to James Buchanan "Buck" Monroe, a prosperous farmer who also ran timber and mining operations, and Melissa Monroe, who kept house and helped pass along dance steps and British-American folksongs to her children. Other musical influences of Bill's youth include the old-time fiddling of his Uncle Pendleton "Uncle Pen" Vandiver and the bluesy guitar playing of ARNOLD SHULTZ, a black musician with whom Bill and Uncle Pen sometimes worked local dances.

Monroe lost both his parents by age sixteen, and subsequently he followed some of his brothers north to the Chicago area, where he labored in a Sinclair Oil refinery, performed as a square dancer on Chicago's WLS *NATIONAL BARN DANCE*, and sang and played mandolin with brothers Charlie (who played guitar) and Birch (who fiddled) on local radio. Birch soon left the trio, and Bill and Charlie decided to pursue music full time as the MONROE BROTHERS, first gaining exposure on stations in Iowa and Nebraska.

The Monroes really hit their stride, however, after moving in 1935 to the Carolinas, where they based themselves mainly at Charlotte, North Carolina's 50,000-watt WBT. Their popularity soon equaled that of any of the era's many duos, and they distinguished themselves by their hard-driving tempos, piercing harmony, and Bill's lightning-fast mandolin solos. In 1936 RCA producer ELI OBERSTEIN recorded them for the first time. Early releases such as "What Would You Give in Exchange for Your Soul" sold well, and before long the team was winning a sizable regional audience with help from WBT's signal and recorded radio shows. However, the headstrong Monroes feuded as brothers will, and the act broke up in 1938. Bill

would record two more sessions for RCA with his new band, the Blue Grass Boys, named for Kentucky, the Bluegrass State.

After rehearsing his group and working Carolina radio, Monroe headed for Nashville to audition for the GRAND OLE OPRY. WSM's GEORGE D. HAY, HARRY STONE, and DAVID STONE, impressed with Monroe's talent and star power, hired him in October 1939 on the strength of his performance of his trademark "Muleskinner Blues," formerly a hit for the legendary JIMMIE RODGERS. WSM's 50,000-watt transmitter and guest spots on the Opry's NBC network portion quickly made Monroe's name a household word. By 1943 he was grossing some $200,000 a year from show dates, many of them staged as part of his own Opry TENT SHOW, which combined music and comedy in delighting rural and small-town audiences throughout the South.

While no one was yet calling Monroe's style "bluegrass" (this would not come until the mid-1950s), many of its basic elements were already present, including its pulsing drive and the intensity of Monroe's high-pitched vocals. During World War II he added the banjo, first played by STRINGBEAN (Dave Akeman), and experimented briefly with the accordion and harmonica, which complemented the basic mandolin-guitar-fiddle-bass combination Monroe would always retain. (Where guitar was concerned, Monroe himself was a formidable instrumentalist and set high benchmarks for his band members through the years.) In 1945 he added the revolutionary three-finger banjo picking of EARL SCRUGGS, which provided bluegrass with its final building block. Monroe's late 1940s recordings for COLUMBIA, made with Scruggs and LESTER FLATT, his singer-guitarist at the time, are now widely regarded as definitive.

In 1948 Scruggs teamed with Flatt to form the Foggy Mountain Boys, and by the early 1950s several bands were playing their own variations of the bluegrass style, including the STANLEY BROTHERS, JIM & JESSE McReynolds, and RENO & SMILEY. Monroe made his band sound higher, bluer, and more lonesome than ever, with help from singer-guitarist JIMMY MARTIN and other expert sidemen, some of whom (including Martin) launched bluegrass bands of their own. As ever, Monroe's repertoire included both sacred and secular material as well as both songs and instrumentals, and he composed much of his material himself or with members of his band. Over the years, Monroe originals such as "Uncle Pen," "Raw Hide," "Blue Moon of Kentucky," "Jerusalem Ridge," "I Want the Lord to Protect My Soul," and dozens of others have formed the basis of the bluegrass canon for professionals and amateurs alike.

Through the 1950s and beyond, Monroe's acoustic sound provided an alternative to honky-tonk, country-pop, and rockabilly. By 1963 he began to attract the attention of the urban folk music audience, with help from folklorist and promoter RALPH RINZLER, who promoted Monroe as the true Daddy of Bluegrass to listeners who thought bluegrass began and ended with Flatt and Scruggs. The year 1965 saw the first multiday bluegrass festival making Monroe the centerpiece, and in 1967 he launched his own annual festival at BEAN BLOSSOM, Indiana, where he had long run a country music park. By 1970, when he won election to the COUNTRY MUSIC HALL OF FAME, he had become the acknowledged patriarch of the bluegrass movement, a cult figure to hordes of fans for whom bluegrass was akin to a religion.

During the last twenty-five years of his life Monroe propagated the gospel of bluegrass to worldwide audiences, appearing in all fifty states and Canada as well as on tours of Japan, England, Ireland, Holland, Switzerland, and Israel. His venues ranged from rural festivals to urban performing arts centers and the White House. He recorded as well, and his career total topped more than 500 selections, most of them made for MCA (formerly DECCA).

Monroe also won recognition for his accomplishments. In 1982 the National Endowment for the Arts gave him its prestigious Heritage Award, and in 1988 he won a Grammy for his album *Southern Flavor*—the first bluegrass Grammy ever bestowed. A 1991 inductee into the International Bluegrass Music Association Hall of Honor, Monroe was also a 1993 recipient of the Lifetime Achievement Award from the National Academy of Recording Arts and Sciences (NARAS), an honor that placed him in the company of Louis Armstrong, CHET ATKINS, RAY CHARLES, Paul McCartney, and other legends. Although bluegrass constitutes a small part of country music's annual sales, such honors testify to the enormous influence Monroe exerted among musicians in many fields.

A stroke suffered in April 1996 ended Monroe's career as a touring artist and hastened his death on September 9 of that year. "We all knew that if he ever got to the point where he couldn't perform that he wasn't going to make it," said EMMYLOU HARRIS. "Music was his life." Memorial services at Nashville's RYMAN AUDITORIUM and later in Monroe's native Rosine, Kentucky, where he is buried, united hundreds of friends and fellow musicians who continue to nurture his legacy as one of country music's great historical personalities. —*John Rumble*

REPRESENTATIVE RECORDINGS

Country Music Hall of Fame (MCA, 1991); *The Essential Bill Monroe* (Columbia, 1992); *The Music of Bill Monroe from 1936–1994* (MCA, 1994)

Charlie Monroe
b. Ohio County, Kentucky, July 4, 1903; d. September 27, 1975

After the dissolution of the MONROE BROTHERS in mid-1938, Charles Pendleton Monroe carried on his musical career with a band initially called the Boys but later known as the Kentucky Pardners. At first Monroe used twin mandolins and a guitar for his basic sound in 1938 and 1939 BLUEBIRD sessions, but he later expanded the group to include fiddle, electric lead guitar, and harmonica, giving him a unique blend of old-time music and just a touch of modernization. Although the Pardners' radio work took them as far north as Wheeling and west to Louisville, they achieved their greatest following in the Carolina Piedmont and in southern Appalachia. He continued recording with RCA VICTOR through 1951, cutting some sixty-two solo sides, including the classic train song "Bringing in the Georgia Mail."

In 1952 and 1956 Charlie waxed some eight numbers for DECCA, including "Old Kentucky Bound," after which he retired to a farm in western Kentucky. During his inactive years he cut two albums with bluegrass accompaniment for the Rem label. In 1972 he emerged from retirement, began working the festival circuit, and recorded for Starday. A bout with cancer, however, curtailed his comeback and ended his life in September 1975.
—*Ivan M. Tribe*

REPRESENTATIVE RECORDINGS

Who's Calling You Sweetheart Tonight (RCA Camden, 1968); *Charlie Monroe's Boys: The Early Years* (Old Homestead, 1981)

Monroe Brothers
Bill Monroe b. Rosine, Kentucky, September 13, 1911; d. September 9, 1996
Charlie Monroe b. Ohio County, Kentucky, July 4, 1903; d. September 27, 1975

Before they started their separate and successful careers, Bill and Charlie Monroe enjoyed a career as a brother duet act in the 1930s. Though fans sometimes regard this period as a sort of rehearsal or apprenticeship for the brothers' later bluegrass and country music, the Monroe Brothers were one of the best-selling and most influential acts of the 1930s, and would have secured their place in history had not either of them established separate careers.

The first incarnation of the Monroe Brothers included Charlie (on guitar), older brother Birch (on fiddle), and young Bill (on mandolin). The time was 1929, and young Bill had just moved to join his brothers in Whiting, Indiana, where they worked in oil refineries and successfully auditioned as square dancers for the WLS NATIONAL BARN DANCE. The trio soon received an offer to go professional, working for Texas Crystals (a patent medicine company); Birch dropped out at this point, leaving Charlie and Bill to forge a duet act and take it to radio in Shenandoah, Iowa, in 1934. The fans loved them, and the company soon transferred them to Omaha, and then to the Carolinas.

Working radio programs and stage shows in places such as Spartanburg, Greensburg, and Charlotte, the brothers drew even more attention both from fans and a new sponsor, CRAZY WATER CRYSTALS, which supported numerous country acts in different states. This led to a contract with RCA-VICTOR's BLUEBIRD RECORDS in 1936. Their first release became their career record: "What Would You Give in Exchange for Your Soul," an old song they had learned in a shape-note singing school years earlier. Bluebird would later claim that this song "out-sold any song ever put on record by an old-time group." It assured the brothers a steady stream of recording sessions, eventually encompassing some sixty sides in three years. Many would become standards: "Drifting Too Far from the Shore" (1936), "New River Train" (1936), "Roll in My Sweet Baby's Arms" (1936), "Roll on Buddy" (1937), "He Will Set Your Fields on Fire" (1937), "Little Joe" (1938), and "A Beautiful Life" (1938). The brothers recorded many of the sides at breakneck speed, with Charlie singing lead and playing powerful rhythm guitar and with Bill singing tenor and playing blistering fiddle-derived mandolin lead parts in a style that had never been heard before. Though many fans, as well as the Bluebird company, thought of the brothers as specializing in gospel songs, they in fact did a number of older country songs and even a few "cover" versions of contemporary material.

During the high point of their career, the brothers toured widely through the Carolinas, often working for Crazy Water Crystals, with announcer Byron Parker, nicknamed the Old Hired Hand. It was a turbulent time, however, since each brother had a strong temper, and the breaking point finally came one morning in 1938 when Charlie stalked over to Bill's trailer and announced, "Bill, we're not doing any good like this," and proceeded to back his own trailer out. In later years, especially during a series of mid-1950s recordings for DECCA, the brothers occasionally reunited in a vain attempt to recapture some of the magic of the early days. —*Charles Wolfe*

Patsy Montana
b. Hope, Arkansas, October 30, 1908; d. May 3, 1996

Patsy Montana achieved a landmark when her 1935 recording of her polka-tempoed composition "I Wanna to Be a Cowboy's Sweetheart" became the first record by a female solo country artist to become a runaway hit. With her energetic voice and sparkling yodeling, and wearing her cowgirl outfit, Montana presented a cheerful image to Depression-era America. The lyrics of her great hit spoke of independence and love and the kind of freedom the cowboy had come to symbolize.

Montana was born Ruby Blevins into a struggling family of ten boys. At seventeen she added an "e" to her first name to make it more sophisticated, and a year later, she left for California. A skilled guitarist and fiddler, she won a talent contest in 1931 singing JIMMIE RODGERS's songs and landed a job on Los Angeles–area radio as Rubye Blevins, the Yodeling Cowgirl from San Antone. Adopting the name Patsy Montana, she also joined with two other female western singers and, as the Montana Cowgirls, worked radio station KMIC with singer-songwriter STUART HAMBLEN and cowboy star Monty Montana.

When the Montana Cowgirls disbanded, Patsy Montana moved back to Arkansas. Then a brief booking on KWKH in Shreveport, Louisiana, brought her to the attention of RCA VICTOR RECORDS star JIMMIE DAVIS. Montana backed Davis in the studio on fiddle and vocals and made her own RCA recording in 1932. A trip with her brothers Kenneth and Claude to the Century of Progress Exposition in

Chicago in 1933 included an audition with WLS for a vocalist slot with the Kentucky Ramblers, a hot, swing-influenced stringband. That year, at twenty-five, Montana joined the Kentucky Ramblers, who became the PRAIRIE RAMBLERS to accommodate their new western image.

Extensive road performances and radio appearances established a reputation for Montana and the band, and even after her marriage to Paul Rose, in 1934, she remained with the group. In 1935 producer ART SATHERLEY took them to New York to record for ARC. This led to the historic recording session that would produce "I Wanna to Be a Cowboy's Sweetheart."

Montana's cowgirl image and material became her stock in trade, with many recordings following. Her exuberant yodeling and sunny singing were backed by sizzling instrumental work on songs such as 1940's "Swing Time Cowgirl."

From 1940, Montana was a solo act. She made a brief appearance in Gene Autry's 1939 film *Colorado Sunset*, but generally she worked on the road. She had her own network radio show during 1946 and 1947, and in 1948 she starred on the LOUISIANA HAYRIDE. Montana continued to book appearances and record until her death. She was elected to the COUNTRY MUSIC HALL OF FAME in 1996. —*Mary A. Bufwack*

REPRESENTATIVE RECORDING
Patsy Montana and the Prairie Ramblers: Columbia Historic Edition (Columbia, 1984)

Bob Montgomery
b. Lampasas, Texas, May 12, 1937

Songwriter, producer, and publisher Bobby LaRoy Montgomery entered show business singing in a duo with BUDDY HOLLY in Lubbock, Texas, when both were in their early teens. In the years since, Montgomery has gone on to a successful executive career in the Nashville music industry, playing an important role in the careers of such artists as BOBBY GOLDSBORO, JOE DIFFIE, and COLLIN RAYE.

Montgomery and Holly played together locally (their business card read "Buddy and Bob, Western and Bop") and recorded several song demos. Montgomery followed Holly to Norman Petty's studio in Clovis, New Mexico, where Montgomery signed on as an engineer and received writer credits on the Holly songs "Wishing," "Love's Made a Fool of You," and "Heartbeat." Montgomery recorded a single for DECCA Records' Coral subsidiary, then moved to Nashville in 1959 to concentrate on songwriting.

As a writer, Montgomery's early credits included "After Awhile" for JIM REEVES, "Back in Baby's Arms" for PATSY CLINE, and "Two of a Kind" for Sue Thompson. But his best-known early copyright is "Misty Blue," a Top Five country hit for Wilma Burgess (Decca, 1966), EDDY ARNOLD (RCA Victor, 1967) and BILLIE JO SPEARS (United Artists, 1976), and a pop hit for Dorothy Moore (Malaco, 1976).

Montgomery's first production credit was MEL TILLIS's "Stateside" (first released on Ric and rereleased on Kapp, 1966). Later, as head of A&R for United Artists Records in Nashville, Montgomery was responsible for hits by JOHNNY DARRELL, DEL REEVES, and BOBBY GOLDSBORO. Montgomery and Goldsboro formed the House of Gold publishing company, which handled such copyrights as "Behind Closed Doors" and "Wind Beneath My Wings." Montgomery moved to the TREE publishing firm and worked

Patsy Montana

there until Tree was sold to Sony; he then joined CBS Records as head of Nashville A&R, signing artists including Joe Diffie, DOUG STONE, and Collin Raye.

In 1992 Montgomery and his wife, Cathy, formed an independent publishing company, Noosa Heads Music, which published the TIM MCGRAW hits "Down on the Farm" and "Maybe We Should Just Sleep on It" (written by Jerry Laseter). Bob and his first wife, Carol (who recorded as a duo for WARNER BROS., ca. 1962), are the parents of singer Kevin Stone, a.k.a. Kevin Montgomery.

—*Todd Everett*

John Michael Montgomery

b. Danville, Kentucky, January 20, 1965

John Michael Montgomery began recording in the midst of the "hat act" stampede of the early 1990s but soon distinguished himself from the herd with the tender balladry of such #1 singles as "I Love the Way You Love Me" (1993), "I Swear" (1994), and "I Can Love You Like That" (1995). In addition, he has carved out a niche for himself turning his manly baritone to such uptempo tongue-twisters as "Be My Baby Tonight" (#1, 1994) and "Sold (The Grundy County Auction Incident)" (#1, 1995).

Montgomery grew up in Nicholasville, Kentucky, and was belting out country classics onstage with his family's band by the time he was five. He bought his first guitar at fifteen and began playing with local bands, continuing to perform with the family group until he was seventeen, when he and his brother Eddy formed their own band. In 1991 ATLANTIC RECORDS executives from Nashville caught his act at Lexington's Austin City Saloon and signed him to a recording contract.

Montgomery's debut album, *Life's a Dance,* reached the

John Michael Montgomery

Top Five on the *Billboard* country album chart and Top Thirty on the pop charts; its title track became his first Top Five single. His next two albums, *Kickin' It Up* and *John Michael Montgomery,* yielded more #1 country singles. Two of Montgomery's #1 hit ballads from these albums—"I Swear" and "I Can Love You Like That"—were covered by pop r&b group All-4-One and became major pop hits for them. Each of Montgomery's first three albums has been certified multiplatinum, with cumulative sales exceeding 12 million units. His 1996 album, *What I Do the Best,* scored Top Five hits with "Friends" and "How Was I to Know." "Angel In My Eyes," from the 1997 *Greatest Hits* album, peaked at #4 in January 1998.

In 1994 Montgomery received two CMA awards (Horizon and Single of the Year for "I Swear"), an ACM award (as 1993's Top New Male Vocalist), and was named the TNN/*Music City News* Star of Tomorrow. In 1995 he picked up an ACM trophy for Single of the Year for "I Swear." In 1994 and 1995 songs he recorded ("I Love the Way You Love Me" and "I Swear," respectively) won ACM Song of the Year honors. Montgomery's recording of "I Can Love You Like That" was named Song of the Year by ASCAP and BMI in 1996.

—*Marjie McGraw*

REPRESENTATIVE RECORDINGS

Life's a Dance (Atlantic, 1992); *Kickin' It Up* (Atlantic, 1994); *John Michael Montgomery* (Atlantic, 1995); *What I Do Best* (Atlantic, 1996); *Greatest Hits* (Atlantic, 1997)

Melba Montgomery

b. Iron City, Tennessee, October 14, 1938

Her note-bending, heavily accented phrasing, and her ineffably country delivery, make Melba Joyce Montgomery perhaps the closest stylistic equivalent to GEORGE JONES among female country singers. She and Jones recorded a series of highly regarded duets during the 1960s, and Montgomery is also known for the 1974 crossover hit "No Charge," as well as for her consistently accomplished songwriting.

Raised near Florence, Alabama, Montgomery initially came to Nashville after winning the GRAND OLE OPRY's 1958 Pet Milk Amateur Contest. She toured as a member of ROY ACUFF's troupe from 1958 to 1962, then set off on a solo career.

Montgomery recorded solo for United Artists, Musicor, Nugget, CAPITOL, and other labels throughout the 1960s but achieved her biggest early hits as the duet partner of Gene Pitney ("Baby Ain't That Fine," 1966), CHARLIE LOUVIN ("Something to Brag About," 1970), and, unforgettably, George Jones. The Jones-Montgomery Top Ten duet "We Must Have Been Out of Our Minds" (1963) was written by Montgomery, as were many of their other 1963–68 efforts.

Solo success eluded Montgomery until she recorded the Harlan Howard–written recitation "No Charge," a celebration of motherhood, for ELEKTRA. Her delivery was so emotion-packed that musicians at the session reportedly wept. The song hit #1 on Mother's Day 1974. Montgomery continued to record throughout the 1970s and sporadically into the 1980s. She reemerged as a songwriter in the 1990s, when a new generation of country stars began recording her collaborations with CARL JACKSON.

—*Robert K. Oermann*

REPRESENTATIVE RECORDINGS

Bluegrass Hootenanny (United Artists, 1964) (with George Jones); *No Charge* (Elektra, 1974)

Montgomery Ward Records
established 1933; ended 1941

The Montgomery Ward retail chain inaugurated its own budget record label in 1933, following the demise of Paramount's Broadway records, which Ward offered through mail-order catalogue sales, much as competitor Sears, Roebuck had offered material on its Supertone, Challenge, and Silvertone labels in the 1920s and would continue to do on CONQUEROR until 1942.

Montgomery Ward's primary arrangement was with RCA VICTOR, which initially attempted to duplicate popular Broadway issues with matching titles from its own catalogue. Thereafter, material from BLUEBIRD sessions was frequently issued on the store's label until 1941, when the arrangement terminated. DECCA also supplied titles from its own catalogue and older GENNETT/Champion matrices in 1935; most Decca CARTER FAMILY titles also appeared on Montgomery Ward in 1937–39. A few titles from the Varsity label lists were also used in 1939–40.   —*Dick Spottswood*

Monument Records
established in Washington, D.C., March 1958

The Monument Records label was launched by FRED FOSTER, an ex-promo man for several record companies and independent distributors. It was named for the Washington Monument. "When I was flying back, I'd see the monument and know I was almost home," said Foster. The first hit, BILLY GRAMMER's "Gotta Travel On," was issued in October 1958.

ROY ORBISON had been recording with only moderate success when Foster acquired him from RCA in 1959, in a deal facilitated by WESLEY ROSE of ACUFF-ROSE. Orbison's third Monument single, "Only the Lonely," peaked at #2 on the pop charts in 1960. In that year both Foster and Orbison relocated to Nashville. Subsequent Orbison hits included "Running Scared," "Crying," "In Dreams," and "Oh, Pretty Woman," all recorded in Nashville. Orbison recorded virtually all his biggest hits for Monument between 1959 and 1965.

Foster expanded his music business interests to include a studio purchased from SUN RECORDS in 1963, COMBINE MUSIC (co-owned with BOB BECKHAM), and an r&b subsidiary, Sound-Stage 7 Records (a joint venture with DJ John "John R." Richbourg), which scored hits with Roscoe Shelton and Joe Simon.

After Orbison, Foster concentrated on country music, signing BOOTS RANDOLPH, BILLY WALKER, HENSON CARGILL, GRANDPA JONES, WILLIE NELSON, JEANNIE SEELY, TONY JOE WHITE, and DOLLY PARTON. The most successful artists after Orbison, though, were KRIS KRISTOFFERSON, LARRY GATLIN, and BILLY SWAN, who scored a #1 hit in 1974 with "I Can Help."

The label ran into financial problems in 1981, and in August 1982 Foster relinquished the presidency to Bob Fead, who ran the label from the West Coast. The label's problems worsened, and it went into Chapter 11 bankruptcy in March 1983 with debts of $7.3 million. In 1985 Foster also lost his controlling 70 percent interest in Com-

bine Music, and all Monument real estate. On April 21, 1987, Monument assets were acquired by CBS Special Products for $810,000. Ten years later, in October 1997, Sony Music (owners of CBS Special Products) reactivated Monument as an imprint of Sony's Nashville division.
—*Colin Escott*

C. E. Moody (*see* Georgia Yellow Hammers)

Clyde Moody
b. Cherokee, North Carolina, September 19, 1915; d. April 7, 1989

Clyde Leonard Moody managed to carve out a career in music that earned him renown in old-time, bluegrass, and newer country. Of partial Native American background, Clyde played music locally with Jay Hugh Hall, and then both joined WADE MAINER's Sons of the Mountaineers. Moody did several recording sessions with Wade Mainer's band, one with his brother J. E. MAINER, and another with Jay Hall and Steve Ledford as the Happy Go Lucky Boys. In 1940 Moody joined BILL MONROE's band and recorded with Monroe for BLUEBIRD, introducing the song "Six White Horses" to the bluegrass idiom. After four years with the Blue Grass Boys, Moody went on his own as a solo vocalist at the GRAND OLE OPRY in 1944. As a singer Moody became an early exponent of the country crooning style typically identified with EDDY ARNOLD.

After brief stints with BULLET and COLUMBIA, Moody signed with KING RECORDS and scored a major success in 1946 with "Shenandoah Waltz." He followed it up with three chart-making hits. Later he went to Washington to work for CONNIE B. GAY's radio and television programs, and then for various radio and TV stations in the Carolinas. Moody left King in the early fifties and signed with DECCA but never had another hit. He later recorded with STARDAY, Wango, Old Homestead, Black Rose, and Longhorn. He appeared as a frequent vocalist on various bluegrass festivals and concerts until his death.
—*Ivan M. Tribe*

REPRESENTATIVE RECORDINGS

The Best of Clyde Moody (King, 1964); *White House Blues* (Wango & Rebel, 1989)

Bob Moore
b. Nashville, Tennessee, November 30, 1932

At fifteen, bassist Bobby L. Moore began working with the GRAND OLE OPRY comedy team JAMUP & HONEY. In 1948 he joined PAUL HOWARD's Arkansas Cotton Pickers, also with the Opry. He went on to back JIMMY DICKENS and CURLY FOX & TEXAS RUBY on tour. Although Moore set out only to play country bass, he became an accomplished jazz player in OWEN BRADLEY's Nashville-based big band in the 1950s. One of Nashville's busiest session bassists from the 1950s on, he contributed to numerous #1 country hits, notably BOBBY HELMS's "Fraulein" (1956), MARTY ROBBINS's "El Paso" (1959), ROGER MILLER's "King of the Road" (1964), LORETTA LYNN's "Coal Miner's Daughter" (1969), and CONWAY TWITTY's "Hello Darlin'" (1969), generally playing string bass. He also played on ELVIS PRESLEY's "It's Now or Never" and PATSY CLINE's "Crazy." As a studio orchestra leader Moore scored a pop instrumental hit via BOUDLEAUX BRYANT's "Mexico" (#7, 1961) and recorded "The Theme from *My Three Sons*," both for MONUMENT RECORDS.

Moore served as ROY ORBISON's orchestra leader and from 1983 to 1985 was a sideman for JERRY LEE LEWIS. A hand injury prompted Moore to retire from his music career in the late 1980s.

—Walt Trott

REPRESENTATIVE RECORDING

Bob Moore—Mexico (Bear Family, 1989)

Charlie Moore

b. Piedmont, South Carolina, February 13, 1935; d. December 24, 1979

Leader of the Dixie Partners from 1957 until his death, Charlie Moore was one of bluegrass music's finest balladeers. Although initially known through the KING recordings he made with Bill Napier in the early 1960s, Moore's easygoing, warm baritone vocals were not widely appreciated until the last years of his life.

Learning guitar as a youth, Charles Benjamin Moore Jr. launched his professional career in 1956 as part of COUSIN WILBUR WESBROOKS's show in Asheville, North Carolina. Later returning to his native South Carolina, Moore organized his first Dixie Partners lineup in 1957. The band soon landed a Sunday afternoon television show in nearby Spartanburg. In 1960 Moore brought in STANLEY BROTHERS sideman Bill Napier as a full partner.

Moore and Napier signed with King Records in 1962 while they were based on WJHG-TV in Panama City, Florida. During next four years they made nine albums for the label; most were hastily produced and failed to capture the band's essence. Eventually returning to Spartanburg, Moore and Napier continued their partnership until late 1966. After fulfilling remaining bookings, Moore quit performing to work as a disc jockey in Fountain City, South Carolina.

Encouraged by the rise of bluegrass festivals, Moore organized a new Dixie Partners in 1970 and began recording for numerous independent labels. He also sharpened his songwriting skills; his best-known composition, "Legend of the Rebel Soldier," reshaped an Irish ballad into a poignant narrative about a dying Confederate soldier.

By the mid-1970s Moore was a familiar fixture on bluegrass circuits. His albums were particularly popular overseas and led to a European tour in 1976. By the time of his second tour three years later, Moore was clearly in poor health, primarily due to advanced alcoholism. In late November 1979 Moore entered a Richmond, Virginia, hospital to relieve problems stemming from an earlier hernia operation. Complications led to his death a month later at age forty-four.

—Dave Samuelson

REPRESENTATIVE RECORDINGS

Charlie Moore Sings Good Bluegrass (Vetco, 1972); *The Fiddler* (Old Homestead, 1975)

Merrill Moore

b. Algona, Iowa, September 26, 1923

Inasmuch as Merrill Moore is known at all, it is for his piano-driven country boogie recordings. He had an assured touch, impeccable taste, but no hits.

Born in rural Iowa, Moore weaned himself on the classic boogie-woogie records of Freddie Slack, Albert Ammons, and their ilk. Moore moved to San Diego in 1948, and in 1950 he started a residency at the Buckaroo Club. He began recording for CAPITOL RECORDS in 1952, and his music was, and remained, a sophisticated blend of boogie woogie and western swing. His vocal timbre bore a certain resemblance to BILL HALEY's, but his phrasing was rooted in the jazz leanings of the western swing vocalists.

Although Moore never scored a charted hit, some of his records apparently sold well. He toured rarely, though, confining himself to nightclubs on the West Coast and to session work for Capitol. For a short period in the late 1960s, he was a cause célèbre in England when Bill Haley fans embraced him. He toured there in 1970.

He continued to record for Capitol until 1958, closing out with an unissued supperclub jazz set. He recorded again in England for B&C Records in 1970, and still works nightclubs on the West Coast.

—Colin Escott

REPRESENTATIVE RECORDING

Boogie My Blues Away (Bear Family, 1990), 2 CDs

Tiny Moore

b. Hamilton County, Texas, May 12, 1920; d. December 15, 1987

Billie "Tiny" Moore popularized the electric mandolin as a jazz instrument in western swing while a member of BOB WILLS's Texas Playboys and during stints with various other western swing and country ensembles. Others had played the instrument in western swing before Moore, but because he gained national exposure with Wills's band Moore became the musician most associated with the mandolin in western swing.

Growing up in Port Arthur, Texas, Moore became a passionate jazz fan, which was the reason he loved to play in the freewheeling Wills band, with whom he was a fixture from 1946 to the early fifties. While with the band he married one of the McKinney Sisters (Dean and Evelyn McKinney), a vocal duo in the Wills band. Moore was married to Dean until his death.

After leaving the Playboys, Moore played in various bands near his home in Sacramento, where he and Dean owned a music store. In the seventies he traveled and recorded with MERLE HAGGARD. At various times Moore also performed with the rock group Commander Cody & the Lost Planet Airmen. A highlight of his life came in 1979 when he and Jethro Burns, backed by other swing musicians, recorded *Tiny Moore and Jethro Burns: Back to Back*, an album that called attention to Moore's jazz mandolin style.

—Charles R. Townsend

REPRESENTATIVE RECORDING

Tiny Moore and Jethro Burns: Back to Back (Kaleidoscope, 1979)

George Morgan

b. Waverly, Tennessee, June 28, 1924; d. July 7, 1975

A fixture on the GRAND OLE OPRY from 1948 until his death in 1975, COUNTRY MUSIC HALL OF FAME member George Thomas Morgan possessed one of the smoothest voices in country music.

Born about fifty miles west of Nashville, Morgan moved a couple of years later with his family to Barberton, Ohio. At age eleven he learned to play guitar, and he made early appearances on radio in Ohio at WAKR-Akron and WWST-Wooster. His career gathered momentum on the *WWVA*

George Morgan

JAMBOREE in the 1940s. In September 1948 EDDY ARNOLD decided to leave the Grand Ole Opry. Morgan, whose singing style was similar, joined the Opry on September 25, 1948, without benefit of a hit record. COLUMBIA RECORDS had signed Morgan just days before, on September 14, but due to the 1948 musicians' strike he didn't record until January 16, 1949.

Recorded at that first session, his composition "Candy Kisses" launched his recording career with a bang, eventually reaching #1 on the country charts. On April 30, 1949, Morgan accounted for half the listings on *Billboard*'s Country Top Ten chart. In addition to his three singles on the chart—"Candy Kisses" (#2), "Rainbow in My Heart" (#8), and "Please, Don't Let Me Love You" (#9)—he was represented by covers of "Candy Kisses" by ELTON BRITT (#8) and RED FOLEY (#10).

That first year proved to be his biggest on the charts, with six singles ultimately hitting the Top Ten in 1949. Of these, "Room Full of Roses" (#4, 1949) was Morgan's only record to cross over onto the pop charts (#25).

Morgan left the Opry in 1956 to host a TV show at Nashville station WLAC but returned to the Opry in 1959 and remained a popular presence there until his death. After seventeen years with Columbia, Morgan left the label in 1965. He moved on to the STARDAY and Stop labels, and then DECCA/MCA in 1971, where he scored his biggest hit in years with "Red Rose from the Blue Side of Town" (#21, 1974). His last recordings were made for FOUR STAR.

In 1973 Morgan watched proudly when youngest daughter LORRIE MORGAN made her Opry debut. Sadly, George Morgan died not long after his fifty-first birthday, from complications following open-heart surgery. Through the wonders of electronics, a posthumous father-daughter duet, "I'm Completely Satisfied With You," charted briefly in 1979.

—*Walt Trott*

REPRESENTATIVE RECORDING

Room Full of Roses: The George Morgan Collection (Razor & Tie, 1996)

Lorrie Morgan
b. Nashville, Tennessee, June 27, 1959

One of the top female country stars of the 1990s, Loretta Lynn Morgan has fashioned a persona and an approach to her music that combine glamor with attention to the concerns of everyday life. Her delivery is often dramatic and torrid, yet has a disarming directness.

The fifth child of GRAND OLE OPRY star GEORGE MORGAN, Lorrie grew up watching her father's performances from backstage. She made her own Opry debut at age thirteen and was working nightclubs when she was fifteen. She became an Opry member in 1984.

After years of performing in Nashville clubs, singing on television, recording for at least four record labels (COLUMBIA, FOUR STAR, ABC/HICKORY, and MCA) with little success, and opening shows on the road for many other performers, Morgan was signed to RCA in 1987. A year earlier she had married KEITH WHITLEY, and in 1989 Morgan was touring Alaska to promote what would become her breakthrough RCA single, "Dear Me," when Whitley drank himself to death. "Dear Me" was followed by three other Top Ten singles from her debut album, *Leave the Light On*, including the #1 hit "Five Minutes." In addition, Morgan added new vocals to an older Whitley recording of " 'Til a Tear Becomes a Rose," creating a duet performance that was recognized as the CMA Vocal Event of the Year in 1990.

Something in Red (1991) was an even stronger album, becoming Morgan's second gold record. Uptempo numbers such as "We Both Walk" were combined with the memorable "Something in Red" and a powerful remake of GEORGE JONES's "A Picture of Me (Without You)." After a switch from RCA to the BNA label, her album *Watch Me* was released in 1992. It included "What Part of No," which became another #1 hit.

In 1993 Morgan made her acting debut in the TNN movie *Proudheart*, a slice-of-life story of a working-class mother. A 1994 TV series featuring Morgan as a police of-

Lorrie Morgan

ficer was not picked up by a network. In 1995 she appeared in a second film, *The Stranger Beside Me.*

"I Didn't Know My Own Strength" (1995), an anthem of independence, could be read as describing Morgan's feelings about her personal life. Four marriages (most recently to singer Jon Randall) and numerous high-profile romances have made her tumultuous love life a constant source of interest to fans.

In 1996, in support of her album *Greater Need,* Morgan toured with PAM TILLIS and CARLENE CARTER. Morgan released the album *Shakin' Things Up* in 1997.

—*Mary A. Bufwack*

REPRESENTATIVE RECORDINGS

Something in Red (RCA, 1991); *Greatest Hits* (RCA, 1995); *Shakin' Things Up* (RCA, 1997)

Gary Morris
b. Fort Worth, Texas, December 7, 1948

This ruggedly handsome Texan, a Grizzly Adams look-alike with a broken nose, entered the country scene as a country heartthrob and moved on quickly to roles on television and in musical theater.

Not everything popularized in that era was of the URBAN COWBOY cut, and Gary Gwyn Morris certainly wasn't. He sang without twang and eschewed cowboy hats and duds. At the end of 1982 he launched a hot streak of romance and vulnerability that included "Velvet Chains," "The Love She Found in Me," "The Wind Beneath My Wings," "Baby, Bye Bye," "100% Chance of Rain," and "Leave Me Lonely."

Morris's voice was stronger in a more classical sense than that of any country artist of his day. He leaped to a string of television soap opera appearances and the Broadway stage, singing the lead in New York productions of *La Bohème* (1984 with LINDA RONSTADT) and *Les Misérables* (1988). These experiences in musical theater accentuated his tendency to hold notes beyond a length appropriate to the average country tune, however. By the late eighties he began to take a ribbing from country radio deejays for oversinging.

Morris's record sales were suffering by the end of 1987, hurt in no small part by a perception among country fans that he was more interested in TV and opera than in country music. Though he released an adventurous acoustic album called *Plain Brown Wrapper,* he was stuck with his image as an artist conflicted. After racking up five #1s and eleven more Top Ten hits between 1980 and 1987, Morris moved back to a touring cast of *Les Misérables,* performances in BRANSON, MISSOURI, and other comfortable theater gigs. Although in 1997, Morris produced the ATLANTIC RECORDS debut of Matt King.

Morris's greatest single contribution to popular music in general may well have been his introduction of "The Wind Beneath My Wings," which was a Top Five country hit for him in 1983, well before it became a multimillion-selling #1 pop hit and a Grammy winner for Bette Midler in 1989.

—*Bob Millard*

REPRESENTATIVE RECORDINGS

Why Lady Why (Warner Bros., 1983); *Plain Brown Wrapper* (Warner Bros., 1986); *Hits* (Warner Bros., 1987)

Lynn Morris
b. Lamesa, Texas, October 8, 1948

Lynn Morris has become a leading woman performer in bluegrass music, a style historically male-dominated. Adept at clawhammer and three-finger-style banjo-playing and at guitar-playing, she sings in a clear, well-placed voice.

After studying guitar under legendary guitarist Johnny Smith while in college in Colorado, she discovered the banjo, working in a folk duo, then City Limits, a Denver-based bluegrass band.

Experience with USO touring groups and Cherokee Rose followed; by 1982 Morris was in State College, Pennsylvania, working in Whetstone Run, which later included her future husband, singer-bassist Marshall Wilborn. When the band folded in 1986, Morris performed with several bands, including Laurie Lewis & Grant Street, while Wilborn worked with the JOHNSON MOUNTAIN BOYS and JIMMY MARTIN.

During the 1988 festival season, the couple formed a band together. Personnel changes due to Morris's vocal range, which requires instrumentalists to play in nontraditional keys, have not altered the character of the group; with two albums to its credit, the Lynn Morris Band is sustained by the constants of Morris and Wilborn. Morris is widely admired among bluegrass fans for her sensitive interpretations of traditional and contemporary material and for her leadership position and advocacy for women in bluegrass music.

—*Frank and Marty Godbey*

REPRESENTATIVE RECORDING

The Lynn Morris Band (Rounder, 1990)

Philip Morris *(see* Philip Morris Country Music Shows, under P)

The Morris Brothers
Wiley Andrew Morris b. Old Fort, North Carolina, February 1, 1919; d. September 22, 1990
Zeke Edward Morris b. Old Fort, North Carolina, May 9, 1916

A spirited duo from western North Carolina, the Morris Brothers had considerable impact on the first generation of bluegrass musicians; they helped shape modern bluegrass performance styles and vocal harmonies, and they contributed songs to the music's repertoire.

After performing locally with his older brother George, Zeke Morris launched his professional career with J. E. MAINER's Mountaineers; Zeke played guitar and sang on the August 1935 BLUEBIRD sessions that produced "Maple on the Hill." In early 1936 WADE MAINER and Zeke left to perform as a duo; when Wiley Morris joined them in 1937, Zeke switched to mandolin.

In late 1937 Wiley and Zeke Morris hired fiddler Homer Sherrill; for the next year they performed as the Smiling Rangers over WPTF-Raleigh. Between 1938 and 1939 the brothers recorded thirty-four titles for Bluebird, including such future bluegrass standards as "Let Me Be Your Salty Dog," "Don't Say Goodbye if You Love Me," and "One Little Word." Between 1939 and 1944 the Morrises were based at WWNC in Asheville; at various times their band featured bluegrass banjo pioneers Hoke Jenkins, DON RENO, and EARL SCRUGGS.

The brothers dissolved their partnership in 1944, shortly after moving to WIRL in Knoxville. Zeke moved to WJHL, Johnson City, where he formed a band that included Bob Millard, Red Rector, and Fred Smith. In November 1945 ELI OBERSTEIN reunited the brothers for a classic RCA VICTOR session that produced "Tragic Romance," "Grave Upon the Green Hillside," "Somebody Loves You, Darling," and the retitled "Salty Dog Blues."

Wiley and Zeke retired from music in the late 1940s, although they made occasional festival appearances until 1983. In 1972 the Morris Brothers and Homer Sherrill recorded an album for ROUNDER, *Wiley, Zeke and Homer.*

—*Dave Samuelson*

Claud Moye (*see* Pie Plant Pete)

MTM Music Group

established in Nashville, Tennessee, October 1984; ended December 1988

A short-lived subsidiary of actress Mary Tyler Moore's MTM Enterprises, Inc., television production company (which began in 1969 in Hollywood), the MTM Music Group opened as a record label, music publisher, and management company in Nashville in October 1984. The label's chairman and chief executive officer was Alan Bernard, formerly vice president of special projects for MTM Enterprises. Howard Stark served as president, and Tommy West served as senior vice president. Offices were located at 21 Music Square East on Nashville's Music Row.

The firm began releasing records in April 1985, distributed via CAPITOL/EMI. During its brief existence, MTM Records was fairly successful in launching several country acts, including HOLLY DUNN, S-K-O, PAUL OVERSTREET, BECKY HOBBS, Judy Rodman, and the Girls Next Door. The label was also home to the alternative rock band In Pursuit and the r&b act the Voltage Brothers. Among the firm's twenty staff songwriters were RADNEY FOSTER, Bill Lloyd, Larry Boone, Becky Hobbs, Holly Dunn, Judy Rodman, and Hugh Prestwood.

Following the July 1988 sale of MTM Enterprises to Great Britain's Television South PLC (TVS) for a reported $325 million, the MTM Music Group was soon up for sale as well. In December 1988 Howard Stark purchased all the assets of the firm, and it ceased to exist as a record company and publishing firm. The MTM publishing catalogue is owned by BMG MUSIC Publishing. —*Paul Kingsbury*

Moon Mullican

b. Corrigan, Texas, March 29, 1909; d. January 1, 1967

In the early 1950s Aubrey Wilson Mullican billed himself King of the Hillbilly Piano Players at a time when he was just about the only headlining country pianist. He was much more than a hillbilly piano player, though; he was as comfortable with jazz, blues, or popular music, and he was instrumental in injecting boogie into country music. Perhaps his enduring contribution was that he extended the sense of what was possible to young would-be pianists such as JERRY LEE LEWIS and FLOYD CRAMER.

Mullican's father bought a pump organ in 1917 so his children could learn religious music, but young Aubrey Mullican's thoughts tended in other directions. When he left home in 1925, it was to play pop music in bars. He had

Moon Mullican

already acquired the nickname "Moon," which may have been a truncation of "Moonshine" or an allusion to his already balding pate. By the late 1930s he was working with LEON "PAPPY" SELPH's Blue Ridge Playboys and CLIFF BRUNER's Texas Wanderers, as well as leading his own groups in Texas and Illinois. He recorded prolifically as a sideman with Bruner (singing on the seminal record of "Truck Driver's Blues"), BUDDY JONES, and others, making more than one hundred recordings between August 1939 and May 1940. In 1939 he appeared with the Texas Wanderers in the movie *Village Barn Dance.*

In the early 1940s Mullican worked with JIMMIE DAVIS at KWKH in Shreveport before forming the Showboys with Cliff Bruner at KLAC–Port Arthur, Texas, in 1943. He left to work with Davis's gubernatorial campaign a few months later (he would continue to work for Davis on and off into the 1960s) but rejoined Bruner soon after. In 1945 he formed his own band, keeping the name Showboys and recording an unissued session for Houston's Gulf Records in 1946. In that same year he described his music as "Texas Socko" or "East Texas Sock." "Technically," his friend, the songwriter Lou Wayne explained, "it is 2/4 rhythm with the accent on the second beat—and when we say accent we mean accent." Mullican asserted that his style had originated in Houston a decade earlier.

In 1946 Mullican signed with KING RECORDS, which would become his most significant recording affiliation. Late that year he recorded "New Pretty Blonde," a nonsense version of the recent Cajun hit "Jole Blon," which became his first hit. For the next few years Mullican was very successful with both boogie numbers and sentimental songs. Among his hits were "Sweeter Than the Flowers" and "I'll Sail My Ship Alone," as well as country versions of such pop hits as "Mona Lisa" and "Goodnight Irene."

Mullican briefly owned several nightclubs in the late 1940s and by 1950 was working in the oil boom town of Odessa, Texas, appearing on KECK. He gave up his own band when HANK WILLIAMS brought him to the GRAND OLE OPRY in June 1951. He and Williams later collaborated on "Jambalaya," a reworking of Papa Cairo's recent Cajun hit "Big Texas." It became one of Williams's biggest hits, but Mullican's recording was less successful.

In 1955 Mullican left Nashville and returned to East Texas. He remained with King until 1956, but his last major hit, "Cherokee Boogie," had come in 1951. Mullican subsequently recorded for Coral, STARDAY, and Hallway Records. His last charted record, "Ragged But Right," was for Starday in 1961.

Mullican's health began failing in the early 1960s. He had a heart attack onstage in Kansas City in 1962 and a fatal one shortly after midnight on New Year's Day 1967.

—*Colin Escott*

REPRESENTATIVE RECORDINGS

Sings His All-Time Greatest Hits (King, ca. 1956); *Moonshine Jamboree* (Ace, 1993)

Joaquin Murphey
b. Hollywood, California, December 30, 1923

Earl Murphey, far better known as "Joaquin," a tag hung on him by SPADE COOLEY, is one of the most legendary musicians in western swing, a vastly influential steel guitarist whose eccentric behavior added to that legend but also limited his career.

Murphey was an unknown when he dazzled Spade Cooley and band during a successful audition. Murphey began recording with Cooley in November 1944 and played on Cooley's huge hits "Shame on You" and "Crazy 'Cause I Love You," quickly becoming a household name among musicians for his sophisticated, acrobatic solos and innovative tunings. He left Cooley in 1946 to work with Andy Parker & the Plainsmen, also recording with T. TEXAS TYLER, Jimmie Widener, and others. Murphey returned to Cooley's band on several occasions over the next decade, at times replacing fellow West Coast steel kingpin NOEL BOGGS. Murphey was working in a quartet with fiddler Buddy Ray in 1956, but by the end of the decade had begun to slip into obscurity, as western swing faded and different, often less sophisticated steel guitar styles prevailed. He was coaxed to record again by DeWitt Scott in 1976 but quit playing for a number of years. He was inducted into the International Steel Guitar Hall of Fame in 1980, and reportedly began recording and playing again in 1997.

—*Kevin Coffey*

REPRESENTATIVE RECORDINGS

Joaquin Murphey (Midland, 1976); *Spadella! The Essential Spade Cooley* (Columbia/Legacy, 1994)

Michael Martin Murphey
b. Oak Cliff, Texas, March 14, 1945

Michael Martin Murphey first came to fame as part of the AUSTIN music scene in the early 1970s. Later he recorded some mainstream country music albums, although he never lived in Nashville and kept close ties to the West. By the end of the 1980s he had begun performing mostly western music, and since then he has recorded several albums of cowboy and western songs.

Murphey grew up in Dallas and wanted to become a Baptist minister, which led to his enrolling in North Texas

State University and studying Greek. At age twenty he moved to Los Angeles, where he studied creative writing at UCLA and began to write songs for Screen Gems. Among these early songs was "What Am I Doing Hanging Around" for the Monkees. In Los Angeles he formed a group, the Lewis & Clark Expedition, with Boomer Castleman (Martin performed under the name Travis Lewis, while Castleman was Boomer Clarke); they had their first pop chart single, "I Feel Good (I Feel Bad)" in 1967.

In 1971 Murphey moved to Austin, Texas, where he joined the alternative music scene and began playing clubs. He was signed to A & M Records and recorded two albums as Michael Murphey, *Geronimo's Cadillac* (1972) and *Cosmic Cowboy Souvenirs* (1973), which featured the underground anthems "Geronimo's Cadillac" and "Cosmic Cowboy."

In 1974 Murphey moved to Colorado and signed with EPIC RECORDS. While there he recorded two albums, *Michael Murphey* (1974) and *Blue Sky, Night Thunder* (1974); the latter included "Wildfire," a #3 pop hit and "Carolina in the Pines," which was #21 pop, both in 1975. In 1979 Murphey moved to Taos, New Mexico, and continued to record for Epic, doing the albums *Swans Against the Sun,* (1975) and *Flowing Free Forever* (1976). Next he signed with the LIBERTY label, where he recorded three mainstream country albums, *Michael Martin Murphey* (1982), *Tonight We Ride* (1985), and *Americana* (1987), all produced by JIM ED NORMAN. The eponymous first Liberty album yielded the #1 country hit (#19 pop) "What's Forever For" *Tonight We Ride* included a remake of "Carolina in the Pines," which became a #9 country hit in 1986.

After Liberty, Murphey signed with WARNER BROS. RECORDS, and his interest in cowboys led him to organize the first West Fest (1986) in Copper Mountain, Colorado, and to record an album, *Cowboy Songs* (1990), which featured a number of old cowboy standards. This led to the formation of Warner Western, an imprint of Warner Bros. Records devoted to western music. Murphey has recorded several albums for the label, including *Sagebrush Symphony* (1995) and *The Horse Legends* (1997). —*Don Cusic*

REPRESENTATIVE RECORDINGS

Blue Sky, Night Thunder (Epic, 1974); *Cowboy Songs* (Warner Bros., 1990); *The Horse Legends* (Warner Western, 1997)

David Lee Murphy
b. Herrin, Illinois, January 7, 1959

By the time his second album came out in 1996, David Lee Murphy was establishing himself as a successor to the OUTLAW, redneck, rock-influenced country of HANK WILLIAMS JR. and WAYLON JENNINGS. Murphy had moved to Nashville nine years before signing with MCA in 1992, and his first album didn't come out until 1994. When it did, Murphy made his name with rowdy anthems: the trade magazine *Radio & Records* named his single "Party Crowd" the most-played song on country radio in 1995. The gold-selling album from which "Party Crowd" was pulled, *Out with a Bang,* produced four other singles as well, including "Dust on the Bottle" and "Just Once." His second album, *Gettin' Out the Good Stuff,* had broader scope, but with mixed results; still, Murphy wrote or co-wrote every song on the album. Murphy released the album *We Can't All be Angels* in 1997.

—*Brian Mansfield*

Out With a Bang (MCA, 1994)

Jimmy Murphy

b. Republic, Alabama, October 11, 1925; d. June 1, 1981

Jimmy Murphy was one of country music's most quirky singer-songwriters, and his reputation largely rests on seven singles released by RCA VICTOR and COLUMBIA between 1951 and 1956. Accompanying himself with a driving finger-picked acoustic guitar, Murphy sang delightfully off-center songs about spirituality, morality, old age, current crazes, and extremely overweight or underweight girlfriends.

While growing up near Birmingham, Alabama, Murphy listened to his father's blues and country records. At age fifteen a neighbor taught him how to play guitar in an open-E tuning; he used that tuning throughout his career. Outside of occasional WBRC-Birmingham radio appearances during the mid-1940s, Murphy began performing professionally in 1950, when he joined ARCHIE CAMPBELL's *Dinner Bell Show* on WROL-Knoxville; Murphy later became part of WNOX's *MIDDAY MERRY-GO-ROUND* cast.

In January 1951 RCA Victor producer STEVE SHOLES recorded Murphy with just his acoustic guitar and Anita Carter on bass. Although "Electricity" and "We Live a Long, Long Time" generated only marginal sales, both are now considered classic recordings. RCA Victor dropped Murphy's contract after the sides from a second, more conventional session failed to click. Signing with Columbia in 1955, Murphy recorded eight tracks with an acoustic rockabilly backing; three singles were issued with little success.

Unable to secure a foothold in the music business, Murphy worked as a brickmason in Knoxville and Birmingham, although he recorded sporadically for small labels. Writer-researcher Richard K. Spottswood tracked him down in the late 1970s; his reemergence led to a critically acclaimed 1978 album on SUGAR HILL, *Electricity*. At the time of his death, Murphy was planning a second album and a European tour. Bear Family reissued Murphy's RCA Victor and Columbia recordings on compact disc in 1990.

—*Dave Samuelson*

Sixteen Tons Rock 'N' Roll (Bear Family, 1990)

Anne Murray

b. Springhill, Nova Scotia, June 20, 1945

If HANK SNOW is the king of Canadian country singers, no one comes closer than Anne Murray to claim the queen's prerogative. In fact, Murray's smooth country-pop style and nonrural clipped Canadian-accented alto spread her music far beyond the country charts from the get-go, making her one of the most popular female crossover artists of all time.

Morna Anne Murray came up in the coal mining region of Nova Scotia, singing for fun while getting her college degree in physical education. She became a high school physical education teacher and had to be coaxed to take a part-time singing job on a Canadian television show, *Sing-Along Jubilee,* in the late 1960s. In 1968, while she was still teaching, the program's musical director, Brian Ahern, pro-

Anne Murray

duced her first album in Toronto, which led to her signing by Capitol/Canada and the eventual release of her first border-crossing hit, "Snowbird," a Top Ten country hit in 1970. That song set the pace for her international and format melding successes to come, becoming a hit in Great Britain as well as a Top Ten American pop hit.

Murray got enormous national exposure when she became a regular on the *Glen Campbell Goodtime Hour,* but she was ultimately unwilling to make the personal sacrifices required to live in Los Angeles and get along with network executives. She was two more years without a significant hit. In 1973 she had her second major country and pop crossover hit, establishing Kenny Loggins's "Danny's Song" as another signature hit, a Top Ten hit on both charts. Her place as the foremost queen of the moderate-tempoed love ballads was clinched in 1973 with "Love Song."

In 1974 Murray made an interesting A-side/B-side singles pairing of the Beatles' *Rubber Soul* album groundbreaker "You Won't See Me," with a distaff version of the GEORGE JONES standard "She Thinks I Still Care." Shipping the 45-rpm disk to both country and pop stations, she netted her first country #1 and a pop Top Ten, more than doubling the single's market performance, as 7-inch vinyl singles were then still a popular sales unit.

Refined yet comfortably down home, Murray toured like crazy until 1975, when she married and decided to start a family with husband Bill Langstroth. For the next couple of years she put her entertainment career on the back burner. In 1978 she refocused on music and had a major comeback hit with the EVERLY BROTHERS' chestnut "Walk Right Back," astutely picking a familiar song by artists who had also successfully bridged the pop and country chasm in their heyday. She later successfully reprised the Monkees' "Daydream Believer" and Bruce Channel's "Hey! Baby!" There followed a long string of hits and awards, repeated Grammys for Best Female Country Vocal

Performance, and the 1985 CMA Duet of the Year Award shared with Dave Loggins. While her vocal influence was heard in early KATHY MATTEA recordings, Murray remained uniquely singular.

Murray maintained her Canadian residence, business headquarters, and her self-directed management, which may help explain how the notoriously suspicious country and pop fans of that era never identified her as exclusively "other." She was never a favorite of either the Nashville or the West Coast awarding organizations, either. Country #1s from the late 1980s through 1986 included "I Just Fall in Love Again," "Blessed Are the Believers," "A Little Good News," "Just Another Woman in Love," "Nobody Loves Me Like You Do," and "Now and Forever (Me and You)." She finished her recording career solidly in the country camp, shut out by younger artists on the pop charts. She remains an icon of country-pop and one of the all-time-favorite artists from the 1970s and 1980s. —*Bob Millard*

REPRESENTATIVE RECORDINGS

Snowbird (Capitol, 1970); *Let's Keep It That Way* (Capitol, 1978); *Anne Murray's Greatest Hits* (Capitol, 1980); *Something to Talk About* (Capitol, 1986); *Christmas* (Capitol, 1988)

Music City USA

The term "Music City USA" had its origin in Nashville radio station WSM's proud tradition of live radio programming. From the mid-1930s to the early 1960s—when TV replaced radio as the nation's variety entertainment medium—WSM originated numerous pop and country network shows, including *Magnolia Blossoms, Sunday Down South,* and the *Prince Albert Show,* the Opry's NBC network segment. Even non-network shows could be heard over most of the nation because of the station's 50,000-watt, clear-channel transmitter. Nashville also boasted stars who came up through the WSM ranks, such as Metropolitan Opera veteran Joseph McPherson and pop singer Dinah Shore.

It was on RED FOLEY's NBC radio show in 1950 that WSM announcer David Cobb coined the phrase "Music City" in a moment of serendipity. By 1953 music trade publications were using it to describe Nashville's recording activity and the hits it yielded. Most sessions were country, but, as in radio, Nashville sessions embraced pop and rhythm & blues as well. In fact, one of the biggest Nashville-produced recordings ever is Francis Craig's #1 pop hit "Near You" (1947). Although country hits prevailed, variety continued; by 1979 nearly half of Nashville sessions were pop, rock, r&b, gospel, or disco.

By 1961 the Nashville music industry had a firm institutional base as well. From ACUFF-ROSE PUBLICATIONS—the only major locally based publisher for a decade after its founding, in 1942—the number of publishers had grown to more than 100. Additionally, there were some 1,100 professional musicians, 200 songwriters, 12 talent agencies, 15 recording studios, and 1,600 artists and sidemen. Nashville's musical ranks also included trade associations such as CMA, promoters, radio syndicators, jingle companies, arrangers, record pressing firms, and performance rights organizations. By 1963 most major labels had built permanent offices in the city. Nashville entrepreneurs were also producing many syndicated TV shows, building a solid audience base for THE NASHVILLE NETWORK (TNN) and COUNTRY MUSIC TELEVISION (CMT) (both headquartered in Nashville) in the eighties and nineties.

Today Nashville boasts some 90 record companies, 24 talent agencies, 104 video and film production companies, nearly 300 music publishers, 174 recording studios, 5,500 union musicians, 17 staffed professional music organizations, and a host of other musical enterprises, constituting an estimated business, with tourism—heavily music-based—making up an additional $2 billion industry. Small wonder that the city's Chamber of Commerce has adopted the Music City logo for its promotional campaigns, a logo that has won Nashville international recognition as a music production center. —*John Rumble*

Music Publishing

As a general rule, music publishing and publishers became more important within the country music business after World War II, as they were becoming *less* important within American popular music as a whole. Country publishing bucked the general trend mainly because its development was slow. The big publishers who were so powerful within America's music industry during the first half of the twentieth century largely ignored country, considering it unworthy of their attention. Much prewar country music was published only if it was recorded, and even some recorded tunes never got published at all. Thus marginalized, new country songs—remember that much early recorded country music consisted of folksongs or older pop music—were published by just a handful of organizations. (M. M. COLE in Chicago was one of the few.) New country tunes were more commonly published, however, not by these publishing firms, which were based where "hillbilly" artists congregated for radio work, but by companies owned by the individual record producers. These savvy business owners realized the profitability of such songs even if many of their artists or writers did not.

ELI OBERSTEIN, DAVE KAPP, W. R. CALAWAY, ART SATHERLEY, and most successfully, RALPH PEER, owned such companies. Only a few prewar writers and artists controlled their own publishing or even exploited the growing appeal for radio songbooks, hawked over the air and sometimes featuring only song lyrics and artist photos. These writers and artists included CARSON ROBISON, ASHER SIZEMORE, BRADLEY KINCAID, and at the very end of the prewar era, GENE AUTRY and ROY ACUFF.

The proliferation of country music publishing companies and a growth in their relative importance within the music industry were spurred by three factors: the birth of BMI in 1940; the boom in country music's national popularity, which came with World War II and the prosperous years thereafter; and increasing business sophistication of the music's singer-songwriters. As Nashville grew as a country recording center, it also became home to many new music publishing ventures: ACUFF-ROSE (1942), launched by Roy Acuff and FRED ROSE; TREE (1951), co-owned by WSM executive JACK STAPP; CEDARWOOD (1954), founded by another WSM executive, JIM DENNY; and Moss-Rose, started by talent manager HUBERT LONG. There were many others, but these came to the fore as major players by the early 1960s and ultimately challenged the immediate postwar strength of the Aberbach Brothers' Los Angeles and New York–based HILL AND RANGE SONGS, founded in the mid-1940s. Soon, not only were singers gravitating to Nashville for their career "breaks," but also songwriters were intent on pitching their songs to the city's growing host of singers and publishers. Of course, some country artists continued to write and/or publish their own material. However, relatively nonperforming songwriters such as DANNY DILL, MARIJOHN WILKIN, CINDY WALKER, HARLAN HOWARD, BOUDLEAUX AND FELICE BRYANT, BOB MCDILL, Jerry Chesnut, CURLY PUTMAN, and JOHN D. LOUDERMILK, who made writing their principal activity, became Music Row powers along with their publishers. Artists and record producers often beat a path to their doors for new material.

Music publishers, finally ensconced as power centers within the country music industry, handled song administration and exploitation as publishers had always done. Even the best publishers today usually hold relatively small staffs of regular writers under contract, because so many well-known writers, no less than artists, have launched their own companies. And one reason why so many artists-writers do so, besides the desire to keep more of a song's income, is that overhead is so low, with only three basic tasks to perform: song administration (securing copyrights, seeing that licenses are issued and the monies collected, and paying outside co-writers or co-publishers), song plugging (working with artists and producers to get songs recorded), and creative work (signing new writers, pairing up writers, and editing their songs).

The monies that publishers and their writers share, now that the sale of printed music (sheet music and songbooks) is fairly negligible, are basically mechanical and performance royalties and synchronization fees. Saving the larger matter of mechanical and performance ROYALTIES for a separate entry, synchronization fees (or "synch" fees) are paid for the use of music in synchronization with visual images. Covered thereby are songs used in motion pictures, television commercials, and home videos, but not songs from live or taped TV variety show performances, which come under performance royalties. Fees paid by these users to publishers for synch licenses vary widely, based on length of a license, length of the song used, and the broadcast audience. Some motion picture uses of songs (usually granted in perpetuity) pay as much as $200,000; for local, short-term television use of part of a song, the cost may be as low as $1,000. One-year national use of a song in a TV commercial, though, is even more profitable than movies, and might bring a publisher as much as $500,000 in synch fees.   —*Ronnie Pugh*

Music Videos

After MTV debuted in 1981, everything about rock music changed dramatically. Videos began to affect record sales and radio airplay, and heartland resistance to new sounds weakened. Trends followed in faster and faster succession, and each seemed to be announced by a landmark video.

It still doesn't work that way in country. The two primary outlets for country music videos, THE NASHVILLE NETWORK and COUNTRY MUSIC TELEVISION, launched within a week of each other in March 1983. They have remained behind MTV in incorporating aesthetic innovation and have been much more conservative about sexual and violent content, reflecting a more mature, mainstream audience. Most importantly, a dozen years after the beginning of country's video age, radio still affects record sales more.

That's not to say that country video hasn't evolved. The RCA and CBS labels produced some of the first promotional clips as early as 1981, but when the country TV networks launched two years later, they still had only about two dozen videos from which to choose. Video didn't really take off until TNN increased its music video programming from three to thirty-one hours per week in 1990 and purchased CMT the next year. By 1995 the networks were adding more than 200 videos per year to their play lists, and country fans were engrossed with country's full-length videos, making them the most popular of any musical genre. For example, seven of the forty-one songs that were featured in music videos and certified gold or platinum in 1993 were country; seventeen of the Top Forty music videos, during the week of February 26, 1994, were country.

Nashville's homegrown production companies, such as Scene Three and Deaton-Flanigen, have mushroomed and been joined by video directors and producers from the coasts who have relocated to Tennessee—Bud Schaetzle, for example, director of several clips for GARTH BROOKS. In recent years, reflecting the higher profile of the genre, the occasional celebrity such as Sean Penn or Burt Reynolds has tried his hand at directing a country video, while other celebrities have made cameo appearances: Huey Lewis in REBA MCENTIRE's "Is There Life Out There?" and David Keith in PATTY LOVELESS's "Blame It on Your Heart." Average budgets for country videos have risen about $20,000 in recent years, and midlevel acts are now spending approximately $80,000.

Among the more notable videos of the medium's first dozen years were HANK WILLIAMS JR.'s computer-generated duet with his father in 1989, "A Tear in My Beer." Two years later the networks wouldn't air Garth Brooks's video for "The Thunder Rolls" due to its "risqué" content, though its depiction of domestic violence would have been unremarkable on MTV. In the following year, 1992, the BILLY RAY CYRUS popularity phenomenon was jump-started by videos of a prefabricated line dance sent to country dance clubs prior to release of the "Achy Breaky Heart" single. More recently, the MAVERICKS and the TRACTORS are among those acts whose careers have been significantly aided by video; an ARISTA executive estimates that half of the double-platinum sales of the Tractors' first album were generated by airplay of the "My Baby Likes to Rock It" video. Videos played on the 9-million-subscriber CMT Europe probably have the strongest sales impact per capita.

Because of country's storytelling tradition, its videos will always be biased in favor of narrative. However, an artform that began with low-budget images of trees and streams has overhauled the visual vocabulary of country. It has also made physical performance and physical appearance more important: Live audiences have become impatient with performers who stand still and sing. In addition, emphasis on artists' attractiveness was apparent from the release of the first videos—among the pioneers were CHARLY MCCLAIN ("Sleeping with the Radio On") and SYLVIA ("The Matador"); videos are often vehicles used to introduce young hunks to female audiences. Accordingly, it has also helped country catch up with pop in a more disturbing way—in some cases a quicker rise to stardom for videogenic young hunks, six months instead of a few years, is matched by an equally steep decent.   —*Mark Schone*

Country Music as Music

Bill Evans

Where is the "country" in country music? It is a question that is debated by each new generation of musicians and listeners. Although the answer has changed through the years, country music has exhibited some remarkable musical continuities through a succession of numerous historical substyles. The sound, the instruments, and the technology used to make country music have changed greatly since the 1920s. Nevertheless, core assumptions related to melody, harmony, meter, song form, ensemble approach, and vocal style have helped to define country music as a unique musical type, even in the face of recent stylistic trends that increasingly incorporate elements from other popular musical styles into the country music sound.

The Historical Background

By the time of country music's first commercial recordings in the 1920s, three centuries of musical exchange had already occurred between Americans of European and those of African ancestry. This interaction was made possible in part by a general compatibility of West African and West European traditional musical systems. Cultural attitudes regarding the basic elements of music—scale types, rhythm, song forms, general instrument and ensemble types, and performance styles and contexts—were largely held in common by musicians of both continents, with different musical results arising from the relative emphasis placed on these shared musical ingredients.

The results of this interaction have distinguished the American music scene from the early nineteenth century forward through a procession of folk and popular music styles that include religious camp meeting songs, ballad and story songs, fiddle and banjo traditions, minstrelsy, spirituals, ragtime, blues, gospel, and early jazz styles. Along with more recently imported sounds, such as the fiddle and accordion traditions of more recent Irish and German immigrants, a wealth of musical styles and resources helped shape early country music in the first decades of the twentieth century.

This legacy of European and African influence has influenced country music in ways that are often taken for granted. Such fundamental characteristics as the predominance of stringed instruments in country ensembles and the ubiquity of song forms built around repetitive verse/chorus structures, as well as country music's unique approach toward harmony and improvisation, all reflect certain underlying attitudes toward musicmaking that have been centuries in the making.

Melody

As in other genres of American folk and popular music, a country song consists of a lyric matched to a sequence of musical notes (a *melody*). This melody is supported by a progression of chords (or *harmony*) played by an accompanying instrument or group of instruments.

Common to both West European and West African traditional music is an understanding of melody as made up of a series of brief phrases related to one another through repetition, elaboration, or variation and that are joined together to form a song. Melodies from the ballad and fiddling traditions of the British Isles were enhanced on American soil by African performance styles, which placed high value on rhythmic vitality and melodic variation, often achieved through bent and/or sliding note choices not usually employed by the West European major and minor scale modes.

Like its traditional and popular predecessors, most country music is vocal music. Therefore, stepwise motion (in which a melody has an abundance of consecutive notes that are adjacent to each other in a scale) and a limited melodic range of an octave or less tend to characterize most country melodies. Of course, exceptions to this generalized rule abound, as in PATSY CLINE's performance of "Crazy," a classic in part because of its leaping melody.

Harmony

One of country music's most distinctive musical features is the straightforward and sturdy way in which harmony is commonly employed to support a melody. The vast majority of country songs are harmonized with major rather than minor chords. However, a few notable exceptions, such as MERLE TRAVIS's "Sixteen Tons," are made memorable in part because of their minor key settings.

Modulation, in which a song moves to a new key, was relatively rare in the first decades of country music history. JOHNNY CASH's 1956 recording of "I Walk the Line" is one remarkable exception, with stanzas sung in the successive keys of F, B-flat, and E-flat before returning once again to B-flat and F. Another example is BOB WILLS's "San Antonio Rose," in which the song's distinctive chorus is in a different key from its verses. Modulation has become much more common in recent years, where, as in rock and pop styles, it functions as a dramatic device intended to bring a sense of climax or finality to an arrangement. In this case, modulation usually shifts the key center up one scale step to the next pitch (as in SHANIA TWAIN's "Any Man of Mine").

The three-chord stereotype of country harmony, in which a song accompaniment is constructed exclusively from chords built on the first, fourth, and fifth notes of the scale, has become something of an signifying cliché for outsiders. As in the blues, often nothing more is really needed in the way of chords for many country pieces, as this famous JIMMIE DAVIS song proves (in the key of C major, the I, IV, and V chords would be played as C, F, and G major chords):

I
You are my sunshine, my only sunshine

IV   I
You make me happy when skies are gray,

IV   I
You'll never know dear how much I love you

V   I
Please don't take my sunshine away.

The thousands of possible melodic and harmonic combinations that have sprung from this seemingly restrictive three-chord palette point to a central tenet of country creativity: to create the maximum emotional effect in the most direct way possible with the most basic of musical means. Nevertheless, country musicians have also employed more complex harmonies since the music's earliest years. Blues and ragtime songs learned by early twentieth-century folk musicians instilled new harmonic ideas, which by the 1920s had become part of the natural resources of early country performers as geographically dispersed as the North Carolina stringband musician CHARLIE POOLE (as in "Don't Let Your Deal Go Down") and western swing bandleader MILTON BROWN (as in his version of W. C. Handy's blues standard "St. Louis Blues"). In this regard, JIMMIE RODGERS, who was greatly influenced by Tin Pan Alley, vaudeville, and early blues and jazz performances, created some of the most complex pieces, harmonically speaking, in country music history.

Basic chord progressions can be made more complex by grafting passing and substitute chords onto the basic I-IV-V framework. Western swing musicians became most adept at this skill, utilizing the harmonic formulas of swing-era jazz to create fast-moving extended choral harmonies in support of the jazzy, improvisational flights of a lead instrumentalist.

While HANK WILLIAMS's classic "I'm So Lonesome I Could Cry" sounds just fine with an accompaniment that uses only the I, IV, and V chords, most modern performances involve a more complex progression originally implied in part by the moving bass line in the first verse of Williams's earliest recording of the piece (transposed here to the key of C with passing chords in parentheses):

C   (C/B)   (Am) (C/G)
Do you hear that lonesome whippoorwill

C   (Am) (Gm) (C7)
He sounds too blue to cry

F   (Dm)   C   (Am)
The midnight train is whining low

C   G   C
I'm so lonesome I could cry

Harmonic embellishments of this kind became increasingly common in country music in the 1940s. However, many of the most distinctive hits of the past two decades maintain a clear relationship to an underlying I-IV-V harmonic foundation in spite of their more complex surface harmonies. REBA MCENTIRE's "Somebody Should Leave" and GARTH BROOKS's "Friends in Low Places" are examples of modern songs in which harmonically elaborate verses suggestive of pop music styles contrast with straightforward choruses that bring the listener firmly back to a country sensibility. In such ways, modern composers blend the traditional with the innovative, bringing new sounds and musical possibilities to the genre.

Meter, Tempo, and Rhythm

Melodies and their accompanying chord progressions are organized in time within a recurring cycle of evenly spaced beats called *meter*. *Tempo* refers to the speed at which a song is performed. *Rhythm* is a much broader musical concept. This term may refer to the metrical arrangement of individual melody notes (as in the *rhythm* of a melody), to the relative stress given to each beat in a metrical cycle (as in the overall *rhythm* of a piece or style), or even to the ways in which the various instruments work together in an ensemble (as in a band's overall sense of *rhythm*). Another legacy of the shared European and African heritage of American folk and popular music is the prevalence of metrical cycles made up of either two *(duple)* or three *(triple)* beats. Duple meters of two- and four-beat cycles predominate in country music. Nevertheless, the waltz, which by definition is performed in triple meter, has developed into something of a sentimental staple, surviving in country music past its diminishing popularity in other American genres. Country waltzes come in a wide variety of tempos, from quite fast (as in MARTY ROBBINS's "El Paso") to very slow (as in JIM REEVES's "He'll Have to Go").

Shifts in meter within a single piece are extremely rare but not altogether unknown (for example, MAC WISEMAN's "'Tis Sweet to Be Remembered" has verses in duple meter with waltz time choruses). Occasionally a composition is sturdy enough to take on a entirely new identity when performed in a different meter, as ELVIS PRESLEY accomplished early in his career with his cover version of "Blue Moon of Kentucky." In this case, Presley transformed the original waltz time of this BILL MONROE composition into a brisk and rocking duple meter.

As with other forms of American popular music, the speed at which country music is performed is often a function of its historical association with a particular dance style. Of even greater importance is the need to establish a tempo that enables the lyric content of a song to be easily understood. As a result, country music tempos tend to occupy a sensible, broad middle ground between the very fast and the very slow. One exception to this rule occurs with country instrumentals, which are often virtuosic displays of musical prowess taken at extremely fast tempos (as in LESTER FLATT & EARL SCRUGGS's banjo showpiece "Foggy Mountain Breakdown").

In addition, each substyle of country music (honky-tonk, western swing, bluegrass) tends to exhibit some internal consistency in regard to a more specific range of acceptable tempos. With the exception of country ballad and heart songs, which are almost always performed at slow tempos, a typical honky-tonk song (such as RAY PRICE's "Crazy Arms") will usually be performed in a medium-fast tempo that is slower than a standard western swing song (such as Bob Wills's "Take Me Back to Tulsa"), which itself is slower in tempo than a fast bluegrass favorite (such as the OSBORNE BROTHERS' "Rocky Top").

An even more important signifier of country music substyle is the unique approach adopted to rhythm and accent by each substyle. MAYBELLE CARTER helped to introduce to country music in the 1920s an accompanimental guitar technique derived from African-American sources in which a bass note struck on the main beat(s) of a measure is followed by a chord brushed across the higher strings on the weaker off beat(s). This separation of main and weak beats in terms of musical role has characterized every subsequent country music style to this day. Some styles, such as western swing and bluegrass, place greater emphasis or accent on the weaker beats of a measure, while other styles, such as honky-tonk and much rock-influenced modern country, tend either to smooth out these differences or to place greater stress on the main beats of each metrical cycle.

Form

The form that has served as a template for the songs of many American genres has its roots in the ballad traditions of the British Isles. It consists of a four-line stanza matched to four melodic phrases of nearly equal length, which are often assembled in such a way that melodic material from the last two phrases brings to a resolution similar material presented in the song's first two lines. Combined with a chorus or refrain of one to four phrases, this is the archetypal song structure of country music.

In reality, a wide variety of song forms are actually used, with much of this variation being the result of ingenious idiosyncratic extensions on the basic four-line format (as in Jimmie Rodgers's six-line stanza form in "Waiting for a Train"). Three-line blues forms with their own variations have always been common, as well as more extended forms (such as Hank Williams's version of "Lovesick Blues") that reflect the enduring legacies of earlier ragtime and classic blues styles. Country instrumentals come in all of these formal varieties but are characteristically multisectional, with contrasting melodic content extending across two or more sections (as in CHUBBY WISE's fiddle breakdown "Orange Blossom Special," which consists of three distinct sections).

The *turnaround* is a formal device common in country music. This is a brief phrase attached to the end of a verse or chorus that brings a sense of completion to a particular section of a tune. Its trademark is a I-V-I chord progression, over which an instrumentalist will play a variation on a set of standardized melodic phrases that have come to be closely associated with the turnaround itself. Turnarounds may also be sung, most memorably in the form of the country yodel, as popularized in different eras by Jimmie Rodgers, Hank Williams, and their admirers.

Some formal devices represent more recent borrowings from other popular styles. One example is the *bridge,* which is a short section of contrasting melodic material usually presented just before a song's climax. As appropriated by modern country songwriters, the lyric content of this penultimate section often provides resolution to a song's lyric or reveals its core sentiment (as in Garth Brooks's "Unanswered Prayers").

Short instrumental interludes, consisting of a brief melody that may or may not be related to the melody of the actual song itself, have provided a special element to some country songs for several decades now. Like the turnaround, these interludes provide an element of musical continuity to a country song, often serving as the introduction and/or ending of a piece. They can be so distinctive as to be a marker of the tune itself (as in the guitar part that opens and closes BOBBY BARE's "Detroit City") or be so memorable that they become virtually synonymous with a song's performer (as is the sonorous, eight-note introduction to Johnny Cash's "Folsom Prison Blues").

Ensemble Approach

It is no historical coincidence that the solo singer accompanied by a guitar occupies a space of great importance in country music. As a social role, the musician-as-storyteller can be traced back many centuries to medieval European minstrel and West African griot traditions. From such roots have emerged on American soil a panoply of styles and genres as disparate as the American broadside ballad, the nineteenth-century parlor song, and rural blues as well as the twentieth-century country song.

In this light, country music history can in large part be traced as the development of various *ensemble* styles in which each successive stylistic innovation presents a new set of musical solutions to the central task of supporting a lead singer (or, as an extension of this principle, multiple singers or one or more lead instrumentalists). While particular instruments, such as the acoustic guitar, fiddle, pedal steel, and banjo, have come to be viewed as closely associated with country music, it is the ways in which these and other instruments are played and how they relate to one another in an ensemble that is ultimately responsible for this genre's unique sound.

Many of the late nineteenth-century and early twentieth-century southern folk music traditions that were the historical precursors of early country music often involved unaccompanied performances in which one or more singers or an instrumentalist performed without the harmonic and rhythmic support of an instrument or group of instruments. By the early decades of the twentieth century, most musicians had incorporated some concept of instrumental accompaniment into their performance practices.

However, different ideas about ensembles, their instrumental makeup, and their sound were developed at varying points in time across widely dispersed southern regions. The spread of national radio programming into rural and small-town locales, along with the growth of the early country recording industry itself, helped to nationalize regional approaches to country music throughout the 1920s and early 1930s. Early country styles became somewhat more standardized as amateur musicians learned the songs and instrumental styles presented on radio and 78-rpm record by such artists as the CARTER FAMILY, Jimmie Rodgers, GENE AUTRY, and UNCLE DAVE MACON.

From these circumstances, a relatively stable model of the country ensemble has emerged whose underlying structural functions have remained more or less consistent to the present day. Central to this concept is a musical division of labor that assigns to each instrument a unique musical function. Instruments are grouped into two main categories: those that primarily supply rhythmic and harmonic support (sometimes collectively referred to as the *rhythm section*) and those that also are capable of executing solos (called *lead instruments*).

Regardless of whether they may be featured in a lead capacity, all instruments spend most of their time in the service of the rhythm section. While the bass and drums are almost always exclusively associated with this supportive role, most other instruments divide their time between the two categories.

Stylistic innovations have often been the result of a talented instrumentalist developing a new performance technique that expands that instrument's potential as a lead instrument within the country band. In this manner, the piano, the resophonic guitar (dobro), the accordion, the lead guitar, the banjo, and even brass instruments, among others, have at various points in country music history helped to fuel the development of new country music sounds and styles.

Ensemble integrity is valued above individual virtuosity in country music. Behind this aesthetic imperative is a concept of musical arrangement in which each instrument maintains its individual voice within the ensemble. This is usually achieved by assigning different rhythmic roles to each instrument such that its unique timbre is experienced as a unique ingredient in a total ensemble sound. This concept has been developed to the greatest extent in bluegrass music, in which each instrument accents different beats and subdivisions of the metrical cycle in precisely executed traditional playing styles.

Another way in which an individual instrument can maintain a unique identity within the country ensemble is through an accompanimental technique known as *back up*. Back up involves a lead instrument performing a second melody behind a lead singer or other instrumentalist, offering in effect a second musical point of interest, which ideally should complement and not overpower a lead singer. Back up is a highly articulated skill in country music. As it is expressed in western swing, honky-tonk, bluegrass, and many modern styles, the exchange of back-up opportunities among the various lead instruments creates a constantly shifting musical landscape which adds great variety to the ensemble sound while also giving the lead instrumentalist additional opportunities to display his or her talents.

Vocal Styles

Vocal styles are without doubt the most significant distinguishing characteristic of country music. While the solo male or female singer is the most ubiquitous presence in country music, group singing in duet, trio, and quartet configurations has been cultivated to a higher degree in country music than in any other American genre, with the possible exception of rhythm & blues and gospel music. The widest possible variety of singing styles has been welcomed under the country music umbrella throughout its history. Much of this variety is the result not only of the music's deep historical roots but also of its close relationship with other twentieth-century American folk and popular genres.

Early country singing styles reveal a dichotomy that is a reflection of the differing assumptions held by musicians of European and of African ancestry regarding singing style and performance technique. Nowhere is this more evident than in the different approaches to singing taken by the two biggest names of early country music history, the Carter Family and Jimmie Rodgers.

Like the ballad singers of the British Isles, the Carter Family is remembered for a plaintive, emotionally detached vocal style designed to draw the listener away from the singer and into the song's lyric. Operating within a musical climate of such overall restraint, emotion and meaning are conveyed by the most subtle of musical means, where a modest ornamental vocal turn or sigh or a slightly bent or delayed note can transmit a world of meaning to listeners who share the worldview of the singer.

In contrast, Jimmie Rodgers's singing style was significantly influenced by both the African-American musicians and the vaudeville and musical theater he encountered as a youth growing up in Mississippi. While he never adopted as declamatory a vocal style as many of the early African-American Delta blues singers, Rodgers's vocals express the widest range of human emotions through an easygoing, conversational vocal style that engages the listener through its unadulterated accessibility, sincerity, and openness.

While there is much common ground between these two approaches, for many years country vocalists felt compelled to follow either one or the other of these artistic paths. It is no small accomplishment that singers such as Hank Williams, LEFTY FRIZZELL, and DOLLY PARTON, among others, managed to bridge this gap with vocal styles that combine the best of both attitudes, managing to be both plaintive *and* conversational at the same time.

In recent years, country vocalists have often too easily worn their musical influences on their sleeves, openly borrowing from the vocal bag of tricks of many different singers. However, unique stylists such as WILLIE NELSON, EMMYLOU HARRIS, and ALISON KRAUSS have continued to emerge in the modern era, each providing fresh variations on established formulas. Today, rock and rhythm & blues singers such as James Taylor, LINDA RONSTADT, the EAGLES, Sam Cooke, and Otis Redding may be as much an influence on today's new singers as Patsy Cline and George Jones.

Conclusion

So where is the "country" in country music? To borrow a well-worn advertising phrase, it might be more a state of mind than any specific set of unique musical characteristics. Country musicians seem to share certain assumptions about melody, harmony, form, and performance technique that together help to shape ideas about the nature of the country sound, its boundaries and its possibilities. This musical road map will change as each succeeding generation introduces new ideas, which are either accepted or rejected as part of the country music landscape. As long as innovative musicians continue to look backward as well as forward in the ongoing process of musical creation, country music will no doubt continue to maintain its unique identity for quite some time to come.

Betty Records

P.O. Box 125   Bellaire, Texas

GLAD MUSIC
BMI

5703
Time: 2:07
(1179)

MAN WITH THE BLUES
(Willie Nelson)
WILLIE NELSON

Narmour & Smith

Will T. Narmour b. Carroll County, Mississippi, May 22, 1889;
d. March 24, 1961
Shell W. Smith b. Carroll County, Mississippi, November 26, 1895;
d. September 1968

Willie Narmour (fiddle) and Shell Smith (guitar) were one of the most popular instrumental duos on record in the late 1920s. According to Mississippi John Hurt, they won a local fiddle contest for which the prize was an opportunity to record for OKEH. Narmour was a neighbor of John Hurt and recommended him to producer Tom Rockwell. The three journeyed from their Avalon, Mississippi, homes to record in Memphis in February 1928. Hurt saw only one coupling released from his session, but the six Narmour & Smith duets were all issued and sold well.

Their 1929 "Carroll County Blues" was a major success and became a tune known by virtually every southern fiddler. Narmour & Smith's last records for OKeh were made in 1930. They journeyed to Atlanta in 1934 to re-record most of the OKeh titles for BLUEBIRD and did not record again.
—*Dick Spottswood*

Murray Nash

b. Campbell, Nebraska, March 5, 1918

Robert Murray Nash was an important business figure in country music from the mid-1940s to the mid-1950s.

During the 1940s, while based in Knoxville, Tennessee, and working in southeastern distribution for RCA RECORDS, he helped sign CLIFF CARLISLE, CHARLIE MONROE, and PEE WEE KING to the label. In 1948, still living in Knoxville, Nash took over the country music department of the newly founded MERCURY label. In 1951, Nashville publisher FRED ROSE hired Nash for ACUFF-ROSE PUBLICATIONS, where he promoted Acuff-Rose songs to record distributors and DJs and worked with WSM to stage the first DJ CONVENTION in 1952. In addition, Nash assisted in launching Acuff-Rose's HICKORY RECORDS.

Shortly before Fred Rose's death in 1954, professional and personality conflicts with WESLEY ROSE led to Nash's departure. In 1955 Nash formed Murray Nash Associates, his own advertising, publicity, promotion, recording, and publishing firm, which he left in 1958. Subsequently Nash became a postman while still running his own publishing company and recording service. He is now retired.
—*John Rumble*

Nashville Bluegrass Band

Alan O'Bryant b. Reidsville, North Carolina, December 26, 1955
Pat Enright b. Huntington, Indiana, April 22, 1945
Roland White b. Madawaska, Maine, April 23, 1938
Stuart Duncan b. Quantico, Virginia, April 14, 1964
Gene Libbea b. Pasadena, California, March 22, 1953

With an emphasis on harmony vocals, well-selected contemporary songs, and stellar instrumental work, the Nashville Bluegrass Band became one of the leading bluegrass groups of the 1980s and 1990s. Collectively and individually the group has received numerous awards (including Entertainer of the Year, Vocal Group of the Year, and Best Fiddler) from the International Bluegrass Music Association.

While rooted in the older traditions of bluegrass, the Nashville Bluegrass Band has employed polished vocal stylings and original songs to give them a contemporary sound. A popular feature of their act is vocal interpretations of gospel songs and spirituals from black traditions. They have recorded and made appearances with the Fairfield Four, a respected black quartet that is considered by many to be one of the oldest a cappella, jubilee-style gospel quartets in the country.

The Nashville Bluegrass Band started in the middle part of 1984 and subsequently released three well-received albums for ROUNDER RECORDS. At the time the band included Pat Enright on guitar and vocals, Alan O'Bryant on banjo and vocals, Mike Compton on mandolin, and Mark Hembree on bass. The inclusion of Compton in the group, with his strong BILL MONROE–influenced mandolin style, gave the ensemble a decidedly traditional feel. The group was further bolstered by the addition of ace fiddler Stuart Duncan.

On July 21, 1988, the band's tour bus was involved in an auto accident outside Roanoke, Virginia, that seriously injured Hembree. Compton and Hembree left the band soon afterward and were replaced by Roland White and Gene Libbea, respectively. The current lineup of the group includes Enright, O'Bryant, White, Duncan, and Libbea. Since 1990 the Nashville Bluegrass Band has recorded for SUGAR HILL RECORDS.
—*Gary B. Reid*

REPRESENTATIVE RECORDINGS

To Be His Child (Rounder, 1987); *Waitin' for the Hard Times to Go* (Sugar Hill, 1993)

The Nashville Bluegrass Band: (from left) Gene Libbea, Pat Enright, Stuart Duncan, Alan O'Bryant, and Roland White

The Nashville Network (*see* TNN)

Nashville Now
established 1983; ended 1993

Nashville Now holds a major distinction not only for country music but for cable television as well. Premiering March 7, 1983, on THE NASHVILLE NETWORK, *Nashville Now* was the first live, prime-time talk show on cable, launching in the 8:00 P.M. to 9:30 P.M. (Central Time) time slot. RALPH EMERY, a well-known radio and television personality in Nashville, hosted the weeknight program, which featured celebrity guests from country music and other fields. Like most other TV talk shows, *Nashville Now* included an in-house band, led by veteran musician Jerry Whitehurst. *Nashville Now* became TNN's flagship program and was largely responsible for introducing fans to country's up-and-coming new talent. In particular, LORRIE MORGAN, who appeared frequently during the show's early days, credits *Nashville Now* with helping her land a record label deal. Other stars, such as RANDY TRAVIS and K. T. OSLIN, received their first national exposure through the program. *Nashville Now* first originated from the Stagedoor Lounge in the Opryland Hotel, then moved to the Gaslight Studio at the Opryland complex. The final live telecast from Nashville aired September 24, 1993. *Nashville Now* concluded its TNN run with a week of programs from San Antonio's Fiesta Texas theme park, October 11–15, 1993.
—*Bob Paxman*

The Nashville Sound

The Nashville Sound is a phrase that denotes a style of country music and an era in which that style was especially influential. The term has also been more generally applied in descriptions of the relaxed, improvisational feel of any recording produced within the informal, good-humored atmosphere that pervades Nashville recording studios. The phrase has been employed to convey the notion of a special mystique surrounding record-making in Nashville,

and in this sense has been an important tool in marketing Nashville as a uniquely creative music center.

The term first appeared in *Music Reporter* in 1958. In November 1960 *Time* magazine published a profile of country music, focusing on the career of JIM REEVES. The *Time* article used "Nashville Sound" as a subheadline, and as a phrase delineating "the essence of C&W," arguing that the absence of written arrangements in Nashville recording sessions imbued country recordings with spontaneous artistry. Quoting DON LAW, then staff producer and head of COLUMBIA RECORDS' Nashville office, *Time* indicates that New York and Los Angeles "let their sound become stereotyped. They write down their arrangements and even read and play the notes."

In 1960 Nashville's morning newspaper, the *Tennessean*, used the phrase, and it appeared in *Broadcasting* magazine the next year. In 1962 *Music Reporter* described a "Magical Nashville Sound" in a headline. By that year the term had become a staple of news accounts describing country music and the Nashville recording scene.

Through the 1960s the Nashville Sound referred to the special magic that could be found in Nashville studios. In 1970, when journalist Paul Hemphill published his examination of the country music business, he titled the book *The Nashville Sound: Bright Lights and Country Music,* and stressed the term's magical connotation: "Even BOB DYLAN and Buffy Sainte-Marie occasionally come to town in search of what is vaguely called 'the Nashville Sound.'"

By the mid-1970s scholars and journalists writing about country music began to employ the term in a different fashion, using it to define a specific substyle of country music, and also as an identifying label for a phase in the evolution of Nashville recording.

Deliberately aimed at broadening country's adult listenership, Nashville Sound recordings are frequently cited as one of the country music's key responses to the popularity of youth-oriented rock & roll in the mid-1950s, which temporarily cut into mainstream country's sales. The Nashville Sound often featured pop-sounding singers such as EDDY ARNOLD, Jim Reeves, and PATSY CLINE, and displayed several distinctive musical characteristics, including string and horn sections and background choruses (most frequently groups such as the JORDANAIRES or the ANITA KERR SINGERS).

Just as significantly, the Nashville Sound tended to exclude the fiddle and banjo, instruments identified with country music's hillbilly heritage. Taken together, the stylistic elements of the Nashville Sound often produced records that sounded more pop than country, and, in fact, many crossed over to become pop hits.

Nashville Sound recordings present an audible stylistic consistency among recordings of various artists produced for different labels. This remarkable consistency derives from both distinctive vocal and instrumental settings and the unique approach to record-making that evolved in Nashville in the late 1950s.

First, Nashville Sound recordings were typically produced by in-house, full-time producers employed by record labels. It was not uncommon for a single producer such as CHET ATKINS or OWEN BRADLEY to spend twelve hours or more each day in the studio, supervising the work of as many as twenty artists. The artistic authority of a handful of staff producers imposed similar elements on a wide variety of recordings.

In a similar fashion, a small number of accompanying musicians performed on a large percentage of recordings. Almost all Nashville recording sessions ran on the same schedule: four three-hour sessions per day, with the first beginning at 10:00 A.M. and the last at 10:00 P.M., each session separated by a one-hour break. In-demand session players sped from studio to studio with guitars stuffed in the trunks of inconspicuous cars to discourage theft, munching sandwiches and downing soft drinks on the fly. It was a demanding life, with the first note sounded in the morning and the last echoing away at 1:00 A.M.

Leading Nashville Sound studio musicians (sometimes referred to as the A-Team) included drummer BUDDY HARMAN; guitarists Ray Edenton, GRADY MARTIN, HANK GARLAND, and HAROLD BRADLEY; bassists BOB MOORE and HENRY STRZELECKI; pianists Floyd Cramer and HARGUS "PIG" ROBBINS; and steel guitarist PETE DRAKE. The Jordanaires and the Anita Kerr Singers provided vocal support, while string and horn players were frequently drawn from the Nashville Symphony.

And the 1960 *Time* account was accurate: Nashville sidemen did not employ formally written arrangements, but developed on-the-spot "head" arrangements in the course of a recording session—often using their own simplified Nashville Number System to jot down chord progressions. This informal approach to arranging executed by a crack team of players who worked together every day, combined with the talented artistic leadership of a handful of producers, provided background instrumentation of remarkable quality and consistency to thousands of country recordings, ranging from a rock & roll stylistic approach to straight country to country-pop.

As a historical period within the history of country music, the Nashville Sound is closely associated with the decade of the 1960s. Representative recordings include Jim Reeves, "He'll Have to Go" (1959; Chet Atkins, producer), Patsy Cline, "Crazy" (1961; Owen Bradley, producer), and Eddy Arnold, "Make the World Go Away" (1965; Atkins, producer). Many Nashville Sound recordings crossed over to become pop hits (Reeves's "He'll Have to Go" rose to # 2 on the *Billboard* pop chart).

Although the Nashville Sound can be seen as the dominant approach to recording in the 1960s, examples of the style can be found as early as 1957 with FERLIN HUSKY's "Gone" and Jim Reeves's "Four Walls." The first use of the phrase "Nashville Sound" in print coincides closely with these early musical efforts.

By the mid-1970s the notion of staff producers handling a stable of artists recording with a select group of accompanying musicians had fallen out of favor. As WILLIE NELSON, WAYLON JENNINGS, and the other OUTLAWS pushed country back toward its hard-edged roots, they demanded—and received—freedom to record in studios of their own choosing, selecting their own, often independent, producers and frequently co-producing their recordings. Nevertheless, important elements of the Nashville Sound remain, including its reliance on a relatively small number of top studio players and a cooperative, relaxed approach to recording that continues to set Nashville apart among music centers worldwide. —*Bill Ivey*

Sydney Nathan
b. Cincinnati, Ohio, April 27, 1903; d. March 5, 1968

Perhaps more than any other record company executive in the history of country music, Syd Nathan fit the stereotype of "the record man" that arose with the new independent labels of the 1940s and 1950s. The founder and president of KING RECORDS was a cigar-chomping tyrant—loud, abrasive, argumentative, crude, willing to take huge risks but always looking for an edge. He was also a genius of sorts who built King into one of the largest and most important independent record companies of the postwar era, changing both the music and the music business in the process.

When Nathan started King Records in 1943, he had behind him a string of failed business ventures impressive mostly for its variety. After dropping out of high school (extremely poor vision convinced him school was futile), Nathan worked in a pawnshop, promoted wrestling matches, ran a shooting gallery, and operated a photo finishing outfit. The turning point came when Nathan began selling used records and realized there was a demand not being met by the major labels.

By concentrating on "the music of the little people" (by which he meant, basically, blacks and southern whites), Nathan built a substantial empire. At its peak, his operation included a half-dozen different labels, publishing companies, a pressing plant, mastering and printing facilities, a national distribution network with thirty-two branch offices, and even his own trucking fleet. Nathan's operation would serve, in varying degrees, as a blueprint for scores of subsequent independent labels.

Nathan's other main contributions were recognizing that the lines between white and black styles of music were arbitrary and artificial, and encouraging his writers, artists, musicians, and staff to blur those lines whenever possible. In that, he anticipated (and helped to create) rock & roll and all that would follow. —*Jon Hartley Fox*

National Barn Dance
established in Chicago, Illinois, April 19, 1924; ended 1960

The *National Barn Dance* was one of the most popular and influential of the radio barn dances and was the first such program to have an extended life on the air. It began on Saturday night, April, 19, 1924, broadcast over Chicago's WLS, a station then owned by Sears, Roebuck and Company.

Originally named the *WLS Barn Dance,* it was the brainchild of WLS executive Edgar L. Bill, and one of its first announcers was GEORGE D. HAY, who would later become famous as the originator and announcer of the GRAND OLE OPRY. The first *WLS Barn Dance* program featured the down-home music of old-time fiddler Tommy Dandurand, who, with square dance caller Tom Owen, re-created the sounds of the old-fashioned country barn dance. Because of the voluminous and enthusiastic response from listeners to the initial broadcast, the *WLS Barn Dance* became a regular Saturday-night feature that was aimed deliberately at both rural and urban listeners. Early on, the program's diverse roster balanced sentimental pop singers such as tenor Henry Burr and contralto Grace Wilson with more rustic acts such as folk balladeer BRADLEY KINCAID and the husband-and-wife team LULU BELLE & SCOTTY.

By October 1, 1928, when Sears sold WLS to *The Prairie Farmer,* a Midwestern farm newspaper, the *WLS Barn Dance*'s Saturday night broadcast time had expanded to almost five and a half hours (7:35 P.M. to 1:00 A.M.). The following year, the program moved to the *Prairie Farmer*'s new office building on Chicago's Washington Boulevard. Burridge D. Butler, publisher of *The Prairie Farmer,* extended his noted paternalistic management style to the operation of WLS, with the result being that the *WLS Barn Dance* became even more folksy, family-oriented, and highly moralistic than ever.

In 1931, WLS became a 50,000-watt powerhouse that reached much of the central United States and southern Canada. When the demand for seats by listeners wanting to watch the weekly broadcast outgrew the studio's capacity, the show was moved from Studio A at the *Prairie Farmer*'s office building to Chicago's Eighth Street Theater, its home from March 19, 1932, to August 31, 1957.

The success of the *WLS Barn Dance* as a radio and stage production led to the sponsorship, beginning September 30, 1933, of a segment of the program on the NBC Blue Network by Miles Laboratories, makers of the then relatively unknown Alka-Seltzer antacid. With the NBC network radio connection, the show was renamed the *National Barn Dance.* When it dropped the show in 1946, Alka-Seltzer was a household word, as were the names of many of the *National Barn Dance* performers who at one time or another were cast members, such as GENE AUTRY, GEORGE GOBEL, PATSY MONTANA, RED FOLEY, the HOOSIER HOT SHOTS, and comedian Pat Buttram.

Following Alka-Seltzer's withdrawal, the *Barn Dance* was without network exposure until 1949, when it went on the ABC network with the Phillips Petroleum Company as its sponsor. In 1960 the *Prairie Farmer* sold WLS to American Broadcasting–Paramount Theaters, which changed the station's musical format to rock & roll, thereby sounding the death knell of the WLS *National Barn Dance.*

Within a few months a similar program featuring many former *National Barn Dance* artists went on the air over Chicago's WGN under the name *WGN Barn Dance;* by 1964, WGN was syndicating the program for television. The radio show lasted until about 1971. —*Wayne Daniel*

Ken Nelson
b. Caledonia, Minnesota, January 19, 1911

As the A&R man in charge of CAPITOL RECORDS' country division for many years, Kenneth F. Nelson played a major part in country music's post–World War II growth. Noted

Ken Nelson

as a generally artist-friendly producer, he brought a host of notable talents—including BUCK OWENS and MERLE HAGGARD—to the fore, showcasing them on record with a singularly crisp production style that helped define the BAKERSFIELD sound and West Coast country in general.

Nelson began his musical career in Chicago in a variety of capacities. He eventually applied for a job at Chicago radio station WJJD, where he wound up as music director, and, due to an avid interest in classical music, became the top announcer for broadcasts by the Chicago Symphony Orchestra. He involved himself with country music after the station put him in charge of their *Suppertime Frolic* hillbilly show, which required that he audition performers as well as schedule them for the program. Scouting talent all over the Midwest and the Southeast, Nelson cemented his connection to country music.

Called to Hollywood by Capitol Records, Nelson first headed the label's transcription department. In 1951 he took over LEE GILLETTE'S position as chief country A&R man when Gillette—an old friend of Nelson's from Chicago days—moved to pop A&R. In December of that year Nelson held a session with HANK THOMPSON that yielded the #1 smash "The Wild Side of Life," a success that set the pattern for Nelson's hit-making career at Capitol. Often working closely with CLIFFIE STONE, Nelson brought to Capitol and recorded the likes of FERLIN HUSKY, JEAN SHEPARD, TOMMY COLLINS, WANDA JACKSON, WYNN STEWART, and JERRY REED. Nelson, Gillette, and Stone also founded CENTRAL SONGS, a publishing company that quickly grew to dominate the West Coast country songwriting industry. (The partners sold the firm to Capitol in 1969.)

In the mid-1950s Nelson was among the powerful country music figures who embraced rock & roll early on, signing Gene Vincent after discovering the singer at Nashville's 1957 DJ CONVENTION. By then dividing his time between Nashville and Hollywood, Nelson continued to bring name talent to Capitol's roster and earned a reputation as one of the best producers in the business. Comfortable taking a laissez-faire approach in the studio, he was ideally suited to work with artists such as Buck Owens and Merle Haggard—those with their own strong, distinct artistic vision. Nelson continued to produce Haggard well into the 1970s, even after Nelson had stepped aside as head of Capitol's country division. Also active in the CMA, he remained involved in recording until his retirement in 1976.

—*Jonny Whiteside*

Rick Nelson
b. Teaneck, New Jersey, May 8, 1940; d. December 31, 1985

Eric Hilliard Nelson was born into a show business family. Dad Ozzie led a big band and mom Harriet Hilliard was the band's "canary," or female singer. Rick gained national attention on his parents' weekly radio show and later on their ABC-TV network series, *The Adventures of Ozzie and Harriet*. As the irrepressible Ricky, he made teenage girls swoon and young boys laugh at his smart-aleck one-liners.

Rick was in his teens when rockabilly hit, and he was a great admirer of ELVIS PRESLEY, CARL PERKINS, and JOHNNY CASH. When Rick expressed his desire to make a record, Ozzie, who had a keen eye for the entertainment business, threw his support behind his son. To test the waters, Ozzie circulated to L.A. record labels a film clip of Rick singing. After twenty-two misses, Ozzie got Verve Records' Barney Kessel to hear the tape. Theorizing that a known personality would be easier to break than an unknown, he agreed to a one-disc deal for the teenager. For the March 1957 session, guitarist MERLE TRAVIS and drummer Earl Palmer were brought on board. His first single was "I'm Walkin' " b/w "Teenager's Romance."

To launch Rick's singing career, Ozzie developed an entire TV episode around him. Titled "Ricky the Drummer," the show aired April 10, 1957. Two weeks later Verve re-leased the single, and within a week the single sold 500,000 copies. With his bargaining power, Ozzie was soon able to land Rick a hefty contract with IMPERIAL RECORDS.

Many consider Rick's work for Imperial some of the best rock & roll ever recorded. His band included guitarist JAMES BURTON, whose name is synonymous with Fender's Telecaster model electric guitar. From his Imperial debut in 1957 through 1962, Rick placed twenty-six singles on *Billboard's* pop chart, including a pair of number ones, "Poor Little Fool" and "Travelin' Man."

Nelson signed with DECCA in 1963, but his hits soon dried up. The onset of the British Invasion did not help the situation either. By the mid-1960s he was in a professional slump despite the quality of his records. His forays into country music with 1966's "Bright Lights and Country Music" and "Country Fever," released in 1967, went largely unnoticed.

Two years later, inspired and encouraged by BOB DYLAN's *Nashville Skyline* album, Nelson formed his Stone Canyon Band. Former Buckaroo pedal steel player Tom Brumley was recruited along with future Eagle Randy Meisner, who brought in guitarist Allen Kemp and Patrick Shanahan on drums. Nelson decided to launch his new band and sound with a live recording, *In Concert at the Troubadour*. The album was a critical success and put him back on the charts with a cover of Dylan's "She Belongs to Me." In 1972 he returned to the charts with a self-composed number, "Garden Party," which recounted his frustration with his identity as a onetime teen idol/oldies artist. For the next few years he enjoyed a limited comeback and guest-hosted an episode of *Saturday Night Live*.

In the 1980s Nelson switched from the country-rock sound he helped to forge to a rawer, rockabilly sound—complete with stand-up bass. His live shows were comprised primarily of his hits of the 1950s and 1960s.

Rick's career came to a sudden and tragic end on New Year's Eve 1985. He and bandmates were en route to a show date in Dallas when their rickety DC-3 airplane experienced heater problems and went down in flames just outside Dekalb, Texas. Nelson; his fiancée, Helen Blair; and his entire band perished in the crash. Rumors surrounded the crash, including one that Rick was free-basing cocaine, which allegedly led to the in-flight explosion. FAA findings cleared Nelson's name, but the stigma remained. In 1986 Nelson was deservedly inducted into the Rock and Roll Hall of Fame alongside his heroes. —*Chris Skinker*

REPRESENTATIVE RECORDINGS
Legendary Master Series, Volume 1 (EMI, 1990); *Legendary Master Series, Volume 2* (EMI, 1991)

Willie Nelson
b. Abbott, Texas, April 30, 1933

Since the mid-1970s Willie Hugh Nelson has emerged as one of the most versatile, enduring, and influential talents in late twentieth-century country music. As a vocal stylist, songwriter, bandleader, and even occasional movie actor, Nelson's long commercial reign (20 #1 hits and 107 chart singles between 1962 and 1993) has been outstripped only by his boundless energy as a performer and songwriter. Between the mid-1950s and the mid-1990s his recorded output has been so vast as to confound all but the most dedicated discographers.

Growing up in central Texas, Nelson came under the

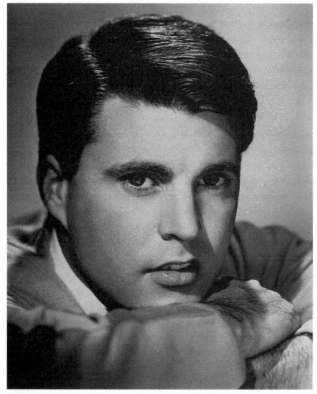

Rick Nelson

Willie Nelson

influence of a wide diversity of abiding musical influences—not just the GRAND OLE OPRY stars of the day, but also more indigenous sounds: the Texas honky-tonk of ERNEST TUBB, the western swing of BOB WILLS, and even the German-American polka bands he often played in as a youth.

Nelson did a brief stint in the air force and married Martha Mathews (the first of four wives) in 1952. He played in various local Texas bands and worked as a DJ at stations in Texas and Vancouver, Washington, where, in the mid-1950s, he made his earliest self-released recordings.

Back in Texas in the late 1950s, Nelson worked at various day jobs and performed extensively in rough-and-tumble honky-tonks in the Houston area. He had begun writing songs as a little boy, and by the 1950s he was starting to turn out fully realized masterpieces such as "Night Life" (recorded by dozens of artists over the years, including Frank Sinatra) and "Family Bible."

In 1960 Nelson relocated to Nashville, where he met songwriter HANK COCHRAN, who connected Nelson with HAL SMITH and his PAMPER MUSIC publishing house. Nelson soon blossomed as one of Music City's most gifted and prolific writers. "Crazy" (first popularized by PATSY CLINE), "Funny How Time Slips Away" (a hit for BILLY WALKER), and "Hello Walls" (FARON YOUNG) are a few of the best known of his compositions from the early 1960s. In 1963 Nelson married his second wife, Shirley Collie (ex-wife of BIFF COLLIE).

In 1962 Nelson signed his first major label recording contract, with LIBERTY RECORDS. In that same year his first two singles—"Touch Me" and "Willingly" (a duet with Shir-

ley Collie)—reached the country Top Ten. In November 1964 he became a member of the Grand Ole Opry. Yet despite numerous single and album releases on Liberty and then RCA RECORDS, it would not be until 1975 that Nelson reached the Top Ten again. His wiry baritone and his manner of phrasing—singing slightly ahead of or behind the beat, which was something he learned listening to Frank Sinatra and other pop singers—were just a bit too far off the beaten path of 1960s mainstream Nashville conventions.

In 1970, with his second marriage over and his house destroyed by fire, Nelson moved back to Texas. He was already a popular performer in his home state, and the looser, more progressive musical atmosphere of AUSTIN proved a freer milieu in which his music could evolve and flourish.

An iconoclast and something of a gypsy, Nelson, a former door-to-door salesman, has always been a brilliant, unabashed self-promoter. Thus it was with great earnestness, much foresight, and a dash of calculation that he developed a countercultural persona replete with long hair, earrings, and worn-out denim, and began courting the youthful audience that had already enabled southern rock to grow from a grassroots phenomenon to a national craze. Allying himself with longtime friend and fellow musician WAYLON JENNINGS, Nelson began laying the groundwork of what, by the mid-1970s, would explode into country music's OUTLAW movement.

In 1973 Nelson was signed to ATLANTIC RECORDS' fledgling country division by Jerry Wexler. Nelson recorded a pair of vivid and surprisingly rustic concept albums, *Shotgun Willie* and *Phases and Stages,* for the label, as well as a gospel album, *The Troublemaker.* Though the singles from these LPs had minimal impact in the charts and the sales were modest, they were still respectable and the critical reception warm.

On July 4, 1973, Nelson held his first annual Willie Nelson Picnic in Dripping Springs, Texas. Within a few years, the festival, with its star-studded cast of Nashville and Texas artists, would become a national media event in and of itself ("Woodstock South of the Brazos" was one writer's description), thus affording Nelson still more exposure.

One of Nelson's many creative high-water marks and his first real commercial breakthrough came with *The Red Headed Stranger.* This 1975 concept album was recorded in a small Texas studio on a shoestring budget. Some of the executives at COLUMBIA RECORDS, Nelson's label at this time, balked at releasing it. (Its raw minimalism, to them, suggested a mere demo record.) Yet it ultimately became the first of many million sellers Nelson would enjoy during the 1970s. From it also came Nelson's first #1 single, "Blue Eyes Cryin' in the Rain," ironically not a song written by Nelson but an ethereal version of a 1945 FRED ROSE composition.

Another milestone came in 1976 with the release of *Wanted! The Outlaws.* This compilation album, released by RCA, Nelson's former label, cleverly repackaged old recordings by Nelson and Jennings, as well as erstwhile Outlaw musician TOMPALL GLASER and Jennings's wife, singer JESSI COLTER. *The Outlaws* also quickly became country music's first LP to be certified platinum (indicating sales of 1 million copies) by the Record Industry Association of American (RIAA) and helped boost both Jennings's and Nelson's national recognition to the point that they were often paired in the public imagination as Waylon & Willie, incidentally the title of one of their LPs. Their #1 country duets include "Good Hearted Woman" (1975) and "Mamas Don't Let Your Babies Grow Up to Be Cowboys" (1978).

Though Nelson has made many fine recordings both before and since, the 1970s constituted his creative and commercial zenith. One of his many uncommon musical gifts has been his ability to assimilate and interpret many different American popular musical styles within the steadfast dimensions of his own rustic yet fluid baritone and his bedrock rural Texas musical instincts. An example of his versatility is seen in a 1977 LP, the album *To Lefty From Willie*, a heartfelt salute to country star LEFTY FRIZZELL and a tribute to Nelson's own Texas honky-tonk roots. Predictably unpredictable, Nelson followed with *Stardust* (1978), an inspired collection of classic pop songs that eventually sold 4 million copies and that is still considered one of his all-time best works.

In the late 1970s, at the height of his stardom, Nelson ventured into feature films and proved a competent actor as well. He played a supporting role with Robert Redford in *The Electric Horseman* (1979) and went on to play the lead in *Honeysuckle Rose* (1980), *The Songwriter* (1984) (with KRIS KRISTOFFERSON), and *Red-Headed Stranger* (1987). But it was in a pair of more obscure films that he really shined. In the western *Barbarosa* (1982), with actor Gary Busey, Nelson even earned accolades from Vincent Canby, film critic of the *New York Times*. Other television films in which Nelson has starred include *Where the Hell's the Gold* (1988) and *Once Upon a Texas Train* (1988).

Unsurprisingly, Nelson's immense creativity and ambition have, at times, wreaked havoc with his personal life. He and his third wife, Connie Koepke, whom he married in 1971, were divorced in 1988. In 1991 he married his fourth and present wife, Ann-Marie D'Angelo. By the early 1990s he had accumulated millions of dollars in debt to the Internal Revenue Service (he has since erased his tax burden), and in the same period of time, his son, Billy, took his own life.

Yet Nelson's passion for music-making has yet to wane. In his sixties, he has continued recording and performing with the energy of a man half his age. In 1993, he was elected to the COUNTRY MUSIC HALL OF FAME. —*Bob Allen*

REPRESENTATIVE RECORDINGS

Red Headed Stranger (Columbia, 1975); *Stardust* (Columbia, 1978); *Across the Borderline* (Columbia, 1993); *The Classic Unreleased Collection* (QVC/Rhino, 1995), 3 discs; *The Essential Willie Nelson* (RCA, 1995)

Bill Nettles

b. Natchitoches, Louisiana, March 13, 1903; d. April 5, 1967

William F. "Bill" Nettles was a noted songwriter and recording artist over a span of three decades.

A disabled navy veteran of World War I, Nettles and his brother Norman were the core of various ensembles in Shreveport—the Dixie Blue Boys, and the Nettles Brothers, for example—popular on KWKH radio, and oft recorded by Vocalion and BLUEBIRD/RCA (1937–45). In addition, Nettles is reported to have written the huge 1934 hit "Nobody's Darling But Mine" for JIMMIE DAVIS.

Nettles's own early recordings often bear Davis's name as co-writer, and in later years Nettles wrote a song about the Davis hit called "The Story of Nobody's Darling."

Nettles's beautiful "Have I Waited Too Long?" was in-troduced at KWKH in 1943 by Radio Dot and Smoky, and later became FARON YOUNG's theme song. Then, inspired by his son Bill Jr.'s navy service in World War II, Nettles wrote the song "God Bless My Darling, He's Somewhere," which became a pop hit by singer Dick Haymes. Along with Harmie Smith, Bob Shelton, Dick Hart, young WEBB PIERCE, and host Hal Burns, Nettles & His Dixie Blue Boys helped to launch a twice-weekly *LOUISIANA HAYRIDE* program on KWKH in the summer of 1945 that predated the more famous auditorium show by almost three years.

Nettles moved to Monroe, Louisiana, in 1946, and except for short performance stays in Jackson, Mississippi, and Orange, Texas, he remained there for the rest of his life. He continued to record, on the BULLET and Imperial labels, and then found perhaps his greatest success with MERCURY RECORDS. A tune he wrote and recorded for that label, "Hadacol Boogie," in a Monroe radio station in 1949, was a celebration of Dudley LeBlanc's restorative elixir. Nettles loved to write "answer" songs, such as "Answer to Blue Eyes," "It's Your Turn to Walk the Floor for Me," "I Hauled Off and Loved Her," and even answered his own songs: "(I Want to Be) Somebody's Darling" and "Hadacol Bounce."

Nettles recorded five sides for STARDAY in 1954, and retired from radio and TV work in 1958. He started his own label in Monroe, Nett Records, for which he made his last recordings during 1965–67. —*Ronnie Pugh*

New Grass Revival

Sam Bush b. Bowling Green, Kentucky, April 15, 1952

Courtney Johnson b. Barren County, Kentucky, December 20, 1939; d. June 7, 1996

Curtis Burch b. Montgomery, Alabama, January 24, 1945

Harry "Ebo Walker" Shelor b. Louisville, Kentucky, October 19, 1941

John Cowan b. Evansville, Indiana, August 24, 1952

Bela Fleck b. New York, New York, July 10, 1959

Pat Flynn b. Los Angeles, California, May 17, 1952

New Grass Revival grew out of Louisville's BLUEGRASS ALLIANCE in 1971, when SAM BUSH (mandolin), Harry "Ebo Walker" Shelor (bass), Courtney Johnson (banjo), and Curtis Burch (guitar) decided to take their music in a different direction. Having grown up under the influence of rhythm & blues and rock & roll as much as bluegrass or country music, they combined elements from these sources into "Newgrass," creating a musical style in which bluegrass instruments, usually electrified, were combined with the heavy rhythm and emotionalism of rock & roll.

New Grass Revival's music stretched beyond tradition but remained connected to earlier styles. Bush's fiddling retained the flavor that had won fiddling competitions, and Johnson's banjo work still reflected the roots of three-finger-style picking.

In performance, the extended rocklike jams on the band's STARDAY RECORDS 1972 debut album (*Arrival of the New Grass Revival*) supplanted the typical sixteen-bar instrumental break. In 1973, rock-influenced electric bassist John Cowan replaced Ebo Walker and became the band's solo vocalist; his powerful tenor, combined with Bush's intense mandolin and fiddle playing, resulted in highly charged performances.

In 1981 Johnson and Burch left, replaced by Bela Fleck on banjo and Pat Flynn on guitar. Fleck's abilities and interests suited him for the instrumental "jam" approach;

long a student of jazz performance, he added lines and phrasings akin to bebop. Flynn, a studio musician with limited road experience, possessed the skill and direction necessary to complement the other members.

With Bush the only remaining original member, the band reached its widest appeal during the 1980s. After many releases on the Flying Fish and SUGAR HILL labels, New Grass Revival signed with CAPITOL RECORDS in 1986, recording four albums. "Callin' Baton Rouge" in 1989 became their only Top Forty single. They reprised the song with Garth Brooks on his 1993 album *The Chase*. They did not fit the prevalent "hot young country" mold, however, and parted company, both with the label and with each other, in 1990.   —*Frank and Marty Godbey*

REPRESENTATIVE RECORDINGS

When the Storm Is Over/Fly Through the Country (Flying Fish, 1977/1975, 1992); *On the Boulevard* (Sugar Hill, 1985, 1989)

The New Lost City Ramblers

Mike Seeger b. New York, New York, August 15, 1933

John Cohen b. New York, New York, August 2, 1932

Tom Paley b. New York, New York, March 19, 1928

Tracy Schwartz b. New York, New York, November 13, 1938

Founded in 1958 by Mike Seeger, John Cohen, and Tom Paley, the New Lost City Ramblers were the first of the folk revival stringbands to introduce northern urban audiences to the old-time music of the rural South. From their base in Washington, D.C., and with a repertoire drawn from 78-rpm recordings and field recordings made by the Library of Congress and others in the 1920s and 1930s, the Ramblers helped to ignite an interest in old-time music that spread throughout the cities and college campuses where the folk revival was in full swing.

The band's appeal derived in part from its academic approach to the music, a welcomed departure from the commercialized representations of the Kingston Trio and other popular performers of the folk revival. Seeger, son of musicologist Charles Seeger and half brother of banjoist Pete Seeger, was steeped in folk music traditions from an early age. Yale-educated Cohen was an active member of the New York City folk scene, while Paley, a mathematician, played in folk clubs in Boston. Tracy Schwartz, another New York folkie, replaced Paley in 1963 and brought a wider range of old-time, bluegrass, Cajun, and ballad influences to the band.

The NLCR's first sixteen albums on the Folkways label served as sources of inspiration and repertoire for old-time stringbands that followed. Although the Ramblers perform only a few concerts each year, their influence can be heard today at folk concerts and square dances, and at fiddlers' conventions throughout the United States.
          —*Jack Bernhardt*

REPRESENTATIVE RECORDINGS

The New Lost City Ramblers (Folkways, 1961); *Modern Times* (Folkways, 1968)

New Riders of the Purple Sage

An important, pioneering country-rock group, the New Riders of the Purple Sage originally grew out of late sixties jam sessions between founder, songwriter-guitarist John "Marmaduke" Dawson and the Grateful Dead's Jerry Garcia, who was then experimenting with steel guitar. The jams soon coalesced into a working group, and the New Riders became the Grateful Dead's popular opening act. By the early seventies, the New Riders were recording for COLUMBIA RECORDS and had branched out on their own.

The New Riders' classic lineup included Dawson, guitarist Dave Nelson, steel guitarist Buddy Cage, drummer Spencer Dryden (formerly with Jefferson Airplane), and a string of bassists including Skip Battin and Stephen Love. The group's early albums spawned the country-rock explosion of the mid-seventies. Hits included "Louisiana Lady," "Henry," "Dead Flowers," and the signature PETER ROWAN–penned anthem "The Adventures of Panama Red," from the band's gold album of the same name. By the time the band signed with MCA RECORDS in 1976, it had begun to lose momentum and direction.

Only Dawson remained from the group's heyday by 1982, but key additions included multi-instrumentalist Rusty Gauthier, and the New Riders have continued to tour and record into the nineties, releasing in 1994 a live album made during a 1993 tour of Japan.   —*Kevin Coffey*

REPRESENTATIVE RECORDINGS

New Riders of the Purple Sage (Columbia, 1971); *The Adventures of Panama Red* (Columbia, 1973)

New Tradition

Danny Roberts b. Louisville, Kentucky, July 30, 1963

Richie Dotson b. Dickson, Tennessee, October 5, 1966

Ken White b. Louisville, Kentucky, February 2, 1965

Ray Cardwell b. Springfield, Missouri, July 11, 1963

Founded in the early 1980s by mandolin player Danny Roberts and banjoist Richie Dotson, New Tradition fashions crisp, hard-driving, contemporary bluegrass gospel music that draws from country, southern gospel, and jazz.

In 1990 the band signed with the newly formed Brentwood Music label and expanded from its regional base in and around Tennessee to a national circuit of festivals, churches, and clubs. The next year New Tradition was named top bluegrass band by the Society for the Preservation of Bluegrass Music in America (SPGMA).

Each of New Tradition's five albums for Brentwood shows a different side of this talented quartet. Early albums emphasized gospel standards, such as "Are You Washed in the Blood," along with original songs featuring lyrics by lead vocalist Daryl Mosely (b. Waverly, Tennessee, September 21, 1964) that reiterate evangelical concerns with atonement, salvation, and family values. Their 1992 release *Love Here Today* is a secular package juxtaposing original songs with pop, country, and bluegrass standards by such artists as the Beatles, MERLE HAGGARD, and BILL MONROE.

New Tradition returned to an all-gospel format in 1993 with *Closer Than It's Ever Been*. In that year, bass player and vocalist Mosley and guitarist Fred Duggin left the band and were replaced by Ray Cardwell and Ken White, respectively. The new lineup released *Old Time Gospel Jamboree*, an instrumental album of gospel standards, in 1994.

The current band lineup includes vocalist and bassist

Mosely, mandolinist Roberts, banjoist Aaron McDaris (b. Springfield, Missouri, December 5, 1975), and guitarist Jamie Clifton (b. Tulsa, Oklahoma, August 29, 1971).

—*Jack Bernhardt*

REPRESENTATIVE RECORDINGS

Closer Than It's Ever Been (Brentwood, 1993); *Old Time Gospel Jamboree* (Brentwood, 1994)

New Traditionalism

The term "new traditionalism" was coined in the mid-1980s to describe the phenomenon of young country artists (such as RICKY SKAGGS, GEORGE STRAIT, and RANDY TRAVIS) deliberately returning to older country styles, such as honky-tonk and bluegrass, and adapting them to the modern commercial environment. This movement back to the past, however, was nothing new for country music. When country music's commercial history began in the 1920s, musicians tended to perform material that was old and familiar, and some of their songs and styles of performance even exhibited the marks of Old World origin. Performers, however, were not resistant to new ideas; songs of more recent vintage—from the worlds of ragtime, blues, jazz, and Tin Pan Alley—also entered their repertories with great frequency. Resistance to change, or the insistence on stylistic purity, was as likely to come from recording directors, radio station executives, or advertisers as from the performers themselves. Occasionally a performer such as BRADLEY KINCAID might hold his own material up as more authentic and more morally edifying than other forms of country music, or BILL MONROE might quietly develop his own stringband style and high-lonesome style of singing as examples of country music "as she should be sung and played" (to use Monroe's famous phrase), but conscious, organized campaigns to resist innovation, or to build conservative alternatives to pop styles, have been rare. No one in country music really resisted the smooth, pop sounds of VERNON DALHART, GENE AUTRY, EDDY ARNOLD, BOB WILLS, RED FOLEY, or JIM REEVES. More traditional musicians, in fact, often borrowed or absorbed elements introduced by these "country-pop" stylists, and performers with widely divergent styles typically performed together at personal appearances or barn dances. Largely in the wake of ELVIS PRESLEY's great impact, however, an increasing number of country fans, musicians, and collectors began to complain about the weakening or disappearance of traditional country music. The complaints grew much stronger with the emergence of country-pop in the sixties, and especially after the country music industry became so infatuated with crossover records. For those who were concerned with the preservation of country music's identity, it was easy to see someone like RAY PRICE, whose honky-tonk recordings stood in such dramatic contrast to the dominant pop sounds of the late fifties, as a savior of country music purity (although he seems never to have viewed himself in this manner).

Not until the the eighties, though, do we find a conscious campaign to bolster the forces of tradition. Ricky Skaggs, for example, sought to build a tradition-based but commercial sound centered around the bluegrass idiom he had grown up with, while also restoring a tone of moral purity within the country music industry. Although Skaggs's overall style represented a synthesis of bluegrass, honky-tonk, and western swing, and was broadly appealing to fans who loved old-time country music, he also utilized an intensely electric and eclectic style of instrumentation that borrowed heavily from contemporary rock music and that clearly exhibited the marks of the time he had spent as front man for EMMYLOU HARRIS's Hot Band. Other singers were not so self-conscious in their attachments to tradition, nor as concerned about the moral image of modern country music as Skaggs, but they nevertheless became identified with the new traditionalist movement. George Strait (whose debut came in 1981, with "Unwound"), drew from western swing, while JOHN ANDERSON exhibited influences drawn from both LEFTY FRIZZELL and rockabilly music. Once it was demonstrated that hard-core country sounds could be commercial, the record labels began looking for young and attractive singers who could perform creditably in styles that seemed to be tradition-based. Consequently, REBA MCENTIRE (who was only marginally traditional, but attractive and immensely talented), and Randy Travis (who was good, handsome, *and* traditional), became the new stars of the movement in the mid-eighties. Since their commercial success paralleled, and largely prompted, country music's great expansion in those years, they encouraged an even greater preoccupation with traditional styles among both musicians and recording companies. Neotraditionalists now flourish in country music, along with those who are friendlier to pop sounds. Few are as assertive about their traditionalism as DWIGHT YOAKAM and MARTY STUART, both of whom proudly flaunt their "hillbilly" credentials and identify with older performers, but a wide range of performers, such as KEITH WHITLEY, PATTY LOVELESS, IRIS DEMENT, MARK CHESNUTT, ALAN JACKSON, and others too numerous to mention, have been identified as neotraditionalists. Few of these performers, however, are unabashed, uncompromising hard-core stylists. Most of them exhibit an awareness of and a liking for much of the youth-oriented music that predominated during the 1970s and 1980s. Marty Stuart, for example, speaks with reverence about such bluegrass mentors as FLATT & SCRUGGS, but also performs with passion music borrowed from rockabilly, southern rock, and soul sources. In country music, tradition is clearly a relative term, and it encompasses a broad range of stylistic preferences.

—*Bill C. Malone*

Mickey Newbury
b. Houston, Texas, May 19, 1940

Like his friend KRIS KRISTOFFERSON, Milton Sim "Mickey" Newbury Jr. was among the first Nashville singer-songwriters who helped broaden the scope of mainstream country writing in the late 1960s. Among his best-known compositions, his semipsychedelic "Just Dropped In (To See What Condition My Condition Was In)" helped launch KENNY ROGERS and the First Edition to stardom in 1968, while "An American Trilogy," his musical montage of "Dixie," "Battle Hymn of the Republic," and "All My Trials," became a staple in the concerts of ELVIS PRESLEY after Newbury himself took it to #26 on the pop charts in 1971–72.

The cultural melting pot of fast-growing Houston provided a varied and rich creative environment for young Newbury, who absorbed the influences of country, r&b, and jazz—all genres that would later be tucked into his soulful lyrics and gentle melodies. His father and uncles leaned toward the country sounds of ERNEST TUBB and JIMMIE RODGERS, but in the mid-1950s Newbury discovered r&b vocal groups such as the Flamingos and the Penguins. His first group, in which Newbury sang tenor harmony, performed such songs as "Annie Had a Baby" and "Earth Angel," and his later heartfelt ballads—many sad and dark—emphasized blues more than country.

During his senior year in high school, Newbury began writing songs. He spent the years 1959 to 1963 in the U.S. Air Force, then later took his songs to Nashville, where he was signed to a writer's contract by WESLEY ROSE of ACUFF-ROSE PUBLICATIONS. Besides "Just Dropped In," Newbury composed "Here Comes the Rain, Baby," which EDDY ARNOLD took to both the country and the pop charts in 1968. DOTTIE WEST and DON GIBSON charted as a duo with Newbury's "Sweet Memories"—a song later recorded by WILLIE NELSON—and ROGER MILLER also recorded Newbury material.

As a performer, Newbury recorded for MERCURY, RCA. ELEKTRA, and other labels, but his only notable chart success was "An American Trilogy," released on Elektra in 1971. Though his delicately crafted records never cracked the country Top Fifty, his significance as a songwriter has remained undiminished. He eventually moved to Eugene, Oregon, where he now resides. —*Gerry Wood*

REPRESENTATIVE RECORDINGS

Looks Like Rain (Mercury, 1969); *Nights When I Am Sane* (Winter Harvest, 1994)

Jimmy C. Newman
b. High Point, Louisiana, August 27, 1927

One of the few Cajun artists to enjoy major success in mainstream country music, Jimmy Yeve Newman grew up on a farm about ten miles from Mamou, in the heart of Cajun country. In his youth he was mostly influenced by country music stars—JIMMIE RODGERS, the CARTER FAMILY, BOB WILLS—and movie cowboys such as ROY ROGERS and GENE AUTRY. It wasn't until Newman began his professional career in 1946 with Cajun fiddler Chuck Guillory that he began to learn Cajun music. During this formative period, he came to admire Cajun artists such as IRY LEJEUNE and HARRY CHOATES. As a member of Guillory's Rhythm Boys, Jimmy sang mostly hillbilly songs in English, along with a few Cajun songs in French.

In 1951 he made his first solo disks for the Feature label, where he cut Cajun-country songs such as "Wondering" and "I Made a Big Mistake." It was also during the early 1950s that he became a regular on the *LOUISIANA HAYRIDE,* before moving to Nashville where he recorded "Cry, Cry, Darlin'," a Top Twenty hit on the DOT label. Newman had become a member of the GRAND OLE OPRY by 1956, and had his biggest hit to date, "A Fallen Star," in 1957. It was during this time that Nashville DJ T. Tommy Cutrer gave Jimmy the middle name Cajun, and the "C" stuck.

Newman moved on to MGM, and then to DECCA, where he enjoyed a long string of hits, including "Alligator Man" (1961), "Bayou Talk" (1962), "Artificial Rose" (1965), and "Born to Love You" (1968). In 1974 Jimmy returned to his Cajun roots and recorded the *Jimmy Newman Sings Cajun* album for the regional La Louisianne label in Lafayette, Louisiana. One cut from that album, "Lache Pas La Patate," sold more than 200,000 copies in French-speaking Canada, qualifying for a gold record. He continues to in-clude strong elements of the Cajun sound—the accordion and fiddle—in his music. —*Charlie Seemann*

REPRESENTATIVE RECORDINGS

Folk Songs of the Bayou Country (Decca, 1963); *Jimmy Newman Sings Country Songs* (Decca, 1966); *Bob a Hula-Diggy Liggy Lo* (Bear Family, 1990)

Roy Newman
b. Santa Anna, Texas, November 12, 1899; d. February 23, 1981

Leader of one of the jazziest western swing bands, Roy Newman began his career in the 1920s as a staff guitarist as Dallas's WRR. He switched to piano in midcareer, with MILTON BROWN's pioneering pianist Fred "Papa" Calhoun as his model. Newman formed the Wanderers in 1931 with multi-instrumentalist-vocalist DICK REINHART and bassist-vocalist Bert Dodson but split with the group in 1933 to form his own band around the Rhythm Aces, a band that included guitarist JIM BOYD, jazz fiddler Thurman Neal, fiddler Art Davis, and tenor banjoist Walker Kirkes. Roy Newman & His Boys shared time with BILL BOYD's Cowboy Ramblers on WRR's *Noon Hour Varieties* and landed a Vocalion contract in 1934. Newman based his style on Brown's Musical Brownies but with even greater jazz emphasis, typically featuring tunes such as "Tiger Rag" and "Weary Blues." The vaudeville clarinetist Holly Horton and the bluesy vocalist Earl Brown were important 1935 additions. Newman's summer 1935 sessions also featured the early electric guitar work of Jim Boyd.

By 1937 Newman's band included former Milton Brown stalwarts fiddler CECIL BROWER and steel guitarist BOB DUNN. Although Jim Boyd left in 1938, Newman added a future star, guitarist-vocalist Gene Sullivan, and replaced Brower with another excellent fiddler, Carroll Hubbard, from W. LEE O'DANIEL's group. Newman made his last recordings in 1939 and gave up his band in 1940. He is remembered, however, for his unusual repertoire, the impeccable musicianship of his bands, and as one of the most important bandleaders of early western swing. —*Kevin Coffey*

REPRESENTATIVE RECORDING

Roy Newman & His Boys, Volume 1, 1934–38 (Origin Jazz Library, 1981)

The Newman Brothers
Henry J. "Hank" Newman b. Cochran, Georgia, April 3, 1905; d. July 25, 1978
Marion Alonzo "Slim" Newman b. Cochran, Georgia, June 18, 1910; d. October 1, 1982
Robert "Bob" Newman b. Cochran, Georgia, October 16, 1915; d. October 8, 1979

The Newman Brothers, also known as the Georgia Crackers, gained fame as the Midwest's answer to the SONS OF THE PIONEERS. Hank and Slim migrated northward from rural Georgia and worked on radio in Ohio and Pennsylvania, cutting a session for Vocalion in 1934 with a sound akin to VERNON DALHART and CARSON ROBISON. After Bob joined in 1935, they worked as a harmony trio. Usually based at WHKC–Columbus, Ohio, the Newmans performed in three Charles Starrett films and recorded for

RCA in the late forties. From 1950 through 1952 Bob recorded twenty-five solo sides for KING RECORDS.

—*Ivan M. Tribe*

REPRESENTATIVE RECORDINGS

The Georgia Crackers (Jewel, 1976); *Bob Newman: Hangover Boogie* (Bear Family, 1984)

Newport Folk Festival

In 1959 producers George Wein and Albert Grossman created a folk music festival at Newport, Rhode Island, which had already been renowned as the site of an annual jazz festival. That summer and in the following year, they brought in the big names of the folk revival (the Kingston Trio, Odetta, Oscar Brand, Jean Ritchie, Pete Seeger, and others), but the festivals were financial failures. The matter would have ended there except for Pete Seeger; his wife, Toshi; his sister, Peggy; and Peggy's husband-to-be, Ewan MacColl, who proposed the establishment of a non-profit foundation as the festival's basis, with minimum payment to all performers, so the big names could underwrite the lesser-known traditional artists. With that premise, the Newport Folk Foundation was established and ran a festival every year between 1963 and 1969.

The 1963 event attracted 40,000—a great improvement over the earlier festivals—and the 1965 attendance was twice as large. Then, in 1970, in response to complaints of Newport's denizens who objected to the crowds, noise, and disruptions, the festival was canceled and was not held again. While Newport featured some of the biggest names in the folk revival, it also served to launch national careers for others, such as Joan Baez, who made her initial Newport appearance as an officially unscheduled guest singer invited by Bob Gibson. More importantly, in its heyday Newport offered a stage on which country, bluegrass, and traditional folk artists were as welcome as the stars of the folk revival. Newport provided the first exposure of many northern college folk fans to bluegrass music, starting with the appearance of EARL SCRUGGS (backed by HYLO BROWN & the Timberliners) and the STANLEY BROTHERS, both at the first 1959 event, followed by other eminent bands in later years, including BILL MONROE, FLATT & SCRUGGS, JIM & JESSE, and the Kentucky Colonels. On the other hand, Newport and similar events made bluegrass musicians, whose performances had been confined principally to the southeastern corner of the United States, aware of potential audiences in other regions of the country. Moreover, bluegrass and mainstream country musicians (including ROY ACUFF and JOHNNY CASH), seeing the interest in traditional folk material, modified their own repertoires accordingly, dusting off older numbers or even devoting entire albums to folk themes.

—*Norm Cohen*

Ernie Newton

b. Hartford, Connecticut, November 7, 1909; d. October 17, 1976

Ernest Newton was probably the most frequently used stand-up acoustic bass player in Nashville recording sessions from 1946 through the late 1950s. Orphaned at five, Newton ran away at fifteen and performed in MINSTREL SHOWS. He performed at WLS in Chicago with Bob Gardner (MAC & BOB) in 1933, recorded with the Hilltoppers (1935), and then joined LES PAUL's Trio. RED FOLEY engaged Newton for the GRAND OLE OPRY when Foley came

to host the *Prince Albert Show* portion of the Opry in 1946. Newton was the first bassist in Nashville to use a drumhead mounted on his bass for rhythmic effect. (Between plucking the strings, Newton would hit the drumhead with a brush held in his right hand.) Newton's touch has enhanced classics such as Foley's "Chattanoogie Shoe Shine Boy," HANK SNOW's "I'm Movin' On," and JOHNNIE & JACK's "Poison Love." On the latter, Newton used maracas to create a Latin beat. During the 1960s he left music to become a golf pro.

—*Walt Trott*

Juice Newton

b. Lakehurst Naval Base, New Jersey, February 18, 1952

During the early 1980s, a time when many country acts were consciously tailoring their sound for potential pop radio airplay, Judy Kay "Juice" Newton crossed over between the two formats naturally with her country-rock hybrid sound. Such hits of hers as "Angel of the Morning," "Queen of Hearts," and "Break It to Me Gently" were among the major successes of that era.

Newton picked up the nickname "Juice" as a child in Virginia Beach and eventually adopted it as her legal name. Spurred by her brother's r&b records and a $120 España guitar that her mother gave her as a gift, Newton decided on music as a career and headed for California after graduation. There she enrolled at Foothill College, where she met up with Otha Young, a guitar-playing songwriter who would become her musical partner. Their first group, Dixie Peach, later became Juice Newton & Silver Spur and recorded for RCA in 1975.

Later signed to CAPITOL as a solo artist, Newton languished on the label until 1981, when her remake of the 1968 Merrilee Rush hit "Angel of the Morning" became a Top Five pop single and broke into the country charts as well. She quickly followed with the format-breaking smashes "Queen of Hearts," "The Sweetest Thing (I've Ever Known)" (written by Young), "Love's Been a Little Bit Hard on Me," and the Grammy-winning "Break It to Me Gently."

Though her pop success turned out to be short-lived, Newton, back on RCA, extended her run on the country charts for several years with such mid-1980s #1 singles as "You Make Me Want to Make You Mine," "Hurt," and "Both to Each Other (Friends and Lovers)," a duet with EDDIE RABBITT.

—*Tom Roland*

REPRESENTATIVE RECORDINGS

Juice (Capitol, 1981); *Old Flame* (RCA, 1985)

Olivia Newton-John

b. Cambridge, England, September 26, 1948

Though far better known as a million-selling pop singer and a star of films such as *Grease* (1978), Olivia Newton-John had such an impact on country radio in the mid-1970s that she was the CMA's controversial choice as Female Vocalist of the Year in 1974.

The daughter of a musically inclined Welshman, Newton-John moved with her family to Australia, where her father became master of Ormond College in Melbourne. She began singing in her early teens, and at age sixteen she won a trip to England in a talent contest. With another Australian singer, Pat Carroll, she appeared as the duet Pat & Olivia on BBC-TV and in cabarets for two years.

In 1971 Newton-John recorded her first single—BOB DYLAN's "If Not for You"—which became an international hit. She toured Europe with the Cliff Richard Show and was voted Best British Girl Singer in 1971 and 1972 by the readers of *Record Mirror*.

Newton-John first hit the U.S. country music charts in 1973 with the Top Ten single "Let Me Be There." She followed this during 1974–75 with "If You Love Me (Let Me Know)," "I Honestly Love You," and "Have You Never Been Mellow"—all of which were huge crossover hits. Nevertheless, her selection as 1974 Female Vocalist of the Year angered many in Nashville and incited a public debate about the merits of the country-pop trends of the era.

In late 1997, after her career had taken her in many other directions, Newton-John signed with MCA Nashville. As of this writing her first MCA album was slated for release in spring 1998. —*Gerry Wood*

REPRESENTATIVE RECORDINGS

Have You Never Been Mellow (MCA, 1975); *Come on Over/Clearly Love* (MCA, 1975)

Roy Nichols
b. Chandler, Arizona, October 21, 1932

One of the most admired and distinctive guitar stylists in all of country music, Roy Nichols and his angular, elegant explorations of a song's melody helped redefine "takeoff," or lead, country guitar from the late 1940s forward. For many years a member of MERLE HAGGARD's backup band, the Strangers—both live and on record—Nichols and his crackling, moody Fender Telecaster also helped create the famous BAKERSFIELD sound.

Arriving in Fresno, California, in 1934, Nichols was accompanying his fiddle-playing father at local dances by age eleven. At fourteen he worked with acts such as Curley Roberts & the Rangers and Elwin Cross, and at one point he led his own band. In 1948 Nichols's already impressive abilities earned him a prestige job as guitarist for MADDOX BROTHERS & ROSE, California's top hillbilly band. (Fred Maddox was named the sixteen-year-old Nichols's guardian.) For the next two years Nichols recorded and toured extensively with the Maddoxes. But fired by their mother, Lula Maddox, during an engagement in Las Vegas, he returned to California and broadcast with Smiley Maxedon on KNGS-Hanford.

In 1953 Nichols toured with LEFTY FRIZZELL and played on some of Frizzell's classic JIMMIE RODGERS tribute recordings. In 1955 Nichols moved to Bakersfield. He joined KERO television's daily *Cousin Herb Henson* show and soon found himself working with WYNN STEWART; in 1960 Nichols moved to Las Vegas to back Stewart at the singer's Nashville Nevada club. Nichols then joined Haggard's Strangers in 1965, thus beginning an artistic alliance that has deeply influenced the overall tone of contemporary country.

Road-weary, Nichols finally left the Strangers in March 1987, though he continued to make sporadic appearances with Fred & Rose Maddox into the early 1990s. He suffered a debilitating stroke in 1996, but at the time of this writing he was slowly recovering. —*Jonny Whiteside*

Nitty Gritty Dirt Band
Jeff Hanna b. Detroit, Michigan, July 11, 1947
Jimmie Fadden b. Long Beach, California, March 9, 1948
John McEuen b. Oakland, California, December 19, 1945
Jim Ibbotson b. Philadelphia, Pennsylvania, January 21, 1947
Bob Carpenter b. Philadelphia, Pennsylvania, December 26, 1946

Originating as a jug band during the 1960s folk movement, the Southern California–based Nitty Gritty Dirt Band quickly evolved into one of America's first successful country-rock groups. Significantly affecting Nashville's country

Nitty Gritty Dirt Band: (from left) Bob Carpenter, John McEuen (seated), Jimmy Ibbotson, Jeff Hanna, and Jimmie Faden

music community, they introduced such veteran artists as ROY ACUFF, JIMMY MARTIN, MOTHER MAYBELLE CARTER, DOC WATSON, and EARL SCRUGGS to a young rock-oriented audience as collaborators on their historic *Will the Circle Be Unbroken* album, a three-disc set released on United Artists in 1972. A sequel, with guests including CHRIS HILLMAN, RICKY SKAGGS, various members of the JOHNNY CASH and Scruggs families, NEW GRASS REVIVAL, and others, was released on Universal Records in 1989. It didn't do nearly as well commercially, though it won a host of industry awards.

More than thirty years after their first gig—May 13, 1966, at the Paradox Club in Orange County, California—the NGDB continues, headed by founding members Jeff Hanna (vocals, guitar) and Jimmie Fadden (drums, harmonica, vocals). The original lineup also included Les Thompson, Bruce Kunkel, Ralph Barr, and singer-guitarist Jackson Browne. Though Browne had left by the time of the band's first album (*The Nitty Gritty Dirt Band*, LIBERTY RECORDS, 1967), the group recorded his compositions, including "Buy for Me the Rain" (their first pop hit, reaching #45), and "Jamaica Say You Will." They were also among the first to record songs by Kenny Loggins ("House at Pooh Corner," 1970), Mike Nesmith, RODNEY CROWELL, JOHN HIATT, and DON SCHLITZ.

Personnel have changed frequently through the years, with singer-songwriter and guitarist Jim Ibbotson having the third-highest current seniority, having joined in 1969. Other members along the way have included John McEuen (whose brother Bill managed the group for many years), Chris Darrow, and, for a while, EAGLES veteran Bernie Leadon. The current lineup, with Hanna, Fadden, Ibbotson, and keyboardist Bob Carpenter (who joined c. 1978), has remained intact as a quartet since 1989. They've been based in Colorado since 1970.

Recording for WARNER BROS., the Nitty Gritty Dirt Band enjoyed a particularly strong hit streak on country radio during 1984–90. Their Top Five singles included "Long Hard Road (the Sharecropper's Dream)," "High Horse," "Modern Day Romance," "Fishin' in the Dark," and "I've Been Lookin'. " The band subsequently moved to Universal, to MCA, back to Liberty, and, in 1996, to Rising Tide.

In 1968 the group spent several months in Oregon filming the musical *Paint Your Wagon,* though much of their contribution wound up on the cutting-room floor. They also appeared in the 1969 exploitation picture *For Singles Only.*

Jeff Hanna married country singer-songwriter Matraca Berg on December 5, 1994. —*Todd Everett*

REPRESENTATIVE RECORDINGS

Will the Circle Be Unbroken (United Artists, 1972); *Twenty Years of Dirt: The Best of the Nitty Gritty Dirt Band* (Warner Bros., 1986); *The Chrismas Album* (Rising Tide, 1997)

Hoyle Nix
b. Azel, Texas, March 22, 1918; d. August 21, 1985

West Texas fiddler, bandleader, and exponent of the BOB WILLS sound, Hoyle Nix helped keep western swing alive on the Texas dance-hall circuit for almost forty years. A longtime resident of Big Spring, Texas, Nix and his younger brother Ben (1920–94) formed the West Texas Cowboys in 1946. The band's first recordings were made for the Dallas-based Star Talent label in 1949. "Big Ball's in Cowtown," the first Star Talent release and a Hoyle Nix

folk-derived re-write, proved to be an enduring standard. He also recorded for Queen, Caprock, Bo-Kay, Stampede, Winston, and Oil Patch. Stampede was his own label, named after his Big Spring dance hall. By the early 1960s Nix's two sons, Larry (b. 1940) and Jody (b. 1952), had become regular members of the band. Throughout his career Nix readily acknowledged the influence of Bob Wills. The two first worked together in 1952 and soon became lifelong friends. The respect that Wills had for Nix was evidenced when he invited Hoyle and Jody to participate on his swan song, the 1974 album *For the Last Time.* After Nix's death Jody took over leadership of the band, thus ensuring that another generation of Texans would be dancing to the music of a Nix fiddle. —*Joe W. Specht*

REPRESENTATIVE RECORDINGS

Hoyle Nix & His West Texas Cowboys (Oil Patch, 1977); *Jody Nix: When It's All Said and Done* (JN, 1995)

Eddie Noack
b. Houston, Texas, April 29, 1930; d. February 5, 1978

Singer-songwriter D. Armona "Eddy" Noack is probably best remembered as the composer of the inspirational classic "These Hands," although his disturbing 1968 recording of LEON PAYNE's "Psycho" on the K-Ark label has long been a cult favorite, covered by, among others, rock singer Elvis Costello.

Noack had already earned a degree in journalism and English from the University of Houston when he decided on a music career. After winning an amateur contest in 1947, he performed on radio for the first time in Baytown, Texas. Two years later, Noack recorded his first single, "Gentlemen Prefer Blondes," for the Gold Star label. However, Noack's big break came in 1956, when HANK SNOW's recording of "These Hands" was released. It reached #5 on the country charts and finally brought Noack recognition. Written the previous year when Noack was in the army, it was originally meant as a statement for the workingman, not a testimony of faith.

Throughout the fifties, Noack continued to drift through various record companies without any success. He signed with PAPPY DAILY's D RECORDS in 1958 and finally had a moderate hit, "Have Blues Will Travel." He also recorded a few rockabilly tunes under the pseudonym Tommy Wood. During the sixties he relocated to Nashville, where he worked for both LEFTY FRIZZELL's and Daily's publishing companies. Also during this time, GEORGE JONES (then produced by Daily) recorded several of Noack's songs as album cuts: "No Blues Is Good News," "For Better or For Worse (But Not For Long)," and "Barbara Joy."

Noack died of an apparent cerebral hemorrhage. —*Don Roy*

Norma Jean
b. near Welliston, Oklahoma, January 30, 1938

Norma Jean Beasler (known professionally as Norma Jean) was a popular recording artist and television star of the 1960s, and a protégée of PORTER WAGONER. Her cheerful, sisterlike smile and uncompromising, woman-oriented songs (written by other writers) created an enduring image of likable femininity.

A farmer's daughter, she moved with her family to

Oklahoma City, where at age twelve she traded her bicycle for a guitar. Her aunt taught her to play, and while still in school she had three weekly radio spots on KLPR. Her chief influence was KITTY WELLS. After working with western swing bands, Norma Jean joined *Jubilee USA* (ABC-TV) in 1958 and before its termination met Porter Wagoner, then a guest on the show.

In 1960 she moved to Nashville, soon joining the *Porter Wagoner Show* on syndicated television, where she was known as Pretty Miss Norma Jean. After an unsuccessful debut on COLUMBIA RECORDS in 1959, she moved to RCA in 1963. Her first hit, "Let's Go All the Way" (#11, 1964), became her best-known song. Of her twenty-two chart records, her highest was "The Game of Triangles" (#5, 1966), recorded with BOBBY BARE and LIZ ANDERSON. On most of her records, Porter Wagoner functioned as de facto producer. Though he and Norma Jean occasionally sang live duets, they never recorded as a duo. She was a member of the GRAND OLE OPRY cast from 1965 through 1969.

She left Wagoner's show in 1967 (and was replaced by DOLLY PARTON) to marry Harold "Jody" Taylor, yet stayed with RCA until 1973. A confessed recovered alcoholic and devout Christian, Norma Jean is again a Nashville entertainer, married to musician George Riddle. —*Steve Eng*

REPRESENTATIVE RECORDINGS

Let's Go All the Way (RCA, 1964); *Jackson Ain't a Very Big Town* (RCA, 1967); *I Guess That Comes from Being Poor* (RCA, 1972)

Jim Ed Norman
b. Fort Myers, Florida, October 16, 1948

Jim Ed Norman is regarded as a music business visionary with a strong sense of community responsibility. He played a major role in the resurgence of traditional country music in the late 1980s by nurturing the careers of RANDY TRAVIS, DWIGHT YOAKAM, and TRAVIS TRITT. As founding president of Leadership Music he has made a major contribution to the Nashville business community.

Norman's preacher father played trumpet; his mother played piano. A keyboard player himself, Norman went to college at North Texas State to become a music teacher. Fellow student Don Henley asked him to join a band, which took the name Shiloh. The group moved to Los Angeles, signed a deal with executive JIMMY BOWEN, and recorded an album, with KENNY ROGERS producing. Shiloh broke up eventually, and Henley went on to form the EAGLES. Though not a member, Norman arranged and conducted strings for the group and played on numerous Eagles classics.

In California, Norman also found arranging work with pop acts LINDA RONSTADT, Kim Carnes, Bob Seger, and America, among others. In 1977, Clive Davis gave Norman the opportunity to produce his first record. "Right Time of the Night" became a Top Ten pop hit for Jennifer Warnes. In great demand, Norman produced the work of Jackie DeShannon. He also began a long association with ANNE MURRAY that yielded nine albums, four Grammys, twenty-four Juno Awards, and the COUNTRY MUSIC ASSOCIATION's 1984 Single of the Year ("A Little Good News") as well as Album of the Year Awards. It was the first time a woman had won both of these awards in a single year.

In 1980 Norman opened Jensing/Jensong, a publishing

Jim Ed Norman

and production company in Los Angeles and Nashville, employing songwriters Chick Rains and Gary Nicholson. Norman continued to rack up production credits with CRYSTAL GAYLE, HANK WILLIAMS JR., JOHNNY LEE, MICKEY GILLEY, and MICHAEL MARTIN MURPHEY, among others.

Norman joined WARNER/REPRISE Nashville in 1983 as vice president of A&R, and in 1984, when company chief Bowen moved to MCA, Norman became executive vice president of Warner. He assumed the title of president in 1989, although he remained involved in A&R and in music production.

Due to the success of Travis, Yoakam, Tritt, and other Warner/Reprise artists, Norman, in the late 1980s, possessed the leverage to establish a progressive, noncountry division in Nashville. He did this for artists such as Take 6 (whom he produced), BELA FLECK & THE FLECKTONES, and Beth Nielsen Chapman (also a production project). In 1989, Norman formed a gospel and contemporary Christian label, Warner Alliance, and in 1992 he started the Warner Western label aimed at audiences of cowboy, Native American, and other western-themed music. In 1994 Warner/Reprise Nashville had its biggest sales year ever, with seven albums going gold or platinum. Norman formed another imprint, Warner Resound, in 1996, to release Christian and pop recordings.

Norman has made important contributions outside the field of music. For his efforts he has received Time/Warner's Andrew Heiskell Community Service Award in 1990, the Anti-Defamation League's Johnny Cash Americanism Award in 1993, and Leadership Music's Bridge Award in 1996, for improving relations between Nashville's music and business communities. —*Jay Orr*

Nudie the Rodeo Tailor
b. Kiev, Ukraine, December 15, 1902; d. May 9, 1984

Nudie Cohn (or Cohen) brought flash and sparkle to the western-wear costumes that became synonymous with

Nudie

country music from the 1940s through the 1960s. From GENE AUTRY to HANK WILLIAMS to ELVIS PRESLEY and GRAM PARSONS, the Brooklyn-bred Jewish tailor outfitted popular music's biggest stars with unique and often outrageous custom designs.

Nudie was quite secretive about his early life, rarely revealing his birth name and origins. The third son of a bootmaker, he was born Nutya Kotlyrenko. The young Ukrainian immigrated to New York City at age eleven (the name Nudie was an Ellis Island corruption of his real name) and first found work as a shoeshine boy on the streets of Brooklyn. After a stint as a boxer, Nudie moved in 1918 to Hollywood to get into the movies. Working sporadically as a film cutter and an extra, he eventually hitchhiked back east in 1932, on the way meeting his future wife, Bobbie Kruger, in a Mankato, Minnesota, boardinghouse. The couple eventually returned to New York, where Nudie found work first as a tailor's apprentice and later making G-strings and pasties for the burlesque queens of New York City.

In 1940 the Cohns decided to try L.A. again, setting up a small tailoring shop in their garage. Nudie's big break came seven years later, when his western designs found a fan in TEX WILLIAMS, who fronted the money for a new sewing machine and commissioned ten costumes for his band. Williams spread the word, and soon business boomed, permitting Nudie, in 1947, to open the store that would become a landmark at 5015 Lankershim Boulevard in North Hollywood. Catering to western film stars and musicians, Nudie stumbled on his signature design when he dreamed up a rhinestone-accented shirt for LEFTY FRIZZELL in late 1951.

Nudie specialized in designing embroidered motifs symbolic of the star's name or repertoire: thus, jail cells for WEBB PIERCE, wagon wheels for PORTER WAGONER, and husky dogs for FERLIN HUSKY. Beginning in the mid-1960s Nudie employed English-born embroidery artisan Rose Clements (b. Rose Grossman, London, August 13, 1919), who brought special machines with her when she moved from Britain to California. Her intricate and original designs required a great amount of skill and encompassed Swiss-, chain-, and satin stitches.

Nudie's designs first crossed over to rock & rollers when COLONEL TOM PARKER commissioned a $2,500 gold lamé suit for Elvis Presley to wear on tour in 1957. In 1968 country-rock pioneer Gram Parsons became a regular client, outfitting himself and his FLYING BURRITO BROTHERS. Nudie's top tailor, MANUEL, actually did the work (which for Parsons included embroidered marijuana leaves and naked women); Manuel would later strike out on his own. Nudie suits became *de rigueur* among California (and British) rockers, and Nudie himself was featured on the June 28, 1969, cover of *Rolling Stone*.

Nudie's personality was as flamboyant as his designs. He spun around town in an extravagantly appointed El Dorado convertible, complete with hundreds of silver dollars embedded in the dashboard and door panels, hand-tooled leather interior, pistol door handles, and an enormous pair of steer horns mounted on the front. Curiously, the gregarious designer always wore two different cowboy boots (never a matching pair) with his lavishly decorated suits and ten-gallon hat. An amateur mandolin player, he recorded one album, which he released himself and sold in his store. The liner notes featured extensive photos of Nudie arm-in-arm with his celebrity clients; these pictures also covered the walls of his shop.

After suffering deteriorating health in the early 1980s, Nudie died of kidney failure at eighty-one. DALE EVANS delivered the eulogy at his star-studded funeral. Bobbie Cohn continued to run the shop, which also stocked belts, saddles, boots, hats, and ready-to-(western)-wear, until 1994, when she retired and closed it down. In 1997 the Autry Museum of Western Heritage purchased Nudie's remaining business records and personal effects. Today Nudie suits are valuable collector's items, some worth tens of thousands of dollars. MARTY STUART is foremost among several contemporary country artists who have amassed significant collections of Nudie's extraordinary designs.

—*Holly George-Warren*

The Center of Music City:
Nashville's Music Row

John Lomax III

A tiny, unique corner of Nashville known as Music Row is the most concentrated creative center in the world. This less-than-two-square-mile area houses all the major components of the music industry: outposts of most of the world's largest recording companies, offices of multinational publishing operations, regional or national headquarters of the nation's three performance rights organizations (ASCAP, BMI, SESAC), dozens of recording studios, and all the other trappings—booking agencies, artist managers, video production companies, and PR firms—that enable Nashville to claim a place as a world music capital along with New York, Los Angeles, and London.

Among the well-known recordings made in Music Row studios have been GARTH BROOKS's multiplatinum albums; Lee Ann Rimes's triple-platinum single, "How Do I Live"; almost all of REBA McENTIRE's hits; VINCE GILL's Grammy-winning efforts; BRENDA LEE's pop smashes; all of PATSY CLINE's recordings; most of the EVERLY BROTHERS classics; SHANIA TWAIN's *The Woman in Me*; many of the classic sides of GEORGE JONES and JOHNNY CASH; and a surprising number of rock and pop hits, such as four BOB DYLAN albums, ROY ORBISON's classic 1960s sides, and many of ELVIS PRESLEY's biggest-selling records.

Though Music Row is the center of power for the industry, the area has strangely never been a popular location for live music. Aside from a couple of failed attempts in the seventies and eighties, the live entertainment industry has looked elsewhere—to the Opryland area, the downtown Broadway/Second Avenue corridor, and the West End Avenue/Elliston Place section, the three major Nashville hot spots for performance venues. It's ironic that in this area, where hundreds of demo singers, studio pickers, and recording artists create music daily, one can find hardly a single public place to hear and see live performances, with the exception of a cramped bar or two.

All the other elements of the industry, however, are found on the Row. Though a bit slow to catch on, many major Nashville banks have specialized branches there, and most of the management and booking companies are now in business on one of the major Row thoroughfares, along with music publishers, TV producers, and a host of others.

Music Row consists of Sixteenth, Seventeenth, Eighteenth, and Nineteenth Avenues South and cross streets McGavock, Roy Acuff Place, Chet Atkins Place, Horton, Edgehill, Hawkins, South Street, and sections of Division and Demonbreun. It is bounded on the south by Wedgewood, on the north by McGavock, on the east by Music Square East (known as Sixteenth after passing Grand), and on the west by Twentieth Avenue South.

The area is located less than two miles from the center of downtown and about a mile from Union Station, until 1974 Nashville's busy passenger train terminal. A tree-lined neighborhood gradually and grudgingly yielding to new office buildings, all of Music Row could fit inside part of New York's Central Park: Music Row stretches just over a mile long and is less than a half mile wide. A tourist's casual walking tour of the major sights requires only about an hour.

Though surrounded by a half million Nashville residents, Music Row today retains much of the charm of a small town or a college campus. And despite plenty of low-rise glass-and-steel office structures, all built during the seventies, eighties, and nineties, Music Row still has a neighborhood flavor, thanks to the many two-story houses that remain, most restored and refurbished into small, homey offices.

No one is sure when the name "Music Row" was coined or who titled it. The area was developed before the turn of the twentieth century as a neighborhood of majestic homes for the wealthy. Seventy-odd years ago the most prominent people in Nashville lived on Music Row: doctors, college presidents, architects, leading merchants, top railroad executives. The northern end of Music Row then featured opulent two- and three-story Victorian mansions, set back from the street, each enclosed inside wrought iron fences. The sidewalks were brick, laid in a herringbone pattern, and magnolia trees dotted the yards. Smaller cottages lined the southern end of Belmont Boulevard, as Sixteenth Avenue South was known, before all the area streets were numbered during the years 1901 to 1908.

Ward-Belmont College, a "finishing school" for young women, presided over the Row from its hillside location on the terminus of Belcourt Street (now Wedgewood). The classically styled building, modeled after a similar structure in Venice, was built in 1850 by the socially prominent Adelicia Acklen, dubbed "Music Row's first superstar" by Nashville historian Libby Fryer.

Fryer, born in 1922, lived on the northwestern corner of the Division–Demonbreun–Music Square East intersection, in a house that later served variously as a funeral parlor, a souvenir shop, a museum for cars of dead celebrities, and Gilley's nightclub. Her family moved from the area in 1928, a few miles south, to the suburb of Green Hills. At the time many believed that the neighborhood was in decline—the once-palatial home next door had become a boardinghouse. Soot from the soft coal everyone burned, smoke from the train station six blocks distant, and effluvia from passing streetcars were so prevalent that "if you went into town or spent much time outside, your underwear would be black when you returned," Fryer recalled.

Unfortunately, the first half of the twentieth century represented one long, gradual decline for the area that would become Music Row. Various economic reversals, capped by the Great Depression, decimated the fortunes of many of the families in residence. Following World War II, the rush to suburbia further diminished the neighborhood's luster. By 1955 Music Row was a blue-collar backwater, filled with decaying homes, rooming houses, duplexes, and a few small retail businesses.

Fortunately, in the postwar years, music came to the rescue. Though records were made in Nashville studios as early as December 1944, downtown locations never really clicked for music business uses owing to parking and other problems. Music Row was born when OWEN BRADLEY and brother HAROLD BRADLEY opened a studio at 804 Sixteenth Avenue South, in a house they renovated. The pair had previously operated recording facilities at Second Avenue South and Lindsley, and in a low-ceilinged room behind a jewelry store on Twenty-first Avenue South ("We didn't have echo at our studio in Hillsboro Village," Harold recalled), but the location at Sixteenth Avenue South proved to be the one that really succeeded.

PAUL COHEN of DECCA RECORDS said he was going to take his business to Dallas, to JIM BECK's studio. "Owen asked him, what if we built a studio here," Harold recalled. Cohen felt this was a good idea, offered to be a silent partner (though he never came up with the promised funds), and offered to schedule a hundred Decca sessions per year to help the Bradleys get established. Economics played a major role as well: The area on Sixteenth Avenue South had been rezoned for commercial use, and land was cheaper there than downtown.

The Bradleys bought the house for $7,500 late in 1954 and began renovation, removing the floor to create a studio with high ceilings. They built a room behind the control room and plastered it in; this became the echo chamber. The studio opened for business in 1955, and by 1956 Bradley Studio was producing such hits as Gene Vincent's "Be Bop a Lula," "Young Love" by SONNY JAMES, and "Singing the Blues" by MARTY ROBBINS. The brothers ambitiously spent another $7,500 to install a surplus army Quonset hut in back for use as a film studio, an early sound stage that became known appropriately as the "Quonset Hut." After a bit of tinkering—the original tile floor was replaced by wood, burlap insulation was installed, mood lighting made its first Nashville appearance, and isolation booths were developed for better sound separation—the sound in the Hut was improved to the point where the studio was believed to have near-magical properties. It certainly far outstripped the original facility in popularity and hits. Today the offices of Sony/ATV Tree Music stand on this spot; if you go into Sony's back parking lot you can still see a part of the old Quonset Hut's roof.

When the Bradleys bought the house at 804 Sixteenth Avenue South and began building their studio, the only music on Music Row was from De Luca's Voice School and at tent revivals held during summers on the empty lot at Sixteenth and Division (today the site of Owen Bradley Park). There were a couple of gas stations farther down Division, and the only other Music Row businesses—Piggly Wiggly, Tillman's and H. G. Hill's groceries, Seligman's 5¢ and 10¢ store, Goodman's Bakery, and Foxall's Pharmacy—were clustered around Sixteenth & Grand.

It was still a blue-collar neighborhood, filled with working people living in duplexes, apartment houses, rooming houses, and single-family dwellings. The streetcars were gone (the steel was ripped up for the war effort), traffic was light, and city buses ran through the area. The Belmont Apartments stood next to the Bradley Studio, and the area's main church was just down Sixteenth, at Grand Avenue. Music Row was racially mixed then, with black families living primarily on South Street, Hawkins, and Grand, while Villa Place, parallel to Sixteenth Avenue and a block east, was racially mixed, as it is today. Longtime resident Ludwig Reinheimer (whose family lived at 804 Sixteenth Avenue South before the Bradley purchase) remembers the area fondly from his childhood: "It was a vibrant neighborhood. It was safe, the streets were lit, we used to walk everywhere after dinner. Kids were on the streets until eight or nine o'clock. Black and white kids played together."

The Bradley Studio opened at a propitious time. In the years following World War II, record labels found it increasingly cheaper and more convenient for country artists to record in Nashville rather than in Chicago, New York, or Hollywood, the centers of the entertainment industry at the time. Paul Cohen at Decca Records in particular had led the way in the use of such Nashville sites as WSM's studios and the CASTLE RECORDING LABORATORY in the Tulane Hotel, and the label's success with such artists as WEBB PIERCE, ERNEST TUBB, RED FOLEY, KITTY WELLS, and others, many of whom were selling to a general audience, soon convinced the company's competitors to follow suit. Thus, when the Bradley Studio became operational in 1955, not only Decca but also the CAPITOL and COLUMBIA labels began booking regular sessions for their country artists at the site, and A&R men from these labels (DON LAW for Columbia and KEN NELSON for Capitol) made frequent trips to Nashville to oversee the sessions.

In 1957 RCA became the first label to open offices on Music Row when it appointed CHET ATKINS to lead its Nashville operation. That fall RCA opened a new studio and headquarters in Nashville, a block west of and around the corner from the Bradley Studio, in the 800 block of Seventeenth Avenue South. RCA had used other Nashville studios for several years, but now it made sense to locate in an area where the industry, such as it was at the time, had already established a beachhead. Thus RCA became the first major label to make a bricks-and-mortar investment in the Row.

In these days, the music business on Music Row was loose and informal. Owen Bradley recalled often deciding to do a session in the morning: "We could usually find the pickers in time to go in and cut that afternoon"—a practice unheard of today, when the top players are often booked weeks, if not months, in advance.

The growth of Music Row into the international center it has now become was an evolutionary process. Flash back to 1961, and "Record Row," as it was then called, consisted of but four business concerns: Bradley Film & Recording Studio, Atlas Artists Bureau (a booking operation), CEDARWOOD PUBLISHING, and RCA's offices. WSM and the Grand Ole Opry were still located downtown, while the ACUFF-ROSE music publishing house and its subsidiary label, HICKORY RECORDS, were on Franklin Road, several miles southeast of Music Row.

Any doubts about the long-term interests of the major labels in Record Row were dispelled early in 1962, when Columbia Records paid $300,000 for the Bradleys' Quonset Hut and surrounding property. The deal included a two-year noncompetition clause, so Owen refrained from building a new studio until that agreement expired; then he opened a new studio, Bradley's Barn, in rural Mount Juliet, some thirty miles northeast of Nashville. By 1963 the trade magazine *Broadcasting* noted that half of all U.S. recordings were being made in Nashville.

At this point the industry moved into high gear. Most other businesses opened up just north of the Bradleys. As of 1965, this area of "Record Row" included several record labels (RCA, Columbia, Decca, Capitol, ABC-Paramount), music publishers (Cedarwood, HILL & RANGE, TREE, AL GALLICO, Moss-Rose, New Keys); talent agencies (Wilhelm, HUBERT LONG), and performing rights organizations (BMI, SESAC). In 1967 the COUNTRY MUSIC HALL OF FAME AND MUSEUM opened on the former site of Rose Park at the northern end of Music Row and was soon attracting hundreds of thousands of tourists to the area. Meanwhile, industry giant ATLANTIC RECORDS, known heretofore primarily for its achievements in black music, opened its first Nashville office in 1971.

A sure sign of growth came in 1973, when Sixteenth and Seventeenth Avenues were converted to one-way thoroughfares, a move that maximized the use of the narrow streets. At that point there were no tall buildings in the area, just four blocks of two- and three-story houses with a couple of two- or three-story office complexes. The biggest building on the Row at that time was RCA's offices and studios, a half-block-long, three-story structure on Seventeenth Avenue South, built on land owned principally by Atkins, Owen Bradley, his brother Harold, and bass player BOB MOORE. Even then, when Music Row had become an acknowledged recording and publishing center, there were still few traffic lights, people parked on both sides of the streets, and most of the labels rented or leased space for their operations, except for, of course, RCA and MCA; the latter built a two-story structure at 35 Music Square West.

Music Row's first two high-rise office buildings rose in the mid-seventies, both proving to be ill-fated efforts for their visionary creators. The dark, octagonal building known as the United Artists Tower (Music Square West at Chet Atkins Place) was originally intended by Gordon Stoker and Neal Matthews as headquarters for the JORDANAIRES and was to be called the City Executive Building. However, escalating costs and other problems forced them to sell. United Artists, a label that folded many years ago, became the biggest early tenant and thus became the building's namesake when the building opened in 1975. Today the U.A. Tower houses a variety of tenants, including a few recording studios, and has been the home for many years of the monthly *Music City News* magazine. Across Music Square West, the five-story FISI Building houses the Nashville offices of *Billboard* magazine and one of the city's major recording studios; it was created as the Four Star building. Owner Joe Johnson envisioned installing recording, mastering, and pressing facilities in the structure so a song could be written on one floor, recorded on another, and emerge as a finished record from a basement manufacturing plant. Four Star went into bankruptcy after completion (wags then dubbed it the "No Star Building") and was converted into general offices. These experiences gave pause to developers—only one major new building was built on the Row between 1975 and 1988.

The fate of Music Row has been tied throughout its existence to the ups and downs of the corporate entities that have operated subsidiary divisions in the city. As the fortunes of those labels and the profits generated by Nashville have ebbed and flowed, so has their support of their "hillbilly" divisions. As long as country remained a consistent, and small, profit center, relationships remained static: Corporate headquarters sent down a budget; Nashville labels sent back more money at year's end and added new masters to the catalogue. But during the first half of the nineties, Nashville and country music's gross revenues quadrupled in just five years, from $500 million in 1989 to more than $2 billion in 1994—and that attracted the attention of the people in corporate headquarters, which by now had evolved into international conglomerates based in Germany (Bertelsmann Music Group, owners of RCA and ARISTA), England (Thorn-EMI, owners of Capitol), the Netherlands (PolyGram, owners of Mercury), Japan (Sony), and Canada (Seagram, owners of MCA). These corporate giants started to look for ways to maximize this income stream.

How did this affect Music Row? Bigger buildings sprouted all over the Row, built by companies heretofore content to rent space in buildings owned by Chet Atkins, RAY STEVENS, or various Bradleys, the chief early landlords on the Row. Music Row's largest expansion phase came during the 1985–95 period. In November 1989 Opryland Music Group, now the owner of the Acuff-Rose catalogue, set up shop in a brand-new brick edifice on Music Square West, bringing HANK WILLIAMS's catalogue of songs to a Music Row address for the first time. In 1990 BMG erected a four-story complex on Music Circle North to house its growing family of labels and publishing operation. In 1992 Mercury took over major offices on Music Square West, while Sony, the new owner of the Columbia and EPIC labels, renovated and enlarged the venerable Columbia building (the site where it all began). In 1994 MCA and WARNER BROS. each opened huge new offices on Music Square East. Meanwhile, publishing giants Warner-Chappell and EMI Music acquired and enlarged existing buildings on Music Square East, while PolyGram Music bought up the Welk Music catalogue and enlarged that building down the street. ASCAP's next-door neighbor, Sony/ATV/Tree Music, also rebuilt in the nineties after

TREE INTERNATIONAL, the city's largest publisher, was acquired in 1989 by Sony for a reported $50 million. In that year CURB RECORDS also relocated, from California to Music Square East.

ASCAP (1992) and BMI (1995) completed ambitious expansions at their existing locations; BMI thereafter moved its national administrative functions to town, going from 33 to more than 400 employees in less than a year, housed in a six-story building behind BMI's original offices on Music Square East. SESAC moved into sparkling new quarters in a two-story steel-and-glass office farther down Sixteenth in 1996. The CMA completed a new building in 1991, at the corner of Music Circle North and East; six years later, NARAS readied a move to the next overflow expansion area, in the 2000 block of Wedgewood. Reba McEntire's multimillion-dollar Starstruck headquarters was completed in 1996, the largest building on the Row devoted to a single artist's enterprises.

Although Capitol Records left the Row for a West End high-rise in 1991 (which the label shared with, among others, a branch office of the FBI), in 1996 Capitol bought property on Music Square West and built a huge structure planned for its headquarters, ironically on the same spot where the label first had rented space. In early 1998, following executive changes, the label put the building up for sale without ever moving into it.

When Capitol's building was opened in 1998, for the first time in history all of the six major multinational recording conglomerates owned buildings on Music Row. Those companies are, in addition to Capitol: Warner Bros. (home also to Reprise and Warner-Alliance), Mercury, BMG (parent to RCA, Arista, and BNA), MCA (also home to Decca), and Sony (which operates the Columbia, Epic, MONUMENT, and Lucky Dog labels).

In 1997 film industry giants Disney and DreamWorks established Nashville operations, promising synergy between their West Coast film divisions and their Music Row offices. Both labels began releasing country recordings in 1998.

By the late nineties many landlords had emerged, but, surprisingly, no one party had become the dominant propertyholder on the Row. As of 1998, many parties owned pieces of the valuable front footage on one of the two major arteries, including a glorious mélange of past and modern industry figures, such as the aforementioned Bradleys and Atkins and Ray Stevens (who began acquiring Row property in 1969), as well as HAROLD SHEDD (ALABAMA's original producer), Dale Morris (Alabama's manager), Pam Lewis (Garth Brooks's original co-manager), Warner Bros., ALAN JACKSON, Ronnie Prophet, Reba McEntire, booking kingpin BUDDY LEE, TIM MCGRAW, LITTLE TEXAS, CRYSTAL GAYLE, Mike Curb, and Barbara Orbison, widow of the late singer.

As the twenty-first century approaches, Music Row shows few signs of slowing down, thus making Nashville's place as the hub of country music more secure than ever.

Oak Ridge Boys

Duane Allen b. Taylortown, Texas, April 29, 1943
Richard Sterban b. Camden, New Jersey, April 24, 1943
Joe Bonsall b. Philadelphia, Pennsylvania, May 18, 1948
William Lee Golden b. Brewton, Alabama, January 12, 1939
Steve Sanders b. Richland, Georgia, September 17, 1952;
d. June 10, 1998

The Oak Ridge Boys injected gospel-based four-part harmonies and exciting live shows into country music and in the process paved the way for all the vocal groups that followed them. From 1977 to 1987—with a lineup of Duane Allen, lead; William Lee Golden, baritone; Richard Sterban, bass; and Joe Bonsall, tenor—they sold millions of records, won every major industry award, and crossed into the pop charts with the 2-million-selling, Grammy-winning single "Elvira" and the million-selling "Bobbie Sue."

Prior to their 1977 breakthrough hit, "Y'All Come Back Saloon," the Oaks had been a controversial gospel act for more than thirty years. They began in 1945 as the Oak Ridge Quartet, a gospel ensemble within WALLY FOWLER's country group, the Georgia Clodhoppers. The original quartet consisted of Fowler, lead vocals; Curly Kinsey, bass; Lon "Deacon" Freeman, baritone; and Johnny New, tenor. They joined the GRAND OLE OPRY in September 1945.

In 1962 they changed their name to the Oak Ridge Boys. Golden joined the group in 1965, Allen in 1966, Sterban in 1972, and Bonsall in 1973. By 1973 they had won a dozen of gospel music's Dove Awards as well as a Grammy. They signed with COLUMBIA RECORDS to broaden their audience, but three albums of "message" music produced two singles that didn't make the country charts and left them ostracized from gospel yet still unknown in country.

Fighting the prevailing industry view that there was room for only one group in country music (the STATLER BROTHERS), the Oaks signed with ABC/DOT (later absorbed by MCA) and hit with with their next single, "Y'All Come Back Saloon" in 1977. Although Allen sang most of the lead parts, all four singers were featured on hits. In 1981 Sterban's thundering bass vocals on a remake of DALLAS FRAZIER's 1966 record "Elvira" took the Oaks to #5 on the *Billboard* pop singles charts.

In 1987 William Lee Golden left the Oaks and was replaced by Steve Sanders, a former child star in gospel music and, at the time, the rhythm guitarist in the Oaks' band. Sanders sang lead on two subsequent hits, "Gonna Take a

The Oak Ridge Boys: (from left)
Duane Allen, Richard Sterban, Joe
Bonsall, and William Lee Golden

Lot of River" (1988) and "Beyond Those Years" (1989), but the group's chart performance soon tapered off. They left MCA for RCA, where they released five chart singles from 1990 to 1992. Then, as in earlier years, their live show carried them through the next few years, when they were without a recording contract. They signed a new agreement with Capitol in 1995. In January 1996 William Lee Golden returned to the Oaks, replacing Steve Sanders, who resigned from the group. —*Walter Carter*

REPRESENTATIVE RECORDINGS

Y'All Come Back Saloon (MCA, 1977); *Fancy Free* (MCA, 1981); *Bobbie Sue* (MCA, 1982); *American Made* (MCA, 1983); *Deliver* (MCA, 1984)

Eli Oberstein

b. New York, December 13, 1901; d. June 12, 1960

A protégé of pioneer A&R man RALPH PEER, Eli Oberstein was responsible for recording most of the country acts for RCA VICTOR's BLUEBIRD line between 1933 and 1939. Often recording in temporary field studios, and frequently making as many as twenty or more masters in one long day, Oberstein oversaw the classic recordings of artists such as J. E. MAINER, the MONROE BROTHERS, the BLUE SKY BOYS, MILTON BROWN, and dozens of others. During this time he also recorded many blues artists, as well as jazz and dance bands; historians also give him credit for helping to create the style of big bands such as Tommy Dorsey and Larry Clinton. It was Oberstein who helped to pioneer the idea of cut-rate labels, first with Bluebird and later with his own labels, such as Varsity, Royale, and Rondo. —*Charles Wolfe*

Tim O'Brien

b. Wheeling, West Virginia, March 16, 1954

Blending bluegrass, folk, country, rock & roll, soul, blues, and gospel, Timothy Page O'Brien has helped to modernize country music's stringband tradition for more than twenty years. Growing up in Wheeling, West Virginia, he learned guitar at age twelve and followed artists based at Wheeling station WWVA and contemporary pop stars such as the Beatles. DOC WATSON's music turned O'Brien to bluegrass and traditional country, and the young singer eventually mastered the fiddle and mandolin as well.

After playing in bands based in Wheeling and Boulder, Colorado, in 1978 O'Brien helped organize the innovative bluegrass group HOT RIZE, known for its humorous alter ego, Red Knuckles and the Trailblazers (with O'Brien as Red). Hot Rize stayed together until 1990, winning the International Bluegrass Music Association (IBMA) Entertainer of the Year Award that year. Along the way, O'Brien wrote hits such as "Untold Stories" for the band and for fellow West Virginian KATHY MATTEA, with whom he dueted on the 1990 Top Ten single "Battle Hymn of Love."

This hit landed O'Brien an RCA solo contract, but when RCA left his recordings unreleased, he formed a new group, the Oh Boys. Subsequent releases on SUGAR HILL RECORDS have included both solo albums and albums recorded with his sister, Mollie, well respected as a blues and folk singer. Tim won IBMA's 1993 Male Vocalist of the Year Award and a Grammy nomination for *Red on Blonde*, a 1996 album of BOB DYLAN tunes. He has appeared frequently on network radio and television, and tours actively in the United States and abroad. —*John Rumble*

REPRESENTATIVE RECORDINGS

Take It Home (Sugar Hill, 1990); *Rock in My Shoe* (Sugar Hill, 1995); *When No One's Around* (Sugar Hill, 1997)

Mark O'Connor

b. Seattle, Washington, August, 5, 1961

Multi-instrumentalist Mark O'Connor is a genuine musical rarity. From his days as a child prodigy who was consistently winning old-time fiddling contests, O'Connor became one of Nashville's busiest and most respected session musicians. As a solo artist he has recorded a series of critically acclaimed albums that combine jazz, country, bluegrass, and other roots music. And then there's Mark O'Connor the classical musician, who wrote and recorded the first-ever *Fiddle Concerto* and who joined classical cellist Yo-Yo Ma and Nashville bassist Edgar Meyer on the classical album *Appalachia Waltz.*

O'Connor started out at age six playing the guitar and began fiddling at age eleven. A few months later he won the twelve-and-under division of the National Old Time Fiddlers' Contest. He gained additional inspiration from Texas fiddling legend Benny Thomasson, who had moved to southwestern Washington. By the time he was in high school, O'Connor had recorded four albums and had won every major fiddle competition in the United States. After graduation he began working with rock-fusion pioneers the Dixie Dregs and jazz greats David Grisman and Stephane Grappelli.

At CHET ATKINS's suggestion, O'Connor moved to Nashville in 1982 and began to forge a career in the studio, playing fiddle, guitar, and mandolin. Although O'Connor had recorded as a solo artist on ROUNDER RECORDS, WARNER BROS. provided him a major label opportunity, and he balanced his studio work for others with three solo albums, *Stone from Which the Arch Was Made* (1987), *Elysian Forest* (1988), and *On the Mark* (1989). By 1990, after appearing on more than 450 recordings, O'Connor had tired of being a studio hired hand. He elected to concentrate on his solo work, which paid large artistic dividends with the Warner Bros. album *New Nashville Cats,* a Grammy-winning musical homage to MUSIC CITY's finest session players. O'Connor continued to pay his respects to his major influences with *Heroes,* a 1994 project that found him performing with Grappelli, Jean-Luc Ponty, Pinchas Zukerman, and DOUG KERSHAW, among others.

O'Connor's connection to the classical world included

Mark O'Connor

a Carnegie Hall appearance with Isaac Stern and Itzhak Perlman, and as a guest soloist with the Boston Pops orchestra. In 1990 the Santa Fe Chamber Music Festival commissioned him to write his *Fiddle Concerto for Violin and Orchestra*. The concerto appeared on a 1995 Warner Bros. recording. His *Fiddle Concerto No. 2* premiered a year later. *Appalachia Waltz*, his project with Yo-Yo Ma and Edgar Meyer, was one of the top-selling classical recordings of 1996.

O'Connor is a six-time winner of the COUNTRY MUSIC ASSOCIATION's Instrumentalist of the Year Award.

—*Calvin Gilbert*

REPRESENTATIVE RECORDINGS

The Championship Years (Country Music Foundation Records, 1990); *New Nashville Cats* (Warner Bros., 1991)

W. Lee "Pappy" O'Daniel
b. Malta, Ohio, March 11, 1890; d. May 12, 1969

One of the most important men in the history of western swing was one who never sang, never played an instrument, and couldn't even read music. Nevertheless, Wilbert Lee "Pass the Biscuits, Pappy" O'Daniel became famous for founding western swing's LIGHT CRUST DOUGHBOYS and for riding its success into a career in Texas politics.

Born in Ohio, O'Daniel grew up on a farm in Kansas. In 1925 he moved to Fort Worth and became sales manager for the Burrus Mill and Elevator Company, manufacturers of Light Crust Flour. In late 1930 Burrus Mill began sponsoring a radio program featuring a stringband consisting of singer MILTON BROWN, fiddler BOB WILLS, and guitarist Herman Arnspiger. Dubbed the Light Crust Doughboys, the trio became a huge success. After Brown and Wills left, O'Daniel added other musicians, acting as their announcer. He also wrote poetry and composed lyrics for songs, including the country standards "Beautiful Texas" and "Put Me in Your Pocket." In 1935 he formed his own company, Hillbilly Flour. Fronting a new band, the Hillbilly Boys, he was elected Texas governor in 1938 and was re-elected in 1940. In 1941 he became a U.S. senator, winning a special election by defeating Congressman Lyndon B. Johnson. After a nonproductive term in the Senate, during which time no O'Daniel proposal received more than four votes, O'Daniel retired, making two halfhearted tries for the governorship of Texas, in 1956 and 1958, and running a poor third in each.

—*Cary Ginell*

REPRESENTATIVE RECORDINGS

W. Lee O'Daniel & His Hillbilly Boys (1935–1938) (Texas Rose, 1982); *White Country Blues (Various Artists)* (Columbia/Legacy, 1993), 2 discs

Molly O'Day
b. McVeigh, Kentucky, July 9, 1923; d. December 5, 1987

Lois LaVerne Williamson, better known as Molly O'Day, was perhaps the most widely admired traditional female country singer of the forties. Her expressive voice had a penetrating quality on sentimental and sacred songs that was virtually unequaled. She first worked on radio with her brother Skeets and Johnnie Bailes at WCHS–Charleston, West Virginia, in 1939, under the stage name Mountain Fern. The next year they worked at WJLS-Beckley and WHIS-Bluefield, where she took the name Dixie Lee and

Molly O'Day

in 1941 married guitarist Lynn Davis. Thereafter, she and Lynn worked as a team, and in 1942 she became known as "Molly O'Day." They subsequently worked for several months each in Birmingham, Louisville, Renfro Valley, and Dallas, making the acquaintance of a young HANK WILLIAMS during their sojourn in Alabama.

In May 1945 the couple came to WNOX in Knoxville and became stars of the *MIDDAY MERRY-GO-ROUND*. When FRED ROSE heard O'Day's rendition of "Tramp on the Street," he persuaded ART SATHERLEY to sign her to COLUMBIA RECORDS. In a related move, Rose signed Hank Williams to ACUFF-ROSE in part because Williams's compositions seemed ideal for O'Day to record. Though she subsequently recorded five of his songs, her biggest numbers, such as "Tramp on the Street," "At the First Fall of Snow," "Matthew 24," and "Don't Sell Daddy Anymore Whiskey," came from other sources.

Unfortunately, the music business placed heavy emotional stress on O'Day, and in 1950 she and her husband both had conversion experiences. They had their last Columbia recording session the following year. Lynn Davis became a Church of God minister-evangelist, and Molly assisted him in his ministry. From the mid-sixties they resided in Huntington, West Virginia. All the while, O'Day steadfastly refused offers to lure her into public performance. She did, however, record gospel albums for Rem and GRS, in 1962 and 1968, respectively. From 1974 until 1987 O'Day and Lynn Davis disc-jockeyed a gospel program on WEMM-FM radio, which he has continued since her death from cancer.

—*Ivan M. Tribe*

REPRESENTATIVE RECORDINGS

Molly O'Day & the Cumberland Mountain Folks (Bear Family, 1992), 2 CDs; *The Soul of Molly O'Day,* (Old Homestead, 1984), 2 vols.

Jamie O'Hara (*see* The O'Kanes)

The O'Kanes

Jamie O'Hara b. Toledo, Ohio, August 8, 1950
Kieran Kane b. Queens, New York, October 7, 1949

With their spare acoustic arrangements and BROTHER DUET–style harmonies, the O'Kanes briefly established themselves as a duo with a difference. Songwriters Jamie O'Hara and Kieran Kane joined forces in 1986, co-writing most of the O'Kanes' songs and creating its signature sound through an often haunting mix of mandolin, fiddle, accordion, acoustic guitar, and banjo.

Kieran Kane began his musical career as a nine-year-old drummer in his brother's rock & roll band. Kane played the northeastern bluegrass and folk circuit in the late 1960s and spent most of the 1970s in Los Angeles as a songwriter and lead guitarist. He moved to Nashville in 1978. In 1982 ELEKTRA RECORDS released his eponymous LP, which charted two Top Twenty country singles. In 1983 he penned Alabama's "Gonna Have a Party" and in 1984 JOHN CONLEE's #1 hit "As Long as I'm Rockin' with You."

Jamie O'Hara had planned to play professional football until he was benched by a college knee injury. He switched his focus to music, moved to Nashville in 1975, and was hired by TREE PUBLISHING as a staff writer. By the mid-1980s his major cuts included RONNIE MCDOWELL's "Older Women" and "Wandering Eyes" and the JUDDS' "Grandpa (Tell Me 'Bout the Good Old Days)," which won O'Hara a 1986 Grammy Award for Best Country Song.

Kane and O'Hara first began collaborating as songwriters in 1985, recording their demos in Kane's attic studio. In 1986 they became a duo and signed with COLUMBIA RECORDS. Their simple studio work tapes became the O'Kanes' self-titled 1986 debut album. In 1987 the duo scored a #1 with "Can't Stop My Heart from Loving You" and three Top Ten hits: "Oh Darlin'," "Daddies Need to Grow Up Too," and "Just Lovin' You." Their second album, *Tired of Runnin'*, yielded "One True Love" (#4, 1988) and "Blue Love" (#10, 1988). In 1989 O'Hara and Kane disbanded to resume their solo writing careers; the following year, Columbia released their third album, *Imagine That*.

Following the O'Kanes' demise, Kane released a 1993 self-titled ATLANTIC album and O'Hara released *Rise Above It*, his debut solo album for RCA RECORDS. In 1994 Kane

and fellow musicians KEVIN WELCH, Tammy Rogers, and Harry Stinson founded DEAD RECKONING RECORDS. The label's first release was Kane's *Dead Rekoning* (*sic*, 1995).

—*Marjie McGraw*

REPRESENTATIVE RECORDINGS

The O'Kanes (Columbia, 1986); *Tired of Runnin'* (Columbia, 1988); *Imagine That* (Columbia, 1990)

OKeh Records

established in New York, New York, 1918; ended 1960s

The OKeh label (pronounced *okay*) grew out of founder Otto Heineman's phonograph accessory business, with an assist from Germany's Lindström company, from whom it leased Odeon and Fonotipia masters. The first vertically cut OKeh records were issued in 1918; lateral discs appeared the following year.

In 1920 Harlem singer Mamie Smith made the first blues records for OKeh; their success engendered immediate competition from other labels. In 1923 the company made the first field trip to the South, to record dance bands and blues singers in Atlanta. A local distributor, Polk Brockman, persuaded producer RALPH PEER to record two sides by colorful local personality and WSB radio star FIDDLIN' JOHN CARSON. Peer did so with reluctance, but the record realized surprising sales and is viewed today as the one that launched the country music industry. HENRY WHITTER, ROBA STANLEY, ERNEST STONEMAN, and KELLY HARRELL soon began recording for OKeh, as did local artists whose work was captured on subsequent trips to Atlanta, Asheville, Dallas, and St. Louis.

In 1926 COLUMBIA purchased OKeh, which was then able to produce electrically made recordings using Columbia's Western Electric process. In the late 1920s, records by NARMOUR & SMITH, FRANK HUTCHISON, and EMMETT MILLER were added to the catalogue.

OKeh went into eclipse in 1932, following the sale of its bankrupt parent company, Columbia. The label was revived briefly in the years 1934–35 and shelved again until it replaced Columbia's low-priced Vocalion label in 1940. The company's country artists, including GENE AUTRY, BOB WILLS, and ROY ACUFF, all appeared on OKeh through 1945, when the label was discontinued again and country artists appeared once more on Columbia.

Columbia revived OKeh briefly in the early 1950s, primarily as a rhythm & blues label, though it also carried some country material briefly in 1953. It was revived once more in the 1960s for r&b releases and a few LP reissues.

—*Dick Spottswood*

Old Dominion Barn Dance

established in Richmond, Virginia, September 1946; ended 1957

This well-known Saturday-night country showcase was broadcast live on WRVA radio, from Lyric Theater at Ninth and Broad Streets, in Richmond, Virginia. The show began in 1946, and several months after its demise in 1957, the *New Dominion Barn Dance* was created by CARLTON HANEY. It, too, was broadcast over WRVA from the same theater, featured more bluegrass acts, and lasted until 1964.

WRVA, which first went on the air in 1925, was owned by Larus and Brothers Tobacco Company, which marketed Edgeworth Pipe Tobacco and Domino Cigarettes. Some of the significant early bands to play at WRVA were the

The O'Kanes: Jamie O'Hara (left) and Kieran Kane

Domino Hillbillies, the Tobacco Tags, and HOYT "SLIM" BRYANT & His Wildcats. The *Old Dominion Barn Dance* originated when C.T. Lucy, general manager of WRVA, obtained the lease to the Lyric Theater, a building suitable for the live show he envisioned. The show was built around the Workman family: SUNSHINE SUE; her husband, John Workman; and his brother Sam, known professionally as Sunshine Sue & the Smiling Rangers.

With Sunshine Sue as hostess, the show drew large crowds to see CHET ATKINS, WILMA LEE & STONEY COOPER, GRANDPA JONES and Ramona, BONNIE LOU and Buster Moore, and JOE MAPHIS. Mary Klick and Rose Lee (later Maphis) appeared as the Saddle Sweethearts, while humor was provided by country comedians Chick Stripling, Quincy Snodgrass, and others. The program's bluegrass acts, including the Farm Hands, Charlie Bailey, RENO & SMILEY, MAC WISEMAN, FLATT & SCRUGGS, and the STANLEY BROTHERS were exceptionally good. WRVA broadcast at 50,000 watts, so the program enjoyed a wide listening audience. In the mid-1950s it was carried nationally on the CBS Radio Network's *Saturday Night Country Style* program, which alternated broadcasts from various radio barn dances, such as the *Tennessee Barn Dance* and the *WWVA JAMBOREE,* from one week to the next.

The demise of the *Old Dominion Barn Dance* came as a result of the rise of rock & roll and its negative impact on much of the country music industry. By 1955 and 1956, attendance at the barn dance had fallen off sharply. With the show losing money, WRVA management reluctantly closed it down. —*Walter V. Saunders*

Old-Time Music

The term "old-time music" is generally used to refer to the styles and repertoires that dominated commercial country music's first decade, roughly from 1924 to 1935. The term seemed to originate with the record companies and publishers of the time, who did not have a clear idea of what to call the music during its early days. "Country" was seldom used this early, and many record companies used the adjective "old-time" to describe the music; one company even put the legend "old-time singing" on its record labels, while another emphasized the adjective "old," calling their product Old Familiar Tunes. In the 1920s the term "old" or "old-time" had positive connotations of nineteenth-century music, in contrast to the jazz and new morality of the 1920s.

Old-time music embraced several diverse styles during this first decade. One was stringband music, either in bands (such as the SKILLET LICKERS) or as a fiddle-guitar duet (such as the KESSINGER BROTHERS). A second was group harmony singing, represented by artists such as the CARTER FAMILY or by the later duet singers, such as the DELMORE BROTHERS. A third was a form of white blues and related yodeling, best represented by JIMMIE RODGERS and CLIFF CARLISLE. A fourth was a solo singing tradition in which artists adapted traditional material to various instrumental accompaniment, such as did BRADLEY KINCAID or UNCLE DAVE MACON.

Throughout the 1930s and 1940s, as other styles of country music developed, the old-time styles fell into a sort of backwater. Exceptions were the vastly popular stringbands of J. E. MAINER in the 1930s, and in the 1940s radio stars such as GRANDPA JONES, STRINGBEAN, and DOC & CHICKIE WILLIAMS. In the 1960s the legendary STONEMAN

FAMILY had a successful syndicated TV show, that kept the old sounds alive in the heart of Nashville.

Starting with the folk music revival of the late 1950s, a number of more modern artists successfully revived many of the old-time styles. In the stringband tradition, the NEW LOST CITY RAMBLERS, whose members sought out and studied with many veterans from the 1920s, influenced thousands with their faithful re-creations of old stringbands during the 1960s. The next decade saw the popularity of groups such as the Highwoods String Band, the Hotmud Family, and the RED CLAY RAMBLERS. Veteran artists such as TOMMY JARRELL and WADE MAINER found new audiences and recorded widely. Carrying on the singing tradition were the remarkable duo of Hazel and Alice, and, in the 1990s, the Whitstein Brothers.

Solo singers included the veteran Roy Harper as well as TNN star David Holt. A new generation of young fiddlers, including Brad Leftwich, Bruce Molsky, Greg Hooven, and Chirps Smith, carried that music into the 1990s. That same decade saw a third generation of new stringbands, such as North Carolina's Freight Hoppers, offering proof positive that the old-time style was a permanent part of country music. —*Charles Wolfe*

Opryland Music Group (*see* Opryland USA, Gaylord Entertainment, Jerry Bradley, and Acuff-Rose)

Opryland USA
opened in Nashville, Tennessee, May 27, 1972

Opryland USA covers a lot of ground, both literally and figuratively. This Nashville-based conglomerate is the cornerstone of GAYLORD ENTERTAINMENT COMPANY and encompasses Nashville's dominant convention hotel, the Opryland theme park, the GRAND OLE OPRY, WSM Radio, the Country Music Radio Network, the RYMAN AUDITORIUM, Opry House theater (home of the Grand Ole Opry), the Springhouse Golf Club, Opryland Music Group (anchored by the incredibly potent ACUFF-ROSE PUBLICATIONS country music catalogue), the $12 million showboat the *General Jackson*, and downtown Nashville's Wildhorse Saloon. From 1983 to 1997 THE NASHVILLE NETWORK (TNN) and later COUNTRY MUSIC TELEVISION (CMT) cable network were part of the Opryland complex as well.

The Opryland USA theme park was created by the National Life and Accident Insurance Company (the parent organization of the Grand Ole Opry) as a new home for the Opry and as an alternative source of revenue for National Life. Plans for the park were first publicly announced on October 18, 1968. Groundbreaking followed on June 30, 1970. The entire park—built on sixty-five acres of land several miles up the Cumberland River from downtown Nashville—cost $66 million. On opening day, May 27, 1972, Opryland staff announced that the park drew 10,000 visitors. The Grand Ole Opry moved to the new Opry House on March 16, 1974, with an opening-night show that included a visit from President Richard M. Nixon. The Opryland Hotel, with 614 rooms, opened adjacent to the park in 1977.

In November 1997 Gaylord officials announced that Opryland would no longer exist as a themed amusement park but would instead be transformed into Opry Mills, a retail entertainment complex, mixing shops, theaters, and restaurants with a few rides. —*Bob Millard*

Roy Orbison

Roy Orbison

b. Vernon, Texas April 23, 1936; d. December 6, 1988

Although his background was in country music, Roy Kelton Orbison left nearly every vestige of it behind to produce perhaps the most completely realized pop records of the early 1960s. They were symphonic in their composition and execution, and at their best conveyed a sense of longing, leaving one with the inescapable feeling that Orbison himself was the lonely man who populated his work.

Orbison grew up in Wink, Texas, and his father was an oil rigger in Jal, New Mexico. Orbison himself was a nearsighted child who turned to music very early. He was playing solo on local radio at age ten, and his first group, the Wink Westerners, played country music on local radio and television. Studying in Odessa in 1955, Orbison assembled another band, the Teen Kings, and, touched by the furor that attended ELVIS PRESLEY's early tours of Texas, plunged into rock & roll.

The Teen Kings' first single, an early version of "Ooby Dooby," was issued on Je-Wel Records. It caught the ear of SAM PHILLIPS at SUN RECORDS, who brought Orbison to Memphis to recut it. For two years Orbison tried hard to rock & roll at Phillips's behest, but nothing, except the remake of "Ooby Dooby," charted. Then, shortly after writing "Claudette" for the EVERLY BROTHERS in 1958, Orbison bought his way off Sun and signed with RCA in Nashville. There followed two undistinguished pop singles on RCA that did little business, and after a year Orbison was dropped.

Music publisher WESLEY ROSE helped sign Orbison with MONUMENT RECORDS in 1959, and the third single, "Only the Lonely," defined the classic Orbison style. Between 1960 and 1965 he became a master of the pop single.

"Running Scared," "Crying," "In Dreams," "Blue Bayou," and "It's Over" were among his hits, all written by Orbison, some co-written with Joe Melson. The biggest hit, "Oh, Pretty Woman," co-written with Bill Dees, was rooted in 1950s rock & roll. Orbison had moved to Nashville in 1960, and all his hits were recorded there with the same session musicians who played on country sessions. One crucial difference, though, was that Monument's FRED FOSTER would not push for the industry norm of recording four songs in a three-hour session but settled instead for one song—if it was *the* one.

Until his death, Orbison's success was worldwide, and he attracted large audiences in Europe and Australia. At home his career went off the rails almost immediately after "Oh, Pretty Woman." His next two Monument singles sold poorly, and then, in July 1965, he signed with MGM RECORDS, where the downward sales pattern continued.

Orbison's personal life was also touched by tragedy in the late 1960s. He had married his high school sweetheart, Claudette Frady, in 1957, but she died in a motorcycle accident in June 1966. Then, in September 1968, two of their sons died in a house fire while Orbison was on tour in England. In March the following year he married a seventeen-year-old German, Barbara Wellhonen.

After leaving MGM in 1973 Orbison went through a succession of contracts, including a short, artistically arid return to Monument in 1976. The movie *Blue Velvet,* which used "In Dreams" to haunting effect, hastened his comeback, as did Bruce Springsteen's speech at Orbison's induction into the Rock & Roll Hall of Fame in 1987. The first Traveling Wilburys album, of which Orbison was a part, climbed to #3 on the pop album charts, and his rehabilitation was completed when "You Got It" on Virgin Records peaked at #9. The album, *Mystery Girl,* posthumously got to #5 on the LP charts. While many of his contemporaries from the 1950s died dreaming of the big comeback, Orbison died at the height of one.

—*Colin Escott*

REPRESENTATIVE RECORDINGS

For the Lonely (Rhino, 1988); *Mystery Girl* (Virgin, 1989); *The Sun Years* (Rhino, 1989); *The Legendary Roy Orbison* (CBS Special Products, 1990), 4 CDs

Oriole Records *(see* American Record Corporation)

Jimmie Osborne

b. Winchester, Kentucky, April 8, 1923; d. December 26, 1957

James Osborne Jr., the singer-songwriter billed as the Kentucky Folk Singer, was one of the more traditional artists to emerge in country music following World War II. His original songs addressed patriotic themes, lost love, and the religious life, but his best numbers were his topical pieces.

In about 1939 Osborne began his career at station WLAP in Lexington, Kentucky. During World War II he worked in defense plants and played on weekends. After the war he returned to WLAP, followed by stints on stations in Asheville, North Carolina, and Texarkana, Arkansas.

In 1947 Osborne moved to KWKH in Shreveport, Louisiana, and later became a regular on the *LOUISIANA HAYRIDE,* subsequently joining the BAILES BROTHERS' band as a featured vocalist. During this period he guested on the

ERNEST TUBB segment of the GRAND OLE OPRY and signed with KING RECORDS. His initial release, "My Heart Echoes," made the country Top Ten in 1948.

Osborne returned to Kentucky, landing a job on WLEX-Lexington. He had his biggest hit in 1949, "The Death of Little Kathy Fiscus," an event ballad that recounts the true-life tragedy of a child who died April 8, 1949, after falling in a deep well-pipe in San Marino, California. The song made #7 on the *Billboard* charts; Osborne donated half of his royalties to the Kathy Fiscus memorial fund.

"God, Please Protect America," a Korean War song that peaked at #9 in *Billboard* in 1950, was Osborne's final hit on the charts. Other songs from that period that did well were the traditional "Hills of Roan County" and his own "Tears of St. Ann." During the early 1950s he appeared on the NATIONAL BARN DANCE at WLS in Chicago and on the MIDWESTERN HAYRIDE at WLW in Cincinnati.

In 1952 Osborne moved to Louisville, Kentucky, where he opened a record store and also had a popular DJ show on WKLO; he later moved to a smaller station, WGRC. Osborne's career was winding down, although he continued recording through May 1955. By this time, however, he was recording other writers' songs and never had another hit. Finally, apparently despondent over a waning musical career and marital problems, Jimmie Osborne took his own life at age thirty-four in Louisville, Kentucky.

—*Walter V. Saunders*

The Osborne Brothers: Bobby (left) and Sonny

REPRESENTATIVE RECORDINGS

Jimmie Osborne Singing Songs He Wrote (Audio Lab, 1959); *The Legendary Jimmie Osborne* (King, 1961)

The Osborne Brothers

Robert Van "Bobby" Osborne Jr. b. Hyden, Kentucky, December 7, 1931

Sonny Roland Osborne b. Hyden, Kentucky, October 29, 1937

Sporting exquisite three-part harmonies and progressive musical ideas, the Osborne Brothers were one of the few bluegrass acts to crack contemporary country radio playlists during the sixties.

Bobby and Sonny Osborne were living in Dayton, Ohio, when they formed their professional partnership in August 1953. Both were seasoned bluegrass professionals: Bob played guitar and mandolin with the LONESOME PINE FIDDLERS, JIMMY MARTIN, and the STANLEY BROTHERS before serving in Korea; teenaged banjo virtuoso Sonny toured with BILL MONROE for two summers.

After working with Jimmy Martin in Detroit and Charlie Bailey in Wheeling, the brothers returned to Dayton in December 1955. Recruiting singer-guitarist RED ALLEN and fiddler Art Stamper, the band worked area clubs as the Osborne Brothers & Red Allen. Publisher-producer WESLEY ROSE signed them to MGM after hearing a demo tape; he was particularly impressed with "Ruby," which was driven by Bobby's pure, high tenor and twin banjo arrangement. The record became a hit in markets where bluegrass traditionally sold well. For their third MGM session, the Osbornes and Allen arranged a novel vocal trio around Dusty Owens's "Once More." Bobby sang lead, pitched higher than the other two harmony parts. "Once More" reached #13 on *Billboard*'s country charts in 1958 and established an unmistakable trademark sound for the band.

When Allen left in April 1958, the Osbornes replaced him with a succession of singer-guitarists, most notably Benny Birchfield and Dale Sledd. Through the efforts of Doyle Wilburn, the brothers landed a DECCA contract in 1963 and joined the GRAND OLE OPRY the following year. The band also changed its musical direction; breaking ranks with bluegrass traditionalists, the Osbornes added steel guitars, a piano, and drums to their records. "Up This Hill and Down," released in February 1966, appealed to country radio programmers who would never otherwise play a bluegrass record. The brothers also benefited from a string of BOUDLEAUX AND FELICE BRYANT–penned hits, particularly "Rocky Top" (1968), "Tennessee Hound Dog" (1969), and "Georgia Pineywoods" (1971). In 1971 the COUNTRY MUSIC ASSOCIATION named them Best Vocal Group of the Year; two years later they became the first bluegrass band to perform at the White House.

Eventually becoming dissatisfied with their commercial direction—the demand for hit singles and the grueling road schedule needed to support them—the Osbornes left MCA RECORDS in 1976 and returned to a more traditional, acoustic bluegrass sound. The move revitalized the brothers' music, and a series of critically acclaimed albums and festival appearances has reinforced their reputation as one of America's premier bluegrass bands. —*Dave Samuelson*

REPRESENTATIVE RECORDINGS

The Osborne Brothers' Bluegrass Collection (CMH, 1978); *The Osborne Brothers: 1956–68* (Bear Family, 1995), 4 CDs

K. T. Oslin

b. Crossett, Arkansas, May 15, 1941

Kay Toinette Oslin came late and didn't stay long, but she left a repertoire of impassioned story songs speaking to her generation of women with a humor and poignance unmatched since LORETTA LYNN at her peak.

Only five when her mother, a onetime professional big band singer, was widowed, Oslin was moved around repeatedly before landing in Houston just as puberty set in. Bitten by the show business "bug," she took ballet at age eleven, and majored in drama in a Texas junior college. She became a contemporary folksinger, working with GUY CLARK for a time. She worked her way to New York City, where she first danced on Broadway in a *West Side Story* revival. She sang jingles, did back-up singing, and toured colleges as a solo, became a Manhattan maven.

Oslin was already well into her thirties, nearly forty, when she began making forays into Nashville as a songwriter. In the mid-1980s DOTTIE WEST recorded one of her tunes, and in 1985 GAIL DAVIES hit with Oslin's "Round The Clock Lovin'." Feints at a recording career were made, but Oslin's material was ahead of its time. In 1986 she arrived to tell with wit and passion the stories of women on the leading edge of the baby boom generation—whom she forever gave identity as "'80's Ladies."

With hits such as "Mary and Willie," "Do Ya," "I'll Always Come Back," "Hold Me," "Hey Bobby," "and "Come Next Monday," Oslin wove little plays into songs, and not always the prescribed "three-minute movies." Oslin made imaginative videos; *'80's Ladies* was practically a feature film in miniature, *Come Next Monday* a high-budget film farce. Along the way she picked up Grammys, ACM, and CMA Awards and garnered a handful of gold and platinum awards for albums. Writing her own sophisticated music, controlling her own themes and image, she was the grand diva of country music for a while, speaking to her cohort as no one had possessed strong enough voice to do before—women are usually cashiered from country radio before the age at which Oslin began.

A noteworthy role in the film *The Thing Called Love* reminded Oslin of her love of acting, not to mention the rigors and loneliness of a traveling concert artist. In the mid-1990s Oslin seemed to quit while she was on top. She spent more time in Los Angeles matriculating in the film-making community. Oslin successfully underwent triple bypass surgery in 1995.
—*Bob Millard*

K. T. Oslin

'80's Ladies (RCA, 1987); *This Woman* (RCA, 1988); *Love in a Small Town* (RCA, 1990); *Songs from an Aging Sex Bomb* (RCA, 1993); *My Roots Are Showing* (RCA, 1996)

Marie Osmond
b. Ogden, Utah, October 13, 1959

It didn't take long for Olive Marie Osmond to start her show business career. At age three she appeared with her brothers on Andy Williams's network TV show, and when she was thirteen she enjoyed her first chart record—the crossover smash "Paper Roses" (MGM, 1973). Arranged and produced by SONNY JAMES, "Paper Roses" spent two weeks at #1 on the country charts, inaugurating a country career that later saw Osmond share in the CMA's Vocal Duo of the Year award on the strength of her chart-topping duet with DAN SEALS, "Meet Me in Montana."

At age fourteen Marie began touring with the Osmond Brothers, and as a teenager she co-hosted with brother Donny a musical TV variety series, *Donny & Marie.* The siblings' duet version of "I'm Leaving It (All) Up to You" (1974) hit the country Top Twenty and peaked at #4 pop, but their duet rendition of "Make the World Go Away" (1975) failed to make an impression in either format.

When the TV series ended, Marie moved to New York and lived there briefly to further her acting career. She wrote a health and fitness book—*Marie Osmond's Guide to Beauty, Health and Style*—and collaborated on an exercise video and two handbooks for expectant mothers. She made little further headway as a recording artist until 1985, when "Meet Me in Montana" hit #1 on the country charts and opened a new chapter in her career as a purveyor of what Osmond (readily acknowledging that she's "not a traditional country singer like TAMMY WYNETTE") has termed "contemporary country." Released later that year, "There's No Stopping Your Heart" also went to #1, as did a 1986 duet with Paul Davis, "You're Still New to Me."

Osmond gained her most recent country chart single in 1990. Since then she has endorsed a line of clothing and now heads the Osmond Foundation for charitable work.
—*Gerry Wood*

I Only Wanted You (Curb/Capitol, 1986); *The Best of Marie Osmond* (Curb/Capitol, 1990)

Outlaws

The term "Outlaw," as applied to an amorphous group of dissident country musicians of the 1970s, was probably first used by Nashville publicist Hazel Smith in 1973. Smith had been asked by a North Carolina radio station to devise an apt designation for music produced at the time by WILLIE NELSON, WAYLON JENNINGS, TOMPALL GLASER, and their comrades. She recalled Jennings's 1972 hit "Ladies Love Outlaws" (written by Lee Clayton) and decided that the term and the image fit. But it wasn't until the release of the 1976 album *Wanted! The Outlaws*—the first country music album to attain platinum status (1 million units sold)— that the Outlaw appellation became widely used to designate a type of country music. The popularity of the term was heightened by the publication in 1978 of journalist Michael Bane's *The Outlaws: Revolution in Country Music*, which profiled the phenomenon and provided candid summaries of the careers of KRIS KRISTOFFERSON, Nelson, Jennings, Glaser, and JESSI COLTER (Jennings's wife).

Until 1976 the most common term in usage was "progressive country," itself originally used to characterize the format of radio station KOKE-FM in Austin, Texas. Texas journalist Jan Reid's book *Redneck Rock* (1974) was an early attempt to coin another term, and some music critics alternately used "cosmic cowboy music," alluding to MICHAEL MARTIN MURPHEY's song title from 1973.

The term "Outlaw" seemed to conjure up the appropriate image for musicians who had been openly critical of the Nashville recording machine and the pop-oriented NASHVILLE SOUND of the 1960s. Some, such as Nelson, moved away from Nashville and recorded. Most wanted to produce their own records and select their own back-up musicians—often the same musicians who backed them on the road. The Outlaws adopted the dress, hairstyles, and lifestyles of rock musicians, including an open identification with drug usage. Experimentation marked their actions, whether presenting a lyrical sexual candor, participating in outdoor rock-styled festivals, hiring agents from New York, or recording outside Nashville.

Much irony lies in the use of the Outlaw persona. DAVID ALLAN COE, an ex-convict and motorcycle gang member, was the only one of the Outlaws who actually approximated true outlawry in his personal life. In fact, at the very time that the term began to catch on, the performers themselves were attaining national commercial success. In addition, the 1976 album *Wanted! The Outlaws* was a Nashville marketing effort from start to finish—a repackaging of old recordings from Nelson, Jennings, Colter, and Glaser that was conceived and executed by RCA executive JERRY BRADLEY.

The Outlaw movement was somewhat short-lived, however. By 1978 Nelson had moved from Texas to Colorado and was beginning to record pop standards; Jennings and Glaser openly split, reportedly over money; Kristofferson was pursuing a Hollywood acting career; Coe's attempts to be outrageous were becoming tiresome; and a hedonistic, drug-oriented lifestyle was beginning to create legal and health problems for each artist. All of this was summed up most effectively by Waylon Jennings in his 1978 hit "Don't You Think This Outlaw Bit's Done Got Out of Hand," a death knell for the Outlaw phenomenon.

—*Stephen R. Tucker*

REPRESENTATIVE RECORDINGS

Wanted! The Outlaws (RCA, 1976); *Waylon and Willie* (RCA, 1978)

Paul Overstreet

b. Antioch, Mississippi, March 17, 1955

Singer-songwriter Paul Overstreet overcame alcoholism and triumphed as a songwriter before moving to a God- and family-oriented emphasis as a solo recording artist.

Inspired as a child by seeing the HANK WILLIAMS' bio movie *Your Cheatin' Heart,* Overstreet recorded for a small Arkansas label at age seventeen and moved to Nashville from Mississippi in 1973. With encouragement from members of DOLLY PARTON's family, he formed a group and spent much of the next five years working the road. Overstreet's marriage in May 1975 to Parton's younger sister Freida ended in divorce in November 1976.

"I did a lot of drinking," Overstreet later recalled.

Paul Overstreet

"Around 1978 I realized that I was going nowhere and could rot in one of those clubs. So one night I said a prayer: 'God, if you get me out of these clubs, I'll quit drinking.'"

Overstreet didn't win his fight with alcohol until 1985, but he started having significant hits as a songwriter in 1982 with GEORGE JONES's recording of "Same Ole Me." During the same year, Overstreet released a self-titled RCA solo album that failed to catch fire. But by the mid-eighties Overstreet's positive, innovative approach to hard-country songs yielded a long string of hits, most notably the 1986 and 1987 CMA Songs of the Year, "On the Other Hand" and "Forever and Ever, Amen," both written with DON SCHLITZ and recorded by RANDY TRAVIS.

In 1986 Overstreet, a moving hard-country singer, recorded one album with the songwriting trio SCHUYLER, KNOBLOCH & OVERSTREET (SKO) before leaving to resume solo work. He recorded the 1987 #1 hit "I Won't Take Less Than Your Love" along with TANYA TUCKER and Paul Davis. Top Ten hits extolling the joys of home and family included 1990's "Richest Man on Earth" and the #1 "Daddy's Come Around," both marketed jointly by RCA and the Christian music Word label. In 1994 Overstreet was voted the TNN/Music City News Christian Country Artist of the Year. As of this writing he had completed recording the album *Time* on the Alabama-based independent Integrity Music, working with producer Jerry Crutchfield.

—*Thomas Goldsmith*

REPRESENTATIVE RECORDINGS

Sowin' Love (RCA, 1989); *Heroes* (RCA, 1990)

Fuzzy Owen

b. Conway, Arkansas, April 30, 1929

One of the pioneers of the country music community in BAKERSFIELD, California, Charles Lee "Fuzzy" Owen owned

Tally Records, the label that first recorded MERLE HAGGARD. Owen has been instrumental in producing Haggard's recordings since the earliest dates and influenced Haggard's songwriting through advice and example. When Haggard signed with CAPITOL, Owen became his manager and helped guide Haggard's career from a virtual unknown to membership in the COUNTRY MUSIC HALL OF FAME.

Growing up in Arkansas, Owen played steel guitar in and around Hot Springs and Little Rock, performing on radio shows before he moved to Bakersfield in 1949 to join his cousin Lewis Talley in a band. In August 1951 Owen was inducted into the army, but after his discharge in 1952 he returned to California, where he performed at the Blackboard, then the Clover Club. This led to a regular job as the steel guitar player on Cousin Herb Henson's local TV show.

Owen co-wrote "A Dear John Letter" with Lewis Talley and Billy Barton and recorded it with BONNIE OWENS for the Mar-Vel label; it was covered by FERLIN HUSKY and JEAN SHEPARD and became a #1 country record in 1953. Owen and Lewis Talley then went into business together with a Bakersfield studio and record label, Tally Records. Fuzzy Owen recorded several self-penned songs for this label, including "Arkie's Got Her Shoes On" and "You're Everything I Wanted Her to Be." In 1959 Owen wrote what became a #1 song for RAY PRICE, "The Same Old Me." When the partnership was dissolved, Owen kept the label and publishing company.

Owen met Merle Haggard while both were performing at the Lucky Spot nightclub in about 1960, just after Haggard was released from San Quentin. Haggard recorded several songs for Tally (including "Singing My Heart Out," written by Owen) and was then signed to Capitol. Owen began to devote more and more time to Haggard's career until he became the singer's full-time manager in 1962.

Since 1962 Owen has played an active role in Haggard's studio recordings, live concerts, and career guidance. Their longtime association has led to Haggard's legendary status but has overshadowed Owen's individual success as a songwriter and musician as well as his own important influence in the development of the Bakersfield sound.

—*Don Cusic*

Bonnie Owens

b. Blanchard, Oklahoma, October 1, 1932

Bonnie Owens was the major female artist to emerge from BAKERSFIELD, California, as that town became the center for the California country movement in the 1950s. Bonnie Campbell met BUCK OWENS when she was fifteen and joined his band, Mac & the Skillet Lickers, on KTYL in Mesa, Arizona. The two married in 1948, and they moved to Bakersfield in 1951. Soon after, their marriage began to fail.

Bonnie was working as a singer and waitress at the Clover Club in September 1953 when Herb Henson began a local TV show, *Cousin Herb's Trading Post Gang*, on KERO. The show's regulars included pianist FUZZY OWEN and guitarist Lewis Talley; the group stayed with the show until 1963, when Herb Henson died.

Owens's first recording was a duet on the Mar-Vel label with Fuzzy Owen, "A Dear John Letter," which preceded the hit version by JEAN SHEPARD and FERLIN HUSKY; next Owens recorded "We Stay Together for the Children's Sake" for Delphi. By this time, Fuzzy Owen and Lewis Talley had built their own studio in the garage at Lewis's home and begun Tally Records.

Owens recorded two songs on Tally, the label begun by Fuzzy Owen and Lewis Talley: "Why Don't Daddy Live Here Anymore" and "Don't Take Advantage of Me," both of which charted. She then recorded a duet with fellow Tally artist MERLE HAGGARD: "Just Between the Two of Us." This was reissued on a CAPITOL duet album after that label acquired Haggard and Owens's contracts.

Between 1965 and 1969 Owens recorded three chart singles for Capitol, including "Number One Heel" and "Consider the Children." In 1965 she won ACM Awards for Top Female and Top Duet (with Merle Haggard). In 1966, she and Merle Haggard again won the Top Duo. This was the peak of her solo career.

From June 28, 1965, when Owens married Merle Haggard, she dedicated herself to him and played a major role in Haggard's career as well as his personal life. She sang harmony on his recordings and toured with him until 1991, even after their 1978 divorce; in 1994 she rejoined Haggard's show and continued to record with him.

—*Don Cusic*

Buck Owens

b. Sherman, Texas, August 12, 1929

Singer, songwriter, and guitarist Alvis Edgar Owens Jr. ruled the country music scene for a period in the mid-1960s, producing a clear, twangy, danceable sound that he repeated across dozens of chart-topping singles. Though he would later become a fixture on television through the success of *HEE HAW*, Owens is best remembered by fans and those younger stars he has influenced for timeless hits such as "Act Naturally" (#1, 1963) and "My Heart Skips a Beat" (#1, 1964).

His early life followed the classic Depression-era Dust Bowl family stereotype. Sharecroppers from North Texas near the Oklahoma border, his family moved west to Arizona in 1937, barely making ends meet. Having experienced the depths of poverty, Owens began playing the honky-tonks of Phoenix and Mesa, Arizona, to make money, learn a trade, and stay away from the harsh conditions of farm labor.

The musical influences on the young Owens were diverse, reflecting both the popular music of the time and places in which he matured and the various styles that he had to learn to play as a working dance-hall musician in the Southwest. He listened to stringband and cowboy music on Mexican border radio stations and learned to play and synthesize western swing, rhythm & blues, and the emerging genre of honky-tonk. In 1947 he met Bonnie Campbell, with whom he worked in a group called Mac & the Skillet Lickers, and the two married in 1948.

In 1951 Buck and his wife, BONNIE OWENS, moved to BAKERSFIELD. California, where Dust Bowl refugees had ended their trip west in fertile farm fields and the burgeoning oil industry. From 1951 to 1958 Buck played at the Blackboard, the center of the vibrant Bakersfield music scene. As lead guitar player and singer for the house band led by BILL WOODS, Buck worked marathon shifts and played anything to get folks dancing, including country, r&b, rockabilly, rhumbas, polkas, and even sambas.

He also took advantage of Bakersfield's proximity to Los Angeles to play sessions at CAPITOL studios, establish-

Buck Owens & the Buckaroos: (from left) Don Rich, Jerry Wiggens, Buck Owens, Doyle Holley, and Tom Brumley

ing himself as a session guitarist for artists such as TOMMY COLLINS and Gene Vincent. He made a few singles for local labels, and even recorded a rockabilly single, "Hot Dog," for Pep Records in 1956, which was released under the name Corky Jones so that Buck's country credibility would not suffer. Capitol producer KEN NELSON signed Owens to Capitol in 1957. Two years later, "Second Fiddle" became Owens's first chart record.

During a period he spent in the Seattle area in the late fifties, Buck struck up a musical relationship and personal friendship with a young fiddler, DON RICH. Their partnership was crucial in Buck's career, and Rich stayed with Owens as musician, guitarist, and leader of Buck's band, the Buckaroos, until his death in 1974.

Owens's first #1 hit, which began a string of six years in which he had at least one #1 and usually had three, was "Act Naturally" in 1963, later covered by the Beatles. Following this with a series of similar singles with a clear sound that seemed literally to jump out of AM transistor radios, Owens hit the top again and again with songs such as the ballad "Together Again" (#1, 1964), "I've Got a Tiger By the Tail" (#1, 1965), "Think of Me" (#1, 1966), and "Sam's Place (#1, 1967).

Unlike most other artists during the heyday of the Nashville Sound, Owens would virtually always record with his road band, giving his records both a distinctive sound and a live feel. From 1963 to 1967, during the peak of Owens's commercial and artistic career, Owens and Rich were joined by pedal steel player Tom Brumley, drummer Willie Cantu, and bassist Doyle Holly on all of Owens's records and on the Buckaroos' own marginally successful releases on Capitol. While Nelson nominally produced his sessions, Owens would shape and control the band's sound and songs. These factors, and Owens's desire to keep the same winning song and arrangement formula, helped to create the conditions for his signature style based on simple storylines, infectious choruses, twangy electric guitar, an insistent rhythm supplied by a drum track placed forward in the mix, and high two-part harmonies featuring Owens and Rich.

Owens's control of his music was reflected in his busi-

ness interests. He established himself as a savvy businessman early in his career with Blue Book, a music publishing company that controlled his own work and that of other Bakersfield writers, such as MERLE HAGGARD. Owens also invested in radio stations throughout the Southwest, and with his manager JACK MCFADDEN established his own management and booking agency, which handled a number of artists.

After many career highlights, including shows at CARNEGIE HALL and the Fillmore in San Francisco, Owens's recording career faded both commercially and artistically in the 1970s, though he kept quite busy with his many business interests and with *Hee Haw*. He was coaxed out of retirement in 1988 by DWIGHT YOAKAM, who helped him return to the top of the charts with the duet "Streets of Bakersfield." Two new albums followed—*Hot Dog!* (1988) and *Act Naturally* (1989), the latter including a duet with Ringo Starr on the title track—neither of which was especially memorable. Yet the classic songs are available again in collections and re-releases, and live on in the countless cover versions with which younger artists pay tribute to Owens's music.
—*Mark Fenster*

REPRESENTATIVE RECORDINGS

On the Bandstand (Capitol, 1963; Sundazed, 1994); *Together Again/My Heart Skips a Beat* (Capitol, 1964; Sundazed, 1994); *Live at Carnegie Hall* (CMF, 1988); *The Buck Owens Collection, 1959–1990* (Rhino, 1992), 4 CDs

Doodle Owens
b. Waco, Texas, November 28, 1930

Like his close friend and frequent co-writer DALLAS FRAZIER, A. L. "Doodle" Owens arrived in Nashville during the mid-1960s and soon established himself as one of the premier hard-country songwriters in town. Among the enduring numbers that he and Frazier wrote together are "All I Have to Offer You (Is Me)" and "(I'm So) Afraid of Losing You Again," both of which hit #1 for CHARLEY PRIDE. But whereas Frazier eventually dropped out of the music business, Owens remained an active songwriter into the 1990s.

Born and raised in Waco, Owens was inspired to become a songwriter by a pair of movies he saw while growing up; one was about the classical composer Frederic Chopin, the other about George Gershwin. As a teenager, Owens hung around local radio stations, paying particular attention to fast-rising star HANK THOMPSON. Owens later played bass with Dallas-based country singer Charlie Adams, and during the mid-1950s performed regularly on a television program hosted by JOHNNY GIMBLE. Owens also recorded a pair of obscure, pop-oriented singles for the MGM and Back Beat labels, respectively.

At RAY PRICE's suggestion, Owens moved with his wife, Mary Ann, to Nashville in 1965. Signed to Forest Hills Music, he enjoyed only modest success at first. But a move to HILL & RANGE gave Owens indirect access to ELVIS PRESLEY, and in 1969 two Owens-Frazier songs appeared on Presley's *From Elvis in Memphis* comeback LP. Besides these and their Pride hits, Owens and Frazier co-wrote such well-known tunes as BRENDA LEE's "Johnny One Time" and STONEY EDWARDS's "Hank and Lefty Raised My Country Soul." In addition, Owens and WHITEY SHAFER co-wrote MOE BANDY's first three chart singles.

Owens's successful run continued with songs such as GEORGE JONES's "Wine Colored Roses" (#10, 1986) and DOUG STONE's "Fourteen Minutes Old" (#6, 1990). But during the early 1990s Owens suffered through heart and kidney problems so severe he was told he had no more than two or three months to live. Miraculously, he survived and picked up his writing again. In 1997 his "Show Me a Woman" (co-written with Doug Johnson) appeared on JOE DIFFIE's *Twice Upon a Time* album. Owens signed with Magnatone Music, also in 1997. —*Daniel Cooper*

Tex Owens
b. Killeen, Texas, June 15, 1892; d. September 9, 1962

Best known for having written the classic western song "Cattle Call," Doie Hensley Owens also was the father of LAURA LEE MCBRIDE (BOB WILLS's first female vocalist) and the brother of TEXAS RUBY, who, with her husband, CURLY FOX, were longtime members of the GRAND OLE OPRY. Tex was a self-taught singer-guitar player; his guitar playing was an easy plucking of basic open chords with his fingers, and his singing was a pleasant western vocal style. He wrote cowboy songs and sentimental songs about mother and love.

The oldest of thirteen children in a Texas sharecropper family, Owens worked on ranches at age fifteen before joining a blackface MINSTREL SHOW. He eventually worked at many occupations, including town marshal in Bridgeport, Oklahoma. In 1932 he landed his own show as the Texas Ranger and became a member of the *Brush Creek Follies* at KMBC, Kansas City, Missouri, where he broadcast for eleven years. He had no band of his own but often appeared with KMBC's Prairie Pioneers and the Texas Rangers. In 1934 Owens recorded "The Dude Ranch Party" (with the Texas Rangers) and "Cattle Call" for DECCA RECORDS, along with three other self-penned songs. In 1936 he recorded for RCA VICTOR, but the label did not issue the songs. After leaving Kansas City, Owens had radio shows on WLW-Cincinnati; KOMA–Oklahoma City; and KHJ-Hollywood. In 1960 he and his wife moved back to Texas. —*Guy Logsdon*

REPRESENTATIVE RECORDING
Cattle Call (Bear Family, 1994)

Vernon Oxford
b. near Rogers, Arkansas, June 8, 1941

Since the mid-1960s, Vernon Paul Oxford has fought a one-man rear-guard action on behalf of what he considers *real* country music. His biggest hit, "Redneck," was probably the most anomalous record he made because it came closest to lampooning the cultural values he holds dear.

Oxford grew up in Arkansas and Kansas, and came to Nashville in May 1964. He found two backers in HARLAN HOWARD and RCA A&R man BOB FERGUSON. He was signed by RCA in October 1965 and was under contract until January 1968 without success. Steady pressure from RCA's British affiliate—topped off by standing ovations at the 1975 International Festival of Country Music in London—persuaded Ferguson to re-sign him in 1975.

Oxford scored several hits after he rejoined RCA, but the biggest by far was "Redneck! (The Redneck National Anthem)," which peaked at #17 in 1976. Two years later, Oxford was off RCA again and has since recorded steadily for smaller labels, including three albums produced by Ferguson for ROUNDER. Still in the Nashville area, Oxford is semiretired from music. —*Colin Escott*

REPRESENTATIVE RECORDING
Keeper of the Flame (Bear Family, 1995), 5 CDs

Ozark Jubilee
established in Springfield, Missouri, 1953

Broadcast from Springfield, Missouri, during the mid- to late-1950s, the *Ozark Jubilee* was the most successful country music network television show of its time, perhaps of all time. The program helped prove the commercial viability of country music as televised entertainment, and it helped make stars of performers such as PORTER WAGONER and BRENDA LEE.

The show's success was all the more remarkable in that the *Ozark Jubilee* started in 1955, while rock & roll was first exploding, and after two ABC-TV shows had already failed (*Hayloft Hoedown*, 1948; and *ABC Barn Dance*, 1949). Still, by 1954 more than half of all American households had a TV set. Fearing that television would undermine its long-running country music radio success (156 live shows per week), Springfield radio station KWTO decided to enter the country TV market. KWTO founder Ralph Foster—with colleagues John Mahaffey and Lester E. Cox—encouraged their protégé, E. E. "SI" SIMAN to spearhead the effort. (Siman had already recruited entertainers CHET ATKINS and Porter Wagoner onto RCA RECORDS.)

In 1953 KWTO had set up the *Ozark Jubilee* on local radio, and then, in 1954, on ABC radio, broadcasting from the Jewell Theater at 216 South Jefferson Street. At this point Siman recruited longtime GRAND OLE OPRY star RED FOLEY, who by then had fallen out with the Opry, to Springfield. Siman then went to New York City, where ABC-TV bought his program idea.

The first show aired on January 22, 1955, and it was a regular Saturday night program for almost five years (except for some Thursday spots in 1956). The televised segment usually lasted one hour, though live in Springfield, it

Red Foley appearing on the Ozark Jubilee

was a two-and-a-half-hour program. Siman had brought special cameras into the theater and hired Don Richardson as a scriptwriter, making the program more progressive than a mere live concert television show. Foley became its perpetual star host.

Other acts began heading to Springfield, such as JEAN SHEPARD, HAWKSHAW HAWKINS, and WEBB PIERCE (once-a-month host, 1955–56). Missouri-based acts included Porter Wagoner and the Foggy River Boys. The "Junior Jubilee" youngsters' segment featured the square-dancing Tadpoles and an eleven-year-old singer from Georgia, Brenda Lee. Eventually Wagoner, and then Lee, left for Nashville, but numerous other *Jubilee* acts arose, becoming national favorites. Among these were BOBBY LORD, MARVIN RAINWATER, WANDA JACKSON, BILLY WALKER, and NORMA JEAN.

As a result of the *Jubilee*'s success, ABC-TV launched three other country music TV programs: the *PEE WEE KING Show* (1955); *Grand Ole Opry* (1955-56); and another Siman production broadcast from Springfield, the *EDDY ARNOLD Show* (1956), which also featured Chet Atkins.

The *Ozark Jubilee* changed its name to *Country Music Jubilee* (1957), then *Jubilee U.S.A.* (1958). Due in part to Foley's Internal Revenue Service tax trial, which scared off sponsors (although Foley eventually won the case), the show closed on September 24, 1960. Then Siman pioneered the color-television *Five Star Jubilee* (NBC-TV, 1961), featuring TEX RITTER, CARL SMITH, JIMMY WAKELY, REX ALLEN, and Nashville pop star Snooky Lanson. RALPH EMERY and his then wife SKEETER DAVIS appeared, as did eleven-year-old BARBARA MANDRELL. According to historian Reta Spears-Stewart, Foley closed the last show (September 22, 1961) saying: "We'll have to do this again someday."

—Steve Eng

Package Shows

During the 1950s, "package show" was the term used to describe a touring country music stage show featuring several performers. Prior to 1940, groups of country entertainers appeared on the vaudeville circuit, and radio station booking offices sent troupes to local schoolhouses, courthouses, and theaters. But the term "package shows" best applies to big-city shows that emerged during World War II. Promoters and booking agents such as OSCAR DAVIS and J. L. FRANK began to stage shows combining up to half a dozen stars from radio programs such as the GRAND OLE OPRY, and sometimes combined talent from several radio barn dances. Meanwhile, J. L. Frank assembled the CAMEL CARAVAN for the R. J. Reynolds Tobacco Company to give free shows to servicemen in the United States and Central America.

During the late 1950s crisis caused by rock & roll, when record sales and gate receipts dropped for many country artists, country entertainers often banded together in units of up to half a dozen acts that could collectively draw sufficient crowds to generate profits. Assisted by the bookers who assembled them and the talent buyers who engaged them, such units remained popular into the 1970s, when the growing popularity of superstars such as KENNY ROGERS and WILLIE NELSON began to make it possible for one or two acts to carry a show date by themselves. Although corporate sponsors have sometimes assembled large troupes, a star-and-opening-act format generally prevails today.

—*John Rumble*

Pamper Music

established in Goodlettsville, Tennessee, January 1, 1959; bought out, April 1969

During its decade of independent existence, Pamper Music developed one of the most heralded song catalogues in the country music business and helped launch the songwriting careers of HANK COCHRAN, HARLAN HOWARD, and WILLIE NELSON.

The firm was founded by principal owners HAL SMITH, RAY PRICE, and Claude Caviness. Smith served as general manager of Pamper, whose Tennessee offices were located at 119 Two Mile Pike in Goodlettsville, twenty miles to the north of Nashville. Caviness headed Pamper's West Coast office, at 9652 Winchell Street, Pico Rivers, California (Caviness's interest in Pamper was purchased by Smith and Price for six figures in 1965).

Hank Cochran (1960–69), Harlan Howard (1962–64), and Willie Nelson (1961–69) wrote many of their classic hits during their Pamper tenure, with Cochran also manning the position of writer relations manager. Ray Pennington, Chuck Howard, Don Rollins, and Fred Carter Jr. also contributed to the wealth and depth of the Pamper catalogue. Standards published by Pamper include "Crazy" (PATSY CLINE, 1961), "Heartaches by the Number" (Ray Price, 1959), "I Fall to Pieces" (Cline, 1961), "Hello Walls" (FARON YOUNG, 1961), and "Make the World Go Away" (EDDY ARNOLD, 1965). In April 1969 Pamper Music was purchased by TREE INTERNATIONAL, and the combination of the two publishing powerhouses ensured Tree's status as a dominant force in the country music publishing field.

—*Kent Henderson*

Colonel Tom Parker

b. Breda, Netherlands, June 26, 1909; d. January 21, 1997

Colonel Tom Parker served as ELVIS PRESLEY's manager from November 1955 until the singer's death in August 1977. Although critics have charged him with having exploited and eroded Presley's talent, the argument can also be made that, without Parker, Elvis might well have remained an obscure rockabilly figure with no national impact.

Born Andreas Cornelis van Kuijk, the fifth of nine children of a Dutch stable manager and his wife, he began an entirely new life after a second trip to America in 1929 (his first brief U.S. sojourn took place in 1927); he never returned to his homeland. In January 1930 he enlisted in the U.S. Army and was stationed in Hawaii with the 64th Coast Artillery, with whom he served three years. After mustering out, he took the name Thomas A. Parker (Thomas R. Parker was the name of his commanding officer in Honolulu); claimed a Huntington, West Virginia, birthplace; and began working with the Royal American Shows traveling carnival in various capacities, including palm reader, sideshow barker, and advance man. He married Marie Mott in 1935 and settled in Tampa, Florida, where he became the field agent for the local Humane Society—an echo of his father's profession as a horseman.

While still working with the Humane Society, Parker also began booking tours for other musical acts, including pop singer Gene Austin, cowboy star Tom Mix, and GRAND OLE OPRY stars ERNEST TUBB, ROY ACUFF, and JAMUP & HONEY. Through doing advance promotion for a Jamup & Honey TENT-SHOW tour in Florida, Parker got to know singer EDDY ARNOLD, and Parker began managing Arnold

Colonel Tom Parker

in the fall of 1945, a job he would hold until September 1953. With Parker's guidance, Arnold became the hottest star in country music, with his own radio shows, movie roles, and a string of #1 records. Along the way, in October 1948, Louisiana governor JIMMIE DAVIS gave Parker an honorary colonel's commission, and thus the new identity was complete. Thereafter he was known as Colonel Parker.

In 1954 Parker began a booking and business partnership with HANK SNOW that brought Elvis Presley into his purview when Presley appeared as an incendiary opening act for Snow and other country stars on tours in 1955. Parker wasted no time attaching himself to Presley, and on August 15, 1955, Parker bought a controlling interest in Presley's management contract from Memphis DJ Bob Neal for $2,500. Parker then engineered a complicated deal among HILL & RANGE MUSIC, RCA RECORDS, and SUN RECORDS to buy out Presley's contract from Sun and sign him to RCA for $40,000—at the time a sum considered astronomical. Presley signed with RCA in November 1955, Neal's management contract with Presley expired in March 1956, and Presley became the biggest star in popular music within weeks. Parker devoted himself almost exclusively to Elvis Presley from that moment on, arranging important TV and concert appearances as well as movie roles.

For his exclusive management services, Parker exacted a high toll. In addition to his basic management fee of 25 percent, Parker received a third of Elvis's concert proceeds after 1972 and half of his record income after 1973. There was, in addition, the toll Parker may well have taken on Presley's creative career by shunting him into limiting arrangements with Hill & Range as his main song suppliers and with producer Hal Wallis on a series of musical movies that rarely rose above the level of pleasant formula.

Following Presley's death, Parker quietly removed himself from the music business, easing into retirement with a $2 million buyout from RCA Records in 1983 for his "right, title, and interest" in all Presley-related contracts. In his later years he split time between homes in Las Vegas and Madison, Tennessee. Among the younger stars he encour-

aged was GEORGE STRAIT, whom Parker urged to consider a movie career. —*Paul Kingsbury*

Linda Parker
b. Covington, Kentucky, January 18, 1912; d. August 12, 1935

A featured member of WLS's *NATIONAL BARN DANCE*, Linda Parker is generally considered the first woman to launch a successful solo career in country music. Her popularity helped open opportunities for other women in the field, most notably PATSY MONTANA.

Genevieve Elizabeth Muenich was an only child raised by working-class parents in Hammond, Indiana. She became interested in music after hearing pop singer Ruth Etting on Chicago radio. Dropping out of high school at age sixteen, Muenich sang at area parks and roadhouses; by late 1929 she was featured on WWAE-Hammond. Moving to Chicago in 1930, she landed a regular fifteen-minute show on WAAF as Jeanne Munich, the Red-Headed Bluebird.

Even though she had no background in folk or country music, promoter JOHN LAIR was impressed by Muenich's personality and talent; in spring 1932 he hired her for his CUMBERLAND RIDGE RUNNERS troupe on WLS. To avoid confusion with her WAAF audience, Lair molded her new persona as Linda Parker, the Sunbonnet Girl from the hills of Kentucky. As Parker she sang ballads and sentimental songs, using the same natural phrasing that reflected her stylistic debt to Etting. Despite her radio success, Parker made only two records during her lifetime; both were issued on Sears, Roebuck & Company's CONQUEROR label.

Parker was stricken with acute appendicitis during an August 3, 1935, show in Elkhart, Indiana. She was rushed to a Mishawaka hospital, where she died nine days later from peritonitis. —*Dave Samuelson*

Lee Roy Parnell
b. Abilene, Texas, December 21, 1956

Lee Roy Parnell has made his mark with dual talents. He's a fine singer, bringing a warm r&b sensibility to his Texas-sized boogie and country tunes. He's also a fine guitarist; his soulful slide guitar work is found on hits from the likes of MARY CHAPIN CARPENTER and PATTY LOVELESS.

Parnell was raised in Stephenville, Texas, and his father was a friend of neighbor and Texas swing pioneer BOB WILLS. His early influences ranged from Wills to the Allman Brothers, Muddy Waters, and Freddy King. Parnell has effectively incorporated both country and blues sounds into his material. Touring since age nineteen, Parnell hit the road from his base in Austin, Texas, and spent twelve years developing his trade. He had tried his skill in Nashville before without success but gave it one more chance in 1987. He then quickly landed a publishing deal with Welk Music (now Polygram).

Parnell and his longtime band the Hot Links became a popular live act, and a sizzling set at the BLUEBIRD CAFE caught the ear of TIM DUBOIS, the head of the newly forming ARISTA-NASHVILLE office. Parnell was signed to a deal, and his eponymous 1990 debut album yielded three singles that failed to climb higher than #54. Parnell's second album, 1992's *Love Without Mercy*, scored with the Top Ten title cut as well as two hits, "What Kind of Fool Do You Think I Am" and "Tender Moment," both of which reached #2. He continued his successful run with "On the Road," a 1993 Top Ten single written by BOB McDILL. Tabbed as the flagship artist for Career Records, Arista's short-lived sister label, Parnell released *We All Get Lucky Sometimes* in 1995 and *Every Night's A Saturday Night* in 1997. He returned to the Arista label when Career Records folded.

His songwriting skills blossomed, and he has gone on to write cuts for JO-EL SONNIER, JOHNNY LEE, COLLIN RAYE, and SWEETHEARTS OF THE RODEO. Parnell's hits have come often in the form of clean, bluesy ballads—sort of a deep-fried Mark Knopfler style. This style is evident on "Givin' Water to a Drownin' Man," a midtempo stomp on his fourth album that was also cut by frequent Parnell collaborator DELBERT McCLINTON. —*Clark Parsons*

REPRESENTATIVE RECORDINGS

Love Without Mercy (Arista, 1992); *On the Road* (Arista, 1993)

Gram Parsons
b. Winter Haven, Florida, November 5, 1946; d. September 19, 1973

Every few years, a country or rock singer or band—among them Elvis Costello, Lone Justice, JIM LAUDERDALE, the KENTUCKY HEADHUNTERS, and the Jayhawks—will point to Gram Parsons, who never had a hit in more than ten years of recording, as a major influence. One will call Parsons the Father of Country-Rock.

Parsons wasn't the first to conceive country-rock, but he was perhaps the most passionate about bringing country music into the increasingly rock & roll world of the 1960s. "It's a beautiful, beautiful idiom that's been overlooked so much," he said in 1972, "and so many people have the wrong idea of it."

Gram Parsons

Born Ingram Cecil Connor III, Parsons was raised in Waycross, Georgia, where he got his first musical ideas from ELVIS PRESLEY and other SUN RECORDS artists. When Gram's father committed suicide in 1958, his family moved to his mother's hometown, Winter Haven, Florida, where she married Robert Parsons, a salesman.

At home, Gram listened to music ranging from pop to r&b and jazz. In school he sang with a rock band as well as a folk group, playing guitar and singing with a thin but emotional voice. He rediscovered country during a brief stay at Harvard in 1965, when he also got into LSD and the Beatles. Saying the best country music was "white soul music," he formed the International Submarine Band, which, after Parsons moved to Los Angeles in 1966, made an album *(Safe at Home)* that included songs by JOHNNY CASH and MERLE HAGGARD. Parsons himself wrote songs about love, about not being understood, about the constant need to move on.

He joined the BYRDS in late 1967, helping take them into country music. By the following spring he had left and co-founded the FLYING BURRITO BROTHERS with CHRIS HILLMAN, his bandmate from the Byrds. Other original members of the Burritos included bassist Chris Ethridge, who'd played briefly with Parsons in the International Submarine Band, and steel guitarist "Sneaky" Pete Kleinow. In an early description of the Burritos, Parsons told *Melody Maker* that the band was "basically a Southern soul group playing country and gospel-oriented music with a steel guitar."

The Flying Burrito Brothers lived up to Parsons's promise of a blend of roots music with a rock & roll attitude. A strong first album earned excellent reviews, especially for songs such as "Sin City" and "Hot Burrito #1." But the album didn't sell. After a train tour wiped out much of the Burritos' promotion budget, the album sank, and a second effort, *Burrito Deluxe*, didn't do any better, despite a superb rendition of the Rolling Stones' "Wild Horses," which Parsons's buddies Mick Jagger and Keith Richards sent him before they themselves recorded it. Soon after an appearance at the Stones' disastrous Altamont rock festival in late 1969, Parsons left the Flying Burrito Brothers.

In late 1971 Parsons heard about EMMYLOU HARRIS, who was singing in Washington, D.C.–area folk clubs. He convinced her to join him for an album featuring back up by several musicians who regularly worked with Parsons's idol Elvis Presley. Parsons and Harris's voices blended exquisitely. The album, *GP*, earned generally good reviews but didn't sell.

After a haphazard tour and another recording session, which resulted in the album *Grievous Angel*, Parsons was found dead of a mixture of alcohol and heroin in a motel room in the desert town of Joshua Tree, California, where he had often visited.

It was in death that Parsons gained his greatest notoriety. Saying they were fulfilling a pact, Parsons's friend and road manager, Phil Kaufman, and another friend spirited Parsons's casket away from a local airport, where it awaited shipment to Parsons's stepfather in Louisiana. Kaufman and his friend drove Parsons's body to Joshua Tree National Monument, where Kaufman tried to set the body on fire. Kaufman was later arrested, and Parsons's remains wound up in a cemetery in New Orleans.

—*Ben Fong-Torres*

REPRESENTATIVE RECORDINGS

The Flying Burrito Brothers: *Gilded Palace of Sin* (A&M, 1969); *GP/Grievous Angel* (Reprise, 1990); *Gram Parsons:*

Warm Evenings, Pale Mornings, Bottled Blues 1963–1973
(Raven, 1991)

Dolly Parton

b. Locust Ridge, Tennessee, January 19, 1946

With their strong feminine stances in the 1960s and 1970s, Dolly Rebecca Parton, along with fellow female pioneers LORETTA LYNN and TAMMY WYNETTE, revolutionized the world of country music for women performers. Then Parton took her crusade a step farther by crossing over to the pop world—landing on the cover of *Rolling Stone,* achieving pop hits, and starring in a series of Hollywood movies. Along the way, however, she ultimately lost much of her core country audience, to the point that in 1996 she sold her Nashville office and in 1997 dissolved her fan club, which had been one of the staunchest in country music.

Parton came from deep in Appalachia, where music was an integral part of life for those who, like the Partons, struggled to make a hard living. Her mother was a singer who taught Dolly church music along with the Elizabethan ballads her ancestors had brought to America. Dolly's grandfather was a fiddling preacher who wrote "Singing His Praise," which was recorded by KITTY WELLS. Several of Dolly's eleven siblings have been active in music, and some worked for a time in her family band.

Parton's childhood figured very strongly in her ambition to escape her circumstances, and in the many frank, unromantic songs she wrote about her experience and about life in Appalachia. For example, "Coat of Many Colors" (#4, 1971) was a straight-ahead account of a humiliating experience she had suffered at school when classmates made fun of her patchwork, homemade coat.

Parton was encouraged in her tentative attempts at music by her uncle Bill Owens, who bought her a guitar and who, by the time she was ten years old, managed to land her a stint on a television variety show in the nearest big town, Knoxville. Nashville soon took note of her, and she made her first guest appearance on the GRAND OLE OPRY at age thirteen in 1959. She also recorded a single for a small Louisiana label, and one for MERCURY RECORDS in Nashville in 1962.

Parton was not daunted by the lack of success of her early recordings, so in 1964 she packed her bags and left for Nashville immediately after graduating from high school. Her first day in town, she met her future husband, contractor Carl Dean, in a Laundromat. Her musical career progressed apace; people began to take note of her as a songwriter, especially after a pair of songs she wrote with Bill Owens became Top Ten hits for BILL PHILLIPS in 1966. Then she recorded for FRED FOSTER's MONUMENT RECORDS from 1965 to 1967, with "Dumb Blonde"—which attacked traditional female stereotypes—becoming her first Top Forty hit.

Parton's pivotal career moment came in 1967, in the form of a phone call from the syndicated television series the *PORTER WAGONER Show.* Wagoner, a flashy-dressing traditional country singer, was looking to replace his duet partner NORMA JEAN. As a team, Wagoner and Parton became immediate audience favorites. Her hourglass figure and outrageous outfits and angelic voice played off perfectly against Wagoner's cornpone humor and old-fashioned country sensibility. RCA RECORDS signed Parton as both Wagoner's duet partner and as a solo recording

Dolly Parton

artist. She became increasingly successful in both personas and soon began to eclipse Wagoner's own star.

Parton's first solo #1 hit was her composition "Joshua" (1971), and that led to three more #1 songs in 1974: "Jolene," "Love Is Like a Butterfly," and "I Will Always Love You." That the latter song was her own personal farewell to partner Wagoner became painfully evident to him when she left his TV show that year. Under contractual obligations, he continued to produce her records until 1976 (including the #1 hit "The Bargain Store" in 1975), but she was soon on her own.

In retrospect, the early to mid-1970s was the most creatively fertile period of Parton's country music career. She was voted the CMA's Female Vocalist of the Year in both 1975 and 1976. Additionally, 1973 yielded what has come to be regarded by some as her most nearly perfect album, *My Tennessee Mountain Home.* It's a bittersweet look backward at a life and a tradition she was bound on leaving. The cover is a picture of the cabin in which she grew up in Sevierville; the songs, especially the title cut, are a matter-of-fact tribute to a people and a way of life that are vanishing. "I wanted to be *free,*" she told *Rolling Stone* in 1977. "I had my songs to sing, I had an ambition and it *burned* inside me. It was something I knew would take me out of the mountains. I knew I could see worlds beyond the Smoky Mountains."

Parton's new life looked beyond Nashville and increasingly upon Hollywood. Her first album after declaring her independence from Wagoner was 1977's *New Harvest, First Gathering,* which yielded the #11 single "Light of a Clear Blue Morning." That same year brought the album *Here*

You Come Again, a glitzy—and successful—attempt at a country-to-pop crossover. The CMA named her Entertainer of the Year in 1978, and it seemed as if Parton could preserve the best of both worlds.

Parton's country career became erratic after that, however, even as her name became a household word and she became a constant presence on network TV, appearing on talk shows, specials, and a brief self-titled series of her own in 1976. Her movie career bounced from stellar *(9 to 5)* to forgettable *(Rhinestone,* which attempted to make Sylvester Stallone a believable country singer). Her recording triumphs included 1987's *Trio* album with EMMYLOU HARRIS and LINDA RONSTADT and the 1993 *Honky Tonk Angels* collaboration with Loretta Lynn and Tammy Wynette. In 1992 the singer Whitney Houston recorded Parton's "I Will Always Love You," which became a #1 smash hit in the pop market, partly due to its inclusion in the soundtrack for the movie *Bodyguard.*

Parton also has demonstrated her business acumen in several ventures, most notably the theme park Dollywood in East Tennessee, near Sevierville. In 1985 she and other investors opened the park, which has become one of the South's leading tourist attractions. Through Dollywood, Parton has contributed in many ways to her home county's economy and to scholarship programs for high school students there. There is now a life-size statue of Parton on the lawn of the Sevier County courthouse.

In 1996 Parton cut *Treasures,* an album of favorites (non-Parton songs), for the new Nashville recording label Rising Tide Entertainment. The album was a critical success but did not fare well commercially. In that same year she and VINCE GILL won the CMA's Vocal Event of the Year Award for their duet recording of "I Will Always Love You."

—*Chet Flippo*

REPRESENTATIVE RECORDINGS

My Tennessee Mountain Home (RCA, 1973); *The World of Dolly Parton, Volume 1* (Monument, 1988); *Eagle When She Flies* (Columbia, 1991); *The Essential Dolly Parton* (RCA, 1995); *The Essential Porter Wagoner and Dolly Parton* (RCA, 1996); *The Essential Dolly Parton, Volume 2* (RCA, 1997)

Patriot Records
founded in Nashville, Tennessee, April 1994; ended April 1995

Patriot Records shared its name with the missiles used by Allied forces during the Persian Gulf War—along with a comparable hit-to-miss ratio. Founded in the spring of 1994 as a subsidiary of LIBERTY RECORDS, at a time when country music's biggest labels were creating or reactivating offshoot labels to expand their artist rosters (MCA's DECCA, Mercury's Polydor), Patriot was headed by Liberty's president/CEO at the time, JIMMY BOWEN. Bowen intended to use the label to develop a half dozen acts during its first year and grow from there.

Unfortunately, Patriot's first signing, young Mississippi singer Bryan Austin, barely dented the charts. Neither did a release from singer Noah Gordon, although the debut American album from Canadian artist Lisa Brokop garnered a Top Forty hit, "Take That." After Bowen retired in April 1995, Liberty and Patriot's parent company, EMI Records Group North America, decided to consolidate both labels under the former Capitol Nashville umbrella, which put an end to Patriot after only a year. Ironically, the fledgling label was just enjoying its first chart success with the second album by platinum-selling Liberty artist JOHN BERRY, *Standing on the Edge,* whose title track gave Patriot its only #1 hit. Berry and Brokop were retained by Capitol Nashville; Austin and Gordon were dropped. —*Jim Ridley*

Les Paul & Mary Ford
Les Paul b. Waukesha, Wisconsin, June 9, 1915
Mary Ford b. Pasadena, California, July 7, 1924; d. September 30, 1977

One of pop music's most imaginative acts during the early 1950s, Les Paul & Mary Ford were respectively rooted in country and western music. While their many hits often featured layers of vocal and guitar overdubs, the couple also recorded relaxed, unadorned covers of country hits and standards.

Born Lester William Polsfuss, Les Paul launched his professional career in 1932, playing guitar, harmonica, and jug with Joe Wolverton as the Ozark Apple Knockers on KMOX, St. Louis, and WBBM, Chicago. In the mid-1930s he was featured on Chicago radio as "Rhubarb Red." Inspired by recordings of Belgian guitarist Django Reinhardt, Paul began playing more jazz; he also experimented with amplifying his guitar. Between 1937 and 1941 he led the Les Paul Trio with singer-guitarist Jimmy Atkins (CHET ATKINS's half brother) and bassist ERNIE NEWTON.

After moving to Los Angeles in 1943, Paul met Iris "Colleen" Summers, a popular western vocalist on KXLA's *Dinner Bell Round-Up Time.* During the first years of their romance, the couple maintained separate careers: Paul with Bing Crosby and the Andrews Sisters; Summers with Art Wenzel, GENE AUTRY, and JIMMY WAKELY. When they began recording together in 1949, Paul gave Summers the name "Mary Ford" to avoid conflicts with her established western music audience.

With their multitracked vocals and crisp electric guitar leads, Les Paul & Mary Ford generated dozens of hits for CAPITOL during the early 1950s, most notably "How High the Moon" and "Vaya con Dios." During these years Paul also made significant contributions to electric guitar and tape recording technologies.

Like other popular artists, Paul & Ford were affected by the rise of rock & roll in the mid-1950s; a jump to COLUMBIA in 1958 failed to rekindle flagging record sales. In 1962 they abandoned their trademark sound to try a contemporary Nashville approach; the resulting albums were musically and commercially unsuccessful. Paul & Ford's professional partnership ended with their 1963 separation and eventual divorce; both later retired from public performance.

In May 1975 Paul and Chet Atkins recorded *Chester & Lester,* an album of guitar duets; it won the 1977 Grammy for Best Country Instrumental Performance. A follow-up album, *Guitar Monsters,* was released in 1978. In 1984 Paul resumed public appearances with a weekly stint at a lower Manhattan jazz club; his re-emergence brought renewed acclaim for his musical and technical achievements. In 1991 Capitol issued a four-CD retrospective covering his years on the label; William Morrow & Company published Mary Alice Shaughnessy's biography *Les Paul: An American Original* in 1992. —*Dave Samuelson*

REPRESENTATIVE RECORDINGS

Chester & Lester (RCA, 1976); *Les Paul: The Legend and the Legacy* (Capitol, 1991), 4 CDs

Johnny Paycheck
b. Greenfield, Ohio, May 31, 1938

In 1977 "Take This Job and Shove It" made Johnny Paycheck a country superstar seemingly overnight. Yet by the time that blue-collar anthem hit the airwaves, Paycheck had been through twenty years' worth of career ups and downs. He had worked as a front man for some of the top talents in the country business, and he had recorded some of the most vigorous, fascinating honky-tonk music ever produced. Along the way he had also co-written such country classics as "Apartment #9" and "Touch My Heart."

Born Donald Eugene Lytle, he received his first guitar when he was six, and he was entering talent contests by age nine. He left home while still a teenager, traveling throughout Ohio and nearby states until he enlisted in the navy. Court-martialed in 1956 for slugging a superior officer, he spent two years in military prison. After his release he took to the highway again, eventually landing in Nashville.

Adopting the professional name Donny Young, he signed as a songwriter with TREE PUBLISHING and as a singer with DECCA RECORDS. He also began a succession of jobs as bass player, front man, and harmony vocalist for such stars as GEORGE JONES, PORTER WAGONER, FARON YOUNG, and RAY PRICE. After recording for MERCURY in 1962, he was discovered by industry veteran Aubrey Mayhew, who took over management of his career, changed his stage name to JOHNNY PAYCHECK, and recorded him for Hilltop Records in New York. Paycheck's first Top Forty single, "A-11," was released on Hilltop in 1965.

Early in 1966 Paycheck and Mayhew started LITTLE DARLIN' RECORDS and moved their operations to Nashville. Paycheck's Little Darlin' catalogue stands out as one of the most musically audacious of its era, typified by such hits as "The Lovin' Machine" and such nonhits as "(Pardon Me) I've Got Someone to Kill." Unfortunately, Paycheck's health and personal well-being were in decline throughout this same period. By the close of the 1960s he and Mayhew had fallen out, and Paycheck had been reduced to living on skid row in Los Angeles.

Tracked down by industry insider Nick Hunter, Paycheck moved to Denver to dry out and eventually hooked up with producer-executive BILLY SHERRILL, who signed him to EPIC RECORDS. In 1971 Paycheck's Epic debut, a cover of the Freddie North r&b hit "She's All I Got," hit #2 on the charts and was nominated for a Grammy. Paycheck stayed with Epic into 1982, marketed first as a love balladeer and later as a so-called OUTLAW. Along the way he scored such memorable hits as "Someone to Give My Love To"; "Slide Off of Your Satin Sheets"; and his career record, "Take This Job and Shove It."

Paycheck's personal life remained tumultuous, however. He had drug problems and legal problems, and on December 19, 1985, he shot a man (not fatally) during a barroom confrontation in Hillsboro, Ohio. Sent to prison in February 1989, he was released two years later. Completely straight, he picked up the pieces of his career and has remained active as a performer ever since. He became a member of the GRAND OLE OPRY in November 1997, and as of early 1998 he was on the verge of signing a new record deal with the Lucky Dog label. —*Daniel Cooper*

REPRESENTATIVE RECORDINGS

Johnny Paycheck's Greatest Hits (Epic, 1974); *Biggest Hits* (Epic, 1982); *The Real Mr. Heartache: The Little Darlin' Years* (Country Music Foundation, 1996)

Leon Payne
b. Alba, Texas, June 15, 1917; d. September 11, 1969

Leon Payne's reputation as one of country music's finest songwriters has unfortunately obscured his considerable talents as a singer. After his graduation from the State School for the Blind in Austin, Texas, in 1935, Payne became a country singer and by 1941 was broadcasting from WRR in Dallas. He recorded for BLUEBIRD RECORDS that April as a solo artist, and as a guest vocalist with BILL BOYD's seminal western swing band, the Cowboy Ramblers. In 1947, while living in Mineola, Texas, he recorded for BULLET RECORDS (with brother-in-law Jack Rhodes's band), and his first release, "Lifetime to Regret," became a hit that would eventually earn him a contract with CAPITOL RECORDS in 1949. The song also brought his songwriting to the attention of other artists, and he became a highly respected songwriter when HANK WILLIAMS recorded his "Lost Highway" and "They'll Never Take Her Love from Me."

Payne's smooth, tenor voice and finely crafted compositions, which numbered in the hundreds by the late 1940s, made him a popular regional performer; he was based in Houston from 1948 to 1952, then moved to San Antonio, where he remained until his death. He also made regular appearances on the *LOUISIANA HAYRIDE* and the GRAND OLE OPRY.

Payne, who sometimes played electric lead guitar and

Johnny Paycheck

trombone in addition to rhythm guitar, followed his stint at Capitol with stays at DECCA, STARDAY (where he tackled rock & roll under the pseudonym Rock Rogers), and several smaller labels. In 1968 EDDIE NOACK recorded Payne's stark and disturbing murder ballad "Psycho," which has since become a cult classic. "I Love You Because," though, has become Payne's most universally admired song. Written for his wife, Myrtie, the song was a hit for Payne himself in 1949 and has since entered the repertoire of virtually everyone, including ELVIS PRESLEY, who has ever tried to sing a country song.   —Bill C. Malone

Rufus Payne (see Tee-Tot and Hank Williams)

Minnie Pearl
b. Centerville, Tennessee, October 25, 1912; d. March 4, 1996

Minnie Pearl was the undisputed queen of country comedy, known for her hopelessly styleless knee-length country dresses, her straw hat decorated with colorful plastic flowers and $1.98 price tag, and her cheerful shout of "Howdee! I'm just so proud to be here!" For fifty years she performed as a member of the GRAND OLE OPRY.

She was born Sarah Ophelia Colley, the youngest of five daughters of a prosperous lumber magnate and his homemaker wife, who lost their fortune in the Great Depression. Aspiring to become an actress, twenty-two-year-old Ophelia (as she was then called) settled for a job as an itinerant community theater director for the Wayne P. Sewell Producing Company, traveling to rural southern cities and staging plays owned by the firm. While on the road in North Alabama she met an elderly woman whose amusing country talk and mannerisms inspired Ophelia Colley to create a comic character that eventually became known as Minnie Pearl.

In April 1939 she made her first professional appearance as the Minnie Pearl character at a women's club function at the Highland Park Hotel in Aiken, South Carolina. In the fall of 1940 a chance opportunity to perform at a banker's convention in Centerville brought her to the attention of executives at WSM in Nashville. On November 30, 1940, she made her debut on the Grand Ole Opry. Less than a week later, more than 300 cards, telegrams, and letters addressed to Minnie Pearl flooded the offices of WSM. On December 7, 1940, the name Minnie Pearl appeared among the Opry cast listing for the first time in the weekly radio guide of the Nashville Tennessean, slotted in the 8:45 P.M. segment.

With the help of her sister Virginia and coaching from the Opry's GEORGE D. HAY, Ophelia Colley gradually developed a fully-fledged comedic character and jokes to go with it. Minnie Pearl became the quintessential small-town spinster, preoccupied with chasing men and gossiping about her family and neighbors in the mythical town of Grinder's Switch—Brother, Uncle Nabob, and sometime boyfriend Hezzie. In the spring of 1942 she graduated into the elite cast of the Opry when she joined the "Prince Albert Show," the half hour of the Opry broadcast over the NBC radio network. Not long after getting this promotion, she added a distinctive new touch to her act: the big "How-DEE!" At the request of the William Esty advertising agency, which had the sponsor's account, she went from a wallflower's shy "Howdy" to a shouted "How-DEE!" that called for an audience response. It quickly became one of her trademarks.

Minnie Pearl

On February 23, 1947, she married Henry Cannon (b. Franklin, Tennessee, August 11, 1917; d. November 7, 1997), a former Army Air Corps pilot and a partner in the charter airplane service Capitol Airways. Before long, he left Capitol Airways and set up his own charter service specializing in the country music business, flying a Beechcraft single-engine plane. Clients included EDDY ARNOLD and his then manager TOM PARKER, HANK WILLIAMS, CARL SMITH, WEBB PIERCE, and eventually ELVIS PRESLEY. Client number one was his wife, who soon became known in Nashville society circles as Sarah Cannon. In addition to transporting his wife, Henry Cannon became her manager as well.

From 1948 to 1958 Minnie worked the Grand Ole Opry with veteran comedian ROD BRASFIELD. They did what was called double comedy, meaning that neither one always played the straight man. Depending on how they felt, one or the other might take the punch line. Their partnership was ended by Brasfield's death in 1958.

Following a May 1, 1957, appearance on NBC-TV's top-rated This Is Your Life, hosted by Ralph Edwards, Minnie Pearl began making many more appearances on NBC-TV shows hosted by TENNESSEE ERNIE FORD and Dinah Shore as well as The Tonight Show. In the sixties she branched out to The Carol Burnett Show and The Jonathan Winters Show, whose producer, Sam Lovullo, recruited her for HEE HAW's cast in 1969. There she reached a wider audience than ever in her various continuing roles as a teacher in a one-room schoolhouse, a house mother in a girls' dormitory, editor of the Grinder's Switch Gazette, and the tough-to-get-along-with passenger in the "Driving Miss Minnie" segments. In the 1980s she began appearing each Friday night on TNN's NASHVILLE NOW joking with host RALPH EMERY for the "Let Minnie Steal Your Joke" segment. She continued to play the Grand Ole Opry as well, frequently teaming in later years with ROY ACUFF.

In her entire career, she had a half dozen albums and about twice as many singles scattered among the BULLET,

KING, RCA, Everest, and STARDAY labels. Most of her records were monologues. When she did sing, she exaggerated the flaws in her voice. She had only one hit, "Giddyup Go—Answer," and that was a maudlin recitation that "answered" a similarly maudlin recitation by RED SOVINE. It did not reflect her comedic style, and she made little mention of it after it became a #10 hit in 1966.

She performed her last show in Joliet, Illinois, on June 15, 1991; two days later she suffered a serious stroke that left her virtually bedridden in a Nashville nursing home for close to five years. When she died following a final series of strokes in 1996, all of Nashville, and indeed the world, mourned her passing.   —*Paul Kingsbury*

Pedal Steel Guitar

In 1939 Alvino Rey, a pop steel guitarist and leader of a big band, teamed with machinist John Moore to design a new type of electric steel guitar—one different from the nonpedal, solid-bodied, electric "lap" steels that were popular for nearly a decade. The Gibson Guitar Company introduced this instrument as the "Electraharp," its pedals and mechanical system able to alter various string pitches to create smoothly voiced and modulated chords.

The first country musician to take the instrument seriously was SPEEDY WEST—an obscure, California-based steel player who approached patternmaker Paul Bigsby to build a three-neck, four-pedal model, which West acquired in February 1948. West first recorded with the instrument on Eddie Kirk's 1949 rendition of "Candy Kisses." From 1950 through 1956 West used the pedal steel guitar on hundreds of country and pop recordings. BUD ISAACS, another buyer of Bigsby's craft, pioneered the instrument in Nashville, and his solo on WEBB PIERCE's 1954 hit recording of "Slowly" inspired steel guitarists across the nation to adopt pedal steels or to adapt their nonpedal instruments to alter string pitches with homemade mechanisms.

In 1955 BUDDY EMMONS, who played a Bigsby pedal steel with LITTLE JIMMY DICKENS's Country Boys, joined SHOT JACKSON to build the first Sho-Bud pedal guitar. Fender began making pedal steels in 1957, designed with the help of Speedy West. Sho-Bud models, however, became a favorite among country steel players due to their quality and the company's Nashville roots.

Pedal steel designs gradually stabilized (though many players had their own variations). Most had two eight-string necks, four or more pedals, and two or three knee levers. Many players tuned one neck to E9 (suitable for commercial country accompaniment) and one to C6 (favored for Western swing or jazz). In Nashville other pedal steel greats emerged, including PETE DRAKE, a Nashville "A-Team" member skilled at playing commercial accompaniment behind singers. Others included Curly Chalker, Hal Rugg, Lloyd Green, Buddy Charleton, Sonny Garrish, Doug Jernigan, PAUL FRANKLIN, Bruce Bouton, and Dan Dugmore. In California, Ralph Mooney, renowned for his work with WYNN STEWART, BUCK OWENS, and MERLE HAGGARD, epitomized the high-pitched BAKERSFIELD style, later using that same technique with WAYLON JENNINGS's Waylors. Many large and small companies manufactured steels, including Gibson; Fender; MSA, founded by Texas steel player Maurice Anderson; and Emmons, founded by Buddy Emmons after he and Shot Jackson parted company. Though pedal steel has risen and fallen in popularity in country's changing trends, it remains one of the music's most identifiable sounds.   —*Rich Kienzle*

Herb Pedersen

b. Berkeley, California, April 27, 1944

As a studio guitarist, banjo player, and harmony singer, Herb Pedersen played a leading role in the emergence of country-rock in the 1970s and 1980s. Pedersen honed his musical skills on the San Francisco Bay area bluegrass circuit. After a short stint in Nashville in the early 1960s, he returned to California in 1963, joining David Grisman in the Smokey Grass Boys. In 1964 he joined VERN GOSDIN and brother Ray Gosdin to play banjo. When EARL SCRUGGS had to undergo hip surgery in 1967, he asked Pedersen to take his place on road bookings. Pedersen recorded two albums with the DILLARDS, *Wheatstraw Suite* (1968) and *Copperfields* (1970), having replaced Doug Dillard on banjo.

Pedersen recorded two albums of his own for EPIC RECORDS: *Southwest* (1975), which yielded his only chart single, "Our Baby's Gone"; and *Sandman* (1976). Meanwhile, as a studio musician, he worked with EMMYLOU HARRIS, LINDA RONSTADT, THE FLYING BURRITO BROTHERS, GRAM PARSONS, JOHN PRINE, KRIS KRISTOFFERSON, and the Doobie Brothers.

In the mid-1980s Pedersen formed the DESERT ROSE BAND with longtime friend CHRIS HILLMAN and guitarist JOHN JORGENSON and recorded for MCA/CURB. "Love Reunited," "He's Back and I'm Blue," and "I Still Believe in You" all cracked *Billboard's* Top Ten country charts, the latter two songs hitting #1. After disbanding in 1993, Pedersen returned to bluegrass with the 1995 formation of the Laurel Canyon Ramblers with ex-Kentucky Colonel band member Billy Ray Lathum.   —*Chris Skinker*

Hap Peebles

b. Anthony, Kansas, January 4, 1913; d. January 8, 1993

Hap Peebles set high standards for show promoters in the entertainment field during the 1950s and 1960s. His accomplishments paved the way to the success that country music is enjoying today.

The Dean of Country Music Promoters was born Harry Alexander Peebles and raised in Anthony, Kansas. In 1931, while working as a newspaper reporter for the *Anthony Republic,* he saw an opportunity to bring shows and sporting events to the town's new auditorium. After years of being a successful promoter, Peebles turned to booking major country acts in 1945. For a time he managed BOB WILLS & HIS TEXAS PLAYBOYS and was the first promoter to provide country music to state and local fairs. He founded the Harry Peebles Agency in Wichita to serve as his headquarters and became the single most important promoter in the Midwest. Moreover, Peeples was one of the first to pair country and rock & roll acts on the same show. He was a founder and lifetime member of the CMA. Peebles also helped organize the International Country Music Talent Buyers Association in 1971 and served as its first president. Peebles received numerous awards and honors over the years, including CMA's first Talent Buyer and Promoter of the Year Award.   —*Don Roy*

Ralph S. Peer

b. Kansas City, Missouri, May 22, 1892; d. January 19, 1960

Ralph Peer was the prominent early businessman in country music. His impact, moreover, on the larger popular mu-

Ralph Peer

sic industry—as a pioneer in recording, music publishing, and artist management—is incalculable. Among the country music innovators whose success can be credited to Peer are JIMMIE RODGERS and the CARTER FAMILY, both of whom Ralph Peer discovered, recorded, and managed.

Ralph Sylvester Peer was born in 1892 in Kansas City, Missouri. His father, a store owner in the Kansas City suburb of Independence, Missouri, sold records and gramophones, among other wares. At age eighteen Peer went to work for the COLUMBIA Phonograph Company. In 1919 he was hired by OKEH RECORDS in New York to assist OKeh's production director, Fred Hagar. Neither the country music nor "race music" industries existed. According to Peer, OKeh's records were manufactured by a button company. "The business then was vocalists making records of 'Silver Threads Among the Gold' and 'Home Sweet Home,'" Peer said in 1959 in one of several taped conversations with Lillian Borgeson (the tapes, from which all subsequent quotes have been taken with permission, are held at the Southern Folklife Collection of the University of North Carolina).

The first moneymaking country-music record, FIDDLIN' JOHN CARSON's "The Little Old Log Cabin in the Lane" b/w "The Old Hen Cackled and the Rooster's Going to Crow" was an accidental success, as was the first race music best-seller three years earlier (Hagar and Peer's production of Mamie Smith's "Crazy Blues"). In June 1923 Peer traveled to Atlanta, looking for a rival to Columbia's race music star, Bessie Smith. (Recording in the field, the decade's major method of obtaining hillbilly and race music records, was a Peer innovation.) Associates persuaded Peer to record Carson, whose music he considered "terrible," but he was quick to capitalize on Carson's unexpected success and recorded a flood of music by the HILL BILLIES, the STONEMAN FAMILY, VERNON DALHART, and other first-generation hillbilly-music stars. Peer always claimed to have supplied country music with the name it wore until af-

ter World War II—"hillbilly." He took credit, too, for the industry's use of the name "race music."

Peer resigned from OKeh in 1925. In 1926 he approached VICTOR RECORDS, which was eager to expand its hillbilly business, with a novel plan. He recalled, "This was a business of recording new copyrights. I would be willing to go to work for nothing with the understanding that there would be no objection if I controlled these copyrights." It was a new way of running the record business, of infusing it with a built-in artistic dynamism. "I insisted on new material," said Peer. "I wouldn't let [artists] record the old stuff, like 'Home Sweet Home.' Painful experience had shown us it just wouldn't sell."

The first stop on Peer's recording trip for Victor, in midsummer 1927, was BRISTOL, Tennessee, a small southern Appalachian city. Jimmie Rodgers, a semiprofessional singer—of blues, primarily—turned up during the last days of the two-week session. Peer later said (inaccurately) that Rodgers "only knew, I think, two chords, on guitar," but he was shrewd enough to see that Rodgers "was an individualist; he had his own style." Peer responded equally quickly to the Carter Family and took charge of both acts' careers. Peer managed Rodgers until his death in 1933.

Even though hillbilly and race music brought him success, Peer said, "I was always trying to get away from hillbilly and into the legitimate music field." By the 1930s he was publishing songs by Hoagy Carmichael, Johnny Mercer, and jazz composer–arranger Don Redman. Peer said he was unconsciously attempting "to take the profits out of the hillbilly and race business and spend that money trying to get established as a pop publisher." He'd founded Southern Music publishers with $1,000 in 1928 and quickly sold it to Victor. Buying it back in 1932, he remained Southern's sole owner until he died.

During and after the Depression he founded a half-dozen branches overseas and started a classical music arm, Serious Music. He claimed to have conceived the idea of a rival publishers' group to ASCAP five years before BMI came into being in 1940; when it did, Peer split his catalogue between ASCAP and BMI (a daring move then but standard practice today), founding Peer International, a BMI affiliate. At Peer's death Peer International was the nation's biggest BMI publisher; Southern was among ASCAP's Top Twenty.

Peer died in Hollywood, California, in 1960 and was elected to the COUNTRY MUSIC HALL OF FAME in 1984.

—*Tony Scherman*

Vito Pellettieri

b. Nashville, Tennessee, November 30, 1889; d. April 14, 1977

To GRAND OLE OPRY performers, Vito Pellettieri's name was synonymous with the show for nearly thirty years. As stage manager and father figure, he became a source of stability and continuity for the Opry staff.

Well before he graduated from high school, he began a twenty-eight-year career as a bandleader, playing dances and parties throughout much of the Southeast, Midwest, and Southwest. A grueling schedule led to a nervous breakdown in 1921, but after his recovery he formed another band with his wife, Kathryn, and began to work at Nashville radio stations WCBQ, WSM, and WLAC.

Early in the 1930s, following a second nervous breakdown, WSM station manager HARRY STONE hired Pellettieri as music librarian; in this role he maintained the files of sheet music used by WSM performers, helped work out musical arrangements, kept logbooks of WSM programs, and made sure that all songs performed were covered under performance rights licenses. In 1934 Stone assigned him to assist GEORGE D. HAY with the Grand Ole Opry, and Pellettieri reluctantly complied. "The performers would come anytime during the evening, do four numbers, and then leave," he recalled. "Some showed up drunk, and some wouldn't even come at all." To bring order out of chaos, Pellettieri brought unruly musicians in line and scheduled them for distinct Opry segments that Stone began to sell to advertisers. Today the Opry retains essentially the same format that Pellettieri helped to shape in the mid-1930s. —*John Rumble*

Ray Pennington (*see* Step One Records)

Hank Penny
b. Birmingham, Alabama, September 18, 1918; d. April 17, 1992

As a band leader, guitarist, and singer, Herbert Clayton "Hank" Penny was an early exponent of western swing. Though based initially in the Southeast, Penny freely admitted to the decidedly southwestern influence of the MILTON BROWN and BOB WILLS sounds, which was apparent from Penny's earliest recordings.

His first professional experience came in 1936 as a member of "Happy" Hal Burns & His Tune Wranglers. To his credit, Penny recognized the importance of high-quality musicianship, and in forming his own group surrounded himself with top-notch players. In 1937 he organized his own band, the Radio Cowboys, which included Sheldon Bennett (fiddle), Louis Dumont (tenor banjo), Carl Stewart (piano, banjo, fiddle, bass), Sammy Forsmark (steel guitar), and Julian Akins (bass, guitar).

In 1938, Penny and his group signed with radio station WSB in Atlanta, Georgia, where their music gained national attention. With the addition in 1939 of two highly skilled performers, NOEL BOGGS (steel guitar) and BOUDLEAUX BRYANT (fiddle), the music of the Radio Cowboys measured up to the high standards that Wills and Brown had set for western swing.

Penny made his first commercial recordings for ARC in 1938, and in 1939 recorded "Won't You Ride in My Little Red Wagon," a REX GRIFFIN song that became closely associated with Penny. Not long after the start of World War II, Penny moved on to Cincinnati, Ohio, where he formed the Plantation Boys, appeared on the *Boone County Jamboree,* and began recording for the KING label. In 1945 Penny departed Cincinnati for Los Angeles, where he formed a group as part of BERT "FOREMAN" PHILLIPS's organization. Following the war, he fronted several more bands, made appearances in a number of western movies, and contributed comedy to the Dude Martin and SPADE COOLEY bands. In the fifties Penny recorded for the RCA and DECCA labels. Penny also opened the Palomino Club in North Hollywood, California, a showcase for country music for some thirty years. Among his five wives were entertainers of note Sue Thompson and Shari Nona. —*Ken Griffis*

Carl Perkins
b. Tiptonville, Tennessee, April 9, 1932; d. January 19, 1998

One of SUN RECORDS' great rockabilly stars, guitarist, singer, and songwriter Carl Lee Perkins personified rocka-

Carl Perkins

billy with his first great hit, "Blue Suede Shoes." Its combination of whiplash guitar, stop-and-start beats, and teen lingo made it a #1 country hit (and a #2 pop hit) for Perkins in 1956; ELVIS PRESLEY recorded the song shortly after Perkins (both versions entered *Billboard*'s pop chart the same day, March 3); and pop bandleader Lawrence Welk cut a version the same month.

As with many of Sun's rockabilly stars, Perkins's childhood musical influences were a mixture of the hillbilly music he heard on the radio (GRAND OLE OPRY broadcasts, most of all) and the blues he heard from fellow sharecroppers in the fields. Along with older brother Clayton (on bass) and younger brother Jay (on guitar), he formed the Perkins Brothers, who concentrated on uptempo honkytonk music.

Perkins married Valda Crider on January 24, 1953, and first approached Sun Records in October 1954, after hearing Presley on the radio and identifying a kindred spirit. Perkins's first single, "Movie Magg" b/w "Turn Around," recorded in October 1954 (and released on Flip, a Sun subsidiary), showcased his range: a sprightly hillbilly number on the A side, a HANK WILLIAMS–derived honky-tonk weeper on the flip.

Throughout 1955 Perkins and his band, anchored by W. S. Holland on drums, performed frequently and developed new material. That December he recorded his third single, "Blue Suede Shoes" b/w "Honey Don't," which made him a star. He continued to record strong material for Sun, such as "Boppin' the Blues" and "Dixie Fried," archetypal rockabilly performances that were both country Top Tens.

On March 21, 1956, en route to a taping of the *Perry Como Show* in New York, the Chrysler Imperial carrying Perkins and band collided with a poultry truck outside Dover, Delaware. The mishap killed the truck driver and sent all three Perkins brothers to the hospital. One month later, Perkins fulfilled his Como show engagement.

Perkins recorded for Sun until December 1957; by then he had become disenchanted with the label as he perceived resources and attention being lavished on JOHNNY CASH and JERRY LEE LEWIS (who started at Sun supporting Perkins on "Matchbox"). Also, the pop market was turning toward sounds more uptown than those provided by Perkins's voice and music.

Perkins followed Cash to COLUMBIA in early 1958, recorded few songs of the quality of his work at Sun, then landed at DECCA in 1963 for a brief stay, the high point being the fiery rocker "Big Bad Blues." Perkins recorded "Big Bad Blues" in London on May 22, 1964, with the Nashville Teens; during his London stay he met the Beatles and attended their recording of "Matchbox," the first of several Beatles covers of Perkins compositions.

Perkins's recordings in the 1960s and 1970s were sparse, characterized by "event" sets such as his collaboration with NRBQ. From 1965 to 1975 Perkins performed as part of Johnny Cash's traveling troupe and supplied the Man in Black with "Daddy Sang Bass," a 1968 chart-topper. Through the 1980s Perkins was involved in many retrospective projects, among them a 1985 cable TV special in which he was supported by high-profile disciples such as George Harrison and Eric Clapton, and *Class of '55* (America/Smash, 1986), an album with Cash, Lewis, and ROY ORBISON. At the same time, his songs were frequently covered by popular country performers such as the JUDDS.

Perkins continued to record into the 1990s, and in 1996 he released a second autobiography, *Go, Cat, Go!* (with David McGee), and a similarly titled CD. He died on January 19, 1998, of complications resulting from a series of strokes.

—Jimmy Guterman

REPRESENTATIVE RECORDINGS

Original Sun Greatest Hits (Rhino, 1986); *The Classic Carl Perkins* (Bear Family, 1990), 5 CDs; *Jive After Five: The Best of Carl Perkins (1958–1978)* (Rhino, 1990)

Philip Morris Country Music Show
established January 1957; ended April 1958

Conceived as a promotional vehicle for the Philip Morris Tobacco Company's tobacco products, the Philip Morris Country Music Show also provided a great boost to country music's popularity in 1957–58.

In 1956 Philip Morris approached JIM DENNY, formerly head of the GRAND OLE OPRY's booking department and now head of his own agency, with the concept of a Philip Morris–sponsored free road show featuring country's top acts. The show was to bring country music to people in southeastern states, with stars traveling in a bus provided and equipped by Philip Morris.

When Denny left the Opry in September 1956 (amid controversy relating to his outside interest in concert promotion) and formed the Jim Denny Artist Bureau, Philip Morris decided to continue dealing with Denny and contracted with his bureau to provide the talent for the road show. When the deal was announced in December 1956 it was called "the largest individual package sale in country music history."

The Philip Morris Country Music Show gave its premiere performance in Richmond, Virginia, in January 1957, then moved on to play to capacity houses in West Virginia, Kentucky, Tennessee, Mississippi, and Louisiana. The cast for the initial series of shows included CARL SMITH,

GOLDIE HILL, RED SOVINE, RONNIE SELF, GORDON TERRY, Bun Wilson, and Carl Smith's band, the Tunesmiths. The lineup eventually grew to include more than twenty top country music names.

Originally designed as a thirteen-week tour of southeastern states, the show grew into a sixteen-month traveling festival of country music that played before 4 million people coast-to-coast. It even spun off a weekly CBS network radio show, which debuted in October 1957.

The Philip Morris Country Music Show's impact on country music's growth over that sixteen-month period was significant. The show brought country music into new areas and played before many people who were experiencing their first taste of country. In addition to the free shows and radio broadcasts, artists gave special shows for veterans' hospitals, military bases, and industrial locations. The Philip Morris Country Music Show concluded in April 1958.

—Al Cunniff

Bill Phillips
b. Canton, North Carolina, January 28, 1936

Bill Clarence Phillips enjoyed his greatest success as a country performer during the mid-1960s. His best-known recording, "Put It Off Until Tomorrow," is remembered not only for his performance of the song, but also for the role it played in a young DOLLY PARTON's career. Parton co-wrote the Phillips hit, and she provided the uncredited—but very audible—harmony vocal part on the recording.

Phillips grew up in North Carolina. While still in high school, he played guitar and sang in local groups around Canton and Asheville. Then he went to Miami for three years, playing on station WMIL's *Ole South Jamboree,* as well as on his own television show (1956–57).

MEL TILLIS invited him to Nashville in 1957, where Phillips signed with CEDARWOOD PUBLISHING, and eventually COLUMBIA RECORDS. In 1958 WEBB PIERCE charted with Phillip's song "Falling Back to You" (#10). The next year Phillips's own record of "Sawmill" went to #27. He shifted to DECCA RECORDS and reached the Top Ten twice in 1966 with songs written by Parton and her uncle, Bill Owens. The first was "Put It Off Until Tomorrow" (#6); the second, "The Company You Keep" (#8).

Phillips appeared on the syndicated television shows of BILL ANDERSON, PORTER WAGONER, and the WILBURN BROTHERS, and he was a regular on the *Kitty Wells–Johnny Wright Family Show.* Phillips also toured with the latter troupe from 1969 until 1984.

In addition to some minor movie roles (*Road to Nashville, Second Fiddle to a Steel Guitar, The Sugarland Express*), Phillips was a guest on the *Dolly* TV show in 1988.

—Steve Eng

REPRESENTATIVE RECORDINGS

Put It Off Until Tomorrow (Decca, 1966); *Bill Phillips's Style* (Decca, 1967)

Foreman Phillips
birthplace, birth date, and death date, unknown

Disc jockey, personal manager, and show promoter Bert "Foreman" Phillips was one of the big wheels of the California country music scene between 1942 and 1952. The first to aggressively exploit the vast audience that had migrated from the Dust Bowl of the Southwest to the humming wartime factories of Southern California, Phillips assembled a stable of talent that included SPADE COOLEY, JIMMY WAKELY, and TEX WILLIAMS. Phillips eventually parlayed that talent into the drawing power behind his legendary World War II–era "swing shift" dances held first at the Venice Pier Ballroom, beginning in the summer of 1942, and soon after at other Southern California venues, such as the Santa Monica Ballroom, the Town Hall Ballroom in Compton, and the Plantation in Culver City. These all-night affairs routinely drew such huge crowds (an average of 5,000 to 7,000 people per show) that a *Time* magazine correspondent attending a Cooley dance expressed fear that the pier itself would collapse.

At his wartime peak, Phillips concurrently ran dances at anywhere from five to seven separate dance halls across the Los Angeles region. Necessarily employing upward of fourteen different bands nightly, Phillips maintained almost dictatorial control over his employees; western swing bandleader HANK PENNY worked for Phillips briefly in 1945, but after one too many improvisatory solos, Phillips fired him and had a large sign reading WHERE'S THE MELODY? posted backstage at the Santa Monica Ballroom.

Hailing from Texas, Phillips had begun his career as a radio ad salesman and had risen to power in the early 1940s as a popular country DJ at KRKD in Los Angeles with his *Western Hit Parade* program and later at KXLA, and he continued on radio into the 1950s. In the postwar years Phillips continued to concentrate on promoting dances as well. By the early 1950s he was producing his own weekday-televised *Foreman Phillips Show*—hosted by WESLEY TUTTLE and his wife, Marilyn—but Phillips never again attained the spectacular degree of success he enjoyed with his swing shift dances. In 1952 he sold the lease on his last ballroom and retired to northern California. —*Jonny Whiteside*

Sam Phillips

b. Florence, Alabama, January 5, 1923

One of the most important non-performers in American music, producer Samuel Cornelius Phillips founded SUN RECORDS and introduced the world to JOHNNY CASH, Howlin' Wolf, B. B. KING, JERRY LEE LEWIS, ROY ORBISON, CARL PERKINS, ELVIS PRESLEY, CHARLIE RICH, and many others. In so doing, he played a lead role in determining many of the directions popular music has taken through the years in the wake of those artists' inspired work.

A blues fan originally from the Florence–Muscle Shoals region of Alabama, Phillips got involved in radio when he was young and wound up at WREC in Memphis in 1945. In October 1949 he decided to supplement his income as a disc jockey for WREC and so signed a lease on a building at 706 Union Avenue, where he was to open his Memphis Recording Service studio. From the beginning, in January 1950, he balanced creative concerns with more pressing worldly ones; he needed to cover the $150 monthly rent, so he focused on for-hire recording rather than the untamed music he loved.

Phillips soon tired of the wedding and bar mitzvah circuit and began documenting the city's tough blues scene. In August 1950 he started the short-lived Phillips label, but soon found a calling in recording blues artists performers and turning the masters over to r&b labels such as RPM and Chess. Phillips often had to stop these artists from trying to smooth their sounds for white producers, insisting—as he did throughout his career—that direct, unfussy pre-

sentation was all that mattered. After Howlin' Wolf moved to Chicago, where he would record directly for Chess, Phillips began another label, Sun Records, and scored many regional and national r&b hits with the likes of Rufus Thomas and Little Junior's Blue Flames.

By early 1954 Phillips was delivering his message of straightforward, soulful presentation to country performers as well as blues singers, and he helped develop rockabilly out of this country-blues mix. For Phillips, wild rockabilly and polite country were part of the same continuum; in either category, he wanted a mood to be established the second a song began, and then for it to intensify and ignite.

His method reached its apotheosis in 1954 and 1955, when Phillips discovered and shepherded Elvis Presley. Phillips sold Presley's contract to RCA for a reported $35,000, which he used to sustain a label whose cash flow was never as solid as its musical grounding. By the early 1960s Phillips supervised fewer and fewer of Sun's day-to-day recordings and made a fortune as an early investor in the Holiday Inn hotel chain. On July 1, 1969, Phillips sold the Sun label to SHELBY SINGLETON and effectively retired, resurfacing only for very rare public appearances and production assignments (he helped out on the 1979 JOHN PRINE album *Pink Cadillac* because his sons Knox and Jerry were producing it).

As Phillips told journalist David Halberstam, "I have one real gift and that gift is to look another person in the eye and be able to tell if he has anything to contribute, and if he does, I have the additional gift to free him from whatever is restraining him." More than merely creating a sound, Phillips initiated a sensibility. —*Jimmy Guterman*

Stu Phillips

b. Montreal, Quebec, Canada, January 19, 1933

Stu Phillips was a best-selling recording artist in Canada and genial television host for the Canadian Broadcasting Company (CBC) before joining the GRAND OLE OPRY in June 1967. He's enjoyed modest success on the country charts in the United States, most notably with RCA's "Vin Rose" (#21, 1967) and "Juanita Jones" (#13, 1967). His experience performing on prime-time Canadian television for five years stood him in good stead as host of the syndicated U.S. variety show *Music Place*. He and HANK SNOW have long been the sole Canadian stars on the Opry. —*Walt Trott*

REPRESENTATIVE RECORDING

Don't Give Up On Me (Broadland, 1993)

Piano

Pianos have been an integral part of country music from the beginning. Even when fiddlers, banjoists, and guitarists were playing at dances, piano was often included for its strong, percussive rhythm. In 1927, for example, RALPH PEER recorded Virginia's Shelor Family String Band, which included piano, at the famous BRISTOL SESSIONS where he first recorded JIMMIE RODGERS, ERNEST STONEMAN, and the CARTER FAMILY.

In Texas, jazz piano became an integral part of western swing music. One of the first musicians MILTON BROWN hired upon forming his Musical Brownies in 1932 was pianist Fred "Papa" Calhoun. Al Stricklin later filled the same role with BOB WILLS & His Texas Playboys in Tulsa, while MOON MULLICAN made his name with CLIFF BRUNER's band and other Houston area swing units. Mullican became the first singer-pianist to make a name in country music after signing with KING RECORDS in 1946 and having a major hit with "New Pretty Blonde" in 1947, which led to his joining the GRAND OLE OPRY in 1949 and subsequent hits. On the West Coast, pianists were common in most country and western swing bands. In the early 1950s, San Diego singer-pianist MERRILL MOORE filled a similar singer-pianist role with his country boogie recordings for CAPITOL. In JIM BECK's Dallas studio, pianist Madge Suttee played a key role in LEFTY FRIZZELL's influential honky-tonk sound of the early 1950s.

In Nashville, DEL WOOD's ebullient 1951 ragtime piano instrumental hit "Down Yonder" made her an Opry mainstay. In the early fifties, veteran pop pianist and bandleader OWEN BRADLEY played on various country records, and publisher FRED ROSE occasionally played the instrument on HANK WILLIAMS's recordings. Other early Nashville session pianists included local pop musicians MARVIN HUGHES and Papa John Gordy. FLOYD CRAMER, a teenage pianist on the *LOUISIANA HAYRIDE*, later became a Nashville studio musician, popularizing the slip-note technique developed by songwriter DON ROBERTSON, which featured chromatic grace notes reminiscent of a pedal steel guitar. It made Cramer as identified with piano as CHET ATKINS was with the guitar.

JERRY LEE LEWIS's profound influence on country piano, derived from his love of black boogie-woogie and blues, was strong in both his early rockabilly days and in his later, successful country career. CHARLIE RICH's piano always reflected the influence of modern jazz. Even such a traditionalist as ROY ACUFF routinely used piano with the Smoky Mountain Boys. JIM REEVES would cancel shows if his pianist wasn't provided a decent instrument. RONNIE MILSAP, MICKEY GILLEY, BECKY HOBBS, and GARY STEWART all use piano as their primary accompaniment. Today, electronic keyboards and synthesizers play greater roles in country recordings, yet acoustic piano remains a mainstay.

—*Rich Kienzle*

Pickard Family

One of the first country singing groups to professionalize their music, and one of the first to appear on national network radio, the Pickard Family was founded by patriarch Obed "Dad" Pickard, a pioneer GRAND OLE OPRY star. Born on July 22, 1874, Obed became proficient on most stringed instruments as a boy, so much so that he had the honor of entertaining Admiral Dewey in the Spanish-American War. From 1900 to 1925, Obed returned to Ashland City, Tennessee, worked as what was referred to then as a commercial traveler, and raised four children: Ruth, Bubb, Charlie, and Ann. In 1926 Obed began working on the Opry as a soloist—dubbed the One-Man Orchestra by GEORGE D. HAY—and made his first records for COLUMBIA.

By 1928 Obed had brought his family into the act, and while visiting Detroit was able to audition for Henry Ford. This led to a forty-week contract with NBC to star in a sort of minstrel show called *The Cabin Door*. A similar job followed the next year, but in 1931, when Mrs. Pickard became ill, the family returned to Tennessee and to a second stint on the Opry. By 1933 they were off again, to stations in Chicago, Philadelphia, New York, New Orleans, and eventually Mexican border station XERA. Their relatively slim number of recordings, for Plaza, BRUNSWICK, and ARC, consisted mostly of familiar folksongs.

In later years the family relocated to California, where Dad (Obed) became the star of one of the first TV series; after his death in 1954, the family continued to work, even recording an LP album for Verve. —*Charles Wolfe*

Pie Plant Pete
b. Ridgeway, Illinois, July 9, 1906; d. February 7, 1988

Claud W. Moye, "Pie Plant Pete," entered show business in 1928 following a successful audition for a spot on the WLS *NATIONAL BARN DANCE*. He reputedly was given his unusual nickname by a WLS announcer who heard him order pie plant pie (better known as rhubarb pie) for dessert in a restaurant. The following Saturday night the announcer introduced him to the *Barn Dance* audience as Pie Plant Pete.

Pete sang novelty and mountain songs and played, simultaneously, a guitar and a harmonica suspended in a wire frame. WLS announcers dubbed this combination of instruments a "two-cylinder cob crusher." After WLS, Pete appeared on radio and television stations in such cities as Cleveland, Syracuse, Fort Wayne, Boston, Rochester, and Detroit. He recorded for GENNETT in the late twenties and early thirties, DECCA and ARC in the mid-thirties, and for the Process label in the forties. After leaving the music business, he formed an advertising agency.

—*Wayne W. Daniel*

REPRESENTATIVE RECORDING
The Old Time Country Music Collection of Pie Plant Pete and Bashful Harmonica Joe (Cattle Mono, 1989)

Don Pierce
b. Ballard, Washington, October 10, 1915

Neither a musician nor a skilled A&R man, Don Pierce was one of the foremost marketers in country music. After he assumed sole control of STARDAY RECORDS in 1958, he showed how music that the major labels ignored (bluegrass, old time) could be successfully marketed on LP.

After discharge from the navy in 1945, Pierce bought a stake in FOUR STAR RECORDS and rose to the position of sales manager. During that time he gained his knowledge of country music, and, after leaving Four Star in 1953, he joined the fledgling Starday label. As the only full-time partner, he was made president. He moved to Nashville in 1957 when Starday was in partnership with MERCURY.

When Pierce took full control of Starday in 1958, he reoriented the company toward acts that the major labels considered marginal and marketed his catalogue on LP using splashily colorful jackets. Utilizing his background in business management, he skillfully exploited the catalogue and built his assets to the point that his share of Starday, bought for $333 in 1953, was worth $2 million when he sold it to Lin Broadcasting in 1968. Since then, Pierce has worked in real-estate development in Hendersonville, Tennessee. —*Colin Escott*

Webb Pierce
b. West Monroe, Louisiana, August 8, 1921; d. February 24, 1991

One of the greatest stars of country music's honky-tonk heyday, the 1950s, Webb Pierce had thirteen singles top

Webb Pierce

the *Billboard* charts in those years—more than any of his illustrious contemporaries. His loud, nasal, high-pitched, and sometimes slightly off-key delivery on hit after hit marked him as one of the music's most distinctive singers in an era of great individualists. A successful investor and wealthy man for much of his life, Pierce knew how to spend money to heighten his image, and he is perhaps as well remembered today for his silver-dollar-studded autos and guitar-shaped swimming pools as for his great music.

Born Webb Michael (or Mike) Pierce in West Monroe, Louisiana, five years earlier than his publicists generally claimed, he grew up with the music of JIMMIE RODGERS, GENE AUTRY, western swing bands of Texas and Oklahoma, and the Cajun bands of his native state. He first sang professionally on KMLB in Monroe, but after a brief army stint in the early days of World War II, he moved to Shreveport in 1944 and found early morning work on KTBS there. For six years he worked for Shreveport's Sears, Roebuck store in the men's furnishings department, the whole time striving for a break in his singing career. Finally he moved to Shreveport's 50,000-watt giant, KWKH, and its Saturday night auditorium broadcast, the *LOUISIANA HAYRIDE*. Building a band around himself with such future legends as FLOYD CRAMER (piano), TILLMAN FRANKS (manager and bass), JIMMY DAY (steel guitar), Tex Grimsley (fiddle), Teddy and Doyle Wilburn and FARON YOUNG (extra vocalists), Webb Pierce was soon the hottest act on that big show. With *Hayride* producer Horace Logan, Pierce launched a record label, Pacemaker, that featured several *Hayride* acts in addition to Pierce himself, who was by then also recording for California's FOUR STAR RECORDS. In late 1951, Pierce moved up to DECCA and the next year scored his first big hit on that label with a version of the 1937 Cajun favorite, "Wondering," which inspired his nickname and band name, the Wondering Boy(s).

Pierce followed "Wondering" with two more #1s, "That Heart Belongs to Me" and BILLY WALLACE's honky-tonk anthem "Back Street Affair," and on the strength of these

joined the GRAND OLE OPRY in mid-1952. "It's Been So Long" and "There Stands the Glass" (the latter banned in some radio markets), his best hits of 1953, established him as the field's biggest honky-tonk star in the wake of HANK WILLIAMS's death, and through 1955, huge hits for Pierce came with regularity: "Slowly" (on which BUD ISAACS's pioneering PEDAL STEEL GUITAR work won countless converts to that instrument), "Even Tho," "More and More," "In the Jailhouse Now," "I Don't Care," "Love, Love, Love," and "Why, Baby, Why." Small wonder that by mid-decade Pierce's concert fee had risen to nearly $1,250 per show, and advance orders for his new singles often reached 200,000 copies.

Pierce closely allied himself with Grand Ole Opry manager JIM DENNY. They launched CEDARWOOD MUSIC in 1953 and later jointly invested earnings from this and other ventures into the purchase of radio stations. But when Denny was fired by WSM in September 1956, for these and other outside interests conflicting with his Opry role, Pierce soon left, too. He was confident that he had outgrown the limits of Grand Ole Opry exposure and was eager to do full-scale, full-paid concerts on Saturday nights instead of working the Opry for union scale wages. Already he had spent most of a year featured on ABC-TV's *OZARK JUBILEE* out of Springfield, Missouri, and soon he would find plenty of TV work and even film roles for producer ALBERT GANNAWAY in addition to his busy touring schedule. Though the rock & roll tide of 1956–59 slowed his record success somewhat, Pierce drew upon the growing stable of talented Cedarwood songwriters (DANNY DILL, WAYNE WALKER, MARIJOHN WILKIN, and especially MEL TILLIS) for good songs to record, and from the late 1950s came the memorable "I'm Tired," "Honky Tonk Song," and "Tupelo County Jail" (all three by Tillis, with whom Pierce even recorded a 1963 duet, "How Come Your Dog Don't Bite Nobody But Me").

After "Honky Tonk Song" in 1957, Top Ten records were fairly common until 1964—indeed, in 1959 "I Ain't Never" hit #2 country and became his only Top Forty pop hit—but Pierce had no more #1s even though his singles regularly charted until 1972. Shortly thereafter he left his twenty-plus-year association with DECCA/MCA, and recorded in the mid-1970s for SHELBY SINGLETON's Plantation Records, including a lament you'd expect from such a wealthy man "The Good Lord Giveth (And Uncle Sam Taketh Away)," which charted poorly, and two unlikely and eminently forgettable duets with stage and film star Carol Channing ("Got You on My Mind" b/w "Love Brought Us Together"), which did not chart at all. By then Webb Pierce was better known for his Curtiswood Lane home and its guitar-shaped swimming pool—a regular stop on bus tours of Nashville—than for new hit records, but soon peace-loving neighbors went to court and took even that away from him.

Pierce's star fared better in the 1980s. In 1982 WILLIE NELSON asked Pierce to sing with him on a remake of "In the Jailhouse Now." It was Pierce's ninety-sixth and last charted record, although young traditionalist RICKY SKAGGS revived two of Webb's hits in that decade: "I Don't Care" (1982) and "I'm Tired" (1987).

Pierce died of pancreatic cancer just as the Persian Gulf War was ending (February 24, 1991). Posthumous reissues have somewhat revived his reputation, and even those irritated by his at times abrasive personality share a widespread recognition of his commercial achievements and superstardom.

—*Ronnie Pugh*

REPRESENTATIVE RECORDINGS

Webb Pierce: The Wondering Boy, 1951–1958 (Bear Family Records, 1991); *Webb Pierce: King of the Honky Tonk, from the Original Decca Masters, 1952–1959* (Country Music Foundation Records, 1991)

Ray Pillow

b. Lynchburg, Virginia, July 4, 1937

Ray Pillow's dark good looks, personality, and pleasing baritone marked him as a real comer in the business back in the mid-1960s. He had a CAPITOL RECORDS contract (signed 1963), tour sponsorship from MARTHA WHITE FLOUR, and a moderately successful single, "Thank You Ma'am" (#17 peak), to welcome in the 1966 New Year. Just ahead was a hit duet with JEAN SHEPARD, "I'll Take the Dog" (#9, 1966), an invitation to join the GRAND OLE OPRY (April 30, 1966), and an award from a national disc jockey poll as Most Programmed New Male Country Artist.

Fortunately, Pillow was prepared for the long dry spell that followed. A navy veteran, he had graduated from Lynchburg College with a business degree. Off-campus, Pillow had honed his talents playing in bands. Despite narrowly losing a WSM Pet Milk talent contest, he had moved his family to Nashville in 1963. When not onstage, he delved in behind-the-scenes activities. Pillow and manager Joe Taylor started a booking agency in 1964 and Pillow had established Sycamore Valley Music, a publishing house. Later, Pillow was instrumental in bringing LEE GREENWOOD to Nashville and signed him to his publishing company. As a result, the firm had the CMA Song of the Year, "God Bless the U.S.A.," in 1985. In January 1990 JIMMY BOWEN engaged Pillow as an A&R man for LIBERTY RECORDS for a few years. As of this writing he still plays his weekend Opry gig.
—*Walt Trott*

REPRESENTATIVE RECORDINGS

One Too Many Memories (Allegiance, 1984); *Ray Pillow* (Dot, 1985)

Pinkard & Bowden

James Sanford "Sandy" Pinkard Jr. b. Abbeville, Louisiana, January 16, 1947

Richard Bowden b. Linden, Texas, September 30, 1945

With album tracks such as "Please Censor Us," Pinkard & Bowden pushed the limits of good taste to extremes never explored by previous duos, such as HOMER & JETHRO, and sometimes crossed these limits unashamedly. Surprisingly, perhaps, Sandy Pinkard and Richard Bowden each had impressive musical credentials when they formed their comedy partnership in 1983. As a Los Angeles–based songwriter, Pinkard's credits included "You're the Reason God Made Oklahoma" (DAVID FRIZZELL & Shelly West), "Coca Cola Cowboy" (MEL TILLIS), "I Can Tell by the Way You Dance" (VERN GOSDIN), and "Blessed Are the Believers" (ANNE MURRAY).

After graduating from high school, Richard Bowden moved to Los Angeles as guitarist in the band Shiloh, whose members included childhood friend Don Henley (of the EAGLES). When the band broke up, Bowden found work recording and touring with LINDA RONSTADT, Roger McGuinn, Dan Fogelberg, Stevie Nicks, and Johnny Rivers.

After meeting in Nashville, Pinkard & Bowden re-corded the relatively tame *Writers in Disguise* (1984), the first of the duo's four WARNER BROS. albums. The content gradually became more risqué with the subsequent releases *PG-13*, *Live*, and *Cousins, Cattle, and Other Love Stories*. Song such as "Drivin' My Wife Away," "Libyan on a Jet Plane," and "Kiss an Angus Good Mornin'" typified parodies of well-known country tunes.

As their language began to become more freewheeling, Pinkard & Bowden began securing bookings in decidedly noncountry settings, including stints opening concert tours for NEIL YOUNG and Don Henley. And while the humor retained a strong country flavor, the duo found itself in greater demand among rock fans. Capitalizing on their X-rated approach, Pinkard & Bowden essentially stopped working country venues to become one of the top-grossing acts at America's mainstream comedy clubs.

Gettin' Stupid, a compilation of Pinkard & Bowden's best material, was marketed through television ads in an arrangement with Warner Special Products.
—*Calvin Gilbert*

REPRESENTATIVE RECORDING

Cousins, Cattle, and Other Love Stories (Warner Bros., 1992)

Pirates of the Mississippi

Bill McCorvey b. Montgomery, Alabama, July 4, 1959
Pat Severs b. Camden, South Carolina, November 10, 1952
Dean Townson b. Battle Creek, Michigan, April 2, 1959
Jimmy Lowe b. Atlanta, Georgia, August 2, 1955
Rich Alves b. Pleasanton, California, May 25, 1953
Greg Trostal b. Elmira, New York, November 10, 1950

When Pirates of the Mississippi found success with their signature single "Feed Jake" in 1991, they unwittingly demonstrated that attitudes within the audience for country music had apparently shifted. While country fans, in general, have traditionally had a conservative bent, "Feed Jake" was accepted despite a verse in which the band shows some tolerance—if not support—for homosexuals: "Now, if you get an ear pierced some will call you gay/But if you drive a pickup, they'll say, 'No, you must be straight'/What we are and what we ain't, what we can and what we can't/does it really matter?"

"Feed Jake" was also something unusual for the Pirates—a restrained, quirky release from an act that more frequently projects a bar band attitude with its raucous approach to country. Aptly, their second album, *Walk the Plank*, was stamped, "This album was mixed to play loud."

The Pirates apparently didn't take themselves seriously before they signed a record deal, either. Originally called the Cloggers, the band consisted of two songwriters, a studio musician, a factory worker, and a computer analyst who played weekends just to "blow off some musical steam." They developed an audience, surprising even themselves when CAPITOL RECORDS came calling, and refused to give up their day jobs until they had their first tour lined up. Unfortunately, though "Feed Jake" rose to #15 on the charts in 1991, subsequent singles failed to reach the Top Twenty. Steel player Pat Severs left the group in 1994 and was replaced by Greg Trostal.
—*Tom Roland*

REPRESENTATIVE RECORDINGS

Pirates of the Mississippi (Capitol, 1990); *A Streetman Named Desire* (Liberty, 1993)

Poco

Richie Furay b. Yellow Springs, Ohio, May 9, 1944

Jim Messina b. Harlingen, Texas, December 5, 1947

Rusty Young b. Long Beach, California, February 23, 1946

George Grantham b. Cordell, Oklahoma, November 20, 1947

Randy Meisner b. Scottsbluff, Nebraska, March 8, 1946

Based in Los Angeles, Poco was formed in 1968 by rhythm guitarist Richie Furay and lead guitarist Jim Messina—two former members of the legendary rock band Buffalo Springfield—and also pedal steel guitarist Rusty Young. Young had played pedal steel guitar on perhaps the first true country-rock song, "Kind Woman" (composed by Furay). Along with the BYRDS, the FLYING BURRITO BROTHERS, Michael Nesmith, Dillard & Clark, and BOB DYLAN, Poco helped pioneer the synthesis of country and rock, combining such numbers as DALLAS FRAZIER's "Honky-Tonk Downstairs" (rendered with a strong satirical edge) with original material such as "You Better Think Twice" (a minor pop hit in 1971).

Poco proved to be one of the most resilient groups in pop music history despite personnel changes: Randy Meisner (later a member of the EAGLES) departed in 1969, leaving a spot for bassist Timothy B. Schmit; Messina left in 1970 and was replaced by Paul Cotton; and Furay left in 1973. Later, Schmit (who joined the Eagles) and drummer George Grantham quit Poco in 1977, and Charlie Harrison, Kim Bullard, and Steve Chapman came aboard. Young was the one original member to say with Poco over the band's lifetime, until 1984, and proved to be a fine songwriter as well as instrumentalist.

Commercially, Poco attracted few country followers but managed to secure moderate success on the rock charts, especially as the group moved toward a more middle-of-the-road pop sound. In addition to "You Better Think Twice," their charted pop singles include "C'mon" (1971), "Rose of Cimarron" (1976), "Indian Summer" (1977), "Crazy Love" (their highest at #17, 1978), "Heart of the Night" (1978), and "Shoot the Moon" (1982). Artistic high points include the albums *Crazy Eyes* (1973), *Legend* (1978), and *Blue and Gray* (1981).

Throughout the years, the band produced consistently fine music. Their influence on more popular bands, especially the Eagles (with whom they shared bassists Randy Meisner and Timothy Schmit) was substantial. In 1989, Young, Furay, Messina, Grantham, and Meisner reunited to make an album with RCA called *Legacy*; they charted with pop singles "Call It Love" (#17) and "Nothin' to Hide."

—*Stephen R. Tucker*

REPRESENTATIVE RECORDINGS

Deliverin' (Epic, 1971); *The Forgotten Trail, 1969–1974* (Epic/Legacy, 1990)

Charlie Poole & the North Carolina Ramblers

b. Randolph County, North Carolina, March 22, 1892; d. May 21, 1931

The August 1927 COLUMBIA RECORDS *Old Familiar Tunes* catalogue describes Charlie Poole as "unquestionably the best known banjo picker and singer in the Carolinas." It was an apt description, for Poole and his band, the North Carolina Ramblers, had already sold more than 250,000 records in the two previous years, and they would double that figure by the time of their final release, in January 1932.

Charles Cleveland Poole grew up in the cotton mill villages of the north-central Piedmont of North Carolina. At an early age he acquired a love of banjo music and learned to play in a three-finger roll that was an adaptation of the then popular style of classical banjo playing. Poole's natural wanderlust led him to such far-flung places as Montana and Canada before 1920.

Joining forces with Posey Rorer, a fiddler from Franklin County, Virginia, Poole formed the North Carolina Ramblers. He eventually married Rorer's sister and settled in Spray, North Carolina. Never happy with cotton mill work, Poole and Rorer quit their jobs in 1925 to try their luck at recording old-time music. They were joined by Spray guitarist Norman Woodlieff in an audition for Columbia on July 27, 1925. The tryout was successful, with two records released from the session. The first record, "Don't Let Your Deal Go Down Blues" backed with "Can I Sleep in Your Barn Tonight Mister?," was a hit, selling more than 102,000 copies. The second release sold another 65,000 copies, though the band received only seventy-five dollars for both records. Poole became a full-time musician, recording more than seventy sides for Columbia, BRUNSWICK, and Paramount records between 1925 and 1931. Among his recordings are songs still performed in old-time music today, including "White House Blues," "There'll Come a Time," "If I Lose," "Sweet Sunny South," and "Budded Rose."

The personnel of the North Carolina Ramblers underwent changes during its five-year recording career. Posey Rorer was replaced first by Lonnie Austin and then Odell Smith, while Norman Woodlieff was replaced by West Virginian Roy Harvey. Poole showed a gift for selecting superb sidemen, and each of the Ramblers was among the best in his field. Both Rorer and Harvey had separate recording careers on their own that included the first old-time recordings of such songs as "I'll Roll in My Sweet Baby's Arms" and "Footprints in the Snow."

Poole's forceful and colorful personality made him a legend in the hill country of his region. Even today his escapades are told as folktales among the people of Blue Ridge. In 1931 he was invited to play back-up in a Hollywood western movie, but by that time his hard living and hard drinking had caught up with him, and he died at age thirty-nine.

—*Kinney Rorer*

REPRESENTATIVE RECORDINGS

Charlie Poole & the North Carolina Ramblers: *Old Time Songs* (County, 1994); Various artists: *White Country Blues* (Columbia, 1993) (contains three recordings by Poole)

Bill Porter

b. St. Louis, Missouri, June 15, 1931

Billy Rhodes Porter was an important recording engineer on the Nashville scene from 1959 to 1966. He grew up in Nashville, worked five years as a television repairman, and moved on to Nashville's WLAC-TV as an audio engineer and cameraman.

In 1959 Porter became chief engineer for RCA RECORDS' Nashville studio, then under the direction of CHET ATKINS. There Porter recorded numerous hits for

RCA country stars, including EDDY ARNOLD ("Tennessee Stud"), JIM REEVES ("He'll Have to Go"), SKEETER DAVIS ("The End of the World"), and HANK LOCKLIN ("Please Help Me I'm Falling"). Porter also recorded RCA pop artists such as Al Hirt ("Java," 1964). His sessions with acts on independent labels included the EVERLY BROTHERS (Cadence, WARNER BROTHERS), ROY ORBISON (MONUMENT), Johnny Tillotson (Cadence), and other country and pop singers.

After a brief stint with COLUMBIA's Nashville studio, in 1964 Porter became manager of the Monument Records studio in Nashville, where he continued his work with Orbison on tunes such as "It's Over" and "Oh, Pretty Woman," and with Joe Tex on r&b hits such as "Hold What You've Got." Technology of the day was limited to three-track machines, with mixing taking place as songs were recorded. Nevertheless, Porter's choice of microphones, skillful mike placement, and sensitivity to blends of voices and instruments produced clean, ambient recordings that remain hallmarks of the NASHVILLE SOUND.

From 1966 to 1973 Porter ran his own studio in Las Vegas, also becoming audioman for ELVIS PRESLEY and other Vegas acts until moving in 1975 to the University of Miami, where Porter developed the nation's first college-level course in studio engineering. From 1970 to 1977 he was the house mixing engineer for Presley's live Vegas shows, as well as his road shows. Subsequently he taught at the University of Colorado at Denver, supervised audio for the Jimmy Swaggart Ministries, and worked with several electronics firms. A 1992 recipient of *Mix* magazines's TEC Award for lifetime technical excellence and achievement, Porter now lives in Hillsboro, Missouri, and teaches at Webster University in St. Louis. —*John Rumble*

Dale Potter
b. Puxico, Missouri, April 28, 1929; d. March 14, 1996

Regarded as one of the best fiddle players of all time in country music, Allen Dale Potter pioneered a use of double stops (playing strings at once in harmony) that has been widely imitated by such well-known pros as BUDDY SPICHER, VASSAR CLEMENTS, Bobby Hicks, and SCOTT STONEMAN.

Potter listened as a youngster to BOB WILLS & His Texas Playboys on the radio. Dale thought that Wills's group had just one fiddle (instead of multiple fiddles, as he later found out) and sought to duplicate the sound. After moving to Nashville in 1948, he began recording with HANK WILLIAMS ("Mind Your Own Business"), LITTLE JIMMY DICKENS, WEBB PIERCE, COWBOY COPAS, and CARL SMITH (he toured with the latter two considerably), as well as GEORGE JONES, HYLO BROWN, MAC WISEMAN, and many others. Potter's twin fiddle work on record with TOMMY JACKSON is some of the country music's finest. One of Potter's finest moments on record occurred at age twenty-three performing "Fiddle Patch" and "Fiddle Sticks" with the Country All-Stars, an RCA RECORDS recording act that included CHET ATKINS and HOMER & JETHRO.

Potter left Nashville in the early 1960s and took a job with singer Judy Lynn in Las Vegas. In the 1970s he headed his own group in Hawaii, and in the 1980s and early 1990s turned up at some bluegrass festivals.

His death came at age sixty-six, following a bout with cancer and a massive stroke. —*Eddie Stubbs*

Don Potter
b. Glens Falls, New York, September 4, 1946

Donald L. Potter's musical arrangements and guitar licks have created distinctive sounds for the JUDDS, jazz trumpeter Chuck Mangione, and 1970s pop singer Dan Hill. Potter signed separate rock, folk, and country recording contracts with CBS Records in the 1960s and 1970s, but he found more success as the featured soloist and co-arranger for Mangione's group, with whom he recorded thirteen albums. In the late seventies and early eighties Potter recorded two solo projects for Mirror Records, released two Myrrh gospel albums, and arranged and played lead guitar on seven Hill albums, including *Longer Fuse*, which yielded "Sometimes When We Touch," a worldwide million-selling pop hit.

In 1983 producer BRENT MAHER hired Potter to play acoustic guitar on the demo recording that ultimately landed the Judds a deal with RCA RECORDS' Nashville division. By using the acoustic guitar as a lead instrument, Potter helped the duo create its energetic sound. He continued to serve as session guitarist, arranger, bandleader, and co-producer for all of the Judds' albums. He also co-wrote their 1991 Top Ten single "One Hundred and Two."

When WYNONNA became a solo artist in 1992, Potter continued his role as co-producer (with TONY BROWN), arranger, and session guitarist on her first three albums. In 1997 Potter left Nashville to go into the ministry. —*Marjie McGraw*

Fiddlin' Cowan Powers
b. Russell County, Virginia, October 1877; d. early 1950s

A farmer and a leatherworker from the hills of southwestern Virginia, James Cowan Powers won regional fame during his early life as a contest fiddler; his fiddling style, inherited from his family, was built around double stops and remarkable bow dexterity. Upon the death of his wife in 1916, he decided to take his family of four children on the road and forge them into a stringband. (The family included Charles, Ada, Ophra, and Carrie, and all were teenagers or younger when they started performing.) The band was soon playing full-time, making a regular five-state circuit through Appalachia, and doing especially well in coal towns of Kentucky and West Virginia. They were one of the first stringbands to turn professional. In August 1924 they traveled to Camden, New Jersey, to make a series of records for the VICTOR COMPANY—the first commercial recordings of a regular mountain stringband that had been performing together outside the studio. The records were commercially successful, and were widely used in Victor's early advertising for old-time music. Later the group did sessions for EDISON and OKEH, but as the family grew up and began their own lives, Powers returned to work as a fiddle soloist. He was still active and playing for the STANLEY BROTHERS when he died onstage at a concert in Saltville, Virginia, in the early 1950s. —*Charles Wolfe*

A Prairie Home Companion
established July 6, 1974

A Prairie Home Companion, syndicated over National Public Radio, was and continues to be a favorite for millions of listeners due to its blend of humor, music, stories, and poems. Humorist Garrison Keillor hosted the original program which aired live on Saturday evenings from July 6, 1974, to June 13, 1987. Keillor 's inspiration for the show came from listening to the GRAND OLE OPRY while in his Nashville hotel room. He had been sent there by *The New Yorker* in March 1974 to cover the Opry's move from the historic RYMAN AUDITORIUM to the OPRYLAND complex. Each episode of *A Prairie Home Companion* revolved around the fictitious town of Lake Wobegon, Minnesota, and its citizens. The site existed primarily as the location for Keillor's stories as well as the centerpiece for imaginary commercial sponsors, including Powdermilk Biscuits and Jack's Fountain Lounge. Keillor, a native of Anoka, Minnesota, based his tales around actual people, and his combination of realism and invention kept the humor homespun yet contemporary. In May 1980 the program began regular live broadcasts via satellite from Minneapolis. In that same year it received a George Peabody Award for excellence in broadcasting. In 1987 Keillor won a Grammy Award for his recording *Lake Wobegon Days,* in the category of Best Spoken Word. The last year of shows and the final performance were televised by The Disney Channel in 1987. Among the guests on the farewell telecast was legendary guitarist CHET ATKINS, a longtime admirer of Keillor.

In November 1989 Keillor began his New York *American Radio Company of the Air* broadcasts, a show produced by Minnesota Public Radio, which had produced the original *A Prairie Home Companion* in its beginnings. In 1992 the show moved back to Minnesota, and in 1993 it reclaimed the name of *A Prairie Home Companion.* Today approximately half the shows are produced in St. Paul, with the remainder being produced in various locations in the United States and sponsored by local public radio stations.
                                                                    —*Bob Paxman*

The Prairie Ramblers

Charles Gilbert "Chick" Hurt b. Willowshade, Kentucky, May 11, 1901; d. October 9, 1967

Jack Taylor b. Summershade, Kentucky, December 7, 1901; d. August 4, 1962

Floyd "Salty" Holmes b. Glasgow, Kentucky, March 6, 1909; d. January 1, 1970

Shelby David "Tex" Atchison b. Rosine, Kentucky, February 5, 1912; d. August 4, 1982

Longtime regulars on WLS's *NATIONAL BARN DANCE,* the Prairie Ramblers put a modern spin on Kentucky stringband music. The band's smooth, propulsive sound influenced a generation of midwestern and southeastern musicians during the early 1930s, most notably BILL MONROE.

Initially called the Kentucky Ramblers, the band launched its professional career in 1932 over WOC–Davenport, Iowa; Ronald Reagan was its announcer. The original members included mandola and tenor banjo player Chick Hurt, bassist Jack Taylor, guitar and harmonica player Salty Holmes, and fiddler Tex Atchison.

Moving to Chicago in January 1933, the band changed its name to reflect WLS's parent company, *The Prairie Farmer.* Besides performing on its own, the Ramblers backed GENE AUTRY on his *National Barn Dance* broadcasts. WLS later hired Arkansas singer PATSY MONTANA to enhance the band's appeal on road shows. In 1934 Montana

and the Ramblers moved to WOR–New York; in January 1935 they began recording for the AMERICAN RECORD CORPORATION. The Ramblers cut risqué novelties under the name "The Sweet Violet Boys," partly to take advantage of the moneymaking jukebox industry.

When the band returned to WLS in 1935, it sported a full western sound. Country/swing fiddler Alan Crockett replaced Atchison in 1938; Ralph "Rusty" Gill replaced Holmes in 1942. WADE RAY joined in about 1947 after Crockett's death. After the Ramblers moved to WLW-Cincinnati, in March 1949, fiddler-guitarist Wally Moore replaced Ray. Moore remained with the band when it returned to Chicago in the summer of 1950.

In early 1956 Hurt and Taylor hired an accordionist as a front man and reemerged as Stan Wolowic and the Polka Chips. From July 1956 to September 1957 the Polka Chips had its own weekly ABC-TV series, *Polka Time;* the band also recorded for ABC Paramount and CAPITOL. Hurt and Taylor dissolved the act in 1960 following a dispute with Wolowic.
                                                                    —*Dave Samuelson*

Elvis Presley
b. Tupelo, Mississippi, January 8, 1935; d. August 16, 1977

Elvis Aron Presley was indisputably the most influential performer in the history of rock & roll, and his life and career have been more thoroughly dissected than any others in popular music. The analysis continues at least partly because of the aura of mystery that even now surrounds him. He never gave an in-depth interview, possibly because of astute media handling but more likely because he found it impossible to account for all that had happened to him.

The one factor usually overlooked in discussions of Elvis Presley is that he came from the country market, and, in a sense, had a more powerful and lasting impact on country music than preeminent country stars such as HANK WILLIAMS or JIMMIE RODGERS. Until Presley's arrival, country music had been considered regional, and only a few artists, such as EDDY ARNOLD, had shaken off this stigma. Presley opened the door for other country singers, such as MARTY ROBBINS, SONNY JAMES, and JOHNNY CASH, to get their music exposed to a broader market. The consensus around Nashville in the mid- to late 1950s was that Elvis Presley was very bad for country music, that he had in fact almost killed it; in truth, he was very good for a younger generation of country musicians, giving them potential access to broader media exposure than their predecessors had enjoyed.

Presley, who was born in Tupelo, Mississippi, but who lived in Memphis from November 1948, developed a true catholicity of taste. The generally accepted notion that he fused country and r&b is essentially true, but he also embraced black and white gospel, mainstream popular music, light opera, and more. Memphis was a good place to hear all this, and by the time Elvis first went to SUN RECORDS to cut a commercial record in July 1954, he had more or less found his style. He was successful in the country market surprisingly quickly. The music of established country artists such as WEBB PIERCE and CARL SMITH was adult in content and execution. Elvis gave younger country fans something of their own. Much of its verve came from r&b, but it was marketed as country music, and the best exposure Elvis got in 1954 and 1955 was on the *LOUISIANA HAYRIDE* and on country stations.

Elvis Presley

Elvis was already starting to show signs of breaking out of the country market when his Sun contract was sold to RCA in November 1955, a deal masterminded by his new manager, COLONEL TOM PARKER. Parker persuaded RCA to pay an unprecedentedly high $35,000 for Presley, a singer of virtually untested appeal outside the country market. RCA, though, was able to catapult him into the national marketplace via television and concentrated promotion. By the end of March 1956 his first RCA single, "Heartbreak Hotel," had sold 1 million copies. In a way that BILL HALEY never could, Presley became both a figurehead for rock & roll and a lightning rod for all those who despised it. In his dress, his stage moves, and his few stage-managed interviews, he projected an image that was at once threatening and vulnerable.

Presley's catholicity of taste and his innate conservatism quickly became apparent in his career direction. He wanted to do movies, Christmas albums, gospel albums, and pop ballads. Perhaps he, too, saw rock & roll as something that might blow over, and he wanted a broad-based career in case it did. The transition was helped by a stint in the army from March 1958 until March 1960. He had made four movies before he went into the army (*Love Me Tender, Loving You, Jailhouse Rock*, and *King Creole*), and movies rather than concerts or television became the medium by which Elvis met his public during the 1960s. There were twenty-seven of them in ten years, most of them frothy and inconsequential. *G.I. Blues* was followed by two quasi-serious dramatic roles in *Flaming Star* and *Wild in the Country*. When the latter two flopped, the pattern was reestablished with *Blue Hawaii*, which was a box-office smash. It was followed by *Follow That Dream; Kid Galahad; Girls, Girls, Girls; It Happened at the World's Fair; Fun in Acapulco; Kissin' Cousins; Viva Las Vegas; Roustabout; Girl Happy; Tickle Me; Harum Scarum; Frankie and Johnny; Paradise Hawaiian Style; Spinout; Easy Come Easy Go; Double Trouble; Clambake; Stay Away Joe; Speedway; Live a Little Love a Little; Charro!; The Trouble With Girls;* and *Change of Habit*.

By the late 1960s Presley's career was in serious trouble. The movies and the accompanying soundtracks had al-

most destroyed his reputation. He hadn't appeared live since March 1961, and so it must have been with some trepidation that he made a live appearance at the NBC studios in Burbank in June 1968 for the taping of a television special that did much to restore his credibility. Apparently reinvigorated, Presley put more effort into song choice and returned to the upper reaches of the charts with "If I Can Dream," "In the Ghetto," and "Suspicious Minds." Some have attributed the new career direction to his marriage to Priscilla Beaulieu on May 1, 1967, although financial pressures and a desire to escape from the stagnant pattern he had established were probably more important.

Presley began performing again in Las Vegas in July 1969, and his two remaining movies were of performances *(Elvis: That's the Way It Is* and *Elvis on Tour)*. He continued performing live until his death eight years later. For an artist of his stature, he seemed to encounter problems in acquiring the best new material, and many of his 1970s recordings were of older songs ("The Wonder of You," "You Don't Have to Say You Love Me," "Promised Land"). It also became clear that Presley himself was starting to suffer from debilitating medical problems, most of them, it was later revealed, stemming from prescription drug abuse. Several posthumous biographies recounted an almost impossible level of drug ingestion. Priscilla divorced him on October 11, 1973, and the last years of his life were tragic indeed as he wrestled with failing health, and a career that once again appeared to stultify him. Presley was elected to the COUNTRY MUSIC HALL OF FAME in 1998.

—*Colin Escott*

REPRESENTATIVE RECORDINGS

Elvis Country (RCA 1971); *The Million Dollar Quartet* (RCA, 1990); *The King of Rock & Roll: The Complete '50s Masters* (RCA, 1992); *From Nashville to Memphis: The Essential '60s Masters* (RCA, 1993); *Amazing Grace* (RCA, 1994)

Frances Preston
b. Nashville, Tennessee, August 27, 1934

Called "one of the true powerhouses in the pop music business" by *Fortune* magazine, Frances Williams Preston could have ended up a schoolteacher. A summer job while a student at the George Peabody School for Teachers in Nashville changed all that. She briefly worked at the National Life and Accident Insurance Company, then at National Life's subsidiary, Nashville radio station WSM, beginning as a receptionist. Rapidly she moved to the center of things at the station; for a period of time she even had her own TV fashion show.

Because of her contacts and all-around ability, she was hired in 1958 by JUDGE ROBERT J. BURTON to open a BMI southern regional office in Nashville. Quickly she led BMI to a position of preeminence in the South, signing and helping countless country writers and publishers and those with roots in other idioms of popular music as well. Behind the scenes she played a major role in building the strength of Nashville as a music center.

In 1964, the year the BMI Building went up on Music Row, Preston became a vice president of BMI—reportedly, the first woman corporate executive in Tennessee. Preston moved to BMI's New York office in 1985, becoming senior vice president for performing rights, and president and CEO the following year. She has been responsible for the

Frances Preston

company's growth in a variety of areas, including domestic licensing, foreign performing rights, legislation for fair compensation for writers, and publishers' and copyright protection.

Nationally prominent in business and political circles, Preston was a member of President Jimmy Carter's Panama Canal Study Committee, on the commission for the White House Record Library, and a member of Vice President Albert Gore Jr.'s National Information Infrastructure Advisory Council.

In 1992, in recognition of her significant role in building Nashville's music industry, she was elected to the COUNTRY MUSIC HALL OF FAME.   —*Burt Korall*

Kenny Price
b. Florence, Kentucky, May 27, 1931; d. August 4, 1987

Rotund singer Kenny Price, known as the Round Mound of Sound, is best known as a longtime cast member of *HEE HAW*, where he sang in the show's gospel quartet and contributed solo numbers and comedy routines.

Price was raised on a farm near Covington, Kentucky, and at fourteen he landed a spot singing on station WZIP in Cincinnati. Following two years of military service in Korea, he appeared on Buddy Ross's *Hometowners* TV show on WLW in Cincinnati and also became a regular on the *MIDWESTERN HAYRIDE*.

He first hit the country charts in 1966 with "Walking on New Grass," a #7 hit on Boone Records. In 1969 he signed with *RCA*, for whom his biggest hit was the #8 "Sheriff of Boone County," released in 1970. In later years he also recorded for the MRC, Dimension, and Broadway labels.
    —*Walt Trott*

REPRESENTATIVE RECORDING

Country Favorites (Broadway, 1987)

Ray Price
b. near Perryville, Texas, January 12, 1926

When Ray Noble Price was inducted into the COUNTRY MUSIC HALL OF FAME in 1996, many noted that the honor was long overdue. Such feelings weren't based so much on the longevity of his career or on the number of major hits he has recorded, for in those regards Price was no different from many other deserving artists awaiting induction. More importantly, Price has been one of country's great innovators. He changed the sound of country music from the late 1950s forward by developing a rhythmic brand of honky-tonk that has been hugely influential ever since. As steel guitarist Don Helms, a veteran of HANK WILLIAMS's Drifting Cowboys, once put it, "Ray Price created an era."

Born near Perryville in East Texas, Price moved with his mother to Dallas after she and his father split up. He was four years old at the time and would spend most of his childhood moving between his mother's house in Dallas and his father's farm. He joined the U.S. Marines during World War II, then afterward enrolled at North Texas Agricultural College, intent on becoming a veterinarian. But while in school he started singing at a place called Roy's House Cafe. He eventually made his way to JIM BECK's recording studio in Dallas, where Beck hooked him up with BULLET RECORDS. Price recorded one single for Bullet in either late 1949 or early 1950.

The Bullet record wasn't successful, but Price began singing on various Dallas-area programs, including the *BIG D JAMBOREE*. He caught the attention of Troy Martin of the Peer-Southern publishing firm, and behind Martin's strong recommendation Price was signed to COLUMBIA RECORDS in March 1951. His first Columbia release was "If You're Ever Lonely, Darling," written by LEFTY FRIZZELL.

Ray Price

Price had little success on Columbia until a fortuitous introduction to Hank Williams in the fall of 1951 changed his fortunes. Williams took Price with him on the road and wrote a song, "Weary Blues (From Waiting)," which he gave to Price to record. Though not a major hit, the song did fairly well for Price, and in January 1952 he moved to Nashville to join the GRAND OLE OPRY. There he roomed with Williams and used the Drifting Cowboys as his back-up band. Many of Price's recordings from this period show him self-consciously adopting Williams's style. This trend would lessen, though, as Price allowed his natural voice more sway on such early hits as the 1954 double-sider "I'll Be There (If You Ever Want Me)" b/w "Release Me."

The pivotal record of Price's career, however, was "Crazy Arms," recorded March 1, 1956. Introduced by TOMMY JACKSON's searing fiddle ("I whistled the sound I wanted Tommy to play," Price recalled) and driven by BUDDY KILLEN's 4/4 bass line, "Crazy Arms" introduced a novel, modernist intensity to what was still an essentially classic honky-tonk sound. The record spent twenty weeks at #1 and established Price as a full-fledged star. For the next several years he continued to tinker with his sound, most importantly emphasizing a shuffle rhythm that was barely perceptible on "Crazy Arms." The 4/4 shuffle, which many artists soon adopted, became so closely identified with Price that it was known in country circles as the "Ray Price Beat."

During this time Price also gave a career leg up to many young musicians and songwriters. WILLIE NELSON, ROGER MILLER, and JOHNNY PAYCHECK all passed through his band, the Cherokee Cowboys, while Nelson, HARLAN HOWARD, and HANK COCHRAN wrote for the publishing company of which Price was part owner, PAMPER MUSIC. Price's 1959 rendition of Howard's "Heartaches by the Number" helped establish Howard in Nashville, while Price's 1958 smash "City Lights" did the same for its writer, BILL ANDERSON. Yet as dominant a hard country artist as Price had become, by the early 1960s he had begun to move into a more pop-oriented direction. This trend culminated with his 1967 hit "Danny Boy." Recorded with full orchestration, the song alienated many of Price's old fans, even as it brought many new ones in from a different direction. Three years later, both sets of fans responded favorably to Price's "For the Good Times." Written by KRIS KRISTOFFERSON, the song was a #1 country hit in 1970 and just barely missed the pop Top Ten.

Price's long association with Columbia ended in 1974, as did his years of chart dominance. Disgruntled with Nashville, he had moved back to Texas by then. Subsequent recordings for Myrrh, ABC/DOT, MONUMENT, and various other labels were often musically unsatisfying, though a 1980 duet album with Willie Nelson showed off Price again in fine form. Through the latter half of the 1980s Price recorded for the Nashville independent STEP ONE, and in 1992 he returned to Columbia for a one-off album that went undeservedly unnoticed. Nevertheless, by the mid-1990s, yet another generation of young country acts—many of them stars of the burgeoning hillbilly music underground—were trumpeting Price's work. To this day, the 4/4 shuffle is so deeply embedded in country music as to be second nature to many. —*Daniel Cooper*

REPRESENTATIVE RECORDINGS

Night Life (Columbia, 1963; reissued Koch, 1996); *The Essential Ray Price 1951–1962* (Columbia/Legacy, 1991)

Charley Pride
b. Sledge, Mississippi, March 18, 1938

Charley Pride's most obvious singularity—that he is the only true country superstar who is also black—tends to obscure the fact that he has been one of the most successful country singers ever. He would be a country legend even without the racial anomaly. With a gritty, southern-accented baritone voice, Pride was able during his remarkably long-lived hit-making heyday (1966–89) to drive even entirely forgettable songs into the Top Ten, if not the #1 position. Given a great song, he typically spent multiple weeks atop the charts.

Pride's background sounds like a classic blues singer's story. The son of a strait-laced sharecropper father, Charley Frank Pride (named "Charl" by his father but spelled "Charley" on his birth certificate) was born on a forty-acre Mississippi cotton farm fifty miles due south of Memphis. Pride picked cotton to buy his first guitar, a ten-dollar Sears, Roebuck model, when he was fourteen. Pride's father was morally opposed to the culture and lyrics of blues music and was a big fan of the GRAND OLE OPRY. So instead of drawing influences from B. B. King's Memphis radio show, Charley Pride was musically schooled on the likes of ERNEST TUBB, PEE WEE KING, and ROY ACUFF.

At age sixteen Pride left home to play professional baseball in the Negro American League. After two years with teams in Memphis and elsewhere he entered the army for a two-year stint, married Rozene Cohran, an ambitious and highly motivated Memphis woman who still oversees the business end of his career, and mustered out of the service in 1958 with every intention of having a big-league baseball career. Pride played briefly in the Pioneer League and

Charley Pride

then worked at a smelting plant in Helena, where he played for the plant ball team. He had tryouts with the California Angels in the early sixties, but by then had injured his throwing arm.

In 1962 RED SOVINE and RED FOLEY discovered Pride in Helena and eventually helped him come to Nashville, where he hooked up with producer JACK CLEMENT. In 1965 Clement's initial demo recordings of Pride caught CHET ATKINS's ear at RCA RECORDS. Atkins flew to Los Angeles to play the sides to top label executives and gained their agreement to sign the remarkable voice before he revealed Pride's color; Pride's first RCA recording session took place in August 1965 and his first single, "The Snakes Crawl at Night," was released in January 1966. Pride's race was likewise shielded from country radio through three single releases until the third, "Just Between You and Me," climbed into the country Top Ten. His gold-selling first album, *Country Charley Pride,* was the first indication many fans had that he was black.

Pride handled the curiosity of fans in dance halls by allowing twenty minutes of stageside gawking before clearing the floor to allow people to dance. As with Jackie Robinson, who broke the color line in big-league baseball, he suffered whatever discrimination he was exposed to in silence, determined that talent was what counted. His work spoke volumes: Between his chart debut in 1966 and 1989, he had twenty-nine #1 country hits, including such enduring classics as "Is Anybody Goin' to San Antone" (1970), "Kiss an Angel Good Mornin'" (1971), and "All I Have to Offer You Is Me" (1969).

He was not, however, the Jackie Robinson of country music, as he has been portrayed. Robinson opened the doors to black players, and the most talented among them rushed in behind him. Although Pride established himself once and for all, no other black country singers came anywhere near equaling his commercial achievements.

In addition to being a talented singer and entertainer, Pride is an astute, conservative businessman. Pride made his home in North Dallas, Texas, becoming an important real-estate and banking investor in that community, as well as setting up a booking and management company, Chardon, which introduced JANIE FRICKE, DAVE & SUGAR, and NEAL MCCOY to stardom. He was a partner in Pi-Gem song publishing with producer TOM COLLINS, all the while cranking out hit after hit and running hard as a nonstop touring artist. He was named CMA's Entertainer of the Year in 1971, and twice Male Vocalist of the Year (1971, 1972). Although invited to join the GRAND OLE OPRY in 1968, he initially declined; he became a cast member in 1993.

—*Bob Millard*

REPRESENTATIVE RECORDINGS

The Best of Charley Pride (RCA, 1985); *Greatest Hits* (RCA, 1988); *The Essential Charley Pride* (RCA, 1997)

Prince Albert Show (see Grand Ole Opry)

John Prine
b. Maywood, Illinois, October 10, 1946

John E. Prine has cited BOB DYLAN, HANK WILLIAMS, and ROGER MILLER as his three main influences. Like Dylan, Prine is a midwesterner who strummed an acoustic guitar

and overcame his small, nasal voice and limited melodic gifts with lyrics that made you sit up and notice. Like Williams, Prine sings about common folks in their own terse vernacular. Like Miller, Prine twists those stories until they yield an absurdist humor.

Though they lived outside Chicago, Prine's parents were from Paradise, Kentucky, and John's childhood summer visits there had a profound influence not only on the subject matter of his songs but also on their sound, which boasted the vocal drawl, honky-tonk two-step, and twangy strum of country music. In the summer of 1971 Steve Goodman, Prine's pal on the Chicago folk-coffeehouse circuit, dragged KRIS KRISTOFFERSON to a deserted Earl of Old Town to hear Prine, who was still working as a mailman at the time. Kristofferson was so impressed he invited Prine to the Bitter End in New York to play for Jerry Wexler of ATLANTIC RECORDS.

Wexler offered Prine a contract the next day, and by the end of the year, *John Prine,* recorded with ELVIS PRESLEY's rhythm section and boasting effusive liner notes by Kristofferson, was in the stores. The album included such future standards as "Hello in There" (a poignant look at old age, soon recorded by Bette Midler), "Angel from Montgomery" (the private thoughts of an Alabama housewife, soon recorded by Bonnie Raitt), "Paradise" (an understated portrait of strip mining in Kentucky), and "Sam Stone" (a devastating portrait of a Vietnam veteran).

Prine soon moved away from the topical material of "Paradise" and "Sam Stone" in favor of quirky vignettes about down-on-their-luck misfits stuck in prison on Christmas, in a bungalow too near the highway, or in a silent marriage. After four albums for Atlantic, he bounced back with some of his finest songs on *Bruised Orange* for Asylum in 1978. After a third Asylum album, Prine and his manager, Al Bunetta, formed their own label, Oh Boy Records, so Prine could take his time writing and recording his songs just the way he wanted. The result was only four studio albums between 1981 and 1995, but each was greeted by hosannas from the music press.

Prine moved to Nashville and enjoyed some modest success writing for such artists as TAMMY WYNETTE ("Unwed Fathers") and DON WILLIAMS ("Love Is on a Roll"). Prine won a Grammy Award for Best Contemporary Folk Recording for his 1991 album *The Missing Years,* produced by Howie Epstein of Tom Petty's Heartbreakers and featuring guest vocals by such admirers as Petty, Raitt, Bruce Springsteen, and Phil Everly.

—*Geoffrey Himes*

REPRESENTATIVE RECORDINGS

John Prine (Atlantic, 1971); *Sweet Revenge* (Atlantic, 1973); *Bruised Orange* (Asylum, 1978); *The Missing Years* (Oh Boy, 1991); *Great Days: The John Prine Anthology* (Rhino, 1993)

Jeanne Pruett
b. Pell City, Alabama, January 30, 1937

Born Norma Jean Bowman, Jeanne Pruett gained her stage name through marriage to guitarist Jack Pruett. The two moved to Nashville in 1956, and Jack held down a job in the road band of MARTY ROBBINS. Jeanne made her first recordings for RCA in 1963. Pruett signed with DECCA RECORDS in 1969 and had enjoyed moderate success with her self-composed song "Hold to My Unchanging Love" in

1971. She also had scored as a staff writer for Marty Robbins Enterprises in 1972 when Robbins hit the Top Ten with a song she wrote called "Love Me."

Her career-making hit came in 1973 when Pruett's producer Walter Haynes remembered a sultry ballad called "Satin Sheets," written by John Volinkaty, and urged Pruett to record it, even though Opry stars BILL ANDERSON and JAN HOWARD had previously recorded the song as a duet in 1973 on their MCA album *Jan and Bill.*

In an unusual promotion gimmick for her single, Pruett personally cut 1,600 pieces of pink, satin sheets and mailed them to everyone on the Country Music Association's membership list. The effort undoubtedly caught the attention of radio station program directors, and the record hit #1 on May 26, 1973. In the wake of the single's success, she joined the GRAND OLE OPRY cast on July 21, 1973.

Among Pruett's other Top Ten hits are "I'm Your Woman" (1973), "Back to Back" (1979), and "Temporarily Yours" (1980). In recent years she has become equally known for her cooking, thanks to appearances on TNN's *NASHVILLE NOW* with host RALPH EMERY and the publication of her cookbook series entitled *Feedin' Friends.*

—*Don Rhodes*

REPRESENTATIVE RECORDINGS

Jeanne Pruett (MCA, 1973); *I'm Your Woman* (MCA, 1974)

Publishing (*see* Music Publishing)

Riley Puckett
b. near Alpharetta, Georgia, May 7, 1894; d. July 13, 1946

A founding member of the seminal old-time stringband known as the SKILLET LICKERS, vocalist-guitarist George Riley Puckett was the principal reason for the band's popularity. Nearly blinded shortly after birth through a faulty eye treatment, Puckett learned to play guitar and banjo in his teens. From then on he made his living playing music, first at dances, parties, and on street corners, and later on radio, at fiddlers' conventions, and on records.

He made his first recordings in 1924 in the company of GID TANNER, his musical associate for many years. Puckett's repertoire was astonishingly varied, ranging from older British ballads to sentimental songs of the late 1800s and contemporary hits of the 1930s. He was featured on more than 200 issued recordings (among them some of the best-selling hits of COLUMBIA's 15000-D hillbilly series), apart from his work with the Skillet Lickers; on at least one occasion he was the uncredited accompanist of a black blues singer. Puckett's idiosyncratic guitar back up was unmistakable on record, and his syncopated bass runs (which did occasion some disparagement from a few of the fiddlers he accompanied) were widely emulated in the 1960s by young guitarists of the urban folksong revival.

Puckett died in an Atlanta hospital of blood poisoning at age fifty-two.

—*Norm Cohen*

REPRESENTATIVE RECORDINGS

Gid Tanner and His Skillet Lickers—with Riley Puckett and Clayton McMichen(Rounder, 1973); *Riley Puckett* (County, 1979)

Pure Prairie League

Country only in the broadest sense of the term when they began in the early seventies, Pure Prairie League would have been right at home on country radio in the post-ALABAMA era. Among the more successful country-rock bands to emerge from the shadow of the BYRDS and Buffalo Springfield, they are best remembered for a handful of singles and a constantly changing personnel that included at various times singer-songwriters Craig Fuller (b. Portsmouth Ohio, July 18, 1949), VINCE GILL, and Gary Burr.

Taking its name from a women's temperance group in the 1939 Errol Flynn western *Dodge City,* the band was formed in Cincinnati, its membership (Fuller, singer-guitarist George Powell, bassist Jim Lanham, steel guitarist John Call, and drummer Tom McGrail) all from the Ohio River valley area. McGrail, who had come up with the group's name, was replaced by Jim Caughlin prior to their first album, *Pure Prairie League* (RCA, 1971). Original lead singer and chief composer Fuller left the band after their second album, *Bustin' Out* (RCA, 1972), to serve two years in a Kentucky hospital as a conscientious objector to the Vietnam War. In his absence, the group was dropped by RCA Records but continued performing as many as 275 shows a year, many of them on college campuses.

FM airplay of "Amie," a concert favorite from *Bustin' Out,* led to an edited version being released and becoming a Top Forty pop hit in 1975. RCA re-signed the group, with only Powell and Call remaining from the original recording lineup, now joined by fellow Cincinnati musicians Billy Hinds (drums), Michael Connor (keyboards), Michael Reilly (bass) from the East Orange Express, and Larry Goshorn from the Goshorn Brothers and Sacred Mushroom.

Goshorn was guitarist and lead singer until the band's 1979 album *Can't Hold Back* (RCA), which featured twenty-two-year-old Vince Gill's debut with the group. Gill sang lead on the band's highest-charting single, "Let Me Love You Tonight," from the album *Firin' Up* (Casablanca, 1980). Though the band's last single to chart was "You're Mine Tonight" in 1981, Pure Prairie League continued to tour under Reilly's leadership, with several more personnel changes, including brief periods with former Loggins & Messina sideman Al Garth on saxophone and the SWEETHEARTS OF THE RODEO (Kristine Arnold and Janis Gill) on backing vocals. Gary Burr, whose songwriting credits already included JUICE NEWTON's "Love's Been a Little Bit Hard on Me" and the OAK RIDGE BOYS' "Make My Life with You," joined as lead singer in 1982, remaining through 1985.

Following a short-lived collaboration with fellow singer-songwriter Eric Justin Kaz (their first album, *American Flyer,* produced by George Martin), Fuller rejoined Pure Prairie League in 1985, sharing leads for three months with Burr. After the group finally disbanded in 1987, Fuller joined rock band Little Feat from 1988 until September 1993, when he left to concentrate on songwriting, with collaborators including Burr and Gary Nicholson.

—*Todd Everett*

REPRESENTATIVE RECORDINGS

Bustin' Out (RCA, 1972); *Firin' Up* (Casablanca, 1980; Mercury, 1993); *Best of the Pure Prairie League* (Polygram, 1995); *Pure Prairie League: If the Shoe Fits* (Renaissance, 1997)

Curley Putman

Curly Putman
b. Princeton, Alabama, November 20, 1930

Songwriter Claude Putman Jr. is responsible for numerous memorable compositions, including "He Stopped Loving Her Today," a massive hit for GEORGE JONES, which Putman co-wrote with BOBBY BRADDOCK and which won the CMA's Song of the Year Award in both 1980 and 1981.

He and Braddock also co-wrote "D-I-V-O-R-C-E" (TAMMY WYNETTE. Additional hits written or co-written by Putman include "Green, Green Grass of Home" (PORTER WAGONER), "My Elusive Dreams" (DAVID HOUSTON), "Blood Red and Goin' Down" (TANYA TUCKER), and "Dumb Blonde" (DOLLY PARTON's first chart single, 1967).

After serving in the navy, Putman worked as a sawmill hand and as a shoe salesman, and played steel guitar in country bands in Huntsville, Alabama. A meeting with BUDDY KILLEN landed Putman a job with TREE MUSIC as a songplugger, and it was not long before he connected as a songwriter. He had minor chart action of his own as a solo artist for the Cherokee and ABC labels in the 1960s.

—*Bob Allen*

Eddie Rabbitt

b. Brooklyn, New York, November 27, 1941; d. May 7, 1998

Edward Thomas Rabbitt brought a smooth, broad-based approach to country music as both songwriter and singer. By far the most significant recent country artist from his part of the world—he grew up in New Jersey—Rabbitt touched millions of fans with a slightly husky, understated vocal technique and craftsmanlike songs that bridged the gap between hard country and a broader pop audience. Some of that contrast emerged from his East Orange upbringing and the Irish roots of his parents, Thomas and Mae. "I've been doing country music for a while, and people ask me, 'What's a kid from New Jersey doing singing country music?'" Rabbitt said in 1990. "I just fell in love with it when I was a kid. I think a lot of it comes from the fact that my mom and dad are from Ireland and my dad plays the violin and the accordion. . . . "

According to an often told story, a Scoutmaster with a hillbilly alter ego inspired a twelve-year-old Rabbitt to play guitar and sing country music. By the mid-1960s Rabbitt began to play professionally on a small scale and released records on the 20th Century-Fox and COLUMBIA labels before hitting the lonesome streets of MUSIC CITY in 1968. His first songwriting success came with the catchy "Working My Way Up from the Bottom," written his first night in Nashville and recorded by ROY DRUSKY. A songwriting deal with ACUFF-ROSE brought a small weekly "draw" to make ends meet and resulted in cuts by GEORGE MORGAN and others. But the turning point came with ELVIS PRESLEY's 1970 hit of Rabbitt's distinctive country-pop tune "Kentucky Rain." With its backwoods imagery and nonstandard chord changes, the song summed up much of what was to become Rabbitt's far-reaching appeal.

It wasn't until 1974 (when he also scored a #1 as a writer with RONNIE MILSAP's "Pure Love") that Rabbitt started his country recording career, for ELEKTRA. But by 1976 he had released his first #1 "Drinkin' My Baby (Off My Mind)." That ode was only the beginning of a hit-crafting mode—often in partnership with Even Stevens—that made Rabbitt a king of the hill during an era when pop-leaning country ruled. Other #1s included 1978's "I Just Want to Love You"; "Every Which Way but Loose," from the 1978 movie starring Clint Eastwood; the Dylanesque "Drivin' My Life Away" and "I Love a Rainy Night (both 1980 and the latter a #1 pop tune); "Step by Step" and "Someone Could Lose a Heart Tonight" (both 1981); and 1982's "You and I," a duet with CRYSTAL GAYLE. Additional Top Ten hits came on WARNER BROS. in 1983 and 1984 with "You Can't Run from Love" and "B-B-B-Burnin' Up With Love," respectively

In 1985 Rabbitt and wife, Janine, suffered a tragedy with the death of their twenty-three-month-old son, Timmy, born with severe birth defects. After at move to RCA and 1986's successful Rabbitt–JUICE NEWTON duet "Both To Each Other (Friends and Lovers)," Rabbitt took a year's hiatus from the charts before returning in 1988 with the energetic #1s "I Wanna Dance with You" and "The Wanderer," the latter a remake of fellow Jersey boy Dion's 1961 pop hit. Rabbitt's eclectic 1990 *Jersey Boy* LP touched his customary bases of pop, r&b, rock, and hard country, but scored its lone #1 single with "On Second Thought."

As a new generation of singers and songwriters led by GARTH BROOKS took ownership of the country peaks, Rabbitt continued to tour nationally and internationally, but

Eddie Rabbitt

he made little further impact in the youth-dominated radio and records scene. In 1995 Rabbitt and Gayle reunited to record a follow-up duet, "I Made a Promise to You," for the soundtrack of the motion picture *Gordy*. Rabbitt was also active in a variety of charitable causes. His death was due to cancer. —*Tommy Goldsmith*

REPRESENTATIVE RECORDINGS

Horizon (Elektra, 1980); *All Time Greatest Hits* (Warner Bros., 1991)

Mose Rager
b. Smallhous, Kentucky, April 2, 1911; d. May 14, 1986

Moses "Mose" Rager, along with his coal-mining colleague Ike Everly, was a crucial link in the musical chain that connected the African-American folk musician ARNOLD SHULTZ with influential guitarists MERLE TRAVIS and CHET ATKINS. In the early 1930s Rager and Everly passed on to Travis a rich tradition of chords, runs, rolls, songs (rags, blues, gospel), and a deep appreciation of black music, as well as a guitar-playing technique they had assimilated from white musician Kennedy Jones, who had learned the style directly from Shultz in the early 1920s. Deriving ultimately from southeastern ragtime-based instrumental methods, this style became widely known in the 1950s and 1960s as "Travis-picking," a technique in which a guitarist, using only the thumb and forefinger, plays melody, harmony, rhythm, and bass simultaneously. This style became enormously popular among country music guitarists during the 1950s, influencing numerous musicians, most notably Chet Atkins.

At various points in the late 1940s Rager worked as a sideman for GRANDPA JONES and CURLY FOX & TEXAS RUBY (with whom he appeared on a few recordings, "Black Mountain Rag" perhaps the best among them), but the guitarist returned to Muhlenberg County in 1950, where he worked as a heavy-equipment operator until his retirement in 1973. Travis readily acknowledged Rager as his mentor, commenting frequently on his "magnetism," once writing that Rager "was a Pied Piper—the kind of guy who could pick up a guitar, walk down the street, and have the whole town following him." —*William E. Lightfoot*

Marvin Rainwater
b. Wichita, Kansas, July 2, 1925

Marvin Karlton Percy, known as Marvin Rainwater (he took his mother's maiden name as a stage moniker), was a maverick performer whose work, though broadly country, distilled many influences and perhaps covered too many bases to find a niche. He wrote and performed one classic country hit, "Gonna Find Me a Bluebird" (1957), and had a #1 hit in England in 1958 with a rock & roll song, "Whole Lotta Woman." He also recorded the original version of "The Pale Faced Indian," later a pop hit (as "Indian Reservation") for Don Fardon and Paul Revere & the Raiders.

Rainwater is one quarter Cherokee and grew up in Kansas studying classical piano. After World War II he moved to the Washington, D.C., area, and launched his career there in country music with ROY CLARK as his guitarist. His first breakthrough was on *Arthur Godfrey's Talent Scouts* TV show in May 1955, and he was signed to MGM RECORDS that year. In 1955 he also joined the *OZARK JUBILEE* and re-

mained a cast member until 1957. Veering between country and rock & roll, he scored hits in both markets but found a permanent home in neither. During the 1950s he played up his part-Indian lineage, which ultimately made him that much more unmarketable.

After leaving MGM in 1961, Rainwater recorded for many labels, including his own Brave Records. He scored a hit in Scandinavia in 1981 with "Henryetta, Oklahoma," and currently lives in rural Minnesota. —*Colin Escott*

REPRESENTATIVE RECORDINGS

Classic Recordings (Bear Family Records, 1992), 4 CDs; *Whole Lotta Woman* (Bear Family Records, 1994)

Willis Alan Ramsey
b. Alabama, 1951

Willis Alan Ramsey is an enigmatic singer-songwriter who released one critically acclaimed album in 1972 at age twenty-one and then virtually disappeared from the music scene. Nevertheless, his songs have been covered by many artists, and he has been cited as an influence by LYLE LOVETT.

Born in Alabama, Willis Alan Ramsey was raised in Dallas. In the summer of 1970 LEON RUSSELL, a partner in the rock & roll label Shelter Records, heard Ramsey in a University of Texas coffee shop and shortly afterward signed him to the label.

His album *Willis Alan Ramsey* was recorded between May 1971 and March 1972 in sessions in Memphis, Nashville, Hollywood, and Tyler, Texas, and was released June 5, 1972. Although the album broke no sales records, its poignant and whimsical songs were widely admired by other artists, and cover records soon appeared by Jimmy Buffett ("The Ballad of Spider John"), WAYLON JENNINGS ("Satin Sheets," not the JEANNE PRUETT song), and America and the Captain & Tennille ("Muskrat Love").

In 1977 Ramsey made an appearance on the public television concert program *AUSTIN CITY LIMITS*. Afterward, like a country J. D. Salinger, he seemed to vanish from the public spotlight. Dissatisfied by his relationship with Shelter Records, he waited out the last eight years of his contract, refusing to record anything for the label. He went through a painful divorce, and his Austin, Texas, recording studio went bankrupt. He made ends meet with royalty checks and payment for a movie soundtrack. In 1987 he moved to England. In 1989, encouraged by friend and admirer Lyle Lovett, Ramsey returned to making occasional live performances in the United States and co-wrote two songs with Lovett that appeared on Lovett's albums: "North Dakota" and "That's Right (You're Not from Texas)." But as of the end of 1997 Ramsey had yet to have another record released. —*Paul Kingsbury*

REPRESENTATIVE RECORDING

Willis Alan Ramsey (Shelter, 1972; DCC, 1990)

Boots Randolph
b. Paducah, Kentucky, June 3, 1927

Homer Louis Randolph III was a key element of the NASHVILLE SOUND, and his saxophone was instrumental in broadening the appeal of country music.

The song that made him well known, however, was a collaborative instrumental he worked up with guitarist James

"Spider" Rich, titled "Yakety Sax" (#35, 1963 pop), which cleverly blended country, jazz, blues, and gospel styles. Originally recorded for RCA, it was the later MONUMENT version that was the hit.

Randolph began playing saxophone in high school groups. In Indiana and Illinois he performed in local bands until Kenneth Burns (HOMER & JETHRO) caught his act and recommended Boots to brother-in-law CHET ATKINS. After hearing Randolph's tape of "Chicken Reel," Atkins invited the young musician to Nashville.

OWEN BRADLEY also admired his talent and engaged him for a 1958 BRENDA LEE session. He quickly became a Nashville session regular, playing on 250 to 300 studio jobs annually for nearly every name artist in Nashville throughout the decade, including ELVIS PRESLEY. In the sixties and seventies Randolph toured with Atkins and FLOYD CRAMER. In 1977, in Nashville's Printer's Alley, Randolph opened his own nightclub, which he closed in 1994. He subsequently co-owned a club with Danny Davis on Music Valley Drive, which lasted until late 1997. —*Walt Trott*

REPRESENTATIVE RECORDING

The Yakin' Sax Man (RCA Camden, 1985)

Wayne Raney
b. Wolf Bayou, Arkansas, August 17, 1920; d. January 23, 1993

Disk jockey, singer, harmonica player, guitarist, recording artist, songwriter, producer, studio owner—Wayne Raney covered all of show business's angles.

Raney taught himself the mouth organ as a five-year-old after hearing a blind hobo playing in the street. At age thirteen Raney had his own program on Mexican BORDER RADIO station XEPN.

In 1936 Raney met his idol, the guitarist and harmonica player LONNIE GLOSSON, and the pair began a twenty-five-year, on-again, off-again partnership highlighted by a long stint at Cincinnati's WCKY beginning in 1941. Their syndicated radio program was eventually carried by some 230 stations, and the popular duo reportedly sold more than 5 million harmonicas (priced at $1.69 each) through the mail.

In 1945, during a stint at WMC in Memphis, Glosson and Raney began recording and touring with the DELMORE BROTHERS. Several of the Delmores' trailblazing country boogie records for KING RECORDS, including their hit "Blues Stay Away from Me," featured the twin harmonica playing of Glosson and Raney.

In 1949 Raney scored a #1 hit and a guest spot on the GRAND OLE OPRY with a King release of his composition, "Why Don't You Haul Off and Love Me." In 1950 he recorded four sides for London Records as Lonesome Willie Evans. After Rabon Delmore's death in 1952, Raney headed west to become a regular member of the *California Hayride* (1953–54). Raney briefly joined LEFTY FRIZZELL's band in about 1953, supplying harmonica, harmony vocals, and co-writing with Frizzell before eventually leaving the honky-tonk star to join the cast of Wheeling, West Virginia's, *WWVA JAMBOREE*. Raney flirted briefly with rockabilly for DECCA before beginning another five-year stint at WCKY. In 1958 he began spending more time on the business end of music, starting his own studio and founding the Rimrock label. His last recordings were released on STARDAY in 1964. In 1976 he started Wayne Raney Cassette Duplication. During this period he also played his har-

monica on *HEE HAW*, with his last performance coming in 1979. In the 1980s, after having already sold his studio and pressing plant to Stax Records, he retired from show business. —*Kim Field*

REPRESENTATIVE RECORDINGS

The Delmore Brothers & Wayne Raney: When They Let the Hammer Down (Bear Family, 1984); *Real Hot Boogie* (Charly, 1986)

Rank & File

In 1983 the Austin-based quartet Rank & File became the poster boys of cowpunk, a description the band's label coined expressly for them and that made the band blanch. Given the band member's backgrounds, the moniker fit: brothers Chip (guitar and vocals) and Tony Kinman (bass and vocals) had previously fronted the Dils, a West Coast punk band known for its 1977 anthem "I Hate the Rich"; guitarist Alejandro Escovedo had been in a band called the Nuns; and drummer Jim "Slim" Evans had been in an outfit called Sharon Tate's Baby.

The Kinman brothers were raised in North Carolina, where they first heard country music. Their family moved to Southern California in their high school years, when they participated in the burgeoning punk scene. The politically minded Dils drew praise as "the American Clash," but the band was short-lived (ca. 1977–79). Moving to New York City from California, the Kinmans teamed with Escovedo, whose father had played in a Norteno band, and in 1981 were inspired to go country by attending a MERLE HAGGARD concert. Rank & File moved to Austin, Texas, later that year, completing its lineup there with drummer Slim Evans. The band's critically acclaimed Slash label debut, *Sundown*, appeared in 1982 and was picked up by WARNER BROS. in 1983. The laudatory notices never translated into commercial success, and college radio was the sole format to embrace Rank & File. Despite initial hopes of finding a country audience for its revved-up covers of such standards as "Ring of Fire," Rank & File eventually gravitated back toward its punk roots. Escovedo left the band in 1985 to found the band True Believers and has been a solo artist since 1992. The Kinmans disbanded Rank & File in 1987 and moved on to a group named Blackbird. —*Mark Humphrey*

REPRESENTATIVE RECORDINGS

Sundown (Slash, 1982); *Long Gone Dead* (Warner Bros., 1984)

Leon Rausch
b. Springfield, Missouri, October 2, 1927

Although his career stretches back to the 1950s, it was not until the 1970s that Edgar Leon Rausch began to receive serious attention as one of most important vocalists in western swing history. Still very active, Rausch may yet emerge as the music's greatest vocal stylist.

Rausch's early career was spent with local bands in Missouri. His mid-1950s recording debut—an excellent "Lost Highway"—was with Waco, Texas–based Clyde Chesser's Village Boys, and by 1958 he was singing with BOB WILLS & His Texas Playboys. When Wills reteamed with TOMMY DUNCAN a year later, Rausch's singing opportunities decreased, but the early sixties found him touring and recording with JOHNNIE LEE WILLS, with whom he first waxed what has become his signature tune, "Milk Cow Blues," for the Sims label.

When Bob Wills gave up bandleading in 1965, Rausch took over the Texas Playboys, appearing and recording with Wills in that capacity during 1965 and 1966. Later in the decade Rausch was leading his own Texas Panthers. Rausch reunited with Bob Wills for his *For the Last Time* in 1973, then joined the reformed Texas Playboys from 1976 to 1986, continuing to lead his own bands and record for small labels such as Derrick and Southland, recording the particularly fine *The Rausch Touch* for the latter in 1985. In the nineties, arguably singing better than ever, Rausch has worked with the JOHNNY GIMBLE–HERB REMINGTON–led Playboys II and recorded prolifically with Tom Morrell and his Time-Warp Top Hands. —*Kevin Coffey*

REPRESENTATIVE RECORDINGS

Leon Rausch: The Rausch Touch (Southland, 1985); *Tom Morrell & the Time-Warp Top Hands: How the West Was Swung, Volume 1* (Priority, 1991)

Eddy Raven
b. August 19, 1944, Lafayette, Louisiana

Edward Garvin Futch, better known as Eddy Raven, has parlayed his direct, soulful singing, skillful songwriting, and Cajun heritage into a career spanning parts of five decades.

Starting as a teenage radio entertainer on a Georgia station, Raven moved in the late 1950s with his family back to Lafayette and the fabulous melting pot of South Louisiana music Legendary singer-songwriter Bobby Charles ("Walking to New Orleans") recorded one of Raven's songs; by 1962 Raven had recorded his own single for Cosmos. Through the 1960s Raven worked with r&b/blues acts including Johnny and Edgar Winter and the regionally famous Boogie Kings. Raven recorded his first LP in 1969, then moved to Nashville the next year with the encouragement of fellow Cajun JIMMY C. NEWMAN.

Raven prospered as a writer, signing with the powerful ACUFF-ROSE publishing house and having tunes recorded by ROY ORBISON, CONNIE SMITH, DON GIBSON, LEFTY FRIZZELL, and even ROY ACUFF, who hit the charts in 1974 with Raven's "Back in the Country." Raven went through a series of record deals for labels including ABC, ABC/DOT, MONUMENT, and Dimension before breaking into the Top Twenty in 1981 with the wistful "I Should Have Called," on ELEKTRA. With popping electric guitar from REGGIE YOUNG and a relaxed Caribbean-flavored groove, the song set the pattern for a string of hits that included "Who Do You Know in California" and the 1984 #1 "I Got Mexico," the latter on RCA. Another milestone for Raven was the OAK RIDGE BOYS' 1982 hit recording of Raven's sentimental but effective composition "Thank God for Kids." "I Got Mexico" kicked off a string of thirteen straight Top Tens for Raven on RCA, including the #1 hits "Shine, Shine, Shine," "I'm Gonna Get You," and "Joe Knows How to Live."

Raven professed dissatisfaction with his sales on RCA, however, and moved in 1989 to the new Universal label, where he was reunited with JIMMY BOWEN, head of Elektra during Raven's stint there. Two more #1s resulted from the *Temporary Sanity* disc—"In a Letter to You" and "Bayou Boys"—but subsequent releases, after CAPITOL had ab-

sorbed nuch of the Universal roster, trended downward. In the mid-1990s Raven was continuing to tour and was signed to the independent Intersound label. —*Thomas Goldsmith*

REPRESENTATIVE RECORDINGS

Best of Eddy Raven (RCA, 1988); *Temporary Sanity* (Universal, 1989)

Wade Ray
b. Griffin, Indiana, April 6, 1918

Western swing fiddler and vocalist Lyman Wade Ray grew up in Arkansas and started playing fiddle at age three. As a child he toured Vaudeville theater circuits as the World's Youngest Violin Player. In 1934 he joined Pappy Cheshire's National Champion Hillbillies in St. Louis, staying with them until 1942, when a two-year army stint interrupted his career.

Then in about 1947, after returning to Cheshire's Hillbillies for a year, he replaced the late fiddler Alan Crockett in the PRAIRIE RAMBLERS at Chicago's WLS *NATIONAL BARN DANCE*. When WLS dropped the Ramblers in 1949, Wade and his friend *Barn Dance* star REX ALLEN moved to Los Angeles that January. By mid-1949 Ray was fronting his own swing band in and around Los Angeles. He recorded for the tiny Cowtown label, briefly for CAPITOL, and then signed with RCA VICTOR in 1951. His best-known RCA singles were the ballads "Walk Softly" and "The Things I Might Have Been."

From 1956 into the early sixties, he led bands in Las Vegas. He later worked with both the SONS OF THE PIONEERS and with ROY ROGERS until moving to Nashville in 1964. There Ray recorded fiddle instrumentals for RCA and became a regular on ERNEST TUBB's syndicated TV show. After spending a year with RAY PRICE's Cherokee Cowboys in 1964, Ray became WILLIE NELSON's touring bass player. From 1967 to 1970 Wade managed the *RENFRO VALLEY BARN DANCE* in Kentucky. Then back in Nashville, he became an artists' representative for Fender Musical Instruments.

In 1979 Ray and his wife, Gracie, moved to St. Louis, and later retired in Sparta, Illinois. —*Rich Kienzle*

REPRESENTATIVE RECORDINGS

Walk Softly & Other Country Songs (RCA Camden, 1966); *A Ray of Country Sun* (ABC Paramount, 1966)

Collin Raye
b. DeQueen, Arkansas, August 22, 1959

Collin Raye made recordings in three different incarnations before his blend of uptempo rockers and unabashedly emotional ballads finally took hold and made him a country star in the 1990s.

Born Floyd Collin Wray, the son of a rockabilly singer named Lois Wray, Collin and his brother Scott formed the Wray Brothers, which recorded for the Oregon independent labels Sasparilla and CIS. In 1986 and 1987, while calling himself Bubba Wray, his group, the Wrays, charted two singles with MERCURY, including "You Lay a Lotta Love on Me," which reached #48 in *Billboard*. During this time Raye played primarily in the Pacific Northwest, working a trail from Oregon to the casinos of Reno, Nevada, where he developed a repertoire that reportedly exceeds 4,000 songs.

Collin Raye

Raye signed with EPIC RECORDS Nashville in 1990 while working in Reno. He later moved to Greenville, Texas, and continued to live there to be with his children.

People who heard the love songs with which Raye made his reputation either dismissed those songs or wrapped their lives around them. Some fans inscribed the lyrics of "Love, Me," Raye's first #1 hit in 1991, on tombstones. "In This Life" became a popular wedding song and was covered by r&b and jazz acts. Raye's other major ballad hits have included "That Was a River," "Little Rock," and "One Boy, One Girl." His sense of entertainment, honed as a Reno cover act, also led him to perform energetic, more rock-oriented songs as well, the most popular of which included "I Want You Bad (and That Ain't Good)," "That's My Story," and "My Kind of Girl." Though Raye's decision to live in Texas rather than Nashville almost certainly dampened both his profile and his record sales, each of his first four albums, *All I Can Be, In My Life, Extremes,* and *I Think About You,* sold more than 1 million copies.

Raye is one of few contemporary country artists to consistently chart well with songs of social commentary, including "Not That Different" (#3, 1996) and "I Think About You" (#3, 1996). Most recently he scored a Top Five hit with "Little Red Rodeo," a track from his 1997 album *The Best of Collin Raye—Direct Hits.* —*Brian Mansfield*

REPRESENTATIVE RECORDINGS

All I Can Be (Epic, 1991); *Extremes* (Epic, 1993); *I Think About You* (Epic, 1995); *The Best of Collin Raye—Direct Hits* (Epic, 1997)

RCA Victor Records
established 1929

RCA Victor Records has perhaps the most distinguished history of involvement in country music of any record la-

bel. Its roots go back to 1901, when the Victor Talking Machine Company, predecessor to RCA, was organized.

In 1922 Victor held what is now considered the first country recording session, with ECK ROBERTSON and Henry Gilliland. Another early benchmark was VERNON DALHART's 1924 recording of "The Prisoner's Song" b/w "Wreck of the Old 97," country's first million-selling disc.

During the late 1920s executive RALPH PEER actively developed the company's country market by making annual trips to southern cities. In a 1927 trip to BRISTOL, TENNESSEE, he supervised the first recordings of both JIMMIE RODGERS and the CARTER FAMILY. Trips by Peer and, later, ELI OBERSTEIN continued after 1929, when RCA purchased Victor, and involved talent as diverse as JIMMIE DAVIS, the ALLEN BROTHERS, and the Stamps Quartet. During the Great Depression these artists were featured on RCA's budget-priced BLUEBIRD label.

After 1940 RCA shared in a dramatic expansion of the music industry sparked by the economic recovery associated with World War II. By the late 1940s STEVE SHOLES was head of country recording for the company, whose foremost country artist was then EDDY ARNOLD. In 1950 Sholes began to record frequently in Nashville, using a succession of local studios. Helping him organize sessions was CHET ATKINS, who assisted in cutting discs by HANK SNOW, PEE WEE KING, GRANDPA JONES, and others.

During the mid-1950s Sholes responded to the challenge of rock & roll by signing ELVIS PRESLEY. Presley's success helped Sholes to convince RCA to build a new studio in Nashville during 1957, the first erected there by a major label. By now, Atkins was RCA's man in Music City, and in this studio he cut such successful acts as DON GIBSON, JIM REEVES, and BOBBY BARE. Together with OWEN BRADLEY's studio, the RCA studio was the birthplace of the smooth, country-pop Nashville Sound.

During the seventies and early eighties RCA often featured country-pop acts such as KENNY ROGERS and RONNIE MILSAP, dropping more traditional acts such as PORTER WAGONER and Hank Snow. However, RCA played a major part in the OUTLAW movement of the mid-1970s, a reaction against the label-controlled studios and sometimes formulaic arrangements of the NASHVILLE SOUND era. Jerry Bradley, who took over the Nashville operation from Atkins in 1974, scored country's first platinum album—titled *Wanted! The Outlaws*—by assembling recordings of WILLIE NELSON, WAYLON JENNINGS, JESSI COLTER, and TOMPALL GLASER.

During the 1980s RCA coped with a mid-decade sales crisis by developing established artists such as ALABAMA and by signing new artists such as the JUDDS, VINCE GILL, and CLINT BLACK, most of whom took traditionalist approaches to their music. These acts were supervised by new Nashville chief JOE GALANTE, who had a strong background in marketing and who established a track record that made RCA an attractive purchase by the German Bertelsmann corporation in 1986.

After a long run of market leadership, however, RCA slipped behind other labels in the country market in the early 1990s. Among the strategies the label has pursued in response are signing new talent such as MARTINA MCBRIDE, Kenny Chesney, and LONESTAR; establishing a companion label, BNA, which shares a core marketing group with RCA; and honing marketing expertise with new technology enabling users to monitor airplay of particular records on individual radio stations. —*John Rumble*

Rebel Records

estalished in Mount Rainier, Maryland, 1959

As the premier independent BLUEGRASS label, Rebel Records helped establish the Washington, D.C., bluegrass scene. It remains a haven for many of the music's most important acts. Rebel was founded in 1959 by Charles R. Freeland and two fellow bluegrass enthusiasts in the Mount Rainier, Maryland, suburb of Washington, then a country-music hotbed for rural migrants who had settled there after World War II. Though its initial releases featured local country performers, Rebel soon focused exclusively on bluegrass at a time when the music was shunned by the major labels. Along with the folk revival, Rebel spurred bluegrass's commercial comeback in the 1960s, culminating with the success of the COUNTRY GENTLEMEN's version of "Bringing Mary Home," which rode the country charts for four weeks in 1965. By the 1970s Rebel boasted such successful acts as the Country Gentlemen (1965–79), the SELDOM SCENE (1970–79), and RALPH STANLEY & the Clinch Mountain Boys (1970–present). In 1979 Freeland sold Rebel to Dave Freeman, the founder of the old-time music reissue and mail-order label County Sales. Now based in Roanoke, Virginia, Rebel has been the home label for such traditionalists as LARRY SPARKS, DEL MCCOURY, and Dave Evans, and has featured such enduring mainstream groups as Lost & Found, the Lonesome River Band, IIIrd Tyme Out, and Blue Highway. —*Eddie Dean*

Red Clay Ramblers

In 1972 the Red Clay Ramblers formed in Chapel Hill, North Carolina, to play traditional stringband music, and they quickly developed a distinctive sound derived from the diverse influences of early jazz, gospel, country, bluegrass, Tin Pan Alley pop, Irish music, and more. Banjo player Tommy Thompson, fiddler Bill Hicks, and guitarist-mandolinist Jim Watson were the group's founding members; pianist Mike Craver joined in 1973.

The Ramblers released their first album, a collaboration with fiddler Al McCanless, on Folkways in 1974, and in January 1975 went to New York to appear for seven months in an off-Broadway musical about Jesse James called *Diamond Studs*—a play co-written by playwright and future band member Bland Simpson. During the show's run the Ramblers met multi-instrumentalist Jack Herrick, a member of the cast who became a member of the band and expanded the group's repertoire with trumpet, pennywhistle, and bouzouki.

The Ramblers have recorded, with the Flying Fish and SUGAR HILL labels, thirteen albums, including a recent live collection. Michelle Shocked and avant-garde musician Eugene Chadbourne both enlisted the group for recording projects, and in recent years the group has distinguished itself with work for theater and film, including the score for playwright Sam Shepard's off-Broadway play *A Lie of the Mind*, and the soundtrack to his first directed feature film, *Far North*. In addition, they played music as the pit band for a pre-Broadway run of ROGER MILLER's *Big River*. Thompson, Herrick, and Simpson composed music and lyrics for *The Merry Wives of Windsor, Texas*, and Thompson and Herrick provided a score for *Ear Ring*, based on author Lee Smith's novel *Oral History*. The Ramblers also appeared in the Broadway production of *Fool Moon*, and they

recently collaborated on *Kudzu,* a musical based on Doug Marlette's popular newspaper cartoon strip.

Thompson, the last original member, left the group in 1994. The current lineup includes Herrick (b. Teaneck, New Jersey, September 19, 1947), Buckner (b. Titusville, Florida, November 10, 1952), Simpson (b. Durham, North Carolina, October 16, 1948), Chris Frank (b. Omaha, Nebraska, April 2, 1952), Mark Roberts (b. Wareham, Massachusetts, April 9, 1957), and Ed Butler (b. Baltimore, Maryland, August 24, 1953). —*Jay Orr*

REPRESENTATIVE RECORDINGS

Music from Sam Shepard's A Lie of the Mind (Sugar Hill, 1986); *Rambler* (Sugar Hill, 1992)

Red River Dave

b. San Antonio, Texas, December 15, 1914

A veteran western entertainer whose career spans seven decades, Red River Dave is best known as a prolific composer of topical, patriotic, and sentimental ballads.

A native of San Antonio, David McEnery toured the rodeo circuits as a youth, winning Texas championships at rope twirling and yodeling. With interest in singing cowboys at a peak, McEnery began his broadcasting career in San Antonio and on BORDER RADIO before moving east in the mid-1930s. After performing on stations in Virginia and Florida, he landed a regular slot on WOR–New York, in 1938; the Mutual Radio Network fed his program to its nationwide affiliates. Encouraged by songwriter-publisher BOB MILLER, McEnery began writing and recording topical songs; "Amelia Earhart's Last Flight" became a country-folk standard. In May 1939 he sang on an experimental television broadcast at the New York World's Fair.

Returning to Texas after World War II, McEnery recorded for numerous postwar labels, appeared in several low-budget westerns, and began performing over WOAI–San Antonio. He also cut transcriptions for Mexican border stations. McEnery was a popular San Antonio television personality through the 1950s and 1960s. In 1967 he largely retired from music to concentrate on his real-estate business, although he continued producing self-accompanied topical singles on his own labels. He returned to music in the late 1970s in Nashville; he then moved to California, where he occasionally performed at Knott's Berry Farm near Anaheim. He now resides in his hometown of San Antonio. —*Dave Samuelson*

Blind Alfred Reed

b. Floyd, Virginia, June 15, 1880; d. January 17, 1956

Although he was born in Virginia, Alfred Reed spent most of his life in West Virginia, mainly near the towns of Princeton, Pipestem, and Hinton. Neither of his parents was musically inclined, but he learned to play fiddle, guitar, banjo, and mandolin at an early age. These abilities, combined with his singing and songwriting, enabled him to earn a living for himself; his wife, Nettie; and their six children. He taught music lessons to youngsters, but the greater portion of his earnings came from performing at dances, meetings, and churches and occasionally from playing on street corners and in city parks for handouts. In the U.S. pre–welfare state, music was one of the few means available to blind people to earn an independent income.

Although he performed in an archaic style, Reed's strong baritone voice was so effectively accompanied by his own fiddling that he became popular locally. His repertoire consisted of songs learned from oral tradition, songbooks, and the radio in addition to the numbers he wrote. It was one of his own compositions that led to a two-year recording career.

On May 24, 1927, a passenger and a freight train on the Virginian Railway collided head-on at Ingleside, West Virginia, killing two and injuring twenty-nine. After hearing radio reports of the accident, Reed composed "The Wreck of the Virginian," a song that became well known in his section of the state. Soon RALPH PEER, a touring talent scout for the Victor Talking Machine Company, heard about the song and contacted Reed. On July 28, 1927, a friend drove the blind singer to BRISTOL, TENNESSEE, where he recorded his train wreck ballad and three religious songs, accompanied only by his own guitar and fiddle. All four sides were issued and produced good sales locally; reportedly, his 78s sold as soon as they reached the stores.

Reed's next session took place in Camden, New Jersey, on December 19, 1927. He was accompanied by his guitar-playing son, Arville, and fiddler Fred Pendleton. Six songs were recorded, including "Always Lift Him Up and Never Knock Him Down," his home community's favorite Reed song; and a critique of the popular flapper hairstyles "Why Do You Bob Your Hair, Girls?" Nearly two years later, on December 3–4, 1929, Reed and Arville made their last recording session, in New York City. Twelve songs were waxed and ten were released, including "Beware," Reed's version of a German folksong first published in the 1860s, and the second recording of "Why Do You Bob Your Hair, Girls?"

Although the Great Depression ended Reed's recording career, he continued to play music for several years thereafter in the Princeton area, by himself, with Arville and Pendleton, and with another locally known blind musician, Richard Harold (who himself cut four sides in 1928 for the COLUMBIA label). By the late 1930s Reed was infrequently playing in public, primarily because of local laws restricting street musicians, but he continued to compose songs, writing them in Braille.   —*W. K. McNeil*

REPRESENTATIVE RECORDING

How Can a Poor Man Stand Such Times and Live?: The Songs of Blind Alfred Reed (Rounder, 1972)

Jerry Reed
b. Atlanta, Georgia, March 20, 1937

Jerry Reed Hubbard brought something highly individual and hot to country music beginning with his 1966 hit "Guitar Man": an infectious sound marked by syncopated, complex fingerstyle guitar and plenty of Deep South attitude. "If you wasn't wearing that black robe, I'd take you out back of this courthouse and I'd try a little bit of Your Honor on! You understand that, you hillbilly?" That's Reed blustering away at a city judge during the fade of his 1971 Grammy winner "When You're Hot, You're Hot." However, Reed's electric mix of picking and grinning grew hot only after years of musical dedication and business dues-paying. The resulting career has brought Reed notable success as a guitarist, recording artist, songwriter, and movie star. He influenced singer-guitarists such as STEVE WARINER and prominent studio guitar players such as

Jerry Reed

BRENT MASON. Reed even influenced CHET ATKINS, who did several Reed tunes on his own albums.

Beginning guitar at age nine, Reed was appearing on shows with the likes of FARON YOUNG and ERNEST TUBB by his early teens. At age seventeen Reed caught the attention of CAPITOL RECORDS executive-producer KEN NELSON during an Atlanta show; the result was a record deal and ten single releases, but little success. After Atlanta music publisher BILL LOWERY encouraged Reed to write songs, he scored tunes recorded by Gene Vincent and by BRENDA LEE ("That's All You Gotta Do," a #6 pop hit). A move to CO-LUMBIA produced the minor 1962 pop hits "Goodnight Irene" and "Hully Gully Guitar."

After serving in the military, Reed took the logical next step, moving to Nashville in 1962 with his wife, Priscilla, (who scored her own #1 record as ROY DRUSKY's duet partner on 1965's "Yes, Mr. Peters"). Reed started playing sessions, appearing on hits by BOBBY BARE and others, and penning hits such as PORTER WAGONER's 1962 #1 "Misery Loves Company." A move to RCA in 1964 brought Reed together with his idol, producer-picker-executive Chet Atkins, who had encouraged a teenage Reed's picking back in Georgia.

Attempts to cast Reed in a standard country mold failed, and by 1966 Atkins was telling Reed simply to be himself on record, to let fly with his funky, down-home wit and hard-earned guitar mastery. "I finally just started writin' exactly what I feel like writin' and not necessarily questionin' it—and that's what comes out," Reed told journalist Jack Hurst. ELVIS PRESLEY recorded Reed's "Guitar Man" and "U.S. Male" with Reed on guitar, as well as tunes from Reed's more reflective side as a writer. Artists from JOHNNY CASH to Engelbert Humperdinck also have recorded Reed's songs.

After "Guitar Man" set the tone, raucous tunes such as "Tupelo Mississippi Flash" (1967), "Alabama Wild Man" (1968), and "Are You From Dixie" (1969) led to two landmark Reed hits: the swampily rhythmic "Amos Moses," a 1970 country hit and pop #8 song, and "When You're Hot, You're Hot," a country #1 for five weeks in 1971. Reed's picking was also setting the woods on fire: He and Atkins earned a 1970 country instrumental Grammy for their duet LP *Me and Jerry.*

Meanwhile, Reed's regular appearances on CBS's *Glen Campbell Goodtime Hour* caught the eye of America and the film industry; hence Reed's wisecracking country boy role in the 1974 Burt Reynolds vehicle *W. W. and the Dixie Dance Kings.* Mostly playing his own wilder side, Reed appeared in *Gator* (1976), *Concrete Cowboys* (a 1977 TV movie that also produced a short-lived 1981 CBS series starring Reed), *Smokey and the Bandit* (1977), *High-Ballin'* (1978), *Hot Stuff* (1979), *Smokey and the Bandit II* (1980), *Smokey and the Bandit III* (1983), and *Survivors* (1983).

As Reed's film career prospered, his records lost steam. After 1973's "Lord, Mr. Ford," he posted only two Top Ten hits—1977's *Smokey* theme, "East Bound and Down," and 1978's tender "I Love You (What Can I Say)—until his pair of 1982 novelty hits, "She Got the Goldmine (I Got the Shaft)" and "The Bird." Reed and WAYLON JENNINGS teamed up for a 1983 hit remake of the Sam and Dave oldie "Hold On, I'm Comin'," but by 1984 Reed was off RCA.

In 1985 Reed produced, directed, and starred in the music-business action flick *What Comes Around,* with dismal box-office results. In 1988 he co-produced, starred in, and wrote songs for the Vietnam action movie *BAT 21,* with Gene Hackman. *Nashville 99,* Reed's TNN police action series, was short-lived.

Reed has kept a low profile in recent years, although he continues to tour and make occasional television appearances. He reunited with Atkins in 1992 for the duo disc *Sneakin' Around* and remains one of popular music's most distinctive and admired guitarists. Reed's "The Claw" has become a standard many players seek to master and has recently been recorded by Dave Edmonds and by the Helecasters. Reed's playing combines complex independent lines in the guitar's bass and treble and also uses rippling combinations of fretted and open strings. "His playing has the complexity of classical music," says scholar-musician John Knowles, "but the rhythmic sense that comes from country, rock, and gospel." —*Thomas Goldsmith*

REPRESENTATIVE RECORDINGS

Me and Jerry (RCA, 1971); *When You're Hot, You're Hot* (RCA, 1971); *The Essential Jerry Reed* (RCA, 1995)

Ola Belle Reed
b. Lansing, North Carolina, August 17, 1916

Ola Belle Reed was one of thirteen children of Arthur Campbell, a schoolteacher who took up music and formed his own band in 1910. She developed an appreciation for old-time country music and learned to play the guitar at an early age. In the early 1930s she taught her brother Alex to play the instrument, and in 1946 the two would join forces to form a band called the New River Boys, named after the river that flowed by their childhood home. Prior to that, though, Alex served in World War II, participating in the Normandy invasion and serving in the same unit with GRANDPA JONES. The group Grandpa Jones & His Munich Mountaineers, of which Alex was a member, was broadcast for eight months after the German surrender.

Upon his return home, Alex and Ola Belle formed their own band, which featured a traditional stringband sound. Initially they broadcasted over WASA in Havre de Grace, Maryland, but soon they moved to Pennsylvania where they developed a strong following over WCOJ in Coatesville, Pennsylvania. They also worked on WBMO in Baltimore, Maryland, and made transcribed (or recorded) radio shows that were aired over several radio stations throughout the United States. Their wide-ranging repertoire included some of the more than 200 original songs that Alex and Ola Belle wrote during their lives.

In 1951 Alex, Ola Belle, and Ola Belle's husband, Bud Reed, established one of the nation's most active country music parks—the New River Ranch near Rising Sun, Maryland. Nine years later, in 1960, they moved to Sunset Park in West Grove, Pennsylvania, where they remained for twenty-six years and broadcasted a regular Sunday radio show from the park. For a brief period in the early 1960s they were featured on station WWVA in Wheeling, West Virginia. They also ran a very successful record store specializing in mail-order sales of country and gospel records. At the same time, Alex worked as an independent DJ operating out of Campbell's Corner Store. Ola Belle also gained the attention of booking agents handling performers on the folk festival circuit, and she appeared at such events as the Smithsonian Folk Festival.
—*W. K. McNeil*

REPRESENTATIVE RECORDINGS

Travel On (Starday, 1965); *Ola Belle Reed* (Rounder, 1973)

Del Reeves
b. Sparta, North Carolina, July 14, 1933

Franklin Delano Reeves made his biggest impact recording uptempo trucker tunes such as "The Girl on the Billboard" (#1, 1965), "Belles of Southern Bell" (#4, 1965), and "Looking at the World Through a Windshield" (#5, 1968), but he is equally well known to GRAND OLE OPRY fans for his humorous impressions of other country singers as he is for his songs.

The youngest of eleven children, he sang on local radio at twelve. After attending Appalachian State College (Boone, North Carolina), he served four years in the air force. While stationed in California, he did TV and made his first recordings for CAPITOL RECORDS in 1957–58. Reeves and wife, Ellen Schiell, co-authored "Sing a Little Song of Heartache," a #3 hit for Capitol artist ROSE MADDOX in 1962.

Reeves recorded for DECCA in 1961–62 and moved to Nashville in 1962 at the urging of songwriter HANK COCHRAN. After short stints with Reprise (1963) and COLUMBIA (1964), Reeves began a fourteen-year association with United Artists Records in 1965 that led to his biggest hits. In 1966 Reeves joined the Grand Ole Opry. He has appeared in eight movies, notably *Sam Whiskey* (1969), and hosted *Del Reeves Country Carnival* TV series (1970–73), enhanced by his impersonations. After leaving United Artists in 1978, he moved on to the Koala and Playback labels. In 1989 Del and Ellen Reeves agreed to promote BILLY RAY CYRUS. Following Cyrus's success with "Achy Breaky Heart" in 1992, Del and Ellen Reeves sued for reimbursement on their investment. Cyrus's camp settled out of court for an undisclosed sum. —*Walt Trott*

REPRESENTATIVE RECORDINGS

Del Reeves—Baby I Love You (Bear Family, 1988); *The Silver Anniversary Album* (Playback, 1990)

Goebel Reeves

b. Sherman, Texas, October 9, 1899; d. January 26, 1959

Goebel Leon Reeves, known as the Texas Drifter, was a genuine hobo who sang hobo and cowboy songs embellished by a distinctive yodel that included a trill, and accompanied himself on the guitar. Among the songs he recorded were "Hobo's Lullaby," "Railroad Boomer," and "The Hobo and the Cop."

One of six siblings, he was born in the Red River valley region of North Texas. When his father was elected to the state legislature, the family moved to Austin, Texas, where Goebel became a legislative page, learned the guitar and trumpet, and first encountered hobos and their songs. He served in World War I, was wounded and discharged, and shortly afterward adopted an itinerant lifestyle.

In the early 1920s Reeves teamed with JIMMIE RODGERS and guitarist Lucien "Piggy" Parks to tour the eastern United States. He also appeared on WFAA in Dallas. He then shipped out to Europe as a merchant seaman. Upon returning in the late 1920s, he found that Rodgers had successfully recorded and determined to do the same. Reeves first recordings were made for OKEH on June 25, 1929, followed by sessions for GENNETT, BRUNSWICK, and other labels, sometimes under pseudonyms. Whenever he needed cash he would appear at a local radio station and convince the manager to put him on the air. He was heard singing in a restaurant by Graham McNamee, who signed him for the *Rudy Vallee Show* on the NBC radio network, but Reeves could not abide urban audiences, who found his songs comical. He later appeared on the GRAND OLE OPRY and *NATIONAL BARN DANCE*. By the advent of World War II, Reeves had retired from active entertaining. He died from a heart condition at the Long Beach (California) Veterans Hospital.   —*Fred Hoeptner*

Jim Reeves

b. Panola County, Texas, August 20, 1923; d. July 31, 1964

Jim Reeves stands as one of the most distinctive singers in the history of country music. His smooth, warm baritone was a major component of the sophisticated, pop-influenced NASHVILLE SOUND that emerged during the late 1950s and early 1960s and that boosted country music to new commercial heights while strengthening Nashville's role as a music center.

James Travis Reeves was the youngest of nine children, and his older brothers were forced to leave school to help support the family after their father died, when Jim was still a baby. Even as a boy, he became fascinated by music; by the time he was twelve he was singing and playing guitar at local dances and playing with a band on Shreveport, Louisiana, radio station KRMD.

After high school in Carthage, Reeves won a baseball scholarship to the University of Texas at Austin, quit to volunteer for military service in World War II, and became a welder after failing his physical. He continued to play baseball in minor leagues in several states while working as a salesman between seasons. By 1947, however, a leg injury ended his baseball career, so he landed announcer's jobs on several East Texas radio stations, slots that allowed him to advertise personal appearances in the area.

In about 1949 Reeves first recorded for the Macy's label in Houston, but his recording career began in earnest when he signed with ABBOTT RECORDS in 1952. Early suc-

Jim Reeves

cess with "Mexican Joe" helped him move up to the 50,000-watt KWKH in Shreveport, where he worked as announcer and performer on the *LOUISIANA HAYRIDE*. From there he graduated to the GRAND OLE OPRY, joining in October 1955 on the strength of early hits on RCA, for whom he began recording the previous May.

At first Reeves generally took a hard country approach to his recordings, but "Four Walls," a #1 country and #11 pop hit, marked his transition to pop-tinged love ballads sung in an intimate, low register, close to the microphone. In doing so, he continued a pattern set by EDDY ARNOLD and RED FOLEY and helped make crossover success a trend for country singers of the day. Between 1957 and 1958 Reeves fronted his own pop radio show, fed from WSM to the ABC network. At about this time Reeves began to reshape his image as well, shifting from cowboy outfits to sport coats and slacks and even tuxedos on occasion.

A demanding perfectionist in the studio, Reeves worked closely with RCA producer CHET ATKINS in choosing material, and their efforts paid off. Hits such as "Blue Boy," "Billy Bayou," "Home," and "Am I Losing You" solidified his stardom while demonstrating his versatility. In 1959–60 he scored his biggest hit, "He'll Have to Go," which topped the country charts and went to #2 pop in the bargain. As the CMA began to push country-pop sounds in converting radio stations to country formats, Reeves became a natural with stations that followed the new Nashville Sound trend. Soon he became an international star to boot, making a 1962 tour to South Africa as well as later trips to England, Ireland, and Europe. Even if fans couldn't understand the lyrics, one journalist wrote, "the resonant purr from the honeyed larynx of Jim Reeves has an almost hypnotic effect."

Although Reeves was killed in a plane crash in 1964, his recordings have continued to sell long after his death. Posthumous hits helped him win election to the COUNTRY

MUSIC HALL OF FAME in 1967, and he charted regularly into the early 1970s.   —*John Rumble*

REPRESENTATIVE RECORDINGS

Live at the Opry (CMF, 1986); *Welcome to My World: The Essential Jim Reeves Collection* (RCA, 1993); *The Essential Jim Reeves* (RCA, 1995)

Mike Reid

b. Aliquippa, Pennsylvania, May 24, 1947

After first achieving stardom as a professional football player, Mike Reid went on to a second career, as a Nashville-based singer and composer, most noted for a string of hits he wrote for RONNIE MILSAP.

Born into a working-class family, Reid gained notoriety as a gridiron star at Penn State. In the 1970s he was an all-pro lineman for the Cincinnati Bengals. He also performed as a classical pianist. He quit football in 1975 and went on the road as a keyboardist-singer.

Reid landed a staff songwriting job with ATV publishing in 1980 and moved to Nashville, where he later signed with Milsap's publishing company. Milsap had eleven hits with Reid tunes, including "Inside," "In Love," "Prisoner of the Highway," and "Lost in the Fifties Tonight (in the Still of the Night)." Reid won a 1983 songwriting Grammy Award for Milsap's "Stranger in My House."

Reid also became a hit source for others, notably the JUDDS ("Born to Be Blue"), LORRIE MORGAN ("He Talks to Me"), BARBARA MANDRELL & LEE GREENWOOD ("To Me"), WILLIE NELSON ("There You Are"), DON WILLIAMS ("One Good Well"), CONWAY TWITTY ("Fallin' for You for Years"), and ALABAMA ("Forever's as Far as I'll Go"). He was AS-CAP's Country Songwriter of the Year in 1985.

Milsap introduced Reid to radio as a singer with the 1988 Top Ten duet "Old Folks." The tunesmith's gospel-tinged baritone attracted admirers at Nashville club showcases, and he was signed by COLUMBIA.

Reid hit the Top Ten with his first solo release, 1990's #1 "Walk on Faith." He was consistently in the Top Twenty with 1991's "Till You Were Gone," "As Simple as That," and "I'll Stop Loving You." But Reid was in his early forties and a soul singer at a time when country turned toward young honky-tonkers. Subsequent singles fared less well.

Reid's renown as a composer continued, nevertheless, especially as Bonnie Raitt had a Top Twenty pop hit with his "I Can't Make You Love Me." He also branched out as the composer of the theater works *A House Divided* (1991), *Tales of Appalachia* (1996), and *Different Fields* (1996). He returned to singing on saxophonist Kirk Whalum's 1995 jazz CD *In This Life*.   —*Robert K. Oermann*

REPRESENTATIVE RECORDINGS

Turning for Home (Columbia, 1991); *Twilight Time* (Columbia, 1992)

Dick Reinhart

b. Tishomingo, Oklahoma, February 17, 1907; d. December 3, 1948

Richard "Dick" Reinhart ranks among the best western swing vocalists. Displaying the versatility typically associated with the genre, Reinhart was an especially fine blues singer, having learned directly from black bluesmen in Dallas's Deep Ellum district. He was also a gifted songwriter ("Fort Worth Jail," "A Broken Heart for a Souvenir") and instrumentalist, playing guitar, mandolin, banjo, and bass.

He was living in Dallas by the late twenties, and 1929 recordings sessions reveal he was already a formidable vocalist. His western ballads for BRUNSWICK hinted at the black influences that were explicit in his falsetto jazz vocal on the Three Virginians' "June Tenth Blues" for OKEH. By 1931 Reinhart had formed the Wanderers with ROY NEWMAN and Bert Dodson, recording for BLUEBIRD in 1935 before joining the LIGHT CRUST DOUGHBOYS late that year, sharing vocal duties with Dodson until the latter's departure. Classic Reinhart performances with the Doughboys included "Ding Dong Daddy" (1936) and "Sittin' on Top of the World" (1938). He departed in 1938 to join the Universal Cowboys, completing a session for Vocalion in 1939 before obtaining his own contract in 1940. He moved to Oklahoma for the first of several stints with JIMMY WAKELY, then headed to the West Coast, where he also worked with GENE AUTRY. Reinhart became more of a crooner as time passed but retained a bluesy tinge until his death, evinced in "Muddy Water" from his final session (COLUMBIA, 1947). Back in Fort Worth, his career on hold, he suffered a fatal heart attack at forty-one.   —*Kevin Coffey*

REPRESENTATIVE RECORDING

Night Spot Blues (Krazy Kat, 1998)

The Reinsmen

For thirty-five years this act has been one of America's most enduring, appealing western singing groups. In 1992 the trio of Dick Goodman (vocal, guitar, bass), Don Richardson (vocal, guitar, bass, banjo), and Jerry Compton (vocal, guitar, steel guitar) passed a milestone as a continuous vocal trio for thirty-one years. Unquestionably, for more than three decades, it was the magnetism of the music written by western music legends—Bob Nolan, Tim Spencer, Stan Jones, MARTY ROBBINS, and others—that inspired the Reinsmen to portray the romance of the West in song.

Goodman and Richardson were products of the Wagonmasters, a very popular musical group at Knotts Berry Farm in Buena Park, California, for a number of years. In 1962 Jerry Compton joined Goodman and Richardson to form the Reinsmen. Bob Wagoner (vocal, guitar), noted for his artistic paintings of the West; Max "Doc" Denning (vocal, fiddle, guitar), one of western music's finest performers; fiddler Harvey Walker; and guitarist/vocalist Johnny Blankenship joined the group at various times.

The Reinsmen have appeared in, and furnished musical background for, motion pictures, made countless appearances with western movie and singing star REX ALLEN, performed at the White House, recorded several albums, and in 1997 made their twenty-eighth consecutive appearance at the very popular Death Valley Encampment in Death Valley, California, which attracts thousands of fans each year.   —*Ken Griffis*

Herb Remington

b. Mishawaka, Indiana, June 9, 1926

One of the kingpins of postwar western swing steel guitar, Herbert Leroy Remington is best known for his four-year stint with BOB WILLS & His Texas Playboys from 1946 to 1950. One of the first important swing steel players not to come from the Southwest, his stylistic origins were in Hawaiian music, a debt still audible in his playing and a musical style that kept him eating in western swing's lean years.

Remington knew little country music when he joined RAY WHITLEY's western swing band in California upon discharge from the service in 1946, but by that summer he had successfully auditioned for Wills. Despite his lack of experience he sounded remarkably assured and mature when he recorded with Wills in September of that year. With the Playboys he produced classic solos on sides such as "Fat Boy Rag" (1946) and his signature tune, "Boot Heel Drag" (1949), and created sophisticated string ensembles with guitarist ELDON SHAMBLIN and mandolinist Tiny Moore. Leaving Wills, Remington worked briefly with HANK PENNY, recording his classic "Remington Ride" in 1950. Remington soon settled in Houston, joining DICKIE AND LAURA LEE McBRIDE's Ranch Hands. Remington became a busy session player, recording countless sessions with artists such as FLOYD TILLMAN, and later toured the country with his own Beachcombers. Today he designs his own steels; co-leads Playboys II, a Wills-revival group, with JOHNNY GIMBLE; and appears with Clyde Brewer's Original River Road Boys.

—*Kevin Coffey*

REPRESENTATIVE RECORDINGS

Herb Remington: Jean Street Swing (Steel Guitar Club of America, 1975), 1946–58 recordings; *Steeling Memories* (Glad Music Co., 1995)

George Reneau
b. Jefferson County, Tennessee, 1901; d. December 1933

Known as the Blind Musician of the Smoky Mountains, George Reneau was one of the few traditional musicians to make the transition from wandering street minstrel to recording artist. He was one of the earliest recording artists, making his first sides in April 1924 and his last in 1927. For a short time in the music's early history, Reneau's records were very popular, rivaling those of FID-DLIN' JOHN CARSON, HENRY WHITTER, and Charlie Oaks in popularity.

Though he was born in the foothills of the Smokies, and apparently blind from birth, Reneau moved to Knoxville as a teenager and learned to play guitar from a niece named Sally. By the start of the 1920s he had become a popular fixture at the train station and on the street corners of Knoxville, where he did "busking" for small change. Gus Nennsteil, a local furniture dealer and talent scout for Vocalion records, heard him and arranged for him to travel to New York to record.

At first Vocalion was interested more in Reneau's guitar and harp playing than his singing: at first Vocalion didn't let Reneau sing on his own records, but had him back young studio singer Gene Austin (who would in a few years became a national star with his recording of "My Blue Heaven"). Reneau's early hit records, which included "Blue Ridge Blues," "Susie Ann," and "Lonesome Road Blues," featured Austin's singing. By February 1925 Reneau began singing on his own records, enjoying success with his version of "The Prisoner's Song," "Woman's Suffrage," and "Wild Bill Jones." In 1927 Reneau teamed with Lester McFarland for a series of duets that were issued under the names the Collins Brothers, the Cramer Brothers, the Lonesome Pine Twins, and half a dozen other aliases. These sides continued to be released on numerous labels over the next five years, including Banner, CHALLENGE, CONQUEROR, Oriole, and Paramount.

During the Depression, Reneau was forced to once again become a street corner singer, and in December 1933 he caught pneumonia and died from it. He was only thirty-two, and his records were his only legacy.

—*Charles Wolfe*

Renfro Valley Barn Dance
established in Cincinnati, Ohio, October 9, 1937

The *Renfro Valley Barn Dance* was heard Saturday nights, mainly in the Midwest and South, for a twenty-year period

Renfro Valley Barn Dance *cast*

beginning October 9, 1937. Created by Kentuckian JOHN LAIR (1894–1985), it was carried at times on the NBC Blue, CBS, and Mutual Networks. Mainly, however, the show's wide audience resulted from access provided by the far, nighttime reach of Cincinnati's WLW and, after 1941, Louisville's WHAS.

On November 4, 1939, after stints first in the Cincinnati Music Hall and later in Dayton's Memorial Auditorium, the show moved to a real barn in Lair's native Renfro Valley, fifty miles south of Lexington, Kentucky. The barn was the centerpiece of a simulated turn-of-the-century village Lair eventually assembled with old and newly built structures. He told listeners they could come to Renfro Valley for a "glimpse of something of the pioneer days in Kentucky not cataloged in musty museums" and have "clean fun on Saturday night we won't be ashamed of on Sunday." The founding partners for the venture were Lair, singer RED FOLEY, and comedian Whitey Ford (the DUKE OF PADUCAH).

Seeking distinctiveness for his program, Lair recruited most of the cast from Kentucky and points south and styled the performers and their music "home folks" rather than "hillbilly." With these "makers of music and distributors of mirth" who also included a few tabloid and minstrel show veterans, Lair crafted a format that initially aired more comedy than WSM's GRAND OLE OPRY and music more rural in flavor than that of WLS's NATIONAL BARN DANCE. Comedy, both musical and spoken, was meted out by the likes of HOMER & JETHRO, fiddler Slim Miller, the Duke of Paducah, Margaret Lillie (Ain't Idy), and Gene "Honey Gal" Cobb.

Over the years, many singers and instrumentalists important to country music appeared on the show. Lair gave equal time to traditional performers such as Lily May Ledford's COON CREEK GIRLS and then-current artists such as Red Foley, the Range Riders, and the Holden Brothers. Gospel music became a regular feature after 1939, with the Crusaders and, later, other quartets. At that time, Lair also began distancing the program from the cowboy-western image, no longer allowing western attire onstage and renaming the Range Riders the Mountain Rangers.

The *Renfro Valley Barn Dance* left the air in 1957 because its sponsors opted for television advertising. However, it continued as an important stage attraction. Beginning in 1989, Lair's successor, Renfro Valley Entertainment, Inc., headed by Warren Rosenthal, rebuilt and expanded the original facility. Several weekly performances and special events, March through December, continue to draw visitors from near and far.   —*Harry S. Rice*

Reno & Smiley

Donald Wesley Reno b. Spartanburg, South Carolina, February 21, 1927; d. October 16, 1984

Arthur Lee "Red" Smiley b. Marshall, North Carolina, May 17, 1925; d. January 2, 1972

The team of Don Reno and Red Smiley was one of the most innovative acts in the early days of bluegrass music. The core of their sound was a bluesy duet that featured rich baritone lead vocals of guitarist Red Smiley paired with the soaring tenor vocals of banjoist Don Reno. Their duet was augmented by Reno's jazzy banjo work.

They first met in 1950 when they both worked in a band called TOMMY MAGNESS & His Tennessee Buddies. While with Magness, they made their first recordings for the

Reno & Smiley: Don Reno (left) and Red Smiley

Cincinnati-based Federal label, a subsidiary of KING RECORDS. Label owner SYD NATHAN was impressed with the talents of Don and Red and soon arranged a recording session for them in their own name. In January 1952 a marathon sixteen-song session was held that launched the classic Reno & Smiley sound. Amazingly, Don Reno composed all of the material recorded. The session produced the first of many hits for the duo, including the now-legendary "I'm Using My Bible for a Road Map," a song that reportedly saved King Records from bankruptcy.

Reno & Smiley were scoring well with radio and record hits but were unable to keep a touring band together. Don Reno soon found himself working in Charlotte, North Carolina, with ARTHUR "GUITAR BOOGIE" SMITH & His Crackerjacks. While working with Smith, Reno helped write and record "Feuding Banjos," the oft-imitated instrumental that was later retitled and was the hit of the 1972 movie *Deliverance.*

Although not working the road as a team, Reno & Smiley continued to record and release material for King. Response to the recordings mounted, and in May 1955 Reno & Smiley organized the classic edition of their Tennessee Cut-Ups, which included fiddler Mack Magaha and bass player John Palmer. They were soon appearing on the OLD DOMINION BARN DANCE on WRVA in Richmond, Virginia. The powerful AM station beamed their sound up and down the East Coast. In 1957 the group settled in Roanoke, Virginia, and secured a daily television program called *Top of the Morning.*

The glory years of Reno & Smiley spanned from 1955 to 1964. During this time they recorded prolifically for King Records. Their hits during this time included "I Know You're Married," "Love, Please Come Home," "Don't Let Your Sweet Love Die," and "Please Remember That I Love You." In the fall of 1964 Reno & Smiley terminated their long-standing partnership. Smiley remained in Roanoke with the *Top of the Morning* show, and Reno moved to Nashville. In the late 1960s, a series of Reno & Smiley reunions led to Smiley's joining Don Reno and his new partner, BILL HARRELL. Several memorable recordings followed. Intact was the classic sound of the old Reno & Smiley duets. The duo met its final demise in January 1972 with the death of Red Smiley, a diabetic who lived most of his life with one lung (the result of a war injury). Don Reno died in October 1984 of complications from a circulatory problem.   —*Gary B. Reid*

REPRESENTATIVE RECORDINGS

Songs from Yesterday (Rebel Records, 1988); *1951–1959* (Highland Music, 1993)

The Reno Brothers
Ronnie Reno b. Buffalo, South Carolina, September 28, 1947
Don Wayne Reno b. Roanoke, Virginia, February 8, 1963
Dale Reno b. Roanoke, Virginia, February 6, 1961

Although the Reno Brothers are heirs to the rich musical legacy established by their father, Don Reno, Ronnie (guitar and lead vocals), Don Wayne (banjo), and Dale (mandolin) are a respected bluegrass ensemble in their own right. As boys, they apprenticed in bands with their father. Ronnie was a member of the RENO & SMILEY band and later worked with the OSBORNE BROTHERS as well as MERLE HAGGARD. Don Wayne and Dale both played in Don Reno's Tennessee Cut-Ups.

The formation of the Reno Brothers occurred in 1984, after the death of their father. For several years they bridged the gap between bluegrass and country by using drums and electric pickups on their instruments. Their show today is structured around conventional bluegrass stylings.

In the early 1990s they benefited from national exposure on *Reno's Old-time Music Festival*, their own show that appeared on the Americana Network. The program was nominated for an Ace Award as part of a series of awards honoring excellence in cable TV broadcasting.

The Renos' most recent recordings appear on the Webco/Pinecastle label. Their recordings regularly appear on the *National Bluegrass Survey*, a monthly chart that ranks the thirty most popular songs in bluegrass. —*Gary B. Reid*

REPRESENTATIVE RECORDINGS

Kentucky Gold (Webco, 1993); *Swing West* (Webco/Pinecastle, 1995)

Republic Records (*see* Gene Autry and Tennessee Records)

Restless Heart
John Dittrich b. Batavia, New York, April 7, 1951
Paul Gregg b. Altus, Oklahoma, December 3, 1954
Dave Innis b. Bartlesville, Oklahoma, April 9, 1959
Greg Jennings b. Nicoma Park, Oklahoma, October 2, 1954
Larry Stewart b. Paducah, Kentucky, March 2, 1959

For eight years prior to the 1993 release of the various artists tribute album *Common Thread: The Songs of the EAGLES*, Restless Heart had already helped to establish the connection between mainstream country and that 1970s supergroup with a light country-rock approach that leaned heavily on a silky-smooth harmonic blend.

Consisting of former session musicians, Restless Heart

formed in 1983 as a means for producer-songwriter TIM DUBOIS and some of his friends to make demo recordings of songs that fell in the cracks between country and pop. Each of the players was already respected within the Nashville music community. Keyboard player Dave Innis, for example, had written the Pointer Sisters hit "Dare Me," while guitarist Greg Jennings had played on several DAN SEALS hits.

The band jelled well enough that they garnered an RCA recording contract. Just before they started making their first album, original lead singer Verlon Thompson left, to be replaced by Larry Stewart. The group met with almost instantaneous success with the 1985 release of their eponymous debut album. Their second single, "I Want Everyone to Cry," began a string of thirteen straight Top Ten hits through 1990, punctuated by six #1 records, including "Why Does It Have to Be (Wrong or Right)," "Wheels," and "Bluest Eyes in Texas." "I'll Still Be Loving You" became a wedding classic and crossed over to the pop Top Forty.

Perhaps in tribute to Restless Heart's success, other country-rock groups with strong harmonies emerged in country music during the latter half of the 1980s, including the DESERT ROSE BAND and SOUTHERN PACIFIC.

In 1992 vocalist Stewart departed for a solo career. Eager to prove they still had something left, the four-man Restless Heart came up with "When She Cries," a massive crossover hit, featuring drummer John Dittrich on lead vocals. But at around the same time, Innis was dismissed.

Operating as a trio, the group put out one more album in 1994, *Matters of the Heart*, which was largely ignored. The threesome took a year off to assess the situation. The original lineup, minus Innis, re-formed in late 1997 and again signed with RCA.   —*Tom Roland*

REPRESENTATIVE RECORDINGS

Restless Heart (RCA, 1985); *The Best of Restless Heart* (RCA, 1991)

Reunion of Professional Entertainers (*see* ROPE)

Jimmie Revard
b. Pawhuska, Oklahoma, November 26, 1909; d. April 12, 1991

Leader of one of the most popular prewar western swing bands, the Oklahoma Playboys, James Osage Revard vied with Buster Coward's TUNE WRANGLERS for supremacy on the competitive 1930s San Antonio scene. One of BLUEBIRD's top country acts during the years 1936–38, Revard scored hits with "Holding the Sack" (1936) and "Tulsa Waltz" (1937).

Descended from a long line of fiddlers, Oklahoma native Revard began violin lessons at twelve but eventually played mostly bass and guitar with his own bands. Formed in about 1935, the Oklahoma Playboys originally included ADOLPH & EMIL HOFNER, on guitar and steel, soon joined by fiddler Ben McKay and two defectors from the Tune Wranglers, guitarist CURLEY WILLIAMS and jazz pianist Eddie Whitley. Revard secured a Bluebird contract in 1936, and his first sessions were dominated by Whitley's piano and bluesy vocals. Whitley left soon after, eventually replaced by another Tune Wrangler, pianist George Timberlake, while vocals chores were divided among Revard, Williams, and Adolph Hofner.

Revard was on 50,000-watt WOAI from 1937 to 1939, with an ill-fated stay in the Midwest during the winter of

1937–38. By 1938 Revard had replaced McKay with the excellent fiddler-vocalist Leon Seago, and Revard began to feature himself on clarinet and added drummer Edmond Franke, solidifying the Oklahoma Playboys as one of the most sophisticated country dance bands of the era. Tiring of the grind, however, Revard disbanded in 1939 (though he recorded again in 1940) and became a San Antonio policeman. After the war, he led bands on a part-time basis, recording for the Everstate label in 1950. In the 1980s, encouraged by new interest in his music, he recorded again. A proposed album remains unissued, though a single was issued on Sarg Records in 1982.   —*Kevin Coffey*

REPRESENTATIVE RECORDING

Jimmie Revard & His Oklahoma Playboys: Oh! Swing It (Rambler, 1982)

Allen Reynolds
b. North Little Rock, Arkansas, August 18, 1938

Although Allen Reynolds has made significant contributions to the careers of DON WILLIAMS, KATHY MATTEA, and CRYSTAL GAYLE, he is likely best known for having produced GARTH BROOKS's albums, which have sold more than 60 million copies. As a producer, Reynolds is highly respected for valuing artistic success as much as commercial potential.

In addition to producing, Reynolds is a successful songwriter, penning such hits as "We Should Be Together"; "Ready for the Times to Get Better"; and "Five O'Clock World," which was a hit for the pop group the Vogues in the 1960s and for HAL KETCHUM in the 1990s. WAYLON JENNINGS, JOHNNY RUSSELL, Don Williams, COLLIN RAYE, and the Cowboy Junkies all have recorded Reynolds's works.

Allen Reynolds

Reynolds began writing songs while earning an English degree at Rhodes College in Memphis. He began writing with collegemate DICKEY LEE, and the two became friends with SUN RECORDS's engineer-producer JACK CLEMENT. Reynolds and Lee moved to Beaumont, Texas, where Clement had opened Gulf Coast Recording Studios, and the two wrote "I Saw Linda Yesterday," which became a Top Fifteen hit for Lee.

The duo moved back to Memphis in 1964 and signed with Screen Gems Publishing Company in Nashville. Then they started their own Memphis production and publishing company, along with producer Stan Kesler, and developed a staff that included writers BOB MCDILL and PAUL CRAFT.

In 1970 Reynolds moved to Nashville and was hired by Clement to produce and manage JMI Records. Reynolds produced two albums for Don Williams before Clement closed the label in 1975. Reynolds became an independent producer and purchased Jack's Tracks Recording Studio. One of the first acts he worked with in the studio was Crystal Gayle. She earned her first Top Ten with the Reynolds-penned "Wrong Road Again," and he produced nineteen more Top Ten hits with her in the next eight years. He produced ten albums for Gayle, including five gold and two platinum successes.

In 1986 Kathy Mattea had made little headway in country music when she teamed up with Reynolds. He overhauled her sound, taking her from overproduced pop-country to more of an acoustic country sound. "Love at the Five and Dime," Mattea's first single with Reynolds as producer, hit the Top Ten.

Reynolds has also produced or co-produced EMMYLOU HARRIS, Hal Ketchum, the CACTUS BROTHERS, the O'KANES, and JOHNNY RODRIGUEZ, among others.

Reynolds made country music history producing nine Garth Brooks albums—including *No Fences, Ropin' the Wind*, and *The Chase*—which together have sold more copies than those of any other act in country history. As a publisher Reynolds's Forerunner Music also contributed "The Thunder Rolls," "Unanswered Prayers," and "That Summer."   —*Beverly Keel*

Michael Rhodes
b. West Monroe, Louisiana, September 16, 1953

A successful studio and touring bassist, Michael Wayne Rhodes's typically huge sound, funky and melodic lines, and strong rhythmic sense have made him one of Nashville's most called-for musicians in recent years. He started playing professionally in Louisiana bands at age fourteen, taking on cover tunes, r&b, and country—"whatever paid," as he recalled in 1995.

He arrived at a firm grasp of a variety of different musical styles during time spent as a musician in Austin, where he moved in the early seventies; in Memphis, where he worked in the mid-seventies with CHARLIE RICH; and in Nashville, where he moved in 1978 and played in the acclaimed local funk band the Nerve.

His session career began as a demo musician for the powerhouse country publisher TREE INTERNATIONAL in Nashville. "Tommy Cogbill [the session bassist-guitarist] was my mentor here in Nashville until he died," Rhodes said. Keyboardist-producer BARRY BECKETT was another key influence. Rhodes has worked on the road and/or recorded with a multitude of stars, including J. J. Cale,

DOLLY PARTON, RODNEY CROWELL, ROSANNE CASH, Steve Winwood, and Larry Carlton. Some signature work includes Crowell's 1988 *Diamonds and Dirt,* Cash's 1987 *King's Record Shop,* and HANK WILLIAMS JR.'s 1987 *Born to Boogie.* In 1997 Rhodes joined Rodney Crowell, STEUART SMITH, and Vince Santoro in the Cicadas. —*Thomas Goldsmith*

REPRESENTATIVE RECORDING

The Cicadas (Warner Bros., 1997)

Speck Rhodes
b. West Plains, Missouri, July 16, 1915

Gilbert "Speck" Rhodes is one of country music's most endearing comedians, with a musical-vaudeville career that dates back to the Great Depression. He was forty-four years old when he joined the syndicated *PORTER WAGONER Show* in 1960, thereafter performing on television as the show's rube comedian for twenty years.

Rhodes's parents moved to Arkansas when he was five years old. Speck played old-fashioned five-string banjo, and in 1931 he and his two brothers and sister would perform on the local town square for five or six dollars. Later, as a touring act, they covered more than thirty states (1933–37). "Maybe the act we followed would be a name tumbling act from Japan. . . . Then maybe you'd follow with a Frank Sinatra–type singer," Rhodes told Paul W. Soelberg.

Rhodes bought a bass fiddle in 1936, and by 1939 he was performing on radio at Poplar Bluff, Missouri. He began to try "clowning"—copying some medicine show techniques—and in 1941 he adopted his famous checkered suit costume. By 1947 the Rhodes family was performing on Memphis radio, and later, on television.

When Rhodes was invited to join the *Porter Wagoner Show,* he updated some of his old Memphis scripts and developed his imaginary telephone character, Sadie. One song he liked to sing was "Sweet Fern." Rhodes also appeared in DOLLY PARTON's *Rhinestone* film in 1984—marking a long rise from his past of picking cotton for fifty cents a day, and singing on the sidewalks for pocket change. —*Steve Eng*

RIAA
established 1952

The Recording Industry Association of America is the lobbying arm of the record business, an organization based in Washington, D.C. and that represents record labels on Capitol Hill. In its role as a governmental liaison, the RIAA has organized defenses for free speech issues, participated in copyright negotiations, and aided the FBI in catching prerecorded music counterfeiters.

But the RIAA's highest-profile achievement is its issuance of gold, platinum, and multiplatinum awards when singles and albums achieve significant sales levels. Six years after the agency's founding, the RIAA instituted its certification policies to provide some basis in reality for the multitude of gold albums that labels were handing out in the 1950s. Independent accountants now audit the sales paperwork submitted by a label when it requests certification, providing an objective confirmation of a company's claims.

Originally, gold records represented $1 million earned in wholesale album sales, or 1 million singles sold. In 1975 the album criterion was altered, requiring sales of 500,000 copies. A year later, the platinum category was added, recognizing sales of 2 million singles or 1 million albums. Multiplatinum albums later came into existence: double-platinum for 2 million albums, triple-platinum for 3 million, etc. In 1989, as the market for singles had slowed substantially, the criterion was changed so that gold singles could be achieved with sales of 500,000.

Among country artists, the first album to be certified gold was TENNESSEE ERNIE FORD's *Hymns* (certified February 20, 1959), and the first gold single was JIMMY DEAN's "Big Bad John" (certified December 14, 1961). Country's first platinum album was the various artists collection *Wanted: The Outlaws* (certified November 24, 1976).

With the development of a new national computer network by a company called SoundScan, the possibility has been raised that direct-sales information—rather than labels' internal paperwork—be used as the basis for gold and platinum certification. —*Tom Roland*

Tandy Rice
b. Franklin, Tennessee, August 16, 1938

Tandy C. Rice Jr. is one of the music industry leaders who helped turn Nashville into a major music business town. "I love sellin' better than anything else," he once told *The Tennessean.* "I'd rather sell than eat."

Rice graduated from The Citadel in Charleston, South Carolina, in 1961, with degrees in business and English. He then joined the air force, serving under General Curtis LeMay of the Strategic Air Command as an information officer.

Back in Nashville in 1963, Rice became a publicist, eventually recruiting stations for the syndicated country television shows operated by Show Biz, Inc., most notably the *PORTER WAGONER Show.* In 1971 Rice bought Show Biz's booking agency, Top Billing, Inc., which represented Wagoner, DOLLY PARTON, and comedian JERRY CLOWER. By 1978 Rice was handling at least eighteen acts, including TOM T. HALL, JIM ED BROWN, Helen Cornelius, and JEANNIE C. RILEY.

Rice became a national celebrity himself during the late 1970s—appearing in *Newsweek* and *Playboy,* for instance—while marketing Billy Carter, brother of President Jimmy Carter, as an unrehearsed but irrepressible comedian. Today he remains active as president and chief executive officer of Top Billing and as a member of numerous professional and charitable organizations. —*Steve Eng*

Tony Rice
b. Danville, Virginia, June 8, 1951

One of the most influential guitar players in bluegrass and related acoustical styles, Anthony David Rice grew up in California. His entire family played bluegrass music, and he was also influenced by DOC WATSON and the late CLARENCE WHITE. Rice's first band was the Haphazards, with his brothers.

After the Rices moved to North Carolina in the 1960s, Tony played and recorded with banjo player Bobby Atkins, then replaced Dan Crary in the BLUEGRASS ALLIANCE in 1970. Relocating to Louisville, Kentucky, Rice worked for a year with SAM BUSH, Courtney Johnson, Lonnie Peerce, and Harry "Ebo Walker" Shelor—three quarters of the band that would become NEW GRASS REVIVAL.

Rice joined J. D. Crowe & the New South for the next four years, initially with his brother Larry Rice (mandolin) and Bobby Slone (fiddle and bass). In 1974 Ricky Skaggs replaced Larry; dobro player Jerry Douglas joined the following April. The resulting five-piece New South became one of the most admired bluegrass bands of all time, although Rice, Skaggs, and Douglas all left in the fall of 1975.

Rice spent the next four years with the David Grisman Quartet, experimenting with everything from classical to jazz, combining these elements into what Grisman called "dawg" music. In 1979 Rice established the Tony Rice Unit as his primary performance vehicle and continued producing projects for himself and other musicians. Notable is *The Bluegrass Album,* a tribute to the music of the 1950s. Intended as a one-time project, this effort was so well received that five sequels followed.

Rice's fluid, highly ornamented guitar work has made him arguably the dominant bluegrass guitarist of his era; his technical command of the instrument is unsurpassed, and each new release explores artistic and technical challenges. Prior to suffering vocal-cord damage, Rice was also a gifted and much-imitated vocal interpreter of bluegrass and introspective modern material.

—*Frank and Marty Godbey*

REPRESENTATIVE RECORDINGS

Manzanita (Rounder, 1978); *The Bluegrass Album* (Rounder, 1981)

The Rice Brothers

Hoke Rice b. near Gainesville, Georgia, January 8, 1909; d. May 26, 1974

Paul Rice b. near Gainesville, Georgia, July 23, 1919; d. January 22, 1988

Hoke and Paul Rice were steeped in the old-time string-band tradition of the Southeast, but when they decided to make their livings as professional musicians, they sought to overcome what they considered the corny hillbilly image. Hoke studied guitar under a classical musician, and by the late 1920s he had settled in Atlanta, where he was a respected musician, admired by hillbilly and jazz musicians working on local radio stations.

Paul later joined Hoke to form a partnership that established them as one of the leading regional BROTHER DUET teams. They hired other musicians, including horn players, and set about developing a hot, syncopated sound that featured pop-oriented material. They worked on radio stations throughout the Southeast before moving to KWKH in Shreveport, Louisiana, where their career peaked just before the brothers were drafted for military duty in World War II.

While working in Shreveport, Paul sold a song to Jimmie Davis and Charles Mitchell for 35 dollars. The song, which Paul claimed to have written a couple of years earlier in Atlanta (there is evidence suggesting that he, too, had bought the song), was "You Are My Sunshine." Prior to selling the song to Davis, the Rice Brothers recorded it for Decca Records, a label for which they ultimately recorded more than fifty sides.

After the war Hoke took a full-time job as a salesman. Paul continued to work as a bass player, mainly in Atlanta, until his retirement from the music business in about 1960.

—*Wayne W. Daniel*

Charlie Rich

Charlie Rich

b. Forrest City, Arkansas, December 14, 1932; d. July 25, 1995

It's probably no exaggeration to say that Charlie Rich was the most eclectic musician ever to be called country. His natural métier was probably supper-club jazz. It's certainly the style with which he began his professional career, and the one to which he periodically reverted. His success, though, came first with rock & roll, then—fleetingly—with white r&b, and finally with countrypolitan country music.

During his enlistment in the air force, Rich played on-and-off-base in a group called the Velvetones; the name alone gives some inkling of their style. Back in Arkansas, Rich tried farming, while doubling as a supper-club pianist in Memphis. He signed with Sun Records in 1957, first as a songwriter and session pianist, and then as a performer. He wrote several songs for Johnny Cash, Jerry Lee Lewis, and other Sun artists. Rich's first record for Sun's Phillips International imprint was cut in August 1958; the third, cut in October 1959, was "Lonely Weekends," a Presleyish rocker that peaked just outside the pop Top Twenty.

Rich recorded a wide variety of tracks for Phillips, including perhaps his most outstanding song, "Who Will the Next Fool Be?" Nothing charted, in part because his music was impossible to pigeonhole. In 1963 he signed with RCA's reactivated Groove Records in Nashville, cutting "Big Boss Man" and several bluesy country records ("There Won't Be Anymore," "I Don't See Me in Your Eyes Anymore") that were later overdubbed and successfully reissued. Then, in 1965, he went with Smash/Mercury Records and scored another Top Thirty pop hit with "Mohair Sam," but once again he couldn't find a follow-up. In 1966 he moved on to Hi Records, where he cut an odd mixture of country and Memphis r&b with no success at all.

In December 1967 Rich signed with Epic Records in Nashville, working under the direction of Billy Sherrill. There were five commercially arid years when Rich seemed to be Sherrill's personal indulgence. Then Rich broke through with "I Take It on Home" and "Behind Closed Doors," the latter a giant pop, country, and international hit in 1973. He was CMA's 1973 Male Vocalist of the Year and 1974 Entertainer of the Year. Rich stayed with Epic until 1978, later seeming to sleepwalk through the increasingly overblown arrangements. He even appeared uncomfortable with success itself, and occasionally exhibited bizarre behavior, such as setting fire to the envelope that announced that JOHN DENVER had won the Entertainer of the Year Award at the nationally televised 1975 CMA Awards ceremony. Together, though, Rich and Sherrill defined crossover country, working the remunerative middle ground between country and easy listening. The #1 hits included "The Most Beautiful Girl," "A Very Special Love Song," "I Love My Friend," and "Rollin' with the Flow."

The chart success began tailing off immediately after Rich left Epic. Subsequent affiliations with United Artists and ELEKTRA produced only minor hits that ended altogether in 1981. Rich then went into semiretirement in Memphis. In 1991 he made an impressive comeback record for Sire that, perhaps more than any other record, captured his sprawling genius. —*Colin Escott*

REPRESENTATIVE RECORDINGS

Greatest Hits (Epic, 1976); *The Complete Smash Sessions* (Mercury, 1992); *Pictures and Paintings* (Sire, 1992); *Lonely Weekends: The Best of the Sun Years* (AVI, 1996); *Feel Like Going Home: The Essential Charlie Rich* (Columbia/Legacy, 1997)

Don Rich
b. Olympia, Washington, August 15, 1941; d. July 17, 1974

Donald Eugene Ulrich—best remembered as lead guitarist and harmony vocalist in BUCK OWENS's band the Buckaroos—began his musical career in 1958 as a sixteen-year-old fiddler playing gigs with Owens in the Seattle area. Together, Owens and Rich honed their partnership and vocal harmonies up and down the West Coast through the early 1960s as Owens's recording career at CAPITOL RECORDS was beginning.

Rich played a crucial role in Owens's career. Having learned to play lead electric guitar from Owens, Rich helped to further develop and solidify the "Buck Owens Sound," a hard-edged and beat-driven honky-tonk style distinct from the smooth pop sounds of country music produced in Nashville at the time. Rich's lead guitar playing in live performances and in most recording sessions from 1961 on enabled Owens to concentrate on his duties as vocalist, MC, and songwriter, as well as on his burgeoning business empire. Rich also wrote songs with Owens, including the classic "Waitin' in Your Welfare Line" (#1, 1966).

Twelve years Owens's junior, Rich became Buck's erstwhile younger brother, both his best friend and musical collaborator. Rich's life ended tragically in a 1974 motorcycle accident, an event that devastated Owens, who has repeatedly explained that Rich's death was an important factor in his withdrawal from recording throughout most of the 1980s. —*Mark Fenster*

Rich-R-Tone Records
established ca. 1946

One of the many regional independent labels to emerge after the war, Rich-R-Tone was founded about 1946 by Johnson City, Tennessee, businessman James Stanton. Using studios of radio stations in the Bristol–Kingsport–Johnson City area, and having his discs pressed in Philadelphia, Stanton issued some 200 titles, generally featuring area artists who focused on grassroots music. Though many never rose much above their regional status, Rich-R-Tone artists did include the STANLEY BROTHERS and WILMA LEE AND STONEY COOPER (first recordings for both groups), who went on to national fame, as well as lesser-known but important acts such as the Bailey Brothers, the Church Brothers, and other bluegrass bands. The label also released numerous records by local favorites, such as Buffalo Johnson. A subsidiary label, Folk Star, was used for "custom" or "vanity press" recordings.

In the 1960s Stanton moved his operations to Nashville, where he opened a studio on Church Street and enjoyed a successful business making custom recordings for bluegrass bands and gospel choirs. For a time he revived Rich-R-Tone as a bluegrass album label. Since Stanton's death the label has remained in possession of his heirs. —*Charles Wolfe*

Ethel Park Richardson
b. Decherd, Tennessee, December 13, 1883; d. April 11, 1968

Ethel Park Richardson journeyed through the southern Appalachians by swayback horse and on foot, gathering material for her 1927 book *American Mountain Songs* and for a network radio career in which she would introduce country music to a city audience.

Singing mountain songs on Chattanooga's WDOD in 1926, Richardson was brought to the attention of NBC Radio in New York, where she auditioned and was given her own program in 1927. She accompanied her singing with an autoharp and was the creator-writer of a dozen different radio series. Writing, her first love, eclipsed her work as a performer.

Hillbilly Heart-Throbs, a weekly program in which Richardson dramatized country songs, began a five-year run on NBC in 1933. FRANK LUTHER, ZORA LAYMAN, CARSON ROBISON, TEX RITTER, TEXAS JIM ROBERTSON, and the Vass Family were among the artists regularly appearing. A later, recorded version of the series was syndicated throughout the 1940s.

In 1955 Richardson was the "folksinging grandmother" who became the first contestant to win the top prize of $100,000 on a TV quiz program (NBC's *The Big Surprise*). Her category was American folk music, prompting a reissue of her book, an offer to do a guest shot on the GRAND OLE OPRY, and recognition for her pioneer efforts in presenting country music to a national audience. —*Jon Guyot Smith*

J. P. Richardson (*see* the Big Bopper)

Kim Richey
b. Zanesville, Ohio, December 1, 1956

By the mid-1990s Kim Richey was proving herself one of the most talented songwriter-performers working out of Nashville. Her co-writing credits include "Nobody Wins" (a #2 hit by RADNEY FOSTER in 1993) and "Believe Me Baby (I Lied)" (a #1 hit by TRISHA YEARWOOD in 1996). In addition, Richey's self-titled 1994 debut album, produced by Richard Bennett, and its 1997 successor, *Bitter Sweet,* both garnered widespread critical acclaim.

Raised in Dayton, Ohio, by her widowed mother and grandmother, Richey attended Western Kentucky University in Bowling Green, where she performed in the band Southern Star with singer-songwriter-guitarist Bill Lloyd (later of the hitmaking duo FOSTER & LLOYD). After a brief stay in Nashville in 1984 that included a job as a short-order cook at the city's songwriting mecca, the BLUEBIRD CAFE, Richey spent time in Europe, South America, Colorado, Boston, and Seattle before returning to MUSIC CITY in the fall of 1988.

Upon her return to Nashville, Richey landed a staff songwriting job at Bluewater Music and later a recording contract with MERCURY RECORDS. A tough-minded individualist, Richey wrote or co-wrote most often with Angelo Petraglia, every song on her two solo albums, both of which feature her clear-eyed explorations of male-female relationships; expressive vocals; and tangy mix of country, rock, and pop music. —*Bill Friskics-Warren*

REPRESENTATIVE RECORDINGS

Kim Richey (Mercury, 1994); *Bitter Sweet* (Mercury, 1997)

Ricochet

Perry "Heath" Wright b. Vian, Oklahoma, April 22, 1967
Duane Mack "Junior" Bryant Jr. b. Pecos, Texas, October 23, 1968
Jeffery Park Bryant b. Pecos, Texas, December 27, 1962
Gregory Charles Cook b. Vian, Oklahoma, January 28, 1965
Edward James Kilgallon b. East Greenbush, New York, May 12, 1965
Teddy Sloan Carr b. Lafayette, Tennessee, July 4, 1960

Fewer than two years after Ricochet made its first serious demo recordings, the band had a gold record for its debut album and was named the ACM's 1996 Top Vocal Group and Top New Vocal Group.

In 1993, drummer Jeff Bryant, whose father once played keyboards for ROY ORBISON and WAYLON JENNINGS, asked singer-guitarist Heath Wright to join him and his brother, ace fiddler Junior Bryant, in a West Texas band called Lariat. A few weeks after Wright signed on, however, Lariat disbanded. At that point the Bryant brothers and Wright regrouped, formed the core of what would become Ricochet, and began auditioning new band members.

They got their first break in the fall of 1993, when Ricochet's original manager convinced veteran Nashville producer Ron Chancey to visit the manager's Columbia, Missouri, nightclub where the band (*sans* Cook and Carr) was performing. Chancey soon convinced COLUMBIA RECORDS to offer the group a four-song development deal.

In early 1994 Wright and the Bryant brothers hired Wright's childhood friend bassist Greg Cook; steel player Teddy Carr; who previously toured with CLAY WALKER; and keyboardist Eddie Kilgallon, owner of an audio/video postproduction studio in upstate New York. Once the band was set, they concentrated on rehearsing smooth four-part harmonies and recording top-quality demos. In February 1995 Columbia added the band to its artist roster and four months later released the band's debut self-titled album.

Ricochet's first single was "What Do I Know," which became a Top Five country hit in early 1996. It was immediately followed by the #1 hit "Daddy's Money" (1996). The band's first two albums were produced by the team of Ron Chancey and Ed Seay. In 1998 Ricochet was again named ACM's Top Vocal group. —*Marjie McGraw*

REPRESENTATIVE RECORDINGS

Ricochet (Columbia, 1995); *Blink of an Eye* (Columbia, 1997)

Riders in the Sky

Douglas Bruce Green b. Great Lakes, Illinois, March 20, 1946
Frederick Owen LaBour b. Grand Rapids, Michigan, June 3, 1948
Paul Woodrow Chrisman b. Nashville, Tennessee, August 23, 1949

Riders in the Sky have played a major role in the renaissance of western music. When they first formed, in 1977, the genre was practically dead; though the SONS OF THE PIONEERS were still performing, there was virtually no new western music being created or performed. Inspired by the classic singing cowboys of the 1935–55 Hollywood era, Riders in the Sky blended crisp harmonies and a good dose of humor to inject renewed vitality into western music.

The group began in 1977 at a listening room. By 1978, founding members Douglas Green, Fred LaBour, and Bill Collins began to take the idea seriously. Collins dropped out later that year, replaced by fiddler Paul "Woody" Chrisman. Along the way the trio acquired some colorful nicknames: Green became Deputy Ranger Doug, Idol of American Youth; LaBour became Too Slim; and Chrisman became King of the Cowboy Fiddlers. The band name came from LaBour after he'd seen a reissue album from the Sons of the Pioneers named *Riders in the Sky*.

In 1979 the Riders recorded the first of their seven albums with ROUNDER, followed by five albums for MCA, and then three albums with COLUMBIA before returning to Rounder in 1995. They also recorded an album for Rhino and another for Rabbit Ears Radio (with ROY ROGERS).

Riders in the Sky: (from left) "Woody" Paul Chrisman, "Ranger" Doug Green, and Fred "Too Slim" LaBour

Billy Lee Riley & the Little Green Men

In addition to their live performances and recordings, they hosted *Tumbleweed Theater* on THE NASHVILLE NETWORK (1983–86); had their own Saturday morning children's show, *Riders in the Sky,* on CBS-TV (August 1991–August 1992); and broadcasted *Riders' Radio Theater* on public radio (1988–1996). Their radio show was taped in Nashville its first season; thereafter the show was taped in Cincinnati. Along the way they added Joey Miskulin ("The Cowpolka King") on accordion and Texas Bix Bender as announcer for their radio shows. Notable honors include joining the GRAND OLE OPRY (June 19, 1982); two Wrangler Awards (1991 and 1993) for Outstanding Western Compositions; and their induction into the Western Music Hall of Fame in 1993, the first contemporary act to be inducted. In 1997 Ranger Doug recorded his first solo album, *Songs of the Sage,* which was composed entirely of his original songs in the classic western style, for the Warner Western label. At this writing, the group's most recent album, *A Great Big Western Howdy from Riders in the Sky,* is set for release on Rounder Records in 1998. —Don Cusic

REPRESENTATIVE RECORDINGS

The Cowboy Way (MCA, 1987); *Riders Radio Theater* (MCA, 1988); *Cowboys in Love* (Columbia, 1994); *Always Drink Upstream from the Herd* (Rounder, 1995)

Billy Lee Riley
b. Pocahontas, Arkansas, October 5, 1933
....

Billy Lee Riley had only six records issued under his own name while at SUN RECORDS, yet he remains one of the most revered rockabilly artists of all time. His group, the Little Green Men, served as the house band for rockabilly sessions at Sun.

A product of Irish and Cherokee ancestry, Riley grew up in poverty in a variety of small towns in Arkansas and Mississippi. His father taught him harmonica; afterward Riley, at age nine, learned how to play guitar from neighboring children on a primarily black plantation. Lying about his age, in 1949 Riley enlisted in the army, where he often performed honky-tonk music along the lines defined by HANK WILLIAMS and LEFTY FRIZZELL. Upon being discharged from the army in 1954, the future rocker relocated to Jonesboro, Arkansas, where he played in a couple of country bands.

Soon after his discharge Riley gave up music, moved to Memphis, and opened a restaurant with his brother-in-law. After the restaurant failed, Riley worked in a variety of jobs and resumed playing, joining Slim Wallace's Dixie Ramblers, whose membership included future engineer, producer, and songwriter JACK CLEMENT. Clement recorded Riley performing three numbers, including two originals, "Trouble Bound" and "Rock with Me, Baby," that he subsequently sold to Sun Records in April 1956. At that point both Riley and Clement began long associations with Sun. Needing to perform in support of his record, Riley formed a road band consisting of Roland Janes (guitar) and J. M. Van Eaton (drums). Riley, Janes, and Van Eaton became the house band at Sun, backing up numerous rockabilly artists through the rest of the decade, the most notable being JERRY LEE LEWIS.

Riley's best-known recordings were "Flyin' Saucer Rock 'n' Roll" and "Red Hot." The former was cut in December 1956 with Riley, Janes, and Van Eaton (dubbed the Little Green Men by SAM PHILLIPS), augmented by Jerry Lee Lewis. "Red Hot," recorded in 1957, was a cover of bluesman Billy the Kid Emerson's Sun original. Both epitomized the raw energy and excitement that was rockabilly at its very finest. As "Red Hot" looked set to explode, Sun released Jerry Lee Lewis's "Great Balls of Fire." As owner of a small independent label with few promotional resources, Sam Phillips opted to give the Lewis record first priority. As a result, Riley's record languished, and his dreams of stardom were dashed. Even if Phillips's decision had been different, it is possible that Riley still would not have been successful, being too primal for national stardom.

Riley would later record under his own name and a variety of pseudonyms for a host of mostly small record companies, having ownership interest in both the Rita and Mojo labels. In the early 1990s Riley came out of a long, self-imposed retirement and began recording for HIGH-TONE RECORDS.   —*Rob Bowman*

REPRESENTATIVE RECORDINGS

Classic Recordings (Bear Family, 1990); *Blue Collar Blues* (HighTone, 1992)

Jeannie C. Riley

b. Anson, Texas, October 19, 1945

Jeannie C. Riley became an overnight sensation in 1968 on the strength of her #1 single "Harper Valley P.T.A."

Born Jeanne Carolyn Stephenson, she grew up in Anson, Texas, singing with the band of her uncle, Johnny Moore. CONNIE SMITH was one of her early country favorites. Her first name change came with her marriage to auto mechanic Mickey Riley before they moved to Nashville in 1966. There she found work as a demo singer and secretary for songwriter Jerry Chesnut's Passkey Music, while Mickey ran a Texaco service station on Nashville's Gallatin Road. Her second name change came just before the release of "Harper Valley P.T.A.," when Plantation Records owner and producer SHELBY SINGLETON added an "i" to Jeanne.

"He really wanted to change my name to Rhonda Renee," Riley has said. "I didn't want that. He used the 'C' from Carolyn because he liked the middle initial of [pop singer] Jaye P. Morgan."

Written by TOM T. HALL, "Harper Valley P.T.A." was recorded on July 26, 1968, and released immediately. The record's moral tale of a single mother who turned the tables on a hypocritical small-town P.T.A. board mirrored the national mood. It topped the *Billboard* country charts for three weeks that September and October, and crossed over to top the pop charts as well. Riley went from earning 50 dollars a week as a secretary to performing on Ed Sullivan's popular CBS network television show the next week. The single also won Riley the 1968 Grammy for Best Country Vocal Performance, Female, as well as the CMA's Single of the Year Award.

Although "Harper Valley P.T.A." was her most enduring hit, Riley went on to place twenty more hits on the country charts between 1968 and 1973, among them "There Never Was a Time,' "The Girl Most Likely," "Country Girl," and "Good Enough to Be Your Wife.' In 1974 she moved on to MERCURY and was recording with WARNER BROS. by 1976.

In the 1980s she turned her attention to her Three Fold Chord Gospel Ministries and to the career of her daughter, Kim Michelle Riley Coyle (who records as Riley Coyle). In 1981 Jeannie C. Riley had an autobiography published, *From Harper Valley to the Mountaintop.*   —*Don Rhodes*

REPRESENTATIVE RECORDING

When Love Has Gone Away (MGM, 1973)

LeAnn Rimes

b. Jackson, Mississippi, August 28, 1982

With the summer 1996 release of "Blue," a BILL MACK song originally intended for PATSY CLINE (though not recorded by her), thirteen-year-old prodigy Margaret LeAnn Rimes

LeAnn Rimes

became an instant star. Since then, her powerful, full-throated vocals and youthful beauty have made her one of the best-selling country artists of the late 1990s.

Rimes won her first song-and-dance competition at five (singing "Getting to Know You") and then told her parents she wanted a career in show business. They soon rearranged their lives to accommodate their talented only child. The following year, the family moved from Jackson, Mississippi, to the Dallas area, where she made her stage debut at seven, portraying Tiny Tim in a local musical production of Dickens's *Christmas Carol.* At age eight she was a two-week winner on the syndicated TV talent show *Star Search,* and a regular at Johnnie High's Country Music Revue stage show in Arlington, Texas.

When she was eleven Rimes recorded her first album, *All That* (Nor Va Jak, 1994). Two years later, she signed with CURB RECORDS in Nashville. In May 1996 Rimes's yodel-inflected rendition of "Blue" (a re-recording of an earlier master) became her first single to appear on country radio station playlists nationwide. Though Rimes was quickly hailed by fans and music press as a second coming of Patsy Cline, the single's classic NASHVILLE SOUND style was judged too archaic by some national radio programmers, and thus "Blue" stalled at #10 on the *Billboard* country singles charts for lack of sufficient airplay. Nevertheless, the public embraced Rimes and the song. The *Blue* album held the #1 position for more than three months on *Billboard*'s country album charts, selling more than 3 million copies by the end of 1996. Rimes's third single from the *Blue* album, "One Way Ticket (Because I Can)," became her first #1 country hit.

In early 1997 Curb Records gathered recordings from Rimes's 1994 *All That* album and repackaged them, with the addition of a new recording of the pop standard "Unchained Melody," as her second Curb album, *Unchained Melody: The Early Years.* The album debuted at #1 on both *Billboard*'s country and Hot 200 pop album charts.

In September 1997 Rimes's third Curb album was released—*You Light Up My Life: Inspirational Songs,* a collection consisting mostly of 1970s ballads ("You Light Up

My Life," "The Rose") and well-known standards ("Amazing Grace," "God Bless America"). The album's first single, "How Do I Live," hit #3 on *Billboard*'s Hot 100 pop singles chart. In late September 1997 *You Light Up My Life* became the first album in the history of *Billboard* magazine to debut simultaneously at #1 on the pop, country, and contemporary Christian album charts. In 1997 Rimes won ACM Awards for Single Record of the Year ("Blue") and Best Female Vocalist. In addition, she became the second country artist (after BOBBIE GENTRY) to earn a Grammy in the Best New Artist category with her 1996 award. In 1998 her Grammy-nominated single "How Do I Live" was the first country single to be certified multiplatinum, and Rimes became the second woman of any musical genre (behind Whitney Houston and her "I Will Always Love You") to have a single certified triple platinum by the RIAA.

For her first three albums, LeAnn's father, Wilbur C. Rimes, served as her record producer, with her mother, Belinda Rimes, filling the role of manager. In the fall of 1997, Wilburn and Belinda Rimes announced their impending divorce and the imminent move of Belinda and LeAnn to Nashville. —*Marjie McGraw*

REPRESENTATIVE RECORDINGS

Blue (Curb/MCG, 1996); *Unchained Melody: The Early Years* (Curb, 1997); *You Light Up My Life: Inspirational Songs* (Curb, 1997)

Nolan "Cowboy Slim" Rinehart
b. near Gustine, Texas, March 11, 1911; d. October 28, 1948

Nolan Arthur Rinehart, often called the King of the BORDER RADIO, was the most popular of the SINGING COWBOYS on border radio. After army service, during which he met JIMMIE RODGERS when the Blue Yodeler entertained troops at Fort Sam Houston, Rinehart began his broadcasting career in the early 1930s. He aired on KSKY–Dallas; XEG–Monterrey, Mexico; and on a small 250-watt station in Brady, Texas, before moving on to the powerful border station XEPN in Eagle Pass, Texas/Piedras Negras, Mexico. After his initial appearances on XEPN, the station was deluged by mail from fans throughout the station's huge broadcast area. As his popularity grew, Rinehart syndicated his transcription programs on all the Mexican border stations. Rinehart teamed up with cowgirl singer PATSY MONTANA for a number of transcription sessions that proved very popular with listeners. During the years he was on border radio, Rinehart did very well selling his songbooks, which included songs such as "Empty Saddles" and his theme song,"Roaming Cowboy," but unfortunately he never made any commercial recordings. He did go to Hollywood for a screen test but never appeared in any movies. Rinehart was killed in an automobile accident in Detroit in 1948, at age thirty-seven, and was buried in Hobbs, New Mexico. Though it has long been rumored that he was on his way to make his first commercial recordings when he was killed, others sources have suggested that he was planning to become an executive in border radio at the time of his death. —*Charlie Seemann*

Ralph Rinzler
b. Passaic, New Jersey, July 20, 1934; d. July 2, 1994

Folklorist, promoter, and musician Ralph Rinzler played a vital role in preserving traditional-style country music and

bringing it to new audiences. Rinzler was fascinated as a boy by a set of Library of Congress folksong recordings and later by Harry Smith's seminal 1951 record collection *The Anthology of American Folk Music.* At Swarthmore College (from which he graduated in 1956), Rinzler became part of the active campus folk scene, teaching himself mandolin, guitar, and banjo. In New York during the late 1950s and early 1960s, Rinzler helped popularize bluegrass and traditional country music by performing and recording with the GREENBRIAR BOYS band, and co-founding that city's Friends of Old Time Music, a group that staged concerts.

As a Folkways Records talent scout and producer, and during a 1961 recording field trip to North Carolina, Rinzler discovered Arthel "DOC" WATSON, who subsequently became an influential flat-picking guitarist and traditional singer. Rinzler also revitalized the career of bluegrass creator BILL MONROE, documenting his accomplishments in a seminal 1963 *Sing Out!* magazine article and (while briefly serving as Monroe's manager) introducing him to the national folk music revival circuit.

From 1964 to 1967 Rinzler was a director of the major NEWPORT (RHODE ISLAND) FOLK FESTIVAL, which showcased many traditional country musicians. He helped country music promoter CARLTON HANEY organize the 1965 all-bluegrass weekend in Fincastle, Virginia, now considered the first true bluegrass festival.

Ralph Rinzler went on to a distinguished career at the Smithsonian Institution in Washington, D.C. In 1967 he founded the Festival of American Folklife, an annual event from which evolved the Smithsonian's Center for Folklife Studies and Cultural Programs. He facilitated the Smithsonian's 1987 acquisition of the important Folkways Records catalogue and archives. He was an assistant secretary Emeritus of the institution at the time of his death. —*Richard D. Smith*

REPRESENTATIVE RECORDING

Bill Monroe & Doc Watson Live Duet Recordings 1963–1980: Off the Record, Volume 2 (Smithsonian/Folkways, 1993)

Tex Ritter
b. Panola County, Texas, January 12, 1905; d. January 2, 1974

The most well-versed western singer of any of Hollywood's singing cowboys was TEX RITTER. Born Woodward Maurice Ritter in Panola County, Texas (the same county where JIM REEVES was born), Ritter was raised with a deep love of western music. When he entered the University of Texas at Austin in 1922 he met J. Frank Dobie, Oscar J. Fox, and John Lomax—three of the most noted authorities on cowboy songs, who added further to his knowledge. While studying law in college Ritter had his own weekly radio program, singing cowboy songs, on KPRC in Houston.

In 1928 Ritter went to New York, where he worked briefly in a Broadway musical production. Returning to college, he entered Northwestern University in Illinois. With the Depression making money hard to come by, he soon returned to New York, where he worked in several more Broadway productions, including *Green Grow the Lilacs*. (A decade later, Rodgers and Hammerstein adapted the play into their *Oklahoma!*.) While in New York, Ritter also worked regularly on a variety of radio programs, and in 1932 he made his first recording.

By mid-decade, the enormous success of GENE AUTRY's films led other studios to look for their own singing cow-

Tex Ritter

boys. One of the first producers to recognize Ritter's potential was Edward Finney. He signed Ritter and released his first starring film, *Song of the Gringo,* in November 1936.

Ritter was well suited to the role of singing cowboy. He looked and acted the part and was singing the type of songs he loved best. Unfortunately, most of his films were made for Grand National and Monogram, two of the so-called poverty row studios. These studios were smaller than the majors and made their films on limited budgets. Although Ritter's films never had the production values of films starring Gene Autry or ROY ROGERS, Ritter still enjoyed considerable success at the box office.

In 1942, after a decade of recording with little success, Ritter became one of the first artists signed by the newly formed CAPITOL RECORDS. He soon began scoring major hits with records such as "Jealous Heart," "Rye Whiskey," "I'm Wastin' My Tears on You," and "You Will Have to Pay." Ritter would record for Capitol for the rest of his life.

A different type of film opportunity came to Ritter in 1952, when he was asked to sing the title song of the Gary Cooper–Grace Kelly western *High Noon.* The song was used as a narrative throughout the film and became Ritter's signature song. He went on to record a number of other western theme songs throughout the decade.

Ritter was one of the first c&w artists to record albums built around a central theme, as he recorded albums of cowboy songs, patriotic songs, hymns, and Mexican songs as well as albums of country music. In 1961 Ritter recorded "I Dreamed of a Hillbilly Heaven," which became one of his biggest hits and displayed the fine way he delivered recitations. Ritter became involved with the formation of the COUNTRY MUSIC ASSOCIATION and was elected its president in 1963.

Ritter's growing involvement in country music led him to move to Nashville in 1965, where he co-hosted the late-night country music radio program on WSM with RALPH

EMERY and joined the GRAND OLE OPRY. In 1970 Ritter ran unsuccessfully for the Republican nomination to the U.S. Senate. Ritter's death on January 2, 1974, marked the passing of one of c&w music's finest and most respected talents. —*Laurence Zwisohn*

REPRESENTATIVE RECORDINGS

An American Legend (Capitol, 1973), 3-record set; *The Best of Tex Ritter* (Curb, 1990); *Country Music Hall of Fame* (MCA, 1991); *Collectors Series* (Capitol, 1992)

The Riverside Rancho
established in Los Angeles, California, ca. 1942; ended 1959

With the onset of World War II, the Riverside Rancho, at 3213 Riverside Drive (near Griffith Park) in Los Angeles, California, became the hub of numerous c&w night spots then rapidly appearing in Southern California.

Owned by Kay and Lou DeRhoda and booked by West Coast promoter Marty Landau (beginning in March 1947), the Rancho featured a 10,000-square-foot dance floor, three bars, dressing facilities downstairs, an upstairs dining hall, and a large veranda. Starting in 1942, BERT "FOREMAN" PHILLIPS, c&w music promoter, placed two of his numerous bands, Bill "Happy" Perryman and SPADE COOLEY, at the Rancho; and upon their departure it became the home of TEX WILLIAMS's Western Caravan for some fifteen years. West Coast artists T. TEXAS TYLER, RAY WHITLEY, HANK PENNY, Dude Martin, JIMMY WAKELY, MERLE TRAVIS, WESLEY TUTTLE, and TEXAS JIM LEWIS made regular appearances there. It was also the preferred Los Angeles venue for out-of-town country acts such as BOB WILLS, HANK WILLIAMS, ROY ACUFF, ERNEST TUBB, LEFTY FRIZZELL, HANK SNOW, PEE WEE KING, WEBB PIERCE, and the MADDOX BROTHERS & ROSE. The Riverside Rancho was an active nightspot until its demolition in 1959. —*Ken Griffis*

Hargus "Pig" Robbins
b. Rhea County, Tennessee, January 18, 1938

Blinded in a knife accident at about age three, Hargus Melvin "Pig" Robbins succeeded FLOYD CRAMER as the leading session pianist in Nashville from the mid-1960s into the 1980s. Although he had classical piano training at the Tennessee School for the Blind from ages seven to fifteen, he built his style from listening to the keyboard work of Floyd Cramer, OWEN BRADLEY, MARVIN HUGHES, RAY CHARLES, and Papa John Gordy on records.

"I got [the nickname] 'Pig' at school," he explained. "I had a supervisor who called me that because I used to sneak in through a fire escape and play when I wasn't supposed to and I'd get dirty as a pig."

His first big Nashville session was for the 1959 GEORGE JONES hit "White Lightnin'." Robbins's work on BOB DYLAN's *Blonde on Blonde* (1966) made Robbins much in demand with pop and rock artists as well. He also contributed distinctive touches to CHARLIE RICH's "Behind Closed Doors" and CRYSTAL GAYLE's "Don't It Make My Brown Eyes Blue." Robbins was CMA's Instrumentalist of the Year in 1976 and ACM's top keyboard player in 1977. He won a Grammy in 1978 as Country Instrumentalist.

Robbins embarked on a brief career as a solo instrumental recording in the late seventies. He recorded for ELEKTRA such solo albums as *Country Instrumentalist of the Year* (1977), *Pig in a Poke* (1978), and *Unbreakable Hearts*

(1979). He remains an influential and active session player, recording recently with RANDY TRAVIS, RICK TREVINO, ALAN JACKSON, TRAVIS TRITT, TRACY BYRD, DOLLY PARTON, and others. —*Bob Millard*

Marty Robbins

b. near Glendale, Arizona, September 26, 1925; d. December 8, 1982

Martin David Robinson was country music's renaissance man. He was a successful recording artist, stage performer, actor, author, songwriter, and stock car racer. His versatile baritone enabled him to handle a wide variety of musical styles, making him one of the more successful crossover artists during the 1950s and 1960s. Throughout his career, he recorded country, western, rockabilly, Hawaiian music, gospel, and pop, with his specialty being pop ballads.

Robbins and his twin sister, Mamie, were born into a poverty-stricken family, and his childhood was difficult. He dropped out of school in his teens, served in the navy during 1943–45, and saw action in the Pacific Theater during World War II.

Robbins's career started in 1947, and he soon had his own radio and television shows on KPHO in Phoenix. On September 27, 1948, he married Marizona Baldwin. They had two children, Ronny and Janet. Robbins's break came in 1951 when JIMMY DICKENS guested on his TV show, and was so impressed that Dickens encouraged his record company to give Robbins a contract. Robbins signed with COLUMBIA RECORDS that year and remained with the label throughout his career, except for the period 1972–74 when he recorded for DECCA/MCA Records.

Robbins joined the GRAND OLE OPRY on January 19, 1953, and moved to Nashville. In 1965 he started performing on the last segment of the Opry so he could race at the Nashville Speedway. During the summer of 1968 he left a

Marty Robbins

race before it ended in order to make his show, only to find that the Opry was running late and he might lose some of his time onstage. That night, he not only stayed onstage for his assigned time period, but he also stayed beyond it. That act of defiance delighted the audience and became a regular occurrence whenever he appeared; thus an enduring Opry tradition was born. Often he would gesture toward the stage manager to signal that he would sing one more song, only to repeat the process for more than an hour, thus cutting into ERNEST TUBB's *Midnight Jamboree.*

Over the course of his career, Robbins had a total of ninety-four chart records, with sixteen going to the #1 position. In 1955 he charted with rockabilly songs and began to establish his crossover capability. In September 1956 Robbins's recording of MELVIN ENDSLEY's "Singing the Blues" hit #1 on *Billboard*'s country chart and placed in the Top Twenty on the pop chart. His crossover success continued with a series of hits he recorded with the Ray Conniff Singers, in 1957 and 1958, aimed at the teen pop market. In April 1957 "A White Sport Coat (and a Pink Carnation)" became his biggest hit. Some other songs from those sessions included "Just Married," "The Story of My Life," and "The Hanging Tree." The year 1957 also saw the release of the first of several of his Hawaiian music albums, *Song of the Islands.*

But Robbins's strongest love was for the music and stories of the Old West. His signature song, the self-penned "El Paso," was released in October 1959 and won Robbins his first Grammy, which was also the first Grammy ever awarded a country song. As a child, his grandfather "Texas Bob" Heckle told him stories of the Old West, and Robbins's most influential hero was GENE AUTRY. Robbins's album *Gunfighter Ballads and Trail Songs* became a hit the same year, and other western albums followed over the years. The one book he wrote was *The Small Man,* a paperback western novel.

Robbins also excelled as a songwriter. In 1952 he signed a songwriting contract with ACUFF-ROSE PUBLICATIONS and in later years established his own music publishing company. A number of Robbins's hits were self-penned, including "A White Sport Coat (and a Pink Carnation)," "El Paso," "You Gave Me a Mountain," and "My Woman, My Woman, My Wife."

Robbins was a genuine showman onstage, not merely a singer. He was especially noted for his relationship with his fans, who called themselves "Marty's Army." Between songs he joked with the audience and allowed them to take photos at any time. Like many country stars, he often stayed around after the concert to sign autographs.

In August 1969 Robbins suffered a heart attack, and on January 27, 1970, he underwent bypass surgery, which was still in the experimental stages then. The operation was a success, and he recovered quickly. On April 13, 1970, he received the Man of the Decade Award from the Academy of Country Music (ACM). On March 16, 1971, he received his second Grammy Award for "My Woman, My Woman, My Wife."

Stock car racing played an important part in Robbins's life. In the 1950s Robbins was racing micromidgets. By the 1960s he was racing modified stock cars at the Nashville Speedway, and in 1966 he entered his first NASCAR Grand National stock car race. Following his heart attack, Robbins was able to pass his physical and return to NASCAR racing in October 1970. However, he again gave up racing briefly after suffering three wrecks in 1974 and 1975. His love for the sport was so strong that he returned to it in

1977, and his final race took place November 7, 1982, a month before his death.

Robbins was one of the few country music artists to star in a number of films and TV series. Beginning in the 1950s Robbins made more than a dozen films with western or country music themes. His TV series included *Western Caravan* (early 1950s), *The Drifter* (1965), *The Marty Robbins Show* (1969), and *Marty Robbins Spotlight* (1977-78).

The last year of Robbins's life was climactic. In May 1982 "Some Memories Just Won't Die" made the country Top Ten, and in October *Billboard* recognized his renewed success by awarding him its "Artist Resurgence Award" as the performer who has seen the greatest career revival during the past year. On October 11, 1982, Robbins was inducted into the COUNTRY MUSIC HALL OF FAME. It was only seven weeks before he suffered a heart attack, on December 2. Robbins died December 8, 1982, at age fifty-seven.

—*Barbara Pruett*

REPRESENTATIVE RECORDINGS

The Song of Robbins (Columbia, 1957; Columbia/Legacy, 1995); *Gunfighter Ballads and Trail Songs* (Columbia, 1959); *Marty After Midnight* (Columbia, 1962; Varese Sarabande, 1997); *The Essential Marty Robbins* (Columbia, 1991), 2 discs; *Marty Robbins, 1951–1958* (Bear Family, 1991), 5 discs

Fiddlin' Doc Roberts
b. Madison County, Kentucky, April 26, 1897; d. August 4, 1978

Dock Phil Roberts, better known as Fiddlin' Doc Roberts, was one of country music's pioneer recorded fiddlers. A Roberts neighbor, talent scout Dennis Taylor, arranged his first recording sessions (with singer Welby Toomey) for GENNETT in Richmond, Indiana, in October 1925, and a prolific decade of country recording began for Roberts. For three different companies, Roberts recorded more than eighty songs and backed other musicians on at least as many more. According to historian Charles Wolfe, only an aversion to travel (ruling out big-city radio and touring) made Roberts less well known than contemporaries ARTHUR SMITH and CLAYTON MCMICHEN. Roberts's fiddling style, as Wolfe has described it, featured a smooth, long-bow technique. A remarkable number of blues songs and tunes local to eastern Kentucky dominated Roberts's repertory.

His partners on records, besides Welby Toomey, included Dick Parman, Ted Chesnut, fiddler Asa Martin, and Roberts's young singing son, James Roberts. Always a popular fiddler for dances in his home area, Roberts was rediscovered by folklorists and other scholars in the 1960s and 1970s and performed frequently in his last years at Kentucky's Berea College. —*Ronnie Pugh*

Kenny Roberts
b. Lenoir City, Tennessee, October 14, 1926

Kenny Roberts, whose spectacular yodeling has prompted standing ovations throughout his half century in show business, continues to tour and record as "America's #1 Yodeler," happily unconcerned with the charts and the changes in mainstream country music.

Born George Kingsbury in Tennessee, he grew up in Massachusetts, learning to yodel by studying the records of WILF CARTER and ELTON BRITT and quitting high school to join the Down Homers on a New Hampshire radio station in 1943. The group next turned up on WOWO's *Hoosier Hop* in Fort Wayne, Indiana, where Roberts emerged as a solo act and the program's headliner at age nineteen. Two years later he had his own daily TV show for children in Cincinnati. Billed as the Jumping Cowboy, his acrobatics and youthful charm made him a hero to local schoolkids, while his singing attracted adult viewers. He was just twenty-two when his Coral recording of "I Never See Maggie Alone" was a Top Ten hit on both the country and pop charts.

In the fifty years since his career began, Roberts has consistently worked in radio and TV and has recorded for a number of labels, including DOT, STARDAY, KING, and Vocalion. His singing voice—like his style—has never changed. "I can still do all my yodels," he has said. "I never smoked, and I'm sure that has helped me."

—*Jonathan Guyot Smith*

REPRESENTATIVE RECORDINGS

Indian Love Call (Starday, 1965); *Traditional Country* (Music Room, 1994)

Don Robertson
b. Peking, China, December 5, 1922

A songwriter and a pianist, Don Robertson left an indelible mark on country music in pioneering the slip-note piano style. Born in China, where his father was a doctor, Robertson moved to the United States in 1927 at age five. He studied music at the University of Chicago, and early in his career worked as a pop pianist in Chicago and then in Hollywood, where he did session for CAPITOL RECORDS beginning in 1947. In 1956 he had a hit record of his own, an infectious novelty called "The Happy Whistler." Though he wrote a number of pop hits starting in the 1950s (including "Hummingbird" for LES PAUL & MARY FORD), during his association with HILL & RANGE music publishers Robertson wrote a number of major songs for country artists. These include "I Really Don't Want to Know" for EDDY ARNOLD in 1954, "I Don't Hurt Anymore" for HANK SNOW in 1954, "You're Free to Go" for CARL SMITH in 1956, and "Ninety Miles an Hour Down a Dead End Street" for Hank Snow in 1963. More importantly, though, Robertson introduced the slip-note technique of piano playing (in which the pianist slides up into a note from the one beneath) on the demo recording of his song "Please Help Me I'm Falling," which HANK LOCKLIN recorded in 1960, with FLOYD CRAMER playing the distinctive piano part in Robertson's style at the instruction of CHET ATKINS. After the record became a #1 country hit, Atkins encouraged Cramer to record piano instrumentals in the slip-note style, popularizing Robertson's sound. —*Stacey Wolfe*

Eck Robertson
b. Madison County, Arkansas, November 20, 1887; d. February 17, 1975

Considered by many historians to be the first southern musician to record what would later be considered country music, Alexander Campbell Robertson was a legendary Texas fiddler who helped to define the so-called long-bow style still used by contest fiddlers today. In spite of a relatively slim recorded output, his work influenced several generations of musicians.

Eck Robertson

Eck Robertson grew up in the town of Hamlin in the Texas panhandle, where his father was a preacher and where he learned his first fiddle tunes from veterans such as Polk Harris and Matt Brown (credited with tunes such as "Ragtime Annie" and "Done Gone"—both of which Robertson would later record). Shortly after the turn of the century, Robertson joined a traveling medicine show, and for the next few years learned not only fiddle tunes but also tricks of showmanship and entertaining. After he married his childhood sweetheart, Jeanetta Levy, the pair continued to tour; as their children grew up, they, too, joined the troupe. (They would eventually number ten.) In the off-season Robertson worked as a piano tuner and frequented the many fiddling contests that were so much a part of the Texas musical landscape.

Inspired by being in a 1922 Fox Movietone newsreel, Robertson became interested in another emerging technology of the day: recordings. In 1922 he and a friend, Civil War veteran Henry Gilliland, attended a Confederate veterans' reunion in Richmond, Virginia. When Gilliland mentioned he had a friend in New York who worked for the Victor Talking Machine Company, the pair caught the next train and appeared in the Victor offices, dressed in western garb, to ask for an audition. The Victor bosses were impressed, and promptly recorded some twelve numbers by the musicians, some as a duo, others solos by Robertson, still others by Robertson with a studio pianist. The high point was Robertson's solo reading of "Sallie Gooden," with its elaborate variations and improvisations—one of the acknowledged masterpieces of old-time music.

Robertson's recordings inspired a generation of other Texas fiddlers to record in the next few years: Red Steeley, Oscar Harper, W. B. Chenoweth, Prince Albert Hunt, and

Samuel Morgan Peacock. Ironically, Robertson himself did not record again until almost the end of this fad: a 1929 session featuring his family and generating important recordings such as "There's a Brown Skin Gal Down the Road Somewhere," "Brown Kelly Waltz," and "Brilliancy Medley." But after this he made no more commercial recordings. A series of radio transcriptions done in 1940 for Sellers has never surfaced, and for most of the 1940s and 1950s Robertson retreated from the mainstream of country music, doing his fiddling at local contests.

In the 1960s Robertson, like so many other stars of the 1920s, was rediscovered by the young enthusiasts of the folk revival; he appeared some at festivals with the NEW LOST CITY RAMBLERS, and let Rambler John Cohen record some of his fiddle solos. (These were released years later as an LP called *Eck Robertson: Famous Cowboy Fiddler*.) In his last years Robertson was often interviewed by fiddling enthusiasts, and was active in contests as late as the 1960s.

—*Charles Wolfe*

Texas Jim Robertson
b. Batesville, Texas, February 27, 1909; d. November 11, 1966

James Battle Robertson was billed as a western singer, but he sang a wide variety of country songs, ranging from "Home on the Range" to "Slipping Around" to "The Old Rugged Cross." While publicity releases always stated that he was from Texas, he started his radio singing career in the 1930s in Charlotte, North Carolina. From there he went to New York, broadcasting over NBC. Texas Jim sang and acted in many radio shows as diverse as the *Death Valley Days* and the *Dick Tracy* series. For many years he enjoyed a vast listening audience for his strong baritone voice and open-chord guitar picking. He recorded for BLUEBIRD, VICTOR, MGM, and lesser-known labels and made personal appearances on GEORGE HAMILTON IV's syndicated television shows. Robertson committed suicide in 1966.

—*Guy Logsdon*

REPRESENTATIVE RECORDINGS

Tales and Songs of the Old West (Strand, 1955); *Texas Jim Robertson Sings the Great Hits of Country & Western Music* (Grand Prix, late 1950s)

Carson Robison
b. Oswego, Kansas, August 4, 1890; d. March 24, 1957

Between 1924 and 1956 Carson Jay Robison had a long and successful career as a country recording artist and as a songwriter specializing in topical songs inspired by news events of the day. Among his best-known compositions are "Carry Me Back to the Lone Prairie," "Barnacle Bill the Sailor," "I'm Goin' Back to Whur I Come From," and "Life Gets Tee-Jus, Don't It." In addition to recording, Robison made numerous appearances on network radio via transcriptions and in movie shorts and published folios of songs.

He was born into a musical family, his father being a fiddler and dance caller, and was reared in Chetopa in southern Kansas near the Oklahoma border. Robison's employment by the railroad and in the Oklahoma oil fields was in addition to his professional singing, whistling, and guitar-playing. He spent the first thirty years of his life in the area, except for army service during World War I.

After working for Kansas City radio station WDAF for about a year, he moved to New York, where he teamed with WENDELL HALL, with whom he had worked earlier in the Midwest, accompanying Hall on guitar and whistling on his records. VICTOR RECORDS noted Robison's talents and signed him as a staff guitarist. He accompanied a number of artists on their records on the guitar, and sang duets with Hall, Gene Austin, and BUELL KAZEE (as Sookie Hobbs).

In late 1924 Robison met the prominent singer VERNON DALHART and became his guitar player. Robison was a gifted composer and in his day had no peer as a writer of topical and event songs, such as "The Mississippi Flood," the type of song that Dalhart specialized in recording. More than sixty of the reported 300-plus songs Robison composed in his lifetime were recorded by Dalhart, and many of them, such as "My Blue Ridge Mountain Home," were big hits. Robison also composed songs for Dalhart under the pseudonyms Carlos B. McAfee ("The John T. Scopes Trial," "Wreck of the 1256"), and Maggie Andrews, his mother's maiden name ("The Engineer's Child," "My Little Home in Tennessee").

Robison sang no vocal solos while associated with Dalhart, but in mid-1926 he began harmonizing with him in duets, and later in trios that included Adelyne Hood. In June 1926 Robison recorded two whistling solos, "Nola" and "Whistleitis," for four different companies, calling himself the Kansas Jayhawk. His ability to whistle two notes in harmony at the same time was a source of amazement to his listeners.

Robison and Dalhart parted in June 1928, due chiefly to a disagreement on splitting the royalties on Robison's compositions. Immediately Robison brought in FRANK LUTHER as his recording partner. They sang almost 300 duets together, released on many labels, chiefly Robison's compositions, until April 1932. Probably their most well-known number was "Barnacle Bill the Sailor," which spawned two sequels. Their chief label credits were as Bud & Joe Billings or Billings & Robison, for Victor, the Carson Robison Trio for many labels, and the Black Brothers for OKEH. Again, as with Dalhart, Robison sang very few solos, with the exception of twenty recordings for the GENNETT label. Two of his most outstanding solos, which he recorded several times through the years, were "Naw I Don't Wanta Be Rich" and "So I Joined the Navy." He also did an event song, "The Ohio Prison Fire," for COLUMBIA and two excellent examples of topical Depression-era songs for ARC: "Prosperity Is Just Around, Which Corner?" and "What Are You Squawkin' About."

After his last session with Frank Luther in April 1932, Robison formed a new act with John, Bill, and Pearl Mitchell, whom he billed as the Buckaroos in the United States; he soon took them to England for a personal appearance tour that included a number of recording sessions, billing them overseas as the Pioneers. Dressed in cowboy costumes, they were an immediate hit. They also made two ensuing trips to England, in 1936 and 1939, recording both times for the Rex label.

Robison continued recording for Victor through the years. In 1936 his five records (ten sides) were released on the MONTGOMERY WARD label. During the years 1941–45 he wrote and recorded a number of wartime numbers, such as "1942 Turkey in the Straw" and "Hitler's Last Letter to Hirohito" (one of a series of funny and insulting imaginary letters from the Axis leaders to one another). He recorded a square dance album for Columbia in 1941 and another for Victor in 1946.

Robison's last recordings were for the MGM label from 1947 through 1956, with his Pleasant Valley Boys, named for the area in New York where he had a 140-acre ranch for many years until his death. The most well-known number from this period was his composition "Life Gets Tee-Jus Don't It." Always trying to keep up with the times, Robison titled one of his last recordings "Rockin' and Rollin' with Grandma"; it was released the year before his death. Robison is a member of the Nashville Songwriters Hall of Fame.

—*Bob Olson*

Fabor Robison

b. Beebe, Arkansas, November 3, 1911; d. September 1986

Fabor Robison was one of the most influential, and controversial, independent record owners and talent scouts of the 1950s. He played a crucial role in developing the early careers of JIM REEVES, JOHNNY HORTON, the BROWNS, MITCHELL TOROK, FLOYD CRAMER, and others. After a tour in the army in World War II, where he had been a cook, Robison settled in California. There he worked for a time as a talent agent with clients such as Johnny Horton and started his record company, ABBOTT RECORDS, primarily to record Horton. Robison also began working as a song hunter for American Music, traveling the country to find new talent and songs.

Robison soon discovered a hotbed of young talent in Shreveport, Louisiana, home of the KWKH *LOUISIANA HAYRIDE*. Not only did he find some of his best singers, but he also used the studios of KWKH and some of its staff musicians to make his records. These regular studio men included a young Floyd Cramer, steel guitarist JIMMY DAY, and fiddlers Big Red and Little Red Hayes. Robison later

Carson Robison

recalled, "Hell, the band was just a bunch of kids, but we cut hits in there that have never been topped." They recorded these two #1 country hits in 1953: "Mexican Joe" by Jim Reeves and "Caribbean" by Mitchell Torok.

In 1953 Robison started the FABOR RECORDS label, on which he recorded important sides by the Browns and Ginny Wright. He soon expanded his recording activities to include his own studio in Southern California, where he used West Coast instrumental greats such as SPEEDY WEST and Roy Lanham. Like most independent record owners, Robison ultimately saw most of his biggest finds move onto major labels. In about 1959 Robison sold off his music publishing and some masters to Jamie/Guyden Records. He left the music business completely in 1965 and sold all remaining masters to the SHELBY SINGLETON Corporation.

—*Stacey Wolfe*

Rock & Roll Trio (*see* Johnny and Dorsey Burnette)

Rockabilly

Rockabilly music was a transition between the HONKY-TONK and country boogie styles and what became rock & roll. Whereas country boogie was a cousin of honky-tonk, centering around a boogie-woogie beat, rockabilly added blues guitar, a heavier dose of r&b tunes, and the driving bluegrass rhythms of BILL MONROE. Instrumentally, rockabilly was not a radical departure, relying as it did mostly on the instruments of honky-tonk: electric and acoustic guitars, string bass, piano, steel guitar, drums, and, on occasion, even fiddles, though many acts used only guitars and bass behind the vocalist. Rock & roll added formalized arrangements (as with Bill Haley's music), while rockabilly's spontaneity, energy and intensity often seemed about to career out of control.

No single artist can claim to have first played rockabilly. In the early 1950s various obscure southern performers were evolving toward that sound. Near Jackson, Tennessee, CARL PERKINS and his band performed in bars, Perkins singing uptempo songs filled with his stinging blues guitar, boogie, and bluegrass rhythms. In Texas, Sid King & His Five Strings mixed honky-tonk with r&b. In Memphis in 1954, ELVIS PRESLEY and Memphis honky-tonk musicians Scotty Moore and Bill Black created a sparse sound built around Presley's hypnotic country-blues vocals; Moore's bluesy, CHET ATKINS–MERLE TRAVIS–influenced electric guitar; and Black's slapped bass. When Elvis became the breakthrough rockabilly artist with his 1954–55 recordings for SUN RECORDS, he proved to be the commercial catalyst for the rockabilly style. He soon attracted others to the label, including Perkins and JERRY LEE LEWIS, who adapted boogie-woogie piano to the new sound. Others had their own variations on the sound. Though horns were seldom used, Sun rockabilly SONNY BURGESS's band the Pacers included a trumpet.

Many major labels signed rockabilly artists, but since older producers rarely understood the music, they often tried too hard to control it, resulting in many failed recordings. A case in point is BUDDY HOLLY's 1956 DECCA session in Nashville, though JOHNNY BURNETTE had greater artistic (if not commercial) success with his Decca recordings with the Rock & Roll Trio, featuring Paul Burlison's wildly distorted, overamplified lead guitar. The music's influence spread nonetheless through the mid- to late fifties. RICK NELSON, who admired Presley and Carl Perkins, made au-

thentic rockabilly music part of his parents' top-rated TV sitcom *The Adventures of Ozzie and Harriet* and recorded hit rockabilly singles for IMPERIAL. Capitol A&R man KEN NELSON made explosive records with both Gene Vincent and WANDA JACKSON. Nonetheless, many of the best and rawest rockabilly singles were primitive performances recorded by obscure performers around the nation and released on tiny regional labels. By the late fifties rockabilly began to vanish nearly as quickly as it appeared, as its original practitioners matured into other, more formalized musical styles. Yet overseas, particularly in England, rockabilly reemerged in the 1970s, attracted younger fans, and inspired extensive European LP reissues from Sun Records and other labels. The revival spread to the United States with the early 1980s popularity of the U.S. revival band Stray Cats. In the mid-1990s U.S. rockabilly revival acts continued to proliferate.

—*Rich Kienzle*

Jesse Rodgers
b. Waynesboro, Mississippi, March 5, 1911; d. December 1973

Born in Mississippi but raised by a Texas uncle (after his mother's untimely passing when he was age twelve), Jesse Otto Rodgers's musical career was influenced early on by the recordings of his superstar cousin JIMMIE RODGERS, and by singing cowboy film stars of the 1930s.

In deference to the power that Jimmie's successful "blue yodel" style had on him, phase one of Jesse's career, beginning in about 1932 on Mexican border stations XEPN and XERA, found him performing in a similar vein. Likewise, upon being signed to record for VICTOR RECORDS' BLUEBIRD label less than a year after his cousin's death, Jesse continued the tradition, as exemplified by "The Rambler's Yodel," "Yodeling the Railroad Blues," and others. Publicity photo autographs were also eagerly prefixed with "Yodelingly yours." But Jesse's cowboy image was beginning to mount, too, and was evident from his first sessions with tunes such as "When the Texas Moon Is Shining" and "The Empty Cot."

An "in deference" posture toward Jimmie's Blue Yodels gradually became one of indifference as Jesse's western image began taking hold. By 1938, as the Jimmie Rodgers influence waned, Jesse began to spell his name "Rogers," without the "d." And, as if to further disassociate himself from his past and to bolster his cowboy figure, his 1946 songbook even proclaims a birthplace of Claremore, Oklahoma, rather than Mississippi.

Jesse's biggest success, however, came after moving in 1944 to Philadelphia, where he became a mainstay for nearly two decades. Starring on WFIL's *Hayloft Hoedown* and cavorting in the 1950s on a children's TV show as Ranger Joe with his trained horse Topaz, Jesse acquired a large regional following, and recordings for Sonora (1946–47), RCA (1948–51), and MGM (1952–54) preserved national recognition as well. But declining health from emphysema forced a move back to Texas in the early 1960s, where he lived in Houston for his final decade.

—*Bob Pinson*

Jimmie Rodgers
b. Meridian, Mississippi, September 8, 1897; d. May 26, 1933

James Charles Rodgers, known professionally as the Singing Brakeman and America's Blue Yodeler, was the first performer inducted into the COUNTRY MUSIC HALL OF

Jimmie Rodgers

FAME. He was honored as the Father of Country Music, "the man who started it all." From many diverse elements—the traditional melodies and folk music of his southern upbringing, early jazz, stage show yodeling, the work chants of railroad section crews, and, most importantly, African-American blues—Rodgers evolved a lasting musical style that made him immensely popular in his own time and a major influence on generations of country artists. GENE AUTRY, ERNEST TUBB, HANK SNOW, LEFTY FRIZZELL, BILL MONROE, JOHNNY CASH, MERLE HAGGARD, TANYA TUCKER, and DOLLY PARTON are only a few of the dozens of stars who have acknowledged the impact of Jimmie Rodgers's music on their careers.

Rodgers was the son of a railroad section foreman but was attracted to show business. At thirteen he won an amateur talent contest and ran away with a traveling medicine show. Stranded far from home, he was retrieved by his father and put to work on the railroad. For a dozen years or so, through World War I and into the 1920s, he rambled far and wide on "the high iron," working as callboy, flagman, baggage master, and brakeman, all the while polishing his musical skills and looking for a chance to earn his living as an entertainer.

After developing tuberculosis in 1924, Rodgers gave up railroading and began to devote full attention to his music, organizing amateur bands, touring with ragtag tent shows, playing on street corners, taking any opportunity he could find to perform. Success eluded him until the summer of 1927. In Asheville, North Carolina, he wangled a regular (but unpaid) spot on the local radio station, WWNC, and persuaded the TENNEVA RAMBLERS, a stringband from BRISTOL, Tennessee-Virginia, to join him as the Jimmie Rodgers Entertainers. When the radio program was abruptly canceled, they found work at a resort in the Blue Ridge Mountains. There they learned that RALPH PEER, an agent for the Victor Talking Machine Company, was making field recordings in Bristol, not far away. Rodgers quickly loaded up the band, went to Bristol, and succeeded in gaining an audition with Peer. Before they could record, however, the group quarreled over billing and broke up. Deserted by the band, Rodgers persuaded Peer to let him record alone, accompanied only by his own guitar.

Prompted by the public's unusually strong response to Rodgers's first release ("Sleep, Baby, Sleep," paired with "The Soldier's Sweetheart"), Peer arranged for Rodgers to record again in November at Victor's home studios in Camden, New Jersey. From this session came the immortal "Blue Yodel (T for Texas)," Rodgers's first big hit. Within months he was on his way to national stardom, playing first-run theaters, broadcasting regularly from Washington, D.C., and signing for a vaudeville tour of major southern cities on the prestigious Loew Circuit.

In the ensuing five years he traveled to Victor's studios in numerous cities nationwide, including New York and Hollywood, eventually recording 110 titles, including such classics as "Waiting for a Train," "Daddy and Home," "In the Jailhouse Now," "Frankie and Johnny," "Treasures Untold," "My Old Pal," "T. B. Blues," "My Little Lady," "The One Rose," "My Blue-Eyed Jane," "Miss the Mississippi and You," and the series of twelve sequels to "Blue Yodel" for which he was most famous. In 1929 Rodgers appeared in a movie, *The Singing Brakeman*, a fifteen-minute short made in Camden by Columbia. He also worked with many other established performers of the time, touring in 1931 with Will Rogers (who jokingly referred to him as "my distant son") and recording with such country music greats as the CARTER FAMILY, CLAYTON McMICHEN, and BILL BOYD, and in at least one instance with a star of major national prominence, Louis Armstrong, who appears with him on "Blue Yodel No. 9." One of the first white stars to work with black musicians, Rodgers also recorded with the fine St. Louis bluesman Clifford Gibson.

Rodgers's career reached its high point during the years 1928 to 1932. By late 1932 the Depression was taking its toll on record sales and theater attendance, and Rodgers's failing health made it impossible for him to pursue the movie projects and international tours he had planned. Through the spring of 1933 he tried, with little success, to book personal appearances. In May he went to New York to fulfill his contract with Victor for twelve more recordings. It took him a week to finish these sessions, resting between takes. Two days later, on May 26, he collapsed on the street and died a few hours later of a massive hemorrhage in his room at the Hotel Taft.

Jimmie Rodgers's impact on country music can scarcely be exaggerated. At a time when emerging "hillbilly music" consisted largely of old-time instrumentals and lugubrious vocalists who sounded much alike, Rodgers brought to the scene a distinctive, colorful personality and a rousing vocal style that in effect created and defined the role of the singing star in country music. His records turned the public's attention away from rustic fiddles and mournful disaster songs to popularize the free-swinging, born-to-lose blues tradition of cheatin' hearts and faded love, whiskey rivers and stoic endurance. Although Rodgers constantly scrabbled for material throughout his career, his recorded repertoire was remarkably broad and diverse, ranging from love songs and risqué ditties to whimsical blues tunes and even gospel hymns. He wrote songs about railroaders and cowboys, cops and robbers, Daddy and Mother, and home—plaintive ballads with all the nostalgic flavor of traditional music but invigorated by a distinctly original approach and punctuated by Rodgers's yodel and unorthodox runs, which became his trademarks. —*Nolan Porterfield*

REPRESENTATIVE RECORDINGS

Jimmie Rodgers: The Early Years (Rounder, 1990); *Jimmie Rodgers: Riding High* (Rounder, 1991); *Jimmie Rodgers: America's Blue Yodeler* (Rounder, 1991); *Jimmie Rodgers: Down the Old Road* (Rounder, 1991); *Jimmie Rodgers, The Singing Brakeman* (Bear Family, 1992), 6 discs

Johnny Rodriguez

b. Sabinal, Texas, December 10, 1951

Juan Raoul Davis "Johnny" Rodriguez was the first mainstream country music star with Hispanic roots. Born into a large music-loving family in rural South Texas, Rodriguez grew up hearing a wide variety of music, including Spanish songs, cowboy ballads, western swing, and commercial country music. In September 1971, while performing at the Alamo Village Resort in Brackettville, Texas, Rodriguez was discovered by TOM T. HALL. In May 1972 Rodriguez joined Hall's band as a guitarist, though MERCURY RECORDS soon signed the young singer to a solo recording contract. By the end of 1972 Rodriguez's first single, "Pass Me By," had climbed the *Billboard* country charts to the #9 position; shortly afterward he had his first #1 hit, "You Always Come Back to Hurting Me." On the strength of both singles, his debut album *(Introducing Johnny Rodriguez)*, and his charismatic stage presence, Rodriguez was nominated for the 1972 CMA Best Male Vocalist Award.

Subsequent albums for Mercury featured high-charting country hits and some interesting album tracks, all of which showcased Rodriguez's eclectic musical personality. Not only did Rodriguez interpret numerous country chestnuts—some (such as "Faded Love" and "Born to Lose") sung in both Spanish and English, reflecting his bilingual background—but he also covered rock & roll and pop music classics (such as the Beatles' "Something" and the

Johnny Rodriguez

EAGLES' "Desperado"). More impressive were Rodriguez's performances of his own original compositions (like "Bossier City Backyard Blues" and "Ridin' My Thumb to Mexico"). After signing with EPIC RECORDS and producer BILLY SHERRILL in 1979, Rodriguez had several more hit singles through the mid 1980s. Some critics have expressed the opinion that Rodriguez never realized his enormous early potential; nevertheless, he remains a hero to the Hispanic people because, while a celebrity in the mainstream Anglo-American world, he retained his native Hispanic identity.
—*Ted Olson*

REPRESENTATIVE RECORDINGS

The Greatest Hits of Johnny Rodriguez (Mercury, 1976); *Biggest Hits* (Epic, 1983); *You Can Say That Again* (HighTone, 1996)

Kenny Rogers

b. Houston, Texas, August 21, 1938

A significant pop star from the mid-1960s to the early 1970s, Kenneth Donald Rogers parlayed gruff musicality and a laid-back sex appeal into country-pop superstardom. Between 1977's "Lucille" and his 1987 duet with RONNIE MILSAP "Make No Mistake, She's Mine," Rogers hit #1 on the *Billboard* country charts with twenty different solo or duet releases.

Rogers entered the country music field with a broad background in a variety of music styles and a high level of entertainment skills. Growing up in federal public housing in Houston, Rogers was exposed to r&b, pop, and jazz as well as country music. His first professional group was a late 1950s vocal act called the Scholars, who had local hits in Houston. A solo hit on Carlton, "That Crazy Feeling" (1958), earned him a shot on *American Bandstand.*

During the early 1960s he developed his studio techniques and a musical sophistication while playing bass, and occasionally singing, in a Houston trio led by jazz pianist Bobby Doyle. Membership in the New Christy Minstrels folk group spurred the founding of First Edition, in which Rogers and other former Minstrels mixed folk, rock, and country sounds. Achieving early success in 1967 with the psychedelic "Just Dropped In (To See What Condition My Condition Was In)," the group scored several additional pop hits on Reprise Records and starred in a syndicated television series.

After the group's breakup in 1974, United Artists executive LARRY BUTLER signed Rogers to the United Artists label, with which he hit the middle of the charts until the stunning success of the mournfully catchy "Lucille" and an album of the same name in 1977. The tune also hit #5 on pop charts. For the next decade or so, Rogers's commercial appeal earned him hit after top hit; just a few highlights were United Artists releases "The Gambler" (1978) written by DON SCHLITZ, "She Believes in Me" (1979), and "Coward of the County" (1979). Butler served to produce these major hits. In 1980, on LIBERTY RECORDS, the crossover smash "Lady"—a romantic ballad written by Commodores kingpin Lionel Richie—topped the pop charts for six weeks.

Duets with DOTTIE WEST included the highly successful "Every Time Two Fools Collide" (1978), "All I Ever Need Is You" (1979), and "What Are We Doin' in Love" (1981). As the country-pop era reached a peak, Rogers piled up honors: three Grammy Awards, eleven People's Choice

Kenny Rogers

Awards, five COUNTRY MUSIC ASSOCIATION Awards, and eight ACADEMY OF COUNTRY MUSIC Awards.

Already a veteran performer in front of the cameras, Rogers gained huge exposure as an actor through the series of four made-for-television treatments of "The Gambler." The 1980s also saw pop-tinged hits including "I Don't Need You" (1981); "Love Will Turn You Around" (1982); the Sheena Easton duet "We've Got Tonight" (1983); and the memorable, melodic DOLLY PARTON duet "Islands in the Stream" (1983), also a #1 pop hit. Rogers appeared front and center in the megastar collaboration "We Are the World" (1985). During the mid-1980s he had additional #1s such as "Crazy, Real Love" and the sensual George Martin–produced "Morning Desire." But the solo hit "Tomb of the Unknown Love" (1986) and the Ronnie Milsap duet "Make No Mistake, She's Mine" (1987) represented Rogers's last appearances at the top of the charts.

Rogers's bland crossover approach began to work against him as pop took on a harder edge and country went back to the music's roots. However, Rogers's career, under the direction of high-powered manager Ken Kragen, remained strong in other areas even as his chart success diminished. He has built an entertainment empire with major investments in the new country mecca of BRANSON, MISSOURI; utilized his longtime hobby of photography to make several well-received books; produced a line of clothing; engaged in major philanthropic endeavors; and even launched, along with former Kentucky governor John Y. Brown, a chain of chicken restaurants. In addition, Rogers continues to tour nationally and internationally and to record; recent releases have included "If Only My Heart Had a Voice" (1993) on GIANT and the David Foster–produced standards collection "Timepiece" (1995) on ATLANTIC RECORDS. After a switch to Magnatone Records, Rogers released 1996's *The Gift*, also the theme of a Christ-

mas TNN special. The disc included "Mary Did You Know," a duet with Magnatone artist WYNONNA. In 1997 Magnatone released his album *Across My Heart*.

—*Thomas Goldsmith*

REPRESENTATIVE RECORDINGS

Kenny Rogers (Liberty, 1976); *The Gambler* (EMI America, 1978); *Greatest Hits* (EMI America, 1980)

Roy Rogers
b. Cincinnati, Ohio, November 5, 1911; d. July 6, 1998

Roy Rogers earned the title King of the Cowboys by becoming the most popular western film star of all time. But before starring in his first film, Rogers earned his eventual place in the COUNTRY MUSIC HALL OF FAME by founding the SONS OF THE PIONEERS.

Leonard Franklin Slye (Rogers's given name) was raised on a farm in Duck Run, Ohio. In June 1930 the Slye family visited one of Roy's sisters in California. The lure of warm weather and the hope of better job prospects led Rogers and his family to move to Los Angeles. Still, the Depression made jobs hard to find. Rogers drove a gravel truck and then worked as a fruit picker in the same central California farm camps John Steinbeck wrote about in *The Grapes of Wrath*.

Rogers had grown up playing mandolin and calling square dances. When his sister encouraged him to appear on a local radio program that featured amateurs, he reluctantly gave it a try. A few days later he was asked to join a country music band called the Rocky Mountaineers, as a singer and guitarist. Before long he convinced them to add another vocalist so they could harmonize together. Bob Nolan was hired, and when he left the group, Tim Spencer replaced him. Over the course of the next two years, Rogers sang with a variety of country music groups, each of which was less successful than the one before. Finally, late in the summer of 1933, he decided to give it one more try by forming a group consisting of himself, Bob Nolan, and Tim Spencer. The Pioneer Trio, as they originally called themselves, worked on their harmonies while Nolan and Spencer began writing the songs that would become the heart of their repertoire.

Radio station KFWB hired the group and a few months later gave them their own program. The Pioneers' unique harmony and their fine original songs—such as "Cool Water" and "Tumbling Tumbleweeds"—led to a series of radio transcriptions, a DECCA record contract, and film appearances in westerns, including two with GENE AUTRY. In October 1937 Rogers heard that Republic Pictures was auditioning for a new singing cowboy. Although he didn't have an appointment, he managed to get into the studio and gain an audition. His screen test led to a contact and a change of name to Roy Rogers.

When Gene Autry walked out on his contract, Rogers was given the starring role in *Under Western Stars*, which had been scheduled to be Autry's next film. The tremendous success of Rogers's first film marked the emergence of a new star. By 1943 Rogers was the top western star at the box office. He retained this rank until he made the transition into television early in the 1950s.

In 1944 DALE EVANS was cast as Rogers's leading lady in *The Cowboy and the Señorita*. The chemistry between them was apparent both to audiences and to the studio. Over the next five years Evans was featured in Rogers's next nineteen films. A little more than a year after the death of his first wife, Rogers and Evans married, on New Year's Eve 1947. A few years later the couple began their television series, which quickly became a favorite with Sunday night family viewers.

Roy Rogers's success in films, radio, television, on records, and in personal appearances was offset by a long series of tragedies. His wife, Arlene, the mother of his first three children, died a week after the birth of their third child, Roy Jr., in 1946. Robin, the only child born to Rogers and Evans, suffered from Down's syndrome and died shortly before her second birthday in 1952. Rogers and Evans eventually adopted four children from different ethnic and social backgrounds, only to lose two of them tragically. Debbie, an orphan they adopted from Korea, died in a church bus accident. Their son Sandy, who had suffered some brain damage due to physical abuse before being adopted by Rogers and Evans, died while serving in the army.

Each of these losses took a tremendous toll on Rogers and Evans, but the couple's religious faith sustained them. Their positive outlook as they confronted life's challenges only added to the public's regard for them.

Roy Rogers was the only person to be elected twice to the Country Music Hall of Fame: first in 1980 as a member of the original Sons of the Pioneers, and then in 1989 as an individual, for his own career achievements. Rogers was a hero to audiences who saw him in films, at rodeos or state fairs, in television appearances, or at visits to his museum in Victorville, California. To fans throughout the world, the King of the Cowboys was one of the most beloved of Americans.

—*Laurence Zwisohn*

Roy Rogers

REPRESENTATIVE RECORDINGS

How Great Thou Art (with Dale Evans) (Capitol, 1961); *The Best of Roy Rogers* (Curb, 1990); *Tribute* (RCA, 1991); *Country Music Hall of Fame* (MCA, 1992)

Smokey Rogers

b. McMinnville, Tennessee, March 23, 1917; d. November 23, 1993

Singer-songwriter-banjoist Eugene "Smokey" Rogers was an important behind-the-scenes figure in the Southern California western swing scene of the 1940s. He began his musical career in Detroit at age thirteen with Jack West & His Circle Star Cowboys. While still in Detroit he became an original member of TEXAS JIM LEWIS's Lone Star Cowboys in 1935.

By the early 1940s Rogers was on the West Coast and in SPADE COOLEY's band. While with Cooley he wrote the 1945 hit "Shame on You." He later left with other band members to form TEX WILLIAMS's Western Caravan, in which he served as Williams's bandleader. At this time Rogers also ran Smokey's Village Music Store in El Cajon, California. As a songwriter he wrote "Gone" for FERLIN HUSKY, a #1 country hit and #4 pop hit in 1957. Another of his well-known compositions is "Spanish Fandango," as recorded by BOB WILLS on MGM RECORDS. Rogers's singing and banjo playing can be heard on his own recordings on FOUR STAR (some billed as Buck Rogers), CAPITOL, Western Caravan (his own label), and STARDAY. He scored his sole Top Ten hit as an artist in 1949 with his Capitol recording "A Little Bird Told Me."

—*Steve Hathaway*

REPRESENTATIVE RECORDINGS

Smokey Rogers: Gone (Starday, 1963); *Smokey Rogers: Western Swing Masterpieces* (Bronco Buster, 1996), Germany

Matt Rollings

b. Bridgeport, Connecticut, December 14, 1964

One of Nashville's most sought-after piano and keyboard players, Matthew C. Rollings has been putting his ivory stamp on thousands of country sessions since 1985. Rollings is also an accomplished jazz musician, a hit songwriter (SUZY BOGGUSS's "Letting Go"), and a producer.

Rollings began receiving piano training under jazz musician Alan Swain at age nine. Rollings made great strides on the instrument when his family moved in 1976 to Phoenix, where music was part of the public school curriculum. By high school he was playing jazz with the school band and was introduced to country music as part of a local honky-tonk ensemble. In 1983 bandleader Billy Williams produced then-unknown LYLE LOVETT and hired Rollings to play piano on the session, the youngster's first exhilarating recording session. With visions of jazz and New York City in his head, Rollings enrolled at Berklee School of Music in Boston, but also accepted invitations for studio work in Nashville. When the offers kept coming and top producer TONY BROWN called him for Lyle Lovett's MCA debut, Matt could no longer resist moving to MUSIC CITY.

Rollings has been voted the ACM Keyboard Player of the Year (1991–96), a Nashville Music Award winner (1995–96), and a *Music Row* magazine Album All-Star (for most of the nineties).

—*Michael Hight*

REPRESENTATIVE RECORDING

Balconies (MCA Master Series, 1990)

Linda Ronstadt

Linda Ronstadt

b. Tucson, Arizona, July 15, 1946

Linda Ronstadt is a renowned interpreter of many kinds of musical material, including rock, soul, operetta, cabaret, show tune, and Mexican mariachi music. But her roots in the folk music revival have often led her to country. She was a pioneer in the Southern California country-rock movement of the late 1960s and early 1970s, and her influence on other country artists is incalculable. Performers from KATHY MATTEA and SUZY BOGGUSS to TRISHA YEARWOOD and PATTY LOVELESS have cited Ronstadt as a major source of inspiration. In 1996 TERRI CLARK gained a hit by reworking Ronstadt's 1978 version of "Poor, Poor Pitiful Me."

The daughter of musically inclined parents, Ronstadt played guitar as a child and performed in a trio with her sister and brother on local television. She quit college at eighteen and headed for Los Angeles, forming the Stone Poneys with folkies Bob Kimmel and Kenny Edwards. They signed to CAPITOL in 1966, and their version of Michael Nesmith's "Different Drum" climbed into the pop charts the following year. When the group dissolved two years after that, Ronstadt went solo with an album (*Hand Sown . . . Home Grown*) that fused country and rock.

Ronstadt recorded her 1970 album *Silk Purse* in Nashville. There she played the GRAND OLE OPRY and appeared on the *JOHNNY CASH Show*. The album included "Long Long Time," which became her first solo hit.

Upon her return to California, Ronstadt hired a band that would later become the EAGLES and released two more country-rock albums. Her 1974 *Heart Like a Wheel* album found commercial success. Her revival of soul singer Betty Everett's "You're No Good" went to #1 on the pop charts that year, and her remake of HANK WILLIAMS's "I Can't Help It (if I'm Still in Love with You)," featuring the harmony vocals of EMMYLOU HARRIS, became a #2 country hit in 1975 and won a Grammy for Best Country Vocal Performance, Female.

Throughout the 1970s Ronstadt succeeded with pop and country material alike. *Prisoner in Disguise* (1975) contained the country hit "Love Is a Rose," DOLLY PARTON's "I Will Always Love You," and a duet with Harris on "The Sweetest Gift (A Mother's Smile)." For *Hasten Down the Wind* (1976) Ronstadt covered PATSY CLINE's "Crazy" and

BUDDY HOLLY's "That'll Be the Day," while *Simple Dreams* (1977) showcased the cowboy standard "Old Paint," as well as Parton's harmonies on the CARTER FAMILY classic "I Never Will Marry." Ronstadt's reading of ROY ORBISON's "Blue Bayou" was a major pop and country smash that same year.

Although Ronstadt later pursued a more overtly rock-oriented style, she maintained her country ties, appearing on Parton's 1976 syndicated TV show and recording songs for *Trio,* a landmark project combining Ronstadt, Harris, and Parton in an album of songs with an unmistakably feminine feel and country flavor. The 1987 album was a massive success, selling 1 million copies, receiving a Grammy and a CMA Award, and containing four major hit records.

Ronstadt's 1991 album of ranchera music could be compared to the romantic cowboy songs of the 1920s and 1930s; her 1995 *Feels Like Home* was a return to folk and country. Since then she has toured with the Pittsburgh Symphony orchestra; released *Dedicated to the One I Love* (ELEKTRA, 1996), an album of rock and pop songs translated into lullabies; and performed at the White House with Aaron Neville. —*Mary A. Bufwack*

REPRESENTATIVE RECORDINGS

Hand Sown . . . Home Grown (Capitol 1969, 1995); *Silk Purse* (Capitol 1970, 1995); *Heart Like a Wheel* (Capitol, 1974); *Trio* (Warner Bros., 1987); *Feels Like Home* (Elektra, 1995)

Jim Rooney

b. Boston, Massachusetts, January 28, 1938

During his forty-year musical career, Jim Rooney has left an indelible impression on folk and country music, enhancing the careers of NANCI GRIFFITH, IRIS DEMENT, and JOHN PRINE along the way. Rooney was a fixture in Boston during the folk revival in the 1960s and played an integral role during its second revival, in the 1980s.

While completing a master's degree in classical literature at Harvard, Rooney teamed up with banjoist BILL KEITH in 1960 to form a partnership that has lasted to this day. Rooney was in the center of the Cambridge folk scene, managing the famous Club 47, an important urban-folk venue that booked Joan Baez, Tom Rush, and others. From 1967 until 1969 he served as talent coordinator and director of the NEWPORT FOLK FESTIVAL, and later he wrote a widely publicized article in *Sing Out!* that defended BOB DYLAN's use of electrical instruments at Newport. Rooney also wrote two books, *Bossmen: Bill Monroe & Muddy Waters*, and *Baby Let Me Follow You Down: The Illustrated Story of the Cambridge Folk Years.*

In 1970 Rooney moved to Woodstock, New York, to supervise the construction of Bearsville Sound Studios. He then managed the studio, which had such clients as the Band, Bonnie Raitt, Van Morrison, Todd Rundgren, and others.

In 1976 Rooney moved to Nashville and soon became associated with "COWBOY" JACK CLEMENT. Rooney began engineering and producing records and played in Cowboy's Ragtime Band. He served as engineer on the first albums of ALISON KRAUSS and Edgar Meyer. During this time he also met ALLEN REYNOLDS. Reynolds and Rooney later formed Forerunner Music Group, which publishes songs by PAT ALGER, HAL KETCHUM, Tony Arata, and others, and the duo produced Ketchum.

Rooney is best known for producing singer-songwriters

who are considered musically left of center, including Griffith, Prine, DeMent, ROBERT EARL KEEN, JERRY JEFF WALKER, TOWNES VAN ZANDT, PETER ROWAN, Dave Olney, and BARRY & HOLLY TASHIAN, among others. Griffith won a Grammy in 1993 for the Rooney-produced *Other Voices, Other Rooms.*
—*Beverly Keel*

ROPE
established in Nashville, Tennessee, 1983

The Reunion of Professional Entertainers (ROPE) is a Nashville-based association created to care for fellow country music entertainers in time of serious illness, death, or other unavoidable distress.

Federally chartered in 1983 as a nonprofit organization, ROPE accepts for membership those who have worked in the music industry at least twenty-five years. Since its beginnings, membership has grown from an initial 70 members to 700. GORDON TERRY, a founder and first president, helped initiate a trust fund and a death, health, and welfare insurance program.

An early mission of ROPE was to build a retirement center for needful seniors. Five-term ROPE president MAC WISEMAN has served on the CMA's steering committee to explore the possibility of making this dream a reality. During Wiseman's tenure a Friends of ROPE program was approved to allow fans and friends of entertainers to contribute as organizational boosters.

ROPE holds quarterly social gatherings, conducts benefit concert fund-raisers, sponsors annual Golden ROPE Awards, and runs an annual Fan Fair booth. Address: ROPE, 50 Music Square West, #700E, Nashville, TN 37203.
—*Walt Trott*

Fred Rose
b. Evansville, Indiana, August 24, 1898; d. December 1, 1954

Knowles Fred Rose was a principal figure in the rise of the Nashville music industry between 1942 and 1954 in his roles as music publisher, songwriter, producer, and talent scout.

Rose's parents separated soon after he was born, and he grew up with relatives in St. Louis. There he supplemented the family income by playing piano for tips in local saloons. By 1917 he had moved to Chicago, where he found similar work in rough-and-tumble clubs and bars of the South Side. During the 1920s Rose made his name as a successful songwriter, authoring or co-authoring pop and jazz hits such as "Red Hot Mama," "Deed I Do," and "Honest and Truly." During these same years he also made piano rolls; broadcast on Chicago radio stations KYW, WLS, and WBBM; and recorded for the BRUNSWICK label.

In 1933, having lost his Chicago radio job because of a drinking problem, Rose moved to Nashville to work on WSM. Between 1933 and 1938 he divided his time mostly among Nashville, Chicago, and New York, performing on live radio shows and shopping his songs to music publishers. While continuing to write pop material, he began to work closely with the VAGABONDS and the DELMORE BROTHERS at WSM and also wrote songs for cowboy singer RAY WHITLEY, then working in New York. In about 1935, in New York, Rose converted to Christian Science, a faith that would guide his personal and professional life from then on.

In 1936 he scored his first pop-western hit, "We'll Rest

Fred Rose

at the End of the Trail," recorded by TEX RITTER, the SONS OF THE PIONEERS, and Bing Crosby. Partly as a result, Rose spent most of the years 1938–42 in Hollywood penning a series of hits for cowboy film stars GENE AUTRY, Ray Whitley, and ROY ROGERS. In 1942 Rose joined ROY ACUFF in founding ACUFF-ROSE PUBLICATIONS, Nashville's first major country publishing house. Rose continued to write or co-write country standards such as "Wait for the Light to Shine," "Afraid," and "Blue Eyes Crying in the Rain" while serving as an expert editor, most notably for his protégé HANK WILLIAMS. Rose also made Acuff-Rose a solid institutional base for aspiring songwriters such as BOUDLEAUX AND FELICE BRYANT. In addition, Rose served as MGM RECORDS' unsalaried, Nashville-based A&R man. For this label he supervised sessions for Williams, the LOUVIN BROTHERS, RED SOVINE, BOB WILLS, and many other acts. Rose's greatest success was recruiting Williams for MGM, but Rose acted as talent scout for other labels as well; for example, he steered both MARTHA CARSON and the LOUVIN BROTHERS to contracts with CAPITOL, and ROSALIE ALLEN to an RCA VICTOR contract. For all these efforts and for his tireless promotion of country music within the American music industry, Rose was elected to the COUNTRY MUSIC HALL OF FAME in 1961—the first year the honor was bestowed by the Country Music Association (CMA).
—*John Rumble*

Wesley Rose
b. Chicago, Illinois, February 11, 1918; d. April 26, 1990

Although he was not initially inclined toward country music, Wesley Herman Rose ascended through his field to become one of the world's top music publishing executives. He received his degree in accounting from Chicago's Walton School of Commerce, and was working as an accountant with Standard Oil Company when his father, FRED ROSE, invited him to join the recently established ACUFF-

ROSE PUBLICATIONS in 1945. The reluctant young man accepted, on the condition that he become general manager, handling most of the business functions of the firm. This freed the elder Rose, a talented songwriter and song editor, to focus on the creative side of the company, working with songwriters on new material and scouting and helping to record new artists on several labels.

Father and son made a good team, especially in promoting the songs and recordings of HANK WILLIAMS in the country market from 1946 to Williams's death in 1953. The Roses also scored hit after hit with pop covers of Williams's songs, and Wesley continued to make the Williams catalogue one of the most valuable in popular music after Fred Rose died in 1954.

By this time Wesley had become a partner in Acuff-Rose and in HICKORY RECORDS, and after 1954 he served as president of Acuff-Rose; Milene Music (Acuff-Rose's companion ASCAP company); Hickory Records; and, beginning in 1959, Acuff-Rose Artists Corporation. Continuing in his father's footsteps, he also served as an independent producer for MGM, WARNER BROTHERS, and other labels. Although Rose played important roles in the careers of the EVERLY BROTHERS, ROY ORBISON, Sue Thompson, and other acts, his primary role was to promote songs written by Acuff-Rose writers, including not only the Everlys and Orbison but also MARTY ROBBINS, BOUDLEAUX AND FELICE BRYANT, DON GIBSON, JOHN D. LOUDERMILK, MICKEY NEWBURY, and EDDY RAVEN. "The object," he said, "is to bring your song to an artist that will make it believable to the public because the public picks the hits." By the time he and Acuff sold the Acuff-Rose catalogues to GAYLORD Broadcasting in 1985, more than thirty songs he published had been performed on radio and TV more than 1 million times each.

Rose was extremely active in making Acuff-Rose a vital part of the music industry's organizational framework. Not only did he set up Acuff-Rose affiliates around the world and help to found CMA, he also served as the first Nashville publisher on the national boards of ASCAP and the Music Publishers Association. On the local scene he served on the boards of the Nashville Area Chamber of Commerce, First American Bank, Belmont College, and the Nashville Symphony. A 1967 recipient of Nashville's prestigious Metronome Award for contributions to the city's music industry, he was elected to the COUNTRY MUSIC HALL OF FAME in 1986. —*John Rumble*

Rounder Records
established in Somerville, Massachusetts, October 1970

Rounder Records, one of the most successful independent labels, was founded in the Boston suburb of Somerville in October 1970 by a group of old-time country music aficionados, including two grad students, Ken Irwin (b. New York, New York, May 23, 1944) and Marian Leighton-Levy (b. Harrington, Maine, August 22, 1948), and a professor of political science, Bill Nowlin (b. Boston, February 14, 1945). Originally a "collective" effort, these three came to the fore, with Irwin involved in producing, Leighton-Levy handling publicity and promotion, and Nowlin taking charge of legal and financial matters. Today, with a large warehouse and office complex in nearby Cambridge, four subsidiary labels, two music publishing companies, co-ownership of a wholesale distribution company, and distribution representation of twenty-five other labels worldwide, Rounder is a $20 million-a-year business.

Initially patterned after COUNTY RECORDS, with two old-timey releases, a newsletter, and a mail-order service, Rounder has since become more like Folkways Records with the diversity of its catalogue. Rounder's first traditional bluegrass album (*One Morning in May*, Joe Val & the New England Bluegrass Boys, 0003) and its first contemporary bluegrass album (*Country Cooking*, 0006) were released in 1971. CAJUN music was first offered in 1974 (*D. L. Menard & the Louisiana Aces*, 6003). Rounder first tried rock in 1977 (*George Thorogood & the Destroyers*, 3013); eventually this genre earned the label its first gold records. And since the 1980s, blues, zydeco, contemporary folk, roots jazz, polka, Tex-Mex, and a wide variety of "world" musics have all been available on Rounder.

In 1995, Rounder released *Now That I've Found You: A Collection* by contemporary bluegrass singer-fiddler ALISON KRAUSS (0345), the label's first platinum record.

Rounder's country artists with ten or more releases include the Dry Branch Fire Squad (1981–96), the JOHNSON MOUNTAIN BOYS (1981–93), TONY RICE and/or the Tony Rice Unit (1977–96), and RIDERS IN THE SKY (1980–96). —*Tom Ewing*

Rouse Brothers
Earl B. Rouse b. November 1, 1911
Ervin Rouse b. Craven County, North Carolina, September 18, 1917; d. July 8, 1981
Gordon Rouse b. July 4, 1914

Though the Rouse Brothers came from a large musical family, it was three of the brothers who really made their mark on country music. Most important was Ervin Rouse, a fiddler and singer best known for his songs "Orange Blossom Special" and "Sweeter Than the Flowers." Often appearing with him was his brother Gordon. In addition, Ervin was something of a child prodigy and joined his brothers on the RKO Keith vaudeville circuit from 1928 to

Wesley Rose

1933. By 1939, he and Gordon were working at the VILLAGE BARN in New York and writing songs for BOB MILLER's company; Ervin even spent a few months as a singer for big band leader Glenn Miller. In later years the brothers played the big resort hotels in Miami.

As early as 1936, the brothers recorded for ARC, and in 1939, a more productive session for BLUEBIRD. In the meantime, they had written a fiddle tune called first "South Florida Blues," later renamed "Orange Blossom Special." Their 1939 Bluebird recording was one of the first in a long line of recordings of the piece—a song that became one of the most played fiddle tunes in modern history.

Ervin Rouse also composed a number of popular pieces, including the mother song "Sweeter Than the Flowers," a hit for MOON MULLICAN (1947), and the bluegrass favorite "Some Old Day" (1936).   —Charles Wolfe

Brent Rowan
b. Waxahachie, Texas, May 28, 1956

As the first Nashville studio guitarist to introduce electronic rack-mount signal-processing gear, Brent Rowan fundamentally changed the recorded sound of country music. Beginning in the mid-1980s his smooth, pop guitar tones on dozens of major hits played a key part in country's massive crossover to pop audiences. Among studio colleagues he's known as "the guy who brought L.A. to Nashville."

After touring for several years with gospel outfits and briefly with GRANDPA JONES, Rowan was only twenty-three years old in 1980 when he cut his first master session, JOHN CONLEE's "Friday Night Blues." Still, his catchy guitar hook helped make it a #1 hit and launched a studio career that averages more than 600 sessions annually.

"The key to my job is interpretation of lyrics," he says. "We're trying to create moods that help songs sell. My personal goal within the ensemble is to create a guitar part so appropriate and important to the record that when somebody covers that tune, they have to play the same licks. You can play the greatest guitar lick in the world, but if it's not appropriate to the song, it doesn't work."

Rowan is a master of taste, restraint, and versatility, and his contributions have garnered one ACM Guitarist of the Year Award (1989) and three CMA Musician of the Year nominations.   —Jon Sievert

Peter Rowan
b. Boston, Massachusetts, July 4, 1942

Peter Hamilton Rowan has long explored traditional, ethnic-based music of the United States and the world. Born into a musical family, he mastered guitar early on and soon learned the mandolin as well. In high school he performed in a rock & roll band, the Cupids, in the New England area.

In 1963 Rowan left Colgate University to pursue music full-time, working folk and bluegrass clubs in the Boston area with JIM ROONEY and banjo innovator BILL KEITH (among others), who intensified Rowan's interest in bluegrass. From 1964 to 1967 Rowan was lead singer-guitarist for bluegrass progenitor BILL MONROE and helped win young, urban converts to the music's cause. Next, with mandolin virtuoso DAVID GRISMAN, Rowan formed Earth Opera, whose drums and horns contrasted sharply with bluegrass. In 1969 Rowan joined SeaTrain, a Bay Area

band fusing folk, rock, and jazz. In 1973 he formed Old and in the Way with Grisman, rock star Jerry Garcia of the Grateful Dead, John Kahn, and fiddler extraordinaire VASSAR CLEMENTS; in that year this group recorded a strong-selling, self-titled live album featuring Rowan's "Panama Red."

Since the mid-1970s the philosophical Rowan has continued to embrace many musical traditions—including bluegrass, blues, Native American, Celtic, Afro-Cuban, and Latin—recording solo and group albums with his brothers Christopher and Lorin, Tex-Mex accordion ace FLACO JIMENEZ, and the NASHVILLE BLUE GRASS BAND, with whom he was a 1988 Grammy finalist for Best Bluegrass Album (*New Moon Rising*, SUGAR HILL). In the mid-1980s Rowan lived in Nashville and wrote songs for country artists such as RICKY SKAGGS and GEORGE STRAIT. Among Rowan's many recent Sugar Hill albums, all showcasing Rowan's songs, are the multiethnic *Awake Me in a New World* (1993), *Dust Bowl Children* (1989)—a compilation reminiscent of Woody Guthrie—and the Grammy-nominated *Bluegrass Boy* (1996), a tribute to Bill Monroe.   —John Rumble

REPRESENTATIVE RECORDINGS
Awake Me in a New World (Sugar Hill, 1993); *Bluegrass Boy* (Sugar Hill, 1996)

Billy Joe Royal
b. Valdosta, Georgia, April 3, 1942

Billy Joe Royal achieved pop success long before his foray into country music, as "Down in the Boondocks" and "Cherry Hill Park" took him to the high reaches of music popularity during the 1960s. But when pop success slid away, Royal migrated to the country music realm, and without significantly changing his style he enjoyed a career resurgence with such Top Ten country hits as "Burned Like a Rocket" (1985–86).

Royal sang on a hometown radio show when he was eleven. Later he joined such budding stars as RAY STEVENS, FREDDY WELLER, JOE SOUTH, and JERRY REED on the *Georgia Jubilee* show broadcast out of Atlanta. Royal's stylistic diversity was further enhanced when he performed at a Savannah, Georgia, nightclub. "They would book both r&b and country acts, and one week we'd be working with RAY PRICE and the next week we'd be working with Sam Cooke," he recalled. "It gave me a chance to watch and listen and learn from all types of singers—the greatest education in the world for a young guy just starting out."

A break came when Royal was working at a club in Cincinnati. Joe South called, pitching a song he had written called "Down in the Boondocks." Royal cut it in an Atlanta school building converted into a three-track studio, with a septic tank used as an echo chamber. Publisher BILL LOWERY took the demo to COLUMBIA RECORDS, where Royal was signed and the single released in 1965. Other hits followed, and Royal hit the touring circuit.

Royal moved back to Georgia in 1980 as his pop music career was running out of steam. Sensing a country feel to his music, he started visiting Nashville, looking for a country song. He found "Burned Like a Rocket," and after being rejected by several record labels, he landed with ATLANTIC RECORDS. The #10 song ignited a string of fifteen country chart records for Royal, including the #2 hits "Tell It Like It Is" and "Till I Can't Take It Anymore." In 1998 Royal signed with Intersound Records, and at this writing the company expected to release his next album in the summer of that year.

—*Gerry Wood*

REPRESENTATIVE RECORDINGS

Down in the Boondocks (Columbia, 1965); *Billy Joe Royal Greatest Hits* (Atlantic, 1991)

Royalties

Writers of country songs derive income mainly from two types of royalties: mechanical royalties from the sale of records; and performance royalties, for most broadcast and concert use of their songs.

Mechanical royalties, the monies paid by record companies for the right to use songs on their recordings, are based on the statutory rate, set by Congress under the latest (1976) Copyright Act. From 1973 to 1993, this rate was adjusted by a Copyright Royalty Tribunal. Since that time, Congress has adjusted the rate, most recently (early 1998) to 7.1 cents for songs under five minutes in length (which practically all country songs are). This royalty covers retail sales through normal distribution channels: songwriters are often asked to take a "rate" (i.e., a rate below the statutory rate) for songs licensed to budget-line or compilation albums, and, of course, they receive no royalties on free goods (promo copies) or store returns. Artists' royalties on record sales are, of course, a separate matter entirely, preset in the contract an artist signs with his record company but subject to no regulation whatsoever.

Although the Nashville-based Copyright Management Inc. (CMI) provides similar services, the New York–based Harry Fox Agency (HFA) is the company most music publishers in the United States use to issue their mechanical licenses to the record companies. Fox acts as the publisher's agent, not only issuing the licenses but also making sure that the users pay, and then accounting for those funds to the publisher. The publisher then pays their songwriters, usually on a semiannual basis. For their work, the Harry Fox Agency keeps 4.5 percent of funds collected. HFA also issues synchronization licenses for publishers (see MUSIC PUBLISHING).

Performance royalties, paid to publishers and songwriters for broadcast and other public performances of their songs (nightclub, concert, elevators, etc.), are set, monitored, and collected for publishers and writers via blanket license fees. Music users pay these fees through the performing rights societies. In the United States the three main societies are ASCAP, BMI, and SESAC. Publishers affiliate with one of these, which then collects performance monies for all their songs nationwide. Writers, too, must affiliate with one (and only one) of these societies: when they do so, performance royalties for their songs come directly from the society to them, bypassing the publisher.

ASCAP and BMI (by far the largest—SESAC, privately owned and for-profit, has only about 1 to 3 percent of the market) are nonprofit corporations, so all monies they collect, after meeting their own expenses, are paid out to their writers and publishers. The amounts are based on complex radio/TV logging procedures; publisher size; and, with ASCAP especially, publisher seniority. BMI pays bonuses for oft-played songs. Both pay performance royalties quarterly, usually a year behind actual performances. Interestingly, U.S. movies do not pay performance royalties—a partial explanation of why their in-perpetuity synch rights for songs are so costly.

Now to put some numbers to this heretofore abstract discussion. Although songwriters' contracts differ, recent informed published estimates of writer earnings on a #1 country hit came in at $25,000 in mechanical royalties and five times that, or $125,000, in performance royalties. Needless to say, the picture wasn't always this rosy: These figures, even for #1s, are historically high. Until the 1950s those few companies that published country songs at all paid low or nonexistent royalties, so certain were they of their ability to exploit or hoodwink their hillbilly talent. Even when BMI came along as competition for ASCAP and instituted an "open-door policy" for what were referred to at the time as "hillbilly" and "race" (blues) writers and publishers, performance royalties stayed comparatively low for years because so very few radio stations played country records or gave prime airtime to their in-studio country talent. On the mechanical royalty front, record companies winked at their producers' moonlighting as song publishers because it kept both salaries and royalty rates low; since the same men would usually get both, the artists and writers were often cut out.

Several factors worked to heighten the level of honesty in the publishing business and to make royalties a more significant part of the performer's income. One was direct confrontation by more sophisticated, astute writers/singers who realized in the days of those first big crossover hits (such as "Tennessee Waltz") how much potential income they were losing. Stories still circulate from those "good old days when times were bad," to borrow DOLLY PARTON's phrase, of SLIM WILLET confronting BILL McCALL of FOUR STAR RECORDS (the infamous "W. S. Stevenson" of Four Star Music as well) with a gun and marching him to the nearest bank for an overdue royalty check on the proceeds of "Don't Let the Stars Get in Your Eyes." JERRY LEE LEWIS, when asked, "You sold 2 million with 'Great Balls of Fire,' didn't you?" replied, "Yeah, and Sam [Phillips] even paid me for one of them."

Another factor was simply the growth of competition. The concentration of so many new, competing publishers in Nashville (ACUFF-ROSE, TREE, CEDARWOOD, Moss-Rose) professionalized the country songwriting business in many ways. For example, a new standard of honesty and fair play to writers came about: Not treated well by one publisher, a writer now had more recourse to take his or her songs elsewhere.

—*Ronnie Pugh*

Johnny Russell
b. Sunflower County, Mississippi, January 23, 1940

Johnny Russell is one of the biggest talents in country music—not only in girth, but also in vocal style, songwriting, humor, and stage presence.

By the time twelve-year-old Johnny Bright Russell's family moved to California, he was already thinking about a performing career. Influenced by the likes of ERNEST TUBB and LEFTY FRIZZELL, Russell spent his teen years winning talent contests. By the late 1950s he was making records for the small Radio label. One of the songs he had written and recorded was "In a Mansion Stands My Love." CHET ATKINS heard it and passed it to JIM REEVES, whose recording became the flip side of the 1960 #1 hit "He'll Have to Go."

Russell plodded along during the early sixties, recording for ABC Records with little success. Then, in 1963, BUCK OWENS recorded his song "Act Naturally" (co-written with Voni Morrison), and the industry began to take notice. Russell moved to Nashville and obtained a job with the WILBURN BROTHERS' publishing company. He soon had songs recorded by the Wilburn Brothers, Patti Page, LORETTA LYNN, and GEORGE HAMILTON IV. Even the Beatles recorded "Act Naturally," in 1965.

Russell signed a recording contract with RCA RECORDS in 1971, and his first Top Twenty hit came two years later, with "Catfish John" (#12, 1973). He had his biggest hit that same year singing the blue-collar anthem "Rednecks, White Socks and Blue Ribbon Beer" (#4). He remained with RCA through 1977, then moved to MERCURY (1978–81) and 16th Avenue Records (1987). Russell joined the GRAND OLE OPRY in 1985 and began appearing as a regular performer on *HEE HAW*. His other songwriting successes include "Making Plans" (PORTER WAGONER & DOLLY PARTON, 1980), "You'll Be Back (Every Night in My Dreams)" (STATLER BROTHERS, 1982), and "Let's Fall to Pieces Together" (GEORGE STRAIT, 1984). —*Don Roy*

REPRESENTATIVE RECORDING

Greatest Hits (Dominion, 1993)

Leon Russell
b. Lawton, Oklahoma, April 2, 1941

The singer-pianist Leon Russell first made his mark as musical director of Joe Cocker's 1970 Mad Dogs and Englishmen tour and as a star of George Harrison's 1971 Concert for Bangladesh. Russell, though, was raised in Oklahoma on honky-tonk and rockabilly, and he periodically returned to those roots.

Hank Wilson (a.k.a. Leon Russell) was playing Tulsa nightclubs with David Gates and J. J. Cale at fourteen, touring with JERRY LEE LEWIS at eighteen, and playing Los Angeles sessions at twenty-two. Russell played on Phil Spector's hits with the Crystals, the Ronettes, the Righteous Brothers, and Tina Turner; he played on the BYRDS' "Mr. Tambourine Man"; and he co-wrote, arranged, and played on most of Gary Lewis's hits. He also formed the Asylum Choir, a duo with Mark Benno, in 1968 and released two critically acclaimed if poor-selling albums. In 1969 Russell formed Shelter Records with former A&M producer Denny Cordell.

In 1971 Russell's self-titled debut solo album was released. It wasn't a big hit, but it included such enduring songs as "Delta Lady" and "A Song for You," both written for Rita Coolidge, KRIS KRISTOFFERSON's future wife. Coolidge toured with Russell and often sang (with Bonnie Bramlett) his composition "Superstar," a 1971 #2 hit for the Carpenters. In that same year he released *Leon Russell and the Shelter People*, which hit #17 on *Billboard*'s pop charts. His third studio album, 1972's *Carney*, went to #2 and yielded the #11 single "Tight Rope." *Carney* also included Russell's "This Masquerade," a Top Ten 1976 hit for George Benson.

In 1973 Russell returned to the country music he loved (and his birth name) with an album called *Hank Wilson's Back*, featuring a cover photo of Russell's back. Recorded with a mix of Nashville session players and Oklahoma pals, it featured raucous, rockabilly arrangements of country standards earlier recorded by the likes of GEORGE JONES and HANK WILLIAMS. Russell's versions of FLATT & SCRUGGS's "Rollin' in My Sweet Baby's Arms" and HANK THOMPSON's "Six Pack To Go" became minor country hits. Russell married his back-up singer Mary McCreary at WILLIE NELSON's house in 1974 and later recorded two

duet albums with her. Russell and Nelson toured together in 1978–79, and their 1979 double-album, *One for the Road*, yielded the #1 country hit "Heartbreak Hotel," a remake of the ELVIS PRESLEY classic.

In 1981 Russell hooked up with the NEW GRASS REVIVAL, the leading progressive-bluegrass band of the time, for *Leon Russell & New Grass Revival: The Live Album*, which mixed Russell's pounding piano and the stringband's picking on country standards and rock oldies. Russell's Hank Wilson persona was resurrected for another country album, 1984's *Volume II*. He spent most of the late eighties running his Paradise Video studio, but in 1992 he released *Anything Can Happen*, co-produced by Bruce Hornsby for Virgin Records. —*Geoffrey Himes*

REPRESENTATIVE RECORDINGS

Hank Wilson's Back (Paradise, 1973); *Leon Russell & New Grass Revival: The Live Album* (Paradise, 1981)

The Ryman Auditorium
established May 12, 1892

Known worldwide as the Mother Church of Country Music, Nashville's Ryman Auditorium was originally named the Union Gospel Tabernacle. It was built by Captain Thomas G. Ryman (1841–1904), the Nashville-based owner of a riverboat fleet, who was inspired by Methodist evangelist Sam Jones to build the red brick hall on Fifth Avenue, just north of Broadway. The building opened for religious services and other public events on May 12, 1892; in 1897 a second-floor gallery was added to accommodate a reunion of Confederate veterans, bringing the seating capacity to 2,579. After Ryman died, the structure was renamed in his honor.

Early in the twentieth century, local citizens formed an association to sponsor New York's Metropolitan Opera, the Chicago Symphony, and similar ensembles. Over the years, the building's magnificent acoustics showcased dozens of top classical and popular artists, including soprano Marian Anderson, tenor Enrico Caruso, cowboy idol GENE AUTRY, Nashville's Fisk Jubilee Singers, and legendary entertainer Bob Hope.

The Ryman hosted country music as early as 1925, with local pickers providing entertainment for police benefit shows. The GRAND OLE OPRY broadcast at least one show

Ryman Auditorium

from the hall in 1942, but did not begin regular broadcasts there until June 5, 1943. At the time, the program was staged at the Tennessee War Memorial Auditorium, but state authorities objected to fans sticking chewing gum under the seats. In desperation, WSM manager HARRY STONE persuaded longtime Ryman manager Lula Naff to rent the hall for Saturday night Opry shows.

During the succeeding twenty years, numerous country greats made their Opry debuts there, including future Hall of Fame members RED FOLEY, HANK WILLIAMS, KITTY WELLS, MARTY ROBBINS, and LITTLE JIMMY DICKENS. Noncountry concerts continued as well, and record producers used the building for sessions by country stars and big bands led by Ray Anthony and Woody Herman. Opry founder GEORGE D. HAY routinely called the Ryman "The Grand Ole Opry House," but the Nashville-based National Life and Accident Insurance Company—which owned WSM—officially endorsed this moniker after purchasing the building from the city of Nashville on September 12, 1963, for a reported $200,000.

In 1968, with crowds growing and estimated repair costs mounting, National Life and WSM executives announced plans to build a new Opry House as the centerpiece for an OPRYLAND theme park north of town. In 1971, a year before the park opened, these officials stated their intention to tear down the Ryman and use its bricks in a new Opryland chapel. Preservationists and entertainers nationwide protested, and the building stood. The Opry's last Ryman show took place on Friday, March 15, 1974, followed by the Reverend Jimmy Snow's *Grand Ole Gospel* program, which concluded with regulars and guests singing the gospel standard "Will the Circle Be Unbroken." The following Saturday saw the first Opry broadcast from the new Opry House at Opryland.

Although the Ryman remained a tourist destination, the facility lay virtually dormant as a concert hall for two decades, largely because it did not meet city fire codes. Movie producers did use it to film scenes for *Nashville* (1975), *Coal Miner's Daughter* (1980), *and Sweet Dreams* (1985), and EMMYLOU HARRIS used the facility to record her critically acclaimed *At the Ryman* album (Reprise, 1992) between April 30 and May 2, 1991, with a select audience and TNN on hand.

After Labor Day weekend in 1993 the building closed, and an $8.5 million renovation project began under GAYLORD ENTERTAINMENT, which had purchased Opryland and related properties in 1983. A new lobby was created, eventually featuring bronze statues of ROY ACUFF and MINNIE PEARL and an interactive video history of the site. On June 4, 1994, the facility officially reopened, with Garrison Keillor hosting a special broadcast of his long-running *A Prairie Home Companion* program before a packed house. That summer, longtime Opry sponsor MARTHA WHITE FLOUR offered its first series of bluegrass shows. Since then, the Ryman has witnessed numerous TNN broadcasts, the popular stage productions *Lost Highway* (on the life of Hank Williams) and *Always . . . Patsy Cline,* as well as concerts by the likes of country legend MERLE HAGGARD and rock stars BOB DYLAN, Bruce Springsteen, and Sheryl Crow.

—*John Rumble*

The Talking Machine:
How Records Shaped Country Music

Colin Escott

Thomas Edison was a visionary who couldn't see far enough. In 1877 he invented the phonograph, but in an article for the *North American Review* the following year, he made it clear that he saw its future in dictation, together with the teaching of elocution, recording the last words of dying persons, and phonographic books for the blind. He even foresaw the phonograph attached to another of his inventions, the telephone, so that calls could be recorded, but he could see no farther than "one-off" recordings on cylinders. The idea of mass-producing recordings didn't occur to him, and it would take another ten years and another inventor, Émile Berliner, to show that it could be done. Berliner also pioneered the flat disc and the "gramophone," with its turntable. So if Edison was the father of recording, Berliner was the father of the record business.

Before World War I, talking machines were the preserve of the urban and the rich. In 1906 the Victor Talking Machine Company (in which Berliner was a partner) introduced its Victrola, retailing at two hundred dollars. Its premium Red Seal records sold for as much as seven dollars each. There were cheaper machines and cheaper records, but they were still out of the reach of most people. That changed swiftly. We don't have sales broken down by market and demographics, but we know that record player sales increased from 550,000 in 1914 to 2 million in 1919. In 1921, record production topped 100 million units, but it fell sharply thereafter as radio stations proliferated. The wider availability of record players, combined with the need to seek out new niche markets in the face of declining sales, sent record companies in search of blues and country performers (as well as other forms of ethnic music) in the hinterlands. That they recorded what we would now call country music in the 1920s shows that the talking machine had penetrated southern rural areas by then.

In a 1938 interview with Kyle Crichton from *Collier's,* A&R man RALPH PEER recalled his first Atlanta field session with FIDDLIN' JOHN CARSON some fifteen years earlier. Even allowing for exaggeration, it showed the pent-up demand for southern rural music. "We didn't even put a serial number on the record," Peer said, referring to "Little Old Log Cabin in the Lane." "[We thought] that when the local dealer got his supply that would be the end of it. We sent him 1,000 records. . . . That night he called New York and ordered 5,000 more by express and 10,000 by freight. When the sales got up to 500,000 we were so ashamed we had Fiddlin' John come up to New York and do a rerecording." The field trip soon became a necessary part of an A&R man's job, and in 1927, Peer—formerly with OKEH, now with Victor—discovered JIMMIE RODGERS and the CARTER FAMILY during famous sessions in BRISTOL, TENNESSEE.

Part of the importance of country records from the 1920s is that they more or less tell us what the first A&R men found when they went in search of country music. Some of the recorded performances were almost certainly more stilted than they would have been in an informal setting and were definitely edited for length and taste. The old British murder ballad "The Wexford Girl," for example, is at least fifteen verses long, and the reason for the murder is implicit ("For the damsel came to me and said 'By you I am with child/I hope dear John you'll marry me for you have me defil'd'"). It was recorded frequently in the United States from 1924 onward as "The Knoxville Girl" or "The Waco Girl," usually with six verses, none of which so much as hint at the reason for the crime. Still, for all their drawbacks, the interwar recordings enable us to experience country music as a variety of discrete regional musics that often had very little in common with one another. As late as 1944, Columbia A&R man ARTHUR SATHERLEY was telling *The Saturday Evening Post*, "I would never think of hiring a Mississippi boy to play in a Texas band. Any Texan would know right off it was wrong." The irony of the record business is that it preserved these regional musics even as it was helping to destroy them.

Arthur Satherley was Columbia's "folk" A&R man, which meant that he not only recorded all the different musics that we would call early forms of country music, but also blues, Cajun, Mexican, and even Québecois music. His circuit took him from his home in Los Angeles to Dallas, Tulsa, San Antonio, New Orleans, Shreveport, and Nashville. Yet, just fifteen years after he spoke to *The Saturday Evening Post*, several developments had overtaken Satherley's world. A country mainstream had evolved from the many different strains of folk and western music, and its ballooning sales distinguished it from all other folk musics. *Billboard* tacitly recognized as much when its charts dropped the term "folk music" in 1949, replacing it with a neologism, "country & western." It was entirely fitting that the "folk music" tag was dropped because country music no longer was folk music; it was a commercial discipline. And, as a country mainstream developed, it quickly became very feasible for a Mississippi boy to play with a Texas band.

Yet another development overtook Satherley's world: The new country music business centered itself on Nashville. Field recordings became things of the past. As late as 1946, a poll of A&R men found that Chicago had the highest concentration of country musicians, and the A&R men considered it the hub of the business. Recordings were made there, and in Dallas, Cincinnati, Los Angeles, and other centers, but by the mid-fifties RCA, COLUMBIA, and DECCA were recording almost all of their country sessions in Nashville.

The development of a country mainstream went hand in hand with the rise of Nashville and the postwar growth of the country record business. "Country and western" embraced old-time fiddling and stringband music, western swing, cowboy music, ERNEST TUBB's honky-tonk music, EDDY ARNOLD's country-pop, ROY ACUFF's hillbilly music, brother duets, and sacred quartets. Ten years later, you could still hear all the different strains that went to make up country music, but now there was a mainstream.

The fact that the nascent country music business centered itself on Nashville played a role in the growth of a mainstream: Because of the GRAND OLE OPRY, most of the major artists were together in one place with a shared pool of session men, and the music industry's infrastructure (music publishers, bookers, etc.) gathered around them. Records helped to forge a mainstream, too. They disseminated music more effectively than 50,000-watt radio stations or any amount of social migration. It was one thing to hear Roy Acuff on the Saturday night Opry; it was quite another to have his records and learn every nuance. Records were so effective at disseminating music that a younger performer such as CARL SMITH, who came from Roy Acuff's hometown, not only had a little Acuff in his style, but also a little Eddy Arnold, HANK WILLIAMS, and TOMMY DUNCAN. Smith carried drums, much like a western dance band, sang the occasional cowboy song, and cut gospel records with the Carter Family. Records probably accounted for the greater part of his musical education.

At the same time, records upped the ante for performers. It was no longer sufficient to be the best fiddler or singer for miles around; now there were records with tangible evidence of someone doing it better—often much better. Records were not only humbling but also a learning tool. They made it possible for ARTHUR SMITH, ZEB AND ZEKE TURNER, and HANK GARLAND to grow up in rural South Carolina and to study Django Reinhardt and Eddie Lang. Records cross-pollinated musics with a speed that was unthinkable before their arrival.

Records came to assume an economic importance as well. Early sales figures are often hard to come by, but it's probably safe to say that the best-selling country record prior to World War II was VERNON DALHART's "Wreck of the Old 97"/"The Prisoner's Song," which sold just over 1 million copies. Jimmie Rodgers's first "Blue Yodel (T for Texas)" was his best-seller, topping out at just over 500,000. Charles Wolfe's research reveals that the Carter Family's "Wildwood Flower" sold about 100,000, as did the DELMORE BROTHERS' "Brown's Ferry Blues," but these were anomalies for hillbilly music in the 1920s and 1930s. More typical were the sales of UNCLE JIMMY THOMPSON's first record, "Karo"/ "Billy Wilson" for Columbia in 1926, which totaled just 9,000 copies, despite his presence on the Grand Ole Opry. And an unknown act in country's early days might sell very little at all. For instance, the Delmores' first record release, which came in 1931 in the depths of the Depression and two years before they joined the Opry, amounted to only 511 copies.

Such low sales figures made it difficult for most country performers to put much stock in record making prior to World War II. Moreover, payment for recording was often strictly in the form of a flat fee, ranging usually from fifteen dollars to fifty dollars per recorded side. Royalties, when paid at all, usually amounted to a half cent per side. At these rates, few country artists earned more than one hundred dollars for any release.

After World War II, the picture began to change. Record sales were no longer incidental to a country musician's career. Earlier, the goal of most country artists had been to get to a major market, such as Dallas, Chicago, or Cincinnati, then work that market for years. Records were little more than self-promotional tools. Now records became a viable source of income, especially after radio was increasingly given over to playing records as opposed to live performances. A landmark decision by the U.S. Court of Appeals in 1940 ruled once and for all that radio stations could play records on the air for free, and pioneering country disc jockeys, like Nelson King at WLW in Cincinnati, did much to elevate the importance of the record.

The old attitude toward records was summed up by the East Texas country singer FRANKIE MILLER in a conversation with researcher Kevin Coffey: "It never really bothered me that much that I didn't get anything for [my] records," he said. "For one thing, I just wanted to have a record out. I would have paid them. And there wasn't any real money in records then. The money was in personal appearances, and having a record out—especially a hit record—boosted crowds, upped your asking price, but you didn't really expect to make anything off the records themselves." Miller was talking about the early fifties, when the situation was already changing. If he had read *Billboard* in September 1947, he would have seen that Ernest Tubb's royalties for the first six months of the year had topped $50,000. In February the following year, *Billboard* reported that Eddy Arnold's 1947 sales had topped 2.7 million records, amounting to more than $70,000 in royalties. Additionally, many of the top stars wrote or acquired a share in the songs they recorded, thereby compounding their earnings.

Most of these sales were to JUKEBOXES. By 1950 there were 400,000 jukeboxes serviced by 5,500 jukebox operators. The ops, as they were called in the music business, bought an average of 150 records a week while the average consumer was still buying fewer than ten a year. WESLEY ROSE is on record as saying that if one of Hank Williams's records sold 250,000 copies, the ops accounted for 150,000 of those sales. Poor distribution to rural areas was partly to blame, and this, incidentally, was a problem that Ernest Tubb boldly aimed to solve when he launched the Ernest Tubb Record Shop in 1947, which offered a mail-order service reaching all areas of the United States (and guaranteed to replace—free of charge—any records damaged in shipping). Meanwhile, the record companies were trying harder to develop a network of branches and subdistributors that would get records to outlets where potential customers could find them.

The profits to be had from records were increasingly on the minds of both musicians and A&R men. If you recorded, there was now an onus on you to compete with everyone else in the marketplace. To do this, you had to stop thinking locally and start thinking nationally. To go coast-to-coast, you needed a mainstream sound. Artists who could only achieve local sales with regional styles were increasingly likely to get shown the door by the major record labels. *Billboard*'s introduction of charts in 1944 added yet another competitive edge and only served to emphasize records that appealed to the broadest possible audience.

Country music, once based in the oral and mostly noncommercial traditions of folk music, was now a commodity, and records hastened its commodification. In a rural setting, country music had been played on the porch, at outdoor gatherings, or in small community centers. Quite suddenly, records made old songs into potential copyrights, they made the band at the local barn dance into potential recording stars, and they drew a line between performers and their audiences. At one time it wasn't unthinkable for everyone to join in or at least feel a part of the performance. That was no longer the case. What had once been a social experience was now a solitary one.

As country music became an integral part of the popular music mix, records came to determine touring schedules, position on a showbill, and the price an artist could charge for shows. It's now almost impossible to sustain a career without a recording contract. If a singer came to Nashville in 1946, it was with the goal of getting on the Grand Ole Opry; fifty years later, the goal was to break into one of the corporate recording monoliths on Music Row. Records now hold the key to everything.

Seventy-eights gave way to 45s and LPs, which have in turn been supplanted by the compact disc. Strangely, though, the country recording business remains locked in one curious anachronism: song length. From the beginning, pop and country 78s timed out at about three minutes, because that was all the discs would allow. Long-playing records were introduced in 1948, and they had a gradual effect on the way most forms of popular music were composed and played. It became possible for songs or suites of songs to last as long as twenty minutes per side. Adult popular music remained singles-driven into the fifties, rock & roll was singles-driven until the mid- to late sixties, but country music remained singles-driven into the era when singles as such had almost ceased to exist. "You just cut a little record and threw it out there" was the way JERRY KENNEDY, president of MERCURY RECORDS, Nashville, during the seventies, characterized the business. Kennedy had started producing in the early sixties and regarded albums as a nuisance at first. "If you cut a hit, it was like a bummer," he said, "because you'd have to find songs enough for an album. The sales weren't there. Six, eight, nine thousand copies wasn't bad."

Even today when six, eight, or nine *hundred* thousand copies isn't bad, the focus is still on assembling an album that contains at least two and ideally three, four, or five songs that can be "pulled" as singles for radio, although singles themselves have become a negligible factor in the sales mix. More than a decade after CDs were introduced, bringing with them a maximum playing time of eighty minutes, country CDs are rarely longer than the old forty-minute LP time limit because the focus is still on singles-length songs.

By the time CDs were introduced in the early 1980s, recording itself had improved dramatically, and the nature of recording was beginning to challenge the very notion of what constituted a performance. Fiddlin' John Carson recorded into an acoustical horn, and the signal (or some of it, anyway) was encrypted onto a wax disc. Human hearing can pick up a range of 10 octaves from 16 to 16,000 cycles per second or Hertz. Acoustic recordings picked up range of roughly 164Hz to 2kHz (2 kilohertz, or 2,000 cycles per second). Electrical recording, widely introduced in 1925, brought with it a range of 30Hz to 8kHz. Engineers at British Decca perfected full-frequency range recording during World War II to detect the difference between Allied and German submarine engines. At the same time, microphone technology improved to the point that sheer lungpower was no longer a prerequisite for singers. Rudy Vallee and Bing Crosby were the first to perfect an intimate singing style. In country music, LEFTY FRIZZELL was probably the first to develop a style in which nuance replaced declamation and for which the microphone was essential.

Recordings were still made onto discs until the widespread introduction of audiotape in 1950. Discs meant that if a performance went off the rails, it was started afresh. Tape led inexorably to splicing, editing, and overdubbing. Multitrack tape was introduced in the mid-1950s, and by the mid-1990s primitive three-track tape had gradually evolved and expanded to four tracks to eight- to sixteen- to thirty-two- to sixty-four-track digital. Before multitrack, a record enshrined a performance. The singer sang; the band played. Everyone hoped that the best vocal performance wouldn't be marred by a flubbed note from the band, or vice versa. Now sixty or more tracks can be recorded separately, and a four-minute recording can be pieced together from them. There need not be an ensemble performance as such. Bad notes can be "repaired"; a flat vocal note can be brought up on key. Technical perfection is easily realizable. The singer and the musicians tend to emerge from a session with a "bed track" (usually the rhythmic skeleton of a song), a "scratch" (or guide) vocal, and weeks of overdubs ahead of them to perfect the final product. The pooling of ideas on the session, once a prized feature of Nashville recordings, hasn't altogether disappeared, but it's rare for a singer and all the musicians to be in the studio at the same time and walk out with a finished recording.

While it's possible to draw a tortuous line from Fiddlin' John to today's country stars, it's tempting to see the earlier forms of country music as somehow purer and less commercial. If records hastened the commercialism of country music, it was a development that didn't need much encouragement. In 1927, when Ralph Peer went to BRISTOL,

Tennessee, and made the first recordings with the Carter Family and Jimmie Rodgers, he didn't get an overwhelming response to his request for performers to audition. Then, as researcher Charles Wolfe discovered, Peer happened to mention that featured performers got one hundred dollars a day, and sidemen received twenty-five dollars. Suddenly he was deluged with requests to audition. And lo! the country record business was born.

YANKEE, GO HOME
(Harlan Howard)
WYNN STEWART and JAN HOWARD
48014

Junior Samples

b. Cumming, Georgia, August 10, 1926; d. November 13, 1983

With only a third-grade education, rotund rural comic Junior Samples became a fixture in country fans' living rooms starting in 1969, as a regular in the colorful world of *HEE HAW*, a popular network and syndicated TV series. Obviously reading from cue cards, Alvin Samples Jr. would speak in a slow southern drawl, often stumbling on his lines for effect. His costume consisted of bibbed overalls, an open-necked shirt with rolled-up sleeves, and boondockers. In a regularly scheduled skit, he would be featured with such cast members as GRANDPA JONES, KENNY PRICE, and an old hound dog—a stereotypical, shiftless hillbilly clan.

Earlier, during the summer of 1967, the nonmusical Samples had a novelty comedy record on the Chart label, "The World's Biggest Whopper" (featuring interviewer Jim Morrison), which garnered enough airplay to spend four weeks on *Billboard*'s country charts. Samples also teamed with comedian ARCHIE CAMPBELL for *Bull Session at Bull's Gap,* a 1968 Chart Records comedy album deriving its name from Campbell's hometown.

Samples's used-car salesman segment on *Hee Haw* always ended with his displaying a sign citing the fictional phone number BR549. The contemporary country band BR5-49 decided it was good enough to borrow for their group name.   —*Walt Trott*

REPRESENTATIVE RECORDINGS

The World of Junior Samples (Chart Records, 1967)*; The Best of Junior Samples* (Chart Records, 1971)

Billy Sanford

b. Natchitoches, Louisiana, January 9, 1940

For more than thirty years, session guitarist William R. Sanford Jr. played on hit country recordings such as "Easy Loving" (1971) and "He Stopped Loving Her Today" (1980), each a CMA Song of the Year two years successively. He also played on such pop hits as ROY ORBISON's "Oh, Pretty Woman" (1964) and Dave Loggins's "Please Come to Boston" (1974).

Self-taught, Sanford started playing as a teenager in Texas nightclubs, then landed a stint as a staff musician on Shreveport's *LOUISIANA HAYRIDE* from 1958 to 1959. Later he played bass in BOB LUMAN's rockabilly road band before Luman invited him to record in Nashville in 1962. After

relocating there in February 1964, Sanford joined Orbison's road ban, the Candy Men, recording pop singles such as "Goodnight" and "You're My Girl."

Sanford also played on ELVIS PRESLEY's Graceland recordings in 1976 and for TV jingles. More recently, Sanford played acoustic and electric guitar on KEITH WHITLEY's 1989 #1 hit "I'm No Stranger to the Rain." Semiretired as of this writing, Sanford played on SAMMY KERSHAW's 1995 recording "What Am I Gonna Do with Her Tattoo."
                                                    —*Walt Trott*

Sarie and Sally

Edna "Sarie" Wilson b. July 15, 1896; d. June 27, 1994
Margaret "Sally" Waters b. Chattanooga, Tennessee, May 2, 1903; d. November 2, 1967

Sarie and Sally were two of the earliest professional comedians on the GRAND OLE OPRY, starring there between 1934 and 1939. The team portrayed two mountain women whose style and repartee caused many fans to see them as a female Lum and Abner, and which anticipated the later comedy of MINNIE PEARL. The creative force behind the act was Edna Wilson (Sarie), born near Chattanooga in 1896. After creating the act in Florida, she and her younger sister, Margaret Waters, auditioned for WSM's daytime schedule in 1934 and won a daily fifteen-minute show that was part rural soap opera, part vaudeville dialogue—but no music. In January 1935 the pair also began appearing on the Opry, attracting sacks of fan mail. Soon they were on the Opry nearly every week and touring with the Dixieliners, PEE WEE KING, and even a young ROY ACUFF. In 1939, after they left the show, they traveled to Hollywood to appear in *In Old Monterey* with GENE AUTRY. Margaret Waters's failing health caused the team to split up in 1941, though Edna Wilson continued to work as a solo act over WSB-Atlanta and WMC-Memphis (where she created a new character, "Aunt Bunie") before returning to Nashville and retirement.   —*Charles Wolfe*

Arthur E. Satherley

b. Bristol, England, October 19, 1889; d. February 10, 1986

"He tried to do a job and he did do a job. He was the recording genius for COLUMBIA RECORDS for a good number of years. . . . [H]e was a good judge of what the market needed."

Such was one record-business pioneer's—RALPH PEER's—estimate of another: Arthur Edward "Uncle Art"

Uncle Art Satherley

Satherley. Producer, talent scout, and salesman, Satherley easily ranks among early country-music's half-dozen essential businessmen. Like his fellow pioneer Peer, he was equally important to the early recording of blues (then called "race music") in the years before World War II, as he was to the recording of early country music (then known as "hillbilly").

An Episcopal minister's son born in Bristol, England, young Satherley shared turn-of-the-century Europe's fascination with the American West. In his midtwenties, he came to the United States and went to work grading lumber for the Wisconsin Chair Company in Port Washington, Wisconsin. When Thomas Edison purchased a subsidiary of Wisconsin Chair, Satherley spent a brief period as one of the inventor's secretaries. In 1918 Satherley joined Wisconsin Chair's new record label, Paramount, first in manufacturing, then as a salesman. By the mid-1920s, after earning a reputation as an expert in the infant genres of hillbilly and race music, Satherley was spending more time scouting and recording talent than working as a salesman.

He left Paramount in 1929 for the AMERICAN RECORD CORPORATION; when COLUMBIA RECORDS bought ARC in 1938, he became Columbia's country and race music A&R chief. "What I was interested in," he would recall, "was the acceptance of the public. Does the public want it? Not what I want, or the artist wanted. Would the public want it?"

The leitmotif in Satherley's self-appraisals is a fierce pride in his empathy, despite his English rearing, with rural Americans. "I was brought up on the farm," he recalled. "I said my prayers on a sheepskin at night on a stone floor [under] a thatched roof. I have shucked wheat with my hands, and oats and barley. I have done much around the farmyard. So you see, I have understood country music from my early childhood days."

Country artists Satherley recorded include the PICKARD FAMILY, CARSON ROBISON, VERNON DALHART, the ALLEN

BROTHERS, the CALLAHAN BROTHERS, CLIFF & BILL CARLISLE, DOC ROBERTS, Asa Martin, AL DEXTER, ROY ACUFF (whom Satherley called a "pure, unadulterated country person, a pure, unadulterated country American"), BILL MONROE, TEX RITTER, RED FOLEY, GEORGE MORGAN, SPADE COOLEY, TED DAFFAN, and JOHNNY BOND (whose records were Satherley's final productions). He recorded blues artists Ma Rainey, Blind Lemon Jefferson, Alberta Hunter, Ida Cox, Big Bill Broonzy, Josh White, Leroy Carr, Memphis Minnie, and others.

Two country stars with whom Satherley worked especially closely were GENE AUTRY and BOB WILLS. Satherley was largely responsible for Autry's recording success—he produced Autry's early hit "That Silver Haired Daddy of Mine." Satherley's persistent lobbying among his movie-business acquaintances helped get the young singer started in films. Satherley also played a large role in securing Autry's cowboy image in radio. Satherley was introduced to Wills in 1935 by his assistant DON LAW (his eventual successor as Columbia Records' country A&R chief) and produced hundreds of Wills's records (and always took credit for naming the bandleader's signature tune, "San Antonio Rose"). Late in life, Wills called his departure from Satherley's stewardship—Wills left Columbia for MGM in October 1947—the worst decision of his career.

Satherley resigned from Columbia as a vice president in 1952, spent a long retirement primarily in Southern California, and died February 10, 1986. He was elected to the COUNTRY MUSIC HALL OF FAME in 1971.

"I'm the only living man who's been through this business with his hands," Satherley said in the late 1970s, "running the factories, making the records, making the formulas, finding the material, seeing that the pressing's done, selling [the records], and finding the artists. Nearly fifty years at it. And always of no fixed abode, just traveling, finding country people to make these recordings. And now considered the daddy of it all. That's what they call me, the daddy of all recordings country: country black, country white."
                                                        —*Tony Scherman*

Mark and Ann Savoy

Mark Savoy b. Eunice, Louisiana, October 1, 1941
Ann Allen Savoy b. St. Louis, Missouri, January 20, 1952

Mark and Ann Savoy, who were married in 1976, have been leaders in the perpetuation of traditional CAJUN music. Mark was born and reared in the heart of Cajun country, which he says "was saturated with old-time Cajun music." He became an accomplished musician, playing both fiddle and accordion, as well as Louisiana's most respected accordion maker. His instruments are highly prized by Cajun musicians. He has performed and recorded with many of Cajun music's greats, including the BALFA BROTHERS, D. L. MENARD, and MICHAEL DOUCET.

Ann, who grew up in Virginia, began playing guitar at age twelve and later became involved in various kinds of folk music. She also studied French, which she later taught. After their marriage, they played together, becoming popular at dances and events in Louisiana as well as much-in-demand ambassadors of traditional Cajun music on the folk music circuit. In addition to her role as musician and mother, Ann is also a scholar of Cajun music, writing numerous articles and the book *Cajun Music: A Reflection of a People.* Today the Savoys operate an accordion factory and music store in Eunice, and continue to actively record and perform locally, nationally, and internationally. —*Charlie Seemann*

Oh What a Night (Arhoolie, 1981); *The Savoy-Smith Cajun Band: Now and Then* (Arhoolie, 1996)

Sawyer Brown

Gregg Hubbard b. Orlando, Florida, October 4, 1960
Mark Miller b. Dayton, Ohio, October 25, 1958
Bobby Randall b. Midland, Michigan, September 16, 1952
Jim Scholten b. Bay City, Michigan, April 18, 1952
Joe Smyth b. Portland, Maine, September 6, 1957
Duncan Cameron b. Utica, New York, July 27, 1956

The country group Sawyer Brown has been well served by the artistic maturation process. When the band established itself nationally with the 1985 hit "Step That Step," they earned a reputation for playing "bubblegum country." Six years later, after the industry had all but left them behind, they re-emerged as an act with considerably more depth and focus.

Revolving around lead singer Mark Miller and keyboard player Gregg (Hobie) Hubbard, who met while attending the University of Central Florida, the group came together after the duo moved to Nashville in 1981. Initially known as Savannah, they took the name Sawyer Brown from a road in suburban Nashville.

In 1984 Sawyer Brown took the $100,000 first prize in the *Star Search* television show, which led to a contract with CURB RECORDS. Live, they presented a wild, colorful stage presence, with outlandish outfits and Miller's propensity for whirling and dancing (Miller was so active onstage he would require four surgeries to repair damaged knees). Buoyed by their youthful worldview and high-energy shows, they scored three straight Top Ten hits before the end of 1985.

But radio and critics cooled on the band. They managed only two more Top Ten records through the end of the decade—"This Missin' You Heart of Mine" and a remake of GEORGE JONES's classic "The Race Is On"—though they remained one of the top-drawing live bands in country music.

"The Walk" changed their reputation in 1991. Drawing on images of a sentimental-but-realistic father-son relationship, the single displayed an understanding of common-man issues not previously addressed in their "bubblegum" fare. Mixing blue-collar themes with the occasional boy-girl ditty, Sawyer Brown became consistent hitmakers in the early 1990s, weighing in with such singles as "The Dirt Road," "The Cafe on the Corner," "All These Years," and "Thank God for You." Ironically, their newfound seriousness emerged at a time when much of the industry became enamored with semi-novelty records.

The group has had only one lineup change in its history: original guitarist Bobby Randall departed in February 1991 and was replaced by former AMAZING RHYTHM ACES member Duncan Cameron. —*Tom Roland*

Greatest Hits (Curb, 1990); *Buick* (Curb, 1991); *Cafe on the Corner* (Curb, 1992)

Don Schlitz

Don Schlitz

b. Durham, North Carolina, August 29, 1952

Don Schlitz is one of the most successful country songwriters of the past two decades, with twenty-four #1 songs to his credit. The first of these was a careermaker—KENNY ROGERS's "The Gambler"—and Schlitz's later chart-toppers have included the JUDDS' "Rockin' with the Rhythm of the Rain" and MICHAEL JOHNSON's "Give Me Wings." Schlitz and his frequent co-writer PAUL OVERSTREET provided RANDY TRAVIS with Travis's first #1 hit, "On the Other Hand," as well as Travis's later blockbuster "Forever and Ever, Amen." With these and other compositions Schlitz helped set the tone for country songwriting during the 1980s NEW TRADITIONALIST era and beyond.

After briefly attending Duke University, Schlitz moved to Nashville in 1973, taking a night-shift job as a computer operator at Vanderbilt University so he could pitch his songs during the day. In 1978 Rogers recorded "The Gambler" (Schlitz had previously recorded his own version), and the Grammy-winning song changed Schlitz's life forever.

Subsequently, Schlitz scored hits for the NITTY GRITTY DIRT BAND, TANYA TUCKER, and the BELLAMY BROTHERS. "On the Other Hand" and "Forever and Ever, Amen" both earned Song of the Year Awards from the CMA and the ACM, and Schlitz was chosen ASCAP's Writer of the Year four times, from 1988 to 1991. His other credits have included KEITH WHITLEY's "When You Say Nothing at All," Travis's "Deeper Than the Holler," and Tanya Tucker's "Strong Enough to Bend."

Schlitz released an album, *Dreamers Matinee,* on CAPITOL RECORDS in 1980. He also joined four other prominent songwriters on the RCA album *Signatures* in 1988. As a writer, his success continued unabated into the 1990s. From 1989 until 1996 he had more than twenty-five country hits to his credit, including GARTH BROOKS's "Learning to Live Again" and MARK CHESNUTT's "Almost Goodbye." Co-writing sessions with MARY CHAPIN CARPENTER produced "I Feel Lucky," "He Thinks He'll Keep Her," and "I Take My Chances."   —*Beverly Keel*

David Lynn Schnaufer
b. Hearne, Texas, September 28, 1952

Soft-spoken Texan David Schnaufer has brought the Appalachian, or mountain dulcimer, to larger audiences than anyone since pioneering Kentucky folksinger Jean Ritchie. Through his session work with such stars as the JUDDS, KATHY MATTEA, JOHNNY CASH, and EMMYLOU HARRIS, his solo recordings, instructional tapes, and two award-winning videos, Schnaufer has reawakened interest in one of America's most important folk instruments.

He lived as a wandering troubadour after taking up the dulcimer in Austin, Texas, in 1973. His travels took him to Colorado, Washington, D.C., and West Virginia before he settled in Nashville in 1984. By this time he had won seven major competitions, including the National Championship title in Winfield, Kansas.

Schnaufer's solo albums and his contributions to the Smoky Mountain series of tapes marketed by Brentwood Music earned him public attention and critical raves, such as these comments by the *Nashville Scene:* "Years from now they'll remember Schnaufer as the man who did for the mountain dulcimer what LES PAUL did for the guitar."

As a founding member of the CACTUS BROTHERS, Schnaufer performed with them until early 1994, when he returned to solo work. Today he continues to tour, conduct workshops nationally, and serve as an adjunct professor at the Blair School of Music of Vanderbilt University in Nashville.   —*John Lomax*

REPRESENTATIVE RECORDINGS

Dulcimer Player Deluxe (S.F.L., 1990); *Dulcimer Sessions* (S.F.L., 1992); *The Cactus Brothers* (Liberty, 1993, out of print); *Tennessee Music Box* (Rivertime Records, 1996)

John Schneider
b. Mount Kisco, New York, April 8, 1960

John Richard Schneider came to wide prominence as Bo Duke, a rural hot-rodder and all-around hero on the popular CBS-TV *Dukes of Hazzard* series (which aired January 26, 1979–July 26, 1985), which featured Tom Wopat as Bo's brother Luke Duke and WAYLON JENNINGS as unseen narrator and theme song singer.

Scotti Bros. Records capitalized on Schneider's popularity with a Top Ten cover of ELVIS PRESLEY's "It's Now or Never" in 1981. Each release, including a dreadful remake of Presley's "Are You Lonesome Tonight," was worse than the last. Schneider was embarrassed with the lounge-Elvis role and wanted to be taken seriously as a country singer, not just exploited as a TV teen idol. He came to Nashville and became friends with JOHNNY CASH, who helped him hone his talents.

Between 1984 and 1987 Schneider established himself on MCA RECORDS as a fairly serious country singer, though still best identified as a television actor. He had a three-year run of hits that included five Top Tens and four #1 singles, his best known being "I've Been Around Enough

to Know." At the end of that string he went back to acting, screenwriting, and directing.   —*Bob Millard*

REPRESENTATIVE RECORDING

Greatest Hits (MCA, 1987)

Thom Schuyler
b. Bethlehem, Pennsylvania, June 10, 1952

Schuyler has been a solo artist, hit songwriter, member of a successful country group, and record company executive, but he is perhaps best known as composer of the songwriter anthem "16th Avenue." A 1982 Top Ten hit for LACY J. DALTON, the tune summed up the highs and lows of Music Row songwriters—"the boys who make the noise on 16th Avenue."

Schuyler had spent much of the seventies trying to make a living as a songwriter in New York City, then came to Nashville in 1977 after hearing striking new sounds on country radio. Success for this folk-tinged, lyrical songwriter came quickly, with hits such as "Hurricane" (Leon Everette, 1981), "Love Will Turn You Around" (KENNY ROGERS, 1982), and "I Don't Know Where to Start" (EDDIE RABBITT, 1982). *Brave Heart,* a 1983 solo album on CAPITOL RECORDS, hit the middle reaches of the country album charts.

In 1986 Schuyler joined songwriter friends Fred Knobloch and Paul Overstreet in the trio S-K-O, which became S-K-B with Overstreet's 1987 departure and his replacement by Craig Bickhardt. After two albums the group disbanded in 1989. Continuing to write hit songs, Schuyler also became involved with music trade organizations including the Nashville Songwriters Association International (NSAI) and the Country Music Association (CMA), where he rose to become president and chairman. In 1992 Schuyler was named head of RCA RECORDS' Nashville division, a position he held until 1994. He signed former O'KANES member Jamie O'Hara and brought WAYLON JENNINGS back to the label. With former Nashville chief JOE GALANTE's return to the city after heading the entire New York–based label from 1990 to 1994, Schuyler became vice president of A & R.   —*Thomas Goldsmith*

Schuyler-Knobloch-Overstreet/Schuyler-Knobloch-Bickhardt (*see* S-K-O/S-K-B)

Ramblin' Tommy Scott
b. Stephens County, Georgia, June 24, 1917

Born Tommy Lee Scott, Ramblin' Tommy Scott has been a singer of country music since the 1930s; he has recorded for KING RECORDS, BULLET RECORDS, FOUR STAR RECORDS, and other labels (though without hits), and has been one of the industry's busiest road performers.

A close associate through the years of CLYDE MOODY and Curly Sechler, Scott became a television pioneer, in 1946, by filming fifty-two quarter-hour shows for syndication. Briefly, he appeared on the GRAND OLE OPRY as a ventriloquist with his dummy Luke McLuke. Scott featured BLACK-FACE comedy in the early years of his touring entourage, and sometimes cowboy stars such as Tim McCoy, Johnny Mack Brown, and Sunset Carson. Scott still tours some 150 days per year from his base in Toccoa, Georgia, leading what he calls America's Last Real Medicine Show.

—Ronnie Pugh

REPRESENTATIVE RECORDINGS

Early Country Favorites (Old Homestead, 1979); *Early Radio, 1941* (Old Homestead, 1980)

Scottdale String Band

East of Atlanta, in DeKalb County, lies the town of Scottdale, home to the popular 1920s Scottdale String Band. An instrumental ensemble unique in instrumentation and with a more varied repertoire than that of other Georgia stringbands, its Atlanta recordings (for OKEH) sold quite well.

The group featured a lead instrument of banjo-mandolin, played by Belvie Freeman prior to 1927 and Charlie Simmons thereafter, and two guitars, by Barney Pritchard (b. June 29, 1904; d. March 1963) and Marvin Head. Performances ranged from traditional folk tunes to jazz and blues pieces to Hawaiian or popular melodies to original material. Better-sellers included the traditional "Chinese Breakdown," originals such as "Scottdale Stomp" and "Stone Mountain Wobble," and a ragtime number, "Carbolic Rag."

The band journeyed to Grafton, Wisconsin, for a last recording session in 1932 for Paramount Records, but sales were practically nonexistent for the resulting two Depression-era releases. Appearances in the Atlanta area continued until the band's demise, in about 1940.

—Bob Pinson

Earl Scruggs & the Earl Scruggs Revue

Earl Scruggs b. Flint Hill, North Carolina, January 6, 1924
Randy Scruggs b. Nashville, Tennessee, August 3, 1953
Gary Scruggs b. Knoxville, Tennessee, May 18, 1949
Steve Scruggs b. Nashville, Tennessee, February 8, 1958;
d. September 23, 1992
Jody Maphis b. August 18, 1954
Bob Wilson b. July 16, 1946

Eager to strengthen his appeal to the emerging youth culture and frustrated by his partner LESTER FLATT's musical inflexibility, bluegrass banjo pioneer Earl Eugene Scruggs recruited his sons RANDY and Gary to form a rock-oriented ensemble in early 1969. The Earl Scruggs Revue initially featured Gary on lead vocals, bass, and harmonica; Randy on electric and acoustic guitar; Bob Wilson on piano; and Jody Maphis on drums. The group's repertoire mixed traditional songs and contemporary folk-rock covers with Earl's instrumental specialties.

During the early 1970s the band included VASSAR CLEMENTS, a bluegrass fiddler with an affinity for blues, who joined Earl, Gary, and Randy Scruggs on the NITTY GRITTY DIRT BAND's 1972 homage to traditional country music, *Will the Circle Be Unbroken.* Bluegrass dobro veteran and blues singer JOSH GRAVES joined the group in March 1972; by then Earl's youngest son, Steve, worked occasional dates and eventually replaced Wilson. Taylor Rhodes (b. February 12, 1953) replaced Maphis in 1978.

Though never embraced by bluegrass or country music purists, the Revue found its niche as a live act playing to college-age audiences. The group recorded for COLUMBIA

throughout the decade and made frequent network television appearances. The group remained a major draw on campuses and in auditoriums as well as other venues until 1980, when persistent back problems forced Earl Scruggs's retirement from the road.

At the time of this writing, a U.K. label, Edsel, planned to release two Earl Scruggs Revue CDs in 1998.

—Dave Samuelson

Randy Scruggs

b. Nashville, Tennessee, August 3, 1953

A son of bluegrass great EARL SCRUGGS, Randy Lynn Scruggs has firmly established his own imprint on contemporary country music. His multifaceted career has included success as a songwriter, instrumentalist, and producer. He earned a CMA Award as producer of the 1989 Album of the Year, the NITTY GRITTY DIRT BAND's *Will the Circle Be Unbroken, Volume 2,* and he won a Grammy (Best Country Instrumental) in 1989 for his recording of "Amazing Grace." As a songwriter, Scruggs's credits include EARL THOMAS CONLEY's "Angel in Disguise" and DEANA CARTER's "We Danced Anyway," among others.

Introduced to the autoharp by Mother Maybelle Carter at age six, Scruggs developed a fascination with that instrument, which led him to learn many of the early songs of the CARTER FAMILY and other traditional artists. At age nine he made his first guest appearance on his father's syndicated television program *Flatt & Scruggs.*

Taking up the guitar, Randy Scruggs spent his childhood summers touring with his father's band. At age thirteen he played on his first recording. Later he teamed up with his older brother Gary to form the Scruggs Brothers, releasing two albums on Vanguard Records. The duo were eventually joined by younger brother Steve and father Earl to form the Earl Scruggs Revue. Meanwhile, Randy continued working as a session player, and he was named one of the nation's top guitarists by *Guitar Player* magazine in 1980. In that same year he opened Scruggs Sound Studio.

Scruggs has produced records by MOE BANDY, BOBBY BARE, Earl Thomas Conley, DEAN DILLON, SKIP EWING, Steve Forbert, WAYLON JENNINGS, SAWYER BROWN, STEVE WARINER, and many others. In 1995 he took home another CMA award as producer of "When You Say Nothing At All," the Single of the Year, recorded by ALISON KRAUSS & Union Station. Scruggs recently signed a recording deal with Reprise Records and has completed the recording of his own album. At the time of this writing, the album was scheduled for release in summer 1998. *—Janet E. Williams*

Dan Seals

b. McCamey, Texas, February 8, 1948

Since 1968, sweet-voiced Danny Wayland Seals has enjoyed hits with a rock band, in a pop duo, and as a solo country singer and duet artist, racking up gold records in the pop and country fields and earning two CMA Awards in 1986. He has also written or co-written about half of his major country hits (usually with BOB MCDILL).

Seals grew up in the oil-field country of West Texas, surrounded by music. His father, Wayland, was an excellent amateur musician good enough to sit in with BOB WILLS, ERNEST TUBB, and JIM REEVES. Seals's older brother, Jim Seals, scored early seventies pop hits with Dash Crofts in Seals & Crofts; a cousin, JOHNNY DUNCAN, tallied several hits on COLUMBIA; while two other cousins, Troy Seals and Chuck Seals, are award-winning songwriters.

Following a minor pop hit with Southwest F.O.B. ("The Smell of Incense," 1968), Seals and bandmate John Ford Coley left their Dallas home for California to become England Dan & John Ford Coley. With KYLE LEHNING as their producer, they created nine Top Forty pop hits between 1976 and 1979, best exemplified by the gentle rock of "I'd Really Like to See You Tonight" (#2 pop, 1976).

When the pair split in 1979, Seals tried a pop solo career as England Dan, then became simply Dan Seals in 1980 with releases for ATLANTIC (1980) and MCA (1981). In 1983 he came to LIBERTY RECORDS, where he immediately began placing country records on the charts. Working once again with Kyle Lehning, Seals issued lovingly crafted pop-country hits such as "My Old Yellow Car"; "Everything That Glitters (Is Not Gold)"; "You Still Move Me"; and "Bop," the catchy 1986 country crossover that earned him CMA Single of the Year honors.

Between 1985 and 1989 he posted nine consecutive #1 singles (for EMI America and then Capitol), which included "Meet Me in Montana," a duet with MARIE OSMOND that won CMA Best Vocal Duo. In the nineties he fell out of favor with radio. In 1995 he signed with the independent Intersound label. —*John Lomax III*

REPRESENTATIVE RECORDINGS

Won't Be Blue Anymore (EMI America, 1985); *The Best* (Capitol, 1987); *In a Quiet Room* (Intersound, 1995)

Jeannie Seely
b. Titusville, Pennsylvania, July 6, 1940

A strong-voiced country singer who emerged in the 1960s, Jeannie Seely is perhaps best known for her 1966 smash "Don't Touch Me." A popular fixture on the GRAND OLE OPRY, she has remained an audience favorite over the years, in large part due to her vibrant onstage personality.

Born Marilyn Jeanne Seely, she was raised in a poor family in western Pennsylvania; her father was a steelworker and farmer. By age eleven she was singing on radio station WMGW in Meadville, Pennsylvania, and by sixteen on television in Erie.

After attending banking school, Seely moved to Los Angeles in 1961. There she combined more financial schooling with songwriting, singing, and working as a disc jockey. In 1965 she shifted to Nashville—at the urging of songwriter HANK COCHRAN—and briefly joined PORTER WAGONER's road (and television) show. She signed with MONUMENT RECORDS, for whom she recorded "Don't Touch Me." Written by Cochran, the ballad shot up the charts to #2, stayed there three weeks, and won her a Grammy. In 1967 Seely joined the Opry, breaking its prudish standards by wearing miniskirts. In that same year, "I'll Love You (More Than You Need)" became her second Top Ten hit.

Seely became a popular figure on television shows (the WILBURN BROTHERS, ERNEST TUBB), and in 1969 she formed a road show with JACK GREENE. Also in 1969, she married Cochran (they later divorced); entertained U.S. military troops in Japan, Taiwan, and Thailand; and signed with DECCA RECORDS. A duet with Greene, "Wish I Didn't Have to Miss You," soon went to #2. Her last Top Ten hit, "Can I Sleep in Your Arms?" (by Cochran), went to #6 in 1973 for MCA RECORDS. In 1978 Seely was injured in a perilous car wreck near Nashville.

A versatile artist, Seely has written songs for NORMA JEAN, CONNIE SMITH, DOTTIE WEST, RAY PRICE, FARON YOUNG, and r&b singer Irma Thomas. She appeared in musicals in the 1980s and even compiled a witty book of earthy epigrams, *Pieces of a Puzzled Mind* (1989). —*Steve Eng*

REPRESENTATIVE RECORDINGS

The Seely Style (Monument, 1966); *Thanks, Hank!* (Monument, 1967); *Can I Sleep in Your Arms* (MCA, 1973)

Seldom Scene

Known for its blend of innovation and traditionalism, the Seldom Scene became one of the bluegrass music's most highly regarded bands despite performing on a part-time basis.

Its mainstay was John Duffey (b. Washington, D.C., March 4, 1934; d. December 10, 1996), who had provided flamboyant mandolin and tenor vocal stylings to another inventive Washington, D.C., area ensemble, the COUNTRY GENTLEMEN, before concentrating on musical instrument repair. In the summer of 1971 Duffey participated in a party jam session with banjo player and mathematician Ben Eldridge; dobro player and commercial artist Mike Auldridge (both former members of Cliff Waldron & the New Shades of Grass); cartographer and former Country Gentlemen bassist Tom Gray; and host John Starling, a U.S. Army surgeon and talented amateur singer-guitarist.

The quintet decided to form a band for fun. Awaiting their debut, Charlie Waller of the Country Gentlemen quipped that they should be called the Seldom Seen, thus inspiring their name.

Starting in November 1971, they began drawing large weekly audiences at Washington-area clubs, became bluegrass festival headliners, and developed a national following.

The outspoken Duffey felt that overperformance of standards was making bluegrass stale. So the band drew material from folk music, rock, country, and the work of songwriter friends. Even when performing bluegrass classics, the Seldom Scene brought a trademark freshness, energy, and drama to its arrangements, achieving a dynamic, near-theatrical performance quality that enthralled listeners.

Despite personnel changes, the Seldom Scene consistently featured accomplished lead singers: Starling, Phil Zimmerman, Lou Reid, Moondi Klein, and finally Dudley Connell (formerly of the JOHNSON MOUNTAIN BOYS). The band's final performance with Duffey was on December 7, 1996, in Englewood, New Jersey, before Duffey died from a heart attack. Seldom Scene was continuing to play at the time this article was written. —*Richard D. Smith*

REPRESENTATIVE RECORDINGS

Live at the Cellar Door (Rebel, 1975); *The Dream Scene* (Sugar Hill, 1996)

Leon "Pappy" Selph
b. Houston, Texas, April 7, 1914

An accomplished fiddler and bandleader, Leon "Pappy" Selph is best known for leading the Blue Ridge Playboys, one of the most popular and influential western swing bands of the 1930s. Some of Selph's band members became pioneers of the embryonic honky-tonk sound. These included pianist MOON MULLICAN, singer/guitarist FLOYD TILLMAN, and songwriter TED DAFFAN.

Selph began playing fiddle when he was five. Initially studying classical violin, he played with the Houston Youth Symphony (1929–1930). Eventually Selph met SHELLY LEE ALLEY, a popular fiddler who had parlayed his talents into songwriting (JIMMIE RODGERS's "Travellin' Blues" and "Gambling Bar Room Blues"). Selph and Alley struck a bargain whereby Alley would teach Selph country fiddle, and Selph would instruct Alley in classical execution. Eventually both would lead successful western swing bands in Houston.

According to Selph, it was BOB WILLS who first brought him to Fort Worth to play fiddle for Papa Sam Cunningham's Crystal Springs Ramblers in 1935. The gig lasted only a few months, but between playing for the Ramblers and observing MILTON BROWN & His Musical Brownies, Selph decided to start his own band. Sponsoring his new band on Houston's KXYZ was station owner Jesse Jones, the oil and real-estate magnate who would later become head of the Reconstruction Finance Corporation under President Franklin D. Roosevelt. It was Jones who named Selph's group the Blue Ridge Playboys, after one of his properties, the Blue Ridge oil patch. Initially calling himself Smilin' Leon, Selph received the nickname Pappy after his first daughter was born, in 1939.

Like many other Texas stringbands, the Blue Ridge Playboys patterned their rhythm after Milton Brown's Musical Brownies. During the late 1930s they played "battle dances" with their South Texas rivals the BAR-X COWBOYS and CLIFF BRUNER & His Texas Wanderers. The Blue Ridge Playboys often shared recording personnel with Shelly Lee Alley & His Alley Cats in a series of recording sessions for the ARC and DECCA labels before World War II.

In 1941 Jesse Jones hired Selph and members of the Blue Ridge Playboys to campaign with then congressman Lyndon B. Johnson in his race against governor W. LEE O'DANIEL for a seat in the U.S. Senate. Johnson lost the controversial election.

World War II ended the Blue Ridge Playboys' career as Selph entered the armed forces. After the war he worked for the fire department, but he resumed his music career, remaining a familiar presence on the Texas music scene into his eighties.
—*Cary Ginell*

REPRESENTATIVE RECORDINGS

Stompin' at the Honky Tonk (String, 1978), one track on various artists' compilation; *Okeh Western Swing* (CBS Special Products, 1989)

SESAC
established 1931

SESAC, originally the Society of European Stage Authors and Composers (now the acronym stands on its own), was formed by Paul Heinecke in 1931 to handle music licensing for various foreign publishers not already affiliated with ASCAP, then the only U.S. music licenser in existence. Largely undisturbed during years of bitter ASCAP-BMI feuding (1940s–1950s), SESAC after 1959 became the target of court action and U.S. Senate investigation for allegedly blackmailing radio stations into signing licenses with threatened litigation, and for refusing to publish a catalogue of SESAC compositions.

SESAC originally represented only publishers (not writ-

ers), and shared all collected mechanical, synchronization, and performing-rights revenues with their affiliated publishers on a 50–50 percentage basis, after deduction of operating expenses. SESAC was and is the only for-profit corporation of the three major U.S. music licensers. By 1960 it had about 320 publishers, and offered an LP Program Service to radio stations that took out SESAC licenses. Its early catalogue was essentially gospel (most of the STAMPS-BAXTER, VAUGHAN, and ALBERT E. BRUMLEY classics), folk, and religious music.

SESAC's Nashville office opened at 806 16th Avenue South in early 1964, the year in which the first SESAC Awards were held. Glenn Ray, C. W. McCALL (Bill Fries), Ted Harris, K.T. OSLIN, Susan Longacre, and Kendal Francheschi, with songs such as "80s Ladies" and "Whoever's in New England," gradually put SESAC on the country map.

For years a family business (passed down from founder Paul Heinecke to his daughter, Alice Prager), SESAC has been owned since 1992 by a New York–based team of investors: Freddie Gershon, Stephen Swid (an owner of *Spin* magazine), and Ira Smith. About 1 to 3 percent of all licensed U.S. music is now handled by SESAC, which has about 5,000 affiliated writers and some 200,000 copyrights. Always with ownership in New York, the national organization has been headquartered, however, in Nashville since its 1985 move to a new building at 55 Music Square East. Dianne Petty, senior vice president and head of the creative department between 1979 and 1995, recently resigned to go back into music publishing. Bill Velez is currently president and CEO. SESAC recently acquired the BOB DYLAN and Neil Diamond catalogues, and recent SESAC-licensed country hits include "I Don't Need Your Rocking Chair," "How Can I Help You Say Goodbye," and "I Got It Honest."
—*Ronnie Pugh*

Whitey Shafer
b. Whitney, Texas, October 24, 1934

Sanger D. "Whitey" Shafer has written or co-written some of the most important country songs of the post-1960s. Hailing from the same central Texas region that produced WILLIE NELSON, Shafer's honky-tonk roots have served him well in providing material for the likes of GEORGE STRAIT ("Does Fort Worth Ever Cross Your Mind," "All My Ex's Live in Texas") and KEITH WHITLEY ("I Never Go Around Mirrors," "I Wonder if You Think of Me"). Shafer is also known for his friendship with LEFTY FRIZZELL, an association that resulted in their co-writing both "I Never Go Around Mirrors" and "That's the Way Love Goes" (a #1 hit for JOHNNY RODRIGUEZ in 1974 and for MERLE HAGGARD in 1984).

Growing up in Whitney, the child of gospel singers, Shafer idolized Frizzell from the moment he first heard Lefty's initial hit in 1950. "I heard that 'If You Got the Money, I Got the Time'—I knew I'd found me a hero," he said. After high school he started singing in local honky-tonks, occasionally sharing the bandstand with young Willie Nelson. Shafer spent three years in the army in California, then returned to Texas, where he held a variety of jobs, including raising turkeys. In 1967 he moved to Nashville and fell in with songwriters A. L. "DOODLE" OWENS and DALLAS FRAZIER. Shafer signed with Blue Crest Music, Frazier's publisher, and had a short-lived artist deal with RCA. GEORGE JONES cut some of his songs, and Frizzell recorded his "You, Babe" in 1972, after which a songwriting partnership developed between them that lasted until Frizzell's death three years later. In the meantime, Shafer and Owens co-wrote "I Just Started Hatin' Cheatin' Songs Today," the 1974 breakthrough record for MOE BANDY.

Eight years before Strait, Bandy also recorded "Does Fort Worth Ever Cross Your Mind," which Shafer wrote with his then wife, Darlene. Ironically, "All My Ex's Live in Texas" was co-written by Shafer's later wife, Lyndia. Both songs were nominated for CMA Song of the Year, for 1985 and 1987, respectively. —*Daniel Cooper*

Eldon Shamblin
b. Weatherford, Oklahoma, April 24, 1916

Of BOB WILLS's myriad Texas Playboys, none had a greater impact on shaping western swing's sound than guitarist-arranger Eldon Shamblin. If not for the Depression, Shamblin would have been a welder in Weatherford, Oklahoma. Hard times drove him to perform in Oklahoma City beer joints in 1934. A short-lived solo spot on Oklahoma City radio station KFXR preceded Shamblin's enlistment in the Tulsa-based Alabama Boys, who recorded for DECCA in 1938 after Shamblin's two-year stint in the group.

On Tulsa's KTUL, Shamblin was a staff guitarist noted for playing swing versions of popular classics. Bob Wills tuned in and hired Shamblin on November 8, 1937. By 1939 Shamblin was arranging for the Texas Playboys; Wills also entrusted him with extensive hiring and firing powers. The evolution of the Texas Playboys from a funky string-band to a horn-heavy big band was in large part Shamblin's doing. The duos he worked out with steel guitarist LEON MCAULIFFE, most notably 1941's "Twin Guitar Special," swung tightly. In 1941 the jazz journal *Metronome* cited Shamblin's electric guitar lead work as "closer than any other white plectrist to getting the solidity and swing and steady flow of ideas of Charlie Christian."

After World War II the emphasis in Shamblin's playing shifted from lead to rhythm in a scaled-down Playboys. Ever the pragmatist, Shamblin has credited his fluid bass lines to the need to "cover for a bad bass man." (In 1974 *Rolling Stone* said he played "the world's best rhythm guitar.") Shamblin left the Playboys in the mid-1950s and, following stints in bands of McAuliffe and fiddler-singer HOYLE NIX, settled in Tulsa to tune pianos. He was recalled to active duty by MERLE HAGGARD, first on the 1974 Wills tribute album *For the Last Time*, and then as a member of Haggard's road band, the Strangers. Since the mid-1970s Shamblin has also been a key figure in various Playboys reunion bands (principally the Original Texas Playboys, 1975–86) and played on ASLEEP AT THE WHEEL's 1994 *Tribute to the Music of Bob Wills & the Texas Playboys*. "Eldon," says Wheel boss Ray Benson, "is like Elvis to us." —*Mark Humphrey*

Kevin Sharp
b. Weiser, Idaho, December 10, 1970

Kevin Sharp, a contemporary country singer who leans toward the pop-country sound, celebrated his first gold album, *Measure of a Man*, in February 1997. However, that accomplishment pales in comparison to Sharp's greatest achievement: surviving cancer.

Sharp, a football player and baritone with the Sacramento Light Opera Association, was an eighteen-year-old senior at Bella Vista High School in Sacramento, California, when he was diagnosed with Ewing's sarcoma, a rare bone cancer. While undergoing chemotherapy and radiation, he was contacted by Make-A-Wish Foundation, and he told them he would most like to meet record producer David Foster. The two met in 1990 and saw each other several times, but didn't really discuss Sharp's musical career.

Sharp's cancer went into remission in 1991, the same year he played his demo tape for Foster, who encouraged him to keep working. Within two years, Sharp was a lead singer in the Great American theme park in California and was singing at restaurants, funerals, and high schools. He began a singing telegram business, auditioned for the TNN show *You Can Be a Star,* and marketed his CD called *You Can Count on Me.* Once again, he turned to Foster for advice. Foster listened to his tape, liked it, and passed it along to his sister, 143 Records executive Jaymes Foster, in 1995. She played the tape for country producer Chris Farren, who offered to produce Sharp. Foster organized a showcase for KYLE LEHNING of ASYLUM RECORDS, which resulted in a record deal.

Sharp released his debut album, *Measure of a Man,* in 1996. Its first single, "Nobody Knows" (a song the Tony Rich Project had already made a hit on the pop charts), was released in September 1996 and went to #1 on the country charts, staying there for four weeks. His second single, "She's Sure Taking It Well," was released in February 1997 and reached #3. —*Beverly Keel*

REPRESENTATIVE RECORDING
Measure of a Man (Asylum, 1996)

Billy Joe Shaver
b. Corsicana, Texas, August 16, 1939

Most country listeners are familiar with Billy Joe Shaver's songs through versions by other performers. Everyone from JOHN ANDERSON to longtime Shaver pal WILLIE NELSON has performed his compositions, as have the Allman Brothers, BOBBY BARE, JOHNNY CASH, BOB DYLAN, TOM T. HALL, WAYLON JENNINGS, KRIS KRISTOFFERSON, JERRY LEE LEWIS, PATTY LOVELESS, ELVIS PRESLEY, JOHNNY RODRIGUEZ, MARTY STUART, and many more. Most of Shaver's songs marry stately acoustic country rhythms with lyrics that veer between plainspoken truths and images that are unimaginable from anyone else; for example: "I'm just an old chunk of coal/But I'm gonna be a diamond someday," from the song of that title, which Anderson turned into a sizable hit in 1981.

Shaver's early songs in the late 1960s and early 1970s were considered part of that era's great explosion of new Nashville songwriting, during which writers such as Kris Kristofferson and GUY CLARK came to the fore. But what attracted other composers to Shaver's material was its distinctive grounding—direct yet poetic, simultaneously self-effacing and boastful.

Shaver was raised in Corsicana, Texas, by his grandmother, and later in Waco by his mother. A stint in the navy led to a series of go-nowhere jobs, including one at a sawmill that cost him most of the index and middle fingers on his right hand. His late 1960s arrival in Nashville led to friendships and alliances with many stars of the day. Shaver had a part in writing all but one number on Waylon Jennings's landmark album *Honky Tonk Heroes* (1973), including "Black Rose," which contains the famous Shaver couplet "The devil made me do it the first time/The second time I done it on my own."

Shaver's recorded debut, *Old Five and Dimers Like Me*, appeared on MONUMENT later the same year. He enjoyed two minor hits in the 1970s ("Georgia on a Fast Train" in 1973 and "You Asked Me To" in 1978) and recorded two albums for Capricorn: the brilliant 1976 *When I Get My Wings*, and the following year's *Gypsy Boy*, which was weighed down by an all-star cast and misguided production decisions. But in part because his songwriting voice is usually stronger than his singing voice, Shaver had little commercial success as a recording artist at that time. His personal and professional life went into a tailspin until Anderson's "I'm Just an Old Chunk of Coal" reinvigorated his career.

Shaver returned to recording with three consistent albums for COLUMBIA in the 1980s, during which time his son, guitarist Eddy Shaver, gradually played a more assertive role in developing lead lines and rhythms as strong as his father's images and aphorisms. Their collaboration reached a peak with 1993's *Tramp on Your Street* (Praxis/Zoo), a spirited set that astonished even longtime fans of the wily songwriter with its rock & roll punch and musical diversity. *Unshaven* (Praxis/Zoo), a companion live set, followed in 1995, and *Highway of Life* (Justice, 1996) returned the Shavers to Billy Joe's original sound.

In 1997 Shaver appeared with leading actor Robert Duvall in the film *The Apostle*.   —*Jimmy Guterman*

REPRESENTATIVE RECORDINGS

Tramp on Your Street (Praxis/Zoo, 1993); *Restless Winder: The Legendary Billy Joe Shaver, 1973–1987* (Razor & Tie, 1995)

Billy Joe Shaver

Victoria Shaw
b. New York, New York, July 13, 1962

Before recording her 1995 debut major label album, *In Full View*, VICTORIA SHAW had gained name recognition in Nashville circles as a bona fide hit songwriter. She has three #1 country songs to her credit: "The River" by GARTH BROOKS, "Too Busy Being in Love" by DOUG STONE, and "I Love the Way You Love Me" by JOHN MICHAEL MONTGOMERY; the latter earned her 1994 Song of the Year honors from the Academy of Country Music (ACM).

Shaw was born in New York City but raised in Los Angeles (she currently maintains residences in Nashville and New York). Both parents worked in the entertainment industry—her father managed the career of her singer mother, who appeared on the *Ed Sullivan Show*. Victoria was writing songs and in a band at age twelve, often playing free mall concerts, where Victoria's sister handed out promotional flyers. Shaw showed up in the *Billboard* Country Singles chart in 1984, barely cracking the Top 100 with "Break My Heart" on the independent MPB label. She opted to concentrate more on songwriting and, by the late 1980s, was collaborating with some of Nashville's top talent, including future superstar Garth Brooks.

—*Michael Hight*

REPRESENTATIVE RECORDINGS

In Full View (Reprise, 1995); *Victoria Shaw* (Reprise, 1997)

Dorothy Shay
b. Jacksonville, Florida, April 11, 1921; d. October 22, 1978

Known as the Park Avenue Hillbilly, Dorothy Shay developed a comedic act by singing humorous hick tunes and dressing in glamorous designer gowns.

Born Dorothy Nell Sims, she rose to fame as a New York supper club attraction during World War II. Shay scored a smash hit on COLUMBIA in 1947 with "Feudin' and Fightin'" and followed it with dozens of similar hokum ditties. By 1951 she was earning $5,000 a night in clubs.

Shay relocated to Los Angeles and appeared in *Comin' Round the Mountain* (1951) with Abbott & Costello. She was a particular favorite of President Dwight D. Eisenhower's and performed at his 1953 inaugural ball. Shay resurfaced in the 1970s with a recurring role as a mountain spinster on the hit TV series *The Waltons*.   —*Robert K. Oermann*

Harold Shedd
b. Bremen, Alabama, November 8, 1931

Harold Shedd's willingness to take risks and his search for innovative sounds made him one of the top country executives of the 1980s. Much of his acclaim revolved around his role as producer for the supergroup ALABAMA.

Shedd was better known for producing jingles for the likes of Shoney's, Bayer aspirin, and McDonald's at the time he began working with Alabama, but he sensed a unique talent when he brought the harmony-laden, country-rock band into his Music Mill Recording Studio in 1979. They emerged as a megaforce, melding southern rock roots with a love of solid country.

Born one of twelve children to a preacher-farmer in rural Alabama, Shedd worked at numerous radio sta-

Harold Shedd

tions—he eventually owned WWCC in his hometown—which probably helped in his ability to find the right songs and the right sounds for Alabama after he began working with them.

"In Alabama's case, we were not lookin' for any beer-drinking, cheatin' kinds of songs," he would explain. "We were lookin' for positive things with positive messages."

Among his production touches, he electronically altered the vocals on 1983's "The Closer You Get," came up with four different versions of "Roll On (Eighteen Wheeler)," and developed a drum sound on "She And I" that utilized reverse echo effects. In the eight years that Shedd produced the group, Alabama notched two dozen Top Ten hits, including twenty-one #1 singles.

Alabama wasn't Shedd's only successful venture. He helped introduce the world to a then forty-six-year-old K. T. OSLIN, and as the head of MERCURY RECORDS in 1992 he developed recording artist BILLY RAY CYRUS and signed SHANIA TWAIN.

Not all of Shedd's moves were successful. He headed Mercury's sister label Polydor when it was opened in 1994, but two years later, after A&M took over Polydor, Shedd left just before the operation closed down. The label had failed to break any new acts.   —*Tom Roland*

Ricky Van Shelton

b. Grit, Virginia, January 12, 1952

....

Ricky Van Shelton lived country music long before he became one of its biggest stars of the late 1980s and early 1990s. Born to a large, religious family, Shelton was singing gospel tunes such as "Supper Time" in public by age three. After a 1960s flirtation with British rock, a teenage Shelton converted to country when his older brother Ronnie offered him use of a 1964 Ford Fairlane if Ricky would join him playing country and bluegrass.

For some fifteen years Shelton bore down on singing and picking guitar, practicing so relentlessly that his family sometimes grew sick of it. His drive to entertain carried him through years in which he made a living the hard way, as he recalled in 1989: "I used to be a pipe fitter and a construction worker and that's hard work, I mean real hard work, and I'd get up at four o'clock in the morning and drive to town and we'd drive an hour and a half to work, work ten hours like a dog and then come home, jump in the shower, eat a little supper and go load up the van and do a gig until two or three o'clock in the morning and get home just in time to change clothes."

Shelton's good looks, golden voice, and intense work ethic formed a firm career foundation when he and future wife, Bettye, moved to Nashville in late 1984. *Tennessean* newspaper columnist Jerry Thompson took on Shelton's management and landed him a COLUMBIA RECORDS deal that produced a debut single by late 1986. The singer's on-the-money vocals during a first studio outing startled the experienced ears of producer STEVE BUCKINGHAM and Music Row session pros. A first LP, 1987's *Wild-Eyed Dream,* combined hard country and rockabilly stylings to produce hits: the rocking "Wild-Eyed Dream" and "Crime of Passion," and the aching country #1's "Somebody Lied," "Life Turned Her That Way," and "Don't We All Have the Right." A follow-up, 1988's *Loving Proof,* produced the #1s "I'll Leave This World Loving You," "From a Jack to a King," and "Living Proof." Suddenly, at thirty-six, Shelton was a full-fledged country star, touring constantly, recording a string of seventeen Top Ten hits, and winning major awards, including the CMA's Horizon Award in 1988 and its male vocalist honor for 1989. Stacking up five platinum and three gold discs, he was also the TNN/*Music City News* Entertainer of the Year and Male Artist of the Year in 1990 and 1991.

In 1990 the hits from the album *RVS III* continued: "Statue of a Fool," "I've Cried My Last Tear for You," "I Meant Every Word He Said," and "Life's Little Ups and Downs." And *Backroads* (1992) scored with a rollicking title

Ricky Van Shelton

track, the DOLLY PARTON duet "Rockin' Years," and the sentimental "Keep It Between the Lines." But, as detailed in Bettye Shelton's co-written 1995 book *She Stays*, the couple had severe marital problems by 1991, problems aggravated by his infidelities and drinking. He had a soul-wrenching religious conversion in early 1992. That year also saw the renewal of Shelton's marriage; the start of a successful series of children's books; and a gospel release, *Don't Overlook Salvation*.

Shelton may have alienated some in the country music industry after a disagreement with show director Irving Waugh over Shelton's role on the 1993 awards show and some frank remarks about country radio consultants. Shelton won the TNN/*Music City News* Christian Country Artist of the Year crown for 1995–1996. Early 1997 found him back in the studio working on a straight-ahead country release for Shelton's own Wal Mart–distributed label.

—*Thomas Goldsmith*

REPRESENTATIVE RECORDINGS

Wild-Eyed Dream (Columbia, 1987); *Loving Proof* (Columbia, 1988); *Greatest Hits Plus* (Columbia, 1992)

The Shelton Brothers

Bob Attlesey (Shelton) b. Reilly Springs, Texas, July 4, 1909; d. November 1986

Joe Attlesey (Shelton) b. Reilly Springs, Texas, January 27, 1911; d. December 26, 1980

....

The Shelton Brothers present fascinating evidence of the changes in southwestern hillbilly music in the 1930s: In a few years they transformed from a traditional southeastern–styled duo into a western swing–influenced, jukebox-friendly, honky-tonk act. Bob handled comedy, vocals, bass, jug, and ukulele, while Joe performed vocals and played mandolin and guitar.

Bob and Joe Attlesey—they later took their mother's maiden name for commercial purposes—formed the Lone Star Cowboys in Tyler, Texas, and played over KGKB, in 1929, with guitarist LEON CHAPPELEAR. From the early 1930s the group performed over KWKH-Shreveport and, in 1933, recorded the classics "Just Because" and "Deep

Elm Blues" for VICTOR. They backed JIMMIE DAVIS in the same sessions.

Splitting from Chappelear, the "Shelton Brothers" followed Davis to DECCA in 1935, by which time they had relocated to New Orleans, where they worked at WWL and teamed with fiddler CURLY FOX. Soon after, they went back to Shreveport and divided their professional time—during the rest of the 1930s and in the early 1940s—between two radio stations: KWKH in Shreveport and WFAA/WBAP in Dallas–Fort Worth. Their group, the Sunshine Boys, became increasingly influenced by western swing as their Decca tenure continued through 1941; traditional tunes such as "Stay in the Wagon Yard" gave way to swing-flavored jukebox fare such as "Parking Meter Blues." The Sunshine Boys (who, without the Sheltons, recorded for OKEH during 1940–41) at times included such swing stalwarts as steel guitarist BOB DUNN and pianist MOON MULLICAN. From 1938, by which time younger brother Merle had joined the group on guitar, Joe Shelton amplified his mandolin and played in a jazzy style reminiscent of pioneering electric mandolinist Leo Raley (who appeared on the band's 1939 sessions, as did fiddler CLIFF BRUNER).

The Sheltons concentrated on show dates rather than dances, though they maintained a top-notch swing band off and on through the late 1940s, waxing sides for KING RECORDS before they disbanded. From the mid-1940s, the brothers began to work separately. For Jimmie Davis, Joe worked bandleader stints, which included Davis's successful 1944 bid for governor. Joe essentially retired from music after 1950, but Bob continued to perform as a comedian—always his stock-in-trade—through the 1970s on such shows as the *BIG D JAMBOREE* and *LOUISIANA HAYRIDE*.

—*Kevin Coffey*

Shenandoah

Ralph Ezell b. Union, Mississippi, June 26, 1953

Mike McGuire b. Haleyville, Alabama, December 28, 1958

Marty Raybon b. Greenville, Alabama, December 8, 1959

Jim Seales b. Hamilton, Alabama, March 20, 1954

Stan Thorn b. Kenosha, Wisconsin, March 16, 1959

....

One of a number of contemporary country bands to emerge in the late 1980s and early 1990s in the aftermath

Shenandoah: (from left) Mike McGuire, Ralph Ezell, Marty Raybon, Stan Thorn, and Jim Seales

of ALABAMA's initial success, the act Shenandoah nearly saw its career scuttled at the outset. The band ultimately endured through major unforeseen legal troubles to maintain a distinct place in country's commercial ranks for nearly a decade.

Originally a quintet formed in Muscle Shoals, Alabama, under the name the MGM Band, the group largely was a live outlet for the members' musical passions, as well as a way to make a few extra dollars. Drummer Mike McGuire, guitarist Jim Seales, and keyboard player Stan Thorn formed the group, and when their lead singer departed, they brought in Marty Raybon. The band added its final piece when bass player Ralph Ezell was imported from a rival group.

McGuire invited record producers Rick Hall and Robert Byrne to hear the band, and a record deal with COLUMBIA ensued. After considering several new names, the final choice came down to Rhythm Rangers or Shenandoah.

Shenandoah established themselves with thick harmonies and a knack for strong melodies on such singles as "Mama Knows," "The Church on Cumberland Road," "Two Dozen Roses," and "Next to You, Next to Me." But they also discovered that three other bands claimed rights to their name, and when they were sued by each of the other acts, they were forced to file for Chapter 11 bankruptcy.

Eventually Shenandoah paid off the other bands and gained permanent rights to the name, continuing to notch such hits as "Rock My Baby"; "I Want to Be Loved Like That"; and a duet with ALISON KRAUSS, "Somewhere in the Vicinity of the Heart," which earned the CMA's Vocal Event of the Year Award in 1995.

Thorn left the band to pursue jazz interests in 1995, and Ezell departed prior to the recording of a 1996 Christmas album. The group disbanded in 1997. Raybon is now in a duo with his brother Tim, the Raybon Brothers. Their first single was "Butterfly Kisses," a country version of the contemporary Christian hit that crossed over to the pop charts for Bob Carlisle.

—*Tom Roland*

REPRESENTATIVE RECORDINGS

The Road Not Taken (Columbia, 1989); *Greatest Hits* (Columbia, 1992)

Jean Shepard
b. Paul's Valley, Oklahoma, November 21, 1933
....

During the 1950s few women managed to break through industry barriers to enjoy full-blown country careers. Even fewer did so singing forthright material in a hardcore honky-tonk style. But one who did was Jean Shepard, whose lively records of the 1950s set the stage for artists such as LORETTA LYNN and TAMMY WYNETTE in the following decade. Shepard continued to score Top Ten hits into the 1970s, and she remains a popular star of the GRAND OLE OPRY as of this writing.

Born Ollie Imogene Shepard, she grew up in rural Oklahoma listening to both Nashville's Grand Ole Opry and BOB WILLS's radio broadcasts out of Tulsa. Just before the end of World War II her family moved to Southern California, settling in Visalia. While in high school, Shepard and some friends formed the Melody Ranch Girls, with whom she both sang and played upright bass. In 1952, as a result of HANK THOMPSON's recommendation, KEN NELSON of CAPITOL RECORDS signed Shepard to his label.

Jean Shepard

Shepard's debut single, on which she was co-billed with steel guitar legend SPEEDY WEST, fared poorly. But her second single, recorded May 19, 1953, was a #1 smash. That record was "A Dear John Letter," to which FERLIN HUSKY contributed the recitation part. The duet crossed over to the pop Top Five and established both singers' careers. From that point forward, Shepard recorded one vibrant honky-tonk single after another, many featuring BILL WOODS's band out of BAKERSFIELD, which included guitarist BUCK OWENS.

In January 1955 Shepard was part of the cast that inaugurated the *OZARK JUBILEE* telecast. But in November that year, coming off successive Top Five hits with "A Satisfied Mind" and "Beautiful Lies," she joined the Grand Ole Opry. The following month she recorded *Songs of a Love Affair,* which is said to have been the first concept album ever recorded by a female country singer.

During the late 1950s Shepard became involved romantically with fellow Opry star HAWKSHAW HAWKINS. On November 26, 1960, the two were married onstage in Wichita, Kansas. Tragically, Hawkins died in the same 1963 plane crash that killed singers PATSY CLINE and COWBOY COPAS. Devastated, Shepard gave up singing for several months. But by the close of the year she had returned to the Opry, and in early 1964 she scored a major comeback hit with "Second Fiddle (to an Old Guitar)." (Since 1968 Shepard has been married to bluegrass musician Benny Birchfield, who was ROY ORBISON's road manager at the time of Orbison's death.)

Through the remainder of the 1960s Shepard enjoyed moderate success, both solo and in duets with RAY PILLOW. Many of her records continued to feature her spunky intolerance of male foibles. In 1973 she switched labels from Capitol to United Artists. She scored an immediate Top Five hit with BILL ANDERSON's "Slippin' Away," but it proved to be her last major success. Like many singers of her generation, she found radio airplay increasingly hard to come by. Her tenure with United Artists ended in 1977, and since then, her infrequent recordings have been issued on a series of small, independent labels. —Daniel Cooper

REPRESENTATIVE RECORDING

Jean Shepard: Honky-Tonk Heroine: Classic Capitol Recordings, 1952–1964 (Country Music Foundation, 1995)

T. G. Sheppard

b. Humbolt, Tennessee, July 20, 1944

T. G. Sheppard had a remarkably long run of chart successes by occupying a musical netherworld somewhere between seventies-style honky-tonk and easy-listening pop crossover, scoring fourteen #1 hits between 1974 and 1991.

Born William Neal Browder, he began singing professionally in Memphis, recording under the name Brian Stacy. He moved into record promotion when that gambit failed. He never gave up on singing, however, working on and off as a background singer and eventually relaunching himself as T. G. Sheppard in 1974 with a #1 hit, "Devil in the Bottle." Between 1974 and 1991 the peripatetic singer recorded for one label after another—Melodyland, Hitsville, WARNER BROS., ELEKTRA, COLUMBIA, and CURB/CAPITOL.

Sheppard's repertoire, while rarely the stuff of classic country music, was most interesting for the breadth of its lyrical directions and sources. In between songs with a honky-tonk ethos such as "Motels and Memories" and "Party Time," he covered pop hits from Neil Diamond, Harry Nilsson, the Turtles, and Elvin Bishop, and turned in duets with Judy Collins, KAREN BROOKS, and Clint Eastwood. Though his best-known hit was SONNY THROCKMORTON's beautiful "Last Cheater's Waltz," Sheppard might ultimately be most significant for pioneering in country the ambivalent contemporary Christian *cum* country-pop lyric when he topped the charts in 1982 with Gary Chapman's "Finally," a song that could be taken as a paean of gratitude either to a woman or to the Messiah.

Sheppard's sales and radio successes with pop-flavored records survived the mid-eighties collapse of Nashville's attempts at compromising country music for pop radio play during the URBAN COWBOY years. While a few of his hits, particularly "Last Cheater's Waltz," seem destined for revival, most are stylistically locked in their own time. The continued rise of new generation artists such as COLLIN RAYE, who can span the pop and country gap, attest to the viability of Sheppard's general musical direction, however. —Bob Millard

REPRESENTATIVE RECORDING

The Best of T. G. Sheppard (Curb, 1992)

Billy Sherrill

b. Phil Campbell, Alabama, November 5, 1936

Billy Norris Sherrill was the most influential producer in country music in the 1970s and, as such, played a far-reaching role in shaping the overall sound and direction of the music's mainstream.

Sherrill's commercial and aesthetic impact is conveyed merely by a partial listing of the artists he produced at EPIC and COLUMBIA Records in Nashville between the late sixties and early nineties. These include, among others, GEORGE JONES, TAMMY WYNETTE, CHARLIE RICH, TANYA TUCKER,

Billy Sherrill

DAVID HOUSTON, BARBARA MANDRELL, JANIE FRICKE, JOHNNY PAYCHECK, JOHNNY RODRIGUEZ, and SHELBY LYNNE.

The son of an evangelist whom he often backed on piano at tent revivals, Sherrill apprenticed in Alabama r&b and rock bands before first breaking into country music as a songwriter. One of his earliest studio assignments in Nashville was as a producer-engineer for former SUN RECORDS producer SAM PHILLIPS in a studio Phillips then had in Nashville. Early on, Sherrill made several records of his own, sometimes playing all the instruments himself. In 1967 he released an album called *Classic Country*, credited to the Billy Sherrill Quintet.

Much of Sherrill's later influence on the country scene had to do with the fact that he was an outsider, an iconoclast who freely drew from pop, r&b, and even rock influences in his country production style. As a youth growing up in Alabama, he had been a big r&b aficionado and had disdained country music. Thus, when he belatedly came to the field, it was with a jaundiced ear and a determination to make his own kind of records.

When Sherrill was first hired by Epic in 1964 he was initially relegated to producing either unknown artists or veterans no one else was interested in producing, often non-country artists such as the r&b act the Staple Singers and the rock band Barry & the Remains. As a producer Sherrill was enamored of rock producer Phil Specter's "Wall of Sound" approach and thus imbued many of his records with a lusher, fuller sound. The end result, more often than not, was unprecedented sales (sometimes in the form of country-to-pop crossover success), along with scorn from critics and purists.

Sherrill's detractors often grumbled that his often lavish production style violated country music's basic tenets of rusticity. Yet particularly in his work with George Jones, Sherrill also produced some of the most credible and traditionally faithful honky-tonk music recorded in Nashville in the seventies and early eighties, such as Jones's "A Picture of Me (Without You)," "Bartender's Blues," and "He Stopped Loving Her Today."

Sherrill often did not content himself with merely producing artists. In the case of some, such as Tammy Wynette, he created entire musical personas for them and wrote or co-wrote songs that enlarged on these personas, such as "Stand By Your Man," "Your Good Girl's Gonna Go Bad," and "I Don't Wanna Play House."

In the case of Charlie Rich, Sherrill took a journeyman white r&b singer and virtually reinvented him as a seventies-style country-pop easy-listening crooner. The result was massive crossover hits such as "Behind Closed Doors," "The Most Beautiful Girl in the World" (which Sherrill co-wrote), and "A Very Special Love Song" (another of his co-compositions). "Almost Persuaded," another Sherrill classic, won him and co-writer Glenn Sutton a 1966 Grammy award for Best Country & Western Song and further established David Houston's career.

By the mid-1970s Sherrill, as vice president of A&R at Epic Records (he would rise to the position of vice president and executive producer at the label in 1980), also began to get some heat for his resistance to the rustic minimalism of the OUTLAW movement, which was, by then, sweeping country music. As a Columbia executive he is said to have resisted releasing Willie Nelson's *Red Headed Stranger,* an austere album completely devoid of the studio refinements and lavish overdubs that Sherrill was so fond of but that eventually sold more than 1 million copies and won numerous awards.

Yet Sherrill himself did occasionally venture far enough out of the commercial mainstream to produce albums with such unlikely artists as RAY CHARLES and British rocker Elvis Costello. Sherrill's often trenchantly sarcastic nature and his tendencies toward seclusion and egocentricity precluded him from winning any popularity contests along Music Row. On the other hand, he succeeded brilliantly where other producers failed when it came to coaxing great music out of temperamental artists such as George Jones, DAVID ALLAN COE, and Johnny Paycheck. Sherrill left Epic and Columbia Records in 1985 but continued for a while as an independent producer, still working with George Jones, among others, and occasionally developing new artists, such as Shelby Lynne. By the early 1990s Sherrill had more or less retired from the music business.

—*Bob Allen*

Steve Sholes

b. Washington, D.C., February 12, 1911; d. April 22, 1968

As a high-level recording executive, Stephen Henry Sholes helped to shepherd country music's commercial growth in the years following World War II. After his family moved near RCA's Camden, New Jersey, plant, where his father worked, Sholes began his RCA career in 1929 as a messenger boy and worked part-time for the firm while attending Rutgers University. In 1935 he joined RCA's radio depart-

ment, but his experience playing saxophone and clarinet in territorial dance bands soon landed him a sales clerk's position in the record department. Under senior executives ELI OBERSTEIN and, after 1939, FRANK WALKER, he assisted in producing pop, country, and ethnic acts, mostly in New York, Chicago, and Atlanta. During the war Sholes worked in the army's V-disc operation, which made recordings for radio broadcast and for personal listening by soldiers.

In 1945 Sholes became head of both country and r&b recording for RCA, based out of New York. Over the next two decades he would sign or develop such country artists as CHET ATKINS, EDDY ARNOLD, THE BROWNS, HANK LOCKLIN, HOMER AND JETHRO, HANK SNOW, JIM REEVES, and PEE WEE KING. At various points in his RCA career the producer also recorded jazz artists such as Jelly Roll Morton, Earl Hines, and Dizzie Gillespie.

Along with producers for other labels, Sholes helped to build Nashville as a music center by recording country talent there. After using a series of local studios (beginning in 1949), he convinced RCA to build its own studio on Seventeenth Avenue South in 1957, just two years after OWEN BRADLEY had opened Nashville's first Music Row studio a block away. Sholes's influence in this decision was greatly enhanced by his signing of ELVIS PRESLEY in 1955, a seminal event in the international rock & roll revolution. As Presley's sales skyrocketed and other Sholes-produced acts gained hits, the rising executive became the company's pop singles manager in 1957, pop singles and albums manager in 1958, and West Coast manager in 1961. In the latter role, Sholes moved to Los Angeles and supervised recording, administration, sales, and marketing aspects. Sholes had installed Chet Atkins (formerly his production assistant) to run RCA's Nashville operation in 1957 but continued to supervise Presley's recordings there and in other cities. In 1963 Sholes became RCA Records' vice president for pop A&R and returned to New York.

During the 1960s Sholes served on the CMA and COUNTRY MUSIC FOUNDATION boards of directors. He died only a year after the opening of the COUNTRY MUSIC HALL OF FAME and Museum, which he and fellow CMA leaders had worked hard to build.

Steve Sholes was elected to the COUNTRY MUSIC HALL OF FAME in 1967.

—*John Rumble*

Jack Shook

b. Decatur, Illinois, September 11, 1910; d. September 23, 1986

A versatile, self-taught guitarist and singer, bridging boundaries between country and pop, Jack Shook played in clubs and on radio stations in the Midwest, Southeast, and Southwest before landing at WSM in 1933. First working solo as a pop act, he soon joined Napoleon "Nap" Bastien and Dee Simmons in a pop trio that became a mainstay of WSM's programming into the late 1940s. (There were brief interruptions while Shook backed pop star Kate Smith on New York–originated CBS network shows in 1934 and served in the marines from 1943 to 1945.)

From 1935 until decade's end, Shook and his partners also played on the GRAND OLE OPRY as the Missouri Mountaineers, with Mack McGar on mandolin and fiddle and Elbert McEwen succeeding Bobby Castlen on accordion. Specializing in harmony vocals and smooth western ballads learned from the SONS OF THE PIONEERS, this aggrega-

Steve Sholes

tion helped add professionalism and country-pop sounds to an Opry roster that still featured many semiprofessional hoedown bands.

Beginning in 1939, Shook became part of the Nashville initial cadre of studio professionals who helped to create the city's recording industry, first by recording radio shows for syndication, then by working on commercially released discs. In this capacity his pop sensibilities and distinctive rhythm playing—enhanced by a left-handed style in which he struck his guitar strings from treble to bass—helped to give a commercial edge to recordings by HANK WILLIAMS ("Lost Highway") and numerous others. As a vocalist, Shook sang on "Blues Stay Away from Me," a 1950 hit for the OWEN BRADLEY quintet, and on eight sides of his own, made for DECCA's Coral label that same year.

Shook continued to work recording sessions into the early 1960s, but until his retirement, in 1982, he mostly played in WSM staff bands for programs such as *The Waking Crew* and *The Noon Show*.

—*Charles Wolfe and John Rumble*

Arnold Shultz

b. Ohio County, Kentucky, 1886; d. 1931

Influential black guitarist Arnold Shultz is widely regarded as a primary source of the thumb-style of guitar playing, also known as Travis picking. The son of a former slave, he came from a musical family and evidently traveled widely as a young man, working on riverboats that traveled the Green River, the Ohio, and the Mississippi to St. Louis, Louisville, Evansville, and other cities. He not only played with black musicians among West-central Kentucky's substantial black population, but also with white musicians such as banjoist Clarence Wilson, bandleader Forrest "Boots" Faught, and Pendleton Vandiver, bluegrass pioneer BILL MONROE's famous "Uncle Pen." Monroe himself worked with Shultz as a young man, playing guitar behind Shultz's fiddle at local house parties that sometimes lasted all night. Between work in the area's coal mines or performing solo or with others, Shultz also played at storefronts, schoolhouses, taverns, and railroad crossings in the Green River area embracing Ohio, Muhlenberg, Butler, and McClean Counties. A short, slightly pudgy man who liked to wear a big black hat, he could play guitar in a variety of styles and sometimes fretted it with a knife or bottleneck in typical blues fashion.

Shultz is best known, however, for his seminal role in the thumb-style guitar. William Lightfoot has succinctly characterized Shultz's style as "alternated bass under a syncopated melody, supported by rich, rhythmic chords and applied to a wide range of music." Central to Shultz's influence as a thumb-picker was white guitarist Kennedy Jones, who learned chords and picking techniques from the black musician. Jones, in turn, transmitted the thumb-style to white guitarist MOSE RAGER, who passed it along to other white guitarists, including Ike Everly (father of the EVERLY BROTHERS) and MERLE TRAVIS. Though Shultz himself evidently never recorded, Travis's records and radio shows ultimately extended Shultz's influence to CHET ATKINS, JERRY REED, Lenny Breau, and a host of other thumb-style pickers who have made this style an essential part of country music. Although official reports cite Shultz's cause of death as an organic "mitral lesion" of the heart, some still believe that jealous white musicians poisoned him with bad whiskey. —*John Rumble*

Shel Silverstein

b. Chicago, Illinois, 1932

Best known first as a cartoonist for *Playboy* magazine and later as illustrator and author of witty children's books, Shelby "Shel" Silverstein also became a celebrated country music songwriter in one of its most innovative and experimental periods.

Musically, Silverstein was influenced by the folk music scenes centered around Chicago's Gate of Horn and New York City's Bitter End. His 1961 album *Inside Folk Songs* included "The Unicorn" and "25 Minutes to Go," which became folk standards. Drawn to Nashville's songwriting circles, he penned JOHNNY CASH's hit "A Boy Named Sue," LORETTA LYNN's "One's on the Way," and "Queen of the Silver Dollar" for DAVE & SUGAR.

A chance meeting with the bar band Dr. Hook & the Medicine Show resulted in Silverstein's penning their breakthrough pop hits: "Sylvia's Mother," and "The Cover of *Rolling Stone*" (which resulted in the group's appearance on the cover of that magazine and also led to a spin-off country version by BUCK OWENS as "On the Cover of the *Music City News*").

Silverstein continued to write for other country artists, especially BOBBY BARE, and their collaboration on Bare's 1975 double-album release *Lullabies, Legends and Lies* was a critical benchmark in modern country songwriting. Silverstein's own albums include *Drain My Brain* in 1980 and *Freakin' at the Freakers' Ball* in 1972. His books include *A Light in the Attic* and *Where the Sidewalk Ends*. —*Chet Flippo*

Si Siman

b. Springfield, Missouri, January 17, 1921; d. December 16, 1994

Ely Earl Siman Jr. was the driving force in Springfield, Missouri's development as a country music center during the 1950s.

After service in the navy during World War II, Siman began to produce radio shows at KWTO in Springfield and serve as MC on road shows featuring KWTO talent. With partners Ralph Foster, Lester E. Cox, and John Mahaffey, he formed RadiOzark Enterprises to produce and distribute syndicated radio shows. In 1954 Siman recruited GRAND OLE OPRY star RED FOLEY to host a new radio barn dance from Springfield, the *OZARK JUBILEE*, which aired on the ABC radio network and, from 1955 to 1960, on ABC-TV. Siman was instrumental in landing the show on ABC-TV. The TV production firm formed by Siman and his partners, Crossroads Television Productions, not only produced the *Jubilee* (sometimes airing as *Jubilee USA* and *Country Music Jubilee*) but also produced the *Eddy Arnold Show* for ABC-TV in 1956, and *Five Star Jubilee* for NBC-TV in 1961. The latter, starring Snooky Lanson, JIMMY WAKELY, REX ALLEN, TEX RITTER, and CARL SMITH, was one of the first country programs to be telecast in color.

All the while, Siman was helping to secure recording contracts for CHET ATKINS, PORTER WAGONER (whom Siman managed), and BRENDA LEE; assisting in running the Top Talent booking operation he formed with his partners; and building the catalogue of Earl Barton Music, a music publishing firm he founded with Mahaffey in 1952. During the sixties Siman managed Red Foley, but increasingly turned his attention to publishing, eventually forming several companion music firms with writers such as Jay Stevens ("Rocky") and Wayne Carson ("The Letter"). In

1987, in anticipation of his retirement, Siman sold these catalogues. His son, Scott Siman, has been an entertainment lawyer, a Sony Nashville senior vice president, and an artist manager (TIM MCGRAW).   —*John Rumble*

Red Simpson
b. Higley, Arizona, March 6, 1934

Best known for his recordings of truck driving songs in the 1960s and 1970s for CAPITOL RECORDS, especially his Top Ten hit "I'm a Truck" in 1971–72, Joe Cecil Simpson was also a successful songwriter. BUCK OWENS recorded about thirty-five of his songs, including "Gonna Have Love," "Sam's Place," and "The Kansas City Song" (all co-written with Owens). Artists such as MERLE HAGGARD, ROY CLARK, FERLIN HUSKY, CONNIE SMITH, and DEL REEVES recorded dozens more.

Simpson and his family had moved to the BAKERSFIELD, California, area in 1937, settling across the river from Oildale in a small community known only as Little Okie. A natural comedian and a versatile musician who played primarily guitar and piano, Simpson first earned his keep performing at most of the nightclubs in Bakersfield. He also appeared on many of Bakersfield's local television shows, such as "Cousin" Herb Henson's *Trading Post Show,* and toured with both Buck Owens and Merle Haggard. Simpson signed with CAPITOL RECORDS in 1965, and in December of that year recorded the album *Roll, Truck, Roll.* The title cut, written by TOMMY COLLINS, became Simpson's first Top Forty country hit. Mostly, though, Red was known around Bakersfield as "Suitcase" Simpson because he could always be found down at the television stations, pitching his suitcase full of songs.

JUNIOR BROWN's 1993 cover of Simpson's "Highway Patrol" led to renewed interest in Simpson's music. In 1996 Brown and Simpson collaborated on both the title track of Brown's *Semi Crazy* album and on a remake of "Nitro Express" for *Rig Rock Deluxe,* a various artists' compilation of truck driving songs.   —*Dale Vinicur*

REPRESENTATIVE RECORDINGS

Roll, Truck, Roll (Capitol, 1966, out of print); *I'm a Truck* (Capitol, 1971, out of print)

Shelby Singleton
b. Waskom, Texas, December 16, 1931

Rockabilly fans know Shelby Singleton as the man who purchased SUN RECORDS of Memphis in July 1969. But long before that, Singleton had established himself as a tremendously successful and colorful country A&R man. As a MERCURY RECORDS executive in the early 1960s, he was involved with the careers of such artists as GEORGE JONES and ROGER MILLER. Later, as head of his own independent label conglomerate, he produced JEANNIE C. RILEY's "Harper Valley P.T.A." Active to this day on the fringes of the country industry, Singleton has, above all else, maintained a reputation as one of the Nashville industry's true characters.

A native of the Texas-Louisiana border region, Singleton was involved with the LOUISIANA HAYRIDE in the 1950s and had worked as a field promotion representative for STARDAY-MERCURY during the 1957–58 union of those two labels. After the Starday-Mercury deal fell apart, Singleton continued working in the field for Mercury. His promo-

Shelby Singleton

tion and sales expertise were all he brought with him, experience-wise, when Mercury promoted him to the creative sector in Nashville in early 1961. As his wife Margie Singleton, a country artist for Mercury, said at the time, "Sometimes he knocks the musicians out—he tells them to play something and there's no such thing."

Nevertheless, Singleton proved to have acute commercial instincts, and in less than a year he was heading the A&R department in New York as well as Nashville. He split his time between the two cities, and, maverick that he was, he brought many of the label's pop and r&b artists, such as Clyde McPhatter, to Nashville to record. Singleton also hired Shreveport guitarist JERRY KENNEDY as his number two man in the Nashville office and eventual successor.

In 1966 Singleton created the Shelby Singleton Corporation and set up his independent operation at 3106 Belmont Boulevard in Nashville. By the end of the decade, the building (to which a studio was added in 1969) housed a bewildering array of Singleton-owned publishing businesses and record labels. Released on Plantation, Riley's "Harper Valley P.T.A." sold 1 million copies in 1968 and, as Sun Records historian Colin Escott has speculated, probably put Singleton into a strong enough position financially to purchase the Sun catalogue. Once he owned the Sun masters, Singleton flooded the market with low-budget LPs featuring the Sun recordings of JERRY LEE LEWIS, JOHNNY CASH, and others. In 1977, though, when Singleton issued some of ELVIS PRESLEY's Sun material, RCA sued him, eventually winning a $45,000 settlement. The whole episode had simply been one of Singleton's many entrepreneurial gambits—no more or less surprising than his having scored one of his empire's biggest hits with C Company's controversial "Battle Hymn of Lt. Calley" (a million seller in 1971), or his firm's having turned out a tribute record to John Lennon just days after Lennon's murder. In 1997 Singleton merged Sun with Brave Entertainment Corporation.   —*Daniel Cooper*

Asher & Little Jimmy Sizemore

Asher Sizemore b. Manchester, Kentucky , June 6, 1906;
d. November 24, 1975

Little Jimmy Sizemore b. Paintsville, Kentucky, January 29, 1928

Country music's premier child star of the 1930s was James L. Sizemore, or Little Jimmy, a cast member of the GRAND OLE OPRY by the time he was five years old. Although he was talented, his success was largely due to the efforts of his father, Asher Sizemore, a pleasant but undistinguished singer who is historically important as one of the great innovators in country music promotion.

Prior to entering the music business full-time, Asher briefly worked as a bookkeeper for a coal mining company in Pike County, Kentucky. After his marriage to Odessa Foley and the birth of their first child, Jimmy, Asher decided to try his hand as a singer. In 1931 he succeeded in getting a show on a Huntington, West Virginia, radio station, where he sang old-time songs and cowboy ballads. He later moved to WCKY in Cincinnati and WHAS in Louisville, by which time Jimmy was performing with his father. By 1933 they were dividing their time between WSM's Grand Ole Opry and WHAS, where Little Jimmy sang such songs as "The Booger Bear," "Has Anybody Seen My Kitty?," and "Little Feet." In 1934 he recorded "Little Jimmy's Goodbye to JIMMIE RODGERS," his best-selling record.

The duo was very popular in the 1930s, due as much to Asher's promotional skills as to Little Jimmy's talent. Asher missed few opportunities to promote his son's musical abilities. In 1933 Asher boasted that the then five-year-old boy could sing more than 200 songs from memory. Besides their appearances on WHAS and WSM, the Sizemores cut fifteen-minute transcriptions that were syndicated throughout the Midwest. These shows proved very profitable because Asher hawked paperback songbooks on each program; he was among the first country performers to use this method of raising additional income. Asher also worked hard to place songs he owned or published with other acts.

In the late 1930s Jimmy's younger brother, Charles Edward, who was called Buddy Boy, was brought into the family act; sister Nancy Louise followed later, though neither child was as popular as Little Jimmy. For a brief period the Sizemores performed on the NBC Network, and then, after leaving the Opry in 1942, they worked mainly in the Midwest throughout the 1940s. The family group appeared on programs over stations KXEL–Waterloo, Iowa; WHO–Des Moines; KMOX–St. Louis; and WSB-Atlanta. By 1950 they were on WKLO-Louisville.

Jimmy and Buddy served in the Korean War, and Buddy was declared lost in action on November 2, 1950. Both Asher and Jimmy eventually moved to Arkansas; Asher settled in DeQueen, where he died in 1975. Jimmy served as an executive with KGMR–Jacksonville, Arkansas, until he moved to Muskogee, Oklahoma, where at last report he still lives.

—*W. K. McNeil*

REPRESENTATIVE RECORDING

Songs of the Soil (Old Homestead, 1984)

Charlie Sizemore

b. Richmond, Kentucky, November 23, 1960

Singer Charlie Sizemore was raised on the music of the STANLEY BROTHERS. Recounts Sizemore, "He (my dad) doesn't much like anything else, so when I was growing up that was all that was allowed in the house. That was about all I listened to and I learned to like it."

At age thirteen, Sizemore joined Lum Patton's group the Half Mountain Boys. After three years Sizemore moved on to the Goins Brothers band, which has been a proving ground for many talented young musicians. In 1977, at sixteen, Sizemore replaced singer KEITH WHITLEY in Ralph Stanley's Clinch Mountain Boys.

Striking out on his own in 1986, Sizemore formed his own band and released his first album, *Congratulations,* for Acoustic Revival Records. In 1993 Sizemore signed with REBEL RECORDS and has released two critically acclaimed albums for the label, 1993's *Back Home* and 1996's *In My View.* The latter features a superb original tune, co-written with JIMMY MARTIN, "Got It Made in the Shade." Sizemore's low-key, understated delivery focuses on the substance of the songs rather than the use of gratuitous hot licks.

—*Chris Skinner*

REPRESENTATIVE RECORDINGS

Back Home (Rebel Records, 1993); *In My View* (Rebel Records, 1996)

Ricky Skaggs

b. Cordell, Kentucky, July 18, 1954

Ricky Lee Skaggs's career falls into three distinct phases. From 1970 to 1980, he was the hottest young picker and singer in bluegrass, both as a sidekick to the reigning legends and as a leader of the New Grass movement. From 1981 to 1989 he adapted his bluegrass sound just enough to become a mainstream country star and scored twenty Top Ten country singles. Since 1990 he has become an elder statesman of country music, more prominent as a TV host, concert attraction, and champion of traditional Appalachian music than as a hitmaker.

He grew up in the mountains of East Kentucky, hearing his parents sing, listening to their bluegrass 78s, and soaking up honky-tonk from WCKY in Cincinnati. Skaggs had been playing mandolin less than a year in 1959 when BILL MONROE invited the five-year-old boy up onstage to sing the OSBORNE BROTHERS' "Ruby." The youngster sang the same song on the FLATT & SCRUGGS television show two years later and had soon mastered fiddle and guitar as well. By 1969 Skaggs had met another fifteen-year-old Kentuckian named KEITH WHITLEY, and they put together a band called the East Kentucky Mountain Boys that did note-perfect imitations of the STANLEY BROTHERS. One night in 1970, Skaggs and Whitley went to see RALPH STANLEY in West Virginia, but when the headliner was late, the club owner asked the two teenagers to entertain the crowd.

"I walked in," Stanley remembered later, "and these two boys were singing the Stanley Brothers' music better than the Stanley Brothers." He hired both of them in the coming year, and Skaggs stayed with the Clinch Mountain Boys through 1974. During that time, Skaggs and Whitley recorded a duo album, *Second Generation Bluegrass,* with support from Stanley and his band; it featured an early version of "Don't Cheat in Our Hometown." Skaggs then decided to try the day-job life in Washington, D.C., but it didn't take, and he was soon playing with the COUNTRY GENTLEMEN and then J. D. CROWE & the New South, both pioneers of the New Grass movement.

Finally Skaggs decided to form his own group, Boone

Ricky Skaggs

Creek, which included dobroist JERRY DOUGLAS. Boone Creek made two albums, one for Rounder in 1977 and another for SUGAR HILL in 1978, and each included a version of Skaggs's favorite gospel number, "Walkin' in Jerusalem." He also released solo albums for REBEL, Sugar Hill, and ROUNDER as well as the duo album *Skaggs & Rice* with guitarist TONY RICE.

In 1977 Skaggs replaced RODNEY CROWELL in EMMYLOU HARRIS's Hot Band and eventually helped her make the 1980 breakthrough bluegrass album *Roses in the Snow.* Harris returned the favor by singing on Skaggs's *Sweet Temptation,* a 1979 solo album that also featured Rice, Douglas, the bluegrass trio known as the WHITES, and such fellow Hot Band members as TONY BROWN, EMORY GORDY, and ALBERT LEE. Both *Roses in the Snow* and *Sweet Temptation* served as blueprints for Skaggs's first major-label project, *Waitin' for the Sun to Shine,* which EPIC released in 1981. The basic sound was still bluegrass, but the banjo had been eliminated; trap drums and electric bass had been added, and the vocal harmonies were sweet and full rather than high and lonesome.

The resulting hybrid was appealing to mainstream country fans and yet exotic enough in its old-fashioned Appalachiana to sound fresh and unusual. *Waitin' for the Sun to Shine* yielded four chart singles, including back-to-back #1s with "Crying My Heart Out Over You" and "I Don't Care." Just as the album was breaking through in the summer of 1981, Skaggs married one of his harmony singers, Sharon White of the WHITES. The Whites would continue to pursue their own career but would contribute to most of Skaggs's studio efforts

Waitin' for the Sun to Shine netted Skaggs two 1982 CMA Awards: the Horizon Award, and the award for Best Male Vocalist. In that same year the singer was inducted as the sixty-first and youngest current member of the GRAND OLE OPRY. He celebrated by releasing the 1982 album *Highways & Heartaches,* which sent three singles to #1—GUY CLARK's "Heartbroke," Jim Eanes's "I Wouldn't Change You if I Could," and Larry Cordle's "Highway 40 Blues."

The 1983 album *Don't Cheat in Our Hometown* also pro-

duced three chart-topping singles: the title tune, MEL TILLIS's "Honey (Open That Door)," and BILL MONROE's "Uncle Pen." In 1984 Skaggs released his fourth straight gold album, *Country Boy,* and saw the title song go to #1. The 1985 concert album *Live in London* featured a special guest appearance by Elvis Costello on "Don't Get Above Your Raising" and sent the single "Cajun Moon" to the top of the charts. In that same year Skaggs won the CMA Entertainer of the Year Award as well as his second Grammy for Best Country Instrumental (for "Wheel Hoss" from *Country Boy*).

After 1985, things slowed down for Skaggs. He still had chart singles from such albums as 1986's *Love's Gonna Get Ya!,* 1987's *Comin' Home to Stay,* 1989's *Kentucky Thunder,* and 1991's *My Father's Son,* but he had only one more #1 hit, 1989's "Lovin' Only Me." He moved to ATLANTIC RECORDS for 1995's *Solid Ground* without much success. He alienated some fans by becoming increasingly outspoken about his fundamentalist Christian beliefs and conservative politics.

At the same time, he emerged as a leading advocate of the traditional elements in country music. He became the performing MC of a popular television program on THE NASHVILLE NETWORK, taped live onstage at the RYMAN AUDITORIUM. His weekly radio show *Simple Life with Ricky Skaggs* was heard on 400 radio stations in the United States and twenty-nine other countries. Beginning in 1991 he hosted the annual Ricky Skaggs Pickin' Party at Wolf Trap Farm Park in Virginia. There he not only presented such top bluegrass acts as Bill Monroe, Ralph Stanley, Tony Rice, Jerry Douglas, J. D. Crowe, DOC WATSON, ALISON KRAUSS, the SELDOM SCENE, and DEL MCCOURY, but also jammed with them in intriguing combinations.

In 1997 Skaggs released his first straight-ahead bluegrass album in twelve years, *Bluegrass Rules!,* on his own label, Skaggs Family Records, distributed by Rounder.

—*Geoffrey Himes*

REPRESENTATIVE RECORDINGS

Keith Whitley & Ricky Skaggs: Second Generation Bluegrass (Rebel, 1971); *Sweet Temptation* (Sugar Hill, 1979); *Waitin' for the Sun to Shine* (Epic, 1981); *Highways & Heartaches* (Epic, 1982); *Don't Cheat in Our Hometown* (Epic, 1983); *Bluegrass Rules!* (Skaggs Family Records/Rounder, 1997)

Skillet Lickers (*see* Gid Tanner)

Jimmie Skinner
b. Blue Lick, Kentucky, April 27, 1909; d. October 28, 1979

James Skinner contributed several standard songs to the bluegrass and country idioms over the years. In addition, his Cincinnati record store provided fans with their favorite discs for twenty-five years.

Natives of the rich musical area surrounding Berea, Kentucky, the Skinners moved to Ohio in 1925, where Jimmie Skinner performed locally until 1945. When Skinner's recordings—first released on the Red Barn label and then Radio Artists Records—began attracting wider attention, he soon moved to such major firms as CAPITOL, DECCA, and MERCURY. His original songs included "Doin' My Time," "Will You Be Satisfied That Way," and "Let's Say Goodbye Like We Said Hello." Ray Lunsford's electric mandolin dominated the instrumentation on his discs.

Although Skinner worked as a radio regular in such locales as Knoxville and Huntington, Cincinnati continued to be his home base until 1974, when he moved to Nashville to further his writing. His Jimmie Skinner Music Center in Cincinnati was a major mail and retail outlet for a quarter century from 1950. Skinner's biggest chart successes, such as "I Found my Girl in the U.S.A." and "Dark Hollow," came on Mercury between 1957 and 1960. Later releases appeared on lesser labels such as STARDAY, Vetco, and RICH-R-TONE, some with bluegrass accompaniment.

—*Ivan M. Tribe*

REPRESENTATIVE RECORDINGS

Songs that Make the Jukebox Play (Mercury, 1957); *Another Saturday Night* (Bear Family, 1988)

S-K-O/S-K-B (Schuyler, Knobloch & Overstreet/Schuyler, Knobloch & Bickhardt)

Out of a group of songwriters who were successfully working Music Row during the day and the BLUEBIRD CAFE at night came the eighties trio of guitarist-vocalists THOM SCHUYLER, Fred Knobloch, and PAUL OVERSTREET.

All three had written numerous hits for other artists—from KENNY ROGERS to RAY CHARLES—and all had attempted solo careers: Schuyler on CAPITOL; Overstreet on RCA; and, most successfully, Knobloch on CBS/Scotti Bros., where he scored a 1980 Top Twenty pop hit with the rueful "Why Not Me." The trio, known as S-K-O for short, carried the acoustic, rotating-vocalists approach of their in-the-round performances at the Bluebird Cafe to an eponymous 1986 debut album, which resulted in hits including the #1 "Baby's Got a New Baby." Overstreet departed to resume a solo career in 1987 and was replaced by Pennsylvania-born Craig Bickhardt, who formerly led his own band and who had had cuts by the JUDDS and KATHY MATTEA. The S-K-B trio hit the road to promote its *No Easy Horses* disc, which had chart hits with the nostalgic "This Old House" and the #8 "Givers and Takers." By March 1989, weary of the road and frustrated by dance-hall crowds who demanded "Cotton Eyed Joe," the songwriter trio had disbanded. —*Thomas Goldsmith*

REPRESENTATIVE RECORDINGS

S-K-O (MTM Records, 1986); *No Easy Horses* (MTM Records, 1988)

Bob Skyles & His Skyrockets

Possessing one of the oddest repertoires and approaches in prewar country music, Bob Skyles & His Skyrockets were a horn-based dance band whose personality was split between corny novelty and more straightforward swing, with the former usually winning out. The group was popular and prolific despite playing in sparsely populated, remote areas for most of its existence.

Originally a family band that grew out of a traveling medicine show, the Skyrockets first formed close to Brady, Texas, in 1935, appearing there on KNEL. Managed by guitarist Brooke "Doc" Kendrick but fronted by his oldest son, multi-instrumentalist Bob, and including sons Sanford and Clifford, the band moved to KIUN-Pecos, in mid-1936. In 1937 Bob Kendrick secured a contract with BLUE-BIRD, changing his name to Skyles at the insistence of A&R man ELI OBERSTEIN, who also insisted that the band exploit its possibilities as a novelty act. The Skyrockets responded

with the hit "Arkansas Bazooka Swing" and other big sellers. For the next two years they were one of Bluebird's hottest hillbilly acts, adding such musicians as multi-instrumentalists Dave Hughs and Frank Wilhelm and pianist-vocalist Max Bennett. Moving to Hobbs, New Mexico, in 1938, the group also was based in San Angelo and El Paso, where it briefly included the legendary MOON MULLICAN. The Skyrockets switched to DECCA in 1940, with much less emphasis on novelty, and moved to BAKERSFIELD, California, before breaking up in 1942. Bob Kendrick became a prize-winning Texas contest fiddler in later years.

—*Kevin Coffey*

REPRESENTATIVE RECORDINGS

Operator's Specials (String, 19800 (various-artists reissue contains two 1938 Skyrockets recordings); *Western Swing, Volume Five* (Old Timey, 1980) (various-artists reissue contains one 1937 Skyrockets recording)

Melvin Sloan Dancers
Ralph Sloan b. Wilson County, Tennessee, March 9, 1925; d. March 12, 1980
Melvin Sloan b. Wilson County, Tennessee, March 27, 1940

The Melvin Sloan Dancers are a SQUARE DANCING troupe that has been performing at the GRAND OLE OPRY since 1952. Formed in about 1949 and named the Cedar Hill Square Dancers, the group reorganized approximately one year later as the Tennessee Travelers. Performances at mid-state county fairs led to a guest spot on the Opry and eventually to full-time membership. The troupe was later known as Ralph Sloan and the Tennessee Travelers until the death of founder and leader Ralph Sloan in 1980. His brother Melvin took over the troupe, and they were renamed the Melvin Sloan Dancers.

Before joining the Opry, the troupe performed on WSM-TV's *Country Junction Show*. The size of the troupe has varied from seventeen to eight members; fewer members allowed them to show off their skills on smaller stages, such as at roller skating rinks. Past members have included Joyce Sloan, Vernon and Jean Huffine, Robbie Gregory, Deborah Shrum, Jackie and Jerry Harper, Carolyn Burris, Debby Harper, Bobby Pardon, and Tommy Harper. In 1988 their Appalachian style of square dancing was officially named the Tennessee state dance. —*Stacey Wolfe*

Ben Smathers & the Stoney Mountain Cloggers
Ben Smathers b. Hendersonville, North Carolina, May 17, 1928; d. September 13, 1990

For thirty-two years to the day, Ben Ray Smathers led the popular Stoney Mountain Cloggers dance troupe at the GRAND OLE OPRY. Organized in the mid-1950s, the group's first appearance on the show came on September 13, 1958; they were hired as regular cast members immediately afterward. Until their appearance at the Grand Ole Opry, CLOGGING, a cross between European folk dancing, buck dancing, and SQUARE DANCING, was rarely seen outside of North Carolina's Dutch-Irish communities.

Largely a family group, the Stoney Mountain Cloggers included in its ranks over the years Ben's wife, Margaret, and their children Hal, Mickey, Candy, Debbie, and Sally. In 1961 the troupe appeared at CARNEGIE HALL with a Grand Ole Opry troupe that included PATSY CLINE and JIM

REEVES. In 1981 the Stoney Mountain Cloggers returned, performing with MERLE HAGGARD and TAMMY WYNETTE. After the death of patriarch Ben Smathers on the thirty-second anniversary of his initial Opry appearance, the group continued until September 11, 1993, when they ended the act.
—*Stacey Wolfe*

Arthur "Guitar Boogie" Smith
b. Clinton, South Carolina, April 1, 1921

An inventive country musician with a flair for 1920s pop tunes, Arthur Smith parlayed his 1945 instrumental hit "Guitar Boogie" into an enduring broadcasting and entrepreneurial career.

Raised in Kershaw, South Carolina, Smith originally played trumpet in his father's brass band. He later formed a traditional jazz ensemble with his two brothers, Ralph and Sonny, and bassist Luke Tucker. By 1938 the Arthur Smith Quartet appeared daily on WSPA-Spartanburg. Frustrated by a lack of success, Smith embraced country music for a BLUEBIRD RECORDS session in 1938. As the Carolina Crackerjacks it offered an appealing mix of country ballads, gospel quartets, and pop standards, usually spotlighting Smith on fiddle. Unlike most country bands, the Crackerjacks relied heavily on written charts.

When World War II broke up the band in fall 1943, Smith briefly worked at WBT-Charlotte, before joining the navy. Returning to Charlotte after the war, he played guitar with the Briarhoppers and CECIL CAMPBELL's Tennessee Ramblers. To wrap up a fall 1945 Campbell session for Super Disc, Smith quickly cut "Guitar Boogie," an acoustic guitar instrumental backed by DON RENO on rhythm guitar and Roy Lear on bass. Credited to the Rambler Trio, it became an enormous regional hit, launched a wave of country boogie records, and established Smith as a recording artist. After signing with MGM in 1947, he recorded country songs and guitar and tenor banjo specialties with his Crackerjacks, and gospel numbers with the Crossroads Quartet. MGM's October 1948 reissue of "Guitar Boogie" eventually rose to #8 on *Billboard*'s country chart. "Feuding Banjos," a 1955 call-and-response novelty featuring Smith's tenor banjo and Reno's five-string, became a bluegrass standard. Renamed "Dueling Banjos," the tune was featured in Warner Bros.' 1972 movie *Deliverance* without crediting Smith; he eventually won a prolonged lawsuit over its use.

In 1951 Smith entered television with daily and weekly shows over WBT-TV; their popularity led him to promote packaged country and gospel shows throughout the South. In 1959 *The Arthur Smith Show* was syndicated to fourteen stations; by 1977 it had appeared in sixty-eight markets across the United States. During the mid-1980s Smith largely retired from performing to concentrate on his business interests.
—*Dave Samuelson*

Arthur Q. Smith
b. Griffin, Georgia, December 11, 1909; d. March 21, 1963

For years during the 1940s and 1950s, the man known as Arthur Q. Smith would stand outside the studios at Knoxville radio station WNOX and peddle songs the way a flea market vendor would peddle hubcaps. For ten dollars or twenty-five dollars a song, young country artists could buy all rights to some of the best songs of the era—pieces such as "Rainbow at Midnight," "If Teardrops Were Pen-

nies," "Wedding Bells," and "I Wouldn't Change You If I Could." Customers included ROY ACUFF, BILL MONROE, MAYBELLE CARTER, CARL SMITH, CARL BUTLER, HANK WILLIAMS, and KITTY WELLS—and dozens of others not yet identified. Smith's name seldom if ever appeared on the song credits, though he kept private notebooks recording who bought which song.

Smith's real name was James Arthur Prichett, and he grew up in Harlan, Kentucky; in the 1940s he tried a singing career, recording for KING and Deluxe, and tried to work with the songwriting establishment by signing with ACUFF-ROSE. Eventually the company let him go, and Prichett soon returned to selling his songs independently. His drinking contributed to an unstable life, though several of his protégés, including HARLAN HOWARD, went on to win recognition for him.
—*Charles Wolfe*

Cal Smith
b. Gans, Oklahoma, April 7, 1932

Born Calvin Grant Shofner, Cal Smith became one of country music's biggest stars of the 1970s. He grew up around San Jose, California, where he first sang in nightclubs with a vocal style similar to HANK THOMPSON's. Smith was the vocalist with Uncle Phil Philley's band when it performed at San Quentin Prison along with JOHNNY CASH and other stars for inmates in early 1958. Smith's first recording, in 1960 for Plaid Records, was even a prison ballad, "Eleven Long Years."

Smith was also by then a popular country music disc jockey with KEEN in San Jose. But he left the West Coast on December 26, 1962, to join ERNEST TUBB's Texas Troubadours as rhythm guitarist and front man, a job he held until July 1968. Tubb boosted Smith's career with featured tracks on Texas Troubadours LPs, performances on the GRAND OLE OPRY and on Tubb's syndicated TV show, and with a Kapp Records contract in 1966. Smith's popularity built slowly (he left Tubb to promote his recording of "Drinking Champagne," a BILL MACK song that made #35 on the *Billboard* chart) until his breakthrough song, BILL ANDERSON's "The Lord Knows I'm Drinking" (1972–73). "Country Bumpkin" and "It's Time to Pay the Fiddler" (both 1974) became his other two #1s, the former earning him CMA's Single of the Year Award.

Onetime part owner of the Nashville Sounds baseball team, Smith lives today in the Missouri Ozarks.
—*Ronnie Pugh*

REPRESENTATIVE RECORDINGS
The Lord Know's I'm Drinking (MCA, 1972); *Country Bumpkin* (MCA, 1974)

Carl Smith
b. Maynardville, Tennessee, March 15, 1927

A second famous son of Maynardville, Tennessee—ROY ACUFF being the first—Carl M. Smith was one of country music's most popular hitmakers of the 1950s and 1960s.

Smith grew up listening to the GRAND OLE OPRY and to daily country broadcasts on Knoxville stations. In 1944 Cas Walker gave him his first radio work, on Knoxville's WROL. As singer, guitarist, and sometimes bass player, Smith worked with the Knoxville band the Brewster Brothers after military service, and then, between 1947 and

Carl Smith

1949, moved many times among Knoxville; Asheville, North Carolina; and Augusta, Georgia. He was back at WROL, working in ARCHIE CAMPBELL's band, when Knoxville dobro player George "Speedy" Krise made a demo of Smith's singing and sent it to Troy Martin in Nashville, the Peer-Southern Music publishing representative in the Music City and a top-flight talent scout for DON LAW of COLUMBIA RECORDS. Martin liked Smith's singing, and arranged an audition with JACK STAPP of WSM. After some WSM guest appearances in March 1950, Stapp gave Smith a six-day-a-week morning show in May, with Opry appearances about every third week. Don Law signed Smith to a Columbia contract on May 5, and six days later Smith held his first session in Nashville's CASTLE STUDIOS.

WSM took time in developing Smith as a young artist. A year passed before his first hit, but then they came with regularity—intense love songs, for the most part, suitably framed by bandsman Johnny Sibert's crying steel guitar. "Let's Live a Little" in 1951 was Smith's first; "Mr. Moon" and "If Teardrops Were Pennies" also made the charts that year.

Friends on the Grand Ole Opry were doing what they could to help Smith's career. HANK WILLIAMS let Smith record his "Me and My Broken Heart" and "There's Nothing as Sweet as My Baby"; ERNEST TUBB, with whom Smith did some of his earliest touring, brought him Jack Henley's "(When You Feel Like You're In Love) Don't Just Stand There." This song became Smith's second #1 hit, preceded by "Let Old Mother Nature Have Her Way," his biggest-selling single.

For the next few years, every one of his records made the Top Twenty—sometimes both sides of a single. The LOUVIN BROTHERS' "Are You Teasing Me" went to #1 in 1952, and its flip side, BOUDLEAUX & FELICE BRYANT's "It's a Lovely, Lovely World," went to #5. This talented couple became favorite Smith song sources after this, supplying "Just

Wait 'Til I Get You Alone" (1953), "Hey Joe!" (1953), and "Back Up Buddy" (1954). Four of his releases, culminating in FREDDIE HART's "Loose Talk," were "Triple Crown Winners," reaching #1 on all three of *Billboard*'s country charts.

Smith left the Grand Ole Opry toward the end of 1956, amid a welter of behind-the-scenes politics, to take star billing on the PHILIP MORRIS COUNTRY MUSIC SHOW, a touring free show sponsored by the cigarette maker, that ran some eighteen months in 1957 and 1958. Television afterward became a favored venue of the handsome Smith. He frequently guested on RED FOLEY's *Jubilee U.S.A.,* and in 1961 was co-host of its follow-up series, *Five Star Jubilee,* also out of Springfield, Missouri. Between 1964 and 1969, Smith's regular TV exposure crossed the border into Canada: He hosted 190 episodes of *Carl Smith's Country Music Hall.*

His recording career was hardly dormant during these years. Carl Smith placed at least one record on the country charts every year between 1951 and 1973, which was virtually his entire time recording with COLUMBIA RECORDS. Briefly coaxed back into recording in the late 1970s for HICKORY RECORDS, Smith gradually gave up touring and recording to live the life of a gentleman horse breeder on his acres near Franklin, Tennessee.

Twice married to country music performers, Smith and first wife, JUNE CARTER (1952–56), are the parents of singing star CARLENE CARTER. Since 1957 Smith has been married to GOLDIE HILL, who was DECCA RECORDS's Golden Hillbilly and, at the time of their wedding, a co-star on the Philip Morris Country Music Show.   —*Ronnie Pugh*

REPRESENTATIVE RECORDINGS

Carl Smith: Columbia Historic Edition (Columbia, 1984); *The Essential Carl Smith, 1950–1956* (Columbia, 1991)

Connie Smith

b. Elkhart, Indiana, August 14, 1941

In November 1964 the talk of the annual disc jockey convention in Nashville was young Connie Smith, whose debut hit "Once a Day" was among the hottest items on the DJs' playlists at that very moment. A year before, Smith had been a small-town housewife in Ohio; now she was a breakout RCA artist with a country voice as powerful as any the seasoned jocks had ever heard. Though not as well known as such contemporaries as LORETTA LYNN and TAMMY WYNETTE, Smith has been cited as a favorite singer of everyone from GEORGE JONES to JUNIOR BROWN. DOLLY PARTON once said, "You know, there's really only three *real* female singers in the world. Streisand, Ronstadt, and Connie Smith. The rest of us are only pretending."

Born Constance June Meador, Smith grew up in West Virginia and Ohio in a family of fourteen children. Her parents were migrant farm workers, her father an abusive alcoholic. As a teenager Smith listened to both the GRAND OLE OPRY and pop radio, paying close attention to KITTY WELLS and JEAN SHEPARD on the former, and to Sarah Vaughan and Nancy Wilson on the latter. Laid up in bed after a lawn mower accident when she was eighteen, Smith taught herself the basics of guitar. Though not serious about a music career, she sang at local square dances and Grange halls. For a time she performed in the traveling band of a man named Floyd Miller, then later with the cast of *Saturday Night Jamboree,* a live TV show carried on WSAZ in Huntington, West Virginia.

On August 4, 1963, Smith won a talent contest that preceded an Opry-troupe concert in Columbus, Ohio. First prize included the chance to sing on the Opry program. Opry headliner BILL ANDERSON took note of Smith's talent, and when the two met up again at a New Year's Day concert in Canton, Ohio, he suggested that she consider coming to Nashville.

At Anderson's invitation, Smith flew to Nashville to sing on the March 28, 1964, edition of the *Ernest Tubb Midnite Jamboree.* In May Anderson invited her back again, this time to make a demo recording of four of his songs. Anderson pitched the tape to CHET ATKINS, who signed Smith to RCA on June 24. On July 16, with BOB FERGUSON producing, she recorded Anderson's "Once a Day," her debut single. It eventually spent eight weeks at #1.

Smith never repeated the spectacular success of "Once a Day," but for the next few years she recorded a succession of albums and Top Ten singles of consistent quality and dramatic impact. As producer, Ferguson sometimes employed standard NASHVILLE SOUND techniques, but Smith's most effective work was usually with straight-ahead country accompaniment highlighted by Weldon Myrick's steel guitar. Her material leaned heavily toward themes of lost love and heartache, as exemplified on Anderson's "Then and Only Then" (#4, 1965) and DALLAS FRAZIER's "Ain't Had No Lovin' "(#2, 1966). But as the end of the decade approached, Smith's song choices (such as "Ribbon of Darkness" and "The Last Letter") seemed to grow more darkly personal. "At that time, I was a sad little girl, and I sang a lot of sad songs," she said.

Never comfortable with the trappings of stardom, Smith was rapidly moving toward a spiritual crisis, and she eventually joined the Rev. Jimmie Snow's Evangel Temple

congregation. In 1973, when she left RCA for COLUMBIA, she had it written into her new contract that she would be allowed to record one gospel album per year along with two country LPs. By then she was retreating from the road and limelight anyway, devoting herself more to home and family. She recorded briefly for MONUMENT in the late 1970s, then disappeared from the charts until 1985, when Columbia recorded her singing "A Far Cry from You"—a song that came from the pen of STEVE EARLE. Since then, Smith has returned to more active work on the road, at the Grand Ole Opry, and in the studio. As of 1998 she had recorded an album of new material, produced by MARTY STUART, due out on WARNER BROS. She and Stuart married on July 8, 1997.   —*Daniel Cooper*

REPRESENTATIVE RECORDINGS

Connie Smith (RCA, 1965 O/P); *The Essential Connie Smith* (BMG, 1996)

Fiddlin' Arthur Smith

b. Bold Springs, Tennessee, April 10, 1898; d. February 28, 1971

Along with CLAYTON MCMICHEN, Fiddlin' Arthur Smith was the most influential fiddler in prewar country music. As a star of the GRAND OLE OPRY and prolific recording artist (for BLUEBIRD RECORDS), he enjoyed wide exposure in the mass media. As a composer he produced dozens of fiddle tunes as well as popular songs such as "More Pretty Girls Than One." As a stylist he helped to popularize the "long bow" style, in which the fiddler used long, smooth bowing strokes as opposed to the older "jiggy bow" style of short, chopping strokes. This long-bow style has dominated modern contest and bluegrass fiddling.

Hailing from Dickson County, in the hills west of Nashville, Smith absorbed some of the distinctive folk fiddle styles of the region before he began to perform with his cousin Homer Smith at the Grand Ole Opry in 1929. After a few years, Opry managers teamed Arthur Smith with SAM & KIRK MCGEE to form an all-star stringband called the Dixieliners (in deference to Smith's work on the Nashville, Chattanooga, & St. Louis Railroad, nicknamed the Dixie Line). The team was enormously popular on the air and on tour, but when Smith started to make records in 1935, he teamed up with the DELMORE BROTHERS. During the next five years he recorded some forty solo sides, including his signature numbers such as "Blackberry Blossom," "Cheatham County Breakdown," and "Fiddler's Dream." The Delmores convinced him to record vocal numbers as well, and he turned out the enduring country favorites "Walking in My Sleep," "Beautiful Brown Eyes," and "Pig at Home in the Pen."

Leaving the Opry in 1938, Smith spent time with the BAILES BROTHERS in West Virginia and then made his way to the West Coast, where he worked for cowboy singer JIMMY WAKELY in the 1940s. By now Smith was introducing the fiddle classic "Orange Blossom Special" to audiences in Las Vegas, on the West Coast, and on radio. He returned to Tennessee in the 1950s, intending to ease into retirement from music, but was coaxed by folklorist Mike Seeger to reunite the Dixieliners (Smith and the McGees) and make their first records, a pair of LPs for Folkways Records. Smith made numerous appearances during the folk revival and eventually cut an album for STARDAY RECORDS. Health problems caught up with him in 1971, and he died in Louisville.   —*Stacey Wolfe*

Connie Smith

Hal Smith
b. Fairview (Cullman County), Alabama, November 21, 1923

Best known as a founding partner of PAMPER MUSIC, James Harrell "Hal" Smith also worked by turns as a Nashville musician, artist manager, and television producer.

After receiving a medical discharge from the army in 1943, Smith moved to Nashville with fiddle in hand. He toured as a sideman with ROY ACUFF, PEE WEE KING, EDDY ARNOLD, ERNEST TUBB, GEORGE MORGAN, CARL SMITH, and others. While working with Tubb in 1948, Smith married guitar player Velma Williams, a former member of Acuff's Smoky Mountain Boys and Girls.

In 1954 Smith began a long career as an entertainment executive, first as manager to RAY PRICE and JIM REEVES and then Carl Smith. Other artists managed by Smith included Ernest Tubb, JIMMY C. NEWMAN, and JACK GREENE. Smith soon expanded into owning and operating talent agencies, publishing companies, and television program productions. One of Smith's most prosperous ventures was the establishment of Pamper Music, publisher of classics by HANK COCHRAN, WILLIE NELSON, and HARLAN HOWARD. Additional companies owned or operated by Smith include Curtis Artists Productions (established in late 1956), Hal Smith Artists Productions, Hal Smith TV Programs, Cullman Records, and Boone Records. Among the syndicated television shows produced by Smith were the *Ernest Tubb Show*, *Wills Family Inspirational Time*, *Country Music Carousel*, and *Skylite Cavalcade*. Significant associates of Smith's entertainment companies included talent agents Jimmy Key and Haze Jones, and television programming personnel A. O. Stinson, Dave White, and Bill Brittain. Smith even owned the Renfro Valley complex for a while in the late 1960s but sold all of his music properties about 1969.
—*Kent Henderson*

Russell Smith (*see* Amazing Rhythm Aces)

Sammi Smith
b. Orange, California, August 5, 1943

Jewel Fay "Sammi" Smith was one of the leading female vocalists of the 1970s and one of the few women performers to have been associated with the OUTLAW phenomenon that peaked near mid-decade. Born in Southern California but reared throughout the Southwest, she began performing in nightclubs (primarily as a rock & roll singer) at age eleven. Smith moved to Nashville in 1967 and signed with COLUMBIA RECORDS. She also became friends with an aspiring songwriter, KRIS KRISTOFFERSON, who would provide her with her biggest hit.

Released early in 1971 on the independent Mega label, "Help Me Make It Through the Night" became a #1 country single and a Top Ten hit on the pop charts. It was a breakthrough recording in many ways, introducing an unprecedented level of sexual candor, which was highlighted by Smith's husky voice and sensual reading of the lyrics. For the song she won a 1971 Grammy for Best Country Vocal Performance, Female. In addition, it secured for Kristofferson his status as Nashville's leading young songwriter on the crest of a new wave of creativity and experimentation.

Unfortunately for Smith, her commercial success peaked with the Grammy-winning effort. Several subsequent releases on Mega generated solid to unspectacular sales, as did two of her compositions for other artists, "Cedartown, Georgia" (for WAYLON JENNINGS) and "Sand-Covered Angels" (for CONWAY TWITTY).

A brief stay in Texas from 1973 to 1975 raised Smith's profile as she appeared regularly with old friends WILLIE NELSON and WAYLON JENNINGS. A move to ELEKTRA RECORDS in 1975, followed by affiliations with three minor companies into the 1980s, did little to revive Smith's career. Her talent usually outperformed her material as she searched for a sequel to one of country music's modern masterpieces.
—*Stephen R. Tucker*

REPRESENTATIVE RECORDINGS
The Best of Sammi Smith (Mega, 1972); *Today I Started Loving You Again* (Mega, 1975)

Steuart Smith
b. Baltimore, Maryland, June 24, 1952

Guitarist-songwriter-producer Smith has made a major impact as a talented, individualistic guitarist, beginning in 1986, as a featured collaborator with RODNEY CROWELL, ROSANNE CASH, and many others.

Smith started his musical career as a keyboardist, but made the switch to guitar in the Washington, D.C., music scene of the mid-seventies. Introduced to country sounds by the honky-tonk efforts of the Beatles and the Rolling Stones, he graduated to listening to country guitar titans ROY NICHOLS and JAMES BURTON and built up startling country chops while retaining rock and r&b influences. Smith's introduction to country session work came circuitously; New York–based CBS Records exec Rick Chertoff heard Smith playing with a "psychobilly" band called Switchblade and kept the guitarist's name for three years before arranging a Crowell session for him in 1986. "Everything sort of snowballed from there," said Smith, who became part of Crowell's highly touted Dixie Pearls band. Smith's highly creative work ranges from the crackling, fresh-sounding country of Crowell's multihit 1988 *Diamonds and Dirt* to the acoustic lyricism of Cash's 1990 *Interiors* to the bluesy sounds of WYNONNA's 1993 *Tell Me Why*. Also active as a pop and folk studio player (Melissa Etheridge, Shawn Colvin), Smith has continued to live in the Washington, D.C. area while commuting to Nashville, New York City, and California. In 1997 Smith joined Rodney Crowell, MICHAEL RHODES, and Vince Santoro in the Cicadas.
—*Thomas Goldsmith*

REPRESENTATIVE RECORDING
The Cicadas (Warner Bros., 1997)

Velma Williams Smith
b. Logan County, Kentucky, July 27, 1924

Velma Elizabeth Williams Smith first gained notice in 1942 when she became a member of ROY ACUFF's Smoky Mountain Boys and Girls. Performing with her sister, Mildred, as the Williams Sisters, Velma Williams played the bass and sang. Following the departure of Rachel Veach from the band, Williams was briefly billed with BASHFUL BROTHER OSWALD as Oswald and his Big Sister. Williams left the Acuff troupe around 1948 and married HAL SMITH, who was then the fiddler for ERNEST TUBB. During the NASHVILLE SOUND era, Williams's distinctive rhythm guitar style earned session appearances on many of CHET ATKINS's

RCA acts, including JIM REEVES, DOTTIE WEST, and SKEETER DAVIS.
—Kent Henderson

Warren Smith
b. Humphreys County, Mississippi, prob. February 7, 1932;
d. January 30, 1980

Although he scored several big country hits in the early 1960s, Warren Smith is better known today for his unsuccessful rockabilly recordings for SUN RECORDS.

He grew up in Louise, Mississippi, and went to West Memphis, Arkansas, in 1955. A local bandleader, Clyde Leoppard, brought him to Sun, and Smith recorded five singles for the label that veered precipitously between country music and rockabilly, the best-known probably being "Ubangi Stomp." Smith acquired the demeanor and mien of the rock & roll star; all he lacked was the hits. His Sun singles were later regarded as quintessential rockabilly.

Smith moved to California in 1959, cut three singles for WARNER BROS., then recorded for LIBERTY (1960–64). "I Don't Believe I'll Fall in Love Today" and "Odds and Ends" were Top Ten country hits, utilizing the hillbilly shuffle that had been so successful for RAY PRICE and others. Smith's career quickly disintegrated, though. There was a serious automobile accident in 1965 and a jail term, both stemming from prescription drug abuse. There were also singles on ever smaller labels, such as Skill and Jubal. He moved to Texas in the mid-1960s and worked outside of music, although he toured Europe to some acclaim as a rockabilly in 1977 and 1978. He died of a heart attack preparing for his third overseas tour.
—Colin Escott

REPRESENTATIVE RECORDINGS

Call of the Wild (Bear Family, 1990); *Classic Recordings 1956–1959* (Bear Family, 1992)

Smith's Sacred Singers

An informal collection of friends and neighbors from northeastern Georgia, Smith's Sacred Singers became the best-selling and most popular gospel group of the 1920s. Their 1926 debut recording of "Pictures from Life's Other Side" b/w "Where We'll Never Grow Old" became the best-selling gospel record in COLUMBIA's 15000 series and one of the best-selling records in old-time music.

A devout Methodist and singing schoolteacher, J. Frank Smith was from Braselton, Georgia, and rehearsed his quartet to sing from the old shape-note books, usually with piano accompaniment. His original group included the Rev. M. L. Thrasher on bass; Clyde Smith (no relation), who played violin and sang baritone; Clarence Cronic (b. September 6, 1902; d. October 22, 1990), who sang tenor and played guitar; and Smith himself singing lead.

Amazed by the sudden and spectacular success of the first Smith record, Columbia rushed the group back into the studio, and soon they had a series of follow-up hits: "Going Down the Valley," "Shouting on the Hills," "The Eastern Gate," and "He Will Set Your Fields On Fire." They would eventually do some sixty-six sides for Columbia between 1926 and 1930 (as well as an additional thirty-eight titles for BLUEBIRD from 1934 to 1936), and their popularity would set off a small boom in gospel music with the major record companies of the time. Smith never tried to professionalize the group—they never toured or did extensive radio work—and the band's personnel shifted rather extensively from session to session.
—Charles Wolfe

Mike Snider
b. Gleason, Tennessee, May 30, 1960

William Michael Snider has taken the venerable country traditions of down-home humor and old-time banjo playing and carried them lovingly into contemporary times. He was one of the first stars created by THE NASHVILLE NETWORK (TNN) via guest spots on RALPH EMERY's *NASHVILLE NOW* (more than a hundred appearances) and the syndicated *HEE HAW* series (he joined the cast in 1987). With his slow-drawling West Tennessee accent, he left an initial impression of a bashful and simple country boy, but he quickly proved to be a shrewd and effective entertainer, mixing old-time tunes with humorous stories about his wife, "Sweetie" (Sabrina). He often generated double the fan mail of famous guests.

At sixteen, Snider received his first banjo. After winning the Mid-South Banjo Championship, he became National Bluegrass Banjo Champion at twenty-three. On January 21, 1984, Snider made his first appearance on the GRAND OLE OPRY. A prouder moment came on June 2, 1990, when he was officially welcomed as a cast member by his comedy idol, MINNIE PEARL. Snider has since added back-up musicians to his act and witty one-liners. In 1989 he hosted TNN's *Fairs & Festivals* series and is in demand for banquets and conventions. He was also a familiar face at the Opryland park. Snider's albums, *Puttin' on the Dog* and *Mike Snider Live at the Opry,* are not available in music stores but instead at his personal appearances. Thanks to TV appearances, Snider says, the releases have sold respectably: "Sometimes you sell a few and sometimes you don't."
—Walt Trott

Glen Snoddy
b. Shelbyville, Tennessee, May 4, 1922

Woodland Sound studio operator Snoddy has played a key role in furthering Nashville's international reputation as a top-quality recording center. He played trombone and piano in his youth but found his calling after World War II as an engineer, working first for Middle Tennessee radio stations and then for the Brown Brothers Recording Service in downtown Nashville. There he engineered hundreds of transcriptions and live radio broadcasts before joining WSM in 1955, where he spent five years broadcasting "everything from big bands to the Opry."

Also active in the new field of TV and in studio recording, Snoddy decided to concentrate on recording in 1960 when he became chief engineer of OWEN BRADLEY's legendary Quonset Hut studio, recording JOHNNY CASH, MARTY ROBBINS, and many others there after COLUMBIA RECORDS took it over in 1962. In 1967 he constructed Woodland out of a former movie theater in East Nashville and made it one of the city's most active and well-regarded studios. Two years later the studio expanded to become a 16,000-square-foot complex. California-based AVI purchased Woodland in 1980; Snoddy worked for the company into the second half of the eighties until retirement. Through Snoddy's tenure there, technologically advanced Woodland hosted such landmark sessions as the NITTY GRITTY DIRT BAND's 1971 *Will the Circle Be Unbroken* album as well as many dozens of name performers: country stars

such as LEFTY FRIZZELL, the OAK RIDGE BOYS, and TAMMY WYNETTE as well as diverse others, including JOHN PRINE, Andy Williams, NEIL YOUNG, Joe Simon, LINDA RONSTADT, and Kansas, whose hit "Dust in the Wind" was cut there.
—*Thomas Goldsmith*

Hank Snow

b. Brooklyn, Nova Scotia, Canada, May 9, 1914

Undeniably the most successful country music star to come out of Canada, Clarence Eugene "Hank" Snow has also emerged as one of the most distinctive stylists, one of the best songwriters, one of the most prolific recording artists, one of the finest guitarists, and one of the most masterful businessmen in the modern industry. Through his career, he has never turned his back on the classic JIMMIE RODGERS style that first made him famous, but he has also experimented with Latin rhythms, jazz, blues, Hawaiian styles, recitations, the mambo, and gospel songs.

The some 840 commercial recordings he made between 1936 and 1985 form one of the largest discographies in the music business. They include folksongs of his Canadian boyhood, Rodgers-styled songs, hobo and railroad songs, cowboy songs, pop standards, and some of the best efforts of Nashville's own songwriters. Hank Snow continually delves back into his early repertoire to resurrect old songs for new audiences. To him, repertoire is a living thing, and his sense of tradition is as sharp and keen as that of any folksinger. His is indeed a valid repertoire: From 1949 to 1980 he saw no fewer than eighty-five of his singles reach *Billboard*'s charts. Nobody was surprised when he was elected to the COUNTRY MUSIC HALL OF FAME in 1979.

His had been a long, torturous road to Nashville; it began far above the northeast boundaries of Maine, in the windswept village of Brooklyn in Nova Scotia. He was one of four children (he had three sisters), and his life became difficult when he was only eight and his parents divorced. That event plunged him into a series of misadventures that resembled something out of a Dickens novel: He was sent off to his paternal grandparents, but he routinely ran away and made his way back to his mother. When she remarried, Snow found himself dealing with a violent stepfather. "I was treated by him . . . like a dog," Snow recalled. "I took many beatings from him and still carry scars across my body that were left by his hamlike hands." To escape from this, as a teenager Snow went to sea working on a fishing trawler in the wild North Atlantic, where he entertained the crew by singing and playing the harmonica. At home, his mother let him listen to Victrola records, first by VERNON DALHART, then by the new singer Jimmie Rodgers.

By 1933 the young singer, armed with a mail-order Timothy Eaton guitar, began singing over CHNS in Halifax; he also met and married a local Dutch-Irish girl named Minnie Blanch Aalders. The young couple soon obtained a serious radio job for the laxative company CRAZY WATER CRYSTALS, and Snow began billing himself Hank the Yodeling Ranger after learning that Jimmie Rodgers had been made an honorary Texas Ranger.

In October 1936 Snow traveled to Montreal to make his first records for Canadian BLUEBIRD: "Lonesome Blue Yodel" and "Prisoned Cowboy." A series of releases followed, including hits such as "Blue Velvet Band," "Galveston Rose," and "My Blue River Rose." All told, he did some ninety recordings for Canadian Bluebird between 1936 and 1949; all but a handful were never released in the United States.

After a couple of abortive stays in Hollywood and West Virginia, Snow finally was able to crack the American market in 1948. An expert rider, he often toured with a trick riding show, featuring his horse Pawnee. He was a modest success in Dallas on the *BIG D JAMBOREE* and contacted ERNEST TUBB, a fellow admirer of Rodgers. Tubb liked his work very much and began to pester the GRAND OLE OPRY staff on Snow's behalf; the Opry finally relented, and invited Snow to join. He was, in fact, introduced onstage by HANK WILLIAMS.

For a time it seemed that Snow's stay would be short; he seemed unable to get a hit or get audience response. Then his first Victor American hit came along: "I'm Movin' On." A piece that Snow's producer had not even wanted to cut, the song rode the charts for forty-four weeks in 1950 and 1951; it was followed by two more #1s: "The Golden Rocket" (1950) and "Rhumba Boogie" (1951). These were his career songs, and for the next five years he averaged two or three Top Ten hits a year, including "I Don't Hurt Anymore" (1954), "The Gold Rush Is Over" (1952), "A Fool Such as I" (1952), "Yellow Roses" (1955), "Conscience, I'm Guilty" (1956), and "I've Been Everywhere" (1962). In addition, he became one of the first country singers to see the LP as the basic creative unit, and created some of the first theme, or concept, albums. He also utilized his considerable skills as a guitarist (his inspiration had been the Farr brothers from the SONS OF THE PIONEERS) to do a series of duets with CHET ATKINS.

Throughout the 1960s and 1970s Snow helped hold the line against rock and pop's assault on traditional country music. He traveled widely (including to Vietnam) and became a fixture on the Opry. In 1977 he recorded his 104th LP for RCA VICTOR RECORDS, *Still Movin' On*, an apt title

Hank Snow

for an artist who gives longevity a new and dramatic meaning. In 1994 he published his autobiography, *The Hank Snow Story,* through the University of Illinois Press. Today, health problems have forced him into semiretirement, and he no longer appears on the Opry. —*Charles Wolfe*

REPRESENTATIVE RECORDINGS

Hank Snow, The Singing Ranger (Bear Family, 1988), 4 CDs; *The Essential Hank Snow* (RCA, 1997)

Society of European Stage Authors and Composers (*see* SESAC)

Leo Soileau

b. Ville Platte, Louisiana, January 19, 1904; d. August 2, 1980

Leo Soileau was one of Cajun music's most innovative and important musicians. As a youngster, Soileau became an accomplished traditional fiddler, learning from old-timers such as DENNIS MCGEE. In 1928 Soileau joined with accordionist Mayuse Lafleur to make the second commercial recording of Cajun music, for VICTOR RECORDS. The next year he and accordionist Moise Robin made recordings for several labels. In November 1929 Soileau recorded some outstanding old-time fiddle duets with his cousin Alius Soileau as the Soileau Couzens. At the same sessions he also recorded with accordionist Oscar "Slim" Doucet.

Soileau was one of the first Cajuns to incorporate elements of commercial country music into Cajun music. In 1934 he formed a stringband, Leo Soileau & His Three Aces. The accordion was dropped from the lineup, and the new sound was Cajun country music. Soileau's Three Aces later became Four Aces, and in 1937 (the last year he recorded), Leo Soileau's Rhythm Boys. He remained active in Louisiana and southeastern Texas playing dances and radio shows until 1953. Later he worked in an oil refinery and as a janitor until he retired in 1968.

—*Charlie Seemann*

Songbooks

Songbooks were once central to country music's popularity, and were basic ingredients of virtually every country singer's professional career. Their origins were rooted in the broadside ballads and song folios hawked on British and American colonial streets in the seventeenth and eighteenth centuries. Early country entertainers, of course, would have been well aware of the pocket songsters sold by BLACKFACE MINSTRELS, circus performers, and vaudevillians, and they would have been familiar with the colorfully illustrated sheet music and song folios that circulated widely in nineteenth-century and early twentieth-century America. Most southerners likely would have encountered wandering folksingers, many of whom were blind, and who peddled their songsheets and "ballet" books in railroad stations and at county fairs, court days, public hangings, and other social gatherings. At least two of these itinerant balladeers, Charlie Oaks and Dick Burnett, made the transition to commercial country music in the 1920s. Burnett, for example, was hawking a small printed booklet of songs at least fourteen years before he made his first recordings, in 1927.

Country singers sold their songbooks at public appearances and advertised them on their radio broadcasts. Published privately by the radio stations and by such publishing houses as M. M. COLE in Chicago, the songbooks usually contained photographs of the musicians and their families, human interest stories, and the lyrics of the entertainers' most popular songs. The earliest of these picture-songbooks has not been conclusively determined, but BRADLEY KINCAID's booklet of 1928, *Favorite Mountain Ballads and Old Time Songs,* was one of the most successful, and an example of the powerful role played by radio in the popularization of country music. Published by WLS in Chicago, the book went through six printings, sold more than 100,000 copies, and was the first of thirteen similar books issued by Kincaid up to approximately 1948. Country entertainers produced a massive array of songbooks, and some performers sometimes made more money from such sales than they did from recordings or personal appearances. The popularity of such material is explained, in part, by the desire of fans to get as close to the personal lives of entertainers as they possibly could, and by the awareness of the performers that a powerful hunger existed in America for old-fashioned entertainment that stressed family values. For example, ASHER SIZEMORE, a Kentucky singer who performed with his young son, LITTLE JIMMIE, on a string of southern radio stations from 1932 to the early 1950s, issued several songbooks with titles such as *Family Circle Songs* and *Hearth and Home Songs.* The sales figures of these songbooks are unknown, but the Sizemores claimed to have received 42,000 letters at WSM on a single day in January 1937. The sale of such songbooks later declined with the fading of live country radio, but commercial publishers have continued to publish material performed by the day's leading artists.

In addition to the songbooks issued individually by country entertainers, fans and fledgling singers also have been able to learn songs from books issued by radio barn dances or by commercial publishers. Likewise, the Renfro Valley publication *Renfro Valley Bugle,* a newspaper, has typically printed old songs that are in the public domain, while the commercial concerns have emphasized newly published items. The most widely circulated commercial song magazine for fans has been *Country Song Roundup,* first published in 1949 in Derby, Connecticut, and still in circulation today. —*Bill C. Malone*

Jo-el Sonnier

b. Rayne, Louisiana, October 2, 1946

Although singer and accordionist Jo-el Sonnier is most often associated with Cajun music, his eclectic repertoire extends to country music, blues, rock, and Gulf Coast swamp-pop. Sonnier unites these styles with powerful, passionate vocals and a formidable upper-register range. Sonnier launched his career with traditional Cajun music. He began playing the accordion at age four, and two years later was a regular live performer on KSIG in Crowley. As a teenager Sonnier began recording prolifically for such regional labels as Swallow, Goldband, and Dupree, cutting some four albums and twelve singles, including "Tes Yeux Bleu" and "Jump Little Frog." Goldband billed him as the Cajun Valentino and released a publicity photo of Sonnier dressed as Rudolph Valentino's character in *The Sheik.*

In the early seventies Sonnier moved to Southern California, worked as a sideman with various bands, and then moved on to a six-year stint in Nashville, where he recorded for MERCURY. Several singles resulted, including

Sons of the Pioneers: (from left) Karl Farr, brother Hugh, Tim Spencer, Len Slye (a.k.a. Roy Rogers), and Bob Nolan with Gus Mack of the Beverly Hill Billies

"I've Been Around Enough to Know"; none did well, though a recent CD reissue reveals some strong material in the Mercury sessions, especially a rousing version of Cleveland Crochet's "Sugar Bee." Sonnier also appeared on ASLEEP AT THE WHEEL's *Wheelin' and Dealin'* before leaving Nashville in 1980. Returning to Louisiana, Sonnier recorded *Cajun Life* for ROUNDER RECORDS, with accompanists including MICHAEL DOUCET. Unfortunately, the album appeared a few years before the early 1980s Cajun craze that popularized such bands as BeauSoleil, but it was nominated for a Grammy in the Best Ethnic or Traditional Recording category.

Returning to California, Sonnier fronted a group known as Friends, which included ex-Band keyboardist Garth Hudson and stellar guitarists ALBERT LEE and David Lindley. Ensuing critical acclaim led to a deal with RCA RECORDS in Nashville and the 1987 album *Come On Joe,* which yielded Top Ten country renditions of "No More One More Time" and Richard Thompson's "Tear Stained Letter," and a Top Forty country hit with Slim Harpo's bluesy swamp-pop classic "Raining in My Heart."

No charted singles followed on follow-up albums for RCA, CAPITOL, and LIBERTY in 1990, 1991, and 1992, but Sonnier's energetic performances have maintained his popularity in both country and Cajun circles. In 1994 he returned to Rounder, releasing a traditional set titled *Cajun Roots,* with accompanists again including Michael Doucet. A similar album, *Cajun Pride,* was released in 1997 and nominated for a Grammy Award in the Traditional Folk category. Besides his career in music, Sonnier has also appeared in several major motion pictures, most notably Peter Bogdanovich's *Mask* (1987).

—*Ben Sandmel*

REPRESENTATIVE RECORDINGS

Come on Joe (RCA, 1987); *The Complete Mercury Sessions* (Mercury, 1992); *Cajun Roots* (Rounder, 1994); *Cajun Pride* (Rounder, 1997); *Here to Stay* (Intersound, 1998)

Sons of the Pioneers

Leonard Franklin Slye [Roy Rogers] b. Cincinnati, Ohio, November 5, 1911; d. July 6, 1998

Robert Clarence Nobles [Bob Nolan] b. New Brunswick, Canada, April 1, 1908; d. June 16, 1980

Lloyd Wilson Perryman b. Ruth, Arkansas, January 29, 1917; d. May 31, 1977

Vernon Tim Spencer b. Webb City, Missouri, July 13, 1908; d. April 26, 1974

Thomas Hubert "Hugh" Farr b. Llano, Texas, December 6, 1903; d. March 17, 1980

Karl Marx Farr b. Rochelle, Texas, April 25, 1909; d. September 20, 1961

America's premier western singing group was formed in 1933 by Ohio-born Leonard Franklin Slye and was initially called the Pioneer Trio. The group included Canadian-born Bob Nolan, and Tim Spencer of Oklahoma. In late 1933 or early 1934 the trio added Hugh Farr, one of the finest country fiddlers of that era, and in mid-1935 guitarist Karl Farr, Hugh's brother, joined the quartet, bringing with him a unique skill that would influence musicians for years to come. Slye, Spencer, Nolan, and Hugh and Karl Farr are referred to by some as the "original" Sons of the Pioneers.

With a new name, Sons of the Pioneers, the group began a series of transcriptions for Standard Radio in late 1934, ushering in an exciting new genre of American folk music that featured unique western themes, a precise "block" singing style where three voices became one, and an impressive instrumental backup. Their smooth harmony was widely admired and was soon emulated by almost every western singing group in America. In addition, they may have been the first western group to feature trio yodeling.

The songs composed by Bob Nolan and Tim Spencer—such as "Tumbling Tumbleweeds," "Cool Water," "Blue Prairie," "Way Out There," "The Everlasting Hills of Oklahoma," "Happy Rovin' Cowboy," "Room Full of Roses," and "A Cowboy Has to Sing"—were decidedly different from what previously had been heard in western music, in lyrical and melodical quality. Many of their compositions were inspired by the Pioneers' participation in a large number of B-western movies, first in 1935 with Charles Starrett, then in 1941 with their old friend Leonard Slye, who now had assumed the studio name of ROY ROGERS and who was rivaling GENE AUTRY for the title of America's favorite SINGING COWBOY star.

The Pioneers were third in order to be signed by the fledging DECCA RECORDS in 1934, following Bing Crosby and cowboy singer-composer STUART HAMBLEN. The Pioneers' Decca recordings proved to be very popular with the fans. In late 1936 tenor Lloyd Perryman joined the group. Meanwhile, comedian-bass player Pat Brady replaced Roy Rogers, who left to join Republic Pictures in 1937.

Signing with RCA VICTOR in 1945, while Ken Carson, Perryman's wartime replacement, was still a member, the Sons of the Pioneers proved to be one of Victor's most popular attractions, remaining with the label until 1969. The early group remained intact until 1949, when both Spencer and Nolan retired and were replaced by KEN CURTIS and Tommy Doss. Upon the departure of Curtis in 1952, Dale Warren joined and presently leads the group. In 1980 the CMA inducted the original Sons of the Pioneers into the COUNTRY MUSIC HALL OF FAME. In 1998 the Pioneers celebrated sixty-five years of continuous performances at their home base in BRANSON, MISSOURI.

—*Ken Griffis*

Sons of the San Joaquin
Joe Hannah b. Marshfield, Missouri, February 1, 1932
Jack Hannah b. Marshfield, Missouri, October 25, 1933
Lon Hannah b. Pasadena, California, April 10, 1956

One of the most popular western music groups active today, the Sons of the San Joaquin are a family trio specializing in western close harmony singing in the style popularized by the SONS OF THE PIONEERS. Brothers Jack and Joe Hannah sang the songs of the Pioneers while growing up, and Joe's son Lon grew up listening to his father and uncle. Eventually it was Lon who convinced them to form a trio.

Prior to turning their full attention to music, the Hannahs had worked as teachers and school counselors. Then in 1989 they were invited to perform at the Cowboy Poetry Gathering in Elko, Nevada, where they were a huge hit. Later that year MICHAEL MARTIN MURPHEY used them as back-up singers on his *Cowboy Songs* album, and their career took off. They became favorites at cowboy music and poetry events throughout the West and released two independent albums, *Bound for the Rio Grande* (1989) and *Great American Cowboy* (1991), before signing with Warner Western, with which they have released two CDs, *A Cowboy Has to Sing* (1992) and *Songs of the Silver Screen* (1993). After leaving Warner Western, the Sons released *Gospel Trails* (1997), their first recording with Western Jubilee Recording Company, featuring a special appearance by DALE EVANS Rogers as lead vocalist on "In the Sweet By and By."

—*Charlie Seemann*

REPRESENTATIVE RECORDINGS
A Cowboy Has to Sing (Warner Western, 1992); *Songs of the Silver Screen* (Warner Western, 1993)

Sony Music (*see* Columbia Records, Epic Records)

Sony Tree (*see* Tree Music)

Joe South
b. Atlanta, Georgia, February 28, 1942

Although he may be best known in country circles as the author of LYNN ANDERSON's 1970 hit "I Never Promised You a Rose Garden," Joe South (born Joseph Souter) has had a colorful and varied career. As a recording artist alone, South had a major impact on the pop charts in the late sixties and early seventies with hits such as "Games People Play," "Walk a Mile in My Shoes," and "Don't It Make You Want to Go Home."

Raised in Atlanta, South started out in the music business at age twelve with his own radio show on WYST. Nurtured by local impresario BILL LOWERY (noted for discovering JERRY REED, RAY STEVENS, Tommy Roe, and BILLY JOE ROYAL, among others), South spent his teenage years working as a novice songwriter and recording artist (for the NRC label, 1958–60). In 1961 he took a stab at making it in Nashville, but he soon returned to Atlanta and hit his stride producing and writing chart records for the Tams ("Untie Me") and Billy Joe Royal ("Down in the Boondocks"). Additional session work as a guitarist for notables such as BOB DYLAN, Simon & Garfunkel, and Aretha Franklin as well as for EDDY ARNOLD and MARTY ROBBINS also raised his profile in the industry.

In the late sixties Bill Lowery secured South a deal with CAPITOL RECORDS, and South recorded his *Introspect* LP. Shortly after the album track "Games People Play" was released as a single in January 1969, South became an overnight sensation, appearing on such prime-time TV variety programs as the *Ed Sullivan Show* and the *Smothers Brothers Show*. The socially relevant lyrics and innovative production style of "Games" established the Joe South sound. Follow-ups "Walk a Mile in My Shoes" and "Don't It Make You Want to Go Home" placed high on both the pop and country charts. Soon his songs were covered by artists as diverse as Ed Ames, Deep Purple, JERRY LEE LEWIS, and Dizzy Gillespie. South released several more albums on Capitol, but following his brother Tommy's suicide in 1971, he retreated to the jungles of Hawaii. He returned in 1975 with one album on Island Records *(Midnight Rainbows)* and has since been living in semiretirement in Atlanta.

—*Ben Vaughn*

REPRESENTATIVE RECORDING
The Best of Joe South (Rhino, 1990)

Southern Pacific
John McFee b. Santa Cruz, California, Nov. 18, 1953
Keith Knudsen b. Ames, Iowa, Oct. 18, 1952
Tim Goodman birthplace and birth date unknown
Stu Cook b. Oakland, California, April 25, 1945
Kurt Howell birthplace and birth date unknown

This country-rock group of the late eighties and early nineties brought together arena-seasoned veterans of major rock bands for four albums, eight Top Twenty singles, major tours, and considerable critical acclaim before splitting in 1991.

Guitarist John McFee, drummer Keith Knudsen, and singer Tim Goodman, formerly a solo artist on CBS, worked together on several country projects before recording their WARNER BROS. debut LP, *Southern Pacific,* in 1984, with famed L.A. sidemen Jerry Scheff on bass and Glenn D. Hardin on piano. Bassist Stu Cook and keyboardist Kurt Howell joined the lineup with the record's release in 1985. Knudsen and McFee's tenures in the Doobie Brothers and Cook's in Creedence Clearwater Revival added star power and experience to the group's crisp musicianship and Goodman's soulful vocals. Early hits included the Tom Petty-penned "Thing About You," with EMMYLOU HARRIS's background vocals, and the exhilarating "Reno Bound." Another rocker, singer David Jenkins from the band Pablo Cruise, became lead singer upon Goodman's departure in 1986. The band enjoyed its greatest commercial success with a third album, 1988's *Zuma,* which included the chart-topping ballad "New Shade of Blue." Southern Pacific recorded its final LP, *County Line,* as a quartet when Jenkins left following two years in the group. The group's entire recording career was on Warner Brothers.

—*Thomas Goldsmith*

REPRESENTATIVE RECORDINGS

Southern Pacific (Warner Bros., 1985); *Zuma* (Warner Bros., 1988); *Greatest Hits* (Warner Bros., 1991)

Red Sovine

b. Charleston, West Virginia, July 17, 1918; d. April 4, 1980

Singer-songwriter-guitarist Woodrow Wilson "Red" Sovine specialized in recitations, and his biggest hits included such self-penned pieces of storytelling as "Little Rosa" (1956), "Phantom 309" (1967), "Giddyup Go" (1965), and "Teddy Bear" (1976). The latter two songs—both trucking numbers—were #1 country hits; "Teddy Bear" was also certified as a million seller.

Sovine started out playing guitar with Jim Pike's Carolina Tarheels in 1935 on WCHS-Charleston. By 1947 Sovine had formed his Echo Valley Boys band, and they were making their mark on the *WWVA JAMBOREE.* In 1949 he signed with MGM RECORDS and moved to Shreveport, Louisiana, where he played the *LOUISIANA HAYRIDE* and hosted KWKH's daily *Johnnie Fair Syrup Show* when HANK WILLIAMS left for the GRAND OLE OPRY.

Sovine joined the Opry himself, in 1954. On January 12, 1954, he did his first DECCA RECORDS session, during which WEBB PIERCE sang harmony on Sovine's "My New Love Affair," the B-side of "How Do You Think I Feel." "Missing You," a song Sovine wrote and recorded, was later cut by Pierce and also JIM REEVES. Sovine's first appearance on *Billboard*'s country chart came in 1955 with "Are You Mine," a duet with GOLDIE HILL; he followed it with another duet, "Why, Baby, Why," with Webb Pierce, a #1 country single.

In 1963 Sovine heard struggling country singer CHARLEY PRIDE in Great Falls, Montana, and encouraged the black balladeer to try his luck in Nashville. Sovine also recommended him to CEDARWOOD, a music publishing firm Webb Pierce co-owned. Pierce introduced Pride to manager Jack Johnson, who landed him an RCA VICTOR RECORDS contract.

Son ROGER SOVINE, a former recording artist, currently heads the Nashville branch of BMI. —*Walt Trott*

REPRESENTATIVE RECORDINGS

Teddy Bear (Starday, 1976); *Woodrow Wilson Sovine* (Starday, 1977)

Roger Sovine

b. Eleanor, West Virginia, February 17, 1943

As vice president of BMI in Nashville, Roger Sovine is in charge of all BMI's activities in the Nashville office. The son of country star RED SOVINE, Roger went to work for CEDARWOOD PUBLISHING in 1965, then moved on to Show-Biz Publishing and South Publishing Productions. In the late 1960s Sovine recorded for IMPERIAL RECORDS and placed two songs on the lower rungs of the country charts— "Culman, Alabam" (1968) and "Little Bitty Nitty Gritty Dirt Town" (1969).

Sovine first worked for BMI in 1972. In 1979 he became vice president of the Welk Music Group, then in 1982 became vice president of TREE INTERNATIONAL. In 1985 he returned to BMI as vice president, Nashville, in charge of all writer/publisher relations. —*Don Cusic*

Larry Sparks

b. Lebanon, Ohio, September 25, 1947

An important player of bluegrass's second generation, Larry Eugene Sparks has forged a deeply personal sound from the influences of blues and honky-tonk as well as the traditional music of his Appalachian roots. Sparks was raised in southern Ohio as the youngest of nine children. He is descended from Kentucky mountain folk who migrated north for work; his grandfather Lewison Dose Russell was a champion old-time fiddler from Jackson County, Kentucky. As a boy, Sparks listened to WAYNE RANEY's nighttime country music radio programs on Cincinnati's WCKY and became a hotshot guitar picker of the local bluegrass scene in an era when the guitar began to challenge the genre's holy triumvirate of banjo, fiddle, and mandolin.

The sixteen-year-old Sparks joined the STANLEY BROTHERS as their lead guitarist in 1964 during one of their frequent excursions to Ohio. In 1965, while still with the Stanleys, Sparks recorded his first single, a cover of Carter Stanley's "It's Never Too Late," for Dayton's Jalyn label. After Carter's death in 1966, Sparks took over as lead singer for RALPH STANLEY & the Clinch Mountain Boys, one of the foremost traditionalist acts in bluegrass. Following a three-year stint with this group, he started his own band, the Lonesome Ramblers, whose numerous alumni include Mike Lilly, banjoist-singer Dave Evans, and fiddler GLEN DUNCAN. The ever-changing aggregation has always featured Sparks's brooding, lonesome vocals, blues-style guitar, and stubbornly old-time sound.

Sparks has recorded for a variety of labels, including Pine Tree, Old Homestead, and STARDAY. His album *You Could Have Called* (King Bluegrass, 1976) boasted three-part fiddle back-up supplied by RICKY SKAGGS, dobro work by Tommy Boyd, and a title track penned for Sparks by r&b legend Charles Brown.

Other career highlights include Spark's masterfully low-key tribute album to HANK WILLIAMS, *Larry Sparks Sings Hank Williams,* with former Bluegrass Boy ROBERT "CHUBBY" WISE on fiddle, and his renditions of such standards as "John Deere Tractor," "A Face in the Crowd,""Love of the Mountains," and the gospel chestnut "Going Up Home (To Live in Green Pastures)." These have become bluegrass classics. Since the 1980s he has been a mainstay on the REBEL roster. Along with mentor Ralph Stanley, Sparks has held the torch for hard-core traditionalist bluegrass."I guess I'm the youngest old-timer around," he says. *—Eddie Dean*

REPRESENTATIVE RECORDINGS

Larry Sparks Sings Hank Williams (Rebel, 1977); *Classic Bluegrass* (Rebel, 1989)

Billie Jo Spears
b. Beaumont, Texas, January 14, 1937

Billie Jo Spears is best known for her sexy 1975 #1 hit "Blanket on the Ground." Although she has not been on the U.S. country charts since 1984, she has enjoyed a considerable following in Great Britain since her first appearance at England's Wembley Festival in 1977.

Born Billie Jean Spears, she began her professional career at age thirteen in 1950, when she appeared at Houston's Keel Auditorium with a number of other country artists. In 1953, as Billie Jean Moore, she made her first recording, "Too Old for Toys, Too Young for Boys," for ABBOTT RECORDS (the flip side was cartoon voice-over master Mel Blanc's "I Dess I Dotta Doe"). She appeared on the LOUISIANA HAYRIDE performing the song.

In 1964, at the urging of songwriter–talent scout Jack Rhodes, she moved to Nashville. Shortly afterward, A&R man Kelso Herston signed her to a recording contract with United Artists Records. In 1966 she followed Herston when he moved to head the Nashville office of CAPITOL RECORDS. During her stint with Capitol from 1966 to 1972, Spears scored her first Top Ten country hit, "Mr. Walker, It's Over," but felt typecast by uptempo, humorous material. Between 1972 and 1974 Spears recovered from problems with her vocal cords and recorded for the small Brite Star and Cutlass labels.

She didn't begin to hit the Top Twenty regularly until after returning to United Artists in 1974. Though Kelso Herston re-signed her to the label, it was LARRY BUTLER (who soon replaced Herston as label head) who produced her fairly successful string of United Artists hits that ran through 1980. "Blanket on the Ground"—with backing vocals from the JORDANAIRES and steel from PETE DRAKE—became her trademark hit, and its success led to her being named the ACADEMY OF COUNTRY MUSIC's Most Promising Female Vocalist in 1976. The following year she began making regular appearances in England, where her strongest following remains. *—Don Rhodes*

REPRESENTATIVE RECORDING

The Best of Billie Jo Spears (Razor & Tie, 1996)

Buddy Spicher
b. Dubois, Pennsylvania, July 28, 1938

At the height of his career as a session fiddler, from the late 1960s through the 1970s, Buddy Spicher backed artists such as CHARLEY PRIDE ("Is Anybody Goin' to San Antone"), DOLLY PARTON ("Coat of Many Colors"), and GENE WATSON ("Love in the Hot Afternoon") on some of country's biggest hits. Later he did studio work with REBA MCEN-TIRE, GEORGE STRAIT, and GARTH BROOKS. His specialty was playing second fiddle (harmony) with fellow fiddlers such as CHUBBY WISE or JOHNNY GIMBLE.

Norman Keith Spicher started playing at age thirteen and progressed to the WWVA JAMBOREE. He first recorded at seventeen with RUSTY & DOUG (Kershaw) at WWVA for Admiral Records. At eighteen, AUDREY WILLIAMS invited him to Nashville. Spicher was most visible on *The Wilburn Brothers Show,* but he was also a sideman for, at various times, HANK SNOW, RAY PRICE, FARON YOUNG, and the OSBORNE BROTHERS. Spicher also backed KITTY WELLS, PATSY CLINE, ROSE MADDOX, and LORETTA LYNN. Initially he lived at MOM UPCHURCH's boardinghouse, forming valued friendships with HANK GARLAND and SHORTY LAVENDER: "TOMMY JACKSON and DALE POTTER also helped me a lot in those early days," he has said.

Spicher proved equally adept on pop or jazz recordings for Rosemary Clooney, Gary Burton, LINDA RONSTADT, and Henry Mancini. He currently performs weekends with CRYSTAL GAYLE and heads a family combo, the Nashville Swing Band, weeknights in downtown Nashville. Sons Matthew and David perform with MARTY STUART and Nashville Mandolin Ensemble, respectively. *—Walt Trott*

REPRESENTATIVE RECORDINGS

Buddies (with Buddy Emmons) (Flying Fish, 1977); *Fiddle Classics* (Flying Fish, 1984)

Carl T. Sprague
b. near Houston, Texas, May 10, 1895; d. February 19,1979

Known as the Original Singing Cowboy, Carl T. Sprague grew up on a ranch near Alvin, Texas, where he worked as a ranch hand and learned many of the cowboy songs he would later record. In 1915 he enrolled at Texas A&M University, where he performed on the campus radio station. He left school to serve in the military during World War I, but returned to graduate after the war, in 1922.

In 1925, inspired by the success of fellow Texan VERNON DALHART, Sprague recorded ten songs for Victor, including Montana cowboy D. J. O'Malley's classic "When the Work's All Done This Fall," which sold an amazing 900,000 copies. Sprague was not the first to record cowboy songs. He was preceded by concert singer Bentley Ball, who recorded "The Dying Cowboy" and "Jessie James" for COLUMBIA in 1919, and Charles Nabell, an obscure performer who recorded *The Great Roundup* and *Utah Carl* for the OKEH label in 1924. However, Sprague was the first person known to come from an authentic ranching background to record cowboy songs, and the popularity of his "When the Work's All Done This Fall" ignited the interest of record companies in the commercial potential of cowboy songs. He made some thirty-three recordings for Victor in nine sessions between 1925 and 1927, including "Following the Cow Trail," "The Last Longhorn," "Is Your Saddle Good and Tight," and "The Cowman's Prayer."

Sprague came out of retirement to appear at a few folk festivals in the 1960s. In 1972, at age seventy-seven, he made his final recordings, an album for the German Folk Variety label titled *Carl T. Sprague: The First Popular Singing Cowboy.* *—Charlie Seemann*

REPRESENTATIVE RECORDINGS

Carl T. Sprague: The First Popular Singing Cowboy (Bear Family, 1978); *Cowboy Songs from Texas* (Bear Family, 1978)

Square Dancing

Square dancing is an American dance form descended from European court and folk dances brought to the United States by colonial settlers. Steps and formations from English contra and Morris dances and French quadrilles and cotillions (as well as the French military drill) evolved into a dance that took hold chiefly in rural and isolated areas of the United States. Appalachian-style square dancing, sometimes called "Dix," was danced to the accompaniment of a single instrument, usually the fiddle. In areas where churches prohibited dancing and fiddle music, a nonaccompanied form of rhythmic dance called "play parties" derived from square dancing.

Square dancing was introduced to a widespread audience in the 1920s, on country radio shows such as the Chicago-based WLS *Barn Dance.* Curiosity about square dancing grew along with a public demand for instruction, and in 1939, Dr. Lloyd ("Pappy") Shaw's book *Cowboy Dances* further popularized this American dance form.

By the 1950s, teachers and callers were instructing hundreds of community groups in the rudiments of square dancing, which had also become a popular part of America's educational curriculum. Eventually, recorded music, specially metered for square dance, began replacing live bands at many gatherings.

As of 1965 there were approximately 30 million square dancers in the United States. By the 1990s, square dancing was bolstered by a resurging interest in country dancing in general. Currently there are thousands of square dance clubs around the world, their members competing for awards and traveling to dance festivals featuring nationally known callers. The square dance has been deemed the national dance of the United States.

Although innovation has played a role, most square dances are generally based on traditional configurations. Each square is made up of four couples; in each the woman stands to the man's right. The squares are directed by a caller, who sings or chants instructions (many of them rhyming) to the music—usually 8- or 16-bar Anglo-American folk tunes, country, or popular rock songs. Calls are arranged so that each man moves around the square, dancing with all four women, until he arrives "home" to his original partner. Traditional square dances include "Bird in the Cage," "The Virginia Reel" ("Sir Roger de Coverly"), "Take a Little Peek," "Solomon Levi," and "Marching Through Georgia."

Many early square dance callers were large-voiced hog farmers or auctioneers. Calling has become a unique art form of approximately 30 basic commands, with more than 5,000 variations. Calls such as "allemande left," "promenade," "do-si-do," and "sashay" are borrowed directly from the French dance terms *allemande, promenade, dos-à-dos,* and *chassez.* Other calls, such as "ladies chain," "split the ring," and "grand right and left" are American originals.

Square dancing helped set the stage for the burgeoning popularity of other country dance forms, such as clogging and line dancing, although their respective roots can be traced to various sources. —*Patricia Hall*

Jim Stafford

b. Eloise, Florida, January 16, 1944

Though known for a series of mid-1970s novelty pop hits, including the million seller "Spiders & Snakes," James

Wayne Stafford never had a record in the Top Fifty on the national country charts. Still, he is often considered a country figure, in part because he used a general country demeanor to become a successful TV personality.

Stafford grew up in a Florida region populated by migrant fruit pickers. He joined a rock group at age fourteen, and at twenty-one he moved to Nashville, intent on becoming a studio musician—with additional plans to join the GRAND OLE OPRY. But he discovered that competition for musicians' jobs was extremely fierce, so two years later, he headed to Atlanta. Eventually he decided to concentrate on singing novelty songs, and by the mid-1970s, Stafford—now based in Los Angeles—had become one of pop music's most successful novelty acts. "Spiders & Snakes" (written by the BELLAMY BROTHERS' David Bellamy) was quickly followed by "My Girl Bill" and "Wildwood Weed."

In 1975 he hosted the *Jim Stafford Show,* a summer replacement series that featured a regular appearance by Rodney the Robot. Stafford became something of a TV regular, replacing JIM ED BROWN as co-host of *Nashville on the Road* (with weekly cast REX ALLEN JR., former DAVE & SUGAR vocalist Sue Powell, and Golly Dang the Wonder Chimp), and joining Burgess Meredith and Priscilla Presley as a co-host for *Those Amazing Animals.*

Stafford was briefly married to singer BOBBIE GENTRY. Now living in BRANSON, MISSOURI, he performs at the Jim Stafford Theater with the Earn As You Learn Band.

—*Tom Roland*

REPRESENTATIVE RECORDING

Jim Stafford (PolyGram, 1974)

Joe Stampley

b. Springhill, Louisiana, June 6, 1943

Following a brief career as a regionally successful rock & roll artist, Joe Stampley turned to country music in the early 1970s. Teamed with producer NORRO WILSON and a team of writers (frequently including himself) from AL GALLICO's firm, Stampley released fifty-three country-charting singles between 1971 and 1989, on the DOT, ABC/Dot, EPIC, and Evergreen labels, plus nine duet singles with MOE BANDY, recorded for COLUMBIA between 1979 and 1985.

Born in Louisiana, Stampley had relocated with his family to Houston (where his father was a salesman) by the early 1950s; before he was ten years old, he'd won a radio station talent contest. Stampley's family moved back to Springhill, and through local promoter and *LOUISIANA HAYRIDE* performer MERLE KILGORE, he was contracted to Los Angeles–based IMPERIAL RECORDS while in the tenth grade. He cut four sides in Los Angeles, with two—including the Stampley-composed "Glenda"—released. A few years later he recorded another original composition, "The Creation of Love," for Chess Records, a deal arranged by Shreveport-based producer Stan Lewis. Still in high school, Stampley was asked to join a rock & roll band from Magnolia, Arkansas, that two years later changed its name to the Uniques. Their first single, for Lewis's Paula label in 1964, was a Stampley-Kilgore original, "Not Too Long Ago." Another Uniques hit was a 1966 cover of New Orleans singer Art Neville's "All These Things," which Stampley later re-recorded for Dot Records with great success.

The Gallico association began with "Not Too Long Ago," and it was the publisher who placed Stampley with

Dot Records in 1970. Stampley's eighteen Top Ten country hits include "If You Touch Me (You've Got to Love Me)" (1972), "Soul Song" (1973), "Roll On Big Mama" (1975), and—with Bandy—"Just Good Ol' Boys" (1979), "Holding the Bag" (1979), "Hey Joe (Hey Moe)" (1981), and "Where's the Dress" (1984).   —*Todd Everett*

REPRESENTATIVE RECORDINGS

The Best of Joe Stampley (Varese Sarabande, 1995); *Good Ol' Boy: Greatest Hits* (Razor and Tie, 1995)

Stamps-Baxter
established in Dallas, Texas, 1926

The Stamps-Baxter Music and Printing Company of Dallas, Texas, emerged as the South's dominant gospel music entity in the 1930s and 1940s. Home of leading religious songwriters—such as ALBERT E. BRUMLEY, Cleavant Derricks, W. Oliver Cooper, Vep Ellis, Eugene Bartlett, James B. Coats, and Luther G. Presley, Stamps-Baxter also invented aggressive and successful song promotional techniques that helped get their songs onto radio and records. Among the many Stamps-Baxter songs that have entered country and bluegrass repertoires are "Rank Stranger to Me," "Just a Little Talk with Jesus," "Precious Memories," "Farther Along," "If We Never Meet Again," "Victory in Jesus," and "I Won't Have to Cross Jordan Alone."

The company was founded in 1926 by Virgil Oliver Stamps and J. R. Baxter Jr. Songwriter-teacher Stamps (1892–1940) was a native of Upshur County, Texas, who began to run singing schools in 1914. After starting his own publishing company in 1924, he had a huge success with his collection *Harbor Bells*, with new editions in print through the 1960s. Needing further capital, Stamps turned to Baxter (1889–1960), a harmony teacher and writer. Advertising that their songs were "new, snappy, and peppy," the pair began a series of annual songbooks. Unlike JAMES D. VAUGHAN, who had started his own gospel record company, Stamps-Baxter supported touring quartets and helped place them on major labels. In 1927, one Stamps Quartet (featuring V. O.'s brother Frank) recorded "Give the World a Smile Each Day" for VICTOR, thereby creating a gospel classic and defining the type of happy, uptempo music the company would come to symbolize. Another innovation the pair achieved was building their own printing plant in Dallas; this allowed them to publish custom gospel songbooks for both country and gospel groups. A third innovation was the development of "all-night singings" at the company's school of music in 1940, thus inaugurating yet another gospel tradition.

After Baxter's death in 1960, his widow, Clarice Howard "Ma" Baxter, ran the company until its sale to the Zondervan conglomerate, a leading publisher of hymns, in 1974.   —*Charles Wolfe*

Ralph Stanley
b. Stratton, Virginia, February 25, 1927

When Carter Stanley's death in 1966 ended the STANLEY BROTHERS' twenty-year professional career, Ralph Stanley reshaped the Clinch Mountain Boys to fit his personal approach to bluegrass. Now pushed to the front of the band, he sang lead more frequently than he ever did with his brother; his vocals reflected the lonesome modality common to the traditional music of western Virginia and eastern Kentucky. Instead of relying exclusively on Carter's songs, Ralph created a fresh repertoire of new and traditional pieces, using the Stanley Brothers' classic mid-1950s sound as a stylistic benchmark. He recruited young LARRY SPARKS as his lead vocalist and guitarist; seasoned LONESOME PINE FIDDLERS members Curly Ray Cline and Melvin Goins played fiddle and rhythm guitar, respectively. The Clinch Mountain Boys' clockwork rhythm was underscored by Cline's unadorned old-time fiddle. Virtually every performance featured one of Stanley's trademark clawhammer banjo specialties.

When Sparks and Goins left to start their own bands in 1970, Stanley assembled what many consider his finest ensemble, with Carter Stanley sound-alike Roy Lee Centers on guitar and former BILL MONROE sideman Jack Cooke on bass. Two eastern Kentucky teenagers, KEITH WHITLEY and RICKY SKAGGS, performed with the band during the 1971–73 festival seasons. During this period Stanley introduced a cappella gospel quartets to his shows; he also began his long affiliation with REBEL RECORDS.

Centers's death in May 1974 disrupted the band's momentum, even though Whitley seamlessly filled his position. After this point Stanley rarely broke new ground stylistically, although he continued to find new songs that fit his musical vision. When Whitley left to join J. D. CROWE in November 1977, seventeen-year-old CHARLIE SIZEMORE replaced him. Sizemore's nine-year tenure sparked the band's return to form: During this period Stanley enjoyed some of his brightest moments onstage and on record.

During the 1980s Stanley's contributions to American culture were acknowledged with a National Heritage fellowship and an honorary doctorate from Lincoln Memorial University. In 1992 numerous bluegrass and country music notables paid homage to Stanley on *Saturday Night and Sunday Morning*, a two-compact disc set produced by Charles R. "Dick" Freeland. Among the participants were Bill Monroe, GEORGE JONES, VINCE GILL, PATTY LOVELESS, EMMYLOU HARRIS, ALISON KRAUSS, DWIGHT YOAKAM, TOM T. HALL, JIMMY MARTIN, and Clinch Mountain Boys alumni Larry Sparks, Ricky Skaggs, and Charlie Sizemore. In 1995 Ralph Stanley II assumed the lead singer-guitar position in his father's band.   —*Dave Samuelson*

REPRESENTATIVE RECORDINGS

Saturday Night and Sunday Morning (Freeland Recording Company, 1992), 2-CD set; *Ralph Stanley and the Clinch Mountain Boys: 1971–73* (Rebel, 1995), 4-CD set

Roba Stanley
b. Gwinnet County, Georgia, 1910; d. June 8, 1986

Though her career in country music lasted only months, Roba Stanley had the distinction of being one of the first woman vocal soloists to record in the genre. She grew up in Dacula, the home of another pioneer, fiddler GID TANNER, and was the daughter of R. M. Stanley, a well-known local fiddler who often competed against Tanner and other early Georgia fiddlers, such as JOHN CARSON. By the time she was twelve, young Stanley was joining her father as they played for dances, political rallies, and in 1924 over WSB radio. This led to a contract with the OKEH RECORDING COMPANY, and in August 1924, at a temporary studio in Atlanta, Stanley recorded a version of the old British ballad "Devilish Mary," in addition to other comical songs.

Stanley, though barely fourteen, had a clear, strong voice and a sense of tradition that gave the records a distinctive style. Later in 1924, and again in 1925, OKeh had her back for more sessions. Among her songs were "All Night Long" and "Single Life," but her entire output totaled only nine sides. She was not interested in touring or following up with her music; in 1925 she met a young man from Florida and retired to marry him and begin a family. For decades she forgot about her early music until she was rediscovered in 1976 by historians; the newspaper feature writers had a field day, and Stanley eventually visited Nashville, where she was saluted from the stage of the GRAND OLE OPRY.
— *Charles Wolfe*

The Stanley Brothers

Carter Glen Stanley b. Stratton, Virginia, August 27, 1925; d. December 1, 1966

Ralph Edmond Stanley b. Stratton, Virginia, February 25, 1927

One of the premier bands from the formative days of bluegrass, the Stanley Brothers and their band, the Clinch Mountain Boys, combined elements from old-time music with the snappy, quick rhythms associated with BILL MONROE's 1945–48 Blue Grass Boys. Guitarist Carter Stanley's emotional lead vocal style was complemented by his younger brother Ralph's soaring tenor, producing a distinctive, haunting duet.

The Stanleys formed their professional partnership in December 1946 after two months backing Roy Sykes over

The Stanley Brothers: Carter (left) and Ralph

WNVA–Norton, Virginia. Recruiting Sykes's mandolin player, Pee Wee Lambert, and a local fiddler, the brothers briefly worked a fifteen-minute morning slot over WNVA before moving to the popular noonday *Farm and Fun Time* over WCYB-Bristol. The station's powerful signal carried their music across a five-state area, helping make the band one of the region's most popular acts. By late 1947 the brothers began recording for RICH-R-TONE, an independent label based in Johnson City, Tennessee. Their second release, "Little Glass of Wine," was a regional hit and resulted in a COLUMBIA RECORDS contract in late 1948. By then Ralph Stanley had abandoned his two-finger banjo style in favor of the three-finger roll popularized by Earl Scruggs (FLATT & SCRUGGS). A striking feature of the Stanley Brothers' Columbia recordings was a unique trio harmony structure that featured the lead vocal of Carter Stanley, the tenor of Ralph Stanley, and an even higher third part by Pee Wee Lambert. It gave a lovely yet haunting effect to songs such as "The Fields Have Turned Brown," "The Lonesome River," and "The White Dove."

From 1953 through 1958 the Stanley Brothers recorded for MERCURY RECORDS. The forty-five songs and instrumentals they recorded for the label are considered by most Stanley fans to be the group's finest. Generally, these recordings showed subtle refinements on the sound established on their Columbia records: tighter, more fluid rhythms and higher vocal pitches, with Ralph's mountain tenor pushed to the forefront.

From 1958 to 1965 the Stanley Brothers recorded primarily for KING RECORDS (though they also recorded in these years for the STARDAY, Blue Ridge, Rimrock, Wango, and Cabin Creek labels). In a span of eight years, King released a total of fifteen albums, making them one of the most recorded bands in bluegrass. With King, the Stanleys recorded their only song to hit the country record charts, a comic novelty ditty called "How Far to Little Rock" (#17, 1960). It was also while with King Records that the duo introduced the lead guitar into their sound. Throughout the 1940s and 1950s, bluegrass bands had used the lead guitar somewhat on sacred recordings, but the Stanleys were the first band to consistently give such prominence to the lead guitar in secular bluegrass settings. The Stanleys' lead guitarists during their King years were Bill Napier, followed by George Shuffler.

During the 1960s, at the height of the folk boom, the Stanley Brothers found much work on college campuses and at folk festivals. Tragically, their twenty-year partnership ended on December 1, 1966, with the death of Carter Stanley at age forty-one. Original songs made up a large percentage of the Stanley Brothers' repertoire, and Carter Stanley composed more than a hundred songs during his lifetime, many of which have become standards in the genre. His songs have been recorded by a host of country artists including PATTY LOVELESS, RICKY SKAGGS, JOHN CONLEE, and EMMYLOU HARRIS. Ralph Stanley continued with a highly successful solo career, and to this day the Stanley Brothers' recordings remain a touchstone for bluegrass players and fans the world over.
— *Gary B. Reid*

REPRESENTATIVE RECORDINGS

The Stanley Brothers and the Clinch Mountain Boys, 1953–1958 & 1959 (Bear Family, 1993), 2 discs; *The Early Starday/King Years* (Highland Music, 1993); *The Complete Columbia Recordings* (Columbia/Legacy, 1996); *Earliest Recordings: Complete Rich-R-Tone 78s, 1947–1952* (Rich-R-Tone, 1997)

Jack Stapp

Jack Stapp

b. Nashville, Tennessee, December 8, 1912; d. December 20, 1980

Jack Stapp served as program director of WSM from 1939 to 1957 and founded TREE PUBLISHING COMPANY, one of Nashville's most successful music publishing firms.

Jack Smiley Stapp was born in Nashville but moved with his family to Atlanta in 1923. At age fifteen he got his first job in radio at Atlanta's Winecoff Hotel, programing a station that was piped into the hotel's rooms. Later he studied at Georgia Tech and became involved with the campus radio station, WGST, which became a commercial station while Stapp moved up and eventually became program manager. Here he met Bert Parks and hired him as an announcer. The two would remain lifelong friends and would go to New York and work for CBS, where Stapp rose to the position of evening network manager. In 1939 Stapp left New York and returned to Nashville to serve as program director for WSM. At WSM Stapp produced NBC network radio shows such as *Sunday Down South, Hospitality Time, Mr. Smith Goes to Town, Riverboat Revels,* and the children's program *Wormwood Forest.* In 1939 a thirty-minute portion of the GRAND OLE OPRY, the *Prince Albert Show,* sponsored by the R. J. Reynolds Tobacco Company, was broadcast over the NBC network for the first time. Stapp worked with an advertising firm, the William Esty Agency, to secure this sponsorship and rehearsed the show every Saturday morning.

Jack Stapp was also a major decision maker in auditioning the talent for the Opry. Along with HARRY STONE, Stapp led the way for the Opry to move from a rural, stringband-based show to one that appealed to a broader audience. During Stapp's tenure at WSM the Opry signed acts such as EDDY ARNOLD, ERNEST TUBB, RED FOLEY, HANK WILLIAMS, and GEORGE MORGAN.

During World War II Stapp enlisted in the army, stud-

ied psychological warfare in New York, then moved on to London, where he worked in radio broadcasting Allied propaganda in support of the war effort (his title was director of the Special Events Department of Psychological Warfare in the European Theater of Operations). At the end of the war he returned to WSM and resumed his duties as program director.

In 1951 Stapp and CBS-TV producer Lou Cowan, with whom he had served in London during World War II, formed Tree Publishing. Nevertheless, Stapp remained at WSM throughout the early 1950s and hired others to run the day-to-day activities of Tree. In July 1957 Stapp left WSM and took the position of program director for WKDA (effective at the beginning of 1958), a rock & roll station in Nashville that became #1 in the market. Stapp also served as president of Tree Publishing during this period, although he did not join the firm full-time until 1964—the year after the publishing company celebrated its first year with more than $1 million in revenues.

Stapp remained head of Tree Publishing throughout that company's biggest period of growth, which included the acquisition of other publishing companies, beginning in 1969 with PAMPER MUSIC, which held many great WILLIE NELSON, HANK COCHRAN, and HARLAN HOWARD songs.

In 1974 an executive realignment at Tree saw Stapp assume the role of chairman of the board and chief executive officer, while his handpicked second in command, BUDDY KILLEN, served as president and chief operating officer. Jack Stapp was elected to the COUNTRY MUSIC HALL OF FAME in October 1989.   *—Don Cusic*

Buddy Starcher

b. near Ripley, West Virginia, March 16, 1906

The Boy from Down Home, as he was frequently billed, was born Oby Edgar Starcher, the oldest of eight children of Homer Francis and Leona Starcher. Shortly after his birth the family made its first of several moves; the constant change of residences came about because Homer frequently built and then sold the houses in which his family lived. In addition to being an expert home builder, Homer was also an excellent fiddler who taught Buddy chords on the five-string banjo, probably to make sure he had an accompanist at dances where he played. Buddy also learned guitar, and by the time he was sixteen, was playing every time he had an opportunity. In 1928 he left the coal mines to make his living as a musician, first working on WFBR-Baltimore. He then moved to WOBY–Charleston, West Virginia, but in 1932 was back in the Baltimore–Washington, D.C., area. That year he wrote "The Bonus Blues," about the World War I Bonus Expeditionary Forces veterans who marched on Washington, a song that got national attention. Its success led to Starcher appearing in a Pathe News short.

After leaving Washington, Starcher worked on stations in several states, most notably WCHS–Charleston, West Virginia. Here he had a hit with a song he introduced several years earlier in Baltimore: "Brown Eyes." It has since been reported as a folksong by some collectors. Starcher later worked in locations ranging from Iowa to Texas to Florida to Pennsylvania. In the 1940s he wrote two songs, "Sweet Thing" and "I'll Still Write Your Name in the Sand," that became country standards. The latter song, recorded for FOUR STAR, became Starcher's first Top Ten hit, in

1949. Also important is another song he wrote during that decade, "You'll Still Be in My Heart," whose melody was used by HANK WILLIAMS for "Cold, Cold Heart." Starcher's 1952 "Love Song of the Waterfall" was SLIM WHITMAN's first #1 hit. However, Starcher's biggest hit, both as a songwriter and performer, came in 1966 with a recitation for the Boone label—"History Repeats Itself," which pointed out similarities and coincidences between the lives of Abraham Lincoln and John F. Kennedy. The record hit #2 on the country charts and crossed over to the pop Top Forty.

After the success of his recording of "History Repeats Itself," Buddy moved to Nashville, leaving a Charleston television show that achieved higher ratings locally than NBC's *Today* show. In 1968 he moved to Florida and then to Albany, New York, where he briefly retired. In the early 1970s he managed radio stations in Texas, including KWBA-Bayton. He eventually moved back to West Virginia, where he worked as a salesman for a Ford dealer. He also appeared at several festivals and country music parks, and was honored by two special programs held in West Virginia parks. In recent years his recordings have been reissued on the Cattle and Bear Family labels.   —*W. K. McNeil*

REPRESENTATIVE RECORDINGS

Country Love Songs (Bear Family, 1978); *Me and My Guitar* (Old Homestead, 1986)

Starday Records
established in Beaumont, Texas, June 1953

Starday Records went through several distinct phases. During the early to mid-1950s it was synonymous with East Texas honky-tonk music, particularly the records of GEORGE JONES, who started with the company. Later, during the 1960s, it tended to emphasize the marginal areas of country music, particularly bluegrass, old-time music, instrumentals, and older artists.

Launched in June 1953, Starday was the creation of JACK STARNES (*Star-*) and HAROLD "PAPPY" DAILY (*-day*). It was an adjunct to both of their businesses, and operated out of Starnes's base in Beaumont and Daily's in Houston. DON PIERCE joined in September and was made president, working out of Los Angeles. The first hit, ARLIE DUFF's "Y'All Come," arrived in late 1953. George Jones, discovered by Starnes, had become the company's biggest seller by 1956. Starnes, though, sold his share in 1955.

As of January 1957 Starday operated MERCURY RECORDS' country division under a joint imprint, Mercury-Starday. The arrangement fell apart in July 1958, and Pierce and Daily also parted ways at that time, dividing the Starday assets between them. Pierce kept the trademark and operated Starday out of Madison, Tennessee. He rebuilt the catalogue, emphasizing bluegrass and old-time music. He also scored some significant hits, such as RED SOVINE's "Giddyup Go," COWBOY COPAS's "Alabam," FRANKIE MILLER's "Blackland Farmer," and JOHNNY BOND's "10 Little Bottles." With the help of Martin Haerle (later the founder of CMH Records), Pierce aggressively marketed Starday product overseas, and via mail order domestically.

Pierce acquired KING RECORDS and sold both companies to Lin Broadcasting of Nashville for $5 million in 1968. Lin sold them to Tennessee Recording and Publishing in 1971, and the masters (without the copyrights) were sold to GML in Nashville in 1975. GML revived the Starday trademark

for new product and scored a #1 hit with Red Sovine's "Teddy Bear" in 1976. Since then, the Starday label has been used for reissues.   —*Colin Escott*

Jack and Neva Starnes
Jack Starnes Jr. birthplace and birth date unknown
Neva Starnes birthplace and birth date unknown

For a time in the early 1950s, Jack Starnes Jr. and his wife Neva were serious movers and shakers in the talent-rich Beaumont, Texas, country music scene. Jack Starnes came to prominence in early 1951 when he took over management of LEFTY FRIZZELL, at that moment the hottest property in country music. Neva Starnes managed a number of acts as well, including, briefly, prestardom RAY PRICE and later JEAN SHEPARD. Jack Starnes was also one of the original partners in STARDAY RECORDS, the label for which GEORGE JONES first recorded.

Before their management odyssey began, the Starneses owned a successful motel and restaurant complex in Voth, north of Beaumont. Looking to expand, Neva bought a Beaumont dance hall, and it was there that the couple met Frizzell. Jack Starnes signed Frizzell to a 50-50 management deal that soon went sour and resulted in a lawsuit in 1952. The lawsuit was settled out of court in June 1953, and within a matter of weeks, Starnes and HAROLD "PAPPY" DAILY started Starday Records. Starnes did not remain with the label for long, and little was heard from him or Neva after the mid-1950s. However, their son Bill (who as a young man served time for bank robbery) went on to manage George Jones and TAMMY WYNETTE, among others.   —*Daniel Cooper*

The Statler Brothers
Harold Wilson Reid b. Augusta County, Virginia, August 21, 1939
Donald Sydney Reid b. Staunton, Virginia, June 5, 1945
Philip Elwood Balsley b. Staunton, Virginia, August 8, 1939
Lewis Calvin DeWitt b. Roanoke, Virginia, March 8, 1938; d. August 15, 1990
Lester James Fortune b. Nelson County, Virginia, March 11, 1955

Along with the OAK RIDGE BOYS, the Statler Brothers have kept the tradition of quartet singing alive in contemporary country music. They have astutely managed their career to the point that they have been one of the top-grossing acts in the business for thirty years, slowly changing their image from that of a hip folk-rock quartet to a middle-of-the-road pop and country television act.

Harold Reid and Lew DeWitt sang in a high school group, the Four Star Quartet, with Phil Balsley and Joe McDorman, in their hometown of Staunton, Virginia. Their first appearance was in 1955. By the time Harold re-formed the group as the Kingsmen in 1961, McDorman had left town, and Harold brought in his younger brother, Don. They sang pop, country, and gospel, but their harmonies were modeled on those of white country gospel quartets such as the Statesmen and the Blackwood Brothers.

In March 1964 they joined JOHNNY CASH's road show and stayed eight and a half years. Early in 1964 they renamed themselves the Statler Brothers (from Statler Tissues) because another group called the Kingsmen was successful then. Cash virtually demanded that COLUMBIA RECORDS sign them, and they began recording in April

The Statler Brothers

1964. Their first hit, "Flowers on the Wall," was cut in March 1965 and became a Top Five country and pop record. Follow-up hits were elusive. A couple of novelty songs ("Ruthless" and "You Can't Have Your Kate and Edith, Too") cracked the country Top Ten in 1967, but the Statlers' career had stalled when they joined MERCURY RECORDS in 1970.

JERRY KENNEDY signed them to Mercury and has been their producer ever since, even after he left the company. Their first Mercury single, "Bed of Rose's," peaked at #9 in country and #58 in pop, and was the first of more than fifty hits on the label. On the second Mercury album, *Pictures of Moments to Remember,* the Statlers tapped into the growing market for 1950s nostalgia. "Do You Remember These?" (a #2 hit) and "Class of '57" (a #6 hit) cemented the direction and helped to win a new audience for the group.

The third Mercury album, *Country Music Then and Now,* contained a segment given over to "Lester 'Roadhog' Moran & His Cadillac Cowboys," an extended parody of a hapless hillbilly band from the last gasp of live radio. That humorous cameo appearance was followed by a complete album, *Lester "Roadhog" Moran & His Cadillac Cowboys: Alive at the Johnny Mack Brown High School* (1974). Then the routine was dropped, and the last word from the Statlers was that Lester was "recovering from an autopsy."

Lew DeWitt's health had never been good; he had suffered from Crohn's disease, a debilitating bowel disorder, and he gave up his place in the group in November 1981. His replacement, at first temporary, then permanent, was Jimmy Fortune, who had much the same background as the others but was ten years younger. Fortune has written "Elizabeth," "More Than Just a Name on the Wall," and "My Only Love" for the group.

Fortune's arrival typified the way in which the Statlers have been able to recharge themselves. Their most successful act of self-renewal came when they agreed to do a weekly television show on TNN. They had always feared overexposure on television and had done only guest ap-

pearances and specials, but starting October 5, 1991, they were on every Saturday night. They modeled the show on 1950s television variety, unapologetically catering to a segment of the market they believe is overlooked by mainstream television. Their consistently high ratings appear to bear them out.

The Statlers are still headquartered in Staunton and run a formidably well-organized business from there, highlighting the fact that they have always been a very self-contained group. They have written most of their own songs, arranged them, managed themselves, and mapped out their own career direction.   —*Colin Escott*

REPRESENTATIVE RECORDINGS

Greatest Hits Volume 1 (Mercury, 1975); *Greatest Hits Volume 2* (Mercury, 1979); *Radio Gospel Favorites* (Mercury, 1986); *The Statler Brothers 30th Anniversary Celebration* (Mercury, 1994), 3 CDs; *The Complete Lester "Roadhog" Moran* (Mercury, 1994)

Red Steagall
b. Gainesville, Texas, December 22, 1937

Russell Steagall, a longtime favorite among western swing and cowboy song fans, is also a songwriter; rodeo performer; producer; and, by act of the Texas legislature, official Cowboy Poet of Texas. He discovered REBA MCENTIRE singing the national anthem at the 1974 PRCA National Finals Rodeo in Oklahoma City and helped her obtain her first recording contract, with MERCURY RECORDS.

Stricken with polio at fifteen and left with diminished use of his left hand and arm, Steagall learned to play mandolin and guitar as part of his physical therapy. He obtained an animal husbandry degree from West Texas State University and while there formed his band, the Coleman County Cowboys. After graduation he worked as a soil chemistry analyst but continued his interest in music.

After RAY CHARLES recorded "Here We Go Again," a song written by Steagall and Don Lanier, Steagall moved to California. He eventually became West Coast representative for Nashville publishing companies TREE and COMBINE, headed United Artists' West Coast office, and formed his own Texas Red Publishing. He concentrated on songwriting, and by 1969 he had cuts by more than sixty artists. Some of his best-known songs include "Miles and Miles of Texas," "Lone Star Beer & Bob Wills Music," and "Bob's Got a Swing Band in Heaven."

A comment during a golf game to friend JOE ALLISON resulted in a 1969 DOT RECORDS recording contract. In 1970 Steagall moved to CAPITOL, where "Party Dolls & Wine" became the first of more than twenty chart hits. In 1976 he returned to ABC/Dot, and his first release, "Lone Star Beer and Bob Wills Music," became his biggest career single. In 1979 he switched to ELEKTRA and currently records for Warner Western. Although his last chart entry was in 1980, Steagall continues to play the rodeo and western poetry circuit, averaging 200 dates per year.   —*William P. Davis*

REPRESENTATIVE RECORDINGS

Lone Star Beer and Bob Wills Music (MCA, 1976); *Born to This Land* (Warner Western, 1993); *Dear Mama, I'm a Cowboy* (Warner Western, 1997)

Steve Stebbins
b. Chico, California, February 17, 1903; d. March 19, 1983

A former Los Angeles policeman who loved country music, Steve Stebbins got into the country talent business in the mid-1940s and wound up running the Americana Corporation. Throughout the 1950s, Americana was among the top booking agencies on the West Coast, its client list including, at various times, such stars as TENNESSEE ERNIE FORD, JOHNNY BOND, and LEFTY FRIZZELL.

Stebbins started Americana in the late 1940s as a partnership with Stuart "Buzz" Carlton and CLIFFIE STONE. Stebbins had met Stone during the war years when Stone had a popular morning radio show on KFVD. Recently retired from the police force, Stebbins had talked Stone into letting him book an appearance for him at a Ventura dance hall. Later, both were involved in *HOMETOWN JAMBOREE,* the country TV program hosted by Stone beginning in 1949, as well as in Americana. Stone got out of Americana to manage Tennessee Ernie Ford full-time, and Carlton also stepped aside, leaving the company to Stebbins.

Though Stebbins, well liked by the artists, had a large stable, he was most closely associated with Frizzell. From late 1952 until about 1962 Stebbins played a role in Frizzell's career that was more than booking agent but less than manager. After Frizzell moved to Nashville, Stebbins never again had such a high-profile artist to handle, though he kept Americana active until his death.
—*Daniel Cooper*

Keith Stegall
b. Wichita Falls, Texas, November 1, 1954

Best known for his production work with multiplatinum sensation ALAN JACKSON, Robert Keith Stegall has had considerable success as a songwriter and a producer. He is also a recording artist with MERCURY RECORDS, where he currently holds the post of senior vice president of A&R.

Stegall's father had played pedal steel for JOHNNY HORTON, so it was no surprise when Keith gravitated to music, mastering piano, guitar, and drums by age fifteen. In high school he toured Canada and Europe with a gospel band, the Cheerful Givers. He earned a B.A. in theology from Centenary College in Shreveport, Louisiana, his home until, on the advice of KRIS KRISTOFFERSON, he moved to Nashville in 1978.

Stegall's first big successes came in the early eighties as the songwriter of country and pop #1s such as "Sexy Eyes" (Dr. Hook), "We're in This Love Together" (Al Jarreau), and "Lonely Nights" (MICKEY GILLEY). Other hits included "Let's Get Over Them Together" (MOE BANDY AND BECKY HOBBS), "Stranger Things Have Happened" (RONNIE MILSAP), and recordings by Johnny Mathis, Helen Reddy, GEORGE STRAIT, REBA MCENTIRE, CHARLEY PRIDE, and many others. More recently Stegall co-wrote the #1 Alan Jackson hits "Don't Rock the Jukebox," "Love's Got a Hold on You," and "Dallas," along with "If I Could Make a Living" (CLAY WALKER) and "Between an Old Memory and Me" (TRAVIS TRITT).

Stegall's career as a producer began in 1985, when he worked with RANDY TRAVIS on his debut WARNER BROS. album. One of the songs Stegall co-produced, "On the Other Hand," was named ACM Single of the Year. In 1989 Stegall produced the demo recordings that landed Alan Jackson his contract with Arista Records and has been retained for every Jackson album since, along with projects by SHENANDOAH and TRACY BYRD.

Stegall hasn't enjoyed the same success as an artist. First with CAPITOL RECORDS, then with EPIC RECORDS, his recording career to date peaked in 1985 with the Top Ten hit "Pretty Lady."   —*Michael Hight*

REPRESENTATIVE RECORDING

Passages (Mercury, 1996)

Step One Records
established in Nashville, Tennessee, February 1984

Step One Records is one of the few independent country labels to have had significant chart success during the post–URBAN COWBOY boom years. While this Nashville label has leaned heavily toward recording such veteran stars as RAY PRICE (1985–91) and FARON YOUNG (1988–91), its most notable success to date was with a younger talent, CLINTON GREGORY (1989–93).

Since its inception, Step One has been guided by songwriter-producer Ray Pennington, a Music Row veteran who had written and been behind the studio boards for WAYLON JENNINGS's "I'm a Ramblin' Man," among other records. In 1984 Pennington had been on the verge of retiring when singer Curtis Potter introduced him to Mel Holt, who became Pennington's partner in Step One. Potter and Ray Price became the first artists on the label. Eventually Pennington decided to experiment with young talent, and in 1991 Clinton Gregory made a splash with "(If It Weren't for Country Music) I'd Go Crazy," which rose to #25 at a time when it was the only independent label release on *Billboard*'s country singles chart. Gregory later signed with a major label, MERCURY RECORDS, but Step One continued to defy the odds by selling records at a time when other independent country labels had a dismal record of survival.   —*Daniel Cooper*

Ray Stevens

Ray Stevens
b. Clarksdale, Georgia, January 24, 1939

Ray Stevens may be known as the Clown Prince of Country Music (he won the TNN *Music City News* Comedian Award for nine years running), but his list of talents is even more impressive: singer, songwriter, arranger, producer, music publisher, multi-instrumentalist, TV star, and entrepreneur.

Born Harold Ray Ragsdale, Stevens grew up listening to country music on local radio. He began piano lessons at age six, and as his musical talents began to blossom, so did his interest in other types of music. The Ragsdale family moved to Atlanta when Stevens was sixteen, and he began working as a DJ and performing in a small combo. It was there that he met Atlanta publishing giant BILL LOWERY. Lowery introduced him to the music business, got him signed to a small record label, and suggested he change his name. (Lowery took Stevens's middle name and his mother's maiden name to give him his new identity.)

While still studying music at Georgia State University, Stevens began recording for MERCURY RECORDS. His first unlikely self-composed release was "Jeremiah Peabody's Poly Unsaturated Quick Dissolving Fast Acting Pleasant Tasting Green and Purple Pills" (#35 pop, 1961). This heralded the string of novelty songs that would be his forte for the next three decades. Though he moved to Nashville in 1962 and became active in the recording industry, his songs did not appear on the country charts until 1969. Throughout the sixties he had his greatest success with off-the-wall compositions such as "Ahab the Arab" (#5 pop, 1962), "Harry the Hairy Ape" (#17 pop, 1963), and "Gitarzan" (#8 pop, 1969). In between the hits he could be found at various recording sessions singing harmony, arranging, and playing various instruments.

In 1970 Stevens had the million-selling and Grammy-winning "Everything Is Beautiful" (#39 country, #1 pop) and hosted a summer replacement TV show for pop singer Andy Williams. Stevens's string of novelty tunes continued with "The Streak" (#3 country, #1 pop, 1974), "Shriner's

Convention" (#7 country, 1980), and "Mississippi Squirrel Revival" (#20 country, 1984–85). Ironically, his biggest country hit was the straight recording of "Misty" (#3 country, 1975), which also garnered him another Grammy.

In 1991 Stevens opened an entertainment center and resort area in BRANSON, MISSOURI, performing there through 1993. His latest venture is successfully selling video classics of his hit songs through direct TV marketing.

—*Don Roy*

REPRESENTATIVE RECORDINGS

The Best of Ray Stevens (Mercury, 1970); *The Ray Stevens Collection* (MCA, 1993)

Gary Stewart
b. Letcher County, Kentucky, May 28, 1945

In the mid-1970s, when many country fans worried that loud, guitar-oriented country-rock was threatening the fine art of honky-tonk singing, Gary Stewart came out of nowhere and proved you could have both. The tall, skinny singer-guitarist combined a rocking band sound with heart-baring hillbilly vocals as no one had, perhaps since JERRY LEE LEWIS.

Stewart was born in Letcher County, Kentucky. When his father was maimed in a mining accident, Stewart's family moved to Fort Pierce, Florida, which remains Stewart's home base even today. He played both rock and country in local bar bands around town, where MEL TILLIS heard him and pointed him toward Nashville. Stewart recorded for the Cory label in 1964 and signed with Kapp in 1968. He wrote hit songs for BILLY WALKER, JIM ED BROWN, and CAL SMITH, but when Stewart heard the Allman Brothers Band in 1971, he went home determined to merge the new southern rock with his love of honky-tonk. Eventually RCA producer Roy Dea called Stewart back to Nashville, and they cut "Drinkin' Thing," a barroom cry of desperation,

Gary Stewart

with Stewart warbling in an over-the-top vibrato reminiscent of Lewis.

It became a Top Ten country hit and was soon followed by two smashes in the same vein, "Out of Hand" (#4) and "She's Actin' Single (I'm Drinkin' Doubles)" (#1). All three found a place on Stewart's 1975 debut album, *Out of Hand*. The cranked-up guitars and drums became even more prominent on the next album, 1976's *Steppin' Out*, which contained the Top Twenty singles "Flat Natural Born Good-Timin' Man" and "In Some Room Above the Street." The title song of the 1977 album *Your Place or Mine*, with its blunt, unromantic approach to saloon sexuality, became a #11 hit. The following year Stewart's album *Little Junior* yielded "Whiskey Trip," his last Top Twenty hit.

Stewart's albums were loud and wild by the standards of mid-1970s Nashville, but his live shows were more so as he played bluesy slide-guitar solos and pushed his vocals into wailing improvisations. This made him a favorite among younger audiences and rock critics (*Rolling Stone* called him a "vintage country boy gone crazy"), but it made the Nashville establishment wary. That wariness, compounded by Stewart's bacchanalian personal habits and indifferent attitude toward stardom, soon sank his career.

There were more albums—1979's *Gary*, 1980's *Cactus and a Rose* with the Allmans, and two duo efforts with fellow singer-songwriter DEAN DILLON; but they produced few hits, and by the mid-1980s Stewart's recording career seemed to be over. Stewart went back to Fort Pierce and played the bar circuits in Florida and Texas. He was remembered only by locals and hard-core collectors. Then the unexpected happened. California's HIGHTONE RECORDS not only re-released his greatest hits and early albums, but also put Stewart back in the studio with Dea for three fine CDs—1988's *Brand New*, 1990's *Battleground*, and 1993's *I'm a Texan*. They weren't as original or as successful as the early RCA albums, but Stewart's voice had deepened and darkened into a knowing awareness of the price of life on the wild side. —*Geoffrey Himes*

REPRESENTATIVE RECORDINGS

Out of Hand (RCA, 1975; reissued HighTone, 1991); *Your Place or Mine* (RCA, 1977); *Gary's Greatest* (HighTone, 1991); *The Essential Gary Stewart* (RCA, 1997)

Redd Stewart
b. Ashland City, Tennessee, May 27, 1921

Henry Redd Stewart spent his formative years in Louisville, Kentucky, a city to which he returned after several years of working as a musician in other parts of the country. The product of a musical family, he formed his own band when he was thirteen years old and began performing on local radio stations. While still in his teens, he went on the road as fiddle player with fellow Kentuckian COUSIN EMMY. In 1937 he joined PEE WEE KING's Golden West Cowboys, a move that took him to the stage of the GRAND OLE OPRY. When King's featured vocalist, EDDY ARNOLD, left the group, Stewart replaced him as lead singer.

While serving in the army, Stewart wrote his first hit song, "Soldier's Last Letter," a World War II hit for ERNEST TUBB in 1944. Stewart's most enduring compositions were the result of his longtime collaboration with Pee Wee King. The most famous song penned by this team is "Tennessee Waltz"—a 1948 hit for King, on which Stewart sang the lead vocal, and subsequently recorded by numerous artists.

In 1950–51, it became a blockbuster crossover hit when recorded by pop artist Patti Page. Other notable songs co-written by King and Stewart include "Bonaparte's Retreat," "Slow Poke," and (co-written with Chilton Price) "You Belong to Me."

In 1947 Stewart and King moved back to Louisville, and for another decade the *Pee Wee King Show* was a regular feature on WAVE-TV. After King's group disbanded, Stewart continued working as a solo artist, sitting in with Louisville bands, and writing songs. Over the years, he recorded his own records for the KING, STARDAY, and HICKORY labels. He had his own TV show at WBBM in Chicago for one season, 1956–57. —*Wayne W. Daniel*

Wynn Stewart
b. Morrisville, Missouri, June 7, 1934; d. July 17, 1985

Though he never attained the career heights of BUCK OWENS or MERLE HAGGARD, Wynnford Lindsey Stewart was, in terms of influence, nearly as important a purveyor of the postwar honky-tonk sound associated with the West Coast. He had a tremendous impact on Owens's style, and he wrote Haggard's first hit, "Sing a Sad Song." At the time Haggard was playing bass with Stewart, and when Haggard formed his own band the Strangers, the nucleus of the band came from Stewart's group. As a singer, Stewart was so committed to hard, West Coast–style country that he once described his "darkest moment" as being "when some country artists recorded pop."

Stewart started playing guitar when he was eight years old, and by the time he turned thirteen he had landed a radio spot on KWTO in Springfield, Missouri. A year later his family moved to Huntington Park, California, where Stewart formed a new band. He first recorded for the Intro label, and in 1956, on the recommendation of SKEETS MC-DONALD, he was signed to CAPITOL RECORDS. He scored his first hit with "Waltz of the Angels" in 1956. Two years later, Stewart's "Above and Beyond," written by a young HARLAN HOWARD, appeared on Jackpot, a subsidiary of the CHALLENGE label. ("Above and Beyond" later became a #3 hit for Buck Owens.) Stewart recorded several lively duets with JAN HOWARD, Harlan's wife, and he had his first Top Ten record with his 1959 Challenge recording of "Wishful Thinking."

Throughout the 1950s Stewart employed top pickers, among them future Strangers ROY NICHOLS and Ralph Mooney. They, and Haggard, worked with Stewart at the Nashville Nevada Club, a Las Vegas nightspot Stewart opened in 1961. In 1964 Capitol executive KEN NELSON saw Stewart in Vegas and re-signed him to the label. Stewart had the only #1 hit of his career with the ballad "It's Such a Pretty World Today," released on Capitol in 1967.

Stewart left Capitol in 1972, and for the next thirteen years he was on the charts only sporadically. He died of a heart attack in 1985, unfortunately too soon for him to have enjoyed the acclaim his steadily rising historic profile has only lately engendered. —*Daniel Cooper*

REPRESENTATIVE RECORDING
Wynn Stewart: The Best of the Challenge Masters (AVI, 1995)

Ocie Stockard
b. Crafton, Texas, May 11, 1909; d. April 23, 1988

A pioneer of western swing, Ocie Blanton Stockard was a charter member of MILTON BROWN & His Musical Brownies. During his career Stockard played tenor banjo, tenor guitar, and fiddle for a variety of western swing bands, including BOB WILLS & his Texas Playboys and TOMMY DUNCAN's Western All-Stars.

Stockard worked as a barber before moving to Fort Worth in 1928. His musical career began in 1929 when he became an original member of the HI FLYERS, one of Fort Worth's earliest stringbands. He also played dances with Bob Wills and Milton Brown at Fort Worth's Crystal Springs Dancing Pavilion. Stockard joined Milton Brown & His Musical Brownies in September 1932, playing tenor banjo on all of their recording sessions. Stockard provided the Musical Brownies with banjo rhythm inspired by New Orleans jazz bands. He would also take occasional improvisational solos and sing harmony. After Brown's death in 1936 Stockard played for Milton's brother Derwood for a year before forming his own band, the Wanderers. Stockard's 1937 and 1941 recording sessions for BLUEBIRD and OKEH are highly regarded by jazz fans. He also recorded for KING RECORDS before joining Bob Wills in California in 1946.
—*Cary Ginell*

REPRESENTATIVE RECORDING

The Famous Fourteen: Ocie Stockard & the Wanderers (Origin Jazz Library, 1981)

Dave Stogner

b. Gainesville, Texas, May 15, 1920; d. May 3, 1989

A western swing bandleader who experienced his greatest success when most of the big names in the genre were struggling, Dave Stogner was also possibly the only bandleader of the 1950s to base his band directly on the pioneering sound of MILTON BROWN's Musical Brownies.

Active in North Texas by his early teens, Stogner concentrated on fiddle, but was capable on a number of instruments. Galvanized by the jazzy music of Brown, Stogner was leading his own band in Ardmore, Oklahoma, by 1937, followed by stints in Oklahoma City and with the Sons of the West in Amarillo. He was in California by the early forties, starting his own band, the Western Rhythmairs, in 1944. Moving to the Fresno area after the war, he worked the San Joaquin Valley circuit and began recording for independent labels such as FOUR STAR and Morgan. Stogner appeared on Fresno television throughout the fifties, but his fame did not spread beyond the area until JIMMY WAKELY helped secure him a DECCA recording contract in 1957. Stogner recorded a fine album featuring former BOB WILLS fiddler Joe Holley, who had also honed his playing from the Musical Brownies and helped Stogner evoke the Brownies spirit. Stogner's heyday was short-lived, and by the late sixties he had disbanded his group. He reorganized it in the 1970s, however, playing and recording into the eighties.
—*Kevin Coffey*

REPRESENTATIVE RECORDINGS

Dave Stogner & His Western Swing Band (Decca, 1957)

Cliffie Stone

b. Stockton, California, March 1, 1917; d. January 17, 1998

In a career that lasted over six decades, Cliffie Stone wore a variety of hats. To the public, he was a radio and TV personality, recording artist, comic straight man, emcee, and bass player. Behind the scenes, he was a record producer,

Cliffie Stone

talent scout, song publisher, and personal manager. All these roles were pivotal in the development of California's thriving postwar country music scene.

Clifford Gilpin Snyder moved with his family at age nine from Stockton to Burbank, then a tiny rural hamlet outside Los Angeles. His father, Herman Snyder, raised dogs and was also the performer Herman the Hermit, nicknamed for his unfashionably long hair and beard. Herman began working with pioneer Los Angeles country radio personality STUART HAMBLEN in the 1930s. In 1935, when Cliffie was eighteen, he also joined Hamblen, on the KFVD *Covered Wagon Jubilee*, as a bass player and comic known as Cliffie Stonehead. Hamblen hosted multiple daily shows on different stations and turned two of them over to Stone in the early 1940s. In 1944 Stone started a third show, *Dinner Bell Round-Up*, over KPAS (later KXLA) in Pasadena, which featured live music and comedy. He also freelanced as a bass player and ran his own record production company, Lariat Records.

Stone's production work at Lariat landed him a job with CAPITOL RECORDS, in 1945, as assistant to country A&R man LEE GILLETTE. As a performer he played bass on Capitol county sessions with TEX RITTER and WESLEY TUTTLE, and was instrumental in signing MERLE TRAVIS to Capitol. He and Travis co-wrote Travis hits such as "Divorce Me C.O.D." (1946) and "So Round! So Firm! So Fully Packed!" (1947). Stone also had several hit records on Capitol: "Silver Stars, Purple Sage, Eyes of Blue" in 1947; and both "Peepin' Through the Keyhole" and "When My Blue Moon Turns to Gold Again" in 1948.

As host of *Dinner Bell Round-Up*, Stone constantly sought new talent, and added KXLA's morning disc jockey, TENNESSEE ERNIE FORD, to the cast as comic and vocalist in 1947. In 1948 the impresario founded a new Saturday night stage show: *HOMETOWN JAMBOREE*, produced at the American Legion Stadium in El Monte, California. The show premiered as a weekly TV broadcast in December 1949 over KCOP-TV in Pasadena. (In 1953 it moved to KTLA-TV, where it ran until its cancellation in 1959.) Along with Ford—the show's star—other regulars at various times included Herman the Hermit, Eddie Kirk, JOHNNY HORTON, Molly Bee, and FERLIN HUSKY.

When Ford was asked to perform in Las Vegas after his 1950 hit country and pop duet "I'll Never Be Free" with Kay Starr, he asked Stone to become his personal manager. In 1956, after Ford landed his prime-time NBC-TV variety series *The Ford Show,* Stone became producer, integrating Ford's down-home flair with the mainstream appeal that a network show required.

At the same time, Stone operated the West Coast song publishing company Central Songs along with Capitol producers Lee Gillette and KEN NELSON. After *The Ford Show* ended in 1961, Stone retired as Ford's manager but kept his hand in radio as a disc jockey and concentrated on Central Songs. The partners sold it to Capitol in 1969. In the 1970s Stone worked for ATV Music and later for GENE AUTRY Music. For his own label, Granite Records, he recorded TEX WILLIAMS and Molly Bee.

Stone's youngest son, Curtis, has been the bass player with HIGHWAY 101 from its beginning to the present. In 1989 Cliffie was elected to the COUNTRY MUSIC HALL OF FAME. After he retired Stone continued to host occasional *Hometown Jamboree* Reunion shows in Southern California. He died of a sudden heart attack on January 17, 1998, at his Saugus, California, home.   —*Rich Kienzle*

David Stone
b. Savannah, Georgia, October 27, 1901; d. August 31, 1995

David P. Stone was instrumental in the early growth of the GRAND OLE OPRY and in promoting country music in the upper Midwest. He grew up in Hamlet, North Carolina, where his father ran a Coca-Cola bottling plant, and in Nashville, where his father later managed an engine repair and distribution company. After high school, David Stone became assistant manager of Loew's Vendôme theater in Nashville, then took the manager's position of another Loew's house in Memphis. Next he became roving relief manager for the Nashville-based Sudekum theater chain, which operated establishments in Tennessee, Kentucky, and Alabama. As the radio boom of the 1920s gradually undercut vaudeville, upon which theaters then relied so heavily, Stone took a job running the radio system of Nashville's Andrew Jackson Hotel, often announcing broadcasts fed from the hotel's ballroom to local radio station WLAC.

It was a natural progression to an announcer's post at WLAC and to a similar position at Nashville's WSM, where David's brother HARRY STONE was station manager. During the 1930s David not only served as a general staff announcer but also handled Grand Ole Opry broadcasts as well, while running the Opry's booking department and traveling with Opry units on the road.

In 1940 Stone moved to St. Paul, Minnesota's, KSTP, where he founded the long-running *Sunset Valley Barn Dance.* The barn dance enjoyed TV exposure for a time, beginning in the 1950s, and spin-off broadcasts included both early morning and noontime radio and TV shows. *Hymn Time,* a Sunday morning TV broadcast hosted by Stone, ran for more than 600 weeks until his retirement, in 1977. Prior to that time Stone also served for many years as

KSTP's farm service director, and in this role hosted special broadcasts from the Minnesota State Fair while also promoting the annual Farm Forum in Minneapolis–St. Paul.   —*John Rumble*

Doug Stone
b. Atlanta, Georgia, June 19, 1956

Doug Stone's promise as a honky-tonk-influenced country singer was threatened by a series of heart problems, including quadruple-bypass surgery in April 1992. By that point, Stone (born Douglas Jackson Brooks) had released seven Top Ten country singles—beginning with 1990's Grammy-nominated ballad "I'd Be Better Off (in a Pine Box)"—and four albums, all ultimately certified gold or platinum.

Stone lists as his influences artists ranging from country singers JIM REEVES and RANDY TRAVIS to pop singer-songwriters James Taylor and Dan Fogelberg, and even progressive rocker Frank Zappa. But his own sound suggests that he may have been listening to GEORGE JONES, LEFTY FRIZZELL, and CONWAY TWITTY, too.

Stone's mother, Gail Menseer, was a singer, and she gave him his first guitar lessons. At age seven, Stone appeared on a bill with LORETTA LYNN. When his parents divorced, Stone moved with his father and two brothers to a mobile home in the small town of Newnan, Georgia, where his father trained him as a mechanic. At sixteen Doug purchased his own mobile home, converting one room to a recording studio. When the mobile home was repossessed, Stone moved into a twelve-foot-by-twelve-foot house, which he continued to improve for several years.

Stone formed a band, Impact, and began playing locally. At the Newnan VFW club some years later he was discovered by his future manager, Phyllis Bennett. Stone's

Doug Stone

Harry Stone

demo tape wound up in the hands of CBS RECORDS' Nashville A&R chief BOB MONTGOMERY, who signed him to the company's EPIC label, changed his last name to Stone (reportedly to avoid confusion with GARTH BROOKS or Kix Brooks of BROOKS & DUNN), and produced "I'd Be Better Off (in a Pine Box)," a song that had been, ironically, rejected by George Jones. Stone's later hits included, among others, the chart-topping "In a Different Light" and "A Jukebox with a Country Song."

In 1995 Stone starred as a widowed country singer in *Gordy,* an independently financed feature film shot in Georgia. He sang five songs in the picture—which also featured appearances by MOE BANDY, BOXCAR WILLIE, ROY CLARK, MICKEY GILLEY, and JIM STAFFORD—but it failed to make much of an impression. —*Todd Everett*

REPRESENTATIVE RECORDINGS

Doug Stone (Epic, 1990); *From the Heart* (Epic, 1992); *Greatest Hits, Volume 1* (Epic, 1995)

Harry Stone
b. Jacksonville, Florida, February 14, 1898; d. October 8, 1968

Harry Leith Stone was one of the most important radio executives in the early history of country music. The son of a Coca-Cola bottling plant operator turned Nashville machinery distributor, he broke into radio at the dawn of the radio age. Stone gained his first experience in radio as an amateur, when he and Jack DeWitt made broadcasts from the DeWitt home, with DeWitt serving as engineer and Stone as announcer. Next, Stone and DeWitt helped operate Nashville station WCBQ for the First Baptist Church, then ran WBAW for the Waldron Drug Company. In 1928 Stone signed with WSM as announcer and quickly became assistant manager.

As station manager GEORGE D. HAY's failing health forced him to take increasingly frequent sick leaves, Stone

replaced him as station manager in 1932 and set about putting WSM on a firm commercial footing. During the 1930s he worked diligently to line up sponsors for a wide variety of pop, country, news, and educational shows. WSM's programming, much of it originated for NBC, continued to diversify after Stone hired JACK STAPP as program director in 1939.

Stone was especially instrumental in gaining advertising sponsors for the GRAND OLE OPRY and, with librarian and Opry stage manager VITO PELLETTIERI, divided the show into the segmented format it retains. WSM announcer and booking department manager DAVID STONE assisted his brother Harry in deliberately building a star system by hiring new professional talent for the show, including ROY ACUFF, PEE WEE KING, and EDDY ARNOLD. Stone also secured NBC network exposure for the Opry by helping to convince the R. J. Reynolds Tobacco Company to sponsor a half-hour segment, the *Prince Albert Show,* beginning in 1939.

Harry Stone was well connected organizationally. He not only worked closely with Nashville's Chamber of Commerce in promoting tourism but also chaired NBC's Station Planning and Advisory Committee and worked with R. J. Reynolds to organize WSM's CAMEL CARAVAN in 1941–42.

By 1950, however, policy and personality clashes with WSM board chairman Edwin Craig and WSM president Jack DeWitt, who was placed over Stone in 1947, led to Stone's resignation. From there he moved on to manage stations in Texas and Arizona and filled a West Coast regional sales slot for ABC. From October 1958 to November 1959 he served as CMA's first executive director, but this organization, still in its infancy, lacked sufficient funds to implement his promotional ideas. From 1960 to 1968 he was advertising manager for *Tennessee* magazine, published by the Tennessee Electric Cooperative Association.
—*John Rumble*

Ernest Stoneman
b. Monarat, Virginia, May 25, 1893; d. June 14, 1968

Ernest Van Stoneman ranked as one of the major figures in country music during the 1925–28 period. After the Great Depression ruined his early career, Stoneman survived several years of dire poverty, then slowly reconstructed a life in music with the support of several of his numerous children. A native of Virginia's Blue Ridge Mountains and a carpenter by trade, Ernest made his first trip to the OKEH recording studio in September 1924, where he cut his arrangement of "The Titanic," a ballad describing the 1912 maritime disaster.

The success of this disc led to more sessions for OKeh as well as EDISON, GENNETT RECORDS, and especially Victor. His repertoire included traditional ballads, Victorian sentimental songs, and mountain sacred numbers. Some were done only with his own guitar and harmonica accompaniment, while others featured a stringband that included such musicians as Kahle Brewer and Eck Dunford on fiddle and cousin George Stoneman on banjo. Still others featured his wife, Hattie, and her siblings Bolen and Irma Frost. Examples of his better known recordings included "The Poor Tramp," "When the Snowflakes Fall Again," "Two Little Orphans," and "The Great Reaping Day."

At BRISTOL, TENNESSEE, in the summer of 1927, Stoneman cut some fourteen Victor masters, compared to six for the CARTER FAMILY and two for JIMMIE RODGERS. After the onset of the Great Depression, however, Stoneman's

Ernest Stoneman with the Dixie Mountaineers

activity declined and he had only one session—with Vocalion—in 1934. Two years earlier, he had moved Hattie and nine children to the Washington, D.C., area, where they endured grinding poverty for some years and increased their family numbers to thirteen.

After World War II "Pop" began to build a band around the children, and they evolved into the STONEMAN FAMILY. After his retirement from carpenter work, he worked with them regularly and participated in their recordings, syndicated TV programs, and earlier triumphs until final illness sidelined the venerable pioneer in mid-April 1968. Continuing interest in his music has resulted in the reissue of several albums containing his earlier recorded works.

—*Ivan M. Tribe*

REPRESENTATIVE RECORDINGS

Ernest V. Stoneman and His Blue Ridge Cornshuckers (Rounder, 1974); *Ernest V. Stoneman: With Family and Friends* (Old Homestead, 1985–89), 3 vols.; *Ernest Stoneman: Edison Recordings: 1928* (County, 1996)

The Stoneman Family

Pattie Inez "Patsy" Stoneman b. Galax, Virginia, May 27, 1925
Calvin Scott Stoneman b. Galax, Virginia, August 4, 1932; d. March 4, 1973
Donna LaVerne Stoneman b. Alexandria, Virginia, February 7, 1934
Oscar James Stoneman b. Washington, D.C., March 8, 1937
Veronica Loretta Stoneman b. Washington, D.C., May 5, 1938
Van Haden Stoneman b. Washington, D.C., December 31, 1940; d. June 3, 1995

The children of country music pioneer ERNEST "POP" STONEMAN forged a career for themselves with a style that fused an exciting blend of bluegrass and country music. Although the Stonemen siblings had started performing together by the late 1940s, the group grew out of a Washington, D.C., band called the Bluegrass Champs, which featured the fiddling talents of Scott Stoneman, sister Donna's exciting mandolin work, brother Jim's bass, and the additional skills of nonfamily members. They emerged as winners on an *Arthur Godfrey's Talent Scouts* CBS-TV show in 1956. By 1961, following the addition of Van Stone-

man on guitar, his sister Veronica (Roni) on banjo, and Pop Stoneman as featured vocalist, the all-family group embarked on an effort to crash the big time.

The Stoneman Family cut a pair of albums for STARDAY in 1962 and 1963, with JACK CLEMENT as their manager. After moving briefly to Texas and then California, they recorded for the World Pacific label and worked at various clubs and Disneyland before finally coming to Nashville late in 1965. In Music City they signed with MGM RECORDS and soon started their own syndicated television program. Their showmanship helped win them the CMA Vocal Group of the Year Award in 1967, but Pop's death the following year left a void. Older sister Patsy replaced him and exercised increasing leadership with the passing of time.

The Stonemans moved to RCA in 1969 but had less success than when with MGM. Roni's departure in 1971 and Donna's in 1972 took some toll on the group's fan appeal, but Patsy, Jimmy, and Van carried on with the help of nonfamily sidemen such as David Dougherty and Johnnie Bellar. Donna later returned and Roni continued to work with them at times, but by the eighties much of their momentum had ebbed. Roni forged an independent image for some eighteen years (1973–1991) as a banjo picker and comedienne on the popular TV show *HEE HAW.* By the time my biography of the group, *The Stonemans,* appeared in 1993, increasing health problems for Jim and Van had rendered the group inactive. Roni continues to work as a solo act, and Donna labors in evangelistic and gospel music endeavors.

—*Ivan M. Tribe*

REPRESENTATIVE RECORDINGS

Those Singin' Swingin' Stompin' Sensational Stonemans (MGM, 1966); *The First Family of Country Music* (CMH, 1982)

Carl Story

b. Lenoir, North Carolina, May 29, 1916; d. March 31, 1995

Carl Moore Story is known as the Father of Bluegrass Gospel, although he recorded on major labels for a decade before using full bluegrass instrumentation and never performed sacred music exclusively.

Story matured in the Carolina Piedmont and started his band the Rambling Mountaineers in the late thirties. For the next three decades he maintained radio—and later television—bases in such locales as Knoxville, Charlotte, and Asheville. Over these years Story's band included such key figures as Red Rector, Claude Boone, Harold Austin, Tater Tate, and the Brewster Brothers. Story himself favored the fiddle in earlier years, for a time fiddling with BILL MONROE at the GRAND OLE OPRY, though Story later switched to guitar.

Story's recording career began in 1947 with MERCURY RECORDS and endured for a decade, although he switched to COLUMBIA briefly (1953–55). Beginning in the late fifties he recorded a series of bluegrass gospel albums for STAR-DAY and then recorded often for smaller companies. As the country music business changed, Carl began working as a disc jockey through the week, taking a band out on weekends. In later years he resided in Greer, South Carolina, and remained active until the last months of his life.

—*Ivan M. Tribe*

REPRESENTATIVE RECORDINGS

Gospel Quartet Favorites (Mercury and Stetson, 1958); *Thank the Lord for Everything* (Pure White Dove, 1994)

George Strait

b. Poteet, Texas, May 18, 1952

Ever since he first came on the contemporary country scene as a voice for NEW TRADITIONALISM in 1981, George Strait's name has become synonymous with "real country." His unadorned Texas rancher's clothes—consisting of cowboy hat, western shirt, and blue jeans—has been copied by a legion of young "hat acts." Strait's albums have been certified either gold or platinum, and he remains a

George Strait

huge concert draw. As much of modern country music includes pop sounds, Strait consistently draws from both the WESTERN SWING and the HONKY-TONK traditions of his native Texas.

Reared in Pearsall, Strait's parents divorced when he was still in grade school. Strait and his older brother Buddy were raised by their father, John Strait, a junior high school math teacher. The boys learned ranch ways early on, helping out on the family's 2,000-acre spread.

The young Strait didn't listen to much country music growing up, but was inspired by the mid-1960s British Invasion rock groups and joined a number of garage bands in high school. He eloped after graduation with longtime sweetheart Norma, then signed up for a stint in the army.

Stationed in Hawaii, Strait found his true calling: country music. In 1973 he auditioned and won the slot as singer in an army base country band. He absorbed the music of HANK WILLIAMS, GEORGE JONES, and MERLE HAGGARD. Haggard's tribute album to the legendary BOB WILLS, *Tribute to the Best Damn Fiddle Player in the World,* was instrumental in turning Strait in the direction of western swing.

Back home, Strait enrolled at Southwest Texas State University to pursue a degree in agriculture but had by then also set his sights seriously on a music career. He hooked up with the Ace in the Hole band and began extensive regional gigging. The band recorded several singles on the D RECORDS label. Despite club success, several trips to Nashville failed to drum up interest in Strait as a major label prospect.

During one fateful club appearance, club owner and former record promotion man Erv Woolsey liked what he heard. In 1981 Woolsey helped Strait sign with MCA. Woolsey would remain Strait's behind-the-scenes advocate before eventually taking on the role of full-time manager.

Strait arrived in Nashville just as the URBAN COWBOY movement was in full swing. His first honky-tonk missive, 1981's "Unwound," went to #6 on the *Billboard* charts. The accompanying album, *Strait Country,* helped to increase hardcore country play on the radio.

As a vocalist, Strait proved a masterful interpreter. His Texas accent came through, but as a singer he avoided over-the-top twang and flashy fillips in favor of subtle phrasing. Through his love of Haggard, he developed both the evocative nuance of LEFTY FRIZZELL and the smooth croon shadings of Bing Crosby and Perry Como.

Strait began his long reign at the top of the charts, and subsequent Top Ten hits displayed his range. Although his roots were in Texas dance-hall music, he also proved he had a way with the pop-influenced tune "If You're Thinking You Want a Stranger (There's One Coming Home)" (#3, 1982) and the smooth ballad "Marina Del Rey" (#6, 1983). Hits that were #1 included his cover of the Bob Wills staple "Right or Wrong" (1983), the sly "All My Ex's Live in Texas" (1987), and the western swing of "Am I Blue" (1987). Albums such as 1984's *Does Fort Worth Ever Cross Your Mind* emphasized Strait's roots in western swing and honky-tonk.

Personal tragedy struck in 1986 when Strait's thirteen-year-old daughter, Jenifer, was killed in a car accident. (Strait's only other child, George Jr., was born in 1981.) When Strait won that year's CMA Male Vocalist of the Year Award, he accepted it in Jenifer's memory.

By 1990 country's ranks had swelled with many young stars who dressed like Strait, but few were able to mimic his keen blend of traditional and contemporary sounds. As evidence of his staying power, his blockbuster hit "Love Without End, Amen" (#1, 1990) topped the charts for five weeks.

Strait hit the big screen in 1992 with *Pure Country,* a film in which he played a disillusioned country star named Dusty Chandler. The soundtrack of the same name became Strait's biggest seller to date, yielding the #1 hits "I Cross My Heart" and the album opener "Heartland."

Although not a songwriter himself, Strait has relied on the cream of the tunesmith crop throughout the years, including stalwart WHITEY SHAFER and youngblood DEAN DILLON. In recent years Strait has leaned on the talents of singer-songwriter JIM LAUDERDALE and Aaron Barker.

In 1995 Strait celebrated his fifteenth year as a recording artist by releasing the boxed-set career retrospective *Strait Out of the Box.* Strait's set flew out of stores in unprecedented numbers. His career remains undiminished. In 1996 the CMA presented him with the Single of the Year Award for "Check Yes or No," and that year he also won Album of the Year *(Blue Clear Sky)* and Male Vocalist of the Year Awards. Strait took away another CMA Male Vocalist of the Year Award in 1997 as well as Album of the Year Award for *Carrying Your Love with Me.* In 1998 he kicked off the George Strait Country Music Festival, a multi-artist nationwide tour sponsored by Nokia and Chevy Trucks.

—*Chris Dickinson*

REPRESENTATIVE RECORDINGS

Strait Country (MCA, 1981); *Does Fort Worth Ever Cross Your Mind* (MCA, 1984); *Ocean Front Property* (MCA, 1987); *Chill of an Early Fall* (MCA, 1991); *Strait Out of the Box* (MCA, 1995); *Blue Clear Sky* (MCA, 1996); *Carrying Your Love with Me* (MCA, 1997)

Mel Street
b. Grundy, Virginia, October 21, 1933; d. October 21, 1978

A gifted hard-country singer, King Malachi "Mel" Street was heavily steeped in the GEORGE JONES honky-tonk influence. Street enjoyed moderate chart success in the 1970s with singles such as "Borrowed Angel" (a Street original that became a Top Ten hit in 1972), "Lovin' on Back Streets" (the highest chart showing of his career, it hit #5 in early 1973), and "I Met a Friend of Yours Today." Street seemed bound for greater stardom when he took his own life on October 21, 1978, on the morning of his forty-fifth birthday.

Street made his radio debut at age sixteen, on a Bluefield, West Virginia, radio station. Later he worked (in West Virginia, Ohio, and in Niagara Falls, New York—where for a time he climbed towers for the Niagara Power Project) in construction, as an electrician, and as an auto body and fender man. He played nightclubs in West Virginia and Niagara, New York, before getting his first significant musical break. This came in 1963 on *Country Jamboree,* a local Saturday night TV show broadcast from Bluefield, West Virginia, on which he appeared regularly until the show's demise in 1968. Another TV show, *Country Showcase,* followed, eventually leading to Street's first local record contract.

Street's earliest chart action—actually, the lion's share of his chart success between his chart debut in 1972 and his death six years later—came on various independent labels: Metromedia, Tandem, Royal American, and GRT.

Street killed himself with a gun just months after signing a major label deal with MERCURY. George Jones, who had admired Street's talent enough to write liner notes for one of his early albums, sang at his funeral. —*Bob Allen*

REPRESENTATIVE RECORDINGS

Borrowed Angel (Metromedia, 1972); *Mel Street's Greatest Hits* (GRT, 1976); *The Very Best of Mel Street* (Sunbird, 1980)

Texas Bill Strength
b. Bessemer, Alabama, August 28, 1928; d. October 1, 1973

William Thomas "Texas Bill" Strength was one of many singers and DJs who have spent years on the fringes of country stardom.

At age sixteen, Strength won an amateur contest in Houston, Texas, where he was raised, and soon began singing on area radio stations. With a style closely resembling those of his two main inspirations—ERNEST TUBB and TEX RITTER—Strength made his first recordings for Houston's small Cireco label, but by 1949 had joined FOUR STAR RECORDS. He worked at stations in St. Joseph, Denver, and Birmingham, and then, in 1950–51, he was hired by the CIO for its *American Folk Songs* radio show and for conventions nationwide. For these performances Strength used as his theme "We Will Overcome," which was appropriate to the labor organization's zeal.

After a stint with Coral Records (1951–54), Strength signed with CAPITOL RECORDS in 1955, and at his first session covered one of that year's big songs, "The Yellow Rose of Texas," recorded by Tubb and others. During these years Strength moved from WEAS in Atlanta (1951–54) to KWEM in West Memphis (1954–55), and there befriended young ELVIS PRESLEY.

Late in 1955 Strength moved to the Minneapolis–St. Paul area, where he spent most of his remaining years. He booked Nashville talent into the popular Flame Supper Club there, worked area radio as a country DJ, and hosted TV kiddie shows. Briefly working California radio in Long Beach and BAKERSFIELD, Strength returned to Minnesota, and during the 1960s and early 1970s recorded sporadically for SUN RECORDS, Toppa, STARDAY, Bangar, Golden Wing, and Brite Star. Probably his best-remembered record (none ever charted) was his 1967 Starday parody "Hillbilly Hades."

A part-time journalist in his last days, Strength published recollections of stars he had known for Minnesota's *Country News-Scene.* Seriously injured in an August 1973 auto accident, he died the following October in a St. Paul hospital, having lived just forty-five years. —*Ronnie Pugh*

Stringband Music

Before the popularity of country vocalists such as JIMMIE RODGERS and the CARTER FAMILY, the most common form of rural, early country music was played by stringbands. As the name implies, these ensembles were comprised of stringed instruments—fiddles, banjos, guitars, and sometimes a mandolin or autoharp.

The first stringbands consisted of fiddle and banjo duets. Early settlers in the American colonies brought the fiddle, and with it fiddle tunes from Ireland, Scotland, and England. The banjo, of African origin, became widespread by the mid-1800s. At about the turn of the twentieth century, rural musicians began to take up the guitar, and it was added to the stringband ensemble, primarily as rhythmic accompaniment. The stringband tradition was well established by the 1920s, when the first country music recordings were being made. Many bands adopted names intended to reflect their country roots: the SKILLET LICKERS, Al Hopkins & the Hillbillies, EARL JOHNSON & His Dixie Clodhoppers, and the Possum Hunters. Repertoires of these groups included old-time fiddle tunes, southern folk songs, and popular nineteenth-century parlor songs.

Old-time stringband music remained popular through the 1930s but was eventually eclipsed by the advent of newer forms of country music, such as electric honky-tonk and western swing. During the mid-1940s BILL MONROE and banjo player EARL SCRUGGS pioneered a new kind of polished, high-energy stringband music that eventually became known as bluegrass. Enclaves of old-time stringband music still thrive. In mountain towns such as GALAX, VIRGINIA, and Mount Airy, North Carolina, many fine old-time fiddlers and banjo players still play for local dances and at banjo and fiddle contests, and people enjoy stringband music alongside their contemporary country music.

—*Charlie Seemann*

Stringbean
b. Annville, Kentucky, June 17, 1916; d. November 10, 1973

Too many country fans remember David "Stringbean" Akeman only as he died—murdered with his wife at their remote Tennessee farm in 1973. Those who saw him perform in person or on *HEE HAW* realized that he was one of the most original comedians in country music as well as a fine clawhammer banjo player and traditional singer. His distinctive striped shirt, low-belted pants, and funny duck-

Stringbean

walk were as familiar as MINNIE PEARL's straw hat. His droll wit and deadpan irony were reflected in signature one-liners such as "Lord, I feel so unnecessary."

Growing up in eastern Kentucky, Akeman worked in Civilian Conservation Corps camps during the Depression before landing his first musical job, as well as his nickname, from country performer Asa Martin. After playing banjo for several bands around the Lexington area, he came to Nashville in about 1942 and became BILL MONROE's first banjo player. Later in the 1940s he teamed with fellow Opry member LEW CHILDRE for a duet act and became a protégé of UNCLE DAVE MACON. The older banjo player taught Stringbean much of his repertoire of old-time banjo songs and even gave him one of his own banjos. By the time of Macon's death in 1952, Stringbean was working as a soloist at the GRAND OLE OPRY and adapting current songs such as "Hillbilly Fever" to his clawhammer style.

Feeling his appeal lay primarily in personal appearances, Stringbean postponed making his own records until 1960, when he began doing a series of EPs and LPs for STARDAY RECORDS. The first of these was *Old Time Banjo Pickin' and Singin'* (1960), but the best-known and most reissued was *A Salute to Uncle Dave Macon* (1963). Stringbean did later albums and singles for the Nugget and Cullman labels. Joining the cast of *Hee Haw* in 1969 rejuvenated his career, though his comedy was featured more than his music. He often teamed with fellow banjoist-comedian GRANDPA JONES, with whom he had become a close friend and neighbor.

In 1973, the brutal murder of Stringbean and his wife, Estelle Stanfill Akeman, at their remote three-room cabin shocked Nashville's music community. The two gunmen, John and Doug Brown, were waiting for Stringbean at home after a Saturday-night Opry performance in hopes of robbing him of cash rumored to be hidden in his cabin; they came away with a few guns and a chainsaw. Though the killers were caught and convicted, many felt an important link with country music's tradition had been senselessly broken. In 1996, police discovered remnants of hundreds of dollars stashed in the walls of the Akemans' cabin.

—*Stacey Wolfe*

Stripling Brothers
Charlie Melvin Stripling b. Pickens County, Alabama, August 8, 1896; d. January 19, 1966
Ira Lee Stripling b. Pickens County, Alabama, June 5, 1898; d. March 11, 1967

This powerful old-time fiddle-guitar duo from rural northwestern Alabama recorded forty-six sides for BRUNSWICK and DECCA between 1928 and 1936. Charlie Stripling had already established his reputation as a formidable contest fiddler when the Brunswick-Balke-Collender Company set up a temporary recording studio in Birmingham. There, in 1928, A&R man JACK KAPP recorded the Striplings' virtuoso performance of "Lost Child." Its success led Brunswick to issue sixteen more Stripling numbers (breakdowns, rags, and waltzes) on the Vocalion label. In 1934 and 1936 Decca issued twenty-four more of their tunes, many of them "ragtime breakdowns" that Charlie Stripling composed for couples who wanted to fox-trot and two-step. The Stripling Brothers are most admired today, however, for their stunning renditions of archaic fiddle tunes such as "Horsehoe Bend," "Big Eyed Rabbit," "Wolves A'Howling," and "Lost Child." Charlie Stripling's recording of the latter is considered the source of the popular fiddle tune "Black Mountain Rag."

Business conditions during the Depression forced Ira, a storeowner, to end his musical career, but Charlie, a cotton farmer, continued to play through the fifties at schoolhouse performances, square dances, and fiddlers' conventions across northwestern Alabama. When recordings by the Stripling Brothers were reissued by COUNTY RECORDS in 1971, their music gained another generation of fans.

—*Joyce Cauthen*

REPRESENTATIVE RECORDINGS

The Stripling Brothers (County, 1971); *Possum Up a Gum Stump* (Alabama Traditions, 1995); *Complete Recorded Works, Volumes I & II* (Document, 1997)

James Stroud

b. Shreveport, Louisiana, July 4, 1949

A drummer by trade, James Stroud emerged as one of the dominant country producers of the 1990s, helping to create the rock-influenced sound that drove the genre to unprecedented mass popularity and record-setting sales. His background in a variety of genres—pop, rock & roll, and r&b—contributed to his ability to surf the expanded borders of the country genre, and his early years on the drumkit influenced his feel for grooves and backbeats, essential in the youth-oriented direction the country idiom took in the 1990s.

Stroud got his start almost by chance, filling in for another drummer at the r&b-oriented Malaco Studios in Jackson, Mississippi, just as he was ending his teen years. His role in Jean Knight's "Mr. Big Stuff" and King Floyd's "Groove Me" cemented a place for him as a session musician. Working in Jackson, Atlanta, and Los Angeles, Stroud played on such 1970s pop hits as the Pointer Sisters' "Yes We Can Can" and Melissa Manchester's "Midnight Blue."

EDDIE RABBITT's producer, David Malloy, took note and called on Stroud to work on Rabbitt's *Horizon* album, which yielded the 1980–81 megahits "Drivin' My Life Away" and "I Love a Rainy Night." Stroud moved to Nashville and became one of the city's most-used session drummers, working on such hits as EDDY RAVEN's "I'm Gonna Get You," TANYA TUCKER's "Highway Robbery," and CONWAY TWITTY's "That's My Job."

Having produced Dorothy Moore's 1976 pop-soul hit "Misty Blue," Stroud took on the producer role in country music after overseeing Fred Knobloch's 1980 minor pop-country success "Why Not Me." As a result, Stroud's name appeared on records by the likes of TIM McGRAW, CLAY WALKER, JOHN ANDERSON, TRACY LAWRENCE, CLINT BLACK, DOUG STONE, and the BELLAMY BROTHERS.

Invariably, producer Stroud built records around the interplay between the drummer and bass player. "I think I concentrate on the foundation of the record," he said. "If the bass and drums sound correct, if they're playin' the right groove and the right feel, it's a lot easier for the musicians around it to play to."

After working in the creative departments at MCA RECORDS and CAPITOL, Stroud took over the top position at GIANT RECORDS when the EAGLES' manager, Irving Azoff, opened the office in 1991. Giant introduced Clay Walker as an artist and sold more than 3 million copies of the tribute album *Common Thread: The Songs of the Eagles,* but in

James Stroud

1994 Stroud's primary recording engineer, Lynn Peterzell, died of a heart attack.

Stroud reconsidered his commitments—he also owned Loud Recording Studio and the Stroudavarious publishing house—and resigned from Giant on April 15, 1997. He joined DreamWorks SKG in June 1997 to head the DreamWorks Records Nashville offices. —*Tom Roland*

Henry Strzelecki

b. Birmingham, Alabama, August 8, 1939

In thirty years as one of the most in-demand bassists in Nashville, Henry P. Strzelecki (pronounced *Struh-lecki*) has performed on at least 500 Top Ten hits, more than 120 of which hit #1. He's on ROY ORBISON's pop millionseller "Oh, Pretty Woman," CONWAY TWITTY's "Happy Birthday, Darlin'," and GEORGE JONES's "He Stopped Loving Her Today."

Strzelecki's idol HANK GARLAND was responsible for landing a teenaged Strzelecki on a 1956 DECCA RECORDS studio session with producer OWEN BRADLEY for newcomer Baker Knight. Meanwhile, with brother Larry and friends, Strzelecki formed the Four Flickers and recorded a Strzelecki original called "Long Tall Texan"; Strzelecki sang, and the record was issued under a pseudonym, Hank Wallis. Though it made no impression on the national charts, a cover by Murry Kellum was a #51 pop hit in 1963. The Beach Boys also covered the song in the sixties, and in 1996 LYLE LOVETT covered it on his *Road to Ensenada* album.

In 1960 Strzelecki moved to Nashville, and CHET ATKINS hired him for an EDDY ARNOLD session. In the busy years that followed, Strzelecki backed ELVIS PRESLEY, Fats Domino, Gordon Lightfoot, Perry Como, and Simon & Garfunkel, in addition to innumerable country artists. After a mild stroke that impaired his hearing, the bassist retired in the late 1980s. —*Walt Trott*

Marty Stuart

b. Philadelphia, Mississippi, September 30, 1958

John Marty Stuart is one country star who has never lost his excitement as a fan. Though he has put several of his own singles in the Top Ten and counts among his friends a long list of Hall of Famers, Stuart still goes out of his way to buy old records and memorabilia, to meet new stars as well as old, and to write articles about his heroes in *Country Music Magazine* and the *Journal of Country Music.* Stuart has one of the world's best collections of country music artifacts (he tours in a bus that for years belonged to ERNEST TUBB) and often loans items from his stash to the COUNTRY MUSIC HALL OF FAME. He has served on the board of the Country Music Foundation since 1991, and he became board president in 1996. He's crazy about hillbilly music, and that enthusiasm feeds every songwriting session, recording session, or concert in which he participates.

Stuart is a top-notch picker on guitar and mandolin, but he possesses only a modest tenor voice and doesn't even attempt big statements or grand drama in his songwriting (which nevertheless reflects solid commercial instincts). He makes his ingrained excitement so contagious, however, that he has surmounted his limitations to become one of country's best-liked performers. His songs have been recorded by WYNONNA JUDD and GEORGE STRAIT, and Stuart has played onstage or in the studio with artists such as BOB DYLAN, WAYLON JENNINGS, NEIL YOUNG, Ernest Tubb, WILLIE NELSON, and EMMYLOU HARRIS.

Stuart's eagerness to explore country music couldn't wait for high school. He was twelve when he toured with Jerry and Tammy Sullivan, a gospel group, to Pentecostal churches throughout the South and Midwest. Stuart was thirteen when bluegrass legend LESTER FLATT hired him as a mandolinist; they played together for six years until Flatt died in 1979. The youngster switched to electric guitar for a tour with VASSAR CLEMENTS's Hillbilly Jazz, then back to acoustic to play with Doc & Merle Watson. For several years Stuart backed his biggest hero of all, JOHNNY CASH. Stuart was even briefly married to Cash's daughter Cindy.

In 1977 Stuart released his debut solo album, *Marty, With a Little Help from My Friends,* on the small bluegrass label Ridge Runner, followed by 1982's *Busy Bee Café* on the slightly larger bluegrass label SUGAR HILL. Dominated by older songs from the repertoires of Flatt, Cash, and BILL MONROE, the latter album featured musical contributions by Cash, DOC WATSON, and Earl Scruggs, but Stuart held his own amid the heady company. He didn't record again as a leader until 1986, when COLUMBIA released the rockabilly-influenced *Marty Stuart.* It didn't sell, and the label decided not to release the more traditional follow-up, *Let There Be Country,* until 1992, when Stuart had scored some hits for MCA.

Stuart's first MCA album was 1989's *Hillbilly Rock.* As the title implies, it was old-fashioned country music with a rhythmic kick. Produced by the STEVE EARLE team of RICHARD BENNETT and TONY BROWN, the arrangements were lean, twangy, and punchy, and propelled the title cut into the Top Ten. The same approach fueled 1991's *Tempted,* which yielded two Top Ten singles: "Burn Me Down" and the title track.

At about this same time, Stuart co-wrote a song called "The Whiskey Ain't Workin'" for an upcoming TRAVIS TRITT album and was invited to play guitar on it. The two musicians hit it off so well in the studio that Tritt asked Stuart to sing a duet vocal on the song, which became a #2 smash in 1991.

The friendship implied in many country duets is sometimes an onstage act rather than an offstage reality, but Tritt and Stuart seemed to have formed a real bond. In 1992 they hit the road on the "No Hats Tour," an irreverent rebuke to the many "hat acts" dominating Nashville at that time. Tritt also sang duets on the title track from Stuart's 1992 album *This One's Gonna Hurt You,* and from *Honky Tonkin's What I Do Best* (1996). Stuart contributed songs to Tritt's next three albums, *T-R-O-U-B-L-E, Ten Feet Tall and Bulletproof,* and *The Restless Kind;* played guitar on two of them; and sang a duet vocal on "Double Trouble" from the latter album.

When the anthology *The Marty Party Hit Pack* was released in 1995, it contained nothing from Stuart's disappointing *Love and Luck* (1994). The new album did contain all his hit singles, his first two Tritt duets, two new songs with the MAVERICKS' producer, DON COOK, a version of "Don't Be Cruel" for an ELVIS PRESLEY tribute, and Stuart's landmark collaboration with the Staple Singers on the band's "The Weight" (*Rhythm, Country & Blues*). The *Hit Pack* remains the single best introduction to Stuart's ability to turn fandom into infectious performance.

In 1997 Stuart tackled some new territory when Discovery Channel Online featured a ten-day cross country tour documenting his day-to-day activities. In that same year he became the third person in the 150-year history of C. F. Martin & Company to have a signature guitar; at this writing, a Fender signature guitar created in his honor is expected in 1998. On July 8, 1997, Stuart married CONNIE SMITH.
　　　　　　　　　　　　　　　　　　—*Geoffrey Himes*

REPRESENTATIVE RECORDINGS

Busy Bee Cafe (Sugar Hill, 1982); *Hillbilly Rock* (MCA, 1989); *Let There Be Country* (Columbia, 1992); *The Marty Party Hit Pack* (MCA, 1995); *Honky Tonkin's What I Do Best* (MCA, 1996)

Marty Stuart

Eddie Stubbs (see Johnson Mountain Boys)

Nat Stuckey
b. Cass County, Texas, December 17, 1933; d. August 24, 1988

Nathan Wright Stuckey II was a successful disc jockey, songwriter, and recording artist. Stuckey earned a degree in radio and TV from Arlington State College, then worked at KALT in Atlanta, Texas, as a disc jockey before spending two years in the army. After his discharge he went back to KALT before joining KWKH in Shreveport, Louisiana, for eight years. KWKH featured the LOUISIANA HAYRIDE barn-dance show, and Stuckey was an announcer for the Hayride when he had his first hit, "Sweet Thang," for Paula Records in 1966.

In 1968 Stuckey's first RCA single, the risqué "Plastic Saddle," reached the Top Ten. He continued to record for RCA until 1976, but had only two other Top Ten recordings, "Sweet Thang and Cisco" in 1969 and "Take Time to Love Her" in 1973. In 1976 he began recording for MCA but never had a major hit.

As a songwriter, however, he achieved success with "Waitin' in Your Welfare Line," a #1 hit for BUCK OWENS in 1965; "Pop-a-Top" (#3, 1967) by JIM ED BROWN; and "Sweet Thang," a chartmaker for ERNEST TUBB and LORETTA LYNN in 1967. After Stuckey's recording career ended he had a successful career singing commercials, including some for Budweiser Beer, before his death, from lung cancer, on August 24, 1988. He is buried in Shreveport, Louisiana.
—Don Cusic

REPRESENTATIVE RECORDINGS
Country Favorites—Stuckey Style (Paula, 1967); The Best of Nat Stuckey (RCA Victor, 1974)

Sugar Hill Records
established in Durham, North Carolina, 1978

Sugar Hill Records, a small but highly respected independent label, was founded in 1978 in Durham, North Carolina, by Barry Poss (b. Brantford, Ontario, Canada, September 7, 1945), who came to Durham in 1968 to study sociology at Duke University. He became interested in old-time country music, and in 1975 joined the staff of David Freeman's COUNTY RECORDS, then newly located in Floyd, Virginia. In 1978 Poss produced the highly successful Mountain Fiddler album by Senator Robert Byrd (County 769) and the Texas Crapshooter album by fiddler Bobby Hicks (County 772). The latter, with electrified accompaniment on one side, was such a radical departure from the traditional music heard previously on County that it caused Freeman to consider a way to record contemporary music without alienating longtime customers. He decided there was need for a label distinct from County and he enlisted Poss, who professed an interest in "newer music," to start it. Rather than being a subsidiary, Sugar Hill (named for an old-time tune) would operate in tandem with County, with warehousing shared at County's Floyd and Roanoke facilities.

Since 1983 the label has won eight Grammy awards: five for Best Bluegrass Album (in 1991: Spring Training by CARL JACKSON, John Starling & the Nash Ramblers [SH-3789]; in 1993: Waitin' for the Hard Times to Go by the NASHVILLE BLUEGRASS BAND [SH-3809]; in 1994: The Great Dobro Sessions by various artists [SH-2206]; in 1995: Unleashed by the Nashville Bluegrass Band [SH-3843]; and in 1996: True Life Blues: The Songs of Bill Monroe by various artists [SH-3752]) and two for Best Traditional Folk Album (in 1987: Riding the Midnight Train [SH-3752] and in 1990: On Praying Ground [SH-3779], both by DOC WATSON).

Currently, Sugar Hill's catalogue lists 232 releases. Artists with ten or more releases include Mike Cross (1981–94), DOYLE LAWSON & QUICKSILVER (1979–96), PETER ROWAN (1981–96), THE SELDOM SCENE (1979–96), and Doc Watson (1984–95).
—Tom Ewing

Gene Sullivan (see Wiley & Gene)

Jerry and Tammy Sullivan
Jerry Sullivan b. Wagarville, Alabama, November 22, 1933
Tammy Sullivan b. Wagarville, Alabama, October 2, 1964

Since 1979, Jerry Sullivan and his daughter Tammy have taken their bluegrass gospel message into the backwoods churches of the rural South. Their ministry continues a family tradition dating to the 1940s, when Jerry's older brother Arthur established a ministry based in Pentecostalism and encouraged his family to play music to accompany their worship services.

Jerry's early influences included the old-time banjo music played by his father, J. B. Sullivan, who learned his drop-thumb technique from Alec Eason, a black resident of Washington County, Alabama. Jerry was also drawn to the music of r&b great Joe Turner and bluesman JERRY REED, and has played professionally in r&b and rockabilly bands, as well as in bluegrass bands with Frank Wakefield, RED ALLEN, James Monroe, and others.

Jerry is a prolific songwriter who often composes with his friend MARTY STUART, and Jerry's eclecticism can be heard in such original compositions as the Cajun-flavored "The Jesus Story," the rockabilly-styled ballad "The Old Man's Prayer," and straightforward bluegrass gospel songs such as "Brand New Church."

Tammy's powerful mezzo-soprano, a complementary counterpart to her father's resonant baritone, can be heard on such personal testimonies as "I Can See God's Moving Hand" and embodies the spirit of Pentecostalism that ignites the family's spiritual quest.
—Jack Bernhardt

REPRESENTATIVE RECORDINGS
A Joyful Noise (Country Music Foundation, 1991); At the Feet of God (New Haven, 1995)

Sun Records
established in Memphis, Tennessee, February 1952

Whether it was JOHNNY CASH's lanky railroad rhythms or ELVIS PRESLEY's shotgun marriage of nearly every form of American music that preceded him, the cast of musicians and producers at Sun Records in Memphis re-imagined what pop music could do. Their efforts in the 1950s have profoundly affected the course of popular music ever since.

Sun was established in 1952 as an outgrowth of producer SAM PHILLIPS's Memphis Recording Service, at 706 Union Avenue. For several years the label's only employee was Phillips's secretary Marion Keisker, whose own understanding of new talent made her an ideal associate. Phillips's brother Jud, and JIM BULLEIT of Nashville, were early investors in the label.

Sam Phillips's earliest blues recordings (e.g., of Bobby Bland, B. B. King, and Howlin' Wolf) had been cut at his Union Avenue studio but released on leading independent labels such as Chess, Duke, and RPM. The first single to actually appear on the Sun label, Johnny London's "Drivin' Slow," was a bluesy instrumental. From 1952 to 1954 Sun released classic r&b records by Rufus Thomas, the Prisonaires, Little Junior's Blue Flames, and Little Milton.

In 1954 Sun released Earl Peterson's "Boogie Blues" and began its move into recording country music just as elemental as its blues catalogue. This interest in mixing country and blues yielded Sun's greatest triumph. In early 1954 Sun released "My Kind of Carrying On," the lone single by Doug Poindexter, whose Starlite Wranglers included bassist Bill Black and guitarist Scotty Moore. Phillips introduced those two to Elvis Presley, whose 1954–55 Sun sessions yielded "That's All Right" (recorded June 5, 1954), a record many consider to have announced the arrival of rock & roll. The top tier of Sun's performers soon included Johnny Cash (1955–58), JERRY LEE LEWIS (1956–63), and CARL PERKINS (1954–58).

When the pop-music market turned away from Sun's hard-edged sound, the label still put out exciting records—Phillips's protégé JACK CLEMENT produced more and more sessions into 1959—but scored fewer hits. By 1960 all its major performers except Lewis had gone, and new discoveries such as CHARLIE RICH (whose records appeared on the affiliated label Phillips International) were more successful artistically than commercially. What's more, crosstown independent-label rivals Hi and Satellite/Stax picked up on Sun's method—mixing country and blues—in new, exciting ways. Phillips opened a second studio, at 639 Madison, in 1960, and soon thereafter bought a studio in Nashville, where BILLY SHERRILL served as his engineer. (Phillips later sold the Nashville studio to FRED FOSTER of MONUMENT RECORDS.)

In 1969 Phillips sold the Sun label and its catalogue to Nashville-based recording executive SHELBY SINGLETON. Under Singleton, Sun has occasionally launched releases by contemporary artists such as Orion (an Elvis impersonator) in the late 1970s, and Jason D. Williams (a Jerry Lee Lewis impersonator) in the early 1990s. But most of Sun's many releases in the past quarter century have been reissues of recordings from the label's 1950s heyday. Since the mid-1970s the label has licensed much of its catalogue to a wide variety of companies, while many of Sun's most popular songs, such as "Whole Lotta Shakin' Goin' On," have been licensed for popular radio and television commercials.

In March 1997 it was announced that Sun was to merge with the Philadelphia-based Brave Entertainment Corporation, with Brave taking on the new name the Sun Music Group, Inc.

—*Jimmy Guterman*

Sunshine Sue

b. Kesauqua, Iowa, November 12, 1912; d. June 13, 1979

Sunshine Sue was the only female star to host a major radio barn dance, serving for ten years as the guiding spirit of the *OLD DOMINION BARN DANCE*, broadcast on Richmond, Virginia, station WRVA.

Born Mary Arlene Higdon, she married musician John Workman, and the pair took their Rock Creek Rangers on the radio barn-dance circuit in the 1930s. After stints at Louisville's WHAS, Chicago's WLS, Cincinnati's WLW, and elsewhere, they arrived at WRVA.

The *Old Dominion Barn Dance* began in Richmond in 1946 with Sunshine Sue at the helm. The show was heard nationally on CBS and traveled to Broadway as part of the 1954 musical *Hayride*. Virginia's governor dubbed Sunshine Sue the Queen of the Hillbillies, and she was also billed as the Sweetheart of the Southland.

Sue was an accordionist, singer, and homey MC. Always more of a personality than a great vocalist, she recorded little. DECCA issued "Blackberry Winter" (1954) and other sides, but her radio signature songs were softly sentimental renditions of "You Are My Sunshine" and "My Mother's Mansions Are Higher Than Mine."

Highly organized, self-disciplined, and prim, Sue invested wisely and retired at age forty-five. After she quit hosting her show in 1957, daughter Ginger took over. Sue continued to make personal appearances until 1963, returning after that only for a 1975 reunion show and record album.

—*Robert K. Oermann*

Doug Supernaw

b. Bryan, Texas, September 26, 1960

Douglas Anderson Supernaw is another in the line of handsome young country "hat acts" to come out of Texas in the 1990s. A self-described "sophisticated redneck," Supernaw grew up in Houston, where his father was a research scientist for Texaco. Although Supernaw began writing songs in high school, his primary passion was sports. He attended the University of St. Thomas on a golf scholarship and briefly tried out for the pro tour. "I missed too many putts," he says.

In the late 1970s Supernaw answered an ad in *Rolling Stone* and spent two years playing "beach music" on the South Atlantic coast. After a year working on an oil rig in Texas, where he says his songwriting started to come together, he took a job as a staff songwriter in Nashville. He stuck it out for four years waiting for a break before returning to Texas in 1991 to form his own band. His 1993 debut album, *Red and Rio Grande*, produced a couple of huge radio hits in "Reno" (#4) and "I Don't Call Him Daddy" (#1). But the follow-up, *Deep Thoughts from a Shallow Mind*, didn't fare well, and Supernaw was dropped by his label, BNA Records. A single from the album, "What'll You Do About Me" (#16, 1995), generated protests from feminists concerned about stalkers in the wake of the O. J. Simpson trial. He jumped to the GIANT label, which released his third album, *You Still Got Me*, in the fall of 1995. A single from this album, "Not Enough Hours in the Night," reached *Billboard*'s country #3 spot.

—*Rick Mitchell*

REPRESENTATIVE RECORDING

Red and Rio Grande (BNA, 1993)

Suppertime Frolic

Suppertime Frolic, a freewheeling radio program that aired six evenings a week on WJJD in Chicago, was an important force in popularizing country music throughout the upper Midwest from the 1930s into the 1950s. Though it was somewhat overshadowed in its own city by the *NATIONAL BARN DANCE* on WLS, the *Frolic* was significant enough to be hailed by *Billboard* magazine in 1944 as a "major country music program." The show had evolved by that point into a distinctive mixture of live performance and recorded music. The two-hour program, heard every night except Sunday, was hosted by Randy Blake, a veteran WJJD air personality and pioneering country music disc jockey.

While the music featured on *Suppertime Frolic* was sometimes a bit more urbane (or at least less Appalachian) than that found on some of its southern counterparts, the long-running show's talent roster also boasted such traditionalists as KARL & HARTY (who joined the show in 1937 after leaving the crosstown rival *National Barn Dance*); banjo picker-singer COUSIN EMMY; the PICKARD FAMILY (led by Obed "Dad" Pickard, an early singing star on the GRAND OLE OPRY); Sally & Billy; and Uncle Henry's Original Kentucky Mountaineers. —*Jon Hartley Fox*

Billy Swan
b. Cape Girardeau, Missouri, May 12, 1942

A rockabilly-styled singer with roots in country and early rock & roll, Billy Swan enjoyed his greatest success in 1974 with "I Can Help," a perky, organ-driven sensation that hit the top of the country and pop charts and sold more than 1 million copies. Yet, even as a teenager, Swan seemed destined to succeed when "Lover Please," a song he wrote at age sixteen, became a Top Ten hit for r&b singer Clyde McPhatter in 1962.

Before moving to Nashville in 1963, Swan recorded with Mirt Mirley & the Rhythm Steppers in Memphis, where he also worked as a gate guard at ELVIS PRESLEY's Graceland mansion. In Nashville he worked as a janitor at the COLUMBIA studio before turning the job over to his friend KRIS KRISTOFFERSON. Swan produced TONY JOE WHITE's first three albums, including White's biggest hit, "Polk Salad Annie," and played in bands with Kristofferson and KINKY FRIEDMAN before hitting it big with "I Can Help."

Swan followed "I Can Help" with several Top Twenty country chart singles, including "Everything's the Same (Ain't Nothing Changed)" (1975), "Do I Have to Draw a Picture" (1981), "I'm Into Loving You" (1981), and "Stuck Right in the Middle of Your Love" (1981). In 1986 he and a former member of the EAGLES, Randy Meisner, formed the band Black Tie, and released the commercially disappointing album *When the Night Falls*. —*Jack Bernhardt*

REPRESENTATIVE RECORDINGS

I Can Help (Monument, 1974); *Billy Swan* (Columbia, 1976)

Sweethearts of the Rodeo
Janis Gill b. Manhattan Beach, California, November 28, 1955
Kristine Arnold b. Manhattan Beach, California, March 1, 1957

Sweethearts of the Rodeo enjoyed a brief run on the country charts between 1986 and 1991. As children growing up in Los Angeles, sisters Janis and Kristine Oliver learned to trade off lead and harmony vocals. In 1973 they began performing a mix of bluegrass, western swing, and country rock as Sweethearts of the Rodeo, a name lifted from the BYRDS' 1968 country-rock LP *Sweetheart of the Rodeo*. In the late 1970s EMMYLOU HARRIS saw the duo win a Long Beach, California, bluegrass talent contest and invited them to appear on a show at the Roxy in Los Angeles. The Sweet-

hearts soon became regulars on the West Coast bluegrass circuit. At a date with PURE PRAIRIE LEAGUE, Janis and Kristine each met their future husbands, respectively—VINCE GILL, then a member of Pure Prairie League, and Leonard Arnold of Blue Steel. Both couples wed and started families in 1980. Janis and Kristine subsequently added back-up harmonies on Pure Prairie League's *Firin' Up* and *Something in the Night* and on Blue Steel's *Nothing But Time*.

In 1983 Janis and Vince moved to Nashville; Kristine and Leonard followed in 1984 (Leonard Arnold subsequently became road manager for TRISHA YEARWOOD). The next year, the Sweethearts won the national finals of the annual Wrangler Country Showdown and signed with COLUMBIA RECORDS. Their first two albums yielded seven Top Ten singles, including "Midnight Girl/Sunset Town" (1986) and "Chains of Gold" (1987). Three of their songs were featured in the 1987 movie *Nadine,* starring Kim Basinger.

In 1993, after their run on the country charts ended, they signed with SUGAR HILL RECORDS, with Janis producing both *Rodeo Waltz* (1994) and *Beautiful Lies* (1996). In 1996, Janis and Kristine, who had always designed and sewn their own stage clothes, opened Gill & Arnold, an upscale boutique in Franklin, Tennessee. Janis Gill filed for divorce from Vince Gill in April 1997. —*Marjie McGraw*

REPRESENTATIVE RECORDINGS

Sweethearts of the Rodeo (Columbia, 1986); *One Time, One Night* (Columbia, 1988); *Beautiful Lies* (Sugar Hill, 1996)

Swift Jewel Cowboys

Founded on April 8, 1933, in Houston, Texas, and disbanded in July 1942, in Memphis, Tennessee, the Swift Jewel Cowboys were named after Swift & Company's Jewel Oil and Shortening products. The original members included Don José Cortes on fiddle, Clifford Zebedee "Kokomo" Crocker on accordion and vocals, Elmer "Slim" Hall on guitar and vocals, and Calvin "Curly" Noland on string bass and vocals. Houston served as the group's home base until fall 1934, when Swift transferred their manager and band mentor, Frank B. Collins, to Memphis. The band soon followed, and their first program aired on WMC on November 4 of that year.

In Memphis, the band's sound also evolved from cowboy toward a hot dance beat approaching western swing with the addition in early 1936 of Farris "Lefty" Ingram, who was capable of playing sax, clarinet, and fiddle. By 1938, when jazz cornetist/pianist David "Pee Wee" Wamble had joined, the band's sound transition was nearing completion.

July 1939 witnessed the Cowboys' only recording activity, with three sessions held at the Gayoso Hotel in Memphis for Vocalion Records. The group's jazz repertoire was in evidence with tunes such as "Memphis Blues," "Fan It," "Coney Island Washboard," and "Dill Pickle Rag," the latter featuring a guest participant, Jimmy Riddle, on harmonica. Riddle would later become well known as one of ROY ACUFF's Smoky Mountain Boys. Another notable alumnus was Wiley Walker, who would later team with Gene Sullivan (of WILEY & GENE) on several hits, including "When My Blue Moon Turns to Gold Again." A child mascot of the band, Bill Justis, would also gain fame for his 1957 performance "Raunchy" and for subsequent record production and arranging achievements. —*Bob Pinson*

Sylvia

b. Kokomo, Indiana, December 9, 1956

Through the early 1980s, Sylvia Kirby had a string of Top Ten country hits that included "Tumbleweed," "Drifter," and especially her 1982 crossover smash "Nobody." All were recorded in a light, airy style she called "prairie music."

Sylvia moved to Nashville in 1975, where she ended up working as a receptionist for producer-publisher TOM COLLINS. Helped out by Collins's early advice, she landed a recording contract with RCA in 1979. By 1982 she already had four Top Ten records to her credit when "Nobody" shot to #1 on the country charts and #15 pop. (A number of her songs, including "Nobody," were written by the prolific songwriting team of Rhonda Kye Fleming and Dennis Morgan.) Sylvia, singing her 1983 hit "Snapshot," also became one of the first country performers to be featured in a modern video clip.

In 1988 she began appearing as Sylvia Hutton, writing and performing family-centered songs designed to encourage children. She also hosted a TNN cooking show and regularly appeared in clubs in Nashville. Her 1996 album *The Real Story* was released by the independent label Red Pony Records. —*Mary A. Bufwack*

REPRESENTATIVE RECORDINGS

Just Sylvia (RCA, 1982); *Snapshot* (RCA, 1983)

It All Begins with a Song:
A Brief History of Country Songwriting

Walter Carter

....

It sounds so easy.

> I heard the wreck on the highway
> But I didn't hear nobody pray
>
> Your cheatin' heart will tell on you
>
> You walk by and I fall to pieces
>
> If drinkin' don't kill me, her memory will
>
> I'm just an old chunk of coal
> But I'm gonna be a diamond someday
>
> Timber, I'm falling in love*

The songs are so simple—especially the good ones. "Three chords and the truth." That's how HARLAN HOWARD, the dean of Nashville songwriters with well over 1,000 songs recorded in his forty-year career, describes country music.

But it's not that easy. Howard himself, on the eve of his induction into the COUNTRY MUSIC HALL OF FAME in 1997, compared songwriting to hitting a baseball. "Mickey Mantle hits .300," he said. "That's hard to do—three out of ten. And out of those hits is a certain percentage of singles, doubles, home runs. He's Hall of Fame, but seven out of ten times he didn't get on base. If I told you I have 3,000 unrecorded songs, you'd say, 'Boy, he wasted his life away.'"

CINDY WALKER, like Harlan Howard, has had hits in five different decades and was inducted into the Hall of Fame in 1997. She said she might write twenty songs or more to come up with a single good one. "Good songs are few and far between," she explained. "It's never easy. It's like digging a ditch. You've got to work at it."

Not only is songwriting hard, even for the best of them, achieving success and recognition is even harder. The Country Music Hall of Fame is filled with record producers and music publishing executives as well as recording stars. But not songwriters. The Hall of Fame was established in 1961, and it took thirty years before FELICE AND BOUDLEAUX BRYANT became the first to be inducted purely on the strength of their songwriting. Cindy Walker and Harlan Howard bring the grand total of "pure songwriters," as Walker calls them, in the Hall of Fame to four.

The competition for country songwriters is brutal. Out of the thousands of writers in Nashville, only a few hundred make a living at it. Only a few dozen make a *good* living. Yet in cities and towns all across America, there are people setting an alarm clock an hour early or staying up after the kids are in bed to polish a few lines of rhyme, strum a chord on a guitar, and dream of being a country songwriter.

Wannabes may get some encouragement from the Nashville Songwriters Association International, but the overriding message from Nashville's music industry is, "Don't give

---

* From, in order: "The Wreck on the Highway" written by Dorsey Dixon, "Your Cheatin' Heart" by Hank Williams, "I Fall to Pieces" by Hank Cochran and Harlan Howard, "If Drinkin' Don't Kill Me (Her Memory Will)" by Harlan Sanders and Rick Beresford, "I'm Just an Old Chunk of Coal (But I'm Gonna Be a Diamond Someday)" by Billy Joe Shaver, "Timber, I'm Falling in Love" by Kostas.

up your day job." That weeds out the undedicated—those who aren't willing to give up careers, families, and responsibilities to move to Nashville, work menial jobs, stand in line for a ten-minute spot on a songwriters night, search for a compatible co-writer, and pray for a publisher who will take a phone call and listen to a song.

And once they're in Nashville, songwriters face a new set of challenges: making the transition from hobbyist to professional, from writing by inspiration to writing by appointment; learning the craft without losing the creativity, balancing originality with commerciality; making contacts, playing the politics of the publishing and recording business.

The motto of the Nashville Songwriters Association is, "It all begins with a song." You'd think, by definition, that means it all begins with a song*writer*, but it hasn't always been that way. Country music as a defined, commercial style of music has been around since the 1920s, but country songwriters—the "boys who make the noise on Sixteenth Avenue," as they were described in a 1982 hit—didn't become prevalent until thirty years later.

Many songwriters can recall a moment of enlightenment when they realized that someone actually wrote songs. Until that moment, they thought songs were somehow just always there. And for a country performer in the early years of the twentieth century, that's the way it was. There were plenty of traditional songs and fiddle tunes to fill up an evening's entertainment. Depending on how isolated a rural musician was, he might also know some popular tunes from the minstrel era, such as "Camptown Races" or "Dem Golden Slippers," whose authorship was known but which were nevertheless well on their way to becoming traditional.

There was no need for new country songs until the late 1920s, when a booming music business produced the first country stars. Through records and radio, their music went out almost instantaneously to a wider audience than they might reach in a lifetime of touring, but national popularity was a beast that demanded constant feeding. They needed new material—lots of it.

VERNON DALHART, who had the first million-selling country record, "The Prisoner's Song," used his star status to attract a writer, CARSON ROBISON. Robison is often cited as the first professional country songwriter, but he was a product of the major songwriting center that existed at that time: Tin Pan Alley in New York. From 1924 to 1928 Robison supplied new, traditional-sounding country songs to Dalhart, until he tired of giving Dalhart half the writing credit and began writing for his own career as a recording artist.

In 1927 the CARTER FAMILY and JIMMIE RODGERS made their first recordings and were immediately pressed for more material. The pressure came from RALPH PEER, the VICTOR RECORDS talent scout who discovered them. Peer had already adopted the philosophy that artists needed original material so it would be (1) new to the ears of record buyers and (2) copyrightable. Publishing royalties were thought to be so insignificant for the hillbilly and race music Peer recorded that Victor let Peer control publishing rights. The standard practice among record companies was either to insist on recording public-domain songs or simply to buy songs for a flat fee, but Peer believed he could build loyalty and long-term relationships with his artists if he shared song royalties with them.

A. P. CARTER and Jimmie Rodgers took Peer's bait and amassed catalogues that would become the foundation of country music. Ironically, neither Carter nor Rodgers was as prolific as their catalogues suggest. They met the demand for material in other ways.

"As the Carters' recording career widened, there were more and more demands on A. P. to find songs from any sources possible, as they gradually ran out of well-known folksongs to record," wrote John Atkins in his contribution to *Stars of Country Music.* "He would often go off for a week at a time on 'song-hunting' trips, and he had, according to his family, an uncanny ability for finding new songs." These "finds" would range from traditional songs to newly written material that he might have purchased. He would then rewrite, rearrange and "work up" these songs for the Carter Family to perform.

Jimmie Rodgers "often found himself scrambling to produce 'original' material to fill the demand," wrote Nolan Porterfield in *Jimmie Rodgers: The Life and Times of America's Blue Yodeler.* "Although some 83 percent of the Blue Yodeler's recordings carry his name as composer or co-composer, he actually wrote very little of the material, and was always dependent on a variety of random sources—his sister-in-law [Elsie McWilliams], amateur composers, Tin Pan Alley hacks—for suitable songs."

Even as country music grew in popularity, songwriting followed the patterns set by

Carter and Rodgers. With country music still emanating from many regional centers—wherever there was a "barn dance" or "a jamboree" radio show—a songwriter would have had to crisscross the country seeking out artists, few of whom had the kind of popularity that would produce significant song royalties. With few professional songwriters, artists were forced to adapt older material or to write their own songs. GENE AUTRY was based at station KVOO in Tulsa in 1931 when he and Jimmy Long wrote Autry's first smash hit, "That Silver-Haired Daddy of Mine." When ROY ACUFF, a star on WNOX in Knoxville, Tennessee, recorded his first "signature" song in 1936, he wrote extra verses to an existing version of "The Great Speckled Bird," a song that used the same melody A. P. Carter had appropriated for "I'm Thinking Tonight of My Blue Eyes." JIMMIE DAVIS of Shreveport, Louisiana, had had some national success by 1940 when he and his steel guitarist Charles Mitchell bought "You Are My Sunshine" from writer Paul Rice and reworked it into Davis's ticket to the Hall of Fame. ERNEST TUBB, singing on KGKO in Fort Worth, Texas, made his breakthrough with his own song, "Walkin' the Floor Over You," in 1941.

While the hillbilly side of country music remained too spread out to make songwriting a viable profession, the rising popularity of western movies with singing stars helped to create a songwriting center in Hollywood by the late 1930s. Although Hollywood would never have a publishing community as geographically centralized as New York's Tin Pan Alley or Nashville's Music Row, it was nevertheless a songwriters' town for country and western writers. In a classic Hollywood scenario, Cindy Walker of Fort Worth, Texas, saw the name Crosby on a building on Sunset Boulevard, walked in with her guitar, talked her way into singing a song for Bing Crosby's brother, and wound up the next day on a movie set singing the song to Bing himself. Crosby had a hit with that song, "Lone Star Trail," in 1941.

Walker moved to Hollywood and lived there for thirteen years, making her living as a country and western songwriter. When BOB WILLS, the king of western swing (who, like other seminal stars of country music, wrote many of his early hits himself), made a series of movies, he recorded thirty-nine of Walker's songs. Hollywood's recording studios attracted all kinds of artists, including country stars. "All the artists used to come out to Hollywood to record—EDDY ARNOLD, Ernest Tubb, HANK SNOW," she said. "Whenever I heard they were coming, well, I'd get busy and start to write something." And with a flourishing live country music scene at places such as the RIVERSIDE RANCHO, the Palomino Ballroom, and the Venice Pier Ballroom, Walker said, "It was just a wonderful place for songwriters."

Hollywood in the 1940s was more than a wonderful place, it was the *only* place for a country songwriter. When asked what was going on in Nashville at the time she moved west, Cindy Walker replied, "I don't have the slightest idea." Indeed, very little was going on in Nashville in 1940 except for the GRAND OLE OPRY on radio. No country publishers. No studios. No record companies.

The publishing void in Nashville was the most serious drawback for a writer. Unless he had an affiliation with a New York, a Chicago, or a Hollywood publisher, he could get no copyright protection for his songs. Furthermore, the AMERICAN SOCIETY OF COMPOSERS, AUTHORS, AND PUBLISHERS (ASCAP) would not admit most writers of hillbilly music (or blues, folk, or jazz), so few country writers made royalties for radio airplay.

That all changed in the 1940s. First, a group of broadcasters, in defiance of ASCAP's proposed doubling of fees, formed BROADCAST MUSIC, INC. (BMI) in 1940 and immediately signed up all the writers who had been snubbed by ASCAP. Now country songwriters had a real financial incentive, because BMI ensured that they would receive royalties from radio airplay of their works.

Then, in 1942, Roy Acuff grew tired of mailing songs to himself in an effort to establish copyright, so he went into partnership with former pop songwriter FRED ROSE to form ACUFF-ROSE PUBLICATIONS. That started the ball rolling in Nashville. Acuff-Rose's success begat more success as songwriters began showing up at the doorstep, foremost among them HANK WILLIAMS in 1946. Williams was not solely a songwriter, of course—he was more like his predecessors, writing songs so Hank Williams the singer would have something to sing—but his music changed the world for country songwriters in three ways:

1. He made country music more personal. In his writing and his singing—which were inseparable—Williams seemed to tear open his heart. When he sang "I'm so lonesome I could cry," he made Jimmie Rodgers's "T for Thelma, that gal made a wreck out of me" or Ernest Tubb's "I'm walking the floor over you" sound like a party record.
2. Williams's songs, coupled with Fred Rose's vision, opened up the lucrative pop market to country songwriters with such hits as "Cold, Cold Heart" by Tony Bennett, "Jambalaya" by Jo Stafford, and "Your Cheatin' Heart" by Joni James.
3. Well into the 1980s, Hank's ghost haunted the songwriters of Nashville. As one frustrated writer said, "Every time I get a good idea, it seems like Hank Williams already wrote it." It seemed that you had to kill yourself to be able to write as good a country song as Hank Williams.

To early songwriters trying to make a living in Nashville, however, Hank Williams was not as important as artists such as Eddy Arnold or WEBB PIERCE—essentially *nonwriting* artists. A songwriter had little chance of getting a song recorded by Hank, since Hank could write his own, but a nonwriting artist was always in need of a good song.

"I looked to the publishers," Arnold recalled. "I always got the best songs from the publishers." The problem was, for Nashville writers anyway, there was only one publisher in Nashville. Arnold looked to a publisher in Chicago, where his record company was based, to find his 1947 #1 hit "I'll Hold You in My Heart (Till I Can Hold You in My Arms)," a song written by Hal Horton and Tommy Dilbeck. His 1948 hit "Bouquet of Roses" was written by Steven Nelson and Bob Hilliard for a publisher in New York, where Arnold also recorded. When more publishing houses opened in Nashville, Arnold said, "I wouldn't wait for them to bring a song out to me. I'd just get in the car and go down to their office. 'Play me something.' I could say yes or no right there. I wanted to have a good rapport with the publishers."

While Arnold did his part in bringing pop audiences to country, Webb Pierce is known for opening up country songwriting in the other direction by singing songs that dealt realistically and unapologetically with such subjects as adultery in "Back Street Affair" (1952) and drinking in "There Stands the Glass" (1953).

It's impossible to say which came first—whether the growth of the songwriting community in Nashville attracted more artists, or whether the increase in artists attracted more writers—but by 1950 there was enough song activity in Nashville to convince Boudleaux and Felice Bryant to move from their home in Georgia. The husband-and-wife team were the first great country writers who came to Nashville for the sole purpose of writing songs. By the end of the 1950s their songs "Bye Bye Love" and "Wake Up, Little Susie," both hits for the EVERLY BROTHERS, had played a monumental role in making Nashville a music center.

Between 1950, when the Bryants arrived, and 1957, when the Everlys hit the country and pop charts, Nashville finally became a songwriter's town. JACK STAPP, who had helped put Nashville on the pop music map by co-writing "Chattanoogie Shoeshine Boy" in 1950, opened TREE PUBLISHING in 1951. Opry manager JIM DENNY partnered with Webb Pierce to open CEDARWOOD PUBLISHING in 1953. Record companies opened offices, and recording studios were built on what would become Music Row. Pop stars such as ELVIS PRESLEY and BRENDA LEE, as well as all the country stars, recorded in Nashville.

By 1960 Nashville looked attractive even to a successful West Coast country songwriter such as Harlan Howard. "I had a couple of hits—'Pick Me Up on Your Way Down' and 'Heartaches by the Number'—before '60," Howard recalled, "so when the publisher sent me a check for one hundred grand, I said 'Wow!' and moved here."

Just as Hollywood had been in the 1940s, Nashville in 1960 was a wonderful place for songwriters, with the demand for songs exceeding the supply of writers. "At that time, all the Opry stars had record deals," Howard recalled. "All of a sudden these singers didn't write their own songs, even if they used to. People like Ernest Tubb and LEFTY FRIZZELL, they became superstars and didn't write like they used to. There came a need for writers, and if there's a need for writers, they'll be there."

"It was easy back then," he added. "There were only eight of us: me, HANK COCHRAN, WILLIE NELSON, MEL TILLIS, Felice and Boudleaux, BILL ANDERSON, and ROGER MILLER."

The country market also expanded, at least for songwriters, in the late fifties with the rise of folk music, which shared the same roots as country. Nashville writers DANNY DILL and MARIJOHN WILKIN wrote "The Long Black Veil" in 1959, and it was immediately embraced by the folk crowd as a traditional song. BOBBY BARE was able to hit the pop charts with songs that were decidedly country, including the Danny Dill–Mel Tillis song "Detroit City," which borrowed the line "I wanna go home" from the folksong "Sloop John B." Lefty Frizzell, who had recorded the original version of "The Long Black Veil," edged onto the pop charts in 1964 with "Saginaw Michigan," written by Bill Anderson and Don Wayne.

The success of Harlan Howard's contemporaries in the early sixties brought a new group of writers to Nashville in the mid-sixties, among them CURLY PUTMAN, DALLAS FRAZIER, and KRIS KRISTOFFERSON. In a replay of Fred Rose's success with Hank Williams's songs in the early fifties, pop artists began finding hits in Nashville publishing houses. Tom Jones gave a straightforward reading to Putman's old-time-sounding (but newly written) country tearjerker "Green Green Grass of Home" in 1966. O. C. Smith, a black singer, had a pop hit with Frazier's "Son of Hickory Holler's Tramp" in 1968 and followed with "Little Green Apples," written by Nashville native Bobby Russell. And in 1969, the First Edition, led by future country superstar KENNY ROGERS, had a pop hit with "Ruby, Don't Take Your Love to Town," Mel Tillis's heartbreaking story of a disabled Vietnam veteran and his straying wife.

Still, despite the ever-widening success of country songwriters, few outside the country music industry knew anything about "C. Putman" or "Howard-Cochran" or "Dill-Tillis"—the names in small print under the song titles on record labels. In 1970, Kris Kristofferson changed that.

In one sense, Kris was an extension of the Hank tradition of self-destruction. He was a hard-drinking, hard-fighting man who had given up a secure career (in the army) and pretty well destroyed his first marriage to pursue his songwriting dream. Williams died at age twenty-nine, Kristofferson arrived in Nashville in 1965 at age twenty-nine, so you could say Kris picked up where Hank left off.

In one monumental year—1970—Kristofferson influenced country songwriting as no one has before or since. "Help Me Make It Through the Night" and "For the Good Times" (recorded by SAMMI SMITH and RAY PRICE, respectively) were, in their most basic form, pleas for mercy sex. The subject was racy, but the lyrics were tender, intimate, and poetic in a way that made the songs about love rather than sex. While the songs had classic, simple structure, straight out of country tradition, the writer was anything but. Kristofferson was schooled in English literature at Oxford—a Rhodes scholar. There had been educated writers in country music before him (Bill Anderson had a college degree, and TOM T. HALL, though self-educated, was as well-read as any English major), but after Kristofferson, education was no longer something a writer needed to hide.

In the tradition of honesty in country music, Kristofferson also opened up a disturbing new window on the life of a songwriter with "Sunday Morning Coming Down," first cut by RAY STEVENS in 1969 but a hit for JOHNNY CASH in 1970. In this depressing confessional, Kristofferson again picked up where Hank left off. When he wrote "Wishing, Lord, that I was stoned," he wasn't talking about booze.

People didn't want to just look in Kristofferson's window; they also wanted to shine a spotlight through it. For the first time, the songwriter was the star. After Janis Joplin's posthumous 1971 pop hit "Me and Bobbie McGee," written by Kristofferson and his publisher FRED FOSTER, Kris was more famous than all but a handful of country artists. He did not die young, as Hank did, but he might as well have. No sooner had he found success than he was gone—by 1973 he had moved to Hollywood to play Billy the Kid in a movie—leaving a second-generation ghost of Hank to haunt Music Row songwriters.

Kristofferson's influence was felt immediately in Nashville. Songwriters poured into town, from college kids who related to the poetry of Kristofferson's lyrics to Vietnam veterans who related to his rejection of his military career. The deluge of writers created a new phenomenon in Nashville nightclubs: Writers Night. It started in late 1971 at the newly opened Exit/In, a small club located a block from the Vanderbilt campus, so named because the entrance was in the back. At the Exit/In's Writers Night, singers counted for nothing. The stage was reserved for songwriters. A typical night might include Jimmy Buffett singing a country song parody "Why Don't We Get Drunk (And Screw)," JOHN HIATT singing "Sure as I'm Sittin' Here" (before it was a pop hit by Three Dog Night), Mac Gayden playing his recent soul music hit "She Shot a Hole in My Soul," and RODNEY CROWELL, newly arrived in town and taking a night off from washing dishes across the street at T.G.I. Friday's restaurant.

The new awareness of songwriters in the 1970s provided the perfect setting for Willie Nelson to become a singing star. A legendary figure in the songwriting community for such standards as "Crazy" and "Ain't It Funny How Time Slips Away," Nelson had been unable to muster a Top Ten record of his own since 1962. With his 1975 album *Red Headed Stranger,* he not only established himself as a singer, he also further opened the window on the life of a songwriter. It wasn't the songs (most of which, ironically, he did not write) so much as the production—so sparse that it was widely criticized within the record industry as being nothing more than a demo, or songwriter's work tape, which is the most basic, original form of a song. To songwriters, there was no better way to present a song, with nothing to focus on but the song itself.

The country song industry had grown from one publisher in 1942 to hundreds in the 1970s, most of them housed in former homes in a six-block area around Sixteenth Avenue South. Record company executive JIMMY BOWEN would describe it as a "horizontal Brill Building," referring to the building that was long the center of New York pop publishing. This was the songwriter's Nashville that THOM SCHUYLER captured in 1982 when he wrote "God bless the boys who make the noise on Sixteenth Avenue" (a hit for LACY J. DALTON).

Along with country music's widening audience in the 1980s and 1990s, the profile of a typical country songwriter widened to the point where there was no longer a prototypical songwriter. At one end of the spectrum there's the traditional country success story of MAX D. BARNES ("Chiseled in Stone"), a former truck driver who waited until his kids were grown before moving to Nashville to try his hand at songwriting. Or DEAN DILLON ("Unwound"), an East Tennessee native who portrayed Hank Williams in an OPRYLAND show and then for a time seemed to be hell-bent on living Hank's self-destructive life. At the other end there's Bob DiPiero ("American Made"), who played guitar in rock bands while he earned a degree in music from Youngstown State University in Ohio. Or Roger Cook ("Talking in Your Sleep"), who came to Nashville after a successful career as a pop writer and producer in England.

BOB McDILL, one of Nashville's most successful songwriters of the past two decades, represents both ends of the spectrum. He grew up in Texas and came to Nashville after an aborted singing career in Memphis. He follows in the footsteps of Kris Kristofferson and Tom T. Hall as a writer with a deep foundation in literature, as he expressed in the line "Those Williams boys, they still mean a lot to me—Hank and Tennessee" (from his song "Good Ole Boys"). And he is equally at home with the decidedly nonliterary crowd immortalized in his first hit, "Red Necks, White Socks and Blue Ribbon Beer."

Just as the prototypical country songwriter disappeared into a variety of writer types, so did the prototypical country song. The most obvious change in country songs came in response to the booming popularity of country dance clubs. For the first time in country music, the music—the beat—was as important as the lyric. "It's got a good beat and you can dance to it"—the famous phrase from the perennial teen dance show *American Bandstand*—now applied to country music.

Country dance songs may have gotten the most consistent exposure but songwriters by no means switched over to a diet of "lite" music. Country writers Frank Myers and Gary Baker produced the love ballad "I Swear," a country smash by JOHN MICHAEL MONTGOMERY that, when recorded by All 4 One, became one of the biggest pop and urban contemporary hits of the 1990s. And in the tradition of "There Stands the Glass" and "Ruby, Don't Take Your Love to Town," country writers took the lead in writing sensitively and honestly about troubling social issues, with such songs as "Where've You Been" (by Jon Vezner and Don Henry) about Alzheimer's disease, and "She Thinks His Name Was John" (by Sandy Knox and Steve Rosen), about AIDS.

As always, artists who could write their own songs had an advantage over the competition, as exemplified by the three superstars most responsible for the country music boom in the 1990s. GARTH BROOKS had a writing hand in his first three hits; after that he wrote about half of them. ALAN JACKSON co-wrote nine out of his first ten. And, except for remakes of older hits, CLINT BLACK has written or co-written virtually every song he ever recorded.

Songwriters followed the country music industry in becoming more businesslike in their approach to writing. The intensity of the competition and the demand from publishers for a consistent flow of new songs forced many songwriters into daily office routines. DON SCHLITZ, who started his long and prolific career with "The Gambler" in 1978, affectionately described the professionalism of his peers: "I always dreamed of a place where songwriters pack their lunchboxes every morning and go off to their offices to work."

Unfortunately, going in to "work" every day can have a stifling effect on creativity, and the great majority of Nashville writers found that the only way to maintain an infusion of fresh ideas day in, day out was through collaboration with other songwriters. Co-writing became a way of life in the Nashville songwriting community of the 1990s, with writers typically filling up their calendars with appointments to write, whether they had a reserve of song ideas or not. For volume and variety, co-writing was the fastest and easiest way to write songs. Gary Burr, for example, wrote his first country hits, "Love's Been a Little Bit Hard on Me" in 1982 and "Make My Life You" in 1985, by himself. But in 1994, when he accomplished the feat of having four artists release singles of his songs simultaneously, three of those songs were co-written—with three different co-writers. The best advertisement for co-writing in 1996 was Mark D. Sanders, who had ten hit songs that year (five of them reaching #1), written with a total of ten different co-writers.

With the phenomenal growth of country music in the 1990s, it would seem that the world has never been better for country songwriters. And in some ways that's true. The mechanical royalty rate, which did not change from 1909 to 1976, tripled in the last quarter of the century. The country music boom produced increased record sales and radio airplay, the two primary sources of royalties for songwriters. With more and more investment at stake in a country record, producers and artists began looking for the best songs, period; the old practice of demanding a piece of the publishing or writer's share of a song in exchange for recording it began to die out.

Not every change in country music worked to the songwriter's advantage, however. Record companies in Nashville started saving a dime in song royalty payments per record by decreasing the number of songs on an average country album from twelve to ten—a figure that did *not* go up with the advent of more expensive CDs that could easily hold twenty songs. ASCAP and BMI quit giving advances to songwriters and publishers. Publishers began recouping the cost of demo sessions from writers' royalties. Publishers for a time forced writers into writer-for-hire agreements, which lengthened the publisher's hold on a copyright but shortened the length of the copyright for the writer and his or her heirs.

By the 1990s, Nashville had earned a reputation as *the* songwriter's town, but at a cost, particularly from the point of view of new songwriters. Well into the 1970s a writer could walk in the front door of a publishing company with a tape, or even just a guitar—just like in the Hank Williams bio movie *Your Cheatin' Heart*—and someone would listen to his song. A few years later, a writer would have to make an appointment or leave a tape. By the 1980s, receptionists at some publishing companies were turning writers away at the door, claiming that the company wasn't accepting new material. One publisher even had an unlisted phone number. In the 1990s, as was accurately portrayed in the 1993 film *This Thing Called Love*, songwriters wanting to play on a writers night at one of Nashville's leading "listening rooms" had to wait in line outside the nightclub, fill out an application, and then audition for the chance to play a few songs for free.

For something that continues to sound so easy, country songwriting seems to have gotten harder and harder through the years. But the writers don't really care about the current mechanical royalty rate or the current "standard" publisher's contract. They don't even care whether the odds against them are a thousand to one or a million to one. They write for the same reason country songwriters have always written—out of a desire to express a simple truth in a new way, to tell an entertaining story, to move people's emotions or move their feet on a dance floor. And, of course, to give a singer something to sing.

For country songwriters, public recognition may come and go, but singers will always need a good song. As Eddy Arnold pointed out, "An artist is only as strong as his songs. I don't care how hot he is, he's always got to have a good song."

The South and Country Music

Bill C. Malone

It may seem foolhardy to attribute a southern identity to country music when we note the music's strength everywhere in the United States and throughout the world. Music, of course, has thrived in every region of rural America, and fiddlers, stringbands, and balladeers could be heard in New England and the Midwest and on the West Coast long before the commercialization of grassroots styles began in the 1920s. Fiddlers abounded from Nova Scotia to California, and it is instructive to note that a Yankee fiddler, Mellie Dunham of Maine, was a finalist in Henry Ford's nationally sponsored fiddle talent contest in 1926. When commercialization did come, the Sears, Roebuck radio station in Chicago, WLS (World's Largest Store), became one of the pioneers of barn dance–style programming, a format that was soon adopted by other stations in the Midwest and Southeast. Since that time, country entertainers have found enthusiastic receptions at state fairs and other personal appearances across America.

Nevertheless, the music has always had a special relationship with the South. Beginning with ECK ROBERTSON and Henry Gilliland's recordings for VICTOR in 1922 and, more crucially, with those made by FIDDLIN' JOHN CARSON for OKEH in 1923, the preponderance of early commercial country entertainers came from the eleven states of the former Confederacy, or from the border states of Kentucky, West Virginia, Missouri, and Oklahoma.

Although performers now come from Canada and other regions of America, the majority of country musicians still come from that region running from Virginia to Texas described by sociologist Richard Peterson as "the fertile crescent." And in that area one still finds the greatest concentration of radio stations that feature nothing but country music. Most of the "influentials," or style setters in country music, such as UNCLE DAVE MACON, JIMMIE RODGERS, THE CARTER FAMILY, BOB WILLS, GENE AUTRY, BILL MONROE, EARL SCRUGGS, HANK WILLIAMS, ELVIS PRESLEY, and a host of others, have come from the South. Hearing these musicians, listeners and critics could not be blamed for assuming that what they were experiencing was a southern phenomenon. Furthermore, the hillbilly image that was attached to the music very early in its commercial infancy conditioned listeners not only to link the music to the South, but also to a stereotypically rural version of southernness. Many people judge the authenticity of country singers by the degree to which their sounds seem to reflect a southern working-class origin, while those who try to burlesque or make fun of country music usually affect what they think is a southern twang.

It might be correct to argue, as some have done, that early recording expeditions would have found comparable rural talent in other parts of the United States if they had chosen to travel there. But, like Cecil Sharp, John Lomax, and other folk music collectors who came before them, RALPH PEER, FRANK WALKER, and other pioneering record talent scouts of the 1920s went south expecting to find a musical land and a musical people. By the time country music's commercial history began in the 1920s, Americans were already preconditioned to think of the South and its music in stereotypical ways. Those perceptions that did so much to inspire folk song collectors and recording A&R men to come south in the first place also influenced the ways in which the music was interpreted. STEPHEN FOSTER, the BLACKFACE MINSTRELS, and the songwriters of Tin Pan Alley had fashioned a musical vision of a placid, romantic South filled with banjo-strumming "darkies" that was hard to extricate from the popular mind.

The music of the South's plain white folk, on the other hand, was either ignored or denigrated, or perceived as an archaic form of Elizabethan culture preserved in the Appalachians. Plain white people, as a whole, were not ignored, but visions of share-cropping, poverty, racism, religious fundamentalism, ignorance, and pellagra prevented a clear or compassionate understanding of their culture. Could such people make music? Early hillbilly musicians, then, labored under the burdens imposed by these prior conceptions. A few musicians bitterly resisted the negative stereotypes, but, like the early African-American entertainers who had to deal with demeaning images, most country entertainers tried to adapt to the various perceptions that clung to their art and profession. Some musicians deliberately played the roles of awkward hillbillies or shy country boys or girls. A few, in fact, projected exaggerated hayseed personas, especially in their humor, which, ironically, came as often from the "rube comedy" of the minstrel or vaudeville stage as from rural culture. Most musicians, though, tried to build positive images within the often embarrassing parameters that defined their music. Over time, most of them have played the role of the cowboy.

Although the powerful role played by mythmaking in the history of country music should not be discounted, the relationship of the music and the South has been more than myth. Not only has country music sounded southern—because of the performers' dialects, vocal inflections, and phrasing—but also its lyric content and tone have reflected southern regional origins. The folk South from which country music evolved, however, should not be viewed as some pristine ethnic or racial culture. The musical South was neither Celtic, Anglo-Saxon, nor Elizabethan (to use only a few of the descriptive terms that still obscure an understanding of the region and its music), nor was it an isolated rural society. The South that nurtured country music has been racially and ethnically diverse, and a society that has vacillated between tradition and modernity. Country music, after all, has been a socially conservative phenomenon that nevertheless could not have existed without the support of radio, recording, and other examples of urban-born media. The music has always embodied the tensions and contradictions felt by the culture that gave it birth—a rural, working-class South that has been persistently transformed by modernity and industrial change.

Two phenomena that historically have contributed most to country music's distinctiveness—African-American culture and evangelical Protestant Christianity—best illustrate the music's rootedness in the southern soil. White and black working-class southerners have lived in uneasy proximity, but they have borrowed musical ideas from each other since the beginnings of southern history. The African-American influence is felt and heard not only in certain songs that have been shared by the two cultures, but above all in the beat and rhythms of many of country music's most distinctive styles. The country entertainers who have gained fame as innovators, and who have taken the music into new and boundary-breaking areas of experimentation, have tended to be those who have effectively fused the traditions of African-American and white rural music: Jimmie Rodgers, Bob Wills, MERLE TRAVIS, Bill Monroe, Hank Williams, and Elvis Presley.

While the blues-tinged melodies and syncopated rhythms of the African-American tradition insinuated themselves into the musical styles of fiddlers and other country musicians, country's evangelical Protestant religious inheritance provided a body of cherished songs, varying styles of performance, and a persistent reminder of mortality and ultimate judgment for the transgressions committed in this world. The conflict between hedonism and moral inhibition has contributed to the tensions that have made country music interesting, just as it provided the basis for the intense vocal stylings of such great singers as Hank Williams, ROSE MADDOX, and GEORGE JONES.

The socioeconomic forces that have transformed the rural South in the decades since the Civil War have also colored the lyrics of country music. In a real sense, with its panorama of songs about railroads, coal mining, textile work, trucking, migration, and the decline of agriculture, country music has documented the industrialization of the South and the transformation of its rural folk into blue collar workers. The nostalgic evocations of place, Mama and the old hometown, and the country church reveal a dislocated people who have been increasingly uprooted from those scenes and symbols of childhood security, and who are consequently conscious of the fragility of all relationships. The songs about ramblers, bad men, and boastful lovers, on the other hand, may recall the deeds of real people, but just as often they appeal to listeners whose lives of toil, social isolation, and poverty have never permitted much more than the thrill of vicarious enjoyment.

Although the country music industry continues to reach for mainstream acceptance by striving to be all things to all people, the music's southernness still manifests itself in a variety of ways. Songs about the South, or about southern places (both real and imagined), actually seem to have increased in the past twenty years or so, and, unlike most earlier items about Dixie, the contemporary songs tend to be written by native southerners. Just as they did during the days of Stephen Foster and his Tin Pan Alley descendants, the songs of the South often find commercial resonance among listeners who cannot claim a southern origin. Country music's popularity north of the Mason-Dixon line may in fact be a facet of what social critic John Egerton has called the "Southernization of the North." The widespread popularity of songs such as HANK WILLIAMS JR.'s "Dixie on My Mind," the BELLAMY BROTHERS' "You Ain't Just Whistling Dixie," and SHENANDOAH's "Sunday in the South" may suggest nothing more than the old and undying fascination with a romantic South, but their appeal probably has been enhanced by the mood of social and political conservatism that after 1968 began to envelop the United States. "Dixie on My Mind," for example, does more than cater to the chauvinistic pride of southerners; with its contempt for New York, it may also appeal to those who equate big-city "liberalism" with many of the nation's social ills. On the other hand, the popularity of such songs as "Rocky Top" and "Luckenbach, Texas," which praise the virtues of mythical communities, suggests the presence of a pervasive and nonideological hunger in America for the down-home rootedness, sense of place, and quiet stability that seem to be slipping from the grasp of most of us. When country singers and songwriters express nostalgia for the South and the alleged virtues of small-town life, listeners everywhere may feel a longing for a domestic security that they never had.

Country songs are by no means the exclusive products of southern writers, but, as a body, contemporary songs still exhibit a preoccupation with themes that, according to sociologist John Shelton Reed, are more strongly embraced by southerners than by other Americans: the sense of place, spirituality, and the acceptance of violence as an appropriate solution for both private and public problems. These traits, Reed argues, indicate the existence of an "enduring South." Songs such as "Carolina, I Knew You," "Lubbock in My Rear View Mirror," "Why Me, Lord," "Sunday in the South," "The Coward of the County," and "A Country Boy Can Survive" might be viewed as the musical illustrations of these persistent southern characteristics. The widespread popularity of these songs, and of country music in general, suggest further that the gap between "southern" and "national" views has narrowed significantly since the sixties.

In stressing the role played by the South in the shaping of the style and content of country music, we must not forget that the music has also done much to shape or reaffirm public perceptions of the South and its people. Whether viewed as a land of placid domestic stability, populated by warm and gentle spirits, or as an exotic region filled with eccentric and violently impulsive people, the publicly perceived South has been, in large part, a musical creation. The outlines of an intriguing and musical South were first drawn by other musicmakers at least a century and a half ago, but country singers and songwriters have preserved and revitalized the tradition with a body of songs that both document and mythologize the region. Country music often merely reaffirms the myths of the South, as do songs such as "A Country Boy Can Survive" or "Amos Moses," but, in songs like "Ode to Billy Joe," "Coat of Many Colors," or "Sunday in the South," the music also captures the texture of the everyday life of average people in a way that no Tin Pan Alley writer was ever able to do. And in songs such as "Hungry Eyes" and "The Roots of My Raising" (written by TOMMY COLLINS), native-born Californian MERLE HAGGARD has lovingly and sensitively recalled the experiences of growing up in a family of transplanted southerners. Whether wedded to older ideas of fantasy and myth, or committed to a realistic depiction of people and places, these songs continue to epitomize the historic relationship between the South and country music.

Joe Talbot

b. Nashville, Tennessee, March 25, 1927

Joseph Hale Talbot, six feet, seven inches tall and salty of tongue, has become a music industry icon in Nashville. Inspired to love country music as a preschooler by the train whistle on a recording of "The Wreck of the Old 97," Talbot learned to play the steel guitar and joined HANK SNOW's Rainbow Ranch Boys in 1950, staying with Snow through his peak years (1950–54). Meanwhile, Talbot earned a Vanderbilt University law degree in 1952, at the insistence of his accountant father. But even with these credentials, he admits that most of his jobs and ventures failed until age forty; his experiences until that age included three years of law practice; traveling sales for Rickenbacker guitars; and work at radio stations, publishers, and record plants. Then, in the mid-1960s, two of his ventures began to pay off. The first was music publishing, a field in which he and partner Ted Harris started Harbot Music in 1965. (Talbot is now sole owner.) Talbot was encouraged and supported by Dr. Russell T. Birmingham and Randall Yearwood to succeed in his second venture—record pressing. Soon Talbot and his partners owned two pressing plants: Precision Record Pressing, Inc., and United Record Pressing, Inc.

Monetary success and his winsome personality soon made Talbot a fixture on the boards of the COUNTRY MUSIC ASSOCIATION and the COUNTRY MUSIC FOUNDATION (lifetime director of the former and past board chairman for both). Between 1967 and 1971 he managed the Nashville office of SESAC. Still pressing 45s through United for small labels and the jukebox market, Talbot and daughter Jana are busiest now in music publishing via an organization they started in the mid-1980s, Talbot Music Group.

—*Ronnie Pugh*

James Talley

b. Tulsa, Oklahoma, November 9, 1943

In the mid-1970s former social worker and carpenter James Talley recorded four critically acclaimed albums for CAPITOL RECORDS (the first of these was self-produced and initially released on Talley's own Torreon label, then picked up by Capitol). Although Talley was marketed as a country singer, he was as influenced by folk music and the blues as he was by country music (Talley held his three biggest musical heroes—WOODY GUTHRIE, B. B. King, and BOB WILLS—in equally high regard). Each of the Capitol albums contained original songs joining socially and politically concerned lyrics to simple melodies; master instrumentalists such as JOHNNY GIMBLE, JOSH GRAVES, and CHARLIE MCCOY provided accompaniment. The music on these albums was serious, idiosyncratic, and often political—qualities that in the mid-1970s doomed a recording artist to little or no airplay on mainstream country radio. Nevertheless, Talley's music reached an enthusiastic, if small, audience. President Jimmy Carter and his wife, Rosalynn Carter, for instance, not only told the American press that Talley was one of their favorite musicians, but also they invited him to perform at the 1977 Presidential Inauguration Ball. By 1978 he was without a recording contract, and his Capitol albums soon fell out of print. Disillusioned with the American music business, Talley went into the real estate business in Nashville in 1983 and eventually signed with Germany's Bear Family Records, which reissued the now legendary Capitol albums and released several new Talley albums.

—*Ted Olson*

REPRESENTATIVE RECORDINGS

Got No Bread, No Milk, No Money, but We Sure Got a Lot of Love (Capitol, 1975); *Tryin' Like the Devil* (Capitol, 1976)

Gid Tanner

b. Thomas Bridge, Georgia, June 6, 1885; d. May 13, 1960

James Gideon Tanner made his living as a chicken farmer in northern Georgia, but in the world of country music he will be remembered as the patriarch of one of the most popular and influential old-time stringbands of the 1920s, the SKILLET LICKERS. By the time he made his first recordings, in 1924, he was already renowned as a perennial principal at the celebrated Atlanta fiddlers' conventions.

Showman first and fiddler second, Tanner regaled crowds with his singing and humorous antics. His prodigious recorded output from 1924 to 1941 reveals a fiddler of modest abilities (he played banjo on his last recordings) but a fine singer and entertainer. Tanner recorded mostly traditional folksongs and fiddle tunes of the nineteenth century or earlier. Though his earliest recordings were solos or duets with RILEY PUCKETT, his most successful discs were those recorded with the Skillet Lickers, a wild, exuberant ensemble whose personnel on COLUMBIA discs generally consisted of Tanner, Puckett, CLAYTON MCMICHEN, and Fate Norris. Tanner and the Skillet Lickers' best-selling discs were made in 1934 for RCA VICTOR, at which time Gid's son, Gordon, played fiddle. Such favorites as "Back Up and Push" and "Down Yonder" (the latter reportedly selling more than 1 million copies) stayed in print for more than two decades. —*Norm Cohen*

Gid Tanner and His Skillet Lickers—with Riley Puckett and Clayton McMichen (Rounder, 1973); *Gid Tanner and His Skillet Lickers: The Kickapoo Medicine Show* (Rounder, 1977)

Barry & Holly Tashian

Barry Tashian b. Oak Park, Illinois, August 5, 1945
Holly P. Kimball Tashian b. New York, New York, January 8, 1946

Husband-and-wife country-bluegrass acoustic duet and Nashville-based Barry & Holly Tashian team up as songwriters and performers on the GRAND OLE OPRY, *A PRAIRIE HOME COMPANION*, and such festivals as Lincoln Center (New York), the Merle Watson Festival, and the Swiss Alps Music Festival. Holly's song "Home" was twice nominated for a bluegrass Grammy, and their *Straw into Gold* album, produced by JIM ROONEY, won the National Association of Independent Record Distributors' award for Album of the Year in 1995. The album's single "Straw into Gold" reached #11 on the *Gavin* AMERICANA chart, and three of their songs hit #1 on the British country charts (1992). The Tashians cite these musical mentors: the EVERLY BROTHERS, the LOUVIN BROTHERS, and JIM & JESSE.

Holly grew up in Westport, Connecticut, studying violin and piano and, vocally, madrigals (1962–64), beginning singing country music as harmony vocalist with the Outskirts (1976–80), a New England, all-women band until Barry joined them as drummer and vocalist.

Barry, who also grew up in Westport, began guitar at age eight (inspired by TV broadcasts of GENE AUTRY), but gravitated to the first-wave rock & roll sounds of CARL PERKINS, Bo Diddley, and Little Richard. As a Boston University student (1963–64) he formed the Remains, a short-lived but highly acclaimed rock band highly successful on the college circuit with TV appearances on *Hullabaloo* and *The Ed Sullivan Show* and four singles released on EPIC collected on their album *The Remains* (1966). The band opened for the Beatles on their last North American tour (August 1966), then disbanded, after which Barry moved to the West Coast (1967) to play with GRAM PARSONS and join the original FLYING BURRITO BROTHERS. Barry recorded with Parsons and EMMYLOU HARRIS on *GP* (1972) and from 1980 to 1989 was a guitarist and lead harmony vocalist in Harris's Hot Band.

Barry & Holly Tashian annually tour throughout the United States, Europe, the United Kingdom, Australia, and New Zealand. Their first album, *Trust in Me* (1989), was released in Germany and England. Their songbook *On the Back Porch with Barry and Holly Tashian* (1995) recaps highlights over four albums. —*Cecelia Tichi*

Ready for Love (Rounder, 1993); *Straw into Gold* (Rounder, 1994)

Tut Taylor

b. Milledgeville, Georgia, November 20, 1923

Dobro virtuoso Robert Arthur "Tut" Taylor rose out of the bluegrass ranks in the 1960s to become a highly regarded session player. At age twelve, having already learned to play

banjo, Taylor began playing mandolin, changing to lap steel, then his primary instrument, dobro, which he plays with a flat pick, rather than the usual thumb and finger picks. Taylor was inspired to play the dobro after hearing ROY ACUFF's famed dobroist BASHFUL BROTHER OSWALD.

During the 1950s and 1960s Tut hosted enormous annual bluegrass jam sessions at Nashville's Disc Jockey convention and became known as a trader and collector of vintage instruments. In 1964 Taylor recorded *Twelve String Dobro*, a World Pacific LP on which GLEN CAMPBELL, CHRIS HILLMAN, and BILL KEITH, among others, all played. In that same year, having met CLARENCE & ROLAND WHITE at the UCLA Folk Festival, he and the Whites along with Billy Ray Lathum and Victor Gaskin joined forces for *Dobro Country*, also a World Pacific release. Other albums featured VASSAR CLEMENTS, Norman Blake, and SAM BUSH.

In 1970, in Nashville, George Gruhn, Taylor, and Randy Wood opened GTR Instruments, forerunner of Nashville's famous Gruhn Guitars instrument store and mail-order house. Taylor left to form a band with JOHN HARTFORD, Clements, and Blake, recording the 1971 Hartford album *Aereo-Plain* for WARNER BROS. Tut also recorded with LEON RUSSELL (*Hank Wilson's Back, Volume I*) and PORTER WAGONER (*The Blue Grass Story*) in 1964.

Tut Taylor Music, his next venture, made stringed instruments under the Tennessee brand, and Ode instruments for Baldwin, which had acquired the Ode Banjo Company.

In 1978 Tut opened a crafts and dulcimer business geared to tourists in Pigeon Forge, Tennessee, then toured arts and crafts fairs for several years before settling in Maryville, Tennessee, in 1992. —*Frank and Marty Godbey*

Tee Tot (Rufus Payne)

birthplace and birth date unknown; d. 1939

Rufus Payne was an itinerant black stringband musician whose existence is all but totally undocumented. In 1935 and 1936 Payne, who probably lived in Greenville, Alabama, gave guitar lessons to a teenaged HANK WILLIAMS, and such fame as he has rests on that.

Payne led a group of musicians who played the sidewalks in the small towns around Greenville. Williams summed up his influence in these terms: "I learned to play the git-tar from an old colored man. . . . He played in a colored street band. . . . I was shinin' shoes, sellin' newspapers, and followin' this old man around to get him to teach me to play the guitar. I'd give him fifteen cents, or whatever I could get hold of for the lesson." —*Colin Escott*

Tennessee/Republic Records

established in Nashville, Tennessee, 1949; ended 1956

Record distributors Alan Bubis and William Beasley, in partnership with Reynold Bubis and Howard Allison, founded Tennessee Records in 1949 and released their first single in January 1950. Located in Nashville, the company had its own studio and publishing company. Though Tennessee's only chart hit was DEL WOOD's "Down Yonder" (#12, 1951), its roster included such notables as HELEN CARTER, GRANT TURNER, RANDY HUGHES, and KIRK MCGEE. As Bubis and Beasley were closing down the Tennessee label in late 1952, possibly as a result of conflict with the musicians' union, they already had Republic Records in full swing. The two labels shared many of the same acts, though Republic (which lasted until 1956) did record pop material such as Pat Boone's debut sides. —*Don Roy*

Tenneva Ramblers

James "Jack" Grant b. Bristol, Tennessee, July 25, 1903; d. March 1968

Claude Grant b. April 17, 1906; d. October 1975

Jack Pierce b. near Bristol, Tennessee, 1908; d. March 1950

Although the Tenneva Ramblers constituted one of the better stringbands of the twenties, their fame derives largely from the brief time (May–August 1927) they were billed as the JIMMIE RODGERS Entertainers, accompanying the Father of Country Music.

Coining their name from the Tennessee-Virginia border that bisects their hometown, the group originated in the early 1920s with guitarist and lead vocalist Claude Grant, his brother Jack on mandolin, and fiddler Jack Pierce. They began by playing square dances and school auditoriums with a repertoire of folk songs, Hawaiian melodies, and current pop tunes. In 1927 they met Jimmie Rodgers in Johnson City, Tennessee, and agreed to join him on his sustaining radio show over WWNC–Asheville, North Carolina. Soon they learned that RALPH PEER was auditioning in Bristol for the Victor Talking Machine Company, but in a disagreement over billing, the Grant brothers and Pierce left Rodgers before they could record together.

As the Tenneva Ramblers once more, they enlisted the services of banjoist Claude Slagle, and on August 4, prior to Rodgers's solo session that afternoon, the group made three sides for Victor. They recorded six more numbers for Victor in February 1928, and, at their final session in October of that year, four sides for COLUMBIA.

As the Ramblers' popularity waned during the Depression, Jack Pierce left to join a Hopkinsville, Kentucky, band known as the Oklahoma Cowboys. The Grant brothers toured locally throughout the 1930s, sometimes joined by Smoky Davis, a blackface comedian. Pierce returned to the group briefly in the late 1940s, but soon after his death in 1950 they no longer appeared professionally.

—*Nolan Porterfield*

Tent Shows

Tent shows form part of a grand tradition of touring shows, embracing circuses, minstrel shows, medicine shows, and dramatic shows, the common denominators being variety and bringing entertainment within reach of rural and small-town audiences as well as urban ones. Although not confined exclusively to the GRAND OLE OPRY (e.g., other tent shows were fielded during the early 1940s by the *RENFRO VALLEY BARN DANCE*), Opry tent shows were by far the most numerous and visible. Evidently the first was assembled about 1941 and headed by JAMUP & HONEY, a blackface comedy team. Also along for this tour was ROY ACUFF, then coming into his own as an Opry star. Soon Acuff was fronting his own unit, and BILL MONROE quickly did the same. Considering the large potential profits, this was hardly surprising; Acuff and Monroe estimated their incomes during 1942 and 1943, respectively, at $200,000 or more, most of which came from gate receipts.

By 1945 the Opry was sending out several tent units each season, which ran from spring to early fall. Routes focused mainly on the Southeast, then country music's principal stronghold. Most tent show schedules consisted of one- or two-day stops in small towns, often of 5,000 or fewer inhabitants, for this is where the bulk of the southern population lived until well after World War II and where many families were slow to buy TV sets. Low admission prices—usually no more than a dollar or so—made tent shows accessible to a large public. Monroe, Acuff, and other troupe leaders played especially hard to their audiences' great love for comedy and often featured band members who did pantomimes and burlesque routines as well as musical numbers. Monroe also pressed his tent unit into service as a baseball team that challenged local athletes at each whistle-stop.

The Opry continued to send out tent shows into the late 1950s, even into New England. But by then rock & roll had cut into country music gate receipts, and Opry stars, like their counterparts elsewhere, were banding together in PACKAGE SHOW units focusing on urban auditoriums.

—*John Rumble*

Al Terry

b. Kaplan, Louisiana, January 14, 1922; d. November 23, 1985

Allison Joseph Theriot Jr. was among the first musicians of Cajun ancestry to succeed in both country and rockabilly. As a teenager he took up guitar and formed a band called the Drifting Cowboys, years before HANK WILLIAMS used the name. The group performed live on KVOL in Lafayette, where Terry was also hired as an announcer.

Terry's recording career began in 1946, when he cut "I'll Be Glad When I'm Free" b/w "If You Want a Broken Heart" for Gold Star. Al and brother Bob Terry toured with Hank Williams in the fall of 1952. In 1954 Al released the original "Good Deal, Lucille"—complete with rockabilly/Cajun swagger and some French lyrics—for HICKORY RECORDS; accompanists included Bob on lap steel and guitarist CHET ATKINS. The record's Top Ten country success led to an appearance on the *LOUISIANA HAYRIDE* (co-billed with ELVIS PRESLEY) and tours with RED FOLEY, RAY PRICE, and MARTY ROBBINS. The song also did well for MOON MULLICAN and CARL SMITH.

Through the late sixties Al Terry recorded for various labels. There were no more hits, but he remained quite popular in Louisiana, appearing on radio and television and running a nightclub in Lafayette. —*Ben Sandmel*

Gordon Terry

b. Decatur, Alabama, October 7, 1931

Gordon Terry once appeared destined for major stardom—the strikingly handsome and versatile entertainer was an actor and musician, fluent in playing bluegrass, modern country, western swing, and rockabilly music. Though he never attained the degree of success many predicted for him, his career achievements have earned him a reputation as a highly respected country musician and performer. Terry is best remembered today as a Nashville recording session fiddler.

After sharpening his skills in his father's band, Terry became fiddler for BILL MONROE's Blue Grass Boys in late 1950. Drafted into the army in 1952, he met FARON YOUNG and worked with his Special Services band, the Circle A Wranglers; he continued working with Young after their 1954 discharge.

Terry launched his singing career in 1956, recording for COLUMBIA, Cadence, and RCA VICTOR; he also appeared in three Republic westerns and the *Sky King* television series. Moving to Los Angeles in fall 1958, Terry toured with the JOHNNY CASH show for four years. Before leaving California, Terry joined guitarist CLARENCE WHITE to back up Eric Weissberg and Marshall Brickman on their groundbreaking progressive bluegrass set *New Dimensions in Banjo and Bluegrass*; WARNER BROS. later used most of its tracks to fill out its *Deliverance* soundtrack album.

Returning to Alabama in 1963, Terry operated Terrytown, a music and amusement complex in Loretta, Tennessee, until 1966. He continued to act, appearing in such cult favorite B-pictures as *Girl from Tobacco Row*. In 1970, under contract to CAPITOL, he recorded his only charted single, "The Ballad of J. C.," a novelty about Johnny Cash. Terry played fiddle on MERLE HAGGARD's 1970 BOB WILLS salute *A Tribute to the Best Damned Fiddle Player in the World*. Terry later toured with Haggard's band the Strangers.

—*Dave Samuelson*

Texas Top Hands

Founded in 1945, the Texas Top Hands are a western swing band that has operated out of San Antonio for more than half a century and that retains a loyal dance-hall following. Over the years the group has recorded for Savoy, Everstate, TNT, and other labels. The band also has backed San Antonian RED RIVER DAVE MCENERY on numerous recordings for Continental and on film shorts for Universal-International. The group's original lineup included Walter Kleypas (piano, accordion, leader), Clarence "Sleepy" Short (fiddle), W. W. "Rusty" Locke (steel guitar, leader), Harrell "Curley" Williams (guitar, fiddle), and George "Knee Hi" Holley (bass).

In 1941 the Top Hands originated as the Texas Tumbleweeds, a band led by guitarist Bob Symons, who had previously recorded extensively with AL DEXTER and the Nite Owls on Vocalion. By the time the band coalesced into the Texas Top Hands, at radio WOAI in 1945, its de facto leader was keyboardist Walter Kleypas. Under Kleypas the band enjoyed its most successful years: moving to KABC, the Top Hands recorded prolifically, appeared in several films with Red River Dave, and enjoyed a major regional hit with fiddler O. B. Easy Adams's "Bandera Waltz." Subsequent bandleaders were steel guitarist Rusty Locke and Adams, who held the band's reins from 1955 to 1979. Since that time the band has been led by vocalist-guitarist Ray Sczepanik, who joined it in 1967.

Some of the band's other key members have included Leonard Brown (banjo, drums, trumpet, fiddle), Louis Glover (guitar), Robert "Buck" Buchanan (fiddle, mandolin), Leon Merritt (guitar, vocals), Cal Berry (fiddle, mandolin), Ernie Elder (piano), Eddie May (drums), Johnny Bush (drums, vocals), Denny Mathis (steel guitar), Jesse "Smitty" Highsmith (piano, bass), Slim Roberts (fiddle, vocals), and Pete Frazier (steel guitar). —*Kevin Coffey*

Texas Tornados (*see* Freddy Fender)

B. J. Thomas
b. Hugo, Oklahoma, August 7, 1942

Billy Joe Thomas began his recording career as a pop singer rendering an old country classic; in later years he moved into country and gospel.

Thomas grew up in Rosenberg, Texas, just outside Houston. He recorded the HANK WILLIAMS classic "I'm So Lonesome I Could Cry" with his group the Triumphs at the Houston studio of Huey Meaux. It was released on the Scepter label in 1966 and became a Top Ten pop hit. Thomas also recorded another Hank Williams song, "I Can't Help It (If I'm Still in Love With You)," which was released in 1967, but it did not have the same degree of success as Thomas's first record.

The success of his first single led to a string of pop hits, including "Billy and Sue," "Eyes of a New York Woman," "Hooked on a Feeling," "I Just Can't Help Believing," and "Mighty Clouds of Joy." His biggest pop hit was "Raindrops Keep Fallin' on My Head" (1969), which was the Academy Award–winning theme song for the movie *Butch Cassidy and the Sundance Kid*.

In 1975 B. J. Thomas had his first country music hit on the ABC label with "(Hey Won't You Play) Another Somebody Done Somebody Wrong Song." Produced by CHIPS MOMAN, the song was #1 in both the country and pop fields. A series of personal problems beset Thomas, who emerged as a born-again Christian in 1976 and began recording for the Christian label Myrrh. In 1977 he released the album *Home Where I Belong*, a commercial success; he also wrote his autobiography, *Home Where I Belong*. (He later wrote another book, *In Tune*, with his wife, Gloria.)

In 1978 he returned to country music, first for MCA, then for Cleveland International (a subsidiary of CBS), where he had two #1 country hits, "Whatever Happened to Old Fashioned Love" (1983) and "New Looks from an Old Lover" (1983). In 1981 Thomas joined the GRAND OLE OPRY on his thirty-ninth birthday.

Thomas won five Grammys for his gospel recordings, one each year between 1977 and 1981; "(Hey Won't You Play) Another Somebody Done Somebody Wrong Song" won the 1975 Grammy for Best Country Song.

—*Don Cusic*

REPRESENTATIVE RECORDING
Greatest Hits (Rhino, 1990)

Ernest Thompson
b. Forsyth County, North Carolina, 1892; d. 1961

Born Ernest Errott Thompson, this blind street singer was one of the earliest country singers to record commercially, cutting thirty-four sides at two sessions for COLUMBIA in 1924. He had an unusually high-pitched vocal quality, reportedly the result of a childhood accident in which his clothing caught fire and resulted in a "scorched throat and voice box." Although born with perfect vision, Thompson lost his sight progressively over a ten-year period. (Some say his vision was impaired during a sawmill accident.) At the North Carolina State School for the Blind he learned piano tuning and broommaking but was more interested in developing his musical talents. He eventually learned enough to play as a one-man band.

Thompson frequently performed at dances, schools, and on the streets until the late 1940s. Generally he accompanied himself on guitar or harmonica, although he was proficient on several stringed instruments. He had a large repertoire consisting of traditional ballads, hymns, pop songs, and instrumental numbers. Thompson usually worked alone, but he sometimes joined a stringband consisting of his sister, Agnes, and a niece, Connie Faw Sides.

Like many other street singers he worked a specific area, and in his case, he covered a rather large one: Forsyth, Surry, and Stokes Counties in North Carolina, and the southern Virginia counties bordering these areas.

From April to September 1924 Thompson went to New York for recording sessions. His first two releases, "Are You from Dixie," a pop song from 1915, and "Wreck of the Southern Old 97," a ballad about a 1903 train wreck, both became standards. (HENRY WHITTER recorded the latter song four months earlier, but the two versions were not identical.) Thompson's repertoire also included the 1896 Gussie Davis sentimental classic "The Baggage Coach Ahead"; the Horatio R. Palmer hymn "Yield Not to Temptation"; and the 1919 comical, Prohibition protest song "How Are You Going to Wet Your Whistle (When the Whole Darn World Goes Dry)." Connie Sides went along on Thompson's second recording session and sang on a few numbers, thereby becoming one of the first country female vocalists on records.

Ernest died at age sixty-nine and was buried in the Fraternity Church of the Brethren Cemetery near Winston-Salem.
—*W. K. McNeil*

Hank Thompson
b. Waco, Texas, September 3, 1925

Few country music artists can claim a longevity and track record to equal that of Hank Thompson. Between 1948 and 1974 he scored no less than twenty-eight Top Ten hits, with another nineteen in the Top Twenty, and continued to chart into the 1980s. Many of these, including "Green Light," "Whoa Sailor," and "Waiting in the Lobby of Your Heart," he penned himself, thus proving his stature in country music's great singer-songwriter tradition. Along the way Thompson forged a potent blend of honky-tonk and western swing that has long served as a source of continuity amid country's experimentation with rock and pop sounds.

Like many country stars, Henry William Thompson took an early interest in music, winning several amateur contests on the harmonica. After he became enthralled by cowboy movie idol GENE AUTRY, however, the guitar became Thompson's instrument of choice. With a Christmas present from his parents, a four-dollar guitar bought at a secondhand store, young Hank was on his way. By the time he finished high school he was broadcasting over radio station WACO as *Hank the Hired Hand,* sponsored by a local flour company.

After graduating, Thompson enlisted in the U.S. Navy. While stationed in San Diego, he persuaded his superiors to let him play area clubs, and after putting out to sea, he entertained his shipmates as well. He kept on broadcasting, too, over a network of small stations organized by American military personnel in the South Pacific. While in the navy he also took advantage of training programs and studied electrical engineering at Southern Methodist University, the University of Texas, and Princeton University—making him one of country music's better-educated stars.

Although he pondered an engineering career after his navy stint was over, radio work and his first hit record, "Whoa Sailor," kept him on a show business track. Assisted by prominent DJ HAL HORTON of the 50,000-watt KRLD in Dallas, this Globe Records release became a minor regional success. Thompson also recorded four sides with the Blue Bonnet label before TEX RITTER, then a promi-

Hank Thompson

nent star on CAPITOL RECORDS, helped him gain a contract with this larger, major label. During 1948–49 Thompson justified Ritter's faith in him with hits such as "Humpty Dumpty Heart" (based on the children's nursery rhyme), "Green Light," and a remake of "Whoa Sailor."

During the 1950s Thompson's songwriting talents, gravelly baritone, precise diction, and powerful combination of western swing and honky-tonk sounds helped him continue his string of hits. The year 1952 brought his first #1 disc, "The Wild Side of Life," a song that inspired the hit that launched KITTY WELLS's career: "It Wasn't God Who Made Honky-Tonk Angels." Subsequent Thompson chartmakers of the 1950s included "Waiting in the Lobby of Your Heart," "Rub-A-Dub-Dub," "Yesterday's Girl, "Wake Up, Irene," "Honky Tonk Girl," "Most of All," "The Blackboard of My Heart," and "Squaws Along the Yukon," all in the Top Ten.

During these years Thompson also made inroads into television, hosting a variety show on WKY-TV in Oklahoma City from 1954 to 1957. In addition, he was one of the earliest country performers to entertain in Las Vegas showrooms, and he recorded one of country's first live albums, *Live at the Golden Nugget,* there in 1960. Meanwhile, he brought his engineering knowledge to bear on his stage show and built top-flight sound and lighting systems that heightened his drawing power at the more than 250 show dates he typically played each year. Thanks to his musical and technical leadership, his Brazos Valley Boys were *Billboard*'s top-ranked band from 1953 to 1965, a record that has yet to be equaled.

Into the 1960s and beyond, Thompson's easy manner made him a welcome guest on network TV variety shows, as did a dynamic stage presence magnified by his size (he stands six feet, two inches tall); a rough-hewn, handsome appearance; and custom-made western outfits for which he became famous. But following "A Six Pack to Go" (#10, 1960) and "Oklahoma Hills" (#7, 1961), he didn't make the Top Ten again until 1968's "On Tap, in the Can, or in the Bottle" and "Smoky the Bar," both recorded early in his association with DOT RECORDS, which he began after a brief stay at WARNER BROS. in the late 1960s. Two more Top Ten hits came in 1974, but the 1970s belonged to country pop, and Thompson's chart success dwindled to the point where he pared down his road schedule and spent more time hunting or tending to his various real-estate, broadcasting, and music publishing interests.

In the 1980s, however, as more traditional sounds enjoyed renewed popularity, Thompson hit the road again in earnest, playing dates in Europe, Africa, Asia, and South America as well as in the United States. He also kept recording, and he signed with Nashville's STEP ONE RECORDS in 1987. In 1997 Curb Records released *Hank Thompson and Friends*, a critically acclaimed collection of duets pairing Thompson with LYLE LOVETT, VINCE GILL, GEORGE JONES, Kitty Wells, and others. Thompson's hard-core honky-tonk–western swing sound—marked by a strong rhythm section of piano, bass, guitar, and drums; lead and fill parts supplied by twin fiddles, electric guitar, and steel; frequent shifts from 2/4 to 4/4 time; and above all his powerful vocals—continues to influence country artists such as GEORGE STRAIT, DWIGHT YOAKAM, ASLEEP AT THE WHEEL, and others among country's newer generation.

Hank Thompson was elected to the COUNTRY MUSIC HALL OF FAME in 1989. He still performs some 120 dates a year throughout the world.   —*John Rumble*

REPRESENTATIVE RECORDINGS

Capitol Collector's Series (Capitol, 1989); *Country Music Hall of Fame* (MCA, 1991); *Here's to Country Music* (Step One, 1997); *Hank Thompson and Friends* (Curb, 1997)

Uncle Jimmy Thompson
b. Smith County, Tennessee, 1848; d. February 17, 1931

Though Uncle Jimmy Thompson had one of the shorter careers in country music—from 1925 until 1931—he had one of the most potent. His defining moment came one night on November 28, 1925, when he played an informal program of fiddle tunes on the newly opened Nashville sta-

Uncle Jimmy Thompson

tion WSM, and started a chain of events that led to the founding of the GRAND OLE OPRY. Cantankerous, hard-drinking, white-bearded, and loquacious, he was a press agent's dream, and the famous pictures of him seated before the microphone with Opry founder GEORGE D. HAY are among the best-known icons in country music history. Behind the legend, though, was a fine musician who represented a long tradition of American fiddling.

Jesse Donald Thompson was born in Smith County, Tennessee, in 1848. Shortly before the Civil War, his family moved to Texas. Here he learned his fiddle style, playing some of the long-bow techniques favored in Texas and learning tunes such as "Flying Clouds" from fiddlers whose styles dated from well before the Civil War. As a young man he traveled widely, eventually marrying and settling back in Smith County, where he took up farming. But not for long, for he took his family back to Texas, where he won, in 1907, a national championship fiddling contest. By 1912 he had returned to Tennessee again, and after his first wife died, he married a Wilson County woman named "Aunt" Ella Manners. By now he was well known as a fiddler, and he traveled the area in a homemade camper, playing for tips while Aunt Ella buck-danced.

Thompson gained his WSM appearance through the offices of his niece, Eva Thompson Jones, who was a staff pianist for the station. A few weeks after this initial appearance, he was asked to become a regular performer on the station, as a founding member of the *Barn Dance,* which soon became the Opry. His fame spread even farther when he became involved with Henry Ford's national fiddling contests in early 1926, and exchanged taunts with Maine's champion fiddler Mellie Dunham.

As the Opry developed and became more structured, Thompson spent less and less time on it; by 1928 he made just two appearances a year. Reasons for this were his unreliability and drinking; another was that he could make more money doing personal appearances. He did make a handful of records: a splendid "Billy Wilson" b/w "Karo" for COLUMBIA in 1926, and a version of "Flying Clouds," replete with dialogue, for Vocalion in 1930. This only hints at his huge repertoire (which he claimed to have held 1,000 items), which was mostly made in the twilight of his career, when he was in his late seventies.   —*Charles Wolfe*

Thrasher Family

This 1920s gospel group was headed by the Rev. M. L. Thrasher, a Congregationalist minister from Braselton, Georgia.

Thrasher began his recording career by preaching and singing bass on some of the best-selling records by SMITH'S SACRED SINGERS, but by mid-1927 he had dropped out, feeling he could do better with his own group. So he recruited some of the original members of Smith's group, including Clarence Cronic, a major singer and guitarist, and his band started a few months later, billed as M. L. Thrasher and his Gospel Singers. Thrasher began a run of some twenty-six COLUMBIA sides, including his best-seller, "When the Roll Is Called Up Yonder" b/w "What Shall We Do with Mother."

In later years he recorded an additional six titles with members of his family as the Thrasher Family. By 1931 his recording career was effectively over, and Rev. Thrasher returned to his original vocation as a preacher.

—*Charles Wolfe*

The Three Little Maids

Eva Alaine Overstake b. Decatur, Illinois, July 23, 1918;
d. November 17, 1951
Evelyn Overstake b. Decatur, Illinois, December 20, 1914; death
date unknown
Lucille Overstake b. Decatur, Illinois, January 13, 1915;
d. December 16, 1978

One of the NATIONAL BARN DANCE's most beloved acts during the early 1930s, the Three Little Maids infused vintage ballads and sentimental songs with sprightly three-part harmonies. Influenced by the Brox Sisters, a popular recording trio of the mid-1920s, their sound was rooted in Evelyn Overstake's soft, low alto vocals and complemented by Eva Overstake's yodels and Lucille Overstake's deft guitar work.

The daughters of two Salvation Army workers, the Overstake Sisters began harmonizing at school functions and mission meetings in Decatur, Illinois. Their popularity led to radio appearances over WJBL in Decatur, and other central Illinois stations; WLS brought them to Chicago in late summer 1931. Renamed the Three Little Maids, the girls sang on the local broadcasts and NBC network feeds of the National Barn Dance; they also appeared on WLS's daily Round-Up and Dinnerbell programs. Like many Barn Dance acts, the Maids signed with the AMERICAN RECORD CORPORATION; they cut four titles in April 1933, all were issued on Sears, Roebuck & Co.'s mail order label CONQUEROR.

On August 9, 1933, Eva married CUMBERLAND RIDGE RUNNERS bassist RED FOLEY, whose wife had died in childbirth earlier that year. The sisters continued performing and recorded four more titles for BLUEBIRD that December. Eva's pregnancy ended the act in early 1934.

Evelyn maintained a solo career on WLS through 1942; her younger sisters sang at occasional midwestern farm meetings until spring 1935, when Lucille moved to Memphis. Eva then formed the Play Party Girls with Jean Davis, which toured that summer with the Cumberland Ridge Runners. Lucille later performed as JENNY LOU CARSON; Eva had a brief solo career as Judy Martin.

—Dave Samuelson

Sonny Throckmorton

b. Carlsbad, New Mexico, April 2, 1941

Every country songwriter dreams about having the kind of hot streak that Sonny Throckmorton had from 1976 to 1980. Signed for a second stretch to country music powerhouse TREE PUBLISHING (he had lost his original deal due to the lack of hits), the affable Texan produced such great hits as "I'm Knee Deep in Loving You" for DAVE & SUGAR, "If We're Not Back in Love by Monday" and "The Way I Am" for MERLE HAGGARD, "Middle Age Crazy" for JERRY LEE LEWIS, "I Wish I Was Eighteen Again" for Lewis and George Burns, "It's a Cheatin' Situation" for MOE BANDY, "Temporarily Yours" for JEANNE PRUETT, and "Trying to Love Two Women" for the OAK RIDGE BOYS.

The son of a Pentecostal preacher, James Fron Throckmorton bounced between San Francisco and Los Angeles before moving to Nashville in 1964 at the urging of steel guitarist–producer–music publisher PETE DRAKE. Throckmorton claimed his first major country success in 1966 with "How Long Has It Been," a #6 hit for Bobby Lewis.

The song's title proved to be prophetic, however. Throckmorton hit a dry spell, and went to Texas in 1975 for a few months. When he returned to Nashville, his luck changed dramatically.

In addition to writing songs, Throckmorton recorded for Starcrest, MERCURY, and MCA with modest success. A double-sided single of "Smooth Sailin'" b/w "Last Cheater's Waltz" went to #47 on Billboard's country charts in 1979. However, both songs were major hits for T. G. SHEPPARD, for which "Last Cheater's Waltz" reached #1. Throckmorton continued to score hits in the 1980s with his writing. His credits include the JUDDS' "Why Not Me," MEL MCDANIEL's "Stand Up," and GEORGE STRAIT's "The Cowboy Rides Away."

The Nashville Songwriters Association International named Throckmorton Songwriter of the Year in 1978, 1979, and 1980, he shared honors as BMI's Songwriter of the Year in 1980; and he was inducted into the Nashville Songwriters Hall of Fame in 1987.

In 1988 he moved to Brownwood, Texas, to care for his now deceased father. He continues to live there, writing songs and performing occasionally.

—Jay Orr

Mel Tillis

b. Pahokee, Florida, August 8, 1932

Lonnie Melvin Tillis, who is gifted with a robust country baritone, parlayed his success as a respected Nashville songwriter in the 1950s and 1960s into a substantial recording career that flourished in the 1970s and early 1980s. Tillis is also famous for his chronic stutter—the result of a childhood bout with malaria—a liability he used to enhance his affable, down-home stage persona. (He even titled his 1984 autobiography Stutterin' Boy.)

Tillis briefly attended the University of Florida, served

Mel Tillis

in the air force, and worked on the railroad before coming to Nashville in 1957. One of his first big successes came that same year when WEBB PIERCE's version of Tillis's "I'm Tired" went to #3 on the country charts. "Detroit City," one of his most famous compositions (co-written with DANNY DILL), was both a Top Ten country hit and a Top Twenty pop hit for BOBBY BARE in 1963. In 1969 KENNY ROGERS & the First Edition had a #6 pop hit and a #39 country single with Tillis's "Ruby, Don't Take Your Love to Town." Other early Tillis-penned hits include "Tupelo County Jail" (co-written and recorded by Webb Pierce), "Heart Over Mind" (RAY PRICE), and "Snakes Crawl at Night" (CHARLEY PRIDE).

Tillis launched his own recording career with COLUMBIA in the late 1950s. In 1963 he and Webb Pierce had a modestly successful duet single, "How Come Your Dog Don't Bite Nobody but Me." He moved on to KAPP Records in the mid-1960s, and on to MGM RECORDS at about the turn of the decade. But it was not until the 1970s that he became a significant player in the charts, on MGM and later MCA. Some of his #1 hits—which stylistically ran the gamut from honky-tonk to light country-pop—include "I Ain't Never," "Good Woman Blues," "Heart Healer," "Coca Cola Cowboy," and "Southern Rains." He won the CMA's Entertainer of the Year Award in 1976 and that same year was inducted into the Nashville Songwriters' Hall of Fame. In 1979 he signed with ELEKTRA RECORDS, and in the early eighties he recorded for MCA RECORDS, and briefly for RCA RECORDS.

Through the years, Tillis has also occasionally ventured into feature films, mostly of the lightweight comedy/action variety. His movie credits include *W.W. and the Dixie Dance Kings* (1975, with Burt Reynolds), *Smokey and the Bandit II* (1980, also with Burt Reynolds), *Murder in Music City* (a 1979 made-for-TV movie), *Cannonball Run* (1982), *Cannonball Run II* (1984), and *Uphill All the Way* (1989, with ROY CLARK).

Though his recording career began to wane by the mid-1980s, Tillis, a shrewd businessman, had by then segued into various business ventures, including management of his extensive music publishing concerns and his theater in BRANSON, MISSOURI, where he frequently performs. He is the father of recording artist PAM TILLIS, who has risen to prominence in the 1990s. —*Bob Allen*

REPRESENTATIVE RECORDINGS

Mel Tillis: American Originals (Columbia, 1990); *Greatest Hits* (Curb, 1991)

Pam Tillis
b. Plant City, Florida, July 24, 1957

Pam Tillis has distinguished herself as a vocal stylist in the 1990s by pairing contemporary country lyrics with traditional country vocals, paving the way for singers such as MINDY MCCREADY. Tillis became one of the few female country singers to write and solely produce her own albums.

The oldest of country star MEL TILLIS's five children, Pam often admitted that she had a love/hate relationship with her dad's career, loving what he did but resenting the time touring demanded. She was eight when she made her GRAND OLE OPRY debut, nervously singing the folksong "Tom Dooley" with a group of children.

Trained as a classical pianist and self-taught on the guitar, Pam performed her first solo gig at Nashville's Exit/In

Pam Tillis

as a teenager. At sixteen, her face was injured in a severe car accident, forcing her to endure many years of surgical reconstruction. When she recovered, she enrolled in the University of Tennessee and formed her first band, performing jug band tunes with a country-rock edge.

In 1976 Tillis briefly returned to Nashville to write songs and work in her father's publishing company, and then headed to San Francisco, performing jazz and rock with her band Freelight and selling Avon cosmetics to supplement her income. After two years she returned to Nashville, supporting herself as a session singer and songwriter, writing songs recorded by CONWAY TWITTY, HIGHWAY 101, JUICE NEWTON, Chaka Khan, and others.

Tillis signed with WARNER BROS. RECORDS and in 1983 released the pop-rock album *Beyond the Doll of Cutey*. After five low-level country chart entries, Tillis left the label and became a staff writer with TREE PUBLISHING. During the next few years she changed her focus from pop to contemporary country.

A 1989 move to ARISTA RECORDS brought Tillis both chart success and a string of gold and platinum albums. Her Arista debut album, *Put Yourself In My Place*, yielded her first Top Five country single, "Don't Tell Me What to Do," as well as the #3 hit "Maybe It Was Memphis." Her third album, *Sweetheart's Dance*, netted Tillis her first #1, "Mi Vida Loca (My Crazy Life)," and also became her first platinum album. *All of This Love*, her first album on which she functioned as the sole producer, yielded more hits, including "The River and the Highway" and "Deep Down." In 1994 Tillis was named the COUNTRY MUSIC ASSOCIATION's Female Vocalist of the Year. That year Warner Bros. took advantage of Tillis's newfound fame by repackaging her old Warner Bros. singles on *The Pam Tillis Collection* album. —*Marjie McGraw*

REPRESENTATIVE RECORDINGS

Put Yourself in My Place (Arista, 1991); *Homeward Looking Angel* (Arista, 1992); *Sweetheart's Dance* (Arista, 1994); *The Pam Tillis Collection* (Warner Bros., 1994); *All of This Love* (Arista, 1996); *Greatest Hits* (Arista, 1997)

Floyd Tillman

Floyd Tillman
b. Ryan, Oklahoma, December 8, 1914

During the thirties and forties, singer-songwriter Floyd Tillman pioneered in the birth of western swing and honky-tonk while penning some of country music's most well-known standards, some of which were among the earliest pop/country crossover hits. WILLIE NELSON has dubbed him the Original OUTLAW for his ability to transcend musical stereotypes and stylistic boundaries.

The son of a sharecropper, Tillman grew up in the cotton mill town of Post, Texas, and as a young man worked as a Western Union telegraph operator while playing mandolin with his brothers at local dances. In about 1934 he began singing as well, forging a distinctive style that has influenced numerous singers, Willie Nelson being the best known. As jazz singers did, he freely interpreted meter and melody, often coming in ahead of or behind the beat; likewise, he often slurred words and bent notes. Later he mastered the resonator guitar, eventually playing jazzy solos on an electrified model, and then played lead electric guitar for ADOLPH HOFNER, a western swing bandleader based in San Antonio. There, listening to other musicians as well as recordings, Tillman absorbed the sounds and styles of numerous pop, jazz, blues, and country musicians.

Tillman's songwriting, singing, and guitar-playing skills led to jobs with Houston pop bandleader Mack Clark and western swing groups fronted by LEON "PAPPY" SELPH and CLIFF BRUNER. Personnel changed frequently in those days, and Tillman worked with many top musicians in these bands, including steel guitarist TED DAFFAN and singer-piano player MOON MULLICAN.

Tillman recorded as a featured vocalist with Selph's Blue Ridge Playboys in 1939, and, later that same year, DECCA recorded him as a solo performer. While his early recordings mainly sought to provide danceable rhythms,

songs such as "Daisy May," recorded in 1940, reveal his trademark half-singing, half-speaking vocals.

By now Tillman had scored his first big songwriting hit, "It Makes No Difference Now," cut by Cliff Bruner in 1938 and pop star Bing Crosby in 1940. Tillman himself did the honors on the multimarket hit "Each Night at Nine" (1944), which appealed to Americans separated from loved ones by military service during World War II. During the conflict Tillman served as a radio operator, and being stationed near Houston allowed him to keep recording. After war's end Tillman's radio and club work helped reinforce Houston's role as a country music center.

Tillman continued to write prolifically and hit the bull's-eye again with "I Love You So Much It Hurts," a love song eventually recorded by RED FOLEY, Andy Williams, and Vic Damone. Tillman himself recorded it for COLUMBIA in 1947. He demonstrated his versatility with "Slippin' Around," possibly country music's most-recognized "cheating" song, and recorded this tune for Columbia in 1949, when JIMMY WAKELY and Margaret Whiting made it a country-pop smash.

At the peak of his career the independent-minded musician decided to retire from grinding road work. In truth, however, Tillman has never quit music altogether. As of this writing, he has continued to record occasionally and to make infrequent TV appearances. He has also kept writing, now counting more than 1,000 songs to his credit. It is estimated that more than 50 million recordings have featured his tunes. Thus, his election to the Nashville Songwriters International Hall of Fame in 1970 and the COUNTRY MUSIC HALL OF FAME in 1984 were well deserved.

—*John Rumble*

REPRESENTATIVE RECORDINGS
Columbia Historic Edition (Columbia, 1985); *Floyd Tillman: Country Music Hall of Fame* (MCA, 1991)

Aaron Tippin
b. Pensacola, Florida, July 3, 1958

Aaron Tippin's bawling, in-your-face delivery made him popular with many country purists in the 1990s. His workingman lyrics, unashamedly redneck attitude, and blue-collar pride were singular during the pretty-cowboy/dance club-ditty Nashville era.

Aaron Tippin

Tippin was raised in the Appalachians of western South Carolina. He initially worked as a private-plane pilot for corporate executives. But following a divorce he decided to try music in Nashville. He competed unsuccessfully on TNN's *You Can Be a Star* in 1986, then moved to Nashville in 1987. He worked as a pipe welder, heavy equipment operator, and truck driver while honing his songwriting abilities. He also became a weight lifter who developed his physique enough to compete in bodybuilding contests.

Tippin was signed as a writer by ACUFF-ROSE, and his tunes were recorded by CHARLEY PRIDE ("Whole Lotta Love on the Line"), the Kingsmen, DAVID BALL, the Mid-South Boys, MARK COLLIE, and others. RCA signed Tippin as a singer. Most of his peers were emulating GEORGE STRAIT, but he reached back to the emotional whine of the HANK WILLIAMS–WEBB PIERCE period.

Tippin had Top Ten hits with "You've Got to Stand For Something" (1991), "There Ain't Nothing Wrong With the Radio" (1992), "I Wouldn't Have It Any Other Way" (1992), "My Blue Angel" (1993), and "Working Man's PhD" (1993), and became noted for his highly physical stage performances. Four consecutive albums of his were million sellers.

Fans wore hard hats and overalls to Tippin's shows, cheering when he championed the working class and asserted his patriotism. He was the first singer to entertain troops during the Persian Gulf War crisis of 1990.

After a career slump in 1994–95 Tippin returned to the Top Ten in 1996 with "That's As Close As I'll Get to Loving You," an album called *Tool Box,* a tool belt as stage attire, his own Tennessee hunting supplies store, and a commercial tie-in with Channelock Tools.   —*Robert K. Oermann*

REPRESENTATIVE RECORDINGS

You've Got to Stand For Something (RCA, 1991); *Read Between the Lines* (RCA, 1992); *Call of the Wild* (RCA, 1993)

TNN: The Nashville Network
established in Nashville, Tennessee, March 7, 1983

The Nashville Network has exerted possibly the greatest influence on the resurgence of country music. The network's programming lineup takes country music themes and the country lifestyle and adapts them to television's most popular formats: concerts, interviews, dance shows, sports, and music videos. On March 7, 1983, TNN premiered to more than 7 million cable households, the largest cable network launch in history. Since that time it has brought newfound prominence to country traditionalists, and opened the doors for younger talents, through its various program concepts. Significant among its milestones are the network's live, exclusive twelve-hour coverage of Farm Aid in September 1985, and the creation of the fan-voted TNN Music City News Country Awards in June 1990. In April 1986 TNN added sports to its lineup. Programming for the eighteen-hours-per-day channel is produced by The Nashville Network and several outside production companies. The Nashville Network is owned by Gaylord Entertainment Company of Nashville, while marketing and distribution are handled by Group W Satellite Communications (GWSC) of Stamford, Connecticut. At its facility in the Opryland complex, TNN produces more than 3,600 hours of original programming each year.

In February 1997 Gaylord Entertainment announced the impending sale of its domestic interests in CMT and TNN to Westinghouse for $1.55 billion in stock, retaining only CMT's international division.   —*Bob Paxman*

Tootsie's Orchid Lounge
established March 1960

Located at 422 Broadway in Nashville, directly across the alley from the RYMAN AUDITORIUM, Tootsie's Orchid Lounge may be the world's most famous country music bar. With its close proximity to the GRAND OLE OPRY until 1974, Tootsie's served as an informal gathering place for singers, musicians, and, most famously, struggling songwriters. WILLIE NELSON supposedly first pitched the song "Hello Walls" to FARON YOUNG while inside Tootsie's, and ROGER MILLER wrote his career breakthrough hit, "Dang Me," by imagining himself at the famous Nashville hangout.

Known as Mom's when run by Louise Hackler, the bar was purchased by Hattie Louise "Tootsie" Bess in March 1960. Hailing from Hohenwald, Tennessee, she and her husband, Big Jeff Bess, a country singer with a popular Nashville radio program, had operated a series of nightclubs during the 1950s. The Besses had divorced by the time Tootsie Bess opened her namesake bar on Broadway, however. Throughout the 1960s she was sole proprietress and unofficial den mother to the ne'er-do-wells who congregated there. (She called them her "funky young'uns.") Famous for her good heart, Bess kept a cigar box full of unpaid tabs that totaled hundreds of dollars. But kind as she was, she was also tough on troublemakers. She had a hat pin she utilized to motivate those who were too casual about leaving their barstool at closing time—an eviction tool in honor of which CHARLEY PRIDE gave her a jeweled version.

Tootsie's was hit hard when the Grand Ole Opry moved from the Ryman to OPRYLAND in 1974. "They ran off and left me, I didn't go off and leave them," Bess said at the time. As business fell off, her health also deteriorated, and she died February 18, 1978. Since then, Tootsie's Orchid Lounge has changed hands numerous times and has been the subject of various legal battles to gain control of it. Though it has always been a popular stop for tourists, its fate has usually been tied to the commercial vicissitudes of Nashville's Lower Broadway district in general. When that district underwent a revival in the early to mid-1990s, Tootsie's became a flash point for an underground, roots-oriented country music scene. TERRI CLARK, Greg Garing, and individual members of BR5-49 (before that band was fully formed) all performed at Tootsie's en route to signing record deals.   —*Daniel Cooper*

Mitchell Torok
b. Houston, Texas, October 28, 1929

Mitchell Torok is remembered as the composer of "Mexican Joe," the song that launched JIM REEVES's rise to stardom. Torok also had a career as a recording artist. The son of Hungarian immigrants, he became interested in country music at age twelve, while growing up in Houston. After high school, Torok flirted briefly with a music career before attending Stephen F. Austin State College, where he graduated with a bachelor of science degree.

In 1953 Torok met FABOR ROBISON, owner of ABBOTT RECORDS, and played "Mexican Joe" for him. Robison produced the Jim Reeves recording, and it became a #1 country song for nine weeks and the top country hit of 1953. In that same year Torok wrote and recorded "Caribbean." Not only did it also reach #1 on the country charts, but also, when a new recording of it was released in 1959, it made it to #27 on the pop charts.

During the 1950s Torok became a regular on the LOUISIANA HAYRIDE, and he placed two other songs on the country charts: "Hootchy Kootchy Henry (From Hawaii)" (#9, 1954) and "Pledge of Love" (#25 pop, 1957). In 1956 his song released on the BRUNSWICK label in England, "When Mexico Gave Up the Rumba," became a #6 pop hit there. Torok recorded for various labels through the years, including DECCA, MERCURY, CAPITOL, RCA, and Reprise. His songs have been recorded by artists ranging from HANK SNOW to Dean Martin and have included VERNON OXFORD's hit "Redneck." —Don Roy

REPRESENTATIVE RECORDING

Mexican Joe in the Caribbean (Bear Family, 1996), 4 discs

Town Hall Party
established in Compton, California, ca. 1952; ended 1960

One of Southern California's most popular country music television programs, Bill Wagnon's *Town Hall Party,* began life as a KFI radio broadcast in 1951 and first hit the small screen either in late 1952 or early 1953. The show lasted until 1960.

Broadcast live from Compton, California, every Saturday night on Los Angeles's KTTV, channel eleven, the three-hour program was emceed by Jay Stewart of the later famous TV show *Let's Make a Deal.* Each segment had its own sponsor (a furniture company, Rheingold beer, Chevrolet), and the show featured a cast of thirty-two, who included the COLLINS KIDS, JOHNNY BOND, JOE & ROSE LEE MAPHIS, Les "Carrot Top" Anderson, SKEETS MCDONALD, and MERLE TRAVIS. Wagnon also booked an average of ten guest performers each week; among those who appeared were EDDIE DEAN, the MADDOX BROTHERS & ROSE, LEFTY FRIZZELL, and JOHNNY CASH. The show helped launch the careers of California-based talent such as FREDDIE HART and BUCK OWENS.

Audiences at the 3,000-capacity Town Hall were not seated, allowing them to crowd around the bandstand, and Wagnon also ran dances there every Friday night. By the mid-1950s the show was being filmed for overseas broadcast by Armed Forces Television. Screen Gems, a Columbia pictures subsidiary, shot thirty-nine half-hour episodes of a show titled *Western Ranch Party* that used much the same cast and that aired in syndication for several years beginning in 1957. —Jonny Whiteside

The Tractors
Ron Getman b. Bristow, Oklahoma, December 13, 1948
Jamie Oldaker b. Centerville, Utah, September 5, 1951
Walt Richmond b. Tulsa, Oklahoma, April 18, 1947
Paul Steve Ripley b. January 5, 1950
Casey Van Beek b. Tulsa, Oklahoma, December 1, 1942

With the gold-level sales of their self-titled debut album, the Tractors disproved one of the traditional axioms of the country music business—that an act can't sell records without going on tour. Released on ARISTA the first week of August 1994, the album, melding numerous strains of roots music, sold 500,000 copies without the Tractors having ever played live together, and without the advent of a Top Ten hit.

The band had, however, made one semi-live appearance along the way, performing "Baby Likes to Rock It" on the televised *CMA Awards Show* October 5. The performance featured only live vocals, while the instrumental tracks were prerecorded, but it gave the band invaluable exposure. By the end of October the Tractors had a gold album. On December 1 they made their first totally live appearance, doing several songs at the GRAND OLE OPRY House for the Country CARES concert. They didn't give their first full concert until the following February.

The Town Hall Party *cast*

That is not to say that the Tractors weren't experienced as musicians. Lead singer Steve Ripley had worked with LEON RUSSELL and BOB DYLAN, keyboard player Walt Richmond spent time with Bonnie Raitt, guitarist Ron Getman hit the road with Janis Ian and Leonard Cohen, bass player Casey Van Beek had worked with LINDA RONSTADT and the EAGLES, and drummer Jamie Oldaker had played with Eric Clapton.

Recording the album at Leon Russell's Church Studio, the Tractors meshed gospel, the blues, swing, country, and roots rock in a raw, rough-and-tumble manner.

"It's a combination of all the things we really loved," Ripley summarized. "We loved Hank Sr. and Elvis and CCR and RAY CHARLES and JERRY LEE LEWIS. It was less a matter of being calculated than just sort of banging away and doing what we loved."

Music Row took notice when the Tractors succeeded while defying the rules. Within two years, SHANIA TWAIN had sold more than 8 million copies of her second album, *The Woman in Me,* without going on tour, and MINDY McCREADY achieved a gold record while likewise avoiding the road. —*Tom Roland*

REPRESENTATIVE RECORDING

The Tractors (Arista, 1994)

Traditional Grass

Paul Mullins b. Menifee County, Kentucky, September 27, 1937

Joe Mullins b. Middletown, Ohio, October 27, 1966

Mark Rader b. Middletown, Ohio, April 21, 1956

Standard-bearers for uncompromising, hard-core bluegrass, Traditional Grass developed a devoted and expanding audience, becoming one of the top-drawing bands on the bluegrass circuit from 1983 to 1995.

Paul Mullins played fiddle with the STANLEY BROTHERS in 1958 before beginning his radio career at WGOH in Grayson, Kentucky. In 1964 he moved to WPFB in Middletown, Ohio, where programming was aimed at Kentuckians and West Virginians in the Dayton area. Mullins promoted concerts and played bluegrass and traditional country music on his popular DJ shows.

After years of playing bluegrass part-time with Earl Taylor, Benny Birchfield, and CHARLIE MOORE, among others, Mullins helped found the Boys from Indiana with Aubrey and Jerry Holt, Harley Gabbard, and banjo virtuoso Noah Crase.

In 1983 Paul, his banjo-player son Joe, and guitarist-lead singer Mark Rader formed Traditional Grass, working part-time with bassists Bill Adams, then Glen "Cookie" Inman. When success allowed expansion, mandolinist/fiddler Gerald Evans Jr. joined, followed, when the band went full-time in 1992, by Mike Clevenger on bass. A series of privately produced cassettes led to a contract with REBEL RECORDS and four high-quality, top-selling projects. In 1995, when Joe was given the opportunity to purchase radio station WBZI–Xenia, Ohio, where he had long hosted a weekday bluegrass gospel show, they disbanded, rather than reorganizing without him.

—*Frank and Marty Godbey*

REPRESENTATIVE RECORDINGS

I Believe in the Old Time Way (Rebel, 1994); *Songs of Love and Life* (Rebel, 1995)

Merle Travis

Merle Travis

b. Rosewood, Kentucky, November 29, 1917; d. October 20, 1983

Merle Travis had an unequaled blend of talents as an innovative guitarist, songwriter, vocalist, guitar designer, and author. His influence on several generations of performers—from CHET ATKINS to Merle's biological son, entertainer Thom Bresh, and hitmakers like MARTY STUART—is beyond question.

Merle Robert Travis, son of local farmer Rob Travis and his wife, Etta, grew up in the heart of western Kentucky coal country. When Rob Travis took a job at a nearby mine in 1925, the family moved to a coal company–owned farm near Ebenezer, Kentucky. At age twelve Merle became obsessed with learning Muhlenberg County's unique guitar finger-picking style, which involved picking syncopated accompaniment on the bass strings with the right thumb while simultaneously playing lead on the treble strings with the index finger. To learn the style, Merle followed coal miners Ike Everly and MOSE RAGER as the two played local parties and dances.

After graduating from high school and serving in the federally sponsored Civilian Conservation Corps program in 1936, Travis moved to Evansville, Indiana, where he worked with two local bands. In 1937 fiddler CLAYTON McMICHEN hired Travis as one of his Georgia Wildcats. Soon Travis joined the Drifting Pioneers, a Chicago-area gospel quartet that moved to WLW radio in Cincinnati, joining the station's *Boone County Jamboree* when it began in 1938. Travis remained at WLW after the group dissolved, and worked with the DELMORE BROTHERS and GRANDPA JONES. In 1943 SYD NATHAN recorded Travis and Jones as the "Sheppard Brothers," the first artists for his Cincinnati-based KING RECORDS.

Travis moved to California in March 1944 and played radio and recording sessions. He also recorded solo material, under his own name and pseudonyms, for various small labels. Signed to CAPITOL as a singer in the spring of 1946, his first single, "Cincinnati Lou," b/w "No Vacancy," became his first hit. Following that he reached #1 with "Divorce Me C.O.D.," which remained at that position for fourteen weeks in 1947. It was one of many songs Travis co-wrote with CLIFFIE STONE, at the time an assistant A&R man at Capitol. Other song successes included 1947's "So Round, So Firm, So Fully Packed" (also a #1 hit for fourteen weeks), a vocal version of "Steel Guitar Rag" with lyrics by Travis and Stone, "Three Times Seven," and "Fat Gal," and in early 1948, "Merle's Boogie Woogie." Travis's and Stone's 1947 composition "Smoke! Smoke! Smoke! (That Cigarette)" became a hit for TEX WILLIAMS and the first million seller for Capitol.

Appreciating the sound of solid-body electric steel guitars, Travis designed an electric Spanish solid-body guitar; in 1948 he had it built by Paul Bigsby, a California pattern-maker and steel guitar builder. Now displayed in the COUNTRY MUSIC HALL OF FAME, the guitar may have inspired Travis's friend Leo Fender to design what was to become the legendary Fender Telecaster electric guitar.

After a brief stay in Richmond, Virginia, in 1949, Travis spent the 1950s in and around California, appearing on local TV, recording, and touring. He landed a cameo role as a guitar-picking soldier in the classic 1953 World War II film *From Here to Eternity*—a picture that starred Montgomery Clift, Burt Lancaster, Frank Sinatra, and Deborah Kerr—and sang "Re-Enlistment Blues," which was used as the movie's *leitmotif*. Then in 1955, TENNESSEE ERNIE FORD's recording of an imaginative coal mining tune Travis had written in 1946, "Sixteen Tons," became a multimillion seller. Travis had recorded this song using acoustic guitar, along with two other folk-flavored originals and a few traditional songs, on the 78-rpm album *Folk Songs of the Hills*, which had drawn little attention at the time. With Ford, "Sixteen Tons" became an American standard and renewed interest in Travis.

Travis and his third wife, Bettie, moved to Nashville in 1968. In 1973 he joined his friend and musical disciple Chet Atkins to record the LP *The Atkins-Travis Traveling Show*, which won a Grammy in 1974 for Best Country Instrumental Performance. Inducted into the COUNTRY MUSIC HALL OF FAME in 1977, Travis spent his later years living in Eastern Oklahoma with his fourth wife, Dorothy, ex-wife of HANK THOMPSON, and often wrote superb memoirs of his career for music magazines. In 1979 he started recording for the Los Angeles–based traditional country label CMH. His 1981 *Travis Pickin'* LP received a Grammy nomination. On October 19, 1983, he suffered a massive coronary and died in an Oklahoma hospital the next morning. His ashes were later interred in Ebenezer, Kentucky, under the Merle Travis monument, which had been dedicated in 1956 to honor both him and his success with the song "Sixteen Tons."

—*Rich Kienzle*

REPRESENTATIVE RECORDINGS

Songs of the Coal Mines (Capitol, 1963); *Travis Pickin'* (CMH, 1981); *Guitar Rags and a Too Fast Past* (Bear Family, 1994), 5 CDs; *Folk Songs of the Hills* (Capitol Nashville, 1996); *Walkin' the Strings* (Capitol Nashville, 1996)

Randy Travis

Randy Travis

b. Marshville, North Carolina, May 4, 1959

A shy North Carolinian, Randy Bruce Traywick eventually became the *de facto* leader of a small band of revolutionaries who dramatically changed the course of country music events beginning in 1986. RICKY SKAGGS, GEORGE STRAIT, and REBA MCENTIRE, and JOHN ANDERSON and EMMYLOU HARRIS before them, had plowed the first furrows of the hard-country regeneration. But Travis's distinctive, understated baritone twang and square-jawed sex appeal endeared him not only to hard-country loyalists but also to millions of fans beyond country's traditional boundaries. The image crystallized in him would soon inspire a raft of good-looking young male stars who sailed into the 1990s.

Born into a country music–loving family, young Randy Traywick had started playing and singing at the family home in tiny Marshville, North Carolina. From the recordings that his guitar-playing father, Harold, bought, Randy spent long hours absorbing the music of HANK WILLIAMS, LEFTY FRIZZELL, and others. Guitar lessons and playing square dances and clubs with brother Ricky gave early vent to Randy's considerable talent. At the same time—from age eleven or twelve to age eighteen—Travis was developing a substance abuse habit that would see him consume LSD, marijuana, speed, alcohol, and other drugs by his midteens. A run of encounters with the law—over everything from speeding to burglary—also marked his rough and rowdy days. "I'm not a person who handles drinking well, to start with," he said years later. "I was one of those, when I drank, I got big. I could whip anybody when I got drunk."

On the brink of doing significant jail time, Travis was saved by the intercession of Elizabeth Lib Hatcher, then the manager of the Country Palace Nightclub in Charlotte, where he had been performing. Hatcher took him in, let the law know he'd be looked after, and made plan after plan for his career. Travis continued to hone his hard-country singing and entertaining skills at the club. He made his record debut as Randy Traywick on the independent Paula label in 1978, hitting #91 on *Billboard*'s country chart in early 1979 with the JOE STAMPLEY–produced "She's My Woman."

Travis and Hatcher made the big move to Nashville in 1981. Known for a time as Randy Ray, Travis put in time both singing and cooking hamburgers at the Nashville Palace, managed by Hatcher and located just minutes from the GRAND OLE OPRY's back door. He recorded an independent live album at the club and gained the friendship of Opry stalwarts such as JIMMY DICKENS and JOHNNY RUSSELL, but had little success storming the pop-laden bastions of Music Row. Even WARNER BROS., the label that was to sign him with such success, turned him down twice. Finally, Warner A&R executive Martha Sharp—who heard in Travis someone who could shepherd traditional-minded country fans back into the fold—gave him a chance to release some singles. Sharp put Travis with producer KYLE LEHNING, whose mastery at complementing the artist's Lefty Frizzell–styled vocals with excellent back-up musicians, combined with Sharp's keen song-spotting sense, helped make Travis a success. The first of the Warner singles, the DON SCHLITZ–PAUL OVERSTREET true-love anthem "On the Other Hand," stiffed in summer 1985, only to reach #1 in spring 1986 after the plaintive, steel-driven "1982" had caught fans' attention and had become Travis's first Top Ten, late in 1985.

Driven by over-the-top fan and radio response, Warner gave Travis a shot at an album, which turned out to be the captivating classic-to-be *Storms of Life* (1986). Fueled by hit singles including "On the Other Hand," "1982," and "Diggin' Up Bones," the album's great song selection and impassioned vocals won it eight weeks at #1 on its way to selling 3 million copies. Its successor *Always and Forever* (1987) stayed at #1 for forty-three weeks on its way to selling 5 million copies—huge numbers for country at that time. It contained Travis's first hit as a writer, "I Told You So," as well as a major career song, "Forever and Ever, Amen," a bouncy Overstreet-Schlitz tune that won the CMA's Single of the Year honor that year. Through the later 1980s Travis kept up his #1 album pace with *Old 8x10* (1988) and *No Holdin' Back* (1989) and a string of #1 singles, broken only, ironically, by his own riveting composition "Promises" (#17), one of his finest releases. Meanwhile, Travis won dozens of awards, including CMA's Horizon Award (1986) and Male Vocalist Award (1987, 1988), and Grammys for Best Country Vocal Performance, Male, in 1987 and 1988.

As everyone from the Rolling Stones to GEORGE JONES became fans, Travis found his personal life, particularly his relationship with Hatcher, becoming grist for the media and the gossip mills. By March 1990 Travis ended up, at a key radio convention, angrily denying rumors that he was homosexual. In May 1990, after years of describing their relationship as one based on business and friendship, Travis and Hatcher married in Hawaii. That year also saw the release of the platinum-selling *Heroes and Friends* album, with the George Jones duet "A Few Ole Country Boys" and the George Bush–inspired single "Point of Light." Even as the spotlight shifted to GARTH BROOKS, Travis continued to make some of the most memorable, high-quality music of the era: the Brook Benton remake "It's Just a Matter of Time" (1989), "Hard Rock Bottom of

Your Heart" (1990), the blue-collar rouser "Better Class of Losers" (1991), "If I Didn't Have You" (1992), "Before You Kill Us All" (1994), and his nostalgic, self-penned "The Box" (1995) are just a few examples of the excellent material from Travis and longtime producer Kyle Lehning. Travis drastically cut down his road schedule in 1992.

He also devoted time to a series of acting roles that included the TV movies *Frank and Jesse*, *Edie & Pen*, *A Dead Man's Revenge*, *Texas*, and *A Holiday to Remember*; the features *The Legend of O. B. Taggert*, *At Risk*, and *Maverick*, as well as television appearances on series including *Matlock* and *Touched By an Angel*. The 1996 release *Full Circle* put Travis back at center stage, yielding the single "Would I" (#25), and reminded media and fans of his indispensable role in country during the decade following his first hit.

In 1997 Travis was released from Warner Bros. and signed with DreamWorks Records Nashville. Travis's debut with this label was the single "Out of My Bones," which entered the *Billboard* charts at #39 on March 7, 1998. The new album, *You and You Alone*, was released in April 1998.

—*Thomas Goldsmith*

REPRESENTATIVE RECORDINGS

Storms of Life (Warner Bros., 1986); *Always and Forever* (Warner Bros., 1987)

Tree Publishing Company
established in New York, New York, and Nashville, Tennessee, 1951

Tree Publishing Company, one of the major independent country music publishing firms in Nashville for almost fifty years, was formed in 1951 by JACK STAPP, then program director at WSM, and Lou Cowan, a CBS broadcasting executive responsible for successful TV game shows such as *The $64,000 Question* and *Break the Bank*. Originally, Cowan put up the money and the administrative offices were in New York; Stapp was in charge of finding songs and songwriters in Nashville.

The name of the company came from Polly Spiegel Cowan, wife of Lou Cowan and heiress to the Spiegel catalogue fortune, who had drawn a tree on the back of her menu in a restaurant as Stapp and Cowan discussed the future firm. (The company would later be known as Tree International and today is known as Sony/ATV Tree.)

In 1953 Stapp hired BUDDY KILLEN, a young bass player who played regularly at the GRAND OLE OPRY, to find songs and songwriters. In 1956 ELVIS PRESLEY, in his first recording session for RCA RECORDS, recorded the Tree song "Heartbreak Hotel," which established Tree as a major publisher. At this point Tree moved into offices in the Cumberland Lodge Building in downtown Nashville.

In 1956 Lou Cowan became president of CBS Television and had to divest himself of Tree. In an agreement, Stapp purchased the company from Cowan and Harry Fleishman in 1957 and gave 30 percent to Killen, and another 10 percent to Joyce Bush, Stapp's longtime secretary.

In 1958 Jack Stapp left WSM to become program director of Nashville rock & roll station WKDA while Buddy Killen handled the day-to-day activities at Tree; in 1964 Stapp left WKDA to assume full-time duties at Tree. In 1963, the year before Stapp came over to Tree full-time, the publishing company had its first million-dollar year.

After "Heartbreak Hotel," Tree's next major success came with ROGER MILLER, who signed with the company in 1958 and who became a superstar when he wrote and recorded such hits as "Dang Me," "Chug-a-Lug," and "King of the Road" in 1964 and 1965. In 1965 Tree also benefited from "Green Green Grass of Home," written by CURLY PUTMAN, which became a pop standard and then a worldwide hit after it was recorded by Tom Jones.

In May 1969 Tree purchased PAMPER MUSIC, owned by HAL SMITH and RAY PRICE, for $1.6 million. Pamper controlled many hit songs of WILLIE NELSON, HANK COCHRAN, and HARLAN HOWARD, such as "Crazy," "Hello Walls," "Make the World Go Away," "Pick Me Up on Your Way Down," and "Funny How Time Slips Away." The purchase doubled the size of Tree, making it the largest independent publisher in Nashville. This began an era when Tree would grow by catalogue acquisitions as well as development of its own writers and songs internally as Tree eventually acquired the publishing companies of DOLLY PARTON, CONWAY TWITTY, JIM ED NORMAN, BUCK OWENS, MERLE HAGGARD, JIM REEVES, NAT STUCKEY, and Jerry Chesnut—in all, more than fifty catalogues.

In 1964 Tree moved into a newly purchased building on Music Row at 905 Sixteenth Avenue South. In 1972 Tree purchased their building at 8 Music Square West.

Tree expanded into the record business in 1965—and the field of rhythm and blues—with the formation of Dial Records. Originally created for singer Joe Tex, the label had success in the 1965–75 period with songs such as "Hold What You've Got," "Show Me," "Skinny Legs and All," "I Gotcha," and "Ain't Gonna Bump No More (With No Big Fat Woman)."

In 1974 Joyce Bush, one of Tree's owners, succumbed to incurable cancer; she was replaced as Stapp's administrative assistant by DONNA HILLEY. Also in 1974 Stapp assumed the role of chief executive officer and board chairman, while Buddy Killen became president and chief operating officer.

On December 20, 1980 Jack Stapp died at age sixty-seven, and Buddy Killen exercised an agreement he and Stapp had made earlier and purchased the company and assumed sole ownership; at Joyce Bush's death, Killen had received her stock, which meant Stapp owned 60 percent of the company and Killen owned 40 percent. The following year Donna Hilley was named executive assistant to the board and in 1978 was named executive vice president.

On January 10, 1989, Sony Music purchased Tree from Buddy Killen for $40 million. After the sale of Tree to Sony, Killen remained head of the company but by the end of the year had stepped down. Donna Hilley remained as senior vice president and chief operating officer. In February 1994 Hilley was named president and chief executive officer of Sony Tree.

In May 1998 Sony Tree further strengthened its position as a Music Row publishing powerhouse with the purchase of Little Big Town Music and Tom Shapiro Music and the signing of Little Big Town's Bob DiPiero, songwriter.
—*Don Cusic*

Buck Trent
b. Spartanburg, South Carolina, February 17, 1938

After first making a name for himself as a sideman, banjo player Charles Wilburn "Buck" Trent became a well-known performer in his own right after progressing from regular televised appearances on the *PORTER WAGONER Show* to appearances on *HEE HAW* and collaborations with *Hee Haw* co-host ROY CLARK.

Trent grew up in the tiny textile town of Arcadia Mills, near Spartanburg. His first love was Hawaiian steel guitar; he then switched to five-string banjo. By age eleven he was playing on Spartanburg's WSPA and WORD radio stations, and then on WLOS-TV in Asheville, North Carolina. He played on California's *TOWN HALL PARTY* television show, but in 1959 moved to Nashville. At MOM UPCHURCH's musicians' rooming home, HANK SNOW's steel guitar player Howard White encouraged Trent to place a special steel bar beneath his banjo strings. It added a certain ring to the sound, which inspired Trent to have the banjo electrified.

Trent had already cut two albums when he joined Porter Wagoner's show in 1962. He traveled (and appeared on TV) as a member of Wagoner's band the Wagonmasters until 1973. Trent also played on many hits recorded in the RCA studio, such as Wagoner's "The Cold Hard Facts of Life" (#2, 1967) and DOLLY PARTON's "Mule Skinner Blues" (Blue Yodel #8)" (#3, 1970). Trent even played music in the film *Nashville Rebel* (1967).

For their work together, Trent and Roy Clark won the CMA's Instrumental Group of the Year award in 1975 and 1976. In recent years Trent has been a star in the BRANSON, MISSOURI, music theater milieu.
—*Steve Eng*

Rick Trevino
b. Houston, Texas, May 16, 1971

When Rick Trevino's "Just Enough Rope" cracked the country Top Forty in late 1993, he became the first nationally recognized country singer of Hispanic descent since JOHNNY RODRIGUEZ and FREDDY FENDER came out of Texas in the 1970s.

Richardo Trevino Jr. was born in Houston's East End, where his father had played with a regionally popular Tejano band. The family moved to a predominantly Anglo neighborhood in Austin when he was five, and Trevino grew up studying classical piano and listening to pop and country music. He began performing solo gigs and singing with country cover bands after graduating from high school, and was signed to SONY by producer STEVE BUCKINGHAM when he was nineteen.

His first album, 1993's *Dos Mundos,* consisted of country songs sung in Spanish and was promoted to the Tejano market. "Just Enough Rope" was recorded in three versions: English, Spanish, and bilingual. The later version might have helped listeners identify Trevino on the playing field of soundalike hat acts. But he insisted he was not "crossing over" to country. "I am a country singer who happens to have a Hispanic background. That's the way I want to be marketed," he said. His faith was justified when a subsequent single from his self-titled English debut album, the ballad "She Can't Say I Didn't Cry," went to the Top Five. The album eventually was certified gold. The follow-up album, *Looking for the Light,* seemed to get lost in the shuffle when it was released on COLUMBIA in the spring of 1995. However, it did produce a *Billboard* #6 single, "Bobbie Ann Mason," and the album reached the #17 country spot. Trevino released a third Columbia album, *Learning as You Go,* in 1996, off which the title track reached #2 and "Running Out of Reasons" hit #1.
—*Rick Mitchell*

REPRESENTATIVE RECORDINGS

Dos Mundos (Sony Discos, 1993); *Rick Trevino* (Columbia, 1994)

Travis Tritt

Travis Tritt
b. Marietta, Georgia, February 9, 1963
·······································

In the 1990s, Travis Tritt's bluesy amalgam of hard-core country and southern rock made him arguably the most significant country-rock vocal stylist since HANK WILLIAMS JR.

James Travis Tritt trained for his vocal career by singing solos in the First Assembly of God's children's choir in Marietta. By age eight he had taught himself to play guitar and by fourteen had penned his first song. Because his family discouraged him from pursuing a career in music, Tritt kept his musical aspirations on a back burner while he worked at a variety of blue-collar jobs. In 1981 he quit a job at an Atlanta heating and air conditioning company and started singing at Atlanta area nightclubs.

In 1982 Tritt met Danny Davenport, a rock radio promoter for WARNER BROS. RECORDS, who also owned a small recording studio on the side. Davenport not only helped Tritt work on demo recordings but more importantly introduced him to Warner Bros.' Nashville division. In 1988, after showcasing in Atlanta for Warner Bros. Records' executives, Tritt was added to the Nashville division's artist roster. The following year he signed a management contract with Ken Kragen, KENNY ROGERS's manager.

Initially signed to a contract specifying the release of only three singles, Tritt shot to stardom with the March 1990 release of his debut album, *Country Club*. The title cut became his first Top Ten single, "Help Me Hold On," his first #1. Tritt's next three albums, *It's All About to Change, T-R-O-U-B-L-E,* and *Ten Feet Tall and Bulletproof,* delivered a string of Top Ten singles, including "Here's a Quarter (Call Someone Who Cares)" (1991) and "Anymore" (1991), both written by Tritt himself. "The Whiskey Ain't Workin'," a rowdy 1991 duet with MARTY STUART, earned the two a 1992 Grammy Award and led to their successful

1992 "No Hats" tour and 1996 "Double Trouble" tour. Subsequent album releases include *A Travis Tritt Christmas: Loving Time of the Year* (1992); *Greatest Hits—From the Beginning* (1995); and *The Restless Kind*, produced by Don Was in 1996.

Tritt's autobiography *Ten Feet Tall and Bulletproof* was published in 1994. The following year he expanded his career to include acting, appearing in the TV movie *Rio Diablo,* HBO series *Tales from the Crypt,* and feature films *The Cowboy Way, Sgt. Bilko,* and *Blues Brothers 2000.* Tritt's songs have appeared on the movie soundtracks of *My Cousin Vinny* (1992), *Honeymoon in Vegas* (1992), and *The Cowboy Way* (1994).

During the course of his career Tritt has received numerous awards, including the CMA's 1991 Horizon Award, 1992 Vocal Event Award (with Marty Stuart), and a share of the 1994 Album of the Year Award for recording "Take It Easy" for *Common Thread: The Songs of the Eagles* album. Tritt was belatedly named Star of Tomorrow at the 1992 fan-voted TNN/*Music City News* Awards. On February 9, 1992, he was inducted into the cast of the GRAND OLE OPRY.
—*Marjie McGraw*

REPRESENTATIVE RECORDINGS

Country Club (Warner Bros., 1990); *It's All About to Change* (Warner Bros., 1991); *T-R-O-U-B-L-E* (Warner Bros., 1992); *Ten Feet Tall and Bulletproof* (Warner Bros., 1994); *The Restless Kind* (Warner Bros., 1996)

Ernest Tubb
b. near Crisp, Texas, February 9, 1914; d. September 6, 1984
·······································

Honky-tonk singer-songwriter, movie actor, record retailer, longtime GRAND OLE OPRY star, and member of the COUNTRY MUSIC HALL OF FAME, Ernest Dale Tubb was among the most influential and important country performers in history. Throughout his own illustrious fifty-year career he gave numerous younger stars invaluable broadcast and concert exposure.

Youngest of five children in a sharecropper's family, Ernest Tubb was born on a cotton farm near Crisp, Texas (thirty-five miles southeast of Dallas) and spent his youth farming in different parts of the state. A fan of early movie cowboys such as Buck Jones and Tom Mix, Tubb first heard the recordings of JIMMIE RODGERS in 1928 and became a huge fan of him and his work. Tubb learned in his spare time to sing, yodel, and play the guitar much like Rodgers did, and shortly after Rodgers's death in 1933, nineteen-year-old Ernest Tubb first worked as a radio singer in San Antonio, city of Jimmie's final residence. Tubb's singing paid little or nothing, so he supported himself digging ditches for the WPA and later clerking in a drugstore in the Alamo City.

In 1936, married now and still enthralled by Rodgers's music and memories, Tubb phoned Rodgers's widow, Mrs. Carrie Rodgers, to ask for an autographed photo. A friendship developed, as Mrs. Rodgers listened to Tubb's radio shows and offered professional advice. Impressed by Tubb's friendly personality and heartfelt singing, Mrs. Rodgers was soon doing much to assist him. She helped to buy him clothes and find new songs, secured a record contract with Jimmie's label (RCA, by then releasing all country recordings on BLUEBIRD), and took him on a regional tour of movie theaters to promote his new recordings.

Both his first records—which were done very much in

the Rodgers vein—and the tour proved unsuccessful. Between 1937 and 1940 Tubb worked for radio stations and at day jobs in various Texas cities (Midland, San Angelo, and Corpus Christi). A 1939 tonsillectomy in San Angelo lowered his voice and effectively eliminated the Rodgers yodel, and hence the Rodgers song repertory, so Tubb became a more energetic and effective songwriter. In 1940 he got a second chance with a major record label, as DAVE KAPP at DECCA agreed to record Tubb during Houston sessions that spring: Of the four songs recorded on April 4, "Blue Eyed Elaine" and its flip side, "I'll Get Along Somehow," became his first success (the former was covered by GENE AUTRY).

Tubb moved to KGKO in Fort Worth during December 1940, and for the first time became a full-time musician. That next June, his sponsor/employer on KGKO became Universal Mills, which gave Tubb his role as the Gold Chain Troubadour. As such, he toured Texas grocery and feed stores and sang on town squares, where such future stars as CHARLIE WALKER and HANK THOMPSON first heard him. On the strength of his sixth Decca release and all-time biggest career hit, "Walking the Floor Over You" (1941), Tubb sang in two Columbia western movies made in 1942, *Fighting Buckaroo* and *Riding West.* He also appeared on Sunday package shows with such stars as BOB WILLS and ROY ACUFF, in far-flung cities such as Shreveport, Little Rock, and Memphis.

Playing in Birmingham during December 1942, Tubb came within the purview of Nashville talent agent and manager J. L. FRANK, who arranged Grand Ole Opry and other personal appearances for Tubb the next month. In February 1943 Tubb joined the regular Opry cast and remained one of its major stars for the rest of his career (thirty-nine more years). At J. L. Frank's behest, Tubb sold a series of radio songbooks via WSM broadcasts, hired his first band, the Texas Troubadours, and continued his film work with periodic trips to California (*Jamboree* for Republic in 1944, and *Hollywood Barndance* for an independent studio in 1947), in addition to ambitious touring. Tubb then was considered one of country music's major stars, regularly appearing on popularity charts with recordings such as "Soldier's Last Letter" (1944), "Tomorrow Never Comes" (1945), "It's Been So Long Darling" (1945), "Rainbow at Midnight" (1946), and "Filipino Baby" (1946). His style—a spare, personalized brand of honky-tonk music that featured a sole electric lead guitar playing straight melody—made him distinctive, recognizable, and, during his heyday, oft-imitated.

In May 1947 Tubb opened the Ernest Tubb Record Shop at 720 Commerce Street in downtown Nashville, the first major all-country record store. Over the next year, *The Midnight Jamboree* show emerged as an outgrowth of the record store, broadcast before a live audience immediately after the Grand Ole Opry and showcasing for the most part deserving young hopefuls and their latest record releases. *The Midnight Jamboree* continues to this day, WSM's second-longest continuous broadcast.

Beneficiary of Mrs. Rodgers's help early in his career, Tubb did all he could as a star to help others: carrying artists on tour with him, putting in a good word with Opry management or record producers, showcasing talent on his *Midnight Jamboree* shows, hiring some for his own Texas Troubadours, and always offering words of advice. The major stars whom Ernest Tubb boosted in these and other ways established his reputation as the industry's most generous and selfless star. HANK WILLIAMS, HANK SNOW, CARL

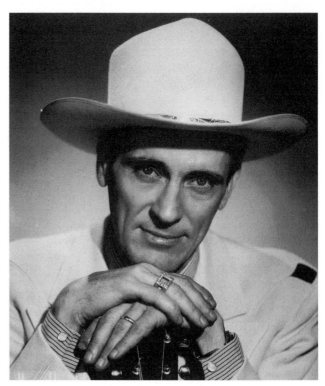

Ernest Tubb

SMITH, Charlie Walker, JUSTIN TUBB (his first child), PATSY CLINE, the WILBURN BROTHERS, JOHNNY CASH, STONEWALL JACKSON, SKEETER DAVIS, GEORGE HAMILTON IV, LORETTA LYNN, JACK GREENE, and CAL SMITH were the main performers who owed various degrees of thanks to Ernest Tubb.

Tubb was the first to bring a Grand Ole Opry show into Carnegie Hall (in September 1947). In keeping with Decca's penchant for recording and promoting duo acts, he became a prolific duet artist over the years, recording with the Andrews Sisters (1949), RED FOLEY (1949–53), the Wilburn Brothers (1957), and Loretta Lynn (1964–69).

While his own career was on an upswing in the early and middle 1960s, honors and accolades came his way, including election in 1965 to the COUNTRY MUSIC HALL OF FAME, the same year he received a gold record for "Walking the Floor Over You." Tubb hosted a syndicated TV show out of Nashville between 1965 and 1968, with WILLIE NELSON his co-star in the early episodes.

No artist toured as much for as long as Ernest Tubb, who worked 150 to 200 shows each year between the early 1960s (when he first turned his Texas Troubadours into a dance band and started playing the nightclub circuit) and 1982, at which time a long-standing battle with emphysema forced him to quit. No artist was better to his fans, and no fans were more loyal to their star: Ernest Tubb had one national fan club with a single president (Norma Winton Barthel) for its entire existence between 1944 and its deactivation in the early 1990s, a few years beyond Tubb's death in September 1984.

—*Ronnie Pugh*

REPRESENTATIVE RECORDINGS

Ernest Tubb: Live, 1965 (Rhino, 1989); *Ernest Tubb: MCA Country Music Hall of Fame* (MCA, 1991); *Let's Say Goodbye Like We Said Hello* (Bear Family, 1991, reissued boxed set of 1947–53 Decca recordings); *The Yellow Rose of Texas* (Bear Family, 1993, reissued boxed set of 1954–60 Decca recordings); *Ernest Tubb & Friends* (LaserLight, 1993); *Walking the Floor Over You* (Bear Family, 1996, reissued boxed set of 1936–47 Bluebird, Decca, and World Transcriptions recordings)

Justin Tubb
b. San Antonio, Texas, August 20, 1935; d. January 24, 1998

The eldest son of ERNEST TUBB, singer-songwriter Justin Wayne Tubb was one of the most underrated talents in country music. Though always mindful of his legacy, the smooth-voiced performer tried hard not to walk in his father's shadow.

Justin Tubb attended schools in Texas and Tennessee, including Castle Heights Military Academy in Lebanon, and the University of Texas at Austin, where he majored in broadcast journalism. Tubb once hoped to be a sports announcer, but by 1953 he was a DJ at WHIN in Gallatin, Tennessee.

At age nine Tubb made his GRAND OLE OPRY debut and at twenty became one of the show's youngest cast members. For his father, Tubb wrote "My Mother Must Have Been a Girl Like You" (1951), which sold about 250,000 copies as a single, thanks to a hit flip side, "Somebody's Stolen My Honey."

Tubb burst onto the national scene via a 1954 duet hit, "Lookin' Back to See," with DECCA RECORDS labelmate GOLDIE HILL. He had a Top Ten country hit again with MARVIN RAINWATER's composition "I've Gotta Go Get My Baby," then hit a career slump.

Songwriting skills, however, helped him forge a comeback. Tubb ballads for other artists included "Big Fool of the Year" (GEORGE JONES), "Lonesome 7-7203" (HAWKSHAW HAWKINS), "Imagine That" (PATSY CLINE), "Keeping Up with the Joneses" (FARON YOUNG & Margie Singleton),

Justin Tubb

"Love Is No Excuse" (DOTTIE WEST & JIM REEVES), "Walkin' Talkin' Cryin' Barely Beatin' Broken Heart" (first for Johnny Wright, later HIGHWAY 101), and "Be Glad" (DEL REEVES).

In 1963, Tubb wrote and sang "Take a Letter, Miss Gray," which put him back in the country Top Ten. For his father he also wrote "Be Better to Your Baby." He managed WSM's *Midnite Jamboree;* founded FOR E.T., a nonprofit agency to promote research on emphysema; and worked on behalf of the American Lung Association of Tennessee.

—*Walt Trott*

REPRESENTATIVE RECORDINGS
Together and Alone, with Lorene Mann (RCA, 1966); *Justin Tubb* (Dot, 1985)

Gabe Tucker
b. Pierce, Kentucky, December 1, 1915

Gaylord Bob "Gabe" Tucker has worn many hats in his long career: musician, comic, show promoter, artist manager, and record producer, among others. Born and raised in Kentucky, Tucker started his own band at seventeen. In Louisville he played bass with Cliff Gross's band and in 1943 came to Nashville as an original member of EDDY ARNOLD's Tennessee Plowboys on bass and trumpet.

Tucker later worked in other Opry bands and developed a solo comedy act. He took his gift of gab to Houston radio in 1951 (KLEE, then KTAL, KNUZ, and Baytown's KRCT), and also emceed live shows there. He made two records for DOT and one for TNT at about this time, then returned to Nashville in May 1955 to manage ERNEST and JUSTIN TUBB and, later, the WILBURN BROTHERS. Tucker severed his ties with the Tubbs and the Wilburns in January 1957, sold his Gaylord Music to HAL SMITH, and returned to Houston. By midyear 1957 Tucker was managing HANK LOCKLIN and the red-hot BOBBY HELMS.

For years employed by Houston impresario PAPPY DAILY, Tucker stayed around country music. A good friend of COLONEL TOM PARKER, Tucker co-authored the book *Up and Down with Elvis Presley* with Marge Crumbaker (1981).

—*Ronnie Pugh*

Tanya Tucker
b. Seminole, Texas, October 10, 1958

Since her 1972 smash hit "Delta Dawn" made her a star at age thirteen, Tanya Denise Tucker has emerged as one of the most successful and popular country singers of the contemporary era. By her thirty-sixth birthday, an age at which many country stars' careers are just becoming established, she had already scored more than fifty chart singles, including (besides "Delta Dawn") such enduring favorites as "San Antonio Stroll" (#1, 1974), "Strong Enough to Bend" (#1, 1988), and "Down to My Last Teardrop" (#2, 1991). Her instantly recognizable husky voice, her extraordinary chart success, her upbringing in the media spotlight, and her wild "Texas Tornado" persona have made Tanya not only a country music superstar but also a full-blown tabloid-magnet household name.

The daughter of Beau and Juanita Tucker, Tanya was born in the West Texas town of Seminole but did not grow up there. Beau Tucker worked a variety of jobs, including prospecting and general contracting, and moved his family around the Southwest while Tanya was young. The

Tanya Tucker

Tuckers settled for a number of years in Willcox, Arizona, then later moved to Phoenix. When Tanya was six years old she shocked and impressed her father by showing off her precocious vocal prowess in the house one day. Over the course of the next few years, with Beau's approval, she started talking her way onto shows headlined by visiting country stars.

"I just remember performing at a lot of the bars at night," she once said. "Like especially the VFW Hall in Willcox, Arizona. Different entertainers would come on, come to town, and I'd sing with them. ERNEST TUBB and LITTLE JIMMY DICKENS being the first two that I remember."

When she was eight or nine years old her father made some primitive, living room recordings of Tanya singing and took the tapes to Nashville, but no one was interested in his talented daughter. In Phoenix she appeared on the *Lew King Show,* a children's TV program, and when the Tuckers moved to Utah she landed a brief spot alongside Robert Redford in the movie *Jeremiah Johnson* (1972). Shortly thereafter Beau Tucker moved the family to Henderson, Nevada, to be close to the Las Vegas entertainment industry. He and Tanya made another demo tape—this one in a real studio—and gave a copy to Dolores Fuller, an actress and songwriter who had penned a number of tunes for the Elvis Presley movies. Through Fuller, Tanya was brought to the attention of BILLY SHERRILL, the chief of EPIC/COLUMBIA RECORDS in Nashville, and he signed her.

On March 17, 1972, at her first Columbia session in Nashville, Tucker recorded "Delta Dawn," with Sherrill producing. The record charted in May, and in July the thirteen-year-old sensation debuted on the GRAND OLE OPRY. Three years shy of receiving her driver's license, Tucker's career was full speed ahead. For the next two and a half years she and Sherrill collaborated on a series of brilliantly layered, melodramatic singles that made the most of the teenage singer's uncanny ability to handle adult material. "What's Your Mama's Name" (1973) was her first #1 record, followed by "Blood Red and Goin' Down" (1973) and the infamous "Would You Lay with Me (In a Field of

Stone)" (1974). The latter song was banned by a few radio stations. "I just think their minds were in the gutter," Tanya said at the time. Still, by then she was being portrayed in the press as some sort of pubescent hillbilly sex goddess, an image that *Rolling Stone* worked to the hilt when they put Tanya on the cover of their September 26, 1974, issue. Less than a month later, Beau Tucker, who had continued to guide his daughter's career, swung a million-dollar deal for her with MCA RECORDS. The contract was signed on her sixteenth birthday.

Tanya's tenure at MCA lasted seven years and yielded the #1 hits "Lizzie and the Rainman" (1975—and also her only song to crack the pop Top Forty), "San Antonio Stroll" (1975), and "Here's Some Love" (1976). In 1978, hoping to expand the scope of her career, she recorded the notorious *T.N.T.* album in Los Angeles. The material was more seventies rock than country, and the album jacket featured Tanya in cheesecake poses. Not long afterward she started dating GLEN CAMPBELL, twenty-two years her senior. The two recorded the duets "Dream Lover" (1980) and "Why Don't We Just Sleep on It Tonight" (1981) and announced their engagement in the press. The relationship fell apart short of the altar, however, and the tabloids had a field day following their breakup. Tucker later sued Campbell amid allegations of physical abuse.

Tucker's career nearly fell apart at the same time. In 1982 she recorded *Changes,* believed to be the first mainstream country album to appear on the ARISTA label. The record, one of Tucker's best, sold poorly, and it was three more years before she was able to secure another record deal. Helping her do so was Nashville producer JERRY CRUTCHFIELD, who had worked with Tucker on a number of her MCA albums. He took her to CAPITOL RECORDS, and in 1986, *Girls Like Me,* Tucker's first album for Capitol Nashville, appeared in stores. The record yielded four Top Ten hits.

With her career back in full swing, the tabloid press began to take a full-time interest in Tucker again. She gave them plenty to work with. In 1988 she checked into the Betty Ford clinic, and on July 5, 1989, her first child, Presley Tanita Tucker, was born out of wedlock. On October 2, 1991, the day of that year's CMA Awards show, Tucker, still unmarried, gave birth to her second child, Beau Grayson Tucker. Tanya was in the hospital, watching the awards show on TV, when it was announced that she had been voted the 1991 Female Vocalist of the Year. After nearly twenty years in the business, it was the first time she had been so honored. Her autobiography, *Nickel Dreams: My Life* (written with Patsi Bale Cox), was published in 1997, the same year that Tucker's album *Complicated* was released.
—*Daniel Cooper*

REPRESENTATIVE RECORDINGS

Delta Dawn (Columbia, 1972); *Tanya Tucker* (MCA, 1975); *T.N.T.* (MCA, 1978); *Changes* (Arista, 1982); *What Do I Do with Me* (Liberty, 1991)

The Tune Wranglers

One of the wildest and most infectious western swing bands, the Tune Wranglers were formed by guitarist Buster Coward and fiddler Tom Dickey in 1934. Claiming to be real cowboys (which may account for the foot-stomping exuberance of their early records), the band was also one of the first western swing groups to wear western attire.

The Wranglers broadcasted on San Antonio's 50,000-watt WOAI and constantly toured central Texas. By their first BLUEBIRD sessions, in February 1936, they had added jazz pianist Eddie Whitley and tenor banjoist-vocalist Red Brown, whose risqué renditions of tunes such as "Red's Tight Like That" dominated the first sessions, though it was Coward's "Texas Sand" that became a huge hit and eventually a country standard.

Subsequent sessions featured the wild electric steel guitar of Eddie Duncan, also an able crooner, but the band tended to get more sophisticated as time went by, except for a September 1937 session for which Brown briefly returned. Tom Dickey left to form his own band in June 1937. Later sessions combined cowboy songs, such as Coward's adaption of the poem "Chopo," with pop and jazz tunes. Important additions included twins Beal (sax and clarinet) and Neal Ruff (tenor banjo), and fiddler-vocalist Leon Seago. Remaining very popular on radio, disc, and in person, the Tune Wranglers scored another major hit with "Hawaiian Honeymoon" in 1939. In that year Coward took the Tune Wranglers to Fort Worth's KFJZ and the new Texas State Network, but he seems to have disbanded his group in 1940.
—*Kevin Coffey*

REPRESENTATIVE RECORDING

The Tune Wranglers, 1936–38 (Texas Rose, 1981)

Nathan Turk
b. Minsk, Poland, May 10, 1895; d. October 24, 1988

The beautiful and lavishly embroidered western-wear designs of Nathan Turk became the signature stagewear of the MADDOX BROTHERS & ROSE, resulting in the group's billing as "the most colorful hillbilly band in the land." From the 1930s to the 1970s, Turk's ready-to-wear and custom western designs became favorites of celluloid cowboys, country artists, and their fans.

At age ten, Nathan Tieg began apprenticing with a tailor in Warsaw, Poland. Eight years later, he immigrated to America and in 1923 opened a shop at 13715 Ventura Boulevard, in Sherman Oaks, where the store remained until 1977. Turk's earliest clients were cowboy stars GENE AUTRY and ROY ROGERS, as well as numerous B-western leading men, and legend has it that NUDIE briefly apprenticed with him. In the 1940s Turk began designing for SPADE COOLEY and HANK THOMPSON, and soon after, he began a relationship with the Maddoxes, which would last until the group disbanded in 1956. The spectacular Turk outfits worn by the Maddox family dazzled with an array of rich hues and eye-catching flowers, hearts, or other organic embroidery designs; many of Rose Maddox's colorful suits featured the flower for which she was named.

Turk's exquisitely well-made designs combined western elements, such as fringe, embroidery, and arrowhead-bordered smile pockets, with tailored men's and women's suit styles. The reportedly polite, soft-spoken tailor often designed embroidery motifs inspired by Dutch, German, and Scandinavian folk art. Turk commissioned much of the delicate, custom embroidery work to a local woman named Viola Grae; his wife, Bessie, perfected the crescent-shaped "smile pocket" detailed with stitched arrowheads; and his nephew did the rhinestone work. His ready-to-wear business made handsome cowboy shirts and suits for men and women. Turk also designed elaborate outfits for riders in Pasadena's Rose Bowl parade.

By the 1970s, Turk's son-in-law, Irving, helped him run the shop, which featured ready-to-wear in the front and custom tailoring in the back. Due to failing health, Nathan Turk retired in 1977, though he continued to do some custom work the following year. After his death at age ninrty-three, his family closed down the business, but his designs live on in the closets of vintage-western-wear enthusiasts, as well as in such museums as the COUNTRY MUSIC HALL OF FAME.
—*Holly George-Warren*

Grant Turner
b. Baird, Texas, May 17, 1912; d. October 19, 1991

Jesse Granderson "Grant" Turner, Texas-born Voice of the GRAND OLE OPRY, served on that show's announcing staff for forty-seven years and is currently the only announcer/disc jockey to be elected to the COUNTRY MUSIC HALL OF FAME.

Growing up in Baird, Texas, near Abilene, Turner was the son of a banker and grandson of a rancher. While still in high school, he performed on Abilene's KFYO as *Ike and His Guitar* in 1928 and first announced for that station in the same year. Turner majored in journalism at college and worked for Texas and Louisiana newspapers during the 1930s, but he returned to radio announcing in 1940 at KFRO in Longview, Texas. In Sherman he held his last Texas radio job, and then moved to Knoxville, Tennessee, in 1942.

Turner rode an all-night bus to Nashville and auditioned for WSM, where he joined the staff on D-Day, the day the Allies invaded Europe in World War II, June 6, 1944. There he first announced early-morning programs, but a few months later joined GEORGE D. HAY's staff of Saturday night Grand Ole Opry announcers. Turner got what he called the "big prize" when he became announcer for R. J. Reynolds's NBC network half hour of the Grand Ole Opry, in the late 1940s: the *Prince Albert Show*, which was piped eventually to some 270 stations and some 10 million

Grant Turner

listeners weekly. Later he hosted WSM's *Mr. DJ, USA* program, featuring guest DJs from around the nation, and in the mid-1950s became the third regular announcer for ERNEST TUBB's WSM *Midnight Jamboree*, a job Turner held until 1977.

Turner's recordings were few and forgettable: four duets with Helen Carter for the Nashville-based TENNESSEE and REPUBLIC labels in 1951–52, and four solo numbers for Chart Records in 1964–65. Turner also made spoken-word LP recordings, including one personal Opry memoir in 1980 for CVS Records.

The genial Turner for years hosted the pre-Opry *Grand Ole Opry Warmup Show*—spinning records and taking requests on the Opry House stage—and worked Friday and Saturday night Opry shows, besides the summer matinees, until the night before he died. Known for his diction, ingratiating personality, and professionalism, Turner was one of three original members to join the Country Disc Jockey Hall of Fame, in 1975, operated by the Federation of International Country Air Personalities. He joined the Country Music Hall of Fame, in 1981.   —*Ronnie Pugh*

Zeb and Zeke Turner

Zeb Turner b. Lynchburg, Virginia, June 23, 1915; d. January 10, 1978

Zeke Turner b. Lynchburg, Virginia, June 18, 1923

Zeke and Zeb Turner were influential instrumentalists and songwriters. Zeke, born James Grishaw, was an electric guitar specialist who became one of country music's first great studio men; older brother Zeb, born William Edward Grishaw, was a guitarist, songwriter, and singer who had a career with KING RECORDS and lesser labels. Both grew up listening to local blues musicians and to pop/jazz guitarists such as George Barnes and Coco Heimal. By 1938 William had adopted the name Zeb Turner and recorded his first solo, "Guitar Fantasy," with a band called the Hi Neighbor Boys.

After jobs on the West Coast and Renfro Valley, Zeb came to Nashville in 1944 to play with WALLY FOWLER's band. In 1946 he recorded "Zeb's Mountain Boogie," the first release on the city's new BULLET label, and watched it become one of the nation's early boogie hits. In the meantime, brother Zeke also moved to town, and became one of the GRAND OLE OPRY headliners, a member of RED FOLEY's Pleasant Valley Boys, and one of Nashville's first session men. In 1947 he began working HANK WILLIAMS sessions (such as "Move It On Over" and "Honky Tonkin'"), where he popularized the dead string technique, muting the guitar strings with the heel of his right hand and turning his amp down so low the guitar almost became a percussion instrument.

The brothers did a handful of sides together (including "Guitar Reel" for Bullet) before they split up. Zeke moved to Cincinnati, where he did studio work for King and other labels, perfecting the famous guitar riff that opens the DELMORE BROTHERS' rendition of "Blues Stay Away From Me." Zeb spent the next few years in the Washington, D.C., area, doing club work and working with JIMMY DEAN. Zeb was publishing his songs by now through ACUFF-ROSE, having a #1 hit with "It's a Sin" (EDDY ARNOLD, 1947). Eventually relocating to Canada, Zeb remained active through the 1960s and died of cancer in January 1978. Zeke stayed in Cincinnati and had dropped out of music by the 1970s. He currently is retired and lives in Florida.   —*Charles Wolfe*

Wesley Tuttle

b. Lamar, Colorado, December 13, 1917

Wesley Tuttle played an important though largely overlooked role in developing and popularizing the California country sound. A presence on California radio beginning in 1933, the San Fernando–based singer-yodeler got into the business after he met CLIFFIE STONE and went to work with STUART HAMBLEN's band.

Despite the fact that he had accidentally lost three fingers in a mishap at his father's Pacoima butcher shop, Tuttle was an accomplished guitarist and yodeled so well that Walt Disney hired him for the *Snow White and the Seven Dwarfs* soundtrack's "Silly Song." Tuttle broadcast steadily, worked with the SONS OF THE PIONEERS for a time, and in 1938 had Leo Fender build him one of the earliest left-handed electric guitars. Tuttle left California in 1940 to work at Cincinnati super station WLW, where he became close with MERLE TRAVIS and was instrumental in Travis's decision to head west.

By 1942 Tuttle was back in San Fernando, specializing in a smooth western style croon and concentrating more on love songs than honky-tonk or swing; he eventually landed a contract with CAPITOL RECORDS and immediately recorded two strong sellers for them: "With Tears in My Eyes" (#1, 1945) and "Detour" (#3, 1946). The label fitted him with a custom-made latex glove to camouflage his damaged hand and sent him on the road with labelmate TEX RITTER. A prolific, sober, and hardworking entertainer, Tuttle also led the house band at Hoot Gibson's Painted Post nightclub, and by the early 1950s had become a fixture on Southern California television via his regular appearances on KTTV's Saturday night *TOWN HALL PARTY* (he also handled director duties) and, with his wife, Marilyn, on KTLA's five-day-a-week *Foreman Phillips Show*.

Tuttle left Capitol in 1949 for a brief stint on Coral, then returned to Capitol and recorded some extraordinary topical ballads ("Heart Sick Soldier on Heartbreak Ridge," "They Locked God Outside the Iron Curtain"). In 1957 he retired from the country music business to become an ordained minister, after which he and Marilyn Tuttle recorded a number of spiritual albums.

—*Jonny Whiteside*

Shania Twain

b. Windsor, Ontario, Canada, August 28, 1965

Shania Twain created a sensation through 1995–96 when her album *The Woman in Me* sold more than 8 million copies, becoming the top-selling album by a female artist in the history of country music. Twain brought a new sensuality to the country female image, and the pop-country sound she crafted with producer-husband Robert John "Mutt" Lange was strikingly original.

Born Eileen Edwards, she was raised in the mining town of Timmins, Ontario. Her father deserted the family when she was two. Mother Sharon married Ojibway Indian Jerry Twain, who raised her. She adopted the Ojibway name "Shania" in his honor.

Twain began singing around her hometown at age eight and was writing songs by age ten. By her teens she was a veteran of Canadian country TV shows. When she wasn't singing, she and her stepfather were reforestation workers in northern Canadian logging camps.

After Twain's mother and stepfather were killed in a car

Shania Twain

accident in 1987, she raised her younger siblings on her own, supporting them by singing at a resort. She came to Nashville with a tape in 1991 and was signed by MERCURY RECORDS.

In 1993 she filmed a flashy video for *What Made You Say That* in Miami Beach, then worked with actors Charles Durning and Sean Penn on a clip for *Dance with the One That Brought You.* Both songs were on her debut CD, which sold in modest numbers but caught Lange's attention. The producer of Foreigner, AC/DC, the Cars, Billy Ocean, Def Leppard, and Bryan Adams, Lange is an avid country fan. He called Mercury to get Twain's number, then came to FAN FAIR in 1993 to meet her. They married on December 21, 1993. A native of South Africa, Lange has stayed in the background throughout Twain's rise to stardom, preferring not to be photographed, interviewed, or to appear in public with his wife. They live on 3,000 acres in the Adirondack wilderness of upstate New York.

When they began to work on *The Woman in Me,* Lange insisted they use the ten Twain originals that had been turned down by the label for her first CD. He co-wrote with her and provided background harmonies.

"Whose Bed Have Your Boots Been Under" began Twain's march to stardom—it won Song of the Year at the 1995 Canadian country awards—and the CD eventually yielded seven hit singles, including the bright, danceable "Any Man of Mine," her first #1. In music industry circles the album's success was deemed all the more astounding in that Twain did not tour in support of it.

In 1996 Jon Landau, known for his long association with Bruce Springsteen, became Twain's manager. Her album *Come on Over* was released in the fall of 1997; in early 1998 its glossy ballad "You're Still the One" became a big pop crossover hit.
—*Robert K. Oermann*

REPRESENTATIVE RECORDINGS

Shania Twain (Mercury, 1993); *The Woman in Me* (Mercury, 1995)

Conway Twitty
b. Friars Point, Mississippi, September 1, 1933; d. June 5, 1993

During his lifetime, Conway Twitty had more #1 country records than any artist in history, his stardom having endured through five decades of changing fashions. He was also one of country music's most diverse stylists and a major songwriting talent: Eleven of his #1 hits were self-penned.

Twitty was born Harold Lloyd Jenkins, the son of a Mississippi ferryboat captain. Taught guitar by his grandfather and a neighborhood blues singer, Twitty went on KFFA radio in Helena, Arkansas, at age twelve. A talented baseball player, he was scouted by the Philadelphia Phillies, then drafted into the armed services during the Korean War. Upon his discharge, he heard the music of ELVIS PRESLEY and headed to SUN RECORDS in Memphis. The sides Twitty recorded for Sun were imitative of Presley and were not issued, but labelmate ROY ORBISON's recording of Twitty's song "Rockhouse" was released.

Twitty then signed with Mercury as a rockabilly performer. At this point he changed his name, combining the names of Conway, Arkansas, and Twitty, Texas, to create his new moniker. Next he signed with MGM, striking paydirt with 1958's million-selling "It's Only Make Believe." "Mona Lisa" (1959), "Danny Boy" (1959), "Lonely Blue Boy" (1960), "What Am I Living For" (1960), and "C'Est Ci Bon" (1961), among others, solidified his status as a teen idol, as did his appearances in *Platinum High School, College Confidential,* and other teen movies. The "Conrad Birdie" character in the Broadway musical *Bye Bye Birdie* parodied Twitty.

Twitty wrote country songs throughout this period and yearned to return to that genre as a performer. Songwriter HARLAN HOWARD was supportive, taking Twitty's "Walk Me to the Door" to COLUMBIA country star RAY PRICE, and urging DECCA's OWEN BRADLEY to sign Twitty in 1965. At first

Conway Twitty

country DJs were skeptical of the former pop star. But in 1968 he finally broke into the country Top Ten with "The Image of Me."

Twitty's follow-up single, "Next in Line," became the first of his forty #1 *Billboard* country hits. His intensely emotional singing and passion-filled lyrics characterized such career-building records as "Hello Darlin'" (1970), "Fifteen Years Ago" (1970), "How Much More Can She Stand" (1971), "Baby's Gone" (1973), "There's a Honky Tonk Angel" (1974), and his steamy "You've Never Been This Far Before" (1973) and "Linda on My Mind" (1975). He and LORETTA LYNN won a Grammy and four CMA Awards for a series of classic duets that included, among others, "After the Fire Is Gone" (1971), "Louisiana Woman, Mississippi Man" (1973), and "Feelin's" (1975).

Twitty's concert performances became like religious revivals, with fervent female followers, leading JERRY CLOWER to dub him "The High Priest of Country Music." Holding to a dramatic, minimalist style, Twitty did not speak on-stage, do interviews, attend music-business parties, appear on TV shows, or perform encores.

In the latter part of the 1970s Twitty began experimenting, adopting elements of rock ("Boogie Grass Band"), soul ("Don't Take It Away"), and OUTLAW sounds ("Play Guitar Play"). He also began producing his own albums and adopted a curly new hairdo in place of his previous pompadour and sideburns. Hits such as "I'd Love to Lay You Down" (1980) and "Tight Fittin' Jeans" (1981) signified a more contemporary sound as well.

Twitty switched from MCA (his label after it absorbed Decca) to WARNER/ELEKTRA in 1981 and recorded country versions of the pop hits "Slow Hand," "The Rose," "Three Times a Lady," and "Heartache Tonight." Other early 1980s hits included "I Don't Know a Thing About Love," penned by Harlan Howard. Twitty opened his $3 million Twitty City tourism complex in Nashville in 1981 and inaugurated the annual "Country Explosion" concerts to kick off FAN FAIR. He was also a co-owner of the minor-league baseball team the Nashville Sounds and of the United Talent booking agency.

VINCE GILL, KATHY MATTEA, NAOMI JUDD, and REBA MCENTIRE were among the many acts whose early careers were boosted by Twitty. His caring about songwriters and their work led to Twitty's billing as "the best friend a song ever had."

Rejoining MCA by 1987, Twitty issued some of his most creative singles to date—"Julia," "Desperado Love," "That's My Job," "Goodbye Time," "She's Got a Single Thing in Mind," and the controversial "Saturday Night Special." He quit smoking and gained new vocal power, made music videos, and began to do interviews and TV appearances. He also published an authorized biography in 1986.

As the 1990s dawned, Twitty was back in the Top Ten with "Crazy in Love" and "I Couldn't See You Leavin.' " His last recording session was a duet with Sam Moore, formerly of the soul hit duo Sam & Dave, on "Rainy Night in Georgia," included in *Rhythm Country & Blues*, released by MCA in 1994. Twitty died suddenly of a stomach aneurysm en route from a show in BRANSON, MISSOURI, to Nashville's 1993 Fan Fair celebration.

In the years since Twitty's death, his widow, Dee Henry Jenkins, has kept his legacy alive, though she also became embroiled in a bitter, prolonged court battle with other members of Twitty's family for control of his estate.

—*Robert K. Oermann*

REPRESENTATIVE RECORDINGS

Conway Twitty's Greatest Hits (MGM, 1960); *Greatest Hits, Volume 1* (MCA, 1974); *The Very Best of Conway and Loretta* (MCA, 1980); *Songwriter* (MCA, 1986); *Greatest Hits, Volume 3* (MCA, 1990); *The Conway Twitty Collection* (MCA, 1994), 4 discs

T. Texas Tyler

b. Mena, Arkansas, June 20, 1916; d. January 23, 1972

David Luke Myrick, better known as T. Texas Tyler, "the Man with a Million Friends," scored his biggest hit in 1948 with the sentimental recitation "Deck of Cards." The record reportedly sold so fast that pressing plants could not meet customer demand. Tyler's almost archaic, trumpet-filigreed recitations were steeped in the Anglo-Celtic tradition but represented nonetheless early country music's vast commercial potential. On the strength of his hit with "Deck of Cards," Tyler appeared at New York's CARNEGIE HALL on April 25, 1948, one of the earlier country acts to do so.

Raised in Philadelphia, Tyler appeared on the *Major Bowes Amateur Hour* radio talent show at age fourteen, then graduated to radio work in West Virginia, Indiana, and on Shreveport, Louisiana's, KWKH in 1942. While in West Virginia and Indiana he nurtured the early career of LITTLE JIMMY DICKENS. Discharged after a year in the army in 1946, Tyler signed with struggling Pasadena, California, independent FOUR STAR RECORDS, the label's first country artist. (Tyler's subsequent success would later attract both MADDOX BROTHERS & ROSE and WEBB PIERCE to the label.) Tyler had another major hit in 1948 with "Dad Gave My Dog Away," after the style of RED FOLEY's sentimental "Old Shep." Tyler's 1949 Los Angeles television show *Range Round Up* was a local favorite, and Tyler had a number of other successful records, including "Filipino Baby" (1946), "Bumming Around" (1953), and "Courting in the Rain" (1954). Unfortunately, Tyler had a serious problem with alcohol and drugs. In the mid-1950s, while on a brief tour

T. Texas Tyler

with HANK SNOW, Tyler was arrested in San Antonio, Texas, for possession of marijuana, and his career never recovered.

In the 1960s STARDAY RECORDS' DON PIERCE (who had recorded Tyler at Four Star years earlier) did an album with Tyler, mostly remakes of past triumphs. Late in life, Tyler turned to a career in the ministry, lived for a time in the Pacific Northwest, and died in Springfield, Missouri.

—*Jonny Whiteside*

Ian Tyson
b. Victoria, British Columbia, Canada, September 25, 1933

Ian Tyson has had two almost completely separate musical careers. First, he was half of the 1960s folk duo Ian & Sylvia; then, from the mid-1980s, he was one of the pioneers of new western (or cowboy) music. His cowboy songs were among the first new songs in that genre for a generation, and they served as a catalyst in the renaissance of cowboy culture.

Tyson grew up on Vancouver Island, the grandson of a British shipping magnate. After art school he went to Toronto, and he met Sylvia Fricker in 1959. They went to New York in 1961 and were taken on by BOB DYLAN's manager, Albert Grossman. They recorded seven albums for Vanguard Records (1961–67), and their original songs included "Four Strong Winds," "Someday Soon," and "You Were on My Mind." They also helped to introduce the work of Gordon Lightfoot. After two albums for MGM RECORDS they recorded a country rock record for Ampex, submerging their own identity into that of the band Great Speckled Bird.

Ian and Sylvia drifted apart personally and professionally in the early 1970s. Tyson hosted a mainstream country television show (*Nashville North,* subsequently *The Ian Tyson Show,* on the CTV network in Canada, 1969–75) and recorded a country album for A&M Canada before he retired in 1977. He moved to Alberta to work on a ranch and didn't record again until 1983, when he began recording a series of cowboy culture albums, first for COLUMBIA RECORDS of Canada, then for his own Eastern Slope Records, licensed to Stony Plain (Canada) and Vanguard in the United States. The third, *Cowboyography,* is generally considered one of the best contemporary cowboy albums, and it reached gold-record status in Canada.

A championship cutting horse rider, Tyson continues to run his ranch near Calgary and has participated in many of the cowboy celebration events in Elko, Nevada, and elsewhere. His work is a powerful evocation of cowboy life in the era of the satellite dish. —*Colin Escott*

REPRESENTATIVE RECORDINGS
Old Corrals and Sagebrush & Other Cowboy Culture Classics (Stony Plain/Bear Family, 1984); *Cowboyography* (Stony Plain/Vanguard, 1986); *Eighteen Inches of Rain* (Stony Plain/Vanguard, 1994)

From Schoolhouses to Arenas: A History of Country Music Touring

Ronnie Pugh

From the time country music became a profession, the main income, be it little or much, has always come from touring: taking one's music in person to the paying customers. In the early years, there weren't many other ways to make money. Recordmaking was a rare privilege, almost a novelty, and radio, though a major entertainment medium, proved most valuable for exposure and publicity. Once most country radio artists had "played out" an area's best venues, they had to move to a distant station and build a brand new following.

Today the industry is larger, and there are more ways for an artist to make money. The country divisions of the major record labels are powers within a multibillion-dollar industry. The national media, broadcast and print, are filled with the faces, the music, and the doings of a growing number of young country stars. Most established country singers own a song publishing venture or two; there are huge sums to be made via product endorsements; and some even have autobiographies that rank on national bestseller lists. But for all that, touring remains the largest and most important slice of this growing pie. It means big dollars for the big stars (GARTH BROOKS, the biggest in 1996, enjoyed sellouts for all 115 of his show dates that year, with gross sales of more than $33 million), survival and needed exposure for newer or midlevel acts.

The essence of country touring remains what MARTY ROBBINS described in the 1960s as the closest modern equivalent to the James boys in the Old West—ride into town, take the money, and ride out. But over these past seventy-plus years the road itself has changed, and so have the venues, those places where traveling performers have found their fans.

A few of the early country music personalities were showmen of the old school, who knew the entertainment business from its pre-electronic era, when it consisted almost entirely of live performing. One such act was OTTO GRAY and his cowboy orchestra; his few 1920s recordings were negligible, but he worked the vaudeville circuits for years and repeatedly got press notices in such entertainment trade papers as *Billboard* and *Variety*. UNCLE DAVE MACON worked mostly as a solo act, with an acceptance in southern theaters unheard of for most country acts. When he gave up his transportation company (hauling freight by wagons) for full-time entertainment, his many contacts came in handy. To book a tour, he'd just write letters to a few of his old friends and line up a supporting act or two to drive him around and share the profits.

Some future country stars (JIMMIE RODGERS, GENE AUTRY, and ROY ACUFF among them) learned their craft with itinerant showmen who barnstormed the country on flatbed trucks to put on minstrel or medicine shows and comedy revues. Rural music became a "business" at the same time the automobile and the open road first captured America's fancy, and since most bands were small and instruments few, the automobile was the preferred means of touring. Except over the worst of winter's roads, cars could generally take a hillbilly entourage anywhere it needed to be in a reasonable time. Trains, though always a favorite early subject of country songs, simply didn't run to most of the remote hamlets and their kerosene-lit schoolhouses, where in winter many of the earliest country shows were staged.

For all its privacy and convenience, touring by car could indeed be crowded, rushed, and dangerous. Besides the bad roads and the bad tires, bad tempers sometimes flared in such close quarters, often over such mundane matters as where to eat or where to bed down. In the Southwest and California, most country bands were larger, used more instruments, and carried early amplifiers and public address systems. Terrain and settlement patterns in those states meant greater distances between show dates but safer (straighter and flatter) highways. Hence it was in Texas and Oklahoma during the 1930s that country music's first tour buses (and even some airplanes) were used by pioneer western swing bands to cover their vast dance-hall circuits—BOB WILLS, MILTON BROWN (in 1936 country music's first major car wreck fatality), the LIGHT CRUST DOUGHBOYS, and others.

These last groups all had home base radio jobs, typical of the successful touring country artists. But for most country acts, radio spots and sponsors did not come easily, and most moved from station to station, working first one territory and then another, plugging show dates on the air. Station management knew what their performers were doing, and established "artist service bureaus" to help with tour booking and promotion (for a per-show fee). Stations with the most successful radio barn dances—WLS in Chicago and WSM in Nashville—kept such bureaus for years, though all hands soon discovered that radio spots alone were inadequate tour promotion. The indispensable on-site promotion was soon taken up by advance men using show posters, handbills, and local radio and newspaper ads. These earliest managers, promoters, and bookers were a mixed lot of honest, dishonest, and indifferent men; but in quest of profits, each made important contributions to the growth of country music's tour business.

Larry Sunbrock promoted all-country shows built around the ever-popular fiddle contest (CURLY FOX, Red Herron, CLAYTON MCMICHEN, or whomever against his regular, Natchee the Indian). But Sunbrock employed the disgraceful tactic of advertising acts he had not booked, then feigned innocence and bewilderment before the local officials and crowds when these acts (naturally) did not appear. OSCAR DAVIS also helped bring country shows into big-city auditoriums. A Rhode Island native whose promotion background included theaters, dance marathons, and walkathons, Davis was convinced by hillbilly radio musician "Happy" Hal Burns to take a chance promoting hillbilly PACKAGE SHOWS in the early 1940s, and their big Sunday "National Championship Hillbilly Jamborees" in such cities as Memphis, Birmingham, Little Rock, Dallas, and Nashville were usually great successes. At first they used such spacious good-weather sites as ballparks or fairgrounds, because many auditorium managers viewed hillbilly artists as unreliable drunks and resented country fans who spat on walls and stuck gum to chairs. But in nine shows during the summer of 1941, Davis's shows made $180,000, using talent such as Roy Acuff, the HOOSIER HOT SHOTS, and ERNEST TUBB, drawn from all parts of the country. That kind of money made a lot of auditorium managers change their minds, and after the war, Davis, the flamboyant "Baron" best known for his white-on-black newspaper ads and fast-talking radio spiels ("Don't You Dare Miss It!"), was booking Ernest Tubb and MINNIE PEARL regularly into 5,000-seat venues such as Detroit's Masonic Auditorium, and into CARNEGIE HALL itself in September 1947.

With civilian tires and autos out of production during World War II, the traveling tent show concept caught on at WSM, pioneered there by blackface comics JAMUP & HONEY in about 1940. David Wilds, son of Lee Davis "Honey" Wilds, remembers that "from the first of April to Labor Day we weren't in Nashville, we lived on the road in a forty-foot house trailer that was towed behind a Pontiac four-door. Anywhere from eight to ten trucks moved the whole thing around." By war's end WSM had several tent shows out at the same time, showcasing the station's growing stable of country talent. First opening in the Northeast and Midwest in the thirties and proliferating in the forties were popular open-air parks such as Sunset Park in West Grove, Pennsylvania, and Buck Lake Ranch in Angola, Indiana, which became regular stopping points for countless country acts over the next twenty-plus years. These were precursors to the weekend-long bluegrass festivals that became so popular after the mid-1960s.

Nationwide talent agencies soon began booking country acts: Jolly Joyce, American Corporation, MCA (Music Corporation of America, which booked its first big Bob Wills tour in November 1944), and William Morris (which booked Ernest Tubb for a 1947 theater tour). This growing business sophistication by the country artist was reflected in the growing number of personal managers, agents, bookers, traveling advance men, and charter pilots, usually clustered around the major radio stations. Some of the older crowd of agents stayed around for years, but a good many of the newer crop were former musicians who loved the music and knew the problems of the road firsthand, such as Frankie More, GABE TUCKER, HAL SMITH, and RANDY HUGHES. A. V. BAMFORD, booking talent out of Nashville, became famous for the huge sweep of his mapped-out tours. TOM PARKER, a former carney advance man from Florida who had helped J. L. FRANK and Oscar Davis promote country shows, signed in succession three choice managerial plums—EDDY ARNOLD, HANK SNOW, and ELVIS PRESLEY. All over the nation, promoters brought acts into their territories and/or developed local talent into national stars. Chief among these promoters were CONNIE B. GAY (Washington, D.C.), HAL HORTON (Dallas), JIM DENNY (Nashville), Cracker Jim Brooker (Miami), TILLMAN FRANKS (Shreveport), SI SIMAN (Springfield), and Ken Ritter (Beaumont and Houston).

The touring performers themselves hardly had time to sort out this burgeoning new business, but they tried. Back in from a hard week of touring for weekend broadcasts, artists exchanged information on the best venues, booking agencies, and road conditions. There was still an air of fun, informality, and cooperation about it all, but that was about to change.

In the mid-1950s came rock & roll, which posed a serious challenge to country music's survival. The tour business for the traditional country artists was hard hit, and one response was the "traveling package show" concept, akin to the older tent shows. The hope was that more names on the marquee would draw more customers. Something of this approach had been tried before with various traveling "caravans": the mixed country-pop entourages like R. J. Reynolds's CAMEL CARAVAN out of WSM in 1941–42 and Dudley LeBlanc's 1951 HADACOL CARAVAN, and one of the earliest all-country rolling tours, 1954's RCA VICTOR Country Caravan. In view of these precedents and a simultaneous competing free show, the PHILIP MORRIS COUNTRY SHOW (1957–58), WSM used the all-Opry, all-in-one touring-package show concept from 1957 until good times came again in the early 1960s. Today there is probably more corporate sponsorship of tours (Marlboro, Fruit of the Loom, Kraft) than ever before; R. J. Reynolds, Hadacol, and Philip Morris were the pioneers.

Better highways (resulting from federal legislation in 1956 that inaugurated the interstate system) and the newly customized tour bus (which could transport in comfort and safety an entire show) helped make the touring package show possible and soon became the preferred mode of travel for individual acts as well. PEE WEE KING, Ernest Tubb, HANK THOMPSON, Marty Robbins, and LESTER FLATT & EARL SCRUGGS were among the acts who pioneered the use of such tour buses. Nearly all of the touring stars of the 1960s and 1970s used buses built with some or all of the comforts of home: bunk beds, refrigerators, card tables, bathrooms, tape decks, record players, hot plates (later microwave ovens), and costume closets. By the 1980s these custom-made travel coaches sold for $300,000 to $350,000, but weren't bad buys: They could be leased out when not in use by the owner, and resold five or six years (and maybe 600,000 miles) later, often for a small profit. Fading by then were memories of country music's highway fatalities (Milton Brown, JOHNNY HORTON, IRA LOUVIN) and many near deaths (T. TOMMY CUTRER, BILL MONROE, Earl Scruggs, Roy Acuff).

While their bands traveled by car or bus, some stars personally preferred (and in some cases needed) the speed and convenience of the private plane. Minnie Pearl's husband, Henry Cannon, pioneered the practice of flying stars such as his wife and Hank Williams to show dates. Hank Thompson and LEON MCAULIFFE were early pilots; LEFTY FRIZZELL owned a plane at his peak; and ROY DRUSKY bought a plane after his first few hits a decade later. Earl Scruggs flew his own plane, as did talent agent Randy Hughes, and singer JIM REEVES. Hughes crashed in March 1963, killing himself and his better-known passengers PATSY CLINE, COWBOY COPAS, and HAWKSHAW HAWKINS; and Reeves, newly licensed at the time, died with his pianist Dean Manuel in 1964, trying (as Hughes had) to get home through bad weather. In 1980 CHARLEY PRIDE's plane landed safely in Dallas after a midair collision in which the other plane was not so lucky. And in 1991 most of REBA MCENTIRE's band perished when their flight struck a mountain moments after takeoff from the San Diego airport. Though major stars such as McEntire frequently use Learjets, the 1963–64 air tragedies for a time cemented the dominance of the custom tour bus, helped, too, by the completed interstate highways and the boom in quality motel construction.

Several trends, pronounced since about 1980, have transformed the world of country touring, which today is certainly bigger (more artists and more dollars) than ever. Travel is safer, the businessmen are generally more honest (less is left to reputation and word of mouth), and the whole process is more scientific and detailed, with little left to chance or improvisation. Road books, which detail a tour day by day, minute by minute, are the touring artist's bible. This growing professionalization of every aspect of touring is reflected in the increasing number of talent agencies, tour managers (the plotters and mappers), and road managers (the traveling advance and on-site people). There are even travel agents whose specialty is tour arrangement, from making the road books to mapping out hotel room locations for an entourage's convenience. In all these respects, country music touring in the 1980s and 1990s has differed little from the touring of rock music acts.

Country music shows now play to a worldwide audience since routine transoceanic flights increased during the 1960s—a far cry indeed from GENE AUTRY's 1939 triumphal ocean liner tour of Ireland, England, and Danzig (days before Hitler invaded). GRAND OLE OPRY acts first went to the Panama Canal Zone in 1942 and traveled to U.S. bases in Germany in 1949. Country acts first toured active war zones in Korea between 1951 and 1953 (GRANDPA JONES, ELTON BRITT, CAROLINA COTTON, Ernest Tubb, Hank Snow) and later visited Vietnam. In more peaceful times, some U.S. country stars have found abroad almost greater fame than at home. Jim Reeves first toured Europe with an RCA VICTOR group in 1957, and later toured South Africa twice, making a movie there on one trip. JOHNNY CASH and SLIM WHITMAN remain British favorites, and GEORGE HAMILTON IV, who once had his own BBC series, is one of the most popular of all U.S. entertainers in Continental Europe. In 1997 LEANN RIMES toured Australia, land of a thriving indigenous country music scene since the days of Jimmie Rodgers.

Here and abroad, the onstage product has changed in recent years. Popular now are concept tours—the "No Hats Tour" of MARTY STUART and TRAVIS TRITT, all-ladies tours, songwriter tours, tours to promote specific albums—and the mechanics and technology of a concert are considerably more complex. By the 1990s, many artists performing in larger arenas—DWIGHT YOAKAM, ALAN JACKSON, BROOKS & DUNN, and others—used big screens to bring music videos to the concert experience. Others, following the BARBARA MANDRELL and Reba McEntire approach, employed strobe lights, smoke, and choreography. Box-office blockbuster Garth Brooks is famous for rock-styled onstage acrobatics.

To mount such spectacles is no mean feat: In 1997, Brooks & Dunn and Reba McEntire teamed up for an eighty-five-city tour that required twenty trucks and nine buses to transport the forty tons of equipment and the hundred-person crew. In addition, the tour hired seventy-five to a hundred additional personnel on a show-by-show basis in each city the tour played.

None of this mounting prosperity and professionalization means that risk and failure have been eliminated from touring. Promoters still go out of business sometimes, and after a few years (fewer and fewer years, it now seems), artists lose some or all of their box-office appeal. Risk can never be banished, but with all these changes, much has been lost. Artist-fan contact is not as close as it was in the smaller venues, and the road, if not as dangerous for the artist, can't be as much fun either. The growing impersonality and "slickness" of the concert experience is one reason why Nashville's annual FAN FAIR has grown so tremendously from its 1972 inception: Fans don't generally get that sort of close contact at shows in their home areas. Early each June, Fan Fair brings to Nashville 25,000 or so of the nation's most dedicated country fans who see most of the stars as informally and personally as all fans once could near home, with autograph booths added to the concert experience.

Any way you choose to measure it, the distance is great from the schoolhouse kerosene lamps of the 1920s and 1930s to the strobe lights of today.

Uncle Tupelo

Uncle Tupelo began as an anomaly, only to become 1990s alternative country icons, the embodiment of yet another rock generation's embrace of its country roots. Natives of Belleville, Illinois—a depressed, blue-collar suburb east of St. Louis—lifelong friends Jay Farrar (b. December 26, 1966) and Jeff Tweedy (b. August 25, 1967) formed Uncle Tupelo in 1988 as an outlet for their shared passion for punk and traditional country music. Wedding these emotionally direct idioms could hardly have made Uncle Tupelo less fashionable amid the irony-besotted rock scene of the day.

Originally a trio featuring Farrar on guitar, Tweedy on bass—both men wrote and sang—and Mike Heidorn on drums, the band worked the midwestern club circuit for a couple of years before releasing its debut album in 1990. *No Depression* and its successor, *Still Feel Gone* (1991)—both issued on the independent Rockville label—won the band a cult following and accolades from the rock music press, including comparisons to the late GRAM PARSONS. Despite such critical hyperbole, Uncle Tupelo nonetheless displayed flashes of brilliance on its next two albums, the mostly acoustic *March 16–20, 1992* (Rockville, 1992) and the largely realized country-rock of *Anodyne* (Sire/Reprise, 1993).

Uncle Tupelo disbanded in 1994, with Farrar forming Son Volt and releasing a pair of albums for WARNER BROS. on which he drinks deeply of the wellspring of old-time country music. Meanwhile, Tweedy recruited drummer Ken Coomer and multi-instrumentalists John Stirratt and Max Johnston—all members of *Anodyne*-era Uncle Tupelo—and launched Wilco, a pop-rock outfit whose two albums on Reprise find Tweedy distancing himself from the alt-country of former bandmate Farrar.

Even if nothing in the catalogues of Uncle Tupelo, Son Volt, or Wilco matches Gram Parsons's best work, Farrar and Tweedy have, in their own way, exerted an influence on their generation comparable to that of Parsons in his day. Uncle Tupelo even inspired the creation of an online discussion folder dedicated to its music and legacy. The title track of the group's debut album, *No Depression*—a cover of an old CARTER FAMILY song—supplied the appellation for the online forum, itself a catalyst for the publication of a bimonthly magazine of the same name. Co-edited by founders Grant Alden and Peter Blackstock, *No Depression* has, since 1995, become the principal document of the alternative country movement of the 1990s.

—*Bill Friskics-Warren*

REPRESENTATIVE RECORDINGS

Uncle Tupelo: *Anodyne* (Sire/Reprise, 1993); Wilco: *A.M.* (Reprise, 1995); Son Volt: *Trace* (Warner Brothers, 1995)

Delia "Mom" Upchurch
b. Gainesboro, Tennessee, August 10, 1891; d. September 1, 1976

For more than twenty years after World War II, Delia "Mom" Upchurch operated a rooming home (as deliberately distinct from rooming house) for struggling country musicians in Nashville. The list of those who stayed in her home at 620 Boscobel Street reads like a street-level hall of fame for the early years in the Nashville country music industry—from rising stars such as CARL SMITH and FARON YOUNG, to famous session musicians such as LLOYD GREEN and BUDDY SPICHER, to legendary songwriters such as HANK COCHRAN and ROGER MILLER. Like Tootsie Bess and a few others, Upchurch came to be regarded as a den mother to the whole community. "They were coming into town with no money, no jobs, and no friends," she said. "They needed someone to give them a place to stay and sort of look after them until they got started. Someone to give them a home." For most rooms Upchurch charged less than ten dollars per week, and she would only rent to country performers. "They don't mix too good with people in other livelihoods," she explained. "And I just like good old hillbilly music."

Upchurch's first roomers were members of PEE WEE KING's Golden West Cowboys. They moved out, however, when her husband, Louis K. Upchurch, died on October 5, 1947. She spent nearly a year coming to terms with his death, then began taking in musicians anew, beginning with the CARTER FAMILY. By the 1950s her home was so well known as a pickers' crash pad that when someone needed a sideman for an upcoming session or tour they would call Mom's to see who was available. "Mom knew how long you were going to be out on tour, and if someone showed up while you were on the road, she had a habit of renting your bed out to them," recalled musician Howard White. Upchurch maintained her East Nashville rooming home into the late 1960s, by which time she was nearly eighty years old.

—*Daniel Cooper*

Urban Cowboy

The term "Urban Cowboy" first gained currency in the summer of 1980, with the release of the Paramount Pictures film *Urban Cowboy*, starring John Travolta and Debra

Urban Cowboy *movie poster*

Winger. The movie that gave a brief country music boom (1980–82) a name was inspired by a nonfiction article in *Esquire* by Aaron Latham ("The Ballad of the Urban Cowboy," September 12, 1978), and it was shot in 1979 at GILLEY's in Pasadena, Texas. The film became the surprise smash hit of 1980, elevating MICKEY GILLEY, JOHNNY LEE, and country music in general to the level of major national fads. Basically an oil-patch-and-trailer-park love story, directed by James Bridges from a screenplay by James Bridges and Aaron Latham, *Urban Cowboy* put a cowboy hat and a Lone Star beer stamp on the American postdisco singles scene that was desperate for a new identity.

The double-LP soundtrack album on Asylum/Full Moon Records featured country-tinged rock artists such as the EAGLES, LINDA RONSTADT, and Bonnie Raitt alongside Mickey Gilley and Johnny Lee. It gave Lee his first #1 country hit—as well as a #5 pop hit—with the movie theme "Lookin' for Love (In All the Wrong Places)." The soundtrack quickly exceeded the million sales mark, and Lee's *Lookin' for Love* album went gold also. Country music got a huge sales boost, nearly doubling its previous high-water mark with $250 million in sales, and by 1981 country was the top-selling genre in America.

Boots, blue jeans, and cowboy garb became the look of the day as dance clubs switched overnight from disco to the cotton-eyed joe. The demand for mechanical bulls was so great that manufacturers couldn't keep up with orders. Most importantly for the art form, country music suddenly had access to adult contemporary (AC) radio.

Perhaps it was the last throes of the NASHVILLE SOUND, but Nashville became so enamored of pop crossover records that it abandoned its southern, rural, working-class roots and promoted a class of AC-ready recording acts typified by JANIE FRICKE, SYLVIA, RAZZY BAILEY, EARL THOMAS CONLEY, T. G. SHEPPARD, and others rising to fame in that era. All of the above had #1 radio hits. Sylvia and Fricke enjoyed a brief flash of gold and platinum record sales, but the Urban Cowboy crossover music devolved into a hybrid misfire, neither good pop nor good country, ultimately failing to satisfy either country or adult contemporary fans.

By 1983 the country sales bubble had burst, with country records sales falling back to previous levels, but it took Nashville a few years to understand that such neotraditionalists as GEORGE STRAIT, RICKY SKAGGS, and RANDY TRAVIS would be its salvation. In January 1985 *Variety* ran the front-page headline "Country Music Sales Turn Sour" and declared "The Urban Cowboy is definitely buried in boot hill." Of all the stars who rose in what is now known as the Urban Cowboy era, only the least identified with pop-crossover mania—ALABAMA—remained a potent force on radio and record racks in the 1990s.   —*Bob Millard*

REPRESENTATIVE RECORDING

Urban Cowboy: Original Soundtrack (Asylum/Full Moon, 1980)

The Vagabonds
Curtis "Curt" Poulton b. Dulaney, West Virginia, 1907
Dean Upson b. November 12, 1900; d. October 1975
Herald Goodman b. August 8, 1900; d. March 1974

Although the Vagabonds were active in country music and on the GRAND OLE OPRY for only four years (1931–34), this smooth-singing vocal trio had a major impact on the Opry and its fans. They were one of the first full-time professional groups to appear on the show, and they were one of the first to publish their own songbooks and establish their own record company. Opry founder JUDGE GEORGE D. HAY referred to them as the first non-southern group on the show, for the group rose to fame in the Midwest. A key member, Curt Poulton, however, was a native of Dulaney, West Virginia.

The trio was formed in 1927 by recent Otterbein College graduates—Dean Upson, brother Paul Upson, and friend Robert Dugan—in Chicago, where they appeared on WLS as a pop and novelty group called the Three Hired Men. A few months later they changed their name to the Vagabonds. They soon made their first records with Charley Straight's orchestra. By 1929 the group had replaced Paul Upson and Dugan with Poulton and Herald Goodman, and had moved to KMOX–St. Louis, which had a fifty-six-station hookup with NBC. Forming their own radio production company, the group broadened their repertoire to include more folk and old-time songs and thus were able to program a greater variety of shows for their radio sponsors. This trend was accelerated when WSM manager HARRY STONE hired them in August 1931 for both pop and country programs, including the Grand Ole Opry.

Unlike many Opry regulars, the Vagabonds were hired as WSM staff musicians, and this gave them more time to develop their own songwriting and publicity. The smooth-singing, pop-influenced trio soon had a huge hit in "When

It's Lamp-Lighting Time in the Valley" and issued their own songbook, *Old Cabin Songs of the Fiddle and Bow.* They sold their book by mail and had to reprint it six times in months due to its success.

In January 1933 the group made a series of custom recordings they sold under their own label, Old Cabin—the first record label to come out of Nashville. A few months later they began recording for Victor's BLUEBIRD label, eventually amassing some thirty-two sides, most of which were either originals or current Tin Pan Alley pieces. After their split in 1934, caused by personal problems and intragroup disputes, Goodman went to Tulsa, Oklahoma, to start KVOO's *Saddle Mountain Roundup* barn dance in 1939. Upson served briefly as head of WSM's booking department in the mid-1940s and then became commercial manager for Shreveport's station KWKH, where he helped to found the LOUISIANA HAYRIDE. Curt Poulton remained to work at WSM for several years, as a soloist and later with the DELMORE BROTHERS.

—*Charles Wolfe*

Leroy Van Dyke

b. Spring Fork, Missouri, October 4, 1929

Velvet-voiced country crooner Leroy Van Dyke had only three Top Ten country hits—and they were his first hits on the charts: "The Auctioneer," a 1956 DOT RECORDS release he co-wrote about his uncle; KENDALL HAYES's bouncy cheating song, "Walk On By," was #1 for nineteen weeks on *Billboard*'s country chart and the strikingly similar follow-up, "If a Woman Answers (Hang Up the Phone)" (#3, 1962). All were pop crossover hits as well.

The son of livestock breeder Frank Van Dyke and Mother Irene, Leroy graduated from the University of Missouri, where he studied journalism and animal husbandry. He also attended livestock auctioneer school in Decatur, Illinois.

Van Dyke served in army intelligence during the Korean War. Following discharge, he performed three years on the OZARK JUBILEE in Springfield, Missouri, and appeared on Arthur Godfrey's CBS-TV broadcasts. After recording with Dot Records from 1956 to 1958, Van Dyke moved on to MERCURY RECORDS, where he recorded his two biggest hits, "Walk On By" and "If a Woman Answers (Hang Up the Phone)," and where he had the bulk of his chart success. He remained with Mercury to 1968.

Darkly handsome, Van Dyke helped usher in a new era of sophisticated country entertainers. He was among the first to perform in tux at posh nightspots such as Playboy Clubs. Grammy-nominated for "Walk On By," he became a big draw in Las Vegas.

In February 1966 his five-year-old son, Ray Leroy, fell through thin ice near his Nashville home and drowned. In the 1967 movie *What Am I Bid?* Van Dyke had a starring role; unfortunately, the low-budget project failed to generate further film offers. Van Dyke continued to place hits on the lower rungs of the country charts through 1977 with recordings for WARNER BROS., KAPP, DECCA, and ABC. In 1989 he moved back to Missouri and performs frequently in BRANSON, MISSOURI.

—*Walt Trott*

REPRESENTATIVE RECORDINGS

Leroy Van Dyke's Greatest Hits (MCA, 1972); *The Original Auctioneer* (Bear Family, 1987); *Walk On By* (Mercury, 1995)

Townes Van Zandt

b. Fort Worth, Texas, March 7, 1944; d. January 1, 1997

An enigmatic, mysterious, compelling troubadour, John Townes Van Zandt virtually defined the term "cult figure" and was a modern link to the wandering minstrel tradition of early bluesmen, WOODY GUTHRIE, and "Ramblin'" Jack Elliott. Born into a well-to-do Texas oil family, Van Zandt spent several weeks during his teenage years in a mental hospital, diagnosed as a manic depressive with schizophrenic tendencies. For much of his life he lived at no fixed address, preferring the road. Influenced by Lightning Hopkins, HANK WILLIAMS, and BOB DYLAN, Van Zandt began in Texas folk clubs in the mid-sixties. MICKEY NEWBURY brought him to Nashville to make his first album, *For the Sake of the Song,* in 1968.

His commercial success was limited due to inconsistent artist management, personal problems, and because his work was issued exclusively by small labels. But Van Zandt's reputation among other songwriters is immense: He has been cited as a major influence by GUY CLARK, STEVE EARLE, NANCI GRIFFITH, LYLE LOVETT, RODNEY CROWELL, ROBERT EARL KEEN, the Cowboy Junkies, HAL KETCHUM, and countless others. *Billboard* magazine referred to him as "the Van Gogh of lyrics," apt because his vibrant poetic imagery recalls the finest expressionist painters.

His best-known songs include "Pancho & Lefty" (recorded by MERLE HAGGARD & WILLIE NELSON), "If I Needed You" (DON WILLIAMS & EMMYLOU HARRIS), and "Tecumseh Valley" (Nanci Griffith, STEVE EARLE).

Van Zandt released fifteen albums in his lifetime, the last, 1995's *No Deeper Blue,* recorded in Ireland. He died of a heart attack at home in Mount Juliet, Tennessee.

—*John Lomax III*

REPRESENTATIVE RECORDINGS

High, Low and in Between (Poppy, 1971; Rhino, 1993); *The Late Great Townes Van Zandt* (Tomato, 1973; Rhino, 1993); *Live at the Old Quarter, Houston, Texas* (Tomato, 1977)

James D. Vaughan

b. Giles County, Tennessee, December 14, 1864; d. February 9, 1941

James David Vaughan was a pioneer gospel songwriter, publisher, and promoter whose work had a major impact on early country music. During the early years of the twentieth century he emerged as the nation's most successful publisher of paperback, shape-note gospel songbooks; he also popularized the idea of the gospel quartet, the use of gospel music on radio and records, and the use of his native South as a center for his musical endeavors.

Shortly after the Civil War, southern gospel music began to emerge from a central location in the Shenandoah Valley of Virginia, under the aegis of the Reubush-Kieffer Company. One of its leading teachers and composers, E. T. Hildebrand, took on young Vaughan as an apprentice and schooled him in songwriting and in how to run music schools. After an abortive stay in Texas, where he ran his own music schools, Vaughan returned to Tennessee, settling in Lawrenceburg in 1902.

However, prior to that, in 1900, he had decided to issue his own songbook, *Gospel Chimes,* and its success guaranteed a series of sequels. By 1909 he had sold some 30,000 songbooks in one year, and by 1910 his figures were double that. He soon hit upon the idea of having workers from his office (in Lawrenceburg) travel across the country as quartets, singing samples from the new books for local churches. This promotion worked so well that the churches soon began to appreciate the quartets more than the songs, and by the 1930s some of the quartets were breaking away to go on their own. Two of the best known were the Speer Family and the John Daniel Quartet, the latter finding fame on the GRAND OLE OPRY.

Vaughan quartets recorded for major labels such as Victor, BRUNSWICK, and Paramount, but Vaughan also started his own record company, Vaughan Records. In 1922 it became the first southern-based record company. He also started the first radio station in Tennessee, WOAN, to broadcast his music.

His various schools of music were training grounds for a number of important country musicians, including the DELMORE BROTHERS and SAM AND KIRK MCGEE. By the 1930s his songs were being widely heard on radio and records. "I Need the Prayers of Those I Love" was a hit by the Delmores and by other duets. "What Would You Give in Exchange (For Your Soul?)" was learned directly from a Vaughan book by BILL AND CHARLIE MONROE. "No Depression in Heaven" was one of a number of Vaughan songs adapted by the CARTER FAMILY.

At his heyday in the 1920s, Vaughan was publishing two new songbooks a year and promoting them with related recordings. The Depression, as well as increasing competition from new outfits such as STAMPS-BAXTER, cut into his sales. In addition, Vaughan's own death in 1941 robbed the company of its leader. But his tradition survived, and as late as the 1990s Vaughan songbooks were still being published by the Church of God Publishing Company in Cleveland, Tennessee.
—*Charles Wolfe*

Victor Talking Machine Company (*see* RCA Victor Records)

Videos (*see* Music Videos)

Jim Vienneau
b. Albany, New York, September 18, 1926

During twenty-six years at MGM RECORDS, James Vienneau helped bring CONWAY TWITTY, Mark Dinning, Sandy Posey, and MARVIN RAINWATER to the label, and he also produced Connie Francis, the Gentrys, BOB LUMAN, SHEB WOOLEY, MEL TILLIS, and HANK WILLIAMS JR. A former insurance broker, James Vienneau was more than happy to follow his uncle FRANK WALKER into the music industry, joining MGM in 1955. Walker was head of MGM and later vice president of its parent company, Loews, Inc.

As a producer, Vienneau was generally praised for electronically teaming HANK WILLIAMS SR. and Jr. on the 1965 LP *Father & Son* but rankled purists by posthumously overdubbing drums and strings onto early Hank Williams tracks, producing four "modernized" albums, including *The Legend Lives Anew* (July 1966). Until he moved his family to Nashville in 1965, Vienneau commuted from his home on Long Island. He encouraged pop stars such as Connie Francis to make the trip and record in Nashville. After departing MGM, he worked briefly with Mike Curb to establish a 20th Century-Fox record label, a less than successful venture. In 1982 Vienneau joined the ACUFF-ROSE

music publishing firm. When Opryland Music Group took over the catalogue, Vienneau joined OMG to work in its creative department.
—*Walt Trott*

The Village Barn
established in New York, New York, October 1929

For more than twenty years, the Village Barn offered club-hopping New Yorkers a curious taste of rural Americana. Located at 52 West Eighth Street in Manhattan's Greenwich Village, the 250-seat nightspot sported a farmyard decor, complete with a live, caged rooster. Its floor show mixed western singers, country performers, novelty acts, vaudeville hoofers, and low comics with ballroom dance bands. Between sets, audiences participated in square dances, musical chairs, and hobby horse and sack races.

Opened by Meyer Horowitz in October 1929, the Village Barn was a springboard for diverse young talent, including hillbilly comedians Anne, Zeke, and JUDY CANOVA, novelty jazz composer Raymond Scott, and pop vocalist Helen O'Connell. Established country or western performers who played there included Zeke Manners, PATSY MONTANA & THE PRAIRIE RAMBLERS, ROSALIE ALLEN, ESMERELDY, RED RIVER DAVE, TEXAS JIM ROBERTSON, CAPTAIN STUBBY & THE BUCCANEERS, and comedian RED INGLE. On May 28, 1948, the Village Barn launched a weekly remote that NBC fed to its television affiliates on the East Coast and eventually the Midwest. The show, which ran for two years, inspired a 1949 low-budget feature film, also called *Village Barn*. On March 25, 1953, Horowitz replaced the club's rustic entertainment policy with a "Gay Nineties" revue.
—*Dave Samuelson*

VOA (*see* The Voice of America)

Vogue Records
established in Detroit, Michigan, 1945

Vogue Records was founded by Tom Saffady, a twenty-nine-year-old Detroit industrialist. Saffady's goal was to invent an unbreakable and unwarpable record that was pleasing to the eye. After years of research, he introduced a picture disc that used a central core of aluminum as a base on which the picture was placed, sealed with a clear-vinyl coating, and then impressed with recorded grooves. The Vogue plant was located near downtown Detroit, while maintaining studios in both Detroit and Chicago. Vogue's general manager was Al Lynas, who arranged sessions, talent, and distributorship, while Seymour Simons served as A&R chief in charge of selecting talent, and songs.

The first Vogue releases went on sale in May 1946 and retailed for $1.05 each, when standard records were selling at 50 cents each. Each disc had multicolored illustrations to represent the song title. Out of the company's sixty-six total releases of mostly popular tunes, six discs contained country music. Veteran performers LULU BELLE & SCOTTY recorded three records, and PATSY MONTANA recorded one. The remaining two discs contained songs by the Downhomers, Nancy Lee & the Hilltoppers, and Judy & Jen. Unfortunately, the Vogue label was not successful, and by August 1947 the company had entered bankruptcy. The files and recording masters were later destroyed, although the records themselves still exist in the hands of collectors and in the archives of the Country Music Foundation (CMF). —*Don Roy*

The Voice of America

The Voice of America holds a broadcasting achievement of historical significance similar to that of WSM in Nashville and WLS in Chicago in the 1920s and 1930s: It has made country music widely available to new audiences who have never heard it before. While those radio stations made the music available at the national level, VOA has been a major force in the development of the international popularity of country music. With its mandate to "tell the world about America," VOA broadcasts country music to approximately 130 million listeners over shortwave transmissions as well as AM and FM radio.

Since 1985, VOA's showcase program, *Country Music USA,* has been hosted by VOA Music Director Judy Massa. Interviews with country artists are an important part of the program format, and this allows VOA to provide something that foreign stations do not—in-depth conversations with artists talking about their music. Massa also has taught the world about the music through the presentation of spe-

cial theme shows, such as a ten-part series about country music instruments, and broadcasts of live concerts. She traveled to the Soviet Union with ROY CLARK in 1988 and broadcast live from Moscow; toured Europe with GARTH BROOKS in 1994 and reported live on that historic tour; covered the Country Gold Festival in Japan; judged international music festivals in Kazakhstan and Bulgaria; and conducted audiovisual seminars on American country music in four cities in China (Chengdu, Shanghai, Beijing, and Guangzhou) in 1993. She has also held special contests for her listeners, with the winner traveling to Washington, D.C., and Nashville. In 1994 Massa was the recipient of the CMA's Media Achievement Award.

Of all the music broadcast worldwide by VOA, country music is ranked first in overall popularity among its listeners, many of whom live in parts of the world where country music records are not even sold and where VOA serves as the sole source for this music. —*Barbara Pruett*

REPRESENTATIVE RECORDINGS

Although there are no commercial recordings available, there is a substantial archive collection of VOA broadcasts available at the Library of Congress, which serves as a repository for VOA's programs.

W·W·W · W·W·W

Porter Wagoner
b. Howell County, Missouri, August 12, 1927

Noted for his onstage jokes, blond pompadour, rhinestone-studded stage wardrobe, and controversial partnership with DOLLY PARTON, Porter Wagoner has become one of country music's elder statesmen in the 1990s. His eighty-one chart records include several country standards, and his television performing since 1955 has culminated in his hosting TNN's *Opry Backstage*, starting in 1992. In the wake of ROY ACUFF's death in November 1992, Wagoner became the unofficial spokesman for the GRAND OLE OPRY.

Wagoner was born in an Ozark Mountains region of Missouri steeped in ancient English balladry. A farm boy, he moved with his family to West Plains, Missouri, where he married in 1946. He formed the Blue Ridge Boys bluegrass band and by 1950 was singing over local radio (KWPM) out of a butcher shop where he cut meat.

Wagoner's big break came when Springfield, Missouri, radio station KWTO hired him in 1951. He signed with RCA RECORDS in 1952, but because his early records didn't

sell well, Wagoner committed himself to a hard-traveling career of playing schoolhouses for gate proceeds only. His act was billed as the Porter Wagoner Trio, with Don Warden on steel guitar and Herschel "Speedy" Haworth on rhythm guitar.

Wagoner's "Trademark," co-written with Gary Walker, went to #2 for CARL SMITH in 1953, and Wagoner's hits penned by other writers, such as "Company's Comin'" (#7, 1954–55) and "A Satisfied Mind" (#1, 1955), kept him on RCA. Wagoner was an early mainstay on the *OZARK JUBILEE* ABC television show (1955–56), but he moved to Nashville with his wife and three children in 1956 and joined the Grand Ole Opry the following year.

In 1960 Wagoner was invited by the Chattanooga Medicine Company to front a syndicated television show. Immediately he broadened his act, adding comedian SPECK RHODES, singer NORMA JEAN, and eventually BUCK TRENT (banjo), Mack Magaha (fiddle), and George McCormick (guitar). The show featured celebrities such as TEX RITTER and COWBOY COPAS, plus newcomers such as WILLIE NELSON and WAYLON JENNINGS. The program ran an impressive two decades, ending in 1981.

As the TV show's reach expanded into nearly one hundred markets, with over three million viewers, Wagoner ran up a string of hits that included "Misery Loves Company" (#1, 1962), "I've Enjoyed As Much of This As I Can Stand" (#7, 1962–1963), "Sorrow on the Rocks" (#5, 1964), "Green, Green Grass of Home" (#4, 1965), "Skid Row Joe" (#3, 1965–1966), "The Cold Hard Facts of Life" (#2, 1967), and "The Carroll County Accident" (#2, 1969). Unlike some of his colleagues, he utilized but never pandered to the NASHVILLE SOUND, and never traded his flashy rhinestone suits for tuxedos. The versatile performer also won three Grammys for sacred recordings with the Blackwood Brothers (1966, 1967, and 1969).

In 1967 Dolly Parton replaced Norma Jean in the show's cast and began recording duets with Wagoner, including fourteen Top Ten hits and one #1, "Please Don't Stop Loving Me" (1974). Wagoner was their de facto producer-arranger on thirteen duet albums, and he also supervised Parton's RCA solo output during this same period. While she eventually outshone Wagoner on the charts, he nevertheless prospered from his tireless efforts in building her career. Although Parton's departure from the show in mid-decade led to angry words and legal action, the two eventually resolved their differences.

Wagoner's post-Parton career upheld his innovative, persistently upbeat persona. He brought James Brown to the Grand Ole Opry, produced r&b sessions for Joe Si-

Porter Wagoner

mon, appeared in the Clint Eastwood film *Honkytonk Man* (1982), and served as an OPRYLAND tourist ambassador in the 1990s. As of early 1998, he continues to co-host (with BILL ANDERSON) the pre-Grand Ole Opry TV show *Opry Backstage*. —*Steve Eng*

REPRESENTATIVE RECORDINGS

Confessions of a Broken Man (RCA, 1966); *The Cold Hard Facts of Life* (RCA, 1967); *The Carroll County Accident* (RCA, 1969); *When I Sing for Him* (P&J Productions, 1979); *Porter Wagoner—The Thin Man from the* [sic] *West Plains—RCA Sessions 1952–1962* (Bear Family, 1993), 4 discs

Jimmy Wakely

b. Mineola, Arkansas, February 16, 1914; d. September 23, 1982

At the height of his career in the 1940s and 1950s, James Clarence Wakely was one of the most prominent West Coast country music performers, with starring roles in movies and on network radio and TV, in addition to a string of big pop crossover hits.

He grew up in Oklahoma and began his professional career in 1937 when he began playing piano with Merle Salathiel (later known as Merle Lindsay) and his Barnyard Boys, and also had a fifteen-minute morning radio show on radio station KTOK. In the summer of 1937 he traveled with the Little Doc Roberts' Medicine Show. Wakely soon began performing on station WKY with a trio called the Bell Boys, a group he eventually reorganized as the Jimmy Wakely Trio.

In the 1940s Wakely and his Trio were regulars on GENE AUTRY's *Melody Ranch* show on CBS network radio. Simultaneously, Wakely began recording for DECCA RECORDS and embarked on a film career, eventually starring in twenty-eight movies and appearing in seventy. He later enjoyed a successful recording career at CAPITOL RECORDS, where he is credited with introducing cheating songs to country music with his 1948 recordings of "One Has My Name, the Other Has My Heart" and "Slipping Around" (a duet with pop singer Margaret Whiting), which hit #1 on both the country and pop charts in 1949. Between 1948 and 1951 he placed twenty-three hits on the country charts, thirteen of which crossed over to the pop charts as well.

In the 1950s and 1960s Wakely appeared on a number of country music television shows, including *Five Star Jubilee* and the *Hollywood Barndance,* which became the *Jimmy Wakely Show*. He continued to perform on a limited basis during the 1970s, often with his children Johnny and Linda Lee. He died in Mission Hills, California, in 1982. —*Charlie Seemann*

REPRESENTATIVE RECORDING

Jimmy Wakely: Vintage Collection (Capitol, 1996)

Bill Walker

b. Sydney, New South Wales, Australia, April 28, 1937

Arranger-conductor William Alfred Walker popularized written, note-for-note arrangements in the Nashville studios of the 1960s. Studio musicians and vocalists had relied mostly on "head" arrangements, but Walker—educated at the Sydney Conservatory—wrote precise, elegant arrangements that further stylized the lush NASHVILLE SOUND. By the late 1960s Walker became Nashville's busiest arranger-conductor.

Before arriving in Nashville, Walker worked for RCA VICTOR's South African franchise and produced one of JIM REEVES's 1963 Johannesburg sessions. Consequently Reeves invited Walker to work for him in Nashville, but, sadly, he arrived on the weekend of Reeves's fatal plane crash in 1964. EDDY ARNOLD employed Walker instead, and through 1968 Walker helped fashion Arnold's uptown, career-rejuvenating musical style.

In the 1970s Walker produced various country acts for his Con Brio label, and independently produced DONNA FARGO's "The Happiest Girl in the Whole U.S.A."—1972's COUNTRY MUSIC ASSOCIATION Song of the Year. Hits featuring Walker's arranging and conducting include Eddy Arnold's "Make the World Go Away" (1965), JOHNNY CASH's "Sunday Morning Coming Down" (1970), and ROY CLARK's "Come Live with Me" (1973). In 1968 Walker joined Cash's network television show as music director, and since, his name has appeared on dozens of Nashville television productions. Today he is the music director of the STATLER BROTHERS' TNN show. —*Michael Streissguth*

Billy Walker

b. Ralls, Texas, January 14, 1929

In a very real sense, the career of Billy Marvin Walker epitomized the changes that overtook country music over a thirty-year period. Starting out with Texas honky-tonk music, he flirted with rock & roll, then went to Nashville just as the NASHVILLE SOUND was a phrase on everyone's lips. Along the way, Walker has both made and witnessed history. He was at HANK WILLIAMS's last show and at ELVIS PRESLEY's first major public appearance. He sat around waiting to record while BUDDY HOLLY was finishing a session in Clovis, New Mexico, and just narrowly missed boarding the plane on which PATSY CLINE, COWBOY COPAS, and HAWKSHAW HAWKINS died.

Walker was inspired by GENE AUTRY to take up music. After getting out of school in 1947, he worked various day jobs before fronting for COLUMBIA artist Jimmy Lawson in 1948. He joined the *BIG D JAMBOREE* in Dallas (where he was billed as the Traveling Texan and performed in a Lone Ranger mask) and worked for HANK THOMPSON in Waco. It was Thompson who got him his first contract, with CAPITOL RECORDS, in 1949. Eighteen months later, Walker switched to Columbia. Several of the early Columbia records, particularly "Anything Your Heart Desires" and the cover version of "Mexican Joe," sold well without charting. The first charted hit was "Thank You for Calling" in 1954.

Walker joined the *LOUISIANA HAYRIDE* in 1952, then went to the *OZARK JUBILEE* in Springfield, Missouri, in 1954. He flirted with rock & roll, and then, in November 1958, returned to Texas to work the country bar circuit. In 1959 he moved to Nashville to join the GRAND OLE OPRY. His records then began charting with more regularity. Walker's original version of "Funny How Time Slips Away" only got up to #23, but the follow-up, "Charlie's Shoes," became Walker's first and only #1 hit, in April 1962. It wasn't until the 1960s that he came into his own, and he continued to chart regularly into the late 1980s.

Walker's records were very much a reflection of changing times and production values. He recorded western-influenced songs such as "Cross the Brazos at Waco" and "Matamoros," country versions of pop songs such as "Ramona," and even tried some of the self-consciously poetic songs that were in vogue in the early 1970s. He left Colum-

Billy Walker

bia in 1965, joined MONUMENT, and then went with MGM in 1970. From that point, he was on RCA (1974–77), and then several smaller labels. His last chart records were on his own label, Tall Texan, in 1988. —*Colin Escott*

REPRESENTATIVE RECORDING

Cross the Brazos at Waco (Bear Family, 1993), 6 CDs

Charlie Walker

b. Copeville, Texas, November 2, 1926

Charles Levi Walker came from the cotton fields of Dallas County, Texas, to become one of country music's most popular disc jockeys and then one of its best shuffle-beat honky-tonk singers. A singer-guitarist with BILL BOYD's Cowboy Ramblers in Dallas from 1943 to 1944, Walker also worked daily remote broadcasts from Sellers Studio to Corpus Christi and other Texas outlets. With the Eighth Army Signal Corps in the Tokyo occupation forces, Walker became the first to broadcast country music to fellow soldiers in the Orient. Discharged in 1947, Walker and his band the Texas Ramblers performed in and around Corpus Christi for several years.

Moving to San Antonio in 1951, Walker became KMAC's country disc jockey and built an enormous listenership with great records and great antics: His sign-on was "This is ol' poke salad, cotton-picking, boll-pulling, corn-shucking, snuff-dipping Charlie Walker." On DECCA RECORDS (1954–56) after a short previous stint with IMPERIAL, Walker had a regional hit, "Tell Her Lies and Feed Her Candy," and his first charted record, "Only You, Only You" (1956). PAPPY DAILY next signed Walker to MERCURY, but it was a chance with COLUMBIA RECORDS (thanks to RAY PRICE) that made possible Walker's first big hit, "Pick Me Up on Your Way Down" (1958), which helped introduce the popular shuffle beat to country music.

Walker remained San Antonio's top country disc jockey

while building his own touring and recording career with a few widely spaced honky-tonk hits: "Who Will Buy the Wine" (1960), "Wild as a Wildcat" (1965), and "Don't Squeeze My Sharmon" (1967). The popularity of the latter convinced Walker (a top-notch golfer as well) to move to Nashville and join the GRAND OLE OPRY, where he remains a member, its staunchest exponent of honky-tonk and western swing styles. Walker portrayed HAWKSHAW HAWKINS in the 1985 film biography of PATSY CLINE, *Sweet Dreams.*
—*Ronnie Pugh*

REPRESENTATIVE RECORDING

Texas Gold (Plantation, 1979)

Cindy Walker

b. Mart, Texas, July 20, 1918

Perhaps the finest female composer in country music history, Cindy Walker became a charter member of the Nashville Songwriters Hall of Fame in 1970 and was elected to the COUNTRY MUSIC HALL OF FAME in 1997. Renowned for her ability to tailor songs for diverse stylists, she has had Top Ten hits during each of the past five decades. Her credits include such country standards as "Cherokee Maiden" and "You Don't Know Me."

Walker's grandfather F. P. Eiland was a hymnwriter of note ("Hold to God's Unchanging Hand"), and her mother, Oree, was an accomplished pianist. After appearing in Texas stage shows, Walker traveled to Hollywood. She successfully pitched tunes to Bing Crosby, landed a 1941 DECCA contract, filmed the first Soundie musical short ("Seven Beers with the Wrong Man," 1941), and scored a Top Ten singing hit ("When My Blue Moon Turns to Gold Again," 1944).

Walker had a star's looks, but set aside her performing career to concentrate on composing. Autry popularized

Cindy Walker

her "Blue Canadian Rockies," AL DEXTER sang "Triflin' Gal," and the Ames Brothers did "China Doll." One of her regular California customers was BOB WILLS, for whom she wrote more than fifty numbers, including "Cherokee Maiden," "Bubbles in My Beer," and "You're From Texas." ERNEST TUBB also relied on her, recording "Warm Red Wine," "Two Glasses Joe," and "Hey Mr. Bluebird," among others.

In 1954 Walker returned to Texas (Mexia) and thereafter divided her time between the town of Mexia and Nashville. Her 1950s classics include EDDY ARNOLD's "You Don't Know Me" and "Take Me in Your Arms and Hold Me," HANK SNOW's "The Gold Rush Is Over" and "The Next Voice You Hear," GEORGE MORGAN's "I Love Everything About You," WEBB PIERCE's "I Don't Care," and JIM REEVES's "Anna Marie."

In the 1960s ROY ORBISON's "Dream Baby (How Long Must I Dream)," Jim Reeves's "Distant Drums," Jerry Wallace's "In the Misty Moonlight," JACK GREENE's "You Are My Treasure," SONNY JAMES's "Heaven Says Hello," Wilma Burgess's "Fifteen Days," and STONEWALL JACKSON's "Leona" all became sizable Walker songwriting hits.

GLEN CAMPBELL, RICKY SKAGGS, RAY CHARLES, LACY J. DALTON, RIDERS IN THE SKY, MICKEY GILLEY, and MERLE HAGGARD are among those who kept her songwriting legacy alive in subsequent decades. Ill health and the death of her accompanist mother in 1991 slowed Walker in the 1990s

—*Robert K. Oermann*

REPRESENTATIVE RECORDING

Words & Music by Cindy Walker (Monument, 1964)

Clay Walker

b. Beaumont, Texas, August 19, 1969

After MARK CHESNUTT and TRACY BYRD, Earnest Clayton Walker was the third singer to emerge from the fertile Beaumont, Texas, country scene in as many years when he debuted in 1993. His career started with quick radio success as his first two singles, "What's It to You" and "Live Until I Die," both hit #1.

Walker grew up on an eighty-acre spread in southeastern Texas informally called "Walkerville." He learned music from his father—a welder who started teaching him guitar at age nine—and his uncle, who in turn had been taught by their father, a professional country singer. Walker attended high school in nearby Vidor, where he played basketball with Tracy Byrd.

Walker began playing professionally at sixteen. He briefly worked as his own manager, agent, music director, and accountant, and he studied business in college with an eye toward becoming his own lawyer as well. Among the venues he played regularly were Beaumont's Neon Armadillo and GEORGE JONES's Jones Country theme park.

Walker signed with GIANT RECORDS, and his first single, "What's It to You," was released in July 1993. Radio warmed to Walker's records from the outset: His first two albums, both of which sold more than 1 million copies, yielded five chart-topping singles, including "Dreaming with My Eyes Open," "If I Could Make a Living," and "This Woman and This Man." During this time he was the most successful artist on Giant's roster and helped give the still young label a significant presence in country music. His hits since then have included "Who Needs You Baby" (#2, 1995) and "Hypnotize the Moon" (#2, 1996), the title track from his

Clay Walker

third platinum-selling album. In 1996 he revealed his recent diagnosis of multiple sclerosis, maintaining that the disease was currently no hindrance to his career.

—*Brian Mansfield*

REPRESENTATIVE RECORDINGS

Clay Walker (Giant, 1993); *If I Could Make a Living* (Giant, 1994); *Hypnotize the Moon* (Giant, 1995); *Rumor Has It* (Giant, 1997)

Frank Walker

b. Fly Summit, New York, October 24, 1889; d. October 15, 1963

For all that he accomplished as a music business executive, Frank B. Walker's reputation rests on the basis of two signings, Bessie Smith and HANK WILLIAMS. It might be fairer, though, to see him as one of the industry's last generalists who knew every facet of the business.

After finishing school in upstate New York, he worked in banking in Albany and New York until 1916. He went into the navy that year and remained there until February 1, 1919. A navy officer found him a job at COLUMBIA RECORDS, where he learned record manufacturing. Then he borrowed $60,000 to buy a controlling interest in the Central Concert Company of Detroit, which booked Enrico Caruso and others. Walker stayed until 1921, when he sold his share and went back to work for Columbia as an A&R man. One of his first assignments was to make field recordings. He traveled throughout the South and later said he would ride horses back into the woods in search of a performer someone had told him about. He would often sell records on his junkets by renting a storefront for a day. Among the country artists he discovered were RILEY PUCKETT, GID TANNER, CHARLIE POOLE, and CLARENCE ASHLEY.

Early in his Columbia career, Walker also took the initiative to sign blues singer Bessie Smith. The precise circumstances are unclear, but it appears that he sent composer and arranger Clarence Williams to Philadelphia to bring her to New York in February 1923.

Rising to the position of vice president at Columbia, Walker created the 14000-D blues series and the 15000-D hillbilly series. Shortly before he left, he made the newly purchased OKEH RECORDS into a low-priced series. He brought the same philosophy of lower pricing on blues and country music to RCA VICTOR when he headed the BLUEBIRD RECORDS subsidiary, listing his product at thirty-five cents instead of the regular price of seventy-five cents when the label began issuing 10-inch records in March 1933. This enabled him to keep sales buoyant throughout the Depression. By the late 1930s he had risen to the rank of vice president within RCA.

During World War II Walker headed the V-Disc program of troop entertainment and resumed with RCA immediately afterward before being recruited by Loew's, Inc., in August 1945 to start a record division for MGM. The label's official launch was in March 1947. By then Walker had arranged for a former munitions plant in Bloomfield, New Jersey, to be converted into a pressing plant, and he personally supervised every aspect of the business, including artist acquisition, manufacturing, and distribution.

MGM Records remained a marginal enterprise throughout the years that Walker remained president, but he will be chiefly remembered for taking a chance on Hank Williams after other major labels had turned him down. Walker remained head of MGM Records until 1956; stayed on as a consultant to and vice president of Loew's, Inc., until his death; and was one of the founders of the Recording Industry Association of American (RIAA).

Walker died at home in Queens, New York. In the *New York Times* obituary, one of his friends recounted that Walker would sometimes write folksy doggerel verse and send it anonymously to friends, suggesting that the artists he had dealt with had had a greater impact on his life than he sometimes let on. —*Colin Escott*

Jerry Jeff Walker
b. Oneonta, New York, March 14, 1942

Perhaps more than any artist besides WILLIE NELSON, Jerry Jeff Walker personified the loose, country-rock hybrid sound and lifestyle of 1970s AUSTIN. The author of "Mr. Bojangles," Walker and his appealingly gruff voice represented everything that was carefree, boozy, and musically alive about Austin's "progressive country." His 1973 album *Viva! Terlingua*, recorded in a dance hall in Luckenbach, Texas, set the era's tone with its mixture of country soul balladry (especially on GUY CLARK's "Desperados Waiting for the Train") and Lone Star party anthems (such as Ray Wylie Hubbard's "Up Against the Wall Red Neck"). As Walker once told a reporter, "I wanted our records to sound like we were having a grand time at a party thrown for a bunch of our best friends—which, I guess, is exactly what it was."

Born Ronald Clyde Crosby in Oneonta, in upstate New York, Walker picked up basic skills on banjo, ukulele, and guitar. While still a teenager he left home and thumbed his way to Florida, and from there to New Orleans, where he sang for tips on the street. He eventually gravitated to New York City and worked his way into the Greenwich Village folk scene. In 1966 he joined a progressive rock group, Circus Maximus (originally the Lost Sea Dreamers), who recorded two albums for Vanguard. Walker left the group after the first album. By this time he had written "Mr. Bojangles," a song inspired by a character Walker had met in a jail cell in New Orleans. Walker sang it one night over an influential live radio program on WBAI in New York, and the song became an instant local hit. Walker signed with ATLANTIC RECORDS, and in 1968 his album *Mr. Bojangles* appeared on the Atlantic subsidiary Atco. Three years later, the song became a major pop hit for the NITTY GRITTY DIRT BAND.

Walker recorded two more albums for Atco and one for Vanguard; he then moved to Austin in 1971. A year later, DECCA released an eponymous Walker album that featured two cuts written by GUY CLARK, including the FM radio hit "L.A. Freeway." Next came *Viva! Terlingua*, on which Walker was backed by the Lost Gonzo Band. The album included their "London Homesick Blues," written by Gary P. Nunn, which became the famous theme song for *AUSTIN CITY LIMITS*.

Into the early 1980s Walker released a series of albums of erratic but intermittently fine quality. During those years he also established a reputation for drunken onstage behavior that sometimes overwhelmed interest in his music. In 1985, determined to turn his life and career fortunes around, he sobered up and started his own label, Tried & True Music, with his wife Susan at the helm. Several albums have since appeared on the label, including *Viva Luckenbach!*, recorded in 1993 in the same dance hall where *Viva! Terlingua* had been made twenty years earlier. —*Daniel Cooper*

REPRESENTATIVE RECORDINGS

Mr. Bojangles (Atco, 1968; reissued Rhino, 1993); *Viva! Terlingua* (MCA, 1973); *Viva Luckenbach!* (Tried & True Music/Rykodisc, 1994)

Frank Walker

Lawrence Walker
b. Duson, Louisiana, September 1, 1907; d. August 15, 1968

Lawrence Walker was the leader of a favorite dance-hall band from the mid-1940s until his death in 1968. He popularized many Cajun classics—for example, "Chère Alice" (La Louisiane, 1960s)—and wrote some of the most lyrical of Cajun songs ,"Yeaux Noir" (La Louisiane, 1960s),"The Unlucky Waltz" (La Louisiane, 1960s) and the "Reno Waltz" (Khoury, early 1950s). The smooth, well-paced sound of his band accounted for its danceability, an important key to local popularity.

Walker's father, Allen Walker, was a popular local fiddler, so young Lawrence was exposed to Cajun music at an early age.Though Lawrence was not a "full-bred " Cajun he spoke Cajun French well. His brother, Elton, played the guitar. When the family moved to Orange, Texas, in 1915, the three formed a band, the Walker Brothers Group, and made two recordings in Dallas in 1929, "La Breakdown la Louisiane" and "La Vie Malheureuse."

The family later moved back to Louisiana, and Walker and his family band continued to play at local dances. In 1935 Walker recorded several songs on the BLUEBIRD label. Six were recorded with a traditional three-piece band with Walker featured on accordion, and two were recorded with Tony Alleman on vocal and Lawrence Walker on violin.

In 1936 Walker appeared at the National Folk Festival in Dallas, Texas, with Aldus "Pop Eye" Broussard and Sidney Broussard on fiddle, Junior Broussard on guitar, Norris Mire on guitar, and Evelyn Broussard on triangle and vocals. Also on the trip was a solo vocalist from Scott, Louisiana, named Elemore Sonnier. This was the first instance of Cajun music being brought to the public's attention on a national level.

The period of post–World War II Louisiana was a high point in Walker's musical career. His band played at all the popular clubs, such as the OST Club in Rayne, the Jolly Rogers Club in Forked Island, the Welcome Club in Crowley, and the Bon Temps Rouler Club in Lafayette. He recorded his most beloved songs in the 1950s and 1960s on the Khoury, La Louisiane, and Swallow labels. His perfectionism plus his wide choice of material made these recordings a strong and unique contribution to the annals of Cajun music.

Walker died of a heart attack in 1968, leaving behind a legendary reputation and scores of beautiful music.

—*Ann Allen Savoy*

REPRESENTATIVE RECORDINGS

A Tribute to the Late Great Lawrence Walker (La Louisiane); *A Legend at Last* (Swallow, 1983)

Wayne Walker
b. Quapaw, Oklahoma, December 13, 1925; d. January 2, 1979

Wayne Paul Walker, one of country music's most prolific songwriters, was raised in Kilgore, Texas. As a performer he played the LOUISIANA HAYRIDE and recorded for various record labels such as DECCA, COLUMBIA, Ric, ABC-Paramount, Everest, and Chess. Though he didn't have success in the recording field, he made up for it in songwriting.

Walker signed with JIM DENNY'S CEDARWOOD PUBLISHING COMPANY shortly after it opened in 1954. Walker, along with WEBB PIERCE, DANNY DILL, JOHN D. LOUDERMILK, MEL

TILLIS, and MARIJOHN WILKIN, would make Cedarwood one of the legendary publishers in Nashville. During the 1950s and 1960s Walker wrote and co-wrote songs that were not only hits for the top artists of the day but that also proved to be hits for other artists years later: "I've Got a New Heartache" (RAY PRICE, 1956; RICKY SKAGGS, 1986), "Are You Sincere" (Andy Williams, 1957; ELVIS PRESLEY, 1979), "Holiday for Love" (Webb Pierce, 1957), "Burning Memories" (Ray Price, 1964; Mel Tillis, 1977), "Leavin' on Your Mind" (PATSY CLINE, 1963), "Little Boy Sad" (JOHNNY BURNETTE, 1961; BILL PHILLIPS, 1969), "Cut Across Shorty" (CARL SMITH, 1960; NAT STUCKEY, 1969), and "All the Time" (KITTY WELLS, 1959; JACK GREENE, 1967).

Walker was married for fifteen years (1958–1973) to Violet Elaine "Scooter Bill" Tubb, the eldest daughter of ERNEST TUBB. Walker was elected into the Nashville Songwriters Hall of Fame in 1975. —*Don Roy*

Wiley Walker (*see* Wiley & Gene)

Jo Walker-Meador
b. Orlinda, Tennessee, February 16, 1924

As executive director of the CMA from 1962 to 1991, Jo Walker-Meador played a direct and influential role in the remarkable growth the country music industry experienced during those years. One year before she took the helm at the CMA, full-time country radio stations numbered fewer than 100 nationwide. By 1995 there were nearly 2,400 such stations.

Born Edith Josephine Denning, she was educated at Peabody College in Nashville and Lambuth College in Jackson, Tennessee. When industry leaders organized the CMA in 1958, they hired Walker-Meador as office manager. She was to do bookkeeping, typing, and general office duties, while former WSM manager HARRY STONE served as executive director. In 1959 she organized a banquet that was to become an annual event and awards program. After Stone's departure, Walker-Meador stayed on and soon assumed his role. Under her direction, the staff eventually grew to more than twenty employees.

The CMA prospered under Walker-Meador's gracious and skillful leadership. Among the organization's well-known programs adopted during her tenure were the launching of a national fund-raising drive to build the COUNTRY MUSIC HALL OF FAME and Museum (the CMA had created the Hall of Fame in 1961) and the CMA's annual awards show, begun in 1967 and televised nationally for the first time in 1968. FAN FAIR, an annual festival of fans and performers, was inaugurated in 1972.

Thanks to the efforts of Walker-Meador and others, the CMA has grown from about 200 members to a membership of more than 7,000 individuals and organizations. Today it is the most important trade organization on the Nashville music scene and among the most active in the world. Walker-Meador has remained involved in events on Music Row since her retirement in 1991. She was elected to the Country Music Hall of Fame in 1995.

—*Mary A. Bufwack*

Chris Wall
b. Los Angeles, California, February 26, 1952

Christopher David Wall is best known as the writer of Confederate Railroad's novelty hit "Trashy Women." But that song, which extolled the virtues of tight jeans and loose morals in a tongue-in-cheek fashion, is hardly representative of the bulk of his work. Like many classic country songwriters, Wall is capable of conveying humor and pathos simultaneously. His "I Drink Therefore I Am" is perhaps the penultimate expression of honky-tonk existentialism.

Christopher David Wall was born and raised in Southern California, where he played high school and college football and graduated from Whittier College with a master's degree in history. He spent summers working on his uncle's ranch in Montana. It wasn't until he was on the far side of thirty that Wall picked up a guitar and started writing songs. He was working as a bartender at the Million Dollar Cowboy Bar in Jackson Hole, Wyoming, when JERRY JEFF WALKER heard him sitting in with a local band. Walker, who recorded "I Feel Like Hank Williams Tonight" as well as "Trashy Women" on his *Live at Gruene Hall* album, persuaded Wall to move to AUSTIN in 1988. Wall has since released three albums of original material and leads a honky-tonk band that, in his words, "plays both kinds of music, country and western."

—*Rick Mitchell*

REPRESENTATIVE RECORDINGS

No Sweat (Rykodisc, 1991); *Cowboy Nation* (Cold Spring, 1994)

Billy Wallace
b. Oklahoma City, Oklahoma, March 26, 1917; d. June 3, 1978

Best known as the writer of "Back Street Affair," Cright "Billy" Wallace wrote several other country hits of the 1950s. Born in Oklahoma City but raised in Alabama, Wallace claimed to have learned guitar from the DELMORE BROTHERS, though he cited ERNEST TUBB and ROY ACUFF as the main influences on his singing style. Wallace's first radio job was in Decatur, Alabama, and he later worked at WSB in Atlanta and WLAC in Nashville. TENNESSEE RECORDS in Nashville first recorded him, though it was for DECCA in 1952 that he recorded "Back Street Affair," his most enduring song. WEBB PIERCE heard it, liked it, and made it a huge hit later that year.

The success of "Back Street Affair," a song based on Wallace's own experiences, opened doors for other Wallace hits, most of them cut by KITTY WELLS—"I'm Paying for That Back Street Affair," "Honky Tonk Waltz," "Cheatin's a Sin," and "Whose Shoulder Will You Cry On." RED FOLEY recorded his "Slaves of a Hopeless Love Affair," while Pierce had another hit with "Don't Throw Your Life Away." As a singer Wallace never had a hit, though he recorded for several labels, including Blue Hen (1955), MERCURY (four rockabilly sides in 1956), Deb (1957), Del-Ray (1962), and Canada's Acadia Records (a 1963 LP). Wallace lived his later life in Huntsville, Alabama.

—*Ronnie Pugh*

Jerry Wallace
b. Guilford, Missouri, December 15, 1928

Aptly nicknamed Mr. Smooth, Jerry Leon Wallace has credited Nat "King" Cole as his primary influence and was a successful pop artist with eleven chart hits for CHALLENGE RECORDS (1958–65) before hitting the country charts. Many of these pop releases, including both "Shutters and Boards" and the million-selling "Primrose Lane," are considered country recordings by many today.

"In the Misty Moonlight," a 1964 release written by country tunesmith CINDY WALKER, was especially popular with country audiences. Although it did not chart country, it provided him with an invitation to appear on the GRAND OLE OPRY several times and presaged his entry on the country charts the following year.

The 1965 MERCURY release "Life's Gone and Slipped Away" marked his first single on the country charts. He was a consistent chart presence for the next fifteen years, recording for Mercury (1965–66), LIBERTY (1967–70), Decca (1971–72), MCA (1973), MGM (1975), and several smaller labels afterward. His most notable release during his country phase was "If You Leave Me Tonight I'll Cry" (1972). Heard as part of the soundtrack for a *Night Gallery* TV program episode titled "The Tune in Dan's Cafe," the DECCA single reached #1 on the country charts and #38 on the pop charts. Released later that year, "Do You Know What It's Like to Be Lonesome" earned him a 1973 CMA nomination as Male Vocalist of the Year. His last chart record was in 1980, but during the 1980s and 1990s Wallace continued to perform in nightclubs.

—*William P. Davis*

REPRESENTATIVE RECORDING

Greatest Hits (Capitol/Curb, 1991)

Don Walser
b. Brownfield, Texas, September 14, 1934

Donald Ray Walser is a country traditionalist from West Texas with a penchant for cowboy songs, Texas swing, and yodel tunes. Among his early yodeling influences he preferred the material of ELTON BRITT to that of SLIM WHITMAN, and began writing his own songs for yodelworthy material. Raised in Lamesa, Texas, near Lubbock, Texas, he started performing in bands when he was fifteen and wrote his signature song, "Rolling Stone from Texas," when he was eighteen. Walser's first recording of it, under the name of his Texas Plainsman band, was released in July 1963 on the tiny Plainsman label. Thirty-one years later, the song became the title cut of his first nationally distributed debut album, co-produced by ASLEEP AT THE WHEEL's Ray Benson for the AUSTIN-based Watermelon label.

During the interim, music had been a sideline for Walser, who continued to write and perform while serving forty-five years in the Texas National Guard. Upon his retirement at age sixty as state auditor for the Texas Guard, he found a receptive audience for the music of his Pure Texas Band among country traditionalists and younger fans alike, though his style was considered an anachronism by contemporary country standards.

"I just like them ol' songs, and I hate to see them die," said Walser, who was named top country act in the 1994–95 Austin Music Awards, and who began touring outside Texas after the favorable response to the debut album.

—*Don McLeese*

Steve Wariner
b. Noblesville, Indiana, December 25, 1954

A high-level gift as an instrumentalist and an enduring dedication to quality have made singer-songwriter-picker Steven Noel Wariner a dependably rewarding artist through years of change in the country music industry. He became one of the few artists with significant chart success during the late 1970s to early 1980s country-pop era to continue to thrive in the dance-hall-driven 1990s. In 1993 superstar GARTH BROOKS called Wariner the Nolan Ryan of country and said, "Guys like Steve are the ones that made country music what it is and what it will eventually become." Fans know Wariner as a painter, close-up magician, athlete, and family man (his wife, Caryn, and sons Ryan and Ross) as well as a strong onstage attraction.

Wariner's country roots reach deep; he was focusing on the music of HANK WILLIAMS, BUCK OWENS, and GEORGE JONES by age ten as he played bass in the country band of his father, Roy, on regional radio and television. While still in his teens, Wariner began fronting his own band and writing his own songs. At age seventeen he was discovered by DOTTIE WEST and toured with her, BOB LUMAN, and hero/mentor CHET ATKINS before landing an RCA contract with Atkins's help in 1976. In those days, albums weren't an immediate perk for a new artist; Wariner put out pop-country singles—including his own touching "I'm Already Taken" (1978)—for two years before releasing his self-titled debut album. Wariner's first #1 hit came in 1981 with "All Roads Lead to You." Releases such as "Kansas City Lights" brought repeated comparisons to major Wariner influence GLEN CAMPBELL. The hot picking of "Midnight Fire" (1983) and the hard-country remake of Bob Luman's "Lonely Women Make Good Lovers" (1983) helped broaden the star's sound.

But it took a move to MCA RECORDS—and a collaboration with executive and producer TONY BROWN—in 1984 to recast Wariner's image for a new country era. A harder country sound and strong song selection produced a string of Top Ten hits, many co-written by Wariner. These include #1s such as the wistful "Some Fools Never Learn"(1985), "You Can Dream of Me" (1985–86), the bluegrassy "Life's Highway" (1986), "Small Town Girl" (1987), "The Weekend" (1987), the rocking "Lynda" (1987), "Where Did I Go Wrong" (1989), and "I Got Dreams" (1989).

Wariner also teamed with Nicolette Larson for the 1986 Top Ten "That's How You Know When Love's Right" and with Campbell for 1987's sentimental #6 hit "The Hand That Rocks the Cradle." Wariner shared in a Grammy and a COUNTRY MUSIC ASSOCIATION Vocal Event of the Year Award for his instrumental and vocal contribution (along with VINCE GILL and RICKY SKAGGS) to MARK O'CONNOR's hot album *Mark O'Connor and the New Nashville Cats* (1991).

A move to ARISTA RECORDS in 1991 produced more Top Ten records, including the BILL ANDERSON–penned "The Tips of My Fingers" in 1992. Although he hasn't joined the multiplatinum ranks of Brooks and others at the time of this writing, Wariner seemed comfortably ensconced as a highly respected, multitalented star possessing a loyal following. His 1996 instrumental album *No More Mr. Nice Guy* featured contributions from Gill, O'Connor, Atkins, rocker Richie Sambora, and others, and demonstrated Wariner's mastery of styles in and outside country. "This will probably be one of the most true-to-me projects I've done," Wariner said while recording it. "Guitar is what got me into doing this in the first place."

Wariner joined the GRAND OLE OPRY in May 1996. Wariner requested and was granted his release from Arista on January 16, 1998. On the strength of recent success as a songwriter, including "Longneck Bottle" on Garth Brooks's *Sevens* album, Wariner signed a recording contract with Capitol Nashville. His first Capitol single, "Holes In the Floor of Heaven" debuted in *Billboard* March 7, 1998.
—*Thomas Goldsmith*

Steve Wariner

REPRESENTATIVE RECORDINGS

Greatest Hits (MCA, 1987); *I Am Ready* (Arista, 1991)

Warner Bros./Reprise Records
established in Hollywood, California, 1958

Though it was one of the last of the major labels to set up shop in Nashville, Warner Bros./Reprise Records steadily grew until, by the mid-1980s, it was clearly one of the city's four most successful labels. Warner Bros. Records, originally a division of the Warner Bros. movie studio, was founded in Los Angeles in 1958. The company acquired Reprise Records from Frank Sinatra in 1963.

Although the company's representation on the country charts goes back to BOB LUMAN and "Let's Think About Living" in 1960, and though the EVERLY BROTHERS began recording for the label in 1960, Warner Bros. did not open a Nashville office until 1975, when Englishman Andy Wickham was hired to run the office, with NORRO WILSON as director of A&R. The label's first big country success was with CMA and Grammy Award winner EMMYLOU HARRIS, the company's most prolific country hitmaker beginning in 1975, although she was signed by the Los Angeles office.

The Nashville branch grew gradually under the aegis of Wickham, Wilson, and FRANK JONES, who ran the Nashville office from 1980 to 1983. Warner Bros. absorbed ELEKTRA RECORDS in 1983; JIMMY BOWEN headed the combined labels in Nashville for a year. He was succeeded by one of his appointees, JIM ED NORMAN. As of 1997, with thirteen years' tenure, Norman was the graybeard of Nashville label bosses.

From the late 1970s to the early 1990s the label's biggest stars were HANK WILLIAMS JR. (1977–78, 1983–91), JOHN

ANDERSON (1977–87), T. G. SHEPPARD (1977–85), the BELLAMY BROTHERS (1976–83), and CRYSTAL GAYLE (1983–89).

In 1986 the company successfully launched the careers of two remarkable stylists: RANDY TRAVIS (1985–97) and DWIGHT YOAKAM (1986–), artists widely credited with expanding country's New Traditionalist movement. In the 1990s TRAVIS TRITT, LITTLE TEXAS, and FAITH HILL were among the company's more successful artists. Meanwhile, the Nashville division diversified beyond country music, enjoying significant sales from a cappella sextet Take 6 and critical acclaim for banjo virtuoso BÉLA FLECK and ace fiddler MARK O'CONNOR. In addition the firm tallied platinum sales from country comic and TV star JEFF FOXWORTHY, who built his career by completing the sentence, "You might be a redneck if . . ." In 1992 the company also created the Warner Western imprint, dedicated to presenting cowboy poets and singers such as the SONS OF THE SAN JOAQUIN and MICHAEL MARTIN MURPHEY. —*John Lomax III*

Country Music in Washington, D.C.

Our nation's capital has always been a popular area for country music and the starting point for some of our top artists. It began in the 1930s and 1940s, when Washington was still a southern town and when people who moved to the city from the South or Appalachia seeking jobs brought their music with them. Live local shows, country bars, and radio programs abounded throughout the area. The biggest influence from the late 1940s through the 1950s was promoter CONNIE B. GAY. In 1946 he entered into country music with local radio programs and patented the name "Town and Country." He held country shows in Constitution Hall and on the steps of the Lincoln Memorial. By the early 1950s he moved into television. Gay also was one of the founders of the COUNTRY MUSIC ASSOCIATION in 1958 and served as first president. He was elected to the COUNTRY MUSIC HALL OF FAME in 1980.

Some of the most successful country singers of the 1950s started their careers on his programs. JIMMY DEAN served in the air force near Washington and stayed after his 1948 discharge. By the early 1950s he caught the attention of Gay, who made him the star of his *Town and Country Time* program on WMAL-TV. This eventually led to a 1957 nationally broadcast CBS-TV morning show that originated on WTOP-TV in Washington. ROY CLARK grew up in the area and was a local boxer at age seventeen before becoming a musician in the 1950s. He joined the Jimmy Dean show briefly in 1954, and jokes about the fact that he was fired for constant lateness. PATSY CLINE, discovered by Gay in 1954 after winning first prize in the Annual National Championship Country Music contest, became a regular on the program until late 1957. GEORGE HAMILTON IV came to D.C. from North Carolina after having a pop hit with "A Rose and a Baby Ruth" in 1956. Gay became his manager, and Hamilton joined Jimmy Dean's program, appearing on both the local and national programs in 1957–58, and briefly had his own national show. He stayed in D.C. until he decided to cross from pop to country and moved to Nashville in 1959. Musician and singer BILLY GRAMMER also started out in the D.C. area in the late 1940s, and eventually joined Jimmy's D.C. show and appeared on the 1957 national show before forming his own band.

By the 1960s things began to change. Gay retired and Dean, Cline, and Hamilton were national stars and moved on. The suburbs grew and attracted the live talent away from the city. And the city itself was changing. It was less influenced by southern culture, and in 1968 race riots had the effect of damaging nighttime business. Places such as the Shamrock (in Georgetown since 1953) closed or moved to the suburbs. In the early 1960s CHARLIE DANIELS made Washington his home when he played in a rock & roll group named the Rockets. In the early 1970s EMMYLOU HARRIS lived in D.C., began her career in local clubs, and eventually put together her Hot Band.

MARY CHAPIN CARPENTER, CLEVE FRANCIS, and JETT WILLIAMS are current artists who began their careers in the area and still live there. Country radio station WMZQ-FM is often the #1 radio station in the geographical area. Bluegrass has always been popular in the area, and two of the top groups called D.C. home. The COUNTRY GENTLEMEN started in 1957, and the SELDOM SCENE formed in 1971 and continues to be a top bluegrass act today. In recent years country music performers have been welcome at the White House under both Democratic and Republican presidents. President Bush was especially cordial to country artists, as was Jimmy Carter. —*Barbara Pruett*

Dale Watson
b. Birmingham, Alabama, October 7, 1963

Since settling in Austin, Texas, in 1993, Kenneth Dale Watson has become an accomplished purveyor of lean, hard-driving honky-tonk music. Watson spent fifteen years playing roadhouses and bars throughout Texas and the South before releasing his debut album, *Cheatin' Heart Attack* (HighTone), in 1995. Nevertheless, his musical apprenticeship began much earlier when, as a boy, he accompanied his truck-driving father when his father sang in the truck stops and cafés of rural West Tennessee.

The younger Watson first made his mark as a performer after moving in 1988 to Los Angeles, where he became a fixture on the *Western Beat Barn Dance*. He then spent a year in Nashville, working as a songwriter and lead guitarist, but his tattoos, pompadour, and maverick spirit never quite agreed with MUSIC CITY. After briefly returning to California, Watson arrived in Austin, where he began to make his mark. Sometimes reminiscent of MERLE HAGGARD, at others of JOHNNY PAYCHECK, Watson's heartrending baritone is an ideal instrument for his plainspoken original songs— real-life tales of work, family, liquor, and heartache. As a list these subjects may read like clichés, but on his last two albums, most notably 1997's *I Hate These Songs* (HIGHTONE), Watson renders them with detail and conviction. —*Bill Friskics-Warren*

REPRESENTATIVE RECORDINGS

Blessed or Damned (HighTone, 1996); *I Hate These Songs* (HighTone, 1997)

Doc Watson
b. Deep Gap, North Carolina, March 2, 1923

Though he has never had a hit single or a gold record award, Arthel Lane "Doc" Watson has nevertheless been an enormously influential performer. His clean, precise, and lightning-fast flat-picking technique on the acoustic guitar has been emulated by innumerable guitar players. In addition, his singing has popularized old country tunes for many fans of folk music and bluegrass.

Born in the Appalachian mountain town of Deep Gap,

Doc Watson

North Carolina, Watson was the sixth of nine children born to General Dixon and Annie Watson. Young Arthel lost his sight to illness somewhere around his first year. But he grew up in a loving and musical family, and with their encouragement he soon graduated from harmonica to banjo and finally to guitar. Watson has said that the first song he ever learned on guitar was the CARTER FAMILY song "When the Roses Bloom in Dixieland." Besides the Carter Family, other early musical influences were JIMMIE RODGERS, the DELMORE BROTHERS, DON RENO, and RILEY PUCKETT.

After a few frustrating years at the School for the Blind in Raleigh, North Carolina, Watson moved toward becoming a professional musician, first busking at taxi stands, and eventually joining the dance band of a local piano player named Jack Williams. During his stint with that band (roughly 1953–62), Watson played a Gibson Les Paul electric exclusively. At age nineteen he was still known by his birth name until an appearance at a radio station remote broadcast at a furniture store in Lenoir, North Carolina. When someone couldn't pronounce his name, a girl in the audience shouted, "Call him Doc!" The nickname stuck.

His career took a major turn in 1960 when Watson met Smithsonian Institution folklorist RALPH RINZLER at a festival near Union Grove, North Carolina. Rinzler was playing with the GREENBRIAR BOYS, and Watson was rhythm guitarist for old-time recording artist "TOM" ASHLEY. As the folk music craze began taking off in the early 1960s, Rinzler booked Ashley's band, including Watson, in New York City. The success of that concert led to a booking at the Ash Grove in Los Angeles. It was there that Ashley caught laryngitis, forcing Watson to become lead singer and group spokesman on show dates.

Eventually Watson began being booked as a solo act and soon had gigs coast to coast, teaming occasionally with BILL MONROE, a teenaged CLARENCE WHITE, and many others, along the way making an incalculable impression on a whole generation of flat-pickers.

Watson recorded for Folkways Records in 1962 and 1963 before moving to Vanguard Records in 1964. Subsequent label affiliations included United Artists, Verve, Poppy, and Flying Fish. His 1990s releases have been on SUGAR HILL RECORDS. Among Watson's recorded works are two standout collaborations: *Strictly Instrumental* (COLUM-BIA, 1967) with FLATT & SCRUGGS and *Will the Circle Be Unbroken* (United Artists, 1972) with the NITTY GRITTY DIRT BAND and many all-star guests, including MAYBELLE CARTER, ROY ACUFF, and MERLE TRAVIS. Watson has won Grammy Awards for his albums *Then and Now, Two Days in November, Live and Pickin', Riding the Midnight Train,* and *On Praying Ground.*

For twenty years Doc Watson's accompanist was his son Eddy Merle Watson (b. Deep Gap, North Carolina, February 8, 1949; d. October 23, 1985), who first joined his father for a road gig at the Berkeley Folk Festival in 1964 at age fifteen. By 1967 Merle was with his father full-time on the road. Though Merle was just a beginner when he teamed with his father, he very quickly developed his own personal, bluesy signature—compatible with but distinct from his father's—on banjo and both fingerstyle and slide guitar. His musical contributions to Doc Watson's stage performances and recordings often have been overlooked and underrated. Their partnership ended in 1985, when Merle died in a tractor accident at his North Carolina farm. Since that time Doc Watson's primary accompanists have been Jack Lawrence and Merle's son, Richard Watson.

—*Don Rhodes*

REPRESENTATIVE RECORDINGS

The Doc Watson Family (Smithsonian/Folkways, 1963); *Southbound* (Vanguard, 1966); *Doc Watson on Stage, Featuring Merle Watson* (Vanguard, 1971); *Memories* (United Artists, 1975); *My Dear Old Southern Home* (Sugar Hill, 1991)

Gene Watson

b. Palestine, Texas, October 11, 1943

The emergence of the neotraditionalists in country music in the 1980s should not make us forget that some singers had been adhering to a no-frills, hard-country style long before that time. Since Gary Gene Watson entered the Top Ten in 1975 with "Love in the Hot Afternoon," a sultry song of passion set in New Orleans, he has been one of country music's greatest voices and song stylists. His tenor voice is smooth and expressive and, as best displayed in his signature song, "Farewell Party," it can soar with intensity and conviction.

Watson came to the CAPITOL label in 1975 after a long and hard apprenticeship in the honky-tonks of Houston and a succession of small regional labels. He worked as an automobile body specialist by day and sang country music at night. "Love in the Hot Afternoon," initially released on the Resco label in 1974, freed him from day labor (but not from his love for automobiles), and he recorded a succession of Top Ten hits for Capitol that included "Paper Rosie," "Nothing Sure Looked Good on You," and "Farewell Party," followed by additional Top Tens for MCA RECORDS ("Fourteen Carat Mind," "Got No Reason Now for Going Home") and EPIC RECORDS ("Memories to Burn") before slipping off the charts in the early 1990s.

The only factors in Watson's career that have changed in the past twenty years are his record labels and his personal grooming style. In the early 1980s a beard and frizzy, permed hair replaced his earlier clean-shaven look and straight, swept-back black hair, but his recordings—on such labels as MCA (1981–85), EPIC (1985–87), WARNER BROS. (1988–91), Broadland (1993), and STEP ONE (1993–present)—have continued to offer the best in bedrock country music.

In the spring of 1997 Watson enjoyed his first appearance on the charts since 1993 with the #45 *Billboard* hit "Change Her Mind" from *The Good Ole Days* on the Step One label. —*Bill C. Malone*

REPRESENTATIVE RECORDINGS

Greatest Hits (MCA, 1985); *Greatest Hits* (Curb/CEMA, 1990); *The Good Ole Days* (Step One, 1997)

Irving Waugh

b. Danville, Virginia, December 8, 1912

Between 1947 and 1992, radio and television executive Irving Cambridge Waugh Jr. played important roles at WSM and with the CMA Awards TV show. He grew up in Norfolk, Virginia, and during high school worked his way around much of the South Pacific on tramp freighters. Later he attended a division of the College of William and Mary in Williamsburg, Virginia. Upon graduation he pursued an interest in drama with the Provincetown Players in New York. While working odd jobs there during the late 1930s he gained early radio exposure on the CBS network program *March of Time,* a dramatization of news of the week. He also worked briefly in Atlanta with a Federal Theater Project company.

After working as a radio announcer in Norfolk, Roanoke, Nashville, and Cleveland, Waugh joined WSM as an announcer in 1941. His first experience with country music came in announcing early morning country broadcasts. During World War II he left WSM temporarily to serve as a special correspondent for NBC radio in the Pacific Theater.

Waugh returned to WSM's commercial department in 1947, became commercial manager the next year, and in 1948 helped to organize the GRAND OLE OPRY's Friday night show. In 1950 he was promoted to commercial manager for WSM's radio and TV operations, and to general manager of WSM-TV in 1957. In 1958 he rose to vice president of WSM, Inc., embracing both radio and TV interests, and in 1968 became president. In this capacity he was instrumental in the planning and building of the OPRYLAND theme park, which opened in 1972.

Waugh also helped to sell the CMA Awards show to NBC-TV in 1968, together with publishing executive JACK STAPP. Although Waugh retired from WSM in 1978, through 1992 he remained executive producer of this program. —*John Rumble*

The Weaver Brothers & Elviry

June Petrie "Elviry" Weaver b. Chicago, Illinois, June 23, 1891; d. November 1977

Leon "Abner" Weaver b. Ozark, Missouri, April 18, 1886; d. December 1962

Frank "Cicero" Weaver b. Ozark, Missouri, February 2, 1891; d. October 1967

Leon "Abner" Weaver liked to bill himself as vaudeville's first rube; he began portraying his hillbilly character in about 1902 in medicine shows. He brought brother Frank, billed as "Cicero," into the act, then the pair joined June Petrie—"Elviry"—in 1913. With her as the front woman, the Weaver Brothers and Elviry rose to headlining status as a $5,000-a-week attraction on the RKO vaudeville circuit after World War I.

Abner and Elviry were married ca. 1916–24; then Elviry married brother Cicero in 1928. Daughters, in-laws, cousins, and other kin were incorporated into a nineteen-member troupe called the Home Folks.

Abner played mandolin, guitar, and fiddle, and is believed to have originated the musical handsaw. Cicero, who never spoke in the act, also played the saw and patented a number of novelty instruments, including a spinning banjo and a one-man-band apparatus. Elviry sang and played piano, ukulele, or mandolin. Her humorous poker-faced delivery and the brothers' shenanigans attracted Hollywood attention. The Weavers appeared in thirteen films from 1937 to 1944, including *GRAND OLE OPRY* (1940).

In the late 1940s the Weaver Brothers and Elviry starred on radio station KWTO in Springfield, Missouri. The act ended with Abner's death in 1962. —*Robert K. Oermann*

Gillian Welch

b. New York, New York, October 2, 1967

Gillian Welch's disarmingly spare debut album, *Revival* (1996), evokes Appalachian music and culture vividly, and a number of country and bluegrass performers have recorded her hauntingly imagistic songs. EMMYLOU HARRIS included Welch's "Orphan Girl" on her influential *Wrecking Ball* album (1995), and TIM & MOLLIE O'BRIEN, the NASHVILLE BLUEGRASS BAND, TRISHA YEARWOOD, and KATHY MATTEA have all cut Welch's material. Somewhat suprisingly, though, Welch didn't grow up in the rural South, but in Los Angeles, where her parents scored music for *The Carol Burnett Show* and sang show tunes around the family piano. After attending college in California, Welch enrolled in Boston's Berklee College of Music and met performing partner David Rawlings. The duo moved to Nashville in 1992, where they soon captivated clubgoers with their close harmony singing and delicately flat-picked guitars, and where Welch's songs began to enthrall other performers. Welch made her debut album for the Almo Sounds label with producer T-Bone Burnett, whose vintage equipment and recording techniques beautifully captured the intimacy and passion of her live duo performances with Rawlings. *Revival* earned Welch *The Gavin Report's* AMERICANA Artist of the Year Award for 1996. —*Bill Friskics-Warren*

REPRESENTATIVE RECORDING

Revival (Almo Sounds, 1996)

Kevin Welch

b. Los Angeles, California, August 17, 1955

Raised in Oklahoma, Kevin Welch moved to Nashville in 1978 and quickly proved himself a promising songwriter. During the 1980s his writing credits included recordings by MOE BANDY, DON WILLIAMS, the JUDDS, SWEETHEARTS OF THE RODEO, RICKY SKAGGS, and CONWAY TWITTY. Toward the end of the decade, however, Welch began attracting attention for his gifts as a performer, ultimately resulting in the phrase "Western Beat" being coined to describe his sophisticated, literate music, and that of a few of his contemporaries. Welch also is co-founder of the independent DEAD RECKONING label.

Released on WARNER BROS., Welch's eponymous 1990 debut (recorded with his band the Overtones) immediately established him as a performer of vision and talent through songs such as "Some Kind of Paradise" and "The Mother Road"—the latter being a paean to Route 66. After overseas audiences came up with the description "Western Beat," Welch released an excellent 1992 album under that title and seemed destined for stardom. But it wasn't to be. After protracted artistic differences with his record company, Welch opted out of his contract with Warner Bros. and joined Kieran Kane, formerly of the late 1980s duo the O'KANES, to form Dead Reckoning. It was for that imprint that Welch released the aptly titled *Life Down Here on Earth* in 1995. Under Welch and Kane's leadership, Dead Reckoning has since earned considerable respect for managing its own affairs and for releasing artistically worthy projects.

—*Bill Friskics-Warren*

REPRESENTATIVE RECORDINGS

Kevin Welch (Warner Bros., 1990); *Western Beat* (Warner Bros., 1992); *Life Down Here on Earth* (Dead Reckoning, 1995)

Freddy Weller
b. Atlanta, Georgia, September 9, 1947

Wilton Frederick "Freddy" Weller came to prominence in the late 1960s and early 1970s as a singer and songwriter who moved easily between the realms of rock & roll and country.

In the early 1960s, fellow Atlantan JOE SOUTH recommended Weller to Atlanta music entrepreneur BILL LOWERY as both guitarist and songwriter when Weller was working regularly at the *Georgia Jubilee* radio show while still in high school. Subsequent work on the road and on sessions with BILLY JOE ROYAL (Weller played on Royal's 1965 hit "Down in the Boondocks") brought Weller to the attention of Paul Revere & the Raiders, who hired him as lead guitarist in 1967. Weller was spotlighted in the Raiders' shows singing a country song, and in 1969 Revere and singer Mark Lindsay helped Weller place his version of Joe South's "Games People Play" with COLUMBIA'S BILLY SHERRILL. Weller's version went to #2 on the country charts in April 1969, the same year Atlanta's Tommy Roe had Top Ten bubblegum pop hits with two songs Weller co-wrote, "Dizzy" and "Jam Up Jelly Tight." Weller remained a Raider through 1971, even though his solo country career yielded three more Top Ten hits before he left the band. His long hair (by the standards of country acts of the early 1970s), youth, and good looks made Weller something of a sex symbol, and his songwriting reflected a then new frankness in country lyrics. "Lonely Women Make Good Lovers," co-written with Spooner Oldham, was a Top Ten country hit for BOB LUMAN in 1972 and for STEVE WARINER in 1983. Weller's own chart success ended in 1980, but he has continued to perform and write songs.

—*Mark Humphrey*

Frank Welling (*see* John McGee & Frank Welling)

Kitty Wells
b. Nashville, Tennessee, August 30, 1919

Kitty Wells was a thirty-three-year-old wife and mother when her immortal 1952 recording of "It Wasn't God Who Made Honky Tonk Angels" suddenly made her a star. Other female country singers of her day were trying their hands at hard-living, honky-tonk sounds, but it was the in-

Kitty Wells

tense and piercing style of Kitty Wells, with her gospel-touched vocals and tearful restraint, that resonated with country audiences of the time and broke the industry barriers for women.

Born Muriel Ellen Deason in Nashville, her country roots went deep. Her father and uncle were country musicians, her mother a gospel singer. In 1934, with the Depression at its height, Wells dropped out of school to work at the Washington Manufacturing Company, where she was paid nine dollars a week to iron shirts. With her two sisters and a cousin, Wells also performed on radio, the four of them broadcasting as the Deason Sisters.

On October 30, 1937, at age eighteen, Wells married Johnnie Wright. The two of them and Wright's sister Louise performed as Johnnie Wright and the Harmony Girls. In 1939 Wright and Jack Anglin formed the duo JOHNNIE & JACK.

Wells performed as the "girl singer" with Johnnie & Jack on radio shows as they traveled throughout the South in the early 1940s. It was during this time that Wright began to refer to his wife as "Kitty Wells," a name taken from an old PICKARD FAMILY tune.

During World War II Anglin served in the army and Wright worked at a DuPont chemical factory north of Nashville. But after the war Johnnie and Jack reunited and Wells traveled with them to join the new LOUISIANA HAYRIDE on KWKH in Shreveport. As "Rag Doll," she spun records and sold quilting supplies.

Wells's recordings for RCA in 1949 and 1950 found no success, but Johnnie & Jack's "Poison Love" took them to the GRAND OLE OPRY in 1952. At this time Wells was persuaded to record an answer song to "The Wild Side of Life," a HANK THOMPSON hit that featured the line "I didn't know God made honky-tonk angels."

Thinking of the $125 recording payment, Wells went into OWEN BRADLEY's studio on May 3, 1952, to record "It Wasn't God Who Made Honky Tonk Angels" for DECCA

RECORDS. The single took off during the summer and sold more than 800,000 copies in its initial release. It also crossed over to *Billboard*'s pop charts, hitting #27.

The song's sentiments are similar to 1894's "She Is More to Be Pitied Than Censured," with its premise that deceitful men are responsible for fallen women. "It Wasn't God Who Made Honky-Tonk Angels" was so controversial that the NBC radio network banned the song as "suggestive," and Wells wasn't allowed to sing it on Opry broadcasts. But audiences couldn't get enough of it.

Her subsequent records followed this pattern of deep emotion, restrained hurt, and a woman's point of view. Her other honky-tonk ballad classics include "Release Me" (1954), "Making Believe" (1955), and "I Can't Stop Loving You" (1958). Contemporary themes and modern ways were highlights of songs such as "Your Wild Life's Gonna Get You Down," "I Heard the Jukebox Playing," "Will Your Lawyer Talk to God?," "Broken Marriage Vows," "Cheatin's a Sin," "Mommy for a Day," and "A Woman Half My Age." On Wells's records, sorrowful men and women acted out their emotional dramas through her plaintive vocals accompanied by a crying steel guitar.

In her stage show Wells was unpretentious, proper, and even old-fashioned in her gingham dresses with full skirts, rickrack, and puffed sleeves. In her private life she was family-oriented and without controversy, crisis, or scandal. But in her songs Wells could be the rejected woman, the barroom sinner, worldly-wise, a victim of her own passion, even morally weak.

As the top female country star of her generation she accumulated thirty-eight *Billboard* Top Ten records and eighty-four charted singles. She starred in her own syndicated TV show in 1968, and her last major hit was in 1971. (Her and Wright's three children—daughters Ruby and Carol Sue, and son Bobby—all became part of *The Kitty Wells–Johnnie Wright Family Show*, which has continued to tour in the 1990s.) She was elected to the COUNTRY MUSIC HALL OF FAME in 1976 and was nominated for a 1989 Grammy Award for her "Honky-Tonk Angels Medley" with K. D. LANG, LORETTA LYNN, and BRENDA LEE. In 1991, during the Grammy show, Wells, along with BOB DYLAN, Marian Anderson, and John Lennon, was presented with a Lifetime Achievement Award. She was the first female country singer to receive the award, and only the third country performer overall, following ROY ACUFF and HANK WILLIAMS.

Ultimately, Wells's great achievement was defying the accepted country music wisdom of her time, which warned that women don't sell records and can't headline shows. Her success led record companies to open their doors to other women, and to experiment with new themes and images for women, thereby indelibly changing country music forever.
—*Mary A. Bufwack*

REPRESENTATIVE RECORDINGS

The Golden Years (Rounder, 1982); *Country Music Hall of Fame* (MCA, 1991); *The Queen of Country* (Bear Family, 1992), 4 discs

E. W. "Bud" Wendell
b. Akron, Ohio, August 17, 1927

As manager of the GRAND OLE OPRY and later president and chief executive officer of the companies that have owned the Opry and OPRYLAND, Bud Wendell has played a major role in the growth of country music in the 1970s, 1980s, and 1990s.

After graduation from Wooster College in Ohio with a degree in economics, Wendell started with the National Life and Accident Insurance Company (then the parent company of WSM and the Opry) in 1950 as a door-to-door insurance salesman in Hamilton, Ohio. After several transfers, he moved to the home office in Nashville in 1962. He worked as an assistant to John H. "Jack" DeWitt, president of WSM, and was named the Opry's manager in April 1968.

As Opry manager, Wendell got off to a shaky start when his very first show was canceled due to the assassination of civil rights leader Martin Luther King Jr., but Wendell soon established himself as a manager who saw the big picture of country music's potential. He smoothed over rifts between the Opry and the country music industry and developed a close relationship with Nashville's business community.

Wendell became vice president of WSM and general manager of the Grand Ole Opry and Opryland theme park in 1974, just as the Opry was being moved from the aging RYMAN AUDITORIUM to the present Opryland grounds. He became president and CEO of WSM in 1978 and chairman in 1980. The GAYLORD company acquired National Life's entertainment interests in 1983, and Wendell was named president and CEO of Gaylord Entertainment in 1991.

The controversial move of the Opry, along with the opening of Opryland (1972) and the development of the Opryland Hotel, had been the visions of IRVING WAUGH (whom Wendell had succeeded as CEO of WSM), but Wendell took Waugh's plan many steps farther. Under Wendell's leadership, Gaylord or its predecessors launched THE NASHVILLE NETWORK (TNN) in 1983, acquired COUNTRY MUSIC TELEVISION (CMT) in 1991, launched CMT Europe in 1992, expanded the Opryland Hotel into Nashville's largest convention facility, and established the Opryland Music Group (which acquired the massive ACUFF-ROSE publishing catalogue). In addition,

E. W. "Bud" Wendell

Wendell oversaw Gaylord's renovation of the Ryman Auditorium and the opening of the Wildhorse Saloon dance club, which helped revive a declining downtown Nashville.

In 1994 Gaylord honored Wendell with the opening of the E. W. Wendell Building, which houses all of Gaylord Entertainment's corporate departments. Wendell retired from Gaylord in 1997 and was elected to the COUNTRY MUSIC HALL OF FAME in 1998. —*Walter Carter*

Bill Wesbrooks (*see* Cousin Wilbur)

Dottie West
b. McMinnville, Tennessee, October 11, 1932; d. September 4, 1991

Country music stylist Dottie West enjoyed one of the longest hitmaking careers of any woman of her generation. Known for her 1964 Grammy-winning recording "Here Comes My Baby," she also was a country pioneer with ad jingles (including the famous Coca-Cola "Country Sunshine" campaign of the 1970s), and she recorded successful duets with JIM REEVES, DON GIBSON, JIMMY DEAN, and KENNY ROGERS.

Born Dorothy Marie Marsh, she grew up in a large, poor family. Her father sexually abused her and was imprisoned. She worked her way through college and married steel guitarist Bill West in 1953. He took a job in Cleveland, Ohio, and she landed a singing slot on that city's *Landmark Jamboree* TV show as half of the Kay-Dots duo with Kathy Dee (Kathy Dearth, 1933–68).

By 1958 West had children Dale, Morris, Kerry, and Shelly, but continued to sing professionally. On weekends the Wests would drive south to Nashville to try to establish contacts in the music industry there. Finally she successfully auditioned for STARDAY in 1959, but little came of the affiliation. In 1961 the family moved to MUSIC CITY. West signed with ATLANTIC, but fared no better than she had at Starday.

Dottie West

She continued to write songs, however, and JIM REEVES had a hit with her composition "Is This Me" in 1963. He brought her to the attention of RCA's CHET ATKINS, who signed West and produced her self-penned "Here Comes My Baby." It earned her GRAND OLE OPRY membership and the first Grammy won by a female country artist. She had other Top Ten singles with "Would You Hold It Against Me" (1966) and "Paper Mansions" (1967), as well as hit duets with Reeves ("Love Is No Excuse," 1964) and Don Gibson ("Rings of Gold," 1969).

PATSY CLINE served as her mentor, and West, in turn, befriended others, boosting the careers of LARRY GATLIN, JEANNIE SEELY, STEVE WARINER, and Tony Toliver, while serving as a den mother for a generation of struggling pickers and writers.

West's own songwriting led to her composing twelve Coca-Cola jingles, including the Clio Award–winning "Country Sunshine," which also became a 1973 Top Ten hit. She moved to United Artists in 1976 and later scored a pair of #1 hits with "A Lesson in Leavin' " (1980) and "Are You Happy Baby?" (1980–81). She also recorded a highly successful string of duets with KENNY ROGERS, including "Everytime Two Fools Collide" (1978), and "What Are We Doin' in Love" (1981), which also became a Top Twenty hit on the pop charts.

Along the way, West shed her gingham/sweetheart image and reemerged as a glamorous, sexy star with a $50,000 wardrobe and a glitzy stage show. After she and Bill West divorced, she married two younger husbands in succession and lived extravagantly.

But bad investments and a lull in West's career in the late 1980s led to bankruptcy in 1990. She died a year later, of injuries from a Nashville car crash. A TV movie of her life aired in 1995.

Son Morris became a member of the national rock act Thunder. Daughter Shelly West became a country star, recording several hits, including duets with DAVID FRIZZELL, in the early 1980s. —*Robert K. Oermann*

REPRESENTATIVE RECORDINGS
The Best of Dottie West (RCA, 1973); *The Best of Dottie West* (Liberty, 1984); *The Essential Dottie West* (RCA, 1996)

Speedy West & Jimmy Bryant
Wesley Webb West b. Springfield, Missouri, January 25, 1924
Ivy Bryant b. Pavo, Georgia, March 5, 1925; d. September 22, 1980

Once billed as the "Flaming Guitars," pedal steel pioneer Speedy West and electric guitarist Jimmy Bryant recorded some of the most spirited instrumental duets in the country genre's history. Their versatility and drive were manifest on thirty-five singles and five albums as well as countless West Coast sessions for everyone from TENNESSEE ERNIE FORD to Frank Sinatra. The freshness of their playing combined speed and technique with a jazzlike improvisational daring. "We sort of had a pact," West recalled. "We agreed to try new things anytime the urge hit us. If it hit our minds, we'd try it right on the session."

West and Bryant were among the midwestern and southern migrant musicians active in the thriving country music scene of post–World War II Los Angeles. They first met (ca. 1947) when playing down the street from one another in competing bars. CLIFFIE STONE teamed them on his *HOMETOWN JAMBOREE* radio and television programs, gave them the "Flaming Guitars" billing and rec-

Speedy West & Jimmy Bryant

ommended them to CAPITOL RECORDS. The duo first recorded together as sidemen backing Tennessee Ernie Ford and Kay Starr on the 1950 hit "I'll Never Be Free," backed with "Ain't Nobody's Business but My Own." The dynamic interplay of West's Bigsby pedal steel (one of the first) and Bryant's electric guitar gave the Ford-Starr hit a fresh sound, one Capitol would use on hundreds of country and pop sessions during the 1950s.

West and Bryant spent eleven years on the *Hometown Jamboree* and recorded prolifically together before parting company in about 1958. They maintained successful separate careers, albeit not always as performers: Bryant was a songwriter best remembered for WAYLON JENNINGS's 1968 hit "Only Daddy That'll Walk the Line"; West, whose session work included LORETTA LYNN's 1960 Zero label debut, became the manager of the Fender Distribution Center in Tulsa, Oklahoma. Steel player and producer PETE DRAKE reunited them for a session on his First Generation label, ultimately issued in 1990 by STEP ONE RECORDS. Earlier in 1975 they performed for the first time in years at Nashville's annual FAN FAIR. Bryant, once billed as the "Fastest Guitar in the Country," died in 1980. A year later a debilitating stroke ended West's zany "crash-bar" playing, but the fun and fury of the 1950s West-Bryant recordings will always mirror the vitality and experimental spirit of the postwar West Coast country scene. —*Mark Humphrey*

REPRESENTATIVE RECORDINGS

For the Last Time (Step One, 1990); *Stratosphere Boogie: The Flaming Guitars of Speedy West and Jimmy Bryant* (Razor & Tie, 1995); *Speedy West, Jimmy Bryant—Flamin' Guitars* (Bear Family, 1997)

Western Swing

Western swing was a style of country music that reached its zenith during the era of big band swing. Like the music of the big bands, western swing was intended for dancing. In fact, the term "western swing" was originally used to distinguish the dance orchestras of traditional swing or dance music from that of western dance bands.

BOB WILLS, best known of all the leaders of western swing bands, combined fiddles, guitars, banjos, piano, bass, and drums with reeds and brass to play a hybrid music that smoothly integrated elements of big band swing, old-time fiddling, Dixieland jazz, blues, and Mexican music. LEON MCAULIFFE, a member of the Wills band and leader of his own band after World War II, told this author that musicians defined this eclectic mixture as simply "a fiddle band that played dance music."

The heyday of western swing paralleled that of the big bands (1930–50). The seeds of this musical style were sown in Fort Worth, Texas, when Bob Wills and singer MILTON BROWN began performing together on radio and at dance clubs. Beginning in the summer of 1930, Wills and Brown, joined by guitarist Herman Arnspiger, began performing over Fort Worth's WBAP as the Aladdin Laddies and later, joined by Brown's brother Derwood on second guitar, as the popular LIGHT CRUST DOUGHBOYS. Two years later Brown left to form his own band, the influential Musical Brownies, and the following year Wills left as well to form his own enormously influential band, the Texas Playboys.

In the Dallas–Fort Worth area during the 1930s, Milton Brown & His Musical Brownies, BILL BOYD, and other pioneering western swing bands spread the regional popularity of western swing through successful recordings and radio shows. The maturation of the genre and national recognition came between 1934 and 1942, when Wills put together his Texas Playboys band in Tulsa, Oklahoma, broadcasting daily over KVOO and recording for COLUMBIA RECORDS. The national record-chart success of such Wills recordings as "San Antonio Rose" (1944), "Texas Playboy Rag" (1945), and "Stay a Little Longer" (1946) attested to the commerciality of the music. In the 1940s and 1950s western swing became a truly national phenomenon, as Bob Wills's brother JOHNNIE LEE WILLS, Leon McAuliffe, and HANK THOMPSON led popular western swing bands in the Southwest and as bandleaders such as HANK PENNY and PAUL HOWARD brought western swing to fans in the Southeast, while SPADE COOLEY challenged Bob Wills for the title King of Western Swing in packed ballrooms across Southern California.

With the rise of television after 1950, Americans no longer went to dances by the thousands, and the big dance orchestras and the western swing bands went into decline or ceased to exist. Only a few outfits could draw crowds large enough to keep large dance bands—which were expensive for bandleaders to pay and transport—on the road. By the mid-1960s, the era of western swing was history.

In the early 1970s, however, there was a revival, sparked in part by MERLE HAGGARD's 1970 tribute album to Bob Wills (*A Tribute to the Best Damn Fiddle Player in the World*) and by the success of Wills's last recording session (captured on the album *For the Last Time*) in 1973, which won a Grammy Award. In addition, a new generation of fans and musicians discovered western swing through contemporary musicians such as WILLIE NELSON, ASLEEP AT THE WHEEL, and GEORGE STRAIT. Though today only Asleep At The Wheel and a few regional groups can be considered genuine western swing bands, many country artists continue to perform occasionally in the western swing style, while evergreen western swing classics such as "San Antonio Rose," "Right or Wrong," "Stay a Little Longer," and "Faded Love" continue to be revived on record and in live performance. —*Charles R. Townsend*

Billy Edd Wheeler
b. Whitesville, West Virginia, December 9, 1932

Although he has received critical acclaim for his own recordings, Wheeler is still primarily regarded as a songwriter. His songs have won twelve ASCAP awards, sold 45 million copies, and have been recorded by artists as varied as ELVIS PRESLEY, Judy Collins, TEX RITTER, CONWAY TWITTY, Nancy Sinatra, MERLE HAGGARD, and KENNY ROGERS, among others. With this success, Wheeler remains humble and credits luck and timing more than his songwriting talent. Even so, he has a good deal of the latter and more education than is regularly associated with a country artist. A graduate of Warren Wilson and Berea Colleges, he also attended Yale Drama School. At various times he has been employed as an editor, music business executive, navy pilot, fund-raiser, and an instructor at Berea College.

In the late 1950s Wheeler started appearing on such programs as *Monitor*, the *Today* show, the *Merv Griffin Show*, and the *WWVA JAMBOREE* in Wheeling, West Virginia. Beginning in 1959 he started recording for the Monitor label, but later moved to United Artists, Kapp, and RCA. He had some success with the LPs *The Wheeler Man* (1963), *Town and Country* (1965), and *Nashville Zodiac* (1969), the latter gaining the greatest critical respect. Still, the biggest portion of his royalties have come from recordings of his songs by others, the notable exception being "Ode to the Little Brown Shack Out Back," his most successful single, which reached #3 on *Billboard* country charts in 1964.

His first major songwriting success was "Reverend Mister Black," with which the Kingston Trio had a Top Ten hit in 1963. JOHNNY CASH and JUNE CARTER had a crossover hit in 1967 with Wheeler's "Jackson," and Kenny Rogers scored big in 1979–80 with his "Coward of the County."

Wheeler is also a collector of folklore and the author of a folk play and several books of folk humor. He is responsible for creating a special music room in the Mountain Hall of Fame in Richwood, West Virginia, and has conducted workshops for songwriters at his alma mater Warren Wilson College. —*W. K. McNeil*

Onie Wheeler
b. Senath, Missouri, November 10, 1921; d. May 26, 1984

Sometimes an artist will carve a little niche for himself, with an obvious debt to no one, yet influencing few. Onie Daniel Wheeler was like that; he had a quirky style, blending his harmonica and strangely inflected vocals, but he never achieved much recognition. He worked alongside FLATT & SCRUGGS, ROY ACUFF, ELVIS PRESLEY, HANK SNOW, and GEORGE JONES, but stubbornness, uncommerciality, and bad luck dogged Wheeler's career.

Wheeler worked on the family farm until he went into the service. After his discharge, he tried for a career in country music, working live radio in Missouri, Arkansas, and Michigan. In August 1953 he signed with OKEH/COLUMBIA RECORDS in Nashville, and his first Columbia session included two of his best-known songs, "Run 'Em Off" and "Mother Prays Loud in Her Sleep." Flatt & Scruggs recorded the latter the day after Wheeler's session, and LEFTY FRIZZELL covered "Run 'Em Off." Starting in 1955,

Wheeler went out on tour with Elvis Presley and other SUN RECORDS artists, and tried recording rockabilly for Columbia and Sun without much conviction.

For the remainder of his career Wheeler flitted in and out of the music business. He recorded for many labels and scored a hit in 1973 with "John's Been Shucking My Corn" on Royal American Records. He was operated on for an aneurysm in January 1984 and started work again a few months later, but he collapsed and died onstage at the Grand Ole Opry House during Jimmie Snow's *Grand Ole Gospel* radio show. —*Colin Escott*

REPRESENTATIVE RECORDING
Onie's Bop (Bear Family Records, 1991)

Bryan White
b. Lawton, Oklahoma, February 17, 1974

When country music began actively seeking a younger demographic in the 1990s, Bryan S. White proved that teen appeal doesn't necessarily have to negate musical substance. And although White certainly attracts his share of screaming adolescent female fans, he's also won the respect of his primary influences, including STEVE WARINER and GLEN CAMPBELL.

White began playing drums at age five, and was seventeen when he switched to guitar and began writing songs. A year later he moved to Nashville and soon secured a staff writer's job at Glen Campbell Music. Signed to ASYLUM RECORDS in 1993, White's self-titled debut album in 1994 was launched with the single "Eugene You Genius," which demonstrated respectable commercial success for a new artist. The follow-up single, "Look At Me Now," fared even better, leading the way for his first two #1s, "Someone Else's Star" and "Rebecca Lynn."

White's second album, *Between Now and Forever*, was re-

Bryan White

leased in 1996, and provided additional hits, including "I'm Not Supposed to Love You Anymore."

Although his first #1s came from the pen of songwriter SKIP EWING, White continues to hone his writing skills. In addition to the songs included in his albums, White wrote the SAWYER BROWN hit "I Don't Believe In Goodbye." White also made a guest appearance on Wariner's 1996 guitar instrumental album *No More Mr. Nice Guy.*

White's list of recognitions include the COUNTRY MUSIC ASSOCIATION's 1996 Horizon Award and the ACADEMY OF COUNTRY MUSIC's 1996 New Male Vocalist honor.

—*Calvin Gilbert*

REPRESENTATIVE RECORDINGS

Bryan White (Asylum, 1994); *Between Now and Forever* (Asylum, 1996); *The Right Place* (Asylum, 1997)

Clarence and Roland White

Clarence White b. Lewiston, Maine, June 7, 1944; d. July 15, 1973
Roland White b. Madawaska, Maine, April 23, 1938

Brothers Roland and Clarence White succeeded in transposing the emotional grit of country's BROTHER DUET tradition to the mandolin and guitar as few others have. Of French-Canadian ancestry, the LeBlanc family, who later changed their name to White, relocated from their native Maine to Southern California in 1954. Father Eric White played guitar, tenor banjo, and harmonica, and his offspring grew up in a house filled with music.

Eventually a family group emerged, featuring brothers Eric on tenor banjo, Roland on mandolin (and sometimes on banjo), guitarist Clarence, and sister Joanne on bass. The group started out singing and playing contemporary country music, but by the mid-1950s—largely due to Roland's influence—the group's emphasis shifted strictly to bluegrass.

Performing as the Country Boys, the group won a talent contest hosted by Carl "Squeakin' Deacon" Moore on radio station KXLA in Pasadena. This soon led to regular appearances on West Coast shows such as the *Country Barndance Jubilee, TOWN HALL PARTY,* and *HOMETOWN JAMBOREE.*

Over the next few years several changes took place in the band. Eric and Joanne dropped out, and Billy Ray Latham (banjo), Leroy Mack (dobro), and Roger Bush (bass) moved into the outfit. The group made two appearances on CBS's popular *THE ANDY GRIFFITH SHOW* in 1961. In 1962 the band changed its name to the Kentucky Colonels and released its first album, *New Sounds of Bluegrass America.*

More importantly, Clarence's guitar work took on a more prominent role in the band. After having seen guitarist DOC WATSON at the L.A. nightclub the Ash Grove, Clarence began to test new possibilities for the guitar's role in bluegrass. At the time, the guitar was considered primarily a rhythm instrument, and few musicians—save for DON RENO, Watson, and EARL SCRUGGS—had bothered to explore the instrument's potential for soloing. In 1964 the group recorded their seminal instrumental album *Appalachian Swing!* for World Pacific Records. Fiddlers Bobby Slone and Scotty Stoneman also did hitches with the group in the 1960s.

By the mid-1960s Clarence's interest shifted to the electric guitar. His work on the BYRDS' "Time Between" in 1966 introduced the now-popular String Bender to rock and country fans. This device, developed by White and Byrds band member Gene Parsons, was a mechanism applied to the B string of the guitar. When activated (by pulling down on the neck), it bent the string, causing the guitar to simulate the crying sound of a pedal steel. Two years later Clarence became a full-time Byrd, remaining until the group's dissolution in February 1973. Until his death that same year (he was hit in a parking lot by a drunk driver), he was a highly sought-after session musician who recorded with LINDA RONSTADT, RICK NELSON, and the EVERLY BROTHERS.

Meanwhile, elder brother Roland continued to nurture his passion for bluegrass. After the Colonels disbanded, he went on to work with bluegrass legends BILL MONROE and LESTER FLATT. In 1973, based in Nashville, he joined the COUNTRY GAZETTE, where he remained until 1987, when he joined the highly successful NASHVILLE BLUEGRASS BAND.

—*Chris Skinker*

REPRESENTATIVE RECORDINGS

Appalachian Swing! (World Pacific Records, 1964; Rounder, 1993); *The Byrds* (Columbia/Legacy, 1990), 4 discs; *Long Journey Home* (Vanguard, 1991)

Joy Lynn White

b. Turrell, Arkansas, October 2, 1961

With a fiery voice to match her flaming red hair, Joy Lynn White has built a cult following on the strength of her powerful, vibrato-laced vocals and mix of uptempo roadhouse country rock and hard-country ballads. Born in Arkansas and raised in the South Bend, Indiana, suburb of Mishawaka, White first sang in public at age four, in her family's Baptist church. She grew up around music—from listening to JIMMIE RODGERS, EMMYLOU HARRIS, and LINDA RONSTADT records to hearing her father, bluegrass guitar player Nathan "Gene" White.

She started out singing in southern-rock bar bands and recorded commercial jingles in Fort Wayne, Indiana, before moving to Nashville in January 1982. She made a living as a waitress and shoeshine girl, then became a much-sought-after demo singer before signing with COLUMBIA RECORDS in 1991. Her first two albums recalled LORETTA LYNN's style, mixing ballad weepers and pumped-up honky-tonk. "They're both me," she once said. "I can't sit and sing one sad country song after another."

Her style went against the early 1990s pop-country grain and found only a limited audience. None of her first five singles reached the Top Forty. Her first album, *Between Midnight & Hindsight* (1992), credited to Joy White, included the singles "Little Tears" (#68), "True Confessions" (#50), and "Cold Day in July" (#71). Her 1994 release *Wild Love* included the singles "Wild Love" (#73) and "Bad Loser," which didn't chart and which marked the end of White's association with Columbia.

She has also sung harmony on recordings by LEE ROY PARNELL, the MAVERICKS, IRIS DeMENT, JAMIE O'HARA, and BOB WOODRUFF and a duet with MARTY BROWN ("I Love Only You" from *Cryin', Lovin', Leavin'*). In addition, she wrote "Big City Bound" for HIGHWAY 101. She was nominated in 1993 for the ACADEMY OF COUNTRY MUSIC's New Female Vocalist Award. In 1997 White signed with PETE ANDERSON's Little Dog label.

—*Bill Hobbs*

REPRESENTATIVE RECORDINGS

Between Midnight & Hindsight (Columbia, 1992); *Wild Love* (Columbia, 1994); *The Lucky Few* (Little Dog, 1997)

Lari White

b. Dunedin, Florida, May 13, 1965

In 1996 Lari White became the poster child for the difficulties facing a recording artist in Nashville. Her label, RCA RECORDS, dropped her, despite both of her two albums having been certified gold (500,000 in sales). The label said the move was strictly a business decision, which underscored the tremendous costs that Nashville labels incurred in the 1990s in promoting acts—costs that frequently can't be recouped without achieving record sales in the millions.

Before then, White had been known only for her boundless talent. Her style of bluesy, gospel-tinged country music owes more to Memphis than to Nashville, and it's best displayed on piano-driven undertows such as "Lead Me Not," off of her 1993 debut album.

White began performing at age four with her parents—she's named for her father, Larry. Despite having lost the little finger of her left hand in an accident when she was one year old, White began playing piano and wrote her first tune at age eight. After playing throughout the Gulf Coast in her teens and studying voice at the University of Miami, White moved to Nashville at age twenty-three with no industry contacts. She won the *You Can Be a Star* contest on TNN in 1988, and began getting cuts as a songwriter. In 1992 White became a back-up singer for RODNEY CROWELL.

Signed to RCA RECORDS, she released her debut in 1993, and her first Top Ten hit came in 1994 with "That's My Baby." When the time came to release White's third album, RCA balked, perhaps because White has never caught on with country radio. Her soulful singing and writing abilities, however, appear to have prepared her for possible success elsewhere in the near future. In the fall of 1997 White signed with Disney Entertainment's newly created Nashville label Lyric Street Records.   —*Clark Parsons*

REPRESENTATIVE RECORDINGS

Lead Me Not (RCA, 1993); *Wishes* (RCA, 1994)

Martha White (*see* Martha White Flour, under M)

Tony Joe White

b. Oak Grove, Louisiana, July 23, 1943

Tony Joe White's spare, southern style of music made him equally at home on the pop charts, in country songwriting circles, and as a European rock idol. Known as the Swamp Fox, he wrote the soul music classic "Rainy Night in Georgia" and had a Top Ten pop hit in 1969 with "Polk Salad Annie." A wide variety of stylists have recorded his tunes, including HANK WILLIAMS JR., GEORGE JONES, RAY CHARLES, JERRY REED, Wilson Pickett, and WAYLON JENNINGS.

As a Louisiana teenager White was deeply influenced by his older brother's blues records. He began performing regionally as Tony & the Mojos, then Tony & the Twilights. He came to Nashville in 1967 and played his songs for COMBINE MUSIC publisher BOB BECKHAM. This led to a staff songwriting job as well as to a MONUMENT RECORDS contract, with BILLY SWAN as his producer.

White's single "Soul Francisco" became a hit in France in 1968 (leading to his European popularity over the next twenty-five years); then, slowly, "Polk Salad Annie" began to climb the U.S. hit parade. "Roosevelt and Ira Lee" and "Save Your Sugar for Me" followed it onto the pop charts in 1969–70.

White's "Rainy Night in Georgia" became a pop and r&b hit for Brook Benton in 1970 and later achieved country notoriety as a 1993 CONWAY TWITTY–Sam Moore duet, the last song Twitty ever recorded. Among White's other notable songwriting successes are ELVIS PRESLEY's "I Got a Thing About You, Baby," Tina Turner's "Steamy Windows," and Dusty Springfield's "Willie and Laura Mae Jones."

White recorded three albums for Monument (1968–70), three for WARNER BROS. (1971–73), and one each for 20th Century (1976), Casablanca (1980), and COLUMBIA (1983). Since 1986 he has been marketing albums on his own label and distributing them overseas.

—*Robert K. Oermann*

REPRESENTATIVE RECORDING

The Best of Tony Joe White (Warner Bros., 1993)

The Whites

Sharon White b. Wichita Falls, Texas, December 17, 1953
Cheryl White b. Wichita Falls, Texas, January 27, 1955
Buck White b. Oklahoma, December 13, 1930

The Whites have a captivating, family-harmony sound, dominated by female voices, that began attracting listeners when Sharon and Cheryl White were barely in their teens. Emerging from the bluegrass field into the country mainstream in 1981, they came to be associated with country's NEW TRADITIONALIST movement through their own work and through their affiliations with EMMYLOU HARRIS and RICKY SKAGGS.

Buck White's musical style reflects his rearing in Oklahoma and Texas. An accomplished honky-tonk pianist and bluegrass mandolinist, he makes music also tinged with western swing, gospel, Mexican, and blues elements. As a teenager and young man he performed on radio with swing bands and bluegrass groups, and even played electric piano for a rock & roll act. In 1962, while Buck worked as a pipefitter in Arkansas, he and his wife, Pat, developed an act with another couple that came to be known as the Down Home Folks. In 1966 Sharon, then thirteen, joined on guitar, while Cheryl, eleven years old, played bass. (By the mid-eighties, the group often included third daughter Rosie on percussion and guitar.) The group initially performed on the bluegrass festival circuit; then in 1971 the Whites moved to Nashville to pursue music full-time. Pat White left the music business in 1973.

The act made their recording debut as Buck White & the Down Home Folks on COUNTY RECORDS in 1972, while the 1980 album *More Pretty Girls Than One,* on SUGAR HILL, captured the family's harmonies at their best. After Emmylou Harris first heard them in 1975, the Whites provided vocals on her "Blue Kentucky Girl" (1979) and joined Harris for a time on tour. Sharon married Harris's then bandleader Ricky Skaggs in 1982.

The Whites' first country chart record, "Send Me the Pillow You Dream On," appeared in 1981. Skaggs began producing them the following year, and Top Ten hits such as "You Put the Blue in Me" (ELEKTRA) followed; Sharon White and Skaggs also recorded successfully as a duo.

The Whites made the gospel album *Doing It by the Book* in 1988 and, in 1996, recorded *Give a Little Back* with STEP

ONE RECORDS. They joined the GRAND OLE OPRY cast in 1984 and continue to perform for audiences regularly.

—*Mary A. Bufwack*

REPRESENTATIVE RECORDING
Greatest Hits (MCA/Curb, 1986)

Whitey & Hogan
Roy "Whitey" Grant b. Shelby, North Carolina, April 7, 1916
Arval Albert Hogan b. Robbinsville, North Carolina, July 24, 1911

Based in Charlotte, North Carolina, Whitey & Hogan were a popular duet harmony team from the late 1930s to the mid-1950s. Both came from working-class origins: Hogan was the son of a western North Carolina lumberman; Whitey was a farm boy. The pair met in about 1936 at a Gastonia, North Carolina, textile mill where both men worked. Discovering their mutual love of music, they built up a repertoire of hymns, folk tunes, contemporary love songs, and novelty tunes, all rendered in the widespread acoustic duet harmony style of the era.

In about 1938 they began broadcasting on radio station WSPA in Spartanburg, South Carolina, then shifted to WGNC in Gastonia in 1939. At this point Charlotte record distributor Vann Sills recruited them for a DECCA recording session in New York. Shortly after World War II they recorded several sides for the New York–based Sonora label, but mostly they remained radio performers, not recording artists.

In 1941 the duo moved to WBT in Charlotte, North Carolina, and worked on *Briarhopper Time,* a daily variety show sponsored by Chicago's Consolidated Drug Trade Products Company, makers of Peruna (a tonic and cold medicine), Kolorbak Hair Dye, and similar products. Whitey & Hogan also worked regional CBS network shows such as the *Dixie Jamboree, Carolina Hayride,* and *Carolina Calling.* Early in the 1950s, local Charlotte TV shows broadened the duo's exposure. In the mid-1950s, with demand for their style fading, the partners became Charlotte mail carriers and bought homes next door to each other. With the bluegrass and old-time music festival movement of the seventies, however, the duet found a new generation of fans.

—*John Rumble*

Keith Whitley
b. Sandy Hook, Kentucky, July 1, 1955; d. May 9, 1989

Hard-country singer Jessie Keith Whitley was just beginning to hit his stride when he died at his Goodlettsville home on May 9, 1989, of alcohol poisoning. He was just thirty-three years old, but he left a powerful musical legacy behind, influencing many young country singers in the 1990s. A songwriter of talent and depth, Whitley wrote compositions that ranged from soulful gospel ("Great High Mountain") to humorous ("I Want My Rib Back").

Steeped in the honky-tonk sounds of LEFTY FRIZZELL and GEORGE JONES and the bluegrass of the STANLEY BROTHERS, Whitley brought a vocal maturity and sensibility to country music far beyond his years. Like his heroes Frizzell, Jones, and Carter Stanley, he struggled with alcoholism for most of his adult life.

By age eight Whitley appeared on singer BUDDY STARCHER's television show broadcast out of Charleston, West Virginia, and was working on local radio shows with his elder brother Dwight. A few years later Whitley met another

Keith Whitley

child prodigy, RICKY SKAGGS from nearby Cordell, at a talent show. Both were contestants, but neither took home first prize. The two became friends and soon formed the East Kentucky Mountain Boys.

In 1970 Whitley and Skaggs were asked to fill in at a nightclub for Ralph Stanley, who was late for the show date due to bus trouble. As Stanley recounted the story some years ago, "I walked in and they were doing the Stanley Brothers *better* than the Stanleys." Although they were still in high school, Ralph hired the two teenagers virtually on the spot. Whitley played guitar and handled some of the vocals, while Ricky was featured on mandolin and vocals. The pair performed in Stanley's Clinch Mountain Boys throughout the next two summer festival seasons and recorded a pair of albums—*Tribute to the Stanley Brothers* (Jayln, 1971) and *Second Generation Bluegrass* (Rebel, 1971).

Whitley left Stanley's outfit in 1972 and joined forces with mandolin player Jimmy Gaudreau and banjoist CARL JACKSON in the Country Store (also dubbed New Tradition). In 1974 Whitley joined the Clinch Mountain Boys for a second hitch. This time he assumed the role of lead vocalist, replacing Roy Lee Centers, who was fatally shot in May of that year. Whitley worked with Stanley until 1978, when he joined J. D. CROWE's New South. While with Crowe, Whitley recorded a handful of albums, including *Live in Japan* (1979) and *Somewhere Between* (1982).

Although successful in bluegrass, Whitley had aspirations far beyond that music's boundaries. In 1984 he moved to Nashville just as the back-to-basics NEW TRADITIONALIST movement was gaining momentum. By September Whitley landed a record contract with RCA RECORDS and had a single on the country charts, "Turn Me to Love," featuring PATTY LOVELESS on background vocals.

Whitley's fourth single, "Miami, My Amy," was his first to crack the country Top Twenty, and his next three singles all broke into the Top Ten. In 1988 Keith hit #1 on the charts with the romantic ballads "Don't Close Your Eyes" and "When You Say Nothing At All." In addition, Whitley's introspective, soul-searching recordings of "I'm No

Stranger to the Rain" and "I Wonder Do You Think of Me" also topped the charts in 1989. The former song was named the CMA's Single of the Year. Several posthumous hits followed, including "It Ain't Nothin' " and a duet with his wife, LORRIE MORGAN, whom he married in 1986, " 'Til a Tear Becomes a Rose." The recording, on which Morgan's vocals were overdubbed onto an existing Whitley track, won the CMA's Vocal Event of the Year Award in 1990.

—*Chris Skinker*

REPRESENTATIVE RECORDINGS

Second Generation Bluegrass (Rebel, 1971); *Don't Close Your Eyes* (RCA, 1988); *I Wonder Do You Think of Me* (RCA, 1989)

Ray Whitley

b. Atlanta, Georgia, December 5, 1901; d. February 21, 1979

Not unlike Hollywood actor Randolph Scott, Georgia-born, Alabama-raised Raymond Otis Whitley remained a quintessential southern gentleman in the heart of the West.

After he appeared on the *WHN Barn Dance* in the mid-1930s, Whitley's baritone voice, bluesy yodeling, considerable charm, and rugged good looks made him a natural for the burgeoning singing cowboy film genre. Beginning in 1936, Whitley starred in sixteen singing cowboy shorts for RKO and appeared in some sixty features overall. His film career ended with a role in the 1956 epic *Giant*.

In addition, he managed the SONS OF THE PIONEERS in their early years, led a western swing band, toured relentlessly, recorded for a number of labels (DECCA, OKEH, and others), and aided the Gibson Guitar Company in developing the J-200 deluxe in 1938. His prototype of the acoustic guitar model so impressed his fellow singing film stars that soon GENE AUTRY, TEX RITTER, and JIMMY WAKELY featured them onscreen, making the jumbo rosewood guitar the sine qua non of the singing cowboy.

An open and generous man, Whitley befriended FRED ROSE in the late 1930s, and while Rose was living with the Whitleys they collaborated on several successful songs, all popularized by Autry: "Lonely River," "I Hang My Head and Cry," and "Ages and Ages Ago." In addition, Whitley wrote one of the most memorable pieces of western music of all time, "Back in the Saddle Again," for one of his films, and the song became Autry's theme song.

With the decline of the singing cowboy and the rise of rock, Ray Whitley quietly phased out of film and music. Rediscovered during the 1970s, he charmed his old fans and a new generation with rope and whip tricks and his still strong voice. He died of diabetic shock while on a fishing trip in Baja California, Mexico, and was sorely missed by a western music community who found him to be the same profoundly decent, unassuming, life-loving gentleman he portrayed onscreen.

—*Douglas B. Green*

Slim Whitman

b. Tampa, Florida, January 20, 1924

Known for his haunting, sky-high falsetto flourishes on sentimental pop songs such as "Indian Love Call" and "Secret Love," Otis Dewey Whitman Jr. also played an early role in popularizing country music in Europe and other foreign lands, making it possible for the international success it enjoys today.

Slim Whitman grew up in the Tampa area, with his

Slim Whitman

main interest in sports, especially baseball. At the outbreak of World War II, he enlisted in the U.S. Navy, and while on board ship he found a guitar and learned to play, adapting his left-handed playing style by stringing the instrument upside down. Several years after his discharge, and after playing minor-league baseball for a time, Whitman decided to try his luck at a music career. In 1948 he began working the nightclubs and radio stations in the Tampa area. In that year, on a recommendation by COLONEL TOM PARKER, he was signed to RCA RECORDS. In 1950 he joined the *LOUISIANA HAYRIDE*.

In late 1951 Whitman signed a contract with IMPERIAL RECORDS (later absorbed by United Artists and then by CAPITOL RECORDS), for whom he would record for twenty-two years. Whitman's first release, "Love Song of the Waterfall," reached #1 on the country charts. His second single, "Indian Love Call" (first popularized by Jeanette MacDonald and Nelson Eddy in the 1936 film *Rose Marie*) became a million seller and remained on the country charts (peaking at #2 country, #9 pop, 1951) for twenty-four weeks. During the next three years, all of his singles charted. Whitman's success spread overseas to England with the 1954 release of "Rose Marie," the title song from the film of the same name. A #4 country hit in the United States, the record went to the #1 spot in England's charts. Not only was Whitman the first country artist to reach the top of the British charts, but he also became the second country performer to play the London Palladium (1956).

At about the time Slim Whitman joined the GRAND OLE OPRY in 1955, he found his career on a downslide. Although Whitman had a dry period in America, his career was still in full swing in England. He returned to the U.S. country charts in 1964 and remained through 1974. In 1979 the Slim Whitman LP *All My Best* was offered through a telemarketing campaign. It was such a success, reportedly selling 4 million copies, that Whitman was signed to the Cleveland International label, where he recorded several moderate hits in 1980 and 1981. Whitman continues to tour, with his son Byron. —*Don Roy*

The Best of Slim Whitman, 1951–1971 (Rhino, 1990); *Greatest Hits* (Curb, 1990); *Slim Whitman: Vintage Collection* (Capitol, 1996)

Bob Whittaker
b. Cookeville, Tennessee, May 10, 1941

On November 1, 1996, the twenty-fifth anniversary of his employment with GAYLORD ENTERTAINMENT, native Tennessean Bob Whittaker became president of the Grand Ole Opry Group, responsible for producing the GRAND OLE OPRY each week.

Whittaker first heard the Saturday night radio show on trips to his grandfather's farm in Baxter, Tennessee, during the mid- to late 1940s. He came to the OPRYLAND USA theme park, in 1971, as its first personnel manager. Four years later he was appointed head of the park's entertainment division, a post he held for thirteen years before assuming responsibility for the *General Jackson* showboat and Gaylord's Fiesta Texas theme park in San Antonio. In 1990 Whittaker was named general manager of Opryland theme park and vice president of Opryland USA. He became general manager of the Opry in September 1993 and worked under president HAL DURHAM until Durham's retirement in 1996.

Whittaker takes an aggressive approach to assembling each week's lineup: working with the cast to choose their songs and occasionally programming a segment centered on a special theme. An accomplished singer himself, Whittaker sometimes joins the harmony group the Carol Lee Singers as a backing vocalist. In addition to the Opry, Whittaker has produced live shows in the theme park (which closed winter 1997 and will be replaced by the planned Opry Mills entertainment/shopping mall). He also hires talent for productions at the Gaylord-owned RYMAN AUDITORIUM and Wildhorse Saloon in Nashville. —*Jay Orr*

Henry Whitter
b. Grayson County, Virginia, April 6, 1892; d. November 17, 1941

One of the first rural folk musicians to make commercial recordings, William Henry Whitter was born near Fries, Virginia, and began playing musical instruments while working in the textile mills. Dissatisfied with his mill job, Whitter turned to music as the road to greater fame, singing and playing his guitar and harmonica in and around Fries. In 1923, possibly in March, Whitter journeyed to New York to visit the General Phonograph Corporation for a recording audition. A more successful session, in December, resulted in his first release: "The Wreck on the Southern Old 97"/"Lonesome Road Blues" (OKEH 40015). It was this recording of "Wreck" that VERNON DALHART later heard, revised, and recorded for the Victor Talking Machine Company, coupled with "The Prisoner's Song"—a disc that became country music's first million-selling hit. Whitter recorded with a number of artists between 1924 and 1930, but his most successful partnership was with blind fiddler Gilliam Banmon "G. B." Gray-

son (b. Ashe County, North Carolina, November 11, 1888; d. August 16, 1930). Together the duo recorded some forty selections—a collection that influenced not only other southeastern musicians during the 1930s but also early bluegrass musicians in the 1950s and then urban folksong revival singers in the 1960s and 1970s. Their recordings ended with Grayson's death in a 1930 automobile accident.

Solo, Whitter's performances were rather lackluster: He was an uninteresting singer with only passable guitar backup and acceptable harmonica work. But with Grayson, something clicked between the two musicians, and the results were outstanding: beautiful, archaic singing and fiddling on Grayson's part, with guitar accompaniment ranging from adequate to very good. Nearly all of the Grayson & Whitter duets have been reissued on LP or CD, but hardly any of Whitter's nearly five dozen solo pieces have been brought out. Whitter's importance rests on his recording of "Old 97," historically one of the most significant in early country music, and in his bringing G. B. Grayson before the microphone, thereby creating one of the finest country music bands to record in the pre-war years. —*Norm Cohen*

Grayson and Whitter (County, 1968); *G. B. Grayson and Henry Whitter: Early Classics, Volume 1 and Volume 2* (Old Homestead, 1984)

John and Audrey Wiggins
John Wayne Wiggins b. Nashville, Tennessee, October 13, 1962
Audrey Lynn Wiggins b. Asheville, North Carolina, December 26, 1967

Brother-and-sister act John and Audrey Wiggins continue a country tradition of family harmony singing reaching back to the CARTER FAMILY and the folk traditions the Carters drew upon. Growing up in Waynesville, North Carolina, the two performers absorbed Appalachian folk music but learned commercial country sounds as well: Their father, Johnny, briefly pursued a country career, moving to Nashville in 1960 and eventually becoming ERNEST TUBB's "Singin' Bus Driver."

Johnny encouraged his children's talents after returning to North Carolina in 1965. John turned semiprofessional by age seventeen, while working for his father's paving business; Audrey appeared with Tubb on a GRAND OLE OPRY spot at age twelve and sang with her brother's band in clubs around Waynesville. From 1979 to 1987 the duo worked out of nearby Maggie Valley, traveling briefly to Nashville in 1984 to make a single and some low-budget videos.

John and Audrey moved to Nashville in 1987, went home, then came back to MUSIC CITY in 1990. In 1994 MERCURY RECORDS released their self-titled debut album, which yielded the chart-making singles "Has Anybody Seen Amy," "She's in the Bedroom Crying," and "Falling out of Love," the latter penned by John. *The Dream* (1997) continued their characteristic mix of rock, pop, and traditional country. By early 1998 Mercury had dropped the brother-sister duo. —*John Rumble*

John & Audrey Wiggins (Mercury, 1994); *The Dream* (Mercury, 1997)

Little Roy Wiggins

b. Nashville, Tennessee, June 27, 1926

Ivan Leroy "Little Roy" Wiggins, the diminutive crying steel guitar wizard best known for his many years with EDDY ARNOLD, was born three miles from the RYMAN AUDITORIUM. Inspired as a child at a party by the steel playing of the GRAND OLE OPRY's Bert Hutcherson, Wiggins first took lessons at age six from Nashville's Robert E. Martin. At thirteen Wiggins got a job with the Opry's PAUL HOWARD and two years later replaced Clell Summey (who left for World War II military service) as steel guitarist with the Golden West Cowboys. Wiggins was lured away in 1943 when singer Eddy Arnold left that band to start his own, the Tennessee Plowboys. Wiggins stayed with Arnold for twenty-five years, long providing the distinctive "ting-a-ling" cry so palatable to country ears in support of Arnold's smooth singing. Wiggins shined on so many Arnold hits that for years the billing read "Eddy Arnold and His Guitar," and everyone knew that the guitar in question was not Arnold's own but Wiggins's steel.

Beginning in the late 1950s Wiggins made instrumental records for DOT RECORDS, STARDAY RECORDS, and afterward for such labels as Midland, Diplomat, Empire Sound, American Sound, Stoneway, and O'Brien. While still playing for Arnold in the early 1960s, Wiggins joined Arnold's partner and accountant Charles Mosley in the insurance and real-estate business in suburban Brentwood, Tennessee. Another business boon came his way through the Tennessee governor's office when Vox Instruments chose Wiggins to endorse its products and also find other country pickers to do the same.

Leaving Arnold's employ in about 1968, Wiggins opened a music store at 427 Broadway near the Ryman and called it Little Roy Wiggins's Music City. At this time he returned to the Grand Ole Opry to play behind the WILLIS BROTHERS, GEORGE MORGAN, ERNIE ASHWORTH, and other acts. After the Opry's 1974 move from the Ryman to the OPRYLAND USA complex, Wiggins closed his music store, and in the 1980s left to perform for Smoky Mountains tourists in Pigeon Forge, Tennessee. He still resides in nearby Sevierville. —*Ronnie Pugh*

Wilburn Brothers (Doyle & Teddy)

Virgil Doyle Wilburn b. Hardy, Arkansas, July 7, 1930; d. October 16, 1982

Thurman Theodore Wilburn b. Hardy, Arkansas, November 30, 1931

Doyle and Teddy Wilburn first performed publicly at ages five and six, respectively, as part of the Wilburn Family, with older siblings Lester, Leslie, and Geraldine. The performance took place Christmas Eve 1937, on a Thayer, Missouri, street corner. In 1940 ROY ACUFF sponsored their debut on the GRAND OLE OPRY, though child labor laws barred their membership. They went on to record for FOUR STAR.

The four brothers performed on KWKH in Shreveport, Louisiana, beginning in about 1948, until by 1951 both Doyle and Teddy had been drafted for the Korean War. During these years the Wilburns invited a relatively unknown WEBB PIERCE to guest on their Shreveport radio show, leading to Pierce's career-launching LOUISIANA HAY-RIDE stint, and eventually Doyle and Teddy played guitar and bass, respectively, on Pierce's first DECCA session. Following military discharge, the duo toured with Pierce, by

The Wilburn Brothers: Teddy and Doyle

now an Opry star. In 1954 Teddy and Doyle signed with Decca and joined the Opry cast two years later as full-fledged members.

During the late 1950s and 1960s the Wilburn Brothers recorded such hits as "I'm So in Love With You," "Trouble's Back in Town," and "Roll, Muddy River" and displayed songwriting talents with recordings such as "Let Me Be the First to Know" and "Somebody's Back in Town." The Wilburns' vocal harmonies enhanced others' recordings as well, notably Pierce's "In the Jailhouse Now" and ERNEST TUBB's "Hey, Mr. Bluebird." Teddy recorded briefly as a Decca duet with Pierce, under the name Rob & Bob.

Equally important were the Wilburns' business achievements, including their Sure-Fire music publishing firm and the Wil-Helm Talent Agency, the latter founded with former HANK WILLIAMS steel player Don Helms. While Sure-Fire published early songs by LORETTA LYNN—whose Decca contract the Wilburns negotiated—Wil-Helm booked top country acts such as JEAN SHEPARD, SONNY JAMES, and the OSBORNE BROTHERS, who eventually covered many Wilburn Brothers hits. In 1963 the Wilburns also began their successful syndicated TV show, which provided Lynn and others with invaluable early exposure. This program was one of the first of its kind to be broadcast in color.

Soon independently wealthy, Teddy studied acting in Hollywood, while Doyle was wed briefly to singer Margie Bowes. Into the 1990s Teddy operated Sure-Fire and still played the Opry on occasion. —*Walt Trott*

REPRESENTATIVE RECORDINGS

Wonderful Wilburn Brothers (King, 1988); *Retrospective* (MCA, 1990)

Wiley & Gene

Wiley Walker b. Laurel Hill, Florida, November 17, 1911; d. May 17, 1966

Gene Sullivan b. Carbon Hill, Alabama, November 6, 1914; d. October 24, 1984

Wiley Walker and Gene Sullivan were country duet singers with a difference. Unlike the many brother acts, who generally employed mandolin and guitar or other acoustic instruments as their basic instruments, Wiley & Gene projected an overall sound and ambience that suggested the emerging honky-tonk environment of the 1940s. Although their popular recordings, such as "Live and Let Live," "When My Blue Moon Turns to Gold Again," and "I Want to Live and Love," showed up in honky-tonks throughout the nation, on jukeboxes, or in the performances of other musicians, Wiley & Gene did not perform in the dance-hall circuit. Instead, they were fixtures on radio stations in Texas and Oklahoma, particularly in Oklahoma City, where they spent most of their career.

Walker was a singer, buck dancer, and fiddler (known especially for his performance of "Rubber Dolly") who traveled for several years with the Harley Sadler Tent Show, where he met and teamed up with the popular entertainer LEW CHILDRE. He and Childre performed as "the Alabama Boys" on WWL in New Orleans and on other southern radio stations. While performing with the Shelton Brothers in Louisiana, Walker began singing duets with Gene Sullivan. Sullivan was a singer, guitarist, and skillful comedian who sometimes recited humorous poetry, including "Sleeping at the Foot of the Bed," which later became a popular recording for LITTLE JIMMY DICKENS. He also recorded the humorous recitation "Wash Your Feet Before Going to Bed." Sullivan played with several Texas country swing bands, including ROY NEWMAN's Boys, with whom he sang and recorded "Kansas City Blues." Sullivan also exhibited considerable talent as a songwriter, and he wrote most of the classic songs that he and Walker recorded. Wiley & Gene inaugurated their popular duet act on KFJZ and the Texas State Network in 1939, but the pinnacle of their career came during the war years, when songs such as "When My Blue Moon Turns to Gold Again" seemed to mirror the loneliness and hope for reconciliation felt by many Americans. Wiley & Gene recorded for COLUMBIA during 1939–47 and again in 1950. Sullivan recorded solo for Columbia in 1951 and 1957.

—*Bill C. Malone*

Marijohn Wilkin
b. Kemp, Texas, July 14, 1920

During the historic NASHVILLE SOUND era, only a handful of women were deeply involved in the country industry in any area other than singing. One was Marijohn Wilkin, a former schoolteacher who became one of the most successful of the first-generation Music Row songwriters. Wilkin cowrote such classic tunes as "The Long Black Veil," "Waterloo," "Cut Across Shorty," and, many years later, the gospel standard "One Day at a Time." She also worked as a songplugger and lead-sheet writer for CEDARWOOD PUBLISHING, and in 1964 she started Buckhorn Music, the company KRIS KRISTOFFERSON wrote for when he arrived in Nashville.

Born Marijohn Melson, she grew up in Sanger, Texas, and learned to play piano at an early age. In college she sang with the Hardin-Simmons University Cowboy Band, a traveling troupe that performed at Franklin D. Roosevelt's third inauguration. Eventually landing in Tulsa, she became a schoolteacher and started writing songs. In 1955, when her eight-year-old musician son, John Buck "Bucky" Wilkin, was discovered by a representative of the *OZARK JUBILEE*, she and her family moved to Springfield, Missouri. Bucky Wilkin worked with BRENDA LEE while his mother sang with RED FOLEY's road show. Foley and others re-

corded her songs, and in 1958, when Nashville booking agent LUCKY MOELLER heard Wilkin at a Springfield piano bar, he convinced her to move to Nashville.

In MUSIC CITY Wilkin initially worked at another piano bar, but soon quit to accept a fifty-dollar-a-week job with Cedarwood, where she was part of an all-star stable of writers who included, among others, JOHN D. LOUDERMILK, DANNY DILL, WAYNE WALKER, and MEL TILLIS. She also recorded two albums, including a collection of Civil War songs that appeared on COLUMBIA in 1961. After Cedarwood chief JIM DENNY died, Wilkin left the company to start Buckhorn Music in partnership with Nashville arranger and saxophonist Bill Justis.

Ironically, Buckhorn's first success was the surf-era rock & roll hit "G.T.O.," which Bucky Wilkin wrote and recorded in 1964 under the name of Ronny & the Daytonas. At about that time Kristofferson arrived in Nashville and contacted Wilkin, having heard of her through mutual acquaintances while he was in the army. Wilkin signed him. Among the songs that Kristofferson wrote during his tenure at Buckhorn was "For the Good Times," a #1 hit for RAY PRICE in 1970.

For all her success, Wilkin grew suicidally depressed during this period, and she embarked on a long, spiritual journey overseas in 1968. She began to write "One Day at a Time" as a prayer, and in 1973 Kristofferson helped her finish the song. Recorded first by Marilyn Sellars, the song became a gospel standard and a hit for CHRISTY LANE.

During the 1970s Wilkin recorded several gospel albums before easing from the limelight. She made headlines anew in 1995 when her "I Just Don't Understand," cowritten with Kent Westberry, appeared on the Beatles' *Live at the BBC* collection. She has lately had success with Seventeenth Avenue Music, another publishing company she co-owns, which has had songs recorded by LEANN RIMES.

—*Daniel Cooper*

Marijohn Wilkin

Slim Willet
b. Victor, Texas, December 1, 1919; d. July 1, 1966

Winston Lee Moore, better known as Slim Willet, is probably best remembered as the writer of "Don't Let the Stars Get in Your Eyes." He adopted his pseudonym while student manager of the radio station at Hardin-Simmons University in Abilene, Texas. After graduation in 1949 he joined Abilene radio station KRBC. In 1950 his recording career began with the release of "I'm a Tool Pusher from Snyder" on the Dallas-based Star Talent label. "Don't Let the Stars Get in Your Eyes," released on FOUR STAR RECORDS in 1952, proved so popular that four different performers, including Willet, had versions in *Billboard*'s Top Ten country jukebox, radio, and record sales at the same time. Perry Como also took the song to #1 on *Billboard*'s pop chart. Although he never had another hit of this magnitude, Willet remained active in the industry. For a brief period he turned his stage name around and established a rock & roll alter ego, Telli W. Mils, the Fat Cat. In addition to his own publishing company and advertising agency, he established the Edmoral and Winston labels to release his recordings and those by area performers such as HOYLE NIX, Dean Beard, Jimmy Seals, Darrell Rhodes, and Curtis Potter. Willet was also a pioneer in live television with a local show featuring new talent such as LARRY GATLIN, and in 1962 Willet was instrumental in the licensing of KCAD, one of the first full-time country music radio stations in the state. Willet's death meant the loss of an important catalyst for live entertainment and recording activity in the Abilene area. *—Joe W. Specht*

REPRESENTATIVE RECORDINGS
Slim Willet (Audio Lab, 1959); *Texas Oil Patch Songs* (Winston, 1962)

Audrey Williams
b. Enon Community, Alabama, February 28, 1923; d. November 4, 1975

As the wife of HANK WILLIAMS, the mother of HANK WILLIAMS JR., and a major force behind both men's rise to stardom, Audrey Mae Sheppard Williams's contributions to the history of country music could easily stand on these facts alone. However, throughout the 1950s and 1960s she established herself as one of Nashville's first female music entrepreneurs, with her own publishing company, booking agency, record label, all-girl band, and movie production company.

She met Hank Williams at a medicine show in the summer of 1943 and married him in December 1944. Audrey's young daughter, Lycrecia, from an earlier marriage, was raised by Hank as his own; their son, Randall Hank Williams, was born in 1949.

Audrey was an integral part of Hank's early career, handling his bookings, collecting money at the door, playing stand-up bass, and singing backup with his band. But theirs was a tempestuous union, marked by a divorce (May 26, 1948), a divorce annulment (August 9, 1949), and a final divorce (April 3, 1952). The anguish in Hank's greatest songs ("Cold, Cold Heart," "I Can't Help It if I'm Still in Love with You," "Your Cheatin' Heart") bears testimony to their rocky relationship.

In the 1950s Audrey recorded briefly for both DECCA and MGM herself (she had previously recorded a few

MGM duets with Hank). After Hank died on January 1, 1953, Audrey never recovered from the guilt and sorrow she felt, and she died of alcoholism. They are buried side by side in Montgomery, Alabama. *—Dale Vinicur*

REPRESENTATIVE RECORDING
Ramblin' Gal (Bear Family Records, 1988)

Curley Williams & His Georgia Peach Pickers
Curley Williams b. near Cairo, Georgia, June 3, 1914; d. September 5, 1970

Curley Williams is principally remembered for writing "Half As Much." Though he recorded the song for COLUMBIA RECORDS in 1951, it became a national hit when HANK WILLIAMS released his version the following year, followed by Rosemary Clooney's pop hit. In his day, Curley Williams was a popular bandleader, starring briefly on the GRAND OLE OPRY (1942–45) and recording for Columbia Records (forty-four sides during his 1945–52 stint with the label).

Born Doc Williams, he grew up on a South Georgia farm listening to his father's fiddling. After forming his first band, Doc Williams & His Santa Fe Trail Riders, in 1940, Williams appeared on radio stations in several small towns in Georgia. In December 1942 the group, renamed Curley Williams & the Georgia Peach Pickers, and consisting of Williams on fiddle; his brothers Sanford and Joseph on bass and guitar, respectively; steel guitarist Boots Harris; pianist Joe Pope; and Jimmy Selph, guitarist and vocalist, made its debut on the Grand Ole Opry.

In 1945 Williams left the Opry for the West Coast, where his group appeared at major dance halls and in a movie, *Riders of the Lone Star,* featuring Charles Starrett. Williams later appeared on radio stations in Louisiana, Tennessee, and Alabama. In 1954 he had his own TV show on WSFA in Montgomery, Alabama. Subsequently, he operated a Montgomery nightclub called The Spur—for which his band provided music—until his death. *—Wayne W. Daniel*

REPRESENTATIVE RECORDING
Radio Favorites (Old Homestead, 1990)

Doc & Chickie Williams
Andrew John Smik Jr. b. Cleveland, Ohio, June 26, 1914
Jessie Wanda Crupe b. Bethany, West Virginia, February 13, 1919

The husband-and-wife duo of Doc & Chickie Williams have been stalwarts of traditional country music in the American Northeast and eastern Canada for more than a half century. They also managed to incorporate some East European ethnic sounds into their style. Andy Smik grew up in the coal mining country of Pennsylvania and got his early radio experience in Cleveland and Pittsburgh—where he adopted the stage name Doc Williams—before joining the *WWVA WHEELING JAMBOREE* in May 1937. He has been associated with the *Jamboree* off and on since then. Doc married Chickie in 1939, and they subsequently had three daughters, but Chickie did not become a regular in the group until 1946. Doc started his own Wheeling Records in 1947, and the initial release, Chickie's rendition of "Beyond the Sunset," was quickly covered by the major labels.

Their band, the Border Riders, carved out a distinct sound, highlighted by Doc's brother Cy on fiddle and Marion Martin on accordion. Although not national stars, the duo have retained popularity in rural areas extending from Ohio to Newfoundland. They recorded numerous singles and albums on the Wheeling label both individually and together. By the late seventies they began to curtail extensive touring but have remained semiactive into the late 1990s. —*Ivan M . Tribe*

REPRESENTATIVE RECORDING

Doc and Chickie Williams: The Golden Years Collection (Wheeling, 1993)

Don Williams
b. Floydada, Texas, May 27, 1939

Country's "Gentle Giant," a crooner in the JIM REEVES tradition, Don Williams was one of country's most consistent hitmakers, scoring at least one Top Five single every year between 1974 and 1991. He was voted Best Male Vocalist at the 1978 CMA Awards and was selected Artist of the Decade in 1980 by the readers of London's *Country Music People* magazine. Between 1972 and 1992 he logged fifty-six chart records, fifty reached Top Twenty, and forty-five hit the Top Ten. Seventeen Williams singles went #1, including such memorable songs as "You're My Best Friend" (1975), "Tulsa Time" (1978), "I Believe in You" (1980), "If Hollywood Don't Need You" (1983), and "That's the Thing About Love" (1984).

Raised in South Texas, Williams had two music careers. The first, as a founding member of folk-pop trio the Pozo Seco Singers, yielded six pop chart records, the most memorable of which was "Time" (#47 pop, 1966). The group disbanded in 1969; Williams worked a variety of nonmusic jobs before venturing to Nashville to give music another try.

Signed as a writer to Jack Music, he made demo recordings with owner JACK "COWBOY" CLEMENT and another

Don Williams

Nashville newcomer, ALLEN REYNOLDS. No outside artists seemed eager to record Williams's songs, suggesting that Don should do them. Thus emboldened, Clement signed Williams to his own JMI Records and released his first album, *Don Williams, Volume One*, in 1972; the album yielded five chart singles, including Don's own song, "The Shelter of Your Eyes" (#14, 1972), and BOB McDILL's "Amanda" (#33, 1973). After a second JMI album Williams then moved to ABC-DOT and continued his hitmaking with "I Wouldn't Want to Live if You Didn't Love Me" (#1, 1974).

An early pioneer in music video and overseas touring, Williams became an even bigger star in England. Eric Clapton and Pete Townsend are big admirers of his easygoing style, and both English rock superstars recorded Williams's songs.

He also became a favorite of actor Burt Reynolds, costarring with him in the feature film *W. W. & the Dixie Dancekings* and appearing in *Smokey & the Bandit II.*

Of all country's major stars, Williams seems the least affected by his many achievements. He never made the Music Row party scene, avoided industry politicking, dodged interviews if possible, and toured sparingly, preferring to spend the maximum time possible on his farm with his wife of thirty-five years, Joy, and their two sons, Gary and Timmy. A rare Williams quote (on superstardom) is instructive: "The only way that I would be comfortable with that sort of title is when people tell me that my music has helped them through some stage of their life. Then I feel that what I'm doing or saying has been meaningful to someone. But as far as that whole approach to special treatment and people carrying on over you, I never have been too big on that." —*John Lomax III*

REPRESENTATIVE RECORDINGS

Don Williams, Volume I (JMI, 1972); *Expressions* (ABC-Dot, 1978); *I Believe In You* (MCA, 1980); *Café Carolina* (MCA, 1984); *An Evening with Don Williams (Best of Live)* (American Harvest Recording Society, 1994)

Hank Williams
b. Mount Olive, Alabama, September 17, 1923; d. January 1, 1953

Hank Williams's legend has long overtaken the rather frail and painfully introverted man who spawned it. Almost single-handedly, Williams set the agenda for contemporary country songcraft, but his appeal rests as much in the myth that even now surrounds his short life. His is the standard by which success is measured in country music on every level, even self-destruction.

Hiram Williams (his name was misspelled "Hiriam" on his birth certificate) came from a rural background. His parents were probably strawberry farmers when he was born, although his father, Lon, later worked for logging companies around Georgiana in South Alabama. Hank was born with a spinal deformity, spina bifida occulta, that would later have a deleterious impact on his life. Lon entered a Veterans Administration hospital in 1930, when Hank was six, and Hank rarely saw him until the early 1940s. Hank's mother, Lillie, moved the family to Greenville, and then to Montgomery, Alabama, in 1937. Hank's musical career was already under way by the mid-1930s, and he formed the first of his DRIFTING COWBOYS bands around 1938.

Hank spent the war years shuttling between Montgomery, where he still tried to play music, and Mobile, where he worked in the shipyards. In December 1944 he married Audrey Mae Sheppard, and, after the war, he reformed the Drifting Cowboys and became the biggest hillbilly music star in Montgomery. His progress was impeded by his drinking, which was already problematical, and by the fact that his music was considered anachronistic.

Music publisher FRED ROSE invited Hank to supply songs for MOLLY O'DAY, and that contact led to Rose offering Hank the chance to record for Sterling Records in December 1946. On the basis of the public response to those records, Rose was able to place Hank with MGM RECORDS, and his first MGM release, "Move It on Over," was a hit in the fall of 1947. Rose tried hard to get Hank out of Montgomery, but the best he could get was an opening on a relatively new radio jamboree, the LOUISIANA HAYRIDE, in Shreveport. Hank moved there in August 1948.

In Shreveport, Hank began performing "Lovesick Blues," a show tune dating back to 1922 that he had learned from either REX GRIFFIN or EMMETT MILLER. The response it got encouraged him to record it after the 1948 recording ban ended. It reached #1 in May 1949 and stayed there sixteen weeks. The success of "Lovesick Blues" and its follow-up, another nonoriginal called "Wedding Bells," convinced the GRAND OLE OPRY that Hank should be hired, despite misgivings about his reliability.

Hank moved to Nashville in June 1949 and swiftly became one of the biggest stars in country music. Increasingly, he decided to stand or fall with his own songs, and, after the success of his own "Long Gone Lonesome Blues" in the spring of 1950, virtually all of his hits were his own compositions.

At the session that produced "Long Gone Lonesome Blues" Hank began to record a series of narrations and talking blues to be issued under the pseudonym Luke the Drifter. Most of them had a strong moral undertone, making them unsuitable for the JUKEBOX trade, which accounted for more than half of his record sales. There was never any serious attempt to hide the identity of Luke the Drifter; it was simply a ploy to avoid jukebox distributors ordering unsuitable records.

The peak years of Hank Williams's career were 1950 and 1951. He was one of the most successful touring acts in country music. Every one of his records charted, except for those issued as Luke the Drifter and his religious duets with Audrey. His songs, which had matured greatly since the demos he had submitted to Molly O'Day, began finding a wider market than his own recordings of them ever could. Starting with "Honky Tonkin'" in 1949, his songs had been covered for the pop market, but it was not until Tony Bennett covered "Cold, Cold Heart" in 1951 that Williams began to be recognized as an important popular songwriter. From that point there was a rush to reinterpret his songs for the pop market. Guy Mitchell, for instance, had a hit with "I Can't Help It," and the duo of Frankie Laine and Jo Stafford took "Hey, Good Lookin'" into the pop Top Ten.

Hank had tried to wrestle down his drinking problem, but career pressures, marital problems, and crippling spinal pain all contributed to make the binges more frequent during 1951. In December he agreed to be operated on, although the operation was not a success. He disbanded his group in December, and, when he started work again in March and April 1952, it was with pickup bands. Audrey had ordered him out of the family home immediately after he came home from the hospital, and he moved into a house with RAY PRICE.

Hank Williams

As 1952 wore on, Hank appeared to care less and less about his career. His appearances were few, and by June he had stopped work altogether. In August he was fired by the Grand Ole Opry, and moved out of Nashville, back to Montgomery. Fred Rose negotiated his return to the *Louisiana Hayride* as of September, and Hank moved back to Shreveport that month. In October he married Billie Jean Jones Eshliman. She was from Shreveport but he had met her in Nashville when she came there with FARON YOUNG. By this point, another girlfriend, Bobbie Jett, was pregnant with his child.

Hank worked in Shreveport from September to December 1952. Most of his bookings were in beer halls, and his drunkenness was now a serious problem compounded by medication prescribed by a bogus doctor, Toby Marshall. Through it all, though, Hank never seemed to strike out in the studio. Even as he played small halls in East Texas, his record of "Jambalaya" was #1. If anything, his hits increased in magnitude as his bookings diminished.

Just before Christmas 1952 Hank took a leave of absence from the *Hayride* and returned to Montgomery to rest. On December 30 he left for two bookings in Charleston, West Virginia, and Canton, Ohio, but died en route. He may have died on December 31, 1952, in the back seat of his chauffered Cadillac, and was pronounced dead early on January 1, 1953, in Oak Hill, West Virginia.

—*Colin Escott*

REPRESENTATIVE RECORDINGS

40 Greatest Hits (Polydor, 1983), 2 CDs; *Rare Demos: First to Last* (CMF Records, 1990); *The Original Singles Collection . . . Plus* (Polydor, 1991), 3 CDs; *The Health & Happiness Shows* (Mercury, 1993), 2 CDs; *Alone and Forsaken* (Mercury, 1995)

Hank Williams Jr.
b. Shreveport, Louisiana, May 26, 1949

For what seems like the greater part of his career, Randall Hank Williams wrestled with the knowledge that it was his lineage that had gotten him his start. He knew that to be taken seriously he needed something uniquely his own. He tried much harder than most offspring who follow a famous parent into the same field, and eventually succeeded in establishing his own identity. His success has been such that there are many who only think of HANK WILLIAMS as the father of Hank Jr.

Hank Jr. has reinterpreted his father's songs consistently since his first recording sessions, but it has been more interesting to chart the changing way he has handled the emotional baggage of being Hank Williams Jr. That burden has been made all the more difficult by the fact that Hank Jr. never really knew his father; he was only three and a half when Hank Williams died. (It was Hank Sr. who gave Hank Jr. the nickname Bocephus, after a ventriloquist's dummy owned by comedian ROD BRASFIELD.)

Hank Jr. grew up in Nashville. He made his stage debut at age eight, his GRAND OLE OPRY debut at eleven, and his recording debut at fourteen. His career was orchestrated by his mother, Audrey, who saw in Hank Jr. an opportunity to sustain the legend in which she had such a huge financial and personal stake. She signed him with his father's label, MGM RECORDS, and the first promotional appearance was scheduled for Canton, Ohio, the town where Hank Sr. was to have performed the day he passed away.

Fans came in droves to see Hank's son, but they didn't buy the records. Also, by recording from an early age, all of Hank Jr.'s growth as an artist has been done in public. He was manipulated by producers who were mostly trying to get a facsimile of Hank Sr. to double their money—hence a series of records as Luke the Drifter Jr. and albums such

Hank Williams Jr.

as *Songs My Father Left Me, The Legend of Hank Williams in Story and Song,* and an album of father-son duets.

Hank Jr. started to assert his independence in the early 1970s. The albums *Living Proof* and *Bocephus* saw him slowly siding with southern rock acts such as the MARSHALL TUCKER BAND and the Allman Brothers. The first clear summation of this direction came with the *Hank Williams Jr. and Friends* album. Its release almost coincided with his death, though; he fell from a mountain in Montana on August 8, 1975, and was very seriously injured. His face was severely damaged, and he could not perform again until May 1976.

The singles drawn from . . . *And Friends* didn't do well, and Hank Jr. left MGM in 1976 to join WARNER BROS. Chart placings were still poor until he signed with ELEKTRA RECORDS in 1979 and once again reexamined his pedigree on "Family Tradition" (a record produced by JIMMY BOWEN, as were all Hank Jr.'s albums through 1985). That song did much to establish the image that Hank Jr. wanted for himself, an image he defined on his next hit, "Whiskey Bent and Hell Bound." He was now the party man living on borrowed time; he was the outlaw, albeit one with a private income. Many of his records were swaggering and self-referential, but at least they had a character that was unique to Hank Jr. He found a new audience with records such as "Dixie on My Mind," "All My Rowdy Friends (Are Coming Over Tonight)," "This Ain't Dallas," and "Gonna Go Huntin' Tonight." Hank Jr. now ranked alongside Lynyrd Skynyrd among fans of southern rock, and Hank Jr.'s music was in fact much closer to rock than to the OUTLAW country acts with whom he identified himself in song and in person.

Occasionally Hank Jr. would reveal his deep musicianship; he can play many instruments, including lead guitar and piano, and he has as thorough a knowledge of American roots music as anyone in the business. "Ain't Misbehavin'," a novel slant on the old Fats Waller tune, displayed that knowledge, and surprised Hank Jr. by reaching #1 on the country charts. In general, though, he has written his own songs to showcase his party animal persona. His autobiography *Living Proof,* completed soon after the accident and subsequently filmed for television in 1983 (with former *Waltons* TV star Richard Thomas playing Hank Jr.), showed a more thoughtful, reflective, and vulnerable man than the songs, but Hank Jr. was careful to let little of that seep into his music during his hot streak in the 1980s, which culminated in his being named Entertainer of the Year by both the ACM and the CMA in 1987. "My fans don't want to hear about family values," he told interviewer Jimmy Guterman. "They want to rock."   —*Colin Escott*

REPRESENTATIVE RECORDINGS

Hank Williams Jr. and Friends (MGM, 1975); *Family Tradition* (Elektra, 1979); *Lone Wolf* (Warner Bros./Curb, 1990); *Living Proof: The MGM Recordings 1963–1975* (Mercury, 1992), 3 CDs; *The Bocephus Box* (Curb/Capricorn, 1992), 3 CDs

Jett Williams
b. Montgomery, Alabama, January 6, 1953

Singer-songwriter Jett Williams was born five days after her father, HANK WILLIAMS, died. Her stage name is a tribute to both of her parents, Bobbie Webb Jett and Hank Williams.

After giving birth to Jett, Bobbie Jett granted legal custody of her daughter to Hank's mother, Lillybelle "Lillie" Stone, who adopted the baby. Stone died about two years later. Jett was given up for adoption again and became a ward of the state of Alabama until February 1956, when she was adopted by Wayne and Louise Deupree; they changed her name from Cathy Yvone Stone to Cathy Louise Deupree, and she was raised by them. Jett received a degree from the University of Alabama in 1975 and began a career as a recreational therapist.

Jett was told of the possibility that she was Hank Williams's daughter at the time of her twenty-first birthday, in 1974, because she was scheduled to receive some money from Lillie Stone's estate. Although the Williams family knew she was his daughter and written documents verified it (a prebirth notarized agreement signed by Hank and Bobbie Jett acknowledged Hank as her father), she went through years of legal action from 1984 to 1992 to receive recognition and her share of her father's estate. The years of court proceedings included a 1989 U.S. Supreme Court ruling upholding a 1988 Alabama court decree that she was "entitled to receive her proportionate share of any proceeds of the estate of her natural father, Hank Williams."

On June 4, 1989, she made her professional debut as a singer. In August of that year she joined with two members of her father's original band, Don Helms and Jerry Rivers, and formed Jett Williams & the Drifting Cowboys Band. She made her GRAND OLE OPRY debut in a guest appearance on New Year's Eve 1993, the evening of the forty-first anniversary of her father's death.

Jett married her attorney, F. Keith Adkinson, on September 28, 1986. They have divided their time between a farm in Tennessee and a yacht named *Jett Stream* on the Potomac River in Washington, D.C. Jett's book, *Ain't Nothin' as Sweet as My Baby: The Story of Hank Williams' Lost Daughter,* has become a best-seller. —*Barbara Pruett*

Lawton Williams
b. Troy, Tennessee, July 24, 1922

Known as Slim Williams early in his career, after boyhood idol COWBOY SLIM RINEHART, Lawton Williams was already a seasoned singer-songwriter when his song "Fräulein" became a mammoth hit for BOBBY HELMS in 1957.

The son of a Tennessee fiddler, Williams began pursuing a musical career in the Detroit area in 1940. He became a military policeman during World War II and found himself stationed around Houston, by 1943, where he became close friends with FLOYD TILLMAN, who taught him the rudiments of songwriting. Williams's earliest recorded songwriting efforts were waxed by CLIFF BRUNER and LAURA LEE MCBRIDE. Williams appeared regularly on Houston's KTRH and Corpus Christi's KEYS before returning to Michigan in 1947, where he made his first recordings for the Sultan and Fortune labels and appeared on WKMH–Dearborn. Returning to Texas by 1950, he became a DJ at Fort Worth's KCNC. An association with HANK LOCKLIN yielded Locklin's hit recording of Williams's "Paper Face" and won Williams a contract with FOUR STAR. He would subsequently record for Coral and IMPERIAL before Locklin hit with his "Geisha Girl" and Helms released "Fräulein" in 1957. From that point Williams was chiefly a songwriter and churned out further classics, such as "Farewell Party" (1962). He continued to perform and record for RCA, MERCURY, and others but later claimed that this aspect of his career limited his songwriting success: Artists thought

he saved his best songs for himself. Retired from performing since 1970, Williams continues to write and has co-owned a publishing company with JIM REEVES's widow, Mary. —*Kevin Coffey*

REPRESENTATIVE RECORDING

Lightning Jones (Bear Family, 1985)

Marc Williams
birthplace and birth date unknown

Little is known about cowboy singer Marc Williams, also known as the Singing Texan. Apparently he was a performer of cowboy songs for about ten years during the 1920s and 1930s, when he made some classic recordings of traditional cowboy songs for BRUNSWICK and DECCA, including "Sioux Indians" (1928 and 1934), "The Night Herding Song" (1930), and "The Cowboy's Dream" (1930). During the 1930s he appeared as Happy Hank on a children's program on radio station WHO in Des Moines, Iowa. A brief article written about him at that time claimed he was a native Texan and actually had been a working cowboy before becoming a professional singer. —*Charlie Seemann*

REPRESENTATIVE RECORDING

Back in the Saddle: American Cowboy Songs, (New World Records, 1983); includes one recording by Williams, "Sioux Indians"

Tex Williams
b. Ramsey, Illinois, August 23, 1917; d. October 11, 1985

Sollie Paul "Tex" Williams took a well-known traditional style known as the "talking blues," used by everyone from CHRIS BOUCHILLON and WOODY GUTHRIE to the GRAND OLE OPRY's ROBERT LUNN and pop singer Phil Harris, and forever made it a part of western swing. One such song gave CAPITOL RECORDS its first million seller. Ironically, that career began in rural Illinois, where Sollie Williams's father was a local blacksmith who played old-time fiddle tunes. A victim of polio, Sollie got his start playing guitar and singing over local radio. He went on to perform around Illinois, then in Washington State and California with various groups.

In 1942 he moved to Los Angeles and joined SPADE COOLEY's western swing band as bass player and vocalist at the Venice Pier Ballroom. It was there that Venice Pier operator FOREMAN PHILLIPS named him "Tex." Williams's smooth vocal on Cooley's 1944 OKEH hit "Shame on You" got Williams a recording contract in 1946 with CAPITOL. That June, after a growing estrangement, Cooley fired Tex, who took most of Cooley's band with him, re-forming them as the Western Caravan. "California Polka" (1946) became Williams's only hit after signing with Capitol; he needed another to keep his contract. MERLE TRAVIS wrote the talking blues "Smoke! Smoke! Smoke! (That Cigarette)" for Tex. Released in the spring of 1947, the song topped the country and pop charts and became Capitol's first million seller.

The talking blues became Williams's trademark, and most of his other hit singles followed that style, including songs such as "That's What I Like About the West," "Never Trust a Woman," "Suspicion," "Who? Me?," "Talking Boogie," and CARSON ROBISON's "Life Gets Tee-Jus, Don't It."

Tex Williams at the Riverside Rancho

Unfortunately, the talking songs eventually stereotyped Williams, obscuring his gifts as a singer. His record sales declined, and he and Capitol parted ways in 1951. Williams also didn't produce hits during his 1952–53 partnering with RCA and his 1953–58 stint with DECCA.

After disbanding the Caravan in 1957, Williams continued to tour and ran a California nightclub until 1965. He recorded an LP for Capitol, two more for LIBERTY, and one for Boone Records, with little success. He had one final Top Thirty single in 1972 with another talking blues tune, "The Night Miss Nancy Ann's Hotel for Single Girls Burned Down," on MONUMENT. Though he worked extensively in Nevada and overseas throughout the 1970s and early 1980s, his health declined, and he died of pancreatic cancer in 1985. —*Rich Kienzle*

REPRESENTATIVE RECORDINGS

Tex Williams in Las Vegas (Liberty, 1962); *Capitol Vintage Collection: Tex Williams* (Capitol Nashville, 1995)

Foy Willing
b. Bosque County, Texas, 1915; d. June 24, 1978

Leader of the popular second-tier western vocal group the Riders of the Purple Sage, who took their name from a Zane Grey novel, Foy Willing, born Willingham, began performing as a teenager around Waco, Texas. His first instrument was the harmonica, but he became proficient on the guitar and the steel guitar as well.

By 1933 Willing was in New York doing a radio show for CRAZY WATER CRYSTALS. He returned to Texas in 1935. By the end of the decade he had joined a cowboy group, Lew Preston & the Men of the Range, at KFJZ, the flagship of the Texas State Network in Fort Worth. Heart problems interrupted his work with the band, which moved to Oklahoma City when TSN faltered in 1940, but Willing made his recording debut at the group's 1940–41 OKEH sessions.

Willing traveled to California and in 1943 formed the Riders of the Purple Sage with Al Sloey and EDDIE DEAN's brother, Jimmie, appearing on the *HOLLYWOOD BARN DANCE* and recording for CAPITOL, scoring a hit with "Texas Blues" in 1944. Willing subsequently recorded for COLUMBIA, DECCA, and Majestic. The band continued to be popular on radio and in western films (backing, among others, ROY ROGERS) until Willing disbanded the group in 1952. Willing appeared and recorded occasionally over the next quarter century, making western film festival appearances until shortly before his death. —*Kevin Coffey*

REPRESENTATIVE RECORDINGS

Hillbilly Music . . . Thank God!, Volume One (Bug/Capitol, 1989), 1 recording on various artists anthology; *Foy Willing & the Riders of the Purple Sage* (ASWT, 1992), 2 CDs; *Songs of the West* (Rhino, 1994), 2 recordings on 4 CD various artists anthology

Kelly Willis
b. Lawton, Oklahoma, October 1, 1968

A talented singer-songwriter with a sweet vibrato voice, Kelly Willis broke into the music world by taking the AUSTIN, TEXAS, music scene by storm in the late 1980s. Having relocated from Virginia to Austin with her husband-to-be, drummer Mas Palermo, Willis (and Palermo) formed the band Radio Ranch and began gigging to wide acclaim. The band's noteworthy 1989 show at Austin's South By Southwest music festival caught the attention of MCA Nashville label vice president–producer TONY BROWN, who signed them to a record deal.

Willis released two albums backed by the group (*Well-Traveled Love* in 1990 and *Bang Bang* in 1991) that featured the electrified, rock-tinged, honky-tonk sound native to many Austin bands. But few had a singer with chops to match Willis's honest, bigger-than-she-looks delivery.

Despite critical acclaim, neither album was a commercial success, and in 1993 Willis made a record for MCA without her band. Willis was divorced from Palermo, and her songwriting continued to shine, but the third Tony Brown and Don Was–produced album didn't create great sales either. Willis was dropped by MCA soon thereafter. Along the way she appeared as an earnest folksinger in actor-director Tim Robbins's movie *Bob Roberts* (1993).

Now married to singer-songwriter Bruce Robison, Willis signed a deal with A&M Records' Los Angeles office in 1996. Willis's perseverance would be rewarded; in 1996 she released an independent, four-song EP (*Fading Fast*) to radio stations, but demand led to a Texas-only retail release. The record made the AMERICANA charts, a middle ground between country and rock.

In 1997 Willis joined pop singers Sarah McLachlan, Jewel, and other female performers in the Lilith Fair concert tour. —*Clark Parsons*

REPRESENTATIVE RECORDINGS

Well-Traveled Love (MCA, 1990); *Bang Bang* (MCA, 1991); *Kelly Willis* (MCA, 1993)

Vic Willis
b. Schulter, Oklahoma, May 31, 1922; d. January 15, 1995

For nearly fifty years, with brothers Guy and Skeeter, John Victor "Vic" Willis entertained as one of the Oklahoma

Wranglers, then as one of the WILLIS BROTHERS. Later he formed the Vic Willis Trio and continued entertaining on the GRAND OLE OPRY.

Willis really had two careers—as performer and as senior country music business statesman. His first career, as performer and musician (accordion and piano), kept him busy until the deaths of brothers Skeeter (1976) and Guy (1981). His second career dominated his last twenty-five years; because of his experience, he sat on boards of directors and executive committees of numerous organizations and served others as officer or official.

For his last thirteen years he was secretary-treasurer of the Nashville AMERICAN FEDERATION OF MUSICIANS (AFM) union chapter, having previously been on its executive board for six years. For two terms he was president of the AFM's southern conference, consisting of some sixty southeastern local unions. Many negotiators commented on how Willis's logic and well-articulated wit defused even the most combative negotiations. Almost single-handedly he created the Musicians' Relief Fund to aid musicians going through temporary hard times.

He also served on the board of ROPE, and for eight years he served the ASSOCIATION OF COUNTRY ENTERTAINERS (ACE) as board member or as executive director, even taking out personal loans to help finance its operations.

Willis's production company, Custom Jingles, serviced national accounts, including beverage companies, banks, and musical instrument manufacturers. He died in a single-vehicle car accident in January 1995. —*Paul W. Soelberg*

The Willis Brothers

James Ulysses Harrod Lyn "Guy" Willis b. Alex, Arkansas, July 5, 1915; d. April 13, 1981
Charles Ray Clayton "Skeeter" Willis b. Coalton, Oklahoma, December 20, 1917; d. January 28, 1976
John Victor "Vic" Willis b. Schulter, Oklahoma, May 31, 1922; d. January 15, 1995

In four decades together, the career of the Willis Brothers embraced hit records, the GRAND OLE OPRY, and contributions to country music history. They were the first musicians to accompany HANK WILLIAMS on record (1946) and with EDDY ARNOLD were in the first presentation of Opry stars at Constitution Hall in Washington, D.C. (1947). Their western-style show took them around the world and onto national radio and television.

Brothers Guy (guitar), Skeeter (fiddle), and Vic (accordion) Willis began performing professionally in 1932 as the Oklahoma Wranglers. Following World War II service they reunited in 1946, adding bass player Chuck "the Indian" Wright, around whom swirled much good-natured onstage hilarity until his retirement in 1960.

In June 1946 they debuted on the Opry and on WSM's *Checkerboard Jamboree* Saturday broadcasts, sponsored by Purina Feed and starring Eddy Arnold and ERNEST TUBB. On December 11, 1946, FRED ROSE recorded four sides by the Wranglers. Following their session, they accompanied newcomer Hank Williams on his first four recordings. In October 1947, with Arnold, they made the historic Constitution Hall appearance. In late 1948 Arnold asked them to join his roadshow, where they remained until 1957. They appeared with Arnold in two 1949 western movies, *Feudin' Rhythm* and *Hoedown*. They ended the 1950s as regulars on the *OZARK JUBILEE* and the *MIDWESTERN HAYRIDE* and on Chat-

tanooga and Birmingham TV stations. By now renamed the Willis Brothers, they returned to Nashville and the Opry in 1960. After Guy died in 1981, Vic formed the Vic Willis Trio and continued to make Opry appearances until his death.

Although they had recorded for MERCURY, Sterling, Coral, RCA VICTOR, Nashville, and CMH Records, their major successes were on STARDAY, which they joined in 1960. Their biggest-selling singles were "Give Me 40 Acres (To Turn This Rig Around)" (1964) and "Bob" (1967). —*Paul W. Soelberg*

REPRESENTATIVE RECORDING

The Best of the Willis Brothers (Starday, 1975)

Billy Jack Wills

b. Hall County, Texas, February 26, 1926; d. March 2, 1991

Western swing bandleader, musician, vocalist, and songwriter Billy Jack Wills was the youngest brother of BOB WILLS. Overshadowed much of his career by his older brothers, Billy Jack left a legacy of song and music that attest to his talent. He played bass and drums for brother JOHNNIE LEE WILLS's band in the early 1940s and after World War II with Bob Wills & His Texas Playboys. With the Playboys he contributed superb vocals and compositions on MGM recordings such as "Rock-A-Bye Baby Blues," "Cadillac in Model 'A,'" and "King Without a Queen." But best known are his lyrics to the classic ballads "Faded Love" and "Lilly Dale." In 1949 Billy Jack and TINY MOORE formed a band based at Wills Point near Sacramento, California. Until it disbanded in 1954, this progressive western swing band experimented with jump blues and the emerging rhythm & blues sound, incorporating a 4/4 beat instead of Bob Wills's usual 2/4 time. With Tiny Moore's tight arrangement and jazzy electric mandolin and hot steel guitarist Vance Terry, they made some superb transcription recordings, which were commercially released on the Western label in the early 1980s. They also recorded for FOUR STAR and MGM Records. —*Steve Hathaway*

REPRESENTATIVE RECORDINGS

Billy Jack Wills & His Western Swing Band (Joaquin, 1996); *Bob Wills: 24 Greatest Hits* (Polydor, 1994)

Bob Wills

b. Kosse, Texas, March 6, 1905; d. May 13, 1975

A bandleader, fiddler, singer, and songwriter, James Robert Wills is the most famous exponent of the popular musical amalgam now known as western swing, which synthesized ragtime, traditional fiddling, New Orleans jazz, blues, Mexican songs, and big band swing. Wills blended it all into a swinging dance music that was wildly popular in the Southwest and on the West Coast from the 1930s into the 1950s. His greatest success was with his Texas Playboys band while based at KVOO in Tulsa, Oklahoma, between 1934 and 1942. Today his compositions, such as "Faded Love," "Maiden's Prayer," "Take Me Back to Tulsa," and "San Antonio Rose," are considered standards of country and pop music.

Wills grew up in a musical family of fiddle players and in an area famous for African-American music that produced Scott Joplin, Victoria Spivey, and Blind Lemon Jefferson.

Bob Wills

From his family, young Jim Rob Wills (as he was then called) learned to play frontier fiddle music; his father had defeated ECK ROBERTSON in fiddle contests on more than one occasion. At age ten young Bob Wills played fiddle for his first ranch dance. From African-American neighbors and migrant workers he learned blues and jazz, which enthralled him. In his late teens he once rode fifty miles on horseback to see the Empress of the Blues, Bessie Smith.

Wills left the family farm at age seventeen and drifted from one job to another across Texas, working in construction and selling insurance in separate stops in Amarillo; preaching in Knox County; barbering in Roy, New Mexico, and in Turkey, Texas; laboring on several farms in various parts of the Lone Star State; and playing ranch house dances and with MEDICINE SHOWS whenever possible.

In November 1929, after joining forces with guitarist Herman Arnspiger, Wills made his first recordings for the BRUNSWICK label, "Gulf Coast Blues" and "Wills Breakdown"; they were never issued and are now presumed lost. In 1930 singer MILTON BROWN and his guitar-playing brother Derwood joined Wills and Arnspiger. In due course they became the Aladdin Lamp Company's "Aladdin Laddies" on WBAP in Fort Worth, and tenor banjoist Sleepy Johnson joined them for dances at the local Crystal Springs pavilion. The five-piece stringband produced the first glimmerings of what would be called western swing a decade later. In late 1930 W. LEE O'DANIEL hired the band to promote Burrus Mill's Light Crust Flour on radio, first at tiny KFJZ and soon at WBAP, where the LIGHT CRUST DOUGHBOYS became a favorite.

After the Browns left the band in September 1932 to form their own outfit, Wills soon exited the Doughboys as well. Taking with him TOMMY DUNCAN (who had replaced Milton Brown as a Doughboy), Wills formed his own Playboys band and tried Waco for three months before heading to Oklahoma City in early 1934. After a short stint there, Wills and his five musicians arrived in Tulsa on February 9 upon being offered a daily program at KVOO on a

trial basis. A daily 12:30 P.M. spot, sponsored first by CRAZY WATER CRYSTALS and soon after by General Mills, launched Wills as the most popular act in the Southwest. During those years he added brass and reeds, drums, and developed a band that by 1940 numbered sixteen members, among them such outstanding players as steel guitarist LEON MCAULIFFE, guitarist ELDON SHAMBLIN, and fiddler JESSE ASHLOCK. The versatile band could play anything from a fiddle breakdown to a George Gershwin composition. Bob Wills & His Texas Playboys enjoyed their greatest success from 1935 to 1947 while recording for ARC/Vocalion/OKeh/Columbia. These recordings sold in the hundreds of thousands and his "San Antonio Rose" probably in the millions. On the strength of his radio and record success, Wills began making musical westerns in Hollywood in 1940.

A December 1942 induction into the army broke up the Texas Playboys, but upon Wills's discharge in 1943 he relocated to Southern California and re-formed the band. There he was more financially successful than at any time in his career. Huge crowds at his dances and big-selling recordings made him one of the highest-paid bandleaders in America.

After the war Wills decided to give up most of the brass and reeds in his band and rely more on fiddles, guitars, steel guitars, and mandolins. This emphasis on strings helped him maintain a fairly strong following well into the 1940s, even after the age of the big bands was over. Unfortunately for Wills, his accomplished vocalist Tommy Duncan left the Texas Playboys in 1948 to form his own unit. After leaving Columbia Records in 1947, Wills worked with a series of labels: MGM (1947–54), DECCA (1955–57), LIBERTY (1960–63), Longhorn (1964), and Kapp (1965–69).

The late 1950s saw a resurging interest in western swing, with Wills returning to Tulsa. The band quickly expanded with the additions of a saxophone section and a new vocalist, LEON RAUSCH. When the band's bookings concentrated in Las Vegas, Wills and the band moved there in late 1959. Tommy Duncan returned briefly (1960–62). By 1967 Wills had disbanded the Texas Playboys. Although he still toured and performed, he did so with house bands and one lone employee, vocalist Gene "Tag" Lambert, who doubled as his driver.

In October 1968 Wills was elected to the COUNTRY MUSIC HALL OF FAME, but the following May he suffered a stroke that marked the end of his performing days. In December 1973, he recorded his final album, *For the Last Time* (United Artists). Other strokes followed, but he held on until May 13, 1975, when pneumonia took his life.

—*Charles R. Townsend*

REPRESENTATIVE RECORDINGS

The Bob Wills Anthology (Columbia, 1973); *Anthology, 1935–1973* (Rhino, 1991); *The Essential Bob Wills* (Columbia, 1992); *Country Music Hall of Fame* (MCA, 1992)

Johnnie Lee Wills
b. Jewett, Texas, September 2, 1912; d. October 25, 1984

Diehard BOB WILLS fans tend to look on Johnnie Lee, his younger brother, as the Wills who stayed home in Tulsa and ran a farm club band for Bob's Texas Playboys after they moved to the West Coast. And though Johnnie Lee indeed started as a tenor banjo player in Bob's mid-1930s band, he soon emerged as an important bandleader in his own right—a longtime fixture on the Tulsa music scene, and an artist who had a number of national hits in the 1940s.

The second of four Wills brothers, Johnnie Lee was especially influenced by their father, Uncle John Wills. After touring with Bob for six years, Johnnie Lee started his own band in 1940 and at once obtained a DECCA recording contract. This resulted in the 1941 hit "Milk Cow Blues," in an arrangement that influenced dozens of later versions. Working from their base at KVOO, Johnnie Lee Wills and His Boys featured musicians such as Guy "Cotton" Thompson (fiddle, vocals), Millard Kelso (piano), Lester "Junior" Barnard (electric guitar), and singer LEON HUFF. The band had an eclectic repertoire, ranging from old-time fiddle breakdowns to modern country songs. In 1949 they signed with the independent label BULLET, and soon had huge novelty hits with two unlikely songs, "Rag Mop" and "Here Comes Peter Cotton Tail."

In later years Wills tried his luck with RCA VICTOR, and in the 1960s did a couple of LPs on the Sims label. By the mid-1960s, though, he broke up his band and devoted much of his energy to running a successful western wear store and a local rodeo, the Tulsa Stampede. He made a comeback of sorts in the 1970s, and in 1978 recorded a splendid *Reunion* album for Flying Fish, a testimony to the many excellent western swing sidemen who had passed through his band.　　　　　　　　　　　　*—Charles Wolfe*

REPRESENTATIVE RECORDING

Reunion (Flying Fish, 1978)

Luke Wills

b. Hall County, Texas, September 10, 1920

Western swing bandleader, musician, and vocalist Luther J. Wills was the next-to-youngest brother of BOB WILLS. Luke began his musical career much like his older brother, accompanying his father, Uncle John Wills, on rhythm guitar at dances. The first band Luke played in was his older brother JOHNNIE LEE WILLS's first aggregation, the Rhythmaires, in 1938. Luke played bass, rhythm guitar, or banjo and chipped in occasional vocals for his older brothers' bands on and off until the Texas Playboys disbanded in 1964. He appeared in several B-western films with the Texas Playboys. His best-known vocal was "Little Star of Heaven." In 1946 he led his own band, originally called the Texas Playboys Number 2. Based in Fresno, California, as was Bob Wills, they played the central and northern California areas when Bob Wills & His Texas Playboys were on tour. Renamed Luke Wills' Rhythm Busters, they recorded for KING and RCA VICTOR RECORDS. The records featured such stellar sidemen as Junior Barnard, Joe Holley, Bobby Bruce, and Cotton Thompson. The band dissolved in 1948. He started another short-lived band 1950, in Oklahoma City. Though Luke limited himself to vocal asides, the bands he fronted were first-rate.　　*—Steve Hathaway*

REPRESENTATIVE RECORDING

High Voltage Gal (Bear Family, 1988)

Norro Wilson

b. Scottsville, Kentucky, April 4, 1938

Norris D. "Norro" Wilson has been involved in the music business since 1956, either as a performer, songwriter, pro-

ducer, A&R executive, or publisher. His long Nashville tenure has afforded him the opportunity to write songs for GEORGE JONES, TAMMY WYNETTE, CHARLIE RICH, and CHARLEY PRIDE. Wilson has also produced projects for CHET ATKINS, EDDY ARNOLD, KEITH WHITLEY, JOHN ANDERSON, MICKEY GILLEY, and SAMMY KERSHAW.

While still in high school, Wilson and three friends formed a barbershop quartet and won a local Kentucky music contest. Wilson's thirst for music was also fueled by frequent family trips to Nashville for the All Night Gospel Review, from which he got a gig as tenor for the Southlanders Quartet. Wilson toured with that group until 1960, then toured with future publishing magnate Don Gant in a duo. In 1967 Wilson accepted a position as a song plugger with AL GALLICO Music. By 1970 Wilson was writing songs for Gallico and receiving the first of many BMI airplay awards (for the Tammy Wynette hit "I'll See Him Through").

During the early 1970s Wilson scored big as a songwriter with #1 hits such as "The Most Beautiful Girl" (1973) and "A Very Special Love Song" (1974), both recorded by Charlie Rich; "He Loves Me all the Way" (1970) and "Another Lonely Song" (1973) for Tammy Wynette; "Night Games" (1983) and "Never Been So Loved in All My Life" (1981) for Charley Pride; and "The Grand Tour" (1974) for George Jones.

The least illustrious of Wilson's achievements have been those as a recording artist. His biggest chart success came with the Top Twenty "Do It to Someone You Love" (MERCURY, 1970). He gave up performing permanently in 1977, two years after he settled into an A&R/producer position with WARNER BROS. RECORDS. He moved to RCA's A&R department in 1982, then took the CEO post for Merit Music in 1987. When Merit was sold in 1990, Wilson started Norro Productions and landed Sammy Kershaw as a production client right off the bat. Wilson and Buddy Cannon produced albums for artists such as George Jones and Kenny Chesney, and together they formed Bud Ro Productions in 1998.　　　　　　　　　　*—Michael Hight*

Jesse Winchester

b. Shreveport, Louisiana, May 17, 1944

Though he first began recording in 1970, Memphis-bred Jesse James Winchester is better known in the country field as a songwriter. His "I'm Gonna Miss You Girl" was a #3 country hit for erstwhile cosmic cowboy MICHAEL MARTIN MURPHEY in 1987, and artists such as WYNONNA JUDD and EMMYLOU HARRIS have also recorded Winchester's songs.

However subtle, Winchester's music demonstrates considerable historical and social reach. Much of this has to do with his childhood exposure to country music, blues, and rockabilly, all of which surface on his records, along with the gospel music he learned to sing and play in church as a boy. Equally important to Winchester's artistic development, though, was his 1967 flight to Canada to avoid serving in the Vietnam War. As an expatriate living in Montreal, Winchester wrote with and longing about the South, especially on songs such as "Biloxi," "Mississippi, You're on My Mind" (a Top Twenty hit for STONEY EDWARDS in 1975), and "L'Air de la Louisiane."

In 1970 Winchester met Robbie Robertson of the Band, who produced and played on Winchester's auspicious self-titled album debut (1970), which includes "Biloxi" as well as "Yankee Lady" and "The Brand New Tennessee Waltz."

Although the album's use of fiddle and mandolin hinted at Winchester's country leanings, his third album, *Learn to Love It* (1974), rendered his down-home roots explicit. Besides featuring a rendition of MARTHA CARSON's "I Can't Stand Up Alone," the album also included the first recorded versions of "Third Rate Romance" and "The End Is Not in Sight." The latter two songs became country hits for writer Russell Smith after he left Winchester's band to front the AMAZING RHYTHM ACES. President Jimmy Carter granted Winchester amnesty in 1977, allowing him to return to the United States (Winchester became a Canadian citizen in 1972). While he has yet to achieve any real commercial success as an artist, his compositions routinely show up on albums made by other artists. Wynonna included two of Winchester's songs on her 1993 album *Tell Me Why*, and his "Oh What a Thrill" was a Top Twenty hit for the MAVERICKS in 1994. —*Bill Friskics-Warren*

REPRESENTATIVE RECORDINGS

Jesse Winchester (Ampex, 1970); *Nothin' But a Breeze* (Bearsville, 1977)

Chubby Wise

b. Lake City, Florida, October 2, 1915; d. January 6, 1996

For more than a half century, Robert Russell Wise built a reputation as one of the greatest fiddlers in country music history. Wise began honing his skills in youth, although he learned the guitar first. By the time he reached voting age, Wise had become a regular performer on the club scene in Jacksonville, Florida, and an associate of Ervin Rouse, from whom he learned or who helped him compose the fiddle classic "Orange Blossom Special." (Historians are still unclear as to the tune's origins, though Rouse owned the copyright.) In 1938 Wise joined a western swing band, the Jubilee Hillbillies, and in the early forties came to Nashville to fiddle with BILL MONROE at the GRAND OLE OPRY and on the road.

His main years with Monroe's Blue Grass Boys (1946–48)—including fiddling on all his COLUMBIA releases (1945–49)—helped make Wise a legend on his instrument. He also recorded some numbers with CLYDE MOODY, such as "Shenandoah Waltz," on which he shared composer credit. In February 1948 Wise and Moody went to Arlington, Virginia, where they began a series of shows for CONNIE B. GAY at WARL. However, by 1949 Wise returned to the Grand Ole Opry and Bill Monroe's band. In 1950 Wise left again and fiddled briefly with the YORK BROTHERS, FLATT & SCRUGGS, and for Connie B. Gay. In 1954 he began a sixteen-year tenure with HANK SNOW's Rainbow Ranch Boys. In addition to many of Snow's RCA VICTOR sessions, Wise recorded with the Snow band for STARDAY, recorded an instrumental album on his own, and backed such performers as HYLO BROWN and MAC WISEMAN in studios.

In 1970 Chubby Wise left Hank Snow and went solo as a freelance fiddler. Having gained some reputation through a recording of "Maiden's Prayer" for the Houston-based Stoneway label, the veteran sideman found that he could earn a living as a guest fiddler at Texas dances. Through the seventies Wise recorded a string of albums for Stoneway and appeared at numerous bluegrass festivals. In 1984 he returned to Florida with some intention of retiring but remained active. Into the nineties, Wise maintained a schedule of solid bookings and recorded two compact discs for Pinecastle before his death from heart failure. —*Ivan M. Tribe*

REPRESENTATIVE RECORDINGS

Chubby Wise in Nashville (Pinecastle, 1994); *Chubby Wise: An American Original* (Pinecastle, 1995)

Mac Wiseman

b. Crimora, Virginia, May 23, 1925

As a popular bluegrass vocalist, Malcolm B. Wiseman is known for his DOT RECORDS recordings of "Shackles and Chains," "Jimmie Brown the Newsboy," "I'll Be All Smiles Tonight," "It Rains Just the Same in Missouri," "Put My Little Shoes Away," and "Love Letters in the Sand." But he has played many other roles in the country music business, including stints as a sideman with FLATT & SCRUGGS and BILL MONROE, as Dot's country A&R director (1956–59), as manager of the *WWVA JAMBOREE* (1966–70), as a founding member and first secretary of the COUNTRY MUSIC ASSOCIATION (1958), and as host of his own annual bluegrass festival at Renfro Valley, Kentucky (1970–83).

Wiseman's first public performances came in the late thirties, while still in high school, singing at WSVA in Harrisonburg, Virginia. His performing days seemed prematurely finished by a teenage bout with polio, but the illness ironically worked to his advantage when the National Foundation for Polio offered him a scholarship that helped him enter the Conservatory of Music in Dayton, Virginia. There he studied piano, musical theory, and radio broadcasting.

Wiseman returned briefly to work at WSVA before being hired in 1946 by MOLLY O'DAY in Knoxville, Tennessee, as a featured vocalist and upright bass fiddle player on her radio show. He played bass on her first recordings for COLUMBIA RECORDS in 1946.

Wiseman left O'Day's group in 1947 and performed that spring over WCYB in Bristol, Virginia. The next year, Lester Flatt also joined the station as a musician. That was the start of a friendship between Wiseman and Flatt that led to Wiseman becoming one of the original members of Flatt & Scruggs's Foggy Mountain Boys in 1948 and to Wiseman and Flatt recording three albums together—*Lester 'N' Mac*, *On the Southbound*, and *Over the Hills to the Poorhouse*—for RCA RECORDS in the early seventies. In between, Wiseman was briefly a member of Bill Monroe's Blue Grass Boys (1949), a longtime recording artist for Dot Records (1951–63), and a featured performer on the *OLD DOMINION BARN DANCE* show in Richmond, Virginia (1953–56).

In the 1990s Wiseman had achieved the status of respected bluegrass elder and continued to be a headliner on the bluegrass festival circuit and in England, where he has long been a favorite. —*Don Rhodes*

REPRESENTATIVE RECORDINGS

The Mac Wiseman Story (CMH Records, 1976); *Twenty Greatest Hits* (Gusto Records, 1983); *Grassroots to Bluegrass* (CMH Records, 1990)

WLS (*see National Barn Dance*)

Da Costa Woltz (*see* Da Costa Woltz's Southern Broadcasters, under D)

Del Wood

b. Nashville, Tennessee, February 22, 1920; d. October 3, 1989

From 1953 to 1989 Del Wood was a fixture at the GRAND OLE OPRY, playing rollicking piano instrumentals from the days of ragtime jazz. She was also one of the few female instrumentalists to make a name for herself in country music.

Polly Adelaide Hendricks began playing piano at age five and gained early experience playing piano in the sheet music sections of Nashville dime stores. She was in her thirties and had been working as a staff pianist at WLBJ in Bowling Green, Kentucky, when she recorded her career record. A producer for Nashville-based TENNESSEE RECORDS hired the pianist to record "Mine All Mine," a potential A side, and L. Wolfe Gilbert's minstrel show tune "Down Yonder" (popularized in 1921 by Ernest Hare & Billy Jones and again by GID TANNER in the middle 1930s) as a flip side. The latter, played in Wood's trademark ragtime style, struck the right chord with fans and hit first on the pop charts on August 24, 1951, peaking at #6. It crossed over to country, reached #5, and sold an estimated 3 million copies. She was the first female instrumentalist to chalk up a million seller. Her gender-neutral stage name—a shortening of her married name, Adelaide Hazelwood—may have helped her avoid the prejudice of male radio programmers against distaff artists.

She joined WSM's Grand Ole Opry November 13, 1953, and recorded more than sixty singles and twenty-five albums for major labels—RCA, DECCA, MERCURY, and COLUMBIA—earning the sobriquets Queen of Ragtime Piano and Queen of the Ivories. She was the first female board member for Nashville's chapter of the AFM, she was also a board member of the Nashville chapter of AFTRA and the fraternal organization ROPE. She made a cameo appearance performing in DOLLY PARTON's 1984 film *Rhinestone*. JERRY LEE LEWIS has credited Wood's piano style as an influence. Wood remained a member of the Opry until the end of her life.

—*Walt Trott*

REPRESENTATIVE RECORDINGS

Flivvers, Flappers & Foxtrots (RCA, 1960, out of print); *Upright, Low-Down & Honky Tonk* (Columbia, 1966, out of print)

Smokey Wood (*see* Modern Mountaineers)

Bob Woodruff

b. Suffern, New York, March 14, 1961

There have been country musicians from New York before—JERRY JEFF WALKER was an upstate New Yorker before he was a Texan—but not too many from Greenwich Village. Robert Woodruff grew up in the heart of New York bohemia and then in the more rustic hippiedom of the Woodstock area.

After fronting a Tom Petty–like New York City band called the Fields during the 1980s, Woodruff signed in 1993 with Nashville-based ASYLUM, as the Time Warner conglomerate resuscitated a dormant label that had earned a reputation for sheltering critically respected, often commercially marginal artists. Woodruff released his first album, *Dreams and Saturday Nights,* in early 1994.

Woodruff, who penned all the songs on the album, is not from the lyin'/cryin' school of writers, as is evident from the intensely personal lyrics of "The Year We Tried to Kill the Pain," a fever chart of a failed relationship. Woodruff tried to crack country radio with the songs "Bayou Girl" and "Hard Liquor, Cold Women, Warm Beer," but despite getting some video airplay with the former, neither single charted above #70. *Dreams and Saturday Nights* sold fewer than 15,000 copies, according to SoundScan. In 1996 Woodruff signed with new Nashville independent label Imprint Records (originally known as Veritas Records), which released his album *Desire Road* in the spring of 1997. Unfortunately, the undercapitalized label withdrew from the record business within scant months of *Desire Road* being issued, and Woodruff once again was left looking for a way to connect with an audience.

—*Mark Schone*

REPRESENTATIVE RECORDINGS

Dreams and Saturday Nights (Asylum, 1994); *Desire Road* (Imprint, 1997)

Bill Woods

b. Denison, Texas, May 12, 1924

Known as the Father of the Bakersfield Sound, Bill Woods moved from Texas to California with his family when he was sixteen, just before the United States entered World War II. As a musician he toured with BOB WILLS & the Texas Playboys, then with TOMMY DUNCAN after Duncan left Wills's band. Woods also toured with JIMMIE DAVIS and in 1950 began a stint as the leader of the Orange Blossom Playboys, the house band at the Blackboard, a club that would become one of the major honky-tonks in BAKERSFIELD. At the Blackboard, Woods hired BUCK OWENS and, later, MERLE HAGGARD as band members, playing an important role in the musical careers of these two country stars. Woods's radio show on KERN featured country music and, as a disc jockey, he was instrumental in Bakersfield radio. He recorded for Modern Records in 1949, and in the 1950s for a variety of small labels, some of which he owned. He was also active as a West Coast session musician, often backing such artists as JEAN SHEPARD in the studio. Woods was a regular on COUSIN HERB HENSON's Bakersfield KERO-TV show *The Trading Post Show,* which began on September 26, 1953. Woods later recorded for CAPITOL and remained active in the Bakersfield country music scene, producing TV shows, and managing acts.

—*Don Cusic*

Sheb Wooley

b. Erick, Oklahoma, April 10, 1921

Shelby F. Wooley is equally well known as an actor and as a recording artist. His most famous musical creations were humorous: "Purple People Eater" (#1 pop, 1958) and "That's My Pa" (#1 country, 1962). Wooley made another name for himself in the guise of Ben Colder, a humorous alter ego character, who first hit the charts with "Almost Persuaded, Number 2" (#6, 1966). In 1968 Ben Colder won the CMA Comedian of the Year Award.

As a youngster in Oklahoma, Wooley learned to ride horses and worked in a few rodeos. That experience served him well in Hollywood, where he made more than sixty films, many of them westerns, beginning with *Rocky Moun-*

tain (1950) and including the award-winning *High Noon* (1954). He also appeared in *Giant* (1955) and *Hoosiers* (1986). He co-starred as Pete Nolan in the popular *Rawhide* TV series.

As an artist Wooley recorded for BULLET RECORDS in 1946, the Bluebonnet label in 1947, and signed in 1948 with MGM RECORDS; he stayed with the label to 1973. As a songwriter Wooley penned "Too Young to Tango," a Top Ten country single for teenaged Sunshine Ruby (#4, 1953) and "Are You Satisfied," a pop success (#11, 1956) for RUSTY DRAPER. Wooley also wrote the *HEE HAW* theme.

Today Wooley remains active through his recordings (some of them marketed on TV and the Internet), occasional film work, and some 125 personal appearances per year. —*Walt Trott*

REPRESENTATIVE RECORDINGS

Country Boogies, Wild 'n' Wooley (Bear Family, 1985); *Sheb Wooley: Blue Guitar* (Bear Family, 1986)

Glenn Worf

b. Dayton, Ohio, January 24, 1954

Glenn Worf began playing the bass after a memorable family vacation to Texas, where he saw a musical group and felt the bass guitar rumbling in his stomach. That event sent Worf on a trip through an endless array of lounges in a number of rock, blues, and country bands. In one group that played original material, Glenn found a joy in creating his own parts, so in 1979 he decided to move to Nashville and try the record business.

Through many a lean year doing all-night club gigs and countless demo sessions, Worf eventually landed a master session gig for FOSTER & LLOYD's first album in 1987. When he was hired to play on KEVIN WELCH's debut album, producers in town discovered an edgy uniqueness in Glenn's playing that got him hired for records by BROOKS & DUNN and for hundreds of sessions since. Some of Worf's recent memorable highlights include albums by GEORGE JONES, Mark Knopfler, and WILLIE NELSON.

In addition, Worf has been a regular on TNN, as part of the *American Music Shop* band and in the series *At the Ryman*. He is also part of the Bluebloods, a MIKE HENDERSON–led blues band whose first album, *First Blood,* appeared on the DEAD RECKONING label in 1996. Worf is also a long-running award winner as the ACM's Bass Player of the Year (1992–97). —*Michael Hight*

REPRESENTATIVE RECORDING

The Bluebloods: First Blood (Dead Reckoning, 1996)

Paul Worley

b. Nashville, Tennessee, February 16, 1950

Paul N. Worley is a triple threat: a player-writer-producer who has made an indelible mark on the sound of modern country music in the past fifteen years. Worley has had a hand in developing or producing many of Nashville's new generation of stars, including BROOKS & DUNN, MARTINA MCBRIDE, COLLIN RAYE, and PAM TILLIS.

Worley has spent decades in and around the Nashville music business. Encouraged by his parents, he began to learn guitar at age thirteen and took guitar lessons at Cotten Music, a small musical instrument shop in Nash-

ville. While a student in philosophy at Vanderbilt University, Worley taught lessons at Cotten, which is located just blocks from the university. After graduation, Worley toured the Southeast as a member of Just Friends, a rock band that was briefly signed to COLUMBIA RECORDS.

Worley's present career began in earnest when he arrived at Odyssey Productions–Audio Media Recording Studio two years after graduation from college. The company specialized in recording remakes of hit songs—using sound a like singers, and occasionally the original artists—for international or special releases. Working with the likes of the Guess Who, TENNESSEE ERNIE FORD, and Little Richard, Worley learned the basic elements of making a great song.

Learning to pick apart a hit song prepared Worley for his next career phase: the session musician. Playing guitar, Worley played on hundreds of songs, backing stars such as REBA MCENTIRE, HANK WILLIAMS JR., EDDY RAVEN, ANNE MURRAY, GLEN CAMPBELL, JOHN ANDERSON, and MICHAEL MARTIN MURPHEY.

In 1981 Worley made his first hit as a producer, Gary Morris's "Headed for a Heartache." Worley has produced literally dozens of #1 recordings, including HIGHWAY 101's "Somewhere Tonight," Pam Tillis's "Don't Tell Me What To Do," and Martina McBride's "Independence Day." In 1989 Worley began work at Sony/TREE PUBLISHING as vice president of creative services. His job was to scout hits and develop talent, and he helped to further the careers of acts such as Brooks & Dunn, TRAVIS TRITT, and Pam Tillis.

In late 1993 Sony revamped its record labels, and Worley became part of a three-man team, with Scott Siman and ALLEN BUTLER, heading the Columbia and EPIC labels. Butler and Worley continue to run the labels, and Worley has served as executive vice president for Sony Nashville. The stable Worley has nurtured includes MARY CHAPIN CARPENTER, PATTY LOVELESS, Collin Raye, and RICK TREVINO. Worley's ascendance is proof that in modern-day Nashville, the ability to craft a hit song is the coin of the realm. —*Clark Parsons*

Mark Wright

b. Fayetteville, Arkansas, September 21, 1957

A multitalented music professional, Mark Wright has found success as a producer, songwriter, and record label executive. A product of the music business program at Nashville's Belmont University, he began his career as an assistant to producer Gary S. Paxton, later working as staff writer for Welk Music and United Artists and as an A&R talent manager for RCA RECORDS. Wright came into his own at RCA, where he was one of the youngest label executives in Nashville and also co-produced CLINT BLACK's multiplatinum breakthrough *Killin' Time* in 1989. Wright continued to produce other artists, most notably MARK CHESNUTT, and ran his own publishing company for five years before becoming DECCA RECORDS' senior vice president in 1994. Wright's songwriting credits include STEVE WARINER's "Why Goodbye" and VERN GOSDIN's "Today My World Slipped Away" (later a hit for GEORGE STRAIT) as well as tunes by the OAK RIDGE BOYS, KENNY ROGERS, EDDIE RABBITT, EARL THOMAS CONLEY, and several by Chesnutt. Wright also has sung jingles for McDonald's, Harley Davidson, Peter Pan Peanut Butter, and Goodyear Tires. —*Brian Mansfield*

Michelle Wright

b. Chatham, Ontario, Canada, July 1, 1961

Released in 1990, Canadian country singer Michelle Wright's first American single, "New Kind of Love," combined her husky, throaty vocals with a song of strength and confidence, signaling a dash of feminism in her music. Her popularity in Canada, where she has been named Entertainer of the Year by the Canadian Country Music Association among other accolades, made a transition to the American market appear possible. Her "Take It Like a Man" hit the Top Ten in 1992, but since then Wright's music has not had a significant impact on U.S. country radio.

Hailing from Merlin, Ontario, Wright grew up around music. Both of her parents were country singers, resulting in a childhood on the road. Raised across the border from Detroit, she was also influenced by the sounds of Diana Ross and other Motown artists. While in college Wright was offered a job in a band and soon found herself working on the road. She spent three years touring with various bands across the United States and Canada before starting her own band and drawing the attention of Savannah Music's Brian Ferriman. Enlisting his aid as her manager, Wright began learning the business aspects of the music industry.

Songwriter Rick Giles saw her perform in Ottawa, Ontario, and brought her to Nashville in 1986 to begin working on some songs. Her first album, *Do Right By Me,* was released in Canada in 1988. One year later she landed on Nashville's ARISTA RECORDS. Her first album for Arista was released in 1990; her most recent, *For Me It's You,* in 1996.

—*Janet Williams*

REPRESENTATIVE RECORDINGS

Do Right By Me (Savannah Music, Canadian release only, 1988); *Michelle Wright* (Arista, 1990); *Now & Then* (Arista, 1992); *For Me, It's You* (Arista, 1996)

WSM

established in Nashville, Tennessee, October 5, 1925

Although known primarily as the home of the GRAND OLE OPRY, Nashville's WSM radio station is significant in its own right as a major influence on country music history, as well as a major force in the development of radio broadcasting per se. During the golden age of radio (1935–50), WSM originated an impressive amount of programming for the various national networks. In later years the station provided the technology and expertise for the founding of the Nashville recording industry. As its early sobriquet "The Air Castle of the South" suggests, the station has been a southern institution, and a powerful presence in the lives of generations of listeners across much of the United States.

Contrary to popular belief, WSM was not the first commercial radio station in Nashville, nor in Tennessee. This honor goes to Nashville's WDAD, operated out of a downtown radio-parts store and which took to the air a month before WSM. The latter had its formal grand opening on Monday, October 5, 1925; its call letters were specially chosen to stand for the slogan "We Shield Millions," the motto of the station's owners, the National Life and Accident Insurance Company. National Life executive Edwin Craig, one of the younger members of the Craigs who had co-founded the insurance firm, pressured the National Life board to open up a radio station in Nashville. A plush,

Radio station WSM's tower, 1930s

state-of-the-art studio was set up on the fifth floor of the newly completed National Life headquarters at Seventh Avenue North and Union Street in downtown Nashville. Although clearly intended to boost sales of National Life insurance policies, programming was designed primarily to entertain Nashville's gentry and middle-class listeners. On the inaugural program there was not a note of the country or folk music that would later become so associated with the station.

The station began broadcasting at 1,000 watts of power—not impressive by modern standards, but at the time stronger than 85 percent of all the other U.S. stations. In those days of uncluttered airwaves, the signals carried for hundreds of miles, and soon the station was receiving letters from as far away as Iowa and Puerto Rico. One of the early favorites on the station was a dance band headed by Francis Craig, also of the National Life Craigs; it would remain a fixture on the station for the next three decades, and in 1947 would enjoy a huge national hit record with "Near You." On November 9, 1925, GEORGE D. HAY arrived to become radio director of the station; one of his first acts would be to start the show that would become the Grand Ole Opry.

By 1927, with its signal now increased to 5,000 watts, WSM had signed with the newly organized NBC network, bringing a bevy of national shows to the area; only on Saturday nights did WSM preempt network fare for the Opry. (The exception was the *Amos and Andy* show, for which WSM interrupted the Opry for 30 minutes.) By 1933 the station had organized a booking service for the increasing number of professional entertainers who were joining the station; in some cases these new professionals worked both on daytime country and pop programs as station staff and the Saturday night Opry. VITO PELLETTIERI was also hired as music librarian to build up the music files and keep track of performing rights problems. By 1934 the station was assigned a coveted "clear channel" status, which meant, in theory, that no other station in the country could operate on the 650 dial slot. The station's superb technology, symbolized by its giant new freestanding tower (which, after its

1932 completion, soon became a favorite of tourist postcards), allowed it to do "remote" broadcasts of network quality. Meanwhile, building on precedents set by HARRY STONE, who became general manager in 1932, a new generation of executives, such as Harry's brother DAVID STONE and JACK STAPP, helped accelerate the movement toward professional talent who could attract new sponsors.

WSM had begun regular network program originations in 1935, and by the closing days of World War II was becoming a major supplier of shows to the national networks, such as NBC, Mutual, and CBS. One of the best and most remembered of these was *Sunday Down South,* a musical variety show built around the excellent big band of Beasley Smith—a band that was essentially the station's studio band for years. The show, which ran well into the 1950s, eventually had a cast that included some sixty entertainers (about as many as the Opry), and was a springboard for nationally known pop singers Kitty Kallen and Snooky Lanson. Other WSM pop programs gave starts to singers Dinah Shore, Phil Harris, and operatic tenor James Melton.

When the station celebrated its silver anniversary in 1950, WSM had become a huge operation, with as many as 200 professional entertainers on the payroll (66 of whom were on the Opry). Its writing staff was by now producing more new live scripts than almost any other single station in America, and WSM was sending seventeen weekly shows to the networks, including children's shows such as *Wormwood Forest* (co-written by Tom Tichenor) and southern-flavored variety shows such as *Riverboat Revels.*

At the same time, though, National Life recognized the monumental changes in store for radio and established WSM-TV in 1950. Television was making traditional radio programming obsolete, and radio was becoming home to a new type of entertainer: the disc jockey. Recognizing this, in 1952 WSM radio sponsored the nation's first annual country DISC JOCKEY CONVENTION coinciding with WSM's birthday celebration, and attracted about a hundred participants. During the next two decades, the switch to the disc jockey format gradually altered WSM to the point where the Opry became its last major live show. In 1968 WSM-FM made its debut, and four years later WSM-AM decided to establish FAN FAIR to accommodate the increasing hordes of fans who were attending the country music trade show that had grown up around the station's birthday festival. A decade later, the station's association with country music was made even stronger when it launched, with the Associated Press, the Music Country Network on satellite. By 1982 National Life sold WSM-TV to Gillette Broadcasting (and renamed the station WSMV-TV). In that same year, National Life and its entertainment properties (WSM radio, OPRYLAND, the Grand Ole Opry, and Opryland Productions) were purchased by the Texas-based American General Insurance Company. In 1983 these entertainment operations, together with THE NASHVILLE NETWORK (recently evolved from Opryland Productions) were acquired by the GAYLORD Broadcasting Company, closing the era of local ownership of WSM.

The 1990s saw the station featuring a music format that emphasized "classic country" of the 1950–70 era. The WSM news operation continued to be one of the largest and best in AM radio, with award-winning features such as *I Love Life.* WSM-FM has been country formatted since 1983 and remains one of the nation's top country stations. With the appointment of Kyle Cantrell as program director in the mid-1990s, the station became even more aware of its own role in American culture and began generating

a series of features that documented this rich heritage. In October 1997 WSM ended its seventy-year affiliation with the NBC radio network, signing with ABC radio.

—*Charles Wolfe*

Roy Wunsch
b. St. Louis, Missouri, June 23, 1945

During the 1980s and 1990s marketing expert Roy Wunsch served as president of Sony Music's Nashville division and as chairman/CEO of Imprint Records. Wunsch began his music career with a summer job at CBS Records' St. Louis Distribution Center, then rapidly advanced through the label's local and regional marketing departments. In 1975 he was promoted to national promotion and sales manager for EPIC RECORDS' Nashville division. He was named vice president of marketing in 1981, second in command of the Nashville division in 1985, and senior vice president and general manager of Nashville operations in 1988 after the Japanese firm Sony Music Entertainment acquired CBS Records (including the Columbia and Epic labels). In 1990 Wunsch was named the Nashville division's first-ever president, a position he held until 1993. Among the artists signed during Wunsch's tenure with Sony Music were JOE DIFFIE, COLLIN RAYE, PATTY LOVELESS, DOUG STONE, and RICK TREVINO.

In July 1995, with Bud Schaetzle, Wunsch co-founded Imprint Records (originally named Veritas Music Entertainment), the first independent country music label founded as a public company and traded on the NASDAQ stock exchange. Wunsch served as chairman and CEO of the company, while Schaetzle, founder of High Five Entertainment, served as president. Its artists included Al Anderson, Charlie Major, Gretchen Peters, Ryan Reynolds, Jeff Wood, and BOB WOODRUFF. In June 1997 the label ceased releasing recordings and underwent a business reorganization.

—*Marjie McGraw*

WWVA Jamboree (Jamboree U.S.A.)
established in Wheeling, West Virginia, January 7, 1933

Under a variety of names—most recently *Jamboree U.S.A.*—the live-audience country music show from WWVA radio in Wheeling, West Virginia, has a record for longevity second only to the GRAND OLE OPRY. Local musicians appeared on the station from the time it went on the air in 1926, but the *Jamboree* as a stage program dates from January 7, 1933, at the Capitol Theater in downtown Wheeling. The site for the broadcast soon was moved to the Wheeling Market Auditorium.

Early stars included the trio of Cap, Andy, & Flip, Silver Yodelin' Bill Jones, the Tweedy Brothers, COUSIN EMMY (Carver), and GRANDPA JONES; and from 1937, DOC WILLIAMS & Big Slim and the Lone Cowboy (HARRY McAULIFFE). George Smith, the program director at WWVA, served as the guiding force in making the *Jamboree* a venerated institution. During its peak years, WWVA was one of several stations owned by Storer Broadcasting. On October 8, 1942, WWVA became a 50,000-watt outlet, a factor that led to the program's growing popularity in rural portions of northeastern states and in eastern Canada.

From December 12, 1942, to July 13, 1946, wartime conditions led to abandonment of the live-audience show, although the *Jamboree* continued as a studio program. It reopened to fans in the Virginia Theater, and over the next

WWVA Jamboree *cast*

decade reached its peak in terms of overall influence. New stars such as HAWKSHAW HAWKINS, WILMA LEE & STONEY COOPER, Roy Scott, and Lee Moore, who also gained renown as the station's all-night DJ, took their places beside veterans such as Williams & Big Slim. The show also had room for several popular female performers, including CHICKIE WILLIAMS, Betty Cody, Milly Wayne, and Bonnie Baldwin, as well as popular rustic comics typified by Hiram Hayseed (W. H. Godwin) and Crazy Elmer (Anthony Slater). For a time in the mid-1950s, a portion of the show was carried by the CBS network.

The coming of widespread TV ownership and rock & roll took some of the luster away form the program's prestige, but it survived even after the demise of the Virginia Theater in 1962. The site moved over to the Rex Theater (1962–66) and to the Wheeling Island Exhibition Center (1966–69) before moving back to its original home, the Capitol, in 1969. Since then it has continued to thrive under the name *Jamboree U.S.A.*

Increasingly, guest stars from Nashville have become the central attraction while *Jamboree* regulars such as Darnell Miller and Junior Norman have been relegated to the status of opening acts. While this move may have permitted the *Jamboree* to avoid the fate of some of the other radio barn dances, some of the older traditions and spontaneity seem to have suffered. Nonetheless, the Wheeling *Jamboree* from WWVA radio has a long and ongoing history in the annals of country music.   —*Ivan M. Tribe*

Tammy Wynette
b. Itawamba County, Mississippi, May 5, 1942; d. April 6, 1998

In the late 1960s and early 1970s the country music charts were dominated by a trio of creative, unique, and defining women: DOLLY PARTON, LORETTA LYNN, and Tammy Wynette. Stylists and songwriters, each articulated women's perspectives with an autobiographical slant that made their lives as much an object of audience interest as their music.

Like her country sisters, Wynette grew up in a hard-scrabble, rural household in the South, but she had big-city dreams. Born Virginia Wynette Pugh, in Itawamba County, Mississippi, she was raised by her cotton-farming grandparents. Her father, William Hollice Pugh, died of a brain tumor when she was less than a year old; he left her a recording of himself and a musical legacy, as he had attempted to be a professional singer rather than a share-cropper. Her mother, Mildred, left for Memphis to work in a defense plant during World War II.

Wynette worked in the cotton fields, played her father's inherited instruments, took music lessons, and followed the careers of many gospel quartets who traveled through Mississippi and Alabama during the southern gospel explosion of the late 1940s and early 1950s. She was one of a trio of friends—"Wynette, Linda, and Imogene"—who performed on a local gospel radio show.

Wynette married Euple Byrd a month before she graduated from high school in 1959. They had two children, and with no steady employment, Byrd moved the family from place to place. Wynette went to beauticians' school and even did a stint as a barmaid and singer in Memphis. Divorced in 1965, at age twenty-three, she was by then the mother of three, working at a beauty salon, singing on a local TV show, living in government housing, and making forty-five dollars a week. But several trips to Nashville and a brief tour with PORTER WAGONER fueled her fantasy of a career in music, and she made the move to MUSIC CITY in 1966.

In that year she walked into the office of producer-songwriter BILLY SHERRILL, of EPIC RECORDS, to pitch some songs. Two weeks later her name was changed to Tammy Wynette, and she was recording for Epic, with Sherrill, who would write many of her songs.

Wynette's first recording, the JOHNNY PAYCHECK–Bobby Austin composition "Apartment #9," earned decent airplay but did not ignite as a hit. But her next release, "Your Good Girl's Gonna Go Bad" (1967), in which she sang of a woman who was going to join her man in his own philandering game, reached the Top Ten. Her first #1, a duet with DAVID HOUSTON, soon followed, and her first solo #1, "I Don't Wanna Play House" (1967), won her a Grammy. Her classic "D-I-V-O-R-C-E" followed in 1968, as Wynette continued to explore the complicated feelings of women

Tammy Wynette

and children faced with the breakup of a family, a theme important personally and musically throughout her career.

Sherrill and Wynette collaborated in writing her signature tune, "Stand By Your Man" (1968), a #1 country smash that also went to #19 on the pop charts. At the height of the women's liberation movement, as bras were being burned in a trash can at the Miss America pageant in Atlantic City, Wynette's song, recommending forgiveness of wayward men, hit the airwaves. A statement of womanly domestic strength, the record nevertheless drew harsh criticism in some quarters (Wynette's critics tended to overlook Janis Joplin's singing of allowing men to take her heart if it made them feel good), but also led to the first of Wynette's three consecutive CMA Female Vocalist of the Year awards (1968–70). "Stand By Your Man" also entered the movies in 1970's *Five Easy Pieces,* starring Jack Nicholson.

Wynette co-wrote her next two hit singles, "Singing My Song" and "The Ways to Love a Man." But songs, no matter who wrote them, were a seamless presentation befitting the "Heroine of Heartbreak." Her gripping, teardrop-in-every-note vocal style seemed to weep with emotion, while her songs elaborated on the theme that suffering ennobles a woman.

Wynette's marriage to singer-songwriter Don Chapel in 1967 was beset by professional jealousy. In 1968 country superstar GEORGE JONES witnessed a fight between the Chapels, and at Jones's urging, Wynette and her daughters drove away with him. Wynette and Jones married on February 16, 1969, and Wynette's fourth daughter, Georgette, was born in 1970.

Jones and Wynette, nicknamed the "President and First Lady" of country music, recorded a string of hit duets that seemed drawn directly from their volatile relationship, which resulted in their divorcing in 1975. Their classic recordings included "Two Story House," "Golden Ring," and the humorous "(We're Not) The Jet Set."

Wynette married Nashville businessman Michael Tomlin within weeks of their meeting, in 1976. The marriage lasted six weeks. In 1978 she married her fifth husband, songwriter-producer GEORGE RICHEY, who had been present in her life for many years, contributing his business acumen and accomplished musicianship. Her 1979 autobiography and a 1981 TV movie based on her life chronicled her personal experiences of frequent illness, often tumultuous relationships, and other hardships—such as being abducted and beaten, having a death threat placed on her life, and being involved in a public bankruptcy case.

By the end of the 1980s Wynette had scored twenty #1 singles and sold more than 30 million records. Her surprising 1992 collaboration with the British duo KLF—which resulted in an international hit with their dance-pop number "Justified and Ancient"—capped a decade of collaboration projects that extended beyond the country field. In 1995 she joined Jones again to make the duet album *One* (MCA), produced by TONY BROWN and NORRO WILSON.

In her career Wynette cultivated being professional, dignified, and ladylike while tough. Her cosmopolitan style had a country-grit soul. Assertively working-class and womanly, Wynette expressed the difficulties facing working women: raising children, holding down a job, and performing domestic roles. Her "steel magnolia" image allowed her to work within a male-dominated environment in which prejudices against women were still strong. If she was the victim, she was also the survivor. Her professional and personal life were indistinguishably interwoven, revealing the reality of only partially realized dreams and painful experience.

Wynette died of a blood clot at age fifty-five and was mourned by the industry and her fans during a nationally televised service, broadcast from the RYMAN AUDITORIUM on April 9, 1998. Appearing at the memorial service were, among others, RANDY TRAVIS, the OAK RIDGE BOYS, Dolly Parton, MERLE HAGGARD, WYNONNA, and LORRIE MORGAN. Later that year Wynette won election to the COUNTRY MUSIC HALL OF FAME.
—*Mary A. Bufwack*

REPRESENTATIVE RECORDINGS

Stand By Your Man (Epic, 1969; reissued Koch, 1997); *Greatest Hits* (Epic, 1977) (with George Jones); *Tears of Fire: The 25th Anniversary Collection* (Epic, 1992), 3 discs

Wynonna (*see* Wynonna Judd, the Judds)

X stations (*see* Border Radio)

Trisha Yearwood
b. Monticello, Georgia, September 19, 1964

Patricia Lynn "Trisha" Yearwood leaped to stardom in 1991 with the release of her hit debut single, "She's in Love with the Boy." Since then, through performances such as her 1996 #1 hit "Believe Me Baby (I Lied)," she has become known as one of country music's strongest vocalists and as one of a number of women who have contributed to redefining the overall sound of country music in the 1990s.

Trisha Yearwood

The younger daughter of a banker and a grade school teacher, Yearwood grew up in the close-knit community of Monticello, Georgia. An avid fan of ELVIS PRESLEY, she also grew up listening to LINDA RONSTADT, whom Yearwood cites as one of her main influences. Following high school she moved to Nashville to attend Belmont University, where she majored in music business.

Her 1987 marriage to Belmont classmate Chris Latham ended in divorce four years later. Before scoring her recording contract with MCA RECORDS, Yearwood worked as a receptionist for now-defunct MTM Records in addition to singing demos. While doing session work, she met producer GARTH FUNDIS, who has been behind the board for all of her MCA albums. She also became acquainted with another aspiring star, GARTH BROOKS, who promised that if he ever made it in the music business, he'd help her in any way he could. True to his word, Brooks invited Yearwood to open his first headlining tour; she has also sung on his albums. In late 1997 there was even talk of a possible Brooks-Yearwood duet album to be released the following year, if circumstances permitted.

Since her 1991 debut album release, *Trisha Yearwood,* her albums have been consistent sellers. She teamed with Don Henley of the EAGLES for "Walkaway Joe," a runaway hit that propelled her 1992 album *Hearts in Armor* to platinum certification. She also shared the CMA's Album of the Year honors with numerous artists for her contribution to *Common Thread: The Songs of the Eagles.*

In 1993 Yearwood was the subject of *Get Hot or Go Home,* a biography written by Lisa Gubernick; in addition, Yearwood was the subject of "The Song Remembers When," a one-hour special for the Disney Channel in 1993. In that same year she made her movie debut, portraying herself in *The Thing Called Love,* directed by Peter Bogdanovich. With her recording of "How Do I Live" from the movie soundtrack *Con Air,* Yearwood won Female Vocalist of the Year honors from the CMA in 1997 as well as a 1997 Grammy Award in the Best Country Female Vocal Performance category. She also shared a Grammy that year with duet partner Garth Brooks for "In Another's Eyes."

In May 1994 Yearwood married Robert Reynolds, bass player for the MAVERICKS. They reside in Hendersonville, Tennessee.
—*Janet Williams*

REPRESENTATIVE RECORDINGS

Trisha Yearwood (MCA, 1991); *Hearts in Armor* (MCA, 1992); *Thinkin' About You* (MCA, 1995); *Everybody Knows* (MCA, 1996); *Songbook—A Collection of Hits* (MCA, 1997)

Dwight Yoakam

b. Pikeville, Kentucky, October 23, 1956

Dwight Yoakam's flashy appearance has distracted attention from his talents as a modern honky-tonk singer and songwriter who has incorporated the expansive harmonies of Beatlesque pop within the old-fashioned narrative and rhythmic structures of BAKERSFIELD country. Stubbornly keeping his distance from Nashville, this California-based artist nonetheless became one of the best-selling country artists of the 1980s and 1990s.

Yoakam was born, as his song put it, "South of Cincinnati," listening to his grandfather's "Miner's Prayer," and was raised north of that city. Like most everyone else in his generation, he grew up on the Beatles and the BYRDS, but he got the bug for hillbilly music from his parents and his church. He banged on doors in Nashville for several years, but in 1978 he headed for California, where GRAM PARSONS and EMMYLOU HARRIS had created an alternative to the Nashville formulas and where MERLE HAGGARD and BUCK OWENS still kept the Bakersfield Sound alive. In Los Angeles Yoakam hooked up with a hot guitarist and producer named PETE ANDERSON, and together they fashioned a unique sound—one that took its structure from the hard-country era of the late 1950s and combined it with ambitious melodies and harmonies.

Because they refused to play Top Forty country, they couldn't work in country clubs, so Yoakam and Anderson opened up for such L.A. roots-rock acts as the Blasters, Los Lobos, and Lone Justice in rock clubs. They started attracting attention, especially when they released a 1984 six-song EP, *Guitars, Cadillacs, Etc.* on the tiny Oak label. Reprise finally took a chance in 1986, and reissued *Guitars, Cadillacs, Etc., Etc.*, with the original six songs plus four new ones (plus an extra "Etc."). Before the year was over, the album had pushed its way to the top of the country charts.

The 1987 follow-up, *Hillbilly Deluxe*, also went #1, yielding four Top Ten country singles, including the originals "Little Ways" and "Please, Please Baby," along with remakes of LEFTY FRIZZELL's "Always Late with Your Kisses" and ELVIS PRESLEY's "Little Sister." Also topping the country album charts was 1988's *Buenos Noches from a Lonely Room*. Yoakam sang a duet with his hero Buck Owens on "Streets of Bakersfield," an obscure track from an old Owens album. The duet became a #1 country single, as did "I Sang Dixie." *Just Lookin' for a Hit* was a 1989 anthology that recycled eight older songs and added two new ones, a duet with K.D. LANG on Gram Parsons's "Sin City" and "Long White Cadillac," the Blasters' song about HANK WILLIAMS's last ride in 1952.

If There Was a Way, released in 1990, only rose to #7 on the country album charts and yielded two Top Ten singles, "You're the One" and "It Only Hurts When I Cry" (co-written with ROGER MILLER). "La Croix d'Amour," which was released only in Europe in 1992, collected such stray tracks as Yoakam's versions of the Grateful Dead's "Truckin'," the Beatles' "Things We Said Today," Elvis Presley's "Suspicious Minds," and Van Morrison's "Here Comes the Night." Yoakam recovered his commercial clout with 1993's *This Time*, which yielded five Top Twenty country singles, including "Ain't That Lonely Yet," which won the 1994 Grammy for Best Male Country Vocal Performance.

In the midst of all this recording and touring, Yoakam found time to pursue his interest in acting. In 1993 Peter

Dwight Yoakam

Fonda directed him in the original play *Southern Rapture* at L.A.'s MET Theatre. In 1994 Yoakam appeared with Nicholas Cage and Dennis Hopper in John Dahl's film *Red Rock West*, and with Martin Sheen in the cable-TV movie *Roswell*. In 1996 Yoakam demonstrated his considerable acting skills in Billy Bob Thornton's film *Slingblade*.

In 1995 Yoakam released his first concert album, *Dwight Live*, which became a showcase for Anderson, who had not only remained Yoakam's producer since the beginning but also his lead guitarist and music director on tour—a most unusual combination. In that same year Yoakam released *Gone*, his most musically ambitious album yet, described by *Rolling Stone* magazine as "cutting-edge country-pop [that] barrels straight ahead like a train out of Bakersfield, California, headed for Liverpool, England." In 1997 Yoakam won praise for his album *Under the Covers*, including fresh interpretations of earlier hits by acts from the Rolling Stones to ROY ORBISON.

Unlike his old roots-rock buddies and unlike his fellow 1986 rookies STEVE EARLE and LYLE LOVETT, Yoakam has flourished on the country charts. There are three reasons for this. For one, he rivals RANDY TRAVIS as the finest honky-tonk singer of his generation; Yoakam's twangy tenor is simply too spellbinding for even country radio to ignore. Two, the prime strength of Yoakam's songwriting is his music, not his lyrics, and mainstream country has found it easier to digest distorted guitars than ironic lyrics. And three, Yoakam has clearly aligned himself with an enduring tradition—the Bakersfield Sound of Owens and Haggard—that has proven its commercial appeal in the past and continues to do so today. —*Geoffrey Himes*

Guitars Cadillacs Etc. Etc. (Reprise, 1986); *Just Lookin' for a Hit* (Reprise, 1989); *This Time* (Reprise, 1993); *Dwight Live* (Reprise, 1995); *Gone* (Reprise, 1995); *Under the Covers* (Reprise, 1997)

The York Brothers

George York b. Louisa, Kentucky, February 10, 1910; d. July 1974

Leslie York b. Louisa, Kentucky, August 23, 1917; d. February 21, 1984

The York Brothers bridged the gap between the older style of harmony duets and more modern country sounds. Natives of eastern Kentucky, the Yorks had varied work and musical experience prior to first working as a team at WPAY in Portsmouth, Ohio. This led to a contract with DECCA RECORDS, for whom they cut six songs in 1941. Later they moved to Detroit, where they recorded "Hamtramck Mama" for Universal. Shortly afterward, they entered military service.

After World War II the York Brothers joined the GRAND OLE OPRY and in 1947 began a decade of recording for KING RECORDS. Many of their discs consisted of country versions of rhythm & blues songs. In 1950 the brothers returned to Detroit and then permanently relocated to the Dallas–Fort Worth area. They continued in music for several more years and had several releases on their own York label. George allegedly had some voice problems with the passing of time, prompting Leslie to carry a disproportionate share of the vocal load. —*Ivan M. Tribe*

The York Brothers, Volumes I & II (King, 1958); *Early Favorites* (Old Homestead, 1987)

Chip Young

b. Atlanta, Georgia, May 19, 1938

Chip Young (Jerry Marvin Stembridge) came of age in the late fifties playing guitar in Atlanta with JERRY REED, JOE SOUTH, and RAY STEVENS. Like many of his contemporaries, Young toured with South and gravitated to LOWERY MUSIC, where Young wrote songs and engineered publishers' demos and commercially released recordings. Following army service (1961–63), he moved to Nashville in 1963, at first to back Reed on tour. Before long Young was playing studio guitar behind stars such as ELVIS PRESLEY, Ann-Margret, EDDY ARNOLD, and GEORGE JONES. Signing as a writer with Bill Justis's Tuneville Music, Young helped Justis build a studio and began producing sessions. Young also recorded instrumentals as a Bell Records artist.

In 1968, he bought a farm near Murfreesboro, Tennessee, and soon built his own studio, Young 'Un Sound. There he produced recordings by acts such as Reed, BILLY SWAN, and r&b artist DELBERT MCCLINTON, while recording others ranging from country/pop singer Jimmy Buffett to pop balladeer Johnny Mathis. By 1978 Young moved his operation to a studio on Seventeenth Avenue South in Nashville, where he produced LARRY GATLIN and recorded such country stars as REBA MCENTIRE, JOHNNY RODRIGUEZ, THE STATLER BROTHERS, and TOM T. HALL.

After selling his studio in 1987, Young remained in demand as a session guitarist until health problems forced him to retire from this field in 1990. Since then he has worked as a song plugger for BMG Publishing while helping to produce new acts such as COLUMBIA's Deryl Dodd. —*John Rumble*

Reba McEntire: *Unlimited* (Mercury, 1982); Chip Young: *Having Thumb Fun with My Friends* (Belle Meade, 1993)

Faron Young

b. Shreveport, Louisiana, February 25, 1932; d. December 10, 1996

From the early 1950s through the mid-1970s, Faron Young was among the top stars and most colorful personalities in all of country music. Signature hits such as "If You Ain't Lovin' (You Ain't Livin')" and "Live Fast, Love Hard, Die Young" marked him as a honky-tonk man in both sound and personal style, while other chart-topping singles, such as "Hello Walls" and "It's Four in the Morning," showed off his versatility as a vocalist. A music industry entrepreneur, he invested in Music Row real estate, and in the 1960s he published the influential trade paper *Music City News*. Though his career did not lack controversy, Young's voluble, outgoing personality was well received, and the entire community was as shocked as it was saddened when he died of a self-inflicted gunshot wound at age sixty-four.

Born in Shreveport and raised on a farm outside of town, Young, as a teenager, was more interested in pop music than in country. But that changed when his high school football coach, who moonlighted in a country band, started Young singing at the local Optimist Club and nursing homes. Young then met WEBB PIERCE and began working with Pierce in clubs and on KWKH. By 1951 Young was appearing on the station's feature program, the LOUISIANA HAYRIDE.

Though he recorded in Shreveport, Young's first sides appeared on Philadelphia's Gotham label. But by February 1952 he had been signed to CAPITOL RECORDS, for which he would record for the next ten years. His first Capitol single appeared that spring, and soon thereafter he moved to Nashville. He recorded his first chart hit, "Goin' Steady," in October 1952, but his career got sidetracked when he was drafted the following month. While in the service, he performed on army recruitment programs and continued to record. He was discharged in November 1954, just as "If You Ain't Lovin' " was hitting the charts.

From 1954 to 1962 Young cut a slew of honky-tonk classics for Capitol, including the first hit version of DON GIBSON's "Sweet Dreams." Most famous was "Hello Walls," a crossover smash for Young in 1961. It was written by WILLIE NELSON, who reportedly pitched the song to Young at TOOTSIE'S ORCHID LOUNGE.

In 1963 Young switched from Capitol to MERCURY RECORDS. Though initially his Mercury catalogue drifted through various bland NASHVILLE SOUND stylings, by the end of the decade he had recaptured much of his hard country fire with hits such as "Wine Me Up." Released in 1971, the waltz-time ballad "It's Four in the Morning" was one of Young's finest records and his last #1 hit. By the mid-1970s his records were becoming overshadowed by his salty persona. For example, he made headlines in 1972 when he spanked a little girl who was in the audience at a concert in Clarksburg, West Virginia.

Young switched labels again in 1979, signing with MCA.

Faron Young

The association lasted only two years, and little was heard from Young after that until the Nashville independent STEP ONE picked him up in 1988. He recorded for Step One into the early 1990s (including a charming, if not particularly exciting, duet album with RAY PRICE), and then withdrew from public view. Though young country acts such as BR5-49 were putting his music before a whole new audience in the mid-1990s, Young apparently felt the industry had turned its back on him. That and despondency over his deteriorating health were cited as possible reasons why Young shot himself on December 9, 1996. He died in Nashville the following day. —*Daniel Cooper*

REPRESENTATIVE RECORDINGS

This Is Faron Young (Capitol, 1959); *Faron Young: Live Fast, Love Hard: Original Capitol Recordings, 1952–1962* (Country Music Foundation, 1995); *Golden Hits* (Mercury Nashville, 1995)

Neil Young
b. Toronto, Ontario, Canada, November 12, 1945

Though best known as a rock singer-songwriter, Neil Young has roots in country music and Nashville. In the mid-1960s he helped to pioneer country-rock as a member of Buffalo Springfield. As part of the seventies rock supergroup Crosby, Stills, Nash, and Young, he recorded country-inspired tracks ("Teach Your Children") for their multimillion seller *Deja Vu*. And Young's songs have provided material for numerous country artists, including EMMYLOU HARRIS, MARTY STUART, WAYLON JENNINGS, and DOLLY PARTON.

His own recordings most closely identify Young with country music. Beginning with his self-titled debut album for Reprise in 1969, he has often blended pedal steel, country rhythms, and rural imagery with distorted, noisy electric guitars. Follow-up albums, including *Everybody Knows This Is Nowhere* and *After the Goldrush*, had country overtones; *Goldrush* even included a cover of DON GIBSON's "Oh, Lonesome Me."

In February 1971 Young was invited to Nashville for a guest spot on JOHNNY CASH's ABC television program. Also booked on the program were pop stars James Taylor and LINDA RONSTADT. With a bunch of new songs in hand—and the help of Taylor and Ronstadt—Young booked time at Nashville's Woodland Sound Studios and brought in some local musicians (including Ben Keith and Kenny Buttrey) to lay down tracks. The album, titled *Harvest*, proved to be one of Young's most successful albums and yielded his only #1 chart single, "Heart of Gold."

In 1978 he released *Comes a Time*, also recorded in Nashville. In addition to Ben Keith, who had by now become a mainstay in Young's outfit, singer-multi-instrumentalist Anthony Crawford, Cajun fiddler Rufus Thibodeaux, and bluegrass guitarist Grant Boatright were enlisted for the project. The album ultimately reached platinum status in sales. Young's composition "Lotta Love" from that album provided singer Nicolette Larsen with her commercial breakthrough later in the same year.

In the early 1980s Young made a concerted effort to tap into the country market and formed the International Harvesters. In addition to Keith, Crawford, and Thibodeaux, Young added legendary Nashville session pianist PIG ROBBINS and songwriter-bass player Joe Allen to the group. In some ways Young's debut album for Geffen Records, *Old Ways*, was a throwback to the NASHVILLE SOUND. Label owner David Geffen fought the release of the album, but Young eventually won. Although it boasted several great pickers and guest artists (including Waylon Jennings and WILLIE NELSON), the album failed to dent the country charts.

In July 1985, though, Young did manage to take the Harvesters to the Live Aid stage in Philadelphia, thus being MUSIC CITY's sole representation at the historic event. On September 22, 1985, Young, along with Willie Nelson and John Mellencamp, launched the first Farm Aid Benefit, in Champaign, Illinois.

Young was inducted into the Roll & Roll Hall of Fame in 1992. In 1997 he was again inducted as a member of Buffalo Springfield. —*Chris Skinker*

REPRESENTATIVE RECORDINGS

Neil Young (Reprise, 1969); *After the Gold Rush* (Reprise, 1970); *Harvest* (Reprise, 1972); *Zuma* (Reprise, 1975); *Comes a Time* (Reprise, 1978)

Reggie Young
b. Caruthersville, Missouri, December 12, 1936

Master guitarist Reggie Grimes Young Jr. has contributed to the rise of Memphis rockabilly in the mid-1950s, the flourishing of CHIPS MOMAN's enormously productive American Studio in Memphis during the 1960s, and the expansion of the Nashville recording scene in the 1970s and beyond. Young started playing guitar in 1951, learning from his father. Influenced by the music of CHET ATKINS and Django Reinhardt, Young played in territorial western swing and country bands, recorded with Memphis rockabilly bands, and worked with country star JOHNNY HORTON out of Shreveport, Louisiana, before returning to Memphis in 1959 to help form the Bill Black Combo, much in demand for road shows and for Royal Recording studio sessions. After a stint in the army (1960–62), Young rejoined the Black unit, which opened for the Beatles on their historic 1964 U.S. tour.

In about 1965 Young began working almost exclusively as a studio player, soon becoming part of American Studio's famous rhythm section. Over the next seven years he played on some 400 chartmaking discs recorded in Memphis by artists ranging from ELVIS PRESLEY and soul singer Wilson Pickett to pop stars Dusty Springfield and Neil Diamond.

As Memphis recording activity slackened, Young moved briefly to Atlanta (1972) and later in the year to Nashville. Immediately he became a "first call" guitarist whose lead and rhythm parts contributed to such hits as Dobie Gray's pop smash "Drift Away," WAYLON JENNINGS's "Luckenbach, Texas," and WILLIE NELSON's "Always on My Mind." Young's stylings have also graced recordings by artists as diverse as Jimmy Buffett, rock star Joe Cocker, jazz innovator Herbie Mann, multimarket singer B. J. THOMAS, and country greats HANK WILLIAMS JR., CONWAY TWITTY, REBA McENTIRE, MERLE HAGGARD, and GEORGE STRAIT. Young continues to play sessions today, while producing sessions, writing songs, and running his own publishing company.

—John Rumble

REPRESENTATIVE RECORDINGS

Elvis Presley: *From Elvis in Memphis* (RCA, 1969); Hank Williams Jr.: *Greatest Hits, Volume 2* (Warner/Curb, 1987); George Strait: *Greatest Hits,* Volume 2 (MCA, 1987)

Steve Young

b. near Newnan, Georgia, July 12, 1942

Steve Young played key roles in the evolution of two historical movements in country music: country-rock and OUTLAW country. Young's first solo album, *Rock, Salt & Nails,* released in 1969 by A&M Records, was one of a handful of late 1960s albums that synthesized the stylistic elements and emotional concerns of country music with those of 1960s rock. By the early 1970s this musical blend—often called country-rock—had become mainstream.

Young's long-standing personal and artistic nonconformity was also an inspiration to so-called Outlaws such as WAYLON JENNINGS and WILLIE NELSON. Jennings once stated that Young "has no earthly idea how great he is." Young recorded two of the most enduring Outlaw albums: *Honky Tonk Man* (Mountain Railroad, 1975) and *Renegade Picker* (RCA, 1976).

Raised in rural and urban settings in Georgia, Alabama, and Texas, Young grew up listening to traditional as well as to commercial country musicians. Accordingly, he has always performed an eclectic mix of songs—powerful interpretations of traditional and contemporary songs alongside compelling original compositions in a wide range of styles. Although his own recordings have never sold widely or received much airplay, other musicians have recognized his talents as a songwriter (e.g., Jennings covered Young's "Lonesome, On'ry, and Mean," and the EAGLES recorded Young's best-known composition, "Seven Bridges Road"); as a vocalist (Jennings once asserted that "Young is the second greatest country music singer—to GEORGE JONES, of course"); and as a guitar virtuoso. —*Ted Olson*

REPRESENTATIVE RECORDINGS

Rock, Salt & Nails (A&M, 1969); *Honky Tonk Man* (Mountain Railroad, 1975); *Switchblades of Love* (Watermelon, 1993)

Joe Zinkan

b. Indianapolis, Indiana, December 16, 1918

Acoustic stand-up bassist Joseph Scudder Zinkan first recorded with the DELMORE BROTHERS for BLUEBIRD RECORDS in September 1938 in Rock Hill, South Carolina. He performed with PEE WEE KING's Golden West Cowboys and then joined ROY ACUFF's Smoky Mountain Boys in 1943 and worked with Acuff into the late 1950s. Zinkan played on Acuff's 1947 recording of "Wabash Cannonball." Although Zinkan generally played bass, on occasion he also sang harmony and played rhythm guitar at sessions. He toured with KITTY WELLS and JOHNNIE & JACK from 1956 to 1959, playing on many of their records, and wrote the duo's "Camel Walk Stroll." He also recorded with JIMMY DICKENS, MARTY ROBBINS, and TAMMY WYNETTE. He retired from music in 1980 and underwent heart surgery in 1990. —*Walt Trott*

APPENDICES

Country Music's All-Time Best-Selling Albums
(as of November 1997)

as certified by the Recording Industry Association of America, Inc. (RIAA)

Artist, Album (Label, Year of Release)

10 million units and above sold in the United States
Garth Brooks, *No Fences* (Capitol, 1990), 13 million sold
Kenny Rogers, *Greatest Hits* (Liberty, 1980), 2 million sold
Garth Brooks, *Ropin' the Wind* (Capitol, 1991), 11 million sold

9 million units sold
Garth Brooks, *The Hits* (Capitol, 1994)
Billy Ray Cyrus, *Some Gave All* (Mercury, 1992)
Shania Twain, *The Woman in Me* (Mercury, 1995)

7 million units sold
Garth Brooks, *Garth Brooks* (Capitol, 1989)
Patsy Cline, *Greatest Hits* (Decca/MCA, 1967)
John Denver, *Greatest Hits* (RCA, 1973)

6 million units sold
Garth Brooks, *The Chase* (Liberty, 1992)
Garth Brooks, *In Pieces* (Liberty, 1993)
Alan Jackson, *A Lot About Livin' (And a Little 'Bout Love)* (Arista, 1992)

5 million units sold
Alabama, *Greatest Hits* (RCA, 1986)
Garth Brooks, *Sevens* (Capitol, 1997)
Brooks & Dunn, *Brand New Man* (Arista, 1991)
Wynonna Judd, *Wynonna* (MCA, 1992)
Tim McGraw, *Not a Moment Too Soon* (Curb, 1994)
Elvis Presley, *Elvis' Golden Records, Volume 1* (RCA, 1957)
Kenny Rogers, *The Gambler* (United Artists, 1978)
Linda Ronstadt, *Greatest Hits* (Asylum, 1977)
George Strait, *Pure Country* (MCA, 1992)
Randy Travis, *Always and Forever* (Warner Bros., 1987)

4 million units sold
Alabama, *The Closer You Get* (RCA, 1983)
Alabama, *Feels So Right* (RCA, 1981)
Alabama, *Mountain Music* (RCA, 1982)
Garth Brooks, *Fresh Horses* (Capitol, 1995)
Brooks & Dunn, *Hard Workin' Man* (Arista, 1993)
Vince Gill, *Still Believe in You* (MCA, 1992)
Alan Jackson, *Don't Rock the Jukebox* (Arista, 1991)
Waylon Jennings, *Greatest Hits* (RCA, 1979)
Kris Kristofferson & Barbra Streisand, *A Star Is Born* (Columbia, 1976)
Reba McEntire, *Greatest Hits, Volume II* (MCA, 1993)
John Michael Montgomery, *John Michael Montgomery* (Atlantic, 1995)
John Michael Montgomery, *Kickin' It Up* (Atlantic, 1994)
Anne Murray, *Greatest Hits* (Capitol, 1980)

Willie Nelson, *Always on My Mind* (Columbia, 1982)
Willie Nelson, *Stardust* (Columbia, 1978)
Willie Nelson & Family, *Willie & Family Live* (Columbia, 1978)
Kenny Rogers, *Ten Years of Gold* (United Artists, 1977)
Kenny Rogers, *Twenty Greatest Hits* (Liberty, 1983)
George Strait, *Strait Out of the Box* (4 CDs) (MCA, 1995)

3 million units sold
Alabama, *Roll On* (RCA, 1984)
Clint Black *Killin' Time* (RCA, 1989)
Clint Black, *Put Yourself in My Shoes* (RCA, 1990)
Garth Brooks, *Beyond the Season* (Liberty, 1992)
Garth Brooks, *The Garth Brooks Collection* (Liberty, 1994)
Brooks & Dunn, *Waitin' on Sundown* (Arista, 1994)
Mary Chapin Carpenter, *Come On, Come On* (Columbia, 1992)
Deana Carter, *Did I Shave My Legs for This?* (Capitol, 1996)
Charlie Daniels Band, *A Decade of Hits* (Epic, 1983)
Charlie Daniels Band, *Million Mile Reflections* (Epic, 1978)
Jeff Foxworthy, *You Might Be a Redneck If . . .* (Warner Bros., 1993)
Vince Gill, *When Love Finds You* (MCA, 1994)
Alan Jackson, *Greatest Hits Collection* (Arista, 1995)
Alan Jackson, *Who I Am* (Arista, 1994)
Reba McEntire, *For My Broken Heart* (MCA, 1991)
Reba McEntire, *Greatest Hits* (MCA, 1987)
Reba McEntire, *It's Your Call* (MCA, 1992)
Reba McEntire, *Read My Mind* (MCA, 1994)
John Michael Montgomery, *Life's a Dance* (Atlantic, 1992)
Willie Nelson, *Greatest Hits (& Some That Will Be)* (Columbia, 1981)
LeAnn Rimes, *Blue* (Curb, 1996)
LeAnn Rimes, *You Light Up My Life: Inspirational Songs* (Curb, 1997)
Kenny Rogers, *Kenny* (United Artists, 1979)
Linda Ronstadt, *Simple Dreams* (Elektra, 1977)
Statler Brothers, *The Best of the Statler Brothers* (Mercury, 1975)
George Strait, *Greatest Hits* (MCA, 1985)
George Strait, *Greatest Hits, Volume II* (MCA, 1987)
Randy Travis, *Storms of Life* (Warner Bros., 1986)
Travis Tritt, *It's All About to Change* (Warner Bros., 1991)
Various artists, *Common Thread: Songs of the Eagles* (Giant, 1993)
Dwight Yoakam, *This Time* (Reprise, 1993)

2 million units sold
Alabama, *Alabama Christmas* (RCA, 1985)
Alabama, *My Home's in Alabama* (RCA, 1980)
John Anderson, *Seminole Wind* (RCA, 1992)
BlackHawk, *BlackHawk* (Arista, 1994)
Brooks & Dunn, *Borderline* (Arista, 1996)
Tracy Byrd, *No Ordinary Man* (MCA, 1994)
Glen Campbell, *Wichita Lineman* (Capitol, 1968)
Johnny Cash, *Johnny Cash at Folsom Prison* (Columbia, 1968)
Johnny Cash, *Johnny Cash at San Quentin* (Columbia, 1969)

Johnny Cash, *Greatest Hits, Volume I* (Columbia, 1967)

Jennings, Nelson, Colter, Glaser, *Wanted! The Outlaws* (RCA, 1976)

Jeff Foxworthy, *Games Rednecks Play* (Warner Bros., 1995)

Vince Gill, *Pocket Full of Gold* (MCA, 1991)

Vince Gill, *When I Call Your Name* (MCA, 1989)

Faith Hill, *It Matters to Me* (Warner Bros., 1995)

Faith Hill, *Take Me as I Am* (Warner Bros., 1993)

Alan Jackson, *Here in the Real World* (Arista, 1990)

Waylon Jennings & Willie Nelson, *Waylon & Willie* (RCA, 1978)

The Judds, *Greatest Hits* (RCA, 1988)

The Judds, *Why Not Me* (RCA, 1984)

Kentucky Headhunters, *Pickin' on Nashville* (Mercury, 1989)

Alison Krauss, *Now That I've Found You* (Rounder, 1995)

Tracy Lawrence, *Alibis* (Atlantic, 1993)

Little Texas, *Big Time* (Warner Bros., 1993)

Neal McCoy, *Another Night* (Arista, 1996)

Reba McEntire, *Rumor Has It* (MCA, 1990)

Tim McGraw, *All I Want* (Curb, 1995)

Tim McGraw, *Everywhere* (Curb, 1997)

Reba McEntire, *Merry Christmas to You* (MCA, 1987)

Ronnie Milsap, *Greatest Hits* (RCA, 1980)

Anne Murray, *Christmas Wishes* (Liberty, 1981)

Willie Nelson, *Red Headed Stranger* (Columbia, 1975)

Willie Nelson & Family, *Original Soundtrack: Honeysuckle Rose* (Columbia, 1980)

Oak Ridge Boys, *Fancy Free* (MCA, 1981)

Dolly Parton & Kenny Rogers, *Once Upon a Christmas* (RCA, 1984)

Elvis Presley, *Aloha from Hawaii Via Satellite* (RCA, 1972)

Elvis Presley, *Blue Hawaii* (RCA, 1961)

Elvis Presley, *Elvis as Recorded at Madison Square Garden* (RCA, 1972)

Elvis Presley, *Elvis' Christmas Album* (RCA, 1957)

Elvis Presley, *Elvis' Golden Records, Volume II* (RCA, 1959)

Elvis Presley, *Elvis Sings the Wonderful World of Christmas* (RCA, 1971)

Elvis Presley, *How Great Thou Art* (RCA, 1966)

Elvis Presley, *Moody Blue* (RCA, 1977)

Kenny Rogers, *Christmas* (Liberty, 1981)

Kenny Rogers, *Eyes That See in the Dark* (RCA, 1983)

Linda Ronstadt, *Heart Like a Wheel* (Capitol, 1974)

George Strait, *Blue Clear Sky* (MCA, 1996)

George Strait, *Carryin' Your Love with Me* (MCA, 1997)

George Strait, *Easy Come, Easy Go* (MCA, 1993)

George Strait, *Ocean Front Property* (MCA, 1987)

The Tractors, *The Tractors* (Arista, 1994)

Randy Travis, *No Holdin' Back* (Warner Bros., 1989)

Randy Travis, *Old 8 x 10* (Warner Bros., 1988)

Travis Tritt, *Country Club* (Warner Bros., 1990)

Travis Tritt, *Ten Feet Tall and Bulletproof* (Warner Bros., 1994)

Travis Tritt, *T-R-O-U-B-L-E* (Warner Bros., 1992)

Hank Williams Jr., *Greatest Hits* (Warner Bros., 1982)

Trisha Yearwood, *Songbook—A Collection* (MCA, 1997)

Trisha Yearwood, *Trisha Yearwood* (MCA, 1991)

1 million units sold

Trace Adkins, *Dreamin' Out Loud* (Capitol, 1996)

Alabama, *40 Hour Week* (RCA, 1985)

Alabama, *Alabama Live* (RCA, 1988)

Alabama, *American Pride* (RCA, 1992)

Alabama, *Cheap Seats* (RCA, 1993)

Alabama, *Greatest Hits, Volume II* (RCA, 1991)

Alabama, *Greatest Hits, Volume III* (RCA, 1994)

Alabama, *In Pictures* (RCA, 1995)

Alabama, *Pass It on Down* (RCA, 1990)

Alabama, *Southern Star* (RCA, 1989)

Alabama, *The Touch* (RCA, 1986)

David Ball, *Thinkin' Problem* (Warner Bros., 1994)

John Berry, *John Berry* (Liberty, 1993)

Clint Black, *Greatest Hits* (RCA, 1996)

Clint Black, *The Hard Way* (RCA, 1992)

Clint Black, *No Time to Kill* (RCA, 1993)

Clint Black, *One Emotion* (RCA, 1994)

Suzy Bogguss, *Aces* (Liberty, 1991)

Brooks & Dunn, *Greatest Hits* (Arista, 1997)

Glen Campbell, *By the Time I Get to Phoenix* (Capitol, 1967)

Glen Campbell, *Galveston* (Capitol, 1969)

Glen Campbell, *Gentle on My Mind* (Capitol, 1967)

Glen Campbell, *Greatest Hits* (Capitol, 1971)

Mary Chapin Carpenter, *Shooting Straight in the Dark* (Columbia, 1990)

Mary Chapin Carpenter, *Stones in the Road* (Columbia, 1994)

Johnny Cash, *The Johnny Cash Portrait* (Columbia, 1976)

Mark Chesnutt, *Almost Goodbye* (MCA, 1993)

Mark Chesnutt, *Longnecks and Short Stories* (MCA, 1992)

Mark Chesnutt, *Too Cold at Home* (MCA, 1990)

Terri Clark, *Terri Clark* (Mercury, 1995)

Patsy Cline, *Patsy Cline Story* (MCA, 1963)

David Allan Coe, *Greatest Hits* (Columbia, 1978)

Confederate Railroad, *Confederate Railroad* (Atlantic, 1992)

Confederate Railroad, *Notorious* (Atlantic, 1994)

Billy Ray Cyrus, *It Won't Be the Last* (Mercury, 1993)

Charlie Daniels Band, *Fire on the Mountain* (Epic, 1974)

Charlie Daniels Band, *Full Moon* (Epic, 1980)

Charlie Daniels Band, *Simple Man* (Epic, 1989)

Mac Davis, *Baby, Don't Get Hooked on Me* (Columbia, 1972)

John Denver, *A Christmas Together* (Windstar, 1988)

John Denver, *I Want to Live* (RCA, 1971)

John Denver, *Spirit* (RCA, 1976)

Diamond Rio, *Diamond Rio* (Arista, 1991)

Diamond Rio, *Love a Little Stronger* (Arista, 1994)

Joe Diffie, *Honky Tonk Attitude* (Epic, 1993)

Joe Diffie, *Third Rock from the Sun* (Epic, 1994)

Tennessee Ernie Ford, *Hymns* (Capitol, 1956)

Tennessee Ernie Ford, *The Star Carol* (Capitol, 1958)

Larry Gatlin & the Gatlin Brothers, *Straight Ahead* (Columbia, 1979)

Crystal Gayle, *We Must Believe in Magic* (United Artists, 1977)

Vince Gill, *The Best of Vince Gill* (RCA, 1989)

Vince Gill, *High Lonesome Sound* (MCA, 1996)

Vince Gill, *Let There Be Peace on Earth* (MCA, 1993)

Lee Greenwood, *Greatest Hits* (MCA, 1985)

Merle Haggard, *Best of the Best of Merle Haggard* (Liberty, 1972)

Merle Haggard, *His Epic Hits: The First 11* (Epic, 1984)

Merle Haggard, *Okie from Muskogee* (Capitol, 1969)

Merle Haggard & Willie Nelson, *Poncho and Lefty* (Epic, 1982)

Emmylou Harris, Dolly Parton, Linda Ronstadt, *Trio* (Warner Bros., 1987)

Johnny Horton, *Greatest Hits* (Columbia, 1961)

Alan Jackson, *Everything I Love* (Arista, 1996)

Waylon Jennings, *Ol' Waylon* (RCA, 1977)

George Jones, *I Am What I Am* (Epic, 1980)

George Jones, *Super Hits* (Epic, 1987)

Wynonna Judd, *Revelations* (MCA/Curb, 1996)

Wynonna Judd, *Tell Me Why* (MCA, 1993)

The Judds, *Christmas Time with the Judds* (RCA, 1987)

The Judds, *Collector's Series* (RCA, 1990)

The Judds, *Heartland* (RCA, 1987)

The Judds, *Love Can Build a Bridge* (RCA, 1990)

The Judds, *Rockin' with the Rhythm* (RCA, 1985)

Toby Keith, *Toby Keith* (Mercury, 1993)

Sammy Kershaw, *Don't Go Near the Water* (Mercury, 1991)

Sammy Kershaw, *Haunted Heart* (Mercury, 1993)

Tracy Lawrence, *I See It Now* (Atlantic, 1994)

Tracy Lawrence, *Sticks and Stones* (Atlantic, 1991)

Tracy Lawrence, *Time Marches On* (Atlantic, 1996)

Little Texas, *Kick a Little* (Warner Bros., 1994)

Patty Loveless, *Honky Tonk Angel* (MCA, 1988)

Patty Loveless, *Only What I Feel* (Epic, 1993)

Patty Loveless, *When Fallen Angels Fly* (Epic, 1994)

Kathy Mattea, *A Collection of Hits* (Mercury, 1990)

The Mavericks, *What a Crying Shame* (MCA, 1994)

Martina McBride, *The Way That I Am* (RCA, 1993)

Neal McCoy, *No Doubt About It* (Atlantic, 1994)

Neal McCoy, *You Gotta Love That* (Atlantic, 1995)

Mindy McCready, *Ten Thousand Angels* (BNA, 1996)

Reba McEntire, *The Last One to Know* (MCA, 1987)

Reba McEntire, *Merry Christmas to You* (MCA, 1987)

Reba McEntire, *Live* (MCA, 1989)

Reba McEntire, *Reba* (MCA, 1988)

Reba McEntire, *Starting Over* (MCA, 1995)

Reba McEntire, *Sweet Sixteen* (MCA, 1989)

Reba McEntire, *What If It's You* (MCA, 1996)

Reba McEntire, *Whoever's in New England* (MCA, 1986)

Ronnie Milsap, *Greatest Hits, Volume II* (RCA, 1985)

Ronnie Milsap, *Greatest Hits, Volume III* (RCA, 1992)

Lorrie Morgan, *Greatest Hits* (BNA, 1995)
Lorrie Morgan, *Leave the Light On* (RCA, 1989)
Lorrie Morgan, *Something in Red* (RCA, 1991)
Lorrie Morgan, *Watch Me* (BNA, 1992)
Anne Murray, *Let's Keep It That Way* (Capitol, 1978)
Anne Murray, *New Kind of Feeling* (Capitol, 1979)
Willie Nelson, *City of New Orleans* (Columbia, 1984)
Willie Nelson, *Pretty Paper* (Columbia,1979)
Willie Nelson, *Somewhere over the Rainbow* (Columbia, 1981)
Willie Nelson, *Willie Nelson Sings Kris Kristofferson* (Columbia, 1979)
Willie Nelson, *Without a Song* (Columbia, 1983)
Juice Newton, *Juice* (Capitol, 1981)
Oak Ridge Boys, *Greatest Hits, Volume 1* (MCA, 1980)
Oak Ridge Boys, *Greatest Hits, Volume 2* (MCA, 1984)
Roy Orbison, *Mystery Girl* (Virgin, 1989)
K. T. Oslin, *80's Ladies* (RCA, 1987)
K. T. Oslin, *This Woman* (RCA, 1988)
Dolly Parton, *Eagle When She Flies* (Columbia, 1991)
Dolly Parton, *Greatest Hits* (RCA, 1982)
Dolly Parton, *Here You Come Again* (RCA, 1977)
Dolly Parton, *Slow Dancing with the Moon* (Columbia, 1993)
Johnny Paycheck, *Take This Job and Shove It* (Epic, 1978)
Elvis Presley, *Elvis in Concert* (RCA, 1977)
Elvis Presley, *G. I. Blues* (RCA, 1960)
Elvis Presley, *His Hand in Mine* (RCA, 1960)
Elvis Presley, *The King of Rock & Roll: Complete 50s Masters* (RCA, 1992), 5 CDs
Elvis Presley, *Pure Gold* (RCA, 1975)
Elvis Presley, *Welcome to My World* (RCA, 1977)
Eddie Rabbitt, *Horizon* (Asylum/Elektra, 1980)
Collin Raye, *All I Can Be* (Epic, 1991)
Collin Raye, *Extremes* (Epic, 1994)
Collin Raye, *I Think About You* (Epic, 1995)
Collin Raye, *In This Life* (Epic, 1992)
Marty Robbins, *Gunfighter Ballads and Trail Songs* (Columbia, 1959)
Kenny Rogers, *Daytime Friends* (United Artists, 1977)
Kenny Rogers, *Duets* (EMI America, 1984)
Kenny Rogers, *Gideon* (United Artists, 1980)
Kenny Rogers, *Kenny Rogers* (United Artists, 1976)
Kenny Rogers, *Love Will Turn You Around* (Liberty, 1982)
Kenny Rogers, *Share Your Love* (Liberty, 1981)
Kenny Rogers, *20 Great Years* (Reprise, 1990)
Kenny Rogers, *We've Got Tonight* (Liberty, 1983)
Kenny Rogers, *What About Me* (RCA, 1984)
Kenny Rogers & Dottie West, *Classics* (United Artists, 1979)
Kenny Rogers & the First Edition, *Greatest Hits* (Reprise, 1971)
Linda Ronstadt, *Greatest Hits, Volume II* (Asylum, 1980)
Linda Ronstadt, *Hasten Down the Wind* (Asylum, 1976)
Linda Ronstadt, *Living in the U.S.A.* (Asylum, 1978)
Linda Ronstadt, *Prisoner in Disguise* (Elektra, 1975)
Dan Seals, *The Best of Dan Seals* (Liberty, 1987)
Ricky Van Shelton, *Backroads* (Columbia, 1991)
Ricky Van Shelton, *Greatest Hits Plus* (Columbia, 1992)
Ricky Van Shelton, *Loving Proof* (Columbia, 1988)
Ricky Van Shelton, *RVS III* (Columbia, 1990)
Ricky Van Shelton, *Wild-Eyed Dream* (Columbia, 1987)
Ricky Skaggs, *Highways and Heartaches* (Epic, 1982)
Soundtrack, *8 Seconds* (MCA, 1994)
Soundtrack, *Honeymoon in Vegas* (Epic, 1992)
Soundtrack, *Urban Cowboy* (Asylum, 1980)
Squirrel Nut Zippers, *Hot* (Mammoth, 1996)
Statler Brothers, *Christmas Card* (Mercury, 1978)
Ray Stevens, *Greatest Hits* (MCA, 1987)
Ray Stevens, *He Thinks He's Ray Stevens* (MCA, 1984)
Doug Stone, *Doug Stone* (Epic, 1990)
Doug Stone, *I Thought It Was You* (Epic, 1991)
George Strait, *Beyond the Blue Neon* (MCA, 1989)
George Strait, *Chill of an Early Fall* (MCA, 1991)
George Strait, *Does Fort Worth Ever Cross Your Mind* (MCA, 1984)
George Strait, *Holding My Own* (MCA, 1992)
George Strait, *If You Ain't Lovin' (You Ain't Livin')* (MCA, 1988)
George Strait, *Lead On* (MCA, 1994)
George Strait, *Livin' It Up (MCA, 1990)*
George Strait, *Merry Christmas Strait to You* (MCA, 1986)
George Strait, *#7* (MCA, 1986)
George Strait, *Something Special* (MCA, 1985)
George Strait, *Strait from the Heart* (MCA, 1982)

George Strait, *Ten Strait Hits* (MCA, 1991)
Pam Tillis, *Homeward Looking Angel* (Arista, 1992)
Pam Tillis, *Sweetheart's Dance* (Arista, 1994)
Aaron Tippin, *Read Between the Lines* (RCA, 1992)
Randy Travis, *Duets—Heroes and Friends* (Warner Bros., 1990)
Randy Travis, *Greatest Hits, Volume I* (Warner Bros., 1992)
Randy Travis, *Greatest Hits, Volume II* (Warner Bros., 1992)
Randy Travis, *High Lonesome* (Warner Bros., 1991)
Travis Tritt, *Greatest Hits—From the Beginning* (Warner Bros., 1995)
Tanya Tucker, *Can't Run from Yourself* (Liberty, 1992)
Tanya Tucker, *Greatest Hits, 1990–1992* (Liberty, 1993)
Tanya Tucker, *Greatest Hits* (Columbia, 1975)
Tanya Tucker, *Greatest Hits, Volume II* (Columbia, 1978)
Tanya Tucker, *What Do I Do with Me* (Liberty, 1991)
Conway Twitty, *Very Best of Conway Twitty* (MCA, 1978)
Various Artists, *Academy of Country Music—101 Greatest Hits* (K-Tel, 1995)
Various Artists, *Rhythm, Country & Blues* (MCA, 1994)
Clay Walker, *Clay Walker* (Giant, 1993)
Clay Walker, *Hypnotize the Moon* (Giant, 1995)
Clay Walker, *If I Could Make a Living* (Giant, 1994)
Bryan White, *Between Now and Forever* (Asylum, 1996)
Bryan White, *Bryan White* (Asylum, 1994)
Keith Whitley, *Greatest Hits* (RCA, 1990)
Hank Williams Jr., *Born to Boogie* (Warner Bros., 1987)
Hank Williams Jr., *Greatest Hits, Volume II* (Warner Bros., 1985)
Hank Williams Jr., *Greatest Hits, Volume III* (Warner Bros., 1989)
Hank Williams Jr., *The Pressure Is On* (Warner Bros., 1981)
Tammy Wynette, *Greatest Hits, Volume I* (Epic, 1969)
Trisha Yearwood, *Hearts in Armor* (MCA, 1992)
Trisha Yearwood, *The Song Remembers When* (MCA, 1993)
Trisha Yearwood, *Thinkin' About You* (MCA, 1995)
Dwight Yoakam, *Buenos Noches from a Lonely Room* (Reprise, 1988)
Dwight Yoakam, *Hillbilly Deluxe* (Reprise, 1987)
Dwight Yoakam, *If There Was a Way* (Reprise, 1990)
Dwight Yoakam, *Just Lookin' for a Hit* (Reprise, 1989)

500,000 units sold
Alabama, *Just Us* (RCA, 1987)
John Anderson, *Greatest Hits* (Warner Bros., 1984)
John Anderson, *Solid Ground* (BNA, 1993)
John Anderson, *Wild and Blue* (Warner Bros., 1982)
Lynn Anderson, *Rose Garden* (Columbia, 1970)
Eddy Arnold, *The Best of Eddy Arnold* (RCA, 1967)
Eddy Arnold, *My World* (RCA, 1965)
Bellamy Brothers, *Greatest Hits* (MCA, 1982)
Clint Black, *Nothin' But the Taillights* (RCA, 1997)
BlackHawk, *Strong Enough* (Arista, 1995)
Suzy Bogguss, *Greatest Hits* (Capitol, 1994)
Suzy Bogguss, *Something Up My Sleeve* (Capitol, 1993)
Suzy Bogguss, *Voices in the Wind* (Liberty, 1992)
Paul Brandt, *Calm Before the Storm* (Reprise, 1996)
Tracy Byrd, *Big Love* (MCA, 1996)
Tracy Byrd, *Tracy Byrd* (MCA, 1993)
Glen Campbell, *Live* (Capitol, 1969)
Glen Campbell, *Rhinestone Cowboy* (Capitol, 1975)
Glen Campbell, *Southern Nights* (Capitol, 1977)
Glen Campbell, *That Christmas Feeling* (Capitol, 1968)
Glen Campbell, *Try a Little Kindness* (Capitol, 1970)
Glen Campbell & Bobbie Gentry, *Glen Campbell and Bobbie Gentry* (Capitol, 1968)
Mary Chapin Carpenter, *A Place in the World* (Columbia, 1996)
Mary Chapin Carpenter, *State of the Heart* (Columbia, 1989)
Johnny Cash, *Hello, I'm Johnny Cash* (Columbia, 1970)
Johnny Cash, *I Walk the Line* (Columbia, 1964)
Johnny Cash, *Johnny Cash Collection—Greatest Hits, Volume II* (Columbia, 1971)
Johnny Cash, *The Johnny Cash Show* (Columbia, 1970)
Johnny Cash, *Ring of Fire—The Best of Johnny Cash* (Columbia, 1963)
Johnny Cash, *The World of Johnny Cash* (Columbia, 1970)
Johnny Cash, Waylon Jennings, Kris Kristofferson, Willie Nelson, *Highwayman* (Columbia, 1985)
Rosanne Cash, *Hits 1979–1989* (Columbia, 1989)
Rosanne Cash, *King's Record Shop* (Columbia, 1987)
Rosanne Cash, *Seven Year Ache* (Columbia, 1981)
Ray Charles, *Modern Sounds in Country & Western Music, Volume II* (ABC, 1962)

Kenny Chesney, *Me and You* (BNA, 1996)

Mark Chesnutt, *Greatest Hits* (Decca, 1996)

Mark Chesnutt, *What a Way to Live* (MCA, 1994)

Terri Clark, *Just the Same* (Mercury, 1996)

Patsy Cline, *Heartaches* (MCA, 1985)

Patsy Cline, *The Patsy Cline Collection* (MCA, 1991), 4 CDs

Patsy Cline, *Sweet Dreams: Original Motion Picture Soundtrack* (MCA, 1985)

Patsy Cline & Jim Reeves, *Remembering* (MCA, 1988)

Jerry Clower, *From Yazoo City (Mississippi Talkin')* (MCA, 1971)

Jerry Clower, *Greatest Hits* (MCA, 1979)

Jerry Clower, *Mouth of the Mississippi* (Decca, 1972)

Jessi Colter & Waylon Jennings, *Leather and Lace* (RCA, 1981)

John Conlee, *Greatest Hits* (MCA, 1983)

Earl Thomas Conley, *Greatest Hits* (RCA, 1988)

Rodney Crowell, *Diamonds and Dirt* (Columbia, 1988)

Billy Ray Cyrus, *Storm in the Heartland* (Mercury, 1994)

Charlie Daniels Band, *Midnight Wind* (Epic, 1977)

Charlie Daniels Band, *Saddle Tramp* (Epic, 1976)

Charlie Daniels Band, *Super Hits* (Epic, 1994)

Charlie Daniels Band, *Windows* (Epic, 1981)

Mac Davis, *All the Love in the World* (Columbia, 1975)

Mac Davis, *Greatest Hits* (Columbia, 1979)

Mac Davis, *It's Hard to Be Humble* (Casablanca, 1980)

Mac Davis, *Stop and Smell the Roses* (Columbia, 1974)

Billy Dean, *Billy Dean* (Liberty, 1991)

Billy Dean, *Fire in the Dark* (Liberty, 1992)

Billy Dean, *Greatest Hits* (Capitol, 1994)

Billy Dean, *Young Man* (Liberty, 1990)

John Denver, *Aerie* (RCA, 1971)

John Denver, *Back Home Again* (RCA, 1974)

John Denver, *An Evening with John Denver* (RCA, 1975)

John Denver, *Farewell Andromeda* (RCA, 1973)

John Denver, *Greatest Hits, Volume II* (RCA, 1983)

John Denver, *John Denver* (RCA, 1978)

John Denver, *Poems, Prayers, and Promises* (RCA, 1971)

John Denver, *Rocky Mountain Christmas* (RCA, 1975)

John Denver, *Rocky Mountain High* (RCA, 1972)

John Denver, *Seasons of the Heart* (RCA, 1982)

John Denver, *Some Days Are Diamonds* (RCA, 1981)

John Denver, *Windsong* (RCA, 1975)

Diamond Rio, *Close to the Edge* (Arista, 1992)

Diamond Rio, *IV* (Arista, 1996)

Joe Diffie, *Life's So Funny* (Epic, 1995)

Joe Diffie, *Regular Joe* (Epic, 1992)

Steve Earle, *Copperhead Road* (Uni, 1988)

Everly Brothers, *The Very Best of the Everly Brothers* (Warner Bros., 1964)

Exile, *Greatest Hits* (Epic, 1986)

Donna Fargo, *Happiest Girl in the Whole U.S.A.* (Dot, 1972)

Freddy Fender, *Before the Next Teardrop Falls* (ABC/Dot, 1975)

Tennessee Ernie Ford, *Nearer the Cross* (Capitol, 1957)

Tennessee Ernie Ford, *Spirituals* (Capitol, 1957)

Jeff Foxworthy, *Crank It Up—The Music Album* (Warner Bros., 1996)

Larry Gatlin & the Gatlin Brothers, *Greatest Hits* (Columbia, 1980)

Crystal Gayle, *Classic Crystal* (EMI-Manhattan, 1979)

Crystal Gayle, *Greatest Hits* (Columbia, 1983)

Crystal Gayle, *Miss the Mississippi* (Liberty, 1979)

Crystal Gayle, *These Days* (Columbia, 1980)

Crystal Gayle, *When I Dream* (United Artists, 1978)

Bobbie Gentry, *Ode to Billy Joe* (Capitol, 1967)

Vince Gill, *Souvenirs* (MCA, 1995)

Mickey Gilley, *Biggest Hits* (Epic, 1982)

Mickey Gilley, *Encore* (Epic, 1980)

Bobby Goldsboro, *Honey* (United Artists, 1968)

Vern Gosdin, *Chiseled in Stone* (Columbia, 1987)

Vern Gosdin, *10 Years of Hits* (Columbia, 1990)

Lee Greenwood, *Inside Out* (MCA, 1981)

Lee Greenwood, *Somebody's Gonna Love You* (MCA, 1983)

Lee Greenwood, *You've Got a Good Love Comin'* (MCA, 1984)

Merle Haggard, *Big City* (Epic, 1981)

Merle Haggard, *The Fightin' Side of Me* (Capitol, 1970)

Tom T. Hall, *Greatest Hits, Volume 2* (Mercury, 1993)

Emmylou Harris, *Blue Kentucky Girl* (Warner Bros., 1979)

Emmylou Harris, *Elite Hotel* (Reprise, 1975)

Emmylou Harris, *Evangeline* (Warner Bros., 1981)

Emmylou Harris, *Luxury Liner* (Warner Bros., 1977)

Emmylou Harris, *Pieces of the Sky* (Reprise, 1975)

Emmylou Harris, *Profile—The Best of Emmylou Harris* (Warner Bros., 1978)

Emmylou Harris, *Quarter Moon in a Ten Cent Town* (Warner Bros., 1978)

Emmylou Harris, *Roses in the Snow* (Warner Bros., 1980)

Freddie Hart, *Easy Loving* (Capitol, 1971)

Wade Hayes, *Old Enough to Know Better* (Columbia, 1994)

Wade Hayes, *On a Good Night* (Columbia, 1996)

Ty Herndon, *Livin' in a Moment* (Epic, 1996)

Ty Herndon, *What Mattered Most* (Epic, 1995)

Highway 101, *Highway 101* (Warner Bros., 1987)

Alan Jackson, *Honky Tonk Christmas* (Arista, 1993)

Waylon Jennings, *Are You Ready for the Country* (RCA, 1976)

Waylon Jennings, *Dreaming My Dreams* (RCA, 1975)

Waylon Jennings, *Greatest Hits* (RCA, 1979)

Waylon Jennings, *I've Always Been Crazy* (RCA, 1978)

Waylon Jennings, *Music Man* (RCA, 1982)

Waylon Jennings, *Waylon Live* (RCA, 1976)

Waylon Jennings, *What Goes Around Comes Around* (RCA, 1979)

Waylon Jennings & Willie Nelson, *Take It to the Limit* (Columbia, 1987)

Waylon Jennings & Willie Nelson, *Waylon and Willie II* (RCA, 1982)

George Jones, *Anniversary—Ten Years of Hits* (Columbia, 1982)

George Jones, *Still the Same Ole Me* (Epic, 1981)

George Jones, *Walls Can Fall* (MCA, 1992)

George Jones, *Wine Colored Roses* (Epic, 1986)

George Jones & Tammy Wynette, *Greatest Hits* (Epic, 1977)

The Judds, *Greatest Hits, Volume II* (RCA, 1991)

The Judds, *River of Time* (RCA, 1989)

The Judds, *Wynonna and Naomi* (RCA, 1984)

Toby Keith, *Blue Moon* (Mercury, 1996)

Toby Keith, *Boomtown* (Mercury, 1994)

The Kendalls, *Heaven's Just a Sin Away* (Ovation, 1977)

Kentucky Headhunter, *Electric Barnyard* (Mercury, 1991)

Sammy Kershaw, *Feeling Good Train* (Mercury, 1994)

Sammy Kershaw, *The Hits/Chapter I* (Mercury, 1995)

Sammy Kershaw, *Politics, Religion and Her* (Mercury, 1996)

Hal Ketchum, *Past the Point of Rescue* (Curb, 1991)

Kris Kristofferson, *Jesus Was a Capricorn* (Monument, 1972)

Kris Kristofferson, *Me and Bobby McGee* (Monument, 1971)

Kris Kristofferson, *The Silver Tongued Devil and I* (Monument, 1971)

Kris Kristofferson, *Songs of Kristofferson* (Monument, 1988)

Kris Kristofferson & Rita Coolidge, *Kris & Rita—Full Moon* (A&M, 1973)

k. d. lang, *Shadowland* (Sire, 1988)

k. d. lang & the reclines, *Absolute Torch and Twang* (Sire, 1989)

Tracy Lawrence, *The Coast Is Clear* (Atlantic, 1997)

Chris LeDoux, *Best of* (Capitol, 1997)

Chris LeDoux, *Whatcha Gonna Do with a Cowboy* (Liberty, 1992)

Little Texas, *First Time for Everything* (Warner Bros., 1992)

Little Texas, *Greatest Hits* (Warner Bros., 1995)

Lonestar, *Lonestar* (RCA, 1995)

Patty Loveless, *Greatest Hits* (MCA, 1993)

Patty Loveless, *Honky Tonk Angel* (MCA, 1988)

Patty Loveless, *On Down the Line* (MCA, 1990)

Patty Loveless, *The Trouble with the Truth* (Epic, 1996)

Lyle Lovett, *Joshua Judges Ruth* (MCA, 1992)

Lyle Lovett, *Lyle Lovett and His Large Band* (MCA, 1989)

Lyle Lovett, *Pontiac* (MCA, 1987)

Loretta Lynn, Dolly Parton, Tammy Wynette, *Honky Tonk Angels* (Columbia, 1993)

Loretta Lynn, *Coal Miner's Daughter* (MCA, 1980)

Loretta Lynn, *Don't Come Home a-Drinkin'* (Decca, 1967)

Loretta Lynn, *Greatest Hits* (MCA, 1968)

Loretta Lynn, *Greatest Hits, Volume II* (MCA, 1974)

Loretta Lynn & Conway Twitty, *Lead Me On* (Decca, 1971)

Loretta Lynn & Conway Twitty, *The Very Best of Loretta & Conway* (MCA, 1979)

Loretta Lynn & Conway Twitty, *We Only Make Believe* (Decca, 1971)

Barbara Mandrell, *The Best of Barbara Mandrell* (MCA, 1979)

Barbara Mandrell, *"Live"* (MCA, 1981)

Kathy Mattea, *Lonesome Standard Time* (Mercury, 1992)

Kathy Mattea, *Time Passes By* (Mercury, 1991)

Kathy Mattea, *Untasted Honey* (Mercury, 1987)

Kathy Mattea, *Walking Away a Winner* (Mercury, 1994)

Kathy Mattea, *Willow in the Wind* (Mercury, 1989)

The Mavericks, *Music for All Occasions* (MCA, 1995)

McBride & the Ride, *Sacred Ground* (MCA, 1992)

Martina McBride, *Wild Angels* (RCA, 1995)

C. W. McCall, *Black Bear Road* (MGM, 1975)

Neal McCoy, *Greatest Hits* (Atlantic, 1997)

Reba McEntire, *The Best of Reba McEntire* (Mercury, 1985)

Reba McEntire, *Have I Got a Deal for You* (MCA, 1985)

Reba McEntire, *My Kind of Country* (MCA, 1984)

Reba McEntire, *What Am I Gonna Do About You?* (MCA, 1986)

Roger Miller, *Dang Me! The Best of Roger Miller* (LaserLight, 1992)

Roger Miller, *Golden Hits* (Smash, 1965)

Roger Miller, *The Return of Roger Miller* (Smash, 1965)

Ronnie Milsap, *It Was Almost Like a Song* (RCA, 1977)

Ronnie Milsap, *Live* (RCA, 1976)

Ronnie Milsap, *Lost in the Fifties Tonight* (RCA, 1986)

Ronnie Milsap, *Only One Love in My Life* (RCA, 1978)

Ronnie Milsap, *There's No Gettin' Over Me* (RCA, 1981)

John Michael Montgomery, *What I Do the Best* (Atlantic, 1996)

Lorrie Morgan, *Greater Need* (RCA, 1996)

Lorrie Morgan, *Greatest Hits* (BNA, 1995)

Lorrie Morgan, *War Paint* (RCA, 1994)

Gary Morris, *Why Lady Why* (Warner Bros., 1983)

Michael Martin Murphey, *Blue Sky—Night Thunder* (Epic, 1975)

David Lee Murphy, *Out with a Bang* (MCA, 1994)

Anne Murray, *Country* (Capitol, 1974)

Anne Murray, *Heart Over Mind* (Capitol, 1984)

Anne Murray, *I'll Always Love You* (Capitol, 1979)

Anne Murray, *A Little Good News* (Liberty, 1983)

Anne Murray, *Snowbird* (Capitol, 1970)

Anne Murray, *Something to Talk About* (Capitol, 1986)

Anne Murray, *Where Do You Go When You Dream* (Capitol, 1981)

Willie Nelson, *Half Nelson* (Columbia, 1985)

Willie Nelson, *The Sound in Your Mind* (Columbia, 1976)

Willie Nelson, *Super Hits* (Columbia, 1994)

Willie Nelson, *The Troublemaker* (Columbia, 1976)

Willie Nelson & Ray Price, *San Antonio Rose* (Columbia, 1980)

Willie Nelson & Leon Russell, *One for the Road* (Columbia, 1979)

Juice Newton, *Greatest Hits* (Capitol, 1987)

Juice Newton, *Quiet Lies* (Capitol, 1982)

Nitty Gritty Dirt Band, *More Great Dirt: The Best of, Volume II* (Warner Bros., 1989)

Nitty Gritty Dirt Band, *Twenty Years of Dirt: The Best of* (Warner Bros., 1986)

Nitty Gritty Dirt Band, *Will the Circle Be Unbroken* (EMI America, 1972)

Oak Ridge Boys, *American Made* (MCA, 1983)

Oak Ridge Boys, *Bobbie Sue* (MCA, 1982)

Oak Ridge Boys, *Deliver* (MCA, 1985)

Oak Ridge Boys, *Oak Ridge Boys Christmas* (MCA, 1985)

Oak Ridge Boys, *The Oak Ridge Boys Have Arrived* (MCA, 1979)

Oak Ridge Boys, *Room Service* (MCA, 1978)

Oak Ridge Boys, *Together* (MCA, 1980)

Oak Ridge Boys, *Ya'll Come Back Saloon* (MCA, 1977)

Roy Orbison, *All Time Greatest Hits, Volume I* (CBS, 1989)

Roy Orbison, *All Time Greatest Hits, Volume II* (CBS, 1989)

Roy Orbison, *Greatest Hits* (Monument, 1976)

Roy Orbison, *In Dreams: Greatest Hits* (Virgin, 1987)

K. T. Oslin, *Love in a Small Town* (RCA, 1990)

Buck Owens, *The Best of Buck Owens* (Capitol, 1964)

Dolly Parton, *The Best of Dolly Parton* (RCA, 1975)

Dolly Parton, *Great Balls of Fire* (RCA, 1979)

Dolly Parton, *Heart Breaker* (RCA, 1978)

Dolly Parton, *Home for Christmas* (Columbia, 1990)

Dolly Parton, *9 to 5 and Odd Jobs* (RCA, 1980)

Dolly Parton, *White Limozeen* (Columbia, 1989)

Johnny Paycheck, *Greatest Hits* (Epic, 1974)

Elvis Presley, *Elvis* (RCA, 1956)

Elvis Presley, *Elvis Country* (RCA, 1971)

Elvis Presley, *Elvis' Golden Records, Volume III* (RCA, 1963)

Elvis Presley, *Elvis' Golden Records, Volume IV* (RCA, 1968)

Elvis Presley, *Elvis: NBC-TV Special* (RCA, 1969)

Elvis Presley, *Elvis Presley* (RCA, 1956)

Elvis Presley, *Elvis—That's the Way It Is* (RCA, 1970)

Elvis Presley, *Elvis: Worldwide 50 Gold Awards Hits, Volume I* (RCA, 1970)

Elvis Presley, *From Elvis in Memphis* (RCA, 1969)

Elvis Presley, *From Elvis Presley Boulevard, Memphis, Tennessee* (RCA, 1976)

Elvis Presley, *From Nashville to Memphis: Essential 60s Masters* (5 CDs) (RCA, 1993)

Elvis Presley, *From Vegas to Memphis* (RCA, 1969)

Elvis Presley, *Girls, Girls, Girls* (RCA, 1962)

Elvis Presley, *A Legendary Performer, Volume I* (RCA, 1973)

Elvis Presley, *A Legendary Performer, Volume II* (RCA, 1976)

Elvis Presley, *A Legendary Performer, Volume III* (RCA, 1978)

Elvis Presley, *Loving You* (RCA, 1957)

Elvis Presley, *Memories at Christmas* (RCA, 1982)

Elvis Presley, *On Stage: February 1970* (RCA, 1970)

Elvis Presley, *Roustabout* (RCA, 1964)

Ray Price, *For the Good Times* (Columbia, 1970)

Charley Pride, *The Best of Charley Pride* (RCA, 1969)

Charley Pride, *The Best of Charley Pride, Volume II* (RCA, 1972)

Charley Pride, *Charley* (RCA, 1975)

Charley Pride, *Charley Pride in Person* (RCA, 1969)

Charley Pride, *Charley Pride Sings Heart Songs* (RCA, 1971)

Charley Pride, *Charley Pride's Tenth Album* (RCA, 1970)

Charley Pride, *The Country Way* (RCA, 1967)

Charley Pride, *Did You Think to Pray* (RCA, 1971)

Charley Pride, *From Me to You (To All My Wonderful Fans)* (RCA, 1971)

Charley Pride, *Just Plain Charley* (RCA, 1970)

Charley Pride, *The Sensational Charley Pride* (RCA, 1969)

Pure Prairie League, *Bustin' Out* (RCA, 1973)

Eddie Rabbitt, *The Best of Eddie Rabbitt* (Elektra, 1979)

Eddie Rabbitt, *Step by Step* (Liberty, 1981)

Boots Randolph, *Boots with Strings* (Monument, 1966)

Boots Randolph, *Yakety Sax* (RCA, 1960)

Collin Raye, *The Best of Collin Raye: Direct Hits* (Epic, 1997)

Jim Reeves, *The Best of Jim Reeves* (RCA, 1964)

Jim Reeves, *Distant Drums* (RCA, 1966)

Jim Reeves, *The Legendary Jim Reeves* (RCA, 1988)

Restless Heart, *Big Dreams in a Small Town* (RCA, 1988)

Restless Heart, *Big Iron Horses* (RCA, 1992)

Restless Heart, *Fast Movin' Train* (RCA, 1990)

Restless Heart, *Wheels* (RCA, 1986)

Charlie Rich, *Behind Closed Doors* (Epic, 1973)

Charlie Rich, *There Won't Be Anymore* (RCA, 1974)

Charlie Rich, *Very Special Love Songs* (Epic, 1974)

Ricochet, *Ricochet* (Columbia, 1996)

Jeannie C. Riley, *Harper Valley P.T.A.* (Plantation, 1968)

Marty Robbins, *Biggest Hits* (Columbia, 1987)

Marty Robbins, *Greatest Hits* (Columbia, 1962)

Marty Robbins, *Greatest Hits, Volume II* (Columbia, 1971)

Marty Robbins, *Greatest Hits, Volume III* (Columbia, 1971)

Marty Robbins, *Marty Robbins All Time Greatest Hits* (Columbia, 1972)

Kenny Rogers, *Best of Kenny Rogers* (Liberty, 1982)

Kenny Rogers, *Christmas in America* (Reprise, 1989)

Kenny Rogers, *The Gift* (Magnatone, 1996)

Kenny Rogers, *Greatest Hits* (RCA, 1988)

Kenny Rogers, *The Heart of the Matter* (RCA, 1985)

Kenny Rogers, *Love Is What We Make It* (Liberty, 1985)

Kenny Rogers, *Love or Something Like It* (United Artists, 1978)

Kenny Rogers, *Something Inside So Strong* (Reprise, 1989)

Kenny Rogers & Dottie West, *Every Time Two Fools Collide* (United Artists, 1978)

Kenny Rogers & the First Edition, *Greatest Hits* (Reprise, 1971)

Billy Joe Royal, *The Royal Treatment* (Atlantic, 1987)

Sgt. Barry Sadler, *Ballads of the Green Berets* (RCA, 1966)

Sawyer Brown, *The Dirt Road* (Curb, 1992)

Sawyer Brown, *Greatest Hits 1990–1995* (Curb, 1995)

Sawyer Brown, *Outskirts of Town* (Curb, 1993)

Dan Seals, *Won't Be Blue Anymore* (EMI America, 1985)

Kevin Sharp, *Measure of a Man* (Asylum, 1996)

Ricky Van Shelton, *A Bridge I Didn't Burn* (Columbia, 1993)

Ricky Van Shelton, *Don't Overlook Salvation* (Columbia, 1992)

Ricky Van Shelton, *Ricky Van Shelton Sings Christmas* (Columbia, 1989)

Shenandoah, *The Extra Mile* (Columbia, 1990)

Shenandoah, *The Road Not Taken* (Columbia, 1989)

Ricky Skaggs, *Country Boy* (Epic, 1984)

Ricky Skaggs, *Don't Cheat in Our Hometown* (Epic, 1983)

Ricky Skaggs, *Live in London* (Epic, 1985)

Ricky Skaggs, *Waitin' for the Sun to Shine* (Epic, 1981)

Soundtrack, *The Buddy Holly Story* (Epic, 1978)
Soundtrack, *Coal Miner's Daughter* (MCA, 1980)
Soundtrack, *Dueling Banjos/Deliverance Soundtrack* (Warner Bros., 1973)
Soundtrack, *The Electric Horseman* (Columbia, 1979)
Soundtrack, *Maverick* (Atlantic, 1994)
Statler Brothers, *Atlanta Blue* (Mercury, 1984)
Statler Brothers, *The Best of the Statler Brothers Rides Again* (Mercury, 1975)
Statler Brothers, *Entertainers . . . On and Off the Record* (Mercury, 1978)
Statler Brothers, *Gospel Favorites* (PolyGram, 1992)
Statler Brothers, *Holy Bible: New Testament* (Mercury, 1975)
Statler Brothers, *Holy Bible: Old Testament* (Mercury, 1975)
Statler Brothers, *The Originals* (Mercury, 1979)
Statler Brothers, *Partners in Rhyme* (Mercury, 1987)
Statler Brothers, *Tenth Anniversary* (Mercury, 1983)
Statler Brothers, *Today* (Mercury, 1983)
Ray Stevens, *Greatest Hits, Volume II* (MCA, 1987)
Ray Stevens, *I Have Returned* (MCA, 1985)
Doug Stone, *From the Heart* (Epic, 1992)
Doug Stone, *Greatest Hits* (Epic, 1994)
Doug Stone, *More Love* (Epic, 1993)
George Strait, *Right or Wrong* (MCA, 1983)
George Strait, *Strait Country* (MCA, 1981)
Marty Stuart, *Hillbilly Rock* (MCA, 1989)
Marty Stuart, *Tempted* (MCA, 1991)
Marty Stuart, *This One's Gonna Hurt You* (MCA, 1992)
Doug Supernaw, *Red and Rio Grande* (RCA, 1993)
Sylvia, *Just Sylvia* (RCA, 1983)
Pam Tillis, *Put Yourself in My Place* (Arista, 1991)
Aaron Tippin, *Call of the Wild* (RCA, 1993)
Aaron Tippin, *Lookin' Back at Myself* (RCA, 1994)
Aaron Tippin, *Tool Box* (RCA, 1995)
Aaron Tippin, *You've Got to Stand for Something* (RCA, 1991)
Randy Travis, *An Old Time Christmas* (Warner Bros., 1989)
Randy Travis, *This Is Me* (Warner Bros., 1994)
Rick Trevino, *Rick Trevino* (Columbia, 1994)
Travis Tritt, *The Restless Kind* (Warner Bros., 1996)
Tanya Tucker, *Greatest Hits* (Liberty, 1989)
Tanya Tucker, *Love Me Like You Used To* (Liberty, 1987)

Tanya Tucker, *Soon* (Liberty, 1993)
Tanya Tucker, *Strong Enough to Bend* (Liberty, 1988)
Tanya Tucker, *Tennessee Woman* (Liberty, 1990)
Tanya Tucker, *TNT* (MCA, 1978)
Tanya Tucker, *What's Your Mama's Name?* (Columbia, 1973)
Tanya Tucker, *Would You Lay with Me* (Columbia, 1974)
Shania Twain, *Shania Twain* (Mercury, 1993)
Conway Twitty, *Greatest Hits, Volume I* (MCA, 1972)
Conway Twitty, *Greatest Hits, Volume II* (MCA, 1976)
Conway Twitty, *Hello Darlin'* (Decca, 1970)
Conway Twitty, *Number Ones* (MCA, 1982)
Conway Twitty, *You've Never Been This Far Before* (MCA, 1973)
Various Artists, *Country Love* (Warner Bros., 1995)
Various Artists, *Keith Whitley: A Tribute Album* (RCA, 1994)
Various Artists, *19 Hot Country Requests, Volume I* (Epic, 1985)
Various Artists, *Skynyrd Frynds* (MCA, 1994)
Clay Walker, *Rumor Has It* (Giant, 1997)
Bryan White, *The Right Place* (Asylum, 1997)
Keith Whitley, *Don't Close Your Eyes* (RCA, 1988)
Don Williams, *The Best of Don Williams, Volume I* (MCA, 1973)
Don Williams, *The Best of Don Williams, Volume II* (MCA, 1979)
Don Williams, *I Believe in You* (MCA, 1980)
Hank Williams, *Greatest Hits* (MGM, 1961)
Hank Williams, *24 of Hank Williams' Greatest Hits* (MGM, 1971)
Hank Williams Jr., *Family Tradition* (Warner Bros., 1979)
Hank Williams Jr., *Five-O* (Warner Bros., 1985)
Hank Williams Jr., *Hank "Live"* (Warner Bros., 1987)
Hank Williams Jr., *High Notes* (Warner Bros., 1982)
Hank Williams Jr., *Lone Wolf* (Warner Bros., 1990)
Hank Williams Jr., *Major Moves* (Curb/Warner Bros., 1984)
Hank Williams Jr., *Man of Steel* (Warner Bros., 1983)
Hank Williams Jr., *Montana Cafe* (Warner Bros., 1986)
Hank Williams Jr., *Rowdy* (Warner Bros., 1981)
Hank Williams Jr., *Strong Stuff* (Warner Bros./Curb, 1983)
Hank Williams Jr., *Whiskey Bent and Hell Bound* (Elektra, 1981)
Hank Williams Jr., *Wild Streak* (Warner Bros., 1988)
Hank Williams Jr., *Your Cheatin' Heart Soundtrack* (MGM, 1964)
Tammy Wynette, *Greatest Hits, Volume II* (Epic, 1971)
Trisha Yearwood, *Everybody Knows* (MCA, 1996)
Dwight Yoakam, *Dwight Live* (Reprise, 1995)
Dwight Yoakam, *Gone* (Reprise, 1995)

The American Society of Composers, Authors & Publishers (ASCAP) Most Performed Country Song of the Year Awards

Year	Song	Writers	Publisher (at Time of Award)
1982	"(There's) No Getting Over Me"	Tom Brasfield–Walt Aldridge	Rick Hall Music
1983	"Love Will Turn You Around"	Kenny Rogers–Even Stevens–David Malloy–Thom Schuyler	Lionsmate Music, DebDave Music, Briarpatch Music
1984	"We've Got Tonight"	Bob Seger	Gear Publishing Co.
1985	"To All the Girls I've Loved Before"	Hal David–Albert Hammond	April Music, Casa David
1986	"Lost in the Fifties Tonight (In the Still of the Night)"	Fred Parris–Mike Reid–Troy Seals	Lodge Hall Music, Two-Sons Music, WB Music Corp.
1987	"Now and Forever (You and Me)"	Randy Goodrum–Jim Vallance–David Foster	California Phase Music, Tom Collins Music Corp., Lodge Hall Music, MCA Music
1988	"I'll Still Be Loving You"	Pat Bunch–Mary Ann Kennedy–Pam Rose–Todd Cerney	Chiswald Music, Hopi-Sound Music, MCA Music
1989	"Too Gone, Too Long"	Gene Pistilli	Almo Music, High Falutin Music
1990	"What's Going on in Your World"	Red Stegall–David Chamberlain–Royce Porter	Ha-Deb Music, Milene Music
1991	"Friends in Low Places"	Earl Bud Lee–Dewayne Blackwell	Chancey Tunes—Music Ridge Music, Careers Music
1992	"Don't Rock the Jukebox"	Roger Murrah–Keith Stegall–Alan Jackson	Mattie Ruth Musick, Seventh Son Music, Tom Collins Music Corp., Murrah Music
1993	"When She Cries"	Marc Beeson–Sonny LeMaire	EMI April Music
1994	"Chattahoochee"	Alan Jackson–Jim McBride	Mattie Ruth Musick, Seventh Son Music, Cross Keys Publishing Co.
1995	"I Swear"	Gary B. Baker–Frank Myers	Rick Hall Music, Morganactive Songs
1996	"I Can Love You Like That"	Steve Diamond–Maribeth Derry–Jennifer Kimball	Criterion Music Corp., Friends & Angels Music, Full Keel Music Co., Second Wave Music, Diamond Cuts
1997	"No News"	Mark D. Sanders	MCA Music Publishing, Starstruck Writers Group

Country's Share of the U.S. Recorded Music Market

Dollars spent (in Millions) and Percent of Total Dollars Spent

Year	Gross Country Sales	Country Portion of Dollars Spent on Recorded Music
1973	$150.2	10.5%
1974	$255.2	11.6%
1975	$276.1	11.7%
1976	$331.2	12.1%
1977	$451.6	12.4%
1978	$426.5	10.2%
1979	$437.5	9.0%
1980	$526.5	12.0%
1981	$529.3	15.0%
1982	$538.8	15.0%
1983	$496.0	13.0%
1984	$393.3	10.0%
1985	$438.8	10.0%
1986	$415.6	10.0%
1987	$528.9	9.5%
1988	$425.3	6.8%
1989	$447.4	6.8%
1990	$663.6	8.8%
1991	$1,002.8	12.8%
1992	$1,570.2	17.4%
1993	$1,878.7	18.7%
1994	$1,967.1	16.3%
1995	$2,056.6	16.7%
1996	$1,837.5	14.7%

(Source: RIAA Annual Reports)

Full-time Country Radio Stations in the U.S.A.

Number of Country Stations and Their Percentage of All U.S. Stations

Year	Full-time Country Stations	Percentage of All U.S. Stations
1961	81	1.7%
1963	97	1.9%
1965	208	3.8%
1969	606	9.0%
1971	525	7.8%
1972	633	8.6%
1973	764	10.2%
1974	856	11.0%
1975	1,116	13.9%
1977	1,140	13.6%
1978	1,150	13.4%
1979	1,434	16.4%
1980	1,534	17.2%
1981	1,785	19.6%
1982	2,114	23.1%
1983	2,266	24.3%
1984	2,265	23.5%
1985	2,289	23.2%
1986	2,275	22.6%
1987	2,212	21.6%
1988	2,169	20.7%
1989	2,086	19.6%
1990	2,108	19.5%
1991	2,140	19.4%
1992	2,203	19.5%
1993	2,402	20.8%
1994	2,427	20.7%
1995	2,346	19.5%
1996	2,321	19.1%

(Sources: RIAA Consumer Profile; *CMA Country Radio Book; Broadcasting & Cable Yearbook 1997*)

BMI's Most Performed Country Song of the Year Awards (The Robert J. Burton Award)

Year	Song	Writers	Publisher (at time of award)
1967	"Almost Persuaded"	Glenn Sutton–Billy Sherrill	Al Gallico Music Corp.
1968	"Release Me"	Eddie Miller–W. S. Stevenson	Four Star Music Co.
1969–1970	"Gentle on My Mind"	John Hartford	Glaser Publications
1971	"(I Never Promised You a) Rose Garden"	Joe South	Lowery Music Co.
1972	"Help Me Make It Through the Night"	Kris Kristofferson	Combine Music Corp.
1973	"The Happiest Girl in the Whole U.S.A."	Donna Fargo	Algee Music Corp., Prima Donna Music Corp.
1974	"Let Me Be There"	John Rostill	Al Gallico Music Corp.
1975	"If You Love Me (Let Me Know)"	John Rostill	Al Gallico Music Corp.
1976	"When Will I Be Loved"	Phil Everly	Acuff-Rose Publications
1977	"Misty Blue"	Bob Montgomery	Talmont Music
1978	"Here You Come Again"	Barry Mann–Cynthia Weil	Screen Gems-EMI Music, Summerhill Songs
1979	"Talking in Your Sleep"	Roger Cook–Bobby Wood	Chriswood Music, Roger Cook Music
1980	"Suspicions"	David Malloy–Randy McCormick–Eddie Rabbitt–Even Stevens	Briarpatch Music, DebDave Music
1981	"9 to 5"	Dolly Parton	Fox Fanfare Music, Velvet Apple Music
1982	"Elvira"	Dallas Frazier	Acuff-Rose Publications
1983	"Nobody"	Rhonda Fleming-Gill–Dennis Morgan	Tom Collins Music Corp.
1984	"Islands in the Stream"	Barry Gibb–Maurice Gibb–Robin Gibb	Gibb Brothers Music
1985	"Mama He's Crazy"	Kenny O'Dell	Kenny O'Dell Music
1986	"Don't Call It Love"	Dean Pitchford–Tom Snow	Careers Music, Pzazz Music, Snow Music
1987	"Hold On"	Rosanne Cash	Atlantic Music Corp., Chelcait Music
1988	"To Know Him Is to Love Him"	Phil Spector	Mother Bertha Music
1989	"Fallin' Again"	Greg Fowler–Teddy Gentry–Randy Owen	Maypop Music
1990	"Cathy's Clown"	Don Everly	Acuff-Rose Music
1991	"Hard Rock Bottom of Your Heart"	Hugh Prestwood	Careers-BMG Music Publishing
1992	"She's in Love with the Boy"	Jon Ims	Rites of Passage Music, Warner/Elektra/Asylum Music
1993	"Achy Breaky Heart"	Don Von Tress	Millhouse Music
1994	"Blame It on Your Heart"	Harlan Howard–Kostas	Harlan Howard Songs, Seven Angels Music, Songs of PolyGram International
1995	"Wink"	Bob DiPiero–Tom Shapiro	American Made Music, Diamond Struck Music, Little Big Town Music, Great Cumberland
1996	"I Can Love You Like That"	Steve Diamond–Jennifer Kimball	Diamond Cuts, Wonderland, Criterion, Second Wave, Full Keel, Friends and Angels
1997	"Nobody Knows"	Dohn DuBosé–Joe Rich	D'Jonsongs, EMI-Blackwood Music, Hitco Music, Joe Shade Music

Grand Ole Opry Members and the Dates They Joined the Show's Cast

Bill Anderson (July 14, 1961)
Ernie Ashworth (March 7, 1964)
Clint Black (January 10, 1991)
Boxcar Willie (February 21, 1981)
Garth Brooks (October 6, 1990)
Jim Ed Brown (August 12, 1963)
The Carlisles (November 14, 1953)
Roy Clark (August 22, 1987)
Jerry Clower (October 27, 1973)
John Conlee (February 7, 1981)
Wilma Lee Cooper (January 12, 1957)
Skeeter Davis (August 4, 1959)
Little Jimmy Dickens (September 25, 1948; rejoined 1975)
Joe Diffie (November 27, 1993)
Roy Drusky (June 13, 1959)
Holly Dunn (October 14, 1989)
The 4 Guys—Sam, Brent, John & Laddie (April 13, 1967)
The Gatlins—Larry, Steve, & Rudy (December 25, 1976)
Don Gibson (April 12, 1958)
Vince Gill (August 10, 1991)
Billy Grammer (February 27, 1959)
Jack Greene (December 23, 1967)
Tom T. Hall (March 28, 1980)
George Hamilton IV (February 8, 1960)

Emmylou Harris (January 25, 1992)
Jan Howard (March 27, 1971)
Alan Jackson (June 7, 1991)
Stonewall Jackson (November 10, 1956; rejoined 1969)
Jim & Jesse (March 7, 1964)
George Jones (August 4, 1956, rejoined January 4, 1969)
Grandpa Jones (March 16, 1946)
Hal Ketchum (January 22, 1994)
Alison Krauss (July 3, 1993)
Hank Locklin (November 9, 1960)
Charlie Louvin (February 26, 1955)
Patty Loveless (June 11, 1988)
Loretta Lynn (September 25, 1962)
Barbara Mandrell (July 29, 1972)
Martina McBride (November 30, 1995)
Mel McDaniel (January 11, 1986)
Reba McEntire (January 17, 1986)
Ronnie Milsap (February 6, 1976)
Lorrie Morgan (June 9, 1984)
Jimmy C. Newman (August 4, 1956)
The Osborne Brothers—Bobby & Sonny (August 8, 1964)
Bashful Brother Oswald (January 21, 1995)
Dolly Parton (January 4, 1969)
Johnny Paycheck (November 8, 1997)

Stu Phillips (June 1, 1967)
Ray Pillow (May 4, 1966)
Charley Pride (May 1, 1993)
Jeanne Pruett (July 21, 1973)
Del Reeves (October 14, 1966)
Riders in the Sky—Doug Green, Fred LaBour & Woody Paul (June 19, 1982)
Johnny Russell (July 6, 1985)
Jeannie Seely (September 16, 1967)
Ricky Van Shelton (June 10, 1988)
Jean Shepard (November 21, 1955)
Ricky Skaggs (May 15, 1982)
Connie Smith (September 18, 1965, rejoined April 21, 1971)
Mike Snider (June 2, 1990)
Hank Snow (January 7, 1950)
Marty Stuart (November 28, 1992)
Randy Travis (December 20, 1986)
Travis Tritt (February 29, 1992)
Justin Tubb (September 10, 1955)
Porter Wagoner (February 23, 1957)
Billy Walker (February 4, 1960)
Charlie Walker (August 17, 1967)
Steve Wariner (May 11, 1996)
The Whites—Buck, Cheryl & Sharon (March 2, 1984)
Teddy Wilburn (November 10, 1956)

Country Music Hall of Fame Members and Their Years of Election

1961
Jimmie Rodgers, Fred Rose, Hank Williams

1962
Roy Acuff

1963
Elections held, but no one candidate had enough votes.

1964
Tex Ritter

1965
Ernest Tubb

1966
Eddy Arnold , James R. Denny, George D. Hay, Uncle Dave Macon

1967
Red Foley, J. L. Frank, Jim Reeves, Stephen H. Sholes

1968
Bob Wills

1969
Gene Autry

1970
Bill Monroe, Original Carter Family

1971
Arthur Edward Satherley

1972
Jimmie Davis

1973
Chet Atkins, Patsy Cline

1974
Owen Bradley, Frank "Pee Wee" King

1975
Minnie Pearl

1976
Paul Cohen, Kitty Wells

1977
Merle Travis

1978
Grandpa Jones

1979
Hubert Long, Hank Snow

1980
Johnny Cash, Connie B. Gay, Original Sons of the Pioneers

1981
Vernon Dalhart, Grant Turner

1982
Lefty Frizzell, Roy Horton, Marty Robbins

1983
Little Jimmy Dickens

1984
Ralph Peer, Floyd Tillman

1985
Lester Flatt & Earl Scruggs

1986
The Duke of Paducah (Whitey Ford), Wesley Rose

1987
Rod Brasfield

1988
Loretta Lynn, Roy Rogers

1989
Jack Stapp, Cliffie Stone, Hank Thompson

1990
Tennessee Ernie Ford

1991
Boudleaux & Felice Bryant

1992
George Jones, Frances Preston

1993
Willie Nelson

1994
Merle Haggard

1995
Roger Miller, Jo Walker-Meador

1996
Patsy Montana, Buck Owens, Ray Price

1997
Harlan Howard, Brenda Lee, Cindy Walker

1998
George Morgan, Elvis Presley, Bud Wendell, Tammy Wynette

Nashville Songwriters Hall of Fame (administered by the Nashville Songwriters Foundation)

1970
Gene Autry, Johnny Bond, Albert Brumley, A. P. Carter, Ted Daffan, Vernon Dalhart, Rex Griffin, Stuart Hamblen, Pee Wee King, Vic McAlpin, Bob Miller, Leon Payne, Jimmie Rodgers, Fred Rose, Redd Stewart, Floyd Tillman, Merle Travis , Ernest Tubb, Cindy Walker, Hank Williams, Bob Wills

1971
Smiley Burnette, Jenny Lou Carson, Wilf Carter, Zeke Clements, Jimmie Davis, Alton & Rabon Delmore, Al Dexter, Vaughan Horton, Bradley Kincaid, Bill Monroe, Bob Nolan, Tex Owens, Tex Ritter, Carson J. Robison, Tim Spencer, Gene Sullivan, Jimmy Wakely, Wiley Walker, Scotty Wiseman

1972
Boudleaux & Felice Bryant, Lefty Frizzell, Jack Rhodes, Don Robertson

1973
Jack Clement, Don Gibson, Harlan Howard, Roger Miller, Steve & Ed Nelson Jr., Willie Nelson

1974
Hank Cochran

1975
Bill Anderson, Danny Dill, Eddie Miller, Marty Robbins, Wayne Walker, Marijohn Wilkin

1976
Carl Belew, Dallas Frazier, John D. Loudermilk, Moon Mullican, Curly Putman, Mel Tillis

1977
Johnny Cash, Woody Guthrie, Merle Haggard, Kris Kristofferson

1978
Joe Allison, Tom T. Hall, Hank Snow, Don Wayne

1979
Rev. Thomas A. Dorsey, Charles & Ira Louvin, Elsie McWilliams, Joe South

1980
Huddie "Leadbelly" Ledbetter, Mickey Newbury, Ben Peters, Ray Stevens

1981
Bobby Braddock, Ray Whitley

1982
Chuck Berry, William J. "Billy" Hill

1983
W. C. Handy, Loretta Lynn, Beasley Smith

1984
Hal David, Billy Sherrill

1985
Bob McDill, Carl Perkins

1986
Otis Blackwell, Dolly Parton

1987
Roy Orbison, Sonny Throckmorton

1988
Hoagy Carmichael, Troy Seals

1989
Rory Michael Bourke, Maggie Cavender, Sanger D. "Whitey" Shafer

1990
Sue Brewer, Ted Harris, Jimmy Webb

1991
Charlie Black, Sonny Curtis

1992
Max D. Barnes, Wayland Holyfield

1993
Red Lane, Don Schlitz, Conway Twitty

1994
Jerry Foster & Bill Rice, Buddy Holly, Richard Leigh, Bobby Russell

1995
Waylon Jennings, Dickey Lee, Dave Loggins

1996
Jerry Chesnut, Kenny O'Dell, Buck Owens, Norro Wilson

1997
Wayne Carson, Roger Cook, Hank Thompson

Grammy Awards Related to Country Music

(Award to artist[s] except in the Best Song and Song of the Year categories. In these cases the award goes to the songwriter[s].)

··

1958

Best Country & Western Performance: "Tom Dooley"—The Kingston Trio (Capitol)

1959

Best Country & Western Performance: "The Battle of New Orleans"—Johnny Horton (Columbia)

Song of the Year: "The Battle of New Orleans" (Jimmy Driftwood)

Best Folk Performance: *The Kingston Trio at Large*—The Kingston Trio (Capitol)

Best Comedy Performance—Musical: "The Battle of Kookamonga"—Homer & Jethro (RCA)

1960

Best Country & Western Performance: "El Paso"—Marty Robbins (Columbia)

1961

Best Country & Western Recording: "Big Bad John"—Jimmy Dean (Columbia)

1962

Best Country & Western Recording: "Funny Way of Laughin'"—Burl Ives (Decca)

Best Rhythm & Blues Recording: "I Can't Stop Loving You"—Ray Charles (ABC-Paramount)

1963

Best Country & Western Recording: "Detroit City"—Bobby Bare (RCA)

Best Rhythm & Blues Recording: "Busted"—Ray Charles (ABC-Paramount)

Best Instrumental Arrangement: "I Can't Stop Loving You"—Count Basie; Arranger: Quincy Jones (Reprise)

1964

Best Country & Western Album: *Dang Me/Chug-a-Lug*—Roger Miller (Smash)

Best Country & Western Single: "Dang Me"—Roger Miller (Smash)

Best Country & Western Song: "Dang Me" (Roger Miller)

Best Country & Western Vocal Performance, Male: "Dang Me"—Roger Miller (Smash)

Best Country & Western Vocal Performance, Female: "Here Comes My Baby"—Dottie West (RCA)

Best New Country & Western Artist: Roger Miller (Smash)

Best Gospel or Other Religious Recording (Musical): *Great Gospel Songs*—Tennessee Ernie Ford (Capitol)

1965

Best Country & Western Album: *The Return of Roger Miller*—Roger Miller (Smash)

Best Country & Western Single: "King of the Road"—Roger Miller (Smash)

Best Country & Western Song: "King of the Road" (Roger Miller)

Best Country & Western Vocal Performance, Male: "King of the Road"—Roger Miller (Smash)

Best Country & Western Vocal Performance, Female: "Queen of the House"—Jody Miller (Capitol)

Best New Country & Western Artist: The Statler Brothers (Columbia)

Best Performance by a Vocal Group: *We Dig Mancini*—Anita Kerr Singers (RCA)

Best Contemporary (R&R) Single: "King of the Road"—Roger Miller (Smash)

Best Contemporary (R&R) Vocal Performance, Male: "King of the Road"—Roger Miller (Smash)

Best Contemporary (R&R) Performance Group (Vocal or Instrumental): "Flowers on the Wall"—The Statler Brothers (Columbia)

Best Gospel or Other Religious Recording (Musical): *Southland Favorites*—George Beverly Shea and the Anita Kerr Singers (RCA)

1966

Best Country & Western Recording: "Almost Persuaded"—David Houston (Epic)

Best Country & Western Song: "Almost Persuaded" (Billy Sherrill–Glenn Sutton)

Best Country & Western Vocal Performance, Male: "Almost Persuaded"—David Houston (Epic)

Best Country & Western Vocal Performance, Female: "Don't Touch Me"—Jeannie Seely (Monument)

Best Performance by a Vocal Group: "A Man and a Woman"—Anita Kerr Singers (Warner Bros.)

Best Sacred Recording (Musical): *Grand Ole Gospel*—Porter Wagoner & the Blackwood Brothers (RCA)

Best Rhythm & Blues Solo Vocal Performance, Male or Female: "Crying Time"—Ray Charles (ABC-Paramount)

Best Rhythm & Blues Recording: "Crying Time"—Ray Charles (ABC-Paramount)

Best Album Cover, Photography: *Confessions of a Broken Man*—Porter Wagoner; Art Direction: Robert Jones; Photographer: Les Leverett (RCA)

1967

Best Country & Western Recording: "Gentle on My Mind"—Glen Campbell (Capitol)

Best Country & Western Song: "Gentle on My Mind" (John Hartford)

Best Country & Western Solo Vocal Performance, Female: "I Don't Wanna Play House"—Tammy Wynette (Epic)

Best Country & Western Solo Vocal Performance, Male: "Gentle on My Mind"—Glen Campbell (Capitol)

Best Country & Western Performance, Duet, Trio, or Group (Vocal or Instrumental): "Jackson"—Johnny Cash & June Carter (Columbia)

Best Vocal Performance, Female: "Ode to Billie Joe"—Bobbie Gentry (Capitol)

Best Vocal Performance, Male: "By the Time I Get to Phoenix"—Glen Campbell (Capitol)

Best Contemporary Female Solo Vocal Performance: "Ode to Billie Joe"—Bobbie Gentry (Capitol)

Best Contemporary Male Solo Vocal Performance: "By the Time I Get to Phoenix"—Glen Campbell (Capitol)

Best New Artist: Bobbie Gentry (Capitol)

Best Sacred Performance: *How Great Thou Art*—Elvis Presley (RCA)

Best Gospel Performance: *More Grand Old Gospel*—Porter Wagoner & the Blackwood Brothers (RCA)

Best Folk Performance: "Gentle on My Mind"—John Hartford (RCA)

Best Instrumental Performance: *Chet Atkins Picks the Best*—Chet Atkins (RCA)

Best Arrangement Accompanying Vocalist(s) or Instrumentalist(s): "Ode to Billie Joe"—Bobbie Gentry; arranger: Jimmie Haskell (Capitol)

Best Album Notes: *Suburban Attitudes in Country Verse*—John D. Loudermilk (RCA)

1968

Best Country Vocal Performance, Female: "Harper Valley P.T.A."—Jeannie C. Riley (Plantation)

Best Country Vocal Performance, Male: "Folsom Prison Blues"—Johnny Cash (Columbia)

Best Country & Western Performance, Duet, Trio or Group (Vocal or Instrumental): "Foggy Mountain Breakdown"—Flatt & Scruggs (Columbia)

Best Country Song: "Little Green Apples" (Bobby Russell)

Album of the Year: *By the Time I Get to Phoenix*—Glen Campbell (Capitol)

Song of the Year: "Little Green Apples" (Bobby Russell)

Best Engineered Recording: "Wichita Lineman"—Glen Campbell; engineers: Joe Polito & Hugh Davies (Capitol)

Best Album Notes: *Johnny Cash at Folsom Prison*; annotator: Johnny Cash (Columbia)

1969

Best Country Vocal Performance, Female: *Stand By Your Man*—Tammy Wynette (Epic)

Best Country Vocal Performance, Male: "A Boy Named Sue"—Johnny Cash (Columbia)

Best Country Song: "A Boy Named Sue" (Shel Silverstein)

Best Country Performance by a Duo or Group: "MacArthur Park"—Waylon Jennings & the Kimberleys (RCA)

Best Country Instrumental Performance: *The Nashville Brass Featuring Danny Davis Play More Nashville Sounds*—Danny Davis & the Nashville Brass (RCA)

Best Rhythm & Blues Vocal Performance, Male: "The Chokin' Kind"—Joe Simon

Song of the Year: "Games People Play" (Joe South)

Best Contemporary Song: "Games People Play" (Joe South)

Best Gospel Performance: *In Gospel Country*—Porter Wagoner & the Blackwood Brothers (RCA)

Best Album Notes: *Nashville Skyline*—Bob Dylan; annotator: Johnny Cash (Columbia)

1970

Best Country Vocal Performance, Female: "Rose Garden"—Lynn Anderson (Columbia)

Best Country Vocal Performance, Male: "For the Good Times"—Ray Price (Columbia)

Best Country Vocal Performance by a Duo or Group: "If I Were a Carpenter"—Johnny Cash & June Carter (Columbia)

Best Country Instrumental Performance: *Me and Jerry*—Chet Atkins & Jerry Reed (RCA)

Best Country Song: "My Woman, My Woman, My Wife" (Marty Robbins)

Best Contemporary Vocal Performance, Male: "Everything Is Beautiful"—Ray Stevens (Barnaby)

Best Gospel Performance (Other Than Soul Gospel): "Talk About the Good Times"—Oak Ridge Boys (Heartwarming)

1971

Best Country Vocal Performance, Female: "Help Me Make It Through the Night"— Sammi Smith (Mega)

Best Country Vocal Performance, Male: "When You're Hot, You're Hot"—Jerry Reed (RCA)

Best Country Vocal Performance by a Duo or Group: "After the Fire Is Gone"— Conway Twitty & Loretta Lynn (Decca)

Best Country Instrumental Performance: "Snowbird"—Chet Atkins (RCA)

Best Country Song: "Help Me Make It Through the Night" (Kris Kristofferson)

Best Sacred Performance: "Did You Think to Pray"—Charley Pride (RCA)

Best Gospel Performance (Other Than Soul Gospel): "Let Me Live"—Charley Pride (RCA)

Lifetime Achievement Award: Elvis Presley

1972

Best Country Vocal Performance, Female: "Happiest Girl in the Whole U. S. A."—Donna Fargo (Dot)

Best Country Vocal Performance, Male: *Charley Pride Sings Heart Songs*—Charley Pride (RCA)

Best Country Vocal Performance by a Duo or Group: "Class of '57"— The Statler Brothers (Mercury)

Best Country Instrumental Performance: *The Real McCoy*—Charlie McCoy (Monument)

Best Country Song: "Kiss an Angel Good Mornin'" (Ben Peters)

Best Inspirational Performance: "He Touched Me"—Elvis Presley (RCA)

Best Album Notes: *Tom T. Hall's Greatest Hits*, Annotator: Tom T. Hall (Mercury)

1973

Best Country Vocal Performance, Female: "Let Me Be There"—Olivia Newton-John (MCA)

Best Country Vocal Performance, Male: "Behind Closed Doors"—Charlie Rich (Epic/Columbia)

Best Country Vocal Performance by a Duo or Group: "From the Bottle to the Bottom"—Kris Kristofferson & Rita Coolidge (A & M)

Best Country Instrumental Performance: "Dueling Banjos"—Eric Weissberg & Steve Mandell (Warner Bros.)

Best Country Song: "Behind Closed Doors" (Kenny O'Dell)

Best Ethnic or Traditional Recording: *Then and Now*—Doc Watson (United Artists)

1974

Best Country Vocal Performance, Female: "Love Song"—Anne Murray (Capitol)

Best Country Vocal Performance, Male: "Please Don't Tell Me How the Story Ends"—Ronnie Milsap (RCA)

Best Country Vocal Performance by a Duo or Group: "Fairytale"—The Pointer Sisters (Blue Thumb)

Best Country Song: "A Very Special Love Song" (Norro Wilson–Billy Sherrill)

Best Country Instrumental Performance: *The Atkins-Travis Traveling Show*—Chet Atkins & Merle Travis (RCA)

Best Traditional or Ethnic Recording: *Two Days in November*—Doc & Merle Watson (United Artists)

Best Gospel Performance: "The Baptism of Jesse Taylor"—Oak Ridge Boys (Columbia)

Best Inspirational Performance: "How Great Thou Art"—Elvis Presley (RCA)

Record of the Year: "I Honestly Love You"—Olivia Newton-John (MCA)

Best Pop Vocal Performance, Female: "I Honestly Love You"—Olivia Newton-John (MCA)

Best Album Notes: *For the Last Time*—Bob Wills; annotator: Charles R. Townsend (United Artists)

1975

Best Country Vocal Performance, Female: "I Can't Help It (If I'm Still in Love with You)"—Linda Ronstadt (Capitol)

Best Country Vocal Performance, Male: "Blue Eyes Crying in the Rain"—Willie Nelson (Columbia)

Best Country Vocal Performance by a Duo or Group: "Lover Please"—Kris Kristofferson & Rita Coolidge (Monument)

Best Country Instrumental Performance: "The Entertainer"—Chet Atkins (RCA)

Best Country Song: "(Hey Won't You Play) Another Somebody Done Somebody Wrong Song" (Chips Moman–Larry Butler)

Best Arrangement Accompanying Vocalists: "Misty"—Ray Stevens; arranger: Ray Stevens (Barnaby)

1976

Best Country Vocal Performance, Female: *Elite Hotel*—Emmylou Harris (Reprise)

Best Country Vocal Performance, Male: "(I'm a) Stand By My Woman Man"—Ronnie Milsap (RCA)

Best Country Vocal Performance by a Duo or Group: "The End Is Not in Sight (The Cowboy Tune)"—Amazing Rhythm Aces (ABC)

Best Country Instrumental Performance: *Chester and Lester*—Chet Atkins & Les Paul (RCA)

Best Country Song: "Broken Lady" (Larry Gatlin)

Best Pop Vocal Performance, Female: *Hasten Down the Wind*—Linda Ronstadt (Asylum)

Best Ethnic or Traditional Recording: *Mark Twang*—John Hartford (Flying Fish)

Best Gospel Performance: "Where the Soul Never Dies"—Oak Ridge Boys (Columbia)

1977

Record of the Year: *Hotel California*—Eagles; Producer: Bill Szymczyk

Best Country Vocal Performance, Female: "Don't It Make My Brown Eyes Blue"—Crystal Gayle (United Artists)

Best Country Vocal Performance, Male: "Lucille"—Kenny Rogers (United Artists)

Best Country Vocal Performance by a Duo or Group:"Heaven's Just a Sin Away"—The Kendalls (Ovation)

Best Country Instrumental Performance: *Country Instrumentalist of the Year*—Hargus "Pig" Robbins (Elektra)

Best Country Song: "Don't It Make My Brown Eyes Blue" (Richard Leigh)

Best Gospel Performance, Traditional: "Just a Little Talk with Jesus"—Oak Ridge Boys (Rockland Road)

Best Inspirational Performance: *Home Where I Belong*—B. J. Thomas (Myrrh/Word)

Best Album Package: *Simple Dreams*—Linda Ronstadt; Art Director: Kosh (Asylum)

1978

Best Country Vocal Performance, Female: *Here You Come Again*—Dolly Parton (RCA)

Best Country Vocal Performance, Male: "Georgia on My Mind"—Willie Nelson (Columbia)

Best Country Vocal Performance by a Duo or Group: "Mamas, Don't Let Your Babies Grow Up to Be Cowboys"—Waylon Jennings & Willie Nelson (RCA)

Best Country Instrumentalist Performance: "One O'clock Jump"—Asleep at the Wheel (Capitol)

Best Country Song: "The Gambler" (Don Schlitz)

Best Pop Vocal Performance, Female: "You Needed Me"—Anne Murray (Capitol)

Best Inspirational Performance: *Happy Man*—B. J. Thomas (Myrrh)

1979

Best Country Vocal Performance, Female: *Blue Kentucky Girl*—Emmylou Harris (Warner Bros.)

Best Country Vocal Performance, Male: "The Gambler"—Kenny Rogers (United Artists)

Best Country Vocal Performance by a Duo or Group: "The Devil Went Down to Georgia"—Charlie Daniels Band (Epic)

Best Country Instrumentalist Performance: "Big Sandy/Leather Britches"—Doc & Merle Watson (United Artists)

Best Country Song: "You Decorated My Life" (Debbie Hupp–Bob Morrison)

Best Rock Vocal Performance by a Duo or Group: "Heartache Tonight"—Eagles (Asylum)

Best Inspirational Performance: *You Gave Me Love (When Nobody Gave Me a Prayer)*—B. J. Thomas (Myrrh)

Producer of the Year (Non-Classical): Larry Butler

1980

Best Country Vocal Performance, Female: "Could I Have This Dance"—Anne Murray (Capitol)

Best Country Vocal Performance, Male: "He Stopped Loving Her Today"—George Jones (Epic)

Best Country Vocal Performance by a Duo or Group: "That Lovin' You Feelin' Again"—Roy Orbison & Emmylou Harris (Warner Bros.)

Best Country Instrumentalist Performance: "Orange Blossom Special/Hoedown"—Gilley's Urban Cowboy Band (Full Moon/Asylum)

Best Country Song: "On the Road Again" (Willie Nelson)

1981

Best Country Vocal Performance, Female: "9 to 5"—Dolly Parton (RCA)

Best Country Vocal Performance, Male: "(There's) No Gettin' Over Me"—Ronnie Milsap (RCA)

Best Country Vocal Performance by a Duo or Group: "Elvira"—Oak Ridge Boys (MCA)

Best Country Instrumental Performance: "After All These Years"—Chet Atkins (RCA)

Best Country Song: "9 to 5" (Dolly Parton)

Best Inspirational Performance: *Amazing Grace*—B. J. Thomas (Myrrh/Word)

Best Recording for Children: *Sesame Country*—The Muppets, Glen Campbell, Crystal Gayle, Loretta Lynn, Tanya Tucker; creator: Jim Henson; album producer: Dennis Scott (Sesame Street)

1982

Best Country Vocal Performance, Female: "Break It to Me Gently"—Juice Newton (Capitol)

Best Country Vocal Performance, Male: "Always on My Mind"—Willie Nelson (Columbia)

Best Country Vocal Performance by a Duo or Group: *Mountain Music*—Alabama (RCA)

Best Country Song: "Always on My Mind" (Johnny Christopher–Mark James–Wayne Carson)

Best Country Instrumental Performance: "Alabama Jubilee"—Roy Clark (Churchill)

Song of the Year: "Always on My Mind" (Johnny Christopher–Mark James–Wayne Carson)

Best Inspirational Performance: *He Set My Life to Music*—Barbara Mandrell (Songbird/MCA)

1983

Best Country Vocal Performance, Female: "A Little Good News"—Anne Murray (Capitol)

Best Country Vocal Performance, Male: "I.O.U."—Lee Greenwood (MCA)

Best Country Vocal Performance by a Duo or Group: *The Closer You Get*—Alabama (RCA)

Best Country Instrumental Performance: "Fireball"—The New South: Ricky Skaggs, Jerry Douglas, Tony Rice, J. D. Crowe, Todd Phillips (Sugar Hill)

Best Country Song: "Stranger in My House" (Mike Reid)

Best Soul Gospel Performance by a Duo or Group: "I'm So Glad I'm Standing Here Today"—Bobby Jones with Barbara Mandrell (Myrrh/Word)

Hall of Fame Award: "Your Cheating Heart"—Hank Williams (MGM, 1953)

1984

Best Country Vocal Performance, Female: "In My Dreams"—Emmylou Harris (Warner Bros.)

Best Country Vocal Performance, Male: "That's the Way Love Goes"—Merle Haggard (Epic/ CBS)

Best Country Vocal Performance by a Duo or Group: "Mama He's Crazy"—The Judds (RCA)

Best Country Instrumental Performance: "Wheel Hoss"—Ricky Skaggs (Columbia)

Best Country Song: "City of New Orleans" (Steve Goodman)

Best Ethnic or Traditional Folk Recording: *Elizabeth Cotten Live!*—Elizabeth Cotten (Arhoolie)

Best Recording for Children: *Where the Sidewalk Ends*—Shel Silverstein; Album Producer: Ron Haffkine (Columbia)

1985

Best Country Vocal Performance, Female: "I Don't Know Why You Don't Want Me"—Rosanne Cash (CBS)

Best Country Vocal Performance, Male: "Lost in the Fifties Tonight (in the Still of the Night)"—Ronnie Milsap (RCA)

Best Country Performance, Duo or Group with Vocal: *Why Not Me*—The Judds (RCA)

Best Country Instrumental Performance: "Cosmic Square Dance"—Chet Atkins & Mark Knopfler (Columbia/CBS)

Best Country Song: "Highwayman" (Jimmy L. Webb)

Hall of Fame Award: "Blue Yodel (T for Texas)"—Jimmie Rodgers (Victor, 1928)

1986

Best Country Vocal Performance, Female: "Whoever's in New England"—Reba McEntire (MCA)

Best Country Vocal Performance, Male: *Lost in the Fifties Tonight*—Ronnie Milsap (RCA)

Best Country Performance, Duo or Group with Vocal: "Grandpa (Tell Me 'Bout the Good Old Days)"—The Judds (RCA)

Best Country Instrumental Performance (Orchestra, Group, or Soloist): "Raisin' the Dickens"—Ricky Skaggs (Epic)

Best Country Song: "Grandpa (Tell Me 'Bout the Good Old Days)" (Jamie O'Hara)

Best Traditional Folk Recording: *Riding the Midnight Train*—Doc Watson (Sugar Hill)

Best Contemporary Folk Album: *Tribute to Steve Goodman*—Various Artists (Red Pajamas)

Best Mexican/American Performance: *Ay Te Dejo en San Antonio*—Flaco Jiminez (Arhoolie)

Best Spoken Word or Nonmusical Recording: *Interviews from "The Class of '55" Recording Sessions*—Carl Perkins, Jerry Lee Lewis, Roy Orbison, Johnny Cash, Sam Phillips, Rick Nelson, and Chips Moman (America Record Corp.)

Hall of Fame Awards: "Blue Suede Shoes"—Carl Perkins (Sun, 1956); "Cool Water"—Sons of the Pioneers (Decca, 1941)

1987

Best Country Vocal Performance, Female: "80's Ladies"—K. T. Oslin (RCA)

Best Country Vocal Performance, Male: *Always and Forever*—Randy Travis (Warner Bros.)

Best Country Performance, Duo or Group with Vocal: *Trio*—Emmylou Harris, Dolly Parton, Linda Ronstadt (Warner Bros.)

Best Country Performance, Duet: "Make No Mistake, She's Mine"—Ronnie Milsap & Kenny Rogers (RCA)

Best Country Instrumental Performance (Orchestra, Group or Soloist): "String of Pars"—Asleep At The Wheel (Epic)

Best Country Song: "Forever and Ever, Amen" (Don Schlitz –Paul Overstreet)

Best Contemporary Folk Recording: *Unfinished Business*—Steve Goodman (Red Pajamas)

Best Album Package: *King's Record Shop*—Rosanne Cash; art director: Bill Johnson (Columbia)

Lifetime Achievement Award: Roy Acuff, Hank Williams, Ray Charles

1988

Best Country Vocal Performance, Female: "Hold Me"—K. T. Oslin (RCA)

Best Country Vocal Performance, Male: *Old 8 x 10*—Randy Travis (Warner Bros.)

Best Country Performance, Duo or Group with Vocal: "Give a Little Love"—the Judds (RCA)

Best Country Instrumental Performance (Orchestra, Group or Soloist): "Sugarfoot Rag"—Asleep At The Wheel (Epic)

Best Country Vocal Collaboration: "Crying"—Roy Orbison & k. d. lang (Virgin)

Best Country Song: "Hold Me" (K. T. Oslin)

Best Bluegrass Recording (Vocal or Instrumental): *Southern Flavor*—Bill Monroe (MCA)

Best Traditional Folk Recording: *Folkways: A Vision Shared—A Tribute to Woody Guthrie & Leadbelly*—various artists; producers: Don DeVito, Joe McEwen, Harold Leventhal, Ralph Rinzler (Columbia)

Best Mexican/American Performance: *Canciónes de Mi Padre*—Linda Ronstadt (Elektra)

Best Album Package: *Tired of the Runnin'*—the O'Kanes; art director: Bill Johnson

Hall of Fame Award: "Hound Dog"—Elvis Presley (RCA, 1956)

1989

Best Country Vocal Performance, Female: *Absolute Torch and Twang*—k. d. lang (Sire)

Best Country Vocal Performance, Male: *Lyle Lovett and His Large Band*—Lyle Lovett (MCA)

Best Country Performance, Duo or Group with Vocal: *Will the Circle Be Unbroken, Volume II*—The Nitty Gritty Dirt Band (Universal)

Best Country Instrumental Performance: "Amazing Grace"—Randy Scruggs (Universal)

Best Country Vocal Collaboration: "There's a Tear in My Beer"—Hank Williams & Hank Williams Jr. (Curb)

Best Country Song: "After All This Time" (Rodney Crowell)

Best Bluegrass Recording: "The Valley Road"—Bruce Hornsby & the Nitty Gritty Dirt Band (Universal)

Record of the Year: "Wind Beneath My Wings"—Bette Midler; Producer: Arif Mardin (Atlantic)

Song of the Year: "Wind Beneath My Wings" (Larry Henley–Jeff Silbar)

Best Rock Performance by a Duo or Group with Vocal: *Traveling Wilburys, Volume One*—Traveling Wilburys: Roy Orbison, George Harrison, Bob Dylan, Tom Petty (Wilbury/Warner Bros.)

Hall of Fame Award: "This Land Is Your Land"—Woody Guthrie (Asch, 1947)

1990

Best Country Vocal Performance, Female: "Where've You Been"—Kathy Mattea (Mercury)

Best Country Vocal Performance, Male: "When I Call Your Name"—Vince Gill (MCA)

Best Country Performance, Duo or Group with Vocal: *Pickin' on Nashville*—The Kentucky Headhunters (Mercury)

Best Country Instrumental Performance: "So Soft, Your Goodbye"—Chet Atkins & Mark Knopfler (Columbia)

Best Country Vocal Collaboration: "Poor Boy Blues"—Chet Atkins & Mark Knopfler (Columbia)

Best Country Song: "Where've You Been" (Jon Vezner–Don Henry)

Best Bluegrass Recording: *I've Got That Old Feeling*—Alison Krauss (Rounder)

Best Traditional Folk Recording: *On Praying Ground*—Doc Watson (Sugar Hill)

Best Mexican/American Performance: "Soy de San Luis"—Texas Tornados (Reprise)

Song of the Year: "From a Distance" (Julie Gold)

Best Pop Vocal Performance, Male: "Oh, Pretty Woman" (track from *A Black & White Night Live*)—Roy Orbison (Virgin)

Best Mexican/American Performance: "Soy de San Luis"—Texas Tornados (Reprise)

Grammy Legend Award: Willie Nelson

1991

Best Country Vocal Performance, Female: "Down at the Twist and Shout"—Mary Chapin Carpenter (Columbia)

Best Country Vocal Performance, Male: *Ropin' the Wind*—Garth Brooks (Capitol)

Best Country Performance, Duo or Group with Vocal: "Love Can Build a Bridge"—the Judds (Curb/ RCA)

Best Country Instrumental Performance: *The New Nashville Cats*—Mark O'Connor, with Steve Wariner, Ricky Skaggs & Vince Gill (Warner Bros.)

Best Country Vocal Collaboration: "Restless"—Steve Wariner, Ricky Skaggs & Vince Gill, from Mark O'Connor's *The New Nashville Cats* (Warner Bros.)

Best Country Song: "Love Can Build a Bridge" (Naomi Judd–John Jarvis–Paul Overstreet)

Best Bluegrass Album: *Spring Training*—Carl Jackson & John Starling (& the Nash Ramblers) (Sugar Hill)

Best Contemporary Folk Album: *The Missing Years*—John Prine (Oh Boy)

Lifetime Achievement Award: Kitty Wells, Bob Dylan

Grammy Legend Award: Johnny Cash

Trustees Award: Sam Phillips

1992

Best Country Vocal Performance, Female: "I Feel Lucky"—Mary Chapin Carpenter (Columbia)

Best Country Vocal Performance, Male: *I Still Believe in You*—Vince Gill (MCA)

Best Country Performance, Duo or Group with Vocal: *At the Ryman*—Emmylou Harris & the Nash Ramblers (Reprise)

Best Country Instrumental Performance: *Sneakin' Around*—Chet Atkins & Jerry Reed (Columbia)

Best Country Vocal Collaboration: "The Whiskey Ain't Workin'"—Travis Tritt & Marty Stuart (Warner Bros.)

Best Country Song: "I Still Believe in You" (Vince Gill–John Barlow Jarvis)

Best Bluegrass Album: *Every Time You Say Goodbye*—Alison Krauss & Union Station (Rounder)

Best Traditional Folk Album: *An Irish Evening at the Grand Opera House, Belfast*—The Chieftains (RCA)

Best Contemporary Folk Album: *Another Country*—The Chieftains (RCA)

Best Mexican/American Performance: *Más Canciónes*—Linda Ronstadt (Elektra)

Hall of Fame Award: "Crazy"—Patsy Cline (Decca, 1961)

Trustees Award: Thomas A. Dorsey

1993

Best Country Vocal Performance, Female: "Passionate Kisses"—Mary Chapin Carpenter (Columbia)

Best Country Vocal Performance, Male: "Ain't That Lonely Yet"—Dwight Yoakam (Reprise)

Best Country Performance, Duo or Group with Vocal: "Hard Workin' Man"—Brooks & Dunn (Arista)

Best Country Instrumental Performance: "Red Wing"—Asleep At The Wheel featuring Eldon Shamblin, Johnny Gimble, Chet Atkins, Vince Gill, Marty Stuart, and Reuben "Lucky Oceans" Gosfield (Liberty)

Best Country Vocal Collaboration: "Does He Love You"—Reba McEntire & Linda Davis (MCA)

Best Country Song: "Passionate Kisses" (Lucinda Williams)

Best Bluegrass Album: *Waitin' for the Hard Times to Go*—The Nashville Bluegrass Band (Sugar Hill)

Best Contemporary Folk Album: *Other Voices/Other Rooms*—Nanci Griffith (Elektra)

Best Southern Gospel, Country Gospel, or Bluegrass Gospel Album: *Good News*—Kathy Mattea (Mercury)

Record of the Year: "I Will Always Love You"—Whitney Houston (Arista)

Best Pop Vocal Performance, Female: "I Will Always Love You"— Whitney Houston (Arista)

Lifetime Achievement Award: Chet Atkins, Bill Monroe, Pete Seeger

1994

Best Female Country Vocal Performance: "Shut Up and Kiss Me"— Mary Chapin Carpenter (Columbia)

Best Male Country Vocal Performance: "When Love Finds You"— Vince Gill (MCA)

Best Country Performance, Duo or Group with Vocal: "Blues for Dixie" (track from *A Tribute to the Music of Bob Wills & the Texas Playboys*)—Asleep At The Wheel with Lyle Lovett (Liberty)

Best Country Instrumental Performance: "Young Thing"—Chet Atkins (Columbia)

Best Country Vocal Collaboration: "I Fall to Pieces"—Aaron Neville & Trisha Yearwood (MCA)

Best Country Album: *Stones in the Road*—Mary Chapin Carpenter (Columbia)

Best Country Song: "I Swear" (Gary Baker–Frank J. Meyers)

Best Bluegrass Album: *The Great Dobro Sessions*—Various Artists (Sugar Hill)

Best Pop Vocal Collaboration: "Funny How Time Slips Away"—Al Green & Lyle Lovett (MCA)

Best Southern Gospel, Country Gospel, or Bluegrass Gospel Album: *I Know Who Holds Tomorrow*—Alison Krauss & the Cox Family (Rounder)

Best Traditional Folk Album: *World Gone Wrong*—Bob Dylan (Columbia)

Best Contemporary Folk Album: *American Recordings*—Johnny Cash (American)

Best Recording Package: *Tribute to the Music of Bob Wills & the Texas Playboys*—Asleep At The Wheel; art director: Buddy Jackson (Liberty)

Best Pop Performance by a Duo or Group with Vocal: "I Swear"— All-4-One (Blitz/Atlantic)

Producer of the Year: Don Was

Hall of Fame Award: "Blowin' in the Wind"—Bob Dylan (Columbia, 1963)

1995

Best Female Country Vocal Performance: "Baby, Now That I've Found You"— Alison Krauss (Rounder)

Best Male Country Vocal Performance: "Go Rest High on That Mountain"— Vince Gill (MCA)

Best Country Performance, Duo or Group with Vocal: "Here Comes the Rain"—The Mavericks (MCA)

Best Country Instrumental Performance: "Hightower"—Asleep At The Wheel featuring Béla Fleck & Johnny Gimble (Capitol)

Best Country Vocal Collaboration: "Somewhere in the Vicinity of the Heart"— Shenandoah & Alison Krauss (Capitol)

Best Country Song: "Go Rest High on That Mountain" (Vince Gill)

Best Country Album: *The Woman in Me*—Shania Twain (Mercury)

Best Bluegrass Album: *Unleashed*—The Nashville Bluegrass Band (Sugar Hill)

Best Contemporary Folk Album: *Wrecking Ball*—Emmylou Harris (Asylum/ Elektra)

Lifetime Achievement Award: Patsy Cline

1996

Best New Artist: LeAnn Rimes (Curb)

Best Female Country Vocal Performance: "Blue"—LeAnn Rimes (Curb)

Best Male Country Vocal Performance: "Worlds Apart"—Vince Gill (MCA)

Best Country Performance by a Duo or Group with Vocal: "My Maria"—Brooks & Dunn (Arista)

Best Country Instrumental Performance: "Jam Man"—Chet Atkins (Columbia)

Best Country Vocal Collaboration: "High Lonesome Sound"—Vince Gill featuring Alison Krauss & Union Station (MCA)

Best Country Song: "Blue" (Bill Mack)

Best Country Album: *The Road to Ensenada*—Lyle Lovett (Curb/ MCA)

Best Bluegrass Album: *True Life Blues: The Songs of Bill Monroe*—various artists (Sugar Hill)

Best Pop Instrumental Performance: "Sinister Minister," from *Live Art*—Béla Fleck & the Flecktones (Warner Bros.)

Lifetime Achievement Award: Everly Brothers, Buddy Holly

1997

Best Female Country Vocal Performance: "How Do I Live"—Trisha Yearwood (MCA)

Best Male Country Vocal Performance: "Pretty Little Adriana"— Vince Gill (MCA)

Best Country Performance by a Duo or Group With Vocal: "Looking In the Eyes of Love"—Alison Krauss & Union Station (Rounder)

Best Country Instrumental Performance: "Little Liza Jane"—Alison Kraus & Union Station

Best Country Vocal Collaboration: "In Another's Eyes"—Trisha Yearwood and Garth Brooks

Best Country Song: "Butterfly Kisses" (Bob Carlisle and Randy Thomas)

Best Country Album: *Unchained*—Johnny Cash (American Recordings)

Best Bluegrass Album: *So Long So Wrong*—Alison Krauss & Union Station

Lifetime Achievement Award: Roy Orbison

Trustees Award: Frances Preston

Country Music Association (CMA) Awards

Entertainer

1967	Eddy Arnold
1968	Glen Campbell
1969	Johnny Cash
1970	Merle Haggard
1971	Charley Pride
1972	Loretta Lynn
1973	Roy Clark
1974	Charlie Rich
1975	John Denver
1976	Mel Tillis
1977	Ronnie Milsap
1978	Dolly Parton
1979	Willie Nelson
1980	Barbara Mandrell
1981	Barbara Mandrell
1982	Alabama
1983	Alabama
1984	Alabama
1985	Ricky Skaggs
1986	Reba McEntire
1987	Hank Williams Jr.
1988	Hank Williams Jr.
1989	George Strait
1990	George Strait
1991	Garth Brooks
1992	Garth Brooks
1993	Vince Gill
1994	Vince Gill
1995	Alan Jackson
1996	Brooks & Dunn
1997	Garth Brooks

Female Vocalist

1967	Loretta Lynn
1968	Tammy Wynette
1969	Tammy Wynette
1970	Tammy Wynette
1971	Lynn Anderson
1972	Loretta Lynn
1973	Loretta Lynn
1974	Olivia Newton-John
1975	Dolly Parton
1976	Dolly Parton
1977	Crystal Gayle
1978	Crystal Gayle
1979	Barbara Mandrell
1980	Emmylou Harris
1981	Barbara Mandrell
1982	Janie Fricke
1983	Janie Fricke
1984	Reba McEntire
1985	Reba McEntire
1986	Reba McEntire
1987	Reba McEntire
1988	K. T. Oslin
1989	Kathy Mattea
1990	Kathy Mattea
1991	Tanya Tucker
1992	Mary Chapin Carpenter
1993	Mary Chapin Carpenter
1994	Pam Tillis
1995	Alison Krauss
1996	Patty Loveless
1997	Trisha Yearwood

Male Vocalist

1967	Jack Greene
1968	Glen Campbell
1969	Johnny Cash
1970	Merle Haggard
1971	Charley Pride
1972	Charley Pride
1973	Charlie Rich
1974	Ronnie Milsap
1975	Waylon Jennings
1976	Ronnie Milsap
1977	Ronnie Milsap
1978	Don Williams
1979	Kenny Rogers
1980	George Jones
1981	George Jones
1982	Ricky Skaggs
1983	Lee Greenwood
1984	Lee Greenwood
1985	George Strait
1986	George Strait
1987	Randy Travis
1988	Randy Travis
1989	Ricky Van Shelton
1990	Clint Black
1991	Vince Gill
1992	Vince Gill
1993	Vince Gill
1994	Vince Gill
1995	Vince Gill
1996	George Strait
1997	George Strait

Musician
(changed from Instrumentalist of the Year in 1988)

1967	Chet Atkins
1968	Chet Atkins
1969	Chet Atkins
1970	Jerry Reed
1971	Jerry Reed
1972	Charlie McCoy
1973	Charlie McCoy
1974	Don Rich
1975	Johnny Gimble
1976	Hargus "Pig" Robbins
1977	Roy Clark
1978	Roy Clark
1979	Charlie Daniels
1980	Roy Clark
1981	Chet Atkins
1982	Chet Atkins
1983	Chet Atkins
1984	Chet Atkins
1985	Chet Atkins
1986	Johnny Gimble
1987	Johnny Gimble
1988	Chet Atkins
1989	Johnny Gimble
1990	Johnny Gimble
1991	Mark O'Connor
1992	Mark O'Connor
1993	Mark O'Connor
1994	Mark O'Connor
1995	Mark O'Connor
1996	Mark O'Connor
1997	Brent Mason

Vocal Group

1967	Stoneman Family
1968	Porter Wagoner & Dolly Parton
1969	Johnny Cash & June Carter
1970	Glaser Brothers
1971	Osborne Brothers
1972	Statler Brothers
1973	Statler Brothers
1974	Statler Brothers
1975	Statler Brothers
1976	Statler Brothers
1977	Statler Brothers
1978	Oak Ridge Boys
1979	Statler Brothers
1980	Statler Brothers
1981	Alabama
1982	Alabama
1983	Alabama
1984	Statler Brothers
1985	Judds
1986	Judds
1987	Judds
1988	Highway 101
1989	Highway 101
1990	Kentucky Headhunters
1991	Kentucky Headhunters
1992	Diamond Rio
1993	Diamond Rio
1994	Diamond Rio
1995	Mavericks
1996	Mavericks
1997	Diamond Rio

Vocal Duo

1970	Porter Wagoner & Dolly Parton
1971	Porter Wagoner & Dolly Parton
1972	Conway Twitty & Loretta Lynn
1973	Conway Twitty & Loretta Lynn
1974	Conway Twitty & Loretta Lynn
1975	Conway Twitty & Loretta Lynn
1976	Waylon Jennings & Willie Nelson
1977	Jim Ed Brown & Helen Cornelius
1978	Kenny Rogers & Dottie West
1979	Kenny Rogers & Dottie West
1980	Moe Bandy & Joe Stampley
1981	David Frizzell & Shelly West
1982	David Frizzell & Shelly West
1983	Merle Haggard & Willie Nelson
1984	Willie Nelson & Julio Iglesias
1985	Anne Murray & Dave Loggins
1986	Dan Seals & Marie Osmond
1987	Ricky Skaggs & Sharon White
1988	Judds
1989	Judds
1990	Judds
1991	Judds
1992	Brooks & Dunn
1993	Brooks & Dunn
1994	Brooks & Dunn
1995	Brooks & Dunn
1996	Brooks & Dunn
1997	Brooks & Dunn

Instrumental Group
(discontinued in 1987)

1967	Buckaroos
1968	Buckaroos
1969	Danny Davis & the Nashville Brass
1970	Danny Davis & the Nashville Brass
1971	Danny Davis & the Nashville Brass
1972	Danny Davis & the Nashville Brass
1973	Danny Davis & the Nashville Brass
1974	Danny Davis & the Nashville Brass
1975	Roy Clark & Buck Trent
1976	Roy Clark & Buck Trent
1977	Original Texas Playboys
1978	Oak Ridge Boys Band
1979	Charlie Daniels Band
1980	Charlie Daniels Band
1981	Alabama
1982	Alabama
1983	Ricky Skaggs Band
1984	Ricky Skaggs Band
1985	Ricky Skaggs Band
1986	Oak Ridge Boys Band

Vocal Event

1988 *Trio*—Emmylou Harris, Dolly Parton & Linda Ronstadt (Warner Bros.)

1989 "There's a Tear in My Beer"—Hank Williams & Hank Williams Jr. (Curb)

1990 "Till a Tear Becomes a Rose"—Lorrie Morgan & Keith Whitley (RCA)

1991 "Restless"—Mark O'Connor & the New Nashville Cats (featuring Vince Gill, Ricky Skaggs & Steve Wariner) (Warner Bros.)

1992 "The Whiskey Ain't Workin'"—Marty Stuart & Travis Tritt (Warner Bros.)

1993 "I Don't Need Your Rocking Chair"—George Jones with Vince Gill, Mark Chesnutt, Garth Brooks, Travis Tritt, Joe Diffie, Alan Jackson, Pam Tillis, T. Graham Brown, Patty Loveless & Clint Black (MCA)

1994 "Does He Love You"—Linda Davis & Reba McEntire (MCA)

1995 "Somewhere in the Vicinity of the Heart"—Shenandoah with Alison Krauss (Liberty)

1996 "I Will Always Love You"—Dolly Parton with special guest Vince Gill (Columbia)

1997 "It's Your Love"—Tim McGraw & Faith Hill (Curb)

Single of the Year

1967 "There Goes My Everything"—Jack Greene (Decca)

1968 "Harper Valley P.T.A."—Jeannie C. Riley (Plantation)

1969 "A Boy Named Sue"—Johnny Cash (Columbia)

1970 "Okie from Muskogee"—Merle Haggard (Capitol)

1971 "Help Me Make It Through the Night"—Sammi Smith (Mega)

1972 "The Happiest Girl in the Whole U.S.A."—Donna Fargo (Dot)

1973 "Behind Closed Doors"— Charlie Rich (Epic)

1974 "Country Bumpkin"—Cal Smith (MCA)

1975 "Before the Next Teardrop Falls"—Freddy Fender (ABC-Dot)

1976 "Good Hearted Woman"—Waylon Jennings & Willie Nelson (RCA)

1977 "Lucille"—Kenny Rogers (United Artists)

1978 "Heaven's Just a Sin Away"—the Kendalls (Ovation)

1979 "The Devil Went Down to Georgia"—Charlie Daniels Band (Epic)

1980 "He Stopped Loving Her Today"—George Jones (Epic)

1981 "Elvira"—Oak Ridge Boys (MCA)

1982 "Always on My Mind"—Willie Nelson (Columbia)

1983 "Swingin'"—John Anderson (Warner Bros.)

1984 "A Little Good News"—Anne Murray (Capitol)

1985 "Why Not Me"—Judds (RCA)

1986 "Bop"—Dan Seals (EMI-America)

1987 "Forever and Ever, Amen"—Randy Travis (Warner Bros.)

1988 "Eighteen Wheels and a Dozen Roses"—Kathy Mattea (Mercury)

1989 "I'm No Stranger to the Rain"—Keith Whitley (RCA)

1990 "When I Call Your Name"—Vince Gill (MCA)

1991 "Friends in Low Places"—Garth Brooks (Capitol)

1992 "Achy Breaky Heart"—Billy Ray Cyrus (Mercury)

1993 "Chattahoochee"—Alan Jackson (Arista)

1994 "I Swear"—John Michael Montgomery (Atlantic)

1995 "When You Say Nothing at All"—Alison Krauss & Union Station (BNA Entertainment)

1996 "Check Yes or No"—George Strait (MCA)

1997 "Strawberry Wine"—Deana Carter (Capitol)

Song of the Year

1967 "There Goes My Everything" (Dallas Frazier)

1968 "Honey" (Bobby Russell)

1969 "Carroll County Accident" (Bob Ferguson)

1970 "Sunday Morning Coming Down" (Kris Kristofferson)

1971 "Easy Loving" (Freddie Hart)

1972 "Easy Loving" (Freddie Hart)

1973 "Behind Closed Doors" (Kenny O'Dell)

1974 "Country Bumpkin" (Don Wayne)

1975 "Back Home Again" (John Denver)

1976 "Rhinestone Cowboy" (Larry Weiss)

1977 "Lucille" (Roger Bowling–Hal Bynum)

1978 "Don't It Make My Brown Eyes Blue" (Richard Leigh)

1979 "The Gambler" (Don Schlitz)

1980 "He Stopped Loving Her Today" (Bobby Braddock–Curly Putman)

1981 "He Stopped Loving Her Today" (Bobby Braddock–Curly Putman)

1982 "Always on My Mind" (Wayne Carson–Johnny Christopher–Mark James)

1983 "Always on My Mind" (Wayne Carson–Johnny Christopher–Mark James)

1984 "Wind Beneath My Wings" (Larry Henley–Jeff Silbar)

1985 "God Bless the U.S.A."(Lee Greenwood)

1986 "On the Other Hand" (Paul Overstreet–Don Schlitz)

1987 "Forever and Ever, Amen" (Paul Overstreet–Don Schlitz)

1988 "80's Ladies" (K. T. Oslin)

1989 "Chiseled in Stone" (Max D. Barnes–Vern Gosdin)

1990 "Where've You Been" (Don Henry–Jon Vezner)

1991 "When I Call Your Name" (Tim DuBois–Vince Gill)

1992 "Look at Us" (Max D. Barnes–Vince Gill)

1993 "I Still Believe in You" (Vince Gill–John Barlow Jarvis)

1994 "Chattahoochee" (Alan Jackson–Jim McBride)

1995 "Independence Day" (Gretchen Peters)

1996 "Go Rest High on That Mountain" (Vince Gill)

1997 "Strawberry Wine" (Matraca Berg–Gary Harrison)

Album of the Year

1967 *There Goes My Everything*—Jack Greene (Decca)

1968 *Johnny Cash at Folsom Prison*—Johnny Cash (Columbia)

1969 *Johnny Cash at San Quentin Prison*—Johnny Cash (Columbia)

1970 *Okie from Muskogee*—Merle Haggard (Capitol)

1971 *I Won't Mention It Again*—Ray Price (Columbia)

1972 *Let Me Tell You About a Song*—Merle Haggard (Capitol)

1973 *Behind Closed Doors*—Charlie Rich (Epic)

1974 *A Very Special Love Song*—Charlie Rich (Epic)

1975 *A Legend in My Time*—Ronnie Milsap (RCA)

1976 *Wanted! The Outlaws*—Waylon Jennings, Willie Nelson, Jessi Colter, Tompall Glaser (RCA)

1977 *Ronnie Milsap Live*—Ronnie Milsap (RCA)

1978 *It Was Almost Like a Song*—Ronnie Milsap (RCA)

1979 *The Gambler*—Kenny Rogers (United Artists)

1980 *Coal Miner's Daughter*—original motion picture soundtrack (MCA)

1981 *I Believe in You*—Don Williams (MCA)

1982 *Always on My Mind*—Willie Nelson (Columbia)

1983 *The Closer You Get*—Alabama (RCA)

1984 *A Little Good News*—Anne Murray (Capitol)

1985 *Does Fort Worth Ever Cross Your Mind*—George Strait (MCA)

1986 *Lost in the Fifties Tonight*—Ronnie Milsap (RCA)

1987 *Always and Forever*—Randy Travis (Warner Bros.)

1988 *Born to Boogie*—Hank Williams Jr. (Warner Bros./Curb)

1989 *Will the Circle Be Unbroken, Volume II*—Nitty Gritty Dirt Band (Universal)

1990 *Pickin' on Nashville*—Kentucky Headhunters (Mercury)

1991 *No Fences*—Garth Brooks (Capitol)

1992 *Ropin' the Wind*—Garth Brooks (Liberty)

1993 *I Still Believe in You*—Vince Gill (MCA)

1994 *Common Thread: The Songs of the Eagles*—various artists (Giant)

1995 *When Fallen Angels Fly*—Patty Loveless (Epic)

1996 *Blue Clear Sky*—George Strait (MCA)

1997 *Carrying Your Love with Me*—George Strait (MCA)

Music Video of the Year

(initiated in 1985; not awarded in 1988)

1985 "All My Rowdy Friends Are Comin' Over Tonight"—Hank Williams Jr.; directed by John Goodhue (Warner Bros.)

1986 "Who's Gonna Fill Their Shoes"—George Jones; directed by Marc Ball (Epic)

1987 "My Name Is Bocephus"—Hank Williams Jr.; directed by Jeff Fisher & Preacher Ewing (Warner Bros.)

1989 "There's a Tear in My Beer"—Hank Williams & Hank Williams Jr.; directed by Ethan Russell (Warner Bros.)

1990 "The Dance"—Garth Brooks; directed by John Lloyd Miller (Capitol)

1991 "The Thunder Rolls"—Garth Brooks; directed by Bud Schaetzle (Capitol)

1992 "Midnight in Montgomery"—Alan Jackson; directed by Jim Shea (Arista)

1993 "Chattahoochee"—Alan Jackson; directed by Martin Kahan (Arista)

1994 "Independence Day"—Martina McBride; directed by Robert Deaton & George J. Flanigen IV (RCA)

1995 "Baby Likes to Rock It"—Tractors; directed by Michael Salomon (Arista)

1996 "My Wife Thinks You're Dead"—Junior Brown; directed by Michael McNamara (Curb)

1997 "455 Rocket"—Kathy Mattea; directed by Steven Goldmann (Mercury)

Comedian
(discontinued in 1971)
1967 Don Bowman
1968 Ben Colder
1969 Archie Campbell
1970 Roy Clark

Horizon Award
1981 Terri Gibbs
1982 Ricky Skaggs
1983 John Anderson

1984 Judds
1985 Sawyer Brown
1986 Randy Travis
1987 Holly Dunn
1988 Ricky Van Shelton
1989 Clint Black
1990 Garth Brooks
1991 Travis Tritt
1992 Suzy Bogguss
1993 Mark Chesnutt
1994 John Michael Montgomery
1995 Alison Krauss
1996 Bryan White
1997 LeAnn Rimes

Academy of Country Music Awards

Entertainer
1970 Merle Haggard
1971 Freddie Hart
1972 Roy Clark
1973 Roy Clark
1974 Mac Davis
1975 Loretta Lynn
1976 Mickey Gilley
1977 Dolly Parton
1978 Kenny Rogers
1979 Willie Nelson
1980 Barbara Mandrell
1981 Alabama
1982 Alabama
1983 Alabama
1984 Alabama
1985 Alabama
1986 Hank Williams Jr.
1987 Hank Williams Jr.
1988 Hank Williams Jr.
1989 George Strait
1990 Garth Brooks
1991 Garth Brooks
1992 Garth Brooks
1993 Garth Brooks
1994 Reba McEntire
1995 Brooks & Dunn
1996 Brooks & Dunn

Female Vocalist
1965 Bonnie Owens
1966 Bonnie Guitar
1967 Lynn Anderson
1968 Cathie Taylor
1969 Tammy Wynette
1970 Lynn Anderson
1971 Loretta Lynn
1972 Donna Fargo
1973 Loretta Lynn
1974 Loretta Lynn
1975 Loretta Lynn
1976 Crystal Gayle
1977 Crystal Gayle
1978 Barbara Mandrell
1979 Crystal Gayle
1980 Dolly Parton
1981 Barbara Mandrell
1982 Sylvia
1983 Janie Fricke
1984 Reba McEntire
1985 Reba McEntire
1986 Reba McEntire
1987 Reba McEntire
1988 K. T. Oslin
1989 Kathy Mattea

1990 Reba McEntire
1991 Reba McEntire
1992 Mary Chapin Carpenter
1993 Wynonna
1994 Reba McEntire
1995 Patty Loveless
1996 Patty Loveless

Male Vocalist
1965 Buck Owens
1966 Merle Haggard
1967 Glen Campbell
1968 Glen Campbell
1969 Merle Haggard
1970 Merle Haggard
1971 Freddie Hart
1972 Merle Haggard
1973 Charlie Rich
1974 Merle Haggard
1975 Conway Twitty
1976 Mickey Gilley
1977 Kenny Rogers
1978 Kenny Rogers
1979 Larry Gatlin
1980 George Jones
1981 Merle Haggard
1982 Ronnie Milsap
1983 Lee Greenwood
1984 George Strait
1985 George Strait
1986 Randy Travis
1987 Randy Travis
1988 George Strait
1989 Clint Black
1990 Garth Brooks
1991 Garth Brooks
1992 Vince Gill
1993 Vince Gill
1994 Alan Jackson
1995 Alan Jackson
1996 George Strait

Vocal Group
(no awards given for 1968, 1971, 1974–76, and 1979–80)
1967 Sons of the Pioneers
1969 Kimberlys
1970 Kimberlys
1972 Statler Brothers
1973 Brush Arbor
1977 Statler Brothers
1978 Oak Ridge Boys
1981 Alabama
1982 Alabama
1983 Alabama

1984 Alabama
1985 Alabama
1986 Forester Sisters
1987 Highway 101
1988 Highway 101
1989 Restless Heart
1990 Shenandoah
1991 Diamond Rio
1992 Diamond Rio
1993 Little Texas
1994 Mavericks
1995 Mavericks
1996 Sawyer Brown

Vocal Duet
(no awards given for 1969–70, 1972–73, 1977–78)
1965 Merle Haggard & Bonnie Owens
1966 Merle Haggard & Bonnie Owens
1967 Merle Haggard & Bonnie Owens
1968 Merle Haggard & Bonnie Owens, Johnny & Jonie Mosby (tie)
1971 Loretta Lynn & Conway Twitty
1974 Loretta Lynn & Conway Twitty
1975 Loretta Lynn & Conway Twitty
1976 Loretta Lynn & Conway Twitty
1979 Moe Bandy & Joe Stampley
1980 Moe Bandy & Joe Stampley
1981 David Frizzell & Shelly West
1982 David Frizzell & Shelly West
1983 Dolly Parton & Kenny Rogers
1984 Judds
1985 Judds
1986 Judds
1987 Judds
1988 Judds
1989 Judds
1990 Judds
1991 Brooks & Dunn
1992 Brooks & Dunn
1993 Brooks & Dunn
1994 Brooks & Dunn
1995 Brooks & Dunn
1996 Brooks & Dunn

Single Record
1968 "Little Green Apples"—Roger Miller (Smash)
1969 "Okie from Muskogee"—Merle Haggard (Capitol)
1970 "For the Good Times"—Ray Price (Columbia)
1971 "Easy Loving"—Freddie Hart (Capitol)

1972 "The Happiest Girl in the Whole U.S.A."—Donna Fargo (Dot)

1973 "Behind Closed Doors"—Charlie Rich (Epic)

1974 "Country Bumpkin"—Cal Smith (MCA)

1975 "Rhinestone Cowboy"—Glen Campbell (Capitol)

1976 "Bring It on Home"—Mickey Gilley (Playboy)

1977 "Lucille"—Kenny Rogers (United Artists)

1978 "Tulsa Time"—Don Williams (ABC)

1979 "All the Gold in California"—Larry Gatlin & the Gatlin Brothers (Columbia)

1980 "He Stopped Loving Her Today"—George Jones (Epic)

1981 "Elvira"—Oak Ridge Boys (MCA)

1982 "Always on My Mind"—Willie Nelson (Columbia)

1983 "Islands in the Stream"—Kenny Rogers & Dolly Parton (RCA)

1984 "To All the Girls I've Loved Before"—Willie Nelson & Julio Iglesias (Columbia)

1985 "Highwayman"—Willie Nelson, Waylon Jennings, Kris Kristofferson, & Johnny Cash (Columbia)

1986 "On the Other Hand"—Randy Travis (Warner Bros.)

1987 "Forever and Ever, Amen"—Randy Travis (Warner Bros.)

1988 "Eighteen Wheels and a Dozen Roses"—Kathy Mattea (PolyGram)

1989 "Better Man"—Clint Black (RCA)

1990 "Friends in Low Places"—Garth Brooks (Capitol)

1991 "Don't Rock the Jukebox"—Alan Jackson (Arista)

1992 "Boot Scootin' Boogie"—Brooks & Dunn (Arista)

1993 "Chattahoochee"—Alan Jackson (Arista)

1994 "I Swear"—John Michael Montgomery (Arista)

1995 "Check Yes Or No"—George Strait (MCA)

1996 "Blue"—LeAnn Rimes (Curb)

Song (Songwriter)

1966 "Apartment #9" (Bobby Austin–Johnny Paycheck)

1967 "It's Such a Pretty World Today" (Dale Noe)

1968 "Wichita Lineman" (Jimmy Webb)

1969 "Okie from Muskogee" (Merle Haggard–Roy Edward Burris)

1970 "For the Good Times" (Kris Kristofferson)

1971 "Easy Loving" (Freddie Hart)

1972 "The Happiest Girl in the Whole U.S.A." (Donna Fargo)

1973 "Behind Closed Doors" (Kenny O'Dell)

1974 "Country Bumpkin" (Don Wayne)

1975 "Rhinestone Cowboy" (Larry Weiss)

1976 "Don't the Girls All Get Prettier at Closing Time" (Baker Knight)

1977 "Lucille" (Roger Bowling–Hal Bynum)

1978 "You Needed Me" (Randy Goodrum)

1979 "It's a Cheatin' Situation" (Sonny Throckmorton–Curly Putman)

1980 "He Stopped Loving Her Today" (Bobby Braddock–Curly Putman)

1981 "You're the Reason God Made Oklahoma" (Sandy Pinkard–Larry Collins)

1982 "Are the Good Times Really Over" (Merle Haggard)

1983 "The Wind Beneath My Wings" (Larry Henley–Jeff Silbar)

1984 "Why Not Me" (Harlan Howard–Sonny Throckmorton–Brent Maher)

1985 "Lost in the Fifties (in the Still of the Night)" (Mike Reid–Troy Seals–Fred Parris)

1986 "On the Other Hand" (Don Schlitz–Paul Overstreet)

1987 "Forever and Ever, Amen" (Don Schlitz–Paul Overstreet)

1988 "Eighteen Wheels and a Dozen Roses" (Paul Nelson–Gene Nelson)

1989 "Where've You Been" (Jon Vezner–Don Henry)

1990 "The Dance" (Tony Arata)

1991 "Somewhere in My Broken Heart" (Billy Dean–Richard Leigh)

1992 "I Still Believe in You" (John Barlow Jarvis–Vince Gill)

1993 "I Love the Way You Love Me" (Victoria Shaw–Chuck Cannon)

1994 "I Swear" (Gary B. Baker–Frank Myers)

1995 "The Keeper of the Stars" (Karen Staley–Dickey Lee–Danny Mayo)

1996 "Blue" (Bill Mack)

Album

1967 *Gentle on My Mind*—Glen Campbell (Capitol)

1968 *Glen Campbell & Bobbie Gentry*—Glen Campbell & Bobbie Gentry (Capitol)

1969 *Okie from Muskogee*—Merle Haggard (Capitol)

1970 *For the Good Times*—Ray Price (Columbia)

1971 *Easy Loving*—Freddie Hart (Capitol)

1972 *Happiest Girl in the Whole U.S.A.*—Donna Fargo (Dot)

1973 *Behind Closed Doors*—Charlie Rich (Epic)

1974 *Back Home Again*—John Denver (RCA)

1975 *Feelin's*—Conway Twitty & Loretta Lynn (MCA)

1976 *Gilley's Smoking*—Mickey Gilley (Playboy)

1977 *Kenny Rogers*—Kenny Rogers (United Artists)

1978 *Y'all Come Back Saloon*—Oak Ridge Boys (MCA)

1979 *Straight Ahead*—Larry Gatlin & the Gatlin Brothers (Columbia)

1980 *Urban Cowboy*—soundtrack (Asylum)

1981 *Feels So Right*—Alabama (RCA)

1982 *Always on My Mind*—Willie Nelson (CBS)

1983 *The Closer You Get*—Alabama (RCA)

1984 *Roll On*—Alabama (RCA)

1985 *Does Forth Worth Ever Cross Your Mind*—George Strait (MCA)

1986 *Storms of Life*—Randy Travis (Warner Bros.)

1987 *Trio*—Dolly Parton, Emmylou Harris, & Linda Ronstadt (Warner Bros.)

1988 *This Woman*—K. T. Oslin (RCA)

1989 *Killin' Time*—Clint Black (RCA)

1990 *No Fences*—Garth Brooks (Capitol)

1991 *Don't Rock the Jukebox*—Alan Jackson (Arista)

1992 *Brand New Man*—Brooks & Dunn (Arista)

1993 *A Lot About Livin' (and a Little 'Bout Love)*—Alan Jackson (Arista)

1994 *Not a Moment Too Soon*—Tim McGraw (Curb)

1995 *The Woman in Me*—Shania Twain (Mercury)

1996 *Blue Clear Sky*—George Strait (MCA)

Video

1984 "All My Rowdy Friends Are Coming Over Tonight"—Hank Williams Jr.

1985 "Who's Gonna Fill Their Shoes"—George Jones

1986 "Whoever's in New England"— Reba McEntire

1987 "80's Ladies"—K. T. Oslin

1988 "Young Country"—Hank Williams Jr.

1989 "There's a Tear in My Beer"—Hank Williams & Hank Williams Jr.

1990 "The Dance"—Garth Brooks

1991 "Is There Life Out There"—Reba McEntire

1992 "Two Sparrows in a Hurricane"—Tanya Tucker

1993 "We Shall Be Free"—Garth Brooks

1994 "The Red Strokes"—Garth Brooks

1995 "The Car"—Jeff Carson

1996 "I Think about You"—Collin Raye

New Female Vocalist (Most Promising)

1965 Kay Adams
1966 Cathie Taylor
1967 Bobbie Gentry
1968 Cheryl Poole
1969 Donna Fargo
1970 Sammi Smith
1971 Barbara Mandrell
1972 Tanya Tucker
1973 Olivia Newton-John
1974 Linda Ronstadt
1975 Crystal Gayle
1976 Billie Jo Spears
1977 Debby Boone
1978 Christy Lane
1979 Lacy J. Dalton
1980 Terri Gibbs
1981 Juice Newton
1982 Karen Brooks
1983 Gus Hardin
1984 Nicolette Larson
1985 Judy Rodman
1986 Holly Dunn
1987 K. T. Oslin
1988 Suzy Bogguss
1989 Mary Chapin Carpenter
1990 Shelby Lynne
1991 Trisha Yearwood
1992 Michelle Wright
1993 Faith Hill
1994 Chely Wright
1995 Shania Twain
1996 LeAnn Rimes

New Male Vocalist (Most Promising)

1965 Merle Haggard
1966 Billy Mize
1967 Jerry Inman
1968 Ray Sanders
1969 Freddy Weller
1970 Buddy Alan
1971 Tony Booth
1972 Johnny Rodriguez
1973 Dorsey Burnette
1974 Mickey Gilley
1975 Freddy Fender
1976 Moe Bandy
1977 Eddie Rabbitt

1978 John Conlee
1979 R. C. Bannon
1980 Johnny Lee
1981 Ricky Skaggs
1982 Michael Martin Murphey
1983 Jim Glaser
1984 Vince Gill
1985 Randy Travis
1986 Dwight Yoakam
1987 Ricky Van Shelton
1988 Rodney Crowell
1989 Clint Black
1990 Alan Jackson
1991 Billy Dean
1992 Tracy Lawrence
1993 John Michael Montgomery
1994 Tim McGraw
1995 Bryan White
1996 Trace Adkins

New Vocal Duo/Group
1989 Kentucky Headhunters
1990 Pirates of the Mississippi
1991 Brooks & Dunn
1992 Confederate Railroad
1993 Gibson Miller Band
1994 The Mavericks
1995 Lonestar
1996 Ricochet

Artist of the Decade
1960–69 Marty Robbins
1970–79 Loretta Lynn
1980–89 Alabama

Fiddle
1965 Billy Armstrong
1966 Billy Armstrong
1967 Billy Armstrong
1968 Billy Armstrong
1969 Billy Armstrong
1970 Billy Armstrong
1971 Billy Armstrong
1972 Billy Armstrong
1973 Billy Armstrong
1974 Billy Armstrong
1975 Billy Armstrong
1976 Billy Armstrong
1977 Billy Armstrong
1978 Johnny Gimble
1979 Johnny Gimble
1980 Johnny Gimble
1981 Johnny Gimble
1982 Johnny Gimble
1983 Johnny Gimble
1984 Johnny Gimble
1985 Johnny Gimble
1986 Mark O'Connor
1987 Johnny Gimble
1988 Mark O'Connor
1989 Mark O'Connor
1990 Mark O'Connor
1991 Mark O'Connor
1992 Mark O'Connor
1993 Mark O'Connor
1994 Mark O'Connor
1995 Rob Hajacos
1996 Stuart Duncan

Steel Guitar
1965 Red Rhodes
1966 Ralph Mooney, Tom Brumley (tie)
1967 Red Rhodes
1968 Red Rhodes
1969 Buddy Emmons
1970 J. D. Maness
1971 J. D. Maness

1972 Buddy Emmons
1973 Red Rhodes
1974 J. D. Maness
1975 J. D. Maness
1976 J. D. Maness
1977 Buddy Emmons
1978 Buddy Emmons
1979 Buddy Emmons
1980 J. D. Maness, Buddy Emmons (tie)
1981 Buddy Emmons
1982 J. D. Maness
1983 J. D. Maness
1984 Buddy Emmons
1985 Buddy Emmons
1986 J. D. Maness
1987 J. D. Maness
1988 J. D. Maness
1989 J. D. Maness
1990 J. D. Maness
1991 Paul Franklin
1992 J. D. Maness
1993 J. D. Maness
1994 Paul Franklin
1995 Paul Franklin
1996 Paul Franklin

Keyboard
1965 Billy Liebert
1966 Billy Liebert
1967 Earl Ball
1968 Earl Ball
1969 Floyd Cramer
1970 Floyd Cramer
1971 Floyd Cramer
1972 Floyd Cramer
1973 Floyd Cramer
1974 Floyd Cramer
1975 Jerry Lee Lewis
1976 Hargus "Pig" Robbins
1977 Hargus "Pig" Robbins
1978 Jimmy Pruett
1979 Hargus "Pig" Robbins
1980 Hargus "Pig" Robbins
1981 Hargus "Pig" Robbins
1982 Hargus "Pig" Robbins
1983 Floyd Cramer
1984 Hargus "Pig" Robbins
1985 Glen D. Hardin
1986 John Hobbs
1987 John Hobbs, Ronnie Milsap (tie)
1988 John Hobbs
1989 Skip Edwards
1990 John Hobbs
1991 Matt Rollings
1992 Matt Rollings
1993 Matt Rollings
1994 Matt Rollings
1995 Matt Rollings
1996 Matt Rollings

Bass
1965 Bob Morris
1966 Bob Morris
1967 Red Wooten
1968 Red Wooten
1969 Billy Graham
1970 Doyle Holly, Billy Graham (tie)
1971 Larry Booth
1972 Larry Booth
1973 Larry Booth
1974 Billy Graham
1975 Billy Graham
1976 Curtis Stone
1977 Larry Booth
1978 Rod Culpepper
1979 Billy Graham
1980 Curtis Stone

1981 Curtis Stone, Joe Osborn (tie)
1982 Red Wooten
1983 Joe Osborn
1984 Joe Osborn
1985 Joe Osborn
1986 Emory Gordy Jr.
1987 Emory Gordy Jr., David Hungate (tie)
1988 Curtis Stone
1989 Michael Rhodes
1990 Bill Bryson
1991 Roy Huskey Jr.
1992 Glenn Worf
1993 Glenn Worf
1994 Glenn Worf
1995 Glenn Worf
1996 Glenn Worf

Guitar
1965 Phil Baugh
1966 Jimmy Bryant
1967 Jimmy Bryant
1968 Jimmy Bryant
1969 Al Bruno, Jerry Inman (tie)
1970 Al Bruno
1971 Al Bruno
1972 Al Bruno
1973 Al Bruno
1974 Al Bruno
1975 Jerry Inman (rhythm), Russ Hansen (lead)
1976 Danny Michaels
1977 Roy Clark
1978 James Burton
1979 Al Bruno
1980 Al Bruno
1981 James Burton
1982 Al Bruno
1983 Reggie Young
1984 James Burton
1985 James Burton
1986 Chet Atkins
1987 Chet Atkins
1988 Al Bruno
1989 Brent Rowan
1990 John Jorgenson
1991 John Jorgenson
1992 John Jorgenson
1993 Brent Mason
1994 Brent Mason
1995 Brent Mason
1996 Brent Mason

Drums
1965 Muddy Berry
1966 Jerry Wiggins
1967 Pee Wee Adams
1968 Jerry Wiggins
1969 Jerry Wiggins
1970 Archie Francis
1971 Jerry Wiggins
1972 Jerry Wiggins
1973 Jerry Wiggins
1974 Jerry Wiggins
1975 Archie Francis
1976 Archie Francis
1977 Archie Francis, George Manz (tie)
1978 Archie Francis
1979 Archie Francis
1980 Archie Francis
1981 Buddy Harman
1982 Archie Francis
1983 Archie Francis
1984 Larrie Londin
1985 Archie Francis
1986 Larrie Londin
1987 Archie Francis

1988	Steve Duncan
1989	Steve Duncan
1990	Steve Duncan
1991	Eddie Bayers
1992	Eddie Bayers
1993	Eddie Bayers
1994	Eddie Bayers
1995	Eddie Bayers
1996	Eddie Bayers

Specialty Instrument

1969	John Hartford, banjo
1977	Charlie McCoy, harmonica
1978	Charlie McCoy, harmonica
1979	Charlie McCoy, harmonica
1980	Charlie McCoy, harmonica
1981	Charlie McCoy, harmonica
1982	James Burton, dobro
1983	Charlie McCoy, harmonica
1984	Ricky Skaggs, mandolin
1985	James Burton, dobro
1986	James Burton, dobro
1987	Ricky Skaggs, mandolin; Jerry Douglas, dobro
1988	Charlie McCoy, harmonica
1989	Jerry Douglas, dobro
1990	Jerry Douglas, dobro
1991	Jerry Douglas, dobro
1992	Jerry Douglas, dobro
1993	Terry McMillan, percussion & harmonica
1994	Terry McMillan, percussion & harmonica
1995	Terry McMillan, percussion & harmonica
1996	Terry McMillan, percussion, harmonica, & cowbells

Touring Band

1965	Buck Owens & the Buckaroos
1966	Buck Owens & the Buckaroos
1967	Buck Owens & the Buckaroos
1968	Buck Owens & the Buckaroos
1969	Merle Haggard & the Strangers
1970	Merle Haggard & the Strangers
1971	Merle Haggard & the Strangers
1972	Merle Haggard & the Strangers
1973	Brush Arbor
1974	Merle Haggard & the Strangers
1975	Merle Haggard & the Strangers
1976	Mickey Gilley & the Red Rose Express
1977	Asleep At The Wheel, Sons of the Pioneers (tie)
1978	Original Texas Playboys
1979	Charlie Daniels Band
1980	Charlie Daniels Band
1981	Merle Haggard & the Strangers
1982	Ricky Skaggs Band
1983	Ricky Skaggs Band
1984	Ricky Skaggs Band
1985	Ricky Skaggs Band
1986	Ricky Skaggs Band
1987	Merle Haggard & the Strangers
1988	Desert Rose Band
1989	Desert Rose Band
1990	Desert Rose Band

Nontouring Band

1970	Tony Booth Band
1971	Tony Booth Band
1972	Tony Booth Band
1973	Ronnie Truhett & the Sound Company
1974	Palomino Riders
1975	Jerry Inman & the Palomino Riders
1976	Possum Holler
1977	Palomino Riders

1978	Rebel Playboys
1979	Midnight Riders
1980	Palomino Riders
1981	Desperados
1982	Desperados
1983	Billy Mize & the Tennesseans
1984	Billy Mize & the Tennesseans
1985	Nashville Now Band
1986	Nashville Now Band
1987	Nashville Now Band
1988	Nashville Now Band
1989	Nashville Now Band
1990	Boy Howdy

Radio Personality/Disk Jockey
(no award given for 1967)

1965	Biff Collie
1966	Biff Collie, Bob Kingsley (tie)
1968	Tex Williams (regional), Larry Scott (Los Angeles)
1969	Dick Haynes
1970	Corky Mayberry
1971	Larry Scott
1972	Larry Scott
1973	Craig Scott
1974	Larry Scott
1975	Billy Parker
1976	Charlie Douglas
1977	Billy Parker
1978	Billy Parker
1979	King Edward IV
1980	Sammy Jackson
1981	Arch Yancey
1982	Lee Arnold
1983	Rhubarb Jones
1984	Coyote Calhoun (large market), Billy Parker (medium market), Don Hollander (small market)
1985	Eddie Edwards
1986	Chris Taylor
1987	Jim Tabor
1988	Jon Conlon
1989	Jon Conlon, Dandalion (tie)
1990	Gerry House
1991	Gerry House
1992	Jon Conlon
1993	Tim Hatrick, Willy D. Loon (tie)
1994	Gerry House
1995	Gerry House
1996	Gerry House

Radio Station

1970	KLAC, Los Angeles, California
1971	KLAC, Los Angeles, California
1972	KLAC, Los Angeles, California
1973	KLAC, Los Angeles, California
1974	KLAC, Los Angeles, California
1975	KLAC, Los Angeles, California
1976	KLAC, Los Angeles, California
1977	KGBS, Los Angeles, California
1978	KVOO, Tulsa, Oklahoma
1979	KFDI, Wichita, Kansas
1980	KLAC, Los Angeles, California
1981	WPLO, Atlanta, Georgia
1982	KIKK, Houston, Texas
1983	KRMD, Shreveport, Louisiana
1984	WCM, Memphis, Tennessee (large market); KVOO, Tulsa, Oklahoma (medium market); WLWI, Montgomery, Alabama (small market)
1985	WAMZ, Louisville, Kentucky
1986	KNIX, Phoenix, Arizona
1987	KNIX, Phoenix, Arizona
1988	WSIX, Nashville, Tennessee
1989	WSIX, Nashville, Tennessee
1990	WSIX, Nashville, Tennessee
1991	WAMZ, Louisville, Kentucky

1992	KNIX, Phoenix, Arizona
1993	KNIX, Phoenix, Arizona
1994	WSIX, Nashville, Tennessee
1995	WSIX, Nashville, Tennessee
1996	WSIX, Nashville, Tennessee

Nightclub

1965	Palomino Club
1966	Palomino Club
1967	Palomino Club
1968	Palomino Club, Gold Nugget
1969	Palomino Club
1970	Palomino Club
1971	Palomino Club
1972	Palomino Club
1973	Palomino Club
1974	Palomino Club
1975	Palomino Club
1976	Palomino Club
1977	Palomino Club
1978	Palomino Club
1979	Palomino Club
1980	Gilley's, Palomino Club (tie)
1981	Billy Bob's, Forth Worth, Texas
1982	Gilley's
1983	Gilley's
1984	Gilley's
1985	Billy Bob's, Forth Worth, Texas
1986	Crazy Horse Steak House & Saloon, Santa Ana, California
1987	Crazy Horse Steak House & Saloon, Santa Ana, California
1988	Crazy Horse Steak House & Saloon, Santa Ana, California
1989	Crazy Horse Steak House & Saloon, Santa Ana, California
1990	Crazy Horse Steak House & Saloon, Santa Ana, California
1991	Crazy Horse Steak House & Saloon, Santa Ana, California
1992	Billy Bob's, Fort Worth, Texas
1993	Toolie's, Phoenix, Arizona
1994	Billy Bob's, Fort Worth, Texas
1995	Crazy Horse Steak House & Saloon, Santa Ana, California
1996	Crazy Horse Steak House & Saloon, Santa Ana, California

Individual Awards
(not awarded every year)

1965	*Billboard*, publication; Central Songs, publisher; Jack McFadden, talent manager; Roger Miller, songwriter & Man of the Year; Billy Mize, TV personality; Ken Nelson, producer/ A& R man
1966	Central Songs, publisher; Dean Martin, Man of the Year; Jack McFadden, talent manager; Billy Mize, TV personality; Ken Nelson, producer/A&R man
1967	Joey Bishop, Man of the Year; Freeway Music, publisher; Billy Mize, TV personality
1968	Glen Campbell, TV personality; Nudie, Director's Award; Tom Smothers, Man of the Year
1969	John Aylesworth, Man of the Year; Johnny Cash, TV personality; Roy Clark, comedy act; Frank Peppiatt, Man of the Year
1970	*Billboard*, publication; Johnny Cash, TV personality; Hugh Cherry, Man of the Year; Roy Clark, comedy act
1971	Glen Campbell, TV personality; Roy Clark, comedy act; Walter Knott, Man of the Year

1972 Roy Clark, TV personality; Lawrence Welk, Man of the Year
1977 Johnny Paycheck, career achievement
1980 George Burns, special achievement
1983 Elvis Presley, Golden Hat Award for contributions to the country music industry
1986 Carl Perkins, career achievement
1993 John Anderson, career achievement; Bill Banchand—Mr. Bill Presents (Phoenix, Arizona), Talent Buyer & Promoter of the Year
1994 George Moffett (Zanesville, Ohio), Talent Buyer & Promoter of the Year
1995 Jeff Foxworthy, Special Achievement Award; George Moffett (Zanesville, Ohio), Talent Buyer & Promoter of the Year
1996 Bob Romeo (Omaha, Nebraska), Talent Buyer & Promoter of the Year

Pioneer Award
1968 Uncle Art Satherley
1969 Bob Wills
1970 Patsy Montana, Tex Ritter
1971 Stuart Hamblen, Bob Nolan, Tex Williams
1972 Gene Autry, Cliffie Stone

1973 Hank Williams
1974 Johnny Bond, Tennessee Ernie Ford, Merle Travis
1975 Roy Rogers
1976 Owen Bradley
1977 Sons of the Pioneers
1978 Eddie Dean
1979 Patti Page
1980 Ernest Tubb
1981 Leo Fender
1982 Chet Atkins
1983 Eddy Arnold
1984 Roy Acuff
1985 Kitty Wells
1986 Minnie Pearl
1987 Roger Miller
1988 Buck Owens
1990 Johnny Cash
1991 Willie Nelson
1992 George Jones
1993 Charley Pride
1994 Loretta Lynn
1995 Merle Haggard
1996 Roy Clark

Jim Reeves Memorial Award
(not awarded every year)
1969 Joe Allison
1970 Bill Boyd

1971 Roy Rogers
1972 Thurston Moore
1973 Sam Lovullo
1974 Merv Griffin
1975 Dinah Shore
1976 Roy Clark
1977 Jim Halsey
1978 Joe Cates
1979 Bill Ward
1980 Ken Kragen
1981 Al Gallico
1982 Jo Walker-Meador
1994 Garth Brooks

Tex Ritter Award (for motion picture soundtrack)
(not awarded every year)
1979 *Electric Horseman*
1980 *Coal Miner's Daughter*
1981 *Any Which Way You Can*
1982 *The Best Little Whorehouse in Texas*
1983 *Tender Mercies*
1984 *Songwriter*
1985 *Sweet Dreams*
1992 *Pure Country*

Music City News/TNN Awards

These awards, founded in 1967, were known as the Music City News Awards up to 1989. In 1990 these awards were merged with The Nashville Network's Viewers' Choice Awards, which had begun in 1988. For those categories where TNN gave an award in 1988 and 1989, we have noted TNN's and MSN's selections; many times they were the same, because, like MSN's awards, TNN's were based on fan voting.

Entertainer
1985 Statler Brothers
1986 Statler Brothers
1987 Statler Brothers
1988 Randy Travis (MCN & TNN)
1989 Randy Travis (MCN & TNN)
1990 Ricky Van Shelton
1991 Ricky Van Shelton
1992 Garth Brooks
1993 Alan Jackson
1994 Alan Jackson
1995 Alan Jackson
1996 Alan Jackson
1997 Alan Jackson

Female Artist
1967 Loretta Lynn
1968 Loretta Lynn
1969 Loretta Lynn
1970 Loretta Lynn
1971 Loretta Lynn
1972 Loretta Lynn
1973 Loretta Lynn
1974 Loretta Lynn
1975 Loretta Lynn
1976 Loretta Lynn
1977 Loretta Lynn
1978 Loretta Lynn
1979 Barbara Mandrell
1980 Loretta Lynn
1981 Barbara Mandrell
1982 Barbara Mandrell
1983 Janie Fricke
1984 Janie Fricke
1985 Reba McEntire
1986 Reba McEntire
1987 Reba McEntire
1988 Reba McEntire (MCN & TNN)
1989 Reba McEntire (MCN & TNN)
1990 Patty Loveless
1991 Reba McEntire
1992 Reba McEntire
1993 Reba McEntire
1994 Lorrie Morgan
1995 Reba McEntire
1996 Lorrie Morgan
1997 Lorrie Morgan

Male Artist
1967 Merle Haggard
1968 Merle Haggard
1969 Charley Pride
1970 Charley Pride
1971 Charley Pride
1972 Charley Pride
1973 Charley Pride
1974 Conway Twitty
1975 Conway Twitty
1976 Conway Twitty
1977 Conway Twitty
1978 Larry Gatlin
1979 Kenny Rogers
1980 Marty Robbins
1981 George Jones
1982 Marty Robbins
1983 Marty Robbins
1984 Lee Greenwood
1985 Lee Greenwood
1986 George Strait
1987 Randy Travis
1988 Randy Travis (MCN & TNN)

1989 Ricky Van Shelton (MCN & TNN)
1990 Ricky Van Shelton
1991 Ricky Van Shelton
1992 Alan Jackson
1993 Alan Jackson
1994 Alan Jackson
1995 Alan Jackson
1996 Alan Jackson
1997 Alan Jackson

Vocal Group
1967 Tompall & the Glaser Brothers
1968 Tompall & the Glaser Brothers
1969 Tompall & the Glaser Brothers
1970 Tompall & the Glaser Brothers
1971 Statler Brothers
1972 Statler Brothers
1973 Statler Brothers
1974 Statler Brothers
1975 Statler Brothers
1976 Statler Brothers
1977 Statler Brothers
1978 Statler Brothers
1979 Statler Brothers
1980 Statler Brothers
1981 Statler Brothers
1982 Statler Brothers
1983 Alabama
1984 Statler Brothers
1985 Statler Brothers
1986 Statler Brothers
1987 Statler Brothers
1988 Statler Brothers (MCN), Oak Ridge Boys (TNN)
1989 Statler Brothers (MCN), Oak Ridge Boys (TNN)
1990 Statler Brothers
1991 Statler Brothers
1992 Statler Brothers
1993 Statler Brothers
1994 Statler Brothers

1995 Statler Brothers
1996 Statler Brothers
1997 Statler Brothers

Vocal Band

1993 Sawyer Brown
1994 Sawyer Brown
1995 Sawyer Brown
1996 Sawyer Brown
1997 Sawyer Brown

Vocal Duo

(award renamed from Vocal Duet in 1988)
1967 Wilburn Brothers
1968 Porter Wagoner & Dolly Parton
1969 Porter Wagoner & Dolly Parton
1970 Porter Wagoner & Dolly Parton
1971 Conway Twitty & Loretta Lynn
1972 Conway Twitty & Loretta Lynn
1973 Conway Twitty & Loretta Lynn
1974 Conway Twitty & Loretta Lynn
1975 Conway Twitty & Loretta Lynn
1976 Conway Twitty & Loretta Lynn
1977 Conway Twitty & Loretta Lynn
1978 Conway Twitty & Loretta Lynn
1979 Kenny Rogers & Dottie West
1980 Conway Twitty & Loretta Lynn
1981 Conway Twitty & Loretta Lynn
1982 David Frizzell & Shelly West
1983 David Frizzell & Shelly West
1984 Kenny Rogers & Dolly Parton
1985 Judds
1986 Judds
1987 Judds
1988 Judds
1989 Judds
1990 Judds
1991 Judds
1992 Judds
1993 Brooks & Dunn
1994 Brooks & Dunn
1995 Brooks & Dunn
1996 Brooks & Dunn
1997 Brooks & Dunn

Vocal Collaboration

1988 *Trio*—Emmylou Harris, Dolly Parton, & Linda Ronstadt (Warner Bros.)
1989 "Streets of Bakersfield"—Dwight Yoakam & Buck Owens (Reprise)
1990 "There's a Tear in My Beer"—Hank Williams & Hank Williams Jr. (Curb)
1991 "'Till a Tear Becomes a Rose"—Lorrie Morgan & Keith Whitley (RCA)
1992 "Rockin' Years"—Dolly Parton & Ricky Skaggs (Columbia)
1993 "The Whiskey Ain't Workin'"—Travis Tritt & Marty Stuart (Warner Bros.)
1994 "Does He Love You"—Reba McEntire & Linda Davis (MCA)
1995 "A Good Year for the Roses"—George Jones & Alan Jackson (MCA)
1996 "Go Rest High on That Mountain"—Vince Gill, Patty Loveless, & Ricky Skaggs (MCA)
1997 "By My Side"—Lorrie Morgan & Jon Randall (RCA)

Single

1978 "Heaven's Just a Sin Away"—the Kendalls (Ovation)
1979 "The Gambler"—Kenny Rogers (EMI-Manhattan)
1980 "Coward of the County"—Kenny Rogers (United Artists)

1981 "He Stopped Loving Her Today"—George Jones (Epic)
1982 "Elvira"—Oak Ridge Boys (MCA)
1983 "Some Memories Just Won't Die"—Marty Robbins (Columbia)
1984 "Elizabeth"—the Statler Brothers (Mercury)
1985 "God Bless the U.S.A."—Lee Greenwood (MCA)
1986 "My Only Love"—Statler Brothers (Mercury)
1987 "On the Other Hand"—Randy Travis (Warner Bros.)
1988 "Forever and Ever, Amen"—Randy Travis (Warner Bros.)
1989 "I'll Leave This World Loving You"—Ricky Van Shelton (Columbia)
1990 "More Than a Name on the Wall"—the Statler Brothers (Mercury)
1991 "When I Call Your Name"—Vince Gill (MCA)
1992 "Don't Rock the Jukebox"—Alan Jackson (Arista)
1993 "I Still Believe in You"—Vince Gill (MCA)
1994 "Chattahoochee"—Alan Jackson (Arista)
1995 "Livin' on Love"—Alan Jackson (Arista)
1996 "Check Yes or No"—George Strait (MCA)
1997 "Trail of Tears"—Billy Ray Cyrus (Mercury)

Song

(not awarded in 1968, 1978–80, 1995–97)
1967 "There Goes My Everything" (Dallas Frazier)
1969 "All I Have to Offer You Is Me" (Dallas Frazier–A. L. "Doodle" Owens)
1970 "Hello Darlin'" (Conway Twitty)
1971 "Help Me Make It Through the Night" (Kris Kristofferson)
1972 "Kiss an Angel Good Mornin'" (Ben Peters)
1973 "Why Me" (Kris Kristofferson)
1974 "You've Never Been This Far Before" (Conway Twitty)
1975 "Country Bumpkin" (Don Wayne)
1976 "Blue Eyes Crying in the Rain" (Fred Rose)
1977 "I Don't Want to Have to Marry You" (Fred Imus–Phil Sweet)
1981 "He Stopped Loving Her Today" (Bobby Braddock–Curly Putman)
1982 "Elvira" (Dallas Frazier)
1983 "I'm Gonna Hire a Wino to Decorate Our Home" (Dewayne Blackwell)
1984 "Swingin'" (John Anderson–Lionel Delmore)
1985 "Elizabeth" (Jimmy Fortune)
1986 "My Only Love" (Jimmy Fortune)
1987 "Too Much on My Heart" (Jimmy Fortune)
1988 "Forever and Ever, Amen" (Don Schlitz–Paul Overstreet)
1989 "I'll Leave This World Loving You" (Wayne Kemp)
1990 "Here in the Real World" (Alan Jackson–Mark Irwin)
1991 "Here's a Quarter (Call Someone Who Cares)" (Travis Tritt)
1992 "I Still Believe in You" (Vince Gill–John Jarvis)
1993 "Chattahoochee" (Alan Jackson–Jim McBride)

1994 "Your Love Amazes Me" (Amanda Hunt Taylor–Chuck Jones)

Album

1976 *When a Tingle Becomes a Chill*—Loretta Lynn (MCA)
1977 *I Don't Want to Have to Marry You*—Jim Ed Brown & Helen Cornelius (RCA)
1978 *Moody Blue*—Elvis Presley (RCA)
1979 *Entertainers . . . on and off the Stage*—The Statler Brothers (Mercury)
1980 *The Originals*—Statler Brothers (Mercury)
1981 *Tenth Anniversary*—the Statler Brothers (Mercury)
1982 *Feels So Right*—Alabama (RCA)
1983 *Come Back to Me*—Marty Robbins (Columbia)
1984 *The Closer You Get*—Alabama (RCA)
1985 *Atlanta Blue*—Statler Brothers (Mercury)
1986 *Partners in Rhyme*—the Statler Brothers (Mercury)
1987 *Storms of Life*—Randy Travis (Warner Bros.)
1988 *Always and Forever*—Randy Travis (Warner Bros.) (MCN & TNN)
1989 *Old 8 x 10*—Randy Travis (Warner Bros.) (TNN); *Loving Proof*—Ricky Van Shelton (Columbia) (MCN)
1990 *Killin' Time*—Clint Black (RCA)
1991 *Here in the Real World*—Alan Jackson (Arista)
1992 *Don't Rock the Jukebox*—Alan Jackson (Arista)
1993 *I Still Believe in You*—Vince Gill (MCA)
1994 *A Lot About Livin' (and a Little 'Bout Love)*—Alan Jackson (Arista)
1995 *Who I Am*—Alan Jackson (Arista)
1996 *Lead On*—George Strait (MCA)
1997 *Blue Clear Sky*—George Strait (MCA)

Video

1985 "Elizabeth"—Statler Brothers (Mercury)
1986 "My Only Love"—Statler Brothers (Mercury)
1987 "Whoever's in New England"—Reba McEntire (MCA)
1988 "Maple Street Memories"—Statler Brothers (Mercury) (MCN); "Forever and Ever, Amen"—Randy Travis (Warner Bros.) (TNN)
1989 "I'll Leave This World Loving You"—Ricky Van Shelton (Columbia) (MCN & TNN)
1990 "Tear in My Beer"—Hank Williams & Hank Williams Jr.; directed by Ethan Russell (Warner Bros.)
1991 "The Dance"—Garth Brooks; directed by John Lloyd Miller (Capitol)
1992 "Rockin' Years"—Dolly Parton & Ricky Van Shelton (Columbia)
1993 "Midnight in Montgomery"—Alan Jackson; directed by Jim Shea (Arista)
1994 "Chattahoochee"—Alan Jackson; directed by Martin Kahan (Arista)
1995 "Independence Day"—Martina McBride (RCA)
1996 "Check Yes or No"—George Strait (MCA)
1997 "Then You Can Tell Me Goodbye"—Neal McCoy (Atlantic)

New Female Artist (Most Promising)

1967 Tammy Wynette
1968 Dolly Parton
1969 Peggy Sue
1970 Susan Raye
1971 Susan Raye
1972 Donna Fargo
1973 Tanya Tucker
1974 Olivia Newton-John
1975 Crystal Gayle
1976 Barbara Mandrell
1977 Helen Cornelius
1978 Debby Boone
1979 Janie Fricke
1980 Charly McClain
1981 Louise Mandrell
1982 Shelly West

New Male Artist (Most Promising)

1967 Tom T. Hall
1968 Cal Smith
1969 Johnny Bush
1970 Tommy Cash
1971 Tommy Overstreet
1972 Billy "Crash" Craddock
1973 Johnny Rodriguez
1974 Johnny Rodriguez
1975 Ronnie Milsap
1976 Mickey Gilley
1977 Larry Gatlin
1978 Don Williams
1979 Rex Allen Jr.
1980 Hank Williams Jr.
1981 Boxcar Willie
1982 T. G. Sheppard

Star of Tomorrow

(award renamed from merged categories
Most Promising Artist, Female & Male, in
1983)
1983 Ricky Skaggs
1984 Ronny Robbins
1985 Judds
1986 John Schneider
1987 Randy Travis
1988 Ricky Van Shelton (MCN & TNN)
1989 Patty Loveless (MCN), Shenandoah (TNN)
1990 Clint Black
1991 Alan Jackson
1992 Travis Tritt
1993 Doug Stone
1994 John Michael Montgomery

Star of Tomorrow, Female

(Star of Tomorrow award divided into three
categories in 1995)
1995 Faith Hill
1996 Terri Clark
1997 LeAnn Rimes

Star of Tomorrow, Male

1995 Tim McGraw
1996 Bryan White
1997 Wade Hayes

Star of Tomorrow, Vocal Group

(discontinued in 1996)
1995 BlackHawk

Instrumentalist of the Year

(not awarded in 1983–87)
1969 Roy Clark
1970 Roy Clark
1971 Roy Clark
1972 Roy Clark
1973 Charlie McCoy
1974 Roy Clark
1975 Buck Owens
1976 Buck Owens
1977 Johnny Gimble
1978 Roy Clark
1979 Roy Clark
1980 Roy Clark
1981 Barbara Mandrell
1982 Barbara Mandrell
1988 Ricky Skaggs
1989 Ricky Skaggs
1990 Ricky Skaggs
1991 Vince Gill
1992 Vince Gill
1993 Vince Gill
1994 Vince Gill

Instrumental Entertainer

1974 Charlie McCoy
1975 Roy Clark
1976 Roy Clark
1977 Roy Clark

Bluegrass Group of the Year

1971 Osborne Brothers
1972 Osborne Brothers
1973 Osborne Brothers
1974 Osborne Brothers
1975 Osborne Brothers
1976 Osborne Brothers
1977 Osborne Brothers
1978 Osborne Brothers
1979 Osborne Brothers
1980 Bill Monroe & the Bluegrass Boys
1981 Bill Monroe & the Bluegrass Boys
1982 Ricky Skaggs
1983 Ricky Skaggs
1984 Ricky Skaggs

Songwriter

1967 Bill Anderson
1968 Bill Anderson
1969 Bill Anderson
1970 Merle Haggard
1971 Kris Kristofferson
1972 Kris Kristofferson
1973 Kris Kristofferson
1974 Bill Anderson
1975 Bill Anderson
1976 Bill Anderson
1977 Larry Gatlin
1978 Larry Gatlin
1979 Eddie Rabbitt
1980 Marty Robbins

Band

1967 Buckaroos
1968 Buckaroos
1969 Buckaroos
1970 Buckaroos
1971 Strangers
1972 Strangers
1973 Po' Boys
1974 Buckaroos
1975 Coalminers
1976 Coalminers
1977 Coalminers
1978 Larry Gatlin, Family & Friends
1979 Oak Ridge Boys Band
1980 Charlie Daniels Band
1981 Marty Robbins Band
1982 Alabama
1983 Alabama

Gospel Artist or Group

1979 Connie Smith
1980 Carter Family
1981 Hee Haw Gospel Quartet
1982 Hee Haw Gospel Quartet
1983 Hee Haw Gospel Quartet
1984 Hee Haw Gospel Quartet
1985 Hee Haw Gospel Quartet
1986 Hee Haw Gospel Quartet
1987 Hee Haw Gospel Quartet
1988 Chuck Wagon Gang
1989 Whites
1990 Chuck Wagon Gang
1991 Chuck Wagon Gang
1992 Chuck Wagon Gang
1993 Chuck Wagon Gang

Christian Country Artist

1994 Paul Overstreet
1995 Ricky Van Shelton
1996 Ricky Van Shelton
1997 Ricky Van Shelton

Country Music TV Show

1969 *Johnny Cash Show, Hee Haw* (tie)
1970 *Hee Haw*
1971 *Hee Haw*
1972 *Hee Haw*
1973 *Hee Haw*
1974 *Hee Haw*
1975 *Hee Haw*
1976 *Hee Haw*
1977 *Hee Haw*
1978 *Fifty Years of Country Music*
1979 *PBS Live from the Grand Ole Opry*
1980 *PBS Live from the Grand Ole Opry*
1981 *Barbara Mandrell & the Mandrell Sisters*
1982 *Barbara Mandrell & the Mandrell Sisters*
1983 *Hee Haw*
1984 *Hee Haw*
1985 *Nashville Now*
1986 *Nashville Now*
1987 *Nashville Now*
1988 *Nashville Now*
1989 *Nashville Now*

Country Music TV Special

1983 *Conway Twitty on the Mississippi*
1984 *Another Evening with the Statler Brothers: Heroes, Legends, & Friends*
1985 *Another Evening with the Statler Brothers: Heroes, Legends, & Friends*
1986 *FarmAid*
1987 *The Statler Brothers' Christmas Present*
1988 *Grand Ole Opry Live*
1989 *A Country Music Celebration*

Comedian

(award renamed from Comedy Act in 1986)
1972 Archie Campbell
1973 Mel Tillis
1974 Mel Tillis
1975 Mel Tillis
1976 Mel Tillis
1977 Mel Tillis
1978 Mel Tillis
1979 Jerry Clower
1980 Statler Brothers
1981 Mandrell Sisters
1982 Statler Brothers
1983 Statler Brothers
1984 Statler Brothers
1985 Statler Brothers
1986 Ray Stevens
1987 Ray Stevens
1988 Ray Stevens
1989 Ray Stevens

1990 Ray Stevens	**Minnie Pearl Award (for charity work)**	1986 Loretta Lynn
1991 Ray Stevens	1988 Minnie Pearl	1987 George Jones
1992 Ray Stevens	1989 Roy Acuff	1988 Conway Twitty
1993 Ray Stevens	1990 Tennessee Ernie Ford	1989 Johnny Cash
1994 Ray Stevens	1991 Barbara Mandrell	1990 Merle Haggard
1995 Jeff Foxworthy	1992 Emmylou Harris	1991 Tammy Wynette
1996 Jeff Foxworthy	1993 Vince Gill	1992 Roy Rogers
1997 Jeff Foxworthy	1994 Dolly Parton	1993 Kitty Wells
	1995 Willie Nelson	1994 Dolly Parton
Founders Award	1996 Amy Grant	1995 Waylon Jennings
1976 Faron Young	1997 George "Goober" Lindsey	1996 Willie Nelson
1977 Ralph Emery		1997 Charley Pride
1978 Ernest Tubb	**Living Legend Award**	
1979 Pee Wee King	1983 Roy Acuff	
1980 Buck Owens	1984 Ernest Tubb	
1981 Betty Cox Adler	1985 Barbara Mandrell	

Contributors

Jonita Aadland
Fiddle Player

Thomas A. Adler
Folklorist and Journalist

Bob Allen
Editor at Large, *Country Music* Magazine

Fred Bartenstein
Musician and Journalist

Jack Bernhardt
Music and Film Editor, *North Carolina Folklore Journal*

Stephen L. Betts
Researcher and Field Producer, The Nashville Network

Rob Bowman
Author, *Soulsville USA: The Story of Stax Records;* 1996 Grammy winner, Best Liner Notes

Mary A. Bufwack
Coauthor, *Finding Her Voice: The Saga of Women in Country Music*

Walter Carter
Author, *The Songwriter's Guide to Collaboration* and other books; Historian, Gibson Guitar Company

Joyce Cauthen
Author, *With Fiddle and Well-Rosined Bow: Old-Time Fiddling in Alabama*

Dale Cockrell
Author, *Demons of Disorder: Early Blackface Minstrels and Their World* and other books

Kevin Coffey
Journalist and Recording Annotator

Norm Cohen
Author, *Long Steel Rail: The Railroad in American Folksong,* and Recording Annotator

Daniel Cooper
Author, *Lefty Frizzell: The Honky-Tonk Life of Country Music's Greatest Singer*

Al Cunniff
Author, *Waylon Jennings*

Don Cusic
Professor of Music Business, Belmont University, and Author

Wayne W. Daniel
Author, *Pickin' on Peachtree: A History of Country Music in Atlanta, Georgia*

Fred Danker
Professor of American Studies, University of Massachusetts

William P. Davis
Former Deputy Director of Collections and Research, Country Music Foundation

Eddie Dean
Senior Writer, *Washington City Paper*

Bryan Di Salvatore
Author and Journalist

Chris Dickinson
Associate Editor, Country Music Foundation

Steve Eng
Author, *A Satisfied Mind: The Country Music Life of Porter Wagoner* and other books

Colin Escott
Author, *Hank Williams* and other books

Dennis Milton Estes
Former Country Disc Jockey

Marilyn A. Estes
Free-Lance Writer

Bill Evans
Bluegrass Banjo Player and Journalist

Todd Everett
Author and Music Journalist

Tom Ewing
Musician and Columnist, *Bluegrass Unlimited*

Mark Fenster
Music Journalist

Kim Field
Author, *Harmonicas, Harps, and Heavy Breathers*

Chet Flippo
Author, *Your Cheatin' Heart: A Biography of Hank Williams* and other books

Ben Fong-Torres
Managing Editor, *Gavin* Magazine

Gene Fowler
Author, *Border Radio* and other books

Jon Hartley Fox
Journalist and Recording Annotator

Bill Friskics-Warren
Music Journalist

Holly George-Warren
Editor, Rolling Stone Press

Calvin Gilbert
Associate Editor, *Radio and Records*

Cary Ginell
Author, *Milton Brown and the Founding of Western Swing*

Frank Godbey
Bluegrass Musician and Journalist

Marty Godbey
Author and Journalist

Thomas Goldsmith
City Editor, Nashville *Tennessean*

Michael Gray
Music Journalist, Country.com

Archie Green
Author, *Only a Miner: Studies in Recorded Coal-Mining Songs* and other books

Douglas B. Green
Founding Member, Riders in the Sky

Sid Griffin
Author, *Gram Parsons: A Music Biography*

Ken Griffis
Author and Music Historian

Jimmy Guterman
Author, *12 Days on the Road*

Patricia Hall
Author and Folklore Consultant

Wade Hall
Author, *Hell-Bent for Music: The Life of Pee Wee King*

Steve Hathaway
Publisher, *Western Swing Newsletter*

Kent Henderson
Researcher and Songwriter

Michael Hight
Music Journalist

Geoffrey Himes
Music Journalist

Bill Hobbs
Music Journalist

Fred Hoeptner
Music Journalist

Mark Humphrey
Radio Writer and Recording Producer

Bill Ivey
Chairman, National Endowment for the Arts

Loyal Jones
Author, *Minstrel of the Appalachians: The Story of Bascom Lamar Lunsford* and other books

Margaret Jones
Author, *Patsy: The Life and Times of Patsy Cline*

Beverly Keel
Assistant Professor of Recording Industry, Middle Tennessee State University, and Music Journalist

Rich Kienzle
Contributing Editor, *Country Music Magazine*; Recording Annotator and Producer

Paul Kingsbury
Author, *The Grand Ole Opry History of Country Music*; Deputy Director of Special Projects, Country Music Foundation

Burt Korall
Author, *Drummin' Men: The Heartbeat of Jazz*

William E. Lightfoot
Professor of Folklore, Appalachian State University

John Lilly
Editor, *Goldenseal*

Pete Loesch
Journalist and Recording Annotator

Guy Logsdon
Author, *"The Whorehouse Bells were Ringing" and Other Songs Cowboys Sing*

John Lomax III
Author, *Nashville: Music City USA*

Bill C. Malone
Author, *Country Music USA* and other books

Brian Mansfield
Music Journalist

Greil Marcus
Author, *Mystery Train* and other books

Jonathan Marx
Editor, *Nashville Scene*

Michael McCall
Author, *Garth Brooks: A Biography*

Brad McCuen
Former Executive, RCA Records

Marjie McGraw
Author, *The Great American Country Music Trivia Book* and other books

Don McLeese
Columnist and Critic at Large, *Austin American Statesman*

W. K. McNeil
Author, *Southern Folk Ballads* and other books

Bob Millard
Contributing Editor, *Country Music Magazine*

Rick Mitchell
Author, *Garth Brooks: One of a Kind, Workin' on a Full House*

Toru Mitsui
Author, *The Story of "You Are My Sunshine"* and other books

Tom Morgan
Musician and Journalist

David C. Morton
Coauthor, *DeFord Bailey: A Black Star in Early Country Music*

Robert K. Oermann
Music Journalist and Coauthor, *Finding Her Voice*

Bob Olson
Record Collector and Discographer

Ted Olson
Author, *Blue Ridge Folklife*

Jay Orr
Music Reporter, *Tennessean*

Clark Parsons
Former Editor, *Nashville Life*

Bob Paxman
Entertainment Journalist

Bob Pinson
Senior Researcher, Country Music Foundation

Nolan Porterfield
Author, *Jimmie Rodgers: The Life and Times of America's Blue Yodeler*

Barbara J. Pruett
Author, *Marty Robbins: Fast Cars and Country Music*

Ronnie Pugh
Author, *Ernest Tubb: The Texas Troubadour*

Gary B. Reid
Owner, Copper Creek Records

Don Rhodes
Music Columnist

Harry Rice
Sound Archivist, Hutchins Library, Berea, Kentucky

Jim Ridley
Senior Writer, *Nashville Scene*

Tom Roland
Author, *The Billboard Book of #1 Country Hits*

David Romvedt
Author, *Windmill: Essays from Four Mile Ranch* and other books

Kinney Rorrer
Author, *Rambling Blues: The Life and Songs of Charlie Poole*

Neil V. Rosenberg
Author, *Bluegrass: A History*

Don Roy
Music Historian and Recording Annotator

John W. Rumble
Historian, Country Music Foundation

Tony Russell
Author, *Blacks, Whites, and Blues*

Dave Samuelson
Music Journalist and Recording Annotator

Ben Sandmel
Drummer, Hackberry Ramblers, and Folklore Researcher

Walt Saunders
Columnist, *Bluegrass Unlimited* Magazine

Ann Savoy
Author, *Cajun Music: A Reflection of a People*

Tony Scherman
Editor, *The Rock Musician*

Mark Schone
Senior Contributing Writer, *SPIN* Magazine

Charlie Seemann
Executive Director, The Western Folklife Center in Nevada

Jon Sievert
Author, *Concert Photography: How to Shoot and Sell Music-Business Photographs*

Chris Skinker
Music Journalist and Recording Annotator

Jon Guyot Smith
Music Historian and Recording Annotator

Richard D. Smith
Author, *Bluegrass: An Informal Guide*

Willie Smyth
Director, Folk Arts Program, The Washington State Arts Commission

Paul Soelberg
Manager, Country Music Forum, Microsoft Network, and Journalist

Joe Specht
Director, McMurry University Library, Abilene, Texas

Dick Spottswood
Author, *Ethnic Music Records*

Michael Streissguth
Author, *Eddy Arnold: Pioneer of the Nashville Sound*

Eddie Stubbs
Announcer, Grand Ole Opry, and Fiddle Player

Cecelia Tichi
Author, *High Lonesome: The American Culture of Country Music* and other books

Jim Bob Tinsley
Author, *He Was Singin' This Song*

Charles Townsend
Author, *San Antonio Rose: The Life and Music of Bob Wills*

Ivan M. Tribe
Author, *Mountain Jamboree: Country Music in West Virginia*

Walt Trott
Author, *The Country Music World of Charlie Lamb*

Stephen R. Tucker
Historian and Journalist

Ben Vaughn
Recording Artist and Record Producer

Dale Vinicur
Coauthor, *Still in Love with You*

Paul F. Wells
Director, Center for Popular Music, Middle Tennessee State University

Jonny Whiteside
Author, *Ramblin' Rose: The Life and Career of Rose Maddox*

Gene Wiggins
Author, *Fiddlin' Georgia Crazy*

Janet E. Williams
Author and Music Journalist

Charles Wolfe
Author, *The Devil's Box: Masters of Southern Fiddling* and other books

Stacey Wolfe
Instructor, Middle Tennessee State University

Gerry Wood
Author, *The Grand Ole Opry Presents the Year in Country Music*

Marshall Wyatt
Director, North Carolina Folklife Institute, and Record Collector and Producer

Laurence Zwisohn
Author, *Loretta Lynn's World of Music*